Why Do You Need This New Edition?

1. *America: Past and Present* (tenth edition) is now tied more closely than ever to the innovative website, *MyHistoryLab*, which helps you learn more in your history course (www.myhistorylab.com). *MyHistoryLab* icons connect the main narrative in each chapter of the book to a powerful array of *MyHistoryLab* resources, including primary source documents, analytical video segments, interactive maps, and more. A *MyHistoryLab Media Assignments* feature now appears at the end of each chapter, capping off the study resources for the chapter. *MyHistoryLab* also includes both eText and audiobook versions of *America: Past and Present*, so that you can read or listen to your textbook any time you have access to the Internet.

2. *America: Past and Present* (tenth edition) now uses the latest *New MyHistoryLab*, which offers the most advanced Study Plan ever. You get personalized study plans for each chapter with content arranged from less complex thinking—like remembering facts—to more complex critical thinking—like understanding connections in history and analyzing primary sources. Assessments and learning applications in the Study Plan link you directly to the *America: Past and Present* eText for reading and review.

3. *America: Past and Present* (tenth edition) includes several new study aids designed to help you improve your understanding of each chapter. Learning Objective Questions now appear at the head of each chapter to help you focus on the most important information. Each chapter closes with a complete Study Resources section, containing a Time Line, Chapter Review, Key Terms and Definitions, and Critical Thinking Questions.

4. In Chapter 5, a new feature essay on Spain and the American Revolution highlights the key military and diplomatic role that the Spanish played in the Revolutionary War.

5. *America: Past and Present* (tenth edition) contains stronger coverage of African American history. A new feature essay in Chapter 16 addresses the short-lived order of "40 Acres and a Mule" for every freedman. A major new section in Chapter 19 describes the spread of Jim Crow in both the South and North after Reconstruction.

6. *America: Past and Present* (tenth edition) includes a new feature essay in Chapter 18 on the rise of the department store in the late nineteenth century and how this affected women and changed the way many Americans shopped.

7. A new feature essay in Chapter 32 discusses why global warming has become such a controversial issue in the United States and how Al Gore's *An Inconvenient Truth* has affected this dispute.

8. Chapter 32 has also been updated to provide a full account of the election of 2008 and the Obama administration through 2011.

PEARSON

AMERICA
Past and Present

COMBINED VOLUME

∎ ∎ ∎

TENTH EDITION

ROBERT A. DIVINE

University of Texas

T. H. BREEN

Northwestern University

R. HAL WILLIAMS

Southern Methodist University

ARIELA J. GROSS

University of Southern California

H. W. BRANDS

University of Texas

PEARSON

Boston Columbus Indianapolis New York San Francisco Upper Saddle River
Amsterdam Cape Town Dubai London Madrid Milan Munich Paris Montréal Toronto
Delhi Mexico City Saõ Paulo Sydney Hong Kong Seoul Singapore Taipei Tokyo

Editorial Director: Craig Campanella
Editor in Chief: Dickson Musslewhite
Executive Editor: Ed Parsons
Editorial Project Manager: Alex Rabinowitz
Editorial Assistant: Emily Tamburri
Director of Marketing: Brandy Dawson
Senior Marketing Manager: Maureen E. Prado Roberts
Marketing Coordinator: Samantha Bennett
Marketing Assistant: Cristina Liva
Senior Managing Editor: Ann Marie McCarthy
Senior Project Manager: Cheryl Keenan
Manufacturing Manager: Mary Fischer
Operations Specialist: Alan Fischer
Manager of Design Development: John Christiana

Senior Art Director: Maria Lange
Interior Design: The Go2Guys, LLc
Cover Design: John Christiana
Cover Art: Capital Cornucopia/Jason E. Powell
Director of Media & Assessment: Brian Hyland
Digital Media Editor: Alison Lorber
Media Editor: Andrea Messineo
Supplements: Project Manager: Emsal Hasan
Composition and Full-Service Project Management: GEX
    Publishing Services
Printer/Binder: Courier/Kendallville
Cover Printer: Courier/Kendallville
Text Font: 10/12 Minion

Credits and acknowledgments borrowed from other sources and reproduced, with permission, in this textbook appear on appropriate page within text or on pages C1–C4.

Many of the designations by manufacturers and seller to distinguish their products are claimed as trademarks. Where those designations appear in this book, and the publisher was aware of a trademark claim, the designations have been printed in initial caps or all caps.

Library of Congress Cataloging-in-Publication Data
America, past and present / Robert A. Divine ... [et al.].—10th ed.
    p. cm.
Includes bibliographical references and index.
ISBN 978-0-205-90520-1 (combined volume)—ISBN 978-0-205-90519-5 (volume 1)—ISBN 978-0-205-90547-8 (volume 2)
1. United States—History—Textbooks. I. Divine, Robert A.
E178.1.A4894 2013
973—dc23

2012018891

10 9 8 7 6 5 4 3

Combined Volume:	ISBN-10: 0-205-90520-X
	ISBN-13: 978-0-205-90520-1
Instructor Review Copy:	ISBN-10: 0-205-90632-X
	ISBN-13: 978-0-205-90632-1
Volume 1:	ISBN-10: 0-205-90519-6
	ISBN-13: 978-0-205-90519-5
Volume 1 A la carte:	ISBN-10: 0-205-91008-4
	ISBN-13: 978-0-205-91008-3
Volume 2:	ISBN-10: 0-205-90547-1
	ISBN-13: 978-0-205-90547-8
Volume 2 A la carte:	ISBN-10: 0-205-91009-2
	ISBN-13: 978-0-205-91009-0

Brief Contents

Contents

Chapter 4

EXPERIENCE OF EMPIRE: EIGHTEENTH-CENTURY AMERICA   78

Chapter 5

THE AMERICAN REVOLUTION: FROM ELITE PROTEST TO POPULAR REVOLT, 1763–1783   104

Chapter 6

THE REPUBLICAN EXPERIMENT   130

Chapter 7

DEMOCRACY AND DISSENT: THE VIOLENCE OF PARTY POLITICS, 1788–1800 156

Chapter 8

REPUBLICAN ASCENDANCY: THE JEFFERSONIAN VISION 178

Chapter 9

NATION BUILDING AND NATIONALISM 202

Chapter 29

AFFLUENCE AND ANXIETY 688

Chapter 30

THE TURBULENT SIXTIES 706

Chapter 31

**THE RISE OF A NEW CONSERVATISM,
1969–1988 736**

Maps, Figures, and Tables

FIGURES

TABLES

Features

New to the Tenth Edition

America: Past and Present (tenth edition) is now tied more closely than ever to the innovative website, *MyHistoryLab*, which helps students learn more in their history course (www.myhistorylab.com). *MyHistoryLab* icons connect the main narrative in each chapter of the book to a powerful array of *MyHistoryLab* resources, including primary source documents, analytical video segments, interactive maps, and more. A *MyHistoryLab Media Assignments* feature now appears at the end of each chapter, capping off the study resources for the chapter. *MyHistoryLab* also includes both eText and audiobook versions of *America: Past and Present*, so that students can read or listen to their textbook any time they have access to the Internet.

America: Past and Present (tenth edition) now uses the latest *New MyHistoryLab*, which offers the most advanced Study Plan ever. Students get personalized study plans for each chapter, with content arranged from less complex thinking—like remembering facts—to more complex critical thinking—like understanding connections in history and analyzing primary sources. Assessments and learning applications in the Study Plan link directly to the *America: Past and Present* eText for reading and review.

America: Past and Present (tenth edition) includes several new study aids designed to help improve student understanding of each chapter. Learning Objective Questions now appear at the head of each chapter to help focus attention on the most important information. Each chapter closes with a complete Study Resources section, containing a Time Line, Chapter Review, Key Terms and Definitions, and Critical Thinking Questions.

In Chapter 5 a new feature essay on Spain and the American Revolution highlights the key military and diplomatic role that the Spanish played in the Revolutionary War.

America: Past and Present (tenth edition) contains stronger coverage of African American history. A new feature essay in Chapter 16 addresses the short-lived order of "40 Acres and a Mule" for every freedman. A major new section in Chapter 19 describes the spread of Jim Crow in both the South and North after Reconstruction.

America: Past and Present (tenth edition) includes a new feature essay in Chapter 18 on the rise of the department store in the late nineteenth century and how this affected women and changed the way many Americans shopped.

A new feature essay in Chapter 32 discusses why global warming has become such a controversial issue in the United States and how Al Gore's *An Inconvenient Truth* has affected this dispute.

Chapter 32 has also been updated to provide a full account of the election of 2008 and the Obama administration through 2011.

About the Authors

ROBERT A. DIVINE

Robert A. Divine, George W. Littlefield Professor Emeritus in American History at the University of Texas at Austin, received his Ph.D. from Yale University in 1954. A specialist in American diplomatic history, he taught from 1954 to 1996 at the University of Texas, where he was honored by both the student association and the graduate school for teaching excellence. His extensive published work includes *The Illusion of Neutrality* (1962); *Second Chance: The Triumph of Internationalism in America During World War II* (1967); and *Blowing on the Wind* (1978). His most recent work is *Perpetual War for Perpetual Peace* (2000), a comparative analysis of twentieth-century American wars. He is also the author of *Eisenhower and the Cold War* (1981) and editor of three volumes of essays on the presidency of Lyndon Johnson. His book, *The* Sputnik *Challenge* (1993), won the Eugene E. Emme Astronautical Literature Award for 1993. He has been a fellow at the Center for Advanced Study in the Behavioral Sciences and has given the Albert Shaw Lectures in Diplomatic History at Johns Hopkins University.

T. H. BREEN

T. H. Breen, William Smith Mason Professor of American History at Northwestern University, received his Ph.D. from Yale University in 1968. He has taught at Northwestern since 1970. Breen's major books include *The Character of the Good Ruler: A Study of Puritan Political Ideas in New England* (1974); *Puritans and Adventurers: Change and Persistence in Early America* (1980); *Tobacco Culture: The Mentality of the Great Tidewater Planters on the Eve of Revolution* (1985); and, with Stephen Innes of the University of Virginia, *"Myne Owne Ground": Race and Freedom on Virginia's Eastern Shore* (1980). His *Imagining the Past* (1989) won the 1990 Historic Preservation Book Award. *Marketplace of Revolution* received the Colonial Wars Book Award for the "best" book on the American Revolution in 2004. In addition to receiving several awards for outstanding teaching at Northwestern, Breen has been the recipient of research grants from the American Council of Learned Societies, the Guggenheim Foundation, the Institute for Advanced Study (Princeton), the National Humanities Center, and the Huntington Library. He has served as the Fowler

Hamilton Fellow at Christ Church, Oxford University (1987–1988); the Pitt Professor of American History and Institutions, Cambridge University (1990–1991); the Harmsworth Professor of American History at Oxford University (2000–2001); and was a recipient of the Humboldt Prize (Germany). His most recent book is *American Insurgents: The Revolution of the People Before Independence* (2010).

R. HAL WILLIAMS

R. Hal Williams is a professor of history at Southern Methodist University. He received his A.B. from Princeton University in 1963 and his Ph.D. from Yale University in 1968. His books include *The Democratic Party and California Politics, 1880–1896* (1973), *Years of Decision: American Politics in the 1890s* (1978), and *The Manhattan Project: A Documentary Introduction to the Atomic Age* (1990). A specialist in American political history, he taught at Yale University from 1968 to 1975 and came to SMU in 1975 as chair of the Department of History. From 1980 to 1988, he served as dean of Dedman College, the School of Humanities and Sciences, at SMU, where he is currently dean of Research and Graduate Studies. In 1980, he was a visiting professor at University College, Oxford University. Williams has received grants from the American Philosophical Society and the National Endowment for the Humanities, and he has served on the Texas Committee for the Humanities. He has recently completed *Realigning America: McKinley, Bryan, and the Remarkable Election of 1896*, which published in 2010. Hal Williams thanks Linda and Lise Williams for support at crucial moments; Susan Harper; Billie Stovall, the core of SMU's Interlibrary Loan system; and above all, Peggy Varghese who helped in every way.

ARIELA J. GROSS

Ariela J. Gross is the John B. and Alice R. Sharp Professor of Law and History at the University of Southern California. She is the author of *Double Character: Slavery and Mastery in the Antebellum Southern Courtroom* (2000) and *What Blood Won't Tell: A History of Race on Trial in America* (2008), winner of the

2009 Willard Hurst Prize for sociolegal history from the Law and Society Association. She has also published numerous law review articles and book chapters, including most recently, "When Is the Time of Slavery? The History of Slavery in Contemporary Legal and Political Argument," in the *California Law Review*. She received her B.A. from Harvard University, her J.D. from Stanford Law School, and her Ph.D. from Stanford University, and she is the recipient of a Guggenheim Fellowship, a National Endowment for the Humanities Long-Term Fellowship at the Huntington Library, and a Frederick J. Burkhardt Fellowship from the American Council for Learned Societies. She has been a visiting professor at Tel Aviv University and the École des Hautes études en Sciences Sociales.

H. W. BRANDS

 H. W. Brands is the Dickson Allen Anderson Centennial Professor of History at the University of Texas at Austin. He is the author of numerous works of history and international affairs, including *The Devil We Knew: Americans and the Cold War* (1993), *Into the Labyrinth: The United States and the Middle East* (1994), *The Reckless Decade: America in the 1890s* (1995), *TR: The Last Romantic (a biography of Theodore Roosevelt)* (1997), *What America Owes the World: The Struggle for the Soul of Foreign Policy* (1998), *The First American: The Life and Times of Benjamin Franklin* (2000), *The Strange Death of American Liberalism* (2001), *The Age of Gold: The California Gold Rush and the New American Dream* (2002), *Woodrow Wilson* (2003), *Andrew Jackson* (2005), *Traitor to His Class: The Privileged Life and Radical Presidency of Franklin Delano Roosevelt* (2008), and *American Colossus: The Triumph of Capitalism, 1865–1900* (2010). His writing has received popular and critical acclaim; several of his books have been bestsellers, and *The First American* and *Traitor to His Class* were finalists for the Pulitzer Prize. He lectures frequently across North America and in Europe. His essays and reviews have appeared in the *New York Times*, the *Wall Street Journal*, the *Washington Post*, the *Los Angeles Times*, *Atlantic Monthly*, and elsewhere. He is a regular guest on radio and television, and has participated in several historical documentary films.

Author Responsibility

Although this book is a joint effort, each author took primary responsibility for writing one section. T. H. Breen contributed the first eight chapters, going from the earliest Native American period to the second decade of the nineteenth century. Ariela J. Gross worked on Chapters 9 through 16, carrying the narrative through the Reconstruction era. R. Hal Williams was responsible for Chapters 17 through 24, focusing on the industrial transformation, urbanization, and the events culminating in World War I. The final eight chapters, bringing the story through the Great Depression, World War II, the Cold War and its aftermath, the wars in Iraq and Afghanistan, and culminating in the historic election of Barack Obama, were the work of H. W. Brands. Each contributor reviewed and revised the work of his or her colleagues and helped shape the material into its final form.

Supplements

Name of Supplement	Supplements for Qualified College Adopters	Name of Supplement	Supplements for Students
MyHistoryLab	MyHistoryLab (www.myhistorylab.com) **The moment you know** Educators know it. Students know it. It's that inspired moment when something that was difficult to understand suddenly makes perfect sense. Our MyLab products have been designed and refined with a single purpose in mind: to help educators create that moment of understanding with their students.	**MyHistoryLab**	MyHistoryLab (www.myhistorylab.com) **The moment you know** Educators know it. Students know it. It's that inspired moment when something that was difficult to understand suddenly makes perfect sense. Our MyLab products have been designed and refined with a single purpose in mind: to help educators create that moment of understanding with their students.
Instructor's Resource Manual with Test Bank	Available at the Instructor's Resource Center, at **www.pearsonhighered.com/ irc**, the Instructor's Resource Manual with Test Bank contains chapter overviews, key points and discussion questions, suggested assignments, and information on audio-visual resources that can be used in developing and preparing lecture presentations. The Test Bank includes multiple choice and essay questions that are both general and text specific. It also contains brief answers to all the questions in the textbook—learning objective questions, review questions, and questions for analysis.	**CourseSmart**	**www.coursemart.com** CourseSmart eTextbooks offer the same content as the printed text in a convenient online format— with highlighting, online search, and printing capabilities. You **save 60% over the list price** of the traditional book.
Annotated Instructor's eText	Housed in the instructor's space within MyHistoryLab, the *Annotated Instructor's eText* for *America Past and Present* (tenth edition) leverages the powerful Pearson eText platform to make it easier than ever for teachers to access subject-specific resources for class preparation.	**Books à la Carte**	Books à la Carte editions feature the exact same content as the traditional printed text in a convenient, three-hole-punched, loose-leaf version at a discounted price—allowing you to take only what you need to class. You'll **save 35% over the net price** of the traditional book. **V1 - ISBN: 0205910084; ISBN-13: 9780205910083; V2 - ISBN: 0205910092; ISBN-13: 9780205910090**
PowerPoint Presentation	Available at the Instructor's Resource Center, at **www.pearsonhighered.com/ irc**, it's text specific and available for download. The PowerPoint slides to accompany *America Past and Present* (tenth edition) include an outline of each chapter and full-color images, maps, and figures from the textbook. All images from the textbook have corresponding teaching notes that provide background information about the image and teaching strategies.	**Library of American Biography Series**	www.pearsonhighered.com/educator/ series/Library-of-American- Biography/10493.page Here you'll find Pearson's renowned series of biographies spotlighting figures who had a significant impact on American history. Included in the series are Edmund Morgan's *The Puritan Dilemma: The Story of John Winthrop*, B. Davis Edmund's *Tecumseh and the Quest for Indian Leadership*, J. William T. Youngs' *Eleanor Roosevelt: A Personal and Public Life*, John R. M. Wilson's *Jackie Robinson and the American Dilemma*, and Sandra Opdycke's *Jane Addams and her Vision for America*.

Name of Supplement	Supplements for Qualified College Adopters	Name of Supplement	Supplements for Students
MyTest	Available at **www.pearsonmytest.com**, MyTest contains a diverse set of over 2,300 multiple-choice, true-false, and essay questions, with a test bank that supports a variety of assessment strategies. The large pool of multiple choice questions for each chapter includes factual, conceptual, and analytical questions, so that instructors may assess students on basic information as well as critical thinking. The MyTest program helps instructors easily create and print quizzes and exams. Questions and tests can be authored online, allowing instructors ultimate flexibility and the ability to efficiently manage assessments anytime, anywhere! Instructors can easily access existing questions and edit, create, and store using simple drag-and-drop and Word-like controls.	**Penguin Valuepacks**	**www.pearsonhighered.com/penguin** A variety of Penguin-Putnam texts is available at discounted prices when bundled with *America Past and Present,* 10/e. Texts include Benjamin Franklin's *Autobiography and Other Writings,* Nathaniel Hawthorne's *The Scarlet Letter,* Thomas Jefferson's *Notes on the State of Virginia,* and George Orwell's *1984.*
Retreiving the American Past	Available through the Pearson Custom Library (**www.pearsoncustom.com, keyword search | rtap**), the *Retrieving the American Past* (RTAP) program lets you create a textbook or reader that meets your needs and the needs of your course. RTAP gives you the freedom and flexibility to add chapters from several best-selling Pearson textbooks, in addition to *America Past and Present (tenth edition)* and/or 100 topical reading units written by the History Department of Ohio State University, all under one cover. Choose the content you want to teach in depth, in the sequence you want, at the price you want your students to pay.	***A Short Guide to Writing About History, 8/e***	Written by Richard A. Marius, late of Harvard University, and Melvin E. Page, Eastern Tennessee State University, this engaging and practical text helps students get beyond merely compiling dates and facts. Covering both brief essays and the documented resource paper, the text explores the writing and researching processes, identifies different modes of historical writing, including argument, and concludes with guidelines for improving style. **ISBN-10: 0205118607; ISBN-13: 9780205118601**
		Longman American History Atlas	This full-color historical atlas designed especially for college students is a valuable reference tool and visual guide to American history. This atlas includes maps covering the scope of American history from the lives of the Native Americans to the 1990s. Produced by a renowned cartographic firm and a team of respected historians, the *Longman American History Atlas* will enhance any American history survey course. **ISBN: 0321004868; ISBN-13: 9780321004864**

America Past and Present
Tenth Edition

MyHistoryLab

The Moment You Know

Educators know it. Students know it. It's that inspired moment when something that was difficult to understand suddenly makes perfect sense. Our MyLab products have been designed and refined with a single purpose in mind—to help educators create that moment of understanding with their students.

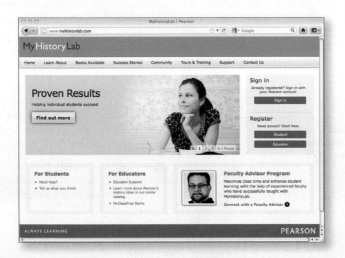

The new MyHistoryLab delivers **proven results** in helping individual students succeed. It provides **engaging experiences** that personalize, stimulate, and measure learning for each student. And, it comes from a **trusted partner** with educational expertise and a deep commitment to helping students, instructors, and departments achieve their goals.

A personalized study plan for each student, based on Bloom's Taxonomy, promotes critical-thinking skills, and helps students succeed in the course and beyond.

Assessment tied to every video, application, and chapter enables both instructors and students to track progress and get immediate feedback—and helps instructors to find the best resources with which to help students.

The **Pearson eText** lets students access their textbook anytime, anywhere, and any way they want. Just like the printed text, students can highlight relevant passages and add their own notes. For even greater flexibility, students can download the eText to an iPad using the free Pearson eText app. And, students can even listen to their text, streaming **full chapter audio** on their computers.

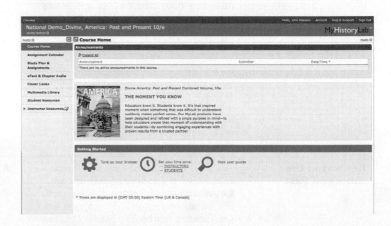

Closer Look tours walk students through key primary sources in detail, helping them to uncover their meaning and understand their context.

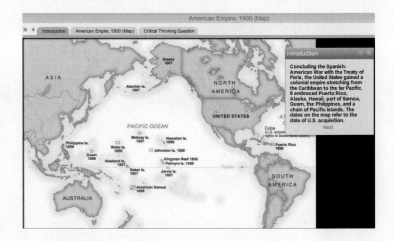

Author Video Lectures with Pearson history authors help students achieve a deeper understanding of key topics and themes. These narrated clips feature documentary images that capture students' attention.

Class Prep collects the very best class presentation resources in one convenient online destination, so instructors can keep students engaged throughout every class.

Writing Assessment

Get your students writing more, and learning more, with automated writing assessment in MyHistoryLab. Although history instructors agree that student writing is the best measure of higher order thinking for their students, less writing is being assigned because the challenge of grading hundreds of student essays is too great. Now MyHistoryLab can help solve the problem. Path-breaking innovations from Pearson have made possible automated scoring and feedback of student essays. Ten writing prompts correlated with *America Past and Present* appear in the text's New MyHistoryLab course.

Key Supplements

Annotated Instructor's eText

Contained within MyHistoryLab, the *Annotated Instructor's eText* for *America Past and Present* (tenth edition), leverages the powerful Pearson eText platform to make it easier than ever for teachers to access subject-specific resources for class preparation. The *AI eText* serves as the hub for all instructor resources, with chapter-by-chapter links to PowerPoint slides, content from the Instructor's Manual, and to *MyHistoryLab's* ClassPrep engine, which contains a wealth of history content organized for classroom use.

Instructor's Manual

The Instructor's Manual contains chapter overview, lecture supplements, discussion questions, suggested assignments, and research resources for each chapter, including both general and text-specific content. It also contains brief answers to all the questions in the textbook—learning objective questions, essay questions for discussion, review questions, and critical thinking questions—along with the text of the questions themselves.

PowerPoint Presentation

The PowerPoint slides to accompany *America Past and Present* (tenth edition), include an outline of each chapter and full-color images, maps, and figures from the textbook.

MyTest Test Bank

Creating a diverse set of multiple choice and essay questions, the MyTest test bank supports a variety of assessment strategies. The large pool of multiple choice questions for each chapter includes factual, conceptual, and analytical questions, so that instructors may assess students on basic information as well as critical thinking.

1 New World Encounters

Contents and Learning Objectives

((•——Listen to the Audio File on myhistorylab   Chapter 1 *New World Encounters*

Clash of Cultures: Interpreting Murder in Early Maryland

New World conquest sparked unexpected, often embarrassing contests over the alleged superiority of European culture. Not surprisingly, the colonizers insisted they brought the benefits of civilization to the primitive and savage peoples of North America. Native Americans never shared this perspective, voicing a strong preference for their own values and institutions. In early seventeenth-century Maryland the struggle over cultural superiority turned dramatically on how best to punish the crime of murder, an issue about which both Native Americans and Europeans had firm opinions.

The actual events that occurred at Captain William Claiborne's trading post in 1635 may never be known. Surviving records indicate that several young males identified as Wicomess Indians apparently traveled to Claiborne's on business, but to their great annoyance, they found the proprietor entertaining Susquehannock Indians, their most hated enemies. The situation deteriorated rapidly after the Susquehannock men

ridiculed the Wicomess youths, "whereat some of Claiborne's people that saw it, did laugh." Unwilling to endure public humiliation, the Wicomess later ambushed the Susquehannock group, killing five, and then returned to the trading post where they murdered three Englishmen.

Wicomess leaders realized immediately that something had to be done. They dispatched a trusted messenger to inform the governor of Maryland that they intended "to offer satisfaction for the harm . . . done to the English." The murder of the Susquehannock was another matter, best addressed by the Native Americans themselves. The governor praised the Wicomess for coming forward, announcing that "I expect that those men, who have done this outrage, should be delivered unto me, to do with them as I shall think fit."

The Wicomess spokesman was dumbfounded. The governor surely did not understand basic Native American legal procedure. "It is the manner amongst

Europeans imagined a New World that often bore little relation to reality. This early engraving depicts the coast of North America as a dangerous place where hostile Indians, bizarre navigational hazards, and sea monsters greeted English sailors.

us Indians, that if any such like accident happens," he explained, "we do redeem the life of a man that is so slain with a 100 Arms length of Roanoke (which is a sort of Beads that they make, and use for money.)" The governor's demand for prisoners seemed doubly impertinent, "since you [English settlers] are here strangers, and coming into our Country, you should rather conform your selves to the Customs of our Country, than impose yours upon us." At this point the governor hastily ended

the conversation, perhaps uncomfortably aware that if the legal tables had been turned and the murders committed in England, he would be the one loudly defending "the Customs of our Country."

Europeans sailing in the wake of Admiral Christopher Columbus constructed a narrative of superiority that survived long after the Wicomess had been dispersed—a fate that befell them in the late seventeenth century. The story recounted first in Europe and then in the United States depicted heroic adventures, missionaries, and soldiers sharing Western civilization with the peoples of the New World and opening a vast virgin land to economic development. The familiar tale celebrated material progress, the inevitable spread of European values, and the taming of frontiers. It was a history crafted by the victors—usually by white leaders such as Maryland's governor—and by the children of the victors to explain how they had come to inherit the land.

This narrative of events no longer provides an adequate explanation for European conquest and settlement. It is not so much wrong as partisan, incomplete, even offensive. History recounted from the perspective of the victors inevitably silences the voices of the victims, the peoples who, in the victors' view, foolishly resisted economic and technological progress. Heroic tales of the advance of Western values only serve to deflect modern attention away from the rich cultural and racial diversity that characterized North American societies for a very long time. More disturbing, traditional tales of European conquest also obscure the sufferings of the millions of Native Americans who perished, as well as the huge numbers of Africans sold in the New World as slaves.

By placing these complex, often unsettling, experiences within an interpretive framework of creative adaptations—rather than of exploration or settlement—we go a long way toward recapturing the full human dimensions of conquest and resistance. While the New World often witnessed tragic violence and systematic betrayal, it allowed ordinary people of three different races and many different ethnic identities opportunities to shape their own lives as best they could within diverse, often hostile, environments.

It should be remembered that neither the Native Americans nor the Africans were passive victims of European exploitation. Within their own families and communities they made choices, sometimes rebelling, sometimes accommodating, but always trying to make sense in terms of their own cultures of what was happening to them. Of course, that was precisely what the Wicomess messenger tried to tell the governor of Maryland.

Native American Histories Before the Conquest

What explains cultural differences among Native American groups before European conquest?

As almost any Native American could have informed the first European adventurers, the peopling of America did not begin in 1492. In fact, although European invaders such as Columbus proclaimed the discovery of a "New World," they really brought into contact three worlds—Europe, Africa, and America—that in the fifteenth century were already old. Indeed, the first migrants reached the North American continent some fifteen to twenty thousand years ago. The precise dating of this great human trek remains a hotly contested topic. Although some archaeologists maintain that settlement began as early as thirty thousand years ago, the scientific evidence in support of this thesis currently is not persuasive. However this debate eventually resolves itself; no one doubts that Native Americans have

recorded a very long history in North America. Their social and cultural development over the period was as complex as any encountered in the so-called Old World.

Environmental conditions played a major part in the story. Twenty thousand years ago the earth's climate was considerably colder than it is today. Huge glaciers, often more than a mile thick, extended as far south as the present states of Illinois and Ohio and covered broad sections of western Canada. Much of the world's moisture was transformed into ice, and the oceans dropped hundreds of feet below their current levels. The receding waters created a land bridge connecting Asia and North America, a region now submerged beneath the Bering Sea that modern archaeologists named **Beringia**.

Even at the height of the last Ice Age, much of the far North remained free of glaciers. Small bands of spear-throwing Paleo-Indians pursued giant mammals (megafauna)—woolly mammoths and mastodons, for example—across the vast tundra of Beringia. These hunters were the first human beings to set foot on a vast, uninhabited continent. Because these migrations took place over a long period of time and involved small, independent bands of highly nomadic people, the Paleo-Indians never developed a sense of common identity. Each group focused on its own immediate survival, adjusting to the opportunities presented by various microenvironments.

The material culture of the Paleo-Indians differed little from that of other Stone Age peoples found in Asia, Africa, and Europe. In terms of human health, however, something occurred on the Beringian tundra that forever altered the history of Native Americans. For reasons that remain obscure, the members of these small migrating groups stopped hosting a number of communicative diseases—smallpox and measles being the deadliest—and although Native Americans experienced illnesses such as tuberculosis, they no longer suffered the major epidemics that under normal conditions would have killed a large percentage of their population every year. The physical isolation of the various bands may have protected them from the spread of contagious disease. Another theory notes that epidemics have frequently been associated with prolonged contact with domestic animals such as cattle and pigs. Since the Paleo-Indians did not domesticate animals, not even horses, they may have avoided the microbes that caused virulent European and African diseases.

Whatever the explanation for this curious epidemiological record, Native Americans lost inherited immunities that later might have protected them from many contagious germs. Thus, when they first came into contact with Europeans and Africans, Native Americans had no defense against the great killers of the Early Modern world. And, as medical researchers have discovered, dislocations resulting from war and famine made the Indians even more vulnerable to infectious disease.

The Environmental Challenge: Food, Climate, and Culture

Some twelve thousand years ago global warming substantially reduced the glaciers, allowing nomadic hunters to pour into the heart of the North American continent. Within just a few thousand years, Native Americans had journeyed from Colorado to the southern tip of South America. Blessed with a seemingly inexhaustible supply of meat, the early migrants experienced rapid population growth. As archaeologists have discovered, however, the sudden expansion of human population coincided with the loss of scores of large mammals, many of them the spear-throwers' favorite sources of food. The animals that died out during this period included mammoths and mastodons; camels and, amazingly, horses were eradicated from the land. The peoples of the Great Plains did not obtain horses until the Spanish reintroduced them in the New World in 1547. Some archaeologists have suggested that the early Paleo-Indian hunters bear responsibility for the mass extinction of so many animals. It is more probable that climatic warming, which transformed well-watered regions into arid territories, put the large mammals under severe stress, and the early humans simply contributed to an ecological process over which they ultimately had little control.

The Indian peoples adjusted to the changing environmental conditions. As they dispersed across the North American continent, they developed new food sources, at first smaller mammals and fish, nuts and berries, and then about five thousand years ago, they discovered how to cultivate certain plants. Knowledge of maize (corn), squash, and beans spread north from central Mexico. The peoples living in the Southwest acquired cultivation skills long before the bands living along the Atlantic Coast. The shift to basic crops—a transformation that is sometimes termed the **Agricultural Revolution**—profoundly altered Native American societies. The availability of a more reliable store of food helped liberate nomadic groups from the insecurities of hunting and gathering. It was during this period that Native Americans began to produce ceramics, a valuable technology for the storage of grain. The vegetable harvest made possible the establishment of permanent villages, that often were governed by clearly defined hierarchies of elders and kings, and as the food supply increased, the Native American population greatly expanded, especially around urban centers in the Southwest and in the Mississippi Valley. Although the evidence is patchy, scholars currently estimate that approximately four million Native Americans lived north of Mexico at the time of the initial encounter with Europeans.

Mysterious Disappearances

Several magnificent sites in North America provide powerful testimony to the cultural and social achievements of native peoples during the final two thousand years before European conquest. One of the more impressive is Chaco Canyon on

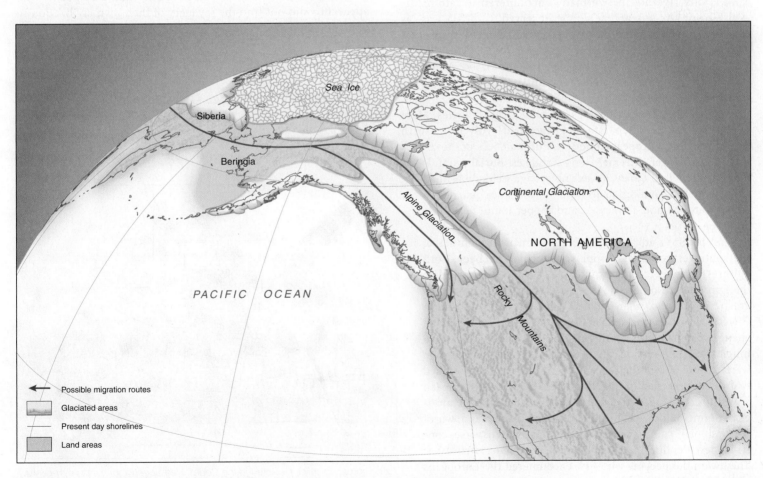

ROUTES OF THE FIRST AMERICANS The peopling of North America began about twenty thousand years ago, during an ice age, and continued for many millennia. Land bridges created by lower sea levels during glaciation formed a tundra coastal plain over what is now the Bering Strait, between Asia and North America.

the San Juan River in present-day New Mexico. The massive pueblo was the center of Anasazi culture, serving both political and religious functions, and it is estimated that its complex structures may have housed as many as fifteen thousand people. The Anasazi sustained their agriculture through a huge, technologically sophisticated network of irrigation canals that carried water long distances. They also constructed a transportation system connecting Chaco Canyon by road to more than seventy outlying villages. Some of the highways were almost a hundred miles long.

During this period equally impressive urban centers developed throughout the Ohio and Mississippi valleys. In present-day southern Ohio, the Adena and Hopewell peoples—names assigned by archaeologists to distinguish differences in material culture—built large ceremonial mounds, where they buried the families of local elites. Approximately a thousand years after the birth of Christ, the groups gave way to the Mississippian culture, a loose collection of communities dispersed along the Mississippi River from Louisiana to Illinois that shared similar technologies and beliefs. Cahokia, a huge fortification and ceremonial site in Illinois that originally rose high above the river, represented the greatest achievement of the Mississippian peoples. Covering almost twenty acres, Cahokia once supported a population of almost twenty thousand, a city rivaling in size many encountered in late medieval Europe. As one archaeologist observed, Cahokia was "as spectacular as any of the magnificent Mexican civilizations that were its contemporaries."

Recent research reveals that the various Native American peoples did not live in isolated communities. To be sure, over the millennia they developed many different cultural and social practices, reflecting the specific constraints of local ecologies. More than three hundred separate languages had evolved in North America before European conquest. But members of the groups traded goods over extremely long distances. Burial mounds found in the Ohio Valley, for example, have yielded obsidian from western Wyoming, shells from Florida, mica quarried in North Carolina and Tennessee, and copper found near Lake Superior.

Yet however advanced the Native American cultures of the southwest and Mississippi Valley may have been, both cultures disappeared mysteriously just before the arrival of the Europeans. No one knows what events brought down the great city of Cahokia or persuaded the Anasazi to abandon Chaco Canyon. Some scholars have suggested that climatic changes coupled with continuing population growth put too much pressure on food supplies; others insist that chronic warfare destabilized the social order. It has even been argued that diseases carried to the New World by the first European adventurers ravaged the cultures. About one point modern commentators are in full agreement: The breakdown of Mississippian culture caused smaller bands to disperse, construct new identities, and establish different political structures. They were the peoples who first encountered the Europeans along the Atlantic coast and who seemed to the newcomers to have lived in the same places and followed the same patterns of behavior since the dawn of time.

Aztec Dominance

The stability resulting from the Agricultural Revolution allowed the Indians of Mexico and Central America to structure their societies in more complex ways. Like the Inca who lived in what is now known as Peru, the Mayan and Toltec peoples of Central Mexico built vast cities, formed government bureaucracies that dominated large tributary populations, and developed hieroglyphic writing as well as an accurate solar calendar. Their cities, which housed several hundred thousand people, greatly impressed the Spanish conquerors. Bernal Díaz del Castillo reported, "When we saw all those [Aztec] towns and villages built in the water, and other great towns on dry land, and that straight and level causeway leading to Mexico, we were astounded. . . . Indeed, some of our soldiers asked whether it was not all a dream."

Not long before Columbus began his first voyage across the Atlantic, the Aztec, an aggressive, warlike people, swept through the Valley of Mexico, conquering the great cities that their enemies had constructed. Aztec warriors ruled by force, reducing defeated rivals to tributary status. In 1519, the Aztecs' main ceremonial center, Tenochtitlán, contained as many as two hundred fifty thousand people as compared with only fifty thousand in Seville, the port from which the early Spaniards had sailed. Elaborate human sacrifice associated with Huitzilopochtli, the Aztec sun god, horrified Europeans, who apparently did not find the savagery of their own civilization so objectionable. The Aztec ritual killings were connected to the agricultural cycle, and the Indians believed the blood of their victims possessed extraordinary fertility powers.

Eastern Woodland Cultures

In the northeast region along the Atlantic coast, the Indians did not practice intensive agriculture. These peoples, numbering less than a million at the time of conquest, generally supplemented

Aztec human sacrifice depicted in the *Codex Magliabechiano*, a sixteenth-century Spanish account of the lives of the native Mexicans. The ritual sacrifices performed by Aztec priests were associated with worship of the sun god—each offering was considered a sacred debt payment.

farming with seasonal hunting and gathering. Most belonged to what ethnographers term the **Eastern Woodland Cultures**. Small bands formed villages during the warm summer months. The women cultivated maize and other crops while the men hunted and fished. During the winter, difficulties associated with feeding so many people forced the communities to disperse. Each family lived off the land as best it could.

Seventeenth-century English settlers were most likely to have encountered the Algonquian-speaking peoples who occupied much of the territory along the Atlantic coast from North Carolina to Maine. Included in this large linguistic family were the Powhatan of Tidewater Virginia, the Narragansett of Rhode Island, and the Abenaki of northern New England.

Despite common linguistic roots, however, the scattered Algonquian communities would have found communication extremely difficult. They had developed very different dialects. A sixteenth-century Narragansett, for example, would have found it hard to comprehend a Powhatan. The major groups of the Southeast, such as the Creek, belonged to a separate language group (Muskogean); the Indians of the eastern Great Lakes region and upper St. Lawrence Valley generally spoke Iroquoian dialects.

Linguistic ties had little effect on Indian politics. Algonquian groups who lived in different regions, exploited different resources, and spoke different dialects did not develop strong ties of mutual identity, and when their own interests were involved, they were more than willing to ally themselves with Europeans or "foreign" Indians against other Algonquian speakers. Divisions among Indian groups would in time facilitate European conquest. Local Native American peoples greatly outnumbered the first settlers, and had the Europeans not forged alliances with the Indians, they could not so easily have gained a foothold on the continent.

However divided the Indians of eastern North America may have been, they shared many cultural values and assumptions. Most Native Americans, for example, defined their place in society through kinship. Such personal bonds determined the character of economic and political relations. The farming bands living in areas eventually claimed by England were often matrilineal, which meant, in effect, that the women owned the planting fields and houses, maintained tribal customs, and had a role in tribal government. Among the native communities of Canada and the northern Great Lakes, patrilineal forms were much more common. In these groups, the men owned the hunting grounds that the family needed to survive.

Eastern Woodland communities organized diplomacy, trade, and war around reciprocal relationships that impressed Europeans as being extraordinarily egalitarian, even democratic. Chains of native authority were loosely structured. Native leaders were such renowned public speakers because

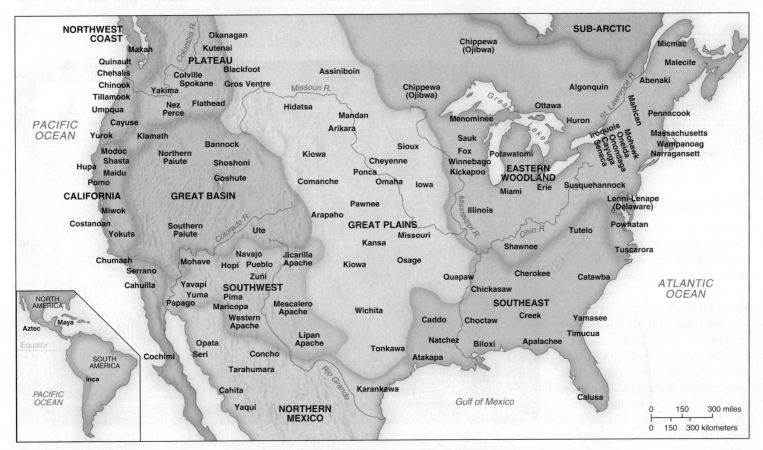

THE FIRST AMERICANS: LOCATION OF MAJOR INDIAN GROUPS AND CULTURE AREAS IN THE 1600s Native Americans had complex social structures, religious systems, and sophisticated agricultural techniques before they came into contact with Europeans.

persuasive rhetoric was often their only effective source of power. It required considerable oratorical skills for an Indian leader to persuade independent-minded warriors to support a certain policy.

Before the arrival of the white settlers, Indian wars were seldom very lethal. Young warriors attacked neighboring bands largely to exact revenge for a previous insult or the death of a relative, or to secure captives. Fatalities, when they did occur, sparked cycles of revenge. Some captives were tortured to death; others were adopted into the community as replacements for fallen relatives.

A World Transformed

How did Europeans and Native Americans interact during the period of first contact?

The arrival of large numbers of white men and women on the North American continent profoundly altered Native American cultures. Change did not occur at the same rates in all places. Indian villages located on the Atlantic coast came under severe pressure almost immediately; inland groups had more time to adjust. Wherever they lived, however, Indians discovered that conquest strained traditional ways of life, and as daily patterns of experience changed almost beyond recognition, native peoples had to devise new answers, new responses, and new ways to survive in physical and social environments that eroded tradition. Historian James Merrell reminded us that the Indians found themselves living in a world that from their perspective was just as "new" as that which greeted the European invaders.

Cultural Negotiations

Native Americans were not passive victims of geopolitical forces beyond their control. So long as they remained healthy, they held their own in the early exchanges, and although they eagerly accepted certain trade goods, they generally resisted other aspects of European cultures. The earliest recorded contacts between Indians and explorers suggest curiosity and surprise rather than hostility. A Southeastern Indian who encountered Hernando de Soto in 1540 expressed awe (at least that is what a Spanish witness recorded): "The things that seldom happen bring astonishment. Think, then, what must be the effect on me and mine, the sight of you and your people, whom we have at no time seen . . . things so altogether new, as to strike awe and terror to our hearts."

What Indians desired most was peaceful trade. The earliest French explorers reported that natives waved from shore, urging the Europeans to exchange metal items for beaver skins. In fact, the Indians did not perceive themselves at a disadvantage in these dealings. They could readily see the technological advantage of guns over bows and arrows. Metal knives made daily tasks much easier. And to acquire such goods they gave up pelts, which to them seemed in abundant supply. "The English have no sense," one Indian informed a French priest. "They give us twenty knives like this for one Beaver skin." Another native announced that "the Beaver does everything perfectly well: it makes kettles, hatchets, swords, knives, bread . . . in short, it makes everything." The man who recorded these observations reminded French readers—in case they had missed the point—that the Indian was "making sport of us Europeans."

Trading sessions along the eastern frontier were really cultural seminars. The Europeans tried to make sense out of Indian customs, and although they may have called the natives "savages," they quickly discovered that the Indians drove hard bargains. They demanded gifts; they set the time and place of trade.

 View the **Closer Look** An Early European Image of Native Americans

Europeans first learned of Native Americans from the sailors who followed Columbus. Images, such as this one from 1505, show the Indians as lustful, scantily-clad, cannibals. The fact that the male subjects in this image have beards—common on European men at the time, but virtually unknown among Native Americans—confirms that the artist had never actually laid eyes on the people he meant to portray.

The Indians used the occasions to study the newcomers. They formed opinions about the Europeans, some flattering, some less so, but they never concluded from their observations that Indian culture was inferior to that of the colonizers. They regarded the beards worn by European men as particularly revolting. As an eighteenth-century Englishman said of the Iroquois, "They seem always to have Looked upon themselves as far Superior to the rest of Mankind and accordingly Call themselves *Ongwehoenwe,* i.e., Men Surpassing all other men."

For Europeans, communicating with the Indians was always an ordeal. The invaders reported having gained deep insight into Native American cultures through sign languages. How much accurate information explorers and traders took from these crude improvised exchanges is a matter of conjecture. In a letter written in 1493, Columbus expressed frustration: "I did not understand those people nor they me, except for what common sense dictated, although they were saddened and I much more so, because I wanted to have good information concerning everything."

In the absence of meaningful conversation, Europeans often concluded that the Indians held them in high regard, perhaps seeing the newcomers as gods. Such one-sided encounters involved a good deal of projection, a mental process of translating alien sounds and gestures into messages that Europeans wanted to hear. Sometimes the adventurers did not even try to communicate, assuming from superficial observation—as did the sixteenth-century explorer Giovanni da Verrazzano—"that they have no religion, and that they live in absolute freedom, and that everything they do proceeds from Ignorance."

Ethnocentric Europeans tried repeatedly to "civilize" the Indians. In practice that meant persuading natives to dress like the colonists, attend white schools, live in permanent structures, and, most important, accept Christianity. The Indians listened more or less patiently, but in the end, they usually rejected European values. One South Carolina trader explained that when Indians were asked to become more English, they said no, "for they thought it hard, that we should desire them to change their manners and customs, since they did not desire us to turn Indians."

To be sure, some Indians were strongly attracted to Christianity, but most paid it lip service or found it irrelevant to their needs. As one Huron told a French priest, "It would be useless for me to repent having sinned, seeing that I never have sinned." Another Huron announced that he did not fear punishment after death since "we cannot tell whether everything that appears faulty to Men, is so in the Eyes of God."

Among some Indian groups, gender figured significantly in a person's willingness to convert to Christianity. Native men who traded animal skins for European goods had more frequent contact with the whites, and they proved more receptive to the arguments of missionaries. But native women jealously guarded traditional culture, a system that often sanctioned polygamy—a husband having several wives—and gave women substantial authority over the distribution of food within the village. French Jesuits seemed especially eager to undermine the independence of Native American women. Among other demands, missionaries insisted on monogamous marriages, an institution based on Christian values but that made little sense in Indian societies where constant warfare against the Europeans killed off large numbers of young males and increasingly left native women without sufficient marriage partners.

The white settlers' educational system proved no more successful than their religion was in winning cultural converts. Young Indian scholars deserted stuffy classrooms at the first chance. In 1744, Virginia offered several Iroquois boys a free education at the College of William and Mary. The Iroquois leaders rejected the invitation because they found that boys who had gone to college "were absolutely good for nothing being neither acquainted with the true methods of killing deer, catching Beaver, or surprising an enemy."

Even matrimony seldom eroded the Indians' attachment to their own customs. When Native Americans and whites married—unions the English found less desirable than did the French or Spanish—the European partner usually elected to live among the Indians. Impatient settlers who regarded the Indians simply as an obstruction to progress sometimes developed more coercive methods, such as enslavement, to achieve cultural conversion. Again, from the white perspective, the results were disappointing. Indian slaves ran away or died. In either case, they did not become Europeans.

Threats to Survival: Trade and Disease

Over time, cooperative encounters between the Native Americans and Europeans became less frequent. The Europeans found it almost impossible to understand the Indians' relation to the land and other natural resources. English planters cleared the forests and fenced the fields and, in the process, radically altered the ecological systems on which the Indians depended. The European system of land use inevitably reduced the supply of deer and other animals essential to traditional native cultures.

Dependency also came in more subtle forms. The Indians welcomed European commerce, but like so many consumers throughout recorded history, they discovered that the objects they most coveted inevitably brought them into debt. To pay for the trade goods, the Indians hunted more aggressively and even further reduced the population of fur-bearing mammals.

Commerce eroded Indian independence in other ways. After several disastrous wars—the Yamasee War in South Carolina (1715), for example—the natives learned that demonstrations of force usually resulted in the suspension of normal trade, on which the Indians had grown quite dependent for guns and ammunition, among other things. A hardened English businessman made the point quite bluntly. When asked if the Catawba Indians would harm his traders, he responded that "the danger would be . . . little from them, because they are too fond of our trade to lose it for the pleasure of shedding a little English blood."

It was disease, however, that ultimately destroyed the cultural integrity of many North American tribes. European adventurers exposed the Indians to bacteria and viruses against which they possessed no natural immunity. Smallpox, measles, and influenza decimated the Native American population. Other diseases such as alcoholism took a terrible toll.

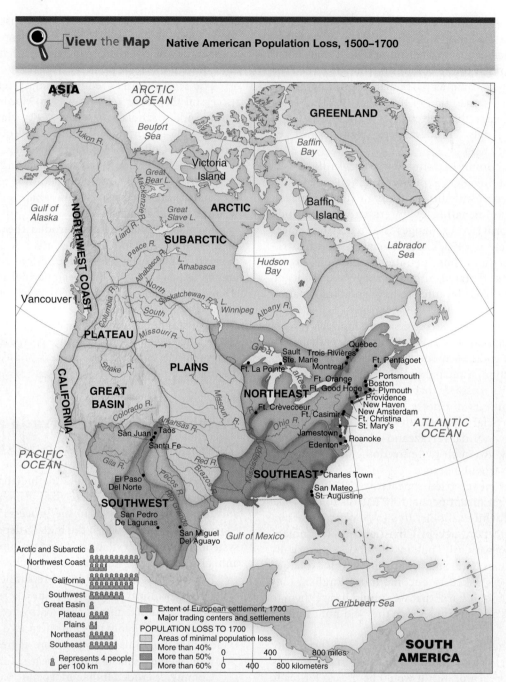

View the Map Native American Population Loss, 1500–1700

NATIVE AMERICAN POPULATION LOSS, 1500–1700 This interactive map demonstrates the pervasive Native American population loss in North America during the first two hundred years of their contact with Europeans. The map further illustrates that the highest percentage of Native American population loss occurred in North American regions initially under Spanish rule.

Within a generation of initial contact with Europeans, the Carib Indians, who gave the Caribbean its name, were virtually extinct. The decimation of Native American peoples was an aspect of ecological transformation known as the **Columbian Exchange**. European conquerors exposed the Indians to several new fatal diseases; the Indians introduced the invaders to marvelous plants such as corn and potatoes, which altered the course of European history. (See the Feature Essay, "The Columbian Exchange and the Global Environment: Ecological Revolution," pp. 12–13.)

The Algonquian communities of New England experienced appalling rates of death. One Massachusetts colonist reported in 1630 that the Indian peoples of his region "above twelve years since were swept away by a great & grievous Plague . . . so that there are verie few left to inhabite the Country." Settlers possessed no knowledge of germ theory—it was not formulated until the mid-nineteenth century—and speculated that a Christian God had providentially cleared the wilderness of heathens.

Historical demographers now estimate that some tribes suffered a 90 to 95 percent population loss within the first century of European contact. The population of the Arawak Indians of Santo Domingo, for example, dropped from about 3,770,000 in 1496 to only 125 in 1570. The death of so many Indians decreased the supply of indigenous laborers, who were needed by the Europeans to work the mines and to grow staple crops such as sugar and tobacco. The decimation of native populations may have persuaded colonists throughout the New World to seek a substitute labor force in Africa. Indeed, the enslavement of blacks has been described as an effort by Europeans to "repopulate" the New World.

Indians who survived the epidemics often found that the fabric of traditional culture had come unraveled. The enormity of the death toll and the agony that accompanied it called traditional religious beliefs and practices into question. The survivors lost not only members of their families, but also elders who might have told them how properly to bury the dead and give spiritual comfort to the living.

Some native peoples, such as the Iroquois, who lived a long way from the coast and thus had more time to adjust to the challenge, withstood the crisis better than did those who immediately confronted the Europeans and Africans. Refugee Indians from the hardest hit eastern communities were absorbed into healthier western groups. However horrific the crisis may have been, it demonstrated powerfully just how much the environment—a source of opportunity as well as devastation—shaped human encounters throughout the New World.

West Africa: Ancient and Complex Societies

What was the character of the West African societies that European traders first encountered?

During the era of the European slave trade, roughly from the late fifteenth through the mid-nineteenth centuries, a number of enduring myths about sub-Saharan West Africa were propagated. Even today, commentators claim that the people who inhabited this region four hundred years ago were isolated from the rest of the world and had a simple, self-sufficient economy. Indeed, some scholars still depict the vast region stretching from the Senegal River south to modern Angola as a single cultural unit, as if at one time all the men and women living there must have shared a common set of African political, religious, and social values.

Sub-Saharan West Africa defies such easy generalizations. The first Portuguese who explored the African coast during the fifteenth century encountered a great variety of political and religious cultures. Many hundreds of years earlier, Africans living in this region had come into contact with Islam, the religion founded by the Prophet Muhammad during the seventh century. Islam spread slowly from Arabia into West Africa. Not until AD 1030 did a kingdom located in the Senegal Valley accept the Muslim religion. Many other West Africans, such as those in ancient Ghana, resisted Islam and continued to observe traditional religions.

As Muslim traders from North Africa and the Middle East brought a new religion to parts of West Africa, they expanded sophisticated trade networks that linked the villagers of Senegambia with urban centers in northwest Africa, Morocco, Tunisia, and Cyrenaica. Great camel caravans regularly crossed the Sahara carrying trade goods that were exchanged for gold and slaves. Sub-Saharan Africa's well-developed links with Islam surprised a French priest who in 1686 observed African pilgrims going "to visit Mecca to visit Mahomet's tomb, although they are eleven or twelve hundred leagues distance from it."

West Africans spoke many languages and organized themselves into diverse political systems. Several populous states, sometimes termed "empires," exercised loose control over large areas. Ancient African empires such as Ghana were vulnerable to external attack as well as internal rebellion, and the oral and written histories of this region record the rise and fall of several large kingdoms. When European traders first arrived, the list of

Artists in West Africa depicted the European traders who arrived in search of gold and slaves. This sixteenth-century Benin bronze relief sculpture shows two Portuguese men.

Feature Essay

The Columbian Exchange and the Global Environment
Ecological Revolution

Modern Americans often speak of the degradation of the global environment in apocalyptic terms, as if the current generation confronts a unique challenge in world history. No doubt, many chemical compounds produced during the twentieth century have proved far more toxic than their inventors ever imagined. But contemporary concerns about the future of the planet should not cause us to lose sight of the historical sweep of these problems. We are certainly not the first society to experience a massive ecological transformation caused by the inevitable intervention of human beings into the processes of nature. Recapturing an earlier moment of environmental history—known as the Columbian Exchange—reminds us that the moral dimensions of change are often a matter of perspective. What one group proclaims as providential progress may strike others as utter disaster.

The first major "ecological revolution" occurred as a direct result of New World exploration during the fifteenth and sixteenth centuries. The earliest explorers had expected America to be an extension of Europe, a place inhabited by familiar plants and animals. They were surprised. The exotic flora of the New World, sketched from sixteenth-century drawings, included the food staple maize and the succulent pineapple. Equally strange to European eyes were buffalo, rattle snakes, catfish, and the peculiar absence of horses and cattle. No domestic animal was common to both sides of the Atlantic except the dog. And perhaps the most striking difference was between the people themselves. Both Native Americans and Europeans found each other to be the most exotic people they had ever encountered.

The most immediate biological consequence of contact between the people of Europe, Africa, and the New World was the transfer of disease. Within a year of Columbus's return from the Caribbean, a new and more virulent strain of syphilis appeared in Europe and became identified as the American disease. By 1505, syphilis had spread all the way to China. The effect of Old World diseases in the Americas was catastrophic. Native Americans had little natural immunity to common African and European diseases because America remained biologically isolated after the reimmersion of the Bering land bridge. When they were exposed to influenza, typhus, measles, and especially smallpox, they died by the millions. Indeed, European exploration of America set off the worst demographic disaster in world history. Within fifty years of the first contact, epidemics had virtually exterminated the native population of Hispaniola and devastated the densely populated Valley of Mexico.

Also unsettling, but by no means as destructive, was the transfer of plants and animals from the Old World to the New. Spanish colonizers carried sugar and bananas across the Atlantic, and in time these crops transformed the economies of Latin America. Even more spectacular was the success of European animals in America. During the sixteenth century, pigs, sheep, and cattle arrived as passengers on European ships, and in the fertile New World environment, they multiplied more rapidly than they had in Europe.

Some animals survived shipwrecks. On Sable Island, a small, desolate island off the coast of Nova Scotia, one can still see the small, longhaired cattle, the successors of the earliest cattle transported to America. Other animals escaped from the ranches of New Spain, generating new breeds such as the fabled Texas longhorn.

No European animal more profoundly affected Native American life than the horse. Once common in North America, the horse mysteriously disappeared from the continent sometime during the last Ice Age. The early Spanish explorers reintroduced the horse to North America, and the sight of this large, powerful animal at first terrified the Indians. Mounted conquistadores discovered that if they could not frighten Indian foes into submission, they could simply outmaneuver them on horseback. The Native Americans of the Southwest quickly adapted the horse to their own use. Sedentary farmers acquired new hunting skills, and soon the Indians were riding across the Great Plains in pursuit of buffalo. The Comanche, Apache, Sioux, and Blackfoot tribes—just to name a few—became dependent on the horse. Mounted Indian warriors galloped into battle, unaware that it was their white adversaries who had brought the horse to America.

Equally dramatic was the effect of American crops on European and African societies. From his first trip to the New World, Columbus brought back a plant that revolutionized the diets of both humans and animals—maize. During the next century, American beans, squash, and sweet potatoes appeared on European tables. The pepper and tomato, other New World discoveries, added a distinctive

Embarcadero de los Cavallos,

flavor to Mediterranean cooking. Despite strong prohibitions on the use of tobacco (in Russia, a user might have his nose amputated), European demand for tobacco grew astronomically during the seventeenth century. The potato caught on more slowly in Europe because of a widespread fear that root crops caused disease. The most rapid acceptance of the white potato came in Ireland, where it became a diet staple in the 1600s. Irish immigrants—unaware of the genealogy of this native American crop—reintroduced the potato into Massachusetts Bay in 1718. And in West Africa, corn gradually replaced traditional animal feeds of low yield.

These sweeping changes in agriculture and diet helped reshape the Old World economies. Partly because of the rich new sources of nutrition from America, the population of Europe, which had long been relatively stable, nearly doubled in the eighteenth century. Even as cities swelled and industries flourished, European farmers were able to feed the growing population. In many ways, the seeds and plants of the New World were far more valuable in Western economic development than all the silver of Mexico and Peru.

QUESTIONS FOR DISCUSSION

1. How did the transfer of diseases, plants, and animals affect the peoples of Europe and the Americas?

2. Why did the reintroduction of the horse transform the Native American societies of the Southwest and the Great Plains?

3. How did American crops affect the Old World?

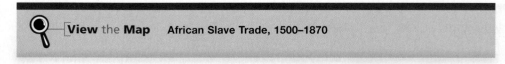

View the Map   African Slave Trade, 1500–1870

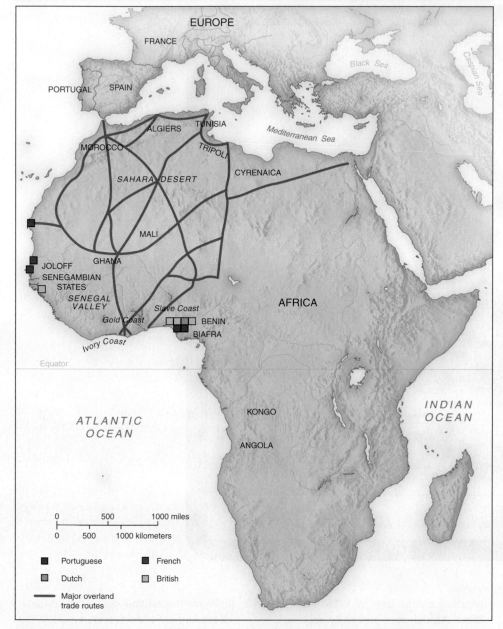

TRADE ROUTES IN AFRICA   African trade routes were well established by the late 1600s. Trade restrictions—and a deadly disease environment—confined European settlements primarily to coastal regions.

were generally settled by clan elders. The senior leaders allocated economic and human resources. They determined who received land and who might take a wife—critical decisions because within the villages of West Africa, women and children cultivated the fields. The communities were economically self-sufficient. Not only were they able to grow enough food to feed themselves, but they also produced trade goods, such as iron, kola, and gum.

The first Europeans to reach the West African coast by sail were the Portuguese. Strong winds and currents along the Atlantic coast moved southward, which meant a ship could sail with the wind from Portugal to West Africa without difficulty. The problem was returning. Advances in maritime technology allowed the Portuguese to overcome these difficulties. By constructing a new type of ship, one uniting European hull design with lateen (triangular) sails from the Middle East, Portuguese caravels were able to navigate successfully against African winds and currents. During the fifteenth century, Portuguese sailors discovered that by sailing far to the west, often as far as the Azores, they could, on their return trips to Europe, catch a reliable westerly wind. Columbus was evidently familiar with the technique. Before attempting to cross the Atlantic Ocean, he sailed to the Gold Coast, and on the way, he undoubtedly studied the wind patterns that would carry his famed caravels to the New World and back again.

The Portuguese journeyed to Africa in search of gold and slaves. Mali and Joloff officials were willing partners in this commerce but insisted that Europeans respect trade regulations established by Africans. They required the Europeans to pay tolls and other fees and restricted the foreign traders to conducting their business in small forts or castles located at the mouths of the major rivers. Local merchants acquired some slaves and gold in the interior and transported them to the coast where they were exchanged for European manufactures. Transactions were calculated in terms of local African currencies: A slave would be offered to a European trader for so many bars of iron or ounces of gold.

European slave traders accepted these terms largely because they had no other choice. The African states fielded formidable armies, and outsiders soon discovered they could not impose their will on the region simply by demonstrations of force.

major states would have included Mali, Benin, and Kongo. Many other Africans lived in what are known as stateless societies, really largely autonomous communities organized around lineage structures. In these respects, African and Native American cultures had much in common.

Whatever the form of government, men and women constructed their primary social identity within well-defined lineage groups, which consisted of persons claiming descent from a common ancestor. Disputes among members of lineage groups

Moreover, local diseases proved so lethal for Europeans—six out of ten of whom would die within a single year's stay in Africa—that they were happy to avoid dangerous trips to the interior. The slaves were usually men and women taken captive during wars; others were victims of judicial practices designed specifically to supply the growing American market. By 1650, most West African slaves were destined for the New World rather than the Middle East.

Even before Europeans colonized the New World, the Portuguese were purchasing almost a thousand slaves a year on the West African coast. The slaves were frequently forced to work on the sugar plantations of Madeira (Portuguese) and the Canaries (Spanish), Atlantic islands on which Europeans experimented with forms of unfree labor that would later be more fully and more ruthlessly established in the American colonies. It is currently estimated that approximately 10.7 million Africans were taken to the New World as slaves. The figure for the eighteenth century alone is about 5.5 million, of which more than one-third came from West Central Africa. The Bight of Benin, the Bight of Biafra, and the Gold Coast supplied most of the others.

The peopling of the New World is usually seen as a story of European migrations. But in fact, during every year between 1650 and 1831, more Africans than Europeans came to the Americas. As historian Davis Eltis wrote, "In terms of immigration alone . . . America was an extension of Africa rather than Europe until late in the nineteenth century."

Europe on the Eve of Conquest

How do you explain Spain's central role in New World exploration and colonization?

In ancient times, the West possessed a mythical appeal to people living along the shores of the Mediterranean Sea. Classical writers speculated about the fate of Atlantis, a fabled Western civilization that was said to have sunk beneath the ocean. Fallen Greek heroes allegedly spent eternity in an uncharted western paradise. But because the ships of Greece and Rome were ill designed to sail the open ocean, the lands to the west remained the stuff of legend and fantasy. In the fifth century, an intrepid Irish monk, St. Brendan, reported finding enchanted islands far out in the Atlantic. He even claimed to have met a talking whale named Jasconius, who allowed the famished voyager to cook a meal on his back.

In the tenth century, Scandinavian seafarers known as Norsemen or Vikings actually established settlements in the New World, but almost a thousand years passed before they received credit for their accomplishment. In the year 984, a band of Vikings led by Eric the Red sailed west from Iceland to a large island in the North Atlantic. Eric, who possessed a fine sense of public relations, named the island Greenland, reasoning that others would more willingly colonize the icebound region "if the country had a good name." A few years later, Eric's son Leif founded a small settlement he named Vinland at a location in northern Newfoundland now called L'Anse aux Meadows. At the time, the Norse voyages went unnoticed by other Europeans.

The hostility of Native Americans, poor lines of communication, climatic cooling, and political upheavals in Scandinavia made maintenance of these distant outposts impossible. At the time of his first voyage in 1492, Columbus seemed to have been unaware of these earlier exploits.

Building New Nation-States

At the time of the Viking settlement, other Europeans were unprepared to sponsor transatlantic exploration. Nor would they be in a position to do so for several more centuries. Medieval kingdoms were loosely organized, and until the early fifteenth century, fierce provincial loyalties, widespread ignorance of classical learning, and dreadful plagues such as the Black Death discouraged people from thinking expansively about the world beyond their own immediate communities.

In the fifteenth century, however, these conditions began to change. Europe became more prosperous, political authority was more centralized, and the Renaissance fostered a more expansive outlook among literate people in the arts and sciences. The Renaissance encouraged—first in Italy and later throughout Europe—bold new creative thinking that challenged the orthodoxies of the Middle Ages. A major element in the shift was the slow but steady growth of population after 1450. Historians are uncertain about the cause of the increase—after all, neither the quality of medicine nor sanitation improved much—but the result was a substantial rise in the price of land, since there were more mouths to feed. Landlords profited from these trends, and as their income expanded, they demanded more of the luxury items, such as spices, silks, and jewels, that came from distant Asian ports. Economic prosperity created powerful new incentives for exploration and trade.

This period also witnessed the centralization of political authority under a group of rulers whom historians refer to collectively as the New Monarchs. Before the mid-fifteenth century, feudal nobles dominated small districts throughout Europe. Conceding only nominal allegiance to larger territorial leaders, the local barons taxed the peasants and waged war pretty much as they pleased. They also dispensed what passed for justice. The New Monarchs challenged the nobles' autonomy. The changes that accompanied the challenges came slowly, and in many areas violently, but the results altered traditional political relationships between the nobility and the crown, and between the citizen and the state. The New Monarchs of Europe recruited armies and supported these expensive organizations with revenues from national taxes. They created effective national courts. While these monarchs were often despotic, they personified the emergent nation-states of Europe and brought a measure of peace to local communities weary of chronic feudal war.

The story was the same throughout most of western Europe. The Tudors of England, represented by Henry VII (r. 1485–1509), ended a long civil war known as the War of the Roses. Louis XI, the French monarch (r. 1461–1483), strengthened royal authority by reorganizing state finances. The political unification of Spain began in 1469 with the marriage of Ferdinand of Aragon and Isabella of Castile, setting off a nation-building process that involved driving both the Jews and Muslims out of Spain. These strong-willed monarchs forged nations out of groups of independent kingdoms. If political centralization had not occurred, the major European countries could not possibly have generated the financial and military resources necessary for worldwide exploration.

A final prerequisite to exploration was reliable technical knowledge. Ptolemy (second century AD) and other ancient geographers had mapped the known world and had even demonstrated that the world was round. During the Middle Ages, however, Europeans lost effective contact with classical tradition. Within Arab societies, the old learning had survived, indeed flourished, and when Europeans eventually rediscovered the classical texts during the Renaissance, they drew heavily on the work of Arab scholars. This "new" learning generated great intellectual curiosity about the globe and about the world that existed beyond the Mediterranean.

The invention of printing from movable type by Johann Gutenberg in the 1440s greatly facilitated the spread of technical knowledge. Indeed, printing sparked a communications revolution whose impact on the lives of ordinary people was as far-reaching as that caused by telephones, television, and computers in modern times. Sea captains published their findings as quickly as they could engage a printer, and by the beginning of the sixteenth century, a small, though growing, number of educated readers throughout Europe were well informed about the exploration of the New World. The printing press invited Europeans to imagine exciting opportunities that they had hardly perceived when the Vikings sailed the North Atlantic.

Imagining a New World

How did Spanish conquest of Central and South America transform Native American cultures?

By 1500, centralization of political authority and advances in geographic knowledge brought Spain to the first rank as a world power. In the early fifteenth century, though, Spain consisted of several autonomous kingdoms. It lacked rich natural resources and possessed few good seaports. In fact, there was little about this land to suggest its people would take the lead in conquering and colonizing the New World.

By the end of the century, however, Spain suddenly came alive with creative energy. The union of Ferdinand and Isabella sparked a drive for political consolidation that, because of the monarchs' fervid Catholicism, took on the characteristics of a religious crusade. Spurred by the militant faith of their monarchs, the armies of Castile and Aragon waged holy war—known as the *Reconquista*—against the independent states in southern Spain that earlier had been captured by Muslims. In 1492, the Moorish (Islamic) kingdom of Granada fell, and, for the first time in centuries, the entire Iberian peninsula was united under Christian rulers. Spanish authorities showed no tolerance for people who rejected the Catholic faith.

During the *Reconquista*, thousands of Jews and Moors were driven from the country. Indeed, Columbus undoubtedly encountered such refugees as he was preparing for his famous voyage. From this volatile social and political environment came the **conquistadores**, men eager for personal glory and material gain,

uncompromising in matters of religion, and unswerving in their loyalty to the crown. They were prepared to employ fire and sword in any cause sanctioned by God and king, and these adventurers carried European culture to the most populous regions of the New World.

Long before Spaniards ever reached the West Indies, they conquered the indigenous peoples of the Canary Islands, a strategically located archipelago in the eastern Atlantic. The harsh labor systems the Spanish developed in the Canaries served as models of subjugation in America. Indeed, the Spanish experience paralleled that of the English in Ireland. An early fifteenth-century Spanish chronicle described the Canary natives as "miscreants . . . [who] do not acknowledge their creator and live in part like beasts." Many islanders quickly died of disease; others were killed in battle or enslaved. The new Spanish landholders introduced sugar, a labor-intensive plantation crop. The landowners forced slaves captured in Africa to provide the labor. This oppressive process was driven by dreams of great wealth, and would be repeated many times by European colonists through the centuries.

Myths and Reality

If it had not been for Christopher Columbus (Cristoforo Colombo), of course, Spain might never have gained an American empire. Little is known about his early life. Born in Genoa in 1451 of humble parentage, Columbus soon devoured the classical learning that had so recently been rediscovered and made available in printed form. He mastered geography, and—perhaps while sailing the coast of West Africa—he became obsessed with the idea of voyaging west across the Atlantic Ocean to reach Cathay, as China was then known.

In 1484, Columbus presented his plan to the king of Portugal. However, while the Portuguese were just as interested as Columbus in reaching Cathay, they elected to voyage around the continent of Africa instead of following the route suggested by Columbus. They suspected that Columbus had substantially underestimated the circumference of the earth and that for all his enthusiasm, he would almost certainly starve before reaching Asia. The Portuguese decision eventually paid off quite handsomely. In 1498, one of their captains, Vasco da Gama, returned from the coast of India carrying a fortune in spices and other luxury goods.

Undaunted by rejection, Columbus petitioned Isabella and Ferdinand for financial backing. They were initially no more interested in his grand design than the Portuguese had been. But time was on Columbus's side. Spain's aggressive New Monarchs envied the success of their neighbor, Portugal. Columbus boldly played on the rivalry between the countries, talking of wealth and empire. Indeed, for a person with little success or apparent support, he was supremely confident. One contemporary reported that when Columbus "made up his mind, he was as sure he would discover what he did discover, and find what he did find, as if he held it in a chamber under lock and key."

Columbus's stubborn lobbying on behalf of the "Enterprise of the Indies" gradually wore down opposition in the Spanish court, and the two sovereigns provided him with a small fleet that contained two of the most famous caravels ever constructed, the *Niña* and the *Pinta*, as well as the square-rigged nao *Santa Maria*. The

● ─[Watch the Video   How Should We Think of Columbus?

Cristoforo Columbo, better known to Americans as Christopher Columbus, was a fifteenth-century sailor from Genoa. Dreaming of reaching the rich markets of Asia by sailing west from Europe, he instead stumbled upon the islands of the Caribbean Sea. In so doing, he ushered in a new age of sustained contact between the peoples of the Americas and the peoples of Europe, Africa, and Asia.

indomitable admiral set sail for Cathay in August 1492, the year of Spain's unification.

Educated Europeans of the fifteenth century knew the world was round. No one seriously believed that Columbus and his crew would tumble off the edge of the earth. The concern was with size, not shape. Columbus estimated the distance to the mainland of Asia to be about 3,000 nautical miles, a voyage his small ships would have no difficulty completing. The actual distance is 10,600 nautical miles, however, and had the New World not been in his way, he and his crew would have run out of food and water long before they reached China, as the Portuguese had predicted.

After stopping in the Canary Islands to refit the ships, Columbus continued his westward voyage in early September. When the tiny Spanish fleet sighted an island in the Bahamas after only thirty-three days at sea, the admiral concluded he had reached Asia. Since his mathematical calculations had obviously been correct, he assumed he would soon encounter the Chinese. It never occurred

to Columbus that he had stumbled upon a new world. He assured his men, his patrons, and perhaps himself that the islands were indeed part of the fabled "Indies." Or if not the Indies themselves, then they were surely an extension of the great Asian landmass. He searched for the splendid cities Marco Polo had described, but instead of meeting wealthy Chinese, Columbus encountered Native Americans, whom he appropriately, if mistakenly, called "Indians."

After his first voyage of discovery, Columbus returned to the New World three more times. But despite his considerable courage and ingenuity, he could never find the treasure his financial supporters in Spain angrily demanded. Columbus died in 1506 a frustrated but wealthy entrepreneur, unaware that he had reached a previously unknown continent separating Asia from Europe. The final disgrace came in 1500 with the publication of a sensationalist account of Amerigo Vespucci's travels across the Atlantic that contained falsified dates to suggest that Vespucci had visited the mainland prior to other explorers such as Columbus and Henry Cabot.

This misleading account convinced German mapmakers that it was Vespucci who had proved America to be a new continent distinct from Asia. Before the misconception could be corrected, the name *America* gained general acceptance throughout Europe.

Only two years after Columbus's first voyage, Spain and Portugal almost went to war over the anticipated treasure of Asia. Pope Alexander VI negotiated a settlement that pleased both kingdoms. Portugal wanted to exclude the Spanish from the west coast of Africa and, what was more important, from Columbus's new route to "India." Spain insisted on maintaining complete control over lands discovered by Columbus, which then still were regarded as extensions of China. The **Treaty of Tordesillas** (1494) divided the entire world along a line located 270 leagues west of the Azores. Any new lands discovered west of the line belonged to Spain. At the time, no European had ever seen Brazil, which turned out to be on Portugal's side of the line. (To this day, Brazilians speak Portuguese.) The treaty failed to discourage future English, Dutch, and French adventurers from trying their luck in the New World.

The Conquistadores: Faith and Greed

Spain's new discoveries unleashed a horde of conquistadores on the Caribbean. These independent adventurers carved out small settlements on Cuba, Hispaniola, Jamaica, and Puerto Rico in the 1490s and early 1500s. They were not interested in creating a permanent society in the New World. Rather, they came for instant wealth, preferably in gold, and were not squeamish about the means they used to obtain it. Bernal Díaz, one of the first Spaniards to migrate to the region, explained he had traveled to America "to serve God and His Majesty, to give light to those who were in darkness, and to grow rich, as all men desire to do." In less than two decades, the Indians who had inhabited the Caribbean islands had been exterminated, victims of exploitation and disease.

For a quarter century, the conquistadores concentrated their energies on the major islands that Columbus had discovered. Rumors of fabulous wealth in Mexico, however, aroused the interest of many Spaniards, including Hernán Cortés, a minor government functionary in Cuba. Like so many members of his class, he dreamed of glory, military adventure, and riches that would transform him from an ambitious court clerk into an honored hidalgo. On November 18, 1518, Cortés and a small army left Cuba to verify the stories of Mexico's treasure. Events soon demonstrated that Cortés was a leader of extraordinary ability.

His adversary was the legendary Aztec emperor, Montezuma. The confrontation between the two powerful personalities is one of the more dramatic of early American history. A fear of competition from rival conquistadores coupled with a burning desire to conquer a vast new empire drove Cortés forward. Determined to push his men through any obstacle, he scuttled the ships that had carried them to Mexico in order to

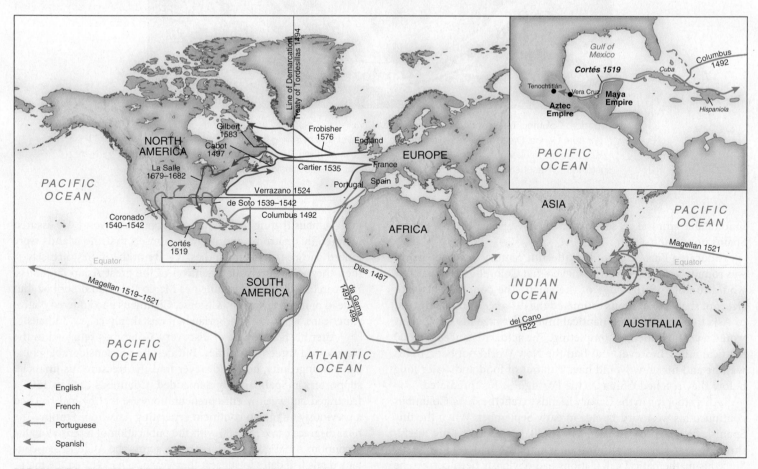

VOYAGES OF EUROPEAN EXPLORATION The routes of the major voyagers to the New World and Asia. Early explorers established land claims for the competing European states.

[Read the Document] Bartolomé de las Casas, "Of the Island of Hispaniola"

The Virgin of Guadalupe is perhaps the best-known religious symbol of Mexico. The image reflects the sixteenth-century encounter between Europeans and Indians. The Virgin Mary was already an important religious figure among the Spanish when they arrived in America. Like the Indian Juan Diego to whom she is said to have appeared and offered hope, comfort, and protection, the Virgin is dark skinned. This 1531 representation shows her clothed in a robe adorned with stars and surrounded by a crown of sunrays. Each year hundreds of thousands of people visit the shrine of the Virgin at Tepeyac, outside Mexico City.

prevent them from retreating. Cortés led his band of six hundred followers across rugged mountains and on the way gathered allies from among the Tlaxcalans, a tributary people eager to free themselves from Aztec domination.

In matters of war, Cortés possessed obvious technological superiority over the Aztec troops. The sound of gunfire initially frightened the Indians. Moreover, Aztec troops had never seen horses, much less armored horses carrying sword-wielding Spaniards. But these elements would have counted for little had Cortés not also gained a psychological advantage over his opponents. At first, Montezuma thought that the Spaniards were gods, representatives of the fearful plumed serpent, Quetzalcoatl. Instead of resisting immediately, the emperor hesitated. When Montezuma's resolve hardened, it was too late. Cortés's victory in Mexico, coupled with other conquests in South America, transformed Spain, at least temporarily, into the wealthiest state in Europe.

From Plunder to Settlement

Following the conquest of Mexico, renamed New Spain, the Spanish crown confronted a difficult problem. Ambitious conquistadores, interested chiefly in their own wealth and glory, had to be brought under royal authority, a task easier imagined than accomplished. Adventurers like Cortés were stubbornly independent, quick to take offense, and thousands of miles away from the seat of imperial government.

The crown found a partial solution in the **encomienda system**. The monarch rewarded the leaders of the conquest with Indian villages. The people who lived in the settlements provided the *encomenderos* with labor tribute in exchange for legal protection and religious guidance. The system, of course, cruelly exploited Indian laborers. One historian concluded, "The first encomenderos, without known exception, understood Spanish authority as provision for unlimited personal opportunism." Cortés alone was granted the services of more than twenty-three thousand Indian workers. The encomienda system made the colonizers more dependent on the king, for it was he who legitimized their title. In the words of one scholar, the new economic structure helped to transform "a frontier of plunder into a frontier of settlement."

Spain's rulers attempted to maintain tight personal control over their American possessions. The volume of correspondence between the two continents, much of it concerning mundane matters, was staggering. All documents were duplicated several times by hand. Because the trip to Madrid took many months, a year often passed before receipt of an answer to a simple request. But somehow the cumbersome system worked. In Mexico, officials appointed in Spain established a rigid hierarchical order, directing the affairs of the countryside from urban centers.

The Spanish also brought Catholicism to the New World. The Dominicans and Franciscans, the two largest religious orders, established Indian missions throughout New Spain. Some friars tried to protect the Native Americans from the worst forms of exploitation. One courageous Dominican, Fra Bartolomé de las Casas, published an eloquent defense of Indian rights, *Historia de las Indias,* which among other things questioned the legitimacy of European conquest of the New World. Las Casas's work provoked heated debate in Spain, and while the crown had no intention of repudiating the vast American empire, it did initiate certain reforms designed to bring greater "love and moderation" to Spanish-Indian relations. It is impossible to ascertain how many converts the friars made. In 1531, however, a newly converted

Christian reported a vision of the Virgin, a dark-skinned woman of obvious Indian ancestry, who became known throughout the region as the **Virgin of Guadalupe**. This figure—the result of a creative blending of Indian and European cultures—served as a powerful symbol of Mexican nationalism in the wars for independence fought against Spain almost three centuries later.

About two hundred fifty thousand Spaniards migrated to the New World during the sixteenth century. Another two hundred thousand made the journey between 1600 and 1650. Most colonists were single males in their late twenties seeking economic opportunities. They generally came from the poorest agricultural regions of southern Spain—almost 40 percent migrating from Andalusia. Since so few Spanish women migrated, especially in the sixteenth century, the men often married Indians and blacks, unions which produced *mestizos* and *mulattos*. The frequency of interracial marriage indicated that, among other things, the people of New Spain were more tolerant of racial differences than were the English who settled in North America. For the people of New Spain, social standing was affected as much, or more, by economic worth as it was by color. Persons born in the New World, even those of Spanish parentage (*criollos*), were regarded as socially inferior to natives of the mother country (*peninsulares*).

Spain claimed far more of the New World than it could possibly manage. Spain's rulers regarded the American colonies primarily as a source of precious metal, and between 1500 and 1650, an estimated 200 tons of gold and 16,000 tons of silver were shipped back to the Spanish treasury in Madrid. This great wealth, however, proved a mixed blessing. The sudden acquisition of so much money stimulated a horrendous inflation that hurt ordinary Spaniards. They were hurt further by long, debilitating European wars funded by American gold and silver. Moreover, instead of developing its own industry, Spain became dependent on the annual shipment of bullion from America, and in 1603, one insightful Spaniard declared, "The New World conquered by you, has conquered you in its turn." This somewhat weakened, although still formidable, empire would eventually extend its territorial claims north to California and the Southwest (see Chapter 4).

The French Claim Canada

What was the character of the French empire in Canada?

French interest in the New World developed slowly. More than three decades after Columbus's discovery, King Francis I sponsored the unsuccessful efforts of Giovanni da Verrazzano to find a short water route to China, via a northwest passage around or through North America. In 1534, the king sent Jacques Cartier on a similar quest. The rocky, barren coast of Labrador depressed the explorer. He grumbled, "I am rather inclined to believe that this is the land God gave to Cain."

Discovery of a large, promising waterway the following year raised Cartier's spirits. He reconnoitered the Gulf of Saint Lawrence, traveling up the magnificent river as far as modern Montreal. Despite his high expectations, however, Cartier got no closer to China, and discouraged by the harsh winters, he headed home in 1542. Not until sixty-five years later did Samuel

de Champlain resettle this region for France. He founded Quebec in 1608.

As was the case with other colonial powers, the French declared they had migrated to the New World in search of wealth as well as in hopes of converting the Indians to Christianity. As it turned out, these economic and spiritual goals required full cooperation between the French and the Native Americans. In contrast to the English settlers, who established independent farms and who regarded the Indians at best as obstacles in the path of civilization, the French viewed the natives as necessary economic partners. Furs were Canada's most valuable export, and to obtain the pelts of beaver and other animals, the French were absolutely dependent on Indian hunters and trappers. French traders lived among the Indians, often taking native wives and studying local cultures.

Frenchmen known as **coureurs de bois** (forest runners), following Canada's great river networks, paddled deep into the heart of the continent in search of fresh sources of furs. Some intrepid traders penetrated beyond the Great Lakes into the Mississippi Valley. In 1673, Père Jacques Marquette journeyed down the

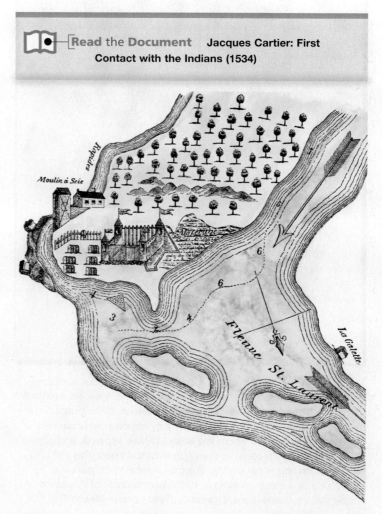

📖 **Read** the **Document**   Jacques Cartier: First Contact with the Indians (1534)

This seventeenth-century woodcut depicts Samuel de Champlain's fortified camp at Quebec on the St. Lawrence River. Champlain founded Quebec for France in 1608.

Source: North Wind Picture Archives.

Mississippi River, and nine years later, Sieur de La Salle traveled all the way to the Gulf of Mexico. In the early eighteenth century, the French established small settlements in Louisiana, the most important being New Orleans. The spreading French influence worried English colonists living along the Atlantic coast, for it appeared the French were about to cut them off from the trans-Appalachian west.

Catholic missionaries also depended on Indian cooperation. Canadian priests were drawn from two orders, the Jesuits and the Recollects, and although measuring their success in the New World is difficult, it seems they converted more Indians to Christianity than did their English Protestant counterparts to the south. Like the fur traders, the missionaries lived among the Indians and learned to speak their languages.

The French dream of a vast American empire suffered from serious flaws. The crown remained largely indifferent to Canadian affairs. Royal officials stationed in New France received limited and sporadic support from Paris. An even greater problem was the decision to settle what seemed to many rural peasants and urban artisans a cold, inhospitable land. Throughout the colonial period, Canada's European population remained small. A census of 1663 recorded a mere 3,035 French residents. By 1700, the figure had reached only 15,000. Men far outnumbered women, thus making it hard for settlers to form new families. Moreover, because of the colony's geography, all exports and imports had to go through Quebec. It was relatively easy, therefore, for crown officials to control that traffic, usually by awarding fur-trading monopolies to court favorites. Such practices created political tensions and hindered economic growth.

The English Enter the Competition

Why did England not participate in the early competition for New World colonies?

The first English visit to North America remains shrouded in mystery. Fishermen working out of Bristol and other western English ports may have landed in Nova Scotia and Newfoundland as early as the 1480s. The codfish of the Grand Banks undoubtedly drew vessels of all nations, and during the summer months some sailors probably dried and salted their catches on Canada's convenient shores. John Cabot (Giovanni Caboto), a Venetian sea captain, completed the first recorded transatlantic voyage by an English vessel in 1497, while attempting to find a northwest passage to Asia.

Cabot died during a second attempt to find a direct route to Cathay in 1498. Although Sebastian Cabot continued his father's explorations in the Hudson Bay region in 1508–1509, England's interest in the New World waned. For the next three-quarters of a century, the English people were preoccupied with more pressing domestic and religious concerns. When curiosity about the New World revived, however, Cabot's voyages established England's belated claim to American territory.

Birth of English Protestantism

At the time of Cabot's death, England was not prepared to compete with Spain and Portugal for the riches of the Orient. Although Henry VII, the first Tudor monarch, brought peace to England after a bitter civil war, the country still contained too many mighty subjects, powerful local magnates who maintained armed retainers and who often paid little attention to royal authority. Henry possessed no standing army; his small navy intimidated no one. To be sure, the Tudors gave nominal allegiance to the pope in Rome, but unlike the rulers of Spain, they were not crusaders for Catholicism.

A complex web of international diplomacy also worked against England's early entry into New World colonization. In 1509, to cement an alliance between Spain and England, the future Henry VIII married Catherine of Aragon. As a result of this marital arrangement, English merchants enjoyed limited rights to trade in Spain's American colonies, but any attempt by England at independent colonization would have threatened those rights and jeopardized the alliance.

By the end of the sixteenth century, however, conditions within England had changed dramatically, in part as a result of the **Protestant Reformation**. As they did, the English began to consider their former ally, Spain, to be the greatest threat to English aspirations. Tudor monarchs, especially Henry VIII (r. 1509–1547) and his daughter Elizabeth I (r. 1558–1603), developed a strong central administration, while England became more and more a Protestant society. The merger of English Protestantism and English nationalism affected all aspects of public life. It helped propel England into a central role in European affairs and was crucial in creating a powerful sense of an English identity among all classes of people.

Popular anticlericalism helped spark religious reformation in England. Although they observed traditional Catholic ritual, the English people had long resented paying monies to a pope who lived in far-off Rome. Early in the sixteenth century, criticism of the clergy grew increasingly vocal. Cardinal Thomas Wolsey, the most powerful prelate in England, flaunted his immense wealth and unwittingly became a symbol of spiritual corruption. Parish priests were objects of ridicule. Poorly educated men for the most part, they seemed theologically ignorant and perpetually grasping. Anticlericalism did not run as deep in England as it had in Martin Luther's Germany, but by the late 1520s, the Catholic Church could no longer take for granted the allegiance of the great mass of the population. The people's growing anger is central to an understanding of the English Reformation. Put simply, if ordinary men and women throughout the kingdom had not accepted separation from Rome, then Henry VIII could not have forced them to leave the church.

The catalyst for Protestant Reformation in England was the king's desire to rid himself of his wife, Catherine of Aragon, who happened to be the daughter of the former king of Spain. Their marriage had produced a daughter, Mary, but, as the years passed, no son. The need for a male heir obsessed Henry. He and his counselors assumed a female ruler could not maintain domestic peace, and England would fall once again into civil war. The answer seemed to be remarriage. Henry petitioned Pope Clement VII for a divorce (technically, an annulment), but the Spanish had other ideas. Unwilling to tolerate the public humiliation of Catherine, they forced the pope to procrastinate. In 1527, time ran out. The passionate Henry fell in love with Anne Boleyn, who later bore him a daughter, Elizabeth. The king decided to divorce Catherine with or without papal consent.

The final break with Rome came swiftly. Between 1529 and 1536, the king, acting through Parliament, severed all ties with the pope, seized church lands, and dissolved many of the monasteries. In March 1534, the Act of Supremacy boldly announced, "The King's Majesty justly and rightfully is supreme head of the Church of England." The entire process, which one historian termed a "state reformation," was conducted with impressive efficiency. Land formerly owned by the Catholic Church passed quickly into private hands, and within a short period, property holders throughout England had acquired a vested interest in Protestantism. Beyond breaking with the papacy, Henry showed little enthusiasm for theological change. Many Catholic ceremonies survived.

The split with Rome, however, opened the door to increasingly radical religious ideas. The year 1539 saw the publication of the first Bible in English. Before then the Scripture had been available only in Latin, the language of an educated elite. For the first time in English history, ordinary people could read the word of God in the vernacular. It was a liberating experience that persuaded some men and women that Henry had not sufficiently reformed the English church.

With Henry's death in 1547, England entered a period of acute political and religious instability. Edward VI, Henry's young son by his third wife, Jane Seymour, came to the throne, but he was still a child and sickly besides. Militant Protestants took advantage of the political uncertainty, insisting the Church of England remove every trace of its Catholic origins. With the death of young Edward in 1553, these ambitious efforts came to a sudden halt. Henry's eldest daughter, Mary, next ascended the throne. Fiercely loyal to the Catholic faith of her mother, Catherine of Aragon, Mary I vowed to return England to the pope.

However misguided were the queen's plans, she possessed her father's iron will. Hundreds of Protestants were executed; others scurried off to the safety of Geneva and Frankfurt, where they absorbed the most radical Calvinist doctrines of the day. When Mary died in 1558 and was succeeded by Elizabeth, the "Marian exiles" flocked back to England, more eager than ever to rid the Tudor church of Catholicism. Mary had inadvertently advanced the cause of Calvinism by creating so many Protestant martyrs, reformers burned for their faith and now celebrated in the woodcuts of the most popular book of the period, John Foxe's *Acts and Monuments*, commonly known as the *Book of Martyrs* (1563). The Marian exiles served as the leaders of the Elizabethan church, an institution that remained fundamentally Calvinist until the end of the sixteenth century.

Militant Protestantism

By the time Mary Tudor came to the throne, the vast popular movement known as the Reformation had swept across northern and central Europe, and as much as any of the later great political revolutions, it had begun to transform the character of the modern world. The Reformation started in Germany when, in 1517, a relatively obscure German monk, Martin Luther, publicly challenged the central tenets of Roman Catholicism. Within a few years, the religious unity of Europe was permanently shattered. The Reformation divided kingdoms, sparked bloody wars, and unleashed an extraordinary flood of religious publication.

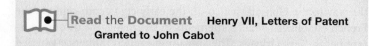 **Read the Document** Henry VII, Letters of Patent Granted to John Cabot

King Henry VII's seizure of the throne of England in 1485 brought an end to a series of civil wars that had torn England apart for almost thirty years. Along with bringing stability to the kingdom, Henry VII also established England's first claims to the Americas by sponsoring the explorations of Captain John Cabot.

Luther's message was straightforward, one ordinary people could easily comprehend. God spoke through the Bible, Luther maintained, not through the pope or priests. Scripture taught that women and men were saved by faith alone. Pilgrimages, fasts, alms, indulgences—none of the traditional ritual observances could assure salvation. The institutional structure of Catholicism was challenged as Luther's radical ideas spread rapidly across northern Germany and Scandinavia.

After Luther, other Protestant theologians—religious thinkers who would determine the course of religious reform in England, Scotland, and the early American colonies—mounted an even more strident attack on Catholicism. The most influential of these was John Calvin, a lawyer turned theologian, who lived most of his adult life in the Swiss city of Geneva. Calvin stressed God's omnipotence over human affairs. The Lord, he maintained, chose some persons for "election," the gift of salvation, while condemning others to eternal damnation. A man or woman could do nothing to alter this decision.

Common sense suggests that such a bleak doctrine—known as predestination—might lead to fatalism or hedonism. After all, why not enjoy the world's pleasures to the fullest if such actions have no effect on God's judgment? But many sixteenth-century Europeans did not share modern notions of what constitutes common sense. Indeed, Calvinists were constantly "up and doing," searching for signs that they had received God's gift of grace. The uncertainty of their eternal state proved a powerful psychological spur, for as long as people did not know whether they were scheduled for heaven or hell, they worked diligently to demonstrate that they possessed at least the seeds of grace.

John Calvin's *Institutes of the Christian Religion* (1536) contained a powerful statement of the new faith, and his teachings spawned religious movements in most northern European countries. In France, the reformed Protestants were known as Huguenots. In Scotland, people of Calvinist persuasion founded the Presbyterian Church. And in seventeenth-century England and America, most of those who put Calvin's teachings into practice were called Puritans.

Woman in Power

Queen Elizabeth demonstrated that Henry and his advisers had been mistaken about the capabilities of female rulers. She was a woman of such talent that modern biographers find little to criticize in her decisions. She governed the English people from 1558 to 1603, an intellectually exciting period during which some of her subjects took the first halting steps toward colonizing the New World.

Elizabeth recognized her most urgent duty as queen was to end the religious turmoil that had divided the country for a generation. She had no desire to restore Catholicism. After all, the pope openly referred to her as a woman of illegitimate birth. Nor did she want to re-create the church exactly as it had been in the final years of her father's reign. Rather, Elizabeth established a unique institution, Catholic in much of its ceremony and government but clearly Protestant in doctrine. Under her so-called Elizabethan settlement, the queen assumed the title "Supreme Head of the Church." Some churchmen who had studied with Calvin in Geneva urged her to drop immediately all Catholic rituals, but she ignored these strident reformers. The young queen understood she could not rule effectively without the full support of her people, and as the examples of Edward and Mary before her demonstrated, neither radical change nor widespread persecution gained a monarch lasting popularity.

The state of England's religion was not simply a domestic concern. One scholar aptly termed this period of European history "the Age of Religious Wars." Catholicism and Protestantism influenced the way ordinary men and women across the continent interpreted the experiences of everyday life. Religion shaped political and economic activities. Protestant leaders, for example, purged the English calendar of the many saints' days that had punctuated the agricultural year in Catholic countries. The Reformation certainly had a profound impact on the economic development of Calvinist countries. Max Weber, a brilliant German sociologist of the early twentieth century, argued in his *Protestant Ethic and Spirit of Capitalism* that a gnawing sense of self-doubt created by the doctrine of "predestination" drove Calvinists to extraordinary diligence. They generated large profits, not because they wanted to become rich, but because they wanted to be doing the Lord's work, to show they might be among God's "elect."

Indeed, it is helpful to view Protestantism and Catholicism as warring ideologies, bundles of deeply held beliefs that divided countries and families much as communism and capitalism did during the late twentieth century. The confrontations between the two faiths affected Elizabeth's entire reign. Soon after she became queen, Pope Pius V excommunicated her, and in his papal bull *Regnans in Exelsis* (1570), he stripped Elizabeth of her "pretended title to the kingdom." Spain, the most fervently Catholic state in Europe, vowed to restore England to the "true" faith, and Catholic militants constantly plotted to overthrow the Tudor monarchy.

Religion, War, and Nationalism

Slowly, but steadily, English Protestantism and English national identity merged. A loyal English subject in the late sixteenth century loved the queen, supported the Church of England, and hated Catholics, especially those who happened to live in Spain. Elizabeth herself came to symbolize this militant new chauvinism. Her subjects adored the Virgin Queen, and they applauded when her famed "Sea Dogs"—dashing figures such as Sir Francis Drake and Sir John Hawkins—seized Spanish treasure ships in American waters. The English sailors' raids were little more than piracy, but in this undeclared state of war, such instances of harassment passed for national victories. There seemed to be no reason patriotic Elizabethans should not share in the wealth of the New World. With each engagement, each threat, each plot, English nationalism took deeper root. By the 1570s, it had become obvious the English people were driven by powerful ideological forces similar to those that had moved the Spanish subjects of Isabella and Ferdinand almost a century earlier.

In the mid-1580s, Philip II, who had united the empires of Spain and Portugal in 1580, decided that England's arrogantly Protestant queen could be tolerated no longer. He ordered the construction of a mighty fleet, hundreds of transport vessels designed to carry Spain's finest infantry across the English channel. When one of Philip's lieutenants viewed the Armada at Lisbon in May 1588, he described it as *la felicissima armada*, the invincible fleet. The king believed that with the support of England's oppressed Catholics, Spanish troops would sweep Elizabeth from power.

It was a grand scheme; it was an even grander failure. In 1588, a smaller, more maneuverable English navy dispersed Philip's Armada, and severe storms finished it off. Spanish hopes for Catholic England lay wrecked along the rocky coasts of Scotland and Ireland. English Protestants interpreted victory in providential terms: "God breathed and they were scattered."

An Unpromising Beginning: Mystery at Roanoke

What role did the Spanish play in the failure of the Roanoke colony?

By the 1570s, English interest in the New World had revived. An increasing number of wealthy gentlemen were in an expansive mood, ready to challenge Spain and reap the profits of Asia and America. Yet the adventurers who directed Elizabethan expeditions were only dimly aware of Cabot's voyages, and their sole experience in settling distant outposts was in Ireland. Over the last three decades of the sixteenth century, English adventurers made almost every mistake one could possibly imagine. They did, however, acquire valuable information about winds and currents, supplies and finance.

Sir Walter Ralegh's experience provided all English colonizers with a sobering example of the difficulties that awaited them in America. In 1584, he dispatched two captains to the coast of present-day North Carolina to claim land granted to him by Elizabeth. The men returned with glowing reports, no doubt aimed in part at potential financial backers. "The soile," declared Captain Arthur Barlow, "is the most plentifull, sweete, fruitfull, and wholesome of all the world."

Ralegh diplomatically renamed this marvelous region Virginia, in honor of his patron, the Virgin Queen. Indeed, highly gendered vocabulary figured prominently in the European conquest of the New World. As historian Kathleen M. Brown explained, "Associations of the land with virgin innocence reinforced the notion that Virginia had been saved from the Spaniard's lust to be conquered by the chaste English." Elizabeth encouraged Ralegh in private conversation but rejected his persistent requests for money. With rumors of war in the air, she did not want to alienate Philip II unnecessarily by sponsoring a colony on land long ago claimed by Spain.

Ralegh finally raised the funds for his adventure, but his enterprise seemed ill-fated from the start. Despite careful planning, everything went wrong. The settlement was poorly situated. Located inside the Outer Banks—perhaps to avoid detection by the Spanish—the Roanoke colony proved extremely difficult to reach. Even experienced navigators feared the treacherous currents and storms off Cape Hatteras. Sir Richard Grenville, the leader of the expedition, added to the colonists' troubles by destroying an entire Indian village in retaliation for the suspected theft of a silver cup.

Grenville hurried back to England in the autumn of 1585, leaving the colonists to fend for themselves. Although they coped quite well, a peculiar series of accidents transformed Ralegh's settlement into a ghost town. In the spring of 1586, Sir Francis Drake was returning from a Caribbean voyage and decided to visit Roanoke. Since an anticipated shipment of supplies was overdue, the colonists climbed aboard Drake's ships and went home.

In 1587, Ralegh launched a second colony. This time he placed in charge John White, a veteran administrator and talented artist, who a few years earlier had produced a magnificent sketchbook of the Algonquian Indians who lived near Roanoke.

Read the Document John White, Letter to Richard Hakluyt and Description of Voyage to the Lost Colony (1590)

John White depicted fishing techniques practiced by the Algonquian Indians of the present-day Carolinas. In the canoe, dip nets and multipronged spears are used. In the background, Indians stab at fish with long spears. At left, a weir traps fish by taking advantage of the river current's natural force.

Once again, Ralegh's luck turned sour. The **Spanish Armada** severed communication between England and America. Every available English vessel was pressed into military service, and between 1587 and 1590, no ship visited the Roanoke colonists. When rescuers eventually reached the island, they found the village deserted. The fate of the "lost" colonists remains a mystery. The best guess is that they were absorbed by neighboring groups of natives, some from as far as the southern shore of the James River.

Conclusion: Campaign to Sell America

Had it not been for Richard Hakluyt the Younger, who publicized explorers' accounts of the New World, the dream of American colonization might have died in England. Hakluyt, a supremely industrious man, never saw America. Nevertheless, his vision of the New World powerfully shaped English public opinion. He interviewed captains and sailors upon their return from distant voyages and carefully collected their stories in a massive book titled *The Principall Navigations, Voyages, and Discoveries of the English Nation* (1589).

The work appeared to be a straightforward description of what these sailors had seen across the sea. That was its strength. In reality, Hakluyt edited each piece so it would drive home the book's central point: England needed American colonies. Indeed, they were essential to the nation's prosperity and independence. In Hakluyt's America, there were no losers. "The earth bringeth fourth all things in aboundance, as in the first creations without toil or labour," he wrote of Virginia. His blend of piety, patriotism, and self-interest proved immensely popular, and his *Voyages* went through many editions.

Hakluyt's enthusiasm for the spread of English trade throughout the world may have blinded him to the aspirations of other peoples who actually inhabited those distant lands. He continued to collect testimony from adventurers and sailors who claimed to have visited Asia and America. In an immensely popular new edition of his work published between 1598 and 1600 and entitled *Voyages*, he catalogued in extraordinary detail the commercial opportunities awaiting courageous and ambitious English colonizers. Hakluyt's entrepreneurial perspective served to obscure other aspects of the European Conquest, which within only a short amount of time would transform the face of the New World. He paid little attention, for example, to the rich cultural diversity of the Native Americans; he said not a word about the pain of the Africans who traveled to North and South America as slaves. Instead, he and many other polemicists for English colonization led the ordinary men and women who crossed the Atlantic to expect nothing less than a paradise on earth. By fanning such unrealistic expectations, Hakluyt persuaded European settlers that the New World was theirs for the taking, a self-serving view that invited ecological disaster and continuous human suffering.

Study Resources

 Take the **Study Plan** for **Chapter 1** *New World Encounters* on **MyHistoryLab**

TIME LINE

24,000–17,000 B.C. Indians cross the Bering Strait into North America

2000–1500 B.C. Agricultural Revolution transforms Native American life

A.D. 1001 Norsemen establish a small settlement in Vinland (Newfoundland)

1030 Death of War Jaabi (king of Takrur), first Muslim ruler in West Africa

1450 Gutenberg perfects movable type

1469 Marriage of Isabella and Ferdinand leads to the unification of Spain

1481 Portuguese build castle at Elmina on the Gold Coast of Africa

1492 Columbus lands at San Salvador

1497 Cabot leads first English exploration of North America

1498 Vasco da Gama of Portugal reaches India by sailing around Africa

1502 Montezuma becomes emperor of the Aztecs

1506 Columbus dies in Spain after four voyages to America

1517 Martin Luther's protest sparks Reformation in Germany

1521 Cortés defeats the Aztecs at Tenochtitlán

1529–1536 Henry VIII provokes English Reformation

1534 Cartier claims Canada for France

1536 Calvin's *Institutes* published

1540 Coronado explores the Southwest for Spain

1558 Elizabeth I becomes queen of England

1585 First Roanoke settlement established on coast of North Carolina

1588 Spanish Armada defeated by the English

1608 Champlain founds Quebec

CHAPTER REVIEW

Native American Histories Before the Conquest

 What explains cultural differences among Native American groups before European conquest?

Paleo-Indians crossed into North America from Asia 20,000 years ago. During the migrations, they divided into distinct groups, often speaking different languages. The Agricultural Revolution sparked population growth, allowing some groups, such as the Aztecs, to establish complex societies. The Eastern Woodland Indians, who lived along the Atlantic coast, had just begun to practice agriculture when the Europeans arrived. (p. 4)

A World Transformed

 How did Europeans and Native Americans interact during the period of first contact?

Native Americans initially welcomed the opportunity to trade with the Europeans. The newcomers insisted on "civilizing" the Indians. Neither Christianity nor European-style education held much appeal for Native Americans, and they resisted efforts to transform their cultures. Contagious Old World diseases, such as smallpox, decimated the Indians, leaving them vulnerable to cultural imperialism. (p. 8)

West Africa: Ancient and Complex Societies

 What was the character of the West African societies that European traders first encountered?

West Africans had learned of Islam long before European traders arrived looking for slaves. The earliest Europeans found powerful local rulers who knew how to profit from commercial exchange. Slaves who had been captured in distant wars were taken to so-called slave factories where they were sold to Europeans and then shipped to the New World. (p. 11)

Europe on the Eve of Conquest

 How do you explain Spain's central role in New World exploration and colonization?

The unification of Spain under Ferdinand and Isabella, and the experience of the *Reconquista*, provided Spain with advantages in its later conquest of the New World. The Spanish crown supported the explorations of Christopher Columbus, who thought he had discovered a new route to Asia. His voyages gave the Spanish a head start in claiming American lands. (p. 15)

Imagining a New World

 How did Spanish conquest of Central and South America transform Native American cultures?

Spanish conquistadores conquered vast territories in the Caribbean, Mexico, and Central and South America during the sixteenth century. Catholic missionaries followed the conquistadores to convert the Indians to Christianity. Although the Spanish conquerors cruelly exploited the Indians as laborers, intermarriage between the groups created a new culture blending Spanish and Indian elements. (p. 16)

The French Claim Canada

 What was the character of the French empire in Canada?

The French in Canada focused on building a trading empire rather than on settlement. The *coureurs de bois* and Catholic missionaries lived among the Indians, learning their languages and customs. French explorers followed the extensive river networks of North America and claimed vast stretches of land along the St. Lawrence and Mississippi Rivers. (p. 20)

The English Enter the Competition

 Why did England not participate in the early competition for New World colonies?

During the early 1500s, religious turmoil preoccupied England's monarchs. After ascending the throne in 1558, Queen Elizabeth I ended internal religious struggle by establishing an English Church that was Protestant in doctrine but Catholic in ceremony. Under Elizabeth, English nationalism merged with anti-Catholicism to challenge Spanish control of the Americas. (p. 21)

An Unpromising Beginning: Mystery at Roanoke

 What role did the Spanish play in the failure of the Roanoke colony?

The second Roanoke colony was founded in 1587, but the following year, the Spanish Armada severed communications between England and America. When an English ship was finally able to reach Roanoke in 1590, the rescuers found the settlement there deserted. (p. 24)

KEY TERMS AND DEFINITIONS

Beringia   Land bridge formerly connecting Asia and North America that is now submerged beneath the Bering Sea. p. 4

Agricultural Revolution   The gradual shift from hunting and gathering to cultivating basic food crops that occurred worldwide from 7,000 to 9,000 years ago. p. 5

Eastern Woodland Cultures   Term given to Indians from the Northeast region who lived on the Atlantic coast and supplemented farming with seasonal hunting and gathering. p. 7

Columbian Exchange   The exchange of plants, animals, and diseases between Europe and the Americas from first contact throughout the era of exploration. p. 10

Conquistadores   Sixteenth-century Spanish adventurers, often of noble birth, who subdued the Native Americans and created the Spanish empire in the New World. p. 16

Treaty of Tordesillas   Treaty negotiated by the pope in 1494 that divided the world along a north–south line in the middle of the Atlantic Ocean, granting Spain all lands west of the line and Portugal lands east of the line. p. 18

Encomienda system   An exploitative system by Spanish rulers that granted conquistadors control of Native American villages and their inhabiatants' labor. p. 19

Virgin of Guadalupe   Apparition of the Virgin Mary that has become a symbol of Mexican nationalism. p. 20

Coureurs de bois   Fur trappers in French Canada who lived among the Native Americans. p. 20

Protestant Reformation   Sixteenth-century religious movement to reform and challenge the spiritual authority of the Roman Catholic Church. p. 21

The Spanish Armada   Spanish fleet sent to invade England in 1588. p. 24

CRITICAL THINKING QUESTIONS

1. How did native American societies experience substantial change prior to European conquest?

2. How would you compare the relationships Europeans formed with West Africans to the ones they formed with Native Americans?

3. How would you contrast the role of religion and economics in the development of the Spanish, French and English empires?

4. How did a relatively small European nation like England rise to a position of world power?

MyHistoryLab Media Assignments

Find these resources in the Media Assignments folder for Chapter 1 on MyHistoryLab

Native American Histories Before the Conquest

- **View** the **Closer Look**   *An Early European Image of Native Americans p. 8*

A World Transformed

View the **Map**   *Native American Population Loss, 1500–1700 p. 10*

West Africa: Ancient and Complex Societies

- **Complete** the **Assignment**   *The Columbian Exchange and the Global Environment: Ecological Revolution p. 12*

- **View** the **Closer Look**   *Columbian Exchange p. 13*

View the **Map**   *African Slave Trade, 1500–1870 p. 14*

Imagining a New World

- **Watch** the **Video**   *How Should We Think of Columbus? p. 17*

- **Read** the **Document**   *Bartolomé de las Casas, "Of the Island of Hispaniola" p. 19*

The French Claim Canada

Read the **Document**   *Jacques Cartier: First Contact with the Indians (1534) p. 20*

The English Enter The Competition

Read the **Document**   *Henry VII, Letters of Patent Granted to John Cabot p. 22*

An Unpromising Beginning: Mystery at Roanoke

Read the **Document**   *John White, Letter to Richard Hakluyt and Description of Voyage to the Lost Colony (1590) p. 24*

■ *Indicates Study Plan Media Assignment*

2 New World Experiments: England's Seventeenth-Century Colonies

Contents and Learning Objectives

Profit and Piety: Competing Visions for English Settlement

In the spring of 1644, John Winthrop, governor of Massachusetts Bay, learned that Native Americans had overrun the scattered tobacco plantations of Virginia, killing as many as five hundred colonists. Winthrop never thought much of the Chesapeake settlements. He regarded the people who had migrated to that part of America as grossly materialistic, and because Virginia had recently expelled several Puritan ministers, Winthrop decided the hostilities were God's way of punishing the tobacco planters for their worldliness. "It was observable," he related, "that this massacre came upon them soon after they had driven out the godly ministers we had sent to them." When Virginians appealed to Massachusetts for military supplies, they received a cool reception. "We were weakly provided ourselves," Winthrop explained, "and so could not afford them any help of that kind."

In 1675, the tables turned. Native Americans declared all-out war against the New Englanders, and soon reports of the destruction of Puritan communities were circulating in Virginia. "The Indians in New England have burned Considerable Villages," wrote one leading tobacco planter, "and have made them [the New Englanders] desert more than one hundred and fifty miles of those places they had formerly seated."

Sir William Berkeley, Virginia's royal governor, was not displeased by news of New England's adversity. He and his friends held the Puritans in contempt. Indeed, the New Englanders reminded them of the religious fanatics who had provoked civil war in England and who in 1649 had executed Charles I. During this particular crisis, Berkeley noted that he might have shown more pity for the beleaguered New Englanders "had they deserved it of the King." The governor, sounding like a Puritan himself, described the warring Indians as the "Instruments" with which God intended "to destroy the King's Enemies." For good measure, Virginia outlawed the export of foodstuffs to their embattled northern neighbors.

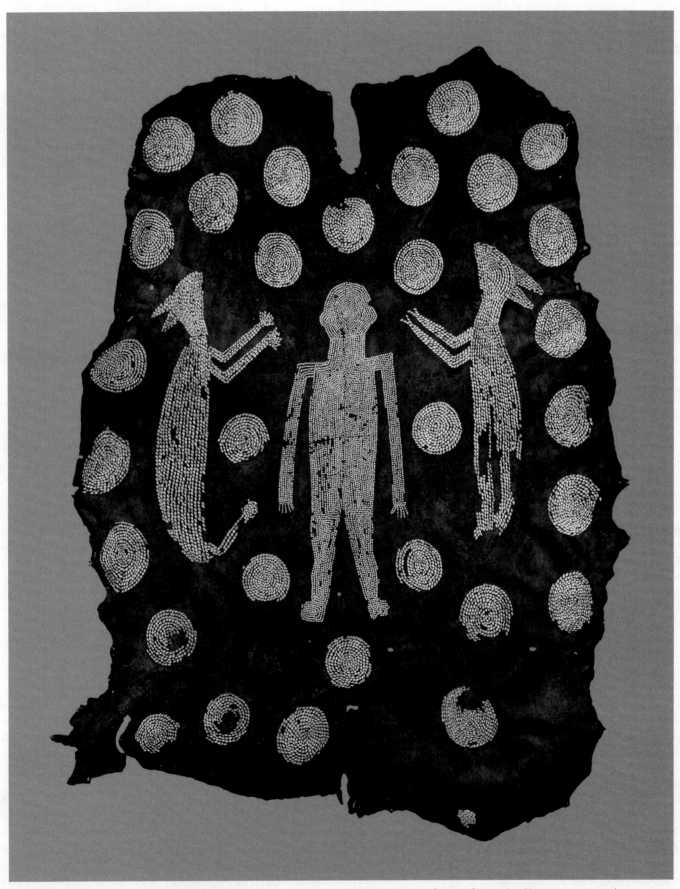

In 1608, Powhatan, the father of Pocahontas, gave this shell-decorated ceremonial cloak to Captain Christopher Newport, commander of the fleet that brought the first English settlers to Jamestown.

Such extraordinary disunity in the colonies—not to mention lack of compassion—comes as a surprise to anyone searching for the roots of modern nationalism in this early period. English colonization in the seventeenth century did not spring from a desire to build a centralized empire in the New World similar to that of Spain or France. Instead, the English crown awarded colonial charters to a wide variety of entrepreneurs, religious idealists, and aristocratic adventurers who established separate and profoundly different colonies. Not only did New Englanders have little in common with the earliest Virginians and Carolinians, but they were often divided among themselves.

Migration itself helps to explain this striking competition and diversity. At different times, different colonies appealed to different sorts of people. Men and women moved to the New World for various reasons, and as economic, political, and religious conditions changed on both sides of the Atlantic during the course of the seventeenth century, so too did patterns of English migration.

Breaking Away

What were some of the social problems facing Britain in the 16th and 17th centuries that helped push English colonists to cross the Atlantic?

English people in the early decades of the seventeenth century experienced what seemed to them an accelerating pace of social change. What was most evident was the rapid growth of population. Between 1580 and 1650, a period during which many men and women elected to journey to the New World, the population of England expanded from about 3.5 million to more than 5 million. Among other things, the expansion strained the nation's agrarian economy. Competition for food and land drove up prices, and people desperate for work took to the roads. Those migrants, many of them drawn into the orbit of London by tales of opportunity, frightened the traditional leaders of English society. To the propertied class, the wandering poor represented a threat to good order, and, particularly during the early decades of the seventeenth century, landholders urged local magistrates throughout the kingdom to enforce the laws against vagrancy.

Even by modern standards, the English population of this period was quite mobile. To be sure, most men and women lived out their days rooted in the tiny country villages of their birth. A growing number of English people, however, were migrant laborers who took seasonal work. Many others relocated from the countryside to London, already a city of several hundred thousand inhabitants by the early seventeenth century. Because health conditions in London were poor, a large number of the new arrivals quickly died, and had their places not been taken by other migrants from the rural villages, the population of London would almost certainly have decreased.

Other, more exotic destinations also beckoned. A large number of English settlers migrated to Ireland, while lucrative employment and religious freedom attracted people to Holland. The Pilgrims, people who separated themselves from the established Church of England, initially hoped to make a new life in Leyden. The migrations within Europe serve as reminders that ordinary people had

choices. A person who was upset about the state of the Church of England or who had lost a livelihood did not have to move to America. That some men and women consciously selected this much more dangerous and expensive journey set them apart from their contemporaries.

English colonists crossed the Atlantic for many reasons. Some wanted to institute a purer form of worship, more closely based on their interpretation of Scripture. Others dreamed of owning land and improving their social position. A few came to the New World to escape bad marriages, jail terms, or the dreary prospect of lifelong poverty. Since most seventeenth-century migrants, especially those who transferred to the Chesapeake colonies, left almost no records of their previous lives in England, it is futile to try to isolate a single cause or explanation for their decision to leave home.

Whatever their reasons for crossing the ocean, English migrants to America in this period left a nation wracked by recurrent, often violent, political and religious controversy. During the 1620s, autocratic Stuart monarchs—James I (r. 1603–1625) and his son Charles I (r. 1625–1649)—who succeeded Queen Elizabeth on the English throne fought constantly with the elected members of Parliament. At stake were rival notions of constitutional and representative government.

Many royal policies—the granting of lucrative commercial monopolies to court favorites, for example—fueled popular discontent, but the crown's hostility to far-reaching religious reform sparked the most vocal protest. Throughout the kingdom, Puritans became adamant in their demand for radical purification of ritual.

Tensions grew so severe that in 1629, Charles attempted to rule the country without Parliament's assistance. The autocratic strategy backfired. When Charles finally was forced to recall Parliament in 1640 because he was running out of money, Parliament demanded major constitutional reforms. Militant Puritans, supported by many members of Parliament, insisted on restructuring the church—abolishing the office of bishop was high on their list. In this angry political atmosphere, Charles took up arms against the supporters of Parliament. The confrontation between Royalists and Parliamentarians set off a long and bloody conflict, known as the English Civil War. In 1649, the victorious Parliamentarians beheaded Charles, and for almost a decade, Oliver Cromwell, a skilled general and committed Puritan, governed England as Lord Protector.

In 1660, following Cromwell's death from natural causes, the Stuarts returned to the English throne. During a period known as the Restoration, neither Charles II (r. 1660–1685) nor James II (r. 1685–1688)—both sons of Charles I—was able to establish genuine political stability. When the authoritarian James lifted some of the restrictions governing Catholics, a Protestant nation rose up in what the English people called the Glorious Revolution (1688) and sent James into permanent exile.

The Glorious Revolution altered the course of English political history and, therefore, that of the American colonies as well. The monarchs who followed James II surrendered some of the prerogative powers that had destabilized English politics for almost a century. The crown was still a potent force in the political life of the nation, but never again would an English king or queen attempt to govern without Parliament.

THE STUART MONARCHS

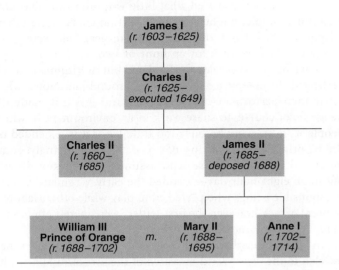

New World. These advocates argued that the North American mainland contained resources of incalculable value. An innovative group, they insisted, might reap great profits and at the same time supply England with raw materials that it would otherwise be forced to purchase from European rivals: Holland, France, and Spain.

Moreover, any enterprise that annoyed Catholic Spain or revealed its weakness in America seemed a desirable end in itself to patriotic English Protestants. Anti-Catholicism and hatred of Spain became an integral part of English national identity during this period, and unless one appreciates just how deeply those sentiments ran in the popular mind, one cannot fully understand

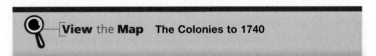

View the **Map**   The Colonies to 1740

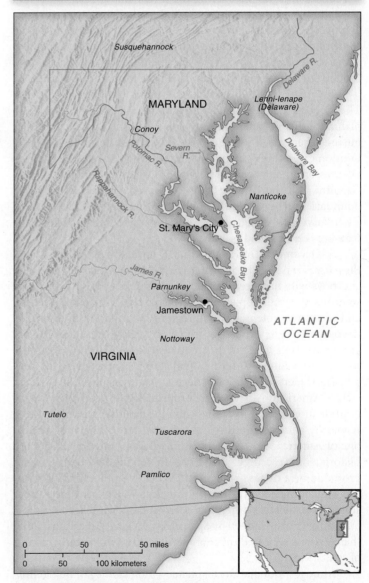

CHESAPEAKE COLONIES, 1640 The many deep rivers flowing into the Chesapeake Bay provided scattered English planters with a convenient transportation system, linking them directly to European markets.

Such political events, coupled with periodic economic recession and religious repression, determined, in large measure, the direction and flow of migration to America. During times of political turmoil, religious persecution, and economic insecurity, men and women thought more seriously about transferring to the New World than they did during periods of peace and prosperity. Obviously, people who moved to America at different times came from different social and political environments. A person who emigrated to Pennsylvania in the 1680s, for example, left an England unlike the one that a Virginian in 1607 or a Bay Colonist in 1630 might have known. Moreover, the young men and women who migrated to London in search of work and who then, in their frustration and poverty, decided to move to the Chesapeake carried a very different set of memories from those people who moved directly to New England from the small rural villages of their homeland.

Regardless of the exact timing of departure, English settlers brought with them ideas and assumptions that helped them make sense of their everyday experiences in an unfamiliar environment. Their values were tested and sometimes transformed in the New World, but they were seldom destroyed. Settlement involved a complex process of adjustment. The colonists developed different subcultures in America, and in each it is possible to trace the interaction between the settlers' values and the physical elements, such as the climate, crops, and soil, of their new surroundings. The Chesapeake, the New England colonies, the Middle Colonies, and the Southern Colonies formed distinct regional identities that have survived to the present day.

The Chesapeake: Dreams of Wealth

Why did the Chesapeake colonies not prosper during the earliest years of settlement?

After the Roanoke debacle in 1590, English interest in American settlement declined, and only a few aging visionaries such as Richard Hakluyt kept alive the dream of colonies in the why ordinary people who had no direct financial stake in the New World so generously supported English efforts to colonize America. Soon after James I ascended to the throne, adventurers were given an opportunity to put their theories into practice in the colonies of Virginia and Maryland, an area known as the Chesapeake, or somewhat later, as the Tobacco Coast.

Entrepreneurs in Virginia

During Elizabeth's reign, the major obstacle to successful colonization of the New World had been raising money. No single person, no matter how rich or well connected, could underwrite the vast expenses a New World settlement required. The solution to this financial problem was the **joint-stock company**, a business organization in which scores of people could invest without fear of bankruptcy. A merchant or landowner could purchase a share of stock at a stated price, and at the end of several years the investor could anticipate recovering the initial amount plus a portion of whatever profits the company had made. Joint-stock ventures sprang up like mushrooms. Affluent English citizens, and even some of more modest fortunes, rushed to invest in the companies and, as a result, some projects were able to amass large amounts of capital, enough certainly to launch a new colony in Virginia.

On April 10, 1606, James issued the first Virginia charter. The document authorized the London Company to establish plantations in Virginia. The London Company was an ambitious business venture. Its leader, Sir Thomas Smith, was reputedly London's wealthiest merchant. Smith and his partners gained possession of the territory lying between present-day North Carolina and the Hudson River. These were generous but vague boundaries, to be sure, but the Virginia Company—as the London Company soon called itself—set out immediately to find the treasures Hakluyt had promised.

In December 1606, the *Susan Constant,* the *Godspeed,* and the *Discovery* sailed for America. The ships carried 104 men and boys who had been instructed to establish a fortified outpost somehundred miles up a large navigable river. The natural beauty and economic potential of the region was apparent to everyone. A voyager on the expedition reported seeing "faire meaddowes and goodly tall trees, with such fresh waters running through the woods, as almost ravished [us] at first sight."

The leaders of the colony selected—without consulting resident Native Americans—what the Europeans considered a promising location more than thirty miles from the mouth of the James River. A marshy peninsula jutting out into the river became the site for one of America's most unsuccessful villages, Jamestown. Modern historians have criticized the choice, for the low-lying ground proved to be a disease-ridden death trap; even the drinking water was contaminated with salt. But the first Virginians were neither stupid nor suicidal. Jamestown seemed the ideal place to build a fort, since surprise attack by Spaniards or Native Americans rather than sickness appeared the more serious threat in the early months of settlement.

Almost immediately, dispirited colonists began quarreling. The adventurers were not prepared for the challenges that confronted them in America. Part of the problem was cultural. Most of them had grown up in a depressed agricultural economy that could not provide full-time employment for all who wanted it. In England, laborers shared what little work was available. One man, for example, might perform a certain chore while others simply watched. Later, the men who had been idle were given an opportunity to work for an hour or two. This labor system may have been appropriate for England, but in Virginia it nearly destroyed the colony. Adventurers sat around Jamestown while other men performed crucial agricultural tasks. It made little sense, of course, to share work in an environment in which people were starving because too little labor was expended on the planting and harvesting of crops. Not surprisingly, some modern historians—those who assumed all workers should put in an eight-hour day—branded the early Virginians as lazy, irresponsible beings who preferred to play while others labored. In point of fact, however, the first settlers were merely attempting to replicate a traditional work experience.

Avarice exacerbated the problems. The adventurers had traveled to the New World in search of the sort of instant wealth they imagined the Spaniards to have found in Mexico and Peru. Published tales of rubies and diamonds lying on the beach probably inflamed their expectations. Even when it must have been apparent that such expectations were unfounded, the first settlers often behaved in Virginia as if they fully expected to become rich. Instead of cooperating for the common good—guarding or farming, for example—individuals pursued personal interests. They searched for gold when they might have helped plant corn. No one was willing to take orders, and those who were supposed to govern the colony looked after their private welfare while disease, war, and starvation ravaged the settlement.

Spinning Out of Control

Virginia might have gone the way of Roanoke had it not been for Captain John Smith. By any standard, he was a resourceful man. Before coming to Jamestown, he had traveled throughout Europe and fought with the Hungarian army against the Turks—and, if Smith is to be believed, he was saved from certain death by various beautiful women. Because of his reputation for boasting, historians have discounted Smith's account of life in early Virginia. Recent scholarship, however, has affirmed the truthfulness of his curious story. In Virginia, Smith brought order out of anarchy. While members of the council in Jamestown debated petty politics, he traded with the local Indians for food, mapped the Chesapeake Bay, and may even have been rescued from execution by a young Indian girl, Pocahontas. In the fall of 1608, he seized control of the ruling council and instituted a tough military discipline. Under Smith, no one enjoyed special privilege. Individuals whom he forced to work came to hate him. But he managed to keep them alive, no small achievement in such a deadly environment.

Leaders of the Virginia Company in London recognized the need to reform the entire enterprise. After all, they had spent considerable sums and had received nothing in return. In 1609, the company directors obtained a new charter from the king, which completely reorganized the Virginia government. Henceforth all commercial and political decisions affecting the colonists rested with the company, a fact that had not been made sufficiently clear in the 1606 charter. Moreover, in

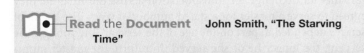

▶ Read the Document   John Smith, "The Starving Time"

CAPTAIN JOHN SMITH.

John Smith (c. 1580–1630) was a professional mercenary and adventurer who fought against both the Spanish and the Ottomans before being hired by the Virginia Company to assist in the establishment of its new colony at Jamestown.

an effort to raise scarce capital, the original partners opened the joint-stock company to the general public. For a little more than £12—approximately one year's wages for an unskilled English laborer—a person or group of persons could purchase a stake in Virginia. It was anticipated that in 1616 the profits from the colony would be distributed among the shareholders. The company sponsored a publicity campaign; pamphlets and sermons extolled the colony's potential and exhorted patriotic English citizens to invest in the enterprise.

Between 1609 and 1611, the remaining Virginia settlers lacked capable leadership, and perhaps as a result, they lacked food. The terrible winter of 1609–1610 was termed the "starving time." A few desperate colonists were driven to cannibalism, an ironic situation since early explorers had assumed that only Native Americans would eat human flesh. In England, Smith heard that one colonist had killed his wife, powdered [salted] her, and "had eaten part of her before it was known; for which he was executed." The captain, who possessed

a droll sense of humor, observed, "Now, whether she was better roasted, broiled, or carbonadoed [sliced], I know not, but such a dish as powdered wife I never heard of." Other people simply lost the will to live.

The presence of so many Native Americans heightened the danger. The first colonists found themselves living—or attempting to live—in territory controlled by what was probably the most powerful Indian confederation east of the Mississippi River. Under the leadership of their *werowance*, Powhatan, these Indians had by 1608 created a loose association of some thirty tribes, and when Captain John Smith arrived to lead several hundred adventurers, the Powhatans (named for their king) numbered some fourteen thousand people, of whom thirty-two hundred were warriors. These people hoped initially to enlist the Europeans as allies against native enemies. When it became clear that the two groups, holding such different notions about labor and property and about the exploitation of the natural environment, could not coexist in peace, the Powhatans tried to drive the invaders out of Virginia, once in 1622 and again in 1644. The failure of the second campaign ended in the complete destruction of the Powhatan empire.

In June 1610, the settlers who had survived despite starvation and conflicts with the Indians actually abandoned Virginia. Through a stroke of luck, however, they encountered a small fleet led by the colony's governor, the Baron De La Warr, just as they commenced their voyage down the James River. De La Warr and the deputy governors who succeeded him, Sir Thomas Gates and Sir Thomas Dale, ruled by martial law. The new colonists, many of them male and female servants employed by the company, were marched to work by the beat of the drum. Such methods saved the colony but could not make it flourish. In 1616, company shareholders received no profits. Their only reward was the right to a piece of unsurveyed land located three thousand miles from London.

"Stinking Weed"

The economic solution to Virginia's problems grew in the vacant lots of Jamestown. Only Indians bothered to cultivate tobacco until John Rolfe, a settler who achieved notoriety by marrying Pocahontas, realized this local weed might be a valuable export. Rolfe experimented with the crop, eventually growing in Virginia a milder variety that had been developed in the West Indies and was more appealing to European smokers.

Virginians suddenly possessed a means to make money. Tobacco proved relatively easy to grow, and settlers who had avoided work now threw themselves into its production with single-minded diligence. In 1617, one observer found that Jamestown's "streets and all other spare places [are] planted with tobacco . . . the Colony dispersed all about planting tobacco." Although King James I originally considered smoking immoral and unhealthy, he changed his mind when the duties he collected on tobacco imports began to mount. He was neither the first nor the last ruler who decided a vice that generates revenue is not really so bad.

The company sponsored another ambitious effort to transform Virginia into a profitable enterprise. In 1618, Sir Edwin

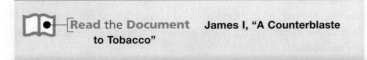 Read the Document   James I, "A Counterblaste to Tobacco"

This tobacco label advertises Virginia's valuable export—tobacco. Despite King James's initial attitude toward the "stinking weed," once the government saw that tobacco made a profit, it dropped its moral criticism of the American crop.

Sandys (pronounced Sands) led a faction of stockholders that began to pump life into the dying organization by instituting a series of sweeping reforms and eventually ousting Sir Thomas Smith and his friends. Sandys wanted private investors to develop their own estates in Virginia. Before 1618, there had been little incentive to do so, but by relaxing Dale's martial law and promising an elective representative assembly called the **House of Burgesses**, Sandys thought he could make the colony more attractive to wealthy speculators.

Even more important was Sandys's method for distributing land. Colonists who covered their own transportation cost to America were guaranteed a **headright**, a 50-acre lot for which they paid only a small annual rent. Adventurers were granted additional headrights for each servant they brought to the colony. This procedure allowed prosperous planters to build up huge estates while they also acquired dependent laborers. This land system persisted long after the company's collapse. So too did the notion that the wealth of a few justified the exploitation many others.

Time of Reckoning

Between 1619 and 1622, colonists arrived in Virginia in record number. Company records reveal that during this short period, 3,570 individuals were sent to the colony. People seldom moved to Virginia in families. Although the first women arrived in Jamestown in 1608, most emigrants were single males in their teens or early twenties who came to the New World as indentured servants. In exchange for transportation across the Atlantic, they agreed to serve a master for a stated number of years. The length of service depended in part on the age of the servant. The younger the servant, the longer he or she served. In return, the master promised to give the laborers proper care and, at the conclusion of their contracts, to provide them with tools and clothes according to "the custom of the country."

Powerful Virginians corrupted the system. Poor servants wanted to establish independent tobacco farms. As they discovered, however, headrights were awarded not to the newly freed servant, but to the great planter who had borne the cost of the servant's transportation to the New World and paid for food and clothing during the indenture. And even though indentured servants were promised land at the moment of freedom, they were most often cheated, becoming members of a growing, disaffected, landless class in seventeenth-century Virginia.

Whenever possible, planters in Virginia purchased able-bodied workers, in other words, persons (preferably male) capable of performing hard agricultural labor. This preference dramatically skewed the colony's sex ratio. In the early decades, men outnumbered women by as much as six to one. As one historian, Edmund S. Morgan, observed, "Women were scarcer than corn or liquor in Virginia and fetched a higher price." Such gender imbalance meant that even if a male servant lived to the end of his indenture—an unlikely prospect—he could not realistically expect to start a family of his own. Moreover, despite apparent legal safeguards, masters could treat dependent workers as they pleased; after all, these people were legally considered property. Servants were sold, traded, even gambled away in games of chance. It does not require much imagination to see that a society that tolerated such an exploitative labor system might later embrace slavery.

Most Virginians then did not live long enough to worry about marriage. Death was omnipresent. Indeed, extraordinarily high mortality was a major reason the Chesapeake colonies developed so differently from those of New England. On the eve of the 1618 reforms, Virginia's population stood at approximately 700. The company sent at least 3,000 more people, but by 1622 only 1,240 were still alive. "It Consequentilie followes," declared one angry shareholder, "that we had then lost 3,000 persons within those 3 yeares." The major killers were contagious diseases. Salt in the water supply also took a toll. And on Good Friday, March 22, 1622, the Powhatan Indians slew 347 Europeans in a well-coordinated surprise attack.

No one knows for certain what effect such a horrendous mortality rate had on the men and women who survived. At the very least, it must have created a sense of impermanence, a desire to escape Virginia with a little money before sickness or violence ended the adventure. The settlers who drank to excess aboard the tavern ships anchored in the James River described the colony "not as a place of Habitacion but only of a short sojourninge."

Corruption and Reform

On both sides of the Atlantic, people wondered who should be blamed. Why had so many colonists died in a land so rich in potential? The burden of responsibility lay in large measure with

📖 **Read the Document**   Wessell Webling, His Indenture (1622)

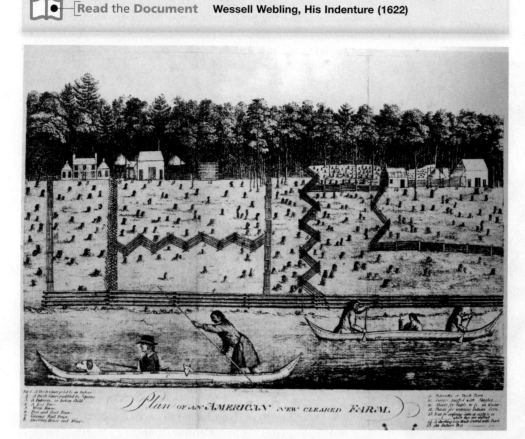

Plan OF AN AMERICAN NEW CLEARED FARM.

Indentured white servants provided much of the labor necessary for the founding of the early colonies. Here, workers are shown clearing lands for agriculture and splitting logs to make boards for building or sale.

area—convened as a court of law as well as a governing body. The "county court" was the most important institution of local government in Virginia, and long after the American Revolution, it served as a center for social, political, and commercial activities.

Changes in government had little impact on the character of daily life in Virginia. The planters continued to grow tobacco, ignoring advice to diversify, and as the Indians were killed, made into tributaries, or pushed north and south, Virginians took up large tracts of land along the colony's many navigable rivers. The focus of their lives was the isolated plantation, a small cluster of buildings housing the planter's family and dependent workers. These were modest wooden structures. Not until the eighteenth century did the Chesapeake gentry build the great Georgian mansions that still attract tourists. The dispersed pattern of settlement retarded the development of institutions such as schools and churches. Besides Jamestown there were no population centers, and as late as 1705, Robert Beverley, a leading planter, reported that Virginia did not have a single place "that may reasonably bear the Name of a Town."

the Virginia Company. Sandys and his supporters were in too great a hurry to make a profit. Settlers were shipped to America, but neither housing nor food awaited them in Jamestown. Weakened by the long sea voyage, they quickly succumbed to contagious disease.

The company's scandalous mismanagement embarrassed the king, and in 1624, he dissolved the bankrupt enterprise and transformed Virginia into a royal colony. The crown appointed a governor and a council. No provision was made, however, for continuing the local representative assembly, an institution the Stuarts heartily opposed. The House of Burgesses had first convened in 1619. While elections to the Burgesses were hardly democratic, the assembly did provide wealthy planters with a voice in government. Even without the king's authorization, the representatives gathered annually after 1629, and in 1639, Charles recognized the body's existence.

He had no choice. The colonists who served on the council or in the assembly were strong-willed, ambitious men. They had no intention of surrendering control over local affairs. Since Charles was having political troubles of his own and lived three thousand miles from Jamestown, he usually allowed the Virginians to have their own way. In 1634, the assembly divided the colony into eight counties. In each one, a group of appointed justices of the peace—the wealthy planters of the

Maryland: A Troubled Refuge for Catholics

The driving force behind the founding of Maryland was Sir George Calvert, later Lord Baltimore. Calvert, a talented and well-educated man, enjoyed the patronage of James I. He was awarded lucrative positions in the government, the most important being the king's secretary of state. In 1625, Calvert shocked almost everyone by publicly declaring his Catholicism; in this fiercely anti-Catholic society, persons who openly supported the Church of Rome were immediately stripped of civil office. Although forced to resign as secretary of state, Calvert retained the crown's favor.

Before resigning, Calvert sponsored a settlement on the coast of Newfoundland, but after visiting the place, the proprietor concluded that no English person, whatever his or her religion, would transfer to a place where the "ayre [is] so intolerably cold." He turned his attention to the Chesapeake, and on June 30, 1632, Charles I granted George Calvert's son, Cecilius, a charter for a colony to be located north of Virginia. The boundaries of the settlement, named Maryland in honor of Charles's queen, were so vaguely defined that they generated legal controversies not fully resolved until the mid-eighteenth century when Charles Mason and Jeremiah Dixon surveyed their famous line between Pennsylvania and Maryland.

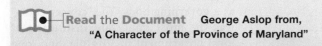

Read the Document George Aslop from, "A Character of the Province of Maryland"

Cecilius Calvert, the second Lord Baltimore, insisted that Maryland tolerate all Christian religions, including Catholicism, something no other colony was willing to do. The young slave in the background reminds us who did the hard labor in the Chesapeake Colonies.

Cecilius, the second Lord Baltimore, wanted to create a sanctuary for England's persecuted Catholics. He also intended to make money. Without Protestant settlers, it seemed unlikely Maryland would prosper, and Cecilius instructed his brother Leonard, the colony's governor, to do nothing that might frighten off hypersensitive Protestants. The governor was ordered to "cause all Acts of the Roman Catholic Religion to be done as privately as may be and . . . [to] instruct all Roman Catholics to be silent upon all occasions of discourse concerning matters of Religion." On March 25, 1634, the *Ark* and *Dove,* carrying about 150 settlers, landed safely, and within days, the governor purchased from the Yaocomico Indians a village that became St. Mary's City, the capital of Maryland.

The colony's charter was an odd document, a throwback to an earlier feudal age. It transformed Baltimore into a "palatine lord," a proprietor with almost royal powers. Settlers swore an oath of allegiance not to the king of England but to Lord Baltimore. In England, such practices had long ago passed into obsolescence. As the proprietor, Lord Baltimore owned outright almost 6 million acres; he possessed absolute authority over anyone living in his domain.

On paper, at least, everyone in Maryland was assigned a place in an elaborate social hierarchy. Members of a colonial ruling class, persons who purchased 6,000 acres from Baltimore, were called lords of the manor. These landed aristocrats were permitted to establish local courts of law. People holding less acreage enjoyed fewer privileges, particularly in government. Baltimore figured that land sales and rents would adequately finance the entire venture.

Baltimore's feudal system never took root in Chesapeake soil. People simply refused to play the social roles the lord proprietor had assigned. These tensions affected the operation of Maryland's government. Baltimore assumed that his brother, acting as his deputy in America, and a small appointed council of local aristocrats would pass necessary laws and carry out routine administration. When an elected assembly first convened in 1635, Baltimore allowed the delegates to discuss only those acts he had prepared. The members of the assembly bridled at such restrictions, insisting on exercising traditional parliamentary privileges. Neither side gained a clear victory in the assembly, and for almost twenty-five years, legislative squabbling contributed to the widespread political instability that almost destroyed Maryland.

The colony drew both Protestants and Catholics, and the two groups might have lived in harmony had civil war not broken out in England. When Cromwell and the Puritan faction executed Charles, transforming England briefly into a republic, it seemed Baltimore might lose his colony. To head off such an event and to placate Maryland's restless Protestants, in 1649, the proprietor drafted the famous "Act concerning Religion," which extended toleration to all individuals who accepted the divinity of Christ. At a time when European rulers regularly persecuted people for their religious beliefs, Baltimore championed liberty of conscience.

However laudable the act may have been, it did not heal religious divisions in Maryland, and when local Puritans seized the colony's government, they promptly repealed the act. For almost two decades, vigilantes roamed the countryside, and during the "Plundering Time" (1644–1646), one armed group temporarily drove Leonard Calvert out of Maryland. In 1655, civil war flared again.

In this troubled sanctuary, ordinary planters and their workers cultivated tobacco on plantations dispersed along riverfronts. In 1678, Baltimore complained that he could not find fifty houses in a space of thirty miles. Tobacco affected almost every aspect of local culture. "In Virginia and Maryland," one Calvert explained, "Tobacco, as our Staple, is our all, and indeed leaves no room for anything Else." A steady stream of indentured servants supplied the plantations with dependent laborers—until they were replaced by African slaves at the end of the seventeenth century.

Europeans sacrificed much by coming to the Chesapeake. For most of the century, their standard of living was primitive when compared with that of people of the same social class who had remained in England. Two-thirds of the planters, for example, lived in houses of only two rooms and of a type associated with the poorest classes in contemporary English society.

Reforming England in America

How did differences in religion affect the founding of the New England colonies?

The Pilgrims enjoy almost mythic status in American history. These brave refugees crossed the cold Atlantic in search of religious liberty, signed a democratic compact aboard the *Mayflower,* landed at Plymouth Rock, and gave us our Thanksgiving Day. As with most legends, this one contains only a core of truth.

The Pilgrims were not crusaders who set out to change the world. Rather, they were humble English farmers. Their story began in the early 1600s in Scrooby Manor, a small community located approximately 150 miles north of London. Many people living in this area believed the Church of England retained too many traces of its Catholic origin. To support such a corrupt institution was like winking at the devil. Its very rituals compromised God's true believers, and so, in the early years of the reign of James I, the Scrooby congregation formally left the established state church. Like others who followed this logic, they were called Separatists. Since English statute required citizens to attend Anglican services, the Scrooby Separatists moved to Holland in 1608–1609 rather than compromise.

The Netherlands provided the Separatists with a good home—too good. The members of the little church feared they were losing their distinct identity; their children were becoming Dutch. In 1617, therefore, a portion of the original Scrooby congregation vowed to sail to America. Included in this group was William Bradford, a wonderfully literate man who wrote *Of Plymouth Plantation,* one of the first and certainly most poignant accounts of an early American settlement.

Poverty presented the major obstacle to the Pilgrims' plans. They petitioned for a land patent from the Virginia Company of London. At the same time, they looked for someone willing to underwrite the staggering costs of colonization. The negotiations went well, or so it seemed. After stopping in England to take on supplies and laborers, the Pilgrims set off for America in 1620 aboard the *Mayflower,* armed with a patent to settle in Virginia and indebted to a group of English investors who were only marginally interested in religious reform.

Because of an error in navigation, the Pilgrims landed not in Virginia but in New England. The patent for which they had worked so diligently had no validity in the region. In fact, the crown had granted New England to another company. Without a patent, the colonists possessed no authorization to form a civil government, a serious matter since some sailors who were not Pilgrims threatened mutiny. To preserve the struggling community from anarchy, forty-one men signed an agreement known as the **Mayflower Compact** to "covenant and combine our selves together into a civil body politick."

Although later praised for its democratic character, the Mayflower Compact could not ward off disease and hunger. During the first months in Plymouth, death claimed approximately half of the 102 people who had initially set out from England. Moreover, debts contracted in England severely burdened the new colony. To their credit, the Pilgrims honored their financial obligations, but it took almost twenty years to satisfy the English investors. Without Bradford, whom they elected as governor, the settlers might have allowed adversity to overwhelm them. Through strength of will and self-sacrifice, however, Bradford persuaded frightened men and women that they could survive in America.

Bradford had a lot of help. Almost anyone who has heard of the Plymouth Colony knows of Squanto, a Patuxt Indian who welcomed the first Pilgrims in excellent English. In 1614, unscrupulous adventurers had kidnapped Squanto and sold him in Spain as a slave. Somehow, this resourceful man escaped bondage, making his way to London, where a group of merchants who owned land in Newfoundland taught him to speak English. They apparently hoped that he would deliver moving public testimonials about the desirability of moving to the New World. In any case, Squanto returned to the Plymouth area just before the Pilgrims arrived. Squanto joined Massasoit, a local Native American leader, in teaching the Pilgrims much about hunting and agriculture, a debt that Bradford freely acknowledged. Although evidence for the so-called First Thanksgiving is extremely sketchy, it is certain that without Native American support the Europeans would have starved.

In time, the Pilgrims replicated the humble little farm communities they had once known in England. They formed Separatist congregations to their liking; the population slowly increased. The settlers experimented with commercial fishing and the fur trade, but the efforts never generated substantial income. Most families relied on mixed husbandry, grain, and livestock. Because Plymouth offered only limited economic prospects, it attracted only a trickle of new settlers. In 1691, the colony was absorbed into its larger and more prosperous neighbor, Massachusetts Bay.

"The Great Migration"

In the early decades of the seventeenth century, an extraordinary spirit of religious reform burst forth in England, and before it had burned itself out, Puritanism had transformed the face of England and America. Modern historians have difficulty comprehending this powerful spiritual movement. Some consider the **Puritans** rather neurotic individuals who condemned liquor and sex, dressed in drab clothes, and minded their neighbors' business.

The crude caricature is based on a profound misunderstanding of the actual nature of this broad popular movement. The seventeenth-century Puritans were more like today's radical political reformers, men and women committed to far-reaching institutional change, than like naive do-gooders or narrow fundamentalists. To their enemies, of course, the Puritans were irritants, always pointing out civil and ecclesiastical imperfections and urging everyone to try to fulfill the commands of Scripture. A great many people, however, shared their vision, and not only did they found several American colonies, but they also sparked the English Civil War, an event that generated bold new thinking about republican government and popular sovereignty.

The Puritans were products of the Protestant Reformation. They accepted a Calvinist notion that an omnipotent God predestined some people to salvation and damned others throughout eternity (see Chapter 1). But instead of waiting passively for Judgment Day, the Puritans examined themselves for signs of grace, for hints that God had in fact placed them among his "elect." A member of this select group, they argued, would try to live according to Scripture, to battle sin and eradicate corruption.

For the Puritans, the logic of everyday life was clear. If the Church of England contained unscriptural elements—clerical vestments, for example—then they must be eliminated. If the pope in Rome was in league with the Antichrist, then Protestant kings had better not form alliances with Catholic states. If God condemned licentiousness and intoxication, then local officials should punish whores and drunks. There was nothing improper about an occasional beer or passionate physical love within marriage, but when sex and drink became ends in themselves, the Puritans thought England's ministers and magistrates should

Read the Document   John Winthrop, "A Model of Christian Charity" (1830)

Voters in Massachusetts who were called "freemen" reelected John Winthrop governor many times, an indication of his success in translating Puritan values into practical policy.

speak out. Persons of this temperament were more combative than the Pilgrims had been. They wanted to purify the Church of England from within, and before the 1630s at least, separatism held little appeal for them.

From the Puritan perspective, the early Stuarts, James I and Charles I, seemed unconcerned about the spiritual state of the nation. James tolerated corruption within his own court; he condoned gross public extravagance. His foreign policy appeased European Catholic powers. At one time, he even tried to marry his son to a Catholic princess. Neither king showed interest in purifying the Anglican Church. In fact, Charles assisted the rapid advance of William Laud, a bishop who represented everything the Puritans detested. Laud defended church ceremonies that they found obnoxious. He persecuted Puritan ministers, forcing them either to conform to his theology or lose their licenses to preach. As long as Parliament met, Puritan voters in the various boroughs and countries throughout England elected men sympathetic to their point of view. These outspoken representatives criticized royal policies and hounded Laud. Because of their defiance, Charles decided in 1629 to rule England without Parliament and four years later named Laud archbishop of Canterbury. The last doors of reform slammed shut. The corruption remained.

John Winthrop, the future governor of Massachusetts Bay, was caught up in these events. Little about his background suggested such an auspicious future. He owned a small manor in Suffolk, one that never produced sufficient income to support his growing family. He dabbled in law. But the core of Winthrop's life was his faith in God, a faith so intense his contemporaries immediately identified him as a Puritan. The Lord, he concluded, was displeased with England. Time for reform was running out. In May 1629, he wrote to his wife, "I am verily perswaded God will bring some heavye Affliction upon this lande, and that speedylye." He was, however, confident that the Lord would "provide a shelter and a hidinge place for us."

Other Puritans, some wealthier and politically better connected than Winthrop, reached similar conclusions about England's future. They turned their attention to the possibility of establishing a colony in America, and on March 4, 1629, their Massachusetts Bay Company obtained a charter directly from the king. Charles and his advisers apparently thought the Massachusetts Bay Company was a commercial venture no different from the dozens of other joint-stock companies that had recently sprung into existence.

Winthrop and his associates knew better. On August 26, 1629, twelve of them met secretly and signed the Cambridge Agreement. They pledged to be "ready in our persons and with such of our severall familyes as are to go with us . . . to embark for the said plantation by the first of March next." There was one loophole. The charters of most joint-stock companies designated a specific place where business meetings were to be held. For reasons not entirely clear—a timely bribe is a good guess—the charter of the Massachusetts Bay Company did not contain this standard clause. It could hold meetings anywhere the stockholders, called "freemen," desired, even America, and if they were in America, the king and his archbishop could not easily interfere in their affairs.

"A City on a Hill"

The Winthrop fleet departed England in March 1630. By the end of the first year, almost two thousand people had arrived in Massachusetts Bay, and before the "**Great Migration**" concluded in the early 1640s, more than sixteen thousand men and women had arrived in the new Puritan colony.

A great deal is known about the background of these particular settlers. A large percentage of them originated in an area northeast of London called East Anglia, a region in which Puritan ideas had taken deep root. London, Kent, and the West Country also contributed to the stream of emigrants. In some instances, entire villages were reestablished across the Atlantic. Many Bay Colonists had worked as farmers in England, but a surprisingly large number came from industrial centers, such as Norwich, where cloth was manufactured for the export trade.

Whatever their backgrounds, they moved to Massachusetts as nuclear families, fathers, mothers, and their dependent children, a form of migration strikingly different from the one that peopled Virginia and Maryland. Moreover, because the settlers had already formed families in England, the colony's sex ratio was more balanced than that found in the Chesapeake colonies. Finally, and perhaps more significantly, once they had arrived in Massachusetts, these men and women survived. Indeed, their life expectancy compares favorably to that of modern Americans. Many factors help explain this phenomenon—clean drinking water and a healthy climate, for example. While the Puritans could not have planned to live longer than did colonists in other parts of the New World, this remarkable accident reduced the emotional shock of long-distance migration.

The first settlers possessed another source of strength and stability. They were bound together by a common sense of purpose. God, they insisted, had formed a special covenant with the people of Massachusetts Bay. On his part, the Lord expected them to live according to Scripture, to reform the church, in other words, to create an Old Testament "city on a hill" that would stand as a beacon of righteousness for the rest of the Christian world. If they fulfilled their side of the bargain, the settlers could anticipate peace and prosperity. No one, not even the lowliest servant, was excused from this divine covenant, for as Winthrop stated, "Wee must be knitt together in this worke as one man." Even as the first ships were leaving England, John Cotton, a popular Puritan minister, urged the emigrants to go forth "with a publicke spirit, looking not on your owne things only, but also on the things of others." Many people throughout the ages have espoused such communal rhetoric, but these particular men and women went about the business of forming a new colony as if they truly intended to transform a religious vision into social reality.

The Bay Colonists gradually came to accept a highly innovative form of church government known as Congregationalism. Under the system, each village church was independent of outside interference. The American Puritans, of course, wanted nothing of bishops. The people (the "saints") were the church, and as a body, they pledged to uphold God's law. In the Salem Church, for example, the members covenanted "with the Lord and with one another and do bind ourselves in the presence of God to walk together in all his ways."

Simply because a person happened to live in a certain community did not mean he or she automatically belonged to the local church. The churches of Massachusetts were voluntary institutions, and in order to join one a man or woman had to provide testimony—a confession of faith—before neighbors who had already been admitted as full members. It was a demanding process. Whatever the personal strains, however, most men and women in early Massachusetts aspired to full membership, which entitled them to the sacraments, and gave some of them responsibility for choosing ministers, disciplining backsliders, and determining difficult questions of theology. Although women and blacks could not vote for ministers, they did become members of the Congregational churches. Over the course of the seventeenth century, women made up an increasingly large share of the membership.

Some aspects of community religiosity in early Massachusetts may, of course, strike modern Americans as morbid. Ministers expected people convicted of capital crimes to offer a full public confession of their sins just before their own execution. Such rituals reinforced everyday moral values by reminding ordinary men and women—those who listened to the confession—of the fatal consequences awaiting those who ignored the teachings of Scripture.

In creating a civil government, the Bay Colonists faced a particularly difficult challenge. Their charter allowed the investors in a joint-stock company to set up a business organization. When the settlers arrived in America, however, company leaders—men like Winthrop—moved quickly to transform the commercial structure into a colonial government. An early step in this direction took place on May 18, 1631, when the category of "freeman" was extended to all adult males who had become members of a Congregational church. This decision greatly expanded the franchise of Massachusetts Bay, and historians estimate that during the 1630s, at least 40 percent of the colony's adult males could vote in elections. While this percentage may seem low by modern or even Jacksonian standards, it was higher than anything the emigrants would have known in England. The freemen voted annually for a governor, a group of magistrates called the Court of Assistants, and after 1634, deputies who represented the interests of the individual towns. Even military officers were elected every year in Massachusetts Bay.

Two popular misconceptions about this government should be dispelled. It was neither a democracy nor a theocracy. The magistrates elected in Massachusetts did not believe they represented the voters, much less the whole populace. They ruled in the name of the electorate, but their responsibility as rulers was to God. In 1638, Winthrop warned against overly democratic forms, since "the best part [of the people] is always the least, and of that best part the wiser is always the lesser." And second, the Congregational ministers possessed no formal political authority in Massachusetts Bay. They could not even hold civil office, and it was not unusual for the voters to ignore the recommendations of a respected minister such as John Cotton.

In New England, the town became the center of public life. In other regions of British America where the county was the focus of local government, people did not experience the same density of social and institutional interaction. In Massachusetts,

Feature Essay

The Children Who Refused to Come Home
Captivity and Conversion

Portrait of Esther Wheelwright as an Ursuline nun.

The spread of terrorism throughout the modern world and reports of journalists and civilian workers captured in war zones have forced many Americans to contemplate a deeply unsettling question: How would they behave if they were kidnapped by members of a group hostile to the fundamental values of the United States? Such concerns are not new. During the colonial period, New Englanders who settled along the frontier with French Canada knew that at any moment they might be carried away to Quebec or Montreal as captives and under fearful conditions might discover the fragility of their own ethnic and religious identities.

Between 1675 and 1763 the French and British empires waged almost constant war. Often the conflicts turned on

dynastic rivalries in Europe, but whatever the causes, the fighting extended to North America, where in an effort to contain the expansion of English settlement, the French and their Indian allies raided exposed communities from the coast of Maine to western Massachusetts. During these years, approximately 1,641 English colonists were taken captive—nearly half of them children—and many other people died in the violent clashes. On the long trek back to Canada, the French and Indians killed those prisoners who resisted or who were too weak to keep up the pace. The Reverend Cotton Mather, New England's most influential late-seventeenth-century minister, invited his parishioners to imagine the terrifying experience of capture: "[The] *Captives* . . . are every minute looking when they shall be roasted alive, to

make a sport and a feast, for the most execrable cannibals . . . *Captives,* that must see their nearest relations butchered before their eyes, and yet be afraid of letting those eyes drop a tear."

Although the French aimed to advance their imperial designs through attacks on English settlements, their Indian allies often entered the frontier wars for different reasons. The Abenaki, for example, harbored grievances against the English colonists from earlier conflicts and hoped with the help of the French to reap vengeance on them. Other Indian groups regarded the English captives as a source of revenue. After all, someone from Massachusetts was sure to offer a ransom for an unfortunate relative, and as one might predict in such a market, the price of liberation rose substantially over time. The Mohawk

Indians, however, viewed the captives as replacements for warriors killed in battle, and whenever possible, they worked to incorporate the New Englanders into their own culture. They knew from experience that children, especially young girls, offered the best prospects for successful adoption.

For the French and many of their Indian allies who had converted to Catholicism, religion served to justify frontier violence. French officials championed the Catholic faith, and they regarded New Englanders, not only as representatives of the British Empire, but also as Protestant heretics. The English gave as good as they got. They accepted as absolute truth that Catholicism was an utterly corrupt religion and that priests, especially Jesuits, could not be trusted in spiritual matters. French religious and political leaders looked upon New England captives as possible converts to Catholicism, for in this ongoing imperial controversy, news that an English Protestant had given up his or her faith for Rome represented a major symbolic victory. As historian James Axtell explained, if the English could not preserve their religious identities as captives, then "their pretensions to the status as God's 'chosen people' . . . would be cast in grave doubt."

The odds of converting young New Englanders to Catholicism in these circumstances must have appeared extraordinarily small. The captives taken in war had come from highly religious communities, where they had received regular instruction in the basic tenets of Reformed Protestantism. As children, Puritans learned to equate the Pope with Satan. Their forefathers had traveled to the New World to cleanse the Church of England from practices associated with Catholicism. And yet, amazingly, once they arrived in Canada, a significant number of prisoners—perhaps as much as fifty percent—accepted the Catholic faith, married French or Indian spouses, and settled comfortably into the routines of life in Canada.

One such convert was Esther Wheelwright. Abenaki Indians captured her in Wells, Maine, in 1703 when she was only seven years old, and adopted her. She was later taken in by nuns who taught her French. She became a keen student of Catholicism. Over time, the sincerity of her new faith won her many admirers, and eventually Esther—renamed Esther Marie Joseph de l'Enfant Jesus—became an Ursuline nun. Some years later, she was appointed Superior of the entire Ursuline order in Canada. When New Englanders attempted to negotiate her release, they discovered that "she does not wish to return" because of the "change of her religion." Esther's mother and father reluctantly accepted their daughter's decision. They even gave money to her convent, and in recognition of their generosity and forgiveness, she sent a portrait of herself as a nun to her bewildered Protestant family.

In the long contest for religious and cultural superiority, Eunice Williams posed an even more difficult challenge for New Englanders. After all, she was the daughter of a leading Congregational minister; no one doubted the quality of her religious instruction. Eunice's ordeal began on February 29, 1704, when a large force of French and Indians over-ran Deerfield, an agricultural community in western Massachusetts. Within a short time the raiders killed many inhabitants, including several members of her family. Her mother died during the long march to Canada. Eventually, the Reverend Williams negotiated his freedom as well as that of several surviving children. Eunice refused to join them. She had fallen in love with an Indian, and although friends and relatives begged her to reject Catholicism and life among the Kahnawake Mohawks, she politely, but firmly, rejected their pleas. Over the next several decades, Eunice and her Indian husband visited New England. On one occasion in 1741, her cousin the Reverend Solomon Williams pointed out in a sermon that Eunice had accepted the "Thickness of *popish* Darkness & Superstition." Lamenting her "pitiful and sorrowful Condition," he urged her to reaffirm the faith of her father. Unhappily for Solomon, Eunice had forgotten all that she once knew of the English language, and so the force of his shrill condemnation was lost on her.

No society easily accepts rejection. New Englanders struggled to comprehend why so many of their children would not come home, and they tried as best they could to explain to themselves why Eunice and the other captives refused to be redeemed. They assured each other that crafty priests had bribed—or even coerced—the children. A few ministers such as Cotton Mather and Eunice's father suggested that God had punished the Protestant communities for their sinful behavior. Whatever contemporaries may have thought of these accounts, modern historians have demonstrated that Catholic priests seldom employed force or promises of worldly goods in winning converts. Some captives may have felt gratitude to the French and Indians who had spared their lives. But undoubtedly, love, marriage, and a growing sense of security in a new society helped sever ties with a New England culture that slowly faded from memory.

The Reverend John Williams's own narrative of the Deerfield captives entitled *The Redeemed Captive Returning to Zion* (1707) addressed the crisis. It became a best-seller in a colony eager to hear the story of those redeemed from captivity, those returned to the fold. At the end of the day, however, the problem of abandoning one's nation and one's faith continued to haunt ordinary men and women who fervently identified with England and Protestantism. By turning their backs on European civilization, English culture, and the Protestant religion, these captives challenged foundational values even more powerfully than did the French and Indians.

QUESTIONS FOR DISCUSSION

1. Why did so many New England captives refuse to return home?

2. Why did the French and Indians view English children, especially young girls, as the most likely converts to their religion and way of life?

groups of men and women voluntarily covenanted together to observe common goals. The community constructed a meetinghouse where religious services and town meetings were held. This powerful sense of shared purpose—something that later Americans have greatly admired—should not obscure the fact that the founders of New England towns also had a keen eye for personal profit. Seventeenth-century records reveal that speculators often made a good deal of money from selling "shares" in village lands. But acquisitiveness never got out of control, and recent studies have shown that entrepreneurial practices rarely disturbed the peace of the Puritan communities. Inhabitants generally received land sufficient to build a house to support a family. Although villagers escaped the kind of feudal dues collected in other parts of America, they were expected to contribute to the minister's salary, pay local and colony taxes, and serve in the militia.

Limits of Religious Dissent

The European settlers of Massachusetts Bay managed to live in peace—at least with each other. This was a remarkable achievement considering the chronic instability that plagued other colonies at this time. The Bay Colonists disagreed over many issues, sometimes vociferously; whole towns disputed with neighboring villages over common boundaries. But the people inevitably relied on the civil courts to mediate differences. They believed in a rule of law, and in 1648 the colonial legislature, called the General Court, drew up the *Lawes and Liberties,* the first alphabetized code of law printed in English. This is a document of fundamental importance in American constitutional history. In clear prose, it explained to ordinary colonists their rights and responsibilities as citizens of the commonwealth. The code engendered public trust in government and discouraged magistrates from the arbitrary exercise of authority.

The Puritans never supported the concept of religious toleration. They transferred to the New World to preserve *their own* freedom of worship; about religious freedom of those deemed heretics, they expressed little concern. The most serious challenges to Puritan orthodoxy in Massachusetts Bay came from two brilliantly charismatic individuals. The first, Roger Williams, arrived in 1631 and immediately attracted a body of loyal followers. Indeed, everyone seemed to have liked Williams as a person.

Williams's *religious ideas,* however, created controversy. He preached extreme separatism. The Bay Colonists, he exclaimed, were impure in the sight of the Lord so long as they remained even nominal members of the Church of England. Moreover, he questioned the validity of the colony's charter, since the king had not first purchased the land from the Indians, a view that threatened the integrity of the entire colonial experiment. Williams also insisted that the civil rulers of Massachusetts had no business punishing settlers for their religious beliefs. It was God's responsibility, not men's, to monitor people's consciences. The Bay magistrates were prepared neither to tolerate heresy nor to accede to Williams's other demands, and in 1636, after attempts to reach a compromise had failed, they banished him from the colony. Williams worked out the logic of his ideas in Providence, a village he founded in what would become Rhode Island.

The magistrates of Massachusetts Bay rightly concluded that the second individual, Anne Hutchinson, posed an even graver threat to the peace of the commonwealth. This extremely intelligent woman, her husband William, and her children followed John Cotton to the New World in 1634. Even contemporaries found her religious ideas, usually termed **Antinomianism**, somewhat confusing.

Whatever her thoughts, Hutchinson shared them with other Bostonians, many of them women. Her outspoken views scandalized orthodox leaders of church and state. She suggested that all but two ministers in the colony had lost touch with the "Holy Spirit" and were preaching a doctrine in the Congregational churches that was little better than that of Archbishop Laud. When authorities demanded she explain her unusual opinions, she suggested that she experienced divine inspiration independently of either the Bible or the clergy. In other words, Hutchinson's teachings could not be tested by Scripture, a position that seemed dangerously subjective. Indeed, Hutchinson's theology called the very foundation of Massachusetts Bay into question. Without clear, external standards, one person's truth was as valid as anyone else's, and from Winthrop's perspective, Hutchinson's teachings invited civil and religious anarchy. But her challenge to authority was not simply theological. As a woman, her aggressive speech sparked a deeply misogynistic response from the colony's male leaders.

When this woman described Congregational ministers—some of them the leading divines of Boston—as unconverted men, the General Court intervened. For two very tense days in 1637, the ministers and magistrates of Massachusetts Bay cross-examined Hutchinson; in this intense theological debate, she more than held her own. She knew as much about the Bible as did her inquisitors.

Hutchinson defied the ministers and magistrates to demonstrate exactly where she had gone wrong. Just when it appeared Hutchinson had outmaneuvered—indeed, thoroughly embarrassed—her opponents, she let down her guard, declaring forcefully that what she knew of God came "by an immediate revelation. . . . By the voice of his own spirit to my soul." Here was what her accusers had suspected all along but could not prove. She had confessed in open court that the Spirit can live without the Moral Law. This antinomian statement fulfilled the worst fears of the Bay rulers, and they were relieved to exile Hutchinson and her followers to Rhode Island.

Mobility and Division

Massachusetts Bay spawned four new colonies, three of which survived to the American Revolution. New Hampshire became a separate colony in 1677. Its population grew very slowly, and for much of the colonial period, New Hampshire remained economically dependent on Massachusetts, its commercial neighbor to the south.

Far more people were drawn to the fertile lands of the Connecticut River Valley. In 1636, settlers founded the villages of Hartford, Windsor, and Wethersfield. No one forced these men and women to leave Massachusetts, and in their new surroundings, they created a society that looked much like the one they had

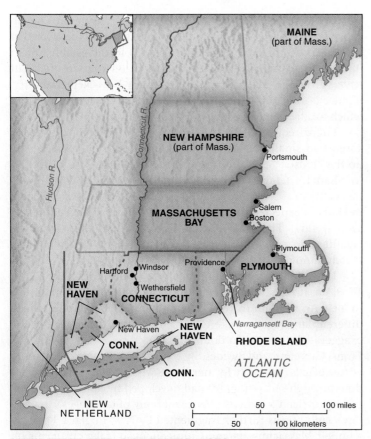

NEW ENGLAND COLONIES, 1650 The early settlers quickly carved up New England. New Haven briefly flourished as a separate colony before being taken over by Connecticut in 1662. Long Island later became part of New York; Plymouth was absorbed into Massachusetts, and in 1677 New Hampshire became a separate colony.

known in the Bay Colony. Through his writings, Thomas Hooker, Connecticut's most prominent minister, helped all New Englanders define Congregational church polity. Puritans on both sides of the Atlantic read Hooker's beautifully crafted works. In 1639, representatives from the Connecticut towns passed the Fundamental Orders, a blueprint for civil government, and in 1662, Charles II awarded the colony a charter of its own.

In 1638, another group, led by Theophilus Eaton and the Reverend John Davenport, settled New Haven and several adjoining towns along Long Island Sound. These emigrants, many of whom had come from London, lived briefly in Massachusetts Bay but then insisted on forming a Puritan commonwealth of their own, one that established a closer relationship between church and state than the Bay Colonists had allowed. The New Haven colony never prospered, and in 1662, it was absorbed into Connecticut.

Rhode Island experienced a wholly different history. From the beginning, it drew people of a highly independent turn of mind, and according to one Dutch visitor, Rhode Island was "the receptacle of all sorts of riff-raff people. . . . All the cranks of New-England retire thither." This description, of course, was an exaggeration. Roger Williams founded Providence in 1636; two years later, Anne Hutchinson took her followers to Portsmouth. Other groups settled around Narragansett Bay.

Not surprisingly, these men and women appreciated the need for toleration. No one was persecuted in Rhode Island for his or her religious beliefs.

One might have thought the separate Rhode Island communities would cooperate for the common good. They did not. Villagers fought over land and schemed with outside speculators to divide the tiny colony into even smaller pieces. In 1644, Parliament issued a patent for the "Providence Plantations," and in 1663, the Rhode Islanders obtained a royal charter. These successes did not calm political turmoil. For most of the seventeenth century, colonywide government existed in name only. Despite their constant bickering, however, the settlers of Rhode Island built up a profitable commerce in agricultural goods.

Allies and Enemies

Puritan expansion in New England did not occur unopposed. During the 1620s, the Pequots, a numerous tribe whose home territory centered on the Thames and Mystic rivers, dominated the trade of southern New England. The Pequots collected furs from other Indian peoples in the region, sold them to the Dutch, and then resold the European goods they obtained to their Indian clients. This middleman status proved highly profitable for the Pequots, giving them first access to the metal weapons, firearms, and other tools sold by the Dutch. Their commercial and military power allowed the Pequots to impose their political control over much of the region and to force their trading partners to pay them tribute.

The founding of the English colonies offered potential new trading partners for the Indians of New England. The Pilgrims and Puritans may have come to New England for religious reasons, but this did not stop them from participating in the region's lucrative fur trade. The Pequots resented this intrusion. They saw the English traders as a threat to their regional power. The English, for their part, saw the Dutch and their Pequot trading partners as a challenge to English control of New England. In 1636, an English trader named John Oldham was killed by unknown Indians. The English eventually came to blame the Pequots, resulting in war. The English allied themselves with the Mohegan Indians, a tribe that had formerly been tributaries to the Pequots, and the Narragansetts, who had recently had some of their land seized by the Pequots.

The Pequot nation was already in decline when the war started. The Pequots had been ravaged by epidemic disease in 1619 and 1633. From a pre-contact population of 13,000, only 3,000 Pequots remained. The Pequot War, as it came to be known, all but destroyed the tribe. The English and their allies quickly routed the Pequots. The English waged an especially vicious campaign. For example, in 1637, English soldiers surrounded a Pequot village on the Mystic River that contained mostly women, children, and old men. The English soldiers set the village on fire and then shot down any Pequots who tried to escape. After the war, the English took most of the surviving Pequots as slaves, giving some to their allies and selling the remainder to the English plantations in the West Indies. The English won the war, but their savage tactics alienated their Indian allies.

Diversity in the Middle Colonies

How did ethnic diversity shape the development of the Middle Colonies?

New York, New Jersey, Pennsylvania, and Delaware were settled for quite different reasons. William Penn, for example, envisioned a Quaker sanctuary; the Duke of York worried chiefly about his own income. Despite the founders' intentions, however, some common characteristics emerged. Each colony developed a strikingly heterogeneous population, men and women of different ethnic and religious backgrounds. This cultural diversity became a major influence on the economic, political, and ecclesiastical institutions of the Middle Colonies. The raucous, partisan public life of the Middle Colonies foreshadowed later American society.

Anglo-Dutch Rivalry on the Hudson

By the early decades of the seventeenth century, the Dutch had established themselves as Europe's most aggressive traders. Holland—a small, loosely federated nation—possessed the world's largest merchant fleet. Its ships vied for the commerce of Asia, Africa, and America. Dutch rivalry with Spain, a fading though still formidable power, was in large measure responsible for the settlement of New Netherland. While searching for the elusive Northwest Passage in 1609, Henry Hudson, an English explorer employed by a Dutch company, sailed up the river that now bears his name. Further voyages led to the establishment of trading posts in New Netherland and on the Connecticut River, although permanent settlement at New Netherland did not occur until 1624. The area also seemed an excellent base from which to attack Spain's colonies in the New World.

The directors of the Dutch West India Company sponsored two small outposts, Fort Orange (Albany) located well up the Hudson River and New Amsterdam (New York City) on Manhattan Island. The first Dutch settlers were not actually colonists. Rather, they were salaried employees, and their superiors in Holland expected them to spend most of their time gathering animal furs. They did not receive land for their troubles. Needless to say, this arrangement attracted relatively few Dutch immigrants.

The colony's population may have been small, only 270 in 1628, but it contained an extraordinary ethnic mix. One visitor to New Amsterdam in 1644 maintained he had heard "eighteen different languages" spoken in the city. Even if this report was exaggerated, there is no doubt the Dutch colony drew English, Finns, Germans, and Swedes. By the 1640s, a sizable community of free blacks (probably former slaves who had gained their freedom through self-purchase) had developed in New Amsterdam, adding African tongues to the cacophony of languages. The colony's culture was further fragmented by New England Puritans who left Massachusetts and Connecticut to stake out farms on eastern Long Island.

New Netherland lacked capable leadership. The company sent a number of director-generals to oversee judicial and political affairs. Without exception, these men were temperamentally unsuited to govern an American colony. They adopted autocratic procedures, lined their own pockets, and, in one case, blundered into a war that needlessly killed scores of Indians and settlers. The company made no provision for an elected assembly. As much as they were able, the scattered inhabitants living along the Hudson River ignored company directives. They felt no loyalty to the trading company that had treated them so shabbily. Long Island Puritans complained bitterly about the absence of representative institutions. The Dutch system has aptly been described as "unstable pluralism."

In August 1664, the Dutch lost their tenuous hold on New Netherland. The English crown, eager to score an easy victory over a commercial rival, dispatched a fleet of warships to New Amsterdam. The commander of this force, Colonel Richard Nicolls, ordered the colonists to surrender. The last director-general, a colorful character named Peter Stuyvesant (1647–1664), rushed wildly about the city urging the settlers to resist the English. But no one obeyed. Even the Dutch remained deaf to Stuyvesant's appeals. They accepted the Articles of Capitulation, a generous agreement that allowed Dutch nationals to remain in the province and to retain their property.

Charles II had already granted his brother, James, the Duke of York, a charter for the newly captured territory and much else besides. The duke became absolute proprietor over Maine, Martha's Vineyard, Nantucket, Long Island, and the rest of New York all the way to Delaware Bay. The king perhaps

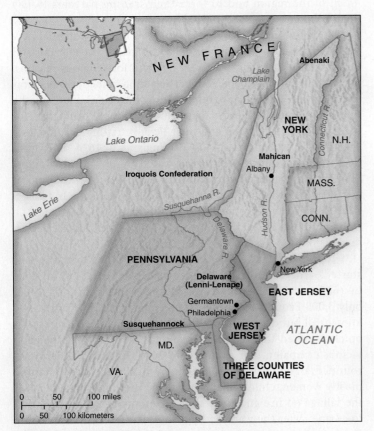

MIDDLE COLONIES, 1685 Until the Revolution, the Iroquois blocked European expansion into Western New York. The Jerseys and Pennsylvania initially attracted English and Irish Quakers, who were soon joined by thousands of Protestant Irish and Germans.

it had been under the Dutch West India Company: a loose collection of independent communities ruled by an ineffectual central government.

Confusion in New Jersey

Only three months after receiving a charter for New York, the Duke of York made a terrible mistake—something this stubborn, humorless man was prone to do. As a gift to two courtiers who had served Charles during the English Civil War, the duke awarded the land lying between the Hudson and Delaware rivers to John, Lord Berkeley, and Sir George Carteret. This colony was named New Jersey in honor of Carteret's birthplace, the Isle of Jersey in the English Channel. When Nicolls heard what the duke had done, he exploded. In his estimation, this fertile region contained the "most improveable" land in all New York, and to give it away so casually seemed the height of folly.

The duke's impulsive act bred confusion. Soon it was not clear who owned what in New Jersey. Before Nicolls had learned of James's decision, the governor had allowed migrants from New England to take up farms west of the Hudson River. He promised the settlers an opportunity to establish an elected assembly, a headright system, and liberty of

Read the Document Father Isaac Jogues, Description of New York, 1640

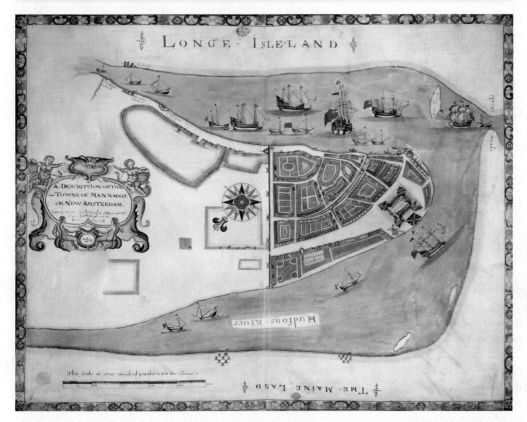

Map of New York City presented to James, Duke of York (the future James II), shortly after the English captured New Amsterdam from the Dutch in 1664.

wanted to encircle New England's potentially disloyal Puritan population, but whatever his aims may have been, he created a bureaucratic nightmare.

During the English Civil War, the duke had acquired a thorough aversion to representative government. After all, Parliament had executed the duke's father, Charles I, and raised up Oliver Cromwell. The new proprietor had no intention of letting such a participatory system take root in New York. "I cannot *but* suspect," the duke announced, that an assembly "would be of dangerous consequence." The Long Islanders felt betrayed. In part to appease these outspoken critics, Governor Nicolls—one of the few competent administrators to serve in the Middle Colonies—drew up in March 1665 a legal code known as the Duke's Laws. It guaranteed religious toleration and created local governments.

There was no provision, however, for an elected assembly or, for that matter, for democratic town meetings. The legal code disappointed the Puritan migrants on Long Island, and when the duke's officers attempted to collect taxes, these people protested that they were "inslav'd under an Arbitrary Power."

The Dutch kept silent. For several decades they remained a large unassimilated ethnic group. They continued to speak their own language, worship in their own churches (Dutch Reformed Calvinist), and eye their English neighbors with suspicion. In fact, the colony seemed little different from what

conscience. In exchange for these privileges, Nicolls asked only that they pay a small annual quitrent to the duke. The new proprietors, Berkeley and Carteret, recruited colonists on similar terms. They assumed, of course, that they would receive the rent money.

The result was chaos. Some colonists insisted that Nicolls had authorized their assembly. Others, equally insistent, claimed that Berkeley and Carteret had done so. Both sides were wrong. Neither the proprietors nor Nicolls possessed any legal right whatsoever to set up a colonial government. James could transfer land to favorite courtiers, but no matter how many times the land changed hands, the government remained his personal responsibility. Knowledge of the law failed to quiet the controversy. Through it all, the duke showed not the slightest interest in the peace and welfare of the people of New Jersey.

Berkeley grew tired of the venture. It generated headaches rather than income, and in 1674, he sold his proprietary rights to a group of surprisingly quarrelsome Quakers. The sale necessitated the division of the colony into two separate governments known as East and West Jersey. Neither half prospered. Carteret and his heirs tried unsuccessfully to turn a profit in East Jersey. In 1677, the Quaker proprietors of West Jersey issued a remarkable democratic plan of government, the Laws, Concessions, and Agreements. But they fought among themselves with such intensity that not even William Penn could bring tranquility to their affairs. Penn wisely turned his attention to the unclaimed territory across the Delaware River. The West Jersey proprietors went bankrupt, and in 1702, the crown reunited the two Jerseys into a single royal colony.

In 1700, the population of New Jersey stood at approximately fourteen thousand. Largely because it lacked a good deepwater harbor, the colony never developed a commercial center to rival New York City or Philadelphia. Its residents lived on scattered, often isolated farms; villages of more than a few hundred people were rare. Visitors commented on the diversity of the settlers. There were colonists from almost every European nation. Congregationalists, Presbyterians, Quakers, Baptists, Anabaptists, and Anglicans somehow managed to live together peacefully in New Jersey.

Quakers in America

How did the Quaker religion influence the development of Pennsylvania?

The founding of Pennsylvania cannot be separated from the history of the Quaker movement. Believers in an extreme form of antinomianism, the **Quakers** saw no need for a learned ministry, since one person's interpretation of Scripture was as valid as anyone else's. This radical religious sect, a product of the social upheaval in England during the Civil War, gained its name from the derogatory term that English authorities sometimes used to describe those who "tremble at the word of the Lord." The name persisted even though the Quakers preferred being called Professors of the Light or, more commonly, Friends.

Quaker Beliefs and Practice

By the time the Stuarts regained the throne in 1660, the Quakers had developed strong support throughout England. One person responsible for their remarkable success was George Fox (1624–1691), a poor shoemaker whose own spiritual anxieties sparked a powerful new religious message that pushed beyond traditional reformed Protestantism. According to Fox, he experienced despair "so that I had nothing outwardly to help me . . . [but] then, I heard a voice which said, 'There is one, even Christ Jesus, that can speak to thy condition.'" Throughout his life, Fox and his growing number of followers gave testimony to the working of the Holy Spirit. Indeed, they informed ordinary men and women that if only they would look, they too would discover they possessed an "Inner Light." This was a wonderfully liberating invitation, especially for persons of lower-class origin. With the Lord's personal assistance, they could attain greater spiritual perfection on earth. Gone was the stigma of original sin; discarded was the notion of eternal predestination. Everyone could be saved.

Quakers practiced humility in their daily lives. They wore simple clothes and employed old-fashioned forms of address that set them apart from their neighbors. Friends refused to honor worldly position and accomplishment or to swear oaths in courts of law. They were also pacifists. According to Fox, all persons were

Read the **Document** William Penn, "Model for Government" (1681)

William Penn (1644 – 1718) received a charter for Pennsylvania from King Charles II in 1681. Penn intended his colony to serve as a religious haven for both his fellow Quakers—who faced persecution both from the Church of England and from the Puritans in New England—and for members of other persecuted Protestant sects.

equal in the sight of the Lord, a belief that generally annoyed people of rank and achievement.

Moreover, the Quakers never kept their thoughts to themselves. They preached conversion constantly, spreading the "Truth" throughout England, Ireland, and America. The Friends played important roles in the early history of New Jersey, Rhode Island, and North Carolina, as well as Pennsylvania. In some places, the "publishers of Truth" wore out their welcome. English authorities harassed the Quakers. Thousands, including Fox himself, were jailed, and in Massachusetts Bay between 1659 and 1661, Puritan magistrates ordered several Friends put to death. Such measures proved counterproductive, for persecution only inspired the martyred Quakers to redouble their efforts.

Penn's "Holy Experiment"

William Penn lived according to the Inner Light, a commitment that led eventually to the founding of Pennsylvania. Penn possessed a curiously complex personality. He was an athletic person who threw himself into intellectual pursuits. He was a bold visionary capable of making pragmatic decisions. He came from an aristocratic family and yet spent his entire adult life involved with a religious movement associated with the lower class.

Precisely when Penn's thoughts turned to America is not known. He was briefly involved with the West Jersey proprietorship. This venture may have suggested the possibility of an even larger enterprise. In any case, Penn negotiated in 1681 one of the more impressive land deals in the history of American real estate. Charles II awarded Penn a charter, making him the sole proprietor of a vast area called Pennsylvania (literally, "Penn's woods"). The name embarrassed the modest Penn, but he knew better than to look the royal gift horse in the mouth.

Why the king bestowed such generosity on a leading Quaker remains a mystery. Perhaps Charles wanted to repay an old debt to Penn's father. The monarch may have regarded the colony as a means of ridding England of its troublesome Quaker population, or, quite simply, he may have liked Penn. In 1682, the new proprietor purchased from the Duke of York the so-called Three Lower Counties that eventually became Delaware. This astute move guaranteed that Pennsylvania would have access to the Atlantic and determined even before Philadelphia had been established that it would become a commercial center.

In designing his government, Penn drew heavily on the writings of James Harrington (1611–1677). This English political philosopher argued that no government could ever be stable unless it reflected the actual distribution of landed property within society. Both the rich and poor had to have a voice in political affairs; neither should be able to overrule the legitimate interests of the other class. The Frame of Government envisioned a governor appointed by the proprietor, a 72-member Provincial Council responsible for initiating legislation, and a 200-person Assembly that could accept or reject the bills presented to it. Penn apparently thought the Council would be filled by the colony's richest landholders, or in the words of the Frame, "persons of most note for their wisdom, virtue and ability." The governor and Council were charged with the routine administration of justice. Smaller landowners spoke through the Assembly. It was a clumsy structure, and in America the entire edifice crumbled under its own weight.

Settling Pennsylvania

Penn promoted his colony aggressively throughout England, Ireland, and Germany. He had no choice. His only source of revenue was the sale of land and the collection of quitrents. Penn commissioned pamphlets in several languages extolling the quality of Pennsylvania's rich farmland. The response was overwhelming. People poured into Philadelphia and the surrounding area. In 1685 alone, eight thousand immigrants arrived. Most of the settlers were Irish, Welsh, and English Quakers, and they generally moved to America as families. But Penn opened the door to men and women of all nations. He asserted that the people of Pennsylvania "are a collection of divers nations in Europe, as French, Dutch, Germans, Swedes, Danes, Finns, Scotch, Irish, and English."

The settlers were by no means all Quakers. The founder of Germantown, Francis Daniel Pastorius, called the vessel that

Read the Document Letter by William Penn to the Committee of the Free Society of Traders (1683)

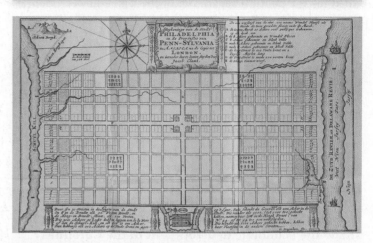

William Penn's plan for Philadelphia shows the city laid out where the Schuylkill and Delaware rivers parallel each other. Four of the five public squares were intended to be parks while the fifth (at the center) was designated for public buildings. Today, it is the site of Philadelphia's city hall.

brought him to the New World a "Noah's Ark" of religions, and within his own household, there were servants who subscribed "to the Roman [Catholic], to the Lutheran, to the Calvinistic, to the Anabaptist, and to the Anglican church, and only one Quaker." Ethnic and religious diversity were crucial in the development of Pennsylvania's public institutions, and its politics took on a quarrelsome quality absent in more homogeneous colonies such as Virginia and Massachusetts.

Penn himself emigrated to America in 1682. His stay, however, was unexpectedly short and unhappy. The Council and Assembly—reduced now to more manageable size—fought over the right to initiate legislation. Wealthy Quaker merchants, most of them residents of Philadelphia, dominated the Council. By contrast, the Assembly included men from rural settlements and the Three Lower Counties who showed no concern for the Holy Experiment.

Penn did not see his colony again until 1699. During his absence, much had changed. The settlement had prospered. Its agricultural products, especially its excellent wheat, were in demand throughout the Atlantic world. Despite this economic success, however, the population remained deeply divided. Even the Quakers had briefly split into hostile factions. Penn's hand-picked governors had failed to win general support for the proprietor's policies, and one of them exclaimed in anger that each Quaker "prays for his neighbor on First Days and then preys on him the other six." As the seventeenth century closed, few colonists still shared the founder's desire to create a godly, paternalistic society.

In 1701, legal challenges in England again forced Penn to depart for the mother country. Just before he sailed, Penn signed the Charter of Liberties, a new frame of government that established a unicameral or one-house legislature (the only one in colonial America) and gave the representatives the right to initiate bills. Penn also allowed the Assembly to conduct its business without proprietary interference. The charter provided for the political separation of the Three Lower Counties (Delaware) from Pennsylvania, something people living in the area had demanded for years. This hastily drafted document served as Pennsylvania's constitution until the American Revolution.

His experience in America must have depressed Penn, now both old and sick. In England, Penn was imprisoned for debts incurred by dishonest colonial agents, and in 1718, Pennsylvania's founder died a broken man.

Planting the Carolinas

How did the Barbadian background of the early settlers shape the economic development of the Carolinas?

In some ways, Carolina society looked much like the one that had developed in Virginia and Maryland. In both areas, white planters forced African slaves to produce staple crops for a world market. But such superficial similarities masked substantial regional differences. In fact, "the South"—certainly the fabled solid South of the early nineteenth century—did not exist during the colonial period. The Carolinas, joined much later by Georgia, stood apart from their northern neighbors. As a historian of colonial Carolina explained, "the southern colonies were never a cohesive section in the same way that New England was. The great diversity of population groups . . . discouraged southern sectionalism."

Proprietors of the Carolinas

Carolina was a product of the restoration of the Stuarts to the English throne. Court favorites who had followed the Stuarts into exile during the Civil War demanded tangible rewards for their loyalty. New York and New Jersey were obvious plums. So too was Carolina. Sir John Colleton, a successful English planter returned from Barbados, organized a group of eight powerful courtiers who styled themselves the True and Absolute Lords Proprietors of Carolina. On March 24, 1663, the king granted these proprietors a charter to the vast territory between Virginia and Florida and running west as far as the "South Seas."

The failure of similar ventures in the New World taught the Carolina proprietors valuable lessons. Unlike the first Virginians, for example, this group did not expect instant wealth. Rather, the proprietors reasoned that they would obtain a steady source of income from rents. What they needed, of course, were settlers to pay those rents. Recruitment turned out to be no easy task. Economic and social conditions in the mother country improved considerably after its civil war, and English people were no longer so willing to transfer to the New World. Even if they had shown interest, the cost of transporting settlers across the Atlantic seemed prohibitively

expensive. The proprietors concluded, therefore, that with the proper incentives—a generous land policy, for example—they could attract men and women from established American colonies and thereby save themselves a great deal of money. Unfortunately for the men who owned Carolina, such people were not easily persuaded. They had begun to take for granted certain rights and privileges, and as the price of settlement, they demanded a representative assembly, liberty of conscience, and a liberal headright system.

Colleton and his associates waited for the money to roll in, but to their dismay, no one seemed particularly interested in moving to the Carolina frontier. A tiny settlement at Port Royal failed. One group of New Englanders briefly considered taking up land in the Cape Fear area, but these people were so disappointed by what they saw that they departed, leaving behind only a sign that "tended not only to the disparagement of the Land . . . but also to the great discouragement of all those that should hereafter come into these parts to settle." By this time, a majority of surviving proprietors had given up on Carolina.

The Barbadian Connection

Anthony Ashley Cooper, later Earl of Shaftesbury, was the exception. In 1669, he persuaded the remaining Carolinian proprietors to invest their own capital in the colony. Without such financial support, Cooper recognized, the project would surely fail. Once he received sufficient funds, this energetic organizer dispatched three hundred English colonists to Port Royal under the command of Joseph West. The fleet put in briefly at Barbados to pick up additional recruits, and in March 1670, after being punished by Atlantic gales that destroyed one ship, the expedition arrived at its destination. Only one hundred people were still alive. The unhappy settlers did not remain long at Port Royal, an unappealing, low-lying place badly exposed to Spanish attack. They moved northward, locating eventually along the more secure Ashley River. Later the colony's administrative center, Charles Town (it did not become Charleston until 1783) was established at the junction of the Ashley and Cooper rivers.

Cooper also wanted to bring order to the new society. With assistance from John Locke, the famous English philosopher (1632–1704), Cooper devised the Fundamental Constitutions of Carolina. Like Penn, Cooper had been influenced by the writings of Harrington. The constitutions created a local aristocracy consisting of proprietors and lesser nobles called *landgraves* and *cassiques,* terms as inappropriate to the realities of the New World as was the idea of creating a hereditary landed elite. Persons who purchased vast tracts of land automatically received a title and the right to sit in the Council of Nobles, a body designed to administer justice, oversee civil affairs, and initiate legislation. A parliament in which smaller landowners had a voice and could accept or reject bills drafted by the council. The very poor were excluded from political life altogether. Cooper thought his scheme maintained the proper "Balance of Government" between aristocracy and democracy, a concept central to Harrington's philosophy. Not surprisingly, the constitutions had little impact on the actual structure of government.

Before 1680, almost half the men and women who settled in the Port Royal area came from Barbados. This small Caribbean island, which produced an annual fortune in sugar, depended on slave labor. By the third quarter of the seventeenth century, Barbados had become overpopulated. Wealthy families could not provide their sons and daughters with sufficient land to maintain social status, and as the crisis intensified, Barbadians looked to Carolina for relief.

These migrants, many of whom were quite rich, traveled to Carolina both as individuals and family groups. Some even brought gangs of slaves with them to the American mainland. The Barbadians carved out plantations on the tributaries of the Cooper River and established themselves immediately as the colony's most powerful political faction. "So it was," wrote historian Richard Dunn, "that these Caribbean pioneers helped to create on the North American coast a slave-based plantation society closer in temper to the islands they fled from than to any other mainland English settlement."

Much of the planters' time was taken up with the search for a profitable crop. The early settlers experimented with a number of plants: tobacco, cotton, silk, and grapes. The most successful items turned out to be beef, skins, and naval stores (especially tar used to maintain ocean vessels). By the 1680s, some Carolinians had built up great herds of cattle—seven or eight hundred head in some cases. Traders who dealt with Indians brought back thousands of deerskins from the interior, and they often returned with Indian slaves as well. These commercial resources, together with tar and turpentine, enjoyed a good market. It was not until the 1690s that

ENGLAND'S PRINCIPAL MAINLAND COLONIES

Name	Original Purpose	Date of Founding	Principal Founder	Major Export	Estimated Population ca. 1700
Virginia	Commercial venture	1607	Captain John Smith	Tobacco	64,560
New Amsterdam (New York)	Commercial venture	1613 (made English colony, 1664)	Peter Stuyvesant, Duke of York	Furs, grain	19,107
Plymouth	Refuge for English Separatists	1620 (absorbed by Massachusetts, 1691)	William Bradford	Grain	Included with Massachusetts
New Hampshire	Commercial venture	1623	John Mason	Wood, naval stores	4,958
Massachusetts	Refuge for English Puritans	1628	John Winthrop	Grain, wood	55,941
Maryland	Refuge for English Catholics	1634	Lord Baltimore (George Calvert)	Tobacco	34,100
Connecticut	Expansion of Massachusetts	1635	Thomas Hooker	Grain	25,970
Rhode Island	Refuge for dissenters from Massachusetts	1636	Roger Williams	Grain	5,894
New Sweden (Delaware)	Commercial venture	1638 (included in Penn grant, 1681; given separate assembly, 1703)	Peter Minuit, William Penn	Grain	2,470
North Carolina	Commercial venture	1663	Anthony Ashley Cooper	Wood, naval stores, tobacco	10,720
South Carolina	Commercial venture	1663	Anthony Ashley Cooper	Naval stores, rice, indigo	5,720
New Jersey	Consolidation of new English territory, Quaker settlement	1664	Sir George Carteret	Grain	14,010
Pennsylvania	Refuge for English Quakers	1681	William Penn	Grain	18,950
Georgia	Discourage Spanish expansion; charity	1733	James Oglethorpe	Rice, wood, naval stores	5,200 (in 1750)

Sources: U.S. Bureau of the Census, *Historical Statistics of the United States: Colonial Times to 1970*, Washington, DC, 1975; John J. McCusker and Russell R. Menard, *The Economy of British America, 1607–1789*, Chapel Hill, 1985.

the planters came to appreciate fully the value of rice, but once they had done so, it quickly became the colony's main staple.

Proprietary Carolina was in a constant political uproar. Factions vied for special privilege. The Barbadian settlers, known locally as the Goose Creek Men, resisted the proprietors' policies at every turn. A large community of French Huguenots located in Craven County distrusted the Barbadians. The proprietors—an ineffectual group following the death of Cooper—appointed a series of utterly incompetent governors who only made things worse. One visitor observed that "the Inhabitants of Carolina should be as free from Oppression as any [people] in the Universe . . . if their own Differences amongst themselves do not occasion the contrary." By the end of the century, the Commons House of Assembly had assumed the right to initiate legislation. In 1719, the colonists overthrew the last proprietary governor, and in 1729, the king created separate royal governments for North and South Carolina.

The Founding of Georgia

How was the founding of the Carolinas different from the founding of Georgia?

The early history of Georgia was strikingly different from that of Britain's other mainland colonies. Its settlement was really an act of aggression against Spain, a country that had as good a claim to this area as did the English. During the eighteenth century, the two nations were often at war (see Chapter 4), and South Carolinians worried that the Spaniards moving up from bases in Florida would occupy the disputed territory between Florida and the Carolina grant.

The colony owed its existence primarily to James Oglethorpe, a British general and member of Parliament who believed that he could thwart Spanish designs on the area south of Charles Town while at the same time providing a fresh start for London's worthy poor, saving them from debtors' prison. Although Oglethorpe envisioned Georgia as an asylum as well as a garrison, the military aspects of his proposal were especially appealing to the leaders of the British government. In 1732, the king granted Oglethorpe and a board of trustees a charter for a new colony to be located between the Savannah and Altamaha rivers and from "sea to sea." The trustees living in the mother country were given complete control over Georgia politics, a condition the settlers soon found intolerable.

During the first years of colonization, Georgia fared no better than had earlier utopian experiments. The poor people of England showed little desire to move to an inclement frontier, and the trustees, in their turn, provided little incentive for emigration. Each colonist received only 50 acres. Another 50 acres could be added for each servant transported to Georgia, but in no case could a settler amass more than 500 acres. Moreover, land could be passed only to an eldest son, and if a planter had no sons at the time of his death, the holding reverted to the trustees. Slavery was prohibited. So too was rum.

Almost as soon as they arrived in Georgia, the settlers complained. The colonists demanded slaves, pointing out to the

THE CAROLINAS AND GEORGIA Caribbean sugar planters migrated to the Goose Creek area where, with knowledge supplied by African slaves, they eventually mastered rice cultivation. Poor harbors in North Carolina retarded the spread of European settlement in that region.

trustees that unless the new planters possessed an unfree labor force, they could not compete economically with their South Carolina neighbors. The settlers also wanted a voice in local government. In 1738, 121 people living in Savannah petitioned for fundamental reforms in the colony's constitution. Oglethorpe responded angrily, "The idle ones are indeed for Negroes. If the petition is countenanced, the province is ruined." The settlers did not give up. In 1741, they again petitioned Oglethorpe, this time addressing him as "our Perpetual Dictator."

While the colonists grumbled about various restrictions, Oglethorpe tried and failed to capture the Spanish fortress at Saint Augustine (1740). This personal disappointment coupled with the growing popular unrest destroyed his interest in Georgia. The trustees were forced to compromise their principles. In 1738, they eliminated all restrictions on the amount of land a man could own; they allowed women to inherit land. In 1750, they permitted the settlers to import slaves. Soon Georgians could drink rum. In 1751, the trustees returned Georgia to the king, undoubtedly relieved to be free of what had become a hard-drinking, slave-owning plantation society much like that in South Carolina. The king authorized an assembly in 1751, but even with these social and political changes, Georgia attracted very few new settlers.

Conclusion: Living with Diversity

Long after he had returned from his adventures in Virginia, Captain John Smith reflected on the difficulty of establishing colonies in the New World. It was a task for which most people were not temperamentally suited. "It requires," Smith counseled, "all the best parts of art, judgment, courage, honesty, constancy, diligence, and industry, [even] to do neere well." On another occasion, Charles I warned Lord Baltimore that new settlements "commonly have rugged and laborious beginnings."

Over the course of the seventeenth century, women and men had followed leaders such as Baltimore, Smith, Winthrop, Bradford, Penn, and Berkeley to the New World in anticipation of creating a successful new society. Some people were religious visionaries; others were hardheaded businessmen. The results of their efforts, their struggles to survive in an often hostile environment, and their interactions with various Native American groups yielded a spectrum of settlements along the Atlantic coast, ranging from the quasifeudalism of South Carolina to the Puritan commonwealth of Massachusetts Bay.

The diversity of early English colonization must be emphasized precisely because it is so easy to overlook. Even though the colonists eventually banded together and fought for independence, persistent differences separated New Englanders from Virginians, Pennsylvanians from Carolinians. The interpretive challenge, of course, is to comprehend how European colonists managed over the course of the eighteenth century to overcome fragmentation and to develop the capacity to imagine themselves a nation.

Study Resources

 Take the **Study Plan** for **Chapter 2** *New World Experiments* on **MyHistoryLab**

TIME LINE

1607 First English settlers arrive at Jamestown

1608–1609 Scrooby congregation (Pilgrims) leaves England for Holland

1609–1611 "Starving time" in Virginia threatens survival of the colonists

1616–1618 Plague destroys Native American populations of coastal New England

1619 Virginia assembly, called House of Burgesses, meets for the first time; First slaves sold at Jamestown

1620 Pilgrims sign the Mayflower Compact

1622 Surprise Indian attack devastates Virginia

1624 Dutch investors create permanent settlements along Hudson River; James I, King of England, dissolves Virginia Company

1625 Charles I ascends English throne

1630 John Winthrop transfers Massachusetts Bay charter to New England

1634 Colony of Maryland is founded

1636 Harvard College is established; Puritan settlers found Hartford and other Connecticut Valley towns

1638 Anne Hutchinson exiled to Rhode Island; Theophilus Eaton and John Davenport lead settlers to New Haven Colony

1639 Connecticut towns accept Fundamental Orders

1644 Second major Indian attack in Virginia

1649 Charles I executed during English Civil War

1660 Stuarts restored to the English throne

1663 Rhode Island obtains royal charter; Proprietors receive charter for Carolina

1664 English soldiers conquer New Netherland

1677 New Hampshire becomes a royal colony

1681 William Penn granted patent for his "Holy Experiment"

1702 East and West Jersey unite to form single colony

1732 James Oglethorpe receives charter for Georgia

CHAPTER REVIEW

Breaking Away

What were some of the social problems facing Britain in the 16th and 17th centuries that helped push English colonists to cross the Atlantic?

Between 1580 and 1650, an expanding population strained England's agrarian economy. Competition for food and land threatened to disrupt law and order and drove many people to migrate from rural areas to London or across the Atlantic. (p. 30)

The Chesapeake: Dreams of Wealth

Why did the Chesapeake colonies not prosper during the earliest years of settlement?

Until tobacco began to be cultivated as a profitable cash crop around 1617, the Virginia colony suffered from disease, hunger, misgovernment, and social dissension. Maryland, which had been founded as a refuge for English Catholics in the late 1630s, and where tobacco also became the economic mainstay, endured decades of political and religious conflict before a stable government was established there in the 1660s. (p. 31)

Reforming England in America

How did differences in religion affect the founding of the New England colonies?

Religious persecution drove thousands of Puritans to New England. John Winthrop hoped the settlers would reform English Protestantism and create a "City on a Hill." The Puritans did not welcome dissent. They exiled Roger Williams and Anne Hutchinson to Rhode Island for their religious beliefs. Stable nuclear families and good health helped Puritans avoid the social turmoil that plagued the Chesapeake colonies. (p. 37)

Diversity in the Middle Colonies

How did ethnic diversity shape the development of the Middle Colonies?

After conquering the Dutch colony of New Netherland in 1664, the English renamed it New York. Despite the conquest, the Dutch remained an influential minority in the colony, and ethnic rivalries shaped the politics of New York for decades. In 1681, Charles II granted William Penn, a Quaker, a charter to establish Pennsylvania. Penn's guarantee to respect all Christian settlers' liberty of conscience drew immigrants from across Northern Europe. (p. 44)

Quakers in America

How did the Quaker religion influence the development of Pennsylvania?

William Penn, the founder of Pennsylvania, was a Quaker, a Protestant sect that emphasized simplicity and the possibility of salvation for all in religious practice and belief and humility and tolerance in daily life. He guaranteed that settlers in Pennsylvania would enjoy liberty of conscience, freedom from persecution, no taxation without representation, and due process of law. (p. 46)

Planting the Carolinas

How did the Barbadian background of the early settlers shape the economic development of the Carolinas?

About half the early settlers of Carolina came from Barbados, a British Caribbean island where the economy depended on the production of sugar by slave labor. In the Carolina colony, these migrants recreated a similar slave-based plantation economy that by the 1690s was based primarily on the cultivation of rice as a cash crop. (p. 48)

The Founding of Georgia

How was the founding of the Carolinas different from the founding of Georgia?

Immigrants from Barbados began settling in the Carolinas in the 1670s. Barbadian immigrants to the Carolinas, many of whom were wealthy planters seeking new lands for plantations, brought slavery with them when they moved. Georgia was founded in 1732 as an alternative to debtors' prison for impoverished Englishmen and as a military outpost to guard against the Spanish in Florida. (p. 50)

KEY TERMS AND DEFINITIONS

Joint-stock company Business enterprise that enabled investors to pool money for commerce and funding for colonies. p. 32

House of Burgesses The elective representative assembly in colonial Virginia. p. 34

Headright System of land distribution in which settlers were granted a 50-acre plot of land from the colonial government for each servant or dependent they transported to the New World. It encouraged the recruitment of a large servile labor force. p. 34

Mayflower Compact Agreement among the Pilgrims aboard the *Mayflower* in 1620 to create a civil government at Plymouth Colony. p. 37

Puritans Members of a reformed Protestant sect in Europe and America that insisted on removing all vestiges of Catholicism from religious practice. p. 37

Great Migration Migration of 16,000 Puritans from England to the Massachusetts Bay Colony during the 1630s. p. 39

Antinomianism Religious belief rejecting traditional moral law as unnecessary for Christians who possess saving grace and affirming that a person could experience divine revelation and salvation without the assistance of formally trained clergy. p. 42

Quakers Members of a radical religious group, formally known as the Society of Friends, that rejects formal theology and stress each person's "inner light," a spiritual guide to righteousness. p. 46

CRITICAL THINKING QUESTIONS

1. Would the first Chesapeake colonies have survived if the settlers had not discovered tobacco as a profitable cash crop?

2. Would the historical development of New England have been different if the Puritans had developed a profitable cash crop like tobacco or rice?

3. How did William Penn's leadership style compare to those of John Winthrop and Captain John Smith?

4. How were the European migrants who were attracted to Georgia and the Carolinas different from the migrants from the Chesapeake and Middle Colonies?

MyHistoryLab Media Assignments

Find these resources in the Media Assignments folder for Chapter 2 on MyHistoryLab

The Chesapeake: Dreams of Wealth

■ **View** the **Map**   *The Colonies to 1740 p. 31*

■ **Read** the **Document**   *John Smith, "The Starving Time" p. 33*

Read the **Document**   *James I, "A Counterblaste to Tobacco" p. 34*

Read the **Document**   *Wessell Webling, His Indenture (1622) p. 35*

Read the **Document**   *George Aslop from, "A Character of the Province of Maryland" p. 36*

Reforming England in America

■ **Read** the **Document**   *John Wintrhrop, "A Model of Christian Charity" (1830) p. 38*

Complete the **Assignment**   *The Children Who Refused to Come Home: Captivity and Conversion p. 40*

Diversity in the Middle Colonies

Read the **Document**   *Father Isaac Jogues, Description of New York, 1640 p. 45*

Quakers in America

■ **Read** the **Document**   *William Penn, "Model for Government" (1681) p. 46*

Read the **Document**   *Letter by William Penn to the Committee of the Free Society of Traders (1683) p. 47*

■ *Indicates Study Plan Media Assignment*

Contents and Learning Objectives

((•●—|**Listen** to the **Audio File** on **myhistorylab**   Chapter 3 *Putting Down Roots*

Families in an Atlantic Empire

The Witherspoon family moved from Great Britain to the South Carolina backcountry early in the eighteenth century. Although otherwise indistinguishable from the thousands of other ordinary families that put down roots in English America, the Witherspoons were made historical figures by the candid account of pioneer life produced by their son, Robert, who was only a small child at the time of their arrival.

The Witherspoons' initial reaction to the New World—at least, that of the mother and children—was utter despondence. "My mother and us children were still in expectation that we were coming to an agreeable place," Robert confessed, "but when we arrived and saw nothing but a wilderness and instead of a fine timbered house, nothing but a very mean dirt house, our spirits quite sunk." For many years, the Witherspoons feared they would be killed by Indians, become lost in the woods, or be bitten by snakes.

The Witherspoons managed to survive the early difficult years on the Black River. To be sure, the Carolina backcountry did not look very much like the world they had left behind. The discrepancy, however, apparently did not greatly discourage Robert's father. He had a vision of what the Black River settlement might become. "My father," Robert recounted, "gave us all the comfort he [could] by telling us we would get all these trees cut down and in a short time [there] would be plenty of inhabitants, [and] that we could see from house to house."

Robert Witherspoon's account reminds us just how much the early history of colonial America was an intimate story of families, and not, as some commentators would have us believe, of individuals. Neither the peopling of the Atlantic frontier, the cutting down of the forests, nor the creation of new communities where one could see from "house to house" was a process that involved what we would today recognize as state policy. Men and women made significant decisions about the character of their lives within families. It was within this primary social unit that most colonists earned their livelihoods, educated their children, defined gender, sustained religious tradition, and nursed each other in sickness. In short, the family was the source of their societal and cultural identities.

Early colonial families did not exist in isolation. They were part of larger societies. As we have already discovered, the

The Mason Children: David, Joanna, and Abigail, c. 1670, an early portrait of three children from a wealthy Massachusetts Bay Colony family. The artist lavished attention on the details of the children's clothing and the objects they hold, marks of their social status and prosperity.

character of the first English settlements in the New World varied substantially (see Chapter 2). During much of the seventeenth century, these initial differences grew stronger as each region responded to different environmental conditions and developed its own traditions. The various local societies in which families like the Witherspoons put down roots reflected several critical elements: supply of labor, abundance of land, unusual demographic patterns, and commercial ties with European markets. In the Chesapeake, for example, an economy based almost entirely on a single staple—tobacco—created an insatiable demand for **indentured servants** and black slaves. In Massachusetts Bay, the extraordinary longevity of the founders generated a level of social and political stability that Virginians and Marylanders did not attain until the very end of the seventeenth century.

By 1660, it seemed regional differences had undermined the idea of a unified English empire in America. During the reign of Charles II, however, a trend toward cultural convergence began. Although subcultures had evolved in strikingly different directions, countervailing forces such as common language and religion gradually pulled English American settlers together. Parliament took advantage of this trend and began to establish a uniform set of rules for the expanding American empire. The process was slow and uneven, often sparking violent colonial resistance. By the end of the seventeenth century, however, England had made significant progress toward transforming New World provinces into an empire that produced needed raw materials and purchased manufactured goods. If a person was black and enslaved, however, he or she was more apt to experience oppression rather than opportunity in British America.

Sources of Stability: New England Colonies of the Seventeenth Century

What factors explain the remarkable social stability achieved in early New England?

Seventeenth-century New Englanders successfully replicated in America a traditional social order they had known in England. The transfer of a familiar way of life to the New World seemed less difficult for these Puritan migrants than it did for the many English men and women who settled in the Chesapeake colonies. Their contrasting experiences, fundamental to an understanding of the development of both cultures, can be explained, at least in part, by the extraordinary strength and resilience of New England families.

Immigrant Families and New Social Order

Early New Englanders believed God ordained the family for human benefit. It was essential to the maintenance of social order, since outside the family, men and women succumbed to carnal temptation. Such people had no one to sustain them or remind them of Scripture. "Without Family care," declared the Reverend Benjamin Wadsworth, "the labour of Magistrates and Ministers for Reformation and Propagating Religion, is likely to be in great measure unsuccessful."

The godly family, at least in theory, was ruled by a patriarch, father to his children, husband to his wife, the source of authority and object of unquestioned obedience. The wife shared responsibility for the raising of children, but in decisions of importance, especially those related to property, she was expected to defer to her spouse.

The New Englanders' concern about the character of the godly family is not surprising. This institution played a central role in shaping their society. In contrast to those who migrated to the colonies of Virginia and Maryland, New Englanders crossed the Atlantic within nuclear families. That is, they moved within established units consisting of a father, mother, and their dependent children rather than as single youths and adults. People who migrated to America within families preserved local English customs more fully than did the youths who traveled to other parts of the continent as single men and women. The comforting presence of immediate family members reduced the shock of adjusting to a strange environment three thousand miles from home. Even in the 1630s, the ratio of men to women in New England was fairly well balanced, about three males for every two females. Persons who had not already married in England before coming to the New World could expect to form nuclear families of their own.

The great migration of the 1630s and early 1640s brought approximately twenty thousand persons to New England. After 1642, the English Civil War reduced the flood of people moving to Massachusetts Bay to a trickle. Nevertheless, by the end of the century, the population of New England had reached almost one hundred twenty thousand, an amazing increase considering the small number of original immigrants.

The explanation for this impressive growth lies in the long lives enjoyed by early New Englanders. Put simply, people who, under normal conditions, would have died in contemporary Europe *lived* in New England. Indeed, the life expectancy of seventeenth-century settlers was not very different from our own. Males who survived infancy might have expected to see their seventieth birthday. Twenty percent of the men of the first generation reached the age of eighty. The figures for women were only slightly lower. Why the early settlers lived so long is not entirely clear. No doubt, pure drinking water, a cool climate that retarded the spread of fatal contagious disease, and a dispersed population promoted general good health.

Longer life altered family relations. New England males lived not only to see their own children reach adulthood but also to witness the birth of grandchildren. One historian, John Murrin, has suggested that New Englanders "invented" grandparents. In other words, this society produced real patriarchs, males of recognized seniority and standing. This may have been one of the first societies in recorded history in which a person could reasonably anticipate knowing his or her grandchildren, a demographic surprise that contributed to social stability. The traditions of particular families and communities literally remained alive in the memories of the colony's oldest citizens.

Commonwealth of Families

The life cycle of the seventeenth-century New England family began with marriage. Young men and women generally initiated courtships. If parents exercised a voice in such matters, it was to discourage union with a person of unsound moral character. In this highly religious society, there was not much chance that young people would stray far from shared community values. The overwhelming majority of the region's population married, for in New England, the single life was not only morally suspect but also physically difficult.

A couple without land could not support an independent and growing family in these agrarian communities. While men generally brought farmland to the marriage, prospective brides were expected to provide a dowry worth approximately one-half what the bridegroom offered. Women often contributed money or household goods.

The household was primarily a place of work—very demanding work. The primary goal, of course, was to clear enough land to feed the family. Additional cultivation allowed the farmer to produce a surplus that could then be sold or bartered, and since agrarian families required items that could not be manufactured at home—metal tools, for example—they usually grew more than they consumed. Early American farmers were not economically self-sufficient; the belief that they were is a popular misconception.

During the seventeenth century, men and women generally lived in the communities of their parents and grandparents. New Englanders usually managed to fall in love with a neighbor, and most marriages took place between men and women living less than 13 miles apart. Moving to a more fertile region might have increased their earnings, but such thoughts seldom occurred to early New Englanders. Religious values, a sense of common purpose, and the importance of family reinforced traditional communal ties.

Towns, in fact, were collections of families, not individuals. Over time, these families intermarried, so the community became an elaborate kinship network. Social historians have discovered that in many New England towns, the original founders dominated local politics and economic affairs for several generations. Not surprisingly, newcomers who were not absorbed into the family system tended to move away from the village with greater frequency than did the sons and daughters of the established lineage groups.

Congregational churches were also built on a family foundation. During the earliest years of settlement, the churches accepted persons who could demonstrate they were among God's "elect." Members were drawn from a broad social spectrum. Once the excitement of establishing a new society had passed, however, New Englanders began to focus more attention on the spiritual welfare of their own families. This quite normal parental concern precipitated a major ecclesiastical crisis. The problem was the status of the children within a gathered church. Sons and daughters of full church members regularly received baptism, usually as infants, but as these people grew to adulthood, they often failed to provide testimony of their own "election." Moreover, they wanted their own children to be baptized. A church synod—a gathering of Congregational ministers—responded to this generational crisis by adopting the so-called Half-Way Covenant (1662). The compromise allowed the grandchildren of persons in full communion to be baptized even though their parents could not demonstrate conversion. Congregational ministers assumed that "God cast the line of election in the loins of godly parents."

Colonists regarded education as primarily a family responsibility. Parents were supposed to instruct children in the principles of Christianity, and so it was necessary to teach boys and girls how to read. In 1642, the Massachusetts General Court reminded the Bay Colonists of their obligation to catechize their families. Five years later, the legislature ordered towns containing at least fifteen families to open an elementary school supported by local taxes. Villages of a hundred or more families had to maintain more advanced grammar schools, which taught a basic knowledge of Latin. At least eleven schools were operating in 1647, and despite their expense, new schools were established throughout the century.

This family-based education system worked. A large majority of the region's adult males could read and write, an accomplishment not achieved in the Chesapeake colonies for another century. The literacy rate for women was somewhat lower, but by the standards of the period, it was still impressive. A printing press operated in Cambridge as early as 1639. *The New-England Primer*, first published in 1690 in Boston by Benjamin Harris, taught children the alphabet as well as the Lord's Prayer. This primer announced:

> He who ne'er learns his ABC,
> forever will a blockhead be.
> But he who to his book's inclined,
> will soon a golden treasure find.

Many New Englanders memorized the entire poem. After 1638, young men could attend Harvard College, the first institution of higher learning founded in England's mainland colonies. The school was originally intended to train ministers, and of the 465 students who graduated during the seventeenth century, more than half became Congregational divines. Harvard had a demanding curriculum. The boys read logic, rhetoric, divinity, and several ancient languages, including Hebrew. Yale College followed Harvard's lead, admitting its first students in 1702.

Women's Lives in Puritan New England

The role of women in the agrarian societies north of the Chesapeake is a controversial subject among colonial historians. Some scholars point out that common law as well as English custom treated women as inferior to men. Other historians, however, depict the colonial period as a "golden age" for women. According to this interpretation, wives worked alongside their husbands. They were not divorced from meaningful, productive labor. They certainly were not transformed into the frail, dependent beings allegedly much admired by middle-class males of the nineteenth century. Both views provide insights into the lives of early American women, but neither fully recaptures their community experiences.

Women's labor and the skilled services that they provided were essential for the economic survival of colonial households. To be sure, women worked on family farms. They did not, however, necessarily do the same jobs that men performed. Women usually handled separate tasks, including cooking, washing, clothes making, dairying, gardening, and caring for young children. Girls began to help their mothers with some of this work as early as age four, beginning their domestic education so that they could one day manage their own household. The average Puritan woman in this period married in her early twenties (compared to the mid-twenties for Puritan men) and it was common for young women who were not yet married to be hired out as servants in other households. Just putting food on the table was an impressive chore in an age before modern conveniences. Women helped butcher meat, harvested garden crops, built and tended cooking fires, and

▷●▶ Read the Document   Prenuptial Agreement (1653)

Puritans viewed marriage as a civil compact rather than a religious sacrament. The families created through marriage formed both the social and economic foundation of Puritan society.

📖●Read the Document **Anne Bradstreet, "Before the Birth of One of Her Children"**

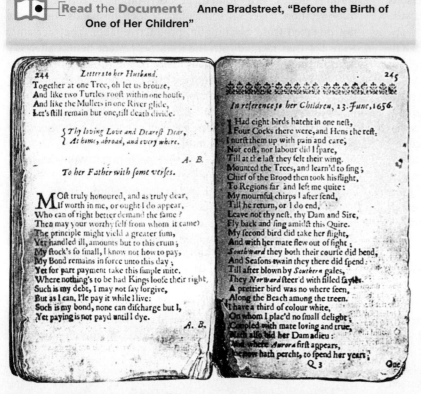

Anne Bradstreet (c.1612–1672) was a Puritan wife, mother, and poet. A collection of her poems entitled *The Tenth Muse Lately Sprung Up in America* was the first work ever published in England's American colonies.

stood for long hours inside large open-hearth fireplaces tending to dishes as they roasted or simmered. This last task sometimes resulted in injury when stray sparks caught clothing on fire.

Often wives—and the overwhelming majority of adult seventeenth-century women were married—raised poultry or performed extra sewing or spinning and thereby achieved some economic independence. When people in one New England community chided a man for allowing his wife to peddle her fowl, he responded, "I meddle not with the geese nor turkeys for they are hers." In fact, during this period women were often described as "deputy husbands," a label that drew attention to their dependence on family patriarchs as well as to their roles as decision makers.

Women also joined churches in greater number than men. Within a few years of founding, many New England congregations contained two female members for every male, a process historians describe as the "feminization of colonial religion." Contemporaries offered different explanations for the gender shift. Cotton Mather, the leading Congregational minister of Massachusetts Bay, argued that God had created "far more *godly Women*" than men. Others thought that the life-threatening experience of childbirth gave women a deeper appreciation of religion. The Quakers gave women an even larger role in religious affairs, which may help to explain the popularity of this sect among ordinary women.

In political and legal matters, society sharply curtailed the rights of colonial women. According to English common law, a wife exercised no control over property. She could not, for example, sell land, although if her husband decided to dispose of their holdings, he was free to do so without her permission. Divorce

was extremely difficult to obtain in any colony before the American Revolution. Indeed, a person married to a cruel or irresponsible spouse had little recourse but to run away or accept the unhappy situation.

Yet most women were neither prosperous entrepreneurs nor abject slaves. Surviving letters indicate that men and women generally accommodated themselves to the gender roles they thought God had ordained. One of early America's most creative poets, Anne Bradstreet, wrote movingly of the fulfillment she had found with her husband. In a piece titled "To my Dear and loving Husband," Bradstreet declared:

> If ever two were one, then surely we.
> If ever man were lov'd by wife, then thee;
> If ever wife was happy in a man,
> Compare with me ye woman if you can.

Although Puritan couples worried that the affection they felt for a husband or a wife might turn their thoughts away from God's perfect love, this was a danger they were willing to risk.

Social Hierarchy in New England

During the seventeenth century, the New England colonies attracted neither noblemen nor paupers. The absence of these social groups meant that the American social structure seemed incomplete by contemporary European standards. The settlers were not displeased that the poor remained in the Old World. The lack of very rich persons—and in this period great wealth frequently accompanied noble title— was quite another matter. According to the prevailing hierarchical view of the structure of society, well-placed individuals were natural rulers, people intended by God to exercise political authority over the rank and file. Migration forced the colonists, however, to choose their rulers from men of more modest status. One minister told a Plymouth congregation that since its members were "not furnished with any persons of *special eminency above the rest*, to be chosen by you into office of government," they would have to make due with neighbors, "not beholding in them the *ordinariness of their persons.*"

The colonists gradually sorted themselves out into distinct social groupings. Persons who would never have been "natural rulers" in England became provincial gentry in the various northern colonies. It helped, of course, if an individual possessed wealth and education, but these attributes alone could not guarantee a newcomer would be accepted into the local ruling elite, at least not during the early decades of settlement. In Massachusetts and Connecticut, Puritan voters expected their leaders to join Congregational churches and defend orthodox religion.

The Winthrops, Dudleys, and Pynchons—just to cite a few of the more prominent families—fulfilled these expectations, and in public affairs they assumed dominant roles. They took their responsibilities quite seriously and certainly did not look kindly on anyone who spoke of their "ordinariness." A colonist who jokingly called a Puritan magistrate a "just ass" found himself in deep trouble with civil authorities.

The problem was that while most New Englanders accepted a hierarchical view of society, they disagreed over their assigned places. Both Massachusetts Bay and Connecticut passed sumptuary laws—statutes that limited the wearing of fine apparel to the wealthy and prominent—to curb the pretensions of those of lower status. Yet such restraints could not prevent some people from rising and others from falling within the social order.

Governor John Winthrop provided a marvelous description of the unplanned social mobility that occurred in early New England. During the 1640s, he recorded in his diary the story of a master who could not afford to pay a servant's wages. To meet this obligation, the master sold a pair of oxen, but the transaction barely covered the cost of keeping the servant. In desperation, the master asked the employee, a man of lower social status, "How shall I do . . . when all my cattle are gone?" The servant replied, "You shall then serve me, so you may have your cattle again." In the margin of his diary next to this account, Winthrop scribbled "insolent."

Most northern colonists were **yeomen** (independent farmers) who worked their own land. While few became rich in America, even fewer fell hopelessly into debt. Their daily lives, especially for those who settled New England, centered on scattered little communities where they participated in village meetings, church-related matters, and militia training. Possession of land gave agrarian families a sense of independence from external authority. As one man bragged to those who had stayed behind in England, "Here are no hard landlords to rack us with high rents or extorting fines. . . . Here every man may be master of his own labour and land . . . and if he have nothing but his hands he may set up his trade, and by industry grow rich."

It was not unusual for northern colonists to work as servants at some point in their lives. This system of labor differed greatly from the pattern of servitude that developed in seventeenth-century Virginia and Maryland. New Englanders seldom recruited servants from the Old World. The forms of agriculture practiced in this region, mixed cereal and dairy farming, made employment of large gangs of dependent workers uneconomic. Rather, New England families placed their adolescent children in nearby homes. These young persons contracted for four or five years and seemed more like apprentices than servants. Servitude was not simply a means by which one group exploited another. It was a form of vocational training program in which the children of the rich as well as the poor participated.

By the end of the seventeenth century, the New England Puritans had developed a compelling story about their own history in the New World. The founders had been extraordinarily godly men and women, and in a heroic effort to establish a purer form of religion, pious families had passed "over the vast ocean into this vast and howling wilderness." Although the children and grandchildren of the first generation sometimes questioned their own ability to please the Lord, they recognized the mission to the New World had been a success: They were "as Prosperous as ever, there is Peace & Plenty, & the Country flourisheth."

The Challenge of the Chesapeake Environment

What factors contributed to political unrest in the Chesapeake region during this period?

An entirely different regional society developed in England's Chesapeake colonies, Virginia and Maryland. This contrast with New England seems puzzling. After all, the two areas were founded at roughly the same time by men and women from the same mother country. In both regions, settlers spoke English, accepted Protestantism, and gave allegiance to one crown. And yet, to cite an obvious example, seventeenth-century Virginia looked nothing like Massachusetts Bay. In an effort to explain the difference, colonial historians have studied environmental conditions, labor systems, and agrarian economies. The most important reason for the distinctiveness of these early southern plantation societies, however, turned out to be the Chesapeake's death rate, a frighteningly high mortality that tore at the very fabric of traditional family life.

Family Life at Risk

Unlike New England's settlers, the men and women who emigrated to the Chesapeake region did not move in family units. They traveled to the New World as young unmarried servants, youths cut off from the security of traditional kin relations. Although these immigrants came from a cross-section of English society, most had been poor to middling farmers. It is now estimated that 70 to 85 percent of the white colonists who went to Virginia and Maryland during the seventeenth century were not free; that is, they owed four or five years' labor in exchange for the cost of passage to America. If the servant was under age 15, he or she had to serve a full seven years. The overwhelming majority of these laborers were males between the ages of 18 and 22. In fact, before 1640, the ratio of males to females stood at 6 to 1. This figure dropped to about 2½ to 1 by the end of the century, but the sex ratio in the Chesapeake was never as favorable as it had been in early Massachusetts.

Most immigrants to the Chesapeake region died soon after arriving. It is difficult to ascertain the exact cause of death in most cases, but malaria and other diseases took a frightful toll. Recent studies also indicate that drinking water contaminated with salt killed many colonists living in low-lying areas. Throughout the entire seventeenth century, high mortality rates had a profound effect on this society. Life expectancy for Chesapeake males was about 43, some ten to twenty years less than for men born in New England! For women, life was even shorter. A full 25 percent of all children died in infancy; another 25 percent did not see their twentieth birthdays. The survivors were often weak or ill, unable to perform hard physical labor.

These demographic conditions retarded normal population increase. Young women who might have become wives and mothers could not do so until they had completed their terms of servitude. They thus lost several reproductive years, and in a society in which so many children died in infancy, late marriage greatly restricted family size. Moreover, because of the unbalanced sex ratio, many adult males simply could not find wives. Migration not only cut them off from their English families but also deprived them of an opportunity to form new ones. Without a constant flow of immigrants, the population of Virginia and Maryland would have actually declined.

High mortality compressed the family life cycle into a few short years. One partner in a marriage usually died within seven years. Only one in three Chesapeake marriages survived as long as a decade. Not only did children not meet grandparents—they often did not even know their own parents. Widows and widowers quickly remarried, bringing children by former unions into their new homes, and it was not uncommon for a child to grow up with persons to whom he or she bore no blood relation. The psychological effects of such experiences on Chesapeake settlers cannot be measured. People probably learned to cope with a high degree of personal insecurity. However they adjusted, it is clear family life in this region was vastly more impermanent than it was in the New England colonies during the same period.

Women's Lives in Chesapeake Society

Women were obviously in great demand in the early southern colonies. Possibly as a result, women married much younger in the South than in New England—with most married by their late teens. Chesapeake men, on the other hand, often married for the first time in their late twenties, if they married at all. Some historians have argued that scarcity heightened the woman's bargaining power in the marriage market. If she was an immigrant, she did not have to worry about obtaining parental consent. She was on her own in the New World and free to select whomever she pleased. If a woman lacked beauty or strength, if she were a person of low moral standards, she could still be confident of finding an American husband. Such negotiations may have provided Chesapeake women with a means of improving their social status.

Nevertheless, liberation from some traditional restraints on seventeenth-century women must not be exaggerated. Most women came to the colonies as indentured servants. Masters often frowned on romantic relationships for fear it would distract from work. If a man and woman wished to marry, and the would-be bride's term of indenture was not up, the prospective groom would have to come up with the money to purchase his intended's contract. As servants, women were also vulnerable to sexual exploitation by their masters.

Once married, a woman in the South took on the same duties as her counterparts in New England, though field work likely took up more of her time as households tried to make a go of it in the tobacco economy. Because of the high mortality rate in the Chesapeake, young women often found themselves caring for children that her husband brought to the family from his first marriage. Moreover, in this unhealthy environment, childbearing was extremely dangerous, and women in the Chesapeake usually died twenty years earlier than their New England counterparts.

The Structure of Planter Society

Colonists who managed somehow to survive grew tobacco—as much tobacco as they possibly could. This crop became the Chesapeake staple, and since it was relatively easy to cultivate, anyone with a few acres of cleared land could harvest leaves for export. Cultivation of tobacco did not, however, produce a society roughly equal in wealth and status. To the contrary, tobacco generated inequality. Some planters amassed large fortunes; others barely subsisted. Labor made the difference, for to succeed in this staple economy, one had to control the labor of other men and women. More workers in the fields meant larger harvests, and, of course, larger profits. Since free persons showed no interest in growing another man's tobacco, not even for wages, wealthy planters relied on white laborers who were not free, as well as on slaves. The social structure that developed in the seventeenth-century Chesapeake reflected a wild, often unscrupulous scramble to bring men and

women of three races—black, white, and Indian—into various degrees of dependence.

Great planters dominated Chesapeake society. The group was small, only a trifling portion of the population of Virginia and Maryland. These ambitious men arrived in America with capital. They invested immediately in laborers, and one way or another, they obtained huge tracts of the best tobacco-growing land. The members of this gentry were not technically aristocrats, for they did not possess titles that could be passed from generation to generation. They gave themselves military titles, sat as justices of the peace on the county courts, and directed local (Anglican) church affairs as members of the vestry. Over time, these gentry families intermarried so frequently that they created a vast network of cousins. During the eighteenth century, it was not uncommon to find a half dozen men with the same surname sitting simultaneously in the Virginia House of Burgesses.

Freemen formed the largest class in Chesapeake society. Their origins were strikingly different from those of the gentry, or for that matter, from those of New England's yeomen farmers. Chesapeake freemen traveled to the New World as indentured servants and, by sheer good fortune, managed to remain alive to the end of their contracts. If they had dreamed of becoming great planters, they were gravely disappointed. Most seventeenth-century freemen lived on the edge of poverty. Some freemen, of course, did better in America than they would have in contemporary England, but in both Virginia and Maryland, historians have found a sharp economic division separating the gentry from the rest of white society.

Below the freemen came indentured servants. Membership in this group was not demeaning; after all, servitude was a temporary status. But servitude in the Chesapeake colonies was not the benign institution it was in New England. Great planters purchased servants to grow tobacco. No one seemed overly concerned whether these laborers received decent food and clothes, much less whether they acquired trade skills. Young people, thousands of them, cut off from family ties, sick often to the point of death, unable to obtain normal sexual release, regarded their servitude as a form of slavery. Not surprisingly, the gentry worried that unhappy servants and impoverished freemen, what the planters called the "giddy multitude," would rebel at the slightest provocation, a fear that turned out to be fully justified.

Sometime after the 1680s—the precise date is impossible to establish—a dramatic demographic shift occurred. Although infant mortality remained high, life expectancy rates for those who survived childhood in the Chesapeake improved significantly, and for the first time in the history of Virginia and Maryland, important leadership positions went to men who had actually been born in America. This transition has been described by one political historian as the "emergence of a creole majority," in other words, as the rise of an indigenous ruling elite. Before this time, immigrant leaders had died without heirs or had returned as quickly as possible to England. The members of the new creole class took a greater interest in local government. Their activities helped give the tobacco colonies the kind of political and cultural stability that had eluded earlier generations of planter adventurers. Not surprisingly, it was during this period of demographic transition that creole leaders founded the College of William and Mary (1693) and authorized the construction of an impressive new capital called Williamsburg. These were changes that, in the words of one creole Virginian, provided the colony "with a sense of permanence and legitimacy . . . it had never before possessed."

The key to success in this creole society was ownership of slaves. Those planters who held more blacks could grow more tobacco and thus could acquire fresh capital needed to purchase additional laborers. Over time, the rich not only became richer; they also formed a distinct ruling elite that newcomers found increasingly difficult to enter.

Opportunities for advancement also decreased for freemen in the region. Studies of mid-seventeenth-century Maryland reveal that some servants managed to become moderately prosperous farmers and small officeholders. But as the gentry consolidated its hold on political and economic institutions, ordinary people discovered it was much harder to rise in Chesapeake society. Those men and women with more ambitious dreams headed for Pennsylvania, North Carolina, or western Virginia.

Social institutions that figured importantly in the daily experience of New Englanders were either weak or nonexistent in the Chesapeake colonies. In part, the sluggish development resulted from the continuation of high infant mortality rates. There was little incentive to build elementary schools, for example, if half the children would die before reaching adulthood. The great planters sent their sons to England or Scotland for their education, and even after the founding of the College of William and Mary in Virginia, the gentry continued to patronize English schools. As a result of this practice, higher education in the South languished for much of the colonial period.

Tobacco influenced the spread of other institutions in the region. Planters were scattered along the rivers, often separated from their nearest neighbors by miles of poor roads. Since the major tobacco growers traded directly with English merchants, they had no need for towns. Whatever items they required were either made on the plantation or imported from Europe. Other than the centers of colonial government, Jamestown (and later Williamsburg) and St. Mary's City (and later Annapolis), there were no villages capable of sustaining a rich community life before the late eighteenth century. Seventeenth-century Virginia did not even possess a printing press. In fact, Governor Sir William Berkeley bragged in 1671, "There are no free schools, nor printing in Virginia, for learning has brought disobedience, and heresy . . . into the world, and printing had divulged them . . . God keep us from both!"

Race and Freedom in British America

How did African American slaves preserve an independent cultural identity in the New World?

Many people who landed in the colonies had no desire to come to the New World. They were Africans taken as slaves to cultivate rice, sugar, and tobacco. As the Native Americans were exterminated and the supply of white indentured servants dried up, European planters demanded ever more African laborers.

Roots of Slavery

A great deal is known about the transfer of African peoples across the Atlantic. During the entire history of this human commerce, between the sixteenth and nineteenth centuries, slave traders carried almost eleven million blacks to the Americas. Most of these men and women

were sold in Brazil or in the Caribbean. A relatively small number of Africans reached British North America, and of this group, the majority arrived after 1700. Slavery existed in each of the thirteen colonies, but the vast majority of slaves lived in the southern colonies where masters put them to work on plantations that grew staple crops for export. Because slaves performed hard physical labor, planters preferred purchasing young males. In many early slave communities, men outnumbered women by a ratio of two to one.

English colonists did not hesitate to enslave black people or, for that matter, Native Americans. While the institution of slavery had long before died out in the mother country, New World settlers quickly discovered how well this particular labor system operated in the Spanish and Portuguese colonies. The decision to bring African slaves to the colonies, therefore, was based primarily on economic considerations.

English masters, however, seldom justified the practice purely in terms of planter profits. Indeed, they adopted a quite different pattern of rhetoric. English writers associated blacks in Africa with heathen religion, barbarous behavior, sexual promiscuity—in fact, with evil itself. From such a racist perspective, the enslavement of Africans seemed unobjectionable. The planters maintained that if black slaves converted to Christianity, shedding their supposedly savage ways, they would benefit from their loss of freedom.

Africans first landed in Virginia in 1619 as a cargo of slaves stolen by a Dutch trader from a Spanish merchant ship in the Caribbean. For the next fifty years, the status of the colony's black people remained unclear. English settlers classified some black laborers as slaves for life, as chattel to be bought and sold at the master's will. But other Africans became servants, presumably for stated periods of time, and it was even possible for a few blacks to purchase their freedom. Several seventeenth-century Africans became successful Virginia planters. These rare exceptions in a long history of oppression remind modern Americans that once, long ago, it was possible to imagine a more open, less racially defined society. (See the Feature Essay, "Anthony Johnson: A Free Black Planter on Pungoteague Creek," pp. 64–65.)

One reason Virginia lawmakers tolerated such confusion was that the black population remained very small. By 1660, fewer than fifteen hundred people of African origin lived in the entire colony (compared to a white population of approximately twenty-six thousand), and it hardly seemed necessary for the legislature to draw up an elaborate slave code to control so few men and women. If the planters could have obtained more black laborers, they certainly would have done so. There is no evidence that the great planters preferred white indentured servants to black slaves.

The problem was supply. During this period, slave traders sold their cargoes on Barbados or the other sugar islands of the West Indies, where they fetched higher prices than Virginians could afford. In fact, before 1680, most blacks who reached England's colonies on the North American mainland came from Barbados or through New Netherland rather than directly from Africa.

By the end of the seventeenth century, the legal status of Virginia's black people was no longer in doubt. They were slaves for life, and so were their children after them. This transformation reflected changes in the supply of Africans to British North America. After 1672, the **Royal African Company** was chartered to meet the colonial planters' demands for black laborers. Historian K. G. Davies terms this organization "the strongest and most effective of all European companies formed exclusively for the African

View the **Closer Look**   African Slave Trade, 1451–1870

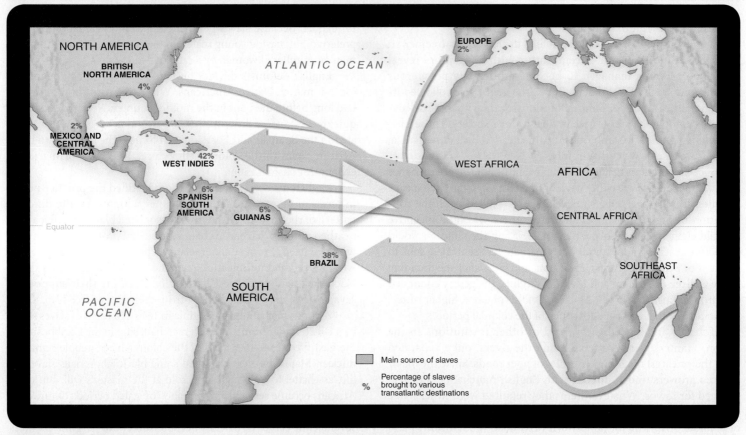

ORIGINS AND DESTINATIONS OF AFRICAN SLAVES, 1619–1760 Although many African slaves were carried to Britain's North American colonies, far more slaves were sold in the Caribbean sugar colonies and Brazil, where because of horrific health conditions, the death rate far exceeded that of the British mainland colonies.

trade." Between 1695 and 1709, more than eleven thousand Africans were sold in Virginia alone; many others went to Maryland and the Carolinas. Although American merchants—most of them based in Rhode Island—entered the trade during the eighteenth century, the British continued to supply the bulk of the slaves to the mainland market for the entire colonial period.

The expanding black population apparently frightened white colonists, for as the number of Africans increased, lawmakers drew up ever stricter slave codes. It was during this period that racism, always a latent element in New World societies, was fully revealed. By 1700, slavery was unequivocally based on the color of a person's skin. Blacks fell into this status simply because they were black. A vicious pattern of discrimination had been set in motion. Even conversion to Christianity did not free the African from bondage. The white planter could deal with his black property as he alone saw fit, and one revolting Virginia statute excused masters who killed slaves, on the grounds that no rational person would purposely "destroy his own estate." Black women constantly had to fear sexual violation by a master or his sons. Children born to a slave woman became slaves regardless of the father's race. Unlike the Spanish colonies, where persons of lighter color enjoyed greater privileges in society, the English colonies tolerated no mixing of the races. Mulattoes and pure Africans received the same treatment.

Constructing African American Identities

The slave experience varied substantially from colony to colony. The daily life of a black person in South Carolina, for example, was quite different from that of an African American who happened to live in Pennsylvania or Massachusetts Bay. The size and density of the slave population determined in large measure how successfully blacks could maintain a separate cultural identity. In the lowlands of South Carolina during the eighteenth century, 60 percent of the population was black. The men and women were placed on large, isolated rice plantations, and their contact with whites was limited. In these areas, blacks developed creole languages, which mixed the basic vocabulary of English with words borrowed from various African tongues. Until the end of the nineteenth century, one creole language, Gullah, was spoken on some of the Sea Islands along the Georgia–South Carolina coast. Slaves on the large rice plantations also were able to establish elaborate and enduring kinship networks that may have helped reduce the more dehumanizing aspects of bondage.

In the New England and Middle Colonies, and even in Virginia, African Americans made up a smaller percentage of the population: 40 percent in Virginia, 8 percent in Pennsylvania, and 3 percent in Massachusetts. In such environments, contact between

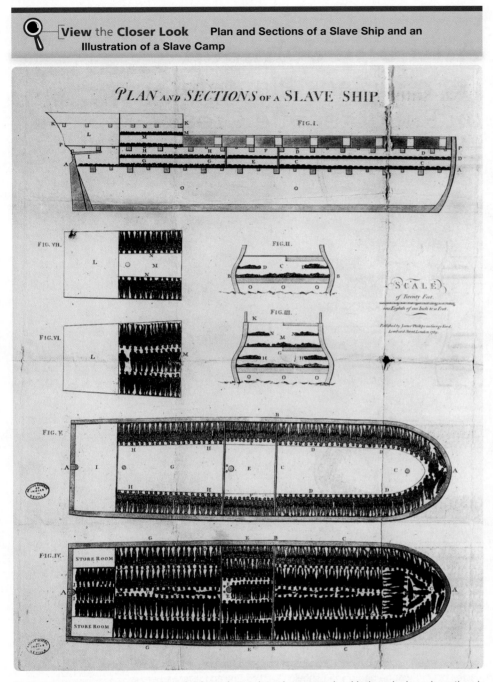

Except for brief excursions on deck for forced exercise, slaves remained below decks, where the air grew foul from the vomit, blood, and excrement in which the terrified victims lay. Some slaves went insane; others refused to eat. On many voyages, between 5 and 20 percent of slaves perished from disease and other causes, which was another reason for captains to pack their ships tightly.

"outlandish" Negroes, as they were called, were forced by blacks as well as whites to accept elements of English culture. It was especially important for newcomers to speak English. Consider, for example, the pain of young Olaudah Equiano, an African sold in Virginia in 1757. This 12-year-old slave declared, "I was now exceedingly miserable, and thought myself worse off than any . . . of my companions; for they could talk to each other [in English], but I had no person to speak to that I could understand. In this state I was constantly grieving and pining, and wishing for death."

Despite such wrenching experiences, black slaves creatively preserved elements of an African heritage. The process of establishing African American traditions involved an imaginative reshaping of African and European customs into something that was neither African nor European. It was African American. The slaves accepted Christianity, but they did so on their own terms—terms their masters seldom fully understood. Blacks transformed Christianity into an expression of religious feeling in which an African element remained vibrant. In music and folk art, they gave voice to a cultural identity that even the most degrading conditions could not eradicate.

A major turning point in the history of African American people occurred during the early decades of the eighteenth century. At this time, blacks living in England's mainland colonies began to reproduce successfully. The number of live births exceeded deaths, and from that date, the expansion of the African American population owed more to natural increase than to the importation of new slaves. Even though thousands of new Africans arrived each year, the creole population was always much larger than that of the immigrant blacks. Not that white masters allowed African American family life to interfere with the work routines of the plantation. Husbands and wives often belonged to different masters and found it hard to find time to visit one another. Difficulties in forming stable families meant that slave women often did not bear children until relatively late

blacks and whites was more frequent than in South Carolina and Georgia. These population patterns had a profound effect on northern and Chesapeake blacks, for while they escaped the physical drudgery of rice cultivation, they found the preservation of an independent African identity difficult. In northern cities, slaves working as domestics and living in the houses of their masters saw other blacks but had little opportunity to develop creole languages or reaffirm a common African past.

In eighteenth-century Virginia, native-born or creole blacks, people who had learned to cope with whites on a daily basis, looked with contempt on slaves who had just arrived from Africa. These

in life. Slave women usually worked in the fields alongside men. Elderly female slaves, often no longer physically fit for field labor, were assigned to watch children while their parents toiled during the long work day. Despite these hardships, North American blacks enjoyed a healthier climate and better diet than did other New World slaves resulting in a demographic shift that did not take place in the Caribbean or South American colonies until a much later date.

Although mainland blacks lived longer than the blacks of Jamaica or Barbados, they were, after all, still slaves. They protested their debasement in many ways, some in individual acts of

Feature Essay

Anthony Johnson
A Free Black Planter on Pungoteague Creek

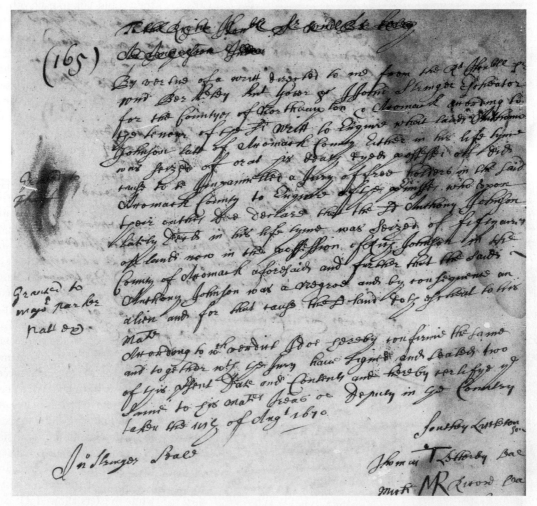

A few months after Anthony Johnson died in 1670, a Virginia court ruled that because "he was a Negro and by consequence an alien," the 250 acres of land that he had owned should revert to England. Shown here is a portion of the court document with that decree.

During the first decades of settlement, a larger proportion of Virginia's black population achieved freedom than at any time until the Civil War ended slavery. Despite considerable obstacles, these free black men and women—their number in these early years was quite small—formed families, acquired property, earned community respect, and helped establish a distinctive African American culture. One member of this group was Anthony Johnson, an immigrant who rose from slavery to prominence on Virginia's Eastern Shore.

Johnson came to Virginia aboard the English vessel *James* in 1621, just two years after the first blacks had arrived in the colony. As a slave known simply as "Antonio a Negro," Johnson found life a constant struggle for survival. Working in the tobacco fields of the Bennett plantation located on the south side of the James River, he endured long hours, poor rations, fearful epidemics, and haunting loneliness—conditions that, more often than not, brought an early death to slaves as well as indentured servants. Johnson, however, was a tough, intelligent, and lucky man.

Exactly how Johnson achieved freedom is not known. Early records reveal that while still living at the Bennett plantation, he took a wife, "Mary a Negro woman." Anthony was fortunate to find her. Because of an exceedingly unequal sex ratio in early Virginia, few males—regardless of color—had an opportunity to form families. Anthony and Mary reared at least four children. Even more remarkable, in a society in which most unions were broken by death within a decade, their marriage lasted more than forty years.

Sometime during the 1630s, Anthony and Mary gained their freedom, perhaps with the help of someone named Johnson. Their bondage probably ended through self-purchase, an arrangement that allowed enterprising slaves to buy their liberty through labor. Later, again under unknown circumstances, the Johnsons migrated to Northampton County on the Eastern Shore of Virginia. During the 1640s, they acquired an estate of 250 acres on Pungoteague Creek, where they raised cattle, horses, and hogs, and cultivated tobacco. To work these holdings, Anthony Johnson apparently relied on the labor of indentured servants and at least one black slave named Casor.

As the "patriarch of Pungoteague Creek," Johnson participated as fully as most whites in Northampton society. He traded with wealthy white landowners and apparently shared their assumptions about the sanctity of property and the legitimacy of slavery. When two white neighbors attempted to steal Casor, Johnson hauled them into court and forced them to return his laborer. On another occasion, Johnson appealed to the court for tax relief after an "unfortunate fire" destroyed much of his plantation.

The Johnsons also maintained close ties with other free blacks, such as Anthony Payne and Emmanuel Driggus, who had similarly attained freedom and prosperity through their own efforts. Johnson's strongest links were with his family. Although his children lived in separate homes after reaching adulthood, his two sons laid out holdings in the 1650s adjacent to their father's plantation, and in times of crisis, parents and children participated in family conferences. These close bonds persisted even after the Johnson clan moved to Somerset County, Maryland, in the 1660s, and Anthony Johnson's subsequent death. When he purchased land in Somerset in 1677, Johnson's grandson, a third-generation free black colonist, named his plantation Angola, perhaps in memory of his grandfather's African homeland.

Interpreting Johnson's remarkable life has proved surprisingly difficult. An earlier generation of historians considered Johnson a curiosity, a sort of black Englishman who did not fit neatly into familiar racial categories. Even some recent writers, concerned about tracing the roots of slavery and prejudice in the United States, have paid scant attention to Johnson and the other free blacks on the Eastern Shore.

Most historians would now agree that Johnson's life illustrated the complexity of race relations in early Virginia. His surprising progression from slave to slaveholder and his easy participation in the world of the white gentry and in a network of black friendships and family ties demonstrated that relations among blacks and whites conformed to no single pattern in the fluid society of mid-seventeenth-century Virginia. Rather, they took a variety of forms—conflict, cooperation, exploitation, accommodation—depending on the goals, status, experience, and environment of the participants. Race was only a single factor—and by no means the decisive one—shaping relations among colonists.

The opportunities that had been available to Anthony Johnson and other Virginia blacks, however, disappeared during the last quarter of the seventeenth century. A growing reliance on slave labor rather than white indentured servitude brought about a rapid increase in the black population of Virginia and an accompanying curtailment of civil liberties on racial grounds. The rise of a group of great planters who dominated the colonial economy soon drove free black farmers into poverty. No longer did they enjoy the security, as had one black farmer in the 1640s, of having "myne owne ground and I will work when I please and play when I please." It is not surprising that after 1706, a time when Virginia's experiment in a genuinely multiracial free society was all but over, the Johnson family disappeared from the colonial records. When modern Americans discuss the history of race relations in the United States, they might consider the factors that allowed some of the first blacks who settled in America to achieve economic and social success.

QUESTIONS FOR DISCUSSION

1. How does the life of Anthony Johnson illustrate the complexity of race relations in early Virginia?

2. Why did the opportunities that free blacks like Anthony Johnson enjoyed disappear in Virginia in the late seventeenth century?

violence, others in organized revolt. The most serious slave rebellion of the colonial period was the Stono Uprising, which took place in September 1739. One hundred fifty South Carolina blacks rose up and, seizing guns and ammunition, murdered several white planters. "With Colours displayed, and two Drums beating," they marched toward Spanish Florida, where they had been promised freedom. The local militia soon overtook the rebellious slaves and killed most of them. Although the uprising was short-lived, such incidents helped persuade whites everywhere that their own blacks might secretly be planning bloody revolt. When a white servant woman in New York City announced in 1741 that blacks intended to burn the town, authorities executed 34 suspected arsonists (30 blacks and 4 whites) and dispatched 72 others either to the West Indies or to Madeira off the north coast of Africa. While the level of interracial violence in colonial society was quite low, everyone recognized that the blacks—in the words of one Virginia governor—longed "to Shake off the fetters of Slavery."

Even within the constraints of slavery, African Americans sometimes found opportunities that afforded a degree of personal freedom. Recent scholarship has discovered, for example, that during the eighteenth century a large number of black men became mariners. It is now estimated that by 1803, African Americans held at least 18 percent of all jobs open to American seamen, and although the number of positions may have been fewer before the Revolution,

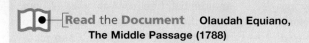

Read the Document Olaudah Equiano, The Middle Passage (1788)

As a young boy, Olaudah Equiano (c.1745–1797) was kidnapped from his home in what is now Nigeria and sold into slavery in America. Equiano eventually earned his freedom by working as a sailor. British abolitionists pointed to the narrative of his extraordinary life to highlight the evils of the slave trade.

Read the Document James Oglethorpe, The Stono Rebellion (1739)

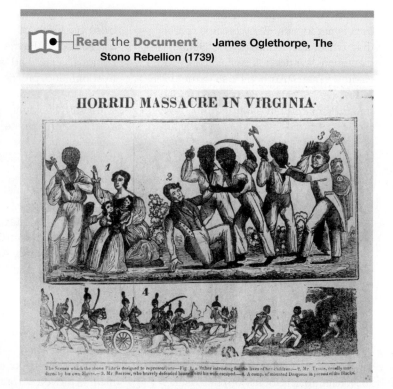

Slave masters often claimed that their slaves loved them and were happy to live in bondage. But events like the Stono Uprising (or Rebellion) of 1739 proved this reassuring fiction to be untrue. Southern whites lived in constant fear that their slaves might one day rise up and repay violence with violence.

black colonial sailors—many of them slaves—sought work on sailing vessels to escape the drudgery of life on rice or tobacco plantations. These African American seamen connected black communities scattered throughout the Caribbean and along the mainland coast, bringing news about distant rebellions and spreading radical political ideologies to slaves who might otherwise not have known much about the transforming events of the eighteenth century.

Rise of a Commercial Empire

Why did England discourage free and open trade in colonial America?

Until the middle of the seventeenth century, English political leaders largely ignored the American colonists. Private companies and aristocratic proprietors had created these societies, some for profit, others for religious sanctuary, but in no case did the crown provide financial or military assistance. After the Restoration of Charles II in 1660, intervention replaced indifference. Englishmen of various sorts—courtiers, merchants, parliamentarians—concluded that the colonists should be brought more tightly under the control of the mother country. The newly restored Stuart monarchy began to establish rules for the entire empire, and the planters of the Chesapeake as well as the Puritans of New England soon discovered they were not as independent as they had imagined. The regulatory policies that evolved during this period formed a framework for an empire that survived with only minor adjustment until 1765.

Response to Economic Competition

By the 1660s, the dominant commercial powers of Europe adopted economic principles that later critics would term **mercantilism**. Proponents of this position argued that since trading nations were engaged in a fierce competition for the world's resources—mostly for raw materials transported from dependent colonies—one nation's commercial success translated directly into a loss for its rivals. It seemed logical, therefore, that England would want to protect its own markets from France or Holland. For seventeenth-century planners free markets made no sense. They argued that trade tightly regulated by the central government represented the only way to increase the nation's wealth at the expense of competitors.

Many discussions of mercantilism suggested that English policy makers during the reign of Charles II had developed a well-integrated set of ideas about the nature of international commerce and a carefully planned set of mercantilist government policies to implement them.

They did nothing of the sort. Administrators responded to particular problems, usually on an individual basis. In 1668, Charles informed his sister, "The thing which is nearest the heart of the nation is trade and all that belongs to it." National interest alone, however, did not shape public policy. Instead, the needs of several powerful interest groups led to the rise of English commercial regulation.

Each group looked to colonial commerce to solve a different problem. For his part, the king wanted money. For their part, English merchants were eager to exclude Dutch rivals from lucrative American markets and needed government assistance to compete successfully with the Dutch, even in Virginia or Massachusetts Bay. From the perspective of the landed gentry who sat in Parliament, England needed a stronger navy, and that in turn meant expansion of the domestic shipbuilding industry. And almost everyone agreed England should establish a more favorable balance of trade, that is, increase exports, decrease imports, and grow richer at the expense of other European states. None of these ideas was particularly innovative, but taken together they provided a blueprint for England's first empire.

Regulating Colonial Trade

After some legislation in that direction during the Commonwealth, Parliament passed a Navigation Act in 1660. The statute was the most important piece of imperial legislation drafted before the American Revolution. Colonists from New Hampshire to South Carolina paid close attention to the details of this statute, which stated (1) that no ship could trade in the colonies unless it had been constructed in either England or America and carried a crew that was at least 75 percent English (for these purposes, colonists counted as Englishmen), and (2) that certain **enumerated goods** of great value that were not produced in England—tobacco, sugar, cotton, indigo, dyewoods, ginger—could be transported from the colonies only to an English or another colonial port. In 1704, Parliament added rice and molasses to the enumerated list; in 1705, rosins, tars, and turpentines needed for shipbuilding were included.

The act of 1660 was masterfully conceived. It encouraged the development of domestic shipbuilding and prohibited European rivals from obtaining enumerated goods anywhere except in England. Since the Americans had to pay import duties in England (for this purpose colonists did not count as Englishmen) on such items as sugar and tobacco, the legislation also provided the crown with another source of income.

In 1663, Parliament passed a second Navigation Act known as the Staple Act, which stated that, with a few noted exceptions, nothing could be imported into America unless it had first been transshipped through England, a process that greatly added to the price ultimately paid by colonial consumers.

The **Navigation Acts** attempted to eliminate the Dutch, against whom the English fought three wars in this period (1652–1654, 1664–1667, and 1672–1674), as the intermediaries of American commerce. Just as English merchants were celebrating their victory, however, an unanticipated rival appeared on the scene: New England merchant ships sailed out of Boston, Salem, and Newport to become formidable world competitors in maritime commerce.

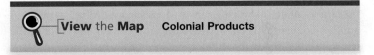

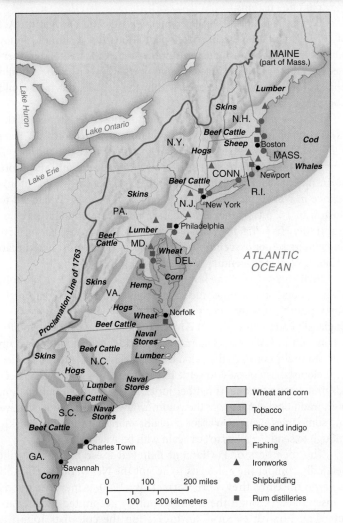

COLONIAL PRODUCTS The above interactive map of colonial products demonstrates the economic reliance of the colonies on exports of certain raw materials, food, and agricultural products.

During the 1660s, the colonists showed little enthusiasm for the new imperial regulations. Reaction to the Navigation Acts varied from region to region. Virginians bitterly protested them. The collection of English customs on tobacco greatly reduced the colonial planters' profits. Moreover, the exclusion of the Dutch from the trade meant that growers often had to sell their crops at artificially low prices. The Navigation Acts hit the small planters especially hard, for they were least able to absorb increased production costs. Even though the governor of Virginia lobbied on the planters' behalf, the crown turned a deaf ear. By 1670, import duties on tobacco accounted for almost £100,000, a sum the king could scarcely do without.

At first, New Englanders simply ignored the commercial regulations. Indeed, one Massachusetts merchant reported in 1664 that Boston entertained "near one hundred sail of ships, this year, of ours and strangers." The strangers, of course, were the Dutch, who had no intention of obeying the Navigation Acts so long as they could reach colonial ports. Some New England merchants found clever ways to circumvent the Navigation Acts. These crafty traders picked up cargoes of enumerated goods such as sugar or tobacco, sailed to another colonial port (thereby technically fulfilling the letter of the law), and then made directly for Holland or France. Along the way they paid no customs.

To plug the loophole, Parliament passed the Navigation Act of 1673. This statute established a plantation duty, a sum of money equal to normal English customs duties to be collected on enumerated products at the various colonial ports. New Englanders could now sail wherever they pleased within the empire, but they could not escape paying customs.

Despite these legal reforms, serious obstacles impeded the execution of imperial policy. The customs service did not have enough effective agents in American ports to enforce the Navigation Acts fully, and some men sent from the mother country did more harm than good. Edward Randolph, head of the imperial customs service in New England, was such a person. He was dispatched to Boston in 1676 to gather information about the conduct of colonial trade. His behavior was so obnoxious, his reports about New Englanders so condescending, that he became the most hated man in late-seventeenth-century Massachusetts.

Parliament passed the last major piece of imperial legislation in 1696. Among other things, the statute tightened enforcement procedures, putting pressure specifically on the colonial governors to keep England's competitors out of American ports. The act of 1696 also expanded the American customs service and for the first time set up vice-admiralty courts in the colonies. This decision eventually rankled the colonists. Established to settle disputes that occurred at sea, vice-admiralty courts required neither juries nor oral cross-examination, both traditional elements of the common law. But they were effective and sometimes even popular for resolving maritime questions quickly enough to send the ships to sea again with little delay.

The members of Parliament believed these reforms would belatedly compel the colonists to accept the Navigation Acts, and in large measure they were correct. By 1700, American goods transshipped through the mother country accounted for a quarter of all English exports, an indication the colonists found it profitable to obey the commercial regulations. In fact, during the eighteenth century, smuggling from Europe to America dried up almost completely.

Colonial Factions Spark Political Revolt, 1676–1691

How did colonial revolts affect the political culture of Virginia and New England?

The Navigation Acts created an illusion of unity. English administrators superimposed a system of commercial regulation on a number of different, often unstable American colonies and called it an empire. But these statutes did not remove long-standing differences. Within each society, men and women struggled to bring order out of disorder, to establish stable ruling elites, to diffuse ethnic and racial tensions, and to cope with population pressures that imperial planners only dimly understood. During the final decades of the seventeenth century, these efforts sometimes sparked revolt.

First, the Virginians rebelled, and then a few years later, political violence swept through Maryland, New York, and Massachusetts Bay, England's most populous mainland colonies.

These events were not in any modern sense of the word ideological. In each colony, the local gentry split into factions, usually the "outs" versus the "ins," and each side proclaimed its political legitimacy.

Civil War in Virginia: Bacon's Rebellion

After 1660, the Virginia economy suffered a prolonged depression. Returns from tobacco had not been good for some time, and the Navigation Acts reduced profits even further. Into this unhappy environment came thousands of indentured servants, people drawn to Virginia, as the governor explained, "in hope of bettering their condition in a Growing Country."

The reality bore little relation to their dreams. A hurricane destroyed one entire tobacco crop, and in 1667, Dutch warships captured the tobacco fleet just as it was about to sail for England. Indentured servants complained about lack of food and clothing. No wonder that Virginia's governor, Sir William Berkeley, despaired of ever ruling "a People where six parts of seven at least are Poor, Endebted, Discontented and Armed." In 1670, he and the House of Burgesses disfranchised all landless freemen, persons they regarded as troublemakers, but the threat of social violence remained.

Enter Nathaniel Bacon. This ambitious young man arrived in Virginia in 1674. He came from a respectable English family and set himself up immediately as a substantial planter. But he wanted more. Bacon envied the government patronage monopolized by Berkeley's cronies, a group known locally as the Green Spring faction. When Bacon attempted to obtain a license to engage in the fur trade, he was rebuffed. This lucrative commerce was reserved for the governor's friends. If Bacon had been willing to wait, he probably would have been accepted into the ruling clique, but as subsequent events would demonstrate, Bacon was not a man of patience.

Events beyond Bacon's control thrust him suddenly into the center of Virginia politics. In 1675, Indians reacting to white encroachment attacked several outlying plantations, killing a few colonists, and Virginians expected the governor to send an army to retaliate. Instead, early in 1676, Berkeley called for the construction of a line of defensive forts, a plan that seemed to the settlers both expensive and ineffective. Indeed, the strategy raised embarrassing questions. Was Berkeley protecting his own fur monopoly? Was he planning to reward his friends with contracts to build useless forts?

📖 ▶ Read the Document   **Nathaniel Bacon's Declaration**
(July 30, 1676)

In 1676, Nathaniel Bacon and about 500 men from the Virginia frontier marched on the colonial capital of Jamestown to demand access to Indian lands. When the House of Burgesses took too long in responding, the rebels set fire to the capital.

While people speculated about such matters, Bacon stepped forward. He boldly offered to lead a volunteer army against the Indians at no cost to the hard-pressed Virginia taxpayers. All he demanded was an official commission from Berkeley giving him military command and the right to attack other Indians, not just the hostile Susquehannocks. The governor steadfastly refused. With some justification, Berkeley regarded his upstart rival as a fanatic on the subject of Indians. The governor saw no reason to exterminate peaceful tribes simply to avenge the death of a few white settlers.

What followed would have been comic had not so many people died. Bacon thundered against the governor's treachery; Berkeley labeled Bacon a traitor. Both men appealed to the populace for support. On several occasions, Bacon marched his followers to the frontier, but they either failed to find the enemy or, worse, massacred friendly Indians. At one point, Bacon burned Jamestown to the ground, forcing the governor to flee to the colony's Eastern Shore. Bacon's bumbling lieutenants chased Berkeley across Chesapeake Bay only to be captured themselves. Thereupon, the governor mounted a new campaign.

As **Bacon's Rebellion** dragged on, it became increasingly apparent that Bacon and his gentry supporters had only the vaguest notion of what they were trying to achieve. The members of the planter elite never seemed fully to appreciate that the rank-and-file soldiers, often black slaves and poor white servants, had serious, legitimate grievances against Berkeley's corrupt government and were demanding substantial reforms, not just a share in the governor's fur monopoly.

Although women had not been allowed to vote in colony elections, they made their political views clear enough during the rebellion. Some were apparently more violent than others. Sarah Glendon, for example, agitated so aggressively in support of Bacon that Berkeley

later refused to grant her a pardon. Another outspoken rebel, Lydia Chiesman, defended her husband before Governor Berkeley, noting that the man would not have joined Bacon's forces had she not persuaded him to do so. "Therefore," Lydia Chiesman concluded, ". . . since what her husband had done, was by her meanes, and so, by consequence, she most guilty, that she might be hanged and he pardoned."

When Charles II learned of the fighting in Virginia, he dispatched a thousand regular soldiers to Jamestown. By the time they arrived, Berkeley had regained full control over the colony's government. In October 1676, Bacon died after a brief illness, and within a few months, his band of rebel followers had dispersed.

Berkeley, now an old and embittered man, was recalled to England in 1677. His successors, especially Lord Culpeper (1680–1683) and Lord Howard of Effingham (1683–1689), seemed interested primarily in enriching themselves at the expense of the Virginia planters. Their self-serving policies, coupled with the memory of near anarchy, helped heal divisions within the Virginia ruling class. For almost a century, in fact, the local gentry formed a united front against greedy royal appointees.

The Glorious Revolution in the Bay Colony

During John Winthrop's lifetime, Massachusetts settlers developed an inflated sense of their independence from the mother country. After 1660, however, it became difficult even to pretend that the Puritan colony was a separate state. Royal officials such as Edward Randolph demanded full compliance with the Navigation Acts. Moreover, the growth of commerce attracted new merchants to the Bay Colony, men who were Anglicans rather than Congregationalists and who maintained close business contacts in London. These persons complained loudly of Puritan intolerance. The Anglican faction was never large, but its presence, coupled with Randolph's unceasing demands, divided Bay leaders. A few Puritan ministers and magistrates regarded compromise with England as treason, a breaking of the Lord's covenant. Other spokesmen, recognizing the changing political realities within the empire, urged a more moderate course.

In 1675, in the midst of this ongoing political crisis, the Indians dealt the New Englanders a terrible setback. Metacomet, a Wampanoag chief the whites called King Philip, declared war against the colonists. The powerful Narragansett Indians, whose lands the settlers had long coveted, joined Metacomet, and in little more than a year of fighting, the Indians destroyed scores of frontier villages, killed hundreds of colonists, and disrupted the entire regional economy. More than one thousand Indians and New Englanders died in the conflict. The war left the people of Massachusetts deeply in debt and more than ever uncertain of their future. As in other parts of colonial America, the defeated Indians were forced off their lands, compelled by events to become either refugees or economically marginal figures in white society.

In 1684, the debate over the Bay Colony's relation to the mother country ended abruptly. The Court of Chancery, sitting in London and acting on a petition from the king, annulled the charter of the Massachusetts Bay Company. In one stroke of a pen, the patent that

Winthrop had so lovingly carried to America in 1630, the foundation for a "city on a hill," was gone. The decision forced the most stubborn Puritans to recognize they were part of an empire run by people who did not share their particular religious vision.

James II, a monarch who disliked representative institutions—after all, Parliament, a representative assembly, had executed his father, Charles I—decided to restructure the government of the entire region in the **Dominion of New England**. In various stages from 1686 to 1689, the Dominion incorporated Massachusetts, Connecticut, Rhode Island, Plymouth, New York, New Jersey, and New Hampshire under a single appointed royal governor. For this demanding position, James selected Sir Edmund Andros (pronounced Andrews), a military veteran of tyrannical temperament. Andros arrived in Boston in 1686, and within a matter of months he had alienated everyone: Puritans, moderates, and even Anglican merchants. Not only did Andros abolish elective assemblies, but he also enforced the Navigation Acts with such rigor that he brought about commercial depression. Andros declared normal town meetings illegal, collected taxes the people never approved, and packed the courts with supporters who detested the local population. Eighteenth-century historian and royal governor Thomas Hutchinson compared Andros unfavorably with the Roman tyrant Nero.

Early in 1689, news of the **Glorious Revolution** reached Boston. The previous fall, the ruling class of England had deposed James II, an admitted Catholic, and placed his Protestant daughter Mary and her husband, William of Orange, on the throne as joint monarchs (see the chart of the Stuart monarchs on p. 31). As part of the settlement, William and Mary accepted a Bill of Rights, a document stipulating the constitutional rights of all Englishmen. Almost immediately, the Bay Colonists overthrew the hated Andros regime. The New England version of the Glorious Revolution (April 18, 1689) was so popular that no one came to the governor's defense. Andros was jailed without a single shot having been fired. According to Cotton Mather, a leading Congregational minister, the colonists were united by the "most Unanimous Resolution perhaps that was ever known to have Inspir'd any people."

However united as they may have been, the Bay Colonists could not take the crown's support for granted. William III could have declared the New Englanders rebels and summarily reinstated Andros. But thanks largely to the tireless lobbying of Increase Mather, Cotton's father, who pleaded the colonists' case in London, William abandoned the Dominion of New England, and in 1691, Massachusetts received a new royal charter. This document differed substantially from the company patent of 1629. The freemen no longer selected their governor. The choice now belonged to the king. Membership in the General Court was determined by annual election, and these representatives in turn chose the men who sat in the council or upper house, subject always to the governor veto. Moreover, the franchise, restricted here as in other colonies to adult males, was determined on the basis of personal property rather than church membership, a change that brought Massachusetts into conformity with general English practice. On the local level, town government remained much as it had been in Winthrop's time.

Contagion of Witchcraft

The instability of the Massachusetts government following Andros's arrest—what Reverend Samuel Willard described as "the short Anarchy accompanying our late Revolution"—allowed what under normal political conditions would have been an isolated, though ugly, local incident to expand into a major colonial crisis. Excessively fearful men and women living in Salem Village, a small, unprosperous farming community, nearly overwhelmed the new rulers of Massachusetts Bay.

Accusations of witchcraft were not uncommon in seventeenth-century New England. Puritans believed that an individual might make a compact with the devil, but during the first decades of settlement, authorities executed only about fifteen alleged witches. Sometimes villagers simply left suspected witches alone. Never before had fears of witchcraft plunged an entire community into panic.

The terror in Salem Village began in early 1692, when several adolescent girls began to behave in strange ways. They cried out for no apparent reason; they twitched on the ground. When concerned neighbors asked what caused their suffering, the girls announced they were victims of witches, seemingly innocent persons who lived in the community. The arrest of several alleged witches did not relieve the girls' "fits," nor did prayer solve the problem. Additional accusations were made, and at least one person confessed, providing a frightening description of the devil as "a thing all over hairy, all the face hairy, and a long nose." In June 1692, a special court convened and began to send men and women to the gallows. By the end of the summer, the court had hanged nineteen people; another was pressed to death. Several more suspects died in jail awaiting trial.

Then suddenly, the storm was over. Led by Increase Mather, a group of prominent Congregational ministers belatedly urged leniency and restraint. Especially troubling to the clergymen was the court's decision to accept **spectral evidence**, that is, reports of dreams and visions in which the accused appeared as the devil's agent. Worried about convicting people on such dubious testimony, Mather declared, "It were better that ten suspected witches should escape, than that one innocent person should be condemned." The colonial government accepted the ministers' advice and convened a new court, which promptly acquitted, pardoned, or released the remaining suspects. After the Salem nightmare, witchcraft ceased to be a capital offense.

No one knows exactly what sparked the terror in Salem Village. The community had a history of religious discord, and during the 1680s, the people split into angry factions over the choice of a minister. Economic tensions played a part as well. Poorer, more traditional farmers accused members of prosperous, commercially oriented families of being witches. The underlying misogyny of the entire culture meant the victims were more often women than men. Terror of attack by Native Americans may also have played a part in this ugly affair. Indians in league with the French in Canada had recently raided nearby communities, killing people related to the families of the bewitched Salem girls, and significantly, during the trials some victims described the Devil as a "tawny man." (For further discussion of the Salem witchcraft trials, see "Witches and the Law," pp. 72–75.)

The Glorious Revolution in New York and Maryland

The Glorious Revolution in New York was more violent than it had been in Massachusetts Bay. Divisions within New York's ruling class ran deep and involved ethnic as well as religious differences. English newcomers and powerful Anglo-Dutch families who had recently risen to commercial prominence in New York City opposed the older Dutch elite.

Much like Nathaniel Bacon, Jacob Leisler was a man entangled in events beyond his control. Leisler, the son of a German minister, emigrated to New York in 1660 and through marriage aligned himself with the Dutch elite. While he achieved moderate prosperity as a merchant, Leisler resented the success of the Anglo-Dutch.

When news of the Glorious Revolution reached New York City in May 1689, Leisler raised a group of militiamen and seized the local fort in the name of William and Mary. As leader of Leisler's Rebellion, he apparently expected an outpouring of popular support, but it was not forthcoming. His rivals waited, watching while Leisler desperately attempted to legitimize his actions. Through bluff and badgering, Leisler managed to hold the colony together, especially after French forces burned Schenectady (February 1690), but he never established a secure political base.

In March 1691, a new royal governor, Henry Sloughter, reached New York. He ordered Leisler to surrender his authority, but when Sloughter refused to prove he had been sent by William

▶ Read the Document Cotton Mather, Memorable Providences Relating to Witchcraft

The publication of Cotton Mather's *Memorable Providences, Relating to Witchcrafts and Possessions* (1689) contributed to the hysteria that resulted in the Salem witchcraft trials of the 1690s, but he did not take part in the trials. He is shown here surrounded by some of the forms a demon assumed in the "documented" case of an English family besieged by witches.

rather than by the deposed James, Leisler hesitated. The pause cost Leisler his life. Sloughter declared Leisler a rebel, and in a hasty trial, a court sentenced him and his chief lieutenant, Jacob Milbourne, to be hanged "by the Neck and being Alive their bodyes be Cutt downe to Earth and Their Bowells to be taken out and they being Alive, burnt before their faces . . . ." In 1695, Parliament officially pardoned Leisler, but he not being "Alive," the decision arrived a bit late. Long after his death, political factions calling themselves Leislerians and Anti-Leislerians struggled to dominate New York government. Indeed, in no other eighteenth-century colony was the level of bitter political rivalry so high.

During the last third of the seventeenth century, the colony of Maryland stumbled from one political crisis to another. Protestants in the colony's lower house resisted Lord Baltimore's Catholic friends in the upper house or council. When news of James's overthrow reached Maryland early in 1689, pent-up antiproprietary and anti-Catholic sentiment exploded. John Coode, a member of the assembly and an outspoken Protestant, formed a group called the Protestant Association, which in August forced Baltimore governor, William Joseph, to resign.

Coode avoided Leisler's fatal mistakes. The Protestant Association, citing many wrongs suffered at the hands of local Catholics, petitioned the crown to transform Maryland into a royal colony. After reviewing the case, William accepted Coode's explanation, and in 1691, the king dispatched a royal governor to Maryland. A new assembly dominated by Protestants declared Anglicanism the established religion. Catholics were excluded from public office on the grounds that they might be in league with French Catholics in Canada. Lord Baltimore lost control of the colony's government, but he and his family did retain title to Maryland's undistributed lands. In 1715, the crown restored to full proprietorship the fourth Lord Baltimore, who had been raised a member of the Church of England, and Maryland remained in the hands of the Calvert family until 1776.

Conclusion: Local Aspirations within an Atlantic Empire

"It is no little Blessing of God," Cotton Mather announced proudly in 1700, "that we are part of the *English* nation." A half century earlier, John Winthrop would not have spoken these words, at least not with such enthusiasm. The two men were, of course, products of different political cultures. It was not so much that the character of Massachusetts society had changed. In fact, the Puritan families of 1700 were much like those of the founding generation. Rather, the difference was in England's attitude toward the colonies. Rulers living more than three thousand miles away now made political and economic demands that Mather's contemporaries could not ignore.

The creation of a new imperial system did not, however, erase profound sectional differences. By 1700, for example, the Chesapeake colonies were more, not less, committed to the cultivation of tobacco and slave labor. Although the separate regions were being pulled slowly into England's commercial orbit, they did not have much to do with each other. The elements that sparked a powerful sense of nationalism among colonists dispersed over a huge territory would not be evident for a very long time. It would be a mistake, therefore, to anticipate the coming of the American Revolution.

Law and Society | Witches and the Law
A Problem of Evidence in 1692

This seventeenth-century house is the former home of Jonathan Corwin, one of the magistrates who presided over the Salem witch trials. Despite having received the nickname of "The Witch House," no accused witches actually resided here, nor were trials ever held within its walls.

The events that occurred at Salem Village in 1692 haunt modern memory. In popular American culture, the incident has come to represent our worst nightmare—a community-sanctioned witch hunt that ferrets out deviants in the name of law. What seems most unsettling about the incident is the failure of allegedly good men and women to bear witness against judicial terror. The ordeal of Salem Village links a distant colonial past with the infamous

McCarthy hearings of the 1950s as well as other, more recent witch hunts. The story of this deeply troubled town challenges us to confront the possibility that we, too, might allow law and authority to become instruments of injustice.

The challenge in exploring law and society is how best to interpret the Salem trials. It would be easy to insist that Puritan magistrates were gross hypocrites, figures who consciously manipulated the law for their own hateful purposes. But such conclusions are simplistic; they fail to place the Salem

nightmare in proper historical context. The participants in this intense social drama acted on a complex set of seventeenth-century assumptions— legal, religious, and scientific—and if judges and jurors wronged innocent people, they did so by the standards of a society very different from our own.

Few New Englanders doubted the existence of witches. For centuries, European communities had identified certain persons as agents of the devil, and when the Puritans migrated to America, they carried these beliefs with them. They recognized no conflict between rational religion and the possible existence of a satanic world populated by witches. Ordinary farmers regarded unusual events—the strange death of a farm animal, for example—as evidence of witchcraft. New England's intellectual leaders sustained popular superstition in impressive scientific publications. In his *Memorable Providences, Relating to Witchcrafts and Possessions* (1689), the Reverend Cotton Mather declared, "I am resolv'd . . . never to use . . . one grain of patience with any man that shall . . . impose upon me a Denial of Devils, or of Witches. I shall . . . count him down-right Impudent if he Assert the Non-Existence of things which we have had such palpable Convictions of."

Colonial New Englanders did more than talk and write about witches; as early as 1647, they executed several. Before the Salem outbreak, ninety-one people had been tried for witchcraft in Massachusetts and Connecticut, and sixteen of them were hanged (not burned as some historians have claimed). In addition, hundreds of people had accused neighbors of witchcraft, but for many reasons—usually lack of convincing evidence—they stopped short of taking such disputes before the court. These were isolated incidents. Before 1692, fear of witches had not sparked mass hysteria.

Salem Village was different. In this instance, charges of witchcraft shattered a community already deeply divided against itself. The predominantly agricultural Salem Village lay a few miles up the Ipswich Road from the bustling commercial port of Salem Town. The farmers of the Village envied their neighbors' prosperity. Even more, they resented the control that Town authorities exerted over the Village church and government. This tension found expression in numerous personal and family rivalries. In 1689, the congregation at Salem Village ordained the Reverend Samuel Parris, a troubled figure who provoked "disquietness" and "restlessness" and who fanned the factionalism that had long plagued the community.

The witchcraft crisis began suddenly in mid-January 1692, when two girls in the Parris household experienced violent convulsions and frightening visions. A local physician examined the afflicted children but found no "natural" cause for their condition. Soon anxious families raised the possibility of witchcraft, a move which set off a storm of accusations that did not abate until October. By that time, 20 people had died and more than 150 prisoners still awaited trial.

Although the witch hysteria affected everyone—men and women, rich and poor, farmers and merchants—the accusers and their targets were not evenly distributed among the population of Salem Village. Twenty of the thirty-four persons who claimed to have been bewitched were girls between the ages of 11 and 20. Women a full generation older than the accusers were most likely to be identified as witches; more than 40 percent of the accused fell into this category. Although men and women from many different backgrounds were accused, one widely shared characteristic was a history of socially unacceptable behavior. Sarah Good, for example, smoked a pipe and was known for cursing her enemies. John Aldin's accusers described him as "a bold fellow . . . who lies with Indian squaws . . . [and stands] with his hat on before the judges." Bridget Bishop ran a scandalous tavern and dressed in a particularly flashy, immodest manner. Those who testified against the supposed witches came from all classes, both genders, and every age group. Indeed, virtually the entire community was drawn into the ugly business of charge and countercharge, fear and betrayal.

New England's intellectual leaders—most of them Harvard-educated clergymen—tried to make sense out of reports coming out of Salem. Since the colonies did not yet have a newspaper, the reflections of these prominent figures significantly shaped how the entire society interpreted the frightening events of 1692. During the spring of that year, accusations of witchcraft mounted while magistrates interrogated everyone touched by the contagion.

Arriving from England in mid-May at the height of the witch hunt, the new royal governor of Massachusetts Bay, William Phips, appointed a special court of law (a court of "oyer and terminer") to try the cases at Salem Village. The seven judges he appointed all had previous experience in the colony's law courts. Phips wanted the trials to be as fair as possible and procedurally correct. A proper jury was impaneled. Despite precautions, however, the court itself soon succumbed to the frenzy. Chief judge and deputy governor William Stoughton, for example, staunchly believed the girls had been bewitched, and he had little doubt that "real" witches were responsible for the trouble at Salem Village. By contrast, Nathaniel Saltonstall was highly skeptical of the witchcraft charges. After witnessing the first round of executions, Saltonstall resigned from the court and turned to alcohol to persuade himself the court had not made a terrible mistake. Although the judges and jury may have felt ambivalent about what was happening, the law stated that persons convicted as witches must die.

Everything turned on evidence. Confession offered the most reliable proof of witchcraft, and it occurred surprisingly often. We will never know what compelled people to confess. Some may have actually believed they had cast spells on their neighbors or had foretold the future. Many women, though believing themselves innocent, may have confessed because of guilt for impure thoughts that they had privately entertained. Perhaps the psychological strain of imprisonment, coupled with intense social scrutiny, convinced them they might have unwittingly entered into a contract with the devil. Regardless, the stories they told undoubtedly mortified those who heard them and fueled the growing frenzy. Imagine the reaction to Ann Foster's July 18 confession:

Ann Foster . . . confessed that the devill in the shape of a black man appeared to her with [Martha] Carrier about six yeare since when they made her a witch and that she promised to serve the devill two years: upon which the Devill promised her prosperity and many things but never performed it, that she and Martha Carrier did both ride on a stick or pole when they went to the witch meeting at Salem Village and that the stick broak: as they were carried in the air above the tops of the trees and they fell but she did hang fast about the neck of [Martha] Carrier and were presently at the village, . . . she further saith that she heard some of the witches say that there was three hundred and five in the whole Country and that they would ruin that place the Village . . .

Most of the accused did not confess, however, forcing the judges to produce tangible evidence of witchcraft. The charge was difficult because the crime of bewitchment was, by nature, an invisible act. Earthly laws and magistrates had difficulty dealing with crimes that occurred in the spiritual world. In this situation, the beleaguered judges used a few customary tests. All witches supposedly had a "witch's teat," usually a flap of skin located anywhere on the body, from which they gave suck to the devil. The judges subjected almost every defendant to a humiliating physical examination in order to find such biological abnormalities. Witches could also be discovered by having them touch a girl in the midst of her torments. If the girl's fits ceased, then the person who touched her was assumed responsible for her agony. Since this form of evidence was immediately observable, judges relied on it heavily, oftentimes parading accused witches before the possessed girls waiting to see whose touch would calm them.

Had the terrible ordeal turned solely on unsightly warts, the trials might have ended without further note. But that did not happen. The judges allowed the jury to entertain a different sort of evidence, "spectral evidence," and it was this material that hanged people at Salem Village. New Englanders believed that witches worked by dispatching a specter, a phantom spirit, to torment their victims. This meant that witches had power over great distances; they were invisible. They entered people's dreams, and dozens of good New Englanders complained of having been bitten, pinched, or even choked by specters that looked a lot like their neighbors. The judges regularly accepted spectral testimony of the sort offered by 18-year-old John Cook:

. . . one morning about sun rising as I was in bed . . . I saw [Bridget] Bishop . . . Standing in the chamber by the window and she looked on me & . . . presently struck me on the Side of the head w'ch did very much hurt me & then I Saw her goe Out under the End window at a little Creviss about So bigg as I Could thrust my hand into. I Saw her again the Same day . . . walke & Cross the roome & having at the time an apple in my hand it flew Out of my hand into my mothers lapp who stood Six or Eight foot distance from me & then She disappeared & though my mother & Severall others were in the Same room yet they affirmed they Saw her not.

As far as the witch hunters were concerned, Bridget Bishop had been caught in the act. To the modern observer, however, the problems with this kind of evidence seem obvious. First, how could one tell whether Cook was lying? The power of his story lay in its inability to be corroborated, for one could never check the authenticity of an intensely private dream or vision. The second problem was that persons accused of being witches had no defense against spectral testimony. When Captain John Aldin stood before his accusers, for example, they immediately fell to the ground, writhing in pain. When asked why he tormented the girls, Aldin firmly denied any wrongdoing, inquiring why the judges "suppose[d he had] no better things to do than to come to Salem to afflict these persons that I never knew or saw before." Aldin's defense did not carry much weight when set against the testimony of the suffering girls, and rather than conclude the accusers manifested a "lying spirit," the judges admitted all spectral evidence as incontestable proof of witchcraft.

Very early in the trials, a few people expressed doubts about the reliability of this particular form of evidence. Cotton Mather and other ministers, for example, issued a statement urging the judges to use spectral evidence with "a very critical and exquisite caution." Some feared the devil could assume the shape of innocent people. If this was the case, then the visions of the afflicted proved nothing but the devil's ability to deceive humans. In the absence of spectral evidence, the cases against most of the witches boiled down to little more than long-standing complaints against obnoxious neighbors. The fury of prosecution silenced the skeptical voices, however, and chief judge William Stoughton continued to accept dreams and visions as proof of witchcraft.

Fantastic testimony about flying witches and pinching specters lent an almost circuslike air to the proceedings at Salem. Before the judges and the members of the jury, the afflicted girls would fall to the ground, convulsing and screaming, claiming to see witches that remained invisible to the court. Hundreds of spectators sat horrified as Satan caused suffering before their own eyes. For seventeenth-century New Englanders who felt the presence of the spiritual world in their everyday lives, the courtroom at Salem offered the opportunity to witness the struggle between the forces of darkness and light. Because of the gravity of the situation, no one expected the judges to deal lightly with those who had sworn allegiance to the devil. Indeed, in the interest of obtaining a confession, the judges conducted harsh interrogations, usually assuming the guilt of the defendant. The intense psychological pressure inflicted on the defendants is revealed in the questioning of Sarah Good, a woman subsequently hanged as a witch:

Judge: Sarah Good, what evil spirit have you familiarity with?

Good: None.

Judge: Why do you hurt these children?

Good: I do not hurt them. I scorn it.

Judge: Who do you employ then to do it?

Good: I employ nobody.

Judge: Have you made a contract with the devil?

Good: No.

Judge: Sarah Good . . . why do you not tell us the truth? Why do you thus torment these poor children?

Good: I do not torment them.

Even the ministers who advised caution applauded the judges' "assiduous endeavors" and encouraged the "vigorous prosecution" of the witches. As the witch hysteria gained momentum, few people dared to defend the witches for fear of being accused themselves. The humble pleas of those who genuinely thought themselves innocent fell on the deaf ears of a community convinced of its own righteousness.

By late September, with twenty people already executed, the emotional intensity that had sustained the witch hunt in its early stages began to ebb. For one thing, the accusations spun wildly out of control as the afflicted girls began naming unlikely candidates as witches: prominent ministers, a judge's mother-in-law, and even the governor's wife! Such accusations discredited the entire procedure by which the witches had been discovered. Also, although the jails could barely hold the 150 people still awaiting trial, the accusations kept coming. The terror was feeding on itself.

In mid-October, Governor Phips dismissed the original court and appointed a new one, this time barring spectral evidence. All remaining defendants were quickly acquitted, although, curiously enough, three women still confessed to having practiced witchcraft. In a letter to the king, Phips explained his decision to end the trials, claiming that "the people" had become "dissatisfied and disturbed." Men and women who had been so eager to purify the community of evil, to murder neighbors in the name of a higher good, now spoke of their fear of divine retribution. Perhaps the dying words of Sarah Good, uttered in response to the assistant minister of Salem Town, echoed in their ears: "I am no more a witch than you are a wizard, and if you take away my life, God will give you blood to drink."

Soon after the trials ended, the witch hunters quickly turned confessors. In 1706, Ann Putnam, one of the most prolific accusers, publicly asked for forgiveness: "I desire to be humbled before God . . . It was a great delusion of Satan that deceived me in that time." Nine years earlier, the Salem jurors had issued a similar statement, asking the community to understand the particular pressures that compelled them to convict so many people:

> *We confess that we . . . were not capable to understand, nor able to withstand the mysterious delusions of the Powers of Darkness . . .; but were for want of Knowledge in our selves, and better Information from others, prevailed with to take up with such Evidence against the Accused, as on further consideration, and better Information, we justly fear was insufficient for the touching the Lives of any . . . whereby we fear we have been instrumental with others, tho Ignorantly and unwittingly, to bring upon our selves, and this People of the Lord, the Guilt of Innocent Blood.*

The state never again executed citizens for witchcraft. The experience at Salem had taught New Englanders that, although witches may have existed, no human court could identify a witch beyond a reasonable doubt. The Reverend Increase Mather summed up the attitude of a post-Salem New England: "It were better that ten suspected witches should escape than that one innocent person should be condemned."

What triggered the tragic events of 1692 remains a mystery. Some historians view the witch hunt as a manifestation of Salem Village's socioeconomic troubles. This interpretation helps explain why the primary accusers came from the agrarian village while the alleged witches either resided in or were somehow connected to the market-oriented town. Perhaps the charge of witchcraft masked a deep resentment for their neighbors' monetary success and the new set of values that accompanied the market economy. Other historians believe the witch hunt reflected a deep ambivalence about gender roles in New England society. Young girls lashed out at older nonconforming women because they symbolized a freedom that was achievable within New England society, yet vehemently criticized. Facing the choice between becoming their husbands' servants or being free, the accusers may have expressed this cultural frustration in lethal ways. Terror of Indian attack may have exacerbated community fear. Some accusers described the devil as a "tawney man," a clear reference to Native Americans. These and many other factors contributed to the witch phenomenon.

Regardless of which interpretation one favors, one must acknowledge that Salem Village had indeed been possessed. The blame rests on the community as a whole, not just on a few vindictive judges. In 1697, another repentant witch hunter, the Reverend John Hale, tried to explain how well-meaning people had caused such harm:

> *I am abundantly satisfyed that those who were most concerned to act and judge in those matters, did not willingly depart from the rules of righteousness. But such was the darkness of that day, . . . that we walked in the clouds, and could not see our way.*

Hale's words ring hollow. They came too late to do much good. As other communities have learned throughout the long history of this nation, it is easier to apologize after the fact than to stand up courageously against the first injustice.

QUESTIONS FOR DISCUSSION

1. Do historians' interpretations of the Salem witch hunt seem adequate to explain the events of 1692? Why or why not?

2. How does your judgment of the ministers and magistrates in charge change if you judge them by modern standards versus the scientific and theological standards of their own time?

3. Should the magistrates who sat in judgment at Salem have been tried later for incompetence or malfeasance?

4. What can modern Americans learn from the events of 1692?

Study Resources

 Take the **Study Plan** for **Chapter 3** *Putting Down Roots* on **MyHistoryLab**

TIME LINE

1619 First blacks arrive in Virginia

1660 Charles II is restored to the English throne; First Navigation Act passed by Parliament

1663 Second Navigation (Staple) Act passed

1673 Plantation duty imposed to close loopholes in commercial regulations

1675 King Philip's (Metacomet's) War devastates New England

1676 Bacon's Rebellion threatens Governor Berkeley's government in Virginia

1681 William Penn receives charter for Pennsylvania

1684 Charter of the Massachusetts Bay Company revoked

1685 Duke of York becomes James II

1686 Dominion of New England established

1688 James II driven into exile during Glorious Revolution

1689 Rebellions break out in Massachusetts, New York, and Maryland

1691 Jacob Leisler executed

1692 Salem Village wracked by witch trials

1696 Parliament establishes Board of Trade

1739 Stono Uprising of South Carolina slaves terrifies white planters

CHAPTER REVIEW

Sources of Stability: New England Colonies of the Seventeenth Century

 What factors explain the remarkable social stability achieved in early New England?

Seventeenth-century New Englanders migrated to America in family groups, ensuring that the ratio of men to women remained roughly even, making it easier for young people to marry and start families. Stable marriage, together with New England's healthy climate, led to rapid population growth. While many young New Englanders served as servants, most seventeenth century colonists eventually acquired property. (p. 56)

The Challenge of the Chesapeake Environment

 What factors contributed to political unrest in the Chesapeake region during this period?

Most immigrants to the early Chesapeake colonies were single young male indentured servants. Disease killed many of them shortly after arriving. Men outnumbered women, making it difficult for freemen to marry. Because of the short life expectancy, marriages did not last long. Economic inequality and family instability contributed to political unrest. (p. 59)

Race and Freedom in British America

 How did African American slaves preserve an independent cultural identity in the New World?

Slaves, especially those in the South, developed new creole languages that blended English with African languages. They established enduring kinship networks that helped mitigate the hardships of slavery. Enslaved Africans also developed new forms of music and folk art that drew upon African roots and adapted the Christianity taught them by their masters to include African religious elements. (p. 61)

Rise of a Commercial Empire

 Why did England discourage free and open trade in colonial America?

During the seventeenth century, Parliament passed mercantilist laws declaring that colonial raw materials and commerce would benefit only the mother country and not a European rival. These commercial regulations represented England's new blueprint for the empire. (p. 66)

Colonial Factions Spark Political Revolt, 1676–1691

 How did colonial revolts affect the political culture of Virginia and New England?

During Bacon's Rebellion, landless freemen rose up against the governor and demanded Indian lands. Although the rebellion failed, it unified Virginia's ruling elite. In 1684, James II restructured the northern colonies to increase crown authority. New Englanders threw off the Dominion of New England in 1689 and negotiated for government charters that allowed significant local autonomy. (p. 68)

KEY TERMS AND DEFINITIONS

Indentured servant Persons who agreed to serve a master for a set number of years in exchange for the cost of transport to America. Indentured servitude was the dominant form of labor in the Chesapeake colonies before slavery. p. 55

Yeomen Southern small landholders who owned no slaves, and who lived primarily in the foothills of the Appalachian and Ozark mountains. p. 59

Royal African Company Slaving company created to meet colonial planters' demands for black laborers. p. 61

Mercantilism Mercantilism assumed that the supply of wealth was fixed. To increase its wealth, a nation needed to export more goods than it imported. Favorable trade and protective economic policies and colonial possessions rich in raw materials were important in achieving this balance. p. 67

Enumerated goods Raw materials, such as tobacco, sugar, and rice, that were produced in the British colonies and under the Navigation Acts had to be shipped only to England or its colonies. p. 67

Navigation Acts Commercial restrictions that regulated colonial commerce to favor England's accumulation of wealth. p. 67

Bacon's Rebellion An armed rebellion in Virginia (1675–1676) led by Nathaniel Bacon against the colony's royal governor, Sir William Berkeley. p. 69

Dominion of New England Incorporation of the New England colonies under a single appointed royal governor that lasted from 1686–1689. p. 70

Glorious Revolution Replacement of James II by William III and Mary II as English monarchs in 1688, marking the beginning of constitutional monarchy in Britain. p. 70

Spectral evidence In the Salem witch trials, the court allowed reports of dreams and visions in which the accused appeared as the devil's agent to be introduced as testimony. The accused had no defense against this kind of "evidence." When the judges later disallowed this testimony, the executions for witchcraft ended. p. 70

CRITICAL THINKING QUESTIONS

1. What factors would have drawn ambitious, young English people in the first half of the seventeenth century to the Chesapeake region rather than to New England?

2. Since living with large numbers of unfree Africans frightened whites, why did colonists continue to import so many slaves?

3. Did the mercantilist system best serve the interests of the English or of the American colonists?

4. Why did colonial rebellions of the seventeenth century not lead to demands for political independence?

MyHistoryLab Media Assignments

Find these resources in the Media Assignments folder for Chapter 3 on MyHistoryLab

Social Stability: New England Colonies of the Seventeenth Century

Read the **Document** *Prenuptial Agreement (1653) p. 57*

Read the **Document** *Anne Bradstreet, "Before the Birth of One of Her Children" p. 58*

Race and Freedom in British America

■ **View** the **Closer Look** *African Slave Trade, 1451–1870 p. 62*

■ **View** the **Closer Look** *Plan and Sections of a Slave Ship and an Illustration of a Slave Camp p. 63*

■ **Complete** the **Assignment** *Anthony Johnson, A Free Black Planter on Pungoteague Creek p. 64*

Read the **Document** *Olaudah Equiano, The Middle Passage (1788) p. 66*

■ **Read** the **Document** *James Oglethorpe, The Stono Rebellion (1739) p. 66*

Rise of a Commercial Empire

View the **Map** *Colonial Products p. 67*

Colonial Factions Spark Political Revolt

■ **Read** the **Document** *Nathaniel Bacon's Declaration (July 30, 1676) p. 69*

Read the **Document** *Cotton Mather, Memorable Providences Relating to Witchcraft p. 71*

Complete the **Assignment** *Witches and the Law: A Problem of Evidence in 1692 p. 72*

■ *Indicates Study Plan Media Assignment*

4

Experience of Empire:
Eighteenth-Century America

Contents and Learning Objectives

((●─┤ **Listen** to the **Audio File** on **myhistorylab**   **Chapter 4** *Experience of Empire*

Constructing an Anglo-American Identity: The Journal of William Byrd

William Byrd II (1674–1744) was a type of British American one would not have encountered during the earliest years of settlement. This successful Tidewater planter was a product of a new, more cosmopolitan environment, and as an adult, Byrd seemed as much at home in London as in his native Virginia. In 1728, at the height of his political influence in Williamsburg, the capital of colonial Virginia, Byrd accepted a commission to help survey a disputed boundary between North Carolina and Virginia. During his long journey into the distant backcountry, Byrd kept a detailed journal, a satiric, often bawdy chronicle of daily events that is now regarded as a classic of early American literature.

On his trip into the wilderness, Byrd met many different people. No sooner had he departed a familiar world of tobacco plantations than he came across a self-styled "Hermit," an Englishman who apparently preferred the freedom of the woods to the constraints of society. "He has no other Habitation but a green Bower or Harbour," Byrd reported, "with a Female Domestick as wild & as dirty as himself."

As the boundary commissioners pushed farther into the backcountry, they encountered highly independent men and women of European descent, small frontier families that Byrd regarded as living no better than savages. He attributed their uncivilized behavior to a diet of too much pork. "The Truth of it is, these People live so much upon Swine's flesh . . . [that it] makes them . . . extremely hoggish in their Temper, & many of them seem to Grunt rather than Speak in their ordinary conversation." The wilderness journey also brought Byrd's party of surveyors into regular contact with Native Americans, whom he properly distinguished as Catawba, Tuscarora, Usheree, and Sapponi Indians.

Byrd's journal invites us to view the rapidly developing eighteenth-century backcountry from a fresh perspective. It was not a vast empty territory awaiting the arrival of European settlers. Maps often sustain this erroneous impression, depicting cities and towns, farms and plantations clustered along the Atlantic coast; they suggest a "line of settlement" steadily pushing outward into a huge blank area with no mark of civilization. The people Byrd met on his journey into the backcountry would not have understood

William Byrd II. Byrd's *History of the Dividing Line: Run in the Year 1728* contains a marvelously satirical account of the culture of poor country farmers in North Carolina.

such maps. After all, the empty space on the maps was their home. They experienced the frontier as populous zones of many cultures stretching from the English and French settlements in the north all the way to the Spanish borderlands in the far southwest.

The point is not to discount the significance of the older Atlantic settlements. During the eighteenth century, Britain's thirteen mainland colonies underwent a profound transformation. The population in the colonies grew at unprecedented rates. German and Scots-Irish immigrants arrived in huge numbers. So too did African slaves.

Wherever they lived, colonial Americans of this period were less isolated from one another than colonists had been during most of the seventeenth century. Indeed, after 1690, men and women expanded their cultural horizons, becoming part of a larger Anglo-American empire. The change was striking. Colonists whose parents or grandparents had come to the New World to confront a "howling wilderness" now purchased imported European manufactures, read English journals, participated in imperial wars, and sought favors from a growing number of resident royal officials. No one—not even the inhabitants of the distant frontiers—could escape the influence of Britain. The cultural, economic, and political links connecting the colonists to the imperial center in London grew stronger with time.

This surprising development raises a difficult question for the modern historian. If the eighteenth-century colonists were so powerfully attracted to Great Britain, then why did they ever declare independence? The answer may well be that as the colonists became more British, they inevitably became more American as well. This was a development of major significance, for it helps to explain the appearance after midcentury of genuine nationalist sentiment. Political, commercial, and military links that brought the colonists into more frequent contact with Great Britain also made them more aware of other colonists. It was within an expanding, prosperous empire that they first began seriously to consider what it meant to be American.

Growth and Diversity

What difficulties did Native Americans face in maintaining their cultural independence on the frontier?

The phenomenal growth of British America during the eighteenth century amazed Benjamin Franklin, one of the first persons to bring mathematical rigor to the study of demography. The population of the English colonies doubled approximately every twenty-five years, and, according to calculations Franklin made in 1751, if the expansion continued at such an extraordinary rate for another century or so, "the greatest Number of Englishmen will be on this Side [of] the water."

Accurate population data from the colonial period are extremely difficult to find. The first national census did not occur until 1790. Still, various sources surviving from prerevolutionary times indicate that the total white population of Britain's thirteen mainland colonies rose from about 250,000 in 1700 to 2,150,000 in 1770, an annual growth rate of 3 percent.

Few societies in recorded history have expanded so rapidly, and if the growth rate had not dropped substantially during the nineteenth and twentieth centuries, the current population of the United States would stand at well more than one billion people. Natural reproduction was responsible for most of the growth. More families bore children who in turn lived long enough to have children of their own. Because of this sudden expansion, the population of the late colonial period was strikingly young; approximately one-half of the populace at any given time was under age 16.

Not only was the total population increasing at a very rapid rate; it also was becoming more dispersed and heterogeneous. Each year witnessed the arrival of thousands of non-English Europeans. Unlike those seventeenth-century English settlers in search of religious sanctuary or instant wealth (see Chapter 2), the newcomers generally transferred in the hope of obtaining their own land and setting up as independent farmers. These people often traveled to the **backcountry**, a region stretching approximately eight hundred miles from western Pennsylvania to Georgia. Although they planned to follow customs they had known in Europe, they found the challenge of surviving on the British frontier far more demanding than they had anticipated. They plunged into a complex, fluid, often violent society that included large numbers of Native Americans and African Americans as well as other Europeans.

Scots-Irish Flee English Oppression

Non-English colonists poured into American ports throughout the eighteenth century, creating rich ethnic diversity in areas originally settled by Anglo-Saxons. The largest group of newcomers consisted of Scots-Irish. The experiences of these people in Great Britain influenced not only their decision to move to the New World but also their behavior once they arrived.

During the seventeenth century, English rulers thought they could thoroughly dominate Catholic Ireland by transporting thousands of lowland Scottish Presbyterians to the northern region of that war-torn country. The plan failed. English officials who were members of the Anglican Church discriminated against the Presbyterians. They passed laws that placed the Scots-Irish at a severe disadvantage when they traded in England; they taxed them at exorbitant rates.

After several poor harvests, many of the Scots-Irish elected to emigrate to America, where they hoped to find the freedom and prosperity that had been denied them in Ireland. "I have seen some of their letters to their friends here [Ireland]," one British agent reported in 1729, ". . . in which after they set forth and recommend the fruitfulness and commodities of the country [America], they tell them, that if they will but carry over a little money with them, they may for a small sum purchase considerable tracts of land." Often entire Presbyterian congregations followed charismatic ministers to the New World, intent on replicating a distinctive, fiercely independent culture on the frontier. It is estimated that one hundred fifty thousand Scots-Irish migrated to the colonies before the Revolution.

Most Scots-Irish immigrants landed initially in Philadelphia, but instead of remaining in that city, they carved out farms on Pennsylvania's western frontier. The colony's proprietors welcomed the influx of new settlers, for it seemed they would form an ideal barrier between the Indians and the older, coastal communities. The Penn family soon had second thoughts, however. The Scots-Irish squatted on whatever land looked best, and when colony officials pointed out that large tracts had already been reserved, the immigrants retorted that "it was against the laws of God and nature that so much land should be idle when so many Christians wanted it to labour on and to raise their bread." Wherever they located, the Scots-Irish challenged established authority.

Read the Document   Benjamin Franklin, "Observations Concerning the Increase of Mankind"

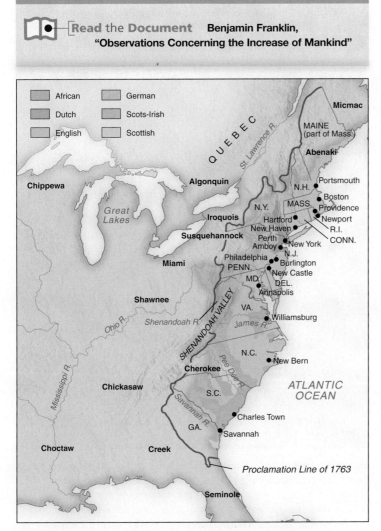

DISTRIBUTION OF EUROPEAN AND AFRICAN IMMIGRANTS IN THE THIRTEEN COLONIES A flood of non-English immigrants swept the British colonies between 1700 and 1775.

Germans Search for a Better Life

A second large body of non-English settlers, more than one hundred thousand people, came from the upper Rhine Valley, the German Palatinate. Some of the migrants, especially those who relocated to America around the turn of the century, belonged to small pietistic Protestant sects whose religious views were somewhat similar to those of the Quakers. These Germans moved to the New World primarily in the hope of finding religious toleration. Under the guidance of Francis Daniel Pastorius (1651–1720), a group of Mennonites established in Pennsylvania a prosperous community known as Germantown.

By midcentury, however, the characteristics of the German migration had begun to change. Large numbers of Lutherans transferred to the Middle Colonies. Unlike members of the pietistic sects, these men and women were not in search of religious freedom. Rather, they traveled to the New World looking to better their material lives. The Lutheran Church in Germany initially tried to maintain control over the distant congregations, but even though the migrants themselves fiercely preserved many aspects of traditional

German culture, they were eventually forced to accommodate to new social conditions. Henry Melchior Mühlenberg (1711–1787), a tireless leader, helped German Lutherans through a difficult cultural adjustment, and in 1748, Mühlenberg organized a meeting of local pastors and lay delegates that ordained ministers of their own choosing, an act of spiritual independence that has been called "the most important single event in American Lutheran history."

The German migrants—mistakenly called Pennsylvania Dutch because the English confused *deutsch* (meaning "German") with *Dutch* ("a person from Holland")—began reaching Philadelphia in large numbers after 1717, and by 1766, persons of German stock accounted for more than one-third of Pennsylvania's total population. Even their most vocal detractors admitted the Germans were the best farmers in the colony.

Ethnic differences in Pennsylvania bred disputes. The Scots-Irish as well as the Germans preferred to live with people of their own background, and they sometimes fought to keep members of the other nationality out of their neighborhoods. The English were suspicious of both groups. They could not comprehend why the Germans insisted on speaking German in America. In 1753, for example, Franklin described these settlers as "the most stupid of their nation." He warned that "unless the stream of [German] importation could be turned from this to other colonies . . . they will soon outnumber us, . . . [and] all the advantages we have, will in my opinion, be not able to preserve our language, and even our government will become precarious." As Franklin's remarks suggest, the pressure on non-English colonists to accommodate to the dominant culture—in other words, to "Anglicize" their manners and behavior—was very great. In comparison to some of his contemporaries, Franklin seemed a moderate critic of the German and Scots-Irish settlers. Others threatened violence against the newcomers who refused to conform to English ways.

Such prejudice may have persuaded members of both groups to search for new homes. After 1730, Germans and Scots-Irish pushed south from western Pennsylvania into the Shenandoah Valley, thousands of them settling in the backcountry of Virginia and the Carolinas. The Germans usually remained wherever they found unclaimed fertile land. By contrast, the Scots-Irish often moved two or three times, acquiring a reputation as a rootless people.

Wherever the newcomers settled, they often found themselves living beyond the effective authority of the various colonial governments. To be sure, backcountry residents petitioned for assistance during wars against the Indians, but most of the time they preferred to be left alone. These conditions heightened the importance of religious institutions within the small ethnic communities. Although the original stimulus for coming to America may have been a desire for economic independence and prosperity, backcountry families—especially the Scots-Irish—flocked to evangelical Protestant preachers, to Presbyterian, and later Baptist and Methodist ministers who not only fulfilled the settlers' spiritual needs but also gave scattered backcountry communities a pronounced moral character that survived long after the colonial period.

Convict Settlers

Since the story of European migration tends to be upbeat—men and women engaged in a largely successful quest for a better material life—it often is forgotten that British courts compelled many people to come to America. Indeed, the African slaves were not the only large group of people coerced into moving to the New World. In 1718, Parliament passed the Transportation Act, allowing judges in England, Scotland, and Ireland to send convicted felons to the American colonies. Between 1718 and 1775, the courts shipped approximately fifty thousand convicts across the Atlantic. Some of these men and women may actually have been dangerous criminals, but the majority seem to have committed minor crimes against property. Although transported convicts—almost 75 percent of whom were young males—escaped the hangman, they found life difficult in the colonies. Eighty percent of them were sold in the Chesapeake colonies as indentured servants. At best they faced an uncertain future, and it is probably not surprising that few former convicts prospered in America.

British authorities lavished praise on this system. According to one writer, transportation drained "the Nation of its offensive Rubbish, without taking away their Lives." Although Americans purchased the convict servants, they expressed fear that these men and women would create a dangerous criminal class. In one irate essay, Benjamin Franklin asked his readers to consider just how the colonists might repay the leaders of Great Britain for shipping so many felons to America. He suggested that rattlesnakes might be the appropriate gift. "I would propose to have them carefully distributed . . .," Franklin wrote, "in the Gardens of all the Nobility and Gentry throughout the Nation; but particularly in the Gardens of the Prime Ministers, *the Lords of Trade* and *Members of Parliament*." The Revolution forced the British courts to redirect the flow of convicts to another part of the world; an indirect result of American independence was the founding of Australia by transported felons.

Native Americans Stake Out a Middle Ground

In some histories of the colonial period, Native Americans make only a brief appearance, usually during the earliest years of conquest and settlement. After initial contact with the first European invaders, the Indians seem mysteriously to disappear from the central narrative of colonization, and it is not until the nineteenth century that they turn up again, this time to wage a last desperate battle against the encroachment of white society.

This obviously inadequate account slights one of the richer chapters of Native American history. During much of the seventeenth century, various Indian groups who contested the English settlers for control of coastal lands suffered terribly, sometimes from war, but more often from the spread of contagious diseases such as smallpox. The two races found it very difficult to live in close proximity. As one Indian informed the members of the Maryland assembly in 1666, "Your hogs & Cattle injure Us, You come too near Us to live & drive Us from place to place. We can fly no farther; let us know where to live & how to be secured for the future from the Hogs & Cattle."

Against such odds the Indians managed to survive. By the eighteenth century, the site of the most intense and creative contact between the races had shifted to the cis-Mississippian west, that is, to the huge territory between the Appalachian Mountains and the Mississippi River, where several hundred thousand Native Americans made their homes.

Tishcohan, chief of the Delaware tribe that lost much of its land in Thomas Penn's Walking Purchase of 1737, is shown here in a 1735 portrait by Gustavus Hesselius. Although treaties and agreements with European settlers were often detrimental to Native Americans, some alliances in the "middle ground" allowed the tribes to play the French against the British. Alliances were often signified by tokens such as certificates, calumets (ceremonial pipes), wampum belts, and medals.

Many Indians had only recently migrated to the area. The Delaware, for example, retreated to far western Pennsylvania and the Ohio Valley to escape almost continuous confrontation with advancing European invaders. Other Indians drifted west in less happy circumstances. They were refugees, the remnants of Native American groups who had lost so many people that they could no longer sustain an independent cultural identity. These survivors joined with other Indians to establish new multiethnic communities. In this respect, the Native American villages may not have seemed all that different from the mixed European settlements of the backcountry. (See the Feature Essay, "Conquest by Other Means: The Pennsylvania Walking Purchase," pp. 84–85.)

Stronger groups of Indians, such as the Creek, Choctaw, Chickasaw, Cherokee, and Shawnee, generally welcomed the refugees. Strangers were formally adopted to take the places of family members killed in battle or overcome by sickness, and it should be appreciated that many seemingly traditional Indian villages of the eighteenth century actually represented innovative responses to rapidly shifting external conditions. As historian Peter Wood explained, "Physically and linguistically diverse groups moved to form loosely organized confederacies, unions of mutual convenience, that effectively restrained interethnic hostilities."

The concept of a ***middle ground***—a term that has only recently entered the interpretive vocabulary—helps us more fully to comprehend how eighteenth-century Indians held their own in the backcountry beyond the Appalachian Mountains. The Native Americans never intended to isolate themselves completely from European contact. They relied on white traders, French as well as English, to provide essential metal goods and weapons. The goal of the Indian confederacies was rather to maintain a strong independent voice in these commercial exchanges, whenever possible playing the French against the British, and so long as they had sufficient military strength— that is, large numbers of healthy armed warriors—they compelled everyone who came to negotiate in the "middle ground" to give them proper respect. It would be incorrect, therefore, to characterize their relations with the Europeans as a stark choice between resistance or accommodation, between total war or abject surrender. Native Americans took advantage of rivals when possible; they compromised when necessary. It is best to imagine the Indians' middle ground as an open, dynamic process of creative interaction.

However desirable they may have appeared, European goods subtly eroded traditional structures of Native American authority. During the period of earliest encounter with white men, Indian leaders reinforced their own power by controlling the character and flow of commercial exchange. If a trader wanted a rich supply of animal skins, for example, he soon learned that he had better negotiate directly with a chief or tribal elder. But as the number of European traders operating within the "middle ground" expanded, ordinary Indians began to bargain on their own account, obtaining colorful and durable manufactured items without first consulting a Native American leader. Independent commercial dealings of this sort tended further to weaken the Indians' ability to resist organized white aggression. As John Stuart, a superintendent of Indian affairs, explained in 1761, "A modern Indian cannot subsist without Europeans; And would handle a Flint Ax or any other rude utensil used by his ancestors very awkwardly; So that what was only convenience at first is now become Necessity."

The survival of the middle ground depended ultimately on factors over which the Native Americans had little control. Imperial competition between France and Great Britain enhanced the Indians' bargaining position, but after the British defeated the French in 1763, the Indians no longer received the same solicitous attention as they had in earlier times. Keeping old allies happy seemed to the British a needless expense. Moreover, contagious disease continued to take a fearful toll. In the southern backcountry between 1685 and 1790, the Indian population dropped an astounding 72 percent. In the Ohio Valley, the numbers suggest similar rates of decline. In fact, there is some evidence that British military officers practiced germ warfare against the Native Americans, giving them blankets contaminated by smallpox. Based on experience, the officers knew that personal belongings such as blankets taken from the sick were contaminated and, thus, that giving these items to the Indians would put them at risk. By the time the United States took control of this region, the middle ground itself had become a casualty of history.

Spanish Borderlands of the Eighteenth Century

Why was the Spanish empire unable to control its northern frontier?

In many traditional histories of North America, the Spanish make only a brief appearance, usually as fifteenth-century conquistadors. But as soon as they have conquered Mexico, they are dropped from the story as if they had no serious part to play in the ongoing development of the continent. This is, of course, a skewed perspective that masks the roots of ethnic diversity in the United States. As anyone who visits the modern American Southwest quickly discovers, Spanish administrators and priests—not to mention ordinary settlers—left a lasting imprint on the cultural landscape of this country.

Until 1821, when Mexico declared independence from Madrid, Spanish authorities struggled to control a vast northern frontier. During the eighteenth century, the Spanish empire in North America included widely dispersed settlements such as San Francisco, San Diego, Santa Fe, San Antonio, and St. Augustine. In these borderland communities, European colonists mixed with peoples of other races and backgrounds, forming multicultural societies. According to historian Ramón A. Gutiérrez, the Spanish provinces present a story of "the

Baroque-style eighteenth-century Spanish mission at San Xavier del Bac in present-day Arizona. Spanish missions dotted the frontier of northern New Spain from Florida to California.

Feature Essay

Conquest by Other Means
The Pennsylvania Walking Purchase

William Penn's Treaty with the Indians, painted by Benjamin West in 1771, presents an idealized picture of relations between the Pennsylvania government and its Indian neighbors. Here the pious William Penn offers the Indians trade goods for their lands.
Source: Courtesy of the Pennsylvania Academy of the Fine Arts, Philadelphia. Gift of Mrs. Sarah Harrison (The Joseph Harrison, Jr. Collection).

European conquest of Native Americans represents a black mark on the history of the New World. Violent dispossession, murder, and near genocide of America's native inhabitants has always fit uneasily into a history of national progress. Colonial writers sought to cover up these disturbing histories by creating myths of "good settlers" who allegedly respected Native American rights and chose to buy Indian lands rather than seize them through force. But such reworkings of history overlook the threats of violence that often surrounded these supposedly "fair" negotiations. Pennsylvania's infamous "Walking Purchase" of 1737 offers a dramatic example of how the myth of a fair deal could cover English self-interest and intimidation.

When he died in 1718, William Penn, the Quaker founder of Pennsylvania, left his sons a legacy of peaceful co-existence between English and Indian. He also burdened them with an imposing debt. During the 1720s, anxious to restore their finances, the Penn heirs began to sell off lands between Pennsylvania and New Jersey, in a region known as the Forks. Settlers coveted the abundant lumber, iron ore, and fertile soil found along the Delaware River and were willing to pay good prices. Only one obstacle stood in the way of their plan to trade frontier lands for English currency. The Penns did not actually own the lands that they were selling. These lands belonged to the region's Native American nation, the Delawares (who referred to themselves as the Lenapes), and they refused to sell.

The Penns' next move surprised the Delawares. Thomas Penn, William Penn's eldest son, produced what he claimed to be an old deed for lands in the Forks purchased by his father in 1686. The document granted to Pennsylvania a tract of land extending along the Delaware River and containing "as much Land as a man could walk in a Day and half" – a very imprecise measure of distance. Since the original deed was incomplete (it had not been signed and did not even list all of the terms of the purchase), Penn had a new "copy" drawn up. He presented this document to the Delawares as proof of a legally binding contract transferring the Indian lands in the Forks to Pennsylvania.

The Delawares were not fooled. Nutimus, leader of the Delawares who lived in the Forks region, challenged the Penns' version of history. The elders among his people remembered that although a land transfer had been discussed, no contract had ever been signed, and William Penn and his agents had never delivered payment. The new deed was a clumsy forgery.

Cries of fraud did not discourage Thomas Penn. He struck up an understanding with the powerful Iroquois Confederacy—an alliance of six Native American nations centered around the Great Lakes. The government of Pennsylvania promised to support the Iroquois in pressing land claims against native tribes to the south and west. The Iroquois in turn pledged to support Pennsylvania in its dealings with the Delawares. As one historian has put it, the Delawares found themselves caught between "an Iroquois hammer and a Pennsylvania anvil." Not powerful enough to challenge both the Pennsylvanians and their Iroquois allies, Nutimus and three other Delaware leaders put their marks on the fraudulent deed.

The Walking of the Boundary occurred on September 19, 1737.

The whole episode was a farce. Thomas Penn had taken the initiative to have a path cleared through the trees for his walkers. Previously, when William Penn had purchased lands from the Delawares, the parties that walked off the boundaries had traveled at a normal traveler's pace winding through the forest and stopping along the way to take meals. Now the three walkers who took off into the Pennsylvania woods set an exhausting pace, each promised a handsome reward if he should be the one that walked the farthest in the allotted day and a half. One dropped out by day's end. A second collapsed the next morning and died from exhaustion a week later. The final walker covered more than 60 miles of wilderness in the 18 hours of daylight allotted for his task.

The Delawares protested this injustice, grumbling about what they named "The Hurry Walk," but could do little about it. In 1740 they filed a complaint with the Pennsylvania Superior Court, warning that "If this Practice must hold why we are No more Brothers and Friends but much more like Open Enemies." The Governor of Pennsylvania dismissed the Delawares' complaint.

When the Delawares refused to concede their claims in the Forks, the Pennsylvania government turned to its Iroquois allies. At a council held in 1742, the Iroquois headman Canasatego told Nutimus and the Delawares "You ought to be taken by the Hair of the Head and skak'd severely till you recover your Senses . . . We conquered you, we made Women of you. . . . This Land that you Claim is gone." Canastego ordered the Delawares to remove north to the Wyoming or Susquehanna Valleys.

Swindled by the Pennsylvanians, betrayed by the Iroquois who they had once called their "cousins," and pressed on every side by encroaching white settlers, Nutimus and his Delawares abandoned the Delaware Valley and withdrew to the west. Peaceful complaints had proven ineffectual. All the Delawares could do now was nurse their grievances and wait.

The waiting ended in 1755, with the beginning of the French and Indian War. The war began in catastrophe for the British and their Iroquois allies in North America, providing what one Delaware described as "a favourable Opportunity for taking revenge." Still seething over the injustice of the Walking Purchase, Delaware warriors and their Shawnee allies fell upon the Pennsylvania settlements along the outskirts of the Walking Purchase lands. Led by Nutimus' nephew Teedyuscung, these warriors burned homes and fields and took over one hundred English lives.

The war soon turned in Britain's favor. As British and Iroquois troops routed their French and Indian enemies in Canada and the Ohio territory, the Delawares realized that they would have to sue for peace. In 1766, the Delawares signed a treaty that relinquished the remainder of their Pennsylvania lands and removed permanently towards the west.

In 1771, Thomas Penn commissioned the great early American artist Benjamin West to create a painting commemorating his father's compassion and fair treatment of Pennsylvania's Indian peoples. The image shows William Penn meeting with Indian leaders, bargaining with them to purchase land where English settlers might farm and raise families. West's painting presents a highly flattering image of Pennsylvania history and of the Penn family. It looks past the violence of 1755 and the underhanded dealings of 1737. It takes as its subject the much revered elder Penn, who had once admonished his children to "let justice have its impartial course . . . fly to no deceits to support or cover injustice." In the end, Thomas Penn betrayed his father's advice. In allowing his greed for land to overpower his sense of propriety and respect for the rights of the Delaware Indians, Thomas Penn set an example emulated far too often throughout American history.

QUESTIONS FOR DISCUSSION

1. Why did Thomas Penn invent a phony deed for Delaware lands?

2. Why did the Delawares side with the French during the French and Indian War?

complex web of interactions between men and women, young and old, rich and poor, slave and free, Spaniard and Indian, all of whom fundamentally depended on the other for their own self-definition."

Conquering the Northern Frontier

Not until late in the sixteenth century did Spanish settlers, led by Juan de Oñate, establish European communities north of the Rio Grande. The Pueblo Indians resisted the invasion of colonists, soldiers, and missionaries, and in a major rebellion in 1680 led by El Popé, the native peoples drove the whites completely out of New Mexico. "The heathen have conceived a mortal hatred for our holy faith and enmity for the Spanish nation," concluded one imperial bureaucrat. Not until 1692 were the Spanish able to reconquer this fiercely contested area. By then, Native American hostility coupled with the settlers' failure to find precious metal had cooled Spain's enthusiasm for the northern frontier.

Concern over French encroachment in the Southeast led Spain to colonize St. Augustine (Florida) in 1565. Although the enterprise never flourished, it claims attention as the first permanent European settlement established in what would become the United States, predating the founding of Jamestown and Plymouth by several decades. Pedro Menéndez de Avilés brought some fifteen hundred soldiers and settlers to St. Augustine, where they constructed an impressive fort, but the colony failed to attract additional Spanish migrants. "It is hard to get anyone to go to St. Augustine because of the horror

with which Florida is painted," the governor of Cuba complained in 1673. "Only hoodlums and the mischievous go there from Cuba."

California never figured prominently in Spain's plans for the New World. Early explorers reported finding only impoverished Indians living along the Pacific coast. Adventurers saw no natural resources worth mentioning, and since the area proved extremely difficult to reach from Mexico City—the overland trip could take months—California received little attention. Fear that the Russians might seize the entire region belatedly sparked Spanish activity, however, and after 1769, two indomitable servants of empire, Fra Junípero Serra and Don Gaspar de Portolá, organized permanent missions and *presidios* (forts) at San Diego, Monterey, San Francisco, and Santa Barbara.

Peoples of the Spanish Borderlands

In sharp contrast to the English frontier settlements of the eighteenth century, the Spanish outposts in North America grew very slowly. A few Catholic priests and imperial administrators traveled to the northern provinces, but the danger of Indian attack as well as a harsh physical environment discouraged ordinary colonists. The European migrants were overwhelmingly male, most of them soldiers in the pay of the empire. Although some colonists came directly from Spain, most had been born in other Spanish colonies such as Minorca, the Canaries, or New Spain, and because European women rarely appeared on the frontier, Spanish males formed relationships with Indian women, fathering large numbers of *mestizos*, children of mixed race.

Read the Document   Testimony by Pedro Naranjo to Spanish Authorities

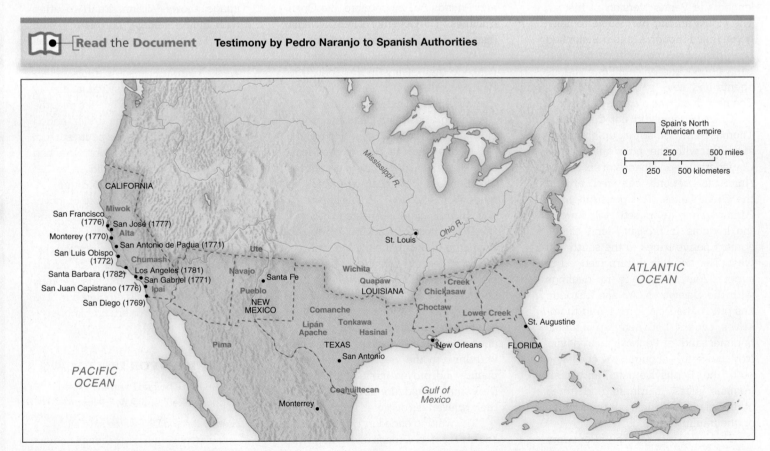

THE SPANISH BORDERLANDS, CA. 1770 In the late eighteenth century, Spain's North American empire extended across what is now the southern United States from Florida through Texas and New Mexico to California.

As in other European frontiers of the eighteenth century, encounters with Spanish soldiers, priests, and traders altered Native American cultures. The experience here was quite different from that of the whites and Indians in the British backcountry. The Spanish exploited Native American labor, reducing entire Indian villages to servitude. Many Indians moved to the Spanish towns, and although they lived in close proximity to the Europeans—something rare in British America—they were consigned to the lowest social class, objects of European contempt. However much their material conditions changed, the Indians of the Southwest resisted strenuous efforts to convert them to Catholicism. The Pueblo maintained their own religious forms—often at great personal risk—and they sometimes murdered priests who became too intrusive. Angry Pueblo Indians at Taos reportedly fed the hated Spanish friars corn tortillas containing urine and mouse meat.

The Spanish empire never had the resources necessary to secure the northern frontier fully. The small military posts were intended primarily to discourage other European powers such as France, Great Britain, and Russia from taking possession of territory claimed by Spain. It would be misleading, however, to overemphasize the fragility of Spanish colonization. The urban design and public architecture of many southwestern cities still reflect the vision of the early Spanish settlers, and to a large extent, the old borderlands remain Spanish speaking to this day.

The Impact of European Ideas on American Culture

How did European ideas affect eighteenth-century American life?

The character of the older, more established British colonies changed almost as rapidly as that of the backcountry. The rapid growth of an urban cosmopolitan culture impressed eighteenth-century commentators, and even though most Americans still lived on scattered farms, they had begun to participate aggressively in an exciting consumer marketplace that expanded their imaginative horizons.

Provincial Cities

Considering the rate of population growth, it is surprising to discover how few eighteenth-century Americans lived in cities. Boston, Newport, New York, Philadelphia, and Charles Town—the five largest cities—contained only about 5 percent of the colonial population. In 1775, none had more than forty thousand persons. The explanation for the relatively slow development of colonial American cities lies in their highly specialized commercial character. Colonial port towns served as entrepôts, intermediary trade and shipping centers where bulk cargoes were broken up for inland distribution and where agricultural products were gathered for export. They did not support large-scale manufacturing. Indeed, the pool of free urban laborers was quite small, since the type of person who was forced to work for wages in Europe usually became a farmer in America.

Yet despite the limited urban population, cities profoundly influenced colonial culture. It was in the cities that Americans were exposed to and welcomed the latest English ideas. Wealthy colonists—merchants and lawyers—tried to emulate the culture of the mother country. They sponsored concerts and plays; they learned to dance. Women as well as men picked up the new fashions quickly, and even though most of them had never been outside the colony of their birth, they sometimes appeared to be the products of London's best families.

It was in the cities, also, that wealthy merchants transformed commercial profits into architectural splendor, for, in their desire to outdo one another, they built grand homes of enduring beauty. Most of these buildings are described as Georgian because they were constructed during the reign of Britain's early Hanoverian kings, who all happened to be named George. Actually these homes were provincial copies of grand country houses of Great Britain. They drew their inspiration from the great Italian Renaissance architect Andrea Palladio (1508–1580), who had incorporated classical themes into a rigidly symmetrical form. Palladio's ideas were popularized in the colonies by James Gibbs, an Englishman whose *Book of Architecture* (1728) provided blueprints for the most spectacular homes of mid-eighteenth-century America.

Their owners filled the houses with fine furniture. Each city patronized certain skilled craftsmen, but the artisans of Philadelphia were known for producing magnificent copies of the works of Thomas Chippendale, Great Britain's most famous furniture designer. These developments gave American cities an elegance they had not possessed in the previous century. One foreign visitor noted of Philadelphia in 1748 that "its natural advantages, trade, riches and power, are by no means inferior to any, even of the most ancient towns of Europe." As this traveler understood, the cultural impact of the cities went far beyond the number of people who actually lived there.

Ben Franklin and American Enlightenment

European historians often refer to the eighteenth century as an Age of Reason. During this period, a body of new, often radical, ideas swept through the salons and universities, altering the way that educated Europeans thought about God, nature, and society. This intellectual revolution, called the **Enlightenment**, involved the work of Europe's greatest minds, men such as Newton and Locke, Voltaire and Hume.

Enlightenment thinkers shared basic assumptions. Philosophers of the Enlightenment replaced the concept of original sin with a much more optimistic view of human nature. A benevolent God, having set the universe in motion, gave human beings the power of reason to enable them to comprehend the orderly workings of his creation. Everything, even human society, operated according to these mechanical rules. The responsibility of right-thinking men and women, therefore, was to make certain that institutions such as church and state conformed to self-evident natural laws. It was possible—or so some philosophers claimed—to achieve perfection in this world. In fact, human suffering had come about only because people had lost touch with the fundamental insights of reason. The writings of these thinkers eventually reached the colonies, where they received a mixed reception. On the whole, the American Enlightenment was a rather tame affair compared to its European counterpart, for while the colonists welcomed experimental science, they defended the tenets of traditional Christianity.

For many Americans, the appeal of the Enlightenment was its focus on a search for useful knowledge, ideas, and inventions

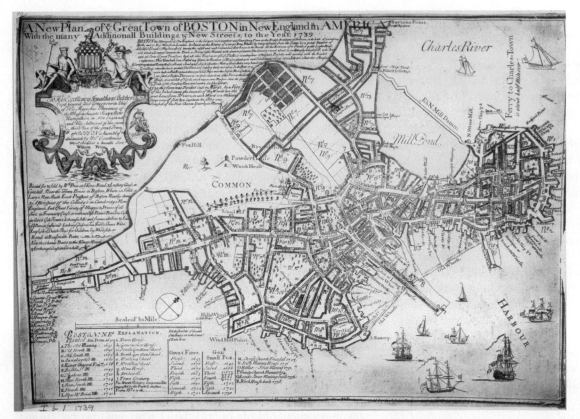

This 1743 map of Boston depicts the port city as an active commercial and cultural center, with many wharves, buildings, churches, and meeting halls.

minister described as "full freighted with Nonesense, Unmannerliness, Railery, Prophaneness, Immorality, Arrogance, Calumnies, Lyes, Contradictions, and what not, all tending to Quarrels and Divisions and to Debauch and Corrupt the Minds and Manners of New England." Franklin got the point; he left Massachusetts in 1723 in search of a less hostile intellectual environment.

After he had moved to Philadelphia, leaving behind an irritable brother as well as New England Puritanism, Franklin devoted himself to the pursuit of useful knowledge, ideas that would increase the happiness of his fellow Americans. Franklin never denied the existence of God. Rather, he pushed the Lord aside, making room for the free exercise of human reason. Franklin tinkered, experimented, and reformed. Almost everything he encountered in his daily life aroused his curiosity. His investigation of electricity brought him world fame, but Franklin was never satisfied with his work in this field until it yielded practical application. In 1756, he invented the lightning rod. He also designed a marvelously efficient stove that is still used today. In modern America, Franklin has become exactly what he would have wanted to be, a symbol of material progress through human ingenuity.

Franklin energetically promoted the spread of reason. In Philadelphia, he organized groups that discussed the latest European literature, philosophy, and science. In 1727, for example, he "form'd most of my ingenious Acquaintances into a Club for mutual Improvement, which we call'd the Junto." Four years later Franklin took a leading part in the formation of the Library Company, a voluntary association that for the first time allowed people like him to pursue "useful knowledge." The members of these societies communicated with Americans living in other colonies, providing them not only with new information but also with models for their own clubs and associations. Such efforts broadened the intellectual horizons of many colonists, especially those who lived in cities.

that would improve the quality of human life. What mattered was practical experimentation. A speech delivered in 1767 before the members of the American Society in Philadelphia reflected the new utilitarian spirit: "Knowledge is of little Use when confined to mere Speculation," the colonist explained, "But when speculative Truths are reduced to Practice, when Theories grounded upon Experiments . . . and the Arts of Living made more easy and comfortable . . . Knowledge then becomes really useful."

The Enlightenment spawned scores of earnest scientific tinkerers, people who dutifully recorded changes in temperature, the appearance of strange plants and animals, and the details of astronomic phenomena. While these eighteenth-century Americans made few earth-shattering discoveries, they did encourage their countrymen, especially those who attended college, to apply reason to the solution of social and political problems.

Benjamin Franklin (1706–1790) absorbed the new cosmopolitan culture. European thinkers regarded him as a genuine philosophe, a person of reason and science, a role that he self-consciously cultivated when he visited England and France in later life. Franklin had little formal education, but as a young man working in his brother's print shop, he managed to keep up with the latest intellectual currents.

In 1721, Franklin and his brother founded the *New England Courant*, a weekly newspaper that satirized Boston's political and religious leaders in the manner of the contemporary British press. Writing under the name Silence Dogood, young Franklin asked his readers "Whether a Commonwealth suffers more by hypocritical Pretenders to Religion, or by the openly Profane?" Proper Bostonians were not prepared for a journal that one

Economic Transformation

The colonial economy kept pace with the stunning growth in population. During the first three-quarters of the eighteenth century, the population increased at least tenfold, and yet even with so many additional people to feed and clothe, the per capita income did not decline. Indeed, with the exception of poor urban dwellers, such as sailors whose employment varied with the season, white

Americans did quite well. An abundance of land and the extensive growth of agriculture accounted for their economic success. New farmers were able not only to provide for their families' well-being but also to sell their crops in European and West Indian markets. Each year, more Americans produced more tobacco, wheat, or rice—to cite just the major export crops—and by this means, they maintained a high level of individual prosperity without developing an industrial base.

At midcentury, colonial exports flowed along well-established routes. More than half of American goods produced for export went to Great Britain. The Navigation Acts (see Chapter 3) were still in effect, and "enumerated" items such as tobacco had to be landed first at a British port. Furs were added to the restricted list in 1722. The White Pines Acts passed in 1711, 1722, and 1729 forbade Americans from cutting white pine trees without a license. The purpose of this legislation was to reserve the best trees for the use of the Royal Navy. The Molasses Act of 1733—also called the Sugar Act—placed a heavy duty on molasses imported from foreign ports; the Hat and Felt Act of 1732 and the Iron Act of 1750 attempted to limit the production of colonial goods that competed with British exports.

These statutes might have created tensions between the colonists and the mother country had they been rigorously enforced. Crown officials, however, generally ignored the new laws. New England merchants imported molasses from French Caribbean islands without paying the full customs; ironmasters in the Middle Colonies continued to produce iron. Even without the Navigation Acts, however, a majority of colonial exports would have been sold on the English market. The emerging consumer society in Great Britain was beginning to create a new generation of buyers who possessed enough income to purchase American goods, especially sugar and tobacco. This rising demand was the major market force shaping the colonial economy.

Colonial merchants operating out of Boston, Newport, and Philadelphia also carried substantial tonnage to the West Indies. In 1768, this market accounted for 27 percent of all American exports. If there was a triangular trade that included the west coast of Africa, it does not seem to have been economically significant. Colonial ships carrying food sailed for the Caribbean and returned immediately to the Middle Colonies or New England with cargoes of molasses, sugar, and rum. In fact, recent research indicates that during the eighteenth century, trade with Africa involved less than 1 percent of all American exports. Slaves were transported directly to colonial ports where they were sold for cash or credit.

The West Indies played a vital role in preserving American credit in Europe. Without this source of income, colonists would not have been able to pay for the manufactured items they purchased in the mother country. To be sure, they exported American products in great quantity to Great Britain, but the value of the exports seldom equaled the cost of British goods shipped back to the colonists. To cover this small but recurrent deficit, colonial merchants relied on profits made in the West Indies.

Birth of a Consumer Society

After midcentury, however, the balance of trade turned dramatically against the colonists. The reasons for this change were complex, but, in simplest terms, Americans began buying more English goods than their parents or grandparents had done. Between 1740 and 1770, English exports to the American colonies increased by an astounding 360 percent, a veritable **consumer revolution** in the colonies.

In part, this shift reflected a fundamental transformation in the British economy. Although the Industrial Revolution was still far in the future, the pace of the British economy picked up dramatically after 1690. Small factories produced certain goods more efficiently and more cheaply than the colonists could. The availability of these products altered the lives of most Americans, even those with modest incomes. Staffordshire china replaced crude earthenware; imported cloth replaced homespun. Franklin noted in his *Autobiography* how changing consumer habits affected his life. For years, he had eaten his breakfast in an earthenware bowl with a pewter spoon, but one morning it was served "in a china bowl, with a spoon of silver." Franklin observed that "this was the first appearance of plate and china in our house which afterwards in the course of years, as our wealth increased, augmented gradually to several hundred pounds in value." In this manner, British industrialization undercut American handicraft and folk art.

To help Americans purchase manufactured goods, British merchants offered generous credit. Colonists deferred settlement by agreeing to pay interest on their debts. The temptation to acquire English finery blinded many people to hard economic realities. They gambled on the future, hoping bumper farm crops would reduce their dependence on the large merchant houses of London and Glasgow. Obviously, some persons lived within their means, but the aggregate American debt continued to grow. Colonial leaders tried various expedients to remain solvent—issuing paper money, for example—and while these efforts delayed a crisis, the balance-of-payments problem was clearly very serious.

The eighteenth century also saw a substantial increase in intercoastal trade. Southern planters sent tobacco and rice to New England and the Middle Colonies, where these staples were exchanged for meat and wheat as well as goods imported from Great Britain. By 1760, approximately 30 percent of the colonists' total tonnage capacity was involved in this extensive "coastwise" commerce. In addition, backcountry farmers in western Pennsylvania and the Shenandoah Valley carried their grain to market along an old Iroquois trail that became known as the Great Wagon Road, a rough, hilly highway that by the time of the Revolution stretched 735 miles along the Blue Ridge Mountains to Camden, South Carolina. Most of their produce was carried in long, gracefully designed Conestoga wagons. These vehicles—sometimes called the "wagons of empire"—had been invented by German immigrants living in the Conestoga River Valley in Lancaster County, Pennsylvania.

The shifting patterns of trade had immense effects on the development of an American culture. First, the flood of British imports eroded local and regional identities. Commerce helped to "Anglicize" American culture by exposing colonial consumers to a common range of British manufactured goods. Deep sectional differences remained, of course, but Americans from New Hampshire to Georgia were increasingly drawn into a sophisticated economic network centered in London. Second, the expanding coastal and overland trade brought colonists of

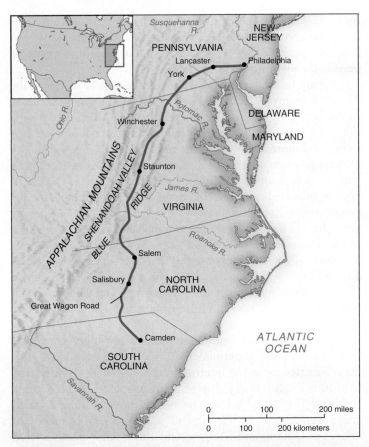

THE GREAT WAGON ROAD By the mid-eighteenth century, the Great Wagon Road had become the major highway for the settlers in the Virginia and Carolina backcountry.

different backgrounds into more frequent contact. Ships that sailed between New England and South Carolina, and between Virginia and Pennsylvania, provided dispersed Americans with a means to exchange ideas and experiences on a more regular basis. Mid-eighteenth-century printers, for example, established several dozen new journals; these were weekly newspapers that carried information not only about the mother country and world commerce but also about events in other colonies.

Religious Revivals in Provincial Societies

How did the Great Awakening transform the religious culture of colonial America?

A sudden, spontaneous series of Protestant revivals known as the **Great Awakening** had a profound impact on the lives of ordinary people. This unprecedented evangelical outpouring altered the course of American history. In our own time, of course, the force of religious revival has been witnessed in different regions throughout the world. It is no exaggeration to claim that a similar populist movement took place in mid-eighteenth-century America, and the new, highly personal appeal to a "new birth" in Christ caused men and women of all backgrounds to rethink basic assumptions about church and state, institutions and society.

The Great Awakening

Only with hindsight does the Great Awakening seem a unified religious movement. Revivals occurred in different places at different times; the intensity of the events varied from region to region. The first signs of a spiritual awakening appeared in New England during the 1730s, but within a decade the revivals in this area had burned themselves out. It was not until the 1750s and 1760s that the Awakening made more than a superficial impact on the people of Virginia. The revivals were most important in Massachusetts, Connecticut, Rhode Island, Pennsylvania, New Jersey, and Virginia. Their effect on religion in New York, Delaware, and the Carolinas was marginal. No single religious denomination or sect monopolized the Awakening. In New England, revivals shattered Congregational churches, and in the South, especially in Virginia, they had an impact on Presbyterians, Methodists, and Baptists. Moreover, there was nothing peculiarly American about the Great Awakening. Mid-eighteenth-century Europe experienced a similar burst of religious emotionalism.

Whatever their origins, the seeds of revival were generally sown on fertile ground. In the early decades of the century, many Americans—but especially New Englanders—complained that organized religion had lost vitality. They looked back at Winthrop's generation with nostalgia, assuming that common people at that time must have possessed greater piety than did later, more worldly colonists. Congregational ministers seemed obsessed with dull, scholastic matters; they no longer touched the heart. And in the Southern Colonies, there were simply not enough ordained ministers to tend to the religious needs of the population.

The Great Awakening arrived unexpectedly in Northampton, a small farm community in western Massachusetts, sparked by Jonathan Edwards, the local Congregational minister. Edwards accepted the traditional teachings of Calvinism (see Chapter 1), reminding his parishioners that their eternal fate had been determined by an omnipotent God, there was nothing they could do to save themselves, and they were totally dependent on the Lord's will. He thought his fellow ministers had grown soft. They left men and women with the mistaken impression that sinners might somehow avoid eternal damnation simply by performing good works. "How dismal will it be," Edwards told his complacent congregation, "when you are under these racking torments, to know assuredly that you never, never shall be delivered from them."

Why this uncompromising message set off several religious revivals during the mid-1730s is not known. Whatever the explanation for the popular response to Edwards's preaching, young people began flocking to the church. They experienced a searing conversion, a sense of "new birth" and utter dependence on God. "Surely," Edwards pronounced, "this is the Lord's doing, and it is marvelous in our eyes." The excitement spread, and evangelical ministers concluded that God must be preparing Americans, his chosen people, for the millennium. "What is now seen in America and especially in New England," Edwards explained, "may prove the dawn of that glorious day."

The Voice of Evangelical Religion

Edwards was an outstanding theologian, but he did not possess the dynamic personality required to sustain the revival. That responsibility fell to George Whitefield, a young, inspiring preacher

⬛▶ Read the Document   Jonathan Edwards,
"Sinners in the Hands of an Angry God"

The Reverend Jonathan Edwards (1703–1858) was an influential author and theologian whose preaching contributed to the Great Awakening.

from England who toured the colonies from New Hampshire to Georgia. While Whitefield was not an original thinker, he was an extraordinarily effective public speaker. And like his friend Benjamin Franklin, he came to symbolize the powerful cultural forces that were transforming the Atlantic world. According to Edwards's wife, Sarah, it was wonderful to witness what a spell Whitefield "casts over an audience . . . I have seen upwards of a thousand people hang on his words with breathless silence, broken only by an occasional half-suppressed sob."

Whitefield's audiences came from all groups of American society: rich and poor, young and old, rural and urban. While Whitefield described himself as a Calvinist, he welcomed all Protestants. He spoke from any pulpit that was available. "Don't tell me you are a Baptist, an Independent, a Presbyterian, a dissenter," he thundered, "tell me you are a Christian, that is all I want."

Whitefield was a brilliant entrepreneur. Like Franklin, with whom he published many popular volumes, the itinerant minister possessed an almost intuitive sense of how this burgeoning consumer society could be turned to his own advantage, and he embraced the latest merchandising techniques. He appreciated, for example, the power of the press in selling the revival, and he regularly promoted his own work in advertisements placed in British and American newspapers. The crowds flocked to hear Whitefield, while his critics grumbled about the commercialization of religion. One anonymous writer in Massachusetts noted that there was "a very wholesome law of the province to discourage Pedlars in Trade" and it seemed high time "to enact something for the discouragement of Pedlars in Divinity also."

Other American-born **itinerant preachers** followed Whitefield's example. The most famous was Gilbert Tennent, a Presbyterian of Scots-Irish background who had been educated in the Middle Colonies. His sermon "On the Danger of an Unconverted Ministry," printed in 1741, set off a storm of protest from established ministers who were understandably insulted. Lesser known revivalists traveled from town to town, colony to colony, challenging local clergymen who seemed hostile to evangelical religion. Men and women who thronged to hear the itinerants were called "New Lights," and during the 1740s and 1750s, many congregations split between defenders of the new emotional preaching and those who regarded the entire movement as dangerous nonsense.

Despite Whitefield's successes, many ministers remained suspicious of the itinerants and their methods. Some complaints may have amounted to little more than sour grapes. One "Old Light" spokesman labeled Tennent "a monster! impudent and noisy." He claimed Tennent told anxious Christians that "they were damned! damned! damned! This charmed them; and, in the most dreadful winter I ever saw, people wallowed in snow, night and day, for the benefit of his beastly brayings; and many ended their days under these fatigues." Charles Chauncy, minister of the prestigious First Church of Boston, raised much more troubling issues. How could the revivalists be certain God had sparked the Great Awakening? Perhaps the itinerants had relied too much on emotion? "Let us esteem those as friends of religion," Chauncy advised, ". . . who warn us of the danger of enthusiasm, and would put us on our guard, that we may not be led aside by it."

Despite occasional anti-intellectual outbursts, the New Lights founded several important centers of higher learning. They wanted to train young men who would carry on the good works of Edwards, Whitefield, and Tennent. In 1746, New Light Presbyterians established the College of New Jersey, which later became Princeton University. Just before his death, Edwards was appointed its president. The evangelical minister Eleazar Wheelock launched Dartmouth (1769); other revivalists founded Brown (1764) and Rutgers (1766).

The Great Awakening also encouraged men and women who had been taught to remain silent before traditional figures of authority to speak up, to take an active role in their salvation. They could no longer rely on ministers or institutions. The individual alone stood before God. Knowing this, New Lights made religious choices that shattered the old harmony among Protestant sects, and in its place, they introduced a noisy, often bitterly fought competition. As one New Jersey Presbyterian explained, "There are so many particular *sects* and *Parties* among professed Christians . . . that we know not . . . in which of these different *paths*, to steer our course for *Heaven*."

Expressive evangelicalism struck a particularly responsive chord among African Americans. Itinerant ministers frequently

Read the **Document**   Benjamin Franklin on
George Whitefield (1771)

The fervor of the Great Awakening was intensified by the eloquence of itinerant preachers such as George Whitefield, the most popular evangelical of the mid-eighteenth century.

course, the New Lights did not sound much different than the mildly rationalist American spokesmen of the Enlightenment. Both groups prepared the way for the development of a revolutionary mentality in colonial America.

Clash of Political Cultures

Why were eighteenth-century colonial assemblies not fully democratic?

The political history of this period illuminates a growing tension within the empire. Americans of all regions repeatedly stated their desire to replicate British political institutions. Parliament, they claimed, provided a model for the American assemblies. They revered the English constitution. However, the more the colonists studied British political theory and practice—in other words, the more they attempted to become British—the more aware they became of major differences. By trying to copy Great Britain, they unwittingly discovered something about being American.

The English Constitution

During the eighteenth century, political discussion began with the British constitution. It was the object of universal admiration. Unlike the U.S. Constitution of 1788, the British constitution was not a formal written document. It was something much more elusive. The English constitution found expression in a growing body of law, court decisions, and statutes, a sense of traditional political arrangements that people of all classes believed had evolved from the past, preserving life, liberty, and property.

In theory, the English constitution contained three distinct parts. The monarch was at the top, advised by handpicked court favorites. Next came the House of Lords, a body of 180 aristocrats who served with 26 Anglican bishops as the upper house of Parliament. And third was the House of Commons, composed of 558 members elected by various constituencies scattered throughout the realm.

Political theorists waxed eloquent on workings of the British constitution. Each of the three parts of government, it seemed, represented a separate socioeconomic interest: king, nobility, and common people. Acting alone, each body would run to excess, even tyranny, but operating within a mixed system, they automatically checked each other's ambitions for the common good. "Herein consists the excellence of the English government," explained the famed eighteenth-century jurist Sir William Blackstone, "that all parts of it form a mutual check upon each other." Unlike the delegates who wrote the Constitution of the United States, eighteenth-century Englishmen did not perceive their constitution as a balance of executive, legislative, and judicial branches.

The Reality of British Politics

The reality of daily political life in Great Britain, however, bore little relation to theory. The three elements of the constitution did not, in fact, represent distinct socioeconomic groups. Men elected to the House of Commons often came from the same social background as

preached to large sympathetic audiences of slaves. Richard Allen (1760–1831), founder of the African Methodist Episcopal Church, reported he owed his freedom in part to a traveling Methodist minister who persuaded Allen's master of the sinfulness of slavery. Allen himself was converted, as were thousands of other black colonists. According to one historian, evangelical preaching "shared enough with traditional African styles and beliefs such as spirit possession and ecstatic expression . . . to allow for an interpenetration of African and Christian religious beliefs."

With religious contention came an awareness of a larger community, a union of fellow believers that extended beyond the boundaries of town and colony. In fact, evangelical religion was one of several forces at work during the mid-eighteenth century that brought scattered colonists into contact with one another for the first time. In this sense, the Great Awakening was a "national" event long before a nation actually existed.

People who had been touched by the Great Awakening shared an optimism about the future of America. With God's help, social and political progress was possible, and from this perspective, of

Read the Document   English Bill of Rights (1689)

This political cartoon, published in London in 1727, denounces corruption in the British electoral system. It warns that if politicians gave into the temptation to use their offices for their own self-interest—one of the chief concerns of Whig ideology—then "Men will be Corrupted and Liberty sold."

publicists whom historians have labeled the Commonwealthmen. These writers decried the corruption of political life, noting that a nation that compromised civic virtue, that failed to stand vigilant against fawning courtiers and would-be despots, deserved to lose its liberty and property. The most famous Commonwealthmen were John Trenchard and Thomas Gordon, who penned a series of essays titled *Cato's Letters* between 1720 and 1723. If England's rulers were corrupt, they warned, then the people could not expect the balanced constitution to save them from tyranny. In one typical article, Trenchard and Gordon observed, "The Appitites . . . of Men, especially of Great Men, are carefully to be observed and stayed, or else they will never stay themselves. The Experience of every Age convinces us, that we must not judge of Men by what they ought to do, but by what they will do."

But, however shrilly these writers protested, they won little support for political reforms. Most eighteenth-century Englishmen admitted there was more than a grain of truth in the commonwealth critique, but they were not willing to tamper with a system of government that had so recently survived a civil war and a Glorious Revolution. Americans, however, took Trenchard and Gordon to heart.

those who served in the House of Lords. All represented the interests of Britain's landed elite. Moreover, there was no attempt to maintain strict constitutional separation. The king, for example, organized parliamentary associations, loose groups of political followers who sat in the House of Commons and who openly supported the monarch's policies in exchange for patronage or pension.

The claim that the members of the House of Commons represented all the people of England also seemed far-fetched. As of 1715, no more than 20 percent of Britain's adult males had the right to vote. Property qualifications or other restrictions often greatly reduced the number of eligible voters. In addition, the size of the electoral districts varied throughout the kingdom. In some boroughs, representatives to Parliament were chosen by several thousand voters. In many districts, however, a handful of electors controlled the result. These tiny, or "rotten," boroughs were an embarrassment. The Methodist leader John Wesley complained that Old Sarum, an almost uninhabited borough, "in spite of common sense, without house or inhabitant, still sends two members to the parliament." Since these districts were so small, a wealthy lord or ambitious politician could easily bribe or otherwise "influence" the entire constituency, something done regularly throughout the century.

Before 1760, few people spoke out against these constitutional abuses. The main exception was a group of radical

Governing the Colonies: The American Experience

The colonists assumed—perhaps naively—that their own governments were modeled on the balanced constitution of Great Britain. They argued that within their political systems, the governor corresponded to the king and the governor's council to the House of Lords. The colonial assemblies were perceived as American reproductions of the House of Commons and were expected to preserve the interests of the people against those of the monarch and aristocracy. As the colonists discovered, however, general theories about a mixed constitution were even less relevant in America than they were in Britain.

By midcentury a majority of the mainland colonies had royal governors appointed by the crown. Many were career army officers who through luck, charm, or family connection had gained the ear of someone close to the king. These patronage posts did not generate income sufficient to interest the most powerful or talented personalities of the period, but they did draw middle-level bureaucrats who were ambitious, desperate, or both. It is perhaps not surprising that most governors decided simply not to "consider any Thing further than how to sit easy."

George Clinton, who served as New York's governor from 1743 to 1753, was probably typical of the men who hoped to "sit easy." Before coming to the colonies, Clinton had compiled an extraordinary record of ineptitude as a naval officer. He gained the governorship more as a means to get him out of England than as a sign of respect. When he arrived in New York City, Clinton ignored the colonists. "In a province given to hospitality," wrote one critic, "he [Clinton] erred by immuring himself in the fort, or retiring to a grotto in the country, where his time was spent with his bottle and a little trifling circle."

Whatever their demerits, royal governors in America possessed enormous powers. In fact, royal governors could do certain things in America that a king could not do in eighteenth-century Britain. Among these were the right to veto legislation and dismiss judges. The governors also served as military commanders in each province.

Political practice in America differed from the British model in another crucial respect. Royal governors were advised by a council, usually a body of about twelve wealthy colonists selected by the Board of Trade in London upon the recommendation of the governor. During the seventeenth century, the council had played an important role in colonial government, but its ability to exercise independent authority declined steadily over the course of the eighteenth century. Its members certainly did not represent a distinct aristocracy within American society.

If royal governors did not look like kings, nor American councils like the House of Lords, colonial assemblies bore little resemblance to the eighteenth-century House of Commons. The major difference was the size of the American franchise. In most colonies, adult white males who owned a small amount of land could vote in colonywide elections. One historian estimates that 95 percent of this group in Massachusetts were eligible to participate in elections. The number in Virginia was about 85 percent. These figures—much higher than those in contemporary England—have led some scholars to view the colonies as "middle-class democracies," societies run by moderately prosperous yeomen farmers who—in politics at least—exercised independent judgment. There were too many of them to bribe, no "rotten" boroughs, and when these people moved west, colonial assemblies usually created new electoral districts.

Colonial governments were not democracies in the modern sense of that term. Possessing the right to vote was one thing, exercising it quite another. Americans participated in elections when major issues were at stake—the formation of banks in mid-eighteenth-century Massachusetts, for example—but most of the time they were content to let members of the rural and urban gentry represent them in the assemblies. To be sure, unlike modern democracies, these colonial politics excluded women and nonwhites from voting. The point to remember, however, is that the power to expel legislative rascals was always present in America, and it was this political reality that kept autocratic gentlemen from straying too far from the will of the people.

Colonial Assemblies

Elected members of the colonial assemblies believed that they had a special obligation to preserve colonial liberties. They perceived any attack on the legislature as an assault on the rights of Americans. The elected representatives brooked no criticism, and several colonial printers landed in jail because they criticized actions taken by a lower house.

So aggressive were these bodies in seizing privileges, determining procedures, and controlling money bills that some historians have described the political development of eighteenth-century America as "the rise of the assemblies." No doubt this is exaggerated, but the long series of imperial wars against the French, demanding large public expenditures, transformed the small, amateurish assemblies of the seventeenth century into the more professional, vigilant legislatures of the eighteenth.

This political system seemed designed to generate hostility. There was simply no reason for the colonial legislators to cooperate with appointed royal governors. Alexander Spotswood, Virginia's governor from 1710 to 1722, for example, attempted to institute a bold new land program backed by the crown. He tried persuasion and gifts and, when these failed, chicanery. But the members of the House of Burgesses refused to support a plan that did not suit their own interests. Before leaving office, Spotswood gave up trying to carry out royal policy in America. Instead, he allied himself with the local Virginia gentry who controlled the House as well as the Council, and because they awarded their new friend with large tracts of land, he became a wealthy man.

A major source of shared political information was the weekly journal, a new and vigorous institution in American life. In New York and Massachusetts especially, weekly newspapers urged readers to preserve civic virtue, to exercise extreme vigilance against the spread of privileged power. In the first issue of the *Independent Reflector*, published in New York (November 30, 1752), the editor announced defiantly that no discouragement shall "deter me from vindicating the *civil and religious RIGHTS* of my Fellow-Creatures: From exposing the peculiar Deformity of publick *Vice*, and *Corruption*; and displaying the amiable Charms of Liberty, with the detestable Nature of *Slavery* and *Oppression*." Through such journals, a pattern of political rhetoric that in Britain had gained only marginal respectability became after 1765 America's normal form of political discourse.

The rise of the assemblies shaped American culture in other, subtler ways. Over the course of the century, the language of the law became increasingly Anglicized. The Board of Trade, the Privy Council, and Parliament scrutinized court decisions and legislative actions from all thirteen mainland colonies. As a result, varying local legal practices that had been widespread during the seventeenth century became standardized. Indeed, according to one historian, the colonial legal system by 1750 "was substantially that of the mother country." Not surprisingly, many men who served in colonial assemblies were either lawyers or persons who had received legal training. When Americans from different regions met—as they frequently did in the years before the Revolution—they discovered that they shared a commitment to the preservation of the English common law.

As eighteenth-century political developments drew the colonists closer to the mother country, they also brought Americans a greater awareness of each other. As their horizons widened, they learned they operated within the same general imperial system, and the problems confronting the Massachusetts House of

Representatives were not too different from those facing Virginia's House of Burgesses or South Carolina's Commons House. Like the revivalists and merchants—people who crossed old boundaries—colonial legislators laid the foundation for a larger cultural identity.

Century of Imperial War

Why did colonial Americans support Great Britain's wars against France?

On paper, at least, the British colonies enjoyed military superiority over the settlements of New France. Louis XIV (r. 1643–1715) possessed an impressive army of 100,000 well-armed troops, but he dispatched few of them to the New World. He left the defense of Canada and the Mississippi Valley to the companies engaged in the fur trade. Meeting this challenge seemed almost impossible for the French outposts strung out along the St. Lawrence River and the Great Lakes. In 1754, New France contained only 75,000 inhabitants as compared to 1.2 million people living in Britain's mainland colonies.

For most of the century, the theoretical advantages enjoyed by the English colonists did them little good. While the British settlements possessed a larger and more prosperous population, they were divided into separate governments that sometimes seemed more suspicious of each other than of the French. When war came, French officers and Indian allies exploited these jealousies with considerable skill. Moreover, although the population of New France was comparatively small, it was concentrated along the St. Lawrence, so that while the French found it difficult to mount effective offensive operations against the English, they could easily mass the forces needed to defend Montreal and Quebec.

King William's and Queen Anne's Wars

Colonial involvement in imperial war began in 1689, when England's new king, William III, declared war on Louis XIV. Europeans called this struggle the War of the League of Augsburg, but to the Americans, it was simply King William's War. Canadians commanded by the Comte de Frontenac raided the northern frontiers of New York and New England, and while they made no territorial gains, they caused considerable suffering among the civilian populations of Massachusetts and New York.

The war ended with the Treaty of Ryswick (1697), but the colonists were drawn almost immediately into a new conflict. Queen Anne's War, known in Europe as the War of the Spanish Succession (1702–1713), was fought across a large geographic area. The bloody combat along the American frontier ended in 1713 when Great Britain and France signed the Treaty of Utrecht. European negotiators showed little interest in the military situation in the New World. Their major concern was preserving a balance of power among the European states. More than two decades of intense fighting had taken a heavy toll in North America, but neither French nor English colonists had much to show for their sacrifice.

Both sides viewed this great contest in conspiratorial terms. From South Carolina to Massachusetts Bay, colonists believed the French planned to "encircle" the English settlements, to confine the English to a narrow strip of land along the Atlantic coast.

The English noted that in 1682, La Salle had claimed for the king of France a territory—Louisiana—that included all the people and resources located on "streams and Rivers" flowing into the Mississippi River. To make good on their claim, the French constructed forts on the Chicago and Illinois rivers. In 1717, they established a military post two hundred miles up the Alabama River, well within striking distance of the Carolina frontier, and in 1718, they settled New Orleans. One New Yorker declared in 1715 that "it is impossible that we and the French can both inhabit this Continent in peace but that one nation must at last give way to the other."

On their part, the French suspected their rivals intended to seize all of North America. Land speculators and frontier traders pushed aggressively into territory claimed by the French and owned by the Native Americans. In 1716, one Frenchman urged his government to hasten the development of Louisiana, since "it is not difficult to guess that their [the British] purpose is to drive us entirely out . . . of North America."

To their great sorrow and eventual destruction, the original inhabitants of the frontier, the Native Americans, were swept up in this undeclared war. The Indians maneuvered to hold their own in the "middle ground." The Iroquois favored the British; the Algonquian peoples generally supported the French. But regardless of the groups to which they belonged, Indian warriors—acting independently and for their own strategic reasons—found themselves enmeshed in imperial policies set by distant European kings.

King George's War and Its Aftermath

In 1743, the Americans were dragged once again into the imperial conflict. During King George's War (1743–1748), known in Europe as the War of the Austrian Succession, the colonists scored a magnificent victory over the French. Louisbourg, a gigantic fortress on Cape Breton Island, the easternmost promontory of Canada, guarded the approaches to the Gulf of St. Lawrence and Quebec. It was described as the Gibraltar of the New World. An army of New England troops under the command of William Pepperrell captured Louisbourg in June 1745, a feat that demonstrated the British colonists were able to fight and to mount effective joint operations.

The Americans, however, were in for a shock. When the war ended with the signing of the Treaty of Aix-la-Chapelle in 1748, the British government handed Louisbourg back to the French in exchange for concessions elsewhere. Such decisions exposed the deep and continuing ambivalence the colonists felt about participation in imperial wars. They were proud to support Great Britain, of course, but the Americans seldom fully understood why the wars were being fought, why certain tactics had been adopted, and why the British accepted treaty terms that so blatantly ignored colonial interests.

The French were not prepared to surrender an inch. But as they recognized, time was running against them. Not only were the English colonies growing more populous, but they also possessed a seemingly inexhaustible supply of manufactured goods to trade with the Indians. The French decided in the early 1750s, therefore, to seize the Ohio Valley before the Virginians could do so. They established forts throughout the region, the most formidable being Fort Duquesne, located at the strategic fork in the Ohio River and later renamed Pittsburgh.

This mid-eighteenth-century lithograph portrays colonial assault troops, under the command of William Pepperrell, establishing a beachhead at Freshwater Cove near Louisbourg. Pepperrell's troops went on to capture the French fortress at Louisbourg.

Although France and England had not officially declared war, British officials advised the governor of Virginia to "repell force by force." The Virginians needed little encouragement. They were eager to make good their claim to the Ohio Valley, and in 1754, militia companies under the command of a promising young officer, George Washington, constructed Fort Necessity not far from Fort Duquesne. The plan failed. French and Indian troops overran the badly exposed outpost (July 3, 1754). Among other things, the humiliating setback revealed that a single colony could not defeat the French.

Albany Congress and Braddock's Defeat

Benjamin Franklin, for one, appreciated the need for intercolonial cooperation. When British officials invited representatives from Virginia and Maryland as well as the northern colonies to Albany (June 1754) to discuss relations with the Iroquois, Franklin used the occasion to present a bold blueprint for colonial union. His so-called **Albany Plan** envisioned the formation of a Grand Council, made up of elected delegates from the various colonies, to oversee matters of common defense, western expansion, and Indian affairs. A President General appointed by the king would preside. Franklin's most daring suggestion involved taxation. He insisted the council be authorized to collect taxes to cover military expenditures.

First reaction to the Albany Plan was enthusiastic. To take effect, however, it required the support of the separate colonial assemblies as well as Parliament. It received neither. The assemblies were jealous of their fiscal authority, and the English thought the scheme undermined the Crown's power over American affairs.

In 1755, the Ohio Valley again became the scene of fierce fighting. Even though there was still no formal declaration of war, the British resolved to destroy Fort Duquesne, and to that end, they dispatched units of the regular army to America. In command was Major General Edward Braddock, an obese, humorless veteran who inspired neither fear nor respect. One colonist described Braddock as "very indolent, Slave to his passions, women & wine, as great an Epicure as could be in his eating, tho a brave man."

On July 9, Braddock led a joint force of twenty-five hundred British redcoats and colonists to humiliating defeat. The French and Indians opened fire as Braddock's army waded across the Monongahela River, about eight miles from Fort Duquesne. Along a narrow road already congested with heavy wagons and confused men, Braddock ordered a counterattack, described by one of his officers as "without any form or order but that of a parcell of school boys coming out of s[c]hool." Nearly 70 percent of Braddock's troops were killed or wounded in western Pennsylvania. The general himself died in battle. The French, who suffered only light casualties, remained in firm control of the Ohio Valley.

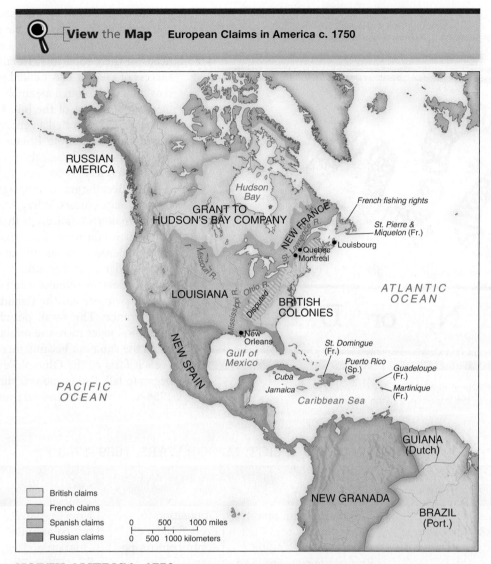

View the Map   European Claims in America c. 1750

NORTH AMERICA, 1750 By 1750, the French had established a chain of settlements southward through the heart of the continent from Quebec to New Orleans. The British saw this development as a threat to their own seaboard colonies, which were expanding westward.

The entire affair profoundly angered Washington, who fumed, "We have been most scandalously beaten by a trifling body of men." The British thought their allies the Iroquois might desert them after the embarrassing defeat. The Indians, however, took the news in stride, observing that "they were not at all surprised to hear it, as they [Braddock's redcoats] were men who had crossed the Great Water and were unacquainted with the arts of war among the Americans."

Seven Years' War

Britain's imperial war effort had hit bottom. No one in England or America seemed to possess the leadership necessary to drive the French from the Mississippi Valley. The cabinet of George II (r. 1727–1760) lacked the will to organize and finance a sustained military campaign in the New World, and colonial assemblies balked every time Britain asked them to raise men and money. On May 18, 1756, the British officially declared war on the French, a conflict called the French and Indian War in America and the **Seven Years' War** in Europe.

Had it not been for William Pitt, the most powerful minister in George's cabinet, the military stalemate might have continued. This supremely self-confident Englishman believed he was the only person capable of saving the British empire, an opinion he publicly expressed. When he became effective head of the ministry in December 1756, Pitt had an opportunity to demonstrate his talents.

In the past, warfare on the European continent had worked mainly to France's advantage. Pitt saw no point in continuing to concentrate on Europe, and in 1757 he advanced a bold new imperial policy, one based on commercial assumptions. In Pitt's judgment, the critical confrontation would take place in North America, where Britain and France were struggling to control colonial markets and raw materials. Indeed, according to Pitt, America was "where England and Europe are to be fought for." He was determined, therefore, to expel the French from the continent, however great the cost.

📖●─┤Read the Document   Albany Plan of Union (1754)

The first political cartoon to appear in an American newspaper was created by Benjamin Franklin in 1754 to emphasize the importance of the Albany Plan.

To effect this ambitious scheme, Pitt took personal command of the army and navy. He mapped strategy. He even promoted young promising officers over the heads of their superiors. He also recognized that the success of the war effort could not depend on the generosity of the colonial assemblies. Great Britain would have to foot most of the bill. Pitt's military expenditures, of course, created an enormous national debt that would soon haunt both Britain and its colonies, but at the time, no one foresaw the fiscal consequences of victory in America.

To direct the grand campaign, Pitt selected two relatively obscure officers, Jeffrey Amherst and James Wolfe. It was a masterful choice, one that a less self-assured man than Pitt would never have risked. Both officers were young, talented, and ambitious, and on July 26, 1758, forces under their direction captured Louisbourg, the same fortress the colonists had taken a decade earlier!

This victory cut the Canadians' main supply line with France. The small population of New France could no longer meet the military demands placed on it. As the situation became increasingly desperate, the French forts of the Ohio Valley and the Great Lakes began to fall. Duquesne was simply abandoned late in 1758 as French and Indian troops under the Marquis

A CENTURY OF CONFLICT: MAJOR WARS, 1689–1763

Dates	European Name	American Name	Major Allies	Issues	Major American Battle	Treaty
1689–1697	War of the League of Augsburg	King William's War	Britain, Holland, Spain, their colonies, and Native American allies against France, its colonies, and Native American allies	Opposition to French bid for control of Europe	New England troops assault Quebec under Sir William Phips (1690)	Treaty of Ryswick (1697)
1702–1713	War of the Spanish Succession	Queen Anne's War	Britain, Holland, their colonies, and Native American allies against France, Spain, their colonies, and Native American allies	Austria and France hold rival claims to Spanish throne	Attack on Deerfield (1704)	Treaty of Utrecht (1713)
1743–1748	War of the Austrian Succession (War of Jenkin's Ear)	King George's War	Britain, its colonies, and Native American allies, and Austria against France, Spain, their Native American allies, and Prussia	Struggle among Britain, Spain, and France for control of New World territory; among France, Prussia, and Austria for control of central Europe	New England forces capture of Louisbourg under William Pepperrell (1745)	Treaty of Aix-la-Chapelle (1748)
1756–1763	Seven Years' War	French and Indian War	Britain, its colonies, and Native American allies against France, its colonies, and Native American allies	Struggle among Britain, Spain, and France for worldwide control of colonial markets and raw materials	British and Continental forces capture Quebec under Major General James Wolfe (1759)	Peace of Paris (1763)

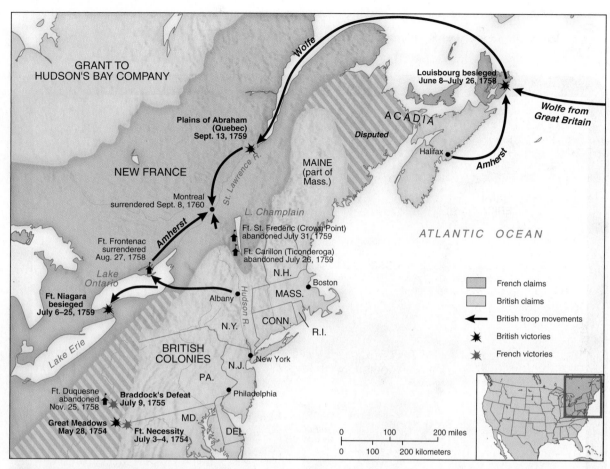

THE SEVEN YEARS' WAR, 1756–1763 Major battle sites. The conflict ended with Great Britain driving the French from mainland North America.

de Montcalm retreated toward Quebec and Montreal. During the summer of 1759, the French surrendered key forts at Ticonderoga, Crown Point, and Niagara.

The climax to a century of war came dramatically in September 1759. Wolfe, now a major general, assaulted Quebec with nine thousand men. But it was not simply force of arms that brought victory. Wolfe proceeded as if he were preparing to attack the city directly, but under cover of darkness, his troops scaled a cliff to dominate a less well-defended position. At dawn on September 13, 1759, they took the French from the rear by surprise. The decisive action occurred on the Plains of Abraham, a bluff high above the St. Lawrence River. Both Wolfe and Montcalm were mortally wounded. When an aide informed Wolfe the French had been routed, he sighed, "Now, God be praised, I will die in peace." On September 8, 1760, Amherst accepted the final surrender of the French army at Montreal.

The **Peace of Paris of 1763** signed on February 10, almost fulfilled Pitt's grandiose dreams. Great Britain took possession of an empire that stretched around the globe. Only Guadeloupe and Martinique, the Caribbean sugar islands, were given back to the French. After a century-long struggle, the French had been driven from the mainland of North America. Even Louisiana passed out of France's control into Spanish hands. The treaty gave Britain title to Canada, Florida, and all the land east of the Mississippi River. Moreover, with the stroke of a diplomat's pen, eighty thousand

French-speaking Canadians, most of them Catholics, became the subjects of George III.

The Americans were overjoyed. It was a time of good feelings and national pride. Together, the English and their colonial allies had thwarted the "Gallic peril." Samuel Davies, a Presbyterian who had brought the Great Awakening to Virginia, announced confidently that the long-awaited victory would inaugurate "a new heaven and a new earth."

Perceptions of War

The Seven Years' War made a deep impression on American society. Even though Franklin's Albany Plan had failed, the military struggle had forced the colonists to cooperate on an unprecedented scale. It also drew them into closer contact with Britain. They became aware of being part of a great empire, military and commercial, but in the very process of waging war, they acquired a more intimate sense of an America that lay beyond the plantation and the village. Conflict had carried thousands of young men across colonial boundaries, exposing them to a vast territory full of opportunities for a booming population. Moreover, the war trained a corps of American officers, people like George Washington, who learned from firsthand experience that the British were not invincible.

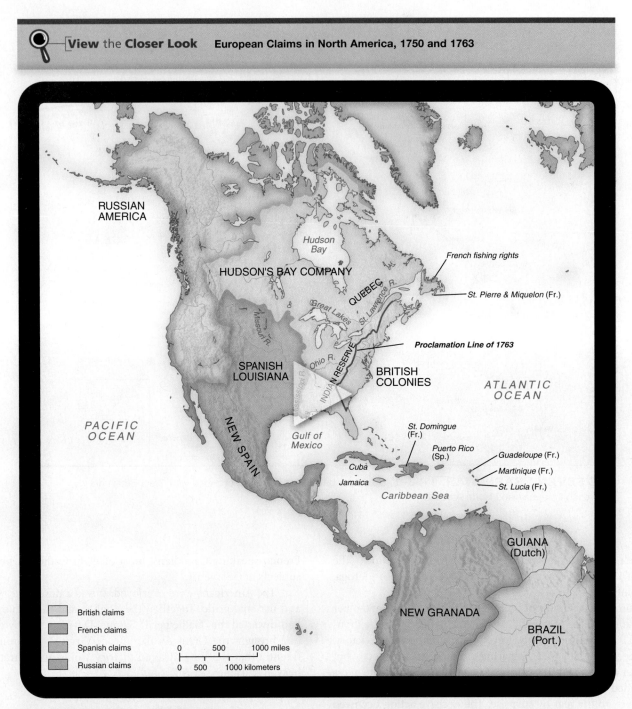

NORTH AMERICA AFTER 1763 The Peace of Paris (1763) redrew the map of North America. Great Britain received all the French holdings except a few islands in the Atlantic and some sugar-producing islands in the Caribbean.

British officials later accused the Americans of ingratitude. England, they claimed, had sent troops and provided funds to liberate the colonists from the threat of French attack. The Americans, appreciative of the aid from England, cheered on the British but dragged their feet at every stage, refusing to pay the bills. These charges were later incorporated into a general argument justifying parliamentary taxation in America.

The British had a point. The colonists were, in fact, slow in providing the men and materials needed to fight the French. Nevertheless, they did make a significant contribution to the war

effort, and it was perfectly reasonable for Americans to regard themselves at the very least as junior partners in the empire. After all, they had supplied almost twenty thousand soldiers and spent well over £2 million. In a single year, in fact, Massachusetts enlisted five thousand men out of an adult male population of about fifty thousand, a commitment that, in the words of one military historian, meant "the war was being waged on a scale comparable to the great wars of modern times." After making such a sacrifice—indeed, after demonstrating their loyalty to the mother country—the colonists would surely have been disturbed to learn that General James

Wolfe, the hero of Quebec, had stated, "The Americans are in general the dirtiest, the most contemptible, cowardly dogs that you can conceive. There is no depending upon them in action. They fall down in their own dirt and desert in battalions, officers and all."

Conclusion: Rule Britannia?

James Thomson, an Englishman, understood the hold of empire on the popular imagination of the eighteenth century. In 1740, he composed words that British patriots have proudly sung for more than two centuries:

> Rule Britannia, rule the waves,
> Britons never will be slaves.

Colonial Americans—at least, those of British background—joined the chorus. By midcentury they took their political and cultural cues from Great Britain. They fought its wars, purchased its consumer goods, flocked to hear its evangelical preachers, and read its many publications. Without question, the empire provided the colonists with a compelling source of identity.

An editor justified the establishment of New Hampshire's first newspaper in precisely these terms. "By this Means," the publisher observed, "the spirited *Englishman*, the mountainous *Welshman*, the brave *Scotchman*, and *Irishman*, and the loyal *American*, may be firmly united and mutually RESOLVED to guard the glorious Throne of BRITANNIA . . . as *British Brothers*, in defending the Common Cause." Even new immigrants, the Germans, Scots-Irish, and Africans, who felt no political loyalty to Great Britain and no affinity to English culture, had to assimilate to some degree to the dominant English culture of the colonies.

Americans hailed Britannia. In 1763, they were the victors, the conquerors of the backcountry. In their moment of glory, the colonists assumed that Britain's rulers saw the Americans as "Brothers," as equal partners in the business of empire. Only slowly would they learn the British had a different perception. For them, "American" was a way of saying "not quite English."

Study Resources

 Take the **Study Plan** for **Chapter 4** *Experience of Empire* on **MyHistoryLab**

TIME LINE

1680 El Popé leads Pueblo revolt against the Spanish in New Mexico

1689 William and Mary accede to the English throne

1706 Birth of Benjamin Franklin

1714 George I of Hanover becomes monarch of Great Britain

1732 Colony of Georgia is established; Birth of George Washington

1734–1736 First expression of the Great Awakening at Northampton, Massachusetts

1740 George Whitefield electrifies listeners at Boston

1745 Colonial troops capture Louisbourg

1748 American Lutheran ministers ordained in Philadelphia

1754 Albany Congress meets

1755 Braddock is defeated by the French and Indians in western Pennsylvania

1756 Seven Years' War is formally declared

1759 British are victorious at Quebec; Wolfe and Montcalm are killed in battle

1760 George III becomes king of Great Britain

1763 Peace of Paris ending French and Indian War is signed

1769 Junípero Serra begins to build missions in California

1821 Mexico declares independence from Spain

CHAPTER REVIEW

Growth and Diversity

What difficulties did Native Americans face in maintaining their cultural independence on the frontier?

Britain's American colonies experienced extraordinary growth during the eighteenth century. German and Scots-Irish migrants poured into the backcountry, where they clashed with Native Americans. The Indians played off French and British imperial ambitions in the "middle ground," but disease and encroachment by European settlers undermined the Indians' ability to resist. (p. 80)

Spanish Borderlands of the Eighteenth Century

Why was the Spanish empire unable to control its northern frontier?

During the late 1600s and early 1700s, the Spanish empire expanded its authority north of Mexico. New settlements were established in the Southwest and California. Although the Spanish constructed missions and forts, a lack of settlers and troops made it impossible for them to impose effective imperial authority. Much of the territory they claimed remained under the control of Indian peoples. (p. 83)

The Impact of European Ideas on American Culture

How did European ideas affect eighteenth-century American life?

During the Enlightenment, educated Europeans and American colonists, like Benjamin Franklin, brought scientific reason to the study of religion, nature, and society. By midcentury, economic growth sparked a consumer revolution that introduced colonists to an unprecedented array of imported manufactured items. New ideas and goods helped integrate the American colonies into mainstream British culture. (p. 87)

Religious Revivals in Provincial Societies

How did the Great Awakening transform the religious culture of colonial America?

The Great Awakening brought a new form of evangelical religion to ordinary Americans. It emphasized personal salvation through a "New Birth" and membership in a large community of believers. Itinerant preachers such as George Whitefield drew huge crowds throughout the colonies. Other ministers followed Whitefield, inviting ordinary Americans to question traditional religious authorities. (p. 90)

Clash of Political Cultures

Why were eighteenth-century colonial assemblies not fully democratic?

Most eighteenth-century colonial governments were comprised of a royal governor, an appointed governor's council, and an elected assembly. Although these representative assemblies did not allow women, blacks, or the poor to vote, they did enfranchise most of the white adult male population. Assemblies guarded their privileges and powers, often conflicting with royal governors who tried to expand their authority. (p. 92)

Century of Imperial War

Why did colonial Americans support Great Britain's wars against France?

France and Britain waged almost constant war in North America. By 1750, Britain's American colonists believed the French in Canada planned to encircle their settlements, cutting them off from the rich lands of the Ohio Valley. The Seven Years' War drove the French from Canada, a victory that generated unprecedented enthusiasm for the British Empire in the colonies. (p. 95)

KEY TERMS AND DEFINITIONS

Backcountry   In the eighteenth century, the edge of settlement extending from western Pennsylvania to Georgia. This region formed the second frontier as settlers moved west from the Atlantic coast into the interior. p. 80

Middle ground   A geographical area where two distinct cultures meet and merge with neither holding a clear upper hand. p. 83

Enlightenment   Philosophical and intellectual movement that began in Europe during the eighteenth century. It stressed the use of reason to solve social and scientific problems. p. 87

Consumer revolution   Period between 1740 and 1770 when English exports to the American colonies increased by 360 percent to satisfy Americans' demand for consumer goods. p. 89

Great Awakening   A sudden, spontaneous, and fervent series of Protestant evangelical revivals beginning in the 1730s and through the 1740s and 1750s that occurred throughout the colonies. The Great Awakening encouraged men and women to take an active role in their salvation and helped connect scattered colonists together with a unifying belief that, with God's assistance, social and political progress was possible in colonial America. p. 90

Itinerant preachers   These charismatic preachers spread revivalism throughout America during the Great Awakening. p. 91

Albany Plan   Plan of intercolonial cooperation proposed by prominent colonists including Benjamin Franklin at a conference in Albany, New York, in 1754. The plan called for a Grand Council of elected delegates from the colonies that would have powers to tax and provide for the common defense. Although rejected by the colonial and British governments, it was a prototype for colonial union. p. 96

Seven Years' War   Worldwide conflict (1756–1763) that pitted Britain against France. With help from the American colonists, the British won the war and eliminated France as a power on the North American continent. Also known as the French and Indian War. p. 97

Peace of Paris of 1763   Treaty ending the French and Indian War by which France ceded Canada to Britain. p. 99

CRITICAL THINKING QUESTIONS

1. What factors ultimately served to undermine the "middle ground"?

2. What impact did the Spanish empire have on the culture of the borderlands?

3. What impact did Enlightenment ideas and commercial goods have on American politics?

4. What are the similarities and differences between the impact of the Enlightenment and the Great Awakening on colonial society?

5. Why did colonists place greater political trust in their elected assemblies than in their royally appointed governors?

MyHistoryLab Media Assignments

Find these resources in the Media Assignments folder for Chapter 4 on MyHistoryLab

Growth and Diversity

Read the **Document**   *William Byrd II, Diary—An American Gentleman p. 79*

■ **Read** the **Document**   *Benjamin Franklin, "Observations Concerning the Increase of Mankind" p. 81*

Spanish Borderlands of the Eighteenth Century

■ **Complete** the **Assignment**   *Conquest by Other Means: The Pennsylvania Walking Purchase p. 84*

Read the **Document**   *Testimony by Pedro Naranjo to Spanish Authorities p. 86*

Religious Revivals in Provincial Societies

■ **Read** the **Document**   *Jonathan Edwards, "Sinners in the Hands of an Angry God" p. 91*

Read the **Document**   *Benjamin Franklin on George Whitfield (1771) p. 92*

Clash of Political Cultures

■ **Read** the **Document**   *English Bill of Rights (1689) p. 93*

Century of Imperial War

View the **Map**   *European Claims in America, c. 1750 p. 97*

Read the **Document**   *Albany Plan of Union (1754) p. 98*

■ **View** the **Closer Look**   *European Claims in North America, 1750 and 1763 p. 100*

■ *Indicates Study Plan Media Assignment*

5 The American Revolution: From Elite Protest to Popular Revolt, 1763–1783

Contents and Learning Objectives

((•—[Listen to the **Audio File** on **myhistorylab**   **Chapter 5** *The American Revolution*

Moment of Decision: Commitment and Sacrifice

Even as the British army poured into Boston in 1774, demanding complete obedience to king and Parliament, few Americans welcomed the possibility of revolutionary violence. For many colonial families, it would have been easier, certainly safer, to accede to imperial demands for taxes enacted without their representation. But they did not do so.

For the Patten family, the time of reckoning arrived in the spring of 1775. Matthew Patten had been born in Ulster, a Protestant Irishman, and with Scots-Irish friends and relatives, he migrated to New Hampshire, where they founded a settlement of fifty-six families known as Bedford. Matthew farmed the unpromising, rocky soil that he, his wife Elizabeth, and their children called home. In time, distant decisions about taxes and representation shattered the peace of Bedford, and the Pattens found themselves drawn into a war not of their own making but which, nevertheless, compelled them to sacrifice the security of everyday life for liberty.

On April 20, 1775, accounts of Lexington and Concord reached Bedford. Matthew noted in his diary,

"I Received the Melancholy news in the morning that General Gage's troops had fired on our Countrymen at Concord yesterday." His son John marched with neighbors in support of the Massachusetts soldiers. The departure was tense. The entire family helped John prepare. "Our Girls sit up all night baking bread and fitting things for him," Matthew wrote.

The demands of war had only just begun. In late 1775 John volunteered for an American march on British Canada. On the long trek over impossible terrain, the boy died. The father recorded his emotions in the diary. John "was shot through his left arm at Bunker Hill fight and now was lead after suffering much fategue to the place where he now lyes in defending the just Rights of America to whose end he came in the prime of life by means of that wicked Tyrannical Brute (nea worse than Brute) of Great Britain [George III]. He was Twenty four years and 31 days old."

The initial stimulus for rebellion came from the gentry, from the rich and wellborn, who resented Parliament's efforts to curtail their rights within the British empire.

Patten family farmstead in Bedford, New Hampshire.

But as these influential planters, wealthy merchants, and prominent clergymen discovered, the revolutionary movement generated a momentum that they could not control. As relations with Britain deteriorated, particularly after 1765, the traditional leaders of colonial society encouraged the ordinary folk to join the protest—as rioters, as petitioners, and finally, as soldiers. Newspapers, sermons, and pamphlets helped transform what had begun as a squabble among the gentry into a mass movement, and once the people had become involved in shaping the nation's destiny, they could never again be excluded.

Had it not been for ordinary militiamen like John Patten in the various colonies, the British would have easily crushed American resistance. Although some accounts of the Revolution downplay the military side of the story, leaving the impression that a few famous "Founding Fathers" effortlessly carried the nation to independence, a more persuasive explanation must recognize the centrality of armed violence in achieving nationhood.

The American Revolution involved a massive military commitment. If common American soldiers had not been willing to stand up to seasoned British troops, to face the terror of the bayonet charge, independence would have remained a dream of intellectuals. Proportionate to the population, a greater percentage of Americans died in military service during the Revolution than in any war in American history, with the exception of the Civil War.

The concept of liberty so magnificently expressed in revolutionary pamphlets was not, therefore, simply an abstraction, an exclusive concern of political theorists such as Thomas Jefferson and John Adams. It also motivated ordinary folk—the Patten family, for example—to take up weapons and risk death. Those who survived the ordeal were never quite the same, for the very experience of fighting, of assuming responsibility in battle and perhaps even of taking the lives of British officers, gave dramatic new meaning to the idea of social equality.

Structure of Colonial Society

Why did Americans resist parliamentary taxation?

Colonists who were alive during the 1760s did not anticipate the coming of national independence. It is only from a modern perspective that we see how the events of this period would lead to the formation of the United States. The colonists, of course, did not know what the future would bring. They would probably have characterized these years as "postwar," as a time of heightened economic and political expectation following the successful conclusion of the Seven Years' War (see Chapter 4).

For many Americans, the period generated optimism. The population continued to grow. Indeed, in 1776, approximately 2.5 million people, black and white, were living in Great Britain's thirteen mainland colonies. The striking ethnic and racial diversity of these men and women amazed European visitors who apparently rated homogeneity more highly than did the Americans. In 1775, for example, a traveler corrected the impression in London that the "colonists are the offspring of Englishmen." To be sure, many families traced their roots to Great Britain, but one also encountered "French, Dutch, Germans innumerable, Indians, Africans, and a multitude of felons." He then asked rhetorically, "Is it possible to tell which are the most turbulent amongst such a mixture of people?"

The American population on the eve of independence was also extraordinarily young, a fact of great importance in understanding the development of effective political resistance. Nearly 60 percent of the American people were under age 21. This is a fact of considerable significance. At any given time, most people in this society were small children, and many of the young men who fought the British during the Revolution either had not been born or had been infants during the Stamp Act crisis. Any explanation for the coming of independence, therefore, must take into account the continuing political mobilization of so many young people.

Postwar Americans also experienced a high level of prosperity. To be sure, some major port cities went through a difficult period as colonists who had been employed during the fighting were thrown out of work. Sailors and ship workers, for example, were especially vulnerable to layoffs of this sort. In general,

however, white Americans did very well. The quality of their material lives was not substantially lower than that of the English. In 1774, the per capita wealth of the Americans—this figure includes blacks as well as whites—was £37.4. This sum exceeds the per capita wealth of many developing countries today. On the eve of revolution, £37.4 would have purchased about 310 bushels of wheat, 1,600 pounds of rice, 11 cows, or 6 horses. A typical white family of five—a father, mother, and three dependent children—not only would have been able to afford decent food, clothing, and housing but also would have had money left over with which to purchase consumer goods. Even the poorest colonists seem to have benefited from a rising standard of living, and although they may not have done as well as their wealthier neighbors, they too wanted to preserve gains they had made.

Wealth, however, was not evenly distributed in this society. Regional variations were striking. The Southern Colonies enjoyed the highest levels of personal wealth in America, which can be explained in part by the ownership of slaves. More than 90 percent of America's unfree workers lived in the South, and they represented a huge capital investment. Even without including the slaves in these wealth estimates, the South did quite well. In terms of aggregate wealth, the Middle Colonies also scored impressively. In fact, only New England lagged noticeably behind, a reflection of its relative inability to produce large amounts of exports for a growing world market.

Breakdown of Political Trust

Ultimate responsibility for preserving the empire fell to George III. When he became king of England in 1760, he was only 22 years of age. The new monarch was determined to play an aggressive role in government. This decision caused considerable dismay among England's political leaders. For decades, a powerful, though loosely associated, group of men who called themselves **Whigs** had set policy and controlled patronage. George II had accepted this situation, and so long as the Whigs in Parliament did not meddle with his beloved army, the king had let them rule the nation.

In one stroke, George III destroyed this cozy relationship. He selected as his chief minister the Earl of Bute, a Scot whose chief qualification for office appeared to be his friendship with the young king. The Whigs who dominated Parliament were outraged. Bute had no ties with the members of the House of Commons; he owed them no favors. It seemed to the Whigs that with the appointment of Bute, George was trying to turn back the clock to the time before the Glorious Revolution, in other words, attempting to reestablish a personal Stuart monarchy free from traditional constitutional restraints. The Whigs blamed Bute for every wrong, real or imagined. George did not, in fact, harbor such arbitrary ambitions, but his actions threw customary political practices into doubt.

By 1763 Bute, despairing of public life, left office. His departure, however, neither restored the Whigs to preeminence nor dampened the king's enthusiasm for domestic politics. Everyone agreed George had the right to select whomever he desired for cabinet posts, but until 1770, no one seemed able to please the monarch. Ministers came and went, often for no other reason than George's personal distaste. Because of this chronic instability, subministers (minor bureaucrats who directed routine colonial affairs) did not know what was expected of them. In the absence of clear long-range policy, some ministers made narrowly based decisions; others did nothing. Most devoted their energies to finding a political patron capable of satisfying the fickle king. Talent played little part in the scramble for office, and incompetent hacks were advanced as frequently as were men of vision. With such turbulence surrounding him, the king showed little interest in the American colonies.

The king, however, does not bear the sole responsibility for England's loss of empire. The members of Parliament who actually drafted the statutes that gradually drove a wedge between the colonies and Britain must share the blame, for they failed to provide innovative answers to the explosive constitutional issues of the day. The problem was not stupidity or even obstinacy, qualities found in equal measure among all peoples.

In part, the impasse resulted from sheer ignorance. Few Englishmen active in government had ever visited America. For those who attempted to follow colonial affairs, accurate information proved extremely difficult to obtain. Packet boats carrying passengers and mail sailed regularly between London and the various colonial ports, but the voyage across the Atlantic required at least four weeks. Furthermore, all correspondence was laboriously copied in longhand by overworked clerks serving in understaffed offices. One could not expect to receive from America an answer to a specific question in less than three months. As a result of the lag in communication between England and America, rumors sometimes passed for true accounts, and misunderstanding influenced the formulation of colonial policy.

But failure of communication alone was not to blame for the widening gap between the colonies and England. Even when complete information was available, the two sides were often unable to understand each other's positions. The central element in this Anglo-American debate was a concept known as **parliamentary sovereignty**. The English ruling classes viewed the role of Parliament from a historical perspective that most colonists never shared. They insisted that Parliament was the dominant element within the constitution. Indeed, this elective body protected rights and property from an arbitrary monarch. During the reign of the Stuarts, especially under Charles I (r. 1625–1649), the authority of Parliament had been challenged, and it was not until the Glorious Revolution of 1688 that the English crown formally recognized Parliament's supreme authority in matters such as taxation. Almost no one, including George III, would have dissented from a speech made in 1766 before the House of Commons, in which a representative declared, "The parliament hath, and must have, from the nature and essence of the constitution, has had, and ever will have a sovereign supreme power and jurisdiction over every part of the dominions of the state, *to make laws in all cases whatsoever*."

The logic of this argument seemed self-evident to the British. In fact, parliamentary leaders could never quite understand why the colonists were so difficult to persuade. In frustration, Lord Hillsborough, the British secretary of state, admonished the colonial agent for Connecticut, "It is essential to the constitution to preserve the supremacy of Parliament inviolate; and tell your friends in America . . . that it is as much their interest to support the constitution and preserve the supremacy of Parliament as it is ours."

Cartoons became a popular means of criticizing government during this period. Here, King George III watches as the kilted Lord Bute slaughters the goose America. A cabinet member holds a basket of golden eggs at rear. At front left, a dog relieves itself on a map of North America.

No Taxation Without Representation: The American Perspective

Americans most emphatically did not see it in their "interest" to maintain the "supremacy of Parliament." The crisis in imperial relations forced the colonists first to define and then to defend principles deeply rooted in their own political culture. For more than a century, their ideas about the colonies' role within the British empire had remained a vague, untested bundle of assumptions about personal liberties, property rights, and representative institutions.

By 1763, however, certain fundamental American beliefs had become clear. From Massachusetts to Georgia, colonists aggressively defended the powers of the provincial assemblies. They drew on a rich legislative history of their own. Over the course of the century, the American assemblies had steadily expanded their authority over taxation and expenditure. Since no one in Britain bothered to clip their legislative wings, these provincial bodies assumed a major role in policy making and routine administration. In other words, by midcentury the assemblies looked like American copies of Parliament. It seemed unreasonable, therefore, for the British suddenly to insist on the supremacy of Parliament, for as the legislators of Massachusetts observed in 1770, "This house has the same inherent rights in this province as the house of commons in Great Britain."

The constitutional debate turned ultimately on the meaning of representation itself. In 1764, a British official informed the colonists that even though they had not elected members to Parliament—indeed, even though they had had no direct contact with the current members—they were nevertheless "virtually" represented by that august body. The members of Parliament, he declared, represented the political interests of everyone who lived in the British empire. It did not really matter whether everyone had cast a vote.

The colonists ridiculed this notion of virtual representation. The only representatives the Americans recognized as legitimate were those actually chosen by the people for whom they spoke. On this crucial point they would not compromise. As John Adams insisted, a representative assembly should actually mirror its constituents: "It should think, feel, reason, and act like them." Since the members of Parliament could not possibly "think" like Americans, it followed logically they could not represent them. And if they were not genuine representatives, the members of Parliament—pretensions to sovereignty notwithstanding—had no business taxing the American people. Thus, in 1764 the Connecticut Assembly declared in bold letters, "NO LAW CAN BE MADE OR ABROGATED WITHOUT THE CONSENT OF THE PEOPLE BY THEIR REPRESENTATIVES."

Ideas About Power and Virtue

Americans expressed their political beliefs in a language they had borrowed from English writers. The person most frequently cited was John Locke, the influential seventeenth-century philosopher whose *Two Treatises of Government* (first published in 1690) seemed, to colonial readers at least, a brilliant description of what was in fact American political practice. Locke claimed that all people possessed natural and inalienable rights. To preserve these God-given rights of life, liberty, and property, for example, free men (the status of women in Locke's work was less clear) formed contracts. These agreements were the foundation of human society as well as civil government, and they required the consent of the people who were actually governed. There could be no coercion. Locke justified rebellion against arbitrary forms of government that were by their very nature unreasonable. Americans delighted in Locke's ability to unite traditional religious values with a spirited defense of popular government, and even when they did not fully understand his technical writings, they seldom missed a chance to quote from the works of "the Great Mr. Locke."

Colonial Americans also enthusiastically subscribed to the so-called Commonwealthman tradition, a body of political assumptions generally identified with two eighteenth-century English publicists, John Trenchard and Thomas Gordon (see Chapter 4). The writings of such figures—most of whom spent their lives in political opposition—helped persuade the colonists that *power* was extremely dangerous, a force that would surely destroy liberty unless it was countered by *virtue*. Persons who shared this highly charged moral outlook regarded bad policy as not simply the result of human error. Rather, it was an indication of sin and corruption.

Insistence on public virtue—sacrifice of self-interest to the public good—became the dominant theme of revolutionary political writing. American pamphleteers seldom took a dispassionate, legalistic approach to their analysis of power and liberty. More commonly, they exposed plots hatched by corrupt courtiers, such as the Earl of Bute. None of them—or their readers—had any doubt that Americans were more virtuous than were the people of England.

During the 1760s, however, popular writers were not certain how long the colonists could hold out against arbitrary taxation, standing armies, Anglican bishops—in other words, against a host of external threats designed to crush American liberty. In 1774, for example, the people of Farmington, Connecticut, declared that "the present ministry, being instigated by the devil and led by their wicked and corrupt hearts, have a design to take away our liberties and properties, and to enslave us forever." Indeed, these Connecticut farmers described Britain's leaders as "pimps and parasites." This highly emotional, conspiratorial rhetoric sometimes shocks modern readers who assume that America's revolutionary leaders were products of the Enlightenment, persons who relied solely on reason to solve social and political problems. Whatever the origins of their ideas may have been, the colonial pamphleteers successfully roused ordinary men and women to resist Britain with force of arms.

Colonial newspapers spread these ideas through a large dispersed population. A majority of adult white males—especially those in the Northern Colonies—were literate, and it is not surprising that the number of journals published in this country increased dramatically during the revolutionary period. For the first time in American history, persons living in various parts of the continent could closely follow events that occurred in distant American cities. Because of the availability of newspapers, the details of Bostonians' confrontations with British authorities were known throughout the colonies, and these shared political experiences drew Americans more closely together, making it possible—in the words of John Adams—for "Thirteen clocks . . . to strike together—a perfection of mechanism which no artist had ever before effected."

Eroding the Bonds of Empire

What events eroded the bonds of empire during the 1760s?

The Seven Years' War saddled Great Britain with a national debt so huge that more than half the annual national budget went to pay the interest on it. Almost everyone in government assumed that with the cessation of hostilities, the troops would be disbanded, thus saving a lot of money. George III had other plans. He insisted on keeping the largest peacetime army in British history on active duty, supposedly to protect Indians from predatory frontiersmen and to preserve order in the newly conquered territories of Florida and Quebec.

Maintaining such a force so far distant from the mother country fueled the budgetary crisis. The growing financial burden weighed heavily on restive English taxpayers and sent government leaders scurrying in search of new sources of revenue.

For their part, colonists doubted the value of this expensive army. Britain did not leave enough troops in America to maintain peace on the frontier effectively. The weakness of the army was dramatically demonstrated during the spring of 1763. The native peoples of the backcountry—the Seneca, Ottawa, Miami, Creek, and Cherokee—had begun discussing how they might turn back the tide of white settlement. The powerful spiritual leader Neolin, known as the Delaware Prophet and claiming vision from the "Master of Life," helped these Indians articulate their fear and anger. He urged them to restore their cultures to the "original state that they were in before the white people found out their country." If moral regeneration required violence, so be it. Neolin converted Pontiac, an Ottawa warrior, to the cause, and he, in turn, coordinated an uprising among the western Indians who had been French allies and who hated all British people—even those sent to protect them from land-grabbing colonists. The formidable Native American resistance was known as Pontiac's Rebellion. In May, Pontiac attacked Detroit; other Indians harassed the Pennsylvania and Virginia frontiers. At the end of the year, after his followers began deserting, Pontiac sued for peace. During even this brief outbreak, the British army proved unable to defend exposed colonial settlements, and several thousand people lost their lives.

From the perspective of the Native Americans who inhabited the Ohio Valley this was a period of almost unmitigated disaster. In fact, more than any other group, the Indians suffered as a direct result of imperial reorganization. The defeat of the French made it impossible for native peoples to play off one imperial power against European rivals (see Chapter 4), and the victorious British made it clear that they regarded their former Indian allies as little more than a nuisance. Diplomatic gifts stopped; humiliating restrictions were placed on trade. But even worse, Pontiac's rising unloosed vicious racism along the colonial frontier, and American colonists often used any excuse to attack local Indians, peaceful or not. Late in 1763, a group of vigilantes known as the Paxton Boys murdered a score of Christian Indians, women and children, living near Lancaster, Pennsylvania. White neighbors treated the killers as heroes, and the atrocity ended only after the Paxton Boys threatened to march on Philadelphia in search of administrators who dared to criticize such cold-blooded crimes. One of the administrators, Benjamin Franklin, observed sadly, "It grieves me to hear that our Frontier People are yet greater Barbarians than the Indians, and continue to murder them in time of Peace."

Whatever happened to the Indians, the colonists fully intended to settle the fertile region west of the Appalachian Mountains. After the British government issued the Proclamation of 1763, which prohibited governors from granting land beyond the headwaters of rivers flowing into the Atlantic, disappointed Americans viewed the army as an obstruction to legitimate economic development, a domestic police force that cost too much money.

Paying Off the National Debt

The task of reducing England's debt fell to George Grenville, the rigid, somewhat unimaginative chancellor of the exchequer who replaced Bute in 1763 as the king's first minister. After carefully reviewing the state of Britain's finances, Grenville concluded that the colonists would have to contribute to the maintenance of the army. The first bill he steered through Parliament was the Revenue Act of 1764, known as the Sugar Act.

This legislation placed a new burden on the Navigation Acts that had governed the flow of colonial commerce for almost a century (see Chapter 3). Those acts had forced Americans to trade almost exclusively with Britain. The statutes were not, however, primarily intended as a means to raise money for the British government. The Sugar Act—and the acts that soon followed—redefined the relationship between America and Great Britain. Parliament now expected the colonies to generate revenue. The preamble of the Sugar Act proclaimed explicitly: "It is just and necessary that

Read the **Document** James Otis, The Rights of the British Colonies Asserted and Proved

James Otis, Jr. (1725-1783) of Massachusetts was a brilliant lawyer, a prolific writer, and a strong supporter of colonial rights. He is credited with being one of the first Patriots to declare that "Taxation Without Representation is Tyranny!"

a revenue be raised . . . in America for defraying the expenses of defending, protecting, and securing the same." The purpose of the Sugar Act was to discourage smuggling, bribery, and other illegalities that prevented the Navigation Acts from being profitable. Parliament reduced the duty on molasses (set originally by the Molasses Act of 1733) from 6 to 3 pence per gallon. At so low a rate, Grenville reasoned, colonial merchants would have little incentive to bribe customs collectors. Much needed revenue would be diverted from the pockets of corrupt officials into the treasury so that it might be used to maintain the army.

Grenville had been too clever by half. The Americans immediately saw through his unconstitutional scheme. According to the members of the Rhode Island Assembly, the Sugar Act taxed the colonists in a manner "inconsistent with their rights and privileges as British subjects." James Otis, a fiery orator from Massachusetts, exclaimed the legislation deprived Americans of "the right of assessing their own taxes."

The act generated no violence. In fact, ordinary men and women were only marginally involved in the drafting of formal petitions. The protest was still confined to the members of the colonial assemblies, to the merchants, and to the well-to-do Americans who had personal interests in commerce.

Popular Protest

Passage of the **Stamp Act of 1765** transformed a debate among gentlemen into a mass political movement. The imperial crisis might have been avoided. Colonial agents had presented Grenville with alternative schemes for raising money in America. But Grenville was a stubborn man, and he had little fear of parliamentary opposition. The majority of the House of Commons assumed that Parliament possessed the right to tax the colonists, and when the chancellor of the exchequer announced a plan to squeeze £60,000 annually out of the Americans by requiring them to purchase special seals or stamps to validate legal documents, the members responded with enthusiasm. The Stamp Act was scheduled to go into effect on November 1, 1765, and in anticipation of brisk sales, Grenville appointed stamp distributors for every colony.

During discussion in Parliament, several members warned that the act would raise a storm of protest in the colonies. Colonel Isaac Barré, a veteran of the Seven Years' War, reminded his colleagues that the Americans were "sons of liberty" and would not surrender their rights without a fight. But Barré's appeal fell on deaf ears.

Word of the Stamp Act reached America in May, and it was soon clear that Barré had gauged the colonists' response correctly. The most dramatic incident occurred in Virginia's House of Burgesses. Patrick Henry, young and eloquent, whom contemporaries compared in fervor to evangelical preachers, introduced five resolutions protesting the Stamp Act on the floor of the assembly. He timed his move carefully. It was late in the session; many of the more conservative burgesses had already departed for their plantations. Even then, Henry's resolves declaring that Virginians had the right to tax themselves as they alone saw fit passed by narrow margins. The fifth resolution, stricken almost immediately from the legislative records, announced that any attempt to collect stamp revenues in America was "illegal, unconstitutional, and unjust, and has a manifest tendency to destroy British as well as American liberty." Henry was carried away by the force of his own rhetoric. He reminded his fellow Virginians that Caesar had had his Brutus, Charles I his Cromwell, and he hoped that "some good American would stand up for his country"—but an astonished speaker of the house cut Henry off in mid-sentence, accusing him of treason.

The Virginia Resolves might have remained a local matter had it not been for the colonial press. Newspapers throughout America printed Henry's resolutions, but, perhaps because editors did not really know what had happened in Williamsburg, they reported that all five resolutions had received the burgesses' full support. Several journals even carried two resolves that Henry had not dared to introduce. A result of this misunderstanding, of course, was that the Virginians appeared to have taken an extremely radical

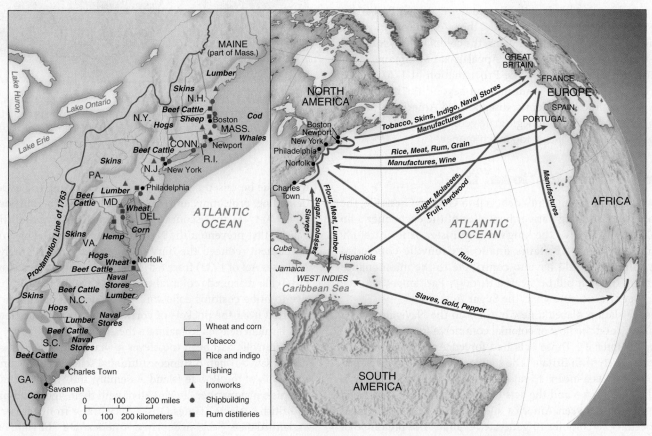

COLONIAL PRODUCTS AND TRADE Although the American colonists produced many agricultural staples that were valuable to Britain, they were dependent on British manufactures such as cloth, metal goods, and ceramics.

Read the Document   Benjamin Franklin, Testimony Against the Stamp Act (1766)

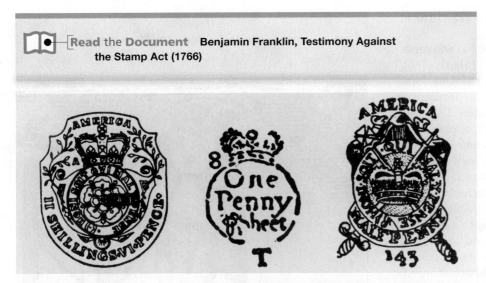

The Stamp Act placed a tax on documents and printed matter—newspapers, marriage licenses, wills, deeds, even playing cards and dice. The stamps (like those shown here) varied in denomination. A tax stamp affixed to a legal document or bill of sale signified that the required tax had been paid.

position on the issue of the supremacy of Parliament, one that other Americans now trumpeted before their own assemblies. No wonder Francis Bernard, royal governor of Massachusetts, called the Virginia Resolves an "alarm bell."

Not to be outdone by Virginia, Massachusetts called a general meeting to protest Grenville's policy. Nine colonies sent representatives to the **Stamp Act Congress** that convened in New York City in October 1765. It was the first intercolonial gathering held since the abortive Albany Congress of 1754; if nothing else, the new congress provided leaders from different regions with an opportunity to discuss common problems. The delegates drafted petitions to the king and Parliament that restated the colonists' belief "that no taxes should be imposed on them, but with their own consent, given personally, or by their representatives." The tone of the meeting was restrained, even conciliatory. The congress studiously avoided any mention of independence or disloyalty to the crown.

Resistance to the Stamp Act soon spread from the assemblies to the streets. By taxing deeds, marriage licenses, and playing cards, the Stamp Act touched the lives of ordinary women and men. Anonymous artisans and seamen, angered by Parliament's apparent insensitivity and fearful that the statute would increase unemployment and poverty, organized mass protests in the major colonial ports.

Imperial politics played out on the streets of American cities as traditional rivalries between neighborhood youths and anti-Catholic sentiment suddenly was redirected against alleged parliamentary oppression. In Boston, the "Sons of Liberty" burned in effigy the local stamp distributor, Andrew Oliver, and when that action failed to bring about his resignation, they tore down one of his office buildings. Even after he resigned, the mob nearly demolished the elegant home of Oliver's close associate, Lieutenant Governor Thomas Hutchinson. The violence frightened colonial leaders, yet evidence suggests that they encouraged the lower classes to intimidate royal officials. Popular participation in these protests was an exciting experience for people who had traditionally deferred to their social betters. After 1765, it was impossible for either royal governors or patriot leaders to take for granted the support of ordinary men and women.

By November 1, 1765, stamp distributors in almost every American port had publicly resigned, and without distributors, the hated revenue stamps could not be sold. The courts soon reopened; most newspapers were published. Daily life in the colonies was undisturbed with one exception: The Sons of Liberty persuaded—some said coerced—colonial merchants to boycott British goods until Parliament repealed the Stamp Act. The merchants showed little enthusiasm for such tactics, but the threat of tar and feathers stimulated cooperation.

The boycott movement was in itself a masterful political innovation. Never before had a resistance movement organized itself so centrally around the market decisions of ordinary consumers. The colonists depended on British imports—cloth, metal goods, and ceramics—and each year they imported more consumer goods than they could possibly afford. In this highly charged moral atmosphere, one in which ordinary people talked constantly of conspiracy and corruption, it is not surprising that Americans of different classes and backgrounds advocated a radical change in buying habits. Private acts suddenly became part of the public sphere. Personal excess threatened to contaminate the entire political community. This logic explains the power of an appeal made in a Boston newspaper: "Save your money and you can save your country."

The boycotts mobilized colonial women. They were excluded from voting and civil office, but such legal discrimination did not mean that women were not part of the broader political culture. Since wives and mothers spent their days involved with household chores, they assumed special responsibility to reform consumption, to root out luxury, and to promote frugality. Indeed, in this realm they possessed real power; they monitored the ideological commitment of the entire family. Throughout the colonies, women altered styles of dress, made homespun cloth, and shunned imported items on which Parliament had placed a tax.

Failed Attempts to Save the Empire

What most Americans did not yet know—after all, communication with Britain required months—was that in July, Grenville had fallen from power. This unexpected shift came about not because the king thought Grenville's policies inept, but rather because George did not like the man. His replacement as first lord of the treasury, Lord Rockingham, was young, inexperienced, and terrified of public speaking, a serious handicap to launching a brilliant parliamentary career. The Rockinghamites—as his followers were called—envisioned a prosperous empire founded on an expanding commerce and local government under the gentle guidance of Parliament. Rockingham wanted to repeal the Stamp Act, but because of the shakiness of his own political coalition, he could not announce such a decision until it enjoyed broad national support. He, therefore, urged merchants and manufacturers throughout England to petition Parliament for repeal of the act, claiming that the American boycott would soon drive them into bankruptcy and spark urban riots.

On March 18, 1766, the House of Commons voted 275 to 167 to rescind the Stamp Act.

Lest its retreat on the Stamp Act be interpreted as weakness, the House of Commons passed the Declaratory Act (March 1766), a shrill defense of parliamentary supremacy over the Americans "in all cases whatsoever." The colonists' insistence on no taxation without representation failed to impress British rulers. England's merchants, supposedly America's allies, claimed sole responsibility for the Stamp Act repeal. The colonists had only complicated the task, the merchants lectured, and if the Americans knew what was good for them, they would keep quiet. To George Mason, a leading political figure in Virginia, such advice sounded patronizing. The British merchants seemed to be saying, "We have with infinite difficulty and fatigue got you excused this one time; pray be a good boy for the future, do what your papa and mama bid you, and hasten to return them your most grateful acknowledgements for condescending to let you keep what is your own." This, Mason snapped, was "ridiculous!"

The Stamp Act crisis also eroded the colonists' respect for imperial officeholders in America. Suddenly, these men—royal governors, customs collectors, military personnel—appeared alien, as if their interests were not those of the people over whom they exercised authority. One person who had been forced to resign the post of stamp distributor for South Carolina noted several years later, "The Stamp Act had introduc'd so much Party Rage, Faction, and Debate that the ancient Harmony, Generosity, and Urbanity for which these People were celebrated is destroyed, and at an End." Similar reports came from other colonies, and it is testimony to the Americans' lingering loyalty to the British crown and constitution that rebellion did not occur in 1765.

Fueling the Crisis

Rockingham's ministry soon gave way to a government headed once again by William Pitt, who was now the Earl of Chatham. The aging Pitt suffered horribly from gout, and during his long absences from London, Charles Townshend, his chancellor of the exchequer, made important policy decisions. Townshend was an impetuous man whose mouth often outran his mind. During a parliamentary debate in January 1767, he surprised everyone by blithely announcing that he knew a way to obtain revenue from the Americans.

The members of the House of Commons were so pleased with the news that they promptly voted to lower English land taxes, an action that threatened fiscal chaos.

A budgetary crisis forced Townshend to make good on his extraordinary boast. His scheme turned out to be a grab bag of duties on American imports of paper, glass, paint, lead, and tea, which collectively were known as the Townshend Revenue Acts (June–July 1767). He hoped to generate sufficient funds to pay the salaries of royal governors and other imperial officers, thus freeing them from dependence on the colonial assemblies.

The chancellor recognized that without tough instruments of enforcement, his duties would not produce the promised revenues. Therefore, he created an American Board of Customs Commissioners, a body based in Boston and supported by reorganized vice-admiralty courts located in Boston, Philadelphia,

((•●—[Listen to the Audio File   "The Liberty Song"

The boycott movement drew many colonial women into popular politics. In this 1774 woodcut, a Daughter of Liberty stands ready to resist British oppression.

and Charles Town. And for good measure, Townshend induced Parliament to order the governor of New York to veto all bills passed by that colony's assembly until it supplied resident British troops in accordance with the Quartering Act (May 1765) that required the colonies to house soldiers in barracks, taverns, and vacant buildings and to provide the army with firewood, candles, and beer, among other items. Many Americans regarded this as more taxation without representation, and in New York, at least, colonists refused to pay.

Colonists showed no more willingness to pay Townshend's duties than they had to buy Grenville's stamps. No congress was called; none was necessary. Recent events had taught people how to coordinate protest, and they moved to resist the unconstitutional revenue acts. In major ports, the Sons of Liberty organized boycotts of British goods. Protest often involved what one historian has termed "rituals of nonconsumption." In some large towns, these were moments of public moral reaffirmation. Men and women took oaths before neighbors promising not to purchase certain goods until Parliament repealed unconstitutional taxation. In Boston, ordinary people were encouraged to sign "Subscription Rolls." "The Selectmen strongly recommend this Measure to Persons of *all ranks*," announced the *Boston Gazette*, "as the most honorable and effectual way of giving public Testimony of their Love to their Country, and of endeavouring to save it from ruin."

On February 11, 1768, the Massachusetts House of Representatives drafted a circular letter, a provocative appeal which it sent directly to the other colonial assemblies. The letter requested suggestions on how best to thwart the Townshend Acts; not surprisingly, legislators in other parts of America, busy with local matters, simply ignored this general appeal. But not Lord Hillsborough, England's secretary for American affairs. This rather mild attempt to create a united colonial front struck him as gross treason, and he ordered the Massachusetts representatives to rescind their "seditious paper." After considering Hillsborough's demand, the legislators voted 92 to 17 to defy him.

Suddenly, the circular letter became a cause célèbre. The royal governor of Massachusetts hastily dissolved the House of Representatives. That decision compelled the other colonies to demonstrate their support for Massachusetts. Assembly after assembly now felt obligated to take up the circular letter, an action Hillsborough had specifically forbidden. Assemblies in other colonies were dissolved, creating a much broader crisis of representative government. Throughout America, the number 92 (the number of legislators who voted against Hillsborough) immediately became a symbol of patriotism. In fact, Parliament's challenge had brought about the very results it most wanted to avoid: a foundation for intercolonial communication and a strengthening of conviction among the colonists of the righteousness of their position.

Fatal Show of Force

In October 1768, British rulers made another mistake, one that raised tensions almost to the pitch they had reached during the Stamp Act riots. The issue at the heart of the trouble was the army. In part to save money and in part to intimidate colonial trouble makers, the ministry transferred four thousand regular troops from Nova Scotia and Ireland to Boston. Most of the army had already been withdrawn from the frontier to the seacoast to save revenue, thereby raising more acutely than ever the issue of why troops were in America at all. The armed strangers camped on the Boston Common, and when citizens passed the site, redcoats shouted obscenities. Sometimes, in accordance with martial law, an errant soldier was whipped within an inch of his life, a bloody sight that sickened Boston civilians. To make relations worse, redcoats—men who were ill treated and underpaid—competed in their spare time for jobs with local dockworkers

and artisans. Work was already in short supply, and the streets crackled with tension.

When colonists questioned why the army had been sent to a peaceful city, pamphleteers responded that it was there to further a conspiracy originally conceived by Bute to oppress Americans, to take away their liberties, and to collect illegal revenues. Grenville, Hillsborough, Townshend: They were all, supposedly, part of the plot. Today such rhetoric may sound excessive, but to Americans who had absorbed the political theories of the Commonwealthmen, a pattern of tyranny seemed obvious.

Colonists had no difficulty interpreting the violence that erupted in Boston on March 5, 1770. In the gathering dusk of that afternoon, young boys and street toughs threw rocks and snowballs at soldiers in a small, isolated patrol outside the offices of the hated customs commissioners in King Street. The details of this incident are obscure, but it appears that as the mob grew and became more threatening, the soldiers panicked. In the confusion, the troops fired, leaving five Americans dead.

Pamphleteers promptly labeled the incident a massacre. The victims of this **Boston Massacre** were seen as martyrs and were memorialized in extravagant terms. In one eulogy, Joseph Warren addressed the dead men's widows and children, dramatically re-creating the gruesome scene in King Street. "Behold

📖▶ Read the Document   *Boston Gazette* Description of the Boston Massacre

Outrage over the Boston Massacre was fanned by propaganda, such as this etching by Paul Revere, which showed British redcoats firing on ordinary citizens. In subsequent editions, the blood spurting from the dying Americans became more conspicuous.

thy murdered husband gasping on the ground," Warren cried, ". . . take heed, ye orphan babes, lest, whilst your streaming eyes are fixed upon the ghastly corpse, your feet slide on the stones bespattered with your father's brains." Apparently, to propagandists like Warren, it mattered little that the five civilians had been bachelors! Paul Revere's engraving of the massacre, appropriately splattered with blood, became an instant best-seller. Confronted with such intense reaction and with the possibility of massive armed resistance, Crown officials wisely moved the army to an island in Boston Harbor.

At this critical moment, the king's new first minister restored a measure of tranquility. Lord North, congenial, well-meaning, but not very talented, became chancellor of the exchequer following Townshend's death in 1767. North was appointed the first minister in 1770, and for the next twelve years—indeed, throughout most of the American crisis—he managed to retain his office. His secret formula seems to have been an ability to get along with George III and to build an effective majority in Parliament.

One of North's first recommendations to Parliament was the repeal of the Townshend duties. Not only had these ill-conceived duties unnecessarily angered the colonists, but they also hurt English manufacturers. By taxing British exports such as glass and paint, Parliament had only encouraged the Americans to develop their own industries; thus, without much prodding, the House of Commons dropped all the Townshend duties—with the notable exception of tea. The tax on tea was retained not for revenue purposes, North insisted, but as a reminder that England's rulers still subscribed to the principles of the Declaratory Act. They would not compromise the supremacy of Parliament. In mid-1770, however, the matter of tea seemed trivial to most Americans. The colonists had drawn back from the precipice, a little frightened by the events of the past two years, and desperately hoped to head off future confrontation with the British.

Last Days of Imperial Rule, 1770–1773

For a short while, American colonists and British officials put aside their recent animosities. Like England's rulers, some colonial gentry were beginning to pull back from protest, especially violent confrontation with established authority, in fear that the lower orders were becoming too assertive. It was probably in this period that Loyalist Americans emerged as an identifiable group. Colonial merchants returned to familiar patterns of trade, pleased no doubt to end the local boycotts that had depressed the American economy. British goods flooded into colonial ports; the level of American indebtedness soared to new highs. In this period of apparent reconciliation, the people of Massachusetts—even of Boston—decided they could accept their new governor, Thomas Hutchinson. After all, he was one of their own, an American.

But appearances were deceiving. The bonds of imperial loyalty remained fragile, and even as Lord North attempted to win the colonists' trust, Crown officials in America created new strains. Customs commissioners whom Townshend had appointed to collect his duties remained in the colonies long after his Revenue Acts had been repealed. If they had been honest, unobtrusive administrators, perhaps no one would have taken notice of their behavior. But the customs commissioners

regularly abused their powers of search and seizure and in the process lined their own pockets. In Massachusetts, Rhode Island, and South Carolina—to cite the most notorious cases—these officials drove local citizens to distraction by enforcing the Navigation Acts with such rigor that a small boat could not cross Narragansett Bay with a load of firewood without first obtaining a sheaf of legal documents. One slip, no matter how minor, could bring confiscation of ship and cargo.

The commissioners were not only corrupt; they were also shortsighted. If they had restricted their extortion to the common folk, they might have avoided becoming a major American grievance. But they could not control their greed. Some customs officers harassed the wealthiest, most powerful men around, men such as John Hancock of Boston and Henry Laurens of Charles Town. The commissioners' actions drove some members of the colonial ruling class into opposition to the king's government. When in the summer of 1772 a group of disguised Rhode Islanders burned a customs vessel, the *Gaspee*, Americans cheered. A special royal commission sent to arrest the culprits discovered that not a single Rhode Islander had the slightest idea how the ship could have come to such an end.

Samuel Adams (1722–1803) refused to accept the notion that the repeal of the Townshend duties had secured American liberty. During the early 1770s, while colonial leaders turned to other matters, Adams kept the cause alive with a drumfire of publicity. He reminded the people of Boston that the tax on tea remained in force. He organized public anniversaries commemorating the repeal of the Stamp Act and the Boston Massacre. Adams was a genuine revolutionary, an ideologue filled with a burning sense of indignation at the real and alleged wrongs suffered by his countrymen. To his contemporaries, this man resembled a figure out of New England's Puritan past. He seemed obsessed with the preservation of public virtue. The American goal, he declared, was the creation of a "Christian Sparta," an ideal commonwealth in which vigilant citizens would constantly guard against the spread of corruption, degeneracy, and luxury.

With each new attempt by Parliament to assert its supremacy over the colonists, more and more Bostonians listened to what Adams had to say. He observed ominously that the British intended to use the tea revenue to pay judicial salaries, thus freeing the judges from dependence on the assembly. When in November 1772 Adams suggested the formation of a **committee of correspondence** to communicate grievances to villagers throughout Massachusetts, he received broad support. Americans living in other colonies soon copied his idea. It was a brilliant stroke. Adams developed a structure of political cooperation completely independent of royal government.

The Final Provocation: The Boston Tea Party

In May 1773, Parliament passed the Tea Act, legislation the Americans might have welcomed. After all, it lowered the price for their favorite beverage. Parliament wanted to save one of Britain's largest businesses, the East India Company, from possible bankruptcy. This commercial giant imported Asian tea into England, where it was resold to wholesalers. The tea was also

Read the **Document**   George R.T. Hewes, "A Retrospect on the Boston Tea Party"

Colonists toss chests of tea overboard while disguised as Mohawk Indians in a historic depiction of the Boston Tea Party of December 16, 1773. At right, a bottle of tea leaves preserved from the protest suggests that one participant or onlooker was mindful of the historical importance of the event.

subject to heavy duties. The company tried to pass these charges on to the consumers, but American tea drinkers preferred the cheaper leaves that were smuggled in from Holland.

The Tea Act changed the rules. Parliament not only allowed the company to sell directly to American retailers, thus cutting out intermediaries, but also eliminated the duties paid in England. If all had gone according to plan, the agents of the East India Company in America would have undersold their competitors, including the Dutch smugglers, and with the new profits would have saved the business.

But Parliament's logic was flawed. First, since the tax on tea, collected in American ports, remained in effect, this new act seemed a devious scheme to win popular support for Parliament's right to tax the colonists without representation. Second, the act threatened to undercut powerful colonial merchants who did a good business trading in smuggled Dutch tea. Considering the American reaction, the British government might have been well advised to devise another plan to rescue the ailing company. At Philadelphia, and then at New York City, colonists turned back the tea ships before they could unload.

In Boston, however, the issue was not so easily resolved. Governor Hutchinson, a strong-willed man, would not permit the vessels to return to England. Local patriots would not let them unload. And so, crammed with the East India Company's tea, the ships sat in Boston Harbor waiting for the colonists to make up their minds. On the night of December 16, 1773, they did so in dramatic

style. A group of men disguised as Mohawk Indians boarded the ships and pitched 340 chests of tea worth £10,000 over the side. Whether Samuel Adams organized the famed **Boston Tea Party** is not known. No doubt he and his allies were not taken by surprise. Even at the time, John Adams, Samuel's distant cousin, sensed the event would have far-reaching significance. "This Destruction of the Tea," he scribbled in his diary, "is so bold, so daring, so firm, intrepid, and inflexible, and it must have so important consequences, and so lasting, that I can't but consider it as an epocha in history."

When news of the Tea Party reached London in January 1774, the North ministry was stunned. The people of Boston had treated parliamentary supremacy with utter contempt, and British rulers saw no humor whatsoever in the destruction of private property by subjects of the Crown dressed in costume. To quell such rebelliousness, Parliament passed a series of laws called the **Coercive Acts**. (In America, they were referred to as the Intolerable Acts.) The legislation (1) closed the port of Boston until the city fully compensated the East India Company for the lost tea; (2) restructured the Massachusetts government by transforming the upper house from an elective to an appointed body and restricting the number of legal town meetings to one a year; (3) allowed the royal governor to transfer British officials arrested for offenses committed in the line of duty to England, where there was little likelihood they would be convicted; and (4) authorized the army to quarter troops wherever they were needed, even if this required the compulsory requisition of uninhabited private buildings. George III enthusiastically supported this tough policy; he appointed

CHRONICLE OF COLONIAL—BRITISH TENSION

Legislation	Date	Provisions	Colonial Reaction
Sugar Act	April 5, 1764	Revised duties on sugar, coffee, tea, wine, other imports; expanded jurisdiction of vice-admiralty courts	Several assemblies protest taxation for revenue
Stamp Act	March 22, 1765; repealed March 18, 1766	Printed documents (deeds, newspapers, marriage licenses, etc.) issued only on special stamped paper purchased from stamp distributors	Riots in cities; collectors forced to resign; Stamp Act Congress (October 1765)
Quartering Act	May 1765	Colonists must supply British troops with housing, other items (candles, firewood, etc.)	Protest in assemblies; New York Assembly punished for failure to comply, 1767
Declaratory Act	March 18, 1766	Parliament declares its sovereignty over the colonies "in all cases whatsoever"	Ignored in celebration over repeal of the Stamp Act
Townshend Revenue Acts	June 26, 29, July 2, 1767; all repealed—except duty on tea, March 1770	New duties on glass, lead, paper, paints, tea; customs collections tightened in America	Nonimportation of British goods; assemblies protest; newspapers attack British policy
Tea Act	May 10, 1773	Parliament gives East India Company right to sell tea directly to Americans; some duties on tea reduced	Protests against favoritism shown to monopolistic company; tea destroyed in Boston (December 16, 1773)
Coercive Acts (Intolerable Acts)	March–June 1774	Closes port of Boston; restructures Massachusetts government; restricts town meetings; troops quartered in Boston; British officials accused of crimes sent to England or Canada for trial	Boycott of British goods; First Continental Congress convenes (September 1774)
Prohibitory Act	December 22, 1775	Declares British intention to coerce Americans into submission; embargo on American goods; American ships seized	Drives Continental Congress closer to decision for independence

General Thomas Gage to serve as the colony's new royal governor. Gage apparently won the king's favor by announcing that in America, "Nothing can be done but by forcible means."

The sweeping denial of constitutional liberties confirmed the colonists' worst fears. To men like Samuel Adams, it seemed as if Britain really intended to enslave the American people. Colonial moderates found their position shaken by the vindictiveness of the Coercive Acts. Edmund Burke, one of America's last friends in Parliament, noted sadly on the floor of Commons, that "This is the day, then, that you wish to go to war with all America, in order to conciliate that country to this."

If in 1774 the House of Commons thought it could isolate Boston from the rest of America, it was in for a rude surprise. Colonists living in other parts of the continent recognized immediately that the principles at stake in Boston affected all Americans. As one Virginian explained, "There were no Heats and Troubles in Virginia till the Blockade of Boston." Few persons advocated independence, but they could not remain passive while Boston was destroyed. They sent food and money and, during the fall of 1774, reflected more deeply than ever on what it meant to be a colonist in the British empire.

The sticking point remained—as it had been in 1765—the sovereignty of Parliament. No one in Britain could think of a way around this constitutional impasse. In 1773, Benjamin Franklin had offered a suggestion. "The Parliament," he observed, "has no right to make any law whatever, binding on the colonies . . . the king, and not the king, lords, and commons collectively, is their sovereign." But so long as it still seemed possible to coerce the Americans into obedience, to punish these errant children, Britain's rulers had little incentive to accept such a humiliating compromise.

Steps Toward Independence

What events in 1775 and 1776 led to the colonists' decision to declare independence?

During the summer of 1774, committees of correspondence analyzed the perilous situation in whic h the colonists found themselves. Something, of course, had to be done. But what? Would the Southern Colonies support resistance in New England? Would Pennsylvanians stand up to Parliament? Not surprisingly, the committees endorsed a call for a Continental Congress, a gathering of fifty-five elected delegates from twelve colonies (Georgia sent none but agreed to support the action taken). This **First Continental Congress** convened in Philadelphia on September 5. It included some of America's most articulate, respected leaders; among them were John Adams, Samuel Adams, Patrick Henry, Richard Henry Lee, Christopher Gadsden, and George Washington.

The delegates were strangers to one another. They knew little about the customs and values, the geography and economy of Britain's other provinces. As John Adams explained on September 18, "It has taken Us much Time to get acquainted with the Tempers, Views, Characters, and Designs of Persons and to let them into the Circumstances of our Province." During the early sessions of the Congress, the delegates eyed each other closely, trying to gain a sense of the strength and integrity of the men with whom they might commit treason.

Differences of opinion soon surfaced. Delegates from the Middle Colonies—Joseph Galloway of Pennsylvania, for example—wanted to proceed with caution, but Samuel Adams and other more radical members pushed the moderates toward confrontation. Boston's master politician engineered congressional commendation of the Suffolk Resolves, a bold statement drawn up in Suffolk County, Massachusetts, that encouraged forcible resistance of the Coercive Acts.

After this decision, the tone of the meeting was established. Moderate spokesmen introduced conciliatory measures, which received polite discussion but failed to win a majority vote. Just before returning to their homes (September 1774), the delegates created the "Association," an intercolonial agreement to halt all commerce with Britain until Parliament repealed the Intolerable Acts. This was a totally revolutionary decision. The Association authorized a vast network of local committees to enforce nonimportation. Violators were exposed, shamed, forced either to apologize publicly for their actions or to be shunned by all their patriot neighbors. In many of the communities, the committees were the government, distinguishing, in the words of James Madison, "Friends from Foes." George III sneered at these activities. "I am not sorry," he confided, "that the line of conduct seems now chalked out . . . the New England Governments are in a state of Rebellion, blows must decide whether they are to be subject to this country or independent."

Shots Heard Around the World

The king was correct. Before Congress reconvened, "blows" fell at Lexington and Concord, two small farm villages in eastern Massachusetts. On the evening of April 18, 1775, General Gage dispatched troops from Boston to seize rebel supplies. Paul Revere, a renowned silversmith and active patriot, warned the colonists that the redcoats were coming. The militia of Lexington, a collection of ill-trained farmers, boys as well as old men, decided to stand on the village green on the following morning, April 19, as the British soldiers passed on the road to Concord. No one planned to fight, but in a moment of confusion, someone (probably a colonist) fired; the redcoats discharged a volley, and eight Americans lay dead.

Word of the incident spread rapidly, and by the time the British force reached its destination, the countryside swarmed with "minutemen," special companies of Massachusetts militia prepared to respond instantly to military emergencies. The redcoats found nothing of significance in Concord and so returned. The long march back to Boston turned into a rout. Lord Percy, a British officer who brought up reinforcements, remarked more in surprise than bitterness that "whoever looks upon them [the American soldiers] as an irregular mob, will find himself much mistaken." On June 17, colonial militiamen again held their own against seasoned troops at the battle of Bunker Hill (actually Breed's Hill). The British finally took the hill, but after this costly "victory" in which he suffered 40 percent casualties, Gage complained that the Americans had displayed "a conduct and spirit against us, they never showed against the French."

Beginning "The World Over Again"

Members of the **Second Continental Congress** gathered in Philadelphia in May 1775. They faced an awesome responsibility. British government in the mainland colonies had almost ceased to function, and with Americans fighting redcoats, the country desperately needed strong central leadership. Slowly, often reluctantly, Congress took control of the war. The delegates formed a Continental Army and appointed George Washington its commander, in part because he seemed to have greater military experience than anyone else available and in part because he looked like he should be commander in chief. The delegates were also eager to select someone who did not come from Massachusetts, a colony that seemed already to possess too much power in national councils. The members of Congress purchased military supplies and, to pay for them, issued paper money. But while they were assuming the powers of a sovereign government, the congressmen refused to declare independence. They debated and fretted, listened to the appeals of moderates who played on the colonists' remaining loyalty to Britain, and then did nothing.

The British government appeared intent on transforming colonial moderates into angry rebels. In December 1775, Parliament passed the Prohibitory Act, declaring war on American commerce. Until the colonists begged for pardon, they could not trade with the rest of the world. The British navy blockaded their ports and seized American ships on the high seas. Lord North also hired German mercenaries (the Russians drove too hard a bargain) to put down the rebellion. And in America, Virginia's royal governor Lord Dunmore further undermined the possibility of reconciliation by urging the colony's slaves to take up arms against their masters. Few did so, but the effort to stir up black rebellion infuriated the Virginia gentry.

Thomas Paine (1737–1809) pushed the colonists even closer to independence. Nothing in this man's background suggested he would write the most important pamphlet in American history. In England, Paine had tried and failed in a number of jobs, and exactly why he elected to move to America in 1774 is not clear. While still in England, Paine had the good fortune to meet Benjamin Franklin, who presented him with letters of introduction to the leading patriots of Pennsylvania. At the urging of his new American friends, Paine produced **Common Sense**, an essay that became an instant best-seller. In only three months, it sold more than 120,000 copies.

Common Sense systematically stripped kingship of historical and theological justification. For centuries, the English had maintained the fiction that the monarch could do no wrong. When the government oppressed the people, the royal counselors received the blame. The Crown was above suspicion. To this, Paine cried nonsense. Monarchs ruled by force. George III was simply a "royal brute," who by his arbitrary behavior had surrendered his claim to the colonists' obedience. The pamphlet also attacked the whole idea of a mixed and balanced constitution. Indeed, *Common Sense* was a powerful democratic manifesto.

Paine's greatest contribution to the revolutionary cause was persuading ordinary folk to sever their ties with Great Britain. It was not reasonable, he argued, to regard England as the mother country. "Europe, and not England," he explained, "is the parent country of America. This new world hath been the asylum for the persecuted lovers of civil and religious liberty from every part of Europe." No doubt that message made a deep impression on Pennsylvania's German population. The time had come for the colonists to form an independent republic. "We have it in our power," Paine wrote in one of his most moving statements, "to begin the world over again . . . the birthday of a new world is at hand."

On July 2, 1776, after a long and tedious debate, Congress finally voted for independence. The motion passed: twelve states for, none against (with New York abstaining). Thomas Jefferson, a young Virginia lawyer and planter who enjoyed a reputation as a graceful writer, drafted a formal declaration that was accepted with alterations two days later. Much of the Declaration of Independence consisted of a list of specific grievances against George III and his government. Like the skilled lawyer he was, Jefferson presented the evidence for independence. The document did not become famous for those passages. Long after the establishment of the new republic, the Declaration challenged Americans to make good on the principle that "all men are created equal." John Adams nicely expressed the patriots' fervor when he wrote on July 3, "Yesterday the greatest question was decided, which ever was debated in America, and a greater perhaps, never was or will be decided among men."

Many revolutionary leaders throughout the modern world—in Europe as in Asia—have echoed Adams's assessment. Of all the documents written during this period, including the Constitution, the Declaration of Independence remains the most powerful and radical invitation to Americans of all backgrounds to demand their equality and full rights as human beings.

Read the Document   Thomas Paine, A Freelance Writer Urges His Readers to Use Common Sense

The message of Thomas Paine's pamphlet *Common Sense* (title page shown) was clear and direct. Paine's powerful argument called for "The Free and Independent States of America." He assured ordinary Americans not only that they could live without a king, but also that they would win the war.

Watch the Video   The American Revolution As Different Americans Saw It

Congress Voting Independence, oil painting by Robert Edge Pine and Edward Savage, 1785. The committee appointed by Congress to draft a declaration of independence included (center, standing) John Adams, Roger Sherman, Robert Livingston, Thomas Jefferson, and (center foreground, seated) Benjamin Franklin. The committee members are shown submitting Jefferson's draft to the speaker.

Fighting for Independence

Why did it take eight years of warfare for the Americans to gain independence?

Only fools and visionaries expressed optimism about America's prospects of winning independence in 1776. The Americans had taken on a formidable military power. The population of Britain was perhaps four times that of its former colonies. England also possessed a strong manufacturing base, a well-trained regular army supplemented by thousands of hired German troops (Hessians), and a navy that dominated the world's oceans. Many British officers had battlefield experience. They already knew what the Americans would slowly learn: Waging war requires discipline, money, and sacrifice.

As later events demonstrated, however, Britain had become involved in an impossible military situation, in some ways analogous to that in which the United States would find itself in Vietnam some two hundred years later. Three separate elements neutralized advantages held by the larger power over its adversary. First, the British had to transport men and supplies across the Atlantic, a logistic challenge of unprecedented complexity. Unreliable lines of communication broke down under the strain of war.

Second, America was too vast to be conquered by conventional military methods. Redcoats might gain control over the major port cities, but as long as the Continental Army remained intact, the rebellion continued. As Washington explained, "the possession of our Towns, while we have an Army in the field, will avail them little . . . It is our Arms, not defenceless Towns, they have to subdue." Even if England had recruited enough soldiers to occupy the entire country, it would still have lost the war. As one Loyalist instructed the king, "if all America becomes a garrison, she is not worth your attention." Britain could only win by crushing the American will to resist.

And third, British strategists never appreciated the depth of the Americans' commitment to a political ideology. In the wars of eighteenth-century Europe, such beliefs had seldom mattered. European troops before the French Revolution served because they were paid or because the military was a vocation, but most certainly not because they hoped to advance a set of constitutional principles. Americans were different. To be sure, some young men were drawn to the military by bounty money or by the desire to escape unhappy families. A few were drafted. But taking such people into account, one still encounters among the American troops a remarkable commitment to republican ideals. One French officer reported from the United

States, "It is incredible that soldiers composed of men of every age, even of children of fifteen, of whites and blacks, almost naked, unpaid, and rather poorly fed, can march so well and withstand fire so steadfastly."

Building a Professional Army

During the earliest months of rebellion, American soldiers—especially those of New England—suffered no lack of confidence. Indeed, they interpreted their courageous stands at Concord and Bunker Hill as evidence that brave yeomen farmers could lick British regulars on any battlefield. George Washington spent the first years of the war disabusing the colonists of this foolishness, for as he had learned during the French and Indian War, military success depended on endless drill, careful planning, and tough discipline—rigorous preparation that did not characterize the minutemen's methods.

Washington insisted on organizing a regular well-trained field army. Some advisers urged the commander in chief to wage a guerrilla war, one in which small partisan bands would sap Britain's will to rule Americans. But Washington rejected that course. He recognized that the Continental Army served not only as a fighting force but also as a symbol of the republican cause. Its very existence would sustain American hopes, and so long as the army survived, American agents could plausibly solicit foreign aid. This thinking shaped Washington's wartime strategy; he studiously avoided "general actions" in which the Continental Army might be destroyed. Critics complained about Washington's caution, but as they soon discovered, he understood better than they what independence required.

If the commander in chief was correct about the army, however, he failed to comprehend the political importance of the militia. These scattered, almost amateur, military units seldom altered the outcome of battle, but they did maintain control over large areas of the country not directly affected by the British army. Throughout the war, they compelled men and women who would rather have remained neutral to actively support the American effort. In 1777, for example, the militia of Farmington, Connecticut, visited a group of suspected Tories, as **Loyalists** (people who sided with the king and Parliament during the Revolution) were called, and after "educating" these people in the fundamentals of republican ideology, a militia spokesman announced, "They were indeed grossly ignorant of the true grounds of the present war with Great Britain . . . [but] They appeared to be penitent of their former conduct, [and] professed themselves convinced . . . that there was no such thing as remaining neuters." Without local political coercion, Washington's task would have been considerably more difficult.

For the half million African American colonists, most of them slaves, the fight for independence took on special poignancy. After all, they wanted to achieve personal as well as political freedom, and many African Americans supported those who seemed most likely to deliver them from bondage. As one historian explained, "The black soldier was likely to join the side that made him the quickest and best offer in terms of those 'unalienable rights' of which Mr. Jefferson had spoken." It is estimated that some five thousand African Americans took up arms to fight against the British. The Continental Army included two all-black units, one from Massachusetts and the other from Rhode Island. In 1778, the legislature of Rhode Island voted to free any slave who volunteered to serve, since, according to the lawmakers, history taught that "the wisest, the freest, and bravest nations . . . liberated their slaves, and enlisted them as soldiers to fight in defence of their country." In the South, especially in Georgia and South Carolina, more than ten thousand African Americans supported the British, and after the patriots had won the war, these men and women left the United States, relocating to Nova Scotia, Florida, and Jamaica, with some eventually resettling in Africa.

Testing the American Will

After the embarrassing defeats in Massachusetts, the king appointed General Sir William Howe to replace the ill-fated Gage. British rulers now understood that a simple police action would not be sufficient to crush the American rebellion. Parliament authorized sending more than fifty thousand troops to the mainland colonies, and after evacuating Boston—an untenable strategic position—the British forces stormed ashore at Staten Island in New York Harbor on July 3, 1776. From this more central location, Howe believed he could cut the New Englanders off from the rest of America. He enjoyed the powerful support of the British navy under the command of his brother, Admiral Lord Richard Howe.

When Washington learned the British were planning to occupy New York City, he transferred many of his inexperienced soldiers to Long Island, where they suffered a major defeat (August 27, 1776). In a series of engagements disastrous for the Americans, Howe drove the Continental Army across the Hudson River into New Jersey. Because of his failure to take full advantage of the situation, however, General Howe lost what seemed in retrospect an excellent opportunity to annihilate Washington's entire army. Nevertheless, the Americans were on the run, and in the fall of 1776, contemporaries predicted the rebels would soon capitulate.

"Times That Try Men's Souls"

Swift victories in New York and New Jersey persuaded General Howe that few Americans enthusiastically supported independence. He issued a general pardon, therefore, to anyone who would swear allegiance to George III. The results were encouraging. More than three thousand men and women who lived in areas occupied by the British army took the oath. This group included one intimidated signer of the Declaration of Independence. Howe perceived that a lasting peace in America would require his troops to treat "our enemies as if they might one day become our friends." A member of Lord North's cabinet grumbled that this was "a sentimental manner of making war," a shortsighted view considering England's experience in attempting to pacify the Irish. The pardon plan eventually failed not because Howe lacked toughness but because his soldiers and officers regarded loyal Americans as inferior provincials, an attitude that did little to promote good relations. In any case, as soon as the redcoats left a pardoned region, the rebel militia retaliated against those who had deserted the patriot cause.

In December 1776, Washington's bedraggled army retreated across the Delaware River into Pennsylvania. American prospects appeared bleaker than at any other time during the war. The Continental Army lacked basic supplies, and many men who had signed up for short-term enlistments prepared to go home. "These are the times that try men's souls," Paine wrote in a pamphlet titled *American Crisis*. "The summer soldier and the sunshine patriot will, in this crisis, shrink from the service of their

View the Map The American Revolution

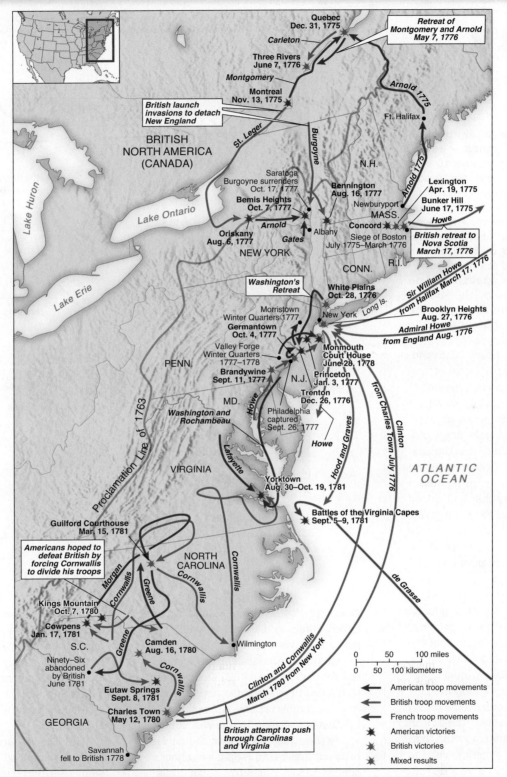

THE AMERICAN REVOLUTION, 1775–1781 The War for Independence ranged over a huge area. Battles were fought in the colonies, on the western frontier, and along the Gulf of Mexico. The major engagements of the first years of the war, from the spontaneous rising at Concord in 1775 to Washington's well-coordinated attack on Trenton in December 1776, were fought in the Northern Colonies. In the middle theater of war, Burgoyne's attempt in 1777 to cut off New England from the rest of the colonies failed when his army was defeated at Saratoga. Action in the final years of the war, from the battles at Camden, Kings Mountain, Cowpens, and Guilford Courthouse to the final victory at Yorktown, occurred in the southern theater of war.

Feature Essay

Spain's Contribution to American Independence

Spain made a significant, although much under-appreciated contribution to the winning of American independence. The decision to support American resistance against Great Britain came in 1779. After an American army had won a stunning victory at the Battle of Saratoga in 1778, Spain joined its ally France in a global contest against Britain that stretched from the banks of the Mississippi River to the islands of the Caribbean and the Straits of Gibraltar.

Spain had little interest in advancing the revolutionary principles of "life, liberty, and the pursuit of happiness." After all, as a traditional monarchy, it was not enthusiastic about championing a radical cause associated with popular rights. Rather, the declaration of war against Britain reflected Spain's desire for revenge against a long-standing enemy that had seized Gibraltar in 1713 and Florida in 1763. Sensing that British military forces around the world were stretched too thin, Spain and France prepared for a conflict designed to regain lost possessions and restore imperial glory.

British leaders appreciated immediately the seriousness of the danger. They knew that it was one thing to fight the insurgent armies of George Washington, quite another to take on two major European powers. Confronting the new threat, Lord George Germain, the British secretary of state, assured the British people that his government would "pursue the war in North America with the utmost vigor." He faced a very difficult

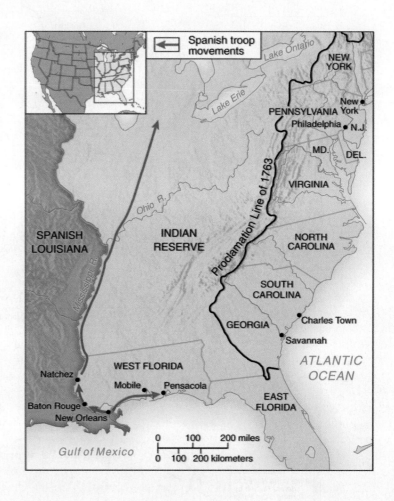

challenge. War with France and Spain forced Britain to reallocate key military resources in ways that took pressure off the struggling American army. Germain ordered half of the 16,000 troops then occupying Philadelphia diverted to other vulnerable regions. Approximately 5,000 were transferred to the West Indies where they guarded against the possibility of French and Spanish attacks against Britain's lucrative sugar trade.

Another 3,000 were posted in Florida, Spain's former colony. In fact, worried that French and Spanish warships might attack vital supply lines, British leaders finally abandoned Philadelphia altogether, a move that allowed Washington to retake the city without having to fire a shot.

Anxious to recapture Florida, the Spanish launched a bold campaign against British forts located along the coast of the Gulf of Mexico. Their success owed a lot to the energy and courage of Bernardo de Gálvez, the Spanish Governor of Louisiana. Before taking this post, he had compiled an impressive military record, having fought against Spain's enemies in Africa and the borderlands of northern Mexico. In fact, he received the governorship of Louisiana as a reward for his extraordinary service.

Gálvez was determined to restore Spain's honor in North America. As he announced, "The king [of Spain] has determined that the principal object of his arms in America during the present war will be to drive [the British] from the Mexican Gulf and the neighborhood of Louisiana." Even before Spain had officially entered the war, Gálvez began sending vital military supplies from St. Louis—then governed by Spain—to American forces operating in the West. These materials helped George Rogers Clark win a string of strategic victories against British forces in the Illinois Territory in 1778. If Clark had failed, the United States could not have creditably claimed all the land east of the Mississippi River during the peace negotiations with Great Britain that ended the Revolution. In 1779, Gálvez moved decisively to drive the British from the region north of New Orleans, and in quick succession, he captured Manchac, Natchez, and Baton Rouge.

Gálvez then turned his attention to regaining Florida. The first obstacle was Mobile. In March 1780, after a two-week siege, the British garrison surrendered to Gálvez's troops. Pensacola presented a much greater military challenge. It served as Britain's administrative and commercial center for West Florida. Moreover, it was well defended. Gálvez's courage and amazing luck allowed the Spanish to carry the day. A Spanish fleet sailing out of Cuba joined ships transporting Gálvez's soldiers in the waters off Pensacola. The admiral of the Cuban fleet was reluctant to enter the port. He feared that his vessels might run aground on sandbars. Gálvez would have none of it. He sailed his own ship boldly into the harbor, and inspired by his example, the captains of the other ships followed his lead. In March 1781, they landed over 7,000 soldiers. The Battle of Pensacola was hard fought. The Spanish siege lasted for over two months, and just as their ammunition was running out, a lucky shot hit the British powder magazine setting off a huge explosion that destroyed much of the fort. The British force—an army made up of British regulars, Native Americans, and American Loyalists—surrendered on May 10.

Gálvez's successful campaign had a major impact on the final year of the American Revolution. The growing military presence of Spain and France in the West Indies compelled the British to station troops in the area that could have been employed against the Continental Army in Yorktown and New York. Moreover, the fall of West Florida made it harder for the British to supply their soldiers and Indian allies operating in the Southern mainland colonies.

Although Spain was unable to retake Gibraltar, Gálvez realized his goal of reclaiming Florida. He had overcome the humiliation of Spain's previous defeats. In 1783 the Spanish Crown invited him to serve on the committee that would draw up the Peace of Paris ending the American Revolution. Even at this moment of triumph, though, Spain refused to recognize the sovereignty of the United States.

It was not long before Spain had second thoughts about its victory over Great Britain. An aggressive new enemy appeared. Every year brought a flood of American settlers into Florida and the Mississippi Valley. They showed not the slightest respect for Spanish authority. In 1787 the Spanish Governor of Florida reported that the American backwoodsmen were "distinguished from savages only in their color, language, and the superiority of their depraved cunning and untrustworthiness." He believed the frontiersmen migrated to Florida "to escape all legal authority." Another Spanish official warned, "A new and independent power has arisen on our continent." He was correct. In 1819 Spain was forced to transfer Florida to the United States.

QUESTIONS FOR DISCUSSION

1. Why did Spain decide to enter the Revolutionary War?

2. Why did the Spanish government have misgivings about American independence?

country, but he that stands it *now* deserves . . . love and thanks . . . ." Before winter, Washington determined to attempt one last desperate stroke.

Howe played into Washington's hands. The British forces were dispersed in small garrisons across the state of New Jersey, and while the Americans could not possibly have defeated the combined British army, they did possess the capacity—with luck—to capture an exposed post. On the night of December 25, Continental soldiers slipped over the ice-filled Delaware River and at Trenton took nine hundred sleeping Hessian mercenaries by complete surprise.

Cheered by success, Washington returned a second time to Trenton, but on this occasion the Continental Army was not so fortunate. A large British force under Lord Cornwallis trapped the Americans. Instead of standing and fighting—really an impossible challenge—Washington secretly, by night, marched his little army around Cornwallis's left flank. On January 3, 1777, the Americans surprised a British garrison at Princeton. Washington then went into winter quarters. The British, fearful of losing more outposts, consolidated their troops, thus leaving much of the state in the hands of the patriot militia.

Victory in a Year of Defeat

In 1777, England's chief military strategist, Lord George Germain, still perceived the war in conventional European terms. A large field army would somehow maneuver Washington's Continental troops into a decisive battle in which the British would enjoy a clear advantage. Complete victory over the Americans certainly seemed within England's grasp. Unfortunately for the men who advocated this plan, the Continental forces proved extremely elusive, and while one British army vainly tried to corner Washington in Pennsylvania, another was forced to surrender in the forests of upstate New York.

In the summer of 1777, General John Burgoyne, a dashing though overbearing officer, descended from Canada with a force of more than seven thousand troops. They intended to clear the Hudson Valley of rebel resistance; join Howe's army, which was to come up to Albany; and thereby cut New England off from the other states. Burgoyne fought in a grand style. Accompanied by a German band, thirty carts filled with the general's liquor and belongings, and two thousand dependents and camp followers, the British set out to thrash the Americans. The campaign was a disaster. Military units, mostly from New England, cut the enemy force apart in the deep woods north of Albany. At the battle of Bennington (August 16), the New Hampshire militia under Brigadier General John Stark overwhelmed a thousand German mercenaries. After this setback, Burgoyne's forces struggled forward, desperately hoping that Howe would rush to their rescue, but when it became clear that their situation at Saratoga was hopeless, the haughty Burgoyne was forced to surrender fifty-eight hundred men to the American General Horatio Gates (October 17).

Soon after Burgoyne left Canada, General Howe unexpectedly decided to move his main army from New York City to Philadelphia. Exactly what he hoped to achieve was not clear, even to Britain's rulers, and of course, when Burgoyne called for assistance, Howe was sitting in the new nation's capital still trying to devise a way to destroy the Continental Army. Howe's campaign began in late July.

The British forces sailed to the head of the Chesapeake Bay and then marched north to Philadelphia. Washington's troops obstructed the enemy's progress, first at Brandywine Creek (September 11) and then at Paoli (September 20), but the outnumbered Americans could not stop the British from entering Philadelphia.

Anxious lest these defeats discourage Congress and the American people, Washington attempted one last battle before the onset of winter. In an engagement at Germantown (October 4), the Americans launched a major counterattack on a fog-covered battlefield, but just at the moment when success seemed assured, they broke off the fight. "When every thing gave the most flattering hopes of victory," Washington complained, "the troops began suddenly to retreat." Bad luck, confusion, and incompetence contributed to the failure. A discouraged Continental Army dug in at Valley Forge, twenty miles outside of Philadelphia, where camp diseases took twenty-five hundred American lives. In their misery, few American soldiers realized their situation was not nearly as desperate as it had been in 1776.

The French Alliance

Even before the Americans declared their independence, agents of the government of Louis XVI began to explore ways to aid the colonists, not so much because the French monarchy favored the republican cause but because it hoped to embarrass the English. The French deeply resented the defeat they had sustained during the Seven Years' War. During the early months of the Revolution, the French covertly sent tons of essential military supplies to the Americans. The negotiations for these arms involved secret agents and fictitious trading companies, the type of clandestine operation more typical of modern times than of the eighteenth century. But when American representatives, Benjamin Franklin for one, pleaded for official recognition of American independence or for outright military alliance, the French advised patience. The international stakes were too great for the king to openly back a cause that had little chance of success.

The American victory at Saratoga convinced the French that the rebels had formidable forces and were serious in their resolve. Indeed, Lord North drew the same conclusion. When news of Saratoga reached London, North muttered, "This damned war." In private conversation, he expressed doubts about England's ability to win the contest, knowing the French would soon enter the fray.

In Paris, Franklin performed brilliantly. In meetings with French officials, he hinted that the Americans might accept a British peace initiative. If the French wanted the war to continue, if they really wanted to embarrass their old rival, then they had to do what the English refused: formally recognize the independence of the United States.

The stratagem paid off handsomely. On February 6, 1778, the French presented American representatives with two separate treaties. The first, called the Treaty of Amity and Commerce, established commercial relations between France and the United States. It tacitly accepted the existence of a new, independent republic. The Treaty of Alliance was even more generous, considering America's obvious military and economic weaknesses. In the event that France and England went to war (they did so on June 14, as everyone expected), the French agreed to reject "either Truce or Peace with Great Britain . . . until the independence of the United States shall have been formally or tacitly assured by the Treaty or Treaties that shall terminate the War." Even more amazing, France surrendered its claim to all territories formerly owned by Great Britain east of the Mississippi River. The Americans pledged they would not sign a separate peace with Britain without first informing their new ally. And in return, France made no claim to Canada, asking only for the right to take possession of certain British islands in the Caribbean. Never had Franklin worked his magic to greater effect.

French intervention instantly transformed British military strategy. What had been a colonial rebellion suddenly became a world conflict, a continuation of the great wars for empire of the late seventeenth century (see Chapter 4). Scarce military resources, especially newer fighting ships, had to be diverted from the American theater to guard the English Channel. In fact, there was talk in London of a possible French invasion. Although the threat of such an assault was not very great until 1779, the British did have cause for concern. The French navy posed a serious challenge to the overextended British fleet. By concentrating their warships in a specific area, the French could hold off or even defeat British squadrons, an advantage that would figure significantly in the American victory at **Yorktown**.

The Final Campaign

British General Henry Clinton replaced Howe, who resigned after the battle of Saratoga. Clinton was a strangely complex individual. As a subordinate officer, he had impressed his superiors as imaginative but easily provoked to anger. When he took command of the British army, his resolute self-confidence suddenly dissolved. Perhaps he feared failure. Whatever the explanation for his vacillation, Clinton's record in America was little better than Howe's or Gage's.

Military strategists calculated that Britain's last chance of winning the war lay in the Southern Colonies, a region largely untouched in the early years of fighting. Intelligence reports reaching London indicated that Georgia and South Carolina contained a sizable body of Loyalists, men who would take up arms for the crown if only they received support and encouragement from the regular army. The southern strategy devised by Germain and Clinton in 1779 turned the war into a bitter guerrilla conflict, and during the last months of battle, British officers worried that their search for an easy victory had inadvertently opened a Pandora's box of uncontrollable partisan furies.

The southern campaign opened in the spring of 1780. Savannah had already fallen, and Clinton reckoned that if the British could take Charles Town, they would be able to control the entire South. A large fleet carrying nearly eight thousand redcoats reached South Carolina in February. Complacent Americans had allowed the city's fortifications to decay, and in a desperate, last-minute effort to preserve Charles Town, General Benjamin Lincoln's forces dug trenches and reinforced walls, but to no avail. Clinton and his second in command, General Cornwallis, gradually encircled the city, and on May 12, Lincoln surrendered an American army of almost six thousand men.

The defeat took Congress by surprise, and without making proper preparations, it dispatched a second army to South Carolina under Horatio Gates, the hero of Saratoga. He too failed. At Camden, Cornwallis outmaneuvered the raw American recruits, capturing or killing 750 during the course of battle (August 16). Poor Gates galloped from the scene and did not stop until he reached Hillsboro, North Carolina, two hundred miles away.

MAJOR BATTLES OF THE AMERICAN REVOLUTION

Battle	Date	Victor
Lexington	Apr. 19, 1775	British
Concord	Apr. 19, 1775	Americans
Bunker Hill	Jun. 17, 1775	Mixed Results
Montreal	Nov. 13, 1775	Americans
Quebec	Dec. 31, 1775	British
Brooklyn Heights	Aug. 27, 1776	British
White Plains	Oct. 28, 1776	British
Trenton	Dec. 26, 1776	Americans
Princeton	Jan. 3, 1777	Americans
Bennington	Aug. 16, 1777	Americans
Brandywine	Sept. 11, 1777	British
Saratoga, First Battle: Freeman's Farm	Sept. 19, 1777	Mixed Results
Philadelphia Captured	Sept. 26, 1777	British
Germantown	Oct 4, 1777	British
Saratoga, Second Battle: Bemis Heights	Oct. 7, 1777	Americans
Charles Town	May 12, 1780	British
Camden	Aug. 16, 1780	British
Kings Mountain	Oct. 7, 1780	Americans
Cowpens	Jan. 17, 1781	Americans
Guilford Courthouse	Mar. 15, 1781	British
Yorktown	Aug. 30- Oct. 18, 1781	Americans and French

Even at this early stage of the southern campaign, the dangers of partisan warfare had become evident. Tory raiders showed little interest in serving as regular soldiers in Cornwallis's army. They preferred night riding, indiscriminate plundering or murdering of neighbors against whom they harbored ancient grudges. The British had unleashed a horde of banditti across South Carolina. Men who genuinely supported independence or who had merely fallen victim to Loyalist guerrillas bided their time. They retreated westward, waiting for their enemies to make a mistake. Their chance came on October 7 at King's Mountain, North Carolina. In the most vicious fighting of the Revolution, the backwoodsmen decimated a force of British regulars and Tory raiders who had strayed too far from base. One witness reported that when a British officer tried to surrender, he was summarily shot down by at least seven American soldiers.

Cornwallis, badly confused and poorly supplied, squandered his strength chasing American forces across the Carolinas. Congress sent General Nathanael Greene to the South with a new army. This young Rhode Islander was the most capable general on Washington's staff. Greene joined Daniel Morgan, leader of the famed Virginia Riflemen, and in a series of tactically brilliant engagements, they sapped the strength of Cornwallis's army, first at Cowpens, South Carolina (January 17, 1781), and later at Guilford Courthouse, North Carolina (March 15). Clinton fumed in New York City. In his estimation, the inept Cornwallis had left "two valuable colonies

The Loyalist Dilemma

Why did so many Loyalists decide to leave the United States during the Revolution?

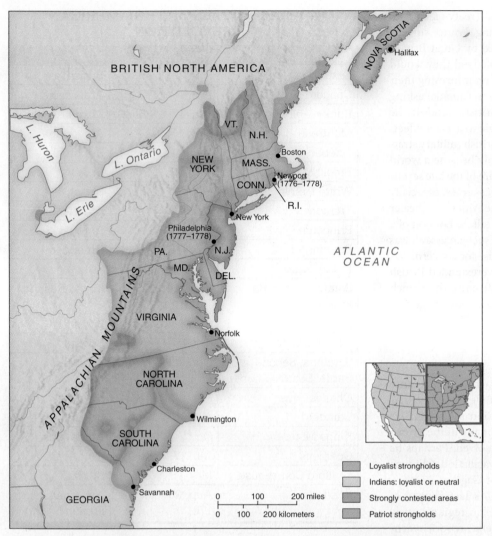

LOYALIST STRONGHOLDS The highest concentrations of Loyalists were in the colonies of New York, North Carolina, South Carolina, and Georgia, especially in the areas around port cities such as New York City, Wilmington, Charleston, and Savannah.

No one knows for certain how many Americans actually supported the Crown during the Revolution. Some Loyalists undoubtedly kept silent and avoided making a public commitment that might have led to banishment or loss of property. But for many persons, neutrality proved impossible. Almost one hundred thousand men and women permanently left America. While a number of these exiles had served as imperial office holders—Thomas Hutchinson, for example—in the main, they came from all ranks and backgrounds. A large number of humble farmers, more than thirty thousand, resettled in Canada. Others relocated to England, the West Indies, or Africa.

The political ideology of the Loyalists was not substantially different from that of their opponents. Like other Americans, they believed that men and women were entitled to life, liberty, and the pursuit of happiness. The Loyalists were also convinced that independence would destroy those values by promoting disorder. By turning their backs on Britain, a source of tradition and stability, the rebels seemed to have encouraged licentiousness, even anarchy in the streets. The Loyalists suspected that Patriot demands for freedom were self-serving, even hypocritical, for as Perserved Smith, a Loyalist from Ashfield, Massachusetts, observed, "Sons of liberty . . . did not deserve the name, for it was evident all they wanted was liberty from oppression that they might have liberty to oppress!"

The Loyalists were caught in a difficult squeeze. The British never quite trusted them. After all, they were Americans. During the early stages of the war, Loyalists organized militia companies and hoped to pacify large areas of the countryside with the support of the regular army. The British generals were unreliable partners, however, for no sooner had they called on loyal Americans to come forward than the redcoats marched away, leaving the Tories exposed to rebel retaliation. And in England, the exiles found themselves treated as second-class citizens. While many of them received monetary compensation for their sacrifice, they were never regarded as the equals of native-born English citizens. Not surprisingly, the Loyalist community in London was gradually transformed into a collection of bitter men and women who felt unwelcome on both sides of the Atlantic.

Americans who actively supported independence saw these people as traitors who deserved their fate of constant, often violent, harassment. In many states—but especially in New York—revolutionary governments confiscated Loyalist property. Other friends of the king received beatings, or as the rebels called them,

behind him to be overrun and conquered by the very army which he boasts to have completely routed but a week or two before."

Cornwallis pushed north into Virginia, planning apparently to establish a base of operations on the coast. He selected Yorktown, a sleepy tobacco market located on a peninsula bounded by the York and James rivers. Washington watched these maneuvers closely. The canny Virginia planter knew this territory intimately, and he sensed that Cornwallis had made a serious blunder. When Washington learned the French fleet could gain temporary dominance in the Chesapeake Bay, he rushed south from New Jersey. With him marched thousands of well-trained French troops under the Comte de Rochambeau. All the pieces fell into place. The French admiral, the Comte de Grasse, cut Cornwallis off from the sea, while Washington and his lieutenants encircled the British on land. On October 19, 1781, Cornwallis surrendered his entire army of six thousand men. When Lord North heard of the defeat at Yorktown, he moaned, "Oh God! It is all over." The British still controlled New York City and Charles Town, but except for a few skirmishes, the fighting ended. The task of securing the independence of the United States was now in the hands of the diplomats.

"grand Toory [sic] rides." A few were even executed. According to one patriot, "A Tory is a thing whose head is in England, and its body in America, and its neck ought to be stretched."

Long after the victorious Americans turned their attentions to the business of building a new republic, Loyalists remembered a receding colonial past, a comfortable, ordered world that had been lost forever at Yorktown. Although many Loyalists eventually returned to their homes, a sizable number could not do so. For them, the sense of loss remained a heavy emotional burden. Perhaps the most poignant testimony came from a young mother living in exile in Nova Scotia. "I climbed to the top of Chipman's Hill and watched the sails disappear in the distance," she recounted, "and such a feeling of loneliness came over me that though I had not shed a tear through all the war I sat down on the damp moss with my baby on my lap and cried bitterly."

Winning the Peace

How did Benjamin Franklin, John Adams, and John Jay secure a better peace treaty than Congress could have expected?

Congress appointed a skilled delegation to negotiate a peace treaty: Benjamin Franklin, John Adams, and John Jay. According to their official instructions, they were to insist only on the recognition of the independence of the United States. On other issues, Congress ordered its delegates to defer to the counsel of the French government.

But the political environment in Paris was much different from what the diplomats had been led to expect. The French had formed a military alliance with Spain, and French officials announced that they could not consider the details of an American settlement until after the Spanish had recaptured Gibraltar from the British. The prospects for a Spanish victory were not good, and in any case, it was well known that Spain coveted the lands lying between the Appalachian Mountains and the Mississippi River. Indeed, there were even rumors afloat in Paris that the great European powers might intrigue to deny the United States its independence.

While the three American delegates publicly paid their respects to French officials, they secretly entered into negotiations with an English agent. The peacemakers drove a remarkable bargain, a much better one than Congress could have expected. The preliminary agreement, the **Treaty of Paris of 1783**, signed on September 3, not only guaranteed the independence of the United States; it also transferred all the territory east of the Mississippi River, except Spanish Florida, to the new republic. The treaty established generous boundaries on the north and south and gave the Americans important fishing rights in the North Atlantic. In exchange, Congress promised to help British merchants collect debts contracted before the Revolution and compensate Loyalists whose lands had been confiscated by the various state governments. Even though the Americans negotiated separately with the British, they did not sign a separate peace. The preliminary treaty did not become effective until France reached its own agreement with Great Britain. Thus did the Americans honor the French alliance. It is difficult to imagine how Franklin, Adams, and Jay could have negotiated a more favorable conclusion to the war. In the fall of 1783, the last redcoats sailed from New York City, ending 176 years of colonial rule.

Conclusion: Preserving Independence

The American people had waged war against the most powerful nation in Europe and emerged victorious. The treaty marked the conclusion of a colonial rebellion, but it remained for the men and women who had resisted taxation without representation to work out the full implications of republicanism. What would be the shape of the new government? What powers would be delegated to the people, the states, the federal authorities? How far would the wealthy, well-born leaders of the rebellion be willing to extend political, social, and economic rights?

For many Americans the challenge of nation building appeared even more formidable than waging war against Great Britain. As Philadelphia physician Dr. Benjamin Rush explained, "There is nothing more common than to confound the terms of American Revolution with those of the late American war. The American war is over, but this is far from being the case with the American Revolution. On the contrary, nothing but the first act of the great drama is closed."

Study Resources

 Take the **Study Plan** for **Chapter 5** *The American Revolution* on **MyHistoryLab**

TIME LINE

1763 Peace of Paris ends the Seven Years' War

1764 Parliament passes Sugar Act to collect American revenue

1765 Stamp Act receives support of House of Commons (March); Stamp Act Congress meets in New York City (October)

1766 Stamp Act repealed the same day that Declaratory Act becomes law (March 18)

1767 Townshend Revenue Acts stir American anger (June–July)

1768 Massachusetts assembly refuses to rescind circular letter (February)

1770 Parliament repeals all Townshend duties except one on tea (March); British troops "massacre" Boston civilians (March)

1772 Samuel Adams forms committee of correspondence

1773 Lord North's government passes Tea Act (May); Bostonians hold Tea Party (December)

1774 Parliament punishes Boston with Coercive Acts (March–June); First Continental Congress convenes (September)

1775 Patriots take stand at Lexington and Concord (April); Second Continental Congress gathers (May); Americans hold their own at Bunker Hill (June)

1776 Congress votes for independence; Declaration of Independence is signed; British defeat Washington at Long Island (August); Americans score victory at Trenton (December)

1777 General Burgoyne surrenders at Saratoga (October)

1778 French treaties recognize independence of the United States (February)

1780 British take Charles Town (May)

1781 Washington forces Cornwallis to surrender at Yorktown (October)

1783 Peace treaty signed (September); British evacuate New York City (November)

CHAPTER REVIEW

Structure of Colonial Society

Why did Americans resist parliamentary taxation?

During the 1760s British rulers claimed that Parliament could make laws for the colonists "in all cases whatsoever." Americans challenged this "parliamentary sovereignty." Drawing on the work of John Locke, the English philosopher, they insisted that God had given them certain natural and inalienable rights. By attempting to tax them without representation, Parliament threatened those rights. (p. 106)

Eroding the Bonds of Empire

What events eroded the bonds of empire during the 1760s?

Wars in America were expensive. Parliament established the Proclamation Line of 1763 to reduce the costs of protecting the frontier, but this angered colonists seeking new lands in the west. Parliament also concluded that the colonists should help reduce the national debt, but when it passed the Stamp Act (1765), Americans protested. Colonists boycotted British manufactured goods. Taken aback, Parliament repealed the hated statute, while maintaining in the Declaratory Act (1766) its complete legislative authority over the Americans. (p. 108)

Steps Toward Independence

What events in 1775 and 1776 led to the colonists' decision to declare independence?

In 1775, following battles at Lexington and Concord, militiamen from throughout New England descended upon Boston, besieging the British troops encamped there. In response, the Continental Congress formed the Continental Army and appointed George Washington commander. In 1776, Thomas Paine's *Common Sense* convinced colonists that a republic was a better form of government than monarchy, and Congress declared independence. (p. 116)

Fighting for Independence

Why did it take eight years of warfare for the Americans to gain independence?

To win their independence, the colonies first had to overcome the formidable military power of Great Britain. Britain had four times the population of the colonies, was the world's leading manufacturer, had a well-trained and experienced army, and the world's best navy. The outgunned colonists had to rely on a war of attrition. It was only after the victory at Saratoga in 1777 convinced the French to enter into an alliance that the colonists were able to win conclusive battles and successfully end the war. (p. 119)

The Loyalist Dilemma

Why did so many Loyalists decide to leave the United States during the Revolution?

Almost 100,000 Loyalists permanently left America during the Revolution. While some Loyalists had held office under the Crown before the Revolution, many others believed that independence from Britain would destroy traditional values and lead to anarchy and new forms of oppression. (p. 126)

Winning the Peace

How did Benjamin Franklin, John Adams, and John Jay secure a better peace treaty than Congress could have expected?

Apart from insisting that Britain recognize the independence of the United States, Congress instructed Franklin, Adams, and Jay to defer to the counsels of the French government during the peace conference. But by conducting secret and separate negotiations with the British, the American delegates were also able to secure all the territory east of the Mississippi River except Spanish Florida for the new republic and to gain important fishing rights for Americans in the North Atlantic. (p. 127)

KEY TERMS AND DEFINITIONS

Whigs   In mid-eighteenth century Britain, the Whigs were a political faction that dominated Parliament. Generally, they opposed royal influence in government and wanted to increase the power of Parliament. In America, a Whig party coalesced in the 1830s in opposition to President Andrew Jackson. The American Whigs supported federal power and internal improvements but not territorial expansion. The Whig party collapsed in the 1850s. p. 106

Parliamentary sovereignty   Principle that emphasized Parliament's power to govern colonial affairs. p. 107

Stamp Act of 1765   Placed a tax on newspapers and printed matter produced in the colonies, causing mass opposition by colonists. p. 110

Stamp Act Congress   Meeting of colonial delegates in New York City in October 1765 to protest the Stamp Act, a law passed by Parliament to raise revenue in America. p. 111

Boston Massacre   A violent clash between British troops and a Boston mob on March 5, 1770. Five citizens were killed when the troops fired into the crowd. The incident inflamed anti-British sentiment in Massachusetts. p. 113

Committee of correspondence   Communication network formed in Massachusetts and other colonies to communicate grievances and provide colonists with evidence of British oppression. p. 114

Boston Tea Party   Raid on British ships in which Patriots disguised as Mohawks threw hundreds of chests of tea owned by the East India Company into Boston Harbor to protest British taxes. p. 115

Coercive Acts   Also known as the Intolerable Acts, the four pieces of legislation passed by Parliament in response to the Boston Tea Party to punish Massachusetts. p. 115

First Continental Congress   A meeting of delegates from 12 colonies in Philadelphia in 1774, the Congress denied Parliament's authority to legislate for the colonies, condemned British actions toward the colonies, created the Continental Association, and endorsed a call to take up arms. p. 117

Second Continental Congress   A gathering of colonial representatives in Philadelphia in 1775 that organized the Continental Army and began requisitioning men and supplies for the war effort. p. 117

Common Sense   Revolutionary tract written by Thomas Paine in 1776. It called for independence and a republican government in America. p. 117

Loyalists   Colonists sided with Britain during the American Revolution. p. 120

Yorktown   Virginia market town on a peninsula bounded by the York and James rivers, where Lord Cornwallis's army was trapped by the Americans and French in 1781. p. 125

Treaty of Paris of 1783   Agreement establishing American independence after the Revolutionary War. It also transferred territory east of the Mississippi River, except for Spanish Florida, to the new republic. p. 127

CRITICAL THINKING QUESTIONS

1. Were British political leaders or American agitators more to blame for the imperial crisis?

2. With more enlightened leadership, could the king and Parliament have preserved Britain's American empire?

3. Did Lexington and Concord make national independence inevitable?

4. Given the logistical problems facing the British, could they have possibly won the Revolutionary War?

MyHistoryLab Media Assignments

Find these resources in the Media Assignments folder for Chapter 5 on MyHistoryLab

Eroding the Bonds of Empire

Read the **Document**   *James Otis, The Rights of the British Colonies Asserted and Proved p. 109*

Read the **Document**   *Benjamin Franklin, Testimony Against the Stamp Act (1766) p. 111*

Listen to the **Audio File**   *"The Liberty Song" p. 112*

■ **Read** the **Document**   *Boston Gazette Description of the Boston Massacre p. 113*

■ **Read** the **Document**   *George R.T. Hewes, "A Retrospect on the Boston Tea Party" p. 115*

Steps Toward Independence

Read the **Document**   *Thomas Paine, A Freelance Writer Urges His Readers to Use Common Sense p. 118*

■ **Watch** the **Video**   *The American Revolution As Different Americans Saw It p. 119*

Fighting for Independence

■ **View** the **Map**   *The American Revolution p. 121*

■ **Complete** the **Assignment**   *Spain's Contribution to American Independence p. 122*

■ *Indicates Study Plan Media Assignment*

6 The Republican Experiment

Contents and Learning Objectives

((•●—[Listen to the **Audio File** on **myhistorylab**   **Chapter 6** *The Republican Experiment*

A New Political Morality

In 1788, Lewis Hallam and John Henry petitioned the General Assembly of Pennsylvania to open a theater. Although a 1786 state law banned the performance of stage plays and other "disorderly sports," many Philadelphia leaders favored the request to hold "representations" in their city. A committee appointed to study the issue concluded that a theater would contribute to "the general refinement of manners and the polish of society." Some supporters even argued that the sooner the United States had a professional theater the sooner the young republic would escape the "foreign yoke" of British culture.

The Quakers of Philadelphia dismissed such claims as out of hand. They warned that such "seminaries of lewdness and irreligion" would quickly undermine "the virtue of the people." They pointed out that "no sooner is a playhouse opened than it becomes surrounded with . . . brothels." Since Pennsylvania was already suffering from a "stagnation of commerce [and] a scarcity of money"—unmistakable signs of God's

displeasure—it seemed unwise to risk divine punishment by encouraging new "hot-beds of vice."

Such rhetoric did not sit well with other citizens who interpreted the revolutionary experience from an entirely different perspective. At issue, they insisted, was not popular morality, but state censorship. If the government silenced the stage, then "the same authority . . . may, with equal justice, dictate the shape and texture of our dress, or the modes and ceremonies of our worship." Depriving those who wanted to see plays of an opportunity to do so, they argued, "will abridge the natural right of every freeman, to dispose of his time and money, according to his own tastes and dispositions."

Throughout post–Revolutionary America everyday matters such as the opening of a new playhouse provoked passionate public debate. These divisions were symptomatic of a new, uncertain political culture struggling to find the proper balance between public morality and private freedom. During the long fight against

Although the words *slave* and *slavery* do not appear in the U.S. Constitution, debate over slavery and the slave trade resulted in a compromise in which both institutions persisted in the new Republic. Not everyone was pleased with the compromise. The Library Company of Philadelphia commissioned this painting, *Liberty Displaying the Arts and Sciences* (1792) by Samuel Jennings. The broken chain at the feet of the goddess Liberty is meant to demonstrate her opposition to slavery.
Source: The Library Company of Philadelphia.

Great Britain, Americans had defended individual rights. The problem was that the same people also believed that a republic that compromised its virtue could not long preserve liberty and independence.

In 1776, Thomas Paine had reminded ordinary men and women that "the sun never shined on a cause of greater worth . . . . 'Tis not the concern of a day, a year, or an age; posterity are virtually involved in the contest, and will be more or less affected, even to the end of time, by the proceedings now." During the 1780s Americans understood their responsibility not only to each other, but also to history. They worried, however, that they might not successfully meet the challenge. The dangers were clear. Individual states seemed intent on looking out for local interests rather than the national welfare. Revolutionary leaders such as George Washington and James Madison concluded that the United States needed a strong central government to protect rights and property. Their creative quest for solutions brought forth a new and enduring constitution.

Defining Republican Culture

What were the limits of equality in the "republican" society of the new United States?

Today, the term *republican* no longer possesses the evocative power it did for most eighteenth-century Americans. For them, it defined not a political party, but rather, an entire political culture. After all, they had done something that no other people had achieved for a very long time. They founded a national government without a monarch or aristocracy; in other words, a genuine republic. Making the new system work was a daunting task. Those Americans who read deeply in ancient and renaissance history knew that most republics had failed, often within a few years, only to be replaced by tyrants who cared not at all what ordinary people thought about the public good. To preserve their republic from such a fate, victorious revolutionaries such as Samuel Adams recast fundamental political values. For them, **republicanism** represented more than a particular form of government. It was a way of life, a core ideology, an uncompromising commitment to liberty and equality.

Adams and his contemporaries certainly believed that creating a new nation-state involved more than simply winning independence from Great Britain. More than did any other form of government, they insisted, a republic demanded an exceptionally high degree of public morality. If American citizens substituted "luxury, prodigality, and profligacy" for "prudence, virtue, and economy," then their revolution surely would have been in vain. Maintaining popular virtue was crucial to success. An innocent stage play, therefore, set off alarm bells. Such "foolish gratifications" seemed to compromise republican goals. It is not surprising that, when confronted by such temptations, Adams thundered, "Rome, Athens, and all the cities of renown, whence came your fall?"

White Americans came out of the Revolution with an almost euphoric sense of the nation's special destiny. This expansive outlook, encountered among so many ordinary men and women, owed much to the spread of Protestant evangelicalism. However skeptical Jefferson and Franklin may have been about revealed religion, the great mass of American people subscribed to an almost utopian vision of the country's future. To this new republic, God had promised progress and prosperity. The signs were visible for everyone. "There is not upon the face of the earth a body of people more happy or rising into consequence with more rapid stride," one man announced in 1786, "than the Inhabitants of the United States of America. Population is increasing, new houses building, new lands clearing, new settlements forming, and new manufactures establishing with a rapidity beyond conception."

Such experience did not translate easily or smoothly into the creation of a strong central government. Modern Americans tend to take for granted the acceptance of the Constitution. Its merits seem self-evident largely because it has survived for two centuries. But in the early 1780s, no one could have predicted that the Constitution as we know it would have been written, much less ratified. It was equally possible that the Americans would have supported a weak confederation or perhaps allowed the various states and regions to go their separate ways.

In this uncertain political atmosphere, Americans divided sharply over the relative importance of *liberty* and *order*. The revolutionary experience had called into question the legitimacy of any form of special privilege. As one republican informed an aristocratic colleague in the South Carolina assembly, "the day is Arrived when *goodness*, and not Wealth, are the only *Criterions of greatness*." A legislative leader in Pennsylvania put the point even more bluntly: "No man has a greater claim of special privilege for his $100,000 than I have for my $5." The man who passionately defended social equality for those of varying economic status, however, may still have resisted the extension of civil rights to women or blacks. Nevertheless, liberty was contagious, and Americans of all backgrounds began to make new demands on society and government. For them, the Revolution had suggested radical alternatives, and in many forums throughout the nation—especially in the elected state assemblies—they insisted on being heard.

In certain quarters, the celebration of liberty met with mixed response. Some Americans—often the very men who had resisted British tyranny—worried that the citizens of the new nation were caught up in a wild, destructive scramble for material wealth. Democratic excesses seemed to threaten order, to endanger the rights of property. Surely a republic could not long survive unless its citizens showed greater self-control. For people concerned about the loss of order, the state assemblies appeared to be the greatest source of instability. Popularly elected representatives lacked what men of property defined as real civic virtue: an ability to work for the common good rather than their private interests.

Working out the tensions between order and liberty, between property and equality, generated an outpouring of political genius. At other times in American history, persons of extraordinary talent have been drawn to theology, commerce, or science, but during the 1780s, the country's intellectual leaders—Thomas Jefferson, James Madison, Alexander Hamilton, and John Adams, among others—focused their creative energies on the problem of how republicans ought to govern themselves.

Living in the Shadow of Revolution

During the 1780s, why were Americans so sensitive to the dangers of "aristocratic display"?

Revolution changed American society, often in ways no one had planned. This phenomenon is not surprising. The great revolutions of modern times produced radical transformations in French, Russian, and Chinese societies. By comparison, the immediate results of the American Revolution appear much tamer, less wrenching. Nevertheless, national independence compelled people to reevaluate hierarchical social relations that they had taken for granted during the colonial period. The faltering first steps of independence raised fundamental questions about the meaning of equality in American society, some of which remain as pressing today as during the 1780s.

Social and Political Reform

Following the war, Americans aggressively ferreted out and, with republican fervor, denounced any traces of aristocratic pretense. As colonists, they had long resented the claims that certain Englishmen made to special privilege simply because of noble birth. Even so committed a republican as George Washington had to be reminded that artificial status was contrary to republican principles. In 1783, he and the officers who had served during the Revolution formed the Society of the Cincinnati, a hereditary organization in which membership passed from father to eldest son. The soldiers meant no harm; they simply wanted to maintain old friendships. But anxious republicans throughout America let out a howl of protest, and one South Carolina legislator, Aedanus Burke, warned that the Society intended to create "an hereditary peerage . . . [which would] undermine the Constitution and destroy civil liberty." After an embarrassed Washington called for appropriate reforms of the Society's bylaws, the Cincinnati crisis receded. The fear of privilege remained, however, and wealthy Americans dropped honorific titles such as "esquire." Lawyers of republican persuasion chided judges who had adopted the English custom of wearing great flowing wigs to court.

The appearance of equality was as important as its actual achievement. In fact, the distribution of wealth in postwar America was more uneven than it had been in the mid-eighteenth century. The sudden accumulation of large fortunes by new families made other Americans particularly sensitive to aristocratic display, for it seemed intolerable that a revolution waged against a monarchy should produce a class of persons legally, or even visibly, distinguished from their fellow citizens.

Republican ferment also encouraged many states to lower property requirements for voting. After the break with Great Britain, such a step seemed logical. As one group of farmers declared, no man can be "free & independent" unless he possesses "a voice . . . in the choice of the most important Officers in the Legislature." Pennsylvania and Georgia allowed all white male taxpayers to participate in elections. Other states were less democratic, but with the exception of Massachusetts, they reduced property qualifications. The reforms, however, did not significantly expand the American electorate. Long before the Revolution, an overwhelming percentage of free white males had owned enough land to vote. In any case, during the 1780s, republican lawmakers were not prepared to experiment with universal manhood suffrage; John Adams observed that if the states pushed the reforms too far, "New claims will arise, women will demand a vote . . . and every man who has not a farthing, will demand an equal vote with any other."

The most important changes in voting patterns were the result of western migration. As Americans moved to the frontier, they received full political representation in their state legislatures, and because new districts tended to be poorer than established coastal settlements, their representatives seemed less cultured, less well trained than those sent by eastern voters. Moreover, western delegates resented traveling so far to attend legislative meetings, and they lobbied successfully to transfer state capitals to more convenient locations. During this period, Georgia moved the seat of its government from Savannah to Augusta, South Carolina from Charles Town to Columbia, North Carolina from New Bern to Raleigh, Virginia from Williamsburg to Richmond, New York from New York City to Albany, and New Hampshire from Portsmouth to Concord.

After gaining independence, Americans also reexamined the relationship between church and state. Republican spokespersons such as Thomas Jefferson insisted that rulers had no right to interfere with the free expression of an individual's religious beliefs. As governor of Virginia, he strenuously advocated the disestablishment of the Anglican Church, an institution that had received tax monies and other benefits during the colonial period. Jefferson and his allies regarded such special privilege not only as a denial of religious freedom—after all, rival denominations did not receive tax money—but also as a vestige of aristocratic society.

In 1786, Virginia cut the last ties between church and state. Other southern states disestablished the Anglican Church, but in Massachusetts and New Hampshire Congregational churches continued to enjoy special status. Moreover, while Americans championed toleration, they seldom favored philosophies that radically challenged Christian values.

African Americans in the New Republic

Revolutionary fervor forced Americans to confront the most appalling contradiction to republican principles—slavery. The Quaker leader John Woolman (1720–1772) probably did more than any other white person of the era to remind people of the evils of this institution. A trip he took through the Southern Colonies as a young man forever impressed upon Woolman "the dark gloominess" of slavery. In a sermon, the outspoken humanitarian declared "that Men having Power too often misapplied it; that though we made Slaves of the Negroes, and the Turks made Slaves of the Christians, I believed that Liberty was the natural Right of all Men equally."

During the revolutionary period, abolitionist sentiment spread. Both in private and in public, people began to criticize slavery in other than religious language. No doubt, the double standard of their own political rhetoric embarrassed many white Americans. They hotly demanded liberation from parliamentary enslavement at the same time that they held several hundred thousand blacks in permanent bondage.

By keeping the issue of slavery before the public through writing and petitioning, African Americans powerfully undermined arguments advanced in favor of human bondage. They demanded freedom, reminding white lawmakers that African American men and women had the same natural right to liberty as did other Americans. In 1779, for example, a group of African Americans living in Connecticut pointedly asked the members of the state assembly "whether it is consistent with the present Claims, of the United States, to hold so many Thousands, of the Race of Adam, our Common Father, in perpetual Slavery." In New Hampshire, nineteen persons who called themselves "natives of Africa" reminded local legislators that "private or public tyranny and slavery are alike detestable to minds conscious of the equal dignity of human nature."

The scientific accomplishments of Benjamin Banneker (1731–1806), Maryland's African American astronomer and mathematician, and the international fame of Phillis Wheatley (1753–1784), Boston's celebrated "African muse," made it increasingly difficult for white Americans to maintain credibly that African Americans could not hold their own in a free society. Wheatley's poems went through many editions, and after reading her work, the great French philosopher Voltaire rebuked a friend who had claimed "there never would be Negro poets." As Voltaire discovered, Wheatley "writes excellent verse in English." Banneker, like Wheatley, enjoyed a well-deserved reputation, in his case for contributions as a scientist. After receiving a copy of an almanac that Banneker had published in Philadelphia, Thomas Jefferson concluded "that nature has given to our black brethren, talents equal to those of the other colors of men."

In the northern states, there was no real economic justification for slavery, and white laborers, often recent European immigrants, resented having to compete in the workplace against slaves. This economic situation, combined with the acknowledgment of the double standard represented by slavery, contributed to the establishment of antislavery societies. In 1775, Franklin helped organize a group in Philadelphia called the Society for the Relief of Free Negroes, Unlawfully Held. John Jay, Alexander Hamilton, and other prominent New Yorkers founded a Manumission Society in 1785. By 1792, antislavery societies were meeting from Virginia to Massachusetts, and in the northern states at least, these groups, working for the same ends as various Christian evangelicals, put slaveholders on the intellectual defensive for the first time in American history.

In several states north of Virginia, the abolition of slavery took a number of different forms. Even before achieving statehood, Vermont drafted a constitution (1777) that specifically prohibited slavery. In 1780, the Pennsylvania legislature passed a law effecting the gradual emancipation of slaves. Although the Massachusetts assembly refused to address the issue directly, the state courts took up the challenge and liberated the African Americans. A judge ruled slavery unconstitutional in Massachusetts because it conflicted with a clause in the state bill of rights declaring "all men . . . free and equal." According to one enthusiast, this decision freed "a Grate number of Blacks . . . who . . . are held in a state of slavery within the bowels of a free and christian Country." By 1800, slavery was well on the road to extinction in the northern states.

These positive developments did not mean that white people accepted blacks as equals. In fact, in the very states that outlawed slavery, African Americans faced systematic discrimination. Free blacks were generally excluded from voting, juries, and militia duty—they were denied rights and responsibilities usually associated with full citizenship. They rarely enjoyed access to education, and in cities such as Philadelphia and New York, where African Americans went to look for work, they ended up living in segregated wards or neighborhoods. Even in the churches—institutions

that had often spoken out against slavery—free African Americans were denied equal standing with white worshipers. Humiliations of this sort persuaded African Americans to form their own churches. In Philadelphia, Richard Allen, a former slave, founded the Bethel Church for Negro Methodists (1793) and later organized the **African Methodist Episcopal Church** (1816), an institution of great cultural as well as religious significance for nineteenth-century American blacks.

Even in the South, where African Americans made up a large percentage of the population, slavery disturbed thoughtful white republicans. Some planters simply freed their slaves, and by 1790 the number of free blacks living in Virginia was 12,766. By 1800, the figure had reached 30,750. There is no question that this trend reflected the uneasiness among white masters. Richard Randolph, one of Virginia's wealthier planters, explained that he freed his slaves "to make restitution, as far as I am able, to an unfortunate race of bond-men, over whom my ancestors have usurped and exercised the most lawless and monstrous tyranny." George Washington also manumitted his slaves. To be sure, most southern slaveholders, especially those living in South Carolina and Georgia, rejected this course of action. Their economic well-being depended on slave labor. Perhaps more significant, however, is the fact that no southern leader during the era of republican experimentation defended slavery as a positive good. Such overtly racist rhetoric did not become part of the public discourse until the nineteenth century.

Despite promising starts in that direction, the southern states did not abolish slavery. The economic incentives to maintain a servile labor force, especially after the invention of the cotton gin in 1793 and the opening up of the Alabama and Mississippi frontier, overwhelmed the initial abolitionist impulse. An opportunity to translate the principles of the American Revolution into social practice had been lost, at least temporarily. Jefferson reported in 1805, "I have long since given up the expectation of any early provision for the extinction of slavery among us." Unlike some contemporary Virginians, the man who wrote the Declaration of Independence condoned slavery on his own plantation, even fathering several children by a woman who, since she was his slave, had little choice in the matter of her pregnancy.

The Challenge of Women's Rights

The revolutionary experience accelerated changes in the way ordinary people viewed the family. At the beginning of the eighteenth century, fathers claimed authority over other members of their families simply on the grounds that they were fathers. As patriarchs, they demanded obedience. If they behaved like brutal despots, so be it; fathers could treat wives and children however they pleased.

A 1797 sketch by architect and engineer Benjamin Henry Latrobe depicting African Americans in Norfolk, Virginia, shaving and dressing in preparation for a Sunday afternoon. Latrobe's drawings of blacks in the American South offer valuable glimpses of daily life in the region.

Read the **Document** **Phillis Wheatley, Religious and Moral Poems**

This engraving of Phillis Wheatley appeared in her volume of verse, *Poems on Various Subjects, Religious and Moral* (1773), the first book published by an African American.

The English philosopher John Locke (1632–1704) powerfully undermined arguments of this sort. In his extremely popular treatise *Some Thoughts Concerning Education* (1693), Locke insisted that the mind was not formed at birth. The child learned from experience, and if the infant witnessed violent, arbitrary behavior, then the baby would become an abusive adult. As Locke warned parents, "If you punish him [the child] for what he sees you practice yourself, he will not think that Severity to proceed from Kindness in you careful to amend a Fault in him; but will be apt to interpret it, as Peevishness and Arbitrary Imperiousness of a Father." Enlightened eighteenth-century mothers and fathers—especially, fathers—condemned tyranny in the home.

At the time of the American Revolution, few seriously accepted the notion that fathers—be they tyrannical kings or heads of ordinary families—enjoyed unlimited powers over women and children. Indeed, people in England as well as America increasingly described the family in terms of love and companionship. Instead of duties, they spoke of affection. This transformation in the way men and women viewed relations of power within the family was most evident in the popular novels of the period. Americans devoured *Pamela* and *Clarissa*, stories by the English writer Samuel Richardson about women who were the innocent victims of unreformed males, usually deceitful lovers and unforgiving fathers.

It was in this changing intellectual environment that American women began making new demands not only on their husbands but also on republican institutions. Abigail Adams, one of the generation's most articulate women, instructed her husband, John, as he set off for the opening of the Continental Congress: "I desire you would Remember the Ladies, and be more generous and favourable to them than your ancestors. Do not put such unlimited power into the hands of the Husbands." John responded in a condescending manner. The "Ladies" would have to wait until the country achieved independence. In 1777, Lucy Knox took an even stronger line with her husband, General Henry Knox. When he was about to return home from the army, she warned him, "I hope you will not consider yourself as commander in chief in your own house—but be convinced . . . that there is such a thing as equal command."

If Knox accepted Lucy's argument, he did so because she was a good republican wife and mother. In fact, women justified their assertiveness largely on the basis of political ideology. If survival of republics really depended on the virtue of their citizens, they argued, then it was the special responsibility of women as mothers to nurture the right values in their children and as wives to instruct their husbands in proper behavior. Contemporaries claimed that the woman who possessed "virtue and prudence" could easily "mold the taste, the manners, and the conduct of her admirers, according to her pleasure." In fact, "nothing short of a general reformation of manners would take place, were the ladies to use their power in discouraging our licentious manners."

During this period, women began to petition for divorce on new grounds. One case is particularly instructive concerning changing attitudes toward women and the family. In 1784, John Backus, an undistinguished Massachusetts silversmith, was hauled before a local court and asked why he beat his wife. He responded that "it was Partly owing to his Education for his father treated his mother in the same manner." The difference between Backus's case and his father's was that Backus's wife refused to tolerate such abuse, and she sued successfully for divorce. Studies of divorce patterns in Connecticut and Pennsylvania show that after 1773 women divorced on about the same terms as men.

The war itself presented some women with fresh opportunities. In 1780, Ester DeBerdt Reed founded a large volunteer women's organization in Philadelphia—the first of its kind in the United States—that raised more than $300,000 for Washington's army. Other women ran family farms and businesses while their husbands fought the British. And in 1790, the New Jersey legislature explicitly allowed women who owned property to vote.

Despite these scattered gains, republican society still defined women's roles exclusively in terms of mother, wife, and homemaker. Other pursuits seemed unnatural, even threatening, and it is perhaps not surprising, therefore, that in 1807 New Jersey lawmakers—angry over a close election in which women voters apparently determined the result—repealed female suffrage in the interests of "safety, quiet, and good order and dignity of the state." Even an allegedly progressive thinker such as Jefferson could not imagine allowing women to participate in serious politics. When in 1807 his secretary of the treasury, Albert Gallatin, called attention

Abigail Adams, wife of President John Adams, was a brilliant woman whose plea to limit the power of husbands gained little sympathetic attention. This portrait of her by Benjamin Blyth is from c. 1766.

to the shortage of educated people to serve in government jobs and suggested recruiting women, Jefferson responded sharply: "The appointment of a woman to office is an innovation for which the public is not prepared, nor am I."

The States: Experiments in Republicanism

Following independence, why did the states insist on drafting *written* constitutions?

In May 1776, the Second Continental Congress invited the states to adopt constitutions. The old colonial charters filled with references to king and Parliament were clearly no longer adequate, and within a few years, most states had taken action. Rhode Island and Connecticut already enjoyed republican government by virtue of their unique seventeenth-century charters that allowed the voters to select both governors and legislators. Eleven other states plus Vermont created new political structures, and their deliberations reveal how Americans living in different regions and reacting to different social pressures defined fundamental republican principles.

Several constitutions were boldly experimental, and some states later rewrote documents that had been drafted in the first

flush of independence. These early constitutions were provisional, but they nevertheless provided the framers of the federal Constitution of 1787 with invaluable insights into the strengths and weaknesses of government based on the will of the people.

Blueprints for State Government

Despite disagreements over details, Americans who wrote the various state constitutions shared certain political assumptions. First, they insisted on preparing written documents. For many of them, of course, this seemed a natural step. As colonists, they had lived under royal charters, documents that described the workings of local government in detail. The Massachusetts Bay charter of 1629, for example (see Chapter 2), guaranteed that the Puritans would enjoy the rights of Englishmen even after they had moved to the New World. And in New England, Congregationalists drew up church covenants stating in clear contractual language the rights and responsibilities of the entire congregation.

However logical the decision to produce written documents may have seemed to the Americans, it represented a major break with English practice. Political philosophers in the mother country had long boasted of Britain's unwritten constitution, a collection of judicial reports and parliamentary statutes. But this highly vaunted system had not protected the colonists from oppression; hence, after declaring independence, Americans demanded that their state constitutions explicitly define the rights of the people as well as the power of their rulers.

Natural Rights and the State Constitutions

The authors of the state constitutions believed men and women possessed certain **natural rights** over which government exercised no control whatsoever. So that future rulers—potential tyrants—would know the exact limits of authority, these fundamental rights were carefully spelled out. Indeed, the people of Massachusetts rejected the proposed state constitution of 1778 largely because it lacked a full statement of their basic rights. They demanded a guarantee of "rights of conscience, and . . . security of persons and property, which every member in the State hath a right to expect from the supreme power."

Eight state constitutions contained specific declarations of rights. The length and character of these lists varied, but, in general, they affirmed three fundamental freedoms: religion, speech, and press. They protected citizens from unlawful searches and seizures; they upheld trial by jury. George Mason, a shrewd political thinker who had written important revolutionary pamphlets, penned the most influential declaration of rights. It was appended to the Virginia Constitution of 1776, and the words were incorporated into other state constitutions as well as the famed Bill of Rights of the federal Constitution.

In almost every state, delegates to constitutional conventions drastically reduced the power of the governor. The constitutions of Pennsylvania and Georgia abolished the governor's office. In four other states, terms such as *president* were substituted for *governor*. Even when those who designed the new state governments provided for a governor, they severely circumscribed his authority.

He was allowed to make almost no political appointments, and while the state legislators closely monitored his activities, he possessed no veto over their decisions (Massachusetts being the lone exception). Most early constitutions lodged nearly all effective power in the legislature. This decision made good sense to men who had served under powerful royal governors during the late colonial period. These ambitious crown appointees had used executive patronage to influence members of the colonial assemblies, and as the Americans drafted their new republican constitutions, they were determined to bring their governors under tight control. In fact, the writers of the state constitutions were so fearful of the concentration of power in the hands of a single person that they failed to appreciate that elected governors—like the representatives themselves—were now the servants of a free people.

The legislature dominated early state government. The constitutions of Pennsylvania and Georgia provided for a unicameral, or one-house, system, and since any male taxpayer could cast a ballot in these states, their legislatures became the nation's most democratic. Other states authorized the creation of two houses, but even as they did so, some of the more demanding republicans wondered why America needed a senate or upper house at all. What social and economic interests, they asked, did that body represent that could not be more fully and directly voiced in the lower house? After all, America had just freed itself of an aristocracy. The two-house form survived the Revolution largely because it was familiar and because some persons had already begun to suspect that certain checks on the popular will, however arbitrary they might have appeared, were necessary to preserve minority rights.

Power to the People

Massachusetts did not adopt a constitution until 1780, several years after the other states had done so. The experience of the people of Massachusetts is particularly significant because in their efforts to establish a workable system of republican government, they hit on a remarkable political innovation. After the rejection of two constitutions drafted by the state legislature, the responsibility fell to a specially elected convention of delegates whose sole purpose was the "formation of a new Constitution."

John Adams took a position of leadership at this convention and served as the chief architect of the governmental framework of Massachusetts. This framework included a house and senate, a popularly elected governor—who, unlike the chief executives of other states, possessed a veto over legislative bills—and property qualifications for officeholders as well as voters. The most striking aspect of the 1780 constitution, however, was the wording of its opening sentence: "We . . . the people of Massachusetts . . . agree upon, ordain, and establish." This powerful statement would be echoed in the federal Constitution. The Massachusetts experiment reminded Americans that ordinary officeholders could not be trusted to define fundamental rights. That important task required a convention of delegates who could legitimately claim to speak for the people.

In 1780, no one knew whether the state experiments would succeed. There was no question that a different type of person had begun to appear in public office, one who seemed, to the local gentry at least, a little poorer and less polished than they would have liked. When one Virginian surveyed the newly elected House of Burgesses in 1776, he discovered it was "composed of men not quite so well dressed, nor so politely educated, nor so highly born as some Assemblies I have formerly seen." This particular Virginian approved of such change, for he believed that "the People's men," however plain they might appear, possessed honesty and sincerity. They were, in fact, representative republicans, people who insisted they were anyone's equal in this burgeoning society.

Other Americans were less optimistic about the nation's immediate prospects. The health of a small republic depended entirely on the virtue of its people. If they or their elected officials succumbed to material temptation, if they failed to comprehend the moral dimensions of political power, or if personal liberty threatened the rights of property, then the state constitutions were no more than worthless pieces of paper. The risk of excess seemed great. In 1778, a group of New Englanders, fearful that unbridled freedom would create political anarchy, observed, "The idea of liberty has been held up in so dazzling colours that some of us may not be willing to submit to that subordination necessary in the freest states."

Stumbling Toward a New National Government

Why did many Americans regard the Articles of Confederation as inadequate?

When the Second Continental Congress convened in 1775, the delegates found themselves waging war in the name of a country that did not yet exist. As the military crisis deepened, Congress gradually—often reluctantly—assumed greater authority over national affairs, but everyone agreed such narrowly conceived measures were a poor substitute for a legally constituted government. The separate states could not possibly deal with the range of issues that now confronted the American people. Indeed, if independence meant anything in a world of sovereign nations, it implied the creation of a central authority capable of conducting war, borrowing money, regulating trade, and negotiating treaties.

Articles of Confederation

The challenge of creating a viable central government proved more difficult than anyone anticipated. Congress appointed a committee to draw up a plan for confederation. John Dickinson, the lawyer who had written an important revolutionary pamphlet titled *Letters from a Farmer in Pennsylvania*, headed the committee. Dickinson envisioned the creation of a strong central government, and the report his committee presented on July 12, 1776, shocked delegates who assumed that the constitution would authorize a loose confederation of states. Dickinson's plan placed the western territories, land claimed by the separate states, under congressional control. In addition, Dickinson's committee called for equal state representation in Congress.

Since some states, such as Virginia and Massachusetts, were more populous than others, the plan fueled tensions between large and small states. Also unsettling was Dickinson's recommendation that taxes be paid to Congress on the basis of a state's total population, black as well as white, a formula that angered Southerners who did not think slaves should be counted. Indeed, even before the British evacuated Boston, Dickinson's committee raised many difficult political questions that would divide Americans for several decades.

Not surprisingly, the draft of the plan—the **Articles of Confederation**—that Congress finally approved in November 1777 bore little resemblance to Dickinson's original plan. The Articles jealously guarded the sovereignty of the states. The delegates who drafted the framework shared a general republican conviction that power—especially power so far removed from the people—was inherently dangerous and that the only way to preserve liberty was to place as many constraints as possible on federal authority.

The result was a government that many people regarded as powerless. The Articles provided for a single legislative body consisting of representatives selected annually by the state legislatures. Each state possessed a single vote in Congress. It could send as many as seven delegates, as few as two, but if they divided evenly on a certain issue, the state lost its vote. There was no independent executive and no veto over legislative decisions. The Articles also denied Congress the power of taxation, a serious oversight in time of war. The national government could obtain funds only by asking the states for contributions, called requisitions, but if a state failed to cooperate—and many did—Congress limped along without financial support. Amendments to this constitution required assent by all thirteen states. The authors of the new system expected the weak national government to handle foreign relations, military matters, Indian affairs, and interstate disputes. They most emphatically did not award Congress ownership of the lands west of the Appalachian Mountains.

The new constitution sent to the states for ratification encountered apathy and hostility. Most Americans were far more interested in local affairs than in the actions of Congress. When a British army marched through a state, creating a need for immediate military aid, people spoke positively about central government, but as soon as the threat had passed, they sang a different tune. During this period, even the slightest encroachment on state sovereignty rankled republicans who feared centralization would inevitably promote corruption.

Western Land: Key to the First Constitution

The major bone of contention with the Articles, however, was the disposition of the vast, unsurveyed territory west of the Appalachians that everyone hoped the British would soon surrender. Although the

📖 Read the Document   The Articles of Confederation (1777)

In 1977, the U.S. Postal Service issued this stamp to commemorate the bicentennial of the drafting of the nation's first constitution—the Articles of Confederation. The Second Continental Congress appointed a thirteen-man committee (one from each state) to draft the document, although only five figures are shown here.

region was claimed by various states, most of it actually belonged to Native Americans. In a series of land grabs that federal negotiators called treaties, the United States government took the land comprising much of modern Ohio, Indiana, Illinois, and Kentucky. Since the Indians had put their faith in the British during the war, they could do little to resist the humiliating treaty agreements at Fort McIntosh (1785), Fort Stanwix (1784), and Fort Finney (1786). As John Dickinson, then serving as the president of the Supreme Executive Council of Pennsylvania, told the Indians, since Great Britain has surrendered "the back country with all the forts . . . that they [the Indians] must now depend upon us for the preservation." If they dared to resist, "we will instantly turn upon them our armies . . . and extirpate them from the land where they were born and now live."

Some states, such as Virginia and Georgia, claimed land all the way from the Atlantic Ocean to the elusive "South Seas," in effect extending their boundaries to the Pacific coast by virtue of royal charters. State legislators—their appetites whetted by aggressive land speculators—anticipated generating large revenues through land sales. Connecticut, New York, Pennsylvania, and North Carolina also announced intentions to seize blocks of western land.

Other states were not blessed with vague or ambiguous royal charters. The boundaries of Maryland, Delaware, and New Jersey had been established many years earlier, and it seemed as if people living in these states would be permanently cut off from the anticipated bounty. In protest, these "landless" states stubbornly refused to ratify the Articles of Confederation. Marylanders were particularly vociferous. All the states had made sacrifices for the common good during the Revolution, they complained, and it appeared only fair that all states should profit from the fruits of victory, in this case, from the sale of western lands. Maryland's spokesmen feared that if Congress did not void Virginia's excessive claims to all of the Northwest Territory (the land west of Pennsylvania and north of the Ohio River) as well as to a large area south of the Ohio, beyond the Cumberland Gap, known as Kentucky, then Marylanders would desert their home state in search of cheap Virginia farms, leaving Maryland an underpopulated wasteland.

Virginians scoffed at the pleas for equity. They suspected that behind the Marylanders' statements of high purpose lay the greed of speculators. Private land companies had sprung up before the Revolution and purchased large tracts from the Indians in areas claimed by Virginia. Their agents petitioned Parliament to legitimize these questionable transactions. Their efforts failed. After the Declaration of Independence, however, the companies shifted the focus of their lobbying to Congress, particularly to the representatives of landless states like Maryland. By liberally distributing shares of stock, officials of the Indiana, Illinois, and Wabash companies gained powerful supporters such as Benjamin Franklin, Robert Morris, and Thomas Johnson, governor of Maryland. These activities encouraged Delaware and New Jersey to modify their

> **Read the Document**   Northwest Ordinance
> (July 3, 1787)

Map shows present-day boundaries.

NORTHWEST TERRITORY The U.S. government auctioned off the land in the Northwest Territory, the region defined by the Ohio River, the Great Lakes, and the Mississippi River. Proceeds from the sale of one section in each township were set aside for the creation and support of public schools.

demands and join the Confederation, while Maryland held out for five years. The leaders of Virginia, though, remained firm. Why, they asked, should Virginia surrender its historic claims to western lands to enrich a handful of selfish speculators?

The states resolved the bitter controversy in 1781 as much by accident as by design. Virginia agreed to cede its holdings north of the Ohio River to the Confederation on condition that Congress nullify the land companies' earlier purchases from the Indians. A practical consideration had softened Virginia's resolve. Republicans such as Jefferson worried about expanding their state beyond the mountains; with poor transportation links, it seemed impossible to govern such a large territory effectively from Richmond. The western settlers might even come to regard Virginia as a colonial power insensitive to their needs. Marylanders who dreamed of making fortunes on the land market grumbled, but when a British army appeared on their border, they prudently accepted the Articles (March 1, 1781). Congress required another three years to work out the details of the Virginia cession. Other landed states followed Virginia's example. These transfers established an important principle, for after 1781, it was agreed that the West belonged not to the separate states but to the United States. In this matter, at least, the national government now exercised full sovereignty.

No one greeted ratification of the Articles with much enthusiasm. When they thought about national politics at all, Americans concerned themselves primarily with winning independence. The new government gradually developed an administrative bureaucracy, and in 1781 it formally created the Departments of War, Foreign Affairs, and Finance. By far the most influential figure in the Confederation was Robert Morris (1734–1806), a freewheeling Philadelphia merchant who was appointed the first superintendent of finance. Although he was a brilliant manager, Morris's decisions as superintendent provoked controversy and deep suspicion. He hardly seemed a model republican. Morris mixed public funds under his control with personal accounts, and he never lost an opportunity to make a profit. While such practices were not illegal, his apparent improprieties undermined his own political agenda. He desperately wanted to strengthen the central government, but highly vocal critics resisted, labeling Morris a "pecuniary dictator."

Northwest Ordinance: The Confederation's Major Achievement

Whatever the weaknesses of Congress may have been, it did score one impressive triumph. Congressional action brought order to western settlement, especially in the Northwest Territory, and incorporated frontier Americans into an expanding federal system. In 1781, the prospects for success did not seem promising. For years, colonial authorities had ignored people who migrated far inland, sending neither money nor soldiers to protect them from Indian attack. Tensions between the seaboard colonies and the frontier regions had sometimes flared into violence. Disorders occurred in South Carolina in 1767, in North Carolina in 1769, and in Vermont in 1777. With thousands of men and women, most of them squatters, pouring across the Appalachian Mountains, Congress had to act quickly to avoid the past errors of royal and colonial authorities.

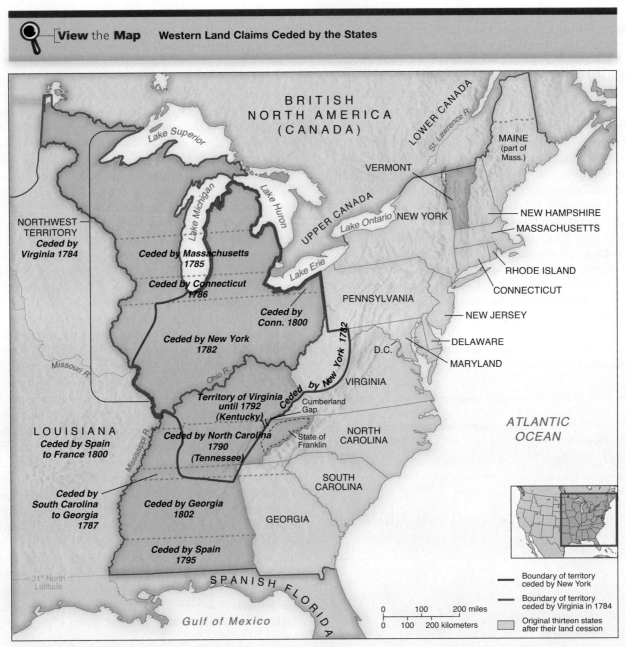

View the Map   Western Land Claims Ceded by the States

WESTERN LAND CLAIMS CEDED BY THE STATES After winning the war, the major issue facing the Continental Congress under the Articles of Confederation was mediating conflicting states' claims to rich western land. By 1802, the states had ceded all rights to the federal government.

The initial attempt to deal with this explosive problem came in 1784. Jefferson, then serving as a member of Congress, drafted an ordinance that became the basis for later, more enduring legislation. Jefferson recommended carving ten new states out of the western lands located north of the Ohio River and recently ceded to the United States by Virginia. He specified that each new state establish a republican form of government. When the population of a territory equaled that of the smallest state already in the Confederation, the region could apply for full statehood. In the meantime, free white males could participate in local government, a democratic guarantee that frightened some of Jefferson's more conservative colleagues.

The impoverished Congress was eager to sell off the western territory as quickly as possible. After all, the frontier represented

a source of income that did not depend on the unreliable generosity of the states. A second ordinance, passed in 1785 and called the Land Ordinance, established an orderly process for laying out new townships and marketing public lands.

Public response disappointed Congress. Surveying the lands took far longer than anticipated, and few persons possessed enough hard currency to make even the minimum purchase. Finally, a solution to the problem came from Manasseh Cutler, a New England minister turned land speculator and congressional lobbyist, and his associates, who included several former officers of the Continental Army.

Cutler and his associates, representing the Ohio and Scioto companies, offered to purchase more than six million

LAND ORDINANCE OF 1785

Grid pattern of a township
36 sections of 640 acres (1 square mile each)

36	30	24	18	12	6
35	29	23	17	11	5
34	28	22	16	10	4
33	27	21	15	9	3
32	26	20	14	8	2
31	25	19	13	7	1

6 miles (vertical)

◄──── 6 miles ────►

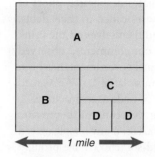

16 · Income of one section reserved for the support of public education

A Half-section   320 acres
B Quarter-section   160 acres
C Half-quarter section   80 acres
D Quarter-quarter section   40 acres

◄──── 1 mile ────►

unsurveyed acres of land located in present-day southeastern Ohio by persuading Congress to accept, at full face value, government loan certificates that had been issued to soldiers during the Revolution. On the open market, the Ohio company could pick up the certificates for as little as 10 percent of their face value; thus, the company stood to make a fortune. Like so many other get-rich-quick schemes, however, this one failed to produce the anticipated millions. Unfortunately for Cutler and his friends, small homesteaders settled wherever they pleased, refusing to pay either government or speculators for the land.

Congress worried about the excess liberty on the frontier. In the 1780s, the West seemed to be filling up with people who by eastern standards were uncultured. Timothy Pickering, a New Englander, declared that "the emigrants to the frontier lands are the least worthy subjects in the United States. They are little less savage than the Indians; and when possessed of the most fertile spots, for want of industry, live miserably." The charge was as old as the frontier itself. Indeed, seventeenth-century Englishmen had said the same things of the earliest Virginians. The lawless image stuck, however, and even a sober observer such as Washington insisted that the West crawled with "banditti." The Ordinance of 1784 placed the government of the territories in the hands of people about whom congressmen and speculators had second thoughts.

These various currents shaped the Ordinance of 1787, one of the final acts passed under the Confederation. The bill, also called the **Northwest Ordinance**, provided a new structure for government of the Northwest Territory. The plan authorized the creation of between three and five territories, each to be ruled by a governor, a secretary, and three judges appointed by Congress. When the population reached five thousand, voters who owned property could elect an assembly, but its decisions were subject to the governor's absolute veto. Once sixty thousand persons resided in a territory, they could write a constitution and petition for full statehood. While these procedures represented a retreat from Jefferson's original proposal, the Ordinance of 1787 contained

several significant features. A bill of rights guaranteed the settlers the right to trial by jury, freedom of religion, and due process of law. In addition, the act outlawed slavery, a prohibition that freed the future states of Ohio, Indiana, Illinois, Michigan, and Wisconsin from the curse of human bondage.

By contrast, settlement south of the Ohio River received far less attention from Congress. Long before the end of the war, thousands of Americans streamed through the Cumberland Gap into a part of Virginia known as Kentucky. The most famous of these settlers was Daniel Boone. In 1775, the population of Kentucky was approximately one hundred; by 1784, it had jumped to thirty thousand. Speculators purchased large tracts from the Indians, planning to resell this acreage to settlers at handsome profits. In 1776, one land company asked Congress to reorganize the company's holdings into a new state called Transylvania. While nothing came of this self-serving request, another, even more aggressive group of speculators in 1784 carved the State of Franklin out of a section of present-day Tennessee, then claimed by North Carolina. Rival speculators prevented formal recognition of Franklin's government. By 1790, the entire region south of the Ohio River had been transformed into a crazy quilt of claims and counterclaims that generated lawsuits for many years to come.

Strengthening Federal Authority

What did the nationalists call for and how did they aim to achieve their initiatives?

Despite its success in bringing order to the Northwest Territory, the Confederation increasingly came under heavy fire from critics who wanted a stronger central government. Complaints varied from region to region, from person to person, but most disappointment reflected economic frustration. Americans had assumed that peace would restore economic growth, but recovery following the Revolution was slow.

The Nationalist Critique

Even before England signed a treaty with America, its merchants flooded American ports with consumer items and offered easy credit. Families that had postponed purchases of imported goods—either because of British blockade or personal hardship—now rushed to buy European finery.

This sudden renewal of trade with Great Britain on such a large scale strained the American economy. Gold and silver flowed back across the Atlantic, leaving the United States desperately short of hard currency. When large merchant houses called in their debts, ordinary American consumers often found themselves on the brink of bankruptcy. "The disagreeable state of our commerce," observed James Wilson, an advocate of strong national government, has been the result "of extravagant and injudicious importation. . . . We seemed to have forgot that to pay was as necessary in trade as to purchase."

To blame the Confederation alone for the economic depression would be unfair. Nevertheless, during the 1780s, many people agreed that a stronger central government could somehow have brought greater stability to the struggling economy. In their rush to acquire imported luxuries, Americans seemed to have deserted republican principles, and a weak Congress was helpless to restore national virtue.

Critics pointed to the government's inability to regulate trade. Whenever a northern congressman suggested restricting British access to American markets, southern representatives, who feared any controls on the export of tobacco or rice, bellowed in protest. Southerners anticipated that navigation acts written by the Confederation would put planters under the yoke of northern shipping interests.

The country's chronic fiscal instability increased public anxiety. While the war was still in progress, Congress printed well over $200 million in paper money, but because of extraordinarily high inflation, the rate of exchange for Continental bills soon declined to a fraction of their face value. In 1781, Congress, facing insolvency, turned to the states for help. They were asked to retire the depreciated currency. The situation was spinning out of control. Several states—pressed to pay their own war-related debts—not only recirculated the Continental bills but also issued nearly worthless money of their own.

A heavy burden of state and national debt compounded the general sense of economic crisis. Revolutionary soldiers had yet to be paid. Women and men who had loaned money and goods to the government clamored for reimbursement. Foreign creditors demanded interest on funds advanced during the Revolution. These pressures grew, but Congress was unable to respond. The Articles specifically prohibited Congress from taxing the American people. It required little imagination to see that the Confederation would soon default on its legal obligations unless something was done quickly.

In response, an aggressive group of men announced that they knew how to save the Confederation. The nationalists—persons such as Alexander Hamilton, James Madison, and Robert Morris—called for major constitutional reforms, the chief of which was an amendment allowing Congress to collect a 5 percent tax on imported goods sold in the states. Revenues generated by the proposed Impost of 1781 would be used by the Confederation to reduce the national debt. On this point the nationalists were adamant. They recognized that whoever paid the public debt would gain the public trust. If the states assumed the responsibility, then the country could easily fragment into separate republics. "A national debt," Hamilton explained in 1781, "if it is not excessive, will be to us a national blessing. It will be a powerful cement to our union." Twelve states accepted the Impost amendment, but Rhode Island—where local interests argued that the tax would make Congress "independent of their constituents"—resolutely refused to cooperate. One negative vote on this proposed constitutional change, and the taxing scheme was dead.

State leaders frankly thought the nationalists were up to no good. The "localists" were especially apprehensive of fiscal plans advanced by Robert Morris. His profiteering as superintendent of finance appeared a threat to the moral fiber of the young republic. Richard Henry Lee and Samuel Adams, men of impeccable patriotic credentials, decried Morris's efforts to create a national bank. Such an institution would bring forth a flock of social parasites, the kind of people that Americans associated with corrupt monarchical government. One person declared that if an impost ever passed, Morris "will have all [the money] in his Pocket."

The nationalists regarded their opponents as economically naive. A country with the potential of the United States required a complex, centralized fiscal system. But for all their pretensions to realism, the nationalists of the early 1780s were politically inept. They underestimated the depth of republican fears, and in their rush to strengthen the Articles, they overplayed their hand.

A group of extreme nationalists even appealed to the army for support. To this day, no one knows the full story of the Newburgh Conspiracy of 1783. Officers of the Continental Army stationed at Newburgh, New York, worried that Congress would disband them without funding their pensions, began to lobby intensively for relief. In March, they scheduled general meetings to protest the weakness and duplicity of Congress. The officers' initial efforts were harmless enough, but frustrated nationalists such as Morris and Hamilton hoped that if the army exerted sufficient pressure on the government, perhaps even threatened a military takeover, then stubborn Americans might be compelled to amend the Articles.

The conspirators failed to take George Washington's integrity into account. No matter how much he wanted a strong central government, he would not tolerate insubordination by the military. Washington confronted the officers directly at Newburgh, intending to read a prepared statement. Fumbling with his glasses before his men, he commented, "Gentlemen, you must pardon me. I have grown gray in your service and now find myself growing blind." The unexpected vulnerability of this great soldier reduced the troops to tears, and in an instant, the rebellion was broken. Washington deserves credit for preserving civilian rule in this country.

Diplomatic Humiliation

In foreign affairs, Congress endured further embarrassment. It could not even enforce the provisions of its own peace treaty. American negotiators had promised Great Britain that its citizens could collect debts contracted before the Revolution. The states, however, dragged their heels, and several even passed laws obstructing the settlement of legitimate prewar claims. Congress was powerless to force compliance. The British responded to this apparent provocation by refusing to evacuate troops from posts located in the Northwest Territory. A strong national government would have driven the redcoats out, but without adequate funds, the weak Congress could not provide soldiers for such a mission.

Congress's postrevolutionary dealings with Spain were equally humiliating. That nation refused to accept the southern boundary of the United States established by the Treaty of Paris. Spain claimed sovereignty over much of the land located between Georgia and the Mississippi River, and its agents schemed with Indian tribes in this region to resist American expansion. On July 21, 1784, Spain fueled the controversy by closing the lower Mississippi River to citizens of the United States.

This unexpected decision devastated western farmers. Free use of the Mississippi was essential to the economic development of the entire Ohio Valley. Because of the prohibitively high cost of transporting freight for long distances over land, western settlers—and southern planters eyeing future opportunities in this area—demanded a secure water link with the world's markets. Their spokesmen in Congress denounced anyone who claimed that navigation of the Mississippi was a negotiable issue.

In 1786, a Spanish official, Don Diego de Gardoqui, opened talks with John Jay, a New Yorker appointed by Congress to obtain rights to navigation of the Mississippi. Jay soon discovered that Gardoqui would not compromise. After making little progress, Jay seized the initiative. If Gardoqui would allow American merchants to trade directly with Spain, thus opening up an important new market to ships from New England and the middle states, then the United States might forgo navigation of the Mississippi for twenty-five years. When southern delegates heard of Jay's concessions, they were outraged. It appeared to them as if representatives of northern commerce were ready to abandon the southern frontier. Angry congressmen accused New Englanders of attempting to divide the United States into separate confederations, for as one Virginian exclaimed, the proposed Spanish treaty "would weaken if not destroy the union by disaffecting the Southern States . . . to obtain a trivial commercial advantage." Congress wisely terminated the negotiations with Spain.

By the mid-1780s, the Confederation could claim several notable achievements. It designed an administrative system that lasted far longer than did the Articles. It also brought order out of the chaos of conflicting western land claims. Still, as anyone could see, the government was struggling. Congress met irregularly. Some states did not even bother to send delegates, and pressing issues often had to be postponed for lack of a quorum. The nation even lacked a permanent capital, and Congress drifted from Philadelphia to Princeton to Annapolis to New York City, prompting one humorist to suggest that the government purchase an air balloon. This newly invented device, he explained, would allow the members of Congress to "float along from one end of the continent to the other" and "suddenly pop down into any of the states they please."

"Have We Fought for This?"

Why did Constitutional delegates compromise on representation and slavery?

By 1785, the country seemed to have lost direction. The buoyant optimism that sustained revolutionary patriots had dissolved into pessimism and doubt. Many Americans, especially those who had provided leadership during the Revolution, agreed something had to be done. In 1786, Washington bitterly observed, "What astonishing changes a few years are capable of producing. Have we fought for this? Was it with these expectations that we launched into a sea of trouble, and have bravely struggled through the most threatening dangers?"

The Genius of James Madison

The conviction of people such as Washington that the nation was indeed in a state of crisis reflected tensions within republican thought. To be sure, they supported open elections and the right of individuals to advance their own economic well-being, but when these elements seemed to undermine social and political order, they expressed the fear that perhaps liberty had been carried too far. The situation had changed quite rapidly. As recently as the 1770s, men of republican persuasion had insisted that the greatest threat to the American people was concentration of power in the hands of unscrupulous rulers. With this principle in mind, they transformed state governors into mere figureheads and weakened the Confederation in the name of popular liberties.

By the mid-1780s, persons of property and standing saw the problem in a different light. Recent experience suggested to them that ordinary citizens did not in fact possess sufficient virtue to sustain a republic. The states had been plagued not by executive tyranny but by an excess of democracy, by a failure of the majority to preserve the property rights of the minority, by an unrestrained individualism that promoted anarchy rather than good order.

As Americans tried to interpret these experiences within a republican framework, they were checked by the most widely accepted political wisdom of the age. Baron de Montesquieu (1689–1755), a French political philosopher of immense international reputation and author of *The Spirit of the Laws* (1748), declared flatly that a republican government could not flourish in a large territory. The reasons were clear. If the people lost direct control over their representatives, they would fall prey to tyrants. Large distances allowed rulers to hide their corruption; physical separation presented aristocrats with opportunities to seize power.

In the United States, most learned men treated Montesquieu's theories as self-evident truths. His writings seemed to demonstrate the importance of preserving the sovereignty of the states, for however much these small republics abused the rights of property and ignored minority interests, it was plainly unscientific to maintain that a republic consisting of thirteen states, several million people, and thousands of acres of territory could long survive.

James Madison rejected Montesquieu's argument, and in so doing, he helped Americans to think of republican government in radical new ways. This soft-spoken, rather unprepossessing Virginian was the most brilliant American political thinker of his generation. One French official described Madison as "a man one must study a long time in order to make a fair appraisal." Those who listened carefully to what Madison had to say, however, soon recognized his genius for translating theory into practice.

Madison delved into the writings of a group of Scottish philosophers, the most prominent being David Hume (1711–1776), and from their works he concluded that Americans need not fear a greatly expanded republic. Madison perceived that "inconveniences of popular States contrary to prevailing Theory, are in proportion not to the extent, but to the narrowness of their limits."

Indeed, it was in small states such as Rhode Island that legislative majorities tyrannized the propertied minority. In a large territory, Madison explained, "the Society becomes broken into a greater variety of interest, of pursuits, of passions, which check each other, whilst those who may feel a common sentiment have less opportunity of communication and contact."

Madison did not, however, advocate a modern "interest group" model of political behavior. The contending parties were incapable of working for the common good. They were too mired in their own local, selfish concerns. Rather, Madison thought competing factions would neutralize each other, leaving the business of running the central government to the ablest, most virtuous persons the nation could produce. In other words, Madison's federal system was not a small state writ large; it was something entirely different, a government based on the will of the people and yet detached from their narrowly based demands. This thinking formed the foundation of Madison's most famous political essay, *The Federalist* No. 10.

Constitutional Reform

A concerted movement to overhaul the Articles of Confederation began in 1786, when Madison and his friends persuaded the Virginia assembly to recommend a convention to explore the creation of a unified system of "commercial regulations." Congress supported the idea. In September, delegates from five states arrived in Annapolis, Maryland, to discuss issues that extended far beyond commerce. The small turnout was disappointing, but the occasion provided strong nationalists with an opportunity to hatch an even bolder plan. The Annapolis delegates advised Congress to hold a second meeting in Philadelphia "to take into consideration the situation of the United States, to devise such further provisions as shall appear to them necessary to render the constitution of the Federal Government adequate to the exigencies of the Union." Whether staunch states' rights advocates in Congress knew what was afoot is not clear. In any case, Congress authorized a grand convention to gather in May 1787.

Events played into Madison's hands. Soon after the Annapolis meeting, an uprising known as **Shays's Rebellion**, involving several thousand impoverished farmers, shattered the peace of western Massachusetts. No matter how hard these men worked the soil, they always found themselves in debt to eastern creditors. They complained of high taxes, of high interest rates, and, most of all, of a state government insensitive to their problems. In 1786, Daniel Shays, a veteran of the Battle of Bunker Hill, and his armed neighbors closed a county courthouse where creditors were suing to foreclose farm mortgages. At one point, the rural insurgents threatened to seize the federal arsenal located at Springfield. Congress did not have funds sufficient to support an army, and the arsenal might have fallen had not a group of wealthy Bostonians raised an army of four thousand troops to put down the insurrection. The victors were in for a surprise. At the next general election, Massachusetts voters selected representatives sympathetic to Shays's demands, and a new liberal assembly reformed debtor law.

Nationalists throughout the United States were not so forgiving. From their perspective, Shays's Rebellion symbolized the breakdown of law and order that they had long predicted. "Great commotions are prevailing in Massachusetts," Madison wrote. "An appeal to the sword is exceedingly dreaded." The time had come for sensible people to speak up for a strong national government. The unrest in Massachusetts persuaded persons who might otherwise have ignored the Philadelphia meeting to participate in drafting a new constitution.

The Philadelphia Convention

In the spring of 1787, fifty-five men representing twelve states traveled to Philadelphia. Rhode Island refused to take part in the proceedings, a decision that Madison attributed to its "wickedness and folly." Thomas Jefferson described the convention as an "assembly of demi-Gods," but this flattering depiction is misleading. However much modern Americans revere the Constitution, they should remember that the individuals who wrote it did not possess divine insight into the nature of government. They were practical people—lawyers, merchants, and planters—many of whom had fought in the Revolution and served in the Congress of the Confederation. The majority were in their thirties or forties. The gathering included George Washington, James Madison, George Mason, Robert Morris, James Wilson, John Dickinson, Benjamin Franklin, and Alexander Hamilton, just to name some of the more prominent participants. Absent were John Adams and Thomas Jefferson, who were conducting diplomacy in Europe; Patrick Henry, a localist suspicious of strong central government, remained in Virginia, announcing he "smelled a rat."

As soon as the Constitutional Convention opened on May 25, the delegates made several procedural decisions of the utmost importance. First, they voted "that nothing spoken in the House be printed, or communicated without leave." The rule was stringently enforced. Sentries guarded the doorways to keep out uninvited visitors, windows stayed shut in the sweltering heat to prevent sound from either entering or leaving the chamber, and members were forbidden to copy the daily journal without official permission. As Madison explained, the secrecy rule saved "both the convention and the community from a thousand erroneous and perhaps mischievous reports." It also has made it extremely difficult for modern lawyers and judges to determine exactly what the delegates had in mind when they wrote the Constitution (see the Feature Essay "The Elusive Constitution: Search for Original Intent," pp. 148–149).

In a second procedural move, the delegates decided to vote by state, but, in order to avoid the kinds of problems that had plagued the Confederation, they ruled that key proposals needed the support of only a majority instead of the nine states required under the Articles.

Inventing a Federal Republic

Madison understood that whoever sets the agenda controls the meeting. Even before all the delegates had arrived, he drew up a framework for a new federal system known as the **Virginia Plan**. Madison wisely persuaded Edmund Randolph, Virginia's popular governor, to present this scheme to the convention on May 29. Randolph claimed that the Virginia Plan merely revised sections of the Articles, but everyone, including Madison, knew better. "My ideas," Madison confessed, "strike . . . deeply at the old Confederation." He was determined to restrain the state assemblies, and in the original Virginia Plan, Madison gave the federal government power to veto state laws.

The Virginia Plan envisioned a national legislature consisting of two houses, one elected *directly* by the people, the other chosen by the first house from nominations made by the state assemblies. Representation in both houses was proportional to the state's

📖 **Read** the **Document**   Military Reports of Shays's Rebellion

This 1787 woodcut portrays Daniel Shays with one of his chief officers, Jacob Shattucks. Shays led farmers in western Massachusetts in revolt against a state government that seemed insensitive to the needs of poor debtors. Their rebellion frightened conservative leaders who demanded a strong new federal government.

population. The Virginia Plan also provided for an executive elected by Congress. Since most delegates at the Philadelphia convention sympathized with the nationalist position, Madison's blueprint for a strong federal government initially received broad support, and the Virginia Plan was referred to further study and debate. A group of men who allegedly had come together to reform the Confederation found themselves discussing the details of "a *national* Government . . . consisting of a *supreme* Legislature, Executive, and Judiciary."

The Virginia Plan had been pushed through the convention so fast that opponents hardly had an opportunity to present their objections. On June 15, they spoke up. William Paterson, a New Jersey lawyer, advanced the so-called New Jersey Plan, a scheme that retained the unicameral legislature in which each state possessed one vote and that at the same time gave Congress extensive new powers to tax and regulate trade. Paterson argued that these revisions, while more modest than Madison's plan, would have greater appeal for the American people. "I believe," he said, "that a little practical virtue is to be preferred to the finest theoretical principles, which cannot be carried into effect." The delegates listened politely and then soundly rejected the New Jersey Plan on June 19. Indeed, only New Jersey, New York, and Delaware voted in favor of Paterson's scheme.

Rejection of this framework did not resolve the most controversial issue before the convention. Paterson and others feared that under the Virginia Plan, small states would lose their separate identities. These delegates maintained that unless each state possessed an equal vote in Congress, the small states would find themselves at the mercy of their larger neighbors.

This argument outraged the delegates who favored a strong federal government. It awarded too much power to the states. "For whom [are we] forming a Government?" Wilson cried. "Is it for men, or for the imaginary beings called States?" It seemed absurd to claim that the sixty-eight thousand people of Rhode Island should have the same voice in Congress as Virginia's seven hundred forty-seven thousand inhabitants.

Compromise Saves the Convention

Mediation clearly offered the only way to overcome what Roger Sherman, a Connecticut delegate, called "a full stop." On July 2, a "grand committee" of one person from each state was elected by the convention to resolve persistent differences between the large and small states. Franklin, at age 81 the oldest delegate, served as chair. The two fiercest supporters of proportional representation based on population, Madison and Wilson, were left off the grand committee, a sure sign that the small states would salvage something from the compromise.

📖 Read the Document   The New Jersey Plan (1787)

William Paterson (1745–1806) was a distinguished lawyer, statesman, and Associate Justice of the U.S. Supreme Court from New Jersey. While serving as a delegate to the Constitutional Convention in Philadelphia in 1787, Paterson proposed the New Jersey Plan for a unicameral legislative body with equal representation from each state. Paterson's legislative proposal was rejected in favor of the Great Compromise, which provided for two legislative bodies: a Senate with equal representation for each state, and a House of Representatives with representation based on population.

The committee recommended that the states be equally represented in the upper house of Congress, while representation was to be proportionate in the lower house. Only the lower house could initiate money bills. Franklin's committee also decided that one member of the lower house should be selected for every thirty thousand inhabitants of a state. Southern delegates insisted that this number include slaves. In the so-called **three-fifths rule**, the committee agreed that for the purpose of determining representation in the lower house, slaves would be counted, but not as much as free persons. For every five slaves, a congressional district received credit for three free voters, a deal that gave the South much greater power in the new government than it would have otherwise received. As with most compromise solutions, the one negotiated by Franklin's committee fully satisfied no one. It did, however, overcome a major impasse, and after the small states gained an assured voice in the upper house, the Senate, they cooperated enthusiastically in creating a strong central government.

Compromising on Slavery

During the final days of August, a deeply disturbing issue came before the convention. It was a harbinger of the great sectional crisis of the nineteenth century. Many northern representatives detested the slave trade and wanted it to end immediately. They despised the three-fifths ruling that seemed to award slaveholders extra power in government simply because they owned slaves. "It seemed now to be pretty well understood," Madison jotted in his private notes, "that the real difference of interest lay, not between the large and small but between the N. and Southn. States. The institution of slavery and its consequences formed a line of discrimination."

Whenever northern delegates—and on this point they were by no means united—pushed too aggressively, Southerners threatened to bolt the convention, thereby destroying any hope of establishing a strong national government. Curiously, even recalcitrant Southerners avoided using the word *slavery*. They seemed embarrassed to call the institution by its true name, and in the Constitution itself, slaves were described as "other persons," "such persons," "persons held to Service or Labour," in other words, as everything but slaves.

A few northern delegates such as Roger Sherman of Connecticut sought at every turn to mollify the Southerners, especially the South Carolinians who spoke so passionately about preserving slavery. Gouverneur Morris, a Pennsylvania representative, would have none of it. He regularly reminded the convention that "the inhabitant of Georgia and S.C. who goes to the Coast of Africa, and in defiance of the most sacred laws of humanity tears away his fellow creatures from their dearest connections and damns them to the most cruel bondage, shall have more votes in a Government instituted for the protection of the rights of mankind, than the Citizen of Pa. or N. Jersey."

Largely ignoring Morris's stinging attacks, the delegates reached an uneasy compromise on the continuation of the slave trade. Southerners feared that the new Congress would pass commercial regulations adversely affecting the planters—taxes on the

👁 Watch the Video   Slavery and the Constitution

Many scholars consider the original U.S. Constitution to be a "pro-slavery document" since its articles protected the international slave trade and, through the "3/5s clause," awarded states extra representation based on the number of slaves that they held.

REVOLUTION OR REFORM? THE ARTICLES OF CONFEDERATION AND THE CONSTITUTION COMPARED

Political Challenge	Articles of Confederation	Constitution
Mode of ratification or amendment	Require confirmation by every state legislature	Requires confirmation by three-fourths of state conventions or legislatures
Number of houses in legislature	One	Two
Mode of representation	Two to seven delegates represent each state; each state holds only one vote in Congress	Two senators represent each state in upper house; each senator holds one vote. One representative to lower house represents every thirty thousand people (in 1788) in a state; each representative holds one vote
Mode of election and term of office	Delegates appointed annually by state legislatures	Senators chosen by state legislatures for six-year term (direct election after 1913); representatives chosen by vote of citizens for two-year term
Executive	No separate executive: delegates annually elect one of their number as president, who possesses no veto, no power to appoint officers or to conduct policy. Administrative functions of government theoretically carried out by Committee of States, practically by various single-headed departments	Separate executive branch: president elected by electoral college to four-year term; granted veto, power to conduct policy and to appoint ambassadors, judges, and officers of executive departments established by legislation
Judiciary	Most adjudication left to state and local courts; Congress is final court of appeal in disputes between states	Separate branch consisting of Supreme Court and inferior courts established by Congress to enforce federal law
Taxation	States alone can levy taxes; Congress funds the Common Treasury by making requisitions for state contributions	Federal government granted powers of taxation
Regulation of commerce	Congress regulates foreign commerce by treaty but holds no check on conflicting state regulations	Congress regulates foreign commerce by treaty; all state regulations must obtain congressional consent

export of rice and tobacco, for example. They demanded, therefore, that no trade laws be passed without a two-thirds majority of the federal legislature. They backed down on this point, however, in exchange for guarantees that Congress would not interfere with the slave trade until 1808 (see Chapter 8). The South even came away with a clause assuring the return of fugitive slaves. "We have obtained," Charles Cotesworth Pinckney told the planters of South Carolina, "a right to recover our slaves in whatever part of America they may take refuge, which is a right we had not before."

Although these deals disappointed many Northerners, they conceded that establishing a strong national government was of greater immediate importance than ending the slave trade. "Great as the evil is," Madison wrote, "a dismemberment of the union would be worse."

The Last Details

On July 26, the convention formed a Committee of Detail, a group that prepared a rough draft of the Constitution. After the committee completed its work—writing a document that still, after so

many hours of debate, preserved the fundamental points of the Virginia Plan—the delegates reconsidered each article. The task required the better part of a month.

During these sessions, the members of the convention concluded that the president, as they now called the executive, should be selected by an electoral college, a body of prominent men in each state chosen by local voters. The number of "electoral" votes held by each state equaled its number of representatives and senators. This awkward device guaranteed that the president would not be indebted to the Congress for his office. Whoever received the second largest number of votes in the electoral college automatically became vice president. In the event that no person received a majority of the votes, the election would be decided by the lower house—the House of Representatives—with each state casting a single vote. Delegates also armed the chief executive with veto power over legislation as well as the right to nominate judges. Both privileges, of course, would have been unthinkable a decade earlier, but the state experiments revealed the importance of having an independent executive to maintain a balanced system of republican government.

Feature Essay

The Elusive Constitution
Search for Original Intent

This nineteenth-century engraving shows how the Pennsylvania State House would have looked in 1776. After the Revolution and the drafting of the Constitution, the building became known as Independence Hall. During the hot summer of 1787, delegates kept the windows closed so that no one on the street could hear the debates.

Many prominent national leaders, alarmed at a perceived "judicial imperialism" in recent activist courts, have urged that judges interpret the Constitution strictly according to the "intent of the Framers." Arguing that a "jurisprudence of original intent" is the "only legitimate basis for constitutional decision making," intentionalists demand that judges measure decisions against a "demonstrable consensus among the Framers and ratifiers as to principles stated or implied in the Constitution."

Yet when one considers circumstances surrounding the Constitution's framing, demonstration of the Founders' intent proves elusive indeed. Delegates to the Constitutional Convention in Philadelphia in 1787 deliberately veiled the purpose of the convention in secrecy to avoid pressure by local constituencies who harbored deep suspicions concerning strong central government. Newspapers, barred from access to the convention, printed only occasional rumors. Delegates refused to speak or correspond with outsiders concerning the proceedings.

The strictness with which delegates observed the rule of secrecy not only restricted contemporary knowledge of what transpired but has also limited the number of sources in which subsequent generations may search for original intent. Only three members preserved complete accounts of convention debates. These records remained unpublished for more than thirty years, forcing the first generation of lawyers and federal judges to rely on the words of the Constitution alone for clues to the Framers' intent.

The publication of the three accounts did not necessarily make the delegates' intent more accessible. The *Journal, Acts and Proceedings of the Convention Assemblies in Philadelphia*, recorded by the convention secretary, William Jackson, provided only a chronological listing of motions, resolutions, and vote tallies. His unpublished manuscript of convention debates, which could have fleshed out the published *Journal*'s "mere skeleton" of the proceedings, was lost.

The notes of New York delegate Robert Yates appeared in 1821 as *Secret Proceedings and Debates of the Convention Assembled at Philadelphia*, but the circumstances of their publication rendered them thoroughly unreliable. Their editor, the former French minister Citizen Edmond Genêt, attained notoriety in the 1790s when he violated American neutrality in the Anglo-French war by commissioning American privateers against British shipping. Genêt supported states' rights and popular government and manipulated Yates's notes to support his views. A comparison of *Secret Proceedings* with the two surviving pages of Yates's manuscript reveals that Genêt altered or deleted more than half the original text.

If the intent of the delegates survives anywhere, Madison's *Notes of Debates in the Federal Convention of 1787* provides its likeliest repository. The "father of the Constitution," as contemporaries called him, carefully preserved notes on convention proceedings and took every measure to ensure their accuracy. Recognizing his own limitations as a stenographer, Madison did not try to record everything said but sought manuscript copies of delegates' speeches that he incorporated into his notes at the end of each day. Madison also waited until the end of each day to record his own speeches, every one of which was extemporaneous, from memory. At the convention's end, he obtained a manuscript copy of secretary Jackson's notes, which he used to supplement and correct his own. Though Madison tinkered at times with his notes over the next thirty years, recent analysis has demonstrated that none of these minor corrections impaired the faithfulness of the text.

Yet in spite of the meticulous care that Madison lavished on his notes, they remain, at best, incomplete repositories of the Framers' original intent. Each day's notes contain only a few minutes of oral discourse, whereas actual delivery occupied between five and seven hours. Furthermore, written manuscripts of speeches may have approximated only roughly what the debaters actually said. Madison's speech on the benefits of a large republic, for example, occupies two closely reasoned pages in his notes. Yet others who took notes seem to have recorded a much shorter and far less impressive oral version. Such discrepancies raise important questions. How did the Framers understand the actual speeches on the convention floor? How did their understanding shape their intentions? How much of their intent is lost in the vast omissions?

These questions take on even greater significance when one considers that the Constitution was forged through a series of compromises among representatives whose interests and intentions differed widely. No delegate was completely satisfied, and the finished document permitted some functions none had intended. Madison himself complained, for example, that the principle of judicial review "was never intended and can never be proper."

Moreover, he thought it would be a mistake to search for the original intent of convention delegates. The delegates' intent could never possibly determine constitutional interpretation, he argued, for "the only authoritative intentions were those of the people of the States, as expressed thro' the Conventions which ratified the Constitution."

Yet the works most commonly cited from the time of state ratification raise problems with the application of this principle as well. Stenographers who recorded the *Debates of the Several State Conventions on the Adoption of the Federal Constitution* did not possess skills adequate to their task, and Federalist partisans edited the speeches with abandon in order to promote their own views. Evidence also suggests that Jonathan Eliot, the journalist who published the debates in 1836, altered them further.

Given the limitations of sources most often cited by modern judges and lawyers, the original intent of most Framers remains as elusive today as it was for the first generation who had no access to those documents. The Constitution's often ambiguous wording, which furnished the sole guide to the Framers' intent in their day, remains the best recourse in our own.

QUESTIONS FOR DISCUSSION

1. Why do some lawyers and politicians still emphasize the Constitution's "original meaning" despite how the country has changed since 1787?

2. How could one try to determine the "original meaning" of the Constitution's Framers?

3. Why did James Madison believe that it would be a mistake to try to search for the original intent of the delegates to the Constitutional Convention?

As the meeting was concluding, some delegates expressed concern about the absence in the Constitution of a bill of rights. Such declarations had been included in most state constitutions, and Virginians such as George Mason insisted that the states and their citizens needed explicit protection from possible excesses by the federal government. While many delegates sympathized with Mason's appeal, they noted that the hour was late and, in any case, that the proposed Constitution provided sufficient security for individual rights. During the hard battles over ratification, the delegates to the convention may have regretted passing over the issue so lightly.

We, the People

The delegates adopted an ingenious procedure for ratification. Instead of submitting the Constitution to the various state legislatures, all of which had a vested interest in maintaining the status quo and most of which had two houses, either of which could block approval, they called for the election of thirteen state conventions especially chosen to review the new federal government. The delegates may have picked up this idea from the Massachusetts experiment of 1780. Moreover, the Constitution would take effect after the assent of only nine states. There was no danger, therefore, that the proposed system would fail simply because a single state like Rhode Island withheld approval.

The convention asked Gouverneur Morris of Pennsylvania, a delegate noted for his urbanity, to make final stylistic changes in the wording of the Constitution. When Morris examined the working draft, he discovered that it spoke of the collection of states forming a new government. This wording presented problems. Ratification required only nine states. No one knew whether all the states would accept the Constitution, and if not, which nine would. A strong possibility existed that several New England states would reject the document. Morris's brilliant phrase "We the People of the United States" eliminated this difficulty. The new nation was a republic of the people, not of the states.

On September 17, thirty-nine men signed the Constitution. A few members of the convention, like Mason, could not support the document. Others had already gone home. For more than three months, Madison had served as the convention's driving intellectual force. He now generously summarized the experience: "There never was an assembly of men, charged with a great and arduous trust, who were more pure in their motives, or more exclusively or anxiously devoted to the object committed to them."

Whose Constitution? Struggle for Ratification

What issues separated Federalists from Antifederalists during debates over ratification?

Supporters of the Constitution recognized that ratification would not be easy. After all, the convention had been authorized only to revise the Articles, but instead it produced a new plan that fundamentally altered relations between the states and the central government. The delegates dutifully dispatched copies of the Constitution to the Congress of Confederation, then meeting in New York City, and that powerless body referred the document to the separate states without any specific recommendation. The fight for ratification had begun.

Federalists and Antifederalists

Proponents of the Constitution enjoyed great advantages over the unorganized opposition. In the contest for ratification, they took no chances. Their most astute move was the adoption of the label **Federalist**. The term cleverly suggested that they stood for a confederation of states rather than for the creation of a supreme national authority. In fact, they envisioned the creation of a strong centralized national government capable of fielding a formidable army. Critics of the Constitution, who tended to be somewhat poorer, less urban, and less well educated than their opponents, cried foul, but there was little they could do. They were stuck with the name **Antifederalist**, a misleading term that made their cause seem a rejection of the very notion of a federation of the states.

The Federalists recruited the most prominent public figures of the day. In every state convention, speakers favoring the Constitution were more polished and more fully prepared than were their opponents. In New York, the campaign to win ratification sparked publication of *The Federalist*, a brilliant series of essays written by Madison, Hamilton, and Jay during the fall and winter of 1787 and 1788. The nation's newspapers threw themselves overwhelmingly behind the new government. In fact, few journals even bothered to carry Antifederalist writings. In some states, the Federalists adopted tactics of questionable propriety in order to gain ratification. In Pennsylvania, for example, they achieved a legal quorum for a crucial vote by dragging several opposition delegates into the meeting from the streets. In New York, Hamilton intimidated upstate Antifederalists with threats that New York City would secede from the state unless the state ratified the Constitution.

In these battles, the Antifederalists articulated a political philosophy that had broad popular appeal. They spoke the language of the Commonwealthmen (see Chapter 4). Like the extreme republicans who drafted the first state constitutions, the Antifederalists were deeply suspicious of political power. During the debates over ratification, they warned that public officials, however selected, would be constantly scheming to expand their authority.

The preservation of individual liberty required constant vigilance. It seemed obvious that the larger the republic, the greater the opportunity for political corruption. Local voters could not possibly know what their representatives in a distant national capital were doing. The government outlined in the Constitution invited precisely the kinds of problems that Montesquieu had described in his famous essay, *The Spirit of the Laws*. "In so extensive a republic," one Antifederalist declared, "the great officers of government would soon become above the control of the people, and abuse their power."

Antifederalists demanded direct, personal contact with their representatives. They argued that elected officials should reflect the character of their constituents as closely as possible. It seemed unlikely that in large congressional districts, the people would be able to preserve such close ties with their representatives. According to the Antifederalists, the Constitution favored persons wealthy enough to have forged a reputation that extended beyond a single community. Samuel Chase told the members of the Maryland

📖 ●▶Read the Document   *Federalist Paper* **No. 51 (Feb. 6, 1788)**

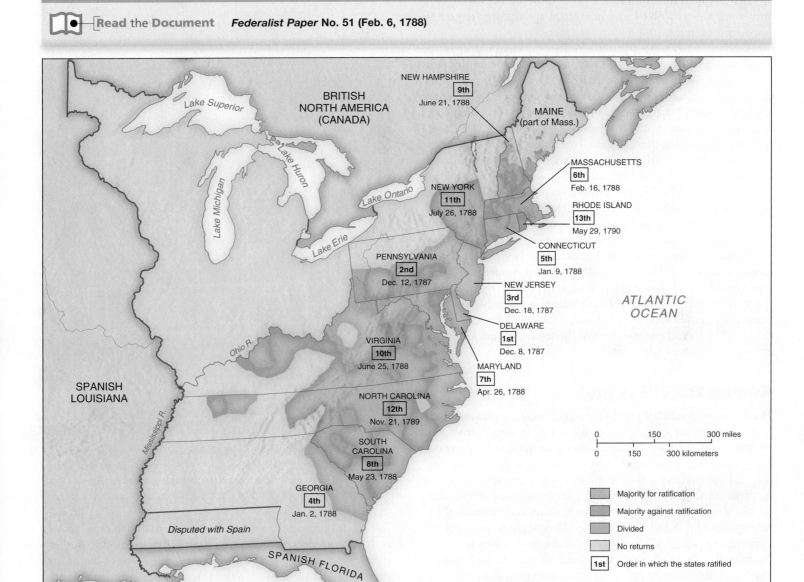

RATIFICATION OF THE CONSTITUTION Advocates of the new Constitution called themselves Federalists, and those who opposed its ratification were known as Antifederalists.

ratifying convention that under the new system, "the distance between the people and their representatives will be so great that there is no probability of a farmer or planter being chosen . . . only the *gentry*, the *rich*, and the well-born will be elected."

Federalist speakers mocked their opponents' localist perspective. The Constitution deserved general support precisely because it ensured that future Americans would be represented by "natural aristocrats," individuals possessing greater insights, skills, and training than did the ordinary citizen. These talented leaders, the Federalists insisted, could discern the interests of the entire population.

Historians have generally accepted the Federalist critique. It would be a mistake, however, to see the Antifederalists as "losers" or as persons who could not comprehend social and economic change. Although their rhetoric echoed an older moral

view of political culture, they accepted more easily than did many Federalists a liberal marketplace in which ordinary citizens competed as equals with the rich and well-born. They believed the public good was best served by allowing individuals like themselves to pursue their own private interests. That is what they had been doing on the local level during the 1780s, and they resented the imposition of elite controls over their affairs. Although the Antifederalists lost the battle over ratification, their ideas about political economy later found many champions in the age of Andrew Jackson.

The Constitution drew support from many different types of people. In fact, historians have been unable to discover sharp correlations between wealth and occupation on the one hand and attitudes toward the proposed system of central government on the other. In general, Federalists lived in more commercialized areas than did their opponents. In the cities, artisans as well as merchants called for ratification, while those farmers who were only marginally involved in commercial agriculture frequently voted Antifederalist.

Despite passionate pleas from Patrick Henry and other Antifederalists, most state conventions quickly adopted the Constitution. Delaware acted first (December 7, 1787), and within eight months of the Philadelphia meeting, eight of the nine states required to launch the government had ratified the document. The contests in Virginia (June 1788) and New York (July 1788) generated bitter debate, but they too joined the union, leaving only North Carolina and Rhode Island outside the United States. Eventually (November 21, 1789, and May 29, 1790), even these states ratified the Constitution. Still, the vote had been very close. The Constitution was ratified in New York by a tally of 30 to 27, in Massachusetts by 187 to 168, and in Virginia by 89 to 79. A swing of a few votes in several key states could have defeated the new government.

While the state conventions sparked angry rhetoric, Americans soon closed ranks behind the Constitution. An Antifederalist who represented one Massachusetts village explained that "he had opposed the adoption of this Constitution; but that he had been overruled . . . by a majority of wise and understanding men [and that now] he should endeavor to sow the seeds of union and peace among the people he represented."

Adding the Bill of Rights

The first ten amendments to the Constitution are the major legacy of the Antifederalist argument. In almost every state convention, opponents of the Constitution pointed to the need for greater protection n of individual liberties, rights that people presumably had possessed in a state of nature. "It is necessary," wrote one Antifederalist, "that the sober and industrious part of the community should be defended from the rapacity and violence of the vicious and idle. A bill of rights, therefore, ought to set forth the purposes for which the compact is made, and serves to secure the minority against the usurpation and tyranny of the majority." The list of fundamental rights varied from state to state, but most Antifederalists demanded specific guarantees for jury trial and freedom of religion. They wanted prohibitions against cruel and unusual punishments. There was also considerable, though not universal, support for freedom of speech and freedom of the press.

Madison and others regarded the proposals with little enthusiasm. In *The Federalist* No. 84, Hamilton bluntly reminded the American people that "the constitution is itself . . . a BILL OF RIGHTS." But after the adoption of the Constitution had been assured, Madison moderated his stand. If nothing else, passage of a bill of rights would appease able men such as George Mason and Edmund Randolph, who might otherwise remain alienated from the new federal system. "We have in this way something to gain," Madison concluded, "and if we proceed with caution, nothing to lose."

The crucial consideration was caution. A number of people throughout the nation advocated calling a second constitutional convention, one that would take Antifederalist criticism into account. Madison wanted to avoid such a meeting, and he feared that some members of the first Congress might use a bill of rights as an excuse to revise the entire Constitution or to promote a second convention.

Read the Document   The Bill of Rights (1789)

The first ten amendments of the U.S. Constitution are known as the Bill of Rights. Proposed by James Madison in 1789, the rights guaranteed in these amendments helped calm the fears of Antifederalists who believed that the new Constitution gave the central government too much power.

Madison carefully reviewed these recommendations as well as the various declarations of rights that had appeared in the early state constitutions, and on June 8, 1789, he placed before the House of Representatives a set of amendments designed to protect individual rights from government interference. Madison told the members of Congress that the greatest dangers to popular liberties came from "the majority [operating] against the minority." A committee compressed and revised his original ideas into ten amendments that were ratified and became known collectively as the **Bill of Rights**. For many modern Americans these amendments are the most important section of the Constitution. Madison had hoped that additions would be inserted into the text of the Constitution at the appropriate places, not tacked onto the end, but he was overruled.

The Bill of Rights protected the freedoms of assembly, speech, religion, and the press; guaranteed speedy trial by an impartial jury; preserved the people's right to bear arms; and prohibited unreasonable searches. Other amendments dealt with legal procedure. Some opponents of the Constitution urged Congress to provide greater safeguards for states' rights, but Madison had no intention of backing away from a strong central government. Only the Tenth Amendment addressed the states' relation to the federal system. This crucial article, designed to calm Antifederalist fears, specified that those "powers not delegated to the United States by the

Constitution, nor prohibited by it to the States, are reserved to the States respectively, or to the people."

On September 25, 1789, the Bill of Rights passed both houses of Congress, and by December 15, 1791, the amendments had been ratified by three-fourths of the states. Madison was justly proud of his achievement. He had effectively secured individual rights without undermining the Constitution. When he asked his friend Jefferson for his opinion of the Bill of Rights, Jefferson responded with typical republican candor: "I like [it] . . . as far as it goes; but I should have been for going further."

Conclusion: Success Depends on the People

By 1789, one phase of American political experimentation had come to an end. During these years, the people gradually, often haltingly, learned that in a republican society, they themselves were sovereign. They could no longer blame the failure of government on inept monarchs or greedy aristocrats. They bore a great responsibility. Americans had demanded a government of the people only

to discover during the 1780s that in some situations, the people could not be trusted with power, majorities could tyrannize minorities, and the best of governments could abuse individual rights.

Contemporaries had difficulty deciding just what had been accomplished. A writer in the *Pennsylvania Packet* thought the American people had preserved order. "The year 1776 is celebrated," the newspaper observed, "for a revolution in favor of liberty. The year 1787 . . . will be celebrated with equal joy, for a revolution in favor of Government." But some aging Patriots grumbled that perhaps order had been achieved at too high a price. In 1788, Richard Henry Lee remarked, "'Tis really astonishing that the same people, who have just emerged from a long and cruel war in defense of liberty, should now agree to fix an elective despotism upon themselves and their posterity."

But most Americans probably would have accepted Franklin's optimistic assessment. As he watched the delegates to the Philadelphia convention come forward to sign the Constitution, he noted that there was a sun carved on the back of George Washington's chair. "I have," the aged philosopher noted, ". . . often in the course of the session . . . looked at [the sun] behind the President without being able to tell whether it was rising or setting; but now at length I have the happiness to know that it is a rising and not a setting sun."

Study Resources

 Take the **Study Plan** for **Chapter 6** *The Republican Experiment* on **MyHistoryLab**

TIME LINE

1776 Second Continental Congress authorizes colonies to create republican governments (May); Eight states draft new constitutions; two others already enjoy republican government by virtue of former colonial charters

1777 Congress accepts Articles of Confederation after long debate (November)

1780 Massachusetts finally ratifies state constitution

1781 States ratify Articles of Confederation following settlement of Virginia's western land claims; British army surrenders at Yorktown (October)

1782 States fail to ratify proposed Impost tax

1783 Newburgh Conspiracy thwarted (March); Society of the Cincinnati raises a storm of criticism; Treaty of peace signed with Great Britain (September)

1785 Land Ordinance for Northwest Territory passed by Congress

1786 Jay-Gardoqui negotiations over Mississippi navigation anger southern states; Annapolis Convention suggests second meeting to revise the Articles of Confederation (September); Shays's Rebellion frightens American leaders

1787–1788 The federal Constitution is ratified by all states except North Carolina and Rhode Island

1791 Bill of Rights (first ten amendments to the Constitution) ratified by states

CHAPTER REVIEW

Defining Republican Culture

What were the limits of equality in the "republican" society of the new United States?

Some Americans worried that the scramble for material wealth would undermine republican values in the new nation. Disparities in wealth made some worry that a hereditary aristocracy might grow up to dominate government. Elites worried that democratic excesses would lead to men without property, and the personal independence and stability that came with it, rising to power. Enslaved African Americans and most women were denied the rights to property and the independence required to become full citizens of a republican society. (p. 131)

Living in the Shadow of Revolution

During the 1780s, why were Americans so sensitive to the dangers of "aristocratic display"?

Although some families had become newly wealthy during the Revolutionary War, most Americans had also become fervent republicans who associated any traces of aristocratic display by the rich with the privileges that British noblemen had claimed during the colonial period. They believed that a revolution waged against monarchy should not produce a new aristocracy that was legally or even visibly distinguished from its fellow citizens. (p. 132)

The States: Experiments in Republicanism

Following independence, why did the states insist on drafting *written* constitutions?

Americans believed that Britain's unwritten constitution had not protected the colonies against oppression. After independence, therefore, they demanded that their state constitutions explicitly define the rights of the people and the power of their rulers. (p. 136)

Stumbling Toward A New National Government

Why did many Americans regard the Articles of Confederation as inadequate?

During the Revolution, Americans showed little interest in establishing a strong national government. Under the Articles of Confederation (1777), an underfunded Congress limped along without direction, while the states competed over western lands. Only after Virginia ceded its claims could Congress draft the Northwest Ordinance, which provided an orderly plan for settling the Ohio Valley. The weak Congress was not even able to force the British to live up to their obligations under the Treaty of Paris of 1783. (p. 137)

Strengthening Federal Authority

What did the nationalists call for and how did they aim to achieve their initiatives?

In the early 1780s, nationalists wanted to persuade the states to amend the Articles of Confederation to create a centralized fiscal system that would allow Congress to levy import taxes and use the revenue to reduce the national debt. Extreme nationalists may even have contemplated using the army to force the states to amend the Articles if necessary. (p. 141)

"Have We Fought for This?"

Why did Constitutional delegates compromise on representation and slavery?

James Madison's Virginia Plan for the Constitution called for representation in both houses of Congress to be proportional to a state's population. Small states objected that this would put them at the mercy of larger states. Southern states feared that more populous northern states might vote to outlaw slavery. To prevent a breakdown, the delegates compromised. Each state would have an equal number of representatives in the Senate and slaves would be counted as three-fifths of a person when determining representation for the federal government. (p. 143)

Whose Constitution? Struggle for Ratification

What issues separated Federalists from Antifederalists during debates over ratification?

During the debates of 1787–1788, Federalists, who favored stronger national government, defended the Constitution against Antifederalists, who opposed centralized authority. By the end of 1791, enough state conventions had endorsed the Constitution for ratification. To appease the Antifederalists, Congress in 1789 added a Bill of Rights to protect the freedoms of citizens against the power of the national government. (p. 150)

KEY TERMS AND DEFINITIONS

Republicanism   Concept that ultimate political authority is vested in the citizens of the nation. p. 132

African Methodist Episcopal Church   Richard Allen founded the African Methodist Episcopal Church in 1816 as the first independent black-run Protestant church in the United States. The AME Church was active in the abolition movement and founded educational institutions for free blacks. p. 134

Natural rights   Fundamental rights over which the government should exercise no control. p. 136

Articles of Confederation   Ratified in 1781, this document was the United States' first constitution, providing a framework for national government. The articles limited central authority by denying the national government any taxation or coercive power. p. 138

Northwest Ordinance   Legislation in 1787 that established governments in America's northwest territories, defined a procedure for their admission to the Union as states, and prohibited slavery north of the Ohio River. p. 141

Shays's Rebellion Armed insurrection of farmers in western Massachusetts led by Daniel Shays. Intended to prevent state courts from foreclosing on debtors unable to pay their taxes, the rebellion was put down by the state militia. Nationalists used the event to call a constitutional convention to strengthen the national government. p. 144

Virginia Plan Offered by James Madison and the Virginia delegation at the Constitutional Convention, this proposal called for a strong executive office and two houses of Congress, each with representation proportional to a state's population. p. 144

Three-fifths rule Constitutional provision that for every five slaves a state would receive credit for three free voters indetermining seats for the House of Representatives. p. 146

Federalist Supporter of the Constitution who advocated its ratification. p. 150

Antifederalists Critics of the Constitution who were concerned that it included no specific provisions to protect natural and civil rights. p. 150

Bill of Rights The first ten amendments to the Constitution, adopted in 1791 to preserve the rights and liberties of individuals. p. 152

CRITICAL THINKING QUESTIONS

1. What factors kept African Americans and women from achieving full political equality in the United States following the Revolution?

2. During the Revolution and immediately afterward, why would so many Americans have opposed the establishment of a strong national government?

3. Why did Thomas Jefferson fear that the new Constitution compromised the republican ideal of government by the people?

4. Since the Federalists and Antifederalists both believed in a republican form of government, why could they not agree on the new Constitution?

MyHistoryLab Media Assignments

Find these resources in the Media Assignments folder for Chapter 6 on MyHistoryLab

Living in the Shadow of Revolution

■ **Read the Document** *Phillis Wheatley,* Religious and Moral Poems *p. 135*

Stumbling Toward a New National Government

Read the Document *The Articles of Confederation (1777) p. 138*

Read the Document *Northwest Ordinance (July 3, 1787) p. 139*

■ **View the Map** *Western Land Claims Ceded by the States p. 140*

"Have We Fought for This?"

■ **Read the Document** *Military Reports of Shays's Rebellion p. 145*

Read the Document *The New Jersey Plan (1787) p. 146*

■ **Watch the Video** *Slavery and the Constitution p. 146*

■ **Complete the Assignment** *The Elusive Constitution: Search for Original Intent p. 148*

Whose Constitution? Struggle for Ratification

Read the Document *Federalist Paper No. 51 (Feb. 6, 1788) p. 151*

Read the Document *The Bill of Rights (1789) p. 152*

■ *Indicates Study Plan Media Assignment*

7 Democracy and Dissent: The Violence of Party Politics, 1788–1800

Contents and Learning Objectives

((•●—[Listen to the **Audio File** on myhistorylab   Chapter 7 *Democracy and Dissent*

Force of Public Opinion

How did the ideas of Jeffersonians differ from those of the Federalists?

While presiding over the first meeting of the U.S. Senate in 1789, Vice President John Adams called the senators' attention to a pressing procedural question: How would they address George Washington, the newly elected president? Adams insisted that Washington deserved an impressive title, a designation lending dignity and weight to his office. The vice president warned the senators that if they called Washington simply "president of the United States," the "common people of foreign countries [as well as] the sailors and soldiers [would] despise him to all eternity." Adams recommended "His Highness, the President of the United States, and Protector of their Liberties," but some senators favored "His Elective Majesty" or "His Excellency."

Adams's initiative caught many persons, including Washington, completely by surprise. They regarded the entire debate as ridiculous. James Madison, a member of the House of Representatives, announced that pretentious European titles were ill suited to the "genius of the people" and "the nature of our Government." Thomas Jefferson, who was then residing in Paris, could not comprehend what motivated the vice president, and in private correspondence, he repeated Benjamin Franklin's judgment that Adams "means well for his

Well-wishers spread flowers in front of George Washington as he rides through Trenton on his way from Virginia to New York for his inauguration as the first president of the United States in 1789.

Country, is always an honest Man, often a wise one, but sometimes, and in some things, absolutely out of his senses." When the senators learned that their efforts embarrassed Washington, they dropped the topic. The leader of the new republic would be called president of the United States. One wag, however, dubbed the portly Adams "His Rotundity."

The comic-opera quality of the debate about how to address Washington should not obscure the participants' serious concern about setting government policy. The members of the first Congress could not take the survival of republican government for granted. All of them, of course, wanted to secure the Revolution. The recently ratified Constitution transferred sovereignty from the states to the people, a bold and unprecedented decision that many Americans feared would generate chronic instability. Translating constitutional abstractions into practical legislation would have been difficult, even under the most favorable conditions. But these were especially trying times. Great Britain and France, rivals in a century of war, put nearly unbearable pressures on the leaders of the new republic and, in the process, made foreign policy a bitterly divisive issue.

Although no one welcomed them, political parties gradually took shape during this period. Neither the Jeffersonians (also called the Republicans) nor the Federalists—as the two major groups were called—doubted that the United States would one day become a great commercial power. They differed, however, on how best to manage the transition from an agrarian household economy to an international system of trade and industry. The Federalists encouraged rapid integration of the United States into a world economy, but however enthusiastic they were about capitalism, they did not trust the people or local government to do the job effectively. A modern economy, they insisted, required strong national institutions that would be directed by a social elite who understood the financial challenge and who would work in the best interests of the people.

Such claims frightened persons who came to identify themselves as Jeffersonians. Strong financial institutions, they thought, had corrupted the government of Great Britain from which they had just separated themselves. They searched for alternative ways to accommodate the needs of commerce and industry. Unlike the Federalists, the Jeffersonians put their faith in the people, defined for the most part politically as white yeoman farmers. The Jeffersonians insisted that ordinary entrepreneurs, if they could be freed from intrusive government regulations, could be trusted to resist greed and crass materialism and to sustain the virtue of the republic.

During the 1790s, former allies were surprised to discover themselves at odds over such basic political issues. One person—Hamilton, for example—would stake out a position. Another, such as Jefferson or Madison, would respond, perhaps speaking a little more extravagantly than a specific issue demanded, goaded by the rhetorical nature of public debate. The first in turn would rebut passionately the new position. By the middle of the decade, this dialectic had almost spun out of control, taking the young republic to the brink of political violence.

Leaders of every persuasion had to learn to live with "public opinion." The revolutionary elite had invited the people to participate in government, but the gentlemen assumed that ordinary voters would automatically defer to their social betters. Instead, the Founders discovered they had created a rough-and-tumble political culture, a robust public sphere of cheap newspapers and street demonstrations. The newly empowered "public" followed the great debates of the period through articles they read in hundreds of highly partisan journals and magazines.

Just as television did in the twentieth century, print journalism opened politics to a large audience that previously might have been indifferent to the activities of elected officials. By the time John Adams left the presidency in 1800, he had learned this lesson well. The ordinary workers and farmers of the United States, feisty individuals who thought they were as good as anyone else and who were not afraid to let their political opinions be known, were not likely to let their president become an "Elective Majesty."

Principle and Pragmatism: Establishing a New Government

Why was George Washington unable to overcome division within the new government?

In 1788, George Washington enjoyed great popularity throughout the nation. The people remembered him as the selfless leader of the Continental Army, and even before the states had ratified the Constitution, everyone assumed he would be chosen president of the United States. He received the unanimous support of the electoral college, an achievement that no subsequent president has duplicated. Adams, a respected Massachusetts lawyer who championed national independence in 1776, was selected vice president. As Washington left his beloved Virginia plantation, Mount Vernon, for New York City, he recognized that the people—now so vocal in their support—could be fickle. "I fear," he explained with mature insight, "if the issue of public measures should not correspond with their sanguine expectations, they will turn the extravagant . . . praise . . . into equally extravagant . . . censures."

Washington owed much of his success as the nation's first president to an instinctive feeling for the symbolic possibilities of political power. Although he possessed only modest speaking abilities and never matched the intellectual brilliance of some contemporaries, Washington sensed that he had come to embody the hopes and fears of the new republic, and thus, without ever quite articulating the attributes necessary to achieve charisma—an instinctive ability that some leaders have to merge their own personality with the abstract goals of the government—he carefully monitored his official behavior. Washington knew that if he did not convincingly demonstrate the existence of a strong republic, people who championed the sovereignty of the individual states would attempt to weaken federal authority before it was ever properly established.

The first Congress quickly established executive departments. Some congressmen wanted to prohibit presidents from dismissing cabinet-level appointees without Senate approval, but James Madison—still a voice for a strong, independent executive—led a successful fight against this restriction on presidential authority. Madison recognized that the chief executive could not function unless he had personal confidence in the people with whom he worked. In 1789, Congress created the Departments of War, State, and the Treasury, and as secretaries, Washington nominated Henry Knox, Thomas Jefferson, and Alexander Hamilton, respectively. Edmund Randolph served as part-time attorney general, a position that ranked slightly lower in prestige than the head of a department. Since the secretary of the treasury oversaw the collection of customs and other future federal taxes, Hamilton could anticipate having several thousand jobs to dispense, an obvious source of political patronage.

To modern Americans accustomed to a huge federal bureaucracy, the size of Washington's government seems amazingly small. When Jefferson arrived in New York to take over the State Department, for example, he found two chief clerks, two assistants, and a part-time translator. With this tiny staff, he not only maintained contacts with the representatives of foreign governments, collected information about world affairs, and communicated with U.S. officials living overseas, but also organized the entire federal census! Since the Constitution tied congressional representation to state population, it was extremely important to count the number of inhabitants fairly and efficiently, a task that strained the resources of the new administration. In 1790, at a cost of only $44,377.28, hundreds of federal enumerators were dispatched to obtain an accurate tally of the nation's inhabitants. Anxious to impress predatory European monarchies with the rapid growth of the United States, Washington hoped the number would be large. The final figure of 3,929,214 people, of which some 700,000 were African American slaves, disappointed the president.

Jefferson immediately recognized that his new job would allow him little leisure for personal interests. The situation in other departments was similar. Overworked clerks scribbled madly just to keep up with the press of correspondence. John Adams, reviewing a bundle of letters and memos, grumbled that "often the handwriting is almost illegible." Considering these working conditions, it is not surprising that the president had difficulty persuading able people to accept positions in the new government. It is even more astonishing that Hamilton and Jefferson were able to accomplish as much as they did with so little assistance.

Congress also provided for a federal court system. The Judiciary Act of 1789, the work primarily of Connecticut Congressman Oliver Ellsworth, created a Supreme Court staffed by a chief justice and five associate justices. In addition, the statute set up thirteen district courts authorized to review the decisions of the state courts. John Jay, a leading figure in New York politics, agreed to serve as chief justice, but since federal judges in the 1790s were expected to travel hundreds of miles over terrible roads to attend sessions of the inferior courts, few persons of outstanding talent and training joined Jay on the federal bench. One who did, Judge James Iredell, complained that service on the Supreme Court had transformed him into a "travelling postboy."

Remembering the financial insecurity of the old Confederation government, the newly elected congressmen passed the tariff of 1789, a tax of approximately 5 percent on imports. The new levy generated considerable revenue for the young republic. Even before it went into effect, however, the act sparked controversy. Southern

planters, who relied heavily on European imports and the northern shippers who could control the flow of imports into the South, claimed that the tariff discriminated against southern interests in favor of those of northern merchants.

Conflicting Visions: Jefferson and Hamilton

Why did Alexander Hamilton and Thomas Jefferson find it so difficult to cooperate as members of Washington's cabinet?

Washington's first cabinet included two extraordinary personalities, Alexander Hamilton and Thomas Jefferson. Both had served the country with distinction during the Revolution, were recognized by contemporaries as men of special genius as well as high ambition, and brought to public office a powerful vision of how the American people could achieve greatness. The story of their opposing views during the decade of the 1790s provides insight into the birth and development of political parties. It also reveals how a common political ideology, republicanism (see Chapter 6), could be interpreted in such vastly different ways that decisions about government policy turned friends into adversaries. Indeed, the falling out of Hamilton and Jefferson reflected deep, potentially explosive political divisions within American society.

Hamilton was a brilliant, dynamic young lawyer who had distinguished himself as Washington's aide-de-camp during the Revolution. Born in the West Indies, the child of an adulterous relationship, Hamilton employed charm, courage, and intellect to fulfill his inexhaustible ambition. He strove not for wealth but for reputation. Men and women who fell under his spell found him almost irresistible, but to enemies, Hamilton appeared a dark, calculating, even evil, genius. He advocated a strong central government and refused to be bound by the strict wording of the Constitution, a document Hamilton once called "a shilly shally thing." While he had fought for American independence, he admired British culture, and during the 1790s, he advocated closer commercial and diplomatic ties with the former mother country, with whom, he said, "we have a similarity of tastes, language, and general manners."

Jefferson possessed a profoundly different temperament. This tall Virginian was more reflective and shone less brightly in society than Hamilton. Contemporaries sometimes interpreted his retiring manner as lack of ambition. They misread Jefferson. He thirsted not for power or wealth but for an opportunity to advance the democratic principles that he had stated so eloquently in the Declaration of Independence. When Jefferson became secretary of state in January 1790, he had just returned from Paris where he witnessed the first exhilarating moments of the French Revolution. These earthshaking events, he believed, marked the beginning of a worldwide republican assault on absolute monarchy and aristocratic privilege. His European experiences biased Jefferson in favor of France over Great Britain when the two nations clashed.

The contrast between these two powerful figures during the early years of Washington's administration should not be exaggerated. They shared many fundamental beliefs. Indeed, both

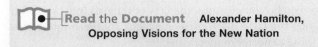

Read the Document   Alexander Hamilton, Opposing Visions for the New Nation

During the first years of Washington's administration, neither Hamilton (top) nor Jefferson (bottom) recognized the full extent of their differences. But as events forced the federal government to make decisions on economic and foreign affairs, the two secretaries increasingly came into open conflict.

Hamilton and Jefferson insisted they were working for the creation of a strong, prosperous republic, one in which commerce would play an important role. Hamilton was publicly accused of being a secret monarchist, but he never repudiated the ideals of the American Revolution. Rather than being spokespersons for competing ideologies, Hamilton and Jefferson were different kinds of republicans who, during the 1790s, attempted as best they could to cope with unprecedented political challenges.

However much these two men had in common, serious differences emerged. Washington's secretaries disagreed on precisely how the United States should fulfill its destiny. As head of the Treasury Department, Hamilton urged his fellow citizens to think in terms of bold commercial development, of farms and factories embedded within a complex financial network that would reduce the nation's reliance on foreign trade. Because Great Britain had already established an elaborate system of banking and credit, the secretary looked to that country for economic models that might be reproduced on this side of the Atlantic.

Hamilton also voiced concerns about the role of the people in shaping public policy. His view of human nature caused him to fear democratic excess. He assumed that in a republican society, the gravest threat to political stability was anarchy rather than monarchy. "The truth," he claimed, "unquestionably is, that the only path to a subversion of the republican system of the Country is, by flattering the prejudices of the people, and exciting their jealousies and apprehensions, to throw affairs into confusion and bring on civil commotion." The best hope for the survival of the republic, Hamilton believed, lay with the country's monied classes. If the wealthiest people could be persuaded that their economic self-interest could be advanced—or at least made less insecure—by the central government, then they would work to strengthen it, and by so doing, bring a greater measure of prosperity to the common people. From Hamilton's perspective, there was no conflict between private greed and public good; one was the source of the other.

On almost every detail, Jefferson challenged Hamilton's analysis. The secretary of state assumed that the strength of the American economy lay not in its industrial potential but in its agricultural productivity. The "immensity of land" represented the country's major economic resource. Contrary to the claims of some critics, Jefferson did not advocate agrarian self-sufficiency or look back nostalgically to a golden age dominated by simple yeomen. He recognized the necessity of change, and while he thought that persons who worked the soil were more responsible citizens than were those who labored in factories for wages, he encouraged the nation's farmers to participate in an expanding international market. Americans could exchange raw materials "for finer manufactures than they are able to execute themselves."

Unlike Hamilton, Jefferson expressed faith in the ability of the American people to shape policy. Throughout this troubled decade, even when the very survival of constitutional government seemed in doubt, Jefferson maintained a boundless optimism in the judgment of the common folk. He instinctively trusted the people, feared that uncontrolled government power might destroy their liberties, and insisted public officials follow the letter of the Constitution, a frame of government he described as "the wisest ever presented to men." The greatest threat to the young republic, he argued, came from the corrupt activities of pseudoaristocrats, persons who placed the protection of "property" and "civil order" above the preservation of "liberty." To tie the nation's future to the selfish interests of a privileged class—bankers, manufacturers, and speculators—seemed cynical as well as dangerous. He despised speculators who encouraged "the rage of getting rich in a day," since such "gaming" activities inevitably promoted the kinds of public vice that threatened republican government. To mortgage the future of the common people by creating a large national debt struck Jefferson as particularly insane. But the responsibility for shaping the economy of the new nation fell mainly to Alexander Hamilton as the first secretary of the treasury.

Hamilton's Plan for Prosperity and Security

Why did many Americans oppose Alexander Hamilton's blueprint for national prosperity?

The unsettled state of the nation's finances presented the new government with a staggering challenge. In August 1789, the House of Representatives announced that "adequate provision for the support of public credit [is] a matter of high importance to the national honor and prosperity." However pressing the problem appeared, no one was prepared to advance a solution, and the House asked the secretary of the treasury to make suggestions.

Congress may have received more than it bargained for. Hamilton threw himself into the task. He read deeply in abstruse economic literature. He even developed a questionnaire designed to find out how the U.S. economy really worked and sent it to scores of commercial and political leaders throughout the country. But when Hamilton's three major reports—on public credit, on banking, and on manufacturers—were complete, they bore the unmistakable stamp of his own creative genius. The secretary synthesized a vast amount of information into an economic blueprint so complex, so innovative that even his allies were slightly baffled. Theodore Sedgwick, a congressman who supported Hamilton's program, explained weakly that the secretary's ideas were "difficult to understand . . . while we are in our infancy in the knowledge of Finance." Certainly, Washington never fully grasped the subtleties of Hamilton's plan.

The secretary presented his *Report on the Public Credit* to Congress on January 14, 1790. His research revealed that the nation's outstanding debt stood at approximately $54 million. This sum represented various obligations that the U.S. government had incurred during the Revolutionary War. In addition to foreign loans, the figure included loan certificates the government had issued to its own citizens and soldiers. But that was not all. The states still owed creditors approximately $25 million. During the 1780s, Americans desperate for cash had been forced to sell government certificates to speculators at greatly discounted prices, and it was estimated that approximately $40 million of the nation's debt was owed to twenty thousand people, only 20 percent of whom were the original creditors.

Funding and Assumption

Hamilton's *Report on the Public Credit* contained two major recommendations covering the areas of funding and assumption. First, under his plan, the United States promised to fund its foreign and domestic obligations at full face value. Current holders of loan certificates, whoever they were and no matter how they obtained them, could exchange the old certificates for new government bonds bearing a moderate rate of interest. Second, the secretary urged the federal government to assume responsibility for paying the remaining state debts.

Hamilton reasoned that his credit system would accomplish several desirable goals. It would significantly reduce the power of the individual states in shaping national economic policy, something Hamilton regarded as essential in maintaining a strong federal government. Moreover, the creation of a fully funded national debt signaled to investors throughout the world that the United States was now solvent, that its bonds represented a good risk. Hamilton argued that investment capital, which might otherwise flow to Europe, would remain in this country, providing a source of money for commercial and industrial investment. In short, Hamilton invited the country's wealthiest citizens to invest in the future of the United States. Critics claimed that the only people who stood to profit from the scheme were Hamilton's friends—some of whom sat in Congress and who had purchased great numbers of public securities at very low prices.

To Hamilton's great surprise, Madison—his friend and collaborator in writing *The Federalist*—attacked the funding scheme in the House of Representatives. The Virginia congressman agreed that the United States should honor its debts. He worried, however, about the citizens and soldiers who, because of personal financial hardship, had been compelled to sell their certificates at prices far below face value. Why should wealthy speculators now profit from their hardship? If the government treated the current holders of certificates less generously, Madison declared, then there might be sufficient funds to provide equitable treatment for the distressed Patriots. Whatever the moral justification for Madison's plan may have been, it proved unworkable on the national level. Far too many records had been lost since the Revolution for the Treasury Department to be able to identify all the original holders. In February 1790, Congress soundly defeated Madison's proposal.

The assumption portion of Hamilton's plan unleashed even greater criticism. Some states had already paid their revolutionary debts, and Hamilton's program seemed designed to reward certain states—Massachusetts and South Carolina, for example—simply because they had failed to put their finances in order. In addition, the secretary's opponents in Congress became suspicious that assumption was merely a ploy to increase the power and wealth of Hamilton's immediate friends. "The Secretary's people scarce disguise their design," observed William Maclay, a crusty Scots-Irish senator from Pennsylvania, "which is to create a mass of debts which will justify them in seizing all the sources of government."

No doubt, Maclay and others expressed genuine fears. Some of those who protested, however, were simply looking after their own speculative schemes. These men had contracted to purchase huge tracts of vacant western lands from the state and federal governments. They anticipated that when settlers finally arrived in these areas, the price of land would skyrocket. In the meantime, the speculators had paid for the land with revolutionary certificates, often purchased on the open market at fifteen cents on the dollar. This meant that one could obtain 1,000 acres for only $150. Hamilton's assumption proposal threatened to destroy these lucrative transactions by cutting off the supply of cut-rate securities. On April 12, a rebellious House led by Madison defeated assumption.

The victory was short-lived. Hamilton and congressional supporters resorted to legislative horse trading to revive his foundering program. In exchange for locating the new federal capital on the Potomac River, a move that would stimulate the depressed economy of northern Virginia, several key congressmen who shared Madison's political philosophy changed their votes on assumption. Hamilton may also have offered to give the state of Virginia more federal money than it actually deserved. Whatever the details of these negotiations may have been, in August, Washington signed assumption and funding into law. The first element of Hamilton's design was now securely in place.

Interpreting the Constitution: The Bank Controversy

The persistent Hamilton submitted his second report to Congress in January 1791. He proposed that the U.S. government charter a national bank. This privately owned institution would be funded in part by the federal government. Indeed, since the **Bank of the United States** would own millions of dollars of new U.S. bonds, its financial stability would be tied directly to the strength of the federal government and, of course, to the success of Hamilton's program. The secretary of the treasury argued that a growing financial community required a central bank to facilitate increasingly complex commercial transactions. The institution not only would serve as the main depository of the U.S. government but also would issue currency acceptable in payment of federal taxes. Because of that guarantee, the money would maintain its value while in circulation.

Madison and others in Congress immediately raised a howl of protest. While they were not oblivious to the many important services a national bank might provide for a growing country, they suspected that banks—especially those modeled on British institutions—might "perpetuate a large monied interest" in the United States. And how was one to interpret the Constitution? That document said nothing specifically about chartering financial corporations, and critics warned that if Hamilton and his supporters were allowed to stretch fundamental law on this occasion, they could not be held back in the future. Popular liberties would be at the mercy of whomever happened to be in office. "To take a single step," Jefferson warned, "beyond the boundaries thus specifically drawn around the powers of Congress is to take possession of a boundless field of power, no longer susceptible to definition." On this issue, Hamilton stubbornly refused to compromise, announcing angrily, "This is the first symptom of a spirit which must either be killed or will kill the constitution of the United States."

This intense controversy involving his closest advisers worried the president. Even though the bank bill passed Congress (February 8), Washington seriously considered vetoing the legislation on constitutional grounds. Before doing so, however, he requested written opinions from the members of his cabinet. Jefferson's rambling, wholly predictable attack on the Bank of the United States was not one of his more persuasive performances. By contrast, in only a few days, Hamilton prepared a masterful essay titled "Defense of the Constitutionality of the Bank." He assured the president that Article I, Section 8 of the Constitution—"The Congress shall have Power . . . To make all Laws which shall be necessary and proper for carrying into Execution the foregoing

Powers"—justified issuing charters to national banks. The "foregoing Powers" on which Hamilton placed so much weight were taxation, regulation of commerce, and making war. He boldly articulated a doctrine of **implied powers**, an interpretation of the Constitution that neither Madison nor Jefferson had anticipated. Hamilton's "loose construction" carried the day, and on February 25, 1791, Washington signed the bank act into law.

Hamilton triumphed in Congress, but the general public looked on his actions with growing fear and hostility. Many persons associated huge national debts and privileged banks with the decay of public virtue. Men of Jefferson's temperament believed that Great Britain—a country Hamilton held in high regard—had compromised the purity of its ancient constitution by allowing speculators to worm their way into positions of political power.

Hamilton seemed intent on reproducing this corrupt system in the United States. When news of his proposal to fund the national debt at full face value leaked out, for example, urban speculators rushed to rural areas, where they purchased loan certificates from unsuspecting citizens at bargain prices. To backcountry farmers, making money without actually engaging in physical labor appeared immoral, unrepublican, and, certainly, un-American. When the greed of a former Treasury Department official led to several serious bankruptcies in 1792, ordinary citizens began to listen more closely to what Madison, Jefferson, and their associates were saying about growing corruption in high places.

Setback for Hamilton

In his third major report, *Report on Manufactures*, submitted to Congress in December 1791, Hamilton revealed the final details of his grand design for the economic future of the United States. This lengthy document suggested ways by which the federal government might stimulate manufacturing. If the country wanted to free itself from dependence on European imports, Hamilton observed, then it had to develop its own industry, textile mills for example. Without direct government intervention, however, the process would take decades. Americans would continue to invest in agriculture. But, according to the secretary of the treasury, protective tariffs and special industrial bounties would greatly accelerate the growth of a balanced economy, and with proper planning, the United States would soon hold its own with England and France.

In Congress, the battle lines were clearly drawn. Hamilton's opponents—not yet a disciplined party but a loose coalition of men who shared Madison's and Jefferson's misgivings about the secretary's program—ignored his economic arguments. Instead, they engaged him on moral and political grounds. Madison railed against the dangers of "consolidation," a process that threatened to concentrate all power in the federal government, leaving the states defenseless. Under the Confederation, of course, Madison had stood with the nationalists against the advocates of extreme states' rights. His disagreements with Hamilton over economic policy, coupled with the necessity of pleasing the voters of his Virginia congressional district every two years, transformed Madison into a spokesman for the states, echoing the substance of Antifederalist arguments he had once hotly rejected (see Chapter 6).

Jefferson attacked the *Report on Manufactures* from a different angle. He assumed—largely because he had been horrified by

Europe's urban poverty—that cities breed vice. The government, Jefferson argued, should do nothing to promote their development. He believed that Hamilton's proposal guaranteed that American workers would leave the countryside and crowd into urban centers. "I think our government will remain virtuous for many centuries," Jefferson explained, "as long as they [the people] are chiefly agricultural. . . . When they get piled upon one another in large cities, as in Europe, they will become corrupt as in Europe." And southern congressmen saw tariffs and bounties as vehicles for enriching Hamilton's northern friends at the planters' expense. The recommendations in the *Report on Manufactures* were soundly defeated in the House of Representatives.

Charges of Treason: The Battle over Foreign Affairs

How did foreign affairs affect domestic politics during the 1790s?

During Washington's second term (1793–1797), war in Europe dramatically thrust foreign affairs into the forefront of American life. The impact of this development on the conduct of domestic politics was devastating. Officials who had formerly disagreed on economic policy now began to identify their interests with either Britain or France, Europe's most powerful nations. Differences of political opinion, however trivial, were suddenly cited as evidence that one group or the other had entered into treasonous correspondence with external enemies eager to compromise the independence and prosperity of the United States. As Jefferson observed during the troubled summer of 1793, European conflict "kindled and brought forward the two parties with an ardour which our own interests merely, could never excite." The spirit of nationalism even spilled over into scientific debate. The normally dispassionate Jefferson reacted very badly when a French writer claimed, among other things, that North American animals were smaller than those found in Europe. (See the Feature Essay, "Defense of Superiority: The Impact of Nationalism on Perceptions of the Environment," pp. 166–167.)

Formal political organizations—the Federalists and Republicans—were born in this poisonous atmosphere. The clash between the groups developed over how best to preserve the new republic. The Republicans (Jeffersonians) advocated states' rights, strict interpretation of the Constitution, friendship with France, and vigilance against "the avaricious, monopolizing Spirit of Commerce and Commercial Men." The Federalists urged a strong national government, central economic planning, closer ties with Great Britain, and maintenance of public order, even if that meant calling out federal troops.

The Peril of Neutrality

Great Britain treated the United States with arrogance. The colonists had defeated the redcoats on land, but on the high seas, the Americans were no match for the British navy, the strongest in the world. Indeed, the young republic could not even compel its old adversary to comply with the Treaty of 1783, in which the British

had agreed to vacate military posts in the Northwest Territory. In 1794, approximately a thousand British soldiers still occupied American land, an obstruction that Governor George Clinton of New York claimed had excluded U.S. citizens "from a very valuable trade to which their situation would naturally have invited them." Moreover, even though 75 percent of American imports came from Great Britain, that country refused to grant the United States full commercial reciprocity. Among other provocations, it barred American shipping from the lucrative West Indian trade.

France presented a very different challenge. In May 1789, Louis XVI, desperate for revenue, authorized a meeting of a representative assembly known as the Estates General. By so doing, the king unleashed explosive revolutionary forces that toppled the monarchy and cost him his life (January 1793). The men who seized power—and they came and went rapidly—were militant republicans, ideologues eager to liberate all Europe from feudal institutions. In the early years of the **French Revolution**, France drew on the American experience, and Thomas Paine and the Marquis de Lafayette enjoyed great popularity. But the French found they could not stop the violence of revolution. Constitutional reform turned into bloody purges, and one radical group, the Jacobins, guillotined thousands of people who were suspected of monarchist sympathies during the so-called Reign of Terror (October 1793–July 1794). These horrific events left Americans confused. While those who shared Jefferson's views cheered the spread of republicanism, others who sided with Hamilton condemned French expansionism and political excess.

In the face of growing international tension, neutrality seemed the most prudent course for the United States. But that policy was easier for a weak country to proclaim than to defend. In February 1793, France declared war on Great Britain—what the leaders of revolutionary France called the "war of all peoples against all kings"—and these powerful European rivals immediately challenged the official American position on shipping: "free ships make free goods," meaning that belligerents should not interfere with the shipping of neutral carriers. To make matters worse, no one was certain whether the Franco-American treaties of 1778 (see Chapter 5) legally bound the United States to support its old ally against Great Britain.

Both Hamilton and Jefferson wanted to avoid war. The secretary of state, however, believed that nations desiring American goods should be forced to honor American neutrality and, therefore, that if Britain treated the United States as a colonial possession, if the Royal Navy stopped American ships on the high seas and forced seamen to serve the king—in other words, if it impressed American sailors—then the United States should award France special commercial advantages. Hamilton thought Jefferson's scheme insane. He pointed out that Britain possessed the largest navy in the world and was not likely to be coerced by American threats. The United States, he counseled, should appease the former mother country even if that meant swallowing national pride.

A newly appointed French minister to the United States, Edmond Genêt, precipitated the first major diplomatic crisis. This incompetent young man arrived in Charleston, South Carolina, in April 1793. He found considerable popular enthusiasm for the French Revolution, and, buoyed by this reception, he authorized privately owned American vessels to seize British ships in the name

📖—[Read the **Document** **Proclamation of Neutrality (1793)**

The execution of Louis XVI by French revolutionaries served to deepen the growing political division in America. Although they deplored the excesses of the Reign of Terror, Jeffersonian Republicans continued to support the French people. Federalists feared that the violence and lawlessness would spread to the United States.

of France. Such actions clearly violated U.S. neutrality and invited British retaliation. When U.S. government officials warned Genêt to desist, he threatened to take his appeal directly to the American people, who presumably loved France more than did members of Washington's administration.

This confrontation particularly embarrassed Jefferson, the most outspoken pro-French member of the cabinet. He described Genêt as "hot headed, all imagination, no judgment, passionate, disrespectful and even indecent towards the President." Washington did not wait to discover whether the treaties of 1778 were still in force. Before he had formally received the impudent French minister, the president issued a Proclamation of Neutrality (April 22). Ironically, after Genêt learned that the Jacobins intended to cut off his head if he returned to France, he requested asylum, married into an extremely wealthy family, and spent the remainder of his life in New York.

Jay's Treaty Sparks Domestic Unrest

Great Britain failed to take advantage of Genêt's insolence. Instead, it pushed the United States to the brink of war. British forts in the Northwest Territory remained a constant source of

tension. In June 1793, a new element was added. The London government blockaded French ports to neutral shipping, and in November, its navy captured several hundred American vessels trading in the French West Indies. The British had not even bothered to give the United States advance warning of a change in policy. Outraged members of Congress, especially those who identified with Jefferson and Madison, demanded retaliation, an embargo, a stoppage of debt payment, even war.

Before this rhetoric produced armed struggle, Washington made one final effort to preserve peace. In May 1794, he sent Chief Justice John Jay to London to negotiate a formidable list of grievances. The effort resulted in a political humiliation known simply as **Jay's Treaty**. Jay's main objectives were removal of the British forts on U.S. territory, payment for ships taken in the West Indies, improved commercial relations, and acceptance of the American definition of neutral rights.

Jefferson's supporters—by now openly called the Republican interest—anticipated a treaty favorable to the United States. After all, they explained, the war with France had not gone well for Great Britain, and the British people were surely desperate for American foodstuffs. Even before Jay departed, however, his mission stood little chance of success. Hamilton, anxious as ever to placate the British, had already secretly informed British officials that the United States would compromise on most issues.

Not surprisingly, when Jay reached London, he encountered polite but firm resistance. The chief justice did persuade the British to abandon their frontier posts and to allow small American ships to trade in the British West Indies, but they rejected out of hand the U.S. position on neutral rights. The Royal Navy would continue to search American vessels on the high seas for contraband and to impress sailors suspected of being British citizens. Moreover, there would be no compensation for the ships seized in 1793 until the Americans paid British merchants for debts contracted before the Revolution. And to the particular annoyance of Southerners, not a word was said about the slaves the British army had carried off at the conclusion of the war. While Jay salvaged the peace, he appeared to have betrayed the national interest.

News of Jay's Treaty—perhaps more correctly called Hamilton's Treaty—produced an angry outcry in the nation's capital. Even Washington was apprehensive. He submitted the document to the Senate without recommending ratification, a sign that the president was not entirely happy with the results of Jay's mission. After an extremely bitter debate, the upper house, controlled by Federalists, accepted a revised version of the treaty (June 1795). The vote was 20 to 10, a bare two-thirds majority.

The details of the Jay agreement soon leaked to the press. This was an important moment in American political history. The popular journals sparked a firestorm of objection. Throughout the country, people who had generally been apathetic about national politics were swept up in a wave of protest. Urban mobs condemned Jay's alleged sellout; rural settlers burned him in effigy. Jay jokingly told friends he could find his way across the country simply by following the light of those fires. Southerners announced they would not pay prerevolutionary debts to British merchants. The Virginia legislature proposed a constitutional amendment reducing the Senate's role in the treaty-making process. As Fisher Ames, a Federalist congressman, noted darkly, "These little whirlwinds of dry leaves and dirt portend a hurricane."

His prediction proved accurate. The storm broke in the House of Representatives. Republican congressmen, led by Madison, thought they could stop Jay's Treaty by refusing to appropriate funds for its implementation. As part of their plan, they demanded that Washington show the House state papers relating to Jay's mission. The challenge raised complex issues of constitutional law. The House, for example, was claiming a voice in treaty ratification, a power explicitly reserved to the Senate. Second, there was the question of executive secrecy in the interest of national security. Could the president withhold information from the public? According to Washington—as well as all subsequent presidents—the answer was yes. He took the occasion to lecture the rebellious representatives that "the nature of foreign negotiations requires caution; and their success must often depend on secrecy."

The president still had a trump card to play. He raised the possibility that the House was really contemplating his impeachment. Such an action was, of course, unthinkable. Even criticizing Washington in public was politically dangerous, and as soon as he redefined the issue before Congress, petitions supporting the president flooded into the nation's capital. The Maryland

Read the **Document**   The Jay Treaty (1794)

John Jay (1745–1829) was a successful lawyer and politician from New York. He served in the Continental Congress during the Revolution, co-authored *The Federalist Papers* with James Madison and Alexander Hamilton, and later became the first Chief Justice of the U.S. Supreme Court.

legislature, for example, declared its "unabated reliance on the integrity, judgment, and patriotism of the President of the United States," a statement that clearly called into question the patriotism of certain Republican congressmen. The Federalists won a stunning tactical victory over the opposition. Had a less popular man than Washington occupied the presidency, however, they would not have fared so well. The division between the two parties was beyond repair. The Republicans labeled the Federalists "the British party"; the Federalists believed that the Republicans were in league with the French.

By the time Jay's Treaty became law (June 14, 1795), the two giants of Washington's first cabinet had retired. Late in 1793, Jefferson returned to his Virginia plantation, Monticello, where, despite his separation from day-to-day political affairs, he remained the chief spokesman for the Republican Party. His rival, Hamilton, left the Treasury in January 1795 to practice law in New York City. He maintained close ties with important Federalist officials, and even more than Jefferson, Hamilton concerned himself with the details of party organization.

Feature Essay

Defense of Superiority
The Impact of Nationalism on Perceptions of the Environment

Nationalism promotes patriotism. However, these expressions of pride can turn malicious. The physical environment of a country can be seen as giving the people who live there special attributes. When claims of superiority seem to have this sort of seemingly scientific justification, the rhetoric of nationalism can become dangerous, often outright racist. Such a situation developed during the earliest years of the American republic.

Even before the Revolution, respected scientists such as Benjamin Franklin resented disparaging remarks about American inferiority. Europeans accepted as fact the notion that New World animals and humans were smaller, slower, and less clever than those found in the Old World. Franklin dismissed the theory as nonsense, and at a dinner party in Paris he took the opportunity to demonstrate that if size really mattered, then the Americans were bigger. When the abbe Raynal, a French naturalist, announced that everything American was substandard compared to European experience, Franklin challenged his host to a test. All the Americans at the table stood; so did the French. Franklin noted with satisfaction that the Americans had the "finest stature and form." Raynal, he observed, was a "mere shrimp."

Although Franklin may have won the battle of the dinner table, other Americans still worried that New World creatures fell short of European standards. The seeds of doubt could be traced to a widely read scientific treatise entitled *Histoire naturelle*, the first volumes of which appeared in 1749.

The author, French philosopher Comte de Buffon, argued that the climate of North America produced animals of smaller size than those encountered in the Old World. As evidence, Buffon cited the absence of elephants, lions, and other large beasts in the New World. The only New World creatures that exceeded their Old World counterparts in size, he declared, were the toads and snakes that thrived in North America's abundant swamps. Worse yet, Buffon asserted that America's climate caused animals found in Europe to "shrink and diminish" when transported to the New World.

For Buffon, Native Americans were a case in point. On the basis of superficial reports of Indian weakness, Buffon announced that conditions in the New World were "pernicious to men, who are degenerated, debilitated, and vitiated in a surprising manner in all parts of their organization." The implications of this idea were not lost on people such as Franklin. If the American environment sapped the Indians of vitality, it was only a matter

A COMPARATIVE VIEW OF THE QUADRUPEDS OF EUROPE AND AMERICA

	Europe lb.	America lb.
Bear	153.7	410.0
Red deer	288.8	273.0
Beaver	18.5	45.0
Otter	8.9	12.0
Cow	763.0	2500.0

Source: Adapted from Thomas Jefferson, *Notes on the State of Virginia* (1787).

Illustration of frogs from Comte de Buffon's *Histoire Naturelle*, 1749. Buffon declared that in the damp American climate only cold-blooded animals such as snakes and frogs flourished and grew larger than their European counterparts.

of time until European settlers who breathed the same air, drank the same water, and cultivated the same land succumbed to sloth. One of Buffon's followers counseled those colonists condemned to live in such an unpromising environment "to know how to make themselves happy . . . with mediocrity," leaving intellectual greatness to those who had wisely remained in the Old World.

American anger over Buffon's theory came to a boil following the American Revolution. The new nation had its honor to defend. If, as the French scientist had maintained, the North American climate caused the physical, mental, and moral abilities of humans to decline, then the republican experiment of the young United States seemed destined to fail. Having already asserted that "all men are created equal" in the Declaration of Independence, Thomas Jefferson set out to prove American equality through science. An uncompromising Patriot, he devoted himself almost entirely to the defense of the fledgling republic, spending much of the 1780s poring over accounts of American animals in search of holes in Buffon's theory.

Jefferson published his results in 1785. In *Notes on the State of Virginia* he countered Buffon with a lengthy series of tables comparing the weight of European and American animals. Not surprisingly, Jefferson always tipped the scale in favor of the New World. While Europe's puny flying squirrels weighed only 2.2 pounds, America could boast of impressive 4-pound squirrels. American bears were three times fatter than Old World bears. And most telling, America had once been the home of huge Ice Age animals called woolly mammoths. They looked a lot like elephants, and one recently unearthed in Kentucky matched the best Old World elephants in terms of size.

Jefferson did not stop there. Determined to use science to improve the international reputation of the United States, Jefferson commissioned the governor of New Hampshire to kill a giant moose, which was then shipped to Paris as a present for Buffon. The plan miscarried. While hunters managed to shoot the moose and drag it from the forest, the unrefrigerated voyage to France made for an extremely foul-smelling gift. For Jefferson, the unlucky moose's decay was a minor problem, since by his own reasoning, he had put to rest misguided European ideas about animal deficiency in the new American republic.

Turning from moose to men, Jefferson took a step that transformed a harmless squabble over the weight of squirrels into something much more alarming. Using the latest scientific research, Jefferson claimed that climate had almost no effect on human beings. Instead, a person's race determined his or her size, vitality, and intelligence. In this scheme, European Americans and Native Americans were equal. And, according to Jefferson, both were vastly superior to Africans. A celebration of national pride had now become a defense of racism.

To make his case, Jefferson first defended Native Americans against Buffon's assertions of climate-induced inferiority. Buffon had suggested that Indians' beardless faces and "lack of ardour for their female" demonstrated their physical inadequacy in comparison to manly Europeans. In response, Jefferson outlined the practice of face plucking. "With them it is disgraceful to be hairy," he claimed of Native Americans, because many believed "it likens them to hogs." Moreover, the Indians did not value French-style womanizing. Jefferson explained that "Their soul is wholly bent upon war," a trait that "procures them glory among men, and makes them the admiration of women." Differences between whites and Indians could be attributed not to the environment, but to culture. Indeed, he saw the two groups as a single race, so closely related that he recommended letting them "intermix, and become one people."

Jefferson rejected completely any notion that Africans in America could be part of this "one people." An unbridgeable biological gulf separated whites and Indians—groups that Jefferson lumped together as "Homo Sapiens Europaeus"—from blacks. Jefferson argued that while Europeans and Native Americans produced fine arts and engaged in brilliant oratory, African slaves exhibited no skill in painting or sculpture, and never "uttered a thought above the level of plain narration." With only anecdotal evidence to support his claims, Jefferson concluded that blacks were "inferior to the whites in the endowments of both body and mind." According to Jefferson, the harsh truth was that whether found in Africa, on Carolina rice plantations, or on the streets of Boston, Africans were a "different species of the same genus." They were a separate race, unworthy of genuine political and social equality.

During the late eighteenth and early nineteenth centuries, American nationalists seized upon Jefferson's ideas, seeing *Notes on the State of Virginia* as a blueprint for a republican society, grounded in rational science and dedicated to racial inequality. In a world still dominated by powerful monarchies and Old World cultures, Americans of all European backgrounds took comfort in being equal to each other and superior to African Americans. In an atmosphere of strident nationalism, few were willing to explain differences between whites and blacks as culturally conditioned. There existed, in Jefferson's words, a "real distinction which nature has made." White Americans were destined by nature to be free, while enslaved blacks, whose labor formed the backbone of the whites' economy, must accept their lesser place in the nation's future. Jefferson's scientific thinking about race—inspired by national insecurity and a Frenchman's musing on New World toads—promoted a divisiveness in American society that continues to trouble the nation.

QUESTIONS FOR DISCUSSION

1. Why were Americans such as Thomas Jefferson so defensive about the size of American animals?

2. What was the relationship between science and racism in Jefferson's thinking?

Read the Document   The Treaty of Greenville

At the Treaty of Greenville in 1795, negotiators shared this calumet, or peace pipe, a spiritually symbolic act for Native Americans. This superficial recognition of the legitimacy of Native American cultures barely disguised the Indians' crushing loss of sovereignty.

Pushing the Native Americans Aside

Before Great Britain finally withdrew its troops from the Great Lakes and Northwest Territory, its military officers encouraged local Indian groups—the Shawnee, Chippewa, and Miami—to attack settlers and traders from the United States. The Indians, who even without British encouragement fully appreciated that the newcomers intended to seize their land, won several impressive victories over federal troops in the area that would become western Ohio and Indiana. In 1790, General Josiah Harmar led his soldiers into an ambush. The following year, an army under General Arthur St. Clair suffered more than nine hundred casualties near the Wabash River. But the Indians were militarily more vulnerable than they realized, for when confronted with a major U.S. army under the command of General Anthony Wayne, they received no support from their former British allies. At the Battle of Fallen Timbers (August 20, 1794), Wayne's forces crushed Indian resistance in the Northwest Territory, and the native peoples were compelled to sign the Treaty of Greenville, formally ceding to the U.S. government the land that became Ohio. In 1796, the last British soldiers departed for Canada.

Shrewd negotiations mixed with pure luck helped secure the nation's southwestern frontier. For complex reasons having to do with the state of European diplomacy, Spanish officials in 1795 encouraged the U.S. representative in Madrid to discuss the navigation of the Mississippi River. Before this initiative, the Spanish government not only had closed the river to American commerce but also had incited the Indians of the region to harass settlers from the United States (see Chapter 6). Relations between the two countries probably would have deteriorated further had the United States not signed Jay's Treaty. The Spanish assumed—quite erroneously—that Great Britain and the United States had formed an alliance to strip Spain of its North American possessions.

To avoid this imagined disaster, officials in Madrid offered the American envoy, Thomas Pinckney, extraordinary concessions: the opening of the Mississippi, the right to deposit goods in New Orleans without paying duties, a secure southern boundary on the 31st parallel (a line roughly parallel to the northern boundary of Florida and running west to the Mississippi), and a promise to stay out of Indian affairs. An amazed Pinckney signed the Treaty of San Lorenzo (also called Pinckney's Treaty) on October 27, 1795, and in March the Senate ratified the document without a single dissenting vote. Pinckney, who came from a prominent South Carolina family, instantly became the hero of the Federalist Party.

A New Revolution in the Americas

Events in the French colony of Saint-Domingue during the 1790s presented the Washington administration with a particularly difficult foreign policy question. Located in the eastern portion of the Caribbean island of Hispaniola, Saint-Dominique was home to a large slave population of African descent. In fact these slaves far outnumbered the white French living in the colony. When these slaves rebelled against their masters in 1791, both sides called upon the United States for assistance. Washington, father of American liberty but also himself a slave owner, had to decide whether to support the rebels in their bid for liberty or the slave masters in their battle to regain control. American popular opinion, especially in the South, favored the white French population. Most white Americans were uncomfortable with the idea of an independent republic governed by free black politicians. Worse yet, a successful slave rebellion in the Caribbean might encourage slaves in the United States to insurrection. Thomas Jefferson called the expulsion of whites from Saint-Domingue a "tragedy" and warned that if something was not done to prevent the contagion of slave rebellion from spreading then "we shall be the murderers of our own children."

Washington ultimately decided to support the slave owners of Saint-Domingue. His government loaned over $700,000 to the French planters trying to restore their authority. American merchants supplied the French with arms and supplies—but also supplied the rebels. Although the southern colonies were spared any large-scale insurrections, slave owners continued to worry throughout the 1790s. The United States became home to an influx of white French refugees. In the end, the rebels succeeded in defeating their French masters. They also drove off invasions by the Spanish and British, who were at war with Revolutionary France and hoped to take advantage of the turmoil to seize the colony. In 1804, the freedom fighters declared the independence of the Republic of Haiti—the second independent republic founded in the Americas after the United States.

▶ Read the Document   The Treaty of San Lorenzo (Pickney's Treaty) (1796)

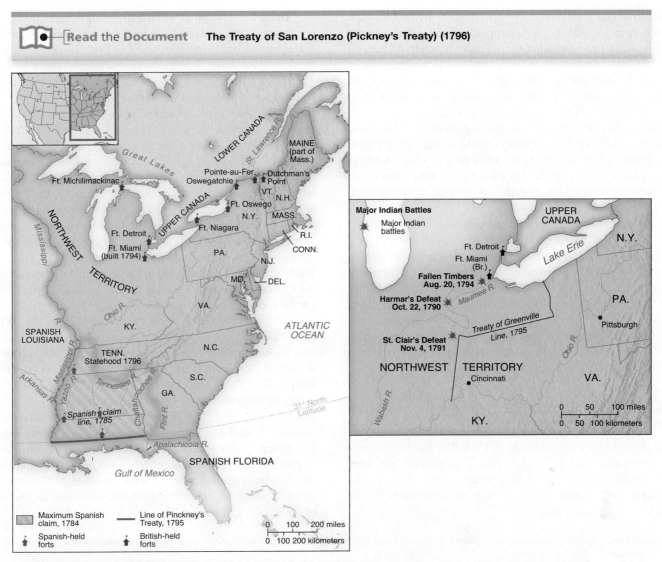

CONQUEST OF THE WEST Withdrawal of the British, defeat of Native Americans, and negotiations with Spain secured the nation's frontiers.

Popular Political Culture

Why was it hard for Americans to accept political dissent as a part of political activity?

More than any other event during Washington's administration, ratification of Jay's Treaty generated intense political strife. Even as members of Congress voted as Republicans or Federalists, they condemned the rising partisan spirit as a grave threat to the stability of the United States. Popular writers equated "party" with "faction" and "faction" with "conspiracy to overthrow legitimate authority." Party conflict also suggested that Americans had lost the sense of common purpose that had united them during the Revolution. Contemporaries did not appreciate the beneficial role that parties could play by presenting alternative solutions to foreign and domestic problems. Organized opposition smacked of disloyalty and therefore had to be eliminated by any means—fair or foul. These intellectual currents coupled with the existence of two parties created an atmosphere that bred suspicion. In the name of national unity, Federalists as well as Republicans advocated the destruction of political adversaries.

Informing the Public: News and Politics

More than any other single element, newspapers transformed the political culture of the United States. Americans were voracious readers. In 1789, a foreign visitor observed, "The common people [here] are on a footing, in point of literature, with the middle ranks of Europe. They all read and write, and understand arithmetic; almost every little town now furnishes a circulating library."

A rapidly expanding number of newspapers appealed to this large literate audience. John Fenno established the *Gazette of the United States* (1789), a journal that supported Hamilton's political philosophy. The Republicans responded in October 1790 with Philip Freneau's influential *National Gazette*. While the format of the publications was similar to that of the colonial papers, their tone was quite different. These fiercely partisan journals presented rumor and opinion as fact. Public officials were regularly dragged through the rhetorical mud. Jefferson, for example, was accused of cowardice; Hamilton, vilified as an adulterer. As party competition became more bitter, editors showed less restraint. One Republican paper even suggested that George Washington had been a British agent during the Revolution. No wonder Fisher Ames announced in 1801, "The newspapers are an overmatch for any government."

This decade also witnessed the birth of political clubs. These "Democratic" or "Republican" associations, as they were called, first appeared in 1793 and were modeled on the political debating societies that sprang up in France during the early years of the French Revolution. Perhaps because of the French connection, Federalists assumed that the American clubs represented the interests of the Republican Party. Their purpose was clearly political indoctrination. The Philadelphia Society announced it would "cultivate a just knowledge of rational liberty." A Democratic club in New York City asked each member to declare himself a "firm and steadfast friend of the EQUAL RIGHTS OF MAN."

By 1794, at least twenty-four clubs were holding regular meetings. How many Americans actually attended their debates is not known, but regardless of the number, the clubs obviously complemented the newspapers in providing the common people with highly partisan political information.

Whiskey Rebellion: Charges of Republican Conspiracy

Political tensions became explosive in 1794. The Federalists convinced themselves that the Republicans were actually prepared to employ violence against the U.S. government. Although the charge was without foundation, it took on plausibility in the context of growing party strife.

The crisis developed when a group of farmers living in western Pennsylvania protested a federal excise tax on distilled whiskey that Congress had originally passed in 1791. These men did not relish paying any taxes, but this tax struck them as particularly unfair. They made a good deal of money distilling their grain into whiskey, and the excise threatened to put them out of business.

Largely because the Republican governor of Pennsylvania refused to suppress the angry farmers, Washington and other leading Federalists assumed that the insurrection represented a direct political challenge. The president called out fifteen thousand militiamen, and, accompanied by Hamilton, he marched against the rebels. The expedition was an embarrassing fiasco. The distillers disappeared, and predictably enough, no one living in the Pittsburgh region seemed to know where the troublemakers had gone. Two supposed rebels were convicted of high crimes against the United States; one was reportedly a "simpleton" and the other insane. Washington eventually pardoned both men. As peace returned to the frontier, Republicans gained much electoral support from voters the Federalists had alienated.

In the national political forum, however, the **Whiskey Rebellion** had just begun. Spokesmen for both parties offered sinister explanations for the seemingly innocuous affair. Washington blamed the Republican clubs for promoting civil unrest. He apparently believed that the opposition party had dispatched French agents to western Pennsylvania to undermine the authority of the federal government. In November 1794, Washington informed Congress that these "self-created societies"—in other words, the Republican political clubs—had inspired "a spirit inimical to all order." Indeed, the Whiskey Rebellion had been "fomented by combinations of men who . . . have disseminated, from an ignorance or perversion of facts, suspicions, jealousies, and accusations of the whole Government."

[📖● **Read the Document** George Washington, Whiskey Rebellion Address to Congress (1794)]

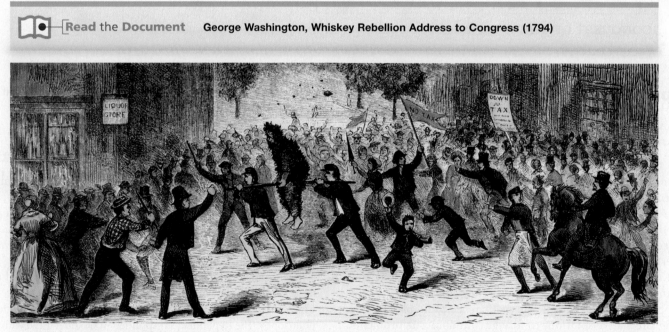

Tarring and feathering federal officials was one way in which western Pennsylvanians protested the tax on whiskey in 1794. Washington's call for troops to put down the insurrection drew more volunteers than he had been able to raise during most of the Revolution.

Source: North Wind Picture Archives.

The president's interpretation of this rural tax revolt was no less charitable than the conspiratorial explanation offered by the Republicans. Jefferson labeled the entire episode a Hamiltonian device to create an army for the purpose of intimidating Republicans. How else could one explain the administration's gross overreaction to a few disgruntled farmers? "An insurrection was announced and proclaimed and armed against," Jefferson noted, "but could never be found." The response of both parties reveals a pervasive fear of some secret evil design to destroy the republic. The clubs and newspapers—as yet unfamiliar tools for mobilizing public opinion—fanned these anxieties, convincing many government officials that the First Amendment should not be interpreted as protecting political dissent.

Washington's Farewell

In September 1796, Washington published his famed **Farewell Address**, formally declaring his intention to retire from the presidency. In the address, which was printed in newspapers throughout the country, Washington warned against all political factions. Written in large part by Hamilton, who drew on a draft prepared several years earlier by Madison, the address served narrowly partisan ends. The product of growing political strife, it sought to advance the Federalist cause in the forthcoming election. By waiting until September to announce his retirement, Washington denied the Republicans valuable time to organize an effective campaign. There was an element of irony in this initiative. Washington had always maintained he stood above party. While he may have done so in the early years of his presidency, events such as the signing of Jay's Treaty and the suppression of the Whiskey Rebellion transformed him in the eyes of many Americans into a spokesman solely for Hamilton's Federalist Party.

Washington also spoke to foreign policy matters in the address. He counseled the United States to avoid making any permanent alliances with distant nations that had no real interest in promoting American security. This statement guided foreign relations for many years and became the credo of later American isolationists, who argued that the United States should steer clear of foreign entanglements.

The Adams Presidency

Why were some Federalists willing to sacrifice political freedoms for party advantage?

The election of 1796 took place in an atmosphere of mutual distrust. Jefferson, soon to be the vice president, informed a friend that "an Anglican and aristocratic party has sprung up, whose avowed object is to draw over us the substance, as they have already done the forms, of British government." On their part, the Federalists were convinced their Republican opponents wanted to hand the government over to French radicals. By modern standards, the structures of both political parties were primitive. Leaders of national stature, such as Madison and Hamilton, wrote letters encouraging local gentlemen around the country to support a certain candidate, but no one attempted to canvass the voters in advance of the election.

During the campaign, the Federalists sowed the seeds of their eventual destruction. Party stalwarts agreed that John Adams should stand against the Republican candidate, Thomas Jefferson. Hamilton, however, could not leave well enough alone. From his law office in New York City, he schemed to deprive Adams of the presidency. His motives were obscure. He apparently feared that an independent-minded Adams would be difficult to manipulate. He was correct.

Hamilton exploited an awkward feature of the Electoral College. In accordance with the Constitution, each elector cast two ballots, and the person who gained the most votes became president. The runner-up, regardless of party affiliation, served as vice president. Ordinarily the Federalist electors would have cast one vote for Adams and one for Thomas Pinckney, the hero of the negotiations with Spain and the party's choice for vice president. Everyone hoped, of course, there would be no tie. Hamilton secretly urged southern Federalists to support only Pinckney, even if that meant throwing away an elector's second vote. If everything had gone according to plan, Pinckney would have received more votes than Adams, but when New Englanders loyal to Adams heard of Hamilton's maneuvering, they dropped Pinckney. When the votes were counted, Adams had 71, Jefferson 68, and Pinckney 59. Hamilton's treachery not only angered the new president but also heightened tensions within the Federalist Party.

Moreover, it forced Adams to work with a Republican vice president. Adams hoped that he and Jefferson could cooperate as they had during the Revolution—they had served together on the committee that drafted the Declaration of Independence—but partisan pressures soon overwhelmed the president's good intentions. Jefferson recorded their final attempt at reconciliation. Strolling home one night after dinner, Jefferson and Adams reached a place "where our road separated, his being down Market Street, mine along Fifth, and we took leave; and he [Adams] never after that . . . consulted me as to any measure of the government."

THE ELECTION OF 1796

Candidate	Party	Electoral Vote
J. Adams	Federalist	71
Jefferson	Republican	68
T. Pinckney	Federalist	59
Burr	Republican	30

The XYZ Affair and Domestic Politics

Foreign affairs immediately occupied Adams's full attention. The French government regarded Jay's Treaty as an affront. By allowing Great Britain to define the conditions for neutrality, the United States had in effect sided with that nation against the interests of France.

Relations between the two countries had steadily deteriorated. The French refused to receive Charles Cotesworth Pinckney, the U.S. representative in Paris. Pierre Adet, the French minister in Philadelphia, openly tried to influence the 1796 election in favor of the Republicans. His meddling in domestic politics not only embarrassed Jefferson, it also offended the American people. The situation then took a violent turn. In 1797, French privateers began seizing American ships. Since neither the United States nor France officially declared war, the hostilities came to be known as the **Quasi-War**.

Hamilton and his friends welcomed a popular outpouring of anti-French sentiment. The High Federalists—as members of

Hamilton's wing of the party were called—counseled the president to prepare for all-out war, hoping that war would purge the United States of French influence. Adams was not persuaded to escalate the conflict. He dispatched a special commission in a final attempt to remove the sources of antagonism. This famous negotiating team consisted of Charles Pinckney, John Marshall, and Elbridge Gerry. They were instructed to obtain compensation for the ships seized by French privateers as well as release from the treaties of 1778.

The commission was shocked by the outrageous treatment it received in France. Instead of dealing directly with Talleyrand, the minister of foreign relations, they met with obscure intermediaries who demanded a huge bribe. The commission reported that Talleyrand would not open negotiations unless he was given $250,000. In addition, the French government expected a "loan" of millions of dollars. The Americans refused to play this insulting game. Pinckney angrily sputtered, "No, no, not a sixpence," and with Marshall he returned to the United States. When they arrived home, Marshall offered his much-quoted toast: "Millions for defense, but not one cent for tribute."

Diplomatic humiliation set off a domestic political explosion. When Adams presented the commission's official correspondence before Congress—the names of Talleyrand's lackeys were labeled X, Y, and Z—the Federalists burst out with a war cry. At last, they would be able to even old scores with the Republicans. In April 1798, a Federalist newspaper in New York City announced ominously that any American who refused to censure France "must have a soul black enough to be *fit for treasons, strategems,* and *spoils.*" Rumors of conspiracy, referred to as the **XYZ Affair**, spread throughout the country. Personal friendships between Republicans and Federalists were shattered. Jefferson described the tense political atmosphere in a letter to an old colleague: "You and I have formerly seen warm debates and high political passions. But gentlemen of different politics would then speak to each other, and separate the business of the Senate from that of society. It is not so now. Men who have been intimate all their lives, cross the streets to avoid meeting, and turn their heads another way, lest they should be obliged to touch their hats."

Crushing Political Dissent

In the spring of 1798, High Federalists assumed that it was just a matter of time until Adams asked Congress for a formal declaration of war. In the meantime, they pushed for a general rearmament, new fighting ships, additional harbor fortifications, and most important, a greatly expanded U.S. Army. About the need for land forces, Adams remained understandably skeptical. He saw no likelihood of French invasion.

The president missed the political point. The army the Federalists wanted was intended not to thwart French aggression but to stifle internal opposition. Indeed, militant Federalists used the XYZ Affair as the occasion to institute what Jefferson termed the "reign of witches." The threat to the Republicans was not simply a figment of the vice president's overwrought imagination. When Theodore Sedgwick, now a Federalist senator from Massachusetts, first learned of the commission's failure, he observed in words that capture the High Federalists' vindictiveness, "It will afford a glorious opportunity to destroy faction. Improve it."

During the summer of 1798, a provisional army gradually came into existence. George Washington agreed to lead the troops, but he would do so only on condition that Adams appoint Hamilton as second in command. This demand placed the president in a terrible dilemma. Several revolutionary veterans—Henry Knox, for example—outranked Hamilton. Moreover, the former secretary of the treasury had consistently undermined Adams's authority, and to give Hamilton a position of real power in the government seemed awkward at best. When Washington insisted, however, Adams was forced to support Hamilton.

The chief of the High Federalists threw himself into the task of recruiting and supplying the troops. No detail escaped his attention. He and Secretary of War McHenry made certain that in this political army only loyal Federalists received commissions. They even denied Adams's son-in-law a post. The entire enterprise took on an air of unreality. Hamilton longed for military glory, and he may have contemplated attacking Spain's Latin American colonies. His driving obsession, however, was the restoration of political order. No doubt, he agreed with a Federalist senator from Connecticut who predicted that the Republicans "never will yield till violence is introduced; we must have a partial civil war . . . and the bayonet must convince some, who are beyond the reach of other arguments."

Hamilton should not have treated Adams with such open contempt. After all, the Massachusetts statesman was still the president, and without presidential cooperation, Hamilton could not fulfill his grand military ambitions. Yet whenever pressing questions concerning the army arose, Adams was nowhere to be found. He let commissions lie on his desk unsigned; he took overlong vacations to New England. He made it quite clear his first love was the navy. In May 1798, the president persuaded Congress to establish the Navy Department. For this new cabinet position, he selected Benjamin Stoddert, a person who did not take orders from Hamilton. Moreover, Adams further infuriated the High Federalists by refusing to ask Congress for a formal declaration of war. When they pressed him, Adams threatened to resign, making Jefferson president. As the weeks passed, the American people increasingly regarded the idle army as an expensive extravagance.

Silencing Political Opposition: The Alien and Sedition Acts

The Federalists did not rely solely on the army to crush political dissent. During the summer of 1798, the party's majority in Congress passed a group of bills known collectively as the **Alien and Sedition Acts**. This legislation authorized the use of federal courts and the powers of the presidency to silence the Republicans. The acts were born of fear and vindictiveness, and in their efforts to punish the followers of Jefferson, the Federalists created the nation's first major crisis over civil liberties.

Congress drew up three separate Alien Acts. The first, the Alien Enemies Law, vested the president with extraordinary wartime powers. On his own authority, he could detain or deport citizens of nations with which the United States was at war and who behaved in a manner he thought suspicious. Since Adams refused to ask for a declaration of war, this legislation never went into effect. A second act, the Alien Law, empowered the president to expel any foreigner from the United States simply by executive decree. Congress limited the acts to two years, and while Adams did not attempt to enforce them, the mere threat of arrest caused some Frenchmen to flee the country. The third act, the Naturalization Law, was the most flagrantly political of

┌◯┤Read the Document   The Alien and Sedition Acts (1798)

In the early years of the republic, political dissent sometimes escalated to physical violence. This fistfight took place on the floor of Congress, February 15, 1798. The combatants are Republican Matthew Lyon and Federalist Roger Griswold.

the group. The act established a fourteen-year probationary period before foreigners could apply for full U.S. citizenship. Federalists recognized that recent immigrants, especially the Irish, tended to vote Republican. The Naturalization Law, therefore, was designed to keep "hordes of wild Irishmen" away from the polls for as long as possible.

The Sedition Law struck at the heart of free political exchange. It defined criticism of the U.S. government as criminal libel; citizens found guilty by a jury were subject to fines and imprisonment. Congress entrusted enforcement of the act to the federal courts. Republicans were justly worried that the Sedition Law undermined rights guaranteed by the First Amendment. When they protested, however, the High Federalists dismissed their complaints. The Constitution, they declared, did not condone "the most groundless and malignant lies, striking at the safety and existence of the nation." They were determined to shut down the opposition press and were willing to give the government what seemed almost dictatorial powers to achieve that end. The Jeffersonians also expressed concern over the federal judiciary's expanded role in punishing sedition. They believed such matters were best left to state officials.

Americans living in widely scattered regions of the country soon witnessed political repression firsthand. District courts staffed by Federalist appointees indicted seventeen people for criticizing the government. Several cases were absurd. In Newark, New Jersey, for example, a drunkard staggered out of a tavern to watch a sixteen-gun salute fired in honor of President Adams. When the man expressed the hope a cannonball might lodge in Adams's ample posterior, he was arrested. No wonder a New York City journal declared that "joking may be very dangerous even to a free country."

The federal courts had become political tools. While the fumbling efforts at enforcement of the Sedition Law did not silence opposition—indeed, they sparked even greater criticism and

created martyrs—the actions of the administration persuaded Republicans that the survival of free government was at stake. Time was running out. "There is no event," Jefferson warned, ". . . however atrocious, which may not be expected."

Kentucky and Virginia Resolutions

By the fall of 1798, Jefferson and Madison were convinced that the Federalists envisioned the creation of a police state. According to Madison, the Sedition Law "ought to produce universal alarm." It threatened the free communication of ideas that he "deemed the only effectual guardian of every other right." Some extreme Republicans such as John Taylor of Virginia recommended secession from the Union; others advocated armed resistance. But Jefferson wisely counseled against such extreme strategies. "This is not the kind of opposition the American people will permit," he reminded his desperate supporters. The last best hope for American freedom lay in the state legislatures.

As the crisis deepened, Jefferson and Madison drafted separate protests known as the **Kentucky and Virginia Resolutions**. Both statements vigorously defended the right of individual state assemblies to interpret the constitutionality of federal law. Jefferson wrote the Kentucky Resolutions in November 1798, and in an outburst of partisan anger, he flirted with a doctrine of nullification as dangerous to the survival of the United States as anything advanced by Hamilton and his High Federalist friends.

In the Kentucky Resolutions, Jefferson described the federal union as a compact. The states transferred certain explicit powers to the national government, but, in his opinion, they retained full authority over all matters not specifically mentioned in the Constitution. Jefferson rejected Hamilton's broad interpretation of the "general welfare" clause. "Every state," Jefferson argued, "has a natural right in cases not within the compact . . . to nullify of their own authority all assumptions of power by others within their limits." Carried to an extreme, this logic could have led to the breakup of the federal government, and in 1798, Kentucky legislators were not prepared to take such a radical stance. While they diluted Jefferson's prose, they fully accepted his belief that the Alien and Sedition Acts were unconstitutional and ought to be repealed.

When Madison drafted the Virginia Resolutions in December, he took a stand more temperate than Jefferson's. Madison urged the states to defend the rights of the American people, but he resisted the notion that a single state legislature could or should have the authority to overthrow federal law.

Adams's Finest Hour

In February 1799, President Adams belatedly declared his independence from the Hamiltonian wing of the Federalist Party. Throughout the confrontation with France, Adams had shown little enthusiasm for war. Following the XYZ debacle, he began to receive informal reports that Talleyrand had changed his tune. The French foreign minister told Elbridge Gerry and other Americans that the bribery episode had been an unfortunate misunderstanding and that if the United States sent new representatives, he was prepared to negotiate in good faith. The High Federalists ridiculed this report.

But Adams, still brooding over Hamilton's appointment to the army, decided to throw his own waning prestige behind peace. In February, he suddenly asked the Senate to confirm William Vans Murray as U.S. representative to France.

The move caught the High Federalists totally by surprise. They sputtered with outrage. "It is solely the President's act," Pickering cried, "and we were all thunderstruck when we heard of it." Adams was just warming to the task. In May, he fired Pickering and McHenry, an action he should have taken months earlier. With peace in the offing, American taxpayers complained more and more about the cost of maintaining an unnecessary army. The president was only too happy to dismantle Hamilton's dream.

When the new negotiators—Oliver Ellsworth and William Davie joined Murray—finally arrived in France in November 1799, they discovered that yet another group had come to power there. This government, headed by Napoleon Bonaparte, cooperated in drawing up an agreement known as the Convention of Mortefontaine. The French refused to compensate the Americans for vessels taken during the Quasi-War, but they did declare the treaties of 1778 null and void. Moreover, the convention removed annoying French restrictions on U.S. commerce. Not only had Adams avoided war, but he had also created an atmosphere of mutual trust that paved the way for the purchase of the Louisiana Territory. The president declared with considerable justification that the second French mission was "the most disinterested, the most determined and the most successful [act] of my whole life." It also cost him reelection.

The Peaceful Revolution: The Election of 1800

What did Jefferson mean when he claimed in his first inaugural address that "We are all republicans; we are all federalists"?

On the eve of the election of 1800, the Federalists were fatally divided. Adams enjoyed wide popularity among the Federalist rank and file, especially in New England, but articulate party leaders such as Hamilton vowed to punish the president for his betrayal of their militant policies. Hamilton even composed a scathing pamphlet titled *Letter Concerning the Public Conduct and Character of John Adams*, an essay that questioned Adams's ability to hold high office.

Once again the former secretary of the treasury attempted to rig the voting in the Electoral College so that the party's vice presidential candidate, Charles Cotesworth Pinckney, would receive more ballots than Adams and America would be saved from "the fangs of Jefferson." As in 1796, the conspiracy backfired. The Republicans gained 73 votes while the Federalists trailed with 65.

To everyone's surprise, however, the election was not resolved in the Electoral College. When the ballots were counted, Jefferson and his running mate, Aaron Burr, had tied. This accident—a Republican elector should have thrown away his second vote—sent the selection of the next president to the House of Representatives, a lame-duck body still controlled by members of the Federalist Party.

As the House began its work on February 27, 1801, excitement ran high. Each state delegation cast a single vote, with nine votes needed for election. On the first ballot, Jefferson received the support of eight states, Burr six, and two states divided evenly.

People predicted a quick victory for Jefferson, but after dozens of ballots, the House had still not selected a president. "The scene was now ludicrous," observed one witness. "Many had sent home for night-caps and pillows, and wrapped in shawls and greatcoats, lay about the floor of the committee-rooms, or sat sleeping in their seats." The drama dragged on for days. To add to the confusion, Burr unaccountably refused to withdraw. Contemporaries thought his ambition had overcome his good sense.

The logjam finally broke when leading Federalists decided that Jefferson, whatever his faults, would make a more responsible president than would the shifty Burr. Even Hamilton labeled Burr "the most dangerous man of the community." On the thirty-sixth ballot, Representative James A. Bayard of Delaware announced he no longer supported Burr. This decision, coupled with Burr's inaction, gave Jefferson the presidency, ten states to four.

THE ELECTION OF 1800

Candidate	Party	Electoral Vote
Jefferson	Republican	73
Burr	Republican	73
J. Adams	Federalist	65
C. Pinckney	Federalist	64

The Twelfth Amendment, ratified in 1804, saved the American people from repeating this potentially dangerous turn of events. Henceforth, the Electoral College cast separate ballots for president and vice president.

((•—[Listen to the **Audio File**   **Jefferson and Liberty**

William Birch's illustration of the partially constructed United States Capitol building in Washington, D.C., in 1800. When Jefferson first took office, the nation's new capital was little more than a swampy and isolated village.

During the final days of his presidency, Adams appointed as many Federalists as possible to the federal bench. Jefferson protested the hasty manner in which these "midnight judges" were selected. One of them, John Marshall, became chief justice of the United States, a post he held with distinction for thirty-four years. But behind the last-minute flurry of activity lay bitterness and disappointment. Adams never forgave Hamilton. "No party," the Federalist president wrote, "that ever existed knew itself so little or so vainly overrated its own influence and popularity as ours. None ever understood so ill the causes of its own power, or so wantonly destroyed them." On the morning of Jefferson's inauguration, Adams slipped away from the capital—now located in Washington, D.C.—unnoticed and unappreciated.

In the address that Adams missed, Jefferson attempted to quiet partisan fears. "We are all republicans; we are all federalists," the new president declared. By this statement, he did not mean to suggest that party differences were no longer important. Jefferson reminded his audience that whatever the politicians might say, the people shared a deep commitment to a federal union based on republican ideals set forth during the American Revolution. Indeed, the president interpreted the election of 1800 as a revolutionary episode, as the fulfillment of the principles of 1776.

The Federalists were thoroughly dispirited by the entire experience. In the end, it had not been Hamilton's foolish electoral schemes that destroyed the party's chances in 1800. Rather, the Federalists had lost touch with a majority of the American people. In office, Adams and Hamilton—whatever their own differences may have been—betrayed their doubts about popular sovereignty too often, and when it came time to marshal broad support, to mobilize public opinion in favor of the party of wealth and privilege, few responded. As Secretary of War Oliver Wolcott observed on hearing of Jefferson's victory, "Have our party shown that they possess the necessary skill and courage to deserve . . . to govern? What have they done? . . . They write private letters. To whom? To each other, but they do nothing to give a proper direction to the public mind."

Conclusion: Danger of Political Extremism

From a broader historical perspective, the election of 1800 seems noteworthy for what did not occur. There were no riots in the streets, no attempted coup by military officers, no secession from the Union, nothing except the peaceful transfer of government from the leaders of one political party to those of the opposition.

Americans had weathered the Alien and Sedition Acts, the meddling by predatory foreign powers in domestic affairs, the shrilly partisan rhetoric of hack journalists, and now, at the start of a new century, they were impressed with their own achievement. As one woman who attended Jefferson's inauguration noted, "The changes of administration which in every government and in every age have most generally been epochs of confusion, villainy and bloodshed, in this our happy country take place without any species of distraction, or disorder." But as she well understood—indeed, as modern Americans must constantly relearn—extremism in the name of partisan political truth can easily unravel the delicate fabric of representative democracy and leave the republic at the mercy of those who would manipulate the public for private benefit.

Study Resources

 Take the **Study Plan** for **Chapter 7** *Democracy and Dissent* on **MyHistoryLab**

TIME LINE

1787 Constitution of the United States signed (September)

1789 George Washington inaugurated (April); Louis XVI of France calls meeting of the Estates General (May)

1790 Congress approves Hamilton's plan for funding and assumption (July)

1791 Bank of the United States is chartered (February); Hamilton's *Report on Manufactures* rejected by Congress (December)

1793 France's revolutionary government announces a "war of all people against all kings" (February); Genêt affair strains relations with France (April); Washington issues Proclamation of Neutrality (April); Spread of "Democratic" clubs alarms Federalists; Jefferson resigns as secretary of state (December)

1794 Whiskey Rebellion put down by U.S. Army (July–November); General Anthony Wayne defeats Indians at the Battle of Fallen Timbers (August)

1795 Hamilton resigns as secretary of the treasury (January); Jay's Treaty divides the nation (June); Pinckney's Treaty with Spain is a welcome surprise (October)

1796 Washington publishes Farewell Address (September); John Adams elected president (December)

1797 XYZ Affair poisons U.S. relations with France (October)

1798–1800 Quasi-War with France

1798 Congress passes the Alien and Sedition Acts (June and July); Provisional army is formed; Virginia and Kentucky Resolutions protest the Alien and Sedition Acts (November and December)

1799 George Washington dies (December)

1800 Convention of Mortefontaine is signed with France, ending Quasi-War (September)

1801 House of Representatives elects Thomas Jefferson president (February)

CHAPTER REVIEW

Force of Public Opinion

How did the ideas of Jeffersonians differ from those of the Federalists?

While both Jeffersonians and Federalists agreed that the new United States would eventually become a great commercial power, they differed on how best to achieve the transition from an agrarian economy to an international system based on trade and industry. The Federalists believed that this would require strong national institutions directed by a social elite, but Jeffersonians distrusted strong financial institutions and put their faith in independent white yeomen farmers who would be free of intrusive government regulations. (p. 156)

Principle and Pragmatism: Establishing a New Government

Why was George Washington unable to overcome division within the new government?

Despite his huge popularity among all segments of the American population, President Washington was unable to bridge the differences between the two most brilliant and strong-willed members of his cabinet: Thomas Jefferson and Alexander Hamilton. These two men fought throughout Washington's presidency over their different visions for the future of the republic. Hamilton imagined an urban commercial nation with a strong central government; Jefferson championed a simple agrarian republic. (p. 158)

Conflicting Visions: Jefferson and Hamilton

Why did Alexander Hamilton and Thomas Jefferson find it so difficult to cooperate as members of Washington's cabinet?

While both Hamilton and Jefferson insisted they were working to create a strong, prosperous republic in which commerce would be important, they differed profoundly on how to achieve that goal. Where Hamilton was pro-British and wanted the American economy to imitate Britain's reliance on trade and industry, Jefferson supported the French Revolution and believed that America's economic strength lay not in developing an industrial workforce but in increasing the country's agricultural productivity, so that farmers could exchange raw materials for imported manufactured goods. (p. 159)

Hamilton's Plan for Prosperity and Security

Why did many Americans oppose Alexander Hamilton's blueprint for national prosperity?

Many citizens—especially farmers and former soldiers—felt that Hamilton's plan to fund state loan certificates at full value would reward the immoral, unrepublican and un-American actions of speculators by allowing them to make money without physical labor. Many also complained that this plan rewarded the financial irresponsibility of states like Massachusetts and South Carolina. Supporters of Jefferson rejected Hamilton's vision of the United States as a commercial and manufacturing nation, feared that his plan for a Bank of the United States would "perpetuate a large monied interest," and protested that his doctrine of implied powers would lead to the steady growth of governmental power. (p. 161)

Charges of Treason: The Battle over Foreign Affairs

How did foreign affairs affect domestic politics during the 1790s?

The French Revolution split American opinion. Republicans cheered it; Federalists condemned it. When France declared war on Britain (1793), the extremely unpopular Jay's Treaty (1794) with Britain provoked heated political debate between its Federalist supporters and Republican opponents. Disagreements over how to deal with French aggression and insults during the Quasi-War and the XYZ Affair drove a wedge between the peace-seeking President John Adams and the High Federalists who called for war and military expansion. This divide helped Jefferson win the election of 1800. (p. 163)

Popular Political Culture

Why was it hard for Americans to accept political dissent as a part of political activity?

In the 1790s, many Americans equated political dissent with disloyalty. During the Whiskey Rebellion (1794), both Federalists and Republicans feared the other party planned to use violence to crush political opposition. In the 1790s, many Americans lamented the loss of unity that had tied them together during the struggle for independence. They feared that partisan politics might lead to a conspiracy to overthrow the legitimately elected government. (p. 169)

The Adams Presidency

Why were some Federalists willing to sacrifice political freedoms for party advantage?

Many Republicans believed that the support of Jeffersonian Republicans for France had compromised American sovereignty. Hamilton and the High Federalists believed that a standing army was necessary to defend against invasion and to silence domestic dissent so that it could not split the republic apart. They rationalized that the sacrifice of political liberties entailed in the Alien and Sedition Acts were necessary to protect the Republic from corrupting foreign (particularly French influences). This was especially important since they anticipated the onset of a war with France. They used the rationale of national security to justify their pursuit of party power. (p. 171)

The Peaceful Revolution: The Election of 1800

What did Jefferson mean when he claimed in his first inaugural address that "we are all Republicans, we are all Federalists"?

Jefferson did not mean that party differences had disappeared or were no longer important after the election of 1800. Instead, he wished to remind his audience that whatever their political differences, the people were united by a deep commitment to a federal union based on republican ideals as set forth in the American Revolution. (p. 174)

KEY TERMS AND DEFINITIONS

Bank of the United States   National bank proposed by Secretary of the Treasury Alexander Hamilton and established in 1791. It served as a central depository for the U.S. government and had the authority to issue currency. p. 162

Implied powers   Powers the Constitution did not explicitly grant the federal government, but that it could be interpreted to grant. p. 162

French Revolution   A social and political revolution in France (1789–1799). p. 163

Jay's Treaty   Treaty with Britain negotiated by Chief Justice John Jay in 1794. Though the British agreed to surrender forts on U.S. territory, the treaty provoked a storm of protest in America. p. 164

Whiskey Rebellion   Protests in 1794 by western Pennsylvania farmers against a federal tax on whiskey. The uprising was suppressed when President George Washington called an army of 15,000 troops to the area. p. 170

Farewell Address   In this 1796 document, President George Washington announced his intention not to seek a third term. He also stressed Federalist interests and warned Americans against political factions and foreign entanglements. p. 171

Quasi-War   Undeclared war between the United States and France in the late 1790s. p. 171

XYZ Affair   A diplomatic incident in which American peace commissioners sent to France by President John Adams in 1797 were insulted with bribe demands from their French counterparts, dubbed X, Y, and Z in American newspapers. The incident heightened war fever against France. p. 172

Alien and Sedition Acts   Collective name given to four laws Congress passed in 1798 to suppress criticism of the federal government and curb liberties of foreigners living in the United States. p. 172

Kentucky and Virginia Resolutions   Statements penned by Thomas Jefferson and James Madison to mobilize opposition to the Alien and Sedition Acts, which they argued were unconstitutional. Jefferson's statement (the Kentucky Resolution) suggested that states could declare null and void congressional acts they deemed unconstitutional. p. 173

CRITICAL THINKING QUESTIONS

1. How were the disagreements between Hamilton and Jefferson a reflection of popular culture in the country during the 1790s?

2. How did American foreign policy during the 1790s influence the growth of political dissent?

3. How important were popular opinion and party politics in poisoning the Adams presidency?

4. How could a constitutional republic justify the passage of highly partisan legislation such as the Alien and Sedition Acts?

MyHistoryLab Media Assignments

Find these resources in the Media Assignments folder for Chapter 7 on MyHistoryLab

Force of Public Opinion

Watch the **Video**   *George Washington: The Father of Our Country p. 157*

Conflicting Visions: Jefferson and Hamilton

Read the **Document**   *Alexander Hamilton, Opposing Visions for the New Nation p. 160*

Charges of Treason: The Battle over Foreign Affairs

Read the **Document**   *Proclamation of Neutrality (1793) p. 164*

Read the **Document**   *The Jay Treaty (1794) p. 165*

Complete the **Assignment**   *Defense of Superiority: The Impact of Nationalism on Perceptions of the Environment p. 166*

Read the **Document**   *The Treaty of Greenville p. 168*

Read the **Document**   *The Treaty of San Lorenzo (Pickney's Treaty) (1796) p. 169*

Popular Political Culture

Read the **Document**   *George Washington, Whiskey Rebellion Address to Congress (1794) p. 170*

The Adams Presidency

Read the **Document**   *The Alien and Sedition Acts (1798) p. 173*

The Peaceful Revolution: The Election of 1800

Listen to the **Audio File**   *Jefferson and Liberty p. 174*

■ *Indicates Study Plan Media Assignment*

8 Republican Ascendancy:
The Jeffersonian Vision

Contents and **Learning Objectives**

((•●—|Listen to the **Audio File** on **myhistorylab**   Chapter 8 *Republican Ascendancy*

Limits of Equality

British visitors often expressed contempt for Jeffersonian society. Wherever they traveled in the young republic, they met ill-mannered people inspired with a ruling passion for liberty and equality. Charles William Janson, an Englishman who lived in the United States for thirteen years, recounted an exchange he found particularly unsettling that had occurred at the home of an American acquaintance. "On knocking at the door," he reported, "it was opened by a servant maid, whom I had never before seen." The woman's behavior astonished Janson. "The following is the dialogue, word for word, which took place on this occasion:—'Is your master at home?'—'I have no master.'—'Don't you live here?'—'I stay here.'—'And who are you then?'—'Why, I am Mr.———'s help. I'd have you know, man, that I am no sarvant [sic]; none but negers [sic] are sarvants.'"

Standing on his friend's doorstep, Janson encountered the authentic voice of Jeffersonian republicanism—self-confident, assertive, blatantly racist, and having no intention of being relegated to low social status. The maid who answered the door believed she was her employer's equal, perhaps not in wealth but surely in character. She may have even dreamed of someday owning a house staffed with "help." American society fostered such ambition. In the early nineteenth century, thousands of settlers poured across the Appalachian Mountains or moved to cities in search of opportunity. Thomas Jefferson and individuals who stood for public office under the banner of the Republican Party claimed to speak for these people.

The limits of the Jeffersonian vision were obvious even to contemporaries. The people who spoke most eloquently about equal opportunity often owned slaves. As early as the 1770s, the famed English essayist Samuel Johnson had chided Americans for their hypocrisy. "How is it," he asked the indignant rebels, "that we hear the loudest yelps for liberty from the drivers of Negroes?" Little had changed since the Revolution. African Americans, who represented one-fifth of the population of the United States, were totally excluded from the new opportunities opening up in the cities and the West. Indeed, the maid in the incident just described insisted—with no apparent sense of inconsistency—that her position was superior to that of blacks, who were brought involuntarily to lifelong servitude.

It is not surprising that in this highly charged racial climate that leaders of the Federalist Party accused the Republicans, especially those who lived in the South, of disingenuousness, and in 1804, one Massachusetts Federalist sarcastically defined "Jeffersonian" as "an Indian word, signifying 'a great tobacco planter, who had herds of black slaves.'" The race issue was always

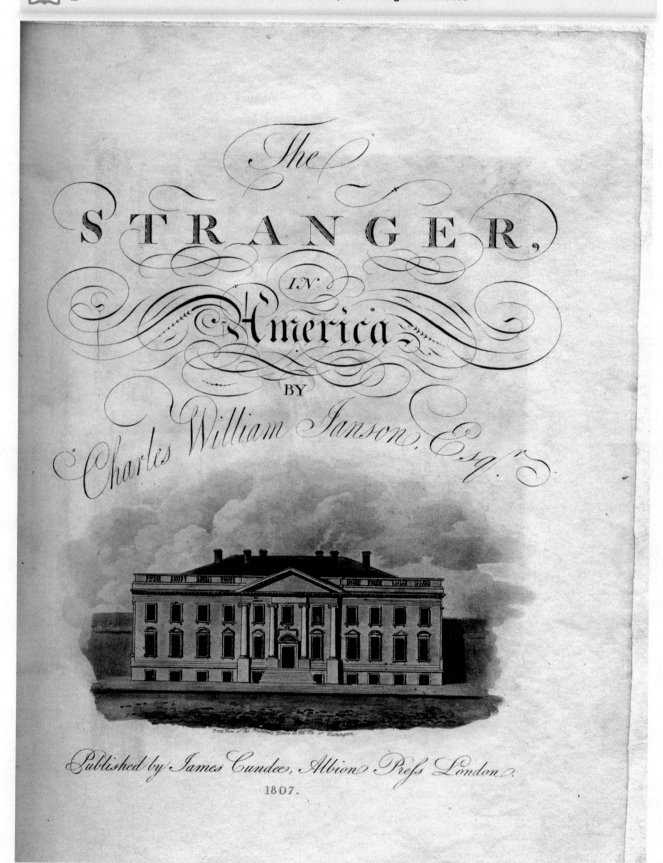

The STRANGER, IN America

BY

Charles William Janson, Esq.

Front View of the President's House in the City of Washington.

Published by James Cundee, Albion Press London
1807.

Charles William Janson published his book, *The Stranger in America* in 1807. In it, he offered a dim view of Jeffersonian America and the passion for liberty and equality it represented.

just beneath the surface of political maneuvering. Indeed, the acquisition of the Louisiana Territory and the War of 1812 fanned fundamental disagreement about the spread of slavery to the western territories.

In other areas, the Jeffersonians did not fulfill even their own high expectations. As members of an opposition party during the presidency of John Adams, they insisted on a strict interpretation of the Constitution, peaceful foreign relations, and a reduction of the role of the federal government in the lives of the average citizens. But following the election of 1800, Jefferson and his supporters discovered that unanticipated pressures, foreign and domestic, forced them to moderate these goals. Before he retired from public office, Jefferson interpreted the Constitution in a way that permitted the government to purchase the Louisiana Territory when the opportunity arose; he regulated the national economy with a rigor that would have surprised Alexander Hamilton; and he led the country to the brink of war. Some Americans praised the president's pragmatism; others felt betrayed. For a man who played a leading role in the revolt against George III, it must have been shocking in 1807 to find himself labeled a "despot" in a popular New England newspaper. "Give ear no longer to the siren voice of democracy and Jeffersonian liberty," the editor shrieked. "It is a cursed delusion, adopted by traitors, and recommended by sycophants."

Regional Identities in a New Republic

How did the Republic's growth shape the market economy and relations with Native Americans?

During the early decades of the nineteenth century, the population of the United States experienced substantial growth. The 1810 census counted 7,240,000 Americans, a jump of almost two million in just ten years. Of this total, approximately 20 percent were black slaves, the majority of whom lived in the South. The large population increase in the nation was the result primarily of natural reproduction, since during Jefferson's presidency few immigrants moved to the New World. The largest single group in this society was children under the age of sixteen, boys and girls who were born after Washington's election and who defined their own futures at a time when the nation's boundaries were rapidly expanding. For

NORTH AMERICA IN 1800 In the 1790s, diplomatic agreements with Britain and Spain and defeat of the Native Americans at the Battle of Fallen Timbers opened the way to U.S. settlement of the land beyond the Appalachian Mountains.

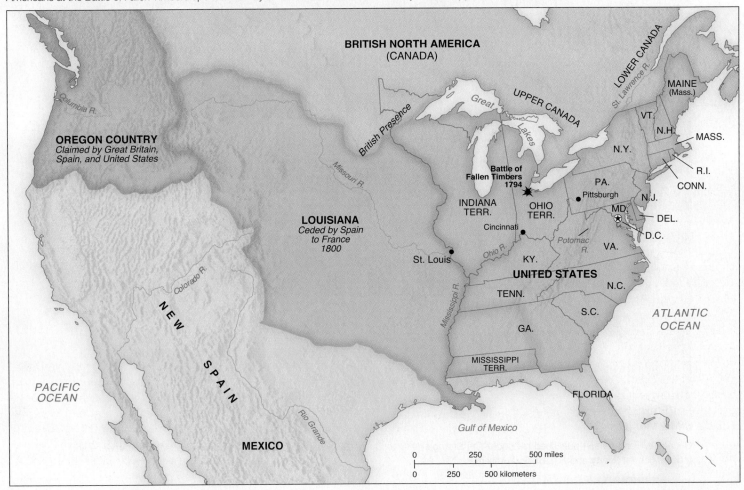

white Americans, it was a time of heightened optimism, and many people possessing entrepreneurial skills or engineering capabilities aggressively made their way in a society that seemed to rate personal merit higher than family background.

Even as Americans defended the rights of individual states, they were forming strong regional identifications. In commerce and politics, they perceived themselves as representatives of distinct subcultures—as Southerners, New Englanders, or Westerners. No doubt, the broadening geographic horizons reflected improved transportation links that enabled people to travel more easily within the various sections. But the growing regional mentality was also the product of defensiveness. While local writers celebrated New England's cultural distinctiveness, for example, they were clearly uneasy about the region's rejection of the democratic values that were sweeping the rest of the nation. Moreover, during this period people living south of the Potomac River began describing themselves as Southerners, not as citizens of the Chesapeake or the Carolinas as they had done in colonial times.

This shifting focus of attention resulted not only from an awareness of shared economic interests but also from a sensitivity to outside attacks on slavery. Several times during the first fifteen years of the nineteenth century, conspirators actually advocated secession, and though the schemes failed, they revealed the powerful sectional loyalties that threatened national unity.

Westward the Course of Empire

The most striking changes occurred in the West. Before the end of the American Revolution, only Indian traders and a few hardy settlers had ventured across the Appalachians. After 1790, however, a flood of people rushed west to stake out farms on the rich soil. Many settlers followed the so-called northern route across Pennsylvania or New York into the old Northwest Territory. Pittsburgh and Cincinnati, both strategically located on the Ohio River, became important commercial ports. In 1803, Ohio joined the Union, and territorial governments were formed in Indiana (1800), Louisiana (1805), Michigan (1805), Illinois (1809), and Missouri (1812). Southerners poured into the new states of Kentucky (1792) and Tennessee (1796). Wherever they located, Westerners depended on water transportation. Because of the extraordinarily high cost of hauling goods overland, riverboats represented the only economical means of carrying agricultural products to distant markets. The Mississippi River was the crucial commercial link for the entire region, and Westerners did not feel secure so long as New Orleans, the southern gate to the Mississippi, remained under Spanish control.

Families that moved west attempted to transplant familiar eastern customs to the frontier. In some areas, such as the Western Reserve, a narrow strip of land along Lake Erie in northern Ohio, the influence of New England remained strong. In general, however, a creative mixing of peoples of different backgrounds in a strange environment generated distinctive folkways. Westerners developed their own heroes, such as Mike Fink, the legendary keelboatman of the Mississippi River; Daniel Boone, the famed trapper and Indian fighter; and the eye-gouging "alligatormen" of Kentucky and Tennessee. Americans who crossed the mountains were ambitious and self-confident, excited by the challenge of almost unlimited geographic mobility. A French traveler observed in 1802 that throughout the region he visited, there was not a single farm "where one cannot with confidence ask the owner from whence he had emigrated, or, according to the light manners of the Americans, 'What part of the world do you come from?'" These rootless people, he explained, "incline perpetually toward the most distant fringes of American settlement."

Native American Resistance

At the beginning of the nineteenth century, a substantial number of Native Americans lived in the greater Ohio Valley; the land belonged to them. The tragedy was that the Indians, many dependent on trade with the white people and ravaged by disease, lacked unity. Small groups of Native Americans, allegedly representing the interests of an entire tribe, sold off huge pieces of land, often for whiskey and trinkets.

Such fraudulent transactions disgusted the Shawnee leaders Tenskwatawa (known as the Prophet) and his brother Tecumseh. Tecumseh rejected classification as a Shawnee and may have been the first native leader to identify himself self-consciously as "Indian." These men desperately attempted to revitalize native cultures, and against overwhelming odds, they briefly persuaded Native Americans living in the Indiana Territory to avoid contact with whites, to resist alcohol, and, most important, to hold on to their land. White intruders saw Tecumseh as a threat to progress, and during the War of 1812, they shattered the Indians' dream of cultural renaissance. The populous Creek nation, located in the modern states of Alabama and Mississippi, also resisted the settlers' advance, but its warriors were crushed by Andrew Jackson's Tennessee militia at the battle of Horseshoe Bend (March 1814).

Well-meaning Jeffersonians disclaimed any intention to destroy the Indians. The president talked of creating a vast reservation beyond the Mississippi River, just as the British had talked before the Revolution of a sanctuary beyond the Appalachian Mountains. He sent federal agents to "civilize" the Indians, to transform them into yeoman farmers. But even the most enlightened white thinkers of the day did not believe the Indians possessed cultures worth preserving. In fact, in 1835, the Democratic national convention selected a vice presidential candidate whose major qualification for high office seemed to be that he had killed Tecumseh. And as early as 1780, Jefferson himself—then serving as the governor of Virginia—instructed a military leader on the frontier, "If we are to wage a campaign against these Indians the end proposed should be their extermination, or their removal beyond the lakes of the Illinois river. The same world will scarcely do for them and us."

Commercial Life in the Cities

Before 1820, the prosperity of the United States depended primarily on its agriculture and trade. Jeffersonian America was by no stretch of the imagination an industrial economy. The overwhelming majority of the population—84 percent in 1810—was directly involved in agriculture. Southerners concentrated on the staple crops of tobacco, rice, and cotton, which they sold on the European market. In the North, people generally produced livestock and cereal crops. Regardless of location, however, the nation's farmers followed a backbreaking work routine that did not differ substantially from that of their parents and grandparents. Except for the cotton gin, important chemical and mechanical inventions did not appear in the fields for another generation.

The merchant marine represented an equally important element in America's preindustrial economy. At the turn of the century, ships flying the Stars and Stripes transported a large share of the world's trade. Merchants in Boston, New York, and Philadelphia received handsome profits from such commerce. Their vessels provided essential links between European countries and their Caribbean colonies. France, for example, relied heavily on American transport for its sugar. These lucrative transactions, coupled with the export of domestic staples, especially cotton, generated impressive fortunes. Between 1793 and 1807, the year Jefferson imposed the embargo against Britain and France, American commerce enjoyed a more than 300 percent increase in the value of exports and in net earnings. Unfortunately, the boom did not last. The success of the "carrying trade" depended in large measure on friendly relations between the United States and the major European powers. When England and France began seizing American ships—as they both did after 1805—national prosperity suffered.

The cities of Jeffersonian America functioned chiefly as depots for international trade. Only about 7 percent of the nation's population lived in urban centers, and most of these people owed their livelihoods either directly or indirectly to the carrying trade. Recent studies revealed that several major port cities of the early republic—New York, Philadelphia, and Baltimore, for example—had some of the highest population densities ever recorded in this country's history. In 1800, more than forty thousand New Yorkers crowded into an area of only 1.5 square miles; in Philadelphia, some forty-six thousand people were packed into less than one square mile. As one historian explained, "The cities contained disproportionate numbers of young white males, free black men and women, and white widows. These people had below-average incomes and also an increasing propensity to live on their own rather than as dependents." As is common today, many city dwellers rented living space, and since the demand for housing exceeded the supply, the rents were high.

The booming carrying trade may actually have retarded the industrialization of the United States. The lure of large profits drew investment capital—a scarce resource in a developing society—into commerce. By contrast, manufacturing seemed too risky. One contemporary complained, "The brilliant prospects held out by commerce, caused our citizens to neglect the mechanical and manufacturing branches of industry."

This man may have exaggerated slightly to make his point. Samuel Slater, an English-born designer of textile machinery, did establish several cotton-spinning mills in New England, but until the 1820s these plants employed only a small number of workers. In fact, during this period far more cloth was produced in individual households than in factories. Another farsighted inventor, Robert Fulton, sailed the first American steamship up the Hudson River in 1807. In time, this marvelous innovation opened new markets for

Before the Industrial Revolution, national prosperity depended on commercial capitalism. Jonathan Budington's painting of *Cannon House and Wharf* (1792), the busy dock area of lower Manhattan, reflects the robust maritime trade of the new republic.

domestic manufacturers, especially in the West. At the end of the War of 1812, however, few people anticipated how greatly power generated by fossil fuel would eventually transform the character of the American economy.

Ordinary workers often felt threatened by the new machines. Skilled artisans who had spent years mastering a trade and who took pride in producing an object that expressed their own personalities found the industrial workplace alienating. Moreover, they rightly feared that innovative technology designed to achieve greater efficiency might throw traditional craftspeople out of work or, if not that, transform independent entrepreneurs into dependent wage laborers. One New Yorker, for example, writing in the *Gazette and General Advertiser* in 1801, warned tradespeople to be on guard against those who "will screw down the wages to the last thread . . . [and destroy] the independent spirit, so distinguished at present in our mechanics, and so useful in republics."

Jefferson as President

How did practical politics challenge Jefferson's political principles?

The District of Columbia seemed an appropriate capital for a Republican president. At the time of Jefferson's first inauguration, Washington was still an isolated rural village, a far cry from the crowded centers of Philadelphia and New York. Jefferson fit comfortably into Washington society. He despised formal ceremony and sometimes shocked foreign dignitaries by meeting them in his slippers or a threadbare jacket. He spent as much time as his official duties allowed in reading and reflection. Isaac, one of Jefferson's slaves, recounted, "Old master had abundance of books: sometimes would have twenty of 'em down on the floor at once; read fust one then tother."

The president was a poor public speaker. He wisely refused to deliver annual addresses before Congress. In personal conversation, however, Jefferson exuded considerable charm. His dinner parties were major intellectual as well as social events, and in this forum, the president regaled politicians with his knowledge of literature, philosophy, and science. According to Margaret Bayard Smith, the wife of a congressman, the president "has more ease than grace—all the winning softness of politeness, without the artificial polish of courts."

Notwithstanding his commitment to the life of the mind, Jefferson was a politician to the core. He ran for the presidency in order to achieve specific goals: the reduction of the size and cost of federal government, the repeal of obnoxious Federalist legislation such as the Alien and Sedition Acts, and the maintenance of international peace. To accomplish his program, Jefferson realized he needed the full cooperation of congressional Republicans, some of whom were fiercely independent men. Over such figures Jefferson exercised political mastery. He established close ties with the leaders of both houses of Congress, and while he seldom announced his plans in public, he made certain his legislative lieutenants knew exactly what he desired. Contemporaries who described Jefferson as a weak president—and some Federalists did just that—did not read the scores of memoranda he sent to political friends or witness the

Read the Document   Margaret Bayard Smith, Reflections upon Meeting Jefferson

Margaret Bayard Smith wrote about life in Washington, D.C. during its early years as the nation's capital. She was a friend of Thomas Jefferson through her husband Samuel Harrison Smith.

informal meetings he held at the executive mansion with important Republicans. In two terms as president, Jefferson never had to veto a single act of Congress.

Jefferson carefully selected the members of his cabinet. During Washington's administration, he had witnessed—even provoked—severe infighting; as president, he nominated only those who enthusiastically supported his programs. James Madison, the leading figure at the Constitutional Convention, became secretary of state. For the Treasury, Jefferson chose Albert Gallatin, a Swiss-born financier who understood the complexities of the federal budget. "If I had the universe to choose from," the president announced, "I could not change one of my associates to my better satisfaction."

Jeffersonian Reforms

A top priority of the new government was cutting the national debt. Throughout American history, presidents have advocated such reductions, but such rhetoric has seldom yielded tangible results. Jefferson succeeded. He and Gallatin regarded a large federal deficit as dangerous to the health of republican institutions. In fact, both men associated debt with Alexander Hamilton's Federalist financial programs, measures they considered harmful to republicanism. Jefferson claimed that legislators elected by the current generation did not have the right to mortgage the future of unborn Americans.

Jefferson also wanted to diminish the activities of the federal government. He urged Congress to repeal all direct taxes, including the tax that had sparked the Whiskey Rebellion in 1794. Secretary Gallatin linked federal income to the carrying trade. He calculated that the entire cost of national government could be borne by customs receipts. As long as commerce flourished, revenues provided sufficient sums. When international war closed foreign markets, however, the flow of funds dried up.

To help pay the debt inherited from the Adams administration, Jefferson ordered substantial cuts in the national budget. The president closed several American embassies in Europe. He also slashed military spending. In his first term, Jefferson reduced the size of the U.S. Army by 50 percent. This decision left only three thousand soldiers to guard the entire frontier. In addition, he retired a majority of the navy's warships. When New Englanders claimed the cuts left the country defenseless, Jefferson countered with a glib argument. As ships of the U.S. Navy sailed the world's oceans, he claimed, they were liable to provoke hostilities, perhaps even war; hence, by reducing the size of the fleet, he promoted peace.

More than budgetary considerations prompted Jefferson's military reductions. He was deeply suspicious of standing armies. In the event of foreign attack, he reasoned, the militia would rise in defense of the republic. No doubt, his experiences during the Revolution influenced his thinking on military affairs, for in 1776, an aroused populace had taken up arms against the British. To ensure that the citizen soldiers would receive professional leadership in battle, Jefferson created the Army Corps of Engineers and the military academy at West Point in 1802.

Political patronage was a great burden to the new president. Loyal Republicans throughout the United States had worked hard for Jefferson's victory, and as soon as he took office, they stormed the executive mansion seeking federal employment. While the president controlled several hundred jobs, he refused to dismiss all the Federalists. To be sure, he acted quickly to remove the so-called midnight appointees, highly partisan selections that Adams had made after learning of Jefferson's election. But to transform federal hiring into an undisciplined spoils system, especially at the highest levels of the federal bureaucracy, seemed to Jefferson to be shortsighted. Moderate Federalists might be converted to the Republican Party, and, in any case, there was a good chance they possessed the expertise needed to run the government. At the end of his first term, half of the people holding office were appointees of Washington and Adams.

Jefferson's political moderation helped hasten the demise of the Federalist Party. This loose organization had nearly destroyed itself during the election of 1800, and following Adams's defeat, prominent Federalist spokesmen such as Fisher Ames and John Jay withdrew from national affairs. They refused to adopt the popular forms of campaigning that the Republicans had developed so successfully during the late 1790s. The mere prospect of flattering the common people was odious enough to drive some Federalists into political retirement.

Many of them also sensed that national expansion worked against their interests. The creation of new states and congressional reapportionment inevitably seemed to increase the number of Republican representatives in Washington. By 1805, the Federalists retained only a few seats in New England and Delaware. "The power of the [Jefferson] Administration," confessed John Quincy Adams in 1802, "rests upon the support of a much stronger majority of the people throughout the Union than the former administrations ever possessed since the first establishment of the Constitution."

The Louisiana Purchase

When Jefferson first took office, he was confident that Louisiana as well as Florida would eventually become part of the United States. After all, Spain owned the territory, and Jefferson assumed he could persuade the rulers of that notoriously weak nation to sell their colonies. If that peaceful strategy failed, the president was prepared to threaten forcible occupation.

In May 1801, however, prospects for the easy or inevitable acquisition of Louisiana suddenly darkened. Jefferson learned that Spain had secretly transferred title to the entire region to France, its powerful northern neighbor. To make matters worse, the French leader Napoleon seemed intent on reestablishing an empire in North America. Even as Jefferson sought additional information concerning the details of the transfer, Napoleon was dispatching a large army to put down a rebellion in France's sugar-rich Caribbean colony, Haiti. From that island stronghold in the West Indies, French troops could occupy New Orleans and close the Mississippi River to American trade.

A sense of crisis enveloped Washington. Some congressmen urged Jefferson to prepare for war against France. Tensions increased when the Spanish officials who still governed New Orleans announced the closing of that port to American commerce (October 1802). Jefferson and his advisers assumed that the Spanish had acted on orders from France, but despite this serious provocation, the president preferred negotiations to war. In January 1803, he asked James Monroe, a loyal Republican from Virginia, to join the American minister, Robert Livingston, in Paris. The president instructed the two men to explore the possibility of purchasing the city of New Orleans. Lest they underestimate the importance of their diplomatic mission, Jefferson reminded them, "There is on the globe one single spot, the possessor of which is our natural and habitual enemy. It is New Orleans." If Livingston and Monroe failed, Jefferson realized he would be forced to turn to Great Britain for military assistance. Dependence on that country seemed repellent, but he recognized that as soon as French troops moved into Louisiana, "we must marry ourselves to the British fleet and nation."

By the time Monroe joined Livingston in France, Napoleon had lost interest in establishing an American empire. The army he sent to Haiti succumbed to tropical diseases. By the end of 1802, more than thirty thousand veteran troops had died. In a fit of disgust, Napoleon announced, "Damn sugar, damn coffee, damn colonies . . . I renounce Louisiana." The diplomats from the United States knew nothing of these developments. They were taken by complete

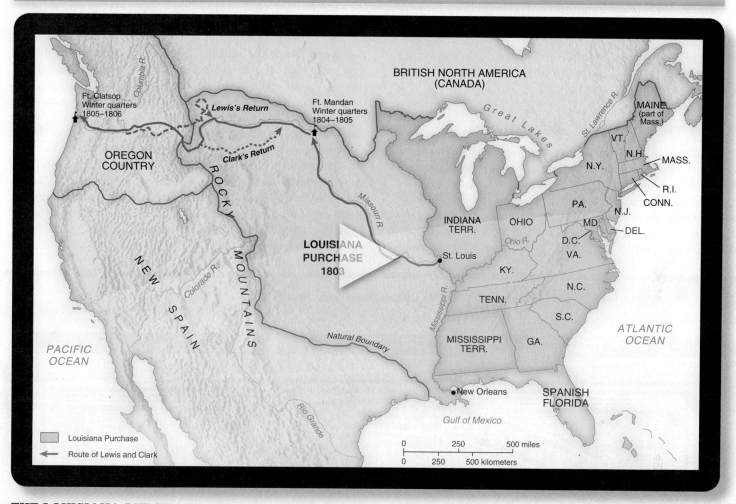

THE LOUISIANA PURCHASE AND THE ROUTE OF LEWIS AND CLARK Not until Lewis and Clark had explored the Far West did citizens of the United States realize just how much territory Jefferson had acquired through the Louisiana Purchase.

surprise, therefore, when they learned that Talleyrand, the French minister for foreign relations, had offered to sell the entire Louisiana Territory in April 1803. For only $15 million, the Americans doubled the size of the United States with the **Louisiana Purchase**. In fact, Livingston and Monroe were not certain how much land they had actually purchased. When they asked Talleyrand whether the deal included Florida, he responded ambiguously, "You have made a noble bargain for yourselves, and I suppose you will make the most of it." Even at that moment, Livingston realized that the transaction would alter the course of American history. "From this day," he wrote, "the United States take their place among the powers of first rank."

The American people responded enthusiastically to news of the Louisiana Purchase. The only criticism came from a few disgruntled Federalists in New England who thought the United States was already too large. Jefferson, of course, was immensely relieved. The nation had avoided war with France. Nevertheless, he worried that the purchase might be unconstitutional. The president

pointed out that the Constitution did not specifically authorize the acquisition of vast new territories and the incorporation of thousands of foreign citizens. To escape this apparent legal dilemma, Jefferson proposed an amendment to the Constitution. Few persons, even his closest advisers, shared the president's scruples. Events in France soon forced Jefferson to adopt a more pragmatic course. When he heard that Napoleon had become impatient for his money, Jefferson rushed the papers to a Senate eager to ratify the agreement, and nothing more was said about amending the Constitution.

Jefferson's fears about the incorporation of this new territory were not unwarranted. The area that eventually became the state of Louisiana (1812) contained many people of French and Spanish background who possessed no familiarity with representative institutions. Their laws had been autocratic, their local government corrupt. To allow such persons to elect a representative assembly struck the president as dangerous. He did not even know whether the population of Louisiana would remain loyal to the United States.

Jefferson, therefore, recommended to Congress a transitional government consisting entirely of appointed officials. In March 1804, the Louisiana Government Bill narrowly passed the House of Representatives. Members of the president's own party attacked the plan. After all, it imposed taxes on the citizens of Louisiana without their consent. According to one outspoken Tennessee congressman, the bill "establishes a complete despotism." Most troubling perhaps was the fact that the legislation ran counter to Jefferson's well-known republican principles.

The Lewis and Clark Expedition

In the midst of the Louisiana controversy, Jefferson dispatched a secret message to Congress requesting $2,500 for the exploration of the Far West (January 1803). How closely this decision was connected to the Paris negotiations is not clear. Whatever the case may have been, the president asked his talented private secretary, Meriwether Lewis, to discover whether the Missouri River "may offer the most direct & practicable water communication across this continent for the purposes of commerce." The president also regarded the expedition as a wonderful opportunity to collect precise data about flora and fauna. He personally instructed Lewis in the latest techniques of scientific observation. While preparing for this great adventure, Lewis's second in command, William Clark, assumed such a prominent role that the effort became known as the **Lewis and Clark Expedition**. The effort owed much of its success to a young Shoshoni woman known as Sacagawea. She served as a translator and helped persuade suspicious Native Americans that the explorers meant no harm. As Clark explained, "A woman with a party of men is a token of peace."

The exploring party set out from St. Louis in May 1804, and after barely surviving crossing the snow-covered Rocky Mountains, with their food supply running dangerously low, the Americans reached the Pacific Ocean in November 1805. The group returned safely the following September. The results of the expedition not only fulfilled Jefferson's scientific expectations but also reaffirmed his faith in the future economic prosperity of the United States.

👁 ─ Watch the Video   Lewis & Clark: What were they trying to accomplish?

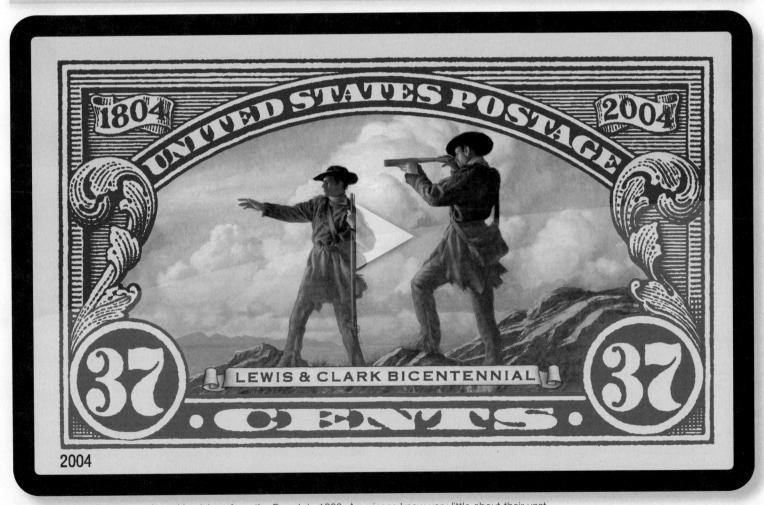

When Thomas Jefferson purchased Louisiana from the French in 1803, Americans knew very little about their vast new territory. The President chose naturalist Meriwether Lewis and William Clark, a soldier and cartographer, to lead a "Voyage of Discovery" to explore these new lands. This stamp commemorates the expedition's 1804 departure up the Missouri River and into the unknown West.

Conflict with the Barbary States

During this period, Jefferson dealt with another problem. For several decades, the North African states of Tangier, Algiers, Tripoli, and Tunis—the Barbary States—had preyed on commercial shipping. (See the Feature Essay, "Barbary Pirates and American Captives: The Nation's First Hostage Crisis," pp. 190–191.) Most European nations paid the pirates tribute, hoping thereby to protect merchants trading in the Mediterranean. In 1801, Jefferson, responding to Tripoli's increased demand for tribute, decided the extortion had become intolerable and dispatched a small fleet to the Barbary Coast, where, according to one commander, the Americans intended to negotiate "through the mouth of a cannon." Tripoli put up stiff resistance, however, and in one mismanaged engagement it captured the U.S. frigate *Philadelphia*. Ransoming the crew cost Jefferson's government another $60,000. An American land assault across the Libyan desert provided inspiration for the words of the "Marines' Hymn"—"to the shores of Tripoli"—but no smashing victory.

Despite a generally unimpressive American military record, a vigorous naval blockade brought hostilities to a conclusion. In 1805, the president signed a treaty formally ending the Barbary War. One diplomat crowed, "It must be mortifying to some of the neighboring European powers to see that the Barbary States have been taught their first lessons of humiliation from the Western World."

Jefferson concluded his first term on a wave of popularity. He had maintained the peace, reduced taxes, and expanded the boundaries of the United States. Not surprisingly, he overwhelmed his Federalist opponent in the presidential election of 1804. In the electoral college, Jefferson received 162 votes to Charles Cotesworth Pinckney's 14. Republicans controlled Congress. John Randolph, the most articulate member of the House of Representatives, exclaimed, "Never was there an administration more brilliant than that of Mr. Jefferson up to this period. We were indeed in 'the full tide of successful experiment!'"

THE ELECTION OF 1804

Candidate	Party	Electoral Vote
Jefferson	Republican	162
C. Pinckney	Federalist	14

Jefferson's Critics

How did Jeffersonians deal with the difficult problems of party politics and slavery?

At the moment of Jefferson's greatest electoral victory, a perceptive person might have seen signs of serious division within the Republican Party and within the country. The president's heavy-handed attempts to reform the federal courts stirred deep animosities. Republicans had begun sniping at other Republicans, and one leading member of the party, Aaron Burr, became involved in a bizarre plot to separate the West from the rest of the nation. Congressional debates over the future of the slave trade revealed the existence of powerful sectional loyalties and profound disagreement on the issue.

THE BARBARY STATES In 1801, President Jefferson refused to continue paying the tribute that pirates of the Barbary States had received for decades.

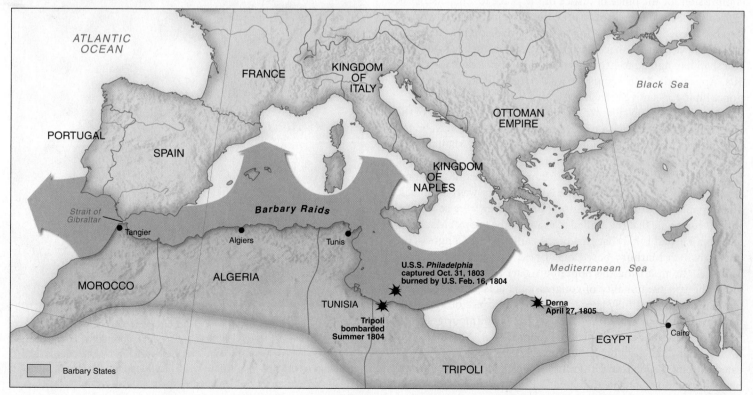

Attack on the Judges

Jefferson's controversy with the federal bench commenced the moment he became president. The Federalists, realizing they would soon lose control over the executive branch, had passed the Judiciary Act of 1801. This bill created several circuit courts and sixteen new judgeships. Through his "midnight" appointments, Adams had quickly filled these positions with stalwarts of the Federalist Party. Such blatantly partisan behavior angered Jefferson. In the courts, he explained, the Federalists hoped to preserve their political influence, and "from that battery all the works of Republicanism are to be beaten down and erased." Even more infuriating was Adams's appointment of John Marshall as the new chief justice. This shrewd, largely self-educated Virginian of Federalist background, whose training in the law consisted of a series of lectures he attended at the College of William and Mary in 1780, was clearly a man who could hold his own against the new president.

In January 1802, Jefferson's congressional allies called for repeal of the Judiciary Act. In public debate, they studiously avoided the obvious political issue. The new circuit courts should be closed not only because they were staffed by Federalists but also, as they argued, because they were needlessly expensive. The judges did not hear enough cases to warrant continuance. The Federalists mounted an able defense. The Constitution, they observed, provided for the removal of federal judges only when they were found guilty of high crimes and misdemeanors. By repealing the Judiciary Act, the legislative branch would in effect be dismissing judges without a trial, a clear violation of their constitutional rights. This argument made little impression on the Republican Party. In March, the House, following the Senate, voted for repeal.

While Congress debated the Judiciary Act, another battle erupted. One of Adams's "midnight" appointees, William Marbury, complained that the new administration would not give him his commission for the office of justice of the peace for the District of Columbia. He sought redress before the Supreme Court, demanding that the federal justices compel James Madison, the secretary of state, to deliver the necessary papers. When they learned that Marshall had agreed to hear this case, the Republicans were furious. Apparently the chief justice wanted to provoke a confrontation with the executive branch.

Marshall was too clever to jeopardize the independence of the Supreme Court over such a relatively minor issue. In his celebrated ***Marbury v. Madison*** decision (February 1803), Marshall berated the secretary of state for withholding Marbury's commission. Nevertheless, he concluded that the Supreme Court did not possess jurisdiction over such matters. Poor Marbury was out of luck. The Republicans proclaimed victory. In fact, they were so pleased with the outcome that they failed to examine the logic of Marshall's decision. He had ruled that part of the earlier act of Congress, the one on which Marbury based his appeal, was unconstitutional. This was the first time the Supreme Court asserted its right to judge the constitutionality of congressional acts, and while contemporaries did not fully appreciate the significance of Marshall's doctrine, *Marbury* v. *Madison* later served as an important precedent for **judicial review** of federal statutes.

Neither Marbury's defeat nor repeal of the Judiciary Act placated extreme Republicans. They insisted that federal judges should be made more responsive to the will of the people. One solution, short of electing federal judges, was impeachment. This clumsy device provided the legislature with a way of removing particularly offensive individuals. Early in 1803, John Pickering, an incompetent judge from New Hampshire, presented the Republicans with a curious test case. This Federalist appointee suffered from alcoholism as well as insanity. While his outrageous behavior on the bench embarrassed everyone, Pickering had not committed any high crimes against the U.S. government. Ignoring such legal niceties, Jefferson's congressional allies pushed for impeachment. Although the Senate convicted Pickering (March 1804), many senators refused to compromise the letter of the Constitution and were conspicuously absent on the day of the final vote.

Jefferson was apparently so eager to purge the courts of Federalists that he failed to heed these warnings. By the spring of 1803, he had set his sights on a target far more important than John Pickering. In a Baltimore newspaper, the president stumbled on the transcript of a speech allegedly delivered before a federal grand jury. The words seemed almost treasonous. The person responsible

> **Read** the **Document**   **Opinion for the Supreme Court for *Marbury* v. *Madison***

William Marbury (1760–1835) was an American lawyer, politician, and banker. In *Marbury* v. *Madision*, Marbury sued the Jefferson administration to follow through on a judge's commission promised him by former President John Adams. Marbury lost, but his case established the doctrine of judicial review—the Supreme Court's authority to declare laws unconstitutional.

was Samuel Chase, a justice of the Supreme Court, who had frequently attacked Republican policies. Jefferson leapt at the chance to remove Chase from office. In a matter of weeks, the Republican-controlled House of Representatives indicted Chase.

Chase's trial before the U.S. Senate was one of the most dramatic events in American legal history. Aaron Burr, the vice president, organized the proceedings. For reasons known only to himself, Burr redecorated the Senate chamber so that it looked more like the British House of Lords than the meeting place of a republican legislature. In this luxurious setting, Chase and his lawyers conducted a masterful defense. By contrast, John Randolph, the congressman who served as chief prosecutor, behaved in an erratic manner, betraying repeatedly his ignorance of relevant points of law. While most Republican senators personally disliked the arrogant Chase, they refused to expand the constitutional definition of impeachable offenses to suit Randolph's argument, and on March 1, 1805, the Senate acquitted the justice of all charges. The experience apparently convinced Chase of the need for greater moderation. After returning to the federal bench, he refrained from attacking Republican policies. His Jeffersonian opponents also learned something important. American politicians did not like tampering with the Constitution in order to get rid of specific judges, even an imprudent one like Chase.

Politics of Desperation

The collapse of the Federalists on the national level encouraged dissension within the Republican Party. Extremists in Congress insisted on monopolizing the president's ear, and when he listened to political moderates, they rebelled. The members of the most vociferous faction called themselves "the good old republicans"; the newspapers labeled them the "Tertium Quids," loosely translated as "nothings" or "no accounts." During Jefferson's second term, the Quids argued that the president's policies, foreign and domestic, sacrificed virtue for pragmatism. Their chief spokesmen were two members from Virginia, John Randolph and John Taylor of Caroline (the name of his plantation), both of whom were convinced that Jefferson had betrayed the republican purity of the Founders. They both despised commercial capitalism. Taylor urged Americans to return to a simple agrarian way of life. Randolph's attacks were particularly shrill. He saved his sharpest barbs for Gallatin and Madison, Republican moderates who failed to appreciate the congressman's self-righteous posturing.

The Yazoo controversy raised the Quids from political obscurity. This complex legal battle began in 1795 when a thoroughly corrupt Georgia assembly sold 35 million acres of western land, known as the Yazoo claims, to private companies at bargain prices. It soon became apparent that every member of the legislature had been bribed, and in 1796, state lawmakers rescinded the entire agreement. Unfortunately, some land had already changed hands. When Jefferson became president, a specially appointed federal commission attempted to clean up the mess. It recommended that Congress set aside 5 million acres for buyers who had unwittingly purchased land from the discredited companies.

Randolph immediately cried foul. Such a compromise, however well-meaning, condoned fraud. Republican virtue hung in the balance. For months, the Quids harangued Congress about the Yazoo business, but in the end, their impassioned oratory accomplished

nothing. The Marshall Supreme Court upheld the rights of the original purchasers in *Fletcher* v. *Peck* (1810). The justices unanimously declared that legislative fraud did not impair private contracts and that the Georgia assembly of 1796 did not have authority to take away lands already sold to innocent buyers. This important case upheld the Supreme Court's authority to rule on the constitutionality of state laws.

Murder and Conspiracy: The Curious Career of Aaron Burr

Vice President Aaron Burr created far more serious difficulties for the president. The two men had never been close. Burr's strange behavior during the election of 1800 raised suspicions that he had conspired to deprive Jefferson of the presidency. Whatever the truth may have been, the vice president entered the new administration under a cloud. He played only a marginal role in shaping policy, a situation extremely frustrating for a person as ambitious as Burr.

In the spring of 1804, Burr decided to run for the governorship of New York. Although he was a Republican, he entered into political negotiations with High Federalists who were plotting the secession of New England and New York from the Union. In a particularly scurrilous contest—and New York politics were always abusive—Alexander Hamilton described Burr as ". . . a dangerous man . . . who ought not to be trusted with the reins of government" and urged Federalists in the state to vote for another candidate.

Whether Hamilton's appeals influenced the voters is not clear. Burr, however, blamed Hamilton for his subsequent defeat and challenged him to a duel. Even though Hamilton condemned this form of violence—his own son had recently been killed in a duel—he accepted Burr's "invitation," describing the foolishness as a matter of personal honor. On July 11, 1804, at Weehawken, New Jersey, the vice president shot and killed the former secretary of the treasury. Both New York and New Jersey indicted Burr for murder. If he returned to either state, he would immediately be arrested. His political career lay in shambles.

In his final weeks as vice president, Burr hatched an audacious scheme. On a trip down the Ohio River in April 1805, after his term as vice president was over, he hinted broadly that he was planning a private military adventure against a Spanish colony, perhaps Mexico. Burr also suggested that he envisioned separating the western states and territories from the Union. The region certainly seemed ripe for secession. The citizens of New Orleans acted as if they wanted no part of the United States. General James Wilkinson, commander of the U.S. Army in the Mississippi Valley, accepted an important role in this vaguely defined conspiracy. The general was a thoroughly corrupt opportunist. Randolph described him as "the only man that I ever saw who was from bark to the very core a villain."

In the late summer of 1806, Burr put his ill-defined plan into action. A small group of volunteers constructed riverboats on a small island in the Ohio River. By the time this armed band set out to join Wilkinson's forces, however, the general had experienced a change of heart. He frantically dispatched letters to Jefferson denouncing Burr. Wilkinson's betrayal destroyed any chance of success. Facing certain defeat, Burr tried to escape to Spanish Florida. It was already too late. Federal authorities arrested Burr in February 1807 and took him to Richmond to stand trial for treason.

Feature Essay

Barbary Pirates and American Captives
The Nation's First Hostage Crisis

AUGUST 1804.

BOMBARDMENT OF TRIPOLI.

Print depicting the bombardment of Tripoli by U.S. naval vessels in 1804.

For more than a quarter-century after independence, terror haunted American sailors and challenged the new republic's influence throughout the world. Pirates from North Africa preyed on commercial vessels in the Mediterranean Sea and along the European Coast. Those unlucky enough to be captured faced enslavement or death. Although such piracy had been going on for a very long time, American entrepreneurs were always willing to risk the dangers to make a profit.

The crew of one ship, the *Polly*, left a record of the horrors awaiting those who encountered the Barbary pirates, North African Muslims based in Algiers, Morocco, Tunis, and Tripoli. Sailing out of Baltimore in autumn 1793, the *Polly* was on its way to a Spanish port when a sailor on watch reported a "strange sail." No one seems to have anticipated trouble.

They were in for a dreadful surprise. When the strange vessel drew alongside the *Polly*, someone "dressed in the Christian habit" hailed the Americans from the deck. Then, without warning, "a great number" of men "dressed in the Turkish habit" poured over the railings brandishing "scimitars and pistols . . . pikes, spears, lances, and knives." The Americans had no defense. The pirates plundered the ship then stripped the Americans of all clothing except "a shirt and a pair of drawers" and chained them in preparation for the voyage to Algiers, reputed to be the cruelest "of any state in all Barbary."

The *Polly*'s crew had become casualties of the young republic's first prolonged hostage crisis involving Muslim states. By the end of the year, Barbary pirates had seized the crews of at least ten other vessels. The captives were thrown into prisons, where they labored in terrible conditions alongside sailors who had been in Algiers for as long as a decade. Algerian guards beat their captives. The enslaved Americans were driven in chains each day to a quarry outside the city of Algiers. Their masters forced them to drag twenty-ton rocks to construction sites. Anyone who attempted escape faced execution.

News of the captives' ordeal offended American pride. Outraged American citizens organized charitable societies pledged to oppose the pirates, send relief to the captives, and lobby Congress to take effective action for their release. Some Americans advocated paying ransom to liberate the prisoners, but others pointed out that such a policy would only encourage more attacks on the nation's merchant marine.

The outpouring of private action and nationalist sentiment forced the U. S. government, which had championed a policy of free trade throughout the world, to adjust to the changing realities of international relations. If the United States allowed itself to be humiliated by the Barbary states— places where "bribery, treachery, rapine, murder, and all the hideous offspring of accursed tyranny, have often drenched the streets with blood"— then it could not expect other, more powerful states to respect its hard-won independence.

U.S. military power frightened no one, especially not the rulers of Barbary states. Neither the French nor the British showed interest in helping the Americans. After all, they viewed them as commercial competitors in the region. In 1795, the federal government finally recognized the seriousness of the problem. President Washington ordered U.S. envoy Joseph Donaldson, Jr., to negotiate release of the captives and to sign treaties ensuring that Algiers would no longer molest American shipping. For these alleged favors, the United States had to promise a humiliating sum totaling nearly $1 million. The combination of debt payments and annual tribute represented about one-sixth of each year's federal budget. Treaties with Tripoli and Tunis also included yearly payments for peace, raising the total even higher.

A policy that essentially condoned blackmail continued until Thomas Jefferson won election as president in 1800. Hoping to extort a larger share of the annual ransom monies, the Pasha of Tripoli forced Jefferson's hand by declaring war on the United States. This preemptive move confirmed belief that attempts to buy off extortionists only generated further greed. It also compelled the United States to back up its world commerce with military might, a decision congressional budget-cutters had tried to avoid.

Vowing not to pay "one penny in tribute," Jefferson dispatched U.S. naval vessels to blockade Tripoli's harbor. Despite brave talk, American intervention proved a failure, at least initially. One battleship went aground and had to be destroyed by marines. Eventually, Commodore Edward Preble and Captain Stephen Decatur showed fighting spirit sufficient to turn defeat into a draw. The American consul at Tunis, William Eaton, even attempted an early form of "regime change," leading a company of Mediterranean mercenaries in an unauthorized effort to depose the Pasha and install his brother. Eaton's mission "to the shores of Tripoli" failed. In 1805, the Pasha, whose power was unshaken, decided that war was becoming too expensive, and he negotiated a peace with the United States that included a payment of $60,000 to ransom the last prisoners.

During the long ordeal with the Barbary pirates, American nationalists portrayed North African states as the opposite of their free republic. Survivors of captivity published narratives containing lurid descriptions of the despotism and cruelty they had endured under their Muslim masters. The popular press castigated Muslims as enemies of civilized society and devoid of human compassion.

Propaganda against Muslim pirates generated its own embarrassing backlash. Shrill nationalist rhetoric reminded many Americans of the uncomfortable similarities between the white slavery of the Barbary states and the African slavery that flourished throughout the southern United States. The African American abolitionist Absalom Jones could discern no real difference between "the unconstitutional bondage in which multitudes of our fellows in complexion are held" and "the deplorable . . . situation of citizens of the United States captured and enslaved . . . in Algiers."

America's first hostage crisis produced a complex legacy. It forced ordinary citizens of the new republic to take stock of themselves within a larger international framework. The war in Tripoli encouraged Jefferson, who had always disfavored a permanent military establishment, to accept a professional navy. Preparedness, he concluded, was the price of maintaining free trade throughout the world. War provided a stark contrast between liberty and tyranny and stimulated the loud celebration of American freedom. In doing so, it also intensified debate over the republic's most glaring domestic contradiction, the persistence of slavery within a nation that was prepared to fight in distant places in the name of liberty.

QUESTIONS FOR DISCUSSION

1. Why did the European powers not eliminate the Barbary pirates?

2. Could U.S. leaders have ignored the challenge of the pirates?

3. How did American nationalists' condemnation of "white slavery" in North Africa affect the debate over the enslavement of African-Americans in the U.S.?

The trial judge was John Marshall, a strong Federalist not likely to do the Republican administration any favors. He refused to hear testimony regarding Burr's supposed intentions. "Troops must be embodied," Marshall thundered, "men must be actually assembled." He demanded two witnesses to each overt act of treason.

Burr, of course, had been too clever to leave this sort of evidence. While Jefferson complained bitterly about the miscarriage of justice, the jurors declared on September 1, 1807, that the defendant was "not proved guilty by any evidence submitted to us." The public was outraged, and Burr prudently went into exile in Europe. The president threatened to introduce an amendment to the Constitution calling for the election of federal judges. Nothing came of his proposal. And Marshall inadvertently helped protect the civil rights of all Americans. If the chief justice had allowed circumstantial evidence into the Richmond courtroom, if he had listened to rumor and hearsay, he would have made it much easier for later presidents to use trumped-up conspiracy charges to silence legitimate political opposition.

The Slave Trade

Slavery sparked angry debate at the Constitutional Convention of 1787 (see Chapter 6). If delegates from the northern states had refused to compromise on this issue, Southerners would not have supported the new government. The slave states demanded a great deal in return for cooperation. According to an agreement that determined the size of a state's congressional delegation, a slave counted as three-fifths of a free white male. This political formula meant that while blacks did not vote, they helped increase the number of southern representatives. The South in turn gave up very little, agreeing only that after 1808 Congress might consider banning the importation of slaves into the United States. Slaves even influenced the outcome of national elections. Had the three-fifths rule not been in effect in 1800, for example, Adams would surely have had the votes to defeat Jefferson in the electoral college.

In an annual message sent to Congress in December 1806, Jefferson urged the representatives to prepare legislation outlawing the slave trade. During the early months of 1807, congressmen debated various ways of ending the embarrassing commerce. It was clear that the issue cut across party lines. Northern representatives

📖▶ Read the **Document**   Congress Prohibits Importation of Slaves, 1807

Although the external slave trade was officially outlawed in 1808, the commerce in humans persisted. An estimated two hundred fifty thousand African slaves were brought illicitly to the United States between 1808 and 1860. The internal slave trade continued as well. Folk artist Lewis Miller sketched this slave coffle marching from Virginia to new owners in Tennessee under the watchful eyes of mounted white overseers.

generally favored a strong bill; some even wanted to make smuggling slaves into the country a capital offense. But there was a serious problem. The northern congressmen could not figure out what to do with black people captured by the customs agents who would enforce the legislation. To sell these Africans would involve the federal government in slavery, which many Northerners found morally repugnant. Nor was there much sympathy for freeing them. Ignorant of the English language and lacking personal possessions, these blacks seemed unlikely to long survive free in the American South.

Southern congressmen responded with threats and ridicule. They explained to their northern colleagues that no one in the South regarded slavery as evil. It appeared naive, therefore, to expect local planters to enforce a ban on the slave trade or to inform federal agents when they spotted a smuggler. The notion that these culprits deserved capital punishment seemed viciously inappropriate. At one point in the debate, Peter Early, a congressman from Georgia, announced that the South wanted "no civil wars, no rebellions, no insurrections, no resistance to the authority of government." All he demanded, in fact, was to let the states regulate slavery. To this, a Republican congressman from western Pennsylvania retorted that Americans who hated slavery would not be "terrified by the threat of civil war."

The bill that Jefferson finally signed in March 1807 probably pleased no one. The law prohibited the importation of slaves into the United States after the new year. Whenever customs officials captured a smuggler, the slaves were to be turned over to state authorities and disposed of according to local custom. Southerners did not cooperate, and for many years African slaves continued to pour into southern ports. Even more blacks would have been imported had Great Britain not outlawed the slave trade in 1807. As part of their ban of the slave trade, ships of the Royal Navy captured American slave smugglers off the coast of Africa, and when anyone complained, the British explained that they were merely enforcing the laws of the United States.

Slavery was both a political and a personal issue for Jefferson. As a political leader during the Revolution, he criticized the institution. But Jefferson also believed that African Americans were inherently inferior to whites. In *Notes on the State of Virginia* (1785) Jefferson insisted as a matter of science that African Americans were not equal to white people "in the endowments both of body and mind," and he worried that the "mixture" of whites and blacks would stain "the blood of the master." It came as a surprise to his admirers when in 1802 a newspaper editor accused Jefferson of having an affair with one of his own slaves. Most historians now agree that Jefferson did indeed have a long-term relationship with Sally Hemings, a slave living at Monticello. Hemings bore Jefferson six children, four of whom survived to adulthood. Jefferson's own life and writings illustrate dramatically the moral contradictions that lay at the heart of slavery in America.

Embarrassments Overseas

Why did the United States find it difficult to avoid military conflict during this period?

During Jefferson's second term (1805–1809), the United States found itself in the midst of a world at war. A brief peace in Europe ended abruptly in 1803, and the two military giants of the age, France and Great Britain, fought for supremacy on land and sea. During the early stages of the war, the United States profited from European adversity. As "neutral carriers," American ships transported goods to any port in the world where they could find a buyer, and American merchants grew wealthy serving Britain and France. Since the Royal Navy did not allow direct trade between France and its colonies, American captains conducted "broken voyages." American vessels sailing out of French ports in the Caribbean would put in briefly in the United States, pay nominal customs, and then leave for France. For several years, the British did little to halt this obvious subterfuge.

Napoleon's successes on the battlefield, however, quickly strained Britain's economic resources. In July 1805, a British admiralty court announced in the Essex decision that henceforth "broken voyages" were illegal. The Royal Navy began seizing American ships in record number. Moreover, as the war continued, the British stepped up the impressment of sailors on ships flying the U.S. flag. Estimates of the number of men impressed ranged as high as nine thousand.

Beginning in 1806, the British government issued a series of trade regulations known as the Orders in Council. These proclamations forbade neutral commerce with the Continent and threatened seizure of any ship that violated these orders. The declarations created what were in effect "paper blockades," for even the powerful British navy could not monitor the activities of every Continental port.

Napoleon responded to Britain's commercial regulations with his own paper blockade called the Continental System. In the Berlin Decree of November 1806 and the Milan Decree of December 1807, he announced the closing of all Continental ports to British trade. Since French armies occupied most of the territory between Spain and Germany, the decrees obviously cut the British out of a large market. The French emperor also declared that neutral vessels carrying British goods were liable to seizure. For the Americans there was no escape. They were caught between two conflicting systems. The British ordered American ships to stop off to pay duties and secure clearances in England on the way to the Continent; Napoleon was determined to seize any vessel that obeyed the British.

This unhappy turn of international events baffled Jefferson. He had assumed that civilized countries would respect neutral rights; justice obliged them to do so. Appeals to reason, however, made little impression on states at war. "As for France and England," the president growled, ". . . the one is a den of robbers, the other of pirates." In a desperate attempt to avoid hostilities for which the United States was ill prepared, Jefferson ordered James Monroe and William Pinckney to negotiate a commercial treaty with Great Britain. The document they signed on December 31, 1806, said nothing about impressment, and an angry president refused to submit the treaty to the Senate for ratification.

The United States soon suffered an even greater humiliation. A ship of the Royal Navy, the *Leopard*, sailing off the coast of Virginia, commanded an American warship to submit to a search for deserters (June 22, 1807). When the captain of the Chesapeake refused to cooperate, the *Leopard* opened fire, killing three men and wounding eighteen. The attack clearly violated the sovereignty of the United States. Official protests received only a perfunctory apology from the British government, and the American people demanded revenge.

Despite the pressure of public opinion, however, Jefferson played for time. He recognized that the United States was unprepared for war against a powerful nation such as Great Britain. The president worried that an expensive conflict with Great Britain would quickly undo the fiscal reforms of his first term. As Gallatin explained, in the event of war, the United States "will be poorer, both as a nation and as a government, our debt and taxes will increase, and our progress in every respect be interrupted."

Embargo Divides the Nation

Jefferson found what he regarded as a satisfactory way to deal with European predators with a policy he called "peaceable coercion." If Britain and France refused to respect the rights of neutral carriers, then the United States would keep its ships at home. Not only would this action protect them from seizure, but it would also deprive the European powers of much needed American goods, especially food. The president predicted that a total embargo of American commerce would soon force Britain and France to negotiate with the United States in good faith. "Our commerce is so valuable to them," he declared, "that they will be glad to purchase it when the only price we ask is to do us justice." Congress passed the **Embargo Act** by large majorities, and it became law on December 22, 1807.

"Peaceable coercion" turned into a Jeffersonian nightmare. The president apparently believed the American people would enthusiastically support the embargo. That was a naive assumption. Compliance required a series of enforcement acts that over fourteen months became increasingly harsh.

By the middle of 1808, Jefferson and Gallatin were involved in the regulation of the smallest details of American economic life. Indeed, in the words of one of Jefferson's biographers, the president assumed the role of "commissar of the nation's economy." The federal government supervised the coastal trade, lest a ship sailing between two states slip away to Europe or the West Indies. Overland trade with Canada was proscribed. When violations still occurred, Congress gave customs collectors the right to seize a vessel merely on suspicion of wrongdoing. A final desperate act, passed in January 1809, prohibited the loading of any U.S. vessel, regardless of size, without authorization from a customs officer who was supported by the army, navy, and local militia. Jefferson's eagerness to pursue a reasonable foreign policy blinded him to the fact that he and a Republican Congress would have had to establish a police state to make it work.

Northerners hated the embargo. Persons living near Lake Champlain in upper New York State simply ignored the regulations, and they roughed up collectors who interfered with the Canadian trade. The administration was determined to stop the smugglers. In a decision that Hamilton might have applauded, Jefferson dispatched federal troops—led by the conspiratorial General Wilkinson—to overawe the citizens of New York.

New Englanders regarded the embargo as lunacy. Merchants of the region were willing to take their chances on the high seas, but for reasons that few people understood, the president insisted that it was better to preserve ships from possible seizure than to make profits. Sailors and artisans were thrown out of work. The popular press maintained a constant howl of protest. One writer observed that embargo in reverse spelled "O grab me!" Not surprisingly, the Federalist Party experienced a brief revival in New England, and a few extremists suggested the possibility of state assemblies nullifying federal law.

By 1809, the bankruptcy of Jefferson's foreign policy was obvious. The embargo never seriously damaged the British economy.

In fact, British merchants rushed to take over the lucrative markets that the Americans had been forced to abandon. Napoleon liked the embargo, since it seemed to harm Great Britain more than it did France. Faced with growing popular opposition, the Republicans in Congress panicked. One newly elected representative declared that "peaceful coercion" was a "miserable and mischievous failure" and joined his colleagues in repealing the embargo a few days before James Madison's inauguration. Relations between the United States and the great European powers were much worse in 1809 than they had been in 1805. During his second term, the pressures of office weighed heavily on Jefferson, and after so many years of public service, he welcomed retirement to Monticello.

A New Administration Goes to War

As president, James Madison suffered from several personal and political handicaps. Although his intellectual abilities were great, he lacked the qualities necessary for effective leadership. In public gatherings, he impressed people as being "exceedingly modest," and one foreign visitor claimed that the new president "always seems to grant that the one with whom he talks is his superior in mind and training." Critics argued that Madison's humility revealed a weak, vacillating character.

During the election of 1808, Randolph and the Quids tried unsuccessfully to persuade James Monroe to challenge Madison's candidacy. Jefferson favored his old friend Madison. In the end, a caucus of Republican congressmen gave the official nod to Madison, the first time in American history that such a congressional group controlled a presidential nomination. The former secretary of state defeated his Federalist rival, Charles Cotesworth Pinckney, in the electoral college by a vote of 122 to 47, with New Yorker George Clinton receiving 6 ballots. The margin of victory was substantially lower than Jefferson's had been in 1804, a warning of political troubles ahead. The Federalists also made impressive gains in the House of Representatives, raising their delegation from 24 to 48.

THE ELECTION OF 1808

Candidate	Party	Electoral Vote
Madison	Republican	122
C. Pinckney	Federalist	47

The new president confronted the same foreign policy problems that had occupied his predecessor. Neither Britain nor France showed the slightest interest in respecting American neutral rights. Threats against either nation rang hollow so long as the United States failed to develop its military strength. Out of weakness, therefore, Madison was compelled to put the Non-Intercourse Act into effect. Congress passed this clumsy piece of legislation at the same time as it repealed the embargo (March 1, 1809). The new bill authorized the resumption of trade between the United States and all nations of the world except Britain and France. Either of these countries could restore full commercial relations simply by promising to observe the rights of neutral carriers.

The British immediately took advantage of this offer. Their minister to the United States, David M. Erskine, informed Madison that the British government had modified its position on a number

Read the Document James Madison, First Inaugural Address (1809)

JAMES MADISON.
President of the United States.

James Madison was a plantation owner and statesman from Virginia. A political protégé of Thomas Jefferson, Madison became the fourth president of the United States and is commonly remembered as the "Father of the United States Constitution."

of sensitive commercial issues. The president was so encouraged by these talks that he publicly announced that trade with Great Britain could resume in June 1809. Unfortunately, Erskine had not conferred with his superiors on the details of these negotiations. George Canning, the British foreign secretary, rejected the agreement out of hand, and while an embarrassed Madison fumed in Washington, the Royal Navy seized the American ships that had already put to sea.

Canning's apparent betrayal led the artless Madison straight into a French trap. In May 1810, Congress passed Macon's Bill Number Two, an act sponsored by Nathaniel Macon of North Carolina. In a complete reversal of strategy, this poorly drafted legislation reestablished trade with both England and France. It also contained a curious carrot-and-stick provision. As soon as either of these European states repealed restrictions upon neutral shipping, the U.S. government promised to halt all commerce with the other.

Napoleon spotted a rare opportunity. He informed the U.S. minister in Paris that France would no longer enforce the hated Berlin and Milan Decrees. Again, Madison acted impulsively. Without waiting for further information from Paris, he announced that unless Britain repealed the Orders in Council by November, the United States would cut off commercial relations. Only later did the president learn that Napoleon had no intention of living up to his side of the bargain; his agents continued to seize American ships. Madison, who had been humiliated by the Erskine experience, decided to ignore the French provocations, to pretend the emperor was behaving in an honest manner. The British could not explain why the United States tolerated such obvious deception. No one in London would have suspected that the president really had no other options left.

Events unrelated to international commerce fueled anti-British sentiment in the newly conquered parts of the United States. Westerners believed—incorrectly, as it turned out—that British agents operating out of Canada had persuaded Tecumseh's warriors to resist the spread of American settlement. According to the rumors that ran through the region, the British dreamed of monopolizing the fur trade. In any case, General William Henry Harrison, governor of the Indiana Territory, marched an army to the edge of a large Shawnee village at the mouth of Tippecanoe Creek near the banks of the Wabash River. On the morning of November 7, 1811, the American troops routed the Indians at the battle of Tippecanoe. Harrison immediately became a national hero, and several decades later the American people rewarded "Tippecanoe" by electing him president. This incident forced Tecumseh—a brilliant leader who was trying to restore the confidence and revitalize tribal cultures of the Indians of the Indiana Territory—to seek British military assistance in battling the Americans, something he probably would not have done had Harrison left him alone.

Fumbling Toward Conflict

In 1811, the anti-British mood of Congress intensified. A group of militant representatives, some of them elected to Congress for the first time in the election of 1810, announced they would no longer tolerate national humiliation. They called for action, for resistance to Great Britain, for any course that promised to achieve respect for the United States and security for its republican institutions. These aggressive nationalists, many of them elected in the South and West, have sometimes been labeled the **War Hawks**. The group included Henry Clay, an earthy Kentucky congressman who served as Speaker of the House, and John C. Calhoun, a brilliant South Carolinian. These fiery orators spoke of honor and pride, as if foreign relations were a sort of duel between gentlemen. While the War Hawks were Republicans, they repudiated Jefferson's policy of peaceful coercion.

Madison surrendered to the War Hawks. On June 1, 1812, he sent Congress a declaration of war against Great Britain. The timing of his action was peculiar. Over the preceding months, tensions between the two nations had relaxed. No new attacks had occurred. Indeed, at the very moment Madison called for war, the British government was suspending the Orders in Council, a conciliatory gesture that in all likelihood would have preserved the peace.

However inadequately Madison communicated his goals, he did seem to have had a plan. His major aim was to force the British to respect American maritime rights, especially in Caribbean waters. The president's problem was to figure out how a small, militarily weak nation like the United States could bring effective pressure on Great Britain. Madison's answer seemed to be Canada.

This colony supplied Britain's Caribbean possessions with much needed foodstuffs. The president reasoned, therefore, that by threatening to seize Canada, the Americans might compel the British to make concessions on maritime issues. It was this logic that Secretary of State James Monroe had in mind when he explained in June 1812 that "it might be necessary to invade Canada, not as an object of the war but as a means to bring it to a satisfactory conclusion."

THE ELECTION OF 1812

Candidate	Party	Electoral Vote
Madison	Republican	128
Clinton	Republican* (antiwar faction)	89

*Clinton was nominated by a convention of antiwar Republicans and endorsed by the Federalists.

Congressional War Hawks, of course, may have had other goals in mind. Some expansionists were probably more concerned about conquering Canada than they were about the impressment of American seamen. For others, the whole affair may have truly been a matter of national pride. Andrew Jackson wrote, "For what are we going to fight? . . . we are going to fight for the reestablishment of our national character, misunderstood and vilified at home and abroad." New Englanders in whose commercial interests the war would supposedly be waged ridiculed such chauvinism. The vote in Congress was close, 79 to 49 in the House, 19 to 13 in the Senate. With this doubtful mandate, the country marched to war against the most powerful maritime nation in Europe. Division over the war question was reflected in the election of 1812. A faction of antiwar Republicans nominated De Witt Clinton of New York, who was endorsed by the Federalists. Nevertheless Madison, the Republican, won narrowly, gaining 128 electoral votes to Clinton's 89.

The Strange War of 1812

Why is the War of 1812 sometimes thought of as a "second war of independence"?

Optimism for the **War of 1812** ran high. The War Hawks apparently believed that even though the United States possessed only a small army and navy, it could easily sweep the British out of Canada. Such predictions flew in the face of political and military realities. Not only did the Republicans fail to appreciate how unprepared the country was for war, but they also refused to mobilize needed resources. The House rejected proposals for direct taxes and authorized naval appropriations only with the greatest reluctance. Indeed, even as they planned for battle, the Republican members of Congress were haunted by the consequences of their political and economic convictions. They did not seem to understand that a weak, highly decentralized government—the one that Jeffersonians championed—was incapable of waging an expensive war against the world's greatest sea power.

New Englanders refused to cooperate with the war effort. In July 1812, one clergyman in Massachusetts urged the people of the region to "proclaim an honourable neutrality." Many persons did just that. New Englanders carried on a lucrative, though illegal,

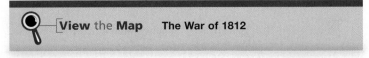

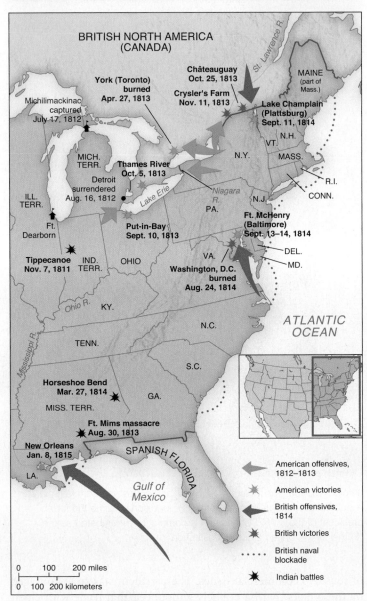

THE WAR OF 1812 Major battles of the War of 1812 brought few lasting gains to either the British or the Americans.

commerce with the enemy. When the U.S. Treasury appealed for loans to finance the war, wealthy northern merchants failed to respond. The British government apparently believed the New England states might negotiate a separate peace, and during the first year of war, the Royal Navy did not bother to blockade the major northern ports.

American military operations focused initially on the western forts. The results were discouraging. On August 16, 1812, Major General William Hull surrendered an entire army to a smaller British force at Detroit. Michilimackinac was lost. Poorly coordinated marches against the enemy at Niagara and Montreal achieved nothing. These experiences demonstrated that the militia, led by aging officers with little military aptitude, no matter how enthusiastic, was no match for well-trained European veterans. On the sea, the United States did much better. In August, Captain Isaac Hull's *Constitution* defeated the HMS *Guerrière* in a fierce battle, and American privateers destroyed or captured a number of British merchant ships. These successes were somewhat deceptive, however. So long as Napoleon threatened the Continent, Great Britain could spare few warships for service in America. As soon as peace returned to Europe in the spring of 1814, Britain redeployed its fleet and easily blockaded the tiny U.S. Navy.

The campaigns of 1813 revealed that conquering Canada would be more difficult than the War Hawks ever imagined. Both sides in this war recognized that whoever controlled the Great Lakes controlled the West. On Lake Erie, the Americans won the race for naval superiority. On September 10, 1813, Oliver Hazard Perry

destroyed a British fleet at Put-in-Bay, and in a much quoted letter written immediately after the battle, Perry exclaimed, "We have met the enemy; and they are ours." On October 5, General Harrison overran an army of British troops and Indian warriors at the battle of Thames River. During this engagement, Tecumseh was killed. On the other fronts, however, the war went badly for the Americans. General Wilkinson suffered an embarrassing defeat near Montreal (battle of Chrysler's Farm, November 11), and the British navy held its own on Lake Ontario.

In 1814, the British took the offensive. Following their victory over Napoleon, British strategists planned to increase pressure on three separate American fronts: the Canadian frontier, Chesapeake coastal settlements, and New Orleans. Sir George Prevost, commander of the British forces in Canada, marched his army south

((•●— Listen to the Audio File   **Star-Spangled Banner**

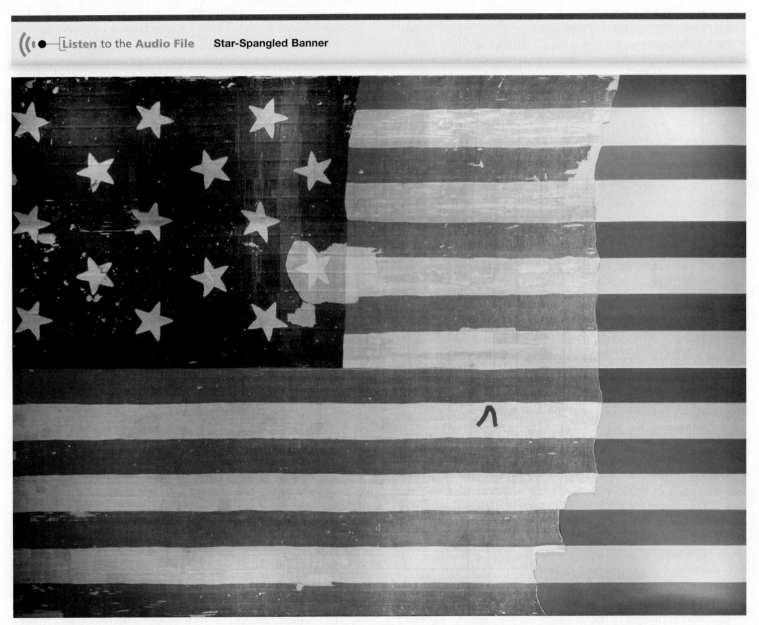

Baltimore lawyer Francis Scott Key viewed the Battle of Ft. McHenry from the deck of a British ship of war. The British bombarded the fort through the night but in the morning Key was thrilled to see that the American "flag was still there." The scene inspired Key to pen a song celebrating this important American victory in the War of 1812—a song that has become America's national anthem. This picture shows that original "Star-Spangled Banner" that flew over Ft. McHenry during the battle.

into upper New York State. A hastily assembled American fleet led by Captain Thomas Macdonough turned back a British flotilla off Plattsburgh on Lake Champlain (September 11, 1814). When Prevost learned of this setback, he retreated quickly into Canada. Although the Americans did not realize the full significance of this battle, the triumph accelerated peace negotiations, for after news of Plattsburgh reached London, the British government concluded that major land operations along the Canadian border were futile.

Throughout the year, British warships harassed the Chesapeake coast. To their surprise, the British found the region almost totally undefended, and on August 24, 1814, in retaliation for the Americans' destruction of the capital of Upper Canada (York, Ontario), a small force of British marines burned the American capital, a victory more symbolic than strategic. Encouraged by their easy success and contemptuous of America's ragtag soldiers, the British launched a full-scale attack on Baltimore (September 13–14). To everyone's surprise, the fort guarding the harbor held out against a heavy naval bombardment, and the British gave up the operation. The survival of Fort McHenry inspired Francis Scott Key to write "The Star-Spangled Banner."

The **Battle of New Orleans** should never have occurred. The British landed a large assault force under General Edward Pakenham at precisely the same time as diplomats in Europe were preparing the final drafts of a peace treaty. The combatants, of course, knew nothing of these distant developments, and on January 8, 1815, Pakenham foolishly ordered a frontal attack against General Andrew Jackson's well-defended positions. In a short time, the entire British force had been destroyed. The Americans suffered only light casualties. The victory not only transformed Jackson into a national folk hero, but it also provided the people of the United States with a much needed source of pride. Even in military terms, the battle was significant, for if the British had managed to occupy New Orleans, they would have been difficult to dislodge regardless of the specific provisions of the peace treaty.

Hartford Convention: The Demise of the Federalists

In the fall of 1814, a group of leading New England politicians, most of them moderate Federalists, gathered in Hartford to discuss relations between the people of their region and the federal government. The **Hartford Convention** delegates were angry and hurt by the Madison administration's seeming insensitivity to the economic interests of the New England states. The embargo had soured New Englanders on Republican foreign policy, but the events of the War of 1812 added insult to injury. When British troops occupied the coastal villages of Maine, then part of Massachusetts, the president did nothing to drive out the enemy. Of course, the self-righteous complaints of convention organizers overlooked New England's tepid support for the war effort.

The men who met at Hartford on December 15 did not advocate secession from the Union. Although people living in other sections of the country cried treason, the convention delegates only recommended changes in the Constitution. They drafted a number of amendments that reflected the New Englanders' growing frustration. One proposal suggested that congressional representation be calculated on the basis of the number of white males living in a state. New England congressmen were tired of the three-fifths rule that gave southern slaveholders a disproportionately large voice in the House. The convention also wanted to limit each president to a single term in office, a reform that New Englanders hoped might end Virginia's monopoly of the executive mansion. And finally, the delegates insisted that a two-thirds majority was necessary before Congress could declare war, pass commercial regulations, or admit new states to the Union. The moderate Federalists of New England were confident these changes would protect their region from the tyranny of southern Republicans.

The convention dispatched its resolutions to Washington, but soon after an official delegation reached the federal capital, the situation became extremely awkward. Everyone was celebrating the victory of New Orleans and the announcement of peace. Republican leaders in Congress accused the hapless New Englanders of disloyalty, and people throughout the country were persuaded that a group of wild secessionists had attempted to destroy the Union. The Hartford Convention accelerated the final demise of the Federalist Party.

Treaty of Ghent Ends the War

In August 1814, the United States dispatched a distinguished negotiating team to Ghent, a Belgian city where the Americans opened talks with their British counterparts. During the early weeks of discussion, the British made impossible demands. They insisted on territorial concessions from the United States, the right to navigate the Mississippi River, and the creation of a large Indian buffer state in the Northwest Territory. The Americans listened to this presentation, more or less politely, and then rejected the entire package. In turn, they lectured their British counterparts about maritime rights and impressment.

Fatigue finally broke the diplomatic deadlock. The British government realized that no amount of military force could significantly alter the outcome of hostilities in the United States. Weary negotiators signed the Treaty of Ghent on Christmas Eve 1814. The document dealt with virtually none of the topics contained in Madison's original war message. Neither side surrendered territory; Great Britain refused even to discuss the topic of impressment. In fact, after more than two years of hostilities, the adversaries merely agreed to end the fighting, postponing the vexing issues of neutral rights until a later date. The Senate apparently concluded that stalemate was preferable to continued conflict and ratified the treaty 35 to 0.

Most Americans—except perhaps the diehard Federalists of New England—viewed the War of 1812 as an important success. Even though the country's military accomplishments had been unimpressive, the people of the United States had been swept up in a contagion of nationalism. The Hartford debacle served to discredit secessionist fantasies for several decades. Americans had waged a "second war of independence" and in the process transformed the Union into a symbol of national destiny. "The war," reflected Gallatin, had made Americans "feel and act more as a nation; and I hope that the permanency of the Union is thereby better secured." That nationalism had flourished in times of war was an irony that Gallatin's contemporaries did not fully appreciate. After the Treaty of Ghent, however, Americans came gradually to realize they had nothing further to fear from Europe, and in an era of peace, the process of sectional divergence began to quicken, threatening to destroy the republic that Jefferson and Madison had worked so hard to preserve.

📖 ⬤ ┤Read the **Document**   **The Treaty of Ghent (1814)**

The Treaty of Ghent ended the War of 1812, but resolved none of the issues—rival territorial claims, impressments, the trading rights of neutral nations—that had led to the war. Still, it presented Americans with a symbolic victory that drew the nation together in its celebration of this "second war of independence." In the center of this painting, U.S. Ambassador (and future President) John Q. Adams shakes hands with members of the British treaty delegation.

Conclusion: Republican Legacy

During the 1820s, it became fashionable to visit retired presidents. These were not, of course, ordinary leaders. Jefferson, Adams, and Madison linked a generation of younger men and women to the heroic moments of the early republic. When they spoke about the Declaration of Independence or the Constitution of the United States, their opinions carried symbolic weight for a burgeoning society anxious about its political future.

A remarkable coincidence occurred on July 4, 1826, the fiftieth anniversary of the Declaration of Independence. On that day, Thomas Jefferson died at Monticello. His last words were, "Is it the Fourth?" On the same day, several hundred miles to the north, John Adams also passed his last day on Earth. His mind was on his old friend and sometimes adversary, and during his final moments, Adams found comfort in the assurance that "Thomas Jefferson still survives."

James Madison lived on at his Virginia plantation, the last of the Founders. Throughout a long and productive career, he had fought for republican values. He championed a Jeffersonian vision of a prosperous nation in which virtuous, independent citizens pursued their own economic interests. He tolerated no aristocratic pretensions. Leaders of a Jeffersonian persuasion—and during his last years, that probably included John Adams—brought forth a democratic, egalitarian society. Although they sometimes worried that the obsessive grubbing for wealth might destroy public virtue, they were justly proud of the republic they had helped to create.

But many visitors who journeyed to Madison's home at Montpelier before he died in 1836 were worried about another legacy of the founding generation. Why, they asked the aging president, had the early leaders of this nation allowed slavery to endure? How did African Americans fit into the republican scheme? Try as they would, neither Madison nor the politicians who claimed the Jeffersonian mantle could provide satisfactory answers. In an open, egalitarian society, there seemed no place for slaves, and a few months before Madison died, a visitor reported sadly, "With regard to slavery, he owned himself almost to be in despair."

Study Resources

 Take the **Study Plan** for **Chapter 8** *Republican Ascendancy* on **MyHistoryLab**

TIME LINE

1800 Thomas Jefferson elected president

1801 Adams makes "midnight" appointments of federal judges

1802 Judiciary Act is repealed (March)

1803 Chief Justice John Marshall rules on *Marbury* v. *Madison* (February); sets precedent for judicial review; Louisiana Purchase concluded with France (May)

1803–1806 Lewis and Clark explore the Northwest

1804 Aaron Burr kills Alexander Hamilton in a duel (July); Jefferson elected to second term

1805 Justice Samuel Chase acquitted by Senate (March)

1807 Burr is tried for conspiracy (August–September); Embargo Act passed (December)

1808 Slave trade is ended (January); Madison elected president

1809 Embargo is repealed; Non-Intercourse Act passed (March)

1811 Harrison defeats Indians at Tippecanoe (November)

1812 Declaration of war against Great Britain (June); Madison elected to second term, defeating De Witt Clinton of New York

1813 Perry destroys British fleet at battle of Put-in-Bay (September)

1814 Jackson crushes Creek Indians at Horseshoe Bend (March); British marines burn Washington, D.C. (August); Hartford Convention meets to recommend constitutional changes (December); Treaty of Ghent ends War of 1812 (December)

1815 Jackson routs British at Battle of New Orleans (January)

CHAPTER REVIEW

Regional Identities in a New Republic

 How did the Republic's growth shape the market economy and relations with Native Americans?

During Jefferson's administration, a rapidly growing population flooded into the Ohio and Mississippi valleys. Family farms produced crops for a robust international market. Cities served as centers, not of industry, but of commerce. When Native Americans such as Tecumseh resisted expansion, the United States government and ordinary white settlers pushed them aside. (p. 180)

Jefferson as President

 How did practical politics challenge Jefferson's political principles?

Jefferson brought to the presidency a commitment to a small, less expensive federal government. In office, however, he discovered that practical politics demanded compromises with Republican principles.

He needed a government capable of responding to unexpected challenges and opportunities throughout the world. Although he worried that the Louisiana Purchase (1803) might exceed his authority under the Constitution, Jefferson accepted the French offer and sent Lewis and Clark to explore this vast territory. (p. 183)

Jefferson's Critics

 How did Jeffersonians deal with the difficult problems of party politics and slavery?

To end Federalist control of the judiciary, Jefferson denied commissions to judges appointed at the end of the Adams administration and attempted to remove others from office. That failed, and the impeachment of Supreme Court Justice Samuel Chase embarrassed the administration. In 1807, after considerable debate and compromise, Jefferson signed into law a bill outlawing the international slave trade. (p. 187)

Embarrassments Overseas

 Why did the United States find it difficult to avoid military conflict during this period?

During Jefferson's second term, Britain and France waged a world war. Both nations tried to manipulate the United States into taking sides. Recognizing that his country possessed only a weak navy and small army, Jefferson supported the Embargo Act (1807), which closed American ports to foreign commerce. This angered New Englanders who regarded open trade as the key to their region's prosperity. (p. 193)

The Strange War of 1812

 Why is the War of 1812 sometimes thought of as a "second war of independence"?

Prior to the war, Britain treated the United States as though it were still a colonial possession and regularly seized sailors on American ships. In 1813, American troops failed to conquer Canada. In 1814, British troops burned Washington, D.C., in retaliation. In 1815, General Andrew Jackson won a stunning victory in the Battle of New Orleans. The resolutions of the Hartford Convention, criticizing the war and the Constitution, proved an embarrassment for the Federalists and accelerated their demise as a political party. (p. 196)

KEY TERMS AND DEFINITIONS

Louisiana Purchase   U.S. acquisition of the Louisiana Territory from France in 1803 for $15 million. The purchase secured American control of the Mississippi River and doubled the size of the nation. p. 185

Lewis and Clark Expedition   Overland expedition to the Pacific coast (1804–1906) let by Meriwether Lewis and William Clark. Commissioned by President Thomas Jefferson, it collected scientific data about the country and its resources. p. 186

Marbury v. Madison   In this 1803 landmark decision, the Supreme Court first asserted the power of judicial review by declaring an act of Congress unconstitutional. p. 188

Judicial review   The authority of the Supreme Court to determine the constitutionality of the statutes. p. 188

Embargo Act   In response to a British attack on an American warship off the coast of Virginia, this 1807 law prohibited foreign commerce. p. 194

War Hawks   Congressional leaders who, in 1811 and 1812, called for war against Britain. p. 195

War of 1812   War between Britain and the United States. U.S. justifications for war included British violations of American maritime rights, impressment of seamen, provocation of the Indians, and defense of national honor. p. 196

Battle of New Orleans   Battle that occurred in 1815 at the end of the War of 1812 when U.S. forces defeated a British attempt to seize New Orleans. p. 198

Hartford Convention   An assembly of New England Federalists who met in Hartford, Connecticut, in December 1814 to protest President James Madison's foreign policy in the War of 1812, which had undermined commercial interests in the North. They proposed amending the Constitution to prevent future presidents from declaring war without a two-thirds majority in Congress. p. 198

CRITICAL THINKING QUESTIONS

1. During a period of international instability and conflict, how was the nation's economy able to expand so impressively?

2. Was Jefferson a weak president, as some Federalists at the time claimed? Provide reasons to support your position.

3. Was Jefferson justified in his attacks on the federal courts?

4. In what way did the resolves of the Hartford Convention contribute to the demise of the Federalist Party?

MyHistoryLab Media Assignments

Find these resources in the Media Assignments folder for Chapter 8 on MyHistoryLab

Regional Identities in a New Republic

Read the Document   Charles William Janson, The Stranger in America p. 179

Read the Document   Margaret Bayard Smith, Reflections upon Meeting Jefferson p. 183

Jefferson as President

■ View the Closer Look   Map of Louisiana Purchase, 1803 p. 185

■ Watch the Video   Lewis & Clark: What were they trying to accomplish? p. 186

Jefferson's Critics

Read the Document   Opinion for the Supreme Court for Marbury v. Madison p. 188

■ Complete the Assignment   Barbary Pirates and American Captives p. 190

■ Read the Document   Congress Prohibits Importation of Slaves 1807 p. 192

Embarrassments Overseas

Read the Document   James Madison, Inaugural Address (1809) p. 195

The Strange War of 1812

■ View the Map   The War of 1812 p. 196

Listen to the Audio File   Star-Spangled Banner p. 197

Read the Document   The Treaty of Ghent (1814) p. 199

■ *Indicates Study Plan Media Assignment*

9 Nation Building and Nationalism

Contents and Learning Objectives

((•—[**Listen** to the **Audio File** on **myhistorylab**   Chapter 9 *Nation Building and Nationalism*

A Revolutionary War Hero Revisits America in 1824

When the Marquis de Lafayette returned to the United States in 1824 he found a peaceful and prosperous nation. For more than a year, the great French hero of the American Revolution toured the country that he had helped to bring into being, and he marveled at how much had changed since he had fought beside George Washington more than forty years before. He was greeted by adoring crowds in places that had been unsettled or beyond the nation's borders four decades earlier. Besides covering the eastern seaboard, Lafayette went west to New Orleans, then up the Mississippi and Ohio rivers by steamboat. He thus sampled a new mode of transportation that was helping to bring the far-flung outposts and settlements of a much enlarged nation into regular contact with each other.

Everywhere Lafayette was greeted with patriotic oratory celebrating the liberty, prosperity, and progress of the new nation. Speaking before a joint session of both houses of Congress, the old hero responded in kind, telling his hosts exactly what they wanted to hear. He hailed "the immense improvements" and "admirable communications" that he had witnessed and declared himself deeply moved by "all the grandeur and prosperity of these happy United States, which . . . reflect on every part of the world the light of a far superior political civilization."

Americans had good reasons to make Lafayette's return the occasion for patriotic celebration and reaffirmation. Since the War of 1812, the nation had been free from serious foreign threats to its independence and way of life. It was growing rapidly in population, size, and wealth. Its republican form of government, which many had considered a risky experiment at the time of its origin, was apparently working well. James Monroe, the current president, had proclaimed in his first inaugural address that "the United States have flourished beyond example. Their citizens individually have been happy and the nation prosperous." Expansion "to the Great Lakes and beyond the sources of the great rivers which communicate through our whole interior" meant that "no country was ever happier with respect to its domain." As for the government, it was so near to perfection that "in respect to it we have no essential improvement to make."

Beneath the optimism and self-confidence, however, lay undercurrents of doubt and anxiety about the future. The visit of the aged Lafayette signified the passing of the Founders. Less than a year after his departure, Jefferson and Adams died

An exuberant crowd celebrates in the square outside Independence Hall in this painting, *Election Day in Philadelphia* (1815), by German American artist John Lewis Krimmel.

Source: Courtesy, The Winterthur Library: Printed Book and Periodical Collection.

within hours of each other on the fiftieth anniversary of the Declaration of Independence, leaving Madison as the last of the great Founders. Some Americans asked whether the Founders' example of republican virtue and self-sacrifice could be maintained in an increasingly prosperous and materialistic society. In fact, many believed public virtue had declined since the heroic age of the Revolution. And what about the place of black slavery in a "perfect" democratic republic? Lafayette himself noted with disappointment that the United States had not yet extended freedom to southern slaves.

But the peace following the War of 1812 did open the way for a great surge of nation building. As new lands were acquired or opened up for settlement, hordes of pioneers often rushed in. Improvements in transportation soon gave many of them access to distant markets, and advances in the processing of raw materials led to the first stirrings of industrialization. Politicians looked for ways to encourage the process of growth and expansion, and an active judiciary handed down decisions that served to promote economic development and assert the priority of national over state and local interests. To guarantee the peace and security essential for internal progress, statesmen

proclaimed a foreign policy designed to insulate America from external involvements. A new nation of great potential wealth and power was emerging.

Expansion and Migration

What key forces drove American expansion westward during this period?

The peace concluded with Great Britain in 1815 allowed Americans to shift their attention from Europe and the Atlantic to the vast lands of North America. The Rush-Bagot Agreement (1817) limited U.S. and British naval forces on the Great Lakes and Lake Champlain and guaranteed that the British would never try to invade the United States from Canada and that the United States would never try to take Canada from the British. The Anglo-American Convention of 1818 set the border between the lands of the Louisiana Purchase and Canada at the 49th parallel and provided for joint U.S. and British occupation of Oregon.

Meanwhile, in the lower Mississippi Valley, the former French colony of Louisiana had been admitted as a state in 1812, and a thriving settlement existed around Natchez in the Mississippi Territory. Elsewhere in the trans-Appalachian west, white settlement was sparse and much land remained in Indian hands. U.S. citizens, eager to expand into lands held by Indian nations as well as Spain, used diplomacy, military action, force, and fraud to "open" lands for U.S. settlement and westward migration.

Extending the Boundaries

Postwar expansionists turned their attention first to Spanish holdings, which included Florida and much of the present-day American West. Their first goal was to obtain Florida from Spain. Between 1810 and 1812, the United States had annexed part of what is now Alabama, claiming that it was part of the Louisiana Purchase. The remainder, known as East Florida, became a prime object of territorial ambition for President James Monroe and his energetic secretary of state, John Quincy Adams. Adams was looking for opportunities to confront Spain for control of the region and put into effect his grand design for continental expansion.

General Andrew Jackson provided such an opening. In 1816, U.S. troops first crossed into East Florida in pursuit of hostile Seminole Indians. This raid touched off a wider conflict, and after taking command in late 1817, Jackson went beyond his official orders and occupied East Florida in April and May of 1818. This operation became known as the First Seminole War. Except for Adams, all the members of Monroe's cabinet privately condemned this aggressive action; so did a report of the House of Representatives. But no disciplinary action was taken, mainly because public opinion rallied behind the hero of New Orleans.

In November 1818, Secretary Adams informed the Spanish government that the United States had acted in self-defense and that further conflict would be avoided only if East Florida were ceded to the United States. The Madrid government, weakened by Latin American revolutions and the breaking up of its empire, was in no position to resist American bullying. As part of the **Adams-Onís Treaty**, signed on February 22, 1819, Spain relinquished Florida to the United States. In return, the United States assumed $5 million of the financial claims of American citizens against Spain.

NORTH AMERICA, 1819 Treaties with Britain following the War of 1812 setting the border between the United States and Canada (British North America) made this border the longest unfortified boundary line in the world.

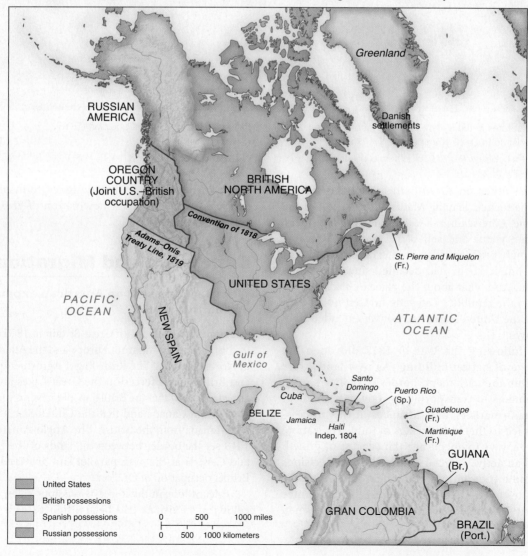

A strong believer that the United States had a continental destiny, Adams also used the confrontation over Florida to make Spain give up its claim to the Pacific coast north of California, thus opening a path for future American expansion. Taking advantage of Spain's desire to keep its title to Texas—a portion of which the United States had previously claimed as part of the Louisiana Purchase—Adams induced the Spanish minister Luis de Onís to agree to the creation of a new boundary between American and Spanish territory that ran north of Texas but extended all the way to the Pacific. Great Britain and Russia still had competing claims to the Pacific Northwest, but the United States was now in a better position to acquire frontage on a second ocean.

Interest in exploitation of the Far West continued to grow during the second and third decades of the nineteenth century. In 1811, a New York merchant, John Jacob Astor, founded the fur-trading post of Astoria at the mouth of the Columbia River in the Oregon Country. Astor's American Fur Company operated out of St. Louis in the 1820s and 1830s, with fur traders working their way up the Missouri to the northern Rockies and beyond. First they limited themselves to trading for furs with the Indians, but later, businesses such as the Rocky Mountain Fur Company, founded in 1822, relied on trappers or "mountain men" who went after game on their own and sold the furs to agents of the company at an annual meeting or "rendezvous."

These colorful characters, who included such legendary figures as Jedediah Smith, Jim Bridger, Kit Carson, and Jim Beckwourth (one of the many African Americans who contributed to the opening of the West as fur traders, scouts, or settlers), accomplished prodigious feats of survival under harsh natural conditions. Following Indian trails, they explored many parts of the Rockies and the Great Basin. Many of them married Indian women and assimilated much of the culture and technology of the Native Americans. The mountain men were portrayed in American literature and popular mythology as exemplars of a romantic ideal of lonely self-reliance in harmony with unspoiled nature.

The Far West, however, remained beyond American dreams of agrarian expansion. The real focus of attention between 1815 and the 1840s was the nearer West, the rich agricultural lands between the Appalachians and the Mississippi that were inhabited by numerous Indian tribes.

Native American Societies under Pressure

Five Indian nations, with a combined population of nearly sixty thousand, occupied much of what later became Mississippi, Alabama, Georgia, and Florida. These nations—the Cherokee, Chickasaw, Choctaw, Creek, and Seminole—became known as the "Five Civilized Tribes" because by 1815 they had adopted many of the features of the surrounding white Southern society: an agricultural economy, a republican form of government, and the institution of slavery. Though these southeastern Indians consciously strategized to respond to Jeffersonian exhortations toward "civilization" and the promise of citizenship that came with it, between 1815 and 1833 it became increasingly clear that most white Americans were not interested in incorporating them into U.S. society, whether as nations or as individuals.

The five nations varied in their responses to white encroachment on their lands. So-called mixed-blood leaders such as John Ross convinced the Cherokee to adopt a strategy of accommodation to increase their chances of survival; the Creek and Seminole, by contrast, took up arms in resistance.

The Cherokee were the largest of the five nations. Traditional Cherokee society had combined hunting by men and subsistence farming by women. In the early nineteenth century, the shift to a more agrarian, market-based economy led to an erosion of the traditional matrilineal kinship system, in which a person belonged to his mother's clan. The new order replaced matrilineal inheritance with the U.S. system of patriarchy in which fathers headed the household and property passed from father to son. An emphasis on the nuclear family with the husband as producer and the wife as domestic caretaker diminished the role of the clan.

The shift toward agriculture also helped introduce American-style slavery to Cherokee society. As the Cherokee adopted plantation-style agriculture, they also began to adopt white attitudes toward blacks. By the time of Indian Removal, a few Cherokee-owned plantations with hundreds of slaves, and there were more than fifteen hundred slaves in the Cherokee Nation. Discrimination against Africans in all five nations grew under pressure of contact with whites. Beginning in the 1820s the Cherokee Council adopted rules regulating slaves. Whereas a few Africans in the eighteenth century had been adopted into the tribe and become citizens, under the new laws slaves could not intermarry with Cherokee citizens, engage in trade or barter, or hold property.

In an effort to head off encroachments by southern states, the Cherokee attempted to centralize power in a republican government in the 1820s as well. Cherokee historian William McLoughlin has described, "a series of eleven laws passed between 1820 and 1823 . . . constituted a political revolution in the structure of Cherokee government. Under these laws the National Council created a bicameral legislature, a district and superior court system, an elective system of representation by geographical district rather than by town, and a salaried government bureaucracy." This process culminated in the 1827 adoption of a formal written constitution modeled on the U.S. Constitution.

At the same time, a renaissance of Cherokee culture was spurred by Sequoyah's invention of a written Cherokee language in 1821–1822. While the alphabet was complicated and lacked punctuation, "Sequoyan" provided the Cherokee a new means of self-expression and a reinvigorated sense of Cherokee identity. The first American Indian newspaper, the *Cherokee Phoenix*, was published in Sequoyan in 1828. By the time of Indian Removal, Cherokee leaders like John Ross and Elias Boudinot could point with pride to high levels of Cherokee acculturation, education, and economic success at American-style "civilization."

The Seminole Nation, the smallest of the five nations, presents perhaps the starkest cultural contrast to the Cherokee, both because the Seminole reacted to pressure from white settlers with armed resistance rather than accommodation, and because their multicultural history gave them a very different relationship to slavery.

The Seminole Nation in Florida formed after the European conquest of America, from the disparate groups of Creek Indians migrating from Georgia and Alabama in the wake of war and disease who mingled with the remnants of native Floridians to form the new tribe. At the same time, Spain had granted asylum to runaway African American slaves from the Carolinas, who created "maroon communities" in Florida, striking up alliances with the Seminole to ward off slave catchers. African Americans and Native Americans intermingled, and by the late eighteenth century, some African Americans were already known as "Seminole Negroes" or "estelusti." The word "Seminole" itself meant "wild" or "runaway" in the Creek language.

Although the Seminoles adopted African slavery at some point in the first decades of the nineteenth century, it was very different from slavery as it existed among whites, or even among the Cherokee and Creek. Seminole "slaves" lived in separate towns, planted and cultivated fields in common, owned large herds of livestock, and paid their "owners" only an annual tribute, similar to that paid by Seminole towns to the *micco* or chief.

During the 1820s and 1830s, the estelusti and the Seminoles were allies in a series of wars against the Americans; however, their alliance came under increasing strain. In 1823, six Seminole leaders, including one of some African ancestry known as "Mulatto King," signed the Treaty of Moultrie Creek, removing the tribe from their fertile lands in northern Florida to swampland south of Tampa. The signers took bribes and believed unfulfilled promises that they would be allowed to stay on their lands. Another provision of the treaty required the Seminoles to return runaway slaves and turn away any future runaways. During the 1830s, Black Seminoles were some of the staunchest opponents of Indian Removal, and played

a major role in the Second Seminole War, fought in resistance to removal from 1835 to 1842. General Thomas W. Jesup, the leader of the U.S. Army, claimed, "This, you may be assured is a negro and not an Indian war."

Treaties like the one signed at Moultrie Creek in 1823 reduced tribal holdings; the federal government used a combination of deception, bribery, and threats to induce land cessions. State governments also began to act on their own, proclaiming state jurisdiction over lands still allotted by federal treaty to Indians within the state's borders. The stage was thus set for the forced removal of the Five Civilized Tribes to the trans-Mississippi West during the administration of Andrew Jackson. (See the Feature Essay, "Confronting a New Environment," pp. 208–209. Jackson's Indian Removal policy is discussed in further detail in Chapter 10.)

Farther north, in the Ohio Valley and the Northwest Territory, Native Americans had already suffered military defeat in the conflict between Britain and the United States, leaving them only a minor obstacle to the ambitions of white settlers and land speculators. When the British withdrew from the Old Northwest in 1815, they left their former Indian allies virtually defenseless before the tide of whites who rushed into the region. Consigned by treaty to reservations outside the main lines of white advance, most of the tribes were eventually forced west of the Mississippi.

The last stand of the Indians in this region occurred in 1831–1832, when a faction of the confederated Sac and Fox Indians under Chief

▶ Read the Document   The Cherokee Treaty of 1817

Mountain men and Native Americans met at a rendezvous to trade their furs to company agents in exchange for food, ammunition, and other goods. Feasting, drinking, gambling, and sharing exploits were also part of the annual event. The painting *Rendezvous* (ca. 1837) by Alfred Jacob Miller.

Black Hawk refused to abandon their lands east of the Mississippi. Federal troops and Illinois state militia pursued Black Hawk's band and drove the Indians back to the river, where they were almost exterminated while attempting to cross to the western bank. Uprooting once populous Indian communities of the Old Northwest was part of a national program for removing Indians of the eastern part of the country to an area beyond the Mississippi.

As originally conceived by Thomas Jefferson, removal would have allowed those Indians who became "civilized" to remain behind on individually owned farms and qualify for American citizenship. This policy would reduce Indian holdings without appearing to violate American standards of justice. Not everyone agreed with Jefferson's belief that Indians, unlike blacks, had the natural ability to adopt white ways and become useful citizens of the republic. During the Monroe era, it became clear that white settlers, many of whom saw Native Americans as irredeemable savages, wanted nothing less than the removal of all Indians, "civilized" or not. Andrew Jackson, who made his name as an Indian fighter in the 1810s, presided over a shift to a far more aggressive Indian removal policy.

Settlement to the Mississippi

While Indians were being hustled or driven beyond the Mississippi, white settlers poured across the Appalachians and filled the agricultural heartland of the United States. In 1810, only about one-seventh of the American population lived beyond the Appalachians; by 1840, more than one-third did. During that period, Illinois grew from a territory with 12,282 inhabitants to a state with 476,183; Mississippi's population of about 40,000 increased tenfold; and Michigan grew from a remote frontier area with fewer than 5000 people into a state with more than 200,000. Eight new western states were added to the Union during this period. Because of the government's removal policies, few settlers actually had to fight Indians. But they did have to obtain possession of land and derive a livelihood from it.

Much of the vast acreage opened up by the westward movement passed through the hands of land speculators before it reached farmers and planters. In the prosperous period following the War of 1812, and again during the boom of the early to mid-1830s, speculation in public lands proceeded at a massive and feverish rate. After a financial panic in 1819 brought ruin to many who had purchased tracts on credit, the minimum price was lowered from $2.00 to $1.25 an acre, but full payment was required in cash. Since few settlers could afford the necessary outlays, wealthy speculators continued to acquire most good land.

Eventually, most of the land did find its way into the hands of actual cultivators. In some areas, squatters arrived before the official survey and formed claims associations that policed land auctions to prevent "outsiders" from bidding up the price and buying their farms out from under them. Squatters also agitated for formal right of first purchase or **preemption** from the government. Between 1799 and 1830, Congress passed a number of special acts that granted squatters in specific areas the right to purchase at the minimum price the land that they had already improved. In 1841, Congress formally acknowledged the right to farm on public lands with the assurance of a *future* preemption right.

Settlers who arrived after speculators had secured title had to deal with land barons. Fortunately for the settlers, most speculators operated on credit and needed a quick return on their investment, selling land at a profit to settlers who had some capital, renting out farms until tenants had earned enough to buy them, or loaning money to squatters who would later pay for the land in installments. As a result, the family farm or owner-operated plantation became the characteristic unit of western agriculture.

Farmers had to produce enough food to subsist and to sell at market to pay off their debts. Not surprisingly, most of the earliest settlement was along rivers that provided a natural means of transportation for flatboats loaded with corn, wheat, cotton, or cured meat. From more remote areas, farmers drove livestock over primitive trails and roads to eastern markets. To turn bulky grain, especially corn, into a more easily transportable commodity, farmers in remote regions often distilled grain into whiskey. Local marketing centers quickly sprang up, usually at river junctions. Some of these grew into small cities virtually overnight, greatly accelerating regional development.

Most frontier people welcomed the opportunity to sell some of their crops in order to acquire the consumer goods they could not produce for themselves. Women especially benefited from the chance to buy some household necessities that they had previously made at home, such as soap, candles, and some articles of clothing. But many of them also valued self-sufficiency and tried to produce enough of the necessities of life to survive when cash crops failed or prices were low.

The People and Culture of the Frontier

Most of the settlers who populated the West were farmers from the seaboard states. Rising land prices and declining fertility of the soil in the older regions often motivated their migration. Most moved in family units and tried to recreate their former ways of life as soon as possible. Women were often reluctant to migrate in the first place, and when they arrived in new areas, they strove valiantly to recapture the comfort and stability they had left behind.

In general, pioneers sought out the kind of terrain and soil with which they were already familiar. People from eastern uplands favored western hill country. Piedmont and Tidewater farmers or planters usually made for the lower and flatter areas. Early settlers avoided the fertile prairies of the Midwest, preferring instead river bottoms or wooded sections because they were more like home and could be farmed by tried-and-true methods. Rather than being the bold and deliberate innovators pictured in American mythology, typical agricultural pioneers were deeply averse to changing their habits.

Yet adjustments were necessary simply to survive under frontier conditions. Initially, at least, isolated homesteads required a high degree of self-sufficiency. Men usually cut down trees, built cabins, broke the soil, and put in crops. Besides cooking, keeping house, and caring for children, women made clothes, manufactured soap and other household necessities, churned butter, preserved food for the winter, and worked in the fields at busy times; at one time or another, women performed virtually all the tasks required by frontier farming. Crops had to be planted, harvested, and readied for home consumption with simple tools brought in wagons from the East—often little more than an axe, a plow, and a spinning wheel.

Feature Essay | Confronting a New Environment

This 1839 satire on western emigration depicts a battered wagon of half-starved pioneers returning to New England after suffering hardships in Illinois, while an optimistic traveler is on his way there.

The era of Indian Removal in the 1830s, during which tens of thousands of Indians were driven from the Southeast to present-day Kansas and Oklahoma, also saw hundreds of thousands of white farmers move to Illinois and Missouri. Despite obvious differences in their experiences, both groups of migrants had to adapt to the same unfamiliar prairie environment.

Seeking to convince Indian tribes to move west and abandon their lands for white settlement, U.S. government officials argued that western lands would afford space and bounty for Indian and European American settlers alike. Indeed, in his address to Congress on December 6, 1830, President Andrew Jackson chided Indians for their resistance to removal:

Our [white] children by thousands yearly leave the land of their birth to seek new homes in distant regions. Does Humanity weep at these painful separations from every thing, animate and inanimate, with which the young heart has become entwined? Far from it. It is rather a source of joy that our country affords scope where our young population may range unconstrained . . . .

Certainly, the new Western environment offered plenty of space. But European Americans and Eastern Indians were woodland people. They lived at the tail end of the "Age of Wood" when forests provided the primary material for building, fencing, and heating, not to mention habitat for game that supplemented their diets. The ideal landscape was a clearing for a farm or small village surrounded by thick forest. In the prairie, emigrants confronted an opposite landscape: huge openings—"barrens"—fringed by trees.

"To one unaccustomed to it, there is something inexpressibly lonely in the solitude of a prairie," wrote Washington Irving. "The loneliness of the forest seems nothing to it." Settlers clustered at the prairie's edge, and only partly for the timber. The grassland had a reputation for fire, dryness, and infertility. James Madison, writing to Thomas Jefferson, expressed the conviction that Illinois was a "miserably poor" country that would never bear "a single bush." Unsurprisingly, therefore, most of the early settlers to the prairie states gravitated to the relatively rare hilly and wooded areas that reminded them from where they had come.

At the time, most Americans believed that vegetation revealed its soil's fertility: The bigger the greenery, the richer the earth. Soil that produced no trees seemed mighty poor indeed. People eventually tried farming the prairie, of course, and discovered the truth: The soil was, in fact, so immensely fertile it supported a thick shield of tangled roots. "Sod-busting" required oxen, tools, and muscle; before the John Deere iron plow became readily available in the mid-nineteenth century, most early settlers were not up to the difficult task.

If Illinois initially seemed barren, the lands of present-day Kansas and Oklahoma seemed positively sterile. In 1820, a government surveyor gave an exaggerated but well-publicized name to this swath of the continent "The Great American Desert." It was here that a diverse assemblage of Indian refugees tried their best to set up new homes in the removal era. In addition to the well-known Five Civilized Tribes from the South, the newcomers included groups from the Northeast and Old Northwest, including the Chippewa, Kickapoo, Miami, Ottawa, Potawatomi, Sac-Fox, Seneca, and Winnebago Indians, among others.

For these woodland peoples, the sea of grass came as a shock. No wonder that many of the relocated Indians complained to the "Great Father"—the federal government. Writing to Indian agent William Clark (of Lewis and Clark fame), Shawnee leaders related that they "traveled three days through prairies and thought we were in the land of the great spirit, for we could see nothing but what was above us and the earth we walked upon." The Wyandot Nation of Ohio decided to send an "unbiased, unprejudiced" exploring expedition to see their promised land on the Missouri-Kansas border. The report was discouraging: "[T]here is but little timber and what there is, is of a low scrubby, knotty and twisted kind and fit for nothing but firewood . . . . [T]here is not good timber sufficient for the purposes of a people that wish to pursue agriculture."

Although many Indian tribes had extensive experience with various forms of agriculture, old methods could not be easily replicated on the prairie, where the soil was too hard to be easily cultivated, and water was scarce. A few Indian groups, such as the Cherokee, had learned to grow marketable crops in their traditional homelands and continued to do so in the new lands after removal. Nonetheless, some Cherokee chose to become seasonal bison hunters on the Southern Plains. Even with changes in their farming and hunting methods, it took decades for the Cherokee to recover from the dispossession of their towns and farms in Georgia. Adaptation was made more difficult by the staggering human losses they suffered on their forced march to the West.

The sickness and death on the Cherokee Trail of Tears—about a fourth of the migrants died on the way—was an extreme form of an experience that European American settlers also faced. For whites and natives alike, moving west meant growing ill; the body became unsettled in its new environment. A spokesperson for tribes removed from upstate New York to Kansas called it "a poor barren unhealthy country where many families have lost all their children in a course of a few years." For both groups, catching the "ague" was an inevitable part of "seasoning" in this new country, which had a reputation for sickliness. Now understood as malaria, the ague commonly presented itself in cycles of shaking. Indeed, the experience was so common that there were essentially two types of settlers: veterans of the "pioneer shakes" and greenhorns. Likewise, it was impossible to completely avoid "the chills" because it could arrive on the very air that permeated wooden cabins.

Antebellum settlers attributed many of their maladies to "miasma." Noah Webster defined it as "infecting substances floating in the air; the effluvia of any putrefying bodies, rising and floating in the atmosphere." According to popular belief, miasma came from rot in humus-rich forests, fertile bottomlands, and well-watered prairie. When settlers broke the prairie in order to "improve" the land, they released foul airs. People attempted to fight miasma by purging the air with coal smoke or wearing strong-smelling bags of herbs around the neck. But the land got sicker before it got healthier. The irony was not lost on settlers. Timothy Flint, who published an influential western guidebook in 1831, wrote that "there appears to be in the great plan of Providence a scale, in which the advantages and disadvantages of human condition are balanced. Where the lands are extremely fertile, it seems to be appended to them, as a drawback to that advantage, that they are generally sickly."

In the antebellum period, many Americans believed that land, like bodies, had intrinsic constitutions or states of health. Ideally, individuals and races could be matched to their "proper" environment (an idea used to defend slavery). Many Northerners and Indians from the North feared for their health when migrating to the hot, humid Mississippi basin. Billy Caldwell, a half-Irish, half-Indian chief from the Great Lakes region, declared that Kansas was "unhealthy for people from a cold climate." There was always the hope that the new Indian homelands would prove unsuitable to white settlers. In 1836, en route to their new home, the Sac and Fox Indians said with bitter sarcasm that "the south side of the Missouri River is intended by the great spirit for the Red skins and for this reason he made so much prairie, that it would not suit . . . the white man, and if this had not been the case the red man would in short time have been without a home." In a matter of time, though, the "white man" would find the prairie suitable and would claim this homeland, too.

Indians removed from the Southeast lost not only their homelands and tribal governments, but a way of life that had depended upon their familiar physical environment. All migrants to the West had to learn new ways of eking out a living from what seemed an inhospitable land.

QUESTIONS FOR DISCUSSION

1. How did the experiences of Native American migrants to the West compare with those of white Americans?

2. Why did so many migrants to the West become sick?

3. Why was it so difficult for Native Americans and whites to adapt to new environments in the West?

But this picture of frontier self-reliance is not the whole story. Most settlers in fact found it extremely difficult to accomplish all the tasks using only family labor. A more common practice was the sharing of work by a number of pioneer families. Except in parts of the South, where frontier planters had taken slaves with them, the normal way to get heavy labor done in newly settled regions was through mutual aid. Assembling the neighbors to raise a house, burn the woods, roll logs, harvest wheat, husk corn, pull flax, or make quilts helped turn collective work into a festive social occasion. Passing the jug was a normal feature of these "bees," and an uproarious good time often resulted from the various contests or competitions that speeded the work along. These communal events represented a creative response to the shortage of labor and at the same time provided a source for community solidarity. They probably tell us more about the "spirit of the frontier" than the conventional image of the pioneer as a lonely individualist.

While some settlers remained in one place and "grew up with the country," many others moved on after a relatively short time. The wandering of young Abraham Lincoln's family from Kentucky to Indiana and finally to Illinois between 1816 and 1830 was fairly typical. The physical mobility characteristic of nineteenth-century Americans in general was particularly pronounced in frontier regions. Improved land could be sold at a profit and the proceeds used to buy new acreage beyond the horizon where the soil was reportedly richer. The temptations of small-scale land speculation and the lure of new land farther west induced a large proportion of new settlers to pull up stakes and move on after only a few years. Few early nineteenth-century American farmers developed the kind of attachment to the land that often characterized rural populations in other parts of the world.

Americans who remained in the East often ignored the frontier farmers and imagined the West as an untamed American wilderness inhabited by Indians and solitary white "pathfinders" who turned their backs on civilization and learned to live in harmony with nature. James Fenimore Cooper, the first great American novelist, fostered this mythic view of the West in his stories of the frontier. He began in 1823 to publish a series of novels featuring Natty Bumppo, or "Leatherstocking"—a character who became the prototype for the western hero of popular fiction. Natty Bumppo was a hunter and scout who preferred the freedom of living in the forest to the constraints of civilization. Through Natty Bumppo, Cooper engendered a main theme of American romanticism—the superiority of a solitary life in the wilderness to the kind of settled existence among the families, schools, and churches to which most real pioneers aspired.

A Revolution in Transportation

How did transportation networks change and improve after the War of 1812?

It took more than the spread of settlements to bring prosperity to new areas and ensure that they would identify with older regions or with the country as a whole. Along the eastern seaboard, land transportation was so primitive that in 1813 it took seventy-five days for one wagon of goods drawn by four horses to make a trip of about a thousand miles from Worcester, Massachusetts, to Charleston, South Carolina. Coastal shipping eased the problem to some extent in the East and stimulated the growth of port cities. Traveling west over the mountains, however, meant months on the trail.

After the War of 1812, political leaders realized that national security, economic progress, and political unity were all more or less dependent on a greatly improved transportation network. Accordingly, President Madison called for a federally supported program of "internal improvements" in 1815. Recommending such a program in Congress, Representative John C. Calhoun described it as a great nationalizing enterprise: "Let us, then, bind the nation together with a perfect system of roads and canals. Let us conquer space." In ensuing decades, Calhoun's vision of a transportation revolution was realized to a considerable extent, although the direct role of the federal government proved to be less important than anticipated.

Roads and Steamboats

Americans who wanted to get from place to place rapidly and cheaply needed, at a bare minimum, new and improved roads. The first great federal transportation project was the building of the National Road between Cumberland, Maryland, on the Potomac and Wheeling, Virginia, on the Ohio (1811–1818). This impressive toll road had a crushed stone surface and immense stone bridges. It was subsequently extended to reach Vandalia, Illinois, in 1838. Another thoroughfare to the West completed during this period was the Lancaster Turnpike connecting Philadelphia and Pittsburgh. Other major cities were also linked by turnpikes—privately owned toll roads chartered by the states. By about 1825, thousands of miles of turnpikes crisscrossed southern New England, upstate New York, much of Pennsylvania, and northern New Jersey.

By themselves, however, the toll roads failed to meet the demand for low-cost transportation over long distances. For the most part, travelers benefited more than transporters of bulky freight, for whom the turnpikes proved expensive.

Even the National Road could not offer the low freight costs required for the long-distance hauling of wheat, flour, and the other bulky agricultural products of the Ohio Valley. For these commodities, water transportation of some sort was required.

The United States's natural system of river transportation was one of the most significant reasons for its rapid economic development. The Ohio-Mississippi system in particular provided ready access to the rich agricultural areas of the interior and a natural outlet for their products. By 1815, large numbers of flatboats loaded with wheat, flour, and salt pork were making a part of the 2,000-mile trip from Pittsburgh to New Orleans. Even after the coming of the steamboat, flatboats continued to carry a major share of the downriver trade.

The flatboat trade, however, was necessarily one-way. A farmer from Ohio or Illinois, or someone hired to do the job, could float down to New Orleans easily enough, but there was generally no way to get back except by walking overland through rough country. Until the problem of upriver navigation was solved, the Ohio-Mississippi could not carry the manufactured goods that farmers desired in exchange for their crops.

Fortunately, a solution was readily at hand: the use of steam power. Late in the eighteenth century, a number of American

🔍 **View** the **Map**   **Expanding America and Internal Improvements**

The Clermont on the Hudson (1830–1835) by Charles Pensee. Although some called his *Clermont* "Fulton's Folly," Robert Fulton immediately turned a profit from his fleet of steamboats, which reduced the cost and increased the speed of river transport.

inventors had experimented with steam-driven riverboats. John Fitch even exhibited an early model to delegates at the Constitutional Convention. But making a commercially successful craft required further refinement. In 1807, inventor Robert Fulton demonstrated the full potential of the steamboat by successfully propelling the *Clermont* 150 miles up the Hudson River. The first steamboat launched in the West was the *New Orleans*, which made the long trip from Pittsburgh to New Orleans in 1811–1812. Besides becoming a principal means of passenger travel on the inland waterways of the East, the river steamboat revolutionized western commerce. In 1815, the *Enterprise* made the first return trip from New Orleans to Pittsburgh. Within five years, sixty-nine steamboats with a total capacity of 13,890 tons were plying western waters.

Steam transport reduced costs, increased the speed of moving goods and people, and allowed a two-way commerce on the Mississippi and Ohio. The steamboat quickly captured the American imagination. Great paddle wheelers became luxurious floating hotels, the natural habitats of gamblers, confidence men, and mysterious women. For the pleasure of passengers and onlookers, steamboats sometimes raced against each other, and their more skillful pilots became folk heroes. But the boats also had a lamentable safety record, frequently running aground, colliding, or blowing up. The most publicized disasters of antebellum America were spectacular boiler explosions that claimed the lives of hundreds of passengers. As a result of such accidents, the federal government began in 1839 to attempt to regulate steamboats and monitor their construction and operation. The legislation, which failed to create an agency capable of enforcing minimum safety standards, stands as virtually the only federal effort in the pre–Civil War period to regulate domestic transportation.

The Canal Boom

A transportation system based solely on rivers and roads had one enormous gap—it did not provide an economical way to ship western farm produce directly east to ports engaged in transatlantic trade or to the growing urban market of the seaboard states. The solution offered by the politicians and merchants of the Middle Atlantic and midwestern states was to build a system of canals that linked seaboard cities directly to the Great Lakes, the Ohio, and ultimately the Mississippi.

The best natural location for a canal connecting a river flowing into the Atlantic with one of the Great Lakes was between Albany and Buffalo, a relatively flat stretch of 364 miles. The potential value of such a project had long been recognized, but when it was actually approved by the New York legislature in 1817, it was justly hailed as an enterprise of breathtaking boldness. At that time, no more than about 100 miles of canal existed in the entire United States, and the longest single canal extended only 26 miles. Credit for the project belongs mainly to New York's vigorous and farsighted governor, De Witt Clinton. He persuaded the New York state legislature to underwrite the project by issuing bonds, and construction began in 1818.

In less than two years, 75 miles were already finished and the first tolls were being collected. In 1825, the entire canal was opened with great public acclaim and celebration.

At 364 miles long, 40 feet wide, and 4 feet deep, and containing 84 locks, the Erie Canal was the most spectacular engineering achievement of the young republic. Furthermore, it was a great economic success. It reduced the cost of moving goods from Buffalo to Albany to one-twelfth the previous rate. It not only lowered the cost of western products in the East but caused an even sharper decline in the price of goods imported from the East by Westerners and helped to make New York City the commercial capital of the nation.

The great success of the Erie Canal inspired other states to extend public credit for canal building. During the 1830s and 1840s, Pennsylvania, Ohio, and Illinois embarked on ambitious canal construction projects, from Philadelphia to Pittsburgh, from the Ohio River to Cleveland, and from Chicago to the Illinois River and the Mississippi.

The canal boom ended when it became apparent in the 1830s and 1840s that most of the waterways were unprofitable. State credit had been overextended, and the panic and depression of the late 1830s and early 1840s forced retrenchment. While some canals continued to be important arteries up to the time of the Civil War and well beyond, railroads were already beginning to compete successfully for the same traffic, and a new phase in the transportation revolution was beginning.

Emergence of a Market Economy

How did developments in transportation support the growth of agriculture, banking, and industry?

The desire to reduce the costs and increase the speed of shipping heavy freight over great distances laid the groundwork for a new economic system. Canals made it less expensive and more profitable for western farmers to ship wheat and flour to New York and Philadelphia and also gave manufacturers in the East ready access to an interior market. Steamboats reduced shipping costs on the Ohio and Mississippi and put farmers in the enviable position of receiving more for their crops and paying less for the goods they needed to import. Hence improved transport increased farm income and stimulated commercial agriculture.

The Beginning of Commercial Agriculture

At the beginning of the nineteenth century, the typical farming household consumed most of what it produced and sold only a small surplus in nearby markets. Most manufactured articles were produced at home. Easier and cheaper access to distant markets caused a decisive change in this pattern. Between 1800 and 1840, agricultural output increased at an annual rate of approximately 3 percent, and a rapidly growing portion of this production consisted of commodities grown for sale rather than consumed at home. The rise in productivity was partly due to technological advances. Iron or steel plows proved better than wooden ones,

the grain cradle displaced the scythe for harvesting, and better varieties or strains of crops, grasses, and livestock were introduced. But the availability of good land and the revolution in marketing were the most important spurs to profitable commercial farming. The existence or extension of transportation facilities made distant markets available and plugged farmers into a commercial network that provided credit and relieved them of the need to do their own selling.

The emerging exchange network encouraged movement away from diversified farming and toward regional concentration on staple crops. Wheat was the main cash crop of the North, and the center of its cultivation moved westward as soil depletion, pests, and plant diseases lowered yields in older regions. In 1815, the heart of the wheat belt was New York and Pennsylvania. By 1839, Ohio was the leading producer and Indiana and Illinois were beginning to come into their own. On the rocky hillsides of New England, sheep raising was displacing the mixed farming of an earlier era. But the prime examples of successful staple production in this era were in the South. Tobacco continued to be a major cash crop of the upper South (despite declining fertility and a shift to wheat in some areas), rice was important in coastal South Carolina, and sugar was a staple of southern Louisiana. Cotton, however, was the "king" crop in the lower South as a whole. In the course of becoming the nation's principal export commodity, it brought wealth and prosperity to a belt of states running from South Carolina to Louisiana. (For more on the rise of "King Cotton," see Chapter 11, pp. 262–264.)

Commerce and Banking

As regions specialized in growing commercial crops, a new system of marketing emerged. During the early stages in many areas, farmers did their marketing personally, even when it required long journeys overland or by flatboat. With the growth of country towns, local merchants took charge of the crops near their sources, bartering clothing and other manufactured goods for produce. These intermediaries shipped the farmers' crops to larger local markets such as Pittsburgh, Cincinnati, and St. Louis. From there the commodities could be sent on to Philadelphia, New York, or New Orleans. Cotton growers in the South were more likely to deal directly with factors or agents in the port cities from which their crop was exported. But even in the South, commission merchants in such inland towns as Macon, Atlanta, Montgomery, Shreveport, and Nashville became increasingly important as intermediaries.

Credit was a crucial element in the whole system. Farmers borrowed from local merchants, who received an advance of their own when they consigned crops to a commission house or factor. The commission agents relied on credit from merchants or manufacturers at the ultimate destination, which might be Liverpool or New York City. The intermediaries all charged fees and interest, but the net cost to the farmers was less than when they had handled their own marketing. The need for credit encouraged the growth of money and banking.

Before the revolutions in transportation and marketing, small-scale local economies could survive to a considerable extent on barter. Under the Constitution, the U.S. government is the only agency authorized to coin money and regulate its value. But in

((•●—[Listen to the **Audio File**   **The Erie Canal**

Illustration of a lock on the Erie Canal at Lockport, New York, 1838. The successful canal facilitated trade by linking the Great Lakes regions to the eastern seaports.

the early to mid-nineteenth century, the government printed no paper money and produced gold and silver coins in such small quantities that it utterly failed to meet the expanding economy's need for a circulating currency.

Private or state banking institutions filled the void by issuing banknotes, promises to redeem their paper in specie—gold or silver—on the bearer's demand. After Congress failed to recharter the Bank of the United States in 1811, existing state-chartered banks took up the slack. Many of them, however, lacked adequate reserves and were forced to suspend specie payments during the War of 1812. The demand for money and credit during the immediate postwar boom led to a vast increase in the number of state banks—from 88 to 208 within two years. The resulting flood of state banknotes caused this form of currency to depreciate well below its face value and threatened a runaway inflation. In an effort to stabilize the currency, Congress established a second Bank of the United States in 1816. The Bank was expected to serve as a check on the state banks by forcing them to resume specie payments.

But it did not perform this task well in its early years. In fact, its own free lending policies contributed to the overextension of credit that led to financial panic and depression in 1819. When the economy collapsed, as it would do again in 1837, many Americans questioned whether the new system of banking and credit was as desirable as it had seemed to be in times of prosperity. As a result, hostility to banks became a prominent feature of American politics.

Early Industrialism

The growth of a market economy also created new opportunities for industrialists. In 1815, most manufacturing in the United States was carried on in households, in the workshops of skilled artisans, or in small mills, which used waterpower to turn wheat into flour or timber into boards. The factory form of production, in which supervised workers tended or operated machines under one roof, was rare. It was found mainly in southern New England, where a number of small spinning mills, relying heavily on the labor of women and children, accomplished one step in the manufacture of cotton textiles. But most spinning of thread, as well as the weaving, cutting, and sewing of cloth, was still done by women working at home.

As late as 1820, about two-thirds of the clothing worn by Americans was made entirely in households by female family members—wives and daughters. A growing proportion, however, was produced for market rather than direct home consumption. Under the "putting-out" system of manufacturing, merchant capitalists provided raw material to people in their own homes, picked up finished or semifinished products, paid the workers, and took charge of distribution. Home manufacturing of this type was centered in the Northeast and often involved farm families making profitable use of their slack seasons.

The making of articles that required greater skill—such as high-quality shoes and boots, carriages or wagons, mill wheels, and barrels or kegs—was mostly carried on by artisans working in small shops in towns. But in the decades after 1815, shops expanded in size, masters tended to become entrepreneurs rather than working artisans, and journeymen often became wage earners rather than aspiring masters. At the same time, the growing market for low-priced goods led to an emphasis on speed, quantity, and standardization in the methods of production. A fully developed factory system emerged first in textile manufacturing. The establishment of the first cotton mills utilizing the power loom as well as spinning machinery—thus making it possible to turn fiber into cloth in a single factory—resulted from the efforts of a trio of Boston merchants: Francis Cabot Lowell, Nathan Appleton, and Patrick Tracy Jackson. On a visit to England in 1810–1811, Lowell succeeded in memorizing the closely guarded industrial secret of how a power loom was constructed. Returning to Boston, he joined with Appleton and Jackson to acquire a water site at nearby Waltham and to obtain a corporate charter for textile manufacturing on a new and expanded scale.

Under the name of the Boston Manufacturing Company, the associates began their Waltham operation in 1813. Its phenomenal success led to the erection of a larger and even more profitable mill at Lowell, Massachusetts, in 1822 and another at Chicopee in 1823. Lowell became the great showplace for early American industrialization. Its large workforce of unmarried young women residing in supervised dormitories, its unprecedented scale of operation, its successful mechanization of almost every stage of the production process—all captured the American middle-class imagination in the 1820s and 1830s. But in the late 1830s and 1840s conditions in the mills changed for the worse as the owners began to require more work for lower pay, and some of the mill girls became militant labor activists. One of these was Sarah Bagley, who helped found the Lowell Female Labor Reform Association in 1844. She subsequently led a series of protests against long hours and changes in the work routine that required more work from each operative. Other mills using similar labor systems sprang up throughout New England, and the region became the first important manufacturing area in the United States.

The shift in textile manufacture from domestic to factory production shifted the locus of women's economic activity. As the New England textile industry grew, the putting-out system rapidly declined. Between 1824 and 1832, household production of textiles dropped from 90 to 50 percent in most parts of New England. The shift to factory production changed the course of capitalist activity in the region. Before the 1820s, New England merchants concentrated mainly on international trade, and Boston mercantile houses

Read the Document The Harbinger, "Female Workers at Lowell" (1836)

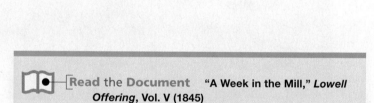

Read the Document "A Week in the Mill," *Lowell Offering*, Vol. V (1845)

Lowell, Massachusetts, became America's model industrial town in the first half of the nineteenth century. In this painting of the town in 1814 (when it was still called East Chelmsford), a multistory brick mill is prominent on the river. Textile mills sprang up throughout Lowell in the 1820s and 1830s, employing thousands of workers, mostly women. The second photograph from c. 1848 shows a Lowell mill worker operating a loom.

made great profits. A major source of capital was the lucrative China trade carried on by fast, well-built New England vessels. When the success of Waltham and Lowell became clear, many merchants shifted their capital away from oceanic trade and into manufacturing. This change had important political consequences, as leading politicians such as Daniel Webster no longer advocated a low tariff that favored importers over exporters. They now became leading proponents of a high duty designed to protect manufacturers from foreign competition.

Although most manufacturing was centered in the Northeast, the West also experienced modest industrial progress. Increasing rapidly in number and size were facilities for processing farm products, such as gristmills, slaughterhouses, and tanneries. Distilleries in Kentucky and Ohio began during the 1820s to produce vast quantities of corn whiskey for a seemingly insatiable public.

One should not assume, however, that America had already experienced an industrial revolution by 1840. In that year, 63.4 percent of the nation's labor force was still employed in agriculture. Only 8.8 percent of workers were directly involved in factory production (others were employed in trade, transportation, and the professions). Although this represented a significant shift since 1810, when the figures were 83.7 and 3.2 percent, respectively, the numbers would have to change a good deal more before it could be said that industrialization had really arrived. The revolution that did occur during these years was essentially one of distribution rather than production. The growth of a market economy of national scope—still based mainly on agriculture but involving a rapid flow of capital, commodities, and services from region to region—was the major economic development of this period. And it was one that had vast repercussions for all aspects of American life.

For those who benefited from it most directly, the market economy provided firm evidence of progress and improvement. But many of those who suffered from its periodic panics and depressions regretted the loss of the individual independence and security that had existed in a localized economy of small producers. These victims of boom and bust were receptive to politicians and reformers who attacked corporations and "the money power."

The Growth of Cities

In 1800, the United States was a rural nation. Only 6 percent of its five million people lived in towns of twenty-five hundred or more, and just two cities (Philadelphia and New York) had populations above fifty thousand. By 1850, one-sixth of the twenty-three million Americans lived in towns of twenty-five hundred or more. This was hardly a complete urbanization of American life, but it did reflect the rise of significant urban centers throughout the Northeast and as far west as Chicago and St. Louis as a result of the transportation revolution and the growing market economy.

The expansion of commerce, banking, and industry in the Northeast drew people to towns like Lowell, Massachusetts, and Albany, New York, which grew to more than twenty-five thousand people, and the growing web of canals and railroads made inland cities like Cincinnati, St. Louis, and Chicago viable and thriving. New York City alone had grown to more than half a million people by 1850. These young cities were magnets for new immigrants from Europe.

Canals and railroads also led to the growth of great cities on the western frontier. From a small town in the 1830s, Chicago grew into the nation's fourth largest city by 1860. It was the hub of a thriving market economy, funneling grain and other farm products from all over the Northwest to cities and towns in the East.

The Politics of Nation Building after the War of 1812

What decisions did the federal government face as the country expanded?

Geographic expansion, economic growth, and the changes in American life that accompanied them were bound to generate political controversy. Farmers, merchants, manufacturers, and laborers were affected by the changes in different ways. So were Northerners, Southerners, and Westerners. Federal and state policies that were meant to encourage or control growth and expansion did not benefit all these groups or sections equally, and unavoidable conflicts of interest and ideology occurred.

But, for a time, these conflicts were not prominently reflected in the national political arena. During the period following the War of 1812, a single party dominated politics. Without a party system in place, politicians did not have to band together to offer the voters a choice of programs and ideologies. A myth of national harmony prevailed, culminating in the **Era of Good Feelings** during James Monroe's two terms as president. Behind this facade, individuals and groups fought for advantage, as always, but without the public accountability and need for broad popular approval that a party system would have required. As a result, popular interest in national politics fell.

The absence of party discipline and programs did not completely immobilize the federal government. Congress did manage to legislate on some matters of national concern. Although the president had little control over congressional action, he could still take important initiatives in foreign policy. The third branch of government—the Supreme Court—was in a position to make far-reaching decisions affecting the relationship between the federal government and the states. The common theme of the public policies that emerged between the War of 1812 and the age of Andrew Jackson, which began in the late 1820s, was an awakening nationalism—a sense of American pride and purpose that reflected the expansionism and material progress of the period.

The Republicans in Power

By the end of the War of 1812, the Federalist Party was no longer capable of winning a national election. The party of Jefferson, now known simply as the Republicans, was so completely dominant that it no longer had to distinguish itself from its opponents. Retreating from their original philosophy of states' rights and limited government, party leaders now openly embraced some of the programs of their former Federalist rivals—policies that seemed dictated by postwar conditions. In December 1815, President Madison proposed to Congress that it consider such measures as the

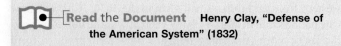

Read the Document   Henry Clay, "Defense of
the American System" (1832)

Senator Henry Clay of Kentucky was the leading proponent of the American System, a series of proposals for the federal government to play a more active role in promoting economic development. These proposals included a national bank, federally financed internal improvements such as roads and canals, and a tariff on imported goods to protect emerging U.S. industries.

reestablishment of a national bank, a mildly protective tariff for industry, and a program of federally financed internal improvements to bind "more closely together the various parts of our extended confederacy." Thus did Jefferson's successor endorse parts of a program enunciated by Alexander Hamilton.

In Congress, Henry Clay of Kentucky took the lead in advocating that the government take action to promote economic development. The keystone of what Clay called the **American System** was a high protective tariff to stimulate industrial growth and provide a "home market" for the farmers of the West, making the nation economically self-sufficient and free from a dangerous dependence on Europe.

In 1816, Congress took the first step toward establishing a neo-Federalist American System. It enacted a tariff raising import duties an average of 25 percent. The legislation was deemed necessary because a flood of British manufactured goods was beginning to threaten the infant industries that had sprung up during the period

when imports had been shut off by the embargo and the war. The tariff had substantial support in all parts of the country, both from a large majority of congressmen from New England and the Middle Atlantic states and from a respectable minority of the southern delegation. In 1816, manufacturing was not so much a powerful interest as a patriotic concern. Many Americans believed the preservation of political independence and victory in future wars required industrial independence for the nation. Furthermore, important sectors of the agricultural economy also felt the need of protection—especially hemp growers of Kentucky, sugar planters of Louisiana, and wool producers of New England.

Later the same year, Congress voted to establish the Second Bank of the United States. The new national bank had a twenty-year charter, an authorized capital of $35 million, and the right to establish branches throughout the country as needed. Organized much like the First Bank, it was a mixed public-private institution, with the federal government owning one-fifth of its stock and appointing five of its twenty-five directors. The Bank served the government by providing a depository for its funds, an outlet for marketing its securities, and a source of redeemable banknotes that could be used to pay taxes or purchase public lands. Legislation dealing with internal improvements made less headway in Congress because it aroused stronger constitutional objections and invited disagreements among sectional groups over who would benefit from specific projects. Except for the National Road, the federal government undertook no major transportation projects during the Madison and Monroe administrations. Both presidents believed that internal improvements were desirable but that a constitutional amendment was required before federal monies could legally be used for the building of roads and canals within individual states. Consequently, public aid for the building of roads and canals continued to come mainly from state and local governments.

Monroe as President

As did Jefferson before him, President Madison chose his own successor in 1816. James Monroe thus became the third successive Virginian to occupy the White House. He served two full terms and was virtually uncontested in his election to each. Monroe was well qualified in terms of experience, having been an officer in the Revolution, governor of Virginia, a special emissary to France, and secretary of state. He was reliable, dignified, and high principled, as well as stolid and unimaginative, lacking the intellectual depth and agility of his predecessors. Nominated, as was the custom of the time, by a caucus of Republicans in the House of Representatives, Monroe faced only nominal Federalist opposition in the general election.

Monroe avoided controversy in his effort to maintain the national harmony that was the keynote of his presidency. His first inaugural address expressed the complacency and optimism of the time, and he followed it up with a goodwill tour of the country, the first made by a president since Washington. A principal aim of Monroe's administrations was to encourage good feelings. He hoped to accommodate or conciliate all the sectional or economic interests of the country and devote his main attention to the task of asserting American power and influence on the world stage. For example, during the Panic of 1819, an economic depression that followed the postwar boom, Congress acted by passing debt relief legislation, but Monroe himself had no program to relieve the economic crisis. He did not feel called on to exert that kind of leadership, and the voters did not seem to have expected it of him.

Monroe prized national harmony even more than economic prosperity. But during his first administration, a bitter controversy developed between the North and the South over the admission of Missouri to the Union. Once again Monroe remained above the battle and suffered little damage to his own prestige. It was left entirely to the legislative branch of the government to deal with the nation's most serious domestic political crisis between the War of 1812 and the late 1840s.

The Missouri Compromise

In 1817, the Missouri territorial assembly applied for statehood. Since there were two to three thousand slaves already in the territory and the petition made no provision for their emancipation or for curbing further introduction of slaves, it was clear that Missouri would enter the Union as a slave state unless Congress took special action. Missouri was slated to be the first state, other than Louisiana, to be carved out of the Louisiana Purchase, and resolution of the status of slavery there would have implications for the rest of the trans-Mississippi West.

THE ELECTION OF 1816

Candidate	Party	Electoral Vote
Monroe	Republican	183
King	Federalist	34

When the question came before Congress in early 1819, sectional fears and anxieties bubbled to the surface. Many Northerners resented southern control of the presidency and the fact that the three-fifths clause of the Constitution, by which every five slaves were counted as three persons in figuring the state's population, gave the South's free population added weight in the House of Representatives and the Electoral College. The South, on the other hand, feared for the future of what it regarded as a necessary balance of power between the sections. Up until 1819, a strict equality had been maintained by alternately admitting slave and free states; in that year, there were eleven of each. But northern population was growing more rapidly than southern, and the North had built up a decisive majority in the House of Representatives. Hence the South saw its equal vote in the Senate as essential for preservation of the balance.

In February 1819, Congressman James Tallmadge of New York introduced an amendment to the statehood bill, banning further introduction of slaves into Missouri and requiring steps toward the gradual elimination of slavery within the state. After a heated debate, the House approved the Tallmadge amendment by a narrow margin. The Senate, however, voted it down. The issue remained unresolved until a new Congress convened in December 1819.

In the great debate that ensued in the Senate, Federalist leader Rufus King of New York argued that Congress was within its rights to require restriction of slavery before Missouri could become a state. Southern senators protested that denying Missouri's freedom in this matter was an attack on the principle of equality among the states and showed that Northerners were conspiring to upset the balance of power between the sections. They were also concerned about the future of African American slavery and the white racial privilege that went with it.

A statehood petition from the people of Maine, who were seeking to be separated from Massachusetts, suggested a way out of the impasse. In February 1820, the Senate passed the **Missouri Compromise**, voting to couple the admission of Missouri as a slave state with the admission of Maine as a free state. A further amendment was also passed prohibiting slavery in the rest of the Louisiana Purchase north of the southern border of Missouri, or above the latitude of 36°30′, and allowing it below that line. The Senate's compromise then went to the House, where it was initially rejected. Through the adroit maneuvering of Henry Clay—who broke the proposal into three separate bills—it eventually won House approval. The measure authorizing Missouri to frame a constitution and apply for admission as a slave state passed by a razor-thin margin of 90 to 87, with most northern representatives remaining opposed.

THE ELECTION OF 1820

Candidate	Party	Electoral Vote
Monroe	Republican	231
J. Q. Adams	No party designation	1

A major sectional crisis had been resolved. But the Missouri affair had ominous overtones for the future of North–South relations. Thomas Jefferson described the controversy as "a fire bell in the night," threatening the peace of the Union. In 1821, he wrote prophetically of future dangers: "All, I fear, do not see the speck on our horizon which is to burst on us as a tornado, sooner or later. The line of division lately marked out between the different portions of our confederacy is such as will never, I fear, be obliterated." The congressional furor had shown that when the issue of slavery or its extension came directly before the people's representatives, regional loyalties took precedence over party or other considerations. An emotional rhetoric of morality and fundamental rights issued from both sides, and votes followed sectional lines much more closely than on any other issue. If the United States were to acquire any new territories in which the status of slavery had to be determined by Congress, renewed sectional strife would be unavoidable.

Postwar Nationalism and the Supreme Court

While the Monroe administration was proclaiming national harmony and congressional leaders were struggling to reconcile sectional differences, the third branch of government—the Supreme Court—was making a more substantial and enduring

View the Map   The Missouri Compromise

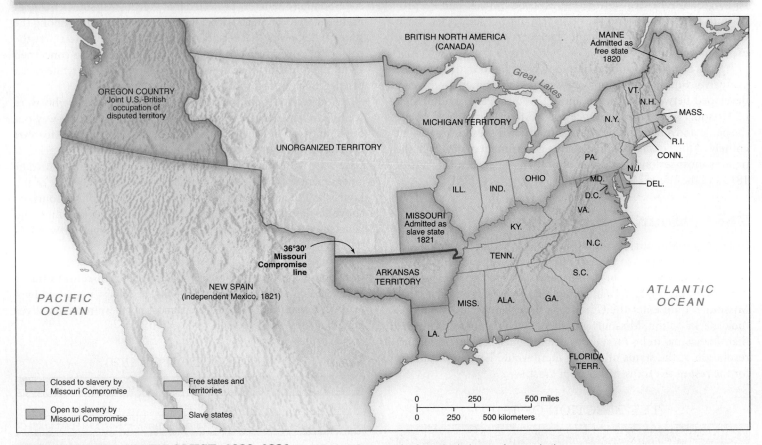

THE MISSOURI COMPROMISE, 1820–1821 The Missouri Compromise kept the balance of power in the Senate by admitting Missouri as a slave state and Maine as a free state. The agreement temporarily settled the argument over slavery in the territories.

contribution to the growth of nationalism and a strong federal government. Much of this achievement was due to the firm leadership and fine legal mind of the chief justice of the United States, John Marshall.

A Virginian, a Federalist, and the devoted disciple and biographer of George Washington, Marshall served as chief justice from 1801 to 1835, and during that entire period he dominated the Court as no other chief justice has ever done. He discouraged dissent and sought to hammer out a single opinion on almost every case that came before the Court.

As the author of most of the major opinions issued by the Supreme Court during its formative period, Marshall gave shape to the Constitution and clarified the crucial role of the Court in the American system of government. He placed the protection of individual liberty, especially the right to acquire property, above the attainment of political, social, or economic equality. Ultimately he was a nationalist, believing that the strength, security, and happiness of the American people depended mainly on economic growth and the creation of new wealth.

The role of the Supreme Court, in Marshall's view, was to interpret and enforce the Constitution in a way that encouraged

economic development, especially against efforts of state legislatures to interfere with the constitutionally protected rights of individuals or combinations of individuals to acquire property through productive activity. To limit state action, he cited the contract clause of the Constitution that prohibited a state from passing a law "impairing the obligation of contracts." As the legal watchdog of an enterprising, capitalist society, the Court could also approve a liberal grant of power for the federal government so that the latter could fulfill its constitutional responsibility to promote the general welfare by encouraging economic growth and prosperity.

In a series of major decisions between 1819 and 1824, the Marshall Court enhanced judicial power and used the contract clause of the Constitution to limit the power of state legislatures. It also strengthened the federal government by sanctioning a broad or loose construction of its constitutional powers and by clearly affirming its supremacy over the states.

In **Dartmouth College v. Woodward** (1819), the Court was asked to rule whether the legislature of New Hampshire had the right to convert Dartmouth from a private college into a state university. Daniel Webster, arguing for the college and against the state, contended that Dartmouth's original charter of 1769 was a valid and irrevocable contract. The Court accepted his argument. Speaking for all the justices, Marshall made the far-reaching determination that any charter granted by a state to a private corporation was fully protected by the contract clause.

In practical terms, the Court's ruling in the Dartmouth case meant that the kinds of business enterprises then being incorporated by state governments—such as turnpike or canal companies and textile manufacturing firms—could hold on indefinitely to any privileges or favors that had been granted in their original charters. The decision therefore increased the power and independence of business corporations by weakening the ability of the states to regulate them or withdraw their privileges. The ruling helped foster the growth of the modern corporation as a profit-making enterprise with only limited public responsibilities.

About a month after the *Dartmouth* ruling, in March 1819, the Marshall Court handed down its most important decision. The case of **McCulloch v. Maryland** arose because the state of Maryland had levied a tax on the Baltimore branch of the Bank of the United States. The unanimous opinion of the Court, delivered by Marshall, was that the Maryland tax was unconstitutional. The two main issues were whether Congress had the right to establish a national bank and whether a state had the power to tax or regulate an agency or institution created by Congress.

In response to the first question, Marshall set forth his doctrine of "implied powers." Conceding that no specific authorization to charter a bank could be found in the Constitution, the chief justice argued that such a right could be deduced from more general powers and from an understanding of the "great objects" for which the federal government had been founded. Marshall thus struck a blow for loose construction of the Constitution and a broad grant of power to the federal government to encourage economic growth and stability.

In answer to the second question—the right of a state to tax or regulate a federal agency—Marshall held that the Bank was indeed such an agency and that giving a state the power to tax it would also give the state the power to destroy it. In an important assertion of the supremacy of the national government, Marshall argued that the American people "did not design to make their government dependent on the states." This opinion ran counter to the view of many Americans, particularly in the South, that the Constitution did not take away sovereignty from the states. The debate over federal–state relations was not resolved until the northern victory in the Civil War decisively affirmed the dominance of federal authority. But Marshall's decision gave great new weight to a nationalist constitutional philosophy.

The **Gibbons v. Ogden** decision of 1824 bolstered the power of Congress to regulate interstate commerce. A steamboat monopoly granted by the state of New York was challenged by a competing ferry service operating between New York and New Jersey. The Court declared the New York grant unconstitutional because it amounted to state interference with Congress's exclusive right to regulate interstate commerce. The Court's ruling went a long way toward freeing private interests engaged in furthering the transportation revolution from state interference.

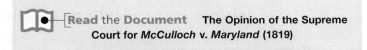

Read the **Document**   **The Opinion of the Supreme Court for** *McCulloch* **v.** *Maryland* **(1819)**

Chief Justice John Marshall affirmed the Supreme Court's authority to overrule state laws and overrule congressional legislation that it held to be in conflict with the Constitution. The portrait is by Chester Harding, ca. 1829.

This case clearly showed the dual effect of Marshall's decision making. It broadened the power of the federal government at the expense of the states while at the same time encouraging the growth of a national market economy. The actions of the Supreme Court provide the clearest and most consistent example of the main nationalistic trends of the postwar period—the acknowledgment of the federal government's major role in promoting the growth of a powerful and prosperous America and the rise of a nationwide capitalist economy.

Nationalism in Foreign Policy: The Monroe Doctrine

The new spirit of nationalism was also reflected in foreign affairs. The main diplomatic challenge facing Monroe after his reelection in 1820 was how to respond to the successful revolt of most of Spain's Latin American colonies after the Napoleonic wars. In Congress, Henry Clay called for immediate recognition of the new republics. In doing so, he expressed the belief of many Americans that their neighbors to the south were simply following the example of the United States in its own struggle for independence.

Before 1822, the administration stuck to a policy of neutrality. Monroe and Secretary of State Adams feared that recognizing the revolutionary governments would antagonize Spain and impede negotiations to acquire Florida. But pressure for recognition grew in Congress, and in 1821, Monroe agreed

Read the Document   The Monroe Doctrine (1823)

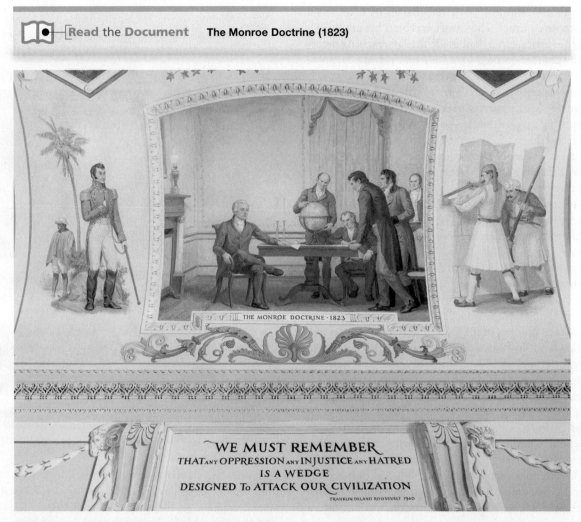

THE MONROE DOCTRINE · 1823

WE MUST REMEMBER
THAT ANY OPPRESSION ANY INJUSTICE ANY HATRED
IS A WEDGE
DESIGNED To ATTACK OUR CIVILIZATION
FRANKLIN DELANO ROOSEVELT 1940

President James Monroe presented this doctrine as part of his annual message to Congress in December 1823. He proposed it at a time when the Old World powers were losing their colonial interests in the New World. The United States had recognized the former colonies of Argentina, Chile, Peru, Mexico, and Colombia as independent nations in 1822. Monroe was in the unenviable position of trying to maintain a strong stance with the European powers, who were struggling over a balance of world power.

to recognize and establish diplomatic ties with the Latin American republics. This action put the United States on a possible collision course with the major European powers. Austria, Russia, and Prussia were committed to rolling back the tides of liberalism, self-government, and national self-determination that had arisen during the French Revolution and its Napoleonic aftermath. After Napoleon's first defeat in 1814, the monarchs of Europe had joined in a "Grand Alliance" to protect "legitimate" authoritarian governments from democratic challenges. Great Britain was originally a member of this concert of nations but withdrew when it found that its own interests conflicted with those of the other members. In 1822, the remaining alliance members, joined now by the restored French monarchy, gave France the green light to invade Spain and restore a Bourbon regime that might be disposed to reconquer the empire. Both Great Britain and the United States were alarmed by this prospect.

The threat from the Grand Alliance pointed to a need for American cooperation with Great Britain, which had its own reasons for wanting to prevent a restoration of Spanish or French power in the New World. Independent nations offered better and more open markets for British manufactured goods than the colonies of other nations, and the spokesmen for burgeoning British industrial capitalism anticipated a profitable economic dominance over Latin America. Monroe welcomed British overtures for cooperation against the Grand Alliance because he believed the United States should take an active role in transatlantic affairs by playing one European power against another. When Monroe presented the question to his cabinet, however, he encountered the opposition of Secretary of State Adams, who distrusted the British and favored a more isolationist policy.

Political ambition also predisposed Adams against joint action with Great Britain; he hoped to be the next president and did not want to give his rivals the chance to label him as pro-British. He therefore advocated unilateral action by the United States. In the end, Adams managed to swing Monroe and the cabinet around to his viewpoint. In his annual message to Congress on December 2, 1823, Monroe included a far-reaching statement on foreign policy that was actually written mainly by Adams, who did become president in 1824. What came to be known as the **Monroe Doctrine** solemnly declared that the United States opposed any further colonization in the Americas or any effort by European nations to extend their political systems outside their own hemisphere. In return, the United States pledged not to involve itself in the internal affairs of Europe or to take part in European wars. The statement envisioned a North and South America composed entirely of independent republics—with the United States preeminent among them.

Although the Monroe Doctrine made little impression on the great powers of Europe at the time it was proclaimed, it signified the rise of a new sense of independence and self-confidence in American attitudes toward the Old World. The United States would now go its own way free of involvement in European conflicts and would energetically protect its own sphere of influence from European interference.

Conclusion: The End of the Era of Good Feelings

The consensus on national goals and leadership that Monroe had represented could not sustain itself. The Era of Good Feelings turned out to be a passing phase and something of an illusion. Although the pursuit of national greatness would continue, there would be sharp divisions over how it should be achieved. A general commitment to settlement of the West and the development of agriculture, commerce, and industry would endure despite serious differences over what role government should play in the process, but the idea that the elite nonpartisan statesmen could define common purposes and harmonize competing elements—the concept of leadership that Monroe and Adams had advanced—would no longer be viable in the more contentious and democratic America of the Jacksonian era.

Study Resources

 Take the **Study Plan** for **Chapter 9** *Nation Building and Nationalism* on **MyHistoryLab**

TIME LINE

1813 Boston Manufacturing Company founds cotton mill at Waltham, Massachusetts

1815 War of 1812 ends

1816 James Monroe elected president

1818 Andrew Jackson invades Florida

1819 Supreme Court hands down far-reaching decision in Dartmouth College case and in *McCulloch v. Maryland*; Adams-Onís treaty cedes Spanish territory to the United States; Financial panic is followed by a depression lasting until 1823

1820 Missouri Compromise resolves nation's first sectional crisis; Monroe reelected president almost unanimously

1823 Monroe Doctrine proclaimed

1824 Lafayette revisits the United States; Supreme Court decides *Gibbons* v. *Ogden*; John Quincy Adams elected president

1825 Erie Canal completed; canal era begins

CHAPTER REVIEW

Expansion and Migration

 What key forces drove American expansion westward during this period?

Westward expansion was fueled by the ambition to expand American territory and to economically exploit and develop the Far West. The First Seminole War gave Monroe and Adams a chance to push Spain from the southeast under the Adams-Onís Treaty, while entrepreneurs established a fur trade in the North and an aggressive "removal" policy forced Indian tribes from the South. (p. 203)

A Revolution in Transportation

 How did transportation networks change and improve after the War of 1812?

New and improved roads were developed, such as the National Road between Cumberland, Maryland and Wheeling, Virginia. Steam power transformed travel along natural rivers with the advent of the steamboat, lowering costs and decreasing transport times. Man-made canals such as the Erie Canal linked seaboard cities directly with the Great Lakes. (p. 210)

Emergence of a Market Economy

 How did developments in transportation support the growth of agriculture, banking, and industry?

Transportation improvements expanded access of producers to regional and even national markets. Farmers began to produce staple crops to sell rather than subsistence crops for their own families. Merchants and banks emerged to connect farm output to distant markets. Textile factories developed to turn Southern cotton into clothing. In the North industrialization increased efficiency but required workers to crowd into factories for long hours. (p. 212)

The Politics of Nation Building after the War of 1812

 What decisions did the federal government face as the country expanded?

The government decided whether new states would allow slavery, how the Supreme Court would function, and how the United States would deal with the European powers. The Missouri Compromise established the 36°30' line dividing slave from free states, while the Court became the supreme constitutional interpreter. The Monroe Doctrine held that the United States and European powers should each control their respective hemispheres. (p. 215)

KEY TERMS AND DEFINITIONS

Adams-Onís Treaty Signed by Secretary of State John Quincy Adams and Spanish minister Luis de Onís in 1819, this treaty allowed for U.S. annexation of Florida. p. 204

Preemption The right of first purchase of public land. Settlers enjoyed this right even if they squatted on the land in advance of government surveyors. p. 207

Era of Good Feelings A description of the two terms of President James Monroe (1817–1823) during which partisan conflict abated and federal initiatives suggested increased nationalism. p. 221

Missouri Compromise A sectional compromise in 1820 that admitted Missouri to the Union as a slave state and Maine as a free state. It also banned slavery in the remainder of the Louisiana Purchase territory above the latitude of 36°30'. p. 217

Dartmouth College* v. *Woodward In this 1819 case, the Supreme Court ruled that the Constitution protected charters given to corporations by states. p. 218

McCulloch* v. *Maryland This 1819 ruling asserted the supremacy of federal power over state power and the legal doctrine that the Constitution could be broadly interpreted. p. 219

Gibbons* v. *Ogden In this 1824 case, the Supreme Court expanded the power of the federal government to regulate interstate commerce. p. 219

Monroe Doctrine A key foreign policy declaration made by President James Monroe in 1823, it declared the Western Hemisphere off limits to new European colonization; in return, the United States promised not to meddle in European affairs. p. 221

CRITICAL THINKING QUESTIONS

1. How did new developments in transportation influence westward expansion?

2. What was the relationship between westward expansion and the institution of slavery?

3. Why do you think some political leaders saw a connection between a growing market economy and a strong national government?

MyHistoryLab Media Assignments

Find these resources in the Media Assignments folder for Chapter 9 on MyHistoryLab

Expansion and Migration

Read the **Document** *The Cherokee Treaty of 1817 p. 206*

■ **Complete** the **Assignment** *Confronting a New Environment p. 208*

A Revolution in Transportation

■ **View** the **Map** *Expanding America and Internal Improvements p. 211*

Emergence of a Market Economy

Listen to the **Audio File** *The Erie Canal p. 213*

■ **Read** the **Document** *The Harbinger, Female Workers at Lowell (1836) p. 214*

Read the **Document** *"A Week in the Mill," Lowell Offering, Vol. V (1845) p. 214*

The Politics of Nation Building after the War of 1812

Read the **Document** *Henry Clay, "Defense of the American System" (1832) p. 216*

■ **View** the **Map** *The Missouri Compromise p. 218*

Read the **Document** *The Opinion of the Supreme Court for McCulloch v. Maryland (1819) p. 219*

■ **Read** the **Document** *The Monroe Doctrine (1823) p. 220*

■ *Indicates Study Plan Media Assignment*

Contents and Learning Objectives

((●—[Listen to the **Audio File** on **myhistorylab** **Chapter 10** *The Triumph of White Men's Democracy*

Democratic Space: The New Hotels

During the 1820s and 1830s the United States became a more democratic country for at least some of its population. The emerging spirit of popular democracy found expression in a new institution—the large hotel with several stories and hundreds of rooms. President-elect Andrew Jackson, the political figure who embodied the spirit of the age, stayed in the recently opened National Hotel when he arrived in Washington in 1829 to prepare for his administration. After a horde of well-wishers made a shambles of the White House during his inaugural reception, Jackson retreated to the hotel for a little peace and a chance to consult with his advisers. The National was only one of several large "first-class" hotels that opened immediately before or during Jackson's presidency. Among the others were the Tremont House in Boston, the Baltimore City Hotel, and New York's Astor House.

The hotel boom responded to the increasing tendency of Americans in the 1820s and 1830s to move about the country. It was to service the rising tides of travelers, transients, and new arrivals that entrepreneurs erected these large places of accommodation. There they provided lodging, food, and drink on an unprecedented scale. These establishments were as different from the inns of the eighteenth century as the steamboat was from the flatboat.

According to historian Doris Elizabeth King, "the new hotels were so obviously 'public' and 'democratic' in their character that foreigners were often to describe them as a true reflection of American society." Their very existence showed that many people, white males in particular, were on the move geographically and socially. Among the hotels' patrons were traveling salesmen, ambitious young men seeking to establish themselves in a new city, and restless pursuers of "the main chance" (unexpected economic opportunities) who were not yet ready to put down roots.

Hotel managers shocked European visitors by failing to enforce traditional social distinctions among their clientele. Under the "American plan," guests were required to pay for their meals and to eat at a common "table d'hôte" with anyone who happened to be there, including servants traveling with their employers. Ability to pay was the only requirement for admission (unless one happened to be an unes-corted woman or dark-skinned), and every white male patron, regardless

New York's Astor House, completed in 1836, was one of the grandest of the new American hotels, offering fine accommodations to travelers who could afford to pay for them.

of social background and occupation, enjoyed the kind of personal service previously available only to a privileged class. Many patrons experienced such amenities as gaslight, indoor plumbing, and steam heat for the first time in their lives. Because a large proportion of the American population stayed in hotels at one time or another—a privilege that was, in Europe, reserved for the elite—foreigners inferred that there was widespread prosperity and a much greater "equality of condition" than existed in Europe.

The hotel culture revealed some of the limitations of the new era of democratic ideals and aspirations. African Americans, Native Americans, and women were excluded or discriminated against, just as they were denied suffrage at a time when it was being extended to all white males. The genuinely poor simply could not afford to patronize the hotels and were consigned to squalid rooming houses. If the social equality *within* the hotel reflected a decline in traditional status distinctions, the broad gulf between

potential patrons and those who could not pay the rates signaled the growth of inequality based on wealth.

Hotel life also reflected the emergence of democratic politics. Professional politicians of a new breed, pursuing the votes of a mass electorate, spent much of their time in hotels as they traveled about. Those elected to Congress or a state legislature often stayed in hotels during the session, and the political deals and bargains required for effective party organization or legislative success were sometimes concluded in these establishments.

The hotel can thus be seen as a fitting symbol for the democratic spirit of the age, one that shows its shortcomings as well as its strengths. The new democracy was first of all political, involving the extension of suffrage to virtually all white males and the rise of modern political parties appealing to a mass electorate. It was also social in that it undermined the habit of deferring to people because of their birth or ancestry and offered a greater expectation that individuals born in relatively humble circumstances could climb the ladder of success. But the ideals of equal citizenship and opportunity did not extend across the lines of race and gender, which actually hardened to some degree during this period.

Democracy in Theory and Practice

How did the relationship between the government and the people change during this time?

During the 1820s and 1830s, the term *democracy* first became a generally accepted term to describe how American institutions were supposed to work. The Founders had defined democracy as direct rule by the people; most of them rejected this concept of a democratic approach to government because it was at odds with their conception of a well-balanced republic led by a "natural aristocracy." For champions of popular government in the Jacksonian period, however, the people were truly sovereign and could do no wrong. "The voice of the people is the voice of God" was their clearest expression of this principle. Conservatives were less certain of the wisdom of the common folk. But even they were coming to recognize that public opinion had to be won over before major policy decisions could be made.

Besides evoking a heightened sense of "popular sovereignty," the democratic impulse seemed to stimulate a process of social leveling. Earlier Americans had usually assumed that the rich and wellborn should be treated with special respect and recognized as natural leaders of the community and guardians of its culture and values. By the 1830s, as the hotel culture revealed, such habits of deference were in decline. The decline of deference meant that "self-made men" of lowly origins could now rise more readily to positions of power and influence. But economic equality, the equitable sharing of wealth, was not part of the mainstream agenda. This was, after all, a competitive capitalist society. The watchword was equality of *opportunity*, not equality of *reward*. Life was a race, and so long as white males appeared to have an equal start, there could be no reason for complaint if some were winners and some were losers. Historians now generally agree that economic inequality—the gap between rich and poor Americans—was actually increasing during this period of political and social democratization.

Democracy and Society

Although some types of inequality persisted or even grew during the age of democracy, they did so in the face of a growing belief that equality was the governing principle of American society. The plain folk were now likely to greet claims for special treatment with indifference or scorn, and to demand equal treatment whatever their place in society.

White domestic workers refused to be called "servants" and instead called themselves "hired help." Household workers often refused to wear livery, agreed to work for only short periods of time, and sometimes insisted on eating at the same table as their employers. As noted in the maid's comments quoted at the beginning of Chapter 8, no true American was willing to be considered a member of a servant class, and those who engaged in domestic work regarded it as a temporary stopgap. Except as a euphemistic substitute for the word *slave*, the term *servant* virtually disappeared from the American vocabulary.

The decline of distinctive modes of dress for upper and lower classes conveyed the principle of equality in yet another way. The elaborate periwigs and knee breeches worn by eighteenth-century gentlemen gave way to short hair and pantaloons, a style that was adopted by men of all social classes. Fashionable dress among women also ceased to be a sure index of gentility; serving girls on their day off wore the same kind of finery as the wives and daughters of the wealthy. Those with a good eye for detail might detect subtle differences, but the casual observer of crowds in a large city could easily conclude that all Americans belonged to a single social class.

In reality, though, inequality based on control of productive resources was increasing during the Jacksonian period. A growing percentage of the population, especially in urban areas, possessed no real estate and little other property. The rise of industrialization was creating a permanent class of low-paid, unorganized wage earners. In rural areas, there was a significant division between successful commercial farmers and small holders, or tenants who subsisted on marginal land, as well as enormous inequality of status between southern planters and their black slaves. But most foreign observers overlooked the widening gap between the propertied middle class and the laboring population; their attention was riveted on the fact that all white males were equal before the law and at the polls, a situation that was genuinely radical by European standards.

Traditional forms of privilege and elitism were also under strong attack, as evidenced by changes in the organization and status of the learned professions. Under Jacksonian pressure, state legislatures abolished the licensing requirements for physicians, previously administered by local medical societies. As a result, practitioners of unorthodox modes of healing were permitted to compete freely with established medical doctors. One popular therapy was Thomsonianism, a form of treatment based entirely on the use of common herbs and roots. Thomsonians argued that their own form of medicine would "make every man his own physician." The democratic tide also struck the legal profession. Local bar associations continued to set the qualifications for practicing attorneys, but in many places they lowered standards and admitted persons with little or no formal training and only the most rudimentary knowledge of the law.

For the clergy, "popular sovereignty" meant being increasingly under the thumb of the laity. The growing dependence of ministers on their congregations forced them to develop a more popular and emotional style of preaching. Ministers had ceased to command respect merely because of their office. They had to please their public, in much the same way as a politician had to satisfy the electorate.

In this atmosphere of democratic leveling, the popular press came to play an increasingly important role as a source of information and opinion. Written and read by common folk, hundreds of newspapers and magazines ushered the mass of white Americans into the political arena. New political views—which in a previous generation might have been silenced by those in power—could now find an audience. Reformers of all kinds could easily publicize their causes, and the press became the venue for the great national debates on issues such as the government's role in banking and the status of slavery in new states and territories. As a profession, journalism was open to those who were literate and thought they had something to say. The editors of newspapers with a large circulation were the most influential opinion makers of the age.

Democratic Culture

The democratic spirit also found expression in the rise of new forms of literature and art directed at a mass audience. The intentions of individual artists and writers varied considerably. Some sought success by pandering to popular taste in defiance of traditional standards of high culture. Others tried to capture the spirit of the age by portraying the everyday life of ordinary Americans rather than the traditional subjects of "aristocratic" art. A notable few hoped to use literature and art as a way of improving popular taste and instilling deeper moral and spiritual values. But all of them were aware that their audience was the broad citizenry of a democratic nation rather than a refined elite.

The romantic movement in literature, which came to the fore in the early nineteenth century in both Europe and America, valued strong feeling and mystical intuition over the calm rationality and appeal to common experience that had prevailed in the writing of the eighteenth century. Romanticism was not necessarily connected with democracy; in Europe, it sometimes went along with a reaffirmation of feudalism and the right of a superior few to rule over the masses. In the American setting, however, romanticism often appealed to the feelings and intuitions of ordinary people: the innate love of goodness, truth, and beauty that all people were thought to possess. Writers in search of popularity and economic success, however, often deserted the high plane of romantic art for crass sentimentalism—a willingness to pull out all emotional stops to thrill readers or bring tears to their eyes.

Literacy and a revolution in the technology of printing enabled a mass market for popular literature. An increase in the number of potential readers and a decrease in publishing costs led to a flood of lurid and sentimental novels, some of which became the first American best sellers. Gothic horror and the perils of virtuous heroines threatened by dastardly villains were among the ingredients that readers came to expect from popular fiction. Many of the new sentimental novels were written by and for women. Some women writers implicitly protested against their situation by portraying men in general as tyrannical, unreliable, or vicious and the women they abandoned or failed to support as resourceful individualists capable of making their own way in a man's world. But the standard happy endings sustained the convention that a woman's place was in the home, for a virtuous and protective man usually turned up and saved the heroine from independence.

In the theater, melodrama became the dominant genre. Despite religious objections, theater-going was a popular recreation in the cities during the Jacksonian era. The standard fare involved the inevitable trio of beleaguered heroine, mustachioed villain, and a hero who asserted himself in the nick of time. Patriotic comedies extolling the common sense of the rustic Yankee who foiled the foppish European aristocrat were also popular and aroused the democratic sympathies of the audience. Men and women of all classes went to the theater, and those in the cheap seats often behaved raucously and even violently when they did not like what they saw. Unpopular actors or plays could even provoke serious riots. In an 1849 incident in New York, twenty-three people were killed in disorders stemming from hostility toward an English actor who was the rival of Edwin Forrest, the most popular American thespian of the time.

 Read the Document   Herman Melville, Excerpt from *Moby-Dick*

In *Moby-Dick*, Herman Melville produced a novel sufficiently original in form and conception to more than fulfill the demand of Young Americans for "a New Literature to fit the New Man in the New Age." But Melville was too deep a thinker not to see the perils that underlay the soaring ambition and aggressiveness of the new age.

The spirit of "popular sovereignty" expressed itself less dramatically in the visual arts, but its influence was still felt. Beginning in the 1830s, painters turned from portraying great events and famous people to depicting everyday life. William Sidney Mount, who painted lively rural scenes, expressed the credo of the democratic artist: "Paint pictures that will take with the public—never paint for the few but the many."

Architecture and sculpture reflected the democratic spirit in a different way; they were viewed as civic art forms meant to glorify the achievements of the republic. In the 1820s and 1830s, the Greek style with its columned facades not only predominated in the architecture of public buildings but was also favored for banks, hotels, and private dwellings. Besides symbolizing an identification of the United States with the democracy of ancient Greece, it achieved monumental impressiveness at a fairly low cost. Even in newly settled frontier communities, it was relatively easy and inexpensive to put up a functional square building and then add a classical facade. Not everyone could live in structures that looked like Greek temples, but almost everyone could admire them from the outside or conduct business within their walls.

Serious exponents of a higher culture and a more refined sensibility sought to reach the new public in the hope of enlightening or uplifting it. The "Brahmin poets" of New England—Henry Wadsworth Longfellow, James Russell Lowell, and Oliver Wendell Holmes—offered lofty sentiments and moral messages to a receptive middle class; Ralph Waldo Emerson carried his philosophy of spiritual self-reliance to lyceums and lecture halls across the country; and great novelists such as Nathaniel Hawthorne and Herman Melville experimented with the popular romantic genres. But Hawthorne and Melville failed to gain a large readership. The ironic and pessimistic view of life that pervaded their work clashed with the optimism of the age. For later generations of American critics, however, the works of Melville and Hawthorne became centerpieces of the American literary "renaissance" of the mid-nineteenth century. Hawthorne's *The Scarlet Letter* (1850) and Melville's *Moby-Dick* (1851) are now regarded as masterworks of American fiction.

The modern ideal of art for art's sake was alien to the instructional spirit of mid-nineteenth-century American culture. The responsibility of the artist in a democratic society, it was assumed, was to contribute to the general welfare by encouraging virtue and proper sentiments. Only Edgar Allan Poe seemed to fit the European image of romantic genius, rebelling against middle-class pieties. But in his own way, Poe exploited the popular fascination with death in his verse and used the conventions of Gothic horror in his tales. The most original of the antebellum poets, Walt Whitman, sought to articulate the rising democratic spirit, but his abandonment of traditional verse forms and his freedom in dealing with the sexual side of human nature left him relatively isolated and unappreciated during his most creative years.

Democratic Political Institutions

The supremacy of democracy was most obvious in the new politics of universal white manhood suffrage and mass political parties. By the 1820s, most states had removed the last remaining barriers to voting participation by all white males. This change was not as radical or controversial as it would be later in nineteenth-century Europe; ownership of land was so common in the United States that a general suffrage did not mean men without property became a voting majority.

Accompanying this broadening of the electorate was a rise in the proportion of public officials who were elected rather than appointed. Increasingly, "the people" chose judges, as well as legislative and executive office holders. A new style of politicking developed. Politicians had to campaign, demonstrating in their speeches on the stump that they could mirror voters' fears and concerns. Electoral politics became more festive and dramatic.

Skillful and farsighted politicians—such as Martin Van Buren in New York—began in the 1820s to build stable statewide political organizations out of what had been loosely organized factions. Before the rise of effective national parties, politicians created true party organizations on the state level by dispensing government jobs to friends and supporters, and by attacking rivals as enemies of popular aspirations. Earlier politicians had regarded parties as a threat to republican virtue and had embraced them only as a temporary expedient, but Van Buren regarded a permanent two-party system as essential to democratic government. In his opinion, parties were an effective check on the temptation to abuse power. The major breakthrough in American political thought during the 1820s and 1830s was the idea of a "loyal opposition," ready to capitalize politically on the mistakes or excesses of the "ins" without denying the right of the "ins" to act the same way when they became the "outs."

Changes in the method of nominating and electing a president fostered the growth of a two-party system on the national level. By 1828, presidential electors were chosen by popular vote rather than by state legislatures in all but two of the twenty-four states. The new need to mobilize grassroots voters behind particular candidates required national organization. Coalitions of state parties that could agree on a single standard-bearer gradually evolved into the great national parties of the Jacksonian era—the Democrats and the Whigs. When national nominating conventions made their appearance in 1831, candidate selection became a matter to be taken up by representative party assemblies, not congressional caucuses or ad hoc political alliances.

New political institutions and practices encouraged a great upsurge of popular interest and participation. In the presidential election of 1824, the proportion of adult white males voting was less than 27 percent. In 1828, it rose sharply to 55 percent; it held at that level for the elections of 1832 and 1836 and then shot up to 78 percent in 1840—the first election in which two fully organized national parties each nominated a single candidate and campaigned for their choices in every state in the Union.

Economic Issues

Economic questions dominated the political controversies of the 1820s and 1830s. The Panic of 1819 and the subsequent depression heightened popular interest in government economic policy, first on the state and then on the national level. No one really knew how to solve the problems of a market economy that went through cycles of boom and bust, but many people thought they had the answer. Some, especially small farmers, favored a return to a simpler and more "honest" economy without banks, paper money, and the easy credit that encouraged speculation. Others, particularly emerging entrepreneurs, saw salvation in government aid and protection for venture capital. Entrepreneurs appealed to state governments for charters that granted special privileges to banks, transportation enterprises, and manufacturing corporations. Politicians attempted to respond to the conflicting views about the best way to restore and maintain prosperity. Out of the economic distress of the early 1820s came a rapid growth of state-level political activity and organization that foreshadowed the rise of national parties organized around economic programs.

The party disputes that arose over corporations, tariffs, banks, and internal improvements involved more than the direct economic concerns of particular interest groups. The republican ideology of the revolutionary period survived through widespread fears of conspiracy against American liberty and equality. Whenever any group appeared to be exerting decisive influence over public policy, people who did not identify with that group's aspirations were quick to charge its members with corruption and the unscrupulous pursuit of power.

The notion that the American experiment was a fragile one, constantly threatened by power-hungry conspirators, eventually took two principal forms. Jacksonians believed that "the money power" endangered the survival of republicanism; their opponents feared that populist politicians like Jackson himself—alleged "rabble-rousers"—would gull the electorate into ratifying high-handed and tyrannical actions contrary to the true interests of the nation.

An object of increasing concern for both sides was the role of the federal government. Should it take positive steps to foster economic growth, as the National Republicans and later the Whigs contended, or should it simply attempt to destroy what Jacksonians decried as "special privilege" or "corporate monopoly"? Almost everyone favored equality of opportunity, but there was serious disagreement over whether this goal could best be achieved by active government support of commerce and industry or by divorcing the government from the economy in the name of laissez-faire and free competition.

Labor Radicalism and Equal Rights

For one group of dissenters, democracy took on a more radical meaning. Working men's parties and trade unions emerged in eastern cities during the late 1820s and early 1830s. Their leaders condemned the growing gap between the rich and the poor. They argued that an expansion of low-paying labor was putting working people under the dominance of their employers to such an extent that the American tradition of "equal rights" was in grave danger. Society, in their view, was divided between "producers"—laborers, artisans, farmers, and small-business owners who ran their own enterprises—and nonproducing "parasites"—bankers, speculators, and merchant capitalists. Working men's parties aimed to give the producers greater control over the fruits of their labor.

These radicals called for a number of reforms to achieve equal rights. Thomas Skidmore, a founder of the New York Working Men's Party, advocated the abolition of inheritance and a redistribution of property. Champions of the rights of labor also demanded greatly extended and improved systems of public education. But education reform, however radical or extensive, could provide equal opportunities only to future generations. To relieve the plight of adult artisans and craftspeople at a time when their economic and social status was deteriorating, labor reformers and trade unionists experimented with cooperative production and called for a ten-hour workday, abolition of imprisonment for debt, and a currency system based exclusively on hard money so workers could no longer be paid in depreciated banknotes.

During the 1830s, federated unions and working men's political parties emerged in several cities. Through mass action these groups were able to achieve better working conditions and shorter workdays. But the depression that began in 1837 wiped out most of these gains. In the 1830s and 1840s, northern abolitionists and early proponents of women's rights made other efforts to extend the meaning and scope of democracy. But Jacksonian America was too permeated with racism and sexism to give much heed to claims that the equal rights prescribed by the Declaration of Independence should be extended to blacks and women. Most of those who advocated democratization explicitly limited its application to white males. In some ways, the civil and political status of blacks and women actually deteriorated during "the age of the common *man*." (See Chapter 12 for a discussion of these movements.)

Jackson and the Politics of Democracy

What political conflicts did President Andrew Jackson face and how did he resolve them?

The public figure who came to symbolize the triumph of democracy was Andrew Jackson, who came out a loser in the presidential election of 1824. His victory four years later, his actions as president, and the great political party that formed around him refashioned national politics in a more democratic mold. No wonder historians have called the spirit of the age Jacksonian Democracy.

The Election of 1824 and J. Q. Adams's Administration

As Monroe's second term ended, the ruling Republican Party was in disarray and could not agree on who should succeed to the presidency. The party's congressional caucus chose William Crawford of Georgia, an old-line Jeffersonian. But a majority of congressmen showed their disapproval of this outmoded method of nominating candidates by refusing to attend the caucus. Monroe himself favored John Quincy Adams of Massachusetts. This gave the New England statesman an important boost but did not discourage others from entering the contest. Supporters of Henry Clay and John C. Calhoun mounted campaigns for their favorites, and a group of local leaders in his home state of Tennessee tossed Jackson's hat into the ring.

Initially, Jackson was not given much of a chance. Unlike other aspirants, he had not played a conspicuous role in national politics; his sole claim to fame was as a military hero, and not even his original supporters believed this would be sufficient to catapult him into the White House. But after testing the waters, Calhoun withdrew and chose instead to run for vice president. Then Crawford suffered a debilitating stroke that weakened his chances. With one Southerner out of the race and another disabled, Jackson began to pick up support in slaveholding states. He also found favor among those in the North and West who were disenchanted with the economic nationalism of Clay and Adams.

In the election, Jackson won a plurality of the electoral votes, but he lacked the necessary majority. The contest was thrown into the House of Representatives, where the legislators were to choose from among the three top candidates. Adams emerged victorious over Jackson and Crawford. Clay, who had just missed making the final three, provided the winning margin by persuading his supporters to vote for Adams. When Adams proceeded to appoint Clay as his secretary of state, the Jacksonians charged that a "corrupt bargain" had deprived their favorite of the presidency. Although there was no evidence that Clay had bartered votes for the promise of a high office, the charge was widely believed. As a result, Adams assumed office under a cloud of suspicion.

Adams had a difficult and frustrating presidency. Adams sought to encourage industrial development, improvements in transportation, and centralized credit. Among the reforms he urged on Congress were federal bankruptcy legislation, debt reduction, road construction, geographical and astronomical exploration, and the creation of a new national university and naval academy. However, the political winds were blowing against nationalistic programs, partly because the country was just recovering from a depression that many thought had been caused or exacerbated by federal banking and tariff policies. Adams refused to bow to public opinion and called for an expansion of federal activity. He had a special interest in government support for science, to which end he advocated the establishment of a national university in Washington. Advocates of states' rights and a strict construction of the Constitution were aghast at such proposals, and the opposition that developed in Congress turned the administration's domestic program into a pipe dream.

In foreign affairs, as well, Adams found himself stymied. International commerce, to Adams, was the cornerstone of foreign policy, and he believed that expanded trade and shipping would strengthen the new nation. While he did not oppose all tariffs, the tariff became the rallying cry of those hostile to his administration. The new Congress elected in 1826 was dominated by men favorable to Andrew Jackson's presidential aspirations. The tariff issue was the main business on their agenda. Pressure for greater protection came not only from manufacturers but also from many farmers, especially wool and hemp growers, who would supply critical votes in the upcoming presidential election. The cotton-growing South—the only section where tariffs of all kinds were unpopular—was assumed to be safely in the general's camp regardless of his stand on the tariff. Therefore, promoters of Jackson's candidacy felt safe in supporting a high tariff to swing critical votes in Jackson's direction. Jackson himself had never categorically opposed protective tariffs so long as they were "judicious."

THE ELECTION OF 1824

Candidate	Party	Popular Vote	Electoral Vote*
J. Q. Adams	No party designations	108,740	84
Jackson		153,544	99
Clay		47,136	37
Crawford		46,618	41

*No candidate received a majority of the electoral votes. Adams was elected by the House of Representatives.

As it turned out, the resulting tariff law was anything but judicious. Congress had operated on a give-and-take principle, trying to provide something for everybody. Those favoring protection for farmers agreed to protection for manufacturers and vice versa. The substantial across-the-board increase in duties that resulted, however, angered southern free traders and became known as the **tariff of abominations**. Historians long erred in explaining the 1828 tariff as a complex Jacksonian plot that backfired; it was in fact an early example of how special-interest groups can achieve their goals in democratic politics by trading votes in the legislative bargaining process known as logrolling.

Jackson Comes to Power

The campaign of 1828 actually began with Adams's election in 1824. Rallying around the charge of a corrupt bargain between Adams and Clay, Jackson's supporters began to organize on the state and local level with an eye to reversing the outcome of the election. By late 1827, a Jackson committee was functioning in virtually every county, town, or city in the nation. Influential state or regional leaders who had supported other candidates in 1824 now rallied behind the Tennessean.

The most significant of these were Vice President Calhoun, who now spoke for the militant states' rights sentiment of the South; Senator Martin Van Buren, who dominated New York politics through the political machine known as the Albany Regency; and two Kentucky editors, Francis P. Blair and Amos Kendall, who worked in the West to mobilize opposition to Henry Clay and his "American System," which advocated government encouragement of economic development through such measures as protective tariffs and federally funded internal improvements. As they prepared themselves for the canvass of 1828, these leaders and their many local followers laid the foundations for the first modern American political party—the Democrats. The fact that the Democratic Party was founded to promote the cause of a particular presidential candidate revealed a central characteristic of the emerging two-party system. From this time on, according to historian Richard P. McCormick, national parties existed primarily "to engage in a contest for the presidency." Without this great prize, there would have been less incentive to create national organizations out of the parties and factions developing in the several states.

The election of 1828 saw the birth of a new era of mass democracy. The mighty effort on behalf of Jackson featured the widespread use of such electioneering techniques as huge public rallies, torchlight parades, and lavish barbecues or picnics paid for by the candidate's supporters. Many historians believe that the massive turnout at such events during much of the rest of the nineteenth century revealed a deeper popular engagement with politics than at other times in American history. But it is also possible, as others have argued, that it merely showed that politicians had learned that providing entertainment and treats could lure people to the polls. Personalities and mudslinging dominated the 1828 campaign. The Democratic Party press and a legion of pamphleteers bombarded the public with vicious personal attacks on Adams and praise of "Old Hickory," as Jackson was called. The supporters of Adams responded in kind; they even sank to the level of accusing Jackson's wife, Rachel, of bigamy and adultery because she had unwittingly married Jackson before being officially divorced from her first husband. The Democrats then came up with the utterly false charge that Adams's wife was born out of wedlock!

What gave Jacksonians the edge was their success in portraying their candidate as an authentic man of the people, despite his substantial fortune in land and slaves. His backwoods upbringing, his record as a popular military hero and Indian fighter, and even his lack of education were touted as evidence that he was a true representative of the common people, especially the plain folk of the South and the West. In the words of one of his supporters, Jackson had "a judgment unclouded by the visionary speculations of the academician." Adams, according to Democratic propagandists, was the exact opposite—an overeducated aristocrat, more at home in the salon than among plain people. Nature's nobleman was pitted against the aloof New England intellectual, and Adams never really had a chance.

Jackson won by a popular vote margin of one hundred fifty thousand and by more than 2 to 1 in the Electoral College. Clearly,

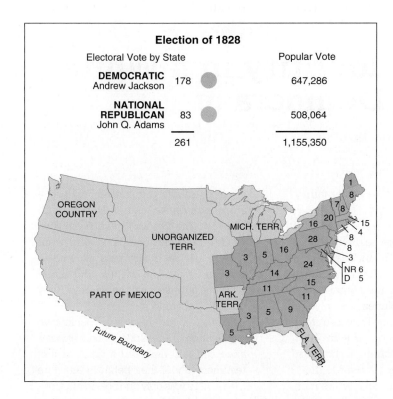

Election of 1828

Electoral Vote by State		Popular Vote
DEMOCRATIC Andrew Jackson	178	647,286
NATIONAL REPUBLICAN John Q. Adams	83	508,064
	261	1,155,350

Jackson's organization had been more effective and his popular appeal substantially greater. He had piled up massive majorities in the Deep South, but the voters elsewhere divided fairly evenly. Adams, in fact, won a majority of the electoral vote in the northern states. Furthermore, it was not clear what kind of mandate Jackson had won. Most of the politicians in his camp favored states' rights and limited government as against the nationalism of Adams and Clay, but the general himself had never taken a clear public stand on such issues as banks, tariffs, and internal improvements. He did, however, stand for the removal of Indians from the Gulf states, and this was a key to his immense popularity in that region.

Jackson turned out to be one of the most forceful and domineering of American presidents. His most striking character traits were an indomitable will, an intolerance of opposition, and a prickly pride that would not permit him to forgive or forget an insult or supposed act of betrayal. It is sometimes hard to determine whether his political actions were motivated by principle or personal spite. As a young man on his own in a frontier environment, he had learned to fight his own battles. Somewhat violent in temper and action, he fought a number of duels and served in wars against the British, the Spanish, and the Indians with a zeal his critics found excessive. His experiences had made him tough and resourceful but had also deprived him of the flexibility normally associated with successful politicians. Jackson's presidency commenced with his open endorsement of rotation of officeholders or what his critics called "the spoils system." Although he did not actually depart radically from his predecessors in the extent to which he removed federal officeholders and replaced them with his supporters, he was the first president to defend this practice as a legitimate application of democratic doctrine. He proclaimed in his first annual message that "the duties of all public officers are . . . so plain and simple that men of intelligence may readily qualify themselves for their performance" and that "no man has any more intrinsic claim to office than another."

Midway through his first administration, Jackson completely reorganized his cabinet, replacing almost all of his original appointees. At the root of this upheaval was a growing feud between Jackson and Vice President Calhoun, but the incident that brought it to a head was the Peggy Eaton affair. Peggy O'Neale Eaton, the daughter of a Washington tavern owner, married Secretary of War John Eaton in 1829. Because of gossip about her moral character, the wives of other cabinet members refused to receive her socially. Jackson became her fervent champion, partly because he found the charges against her reminiscent of the slanders against his late wife, who had died in 1828. When he raised the issue of Mrs. Eaton's social status at a cabinet meeting, only Secretary of State Van Buren, a widower, supported his stand. This seemingly trivial incident led to the resignation of all but one of the cabinet members, and the president was able to begin again with a fresh slate. Although Van Buren resigned with

Read the **Document**   **Andrew Jackson, First Annual Message to Congress (1829)**

Jackson's resigning cabinet members were, according to this cartoon, rats deserting a falling house. Jackson is seated on a collapsing chair, while the "altar of reform" and "public confidence in the stability of this administration" pillars topple to his left, and several "resignations" flutter behind him. The president's foot is on the tail of the Secretary of State Martin Van Buren rat.

Feature Essay | Racial Identity in a White Man's Democracy

In mid-nineteenth-century Georgia, like most American states, racial identity was defined by statute: a "negro" was a person with at least one grandparent of African origin. But in practice, statutory rules about ancestry could not decide whether a person was black or white. Across the American South (and occasionally in the North as well), trials were held in which a person's race was determined according to how he appeared and behaved, with whom he associated, and whether he performed acts of citizenship.

The Jacksonian movement revolutionized Southern life by extending full rights of citizenship to all white men—voting, holding public office, participating in party politics. These political acts were reserved for white men and also became the emblems and markers of white manhood. Honor, which had once been seen as the exclusive concern of the gentleman, was democratized. Southern politics increasingly depended on a belief that all white men were equals, that only blacks constituted the "mudsill" class. This "white man's democracy" helped to mobilize ordinary white people under the planters' banner, and white supremacy helped to justify slavery in a free republic.

Bryan v. *Walton (1864)* was a case that became somewhat famous for the Georgia Supreme Court's pronouncements on the "social and civil degradation" of black people, and the idea that "the prejudice . . . of caste, is unconquerable," so that black people could never be citizens. The case went to trial three times between 1848 and 1863, and those trials turned on the prior question of whether the men of the Nuñez family were in fact black or white.

Joseph Nuñez was the son of Lucy, a white woman. Before he died, he sold six slaves to Seaborn Bryan. The administrator of his estate, Hughes Walton, sued Bryan to recover the human property, claiming that Nuñez was a man of color and so was legally barred from selling slaves. The first trial in 1848 was decided on technical grounds, but as the case went forward, there was no doubt that only as a white man did Joseph Nuñez have the right to do what he would with his property. So the second and third trials focused on the racial identity of Joseph and his father James. Dozens of their neighbors testified about them—and remarkably, they could agree on very little.

Bryan's witnesses agreed that James had a dark complexion—some thought he might be Indian; others considered him Portuguese. Mary Rogers described James: "straight long nose, thin lips, straight and very black hair, rather a narrow, long face and of a red complexion; he was not a large man, walked trim and nice." She went on to report that "Jim was always among respectable white people in the neighborhood in their dances, parties, &c. and was received by them as on a footing with whites." Stephen Newman and Mary Harrel testified that Jim Nuñez looked more Indian than "negro," and that "his action and movements were as genteel as any man witnesses have known; there was no clumsiness about him." They "well remembered Jim Nuñez's dancing, which was very graceful; many persons tried to catch his step, and nearly all admired its style." (Contrary to modern stereotypes, this evidence of good dancing style went to prove Jim's whiteness.) Mary Harrel testified that Jim Nuñez "never kept low, trifling, or rakish company" and went "where no free negro was allowed to associate with the whites, and dined with the whites just the same as any gentleman would have done."

Bryan had offered a persuasive explanation of the Nuñez men's appearance and had amassed a great deal of testimony about their behavior as white men. There was only one hole in his argument: No one presented any evidence of either Nuñez exercising political or legal rights. Indeed, Harriet Kilpatrick testified that as far as she knew, "neither Jim [n]or Joe Nuñez ever voted or exercised any of the rights of citizenship." At the third trial, William C. Bates, testified that James Nuñez "was treated by his neighbors as a gentleman, recognized as a gentleman, and enjoyed the privileges of a gentleman and a free citizen." Yet on cross-examination, Bates explained that he "was too young, when I knew James Nuñez, to answer whether he voted, mustered, or served on juries." James Nuñez had never been seen performing the specific acts of white manhood—a serious omission.

Only one witness gave testimony alleging James Nuñez's exercise of his civic rights. The deposition of South Carolinian Matthew Alexander suggested that before James had moved to Georgia, he had a "fine dancer— quite a gentleman in manners and appearance," with long straight black hair. More importantly, "he enjoyed all the privileges of a free man . . . James Nuñez voted, mustered, and did jury duty, and exercised the usual privileges and duties of free white citizens." But he could give none of the details.

An attorney in a nineteenth-century trial addresses an all white jury in the jury box.

On the opposite side of the courtroom, Walton's witnesses testified exactly the opposite. Charles Cosnahan believed Nuñez was a mulatto based on appearance ("tolerable kinky hair . . . did not have a fair complexion"), reputation ("they passed in the neighborhood as free colored persons"), and the fact that neither Jim nor Joseph "voted or performed military duty; they exercised no other rights than those of free negroes." Joseph Cosnahan explained that he "never knew of [James and Joseph] exercising the usual rights of white citizens," although "James Nuñez was an educated man and mixed sometimes with white men; they were regarded in the neighborhood as mulattoes; the white citizens associated with them and regarded them as mulattoes." Several other witnesses corroborated this version of Joseph and James's racial identity, and the jury gave a verdict to Walton, ratifying the view that Nuñez was not white.

At the end of the third trial, juries had heard conflicting testimony on every aspect of Joseph Nuñez's white identity: appearance, self-presentation, reputation and acceptance among blacks and whites, white ancestry, white conduct, white character—and on his failure to exercise the rights and privileges of whiteness. While no one could agree whether James and Joseph had straight or curly hair, almost everyone agreed on this latter point: they had not performed the civic duties of white manhood. The jury was persuaded: they found for Hughes Walton.

Judge Lumpkin, for the Supreme Court of Georgia, sought to set the matter to rest at the case's final disposition in 1864. Lumpkin disparaged all testimony in favor of Nuñez's whiteness as given by dupes who had been fooled by appearances, and found that Joseph was a man of color who had no right to sell slaves.

Yet despite the community's disagreement over the Nuñezes' identity, they did agree on one point: the Nuñezes' race could be known through their performances. Race was not only something Joseph and James *were*, it was something they *did*. Who was a white man? A civic being who voted, served on juries, and mustered in the militia. Degraded black men were not capable of such things, while honorable white men could not keep from doing them. In racial identity trials across the South, judges made clear that, as one South Carolina judge put it, a man could be found white "although of a dark complexion," if he "had been recognized as a white man, received into society, and exercised political privileges as such."

The law was involved not only in recognizing racial identity, but in creating it; the state itself—through its legal and military institutions—helped make people white. In allowing men of low social status to participate in white men's democracy by voting, serving on juries, and mustering in the militia, the state welcomed every white man into symbolic equality with the wealthy Southern slaveholder.

QUESTIONS FOR DISCUSSION

1. Why did political changes emphasize the social importance of slavery?

2. How did the circumstances of Joseph and James Nuñez lives decide what rights they should have?

the rest to promote a thorough reorganization, his loyalty was rewarded by his appointment as minister to England and strong prospects of future favor.

Indian Removal

The first major policy question facing the Jackson administration concerned the fate of Native Americans. Jackson had long favored removing eastern Indians to lands beyond the Mississippi. In his military service on the southern frontier, he had been directly involved in persuading and coercing tribal groups to emigrate. Jackson's support of removal was no different from the policy of previous administrations. The only real issues to be determined were how rapidly and thoroughly the process should be carried out and by what means. At the time of Jackson's election, the states of Georgia, Alabama, and Mississippi, distressed by the federal government's failure to eliminate the substantial Indian enclaves remaining within their boundaries, were clamoring for quick action. Since Adams seemed to have dragged his feet on the issue, voters in these states turned overwhelmingly to Jackson, who promised to expel the Indians without delay.

Immediately after Jackson's election, Georgia extended its state laws over the Cherokee within its borders. Georgia declared that all Cherokee laws and customs were null and void, made all white people living in the Cherokee Nation subject to Georgia's laws, declared the Cherokee mere tenants at will on their land, and made it a crime for any Cherokee to try to influence another Cherokee to stay in Georgia. At the same time, state officials authorized the Georgia militia to conduct a campaign of violence against the Cherokee to increase pressure on them to give up their land and move west. Before Jackson's inauguration, Alabama and Mississippi took similar action, abolishing the sovereignty of the Creeks and Choctaw, and declaring state control of the tribes.

This legislation defied both the Constitutional provisions giving the federal government exclusive jurisdiction over Indian affairs and specific treaties. Jackson endorsed the state actions. He regarded Indians as that they were children when they did the white man's bidding and savage beasts when they resisted. He was also aware of his political debt to the land-hungry states of the South. Consequently, in December 1829, he advocated a new and more coercive removal policy. Denying Cherokee autonomy, he asserted the primacy of states' rights over Indian rights, and called for the speedy and thorough removal of all eastern Indians to designated areas beyond the Mississippi. Chief John Ross warned his people that "the object of the President is . . . to create divisions among ourselves." President Jackson rejected Ross's appeal against Georgia's violation of federal treaty, and in 1830, the president's congressional supporters introduced a bill to implement the removal policy. Opponents charged that the president had defied the Constitution by removing federal protection from the southeastern tribes. But Jackson and his supporters were determined to ride roughshod over humanitarian or constitutional objections to Indian dispossession. With strong support from the South and the western border states, the removal bill passed the Senate by a vote of 28 to 19 and the House by the narrow margin of 102 to 97.

Jackson then moved quickly to conclude the necessary treaties, using the threat of unilateral state action to bludgeon the tribes into submission. The treaty for Cherokee removal was negotiated with 75 out of 17,000 Cherokees, and none of the tribal officers was present. By 1833, all the southeastern tribes except the Cherokee had agreed to evacuate their ancestral homelands. Choctaw Chief David Folsom wrote, "We are exceedingly tired. We have just heard of the ratification of the Choctaw Treaty. Our doom is sealed. There is no course for us but to turn our faces to our new homes in the setting sun." Alexis de Tocqueville, the French author of *Democracy in America*, watched the troops driving the Choctaws across the Mississippi River in the winter of 1831. He wrote that Americans had deprived Indians of their rights "with singular felicity, tranquilly, legally, philanthropically . . . It is impossible to destroy men with more respect for the laws of humanity."

Yet President Jackson was not always concerned with respect for the law. In 1832, he condoned Georgia's defiance of a Supreme Court decision (*Worcester* v. *Georgia*) that denied a state's right to extend its jurisdiction over tribal lands. Georgia had arrested and sentenced to four years' hard labor a missionary who violated state law by going on tribal land without Georgia's permission; the Supreme Court declared the law unconstitutional. Jackson's legendary declaration that Chief Justice Marshall had "made his decision, now let him enforce it," is almost certainly apocryphal, as there was nothing for either Jackson or Marshall to "enforce"; the decision only required the state of Georgia to release Worcester from custody, which it did several months later. But the story reflects Jackson's general attitude towards the Court's decisions on federal jurisdiction. He would not protect Indians from state action, no matter how violent or coercive, and he put the weight of the federal government behind removal policy.

By 1833, all the southeastern tribes except the Cherokee had agreed to evacuate their ancestral homes. A stubbornly resisting majority faction of the Cherokee held out until 1838 when military pressure forced them to march to Oklahoma. This trek—known as the **Trail of Tears**—was made under such harsh conditions that almost four thousand of approximately sixteen thousand marchers died on the way. The final chapter of Indian Removal was the Second Seminole War, which lasted from 1834 to 1841. Although the government had convinced a small group of Seminoles to sign a treaty in 1834 agreeing to removal, most Seminoles renounced the treaty and resisted for years, making the bloody conflict the most expensive Indian war in U.S. history. The removal of the southeastern Indians exposed the prejudiced and greedy side of Jacksonian democracy. (See the discussion of the background of Indian Removal in Chapter 9.)

The Nullification Crisis

During the 1820s, Southerners became increasingly fearful of federal encroachment on the rights of the states. Behind this concern, in South Carolina at least, was a strengthened commitment to the preservation of slavery and a resulting anxiety about possible uses of federal power to strike at the "peculiar institution." Hoping to keep the explosive slavery issue out of the political limelight, South Carolinians seized on another genuine grievance—the protective tariff—as the issue on which to take their stand in favor of a state veto power over federal actions they viewed as contrary to their interests. As a staple-producing and exporting region, the

View the **Closer Look**   The Trail of Tears

Robert Lindneux, *The Trail of Tears* (1942). Cherokee Indians, carrying their few possessions, are prodded along by U.S. soldiers on the Trail of Tears. Several thousand Native Americans died on the ruthless forced march from their homelands in the East to the newly established Indian Territory in Oklahoma.

South had sound economic reasons for favoring free trade. Tariffs increased the prices that southern agriculturists paid for manufactured goods and threatened to undermine their foreign markets by inciting counterprotection. An economic crisis in the South Carolina upcountry during the 1820s made that state particularly receptive to extreme positions on the tariff and states' rights.

Vice President John C. Calhoun emerged as the leader of the states' rights insurgency in South Carolina, abandoning his earlier support of nationalism and the American system. After the passage of the tariff of abominations in 1828, the state legislature declared the new duties unconstitutional and endorsed a lengthy statement—written anonymously by Calhoun—that affirmed **nullification**, or the right of an individual state to set aside federal law. Calhoun supported Jackson in 1828 and planned to serve amicably as his vice president, expecting Jackson to support his native region on questions involving the tariff and states' rights. He also entertained hopes of succeeding Jackson as president.

Early in his administration, Jackson appeared well attuned to the southern slaveholding position on state versus federal authority. Besides acquiescing in Georgia's de facto nullification of federal treaties upholding Indian tribal rights, he vetoed a major internal improvements bill in 1830, invoking a strict construction of the

Constitution to deny federal funds for the building of the Maysville Road in Kentucky.

Meanwhile, a bitter personal feud developed between Jackson and Calhoun. Jackson viewed the vice president and his wife as prime movers in the ostracism of Peggy Eaton. Furthermore, evidence came to light that Calhoun, as secretary of war in Monroe's cabinet in 1818, had privately advocated punishing Jackson for his incursion into Florida. As Calhoun lost favor with Jackson, it became clear that Van Buren, rather than the vice president, would be Jackson's designated successor. The personal breach between Jackson and Calhoun colored and intensified their confrontation over nullification and the tariff.

The two men differed on matters of principle as well. Although generally a defender of states' rights and strict construction of the Constitution, Jackson opposed the theory of nullification as a threat to the survival of the Union. In his view, federal power should be held in check, but this did not mean the states were truly sovereign. His nationalism was that of a military man who had fought for the country against foreign enemies, and he was not about to permit the nation's disintegration at the hands of domestic dissidents. The differences between Jackson and Calhoun came into the open at the Jefferson Day dinner in 1830, when Jackson offered the toast

"Our Union: It must be preserved," to which Calhoun responded, "The Union. Next to Liberty, the most dear. May we always remember that it can only be preserved by distributing equally the benefits and the burdens of the Union."

In 1830 and 1831, the movement against the tariff gained strength in South Carolina. Calhoun openly took the lead, elaborating further on his view that states had the right to set aside federal laws. In 1832, Congress passed a new tariff that lowered the rates slightly but retained the principle of protection. Supporters of nullification argued that the new law simply demonstrated that no genuine relief could be expected from Washington. They then succeeded in persuading the South Carolina state legislature to call a special convention. When the convention met in November 1832, the

members voted overwhelmingly to nullify the tariffs of 1828 and 1832 and to forbid the collection of customs duties within the state.

Jackson reacted with characteristic decisiveness. He alerted the secretary of war to prepare for possible military action, issued a proclamation denouncing nullification as treasonous, and asked Congress to vote him the authority to use the army to enforce the tariff. At the same time, he sought to pacify the nullifiers somewhat by recommending a lower tariff. Congress responded by enacting the Force Bill—which gave the president the military powers he sought—and the compromise tariff of 1833. The latter was primarily the work of Jackson's political enemy Henry Clay, but the president signed it anyway. Faced with Jackson's clear intention to use force if necessary and somewhat appeased by the prospect of a lower tariff, South Carolina suspended

 View the **Closer Look** Indian Removal

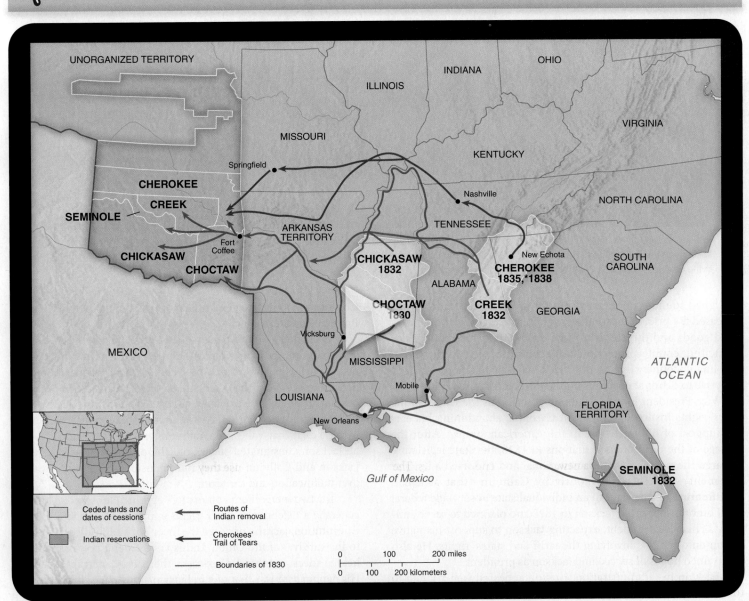

INDIAN REMOVAL Because so many Native Americans, uprooted from their lands in the East, died on the forced march to Oklahoma, the route they followed became known as the Trail of Tears.

*Treaty signed in 1835 by a minority faction was met with defiance from the majority, but removal was forced in 1838.

the nullification ordinance in late January 1833 and formally rescinded it in March, after the new tariff had been enacted. To demonstrate that they had not conceded their constitutional position, the convention delegates concluded their deliberations by nullifying the Force Bill.

The nullification crisis revealed that South Carolinians would not tolerate any federal action that seemed contrary to their interests or raised doubts about the institution of slavery. The nullifiers' philosophy implied the right of secession as well as the right to declare laws of Congress null and void. A fear of northern meddling with slavery was the main spur to the growth of a militant doctrine of state sovereignty in the South. At the time of the nullification crisis, the other slave states had not yet developed such strong anxieties about the future of the "peculiar institution" and had not embraced South Carolina's radical conception of state sovereignty. Jackson was himself a Southerner and a slaveholder, a man who detested abolitionists. In general, he was a proslavery president; later he would use his executive power to stop antislavery literature from being carried by the U.S. mail.

Some farsighted southern loyalists, however, were alarmed by the Unionist doctrines that Jackson propounded in his proclamation against nullification. More strongly than any previous president, he had asserted that the federal government was supreme over the states and that the Union was indivisible. He had further justified the use of force against states that denied federal authority.

📖─ **Read the Document**   **South Carolina's Ordinance of Nullification**

Vice President John C. Calhoun emerged as a champion of states' rights during the nullification crisis, when cartoons such as this example depicted the emaciated South burdened by tariffs while the North grew fat at the southerners' expense.

The Bank War and the Second Party System

What were the arguments for and against the Bank of the United States?

Jackson's most important and controversial use of executive power was his successful attack on the Bank of the United States. The **Bank war** revealed some of the deepest concerns of Jackson and his supporters and dramatically expressed their concept of democracy. It also aroused intense opposition to the president and his policies, an opposition that crystallized in a new national party—the Whigs. The destruction of the Bank and the economic disruption that followed brought to the forefront the issue of the government's relationship to the nation's financial system. Differences on this question helped to sustain and strengthen the new two-party system.

Mr. Biddle's Bank

The Bank of the United States had long been embroiled in public controversy. Its role in precipitating the Panic of 1819 by first extending credit freely and then suddenly calling in its loans had led many, especially in the South and the West, to blame the Bank

for the subsequent depression. But after Nicholas Biddle took over the Bank's presidency in 1823, the institution regained public confidence. Biddle was an able manager who probably understood the mysteries of banking and currency better than any other American of his generation. A Philadelphia gentleman of broad culture, extensive education, and some political experience, he was also arrogant and vain. He was inclined to rely too much on his own judgment and refused to admit his mistakes. But his record prior to the confrontation with Jackson was a good one. In 1825 and again in 1828, he acted decisively to curb an overextension of credit by state banks and helped avert a recurrence of the boom-and-bust cycle.

The actual performance of the Bank was not the only target of criticism about it. Old-line Jeffersonians had always opposed it on principle, both because they viewed its establishment as unconstitutional and because it placed too much power in the hands of a small, privileged group. The Bank was a chartered monopoly, an essentially private corporation that performed public services in return for exclusive economic rights. Because of its great influence, the Bank tended to be blamed for any economic problems. For those who had misgivings about the rise of the national market, the Bank epitomized the forces threatening the independence and prosperity of small producers. In an era of rising white men's democracy, an obvious and telling objection to the Bank was simply that it possessed great power and privilege without being under popular control.

The Bank Veto and the Election of 1832

Jackson came into office with strong reservations about banking and paper money in general—in part as a result of his own brushes with bankruptcy after accepting promissory notes that depreciated in value. He also harbored suspicions that branches of the Bank of the United States had illicitly used their influence on behalf of his opponent in the presidential election. In his annual messages in 1829 and 1830, Jackson called on Congress to begin discussing "possible modification of a system which cannot continue to exist in its present form without . . . perpetual apprehensions and discontent on the part of the States and the People."

Biddle began to worry about the fate of the Bank's charter when it came up for renewal in 1836. At the same time, Jackson was listening to the advice of close friends and unofficial advisers—members of his "Kitchen Cabinet"—especially Amos Kendall and Francis P. Blair, who thought an attack on the Bank would provide a good party issue for the election of 1832. Biddle then made a fateful blunder. Panicked by the presidential messages and the anti-Bank oratory of congressional Jacksonians such as Senator Thomas Hart Benton of Missouri, he determined to seek recharter by Congress in 1832, four years early. Senator Henry Clay, leader of the antiadministration forces on Capitol Hill, encouraged this move because he was convinced that Jackson had chosen the unpopular side of the issue and would be embarrassed or even discredited by a congressional endorsement of the Bank.

The bill to recharter, introduced in the House and Senate in early 1832, aroused Jackson and unified his administration and party against renewal. The bill found many supporters in Congress, however. A number of legislators had received loans from the Bank, and the economy seemed to be prospering under the Bank's guidance. As a result, the bill to recharter passed Congress with ease.

THE ELECTION OF 1832

Candidate	Party	Popular Vote	Electoral Vote
Jackson	Democratic	688,242	219
Clay	National Republican	473,462	49
Wirt	Anti-Masonic	101,051	7
Floyd	Independent Democratic	*	11

*Delegates chosen by South Carolina legislature

The next move was Jackson's, and he made the most of the opportunity by vetoing the bill. After repeating his opinion that the Bank was unconstitutional, notwithstanding the Supreme Court's ruling on the issue, he went on to argue that it violated the fundamental rights of the people in a democratic society: "In the full enjoyment of the gifts of Heaven and the fruits of superior industry, economy, and virtue, every man is equally entitled to protection by law; but when the laws undertake to add to those natural and just advantages artificial distinctions, to grant . . . exclusive privileges, the humble members of society—the farmers, mechanics, and laborers—who have neither the time nor the means of securing like

favors to themselves, have a right to complain of the injustice of their government." Government, he added, should "confine itself to equal protection."

Jackson thus called on the common people to join him in fighting the "monster" corporation. His veto message was the first ever to use more than strictly constitutional arguments and to deal directly with social and economic issues. Congressional attempts to override the veto failed, and Jackson resolved to take the entire issue to the people in the upcoming presidential election.

The 1832 election, the first in which candidates were chosen by national nominating conventions, pitted Jackson against Henry Clay, standard-bearer of the National Republicans. Although the Democrats did not adopt a formal platform, the party stood firmly behind Jackson in his opposition to rechartering the Bank. Clay and the National Republicans attempted to marshal the pro-Bank sentiment that was strong in many parts of the country. But Jackson won a great personal triumph, garnering 219 electoral votes to 49 for Clay. His share of the popular vote was not quite as high as it had been in 1828, but it was substantial enough to be interpreted as a mandate for continuing the war against the Bank.

Killing the Bank

Not content with preventing the Bank from getting a new charter, the victorious Jackson now resolved to attack it directly by removing federal deposits from Biddle's vaults. Jackson told Van Buren, "The bank . . . is trying to kill me, but I will kill it." The Bank had indeed used all the political influence it could muster in an attempt to prevent Jackson's reelection, in an act of self-defense. Old Hickory regarded Biddle's actions as a personal attack, part of a devious plot to destroy the president's reputation and deny him the popular approval he deserved. Although he presided over the first modern American political party, Jackson did not really share Van Buren's belief in the legitimacy of a competitive party system. In his view, his opponents were not merely wrong; they were evil and deserved to be destroyed. Furthermore, the election results convinced him that he was the people's chosen instrument in the struggle against corruption and privilege, the only man who could save the pure republicanism of Jefferson and the Founders from the "monster bank."

To remove the deposits from the Bank, Jackson had to overcome strong resistance in his own cabinet. When one secretary of the treasury refused to support the policy, he was shifted to another cabinet post. When a second balked at carrying out removal, he was replaced by Roger B. Taney, a Jackson loyalist and dedicated opponent of the Bank. Beginning in late September 1833, Taney ceased depositing government money in the Bank of the United States and began to withdraw the funds already there. Although Jackson had earlier suggested that the government keep its money in some kind of public bank, he had never worked out the details or made a specific proposal to Congress. The problem of how to dispose of the funds was therefore resolved by an ill-advised decision to place them in selected state banks. By the end of 1833, twenty-three state banks had been chosen as depositories. Opponents charged that the banks had been selected for political rather than fiscal reasons and dubbed them Jackson's "pet banks." Since Congress refused to approve administration proposals to regulate the credit policies of these banks, Jackson's effort to shift to a hard-money economy was quickly nullified by the use the state banks made of the new deposits. They extended credit more recklessly than before and increased the amount of paper money in circulation.

The Bank of the United States counterattacked by calling in outstanding loans and instituting a policy of credit contraction that helped bring on an economic recession. Biddle hoped to win support for recharter by demonstrating that weakening the Bank's position would be disastrous for the economy. With some justification, the president's supporters accused Biddle of deliberately and unnecessarily causing economic distress out of personal resentment and a desire to maintain his unchecked powers and privileges. The Bank never regained its charter.

Strong opposition to Jackson's fiscal policies developed in Congress. Henry Clay and his supporters contended that the president had violated the Bank's charter and exceeded his constitutional authority when he removed the deposits. They eventually persuaded the Senate to approve a motion of censure. Jacksonians in the House were able to block such action, but the president was further humiliated when the Senate refused to confirm Taney as secretary of the treasury. Not all of the criticism and obstructionism

can be attributed to bitterness on the part of pro-Bank politicians. Some congressmen who originally defended Jackson's veto became disenchanted with the president because they thought he had gone too far in asserting the powers of his office.

The Emergence of the Whigs

The coalition that passed the censure resolution in the Senate provided the nucleus for a new national party—the Whigs. The leadership of the new party and a majority of its support came from National Republicans associated with Clay and New England ex-Federalists led by Senator Daniel Webster of Massachusetts. The Whigs also picked up critical support from southern proponents of states' rights who had been upset by Jackson's stand on nullification and then saw an unconstitutional abuse of power in his withdrawal of federal deposits from the Bank of the United States. Even Calhoun and his nullifiers occasionally cooperated with the Whig camp. The initial rallying cry for this diverse anti-Jackson coalition was "executive usurpation." The Whig label was chosen because of its associations with both English and American revolutionary opposition to royal power and prerogatives. In their propaganda, the Whigs portrayed the tyrannical designs of "King Andrew" and his court.

The Whigs also gradually absorbed the Anti-Masonic Party, a surprisingly strong political movement that had arisen in the northeastern states in the late 1820s and early 1830s. Capitalizing on the hysteria aroused by the 1826 disappearance and apparent murder of a New Yorker who had threatened to reveal the secrets of the Masonic order, the Anti-Masons exploited traditional American fears of secret societies and conspiracies. They also appealed successfully to the moral concerns of the northern middle class under the sway of an emerging evangelical Protestantism. Anti-Masons detested Jacksonianism mainly because it stood for a toleration of diverse lifestyles. Democrats did not think government should be concerned about people who drank, gambled, or found better things to do than go to church on Sundays. Their opponents from the Anti-Masonic tradition believed government should restrict such "sinful" behavior. This desire for moral and religious uniformity contributed an important cultural dimension to northern Whiggery.

As the election of 1836 approached, the government's fiscal policies also provoked a localized rebellion among the urban working-class elements of the Democratic coalition. In New York City, a dissident faction broke with the regular Democratic organization mainly

Read the Document   Andrew Jackson, Veto of the Bank Bill

Aided by Van Buren (center), Jackson wields his veto rod against the Bank of the United States, whose heads represent the directors of the state branches. Bank president Nicholas Biddle is wearing the top hat.

Source: Collection of The New-York Historical Society, Negative 42459.

((●━━[Listen to the **Audio File**   Van Buren

Martin Van Buren, only five feet six inches tall, was known as the "Little Magician" when he became president in 1836. He was unlucky to preside over the country during the Panic of 1837, and his deflationary policies were unsuccessful in alleviating the economic crisis. He served only one term in office.

over issues involving banking and currency. These radicals favored a strict hard-money policy and condemned Jackson's transfer of federal deposits to the state banks as inflationary. Because they wanted working people to be paid in specie rather than banknotes, they went beyond opposition to the Bank of the United States and attacked state banks as well. Seeing no basis for cooperation with the Whigs, they established the independent Equal Rights Party and nominated a separate state ticket for 1836.

Jackson himself had hard-money sentiments and regarded the "pet bank" solution as a stopgap measure rather than a final solution to the money problem. He reluctantly surrendered to congressional pressure in early 1836 and signed legislation allocating surplus federal revenues to the deposit banks, increasing their numbers, and weakening federal controls over them. The result was runaway inflation. State banks in the South and West responded to demands from land-speculating interests by issuing a new flood of paper money. Reacting somewhat belatedly to the speculative

mania he had inadvertently helped to create, Jackson pricked the bubble on July 11, 1836. He issued his specie circular, requiring that after August 15 only gold and silver would be accepted in payment for public lands. The action served to curb inflation and land speculation but did so in such a sudden and drastic way that it helped precipitate the financial panic of 1837.

The Rise and Fall of Van Buren

As his successor, Jackson chose Martin Van Buren, who had served him loyally as vice president during his second term. Van Buren was the greatest master of practical politics in the Democratic Party, and the Democratic national convention of 1835 unanimously confirmed Jackson's choice. In accepting the nomination, Van Buren promised to "tread generally in the footsteps of General Jackson."

The newly created Whig Party, reflecting the diversity of its constituency, did not try to decide on a single standard-bearer. Instead, each region chose candidates—Daniel Webster in the East, William Henry Harrison of Ohio (also the Anti-Masonic nominee) in the Old Northwest, and Hugh Lawson White of Tennessee (a former Jackson supporter) in the South. Whigs hoped to deprive Van Buren of enough electoral votes to throw the election into the House of Representatives where one of the Whigs might stand a chance.

The stratagem proved unsuccessful. Van Buren carried fifteen of the twenty-six states and won a clear majority in the electoral college. But the election foreshadowed future trouble for the Democrats, particularly in the South. There the Whigs ran virtually even, erasing the enormous majorities that Jackson had run up in 1828 and 1832. The emergence of a two-party system in the previously solid Deep South resulted from two factors—opposition to some of Jackson's policies and the image of Van Buren as an unreliable Yankee politician. The division did not reflect basic disagreement on the slavery issue. Southern Whigs and Democrats shared a commitment to protecting slavery, and each tried to persuade the electorate they could do the job better than the opposition.

As he took office, Van Buren was immediately faced with a catastrophic depression. The price of cotton fell by almost 50 percent, banks all over the nation suspended specie payments, many businesses went bankrupt, and unemployed workers demonstrated in several cities. The sale of public lands fell off so drastically that the federal surplus, earmarked in 1836 for distribution to the states, became a deficit.

The **Panic of 1837**, economic historians have concluded, was not exclusively, or even primarily, the result of government policies. It was in fact international in scope and reflected some complex changes in the world economy that were beyond the control of American policymakers. But the Whigs were quick to blame the state of the economy on Jacksonian finance, and the administration had to make a politically effective response. Since Van Buren and his party were committed to a policy of laissez-faire on the federal level, there was little or nothing they could do to relieve economic distress through subsidies or relief measures. But Van Buren could at least try to salvage the federal funds deposited in shaky state banks and devise a new system of public finance that would not contribute to future panics by fueling speculation and credit expansion.

Van Buren's solution was to establish a public depository for government funds with no connections whatsoever to commercial

View the **Closer Look**   General Harrison's Log Cabin March—Sheet Music

In this image, William Henry Harrison's log cabin and the flag beside it are composed of sheet music for a march. A march is a military tune; it would have been chosen to communicate Harrison's heroism as an Indian fighter and protector of frontier families.

banking. His proposal for such an "independent subtreasury" aroused intense opposition from the congressional Whigs, who strongly favored the reestablishment of a national bank as the only way to restore economic stability. Whig resistance stalled the Independent Subtreasury Bill for three years; it was not until 1840 that it was enacted into law. In the meantime, the economy had temporarily revived in 1838, only to sink again into a deeper depression the following year.

THE ELECTION OF 1836

Candidate	Party	Popular Vote	Electoral Vote
Van Buren	Democratic	764,198	170
Harrison	Whig	549,508	73
White	Whig	145,342	26
Webster	Whig	41,287	14
Mangum	Independent Democratic	*	11

*Delegates chosen by South Carolina legislature

Van Buren's chances for reelection in 1840 were undoubtedly hurt by the state of the economy. The Whigs had the chance to offer alternative policies that promised to restore prosperity. In 1836, the Whigs had been disorganized and had not fully mastered the new democratic politics. But in 1840, they settled on a single nominee and matched the Democrats in grassroots organization and popular electioneering. The Whigs passed over the true leader of their party, Henry Clay. Instead they found their own Jackson in William Henry Harrison, a military hero of advanced age who was associated in the public mind with the battle of Tippecanoe and the winning of the West. To balance the ticket and increase its appeal in the South, they chose John Tyler of Virginia, a converted states' rights Democrat, to be Harrison's running mate.

Using the slogan "Tippecanoe and Tyler, too," the Whigs pulled out all stops in their bid for the White House. Rallies and parades took place in every locality, complete with posters, placards, campaign hats and emblems, special songs, and even movable log cabins filled with coonskin caps and barrels of cider for the faithful. Imitating the Jacksonian propaganda against Adams in 1828, they portrayed Van Buren as a luxury-loving aristocrat and

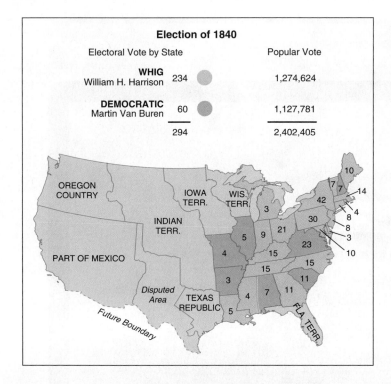

Election of 1840

	Electoral Vote by State		Popular Vote
WHIG William H. Harrison	234		1,274,624
DEMOCRATIC Martin Van Buren	60		1,127,781
	294		2,402,405

compared him with their own homespun candidate. There was an enormous turnout on election day—78 percent of those eligible to vote. When it was over, Harrison had parlayed a narrow edge in the popular vote into a landslide in the electoral college. He carried 19 of the 26 states and won 234 electoral votes to 60 for Van Buren. Buoyed by the electorate's belief that their policies might revive the economy, the Whigs also won control of both houses of Congress.

Contrary to what most historians used to believe, personalities and hoopla did not decide the election of 1840. The economy was in dire straits, and the Whigs, unlike the Democrats, had a program that seemed to offer hope for a solution—the latest version of Henry Clay's American System. Whigs proposed to revive the Bank of the United States in order to restore fiscal stability, raise tariffs to protect manufacturers and manufacturing jobs, and distribute federal revenues to the states for internal improvements that would stimulate commerce and employment. Whig victories in the state and local elections of 1840, many of which preceded the presidential vote, strongly suggest that voters were responding to the party and its program.

Heyday of the Second Party System

What was the two-party system, and how were the parties different?

America's **second party system** came of age in the election of 1840. Unlike the earlier competition between Federalists and Jeffersonian Republicans, the rivalry of Democrats and Whigs made the two-party pattern a normal feature of electoral politics. During the 1840s, the two national parties competed on fairly equal terms for the support of the electorate. Allegiance to one party or the other became an important source of personal identity for many Americans and increased their interest and participation in politics.

In addition to drama and entertainment, the parties offered the voters a real choice of programs and ideologies. Whigs stood for a "positive liberal state"—which meant government had the right and duty to subsidize or protect enterprises that could contribute to general prosperity and economic growth. Democrats normally advocated a "negative liberal state." According to them, government should keep its hands off the economy; only by doing nothing could it avoid favoring special interests and interfering with free competition. They charged that granting subsidies or special charters to any group would create pockets of privilege or monopoly and put ordinary citizens under the thumb of the rich and powerful.

Conflict over economic issues helped determine each party's base of support. In the Whig camp were industrialists who wanted tariff protection, merchants who favored internal improvements as a stimulus to commerce, and farmers and planters who had adapted successfully to a market economy. Democrats appealed mainly to smaller farmers, workers, declining gentry, and emerging entrepreneurs who were excluded from the established commercial groups that stood to benefit most from Whig programs. Democratic rhetoric about monopoly and privilege appealed to those who had mixed or negative feelings about the rise of a national market economy. To some extent, this division pitted richer, more privileged Americans against those who were poorer and less economically or socially secure. But it did not follow class lines in any simple or direct way. Many businessmen were Democrats, and large numbers of wage earners voted Whig. Merchants engaged in the import trade had no use for Whiggish high tariffs, whereas workers in industries clamoring for protection often concluded that their jobs depended on such duties.

Lifestyles and ethnic or religious identities also strongly affected party loyalties. In the northern states, one way to tell the typical Whig from the typical Democrat was to see what each did on Sunday. A person who went to one of the evangelical Protestant churches was very likely to be a Whig. On the other hand, the person who attended a ritualized service—Catholic, Lutheran, or Episcopalian—or did not go to church at all was most probably a Democrat.

The Democrats were the favored party of immigrants, Catholics, freethinkers, backwoods farmers, and those of all classes who enjoyed traditional amusements condemned by the new breed of moral reformers. One thing all these groups had in common was a desire to be left alone, free of restrictions on their freedom to think and behave as they liked. The Whigs enjoyed particularly strong support among Protestants of old stock living in smaller cities, towns, and prosperous rural areas devoted to market farming. In general, the Whigs welcomed a market economy but wanted to restrain the individualism and disorder it created by enforcing cultural and moral values derived from the Puritan tradition.

Nevertheless, party conflict in Congress continued to center on national economic policy. Whigs stood firm for a loose construction of the Constitution and federal support for business and economic development. The Democrats persisted in their defense of strict construction, states' rights, and laissez-faire. Debates over tariffs, banking, and internal improvements remained vital and vigorous during the 1840s.

True believers in both parties saw a deep ideological or moral meaning in the clash over economic issues. Whigs and Democrats had conflicting views of the good society, and their policy positions reflected these differences. The Democrats were the party of white male equality and personal liberty. They perceived the American people as a collection of independent and self-sufficient white men. The role of government was to see to it that the individual was not interfered with—in his economic activity, in his personal habits, and in his religion (or lack of it). Democrats were ambivalent about the rise of the market economy because of the ways it threatened individual independence. The Whigs, on the other hand, were the party of orderly progress under the guidance of an enlightened elite. They believed that the propertied, the well-educated, and the pious were responsible for guiding the masses toward the common good. Believing sincerely that a market economy would benefit everyone in the long run, they had no qualms about the rise of a commercial and industrial capitalism.

Conclusion: Tocqueville's Wisdom

The French traveler Alexis de Tocqueville, author of the most influential account ever written of the emergence of American democracy, visited the United States in 1831 and 1832. He departed well before the presidential election and had relatively little to say about national politics and the formation of political parties. For him, the essence of American democracy was local self-government, such as he observed in the town meetings of New England. The participation of ordinary citizens in the affairs of their communities impressed him greatly, and he praised Americans for not conceding their liberties to a centralized state, as he believed the French had done.

However, Tocqueville was acutely aware of the limitations of American democracy. He knew that the kind of democracy men were practicing was not meant for women. Observing how women were strictly assigned to a separate domestic sphere, he concluded that Americans had never supposed "that democratic principles should undermine the husband's authority and make it doubtful who is in charge of the family." He also believed the nullification crisis foreshadowed destruction of the Union and predicted the problem of slavery would lead eventually to civil war and racial conflict. He noted the power of white supremacy, providing an unforgettable firsthand description of the sufferings of an Indian community in their forced migration to the West, as well as a graphic account of the way free blacks were segregated and driven from the polls in northern cities such as Philadelphia. White Americans, he believed, were deeply prejudiced against people of color, and he doubted it was possible "for a whole people to rise . . . above itself." Perhaps a despot could force the equality and mingling of the races, but

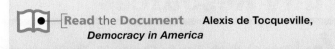 Read the Document   Alexis de Tocqueville, *Democracy in America*

Alexis de Tocqueville (1805–1859) is credited with creating one of the most perceptive and enduring portraits of the American people and their political institutions, and his observations, Democracy in America (2 volumes, 1835–1840), are still read and discussed by Americans today.

"while American democracy remains at the head of affairs, no one would dare attempt any such thing, and it is possible to foresee that the freer the whites in America are, the more they will seek to isolate themselves." His observations have value because of their clear-sighted insistence that the democracy and equality of the Jacksonian era were meant for only some of the people. His belief that problems associated with slavery would endanger the union was keenly prophetic.

Study Resources

 Take the **Study Plan** for **Chapter 10** *The Triumph of White Men's Democracy* on **MyHistoryLab**

TIME LINE

1824 House of Representatives elects John Quincy Adams president

1828 Congress passes "tariff of abominations"; Jackson elected president over J. Q. Adams

1830 Jackson vetoes the Maysville Road bill; Congress passes Indian Removal Act

1831 Jackson reorganizes his cabinet; First national nominating conventions meet

1832 Jackson vetoes the bill rechartering the Bank of the United States; Jackson reelected, defeating Henry Clay (National Republican candidate)

1832–1833 Crisis erupts over South Carolina's attempt to nullify the tariff of 1832

1833 Jackson removes federal deposits from the Bank of the United States

1834 Whig Party comes into existence

1836 Jackson issues "specie circular"; Martin Van Buren elected president

1837 Financial panic occurs, followed by depression lasting until 1843

1840 Congress passes the Independent Subtreasury Bill; Harrison (Whig) defeats Van Buren (Democrat) for the presidency

CHAPTER REVIEW

Democracy in Theory and Practice

 How did the relationship between the government and the people change during this time?

The federal government grew more accountable to the people it represented. "Popular sovereignty" meant that men of modest backgrounds could attain new social status, while cultural expression reflected this "decline in deference." More public officials now had to seek popular election, but public opinion divided over the role of government in the economy. (p. 226)

Jackson and the Politics of Democracy

 What political conflicts did President Andrew and Jackson face and how did he resolve them?

Jackson resolved political conflicts with iron-fisted authority. During the Peggy Eaton affair, he sacked his entire cabinet, and he handled the Indian dilemma by evicting Native Americans from their homeland. During the nullification crisis, he threatened South Carolina with military force. (p. 229)

The Bank War and the Second Party System

 What were the arguments for and against the Bank of the United States?

Nicholas Biddle believed that the Bank of the United States was essential to American economic stability. Jackson believed the federal bank to be unconstitutional and saw it as a personal enemy and "monster corporation." Bank proponents believed that Jackson's "Bank War" exceeded his constitutional authority, and the Whig Party emerged in opposition to his policies. (p. 237)

Heyday of the Second Party System

 What was the two-party system, and how were the parties different?

The "second party system" was the rivalry between Whigs and Democrats. The Whigs included industrialists, merchants, and farmers who favored stimulus to commerce. Democrats included smaller farmers, wage workers, and declining gentry—individuals the new market economy had left behind. The division also marked cultural differences in religion, ethnicity, and lifestyle. (p. 242)

KEY TERMS AND DEFINITIONS

Tariff of abominations   An 1828 protective tariff, or tax on imports, that angered southern free traders. p. 230

Trail of Tears   In the winter of 1838–1839, the Cherokee were forced to evacuate their lands in Georgia and travel under military guard to present-day Oklahoma. Exposure and disease killed roughly one-quarter of the 16,000 forced migrants en route. p. 234

Nullification   The supposed right of any state to declare a federal law inoperative within its boundaries. In 1832, South Carolina nullified the federal tariff. p. 235

Bank War   Between 1832–1836, Andrew Jackson used his presidential power to fight and ultimately destroy the second Bank of the United States. p. 237

Panic of 1837   A financial depression that lasted until the 1840s. p. 240

Second party system   Historians' term for the national two-party rivalry between Democrats and Whigs. The second party system began in the 1830s and ended in the 1850s with the demise of the Whigs and the rise of the Republican Party. p. 242

CRITICAL THINKING QUESTIONS

1. What do you think was the relationship between the new democratic culture and the emergence of the second party system?

2. Do you think Jackson's forceful style of leadership was a good model for the presidency? Should he have deferred more to the states or to Congress in pursuing his policies?

3. Why do you think the people the Democratic Party appealed to were so worried about a national bank?

MyHistoryLab Media Assignments

Find these resources in the Media Assignments folder for Chapter 10 on MyHistoryLab

Democracy in Theory and Practice

Read the **Document**   *Herman Melville, Excerpt from Moby-Dick p. 227*

Jackson and the Politics of Democracy

Read the **Document**   *Andrew Jackson, First Annual Message to Congress (1829) p. 231*

■ **Complete** the **Assignment**   *Racial Identity in a White Man's Democracy p. 232*

View the **Closer Look**   *The Trail of Tears p. 235*

■ **View** the **Closer Look**   *Indian Removals p. 236*

■ **Read** the **Document**   *South Carolina's Ordinance of Nullification p. 237*

The Bank War and the Second Party System

■ **Read** the **Document**   *Andrew Jackson, Veto of the Bank Bill p. 239*

Listen to the **Audio**   *Van Buren p. 240*

■ **View** the **Closer Look**   *General Harrison's Log Cabin March—Sheet Music p. 240*

Heyday of the Second Party System

Read the **Document**   *Alexis de Tocqueville, Democracy in America p. 243*

■ *Indicates Study Plan Media Assignment*

11 Slaves and Masters

Contents and **Learning Objectives**

((•●—[**Listen** to the **Audio File** on **myhistorylab**   Chapter 11 *Slaves and Masters*

Nat Turner's Rebellion: A Turning Point in the Slave South

On August 22, 1831, the worst nightmare of southern slaveholders became reality. A group of slaves in Southampton County, Virginia, rose in open and bloody rebellion. Their leader was Nat Turner, a preacher and prophet who believed God had given him a sign that the time was ripe to strike for freedom; a vision of black and white angels wrestling in the sky had convinced him that divine wrath was about to be visited upon the white oppressor.

Beginning with a few followers and rallying others as he went along, Turner led his band from plantation to plantation and oversaw the killing of nearly sixty whites. After only forty-eight hours, white forces dispersed the rampaging slaves. The rebels were then rounded up and executed, along with dozens of other slaves who were vaguely suspected of complicity. Nat Turner was the last to be captured, and he went to the gallows unrepentant, convinced he had acted in accordance with God's will.

After the initial panic and rumors of a wider insurrection had passed, white Southerners went about making sure such an incident would never happen again. Their anxiety and determination were strengthened by the fact that 1831 also saw the emergence of a more militant northern abolitionism. Just two years after African American abolitionist David Walker published his *Appeal to the Colored Citizens of the World*, calling for blacks to take up arms against slavery, William Lloyd Garrison put out the first issue of his newspaper, *The Liberator*, the first publication by a white author to demand immediate abolition of slavery rather than gradual emancipation. Nat Turner and William Lloyd Garrison were viewed as two prongs of a revolutionary attack on the southern way of life. Although no evidence came to light that Turner was directly influenced by abolitionist propaganda, many whites believed that he must have been or that future rebels might be. Consequently, they launched a massive campaign to quarantine the slaves from possible exposure to antislavery ideas and attitudes.

A series of new laws severely restricted the rights of slaves to move about, assemble without white supervision, or learn to read and write. The wave of repression did not stop at the color line; laws and the threat of mob action prevented white dissenters from

A Ride for Liberty—The Fugitive Slaves by Eastman Johnson depicts a slave family in flight to the North.

Source: Brooklyn Museum of Art. Gift of Gwendolyn O.L. Conkling—40.59a—*A Ride for Liberty—The Fugitive Slaves* by Eastman Johnson, ca. 1862. Oil on paper board, 22 × 26 1/4 in.

publicly criticizing or even questioning the institution of slavery. Loyalty to the region was firmly identified with defense of it, and proslavery agitators sought to create a mood of crisis and danger requiring absolute unity and single-mindedness among the white population. This embattled attitude lay behind the growth of a more militant sectionalism and inspired threats to secede from the Union unless the South's peculiar institution could be made safe from northern or abolitionist attack.

The campaign for repression after the Nat Turner rebellion apparently achieved its original aim. Between 1831 and the Civil War, there were no further uprisings resulting in the mass killing of whites. This fact once led some historians to conclude that African American slaves were brainwashed into a state of docility. But resistance to slavery simply took less dangerous forms. The brute force employed in response to the Turner rebellion and the elaborate precautions taken against its recurrence provided slaves with a more realistic sense of the odds against direct confrontation with white power. As a result, they sought and perfected other methods of asserting their humanity. The heroic effort to endure slavery without surrendering to it gave rise to an African American culture of lasting value.

This culture combined unique family arrangements, religious ideas of liberation, and creative responses to the oppression of servitude. Among white Southerners, the need to police and control the huge population of enslaved people influenced every aspect of daily life and produced an increasingly isolated, divided, and insecure society. While long-standing racial prejudice contributed to the divided society, the determination of whites to preserve the institution of slavery derived in large part from the important role slavery played in the southern economy.

The Divided Society of the Old South

What were the divisions within black society in the Old South?

Slavery would not have lasted as long as it did—and Southerners would not have reacted so strongly to real or imagined threats to its survival—if an influential class of whites had not had a vital and growing economic interest in this form of human exploitation. Since the early colonial period, forced labor had been considered essential to the South's plantation economy. In the period between the 1790s and the Civil War, plantation agriculture expanded enormously, and so did dependence on slave labor; unfree blacks were the only workers readily available to landowners who sought to profit from expanding market opportunities by raising staple crops on a large scale. As slavery increased in its importance to the southern economy and society, the divisions within that society grew increasingly apparent.

Most fundamentally, the fact that all whites were free and most blacks were slaves created a sharp cleavage between the races in southern society. Indeed, during the last decades before the Civil War, the racial divide grew ever more congruent with the split between free and unfree. Yet the overwhelming importance of race gives an impression of a basic equality within the "master race" that some would say is an illusion. The truth may lie somewhere in between. In the language of sociologists, inequality in the **Old South** was determined in two ways: by class (differences in status resulting from unequal access to wealth and productive resources) and by caste (inherited advantages or disadvantages associated with racial ancestry). Awareness of both systems of social ranking is necessary for an understanding of southern society.

White society was divided by class and by region; both were important for determining a white Southerner's relationship to the institution of slavery. The large planters were the dominant class, and nonslaveholders were of lower social rank. Planters (defined as those who owned twenty or more slaves) tended to live in the plantation areas of the "Cotton Belt" stretching from Georgia across Alabama, Mississippi, Louisiana, and Texas, as well as the low country of South Carolina. In upcountry and frontier areas lived yeoman farmers who owned few or no slaves.

In 1860, only one-quarter of all white Southerners belonged to families owning slaves. Even in the Cotton Belt, slaveholders were a minority of whites on the eve of the Civil War—about 40 percent. Planters were the minority of a minority, just 4 percent of the total white population of the South in 1860. Twenty percent of whites owned twenty slaves or less, and the remaining majority, three-fourths of all whites, owned no slaves at all. Thus, southern society was dominated by a planter class that was a numerical and geographically isolated minority; inequalities of class created regional divisions.

There were also divisions within black society. Most African Americans in the South were slaves, but a small number, about 6 percent, were free. Even free blacks faced increasing restrictions on their rights during the antebellum era. Among slaves, the great majority lived on plantations and worked in agriculture, but a small number worked either in industrial jobs or in a variety of tasks in urban settings. Even on plantations, there were some differences in status and experience between field hands and servants who worked in the house or in skilled jobs such as carpentry or blacksmithing. Yet because all blacks, even those who were free, suffered under the yoke of racial prejudice and legal inequality, these diverse experiences did not translate into the kind of class divisions that caused rifts within white southern society. Rather, most blacks shared the goal of ending slavery.

The World of Southern Blacks

What factors made living conditions for southern blacks more or less difficult?

The majority of slaves lived on units of land owned by planters who had twenty or more slaves. On the other hand, only 2.4 percent lived on very large plantations of more than two hundred slaves. Few slaves lived in all-black worlds like those of some Caribbean plantations, where it was possible to create autonomous black communities with little white intervention in daily life. Most Southern slaves lived in close contact with their masters and suffered their masters' strenuous efforts to maintain control over all aspects of their lives.

The masters of these agrarian communities sought to ensure their personal safety and the profitability of their enterprises by using physical and psychological means to make slaves docile and obedient. By word and deed, they tried to convince the slaves that whites were superior and had a right to rule over blacks. Masters also drew constant attention to their awesome power and ability to deal harshly with rebels and malcontents. As increasing numbers of slaves were converted to Christianity and attended white-supervised services, they were forced to hear, repeatedly, that God had commanded slaves to serve and obey their masters.

Despite these pressures, most African Americans managed to retain an inner sense of their own worth and dignity. When conditions were right, they openly asserted their desire for freedom and equality and showed their disdain for white claims that slavery was a "positive good."

Some historians have argued that a stress on the strength of slave culture obscures the harshness and cruelty of the system and its damaging effect on the African American personality. Slavery was often a demoralizing and even brutalizing experience, providing little opportunity for learning about the outside world, developing mental skills, and exercising individual initiative. Compared with serfs in Russia or even with slaves on some of the large sugar plantations of the Caribbean, slaves on the relatively small southern plantations or farms, with their high turnover of personnel, had less chance to develop communal ties of the kind associated with peasant villages. Nevertheless, their sense of being part of a distinctive group with its own beliefs and ways of doing things, fragile and precarious though it may have been, made *psychic survival* possible and helped engender an African American ethnicity that would be a source of strength in future struggles.

Although slave culture did not normally provoke violent resistance to the slaveholders' regime, the inner world that slaves made for themselves gave them the spiritual strength to thwart the masters' efforts to take over their hearts and minds. After emancipation, this resilient cultural heritage would combine with the tradition of open protest created by rebellious slaves and free black abolitionists to inspire and sustain new struggles for equality.

Slaves' Daily Life and Labor

Slaves' daily life varied enormously depending on the region in which they lived and the type of plantation or farm on which they worked. By the time of the Civil War, 90 percent of the South's four million slaves worked on plantations or farms, with the remainder working in industry or in cities. Slaves were close to half of the total population in the "Black Belt" or "Cotton Belt" of the lower South—South Carolina, Georgia, Alabama, Mississippi, Louisiana, Arkansas, and Texas—and many lived in plantation regions with a slave majority. In the upper South—North Carolina, Virginia, Maryland, Delaware, Kentucky, Tennessee, and Missouri—whites outnumbered slaves by more than three to one, and slaves were far more likely to live on farms where they worked side by side with an owner.

On large plantations in the Cotton Belt, most slaves worked in "gangs" under an overseer. White overseers, sometimes helped by black "drivers," enforced a workday from sunup to sundown, six days a week. Cotton cultivation required year-round labor, so there was never a slack season under "King Cotton." Enslaved women and children were expected to work in the fields as well, often bringing babies and young children to the fields where they could be cared for by older children, and nursed by their mothers during brief breaks. Some older children worked in "trash gangs," doing lighter tasks such as weeding and yard cleaning. Life on the sugar plantations was even harsher, sometimes entailing work well into the night during the harvest season. Mortality rates in some parts of sugar-growing Louisiana were very high.

In the low country of South Carolina and Georgia, slaves who cultivated rice worked under a "task system" that gave them more control over the pace of labor. With less supervision, many were able to complete their tasks within an eight-hour day. Likewise, slaves who lived on small farms often worked side by side with their masters rather than in large groups of slaves, although such intimacy did not necessarily mean a leveling of power relationships. Yet despite masters' efforts to control the pace of work, even under the gang system, slaves resisted working on "clock" time, enforcing customary rights to take breaks and especially to take Sunday off completely.

While about three-quarters of slaves were field workers, slaves performed many other kinds of labor. They dug ditches, built houses, worked on boats and in mills (often hired out by their masters for a year at a time), and labored as house servants. Some slaves also worked within the slave community as preachers, caretakers of children, and healers, especially women. While white masters sometimes treated domestic workers or other personal servants as having a special status, it would be a mistake to assume that slaves shared their ranking system. Evidence suggests that those with the highest status within slave communities were preachers and healers, people whose special skills and knowledge directly benefited their communities.

A small number of slaves, about 5 percent, worked in industry in the South. The closest thing to a factory in the Old South was the Tredegar Iron Works in Richmond, Virginia, staffed almost entirely by slaves. Slaves also built most of the railroads that existed in the southern states, but these were few relative to the North before the Civil War. Overall, the South remained predominantly agricultural throughout the antebellum era, and most slaves worked in the fields.

Slaves in cities took on a wider range of jobs than plantation slaves, and in general enjoyed more autonomy. Some urban slaves even lived apart from their masters and hired out their own time, returning a portion of their wages to their owners. They also worked in eating and drinking establishments, hotels, and as skilled laborers in tradesmen's shops.

In addition to the work they did for their masters in the fields or in other jobs, most slaves kept gardens or small farm plots to supplement their daily food rations. They also fished, hunted, and trapped animals. Many slaves also worked "overtime" for their own masters on Sundays or holidays in exchange for money or goods, or hired out their overtime hours to others. This "underground economy" suggests slaves' overpowering desire to provide for their families, sometimes even raising enough funds to purchase their freedom.

Slave Families, Kinship, and Community

More than any other, the African American family was the institution that prevented slavery from becoming utterly demoralizing. Contrary to what historians and sociologists used to believe, slaves had a strong and abiding sense of family and kinship. The nature of the families or households that predominated on particular plantations or farms varied. On large plantations with relatively stable slave populations, a substantial majority of slave children lived in two-parent households, and many marriages lasted for as long as twenty to thirty years. They were more often broken up by the death or sale of one of the partners than by voluntary dissolution of the union. Here mothers, fathers, and children were closely bonded, and parents shared child-rearing responsibilities (within the limits allowed by the masters). Marital fidelity was encouraged by masters who believed that stable unions produced more offspring and by Christian churches that viewed adultery and divorce as sinful.

📖 Read the Document   Overseer's Report from
Chicora Wood Plantation

Chicora Wood was an extremely successful rice plantation in South Carolina owned by Robert Allston. Allston owned several plantations and, of course, many slaves. In 1850 he owned 401 slaves; by 1860 that number had increased to 603.

But in areas where most slaves lived on farms or small plantations, and especially in areas of the upper South where the trading and hiring out of slaves was frequent, a different pattern seems to have prevailed. Under these circumstances, slaves frequently had spouses who resided on other plantations or farms, often some distance away, and ties between husbands and wives were looser and more fragile. The result was that female-headed families were the norm, and responsibility for child rearing was vested in mothers, assisted in most cases by female relatives and friends. Mother-centered families with weak conjugal ties were a natural response to the infrequent presence of fathers and to the prospect of their being moved or sold beyond visiting distance. Where the breakup of unions by sale or relocation could be expected at any time, it did not pay to invest all of one's emotions in a conjugal relationship. But whether the basic family form was nuclear or matrifocal (female-headed), the ties that it created were infinitely precious to its members. Masters acquired great leverage over the behavior of slaves by invoking the threat of family breakup through sale.

The terrible anguish that usually accompanied the breakup of families through sale showed the depth of kinship feelings. Masters knew that the first place to look for a fugitive was in the neighborhood of a family member who had been sold away. Indeed, many slaves tried to shape their own sales in order to be sold with family members or to the same neighborhood. These efforts were fraught with danger. As one ex-slave recalled, "The mistress asked her which she loved the best her mammy or her daddy and she thought it would please her daddy to say that she loved him the best so she said 'my daddy' but she regretted it very much when she found this caused her to be sold [along with her father] the

next day." Harriet Jacobs, an escaped slave famous for her published autobiography, hid in her grandmother's attic for seven years while attempting to secure her children's freedom. (For more on Harriet Jacobs, see the Feature Essay "Harriet Jacobs and Maria Norcom: Women of Southern Households," pp. 252–253.)

Feelings of kinship and mutual obligation extended beyond the primary family. Grandparents, uncles, aunts, and even cousins were often known to slaves through direct contact or family lore. A sense of family continuity over three or more generations was revealed in the names that slaves gave to their children or took for themselves. Infants were frequently named after grandparents, and those slaves who assumed surnames often chose that of an ancestor's owner rather than the family name of a current master.

Kinship ties were not limited to blood relations. When families were broken up by sale, individual members who found themselves on plantations far from home were likely to be "adopted" into new kinship networks. Orphans or children without responsible parents were quickly absorbed without prejudice into new families. Soon after the Civil War, one Reconstruction official faced an elderly ex-slave named Roger, who demanded land "to raise crop on" for his "family of sixty 'parents,' that is, relations, children included." A family with sixty parents made no sense to this official, but it made sense in a community in which families were defined by ties of affection and cooperation rather than "blood" relation.

For some purposes, all the slaves on a plantation were in reality members of a single extended family, as their forms of address clearly reveal. Elderly slaves were addressed by everyone else as "uncle" and "aunty," and younger unrelated slaves commonly called each other "brother" or "sister." Strong kinship ties, whether real or fictive, meant slaves could depend on one another. The kinship network also provided a vehicle for the transmission of African American folk traditions from one generation to the next.

African American Religion

From the realm of culture and fundamental beliefs, African Americans drew the strength to hold their heads high and look beyond their immediate condition. Religion was the cornerstone of this emerging African American culture. Black Christianity may have owed its original existence to the efforts of white missionaries, but it was far from a mere imitation of white religious forms and beliefs. This distinctive variant of evangelical Protestantism incorporated elements of African religion and emphasized those portions of the Bible that spoke to the aspirations of an enslaved people thirsting for freedom.

Most slaves did not encounter Christianity in a church setting. There were a few independent black churches in the antebellum South, which mainly served free blacks and urban slaves with indulgent masters. Free blacks who seceded from white congregations that discriminated against them formed a variety of autonomous Baptist groups as well as southern branches of the highly successful **African Methodist Episcopal (AME) Church**, organized as a national denomination under the leadership of the Reverend Richard Allen of Philadelphia in 1816. But the mass of blacks did not have access to the independent churches.

Plantation slaves who were exposed to Christianity either attended the neighboring white churches or worshiped at home.

On large estates, masters or white missionaries often conducted Sunday services. But the narratives and recollections of ex-slaves reveal that white-sanctioned religious activity was only a superficial part of the slaves' spiritual life. The true slave religion was practiced at night, often secretly, and was led by black preachers. Historian Albert J. Raboteau has described this underground black Christianity as "the invisible institution."

This covert slave religion was a highly emotional affair that featured singing, shouting, and dancing. In some ways, the atmosphere resembled a backwoods revival meeting. But much of what went on was actually an adaptation of African religious beliefs and customs. The chanting mode of preaching—with the congregation responding at regular intervals—and the expression of religious feelings through rhythmic movements, especially the counterclockwise movement known as the ring shout, had clear African origins. The black conversion experience was normally a state of ecstasy more akin to possession by spirits—a major form of African religious expression—than to the agony of those

"struck down" at white revivals. The emphasis on sinfulness and fear of damnation that were core themes of white evangelicalism played a lesser role among blacks. For them, religion was more an affirmation of the joy of life than a rejection of worldly pleasures and temptations.

Slave sermons and religious songs spoke directly to the plight of a people in bondage and implicitly asserted their right to be free. The most popular of all biblical subjects was the deliverance of the children of Israel from slavery in Egypt in the book of Exodus. In one moving spiritual, God commands Moses to "tell Old Pharaoh" to "let my people Go." Many sermons and songs refer to the crossing of Jordan and the arrival in the Promised Land. "Oh Canaan, sweet Canaan, I am bound for the land of Canaan" and "Oh brothers, don't get weary. . . . We'll land on Canaan's shore" are typical of lines from spirituals known to have been sung by slaves. Other songs invoke the liberation theme in different ways. One recalls that Jesus had "set poor sinners free," and another prophesies, "We'll soon be free, when the Lord will call us home."

📖⊙ **Read** the **Document**   **Frances E. W. Harper, "The Slave Mother"**

On large plantations, slave men and women formed stable monogamous unions that often lasted until the couple was broken up by the death or sale of one of the partners. This painting by Christian Mayr portrays a slave wedding celebrated in White Sulphur Springs, Virginia, in 1838. The wedding couple wears white attire.

Feature Essay

Harriet Jacobs and Maria Norcom
Women of Southern Households

This 1836 engraving from an antislavery novel depicts a plantation mistress scolding a slave woman while the master looks on. Though white women were also subjugated to the authority of white men in southern society, the divide of race prevented plantation ladies and slaves from finding potential solidarity as women.

Harriet Jacobs, born enslaved in North Carolina in 1813, became a slave in James and Maria Norcom's household in 1825. James began to "whisper foul words" in Harriet's ears when she was a young teenager. Harriet had no one to whom she could turn, except for her free black grandmother, who lived in the town. Although her grandmother had been a slave, Harriet's master "dreaded her scorching rebukes" and furthermore "he did not wish to have his villainy made public." For a time, this wish to "keep up some outward show of decency" protected Harriet.

Harriet Jacobs's grandmother was an unusual woman, who had worked extra for years to buy her children's freedom, only to be cheated out of her earnings at the end. Like most free black women, Harriet's grandmother was the unmarried head of her own household, separated long ago from the father of her children. Running their own households gave some free black women a measure of autonomy, but also left them with little support in the daily struggle against poverty and racism.

Maria Norcom, as the wife of a prominent doctor and large plantation owner, lived a life very different from Harriet's or her grandmother's. Yet it was not the life of carefree luxury sometimes portrayed in movies and books about the Old South. Compared to poorer women in the South, Maria had more access to education and periods of recreation and relaxation. But as a lady of the upper class, she was expected to master strict rules of womanhood that demanded moral purity and virtue. She also had to learn the personal and managerial skills necessary to oversee a household staffed by slaves.

Most southern white women worked hard to keep households and families together, and they all lived within a social system that denied them legal rights by placing them under the domination of husbands and fathers. James Norcom's behavior, while it certainly violated his vows of marriage, was not egregious enough to have won Maria a divorce under the laws of North Carolina.

Whether they were rich or poor, free or enslaved, women were, to a large degree, defined by their relationship to the head of the household, nearly always a white man. Although there were expectations that husbands would protect and care for their wives, women had little recourse against husbands who departed from those expectations. For example, Marion S. D. Converse, a woman from a prominent South Carolina family, dreaded her abusive second husband, Augustus. Through years of beatings and jealous tirades, Marion was unable to escape the bonds of marriage because Augustus's deplorable conduct fell short of legal grounds for divorce in South Carolina (only abandonment or impotence). Yet Marion Converse was able to gain aid and protection from her prominent family, who shielded her from the worst consequences of an abusive marriage.

When Maria Norcom discovered her husband's overtures toward Harriet, she was distraught and took Harriet to sleep in her own room. Yet, as Harriet later described it, Maria "pitied herself as a martyr; but she was incapable of feeling for the condition of shame and misery in which her unfortunate, helpless slave was placed." Harriet often woke to find Maria bending over her, and came to fear for her safety around this "jealous mistress." Harriet Jacobs's and Maria Norcom's story illustrates that planters ruled their wives as well as their slaves. All southern women were embedded in a social system that gave authority over their lives and choices to men. Despite this commonality, few women were able to reach across the divides of race and class to recognize these similarities. Tormented by jealousy and humiliation, Maria came to blame the slave rather than her husband for their intimacy, imagining that Harriet herself had seduced him.

Harriet managed to elude her master's advances, in part due to Maria's vigilance. Enslaved women such as Harriet Jacobs were the most vulnerable of southern women. They were subject to a level of violence and sexual assault that was unknown to other women in the South; and when they were victims of violence, they lacked even the limited legal defenses that were open to poor white women. Because black women were considered unable to give or withhold consent, it was not a crime to rape a black woman. And had Harriet fought back physically against her master's advances, she risked criminal prosecution and even death. When the slave Celia killed the master who had been raping her for years, her court-appointed lawyer argued that she should not be criminally liable, based on a Georgia statute allowing women to use force to defend their "honor" against a rapist. The court, however, decreed that black women were not "women" within the meaning of the statute. Celia had no honor that the law recognized. She was thus convicted of murder, sentenced to death, and hanged.

Excluding black women from the laws of rape also reinforced common images of black women as either sexually aggressive "Jezebels" or sexless, nurturing "Mammies." The first stereotype justified the sexual exploitation of slave women and the second fed the slaveowners' fantasy that their slaves loved and cared for them. Of course, neither of these images corresponded to the realities and hardships of slave life. Enslaved women were often assigned backbreaking labor that paid little attention to common distinctions about "women's work." They were expected to do all of the normal tasks assigned to women—sewing, washing, child care—as well as working a full day in the fields. Despite these brutal conditions, slave women organized communities and households, and tried to protect them against the worst excesses of the slave system. Harriet and her grandmother were involved in a complicated network of extended kin, and invested a great deal of energy in protecting brothers and sons from sale "up the river."

Harriet eventually escaped from the Norcoms in 1835, hiding in her grandmother's attic for seven years. Escaped from the bonds of slavery, Harriet eventually joined the battle to abolish it. Her book, *Incidents in the Life of a Slave Girl, the Autobiography of Linda Brent*, was published in 1861, with the help of abolitionist novelist Lydia Maria Child. For many years, critics dismissed the narrative as either a work of fiction or the product of Child's own pen; but historians today have laid those charges to rest, recognizing Harriet Jacobs's important contribution to the struggle against slavery and to American literature.

We know much less about what happened to Maria Norcom, who neither kept a diary nor wrote her own story. All that we know is that she continued in her unhappy marriage to James Norcom. Her daughter Mary Matilda, when she came of age, pursued and attempted to reclaim Harriet as her slave under the Fugitive Slave Act. To thwart this effort, Harriet allowed an abolitionist friend to buy her and set her free.

In slaveholding households like that of the Norcoms, all the women, whether white or black, free or enslaved, were subject to the will of the master of the household. Most southern women depended on white men legally and socially, giving them little recourse against men like James Norcom, who burst the bounds of "decency." Despite their shared submission to James, an impassable gulf separated Harriet and Maria, and its name was race. After the Civil War, southern women, white and black, reorganized their households in a changed society, but it would still be another century before they began to bridge that gulf.

QUESTIONS FOR DISCUSSION

1. How did race affect the lives of southern women like Harriet Jacobs and Maria Norcom?

2. Why did slaveholding white men like James Norcom have so much power over their slaves and wives?

3. Why were male slaveholders able to sexually abuse black women without having to face legal consequences in the South?

((•●—| Listen to the **Audio File**   **When the Roll is Called up Yonder**

Free blacks in the North established African Methodist Episcopalian churches like the Bethel A.M.E. Church in Philadelphia, founded by the minister Richard Allen. Today, it is the oldest church property continuously owned by African Americans.

Most of the songs of freedom and deliverance can be interpreted as referring exclusively to religious salvation and the afterlife—and this was undoubtedly how slaves hoped their masters would understand them. But the slaves did not forget that God had once freed a people from slavery in this life and punished their masters. The Bible thus gave African Americans the hope that they, as a people, would repeat the experience of the Israelites and be delivered from bondage. Besides being the basis for a deep-rooted hope for eventual freedom, religion helped the slaves maintain their sense of inner worth. Unless their masters were unusually pious, religious slaves could regard themselves as superior to their owners. Some slaves even believed that all whites were damned because of their unjust treatment of blacks, while all slaves would be saved because any sins they committed were the involuntary result of their condition.

More important, the "invisible institution" of the church gave African Americans a chance to create and control a world of their own. Preachers, elders, and other leaders of slave congregations could acquire a sense of status within their own community that had not been conferred by whites; the singers who improvised the spirituals found an outlet for independent artistic expression. Although religion seldom inspired slaves to open rebellion, it must be regarded as a prime source of resistance to the dehumanizing effects of enslavement.

Resistance and Rebellion

Open rebellion, the bearing of arms against the oppressors by organized groups of slaves, was the most dramatic and clear-cut form of slave resistance. In the period between 1800 and 1831, a number of slaves participated in revolts that showed their willingness to risk their lives in a desperate bid for liberation. In 1800,

a Virginia slave named Gabriel Prosser mobilized a large band of his fellows to march on Richmond. But a violent storm dispersed "Gabriel's army" and enabled whites to suppress the uprising without any loss of white life.

In 1811, several hundred Louisiana slaves marched on New Orleans brandishing guns, waving flags, and beating drums. It took three hundred soldiers of the U.S. Army, aided by armed planters and militiamen, to stop the advance and to end the rebellion. In 1822, whites in Charleston, South Carolina, uncovered an extensive and well-planned conspiracy, organized by a free black man named Denmark Vesey, to seize local armories, arm the slave population, and take possession of the city. Although the **Vesey conspiracy** was nipped in the bud, it convinced South Carolinians that blacks were "the Jacobins of the country [a reference to the militants of the French Revolution] against whom we should always be on guard."

Only a year after the Vesey affair, whites in Norfolk County, Virginia, complained of the activities of a marauding band of runaway slaves that had killed several whites. The militia was sent out and captured the alleged leader—a fugitive of several years' standing named Bob Ferebee. Groups of runaways, who hid for years in places such as the Great Dismal Swamp of Virginia, continued to raid plantations throughout the antebellum period and were inclined to fight to the death rather than be recaptured.

As we have already seen, the most bloody and terrifying of all slave revolts was the Nat Turner insurrection of 1831. Although it was the last slave rebellion of this kind during the pre–Civil War period, armed resistance had not ended. Indeed, the most sustained and successful effort of slaves to win their freedom by force of arms took place in Florida between 1835 and 1842, when hundreds of black fugitives fought in the Second Seminole War alongside the Indians who had given them a haven. The Seminoles were resisting removal to Oklahoma, but for the blacks who took part, the war was a struggle for their own freedom, and when it ended, most of them were allowed to accompany their Indian allies to the trans-Mississippi West.

Only a tiny fraction of all slaves ever took part in organized acts of violent resistance. Most realized that the odds against a successful revolt were very high, and bitter experience had shown them that the usual outcome was death to the rebels. As a consequence, they characteristically devised safer or more ingenious ways to resist white dominance.

One way of protesting against slavery was to run away, and thousands of slaves showed their discontent and desire for freedom in this fashion. Most fugitives never got beyond the neighborhood of the plantation; after "lying out" for a time, they would return, often after negotiating immunity from punishment. But many escapees remained free for years by hiding in swamps or other remote areas, and a fraction made it to freedom in the North or Mexico. Some fugitives stowed away aboard ships heading to northern ports; others traveled overland for hundreds of miles, avoiding patrols and inquisitive whites by staying off the roads and moving only at night. Some were able to escape with the help of the **Underground Railroad**, an informal network of sympathetic free blacks (and a few whites) who helped fugitives make their way North. Light-skinned blacks sometimes made it to freedom by passing for white, and one resourceful slave even had himself packed in a box and shipped to the North.

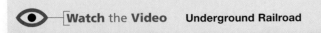

Watch the Video   Underground Railroad

NEGROES ESCAPING OUT OF SLAVERY—Sketched by A. R. Waud.—

Between 1815 and 1860, it is estimated that 130,000 refugees (out of 4 million slaves) escaped the slave South on the "Underground Railroad." The railroad had as many as 3,200 active workers. By the 1850s, substantial numbers of Northerners had been in open violation of federal law by hiding runaways for a night.

The typical fugitive was a young, unmarried male from the upper South. For the majority of slaves, however, flight was not a real option. Either they lived too deep in the South to have any chance of reaching free soil, or they were reluctant to leave family and friends behind. Slaves who did not or could not leave the plantation had to register their opposition to the masters' regime while remaining enslaved.

The normal way of expressing discontent was engaging in a kind of indirect or passive resistance. Many slaves worked slowly and inefficiently, not because they were naturally lazy (as whites supposed) but as a gesture of protest or alienation as conveyed in the words of a popular slave song, "You may think I'm working/But I ain't." Others withheld labor by feigning illness or injury. Stealing provisions—a very common activity on most plantations—was another way to show contempt for authority. According to the code of ethics prevailing in the slave quarters, theft from the master was no sin; it was simply a way for slaves to get a larger share of the fruits of their own labors.

Substantial numbers of slaves committed acts of sabotage. Tools and agricultural implements were deliberately broken, animals were willfully neglected or mistreated, and barns or other outbuildings were set afire. Often masters could not identify the culprits because slaves did not readily inform on one another. The ultimate act of clandestine resistance was poisoning the master's food. Some slaves, especially the "conjure" men and women who practiced a combination of folk medicine and witchcraft, knew how to mix rare, virtually untraceable poisons; and a suspiciously large number of plantation whites became suddenly and mysteriously ill. Sometimes whole families died from obscure "diseases" that did not infect the slave quarters.

The basic attitude behind such actions was revealed in the folktales that slaves passed down from generation to generation. The famous Brer Rabbit stories showed how a small, apparently defenseless animal could overcome a bigger and stronger one through cunning and deceit. Although these tales often had an African origin, they also served as an allegory for the black view of the master-slave relationship. Other stories—which were not told in front of whites—openly portrayed the slave as a clever trickster outwitting the master. In one such tale, a slave reports to his master that seven hogs have died of "malitis." Thinking this is a dread disease, the master agrees to let the slaves have all the meat. What really happened, so the story goes, was this: "One of the strongest Negroes got up early in the morning" and "skitted to the hog pen with a heavy mallet in his hand. When he tapped Mister Hog 'tween the eyes with that mallet, 'malitis' set in mighty quick."

Free Blacks in the Old South

Free blacks occupied an increasingly precarious position in the antebellum South. White Southerners' fears of free blacks inciting slave revolts, and their reaction to attacks by abolitionists, led slaveholders after 1830 increasingly to defend slavery as a positive good rather than a necessary evil. Southerners articulated this defense of slavery in terms of race, emphasizing a dual image of the black person: Under the "domesticating" influence of a white master, the slave was a child, a happy Sambo; outside of this influence, he was a savage beast.

Beginning in the 1830s, all of the southern states passed a series of laws cracking down on free blacks. These laws forced free people of color to register or have white guardians who were responsible for their behavior. Invariably, free blacks were required to carry papers proving their free status, and in some states, they had to obtain official permission to move from one county to another. Licensing laws were invoked to exclude blacks from several occupations, and attempts by blacks to hold meetings or form organizations were frequently blocked by the authorities. Sometimes vagrancy and apprenticeship laws were used to force free blacks into a state of economic dependency barely distinguishable from outright slavery.

Although beset by special problems of their own, most free blacks identified with the suffering of the slaves; when circumstances allowed, they protested against the peculiar institution and worked for its abolition. Many of them had once been slaves themselves or were the children of slaves; often they had close relatives who were still in bondage. Furthermore, they knew that the discrimination from which they suffered was rooted in slavery and the racial attitudes that accompanied it. So long as slavery existed, their own rights were likely to be denied, and even their freedom was at risk; former slaves who could not prove they had been legally freed were subject to reenslavement. This threat existed even in the North: Under federal fugitive slave laws, escaped slaves could be returned to bondage. Even blacks who were born free were not perfectly safe. Kidnapping or fraudulent seizure by slave catchers was always a possibility.

Because of the elaborate system of control and surveillance, free blacks in the South were in a relatively weak position to work against slavery. The case of Denmark Vesey showed that a prosperous and well-situated free black might make a stand in the struggle for freedom, but it also revealed the dangers of revolutionary activity and the odds against success. The wave of repression against the free black population that followed the Vesey conspiracy heightened the dangers and increased the odds. Consequently, most free blacks found that survival depended on creating the impression of loyalty to the planter regime. In some parts of the lower South, groups of relatively privileged free people of color, mostly of racially mixed origin, were sometimes persuaded that it was to their advantage to preserve the status quo. As skilled artisans and small-business owners dependent on white favors and patronage, they had little incentive to risk

Henry "Box" Brown emerges from the crate in which he escaped from slavery in Richmond, Virginia, to freedom in Philadelphia.

everything by taking the side of the slaves. In southern Louisiana, there was even a small group of mulatto planters who lived in luxury, supported by the labor of other African Americans.

However, although some free blacks were able to create niches of relative freedom, their position in southern society became increasingly precarious. Beginning in the 1830s, southern whites sought to draw the line between free and unfree more firmly as a line between black and white. Free blacks were an anomaly in this system; increasingly, the southern answer was to exclude, degrade, and even enslave those free people of color who remained within their borders. Just before the outbreak of the Civil War, a campaign developed in some southern states to carry the pattern of repression and discrimination to its logical conclusion: Several state legislatures proposed laws giving free people of color the choice of emigrating from the state or being enslaved.

White Society in the Antebellum South

What divided and united white southern society?

Those who know the Old South only from modern novels, films, and television programs are likely to envision a land filled with majestic plantations. Pillared mansions behind oak-lined carriageways are portrayed as scenes of aristocratic splendor, where courtly gentlemen and elegant ladies, attended by hordes of uniformed black servants, lived in refined luxury. It is easy to conclude from such images that the typical white Southerner was an aristocrat who belonged to a family that owned large numbers of slaves.

The great houses existed and some wealthy slaveholders did maintain as aristocratic a lifestyle as was ever seen in the United States. But census returns indicate that this was the world of only a small percentage of slaveowners and a minuscule portion of the total white population. The number of large planters who had the means to build great houses and entertain lavishly, those who owned at least fifty slaves, comprised fewer than 1 percent of all whites.

Most southern whites were nonslaveholding yeoman farmers. Yet even those who owned no slaves grew to depend on slavery in other ways, whether economically, because they hired slaves, or psychologically, because having a degraded class of blacks below them made them feel better about their own place in society. However, the class divisions between slaveholders and nonslaveholders did contribute to the political rifts that became increasingly apparent on the eve of the Civil War.

The Planters' World

The great planters, although few in number, had a weighty influence on southern life. They set the tone and values for much of the rest of society, especially for the less wealthy slaveowners who sought to imitate the planters' style of living to the extent that resources allowed. Although many of them were too busy tending to their plantations to become openly involved in politics, wealthy planters held more than their share of high offices and often exerted a decisive influence on public policy. Within those regions of the South in which plantation agriculture predominated, they were a ruling class in every sense of the term.

Contrary to legend, a majority of the great planters of the pre–Civil War period were self-made rather than descendants of the old colonial gentry. Some were ambitious young men who married planters' daughters. Others started as lawyers and used their fees and connections to acquire plantations.

As the Cotton Kingdom spread westward to Alabama, Mississippi, and Louisiana, a greater proportion of the largest slaveholders were men who began their careers in commerce, land speculation, banking, and even slave trading. Stephen Duncan of Mississippi, probably the most prosperous cotton planter in the South during the 1850s (he owned eight plantations and 1018 slaves), had invested the profits from his banking operations. Among the largest sugar planters of southern Louisiana at this time were Maunsel White and John Burnside, Irish immigrants who had prospered as New Orleans merchants, and Isaac Franklin, former king of the slave traders.

To be successful, a planter had to be a shrewd entrepreneur who kept a careful eye on the market, the prices of slaves and land, and the extent of his indebtedness. Reliable "factors"—the agents who marketed the crop and provided advances against future sales—could assist him in making decisions, but a planter who failed to spend a good deal of time with his account books could end up in serious trouble. Managing the slaves and plantation production was also difficult and time consuming, even when overseers were available to supervise day-to-day activities. Hence few planters could be the men of leisure featured in the popular image of the Old South.

Likewise, despite typical images of women in the Old South—full hoop skirts and wide front porches, elaborate parties in plantation houses dripping with Spanish moss, elegant ladies gossiping over tea—few women fit the stereotype of the southern belle. Not only were plantation mistresses a tiny minority of the women who lived and worked in the slave states before the Civil War, but even those who were part of the planter elite rarely lived lives of leisure. (See the Feature Essay "Harriet Jacobs and Maria Norcom: Women of Southern Households," pp. 252–253.)

Some of the richest and most secure plantation families did aspire to live in the manner of a traditional landed aristocracy. A few were so successful that they were accepted as equals by visiting English nobility. Big houses, elegant carriages, fancy-dress balls, and excessive numbers of house servants all reflected aristocratic aspirations. The romantic cult of chivalry, described in the popular novels of Sir Walter Scott, was in vogue in some circles and even led to the nonviolent reenactment of medieval tournaments. Dueling, despite efforts to repress it, remained the standard way to settle "affairs of honor" among gentlemen. Another sign of gentility was the tendency of planters' sons to avoid "trade" as a primary or secondary career in favor of law or the military. Planters' daughters were trained from girlhood to play the piano, speak French, dress in the latest fashions, and sparkle in the drawing room or on the dance floor. The aristocratic style originated among the older gentry of the seaboard slave states, but by the 1840s and 1850s it had spread southwest as a second generation of wealthy planters began to displace the rough-hewn pioneers of the Cotton Kingdom.

Planters, Racism, and Paternalism

No assessment of the planters' outlook or "worldview" can be made without considering their relations with their slaves. Planters, by the census definition, owned more than half of all the slaves in the South and set standards for treatment and management. It is clear from their private letters and journals, as well as from proslavery propaganda, that most planters liked to think of themselves as benevolent masters. Rather than seeing slavery as a brutal form of economic exploitation, they argued that blacks needed the slave system to ensure that they were cared for and protected. Often they referred to their slaves as if they were members of an extended patriarchal family—a favorite phrase was "our people." According to this ideology of paternalism, blacks were a race of perpetual children requiring constant care and supervision by superior whites. Paternalistic rhetoric increased greatly after abolitionists began to charge that most slaveholders were sadistic monsters.

Paternalism went hand in hand with racism. In a typical proslavery apology, Georgia lawyer Thomas Reade Cobb wrote that "a state of bondage, so far from doing violence to the law of [the African's] nature, develops and perfects it; and that, in that state, he enjoys the greatest amount of happiness, and arrives at the greatest degree of perfection of which his nature is capable." Slaveholders justified slavery by the supposed mental and moral inferiority of Africans. It was only in the 1830s and 1840s that a full-blown modern racism developed on both sides of the Atlantic. Racial "scientists" developed theories relating skull size to mental ability, and some proslavery apologists even developed religious theories of "polygenesis," arguing that blacks were not descended from Adam and Eve. This racial ideology helped slaveholders believe that a benevolent Christian could justly enslave another human being.

While some historians have argued that paternalism was part of a social system that was organized like a family hierarchy rather than a brutal, profit-making arrangement, there was no inconsistency between planters' paternalism and capitalism. Slaves were themselves a form of capital; that is, they were both the main tools of production for a booming economy as well as an asset in themselves valuable for their rising prices, like shares in the stock market today. The ban on the transatlantic slave trade in 1808 was effective enough to make it economically necessary to the continuation of slavery for the slave population to reproduce itself. Rising slave prices also inhibited extreme physical abuse and deprivation. It was in the interest of masters to see that their slave property remained in good enough condition to work hard and produce large numbers of children. Furthermore, a good return on their investment enabled southern planters to spend more on slave maintenance than could masters in less prosperous plantation economies.

Much of the slaveholders' "paternalist" writing discussed "the coincidence of humanity and interest," by which they meant that treating slaves well (including firm discipline) was in their best economic interest. Thus, there was a grain of truth in the planters' claim that their slaves were relatively well provided for. Recent comparative studies have suggested that North American slaves of the pre–Civil War period enjoyed a somewhat higher standard of living than those in other New World slave societies, such as Brazil and the West Indian sugar islands. Their food, clothing, and shelter were normally sufficient to sustain life and labor at slightly above a bare subsistence level, and the rapid increase of the slave population in the Old South stands in sharp contrast to the usual failure of slave populations to reproduce themselves.

But some planters did not behave rationally. They failed to control their tempers or tried to work more slaves than they could afford to maintain. Consequently, there were more cases of physical abuse and undernourishment than a purely economic calculation would lead us to expect.

The testimony of slaves themselves and of some independent white observers suggests that masters of large plantations generally did not have close and intimate relationships with the mass of field slaves. The kind of affection and concern associated with a father figure appears to have been limited mainly to relationships with a few favored house servants or other elite slaves, such as drivers and highly skilled artisans. The field hands on large estates dealt mostly with overseers who were hired or fired because of their ability to meet production quotas.

The limits of paternalism were revealed in the slave market. Planters who looked down on slave traders as less than respectable gentlemen nevertheless broke apart families by selling slaves "down river" when they found themselves in need of money. Even slaveholders who claimed not to participate in the slave market themselves often mortgaged slaves to secure debts; as many as one-third of all slave sales in the South were court-ordered sheriff's auctions when such masters defaulted on their debts.

While paternalism may have moderated planters' behavior to some extent, especially when economic self-interest reinforced "humanity," it is important to remember that most departures from unremitting labor and harsh conditions were concessions wrested from owners through slaves' defiance and resistance, at great personal risk.

Furthermore, when they were being most realistic, planters conceded that the ultimate basis of their authority was the slaves' fear of force and intimidation, rather than the natural obedience resulting from a loving parent-child relationship. Scattered among

their statements are admissions that they relied on the "principle of fear," "more and more on the power of fear," or—most graphically—that it was necessary "to make them stand in fear." Devices for inspiring fear included whipping and the threat of sale away from family and friends. Planters' manuals and instructions to overseers reveal that certain and swift punishment for any infraction of the rules or even for a surly attitude was the preferred method for maintaining order and productivity.

When masters did abuse their power by torturing, killing, or raping their slaves, the victims had little recourse. Slaves lacked legal protection against such cruelty because their testimony was not accepted in court. Abolitionists were correct in condemning slavery on principle because it gave one human being nearly absolute power over another. This system was bound to result in atrocities and violence.

Small Slaveholders

As we have seen, the great majority of slaveholders were not planters. Some of the small slaveholders were urban merchants or professional men who needed slaves only for domestic service, but more typical were farmers who used one or two slave families to ease the burden of their own labor. Relatively little is known about life on these small slaveholding farms; unlike the planters, the owners left few records behind. We do know that life was relatively spartan. Masters lived in log cabins or small frame cottages, and slaves lived in lofts or sheds that were not usually up to plantation housing standards.

For better or worse, relations between owners and their slaves were more intimate than on larger estates. These farmers often worked in the fields alongside their slaves and sometimes ate at the same table or slept under the same roof. But such closeness did not necessarily result in better treatment. Slave testimony reveals that both the best and the worst of slavery could be found on these farms, depending on the master. Given a choice, most slaves preferred to live on plantations because they offered the sociability, culture, and kinship of the slave quarters, as well as better prospects for adequate food, clothing, and shelter. Marginal slaveholders often sank into poverty and were forced either to sell their slaves or give them short rations.

Yeoman Farmers

Just below the small slaveholders on the social scale was a substantial class of **yeoman farmers** who owned land they worked themselves. Contrary to another myth about the Old South, most of these people did not fit the image of the degraded, shiftless poor white. While there were impoverished white squatters on stretches of barren or sandy soil that no one else wanted, and a significant number of tenant farmers, most were ambitious young men seeking to accumulate the capital to become landowners. The majority of the nonslaveholding rural population were proud, self-reliant farmers. If they were disadvantaged in comparison with farmers elsewhere in the United States, it was because the lack of economic development and urban growth perpetuated frontier conditions and denied them the opportunity to produce a substantial surplus for market.

The yeomen were mostly concentrated in the backcountry where slaves and plantations were rarely seen. In every southern state, white farmers without slaves populated hilly sections unsuitable for plantation agriculture, like the foothills of the Appalachians and the Ozarks, and long stretches of piney barrens along the Gulf Coast. A somewhat distinct group were the genuine mountaineers, who lived too high up to succeed at farming and relied heavily on hunting, lumbering, and distilling whiskey.

Yeoman women, much more than their wealthy counterparts, participated in every dimension of household labor. They worked in the garden, made handicrafts and clothing, and even labored in the fields when necessary. Women in the most dire economic circumstances even worked for wages in small businesses or on nearby farms. They also raised much larger families than their wealthier neighbors because having many children supplied a valuable labor pool for the family farm. There were also a greater number of lower-class women who lived outside of male-headed households. Despite the pressures of respectability, there was a greater acceptance and sympathy in less affluent communities for women who bore illegitimate children or were abandoned by their husbands. Working women created a broader definition of "proper households" and navigated the challenges of holding families together in precarious economic conditions. The lack of transportation facilities, more than some failure of energy or character, limited the prosperity of the yeomen. A large part of their effort was devoted to growing subsistence crops, mainly corn. They raised a small percentage of the South's cotton and tobacco, but production was severely limited by the difficulty of marketing. Their main source of cash was livestock, especially hogs. Hogs could be walked to market over long distances, and massive droves from the backcountry to urban markets were commonplace. But southern livestock, which was generally allowed to forage in the woods rather than being fattened on grain, was of poor quality and did not bring high prices or big profits to raisers.

Although they did not benefit directly from the peculiar institution, most yeomen and other nonslaveholders tolerated slavery and fiercely opposed abolitionism in any form. A few antislavery Southerners, most notably Hinton R. Helper of North Carolina, tried to convince the yeomen that they were victimized by planter dominance and should work for its overthrow, but they made little headway. Most yeomen were staunch Jacksonians who resented aristocratic pretensions and feared concentrations of power and wealth in the hands of the few. When asked about the gentry, they commonly voiced their disdain of "cotton snobs" and rich planters generally. In state and local politics, they sometimes expressed such feelings by voting against planter interests on issues involving representation, banking, and internal improvements. Why, then, did they fail to respond to antislavery appeals that called on them to strike at the real source of planter power and privilege?

One reason was that some nonslaveholders hoped to get ahead in the world, and in the South this meant acquiring slaves of their own. Just enough of the more prosperous yeomen broke

📖● Read the Document   George Fitzhugh, The Blessings of Slavery (1857)

This proslavery cartoon of 1841 contends that the slave in America had a better life than did the working-class white in England. Supposedly, the grateful slaves were clothed, fed, and cared for in their old age by kindly and sympathetic masters, while starving English workers were mercilessly exploited by factory owners.
Source: Collection of The New-York Historical Society, negative no. 3087.

into the slaveholding classes to make this dream seem believable. Planters, anxious to ensure the loyalty of nonslaveholders, strenuously encouraged the notion that every white man was a potential master.

Even if they did not aspire to own slaves, white farmers often viewed black servitude as providing a guarantee of their own liberty and independence. A society that gave them the right to vote and the chance to be self-sufficient on land of their own encouraged the feeling they were fundamentally equal to the largest slaveholders. In part, their anxieties were economic; freed slaves would compete with them for land or jobs. But an intense racism deepened their fears and made their opposition to black freedom implacable. "Now suppose they was free," a nonslaveholder told a northern traveler, "you see they'd think themselves just as good as we ... just suppose you had a family of children, how would [you] like to hev a niggar feeling just as good as a white man? How'd you like to hev a niggar steppin' up to your darter?" Emancipation was unthinkable because it would remove the pride and status that automatically went along with a white skin in this acutely race-conscious society. Slavery, despite its drawbacks, served to keep blacks "in their place" and to make all whites, however poor and uneducated, feel they were free and equal members of a master race.

A Closed Mind and a Closed Society

Despite the tacit assent of most nonslaveholders, the dominant planters never lost their fear that lower-class whites would turn against slavery. They felt threatened from two sides: from the slave quarters where a new Nat Turner might be gathering his forces, and from the backcountry where yeomen and poor whites might heed the call of abolitionists and rise up against planter domination. Beginning in the 1830s, the ruling element tightened the screws of slavery and used their control of government and communications to create a mood of impending catastrophe designed to ensure that all southern whites were of a single mind on the slavery issue.

Before the 1830s, open discussion of the rights or wrongs of slavery had been possible in many parts of the South. Apologists commonly described the institution as "a necessary evil." In the upper South, as late as the 1820s, there had been significant support for the **American Colonization Society**, with its program of gradual voluntary emancipation accompanied by deportation of the freedmen. In 1831 and 1832—in the wake of the Nat Turner uprising—the Virginia state legislature debated a gradual emancipation plan. Major support for ensuring white safety by getting rid of both slavery and blacks came from representatives of the yeoman farmers living west of the Blue Ridge Mountains. But the defeat of the proposal effectively ended the discussion. The argument that slavery was "a positive good"—rather than an evil slated for gradual elimination—won the day.

The "positive good" defense of slavery was an answer to the abolitionist charge that the

institution was inherently sinful. The message was carried in a host of books, pamphlets, and newspaper editorials published between the 1830s and the Civil War. Partly, the argument was aimed at the North, as a way of bolstering the strong current of antiabolitionist sentiment. But Southerners themselves were a prime target; the message was clearly calculated to resolve the kind of doubts and misgivings that had been freely expressed before the 1830s. Much of the message may have been over the heads of nonslaveholders, many of whom were semiliterate, but some of the arguments, in popularized form, were used to arouse racial anxieties that tended to neutralize antislavery sentiment among the lower classes.

The proslavery argument was based on three main propositions. The first and foremost was that enslavement was the natural and proper status for people of African descent. Blacks, it was alleged, were innately inferior to whites and suited only for slavery. Biased scientific and historical evidence was presented to support this claim. Second, slavery was held to be sanctioned by the Bible and Christianity—a position made necessary by the abolitionist appeal to Christian ethics. Ancient Hebrew slavery was held up as a divinely sanctioned model, and Saint Paul was quoted endlessly on the duty of servants to obey their masters. Southern churchmen took the lead in reconciling slavery with religion and also made renewed efforts to convert the slaves as a way of showing that enslavement could be a means for spreading the gospel.

Finally, efforts were made to show that slavery was consistent with the humanitarian spirit of the nineteenth century. The premise that blacks were naturally dependent led to the notion that they

Read the Document Poem, "The Slave Auction"

This illustration of a public auction of slaves in Charleston, South Carolina in 1856 was representative of the horrific treatment of slaves including the separation of the parents of slaves from their young children. Literary and visual depictions of slave auctions were produced and widely disseminated to mobilize abolitionist sentiment among slavery opponents based in the North and in England.

needed some kind of "family government" or special regime equivalent to the asylums that existed for the small numbers of whites who were also incapable of caring for themselves. The plantation allegedly provided such an environment, as benevolent masters guided and ruled this race of "perpetual children."

By the 1850s, the proslavery argument had gone beyond mere apology for the South and its peculiar institution and featured an ingenious attack on the free-labor system of the North. According to Virginian George Fitzhugh, the master-slave relationship was more humane than the one prevailing between employers and wage laborers in the North. Slaves had security against unemployment and a guarantee of care in old age, whereas free workers might face destitution and even starvation at any time. Worker insecurity in free societies led inevitably to strikes, bitter class conflicts, and the rise of socialism; slave societies, on the other hand, could more effectively protect property rights and maintain other traditional values because their laboring class was better treated and, at the same time, more firmly controlled.

Proslavery Southerners attempted to seal off their region from antislavery ideas and influences. Whites who were bold enough to criticize slavery publicly were mobbed or persecuted. One of the last and bravest of the southern abolitionists, Cassius M. Clay of Kentucky, armed himself with a brace of pistols when he gave speeches, until the threat of mob violence finally forced him across the Ohio River. In 1856, a University of North Carolina professor was fired because he admitted he would vote for the moderately antislavery Republican Party if he had a chance. Clergymen who questioned the morality of slavery were driven from their pulpits, and northern travelers suspected of being abolitionist agents were tarred and feathered. When abolitionists tried to send their literature through the mail during the 1830s, it was seized in southern post offices and publicly burned.

Such flagrant denials of free speech and civil liberties were inspired in part by fears that non-slaveholding whites and slaves would get subversive ideas about slavery. Hinton R. Helper's book *The Impending Crisis of the South*, an 1857 appeal to nonslaveholders to resist the planter regime, was suppressed with particular vigor; those found with copies were beaten up or even lynched. But the deepest fear was that slaves would hear the abolitionist talk or read antislavery literature and be inspired to rebel. Such anxieties rose to panic pitch after the Nat Turner rebellion. Consequently, new laws were passed making it a crime to teach slaves to read and write. Other repressive legislation aimed at slaves banned meetings unless a white man was present, severely restricted the activities of black preachers, and suppressed independent black churches. Free blacks, thought to be possible instigators of slave revolt, were denied basic civil liberties and were the object of growing surveillance and harassment.

All these efforts at thought control and internal security did not allay planters' fears of abolitionist subversion, lower-class white dissent, and, above all, slave revolt. The persistent barrage of proslavery propaganda and the course of national events in the 1850s created a mood of panic and desperation. By this time, an increasing number of Southerners had become convinced that safety from abolitionism and its associated terrors required a formal withdrawal from the Union—secession.

Slavery and the Southern Economy

How was slavery related to economic success in the South?

Southern society transformed itself according to the needs of the slave system because slavery played such a crucial role in the economic life of the South. Despite the internal divisions of southern society, white Southerners from all regions and classes came to perceive their interests tied up with slavery, whether because they owned slaves themselves or because they believed in slavery as essential to the "southern way of life" or "white men's democracy." And because slavery was the cornerstone of the southern economy, it affected white Southerners' attitudes toward landholding and toward industrialization.

For the most part, the expansion of slavery—the number of slaves in the South more than tripled between 1810 and 1860 to nearly four million—can be attributed to the rise of "King Cotton." The cotton-growing areas of the South were becoming more and more dependent on slavery, at the same time that agriculture in the upper South was actually moving away from the institution. Yet slavery continued to remain important to the economy of the upper South in a different way, through the slave trade.

 View the **Closer Look**   Slave Auction in Richmond, Virgina

A SLAVE AUCTION IN VIRGINIA.—FROM A SKETCH BY OUR SPECIAL ARTIST.

The spectacle of a slave market was commonplace in the cities of the antebellum South. Here, the correspondent has depicted a relaxed scene as if to evoke the prosaic nature of the event.

View the Map Slavery in the South

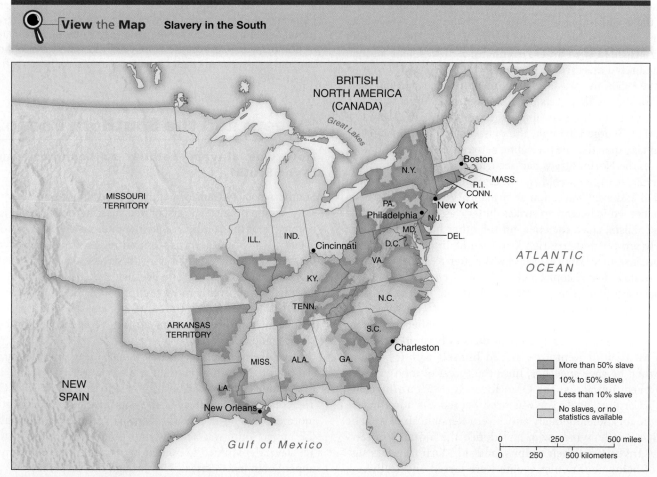

SLAVE CONCENTRATION, 1820 In 1820, most slaves lived in the eastern seaboard states of Virginia and South Carolina and in Louisiana on the Gulf of Mexico.

The Internal Slave Trade

Tobacco, the original plantation crop of the colonial period, continued to be the principal slave-cultivated commodity of the upper tier of southern states during the pre–Civil War era. But markets were often depressed, and profitable tobacco cultivation was hard to sustain for very long in one place because the crop rapidly depleted the soil. During the lengthy depression of the tobacco market that lasted from the 1820s to the 1850s, tobacco farmers in Virginia and Maryland experimented with fertilizer use, crop rotation, and diversified farming, all of which increased the need for capital but reduced the demand for labor.

As slave prices rose (because of high demand in the lower South) and demand for slaves in the upper South fell, the "internal" slave trade took off. Increasingly, the most profitable business for slaveholders in Virginia, Kentucky, Maryland, and the Carolinas was selling "surplus" slaves from the upper South to regions of the lower South, where staple crop production was more profitable. This interstate slave trade sent an estimated six to seven hundred thousand slaves in a southwesterly direction between 1815 and 1860. Historian Michael Tadman estimates that the chances of a slave child in the Upper South in the 1820s being "sold South" by 1860 were as high as 30 percent. Such sales were wrenching, not only splitting families, but making it especially unlikely that the slaves sold would ever see friends or family again.

Some economic historians have concluded that the most important crop produced in the tobacco kingdom was not the "stinking weed" but human beings cultivated for the auction block. Respectable planters did not like to think of themselves as raising slaves for market, but few would refuse to sell some of their "people" if they needed money to get out of debt or make expensive improvements. For the region as a whole, the slave trade provided a crucial source of capital in a period of transition and innovation.

Nevertheless, the fact that slave labor was declining in importance in the upper South meant the peculiar institution had a weaker hold on public loyalty there than in the cotton states. Diversification of agriculture was accompanied by a more rapid rate of urban and industrial development than was occurring elsewhere in the South. As a result, Virginians, Marylanders, and Kentuckians were seriously divided on whether their ultimate future lay with the Deep South's plantation economy or with the industrializing free-labor system that was flourishing just north of their borders.

The Rise of the Cotton Kingdom

The warmer climate and good soils of the lower tier of southern states made it possible to raise crops more naturally suited than tobacco or cereals to the plantation form of agriculture and the heavy use of slave labor. Since the colonial or revolutionary

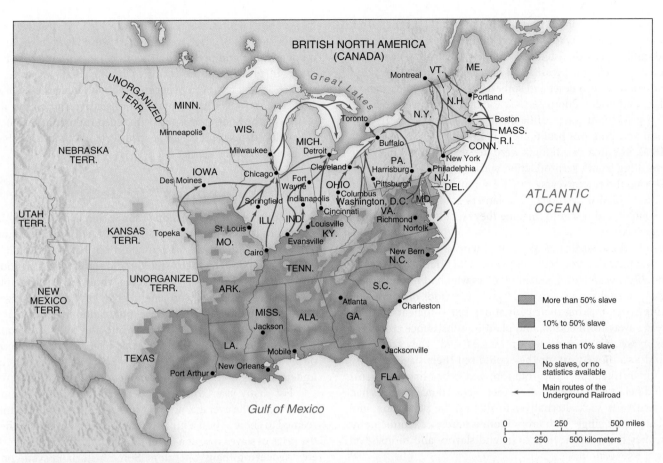

SLAVE CONCENTRATION, 1860 In 1860, slavery had extended throughout the southern states, with the greatest concentrations of slaves in the states of the Deep South. There were also sizable slave populations in the new states of Missouri, Arkansas, Texas, and Florida.

periods, rice and a special long-staple variety of fine cotton had been grown profitably on vast estates along the coast of South Carolina and Georgia. In lower Louisiana, between New Orleans and Baton Rouge, sugar was the cash crop. As in the West Indies, sugar production required a large investment and a great deal of backbreaking labor: in other words, large, well-financed plantations and small armies of slave laborers. Cultivation of rice, long-staple cotton, and sugar was limited by natural conditions to peripheral, semitropical areas. It was the rise of short-staple cotton as the South's major crop that strengthened the hold of slavery and the plantation on the southern economy.

Short-staple cotton differed from the long-staple variety in two important ways: Its bolls contained seeds that were much more difficult to extract by hand, and it could be grown almost anywhere south of Virginia and Kentucky—the main requirement was a guarantee of two hundred frost-free days. Before the 1790s, the seed extraction problem had prevented short-staple cotton from becoming a major market crop. The invention of the **cotton gin** in 1793 resolved that difficulty, however, and the subsequent westward expansion opened vast areas for cotton cultivation. Unlike rice and sugar, cotton could be grown on small farms as well as on plantations. But large planters enjoyed certain advantages that made them the main producers. Only relatively large operators could afford their own gins or possessed the capital to acquire the fertile bottomlands that brought the highest yields. They also had lower transportation costs because they were able

to monopolize land along rivers and streams that were the South's natural arteries of transportation.

The first major cotton-producing regions were inland areas of Georgia and South Carolina, but the center of production shifted rapidly westward during the nineteenth century. By the 1830s, Alabama and Mississippi had surpassed Georgia and South Carolina as cotton-growing states. By the 1850s, Arkansas, northwest Louisiana, and east Texas were the most prosperous and rapidly growing plantation regions. The rise in total production that accompanied this geographic expansion was phenomenal. Between 1792 and 1817, the South's output of cotton rose from about 13,000 bales to 461,000; by 1840, it was 1.35 million; and in 1860, production peaked at the colossal figure of 4.8 million bales. Most of the cotton went to supply the booming textile industry of Great Britain. Lesser proportions went to the manufacturers of continental Europe and the northeastern United States.

"Cotton is king!" proclaimed a southern orator in the 1850s, and he was right. By that time, three-quarters of the world's supply of cotton came from the American South, and this single commodity accounted for more than half the total dollar value of American exports. Cotton growing and the network of commercial and industrial enterprises that marketed and processed the crop constituted the most important economic interest in the United States on the eve of the Civil War. Since slavery and cotton seemed inextricably linked, it appeared obvious to many Southerners that their peculiar institution was the keystone of national wealth and economic progress.

However, the rise of the Cotton Kingdom did not bring a uniform or steady prosperity to the lower South. Many planters worked the land until it was exhausted and then took their slaves westward to richer soils, leaving depressed and ravaged areas in their wake.

Planters were also beset and sometimes ruined by fluctuations in markets and prices. Boom periods and flush times were followed by falling prices and waves of bankruptcies. The great periods of expansion and bonanza profits were 1815–1819, 1832–1837, and 1849–1860. The first two booms were deflated by a fall in cotton prices resulting from overproduction and depressed market conditions. During the eleven years of rising output and high prices preceding the Civil War, however, the planters gradually forgot their earlier troubles and began to imagine they were immune to future economic disasters.

Despite the insecurities associated with cotton production, most of the time the crop represented the Old South's best chance for profitable investment. Prudent planters who had not borrowed too heavily during flush times could survive periods of depression by cutting costs, making their plantations self-sufficient by shifting acreage away from cotton, and planting subsistence crops. For those with worn-out land, two options existed: They could sell their land and move west, or they could sell their slaves to raise capital for fertilization, crop rotation, and other improvements that could help them survive where they were. Hence planters had little incentive to seek alternatives to slavery, the plantation, and dependence on a single cash crop. From a purely economic point of view, they had every reason to defend slavery and to insist on their right to expand it.

Slavery and Industrialization

As the sectional quarrel with the North intensified, Southerners became increasingly alarmed by their region's lack of economic self-sufficiency. Dependence on the North for capital, marketing facilities, and manufactured goods was seen as evidence of a dangerous subservience to "external" economic interests. Southern nationalists such as J. D. B. DeBow, editor of the influential *DeBow's Review*, called during the 1850s for the South to develop its own industries, commerce, and shipping. As a fervent defender of slavery, DeBow did not believe such diversification would require a massive shift to free wage labor. He saw no reason for slaves not to be used as the main workforce in an industrial revolution. But his call for a diversified economy went unanswered. Men with capital were doing too well in plantation agriculture to risk their money in other ventures.

It is difficult to determine whether the main factor that kept most slaves working on plantations and farms was some inherent characteristic of slavery as a labor system or simply the strong market demand for cotton and the South's capacity to meet it. A minority of slaves—about 5 percent during the 1850s—were, in fact, successfully employed in industrial tasks such as mining, construction, and mill work. In the 1840s and 1850s, a debate raged among white capitalists over whether the South should use free whites or enslaved blacks as the labor supply for industry. William Gregg of South Carolina, the foremost promoter of cotton mills in the Old South, defended a white labor policy, arguing that factory work would provide new economic opportunities for a degraded class of poor whites. But other advocates of industrialization feared that the growth of a free working class would lead to social conflict among whites and preferred using slaves for all supervised manual labor. In practice, some factories employed slaves, others white workers, and a few even experimented with integrated workforces. It is clear, however, that the union of slavery and cotton that was central to the South's prosperity impeded industrialization and left the region dependent on a one-crop agriculture and on the North for capital and marketing.

The "Profitability" Issue

Some Southerners were making money, and a great deal of it, using slave labor to raise cotton. The great mansions of the Alabama "black belt" and the lower Mississippi could not have been built if their owners had not been successful. But did slavery yield a good return for the great majority of slaveholders who were not large planters? Did it provide the basis for general prosperity and a relatively high standard of living for the southern population in general, or at least for the two-thirds of it who were white and free? These questions have been hotly debated by economic historians. Some knowledge of the main arguments regarding its "profitability" is helpful to an understanding of the South's attachment to slavery.

For many years, historians believed that slave-based agriculture was, on the average, not very lucrative. Planters' account books seemed to show at best a modest return on investment. In the 1850s, the price of slaves rose at a faster rate than the price of cotton, allegedly squeezing many operators. Some historians even concluded that slavery was a dying institution by the time of the Civil War. Profitability, they argued, depended on access to new and fertile land suitable for plantation agriculture, and virtually all such land within the limits of the United States had already been taken up by 1860. Hence slavery had allegedly reached its natural limits of expansion and was on the verge of becoming so unprofitable that it would fall of its own weight in the near future.

A more recent interpretation, based on modern economic theory, holds that slavery was in fact still an economically sound institution in 1860 and showed no signs of imminent decline. A reexamination of planters' records using modern accounting methods shows that during the 1850s, planters could normally expect an annual return of 8 to 10 percent on capital invested. This yield was roughly equivalent to the best that could then be obtained from the most lucrative sectors of northern industry and commerce.

Furthermore, it is no longer clear that plantation agriculture had reached its natural limits of expansion by 1860. Production in Texas had not yet peaked, and construction of railroads and levees was opening up new areas for cotton growing elsewhere in the South. With the advantage of hindsight, economic historians have pointed out that improvements in transportation and flood control would enable the post–Civil War South to double its cotton acreage. Those who now argue that slavery was profitable and had an expansive future have made a strong and convincing case.

But the larger question remains: What sort of economic development did a slave plantation system foster? The system may have made slaveholders wealthy, but did the benefits trickle down to the rest of the population—to the majority of whites who owned no slaves and to the slaves themselves? Did it promote efficiency and progressive change? Economists Robert Fogel and Stanley Engerman have argued that the plantation's success was due to an internally efficient enterprise with good managers and industrious, well-motivated workers. Other economic historians have attributed the profitability almost exclusively to favorable market conditions.

Large plantation owners were the only segment of the population to enjoy the full benefits of the slave economy. Small slaveholders and nonslaveholders shared only to a very limited extent in the bonanza profits of the cotton economy. Because of various insecurities—lack of credit, high transportation costs, and a greater vulnerability to market fluctuations—they had to devote a larger share of their acreage to subsistence crops, especially corn and hogs, than did the planters. They were thus able to survive, but their standard of living was lower than that of most northern farmers. Slaves received sufficient food, clothing, and shelter for their subsistence and to make them capable of working well enough to keep the plantation afloat economically, but their living standard was below that of the poorest free people in the United States. It was proslavery propaganda rather than documented fact, to maintain that slaves were better off than northern wage laborers.

The South's economic development was skewed in favor of a single route to wealth, open only to the minority possessing both a white skin and access to capital. The concentration of capital and business energies on cotton production foreclosed the kind of diversified industrial and commercial growth that would have provided wider opportunities. Thus, in comparison to the industrializing North, the South was an underdeveloped region in which much of the population had little incentive to work hard. A lack of public education for whites and the denial of even minimal literacy

to slaves represented a critical failure to develop human resources. The South's economy was probably condemned so long as it was based on slavery.

Conclusion: Worlds in Conflict

If slaves lived to some extent in a separate and distinctive world of their own, so did planters, less affluent whites, and even free blacks. The Old South was thus a deeply divided society. The northern traveler Frederick Law Olmsted, who made three journeys through the slave states in the 1850s, provided a vivid sense of how diverse in outlook and circumstances southern people could be. Visiting a great plantation, he watched the slaves stop working as soon as the overseer turned away; on a small farm, he saw a slave and his owner working in the fields together. Treatment of slaves, he found, ranged from humane paternalism to flagrant cruelty. Olmsted heard nonslaveholding whites damn the planters as "cotton snobs" but also talk about blacks as "niggars" and express fear of interracial marriages if slaves were freed. He received hospitality from poor whites living in crowded one-room cabins as well as from fabulously wealthy planters in pillared mansions, and he found life in the backcountry radically different from that in the plantation belts.

He showed that the South was a kaleidoscope of groups divided by class, race, culture, and geography. What held it together and provided some measure of unity were a booming plantation economy and a web of customary relationships and loyalties that could obscure the underlying cleavages and antagonisms. The fractured and fragile nature of this society would soon become apparent when it was subjected to the pressures of civil war.

Study Resources

 Take the **Study Plan** for **Chapter 11** *Slaves and Masters* on **MyHistoryLab**

TIME LINE

1793 Eli Whitney invents the cotton gin

1800 Gabriel Prosser leads abortive slave rebellion in Virginia

1811 Slaves revolt in Point Coupée section of Louisiana

1822 Denmark Vesey conspiracy uncovered in Charleston, South Carolina

1829 David Walker publishes *Appeal* calling for slave insurrection

1830 First National Negro Convention meets

1831 Slaves under Nat Turner rebel in Virginia, killing almost sixty whites

1832 Virginia legislature votes against gradual emancipation

1835–1842 Blacks fight alongside Indians in the Second Seminole War

1837 Panic of 1837 is followed by major depression of the cotton market

1847 Frederick Douglass publishes the *North Star*, a black antislavery newspaper

1849 Cotton prices rise, and a sustained boom commences

1851 Group of free blacks rescues escaped slave Shadrack from federal authorities in Boston

1852 Harriet Beecher Stowe's antislavery novel *Uncle Tom's Cabin* is published and becomes a best seller

1857 Hinton R. Helper attacks slavery on economic grounds in *The Impending Crisis of the South*; the book is suppressed in the southern states

1860 Cotton prices and production reach all-time peak

CHAPTER REVIEW

The Divided Society of the Old South

 What were the divisions within black society in the Old South?

Most African Americans in the Old South were slaves who worked on plantations and farms as agricultural laborers, domestic servants, and skilled craftsmen. Although slave servants and craftsmen enjoyed higher status than field hands, all southern blacks, even the six percent who were free, suffered from racial prejudice and severe legal inequality. (p. 248)

The World of Southern Blacks

 What factors made living conditions for southern blacks more or less difficult?

Living conditions were difficult because slaves performed many types of labor. Some worked from sunup to sundown in gangs; others maintained more work control through the "task system"; urban slaves and free blacks had more autonomy. Family and community helped ease slave life, while some slaves resisted oppression by running away, sabotage, and even armed rebellion. (p. 248)

White Society in the Antebellum South

 What divided and united white southern society?

While great planters were a tiny minority of the population, they set the tone for white southern society, propagating the ideology of "paternalism," that slaves were children who required a stern but loving parent. Most whites owned few or no slaves, but a political system of "white man's democracy" and the ideology of white supremacy united them with large slaveholders. (p. 256)

Slavery and the Southern Economy

 How was slavery related to economic success in the South?

Slavery dominated the economy of the South: Tobacco gave way to the internal slave trade as the biggest business in the upper South, while the cotton gin made large-scale staple agriculture a booming economic machine in the Deep South, fueling the growth of a world textile industry and enriching the planter class. (p. 261)

KEY TERMS AND DEFINITIONS

Old South The term refers to the slaveholding states between 1830 and 1860, when slave labor and cotton production dominated the economies of the southern states. This period is also known as the "antebellum era." p. 248

Vesey conspiracy An unsuccessful 1822 plot to burn Charleston, South Carolina, and initiate a general slave revolt, led by a free African American, Denmark Vesey. p. 254

Underground Railroad A network of safe houses organized by abolitionists (usually free blacks) to help slaves escape to the North or Canada. p. 254

Yeoman farmers Southern small landholders who owned no slaves, and who lived primarily in the foothills of the Appalachian and Ozark mountains. They were self-reliant and grew mixed crops, although they usually did not produce a substantial amount to be sold on the market. p. 258

American Colonization Society Founded in 1817, the society advocated the relocation of free blacks and freed slaves to the African colony of Monrovia, present-day Liberia. p. 260

Cotton gin Invented by Eli Whitney in 1793, this device for separating the seeds from the fibers of short-staple cotton enabled a slave to clean fifty times more cotton as by hand, which reduced production costs and gave new life to slavery in the South. p. 263

CRITICAL THINKING QUESTIONS

1. Do you think the booming cotton economy benefited all members of southern society, or only certain segments?

2. What difference did it make in a slave's life if he or she belonged to a great planter or to a small farmer?

3. What do you think is the connection between slavery and racism? Why did slaveholders begin defending slavery in racial terms in the 1830s?

MyHistoryLab Media Assignments

Find these resources in the Media Assignments folder for Chapter 11 on MyHistoryLab

The Divided Society of the Old South

■ **Read** the **Document**   *Confessions of Nat Turner (1831)* p. 247

The World of Southern Blacks

Read the **Document**   *Overseer's Report from Chicora Wood Plantation* p. 250

Read the **Document**   *Frances E.W. Harper, "The Slave Mother"* p. 251

Listen to the **Audio File**   *When the Roll is Called up Yonder* p. 254

■ **Complete** the **Assignment**   *Harriet Jacobs and Maria Norcom: Women of Southern Households* p. 252

Watch the **Video**   *Underground Railroad* p. 255

White Society in the Antebellum South

■ **Read** the **Document**   *George Fitzhugh, The Blessings of Slavery (1857)* p. 259

Read the **Document**   *Poem, "The Slave Auction"* p. 260

Slavery and the Southern Economy

■ **View** the **Closer Look**   *Slave Auction in Richmond, Virginia* p. 261

■ **View** the **Map**   *Slavery in the South* p. 262

■ Indicates Study Plan Media Assignment

12 The Pursuit of Perfection

Contents and Learning Objectives

((•●—[Listen to the **Audio File** on **myhistorylab**   **Chapter 12** *The Pursuit of Perfection*

Redeeming the Middle Class

In the winter of 1830 to 1831, a wave of religious revivals swept the northern states. The most dramatic and successful took place in Rochester, New York. Large audiences, composed mostly of respectable and prosperous citizens, heard Presbyterian evangelist Charles G. Finney preach that every man or woman had the power to choose Christ and a godly life. Finney broke with his church's traditional belief that it was God's inscrutable will that decided who would be saved when he preached that "sinners ought to be made to feel that they have something to do, and that something is to repent. That is something that no other being can do for them, neither God nor man, and something they can do and do now."

For six months, Finney held prayer meetings almost daily, putting intense pressure on those who had not experienced salvation. Hundreds came forth to declare their faith, and church membership doubled during his stay. The newly awakened Christians of Rochester were urged to convert relatives, neighbors, and employees. If enough people enlisted in the evangelical crusade, Finney proclaimed, the millennium would be achieved within months.

Finney's call for religious and moral renewal fell on fertile ground in Rochester. The bustling boomtown on the Erie Canal was suffering from severe growing pains

and tensions arising from rapid economic development. Leading families were divided into quarreling factions, and workers were threatening to break free from the control their employers had previously exerted over their daily lives. Most of the early converts were from the middle class. Businessmen who had been heavy drinkers and irregular churchgoers now abstained from alcohol and went to church at least twice a week. They also pressured the employees in their workshops, mills, and stores to do likewise. More rigorous standards of proper behavior and religious conformity unified Rochester's elite and increased its ability to control the rest of the community. As in other cities swept by the revival, evangelical Protestantism provided the middle class with a stronger sense of identity and purpose.

But the war on sin was not always so unifying. Among those converted in Rochester and elsewhere were some who could not rest easy until the nation as a whole conformed to the pure Christianity of the Sermon on the Mount. Finney expressed such a hope himself, but he concentrated on religious conversion and moral uplift of the individual, trusting that the purification of American society and politics would automatically follow. Other religious and moral reformers were inspired to crusade against those social and political institutions that failed to measure up to the standards of Christian perfection. They proceeded to attack such collective "sins" as the liquor traffic, war, slavery, and even government.

Jeremiah Paul, *Revival Meeting*

Religiously inspired reformism cut two ways. On the one hand, it imposed a new order and cultural unity to previously divided and troubled communities like Rochester. But it also inspired a variety of more radical movements that threatened to undermine established institutions that failed to live up to the principles of the more idealistic reformers. One of these movements—abolitionism—challenged the central social and economic institution of the southern states and helped trigger political upheaval and civil war.

The Rise of Evangelicalism

How did the evangelical revivalism of the early nineteenth century spur reform movements?

American Protestantism was in a state of constant ferment during the early nineteenth century. The separation of church and state, a process that began during the Revolution, was now complete. Government sponsorship and funding had ended, or would soon end, for the established churches of the colonial era, such as the Congregationalists of New England and the Episcopalians of the South. Dissenting groups, such as Baptists and Methodists, welcomed full religious freedom because it offered a better chance to win new converts. All pious Protestants, however,

worried about the spread of "infidelity"—a term they applied to Catholics, freethinkers, Unitarians, Mormons, and any nonevangelical Christian. But they faced opposition to their effort to make the nation officially Protestant. Secular ideas drawn from the Enlightenment of the late eighteenth century had achieved wide acceptance as a basis for the establishment of a democratic republic, and opposition to mixing religion with public life remained strong during the age of Jackson. As deism—the belief in a God who expressed himself through natural laws accessible to human reason—declined in popularity in the early to mid-nineteenth century, Catholic immigration increased, and the spread of popery became the main focus of evangelical concern. Both Catholics and Unitarians (who quietly carried forward the rationalistic traditions of the eighteenth century) resented and resisted the evangelicals' efforts to convert them to "the Christianity of the heart." Most of those who accepted Christ as their personal savior in revival meetings previously had been indifferent to religion rather than adhering to an alternative set of beliefs.

Revivalism proved to be a very effective means to extend religious values and build up church membership. The Great Awakening of the mid-eighteenth century had shown the wonders that evangelists could accomplish, and new revivalists repeated this success by greatly increasing membership in Protestant churches.

They also capitalized on the growing willingness of Americans to form voluntary organizations. Spiritual renewals were often followed by mobilization of the faithful into associations to spread the gospel and reform American morals.

According to some historians, evangelical revival and the reform movements it inspired reflected the same spirit as the new democratic politics. In a sense this is true: Jacksonian politicians and evangelists both sought popular favor and assumed that individuals were free agents capable of self-direction and self-improvement. But leaders of the two types of movements made different kinds of demands on ordinary people. Jacksonians idealized common folk as they found them and saw no danger to the community if individuals pursued their worldly interests. Evangelical reformers, who tended to support the Whigs or to reject both parties, believed that the common people, and not just the elite, needed to be redeemed and uplifted—committed to a higher goal than self-interest. The republic would be safe, they insisted, only if a right-minded minority preached, taught, and agitated until the mass of ordinary citizens was reborn into a higher life.

The Second Great Awakening: The Frontier Phase

The **Second Great Awakening** began on the southern frontier around the turn of the century. In 1801, a crowd estimated at nearly fifty thousand gathered at Cane Ridge, Kentucky. According to a contemporary observer:

> The noise was like the roar of Niagara. The vast sea of human beings seemed to be agitated as if by a storm. I counted seven ministers all preaching at once.... Some of the people were singing, others praying, some crying for mercy ...while others were shouting most vociferously.... At one time I saw at least five hundred swept down in a moment, as if a battery of a thousand guns had been opened upon them, and then followed immediately shrieks and shouts that rent the heavens.

Highly emotional camp meetings, organized usually by Methodists or Baptists but sometimes by Presbyterians, became a regular feature of religious life in the South and the lower Midwest. On the frontier, the camp meeting met social as well as religious needs. In the sparsely settled southern backcountry, it was difficult to sustain local churches with regular ministers. Methodists solved part of the problem by sending out circuit riders. Baptists licensed uneducated farmers to preach to their neighbors. But for many people, the only way to get baptized or married or to have a communal religious experience was to attend a camp meeting.

Rowdies and scoffers also attended, drinking whiskey, carousing, and fornicating on the fringes of the small city of tents and wagons. Sometimes they were "struck down" by a mighty blast from the pulpit. Evangelists loved to tell stories of such conversions or near conversions. According to Methodist preacher Peter Cartwright, one scoffer was seized by the "jerks"—a set of involuntary bodily movements often observed at camp meetings. Normally such an exercise would lead to conversion, but this particular sinner was so hard-hearted that he refused to surrender to God. The result was that he kept jerking until his neck was broken.

Camp meetings provided an emotional outlet for rural people whose everyday lives were often lonely and tedious. They could also promote a sense of community and social discipline. Conversion at a camp meeting could be a rite of passage, signifying that a young man or woman had outgrown wild or antisocial behavior and was now ready to become a respectable member of the community.

In the southern states, Baptists and Presbyterians eventually deemphasized camp meetings in favor of "protracted meetings" in local churches, which featured guest preachers holding forth day after day for up to two weeks. Southern evangelical churches, especially Baptist and Methodist, grew rapidly in membership and influence during the first half of the nineteenth century and became the focus of community life in rural areas. Although they fostered societies to improve morals—to encourage temperance and discourage dueling, for example—they generally shied away from social reform. The conservatism of a slaveholding society discouraged radical efforts to change the world.

The Second Great Awakening in the North

Reformist tendencies were more evident in the distinctive kind of revivalism that originated in New England and western New York. Northern evangelists were mostly Congregationalists and Presbyterians, strongly influenced by New England Puritan traditions. Their greatest successes were not in rural or frontier areas but in small- to medium-sized towns and cities. Their revivals could be stirring affairs but were less extravagantly emotional than the camp meetings of the South. Northern evangelists formed societies devoted to the redemption of the human race in general and American society in particular.

The reform movement in New England began as an effort to defend Calvinism against the liberal views of religion fostered by the Enlightenment. The Reverend Timothy Dwight, who became president of Yale College in 1795, was alarmed by the younger generation's growing acceptance of the belief that the Deity was the benevolent master architect of a rational universe rather than an all-powerful, mysterious God. Dwight was particularly disturbed by those religious liberals whose rationalism reached the point of denying the doctrine of the Trinity and who proclaimed themselves to be "Unitarians."

To Dwight's horror, Unitarians captured some fashionable and sophisticated New England congregations and even won control of the Harvard Divinity School. He fought back by preaching to Yale undergraduates that they were "dead in sin" and succeeded in provoking a series of campus revivals. But the harshness and pessimism of orthodox Calvinist doctrine, with its stress on original sin and predestination, had limited appeal in a republic committed to human freedom and progress.

A younger generation of Congregational ministers reshaped New England Puritanism to increase its appeal to people who shared the prevailing optimism about human capabilities. The main theologian of early nineteenth-century neo-Calvinism was Nathaniel Taylor, a disciple of Dwight, who also held forth at Yale. Taylor softened the doctrine of predestination almost out of existence by contending that every individual was a free agent who had the ability to overcome a natural inclination to sin.

The first great practitioner of the new evangelical Calvinism was Lyman Beecher, another of Dwight's pupils. In the period just before and after the War of 1812, Beecher helped promote a

View the **Closer Look**   Methodist Camp Meeting, 1819

The Second Great Awakening swept across the United States in the early decades of the 19th century, bringing religious camp meetings such as the one depicted here to rural and urban areas alike. Held outdoors, these gatherings allowed huge audiences to share in a highly emotional experience as they expressed their faith.

series of revivals in the Congregational churches of New England. Using his own homespun version of Taylor's doctrine of free agency, Beecher induced thousands to acknowledge their sinfulness and surrender to God.

During the late 1820s, Beecher was forced to confront the new and more radical form of revivalism being practiced in western New York by Charles G. Finney. Upstate New York was a seedbed for religious enthusiasms of various kinds. A majority of its population were transplanted New Englanders who had left behind their close-knit village communities and ancestral churches but not their Puritan consciences. Troubled by rapid economic changes and the social dislocations that went with them, they were ripe for a new faith and a fresh moral direction.

Although he worked within Congregational and Presbyterian churches (which were then cooperating under a plan of union established in 1804), Finney departed radically from Calvinist doctrines. In his hands, free agency became unqualified free will. One of his sermons was titled "Sinners Bound to Change Their Own Hearts." Finney was relatively indifferent to theological issues. His appeal was to emotion rather than to doctrine or reason.

He wanted converts to feel the power of Christ and become new men and women. He eventually adopted the extreme view that redeemed Christians could be totally free of sin—as perfect as their Father in Heaven.

Beginning in 1823, Finney conducted a series of highly successful revivals in towns and cities of western New York, culminating in the aforementioned triumph in Rochester in 1830–1831. Finney sought instantaneous conversions through a variety of new and controversial methods. These included holding protracted meetings that lasted all night or several days in a row, placing an "anxious bench" in front of the congregation where those in the process of repentance could receive special attention, and encouraging women to pray publicly for the souls of male relatives.

The results could be dramatic. Sometimes listeners fell to the floor in fits of excitement. "If I had had a sword in my hand," Finney recalled, "I could not have cut them off as fast as they fell." Although he appealed to emotion, Finney had a practical, almost manipulative, attitude toward the conversion process: It "is not a miracle or dependent on a miracle in any sense…. It is purely a philosophical result of the right use of constituted means."

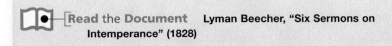

Read the Document Lyman Beecher, "Six Sermons on Intemperance" (1828)

The Beecher family, shown here in a photograph by Mathew Brady, contributed four influential members to the reform movement. Lyman Beecher (seated center) was a successful preacher and a master strategist in the organized campaign against sin and "infidelity." His eldest daughter, Catharine (on his right), was a leader in the movement supporting higher education for women. Another daughter, Harriet (seated far right), wrote the novel *Uncle Tom's Cabin*. Lyman's son, Henry Ward Beecher (standing far right), was an ardent antislavery advocate and later became one of the most celebrated preachers of the post–Civil War era. He also became involved in a notorious scandal and trial.

Lyman Beecher and eastern evangelicals were disturbed by Finney's new methods and by the emotionalism that accompanied them. They were also upset because he violated long-standing Christian tradition by allowing women to pray aloud in church. An evangelical summit meeting between Beecher and Finney, held at New Lebanon, New York, in 1827, failed to reach agreement on this and other issues. Beecher even threatened to stand on the state line if Finney attempted to bring his crusade into Connecticut. But it soon became clear that Finney was not merely stirring people to temporary peaks of excitement; he also was leaving strong and active churches behind him, and eastern opposition gradually weakened. Finney eventually founded a tabernacle in New York City that became a rallying point for evangelical efforts to reach the urban masses.

From Revivalism to Reform

The northern wing of the Second Great Awakening, unlike the southern, inspired a great movement for social reform. Converts were organized into voluntary associations that sought to stamp out sin and social evil and win the world for Christ. An activist and

outgoing Christianity was being advanced, not one that called for withdrawal from a sinful world. Most of the converts of northern revivalism were middle-class citizens already active in the lives of their communities. They were seeking to adjust to the bustling world of the market revolution without violating their traditional moral and social values. Their generally optimistic and forward-looking attitudes led to hopes that a wave of conversions would save the nation and the world.

In New England, Beecher and his evangelical associates established a great network of missionary and benevolent societies. In 1810, Presbyterians and Congregationalists founded a Board of Commissioners for Foreign Missions and soon dispatched two missionaries to India. In 1816, the Reverend Samuel John Mills took the leading role in organizing the American Bible Society. By 1821, the society had distributed one hundred forty thousand Bibles, mostly in parts of the West where churches and clergymen were scarce.

Another major effort went into publication and distribution of religious tracts, mainly by the American Tract Society, founded in 1825. Special societies targeted groups beyond the reach of regular churches, such as seamen, Native Americans, and the urban poor. In 1816 to 1817, middle-class women in New York, Philadelphia, Charleston, and Boston formed societies to spread the gospel in lower-class wards—where, as one of their missionaries put it, there was "a great mass of people beyond the restraints of religion."

Evangelicals founded moral reform societies as well as missions. Some of these aimed at curbing irreligious activity on the Sabbath; others sought to stamp out dueling, gambling, and prostitution. In New York in 1831, a zealous young clergyman published a sensational report claiming there were ten thousand prostitutes in the city. As a result of this exposé, an asylum was established for the redemption of "abandoned women." When middle-class women became involved in this crusade, they shifted its focus to the men who patronized prostitutes, and they proposed that teams of observers record and publish the names of men seen entering brothels. The plan was abandoned because it offended those who thought the cause of virtue would be better served by suppressing public discussion and investigation of sexual vices.

Beecher was especially influential in the **temperance movement**, the most successful reform crusade; his published sermons were the most important and widely distributed of the early tracts calling for total abstinence from "demon rum." The temperance movement was directed at a real social evil. Since the Revolution, whiskey had become the most popular American beverage. Made from corn by individual farmers or, by the 1820s, in commercial distilleries, it was cheaper than milk or beer and safer than water (which was

Watch the Video   Drinking and the Temperance Movement in Nineteenth-Century America

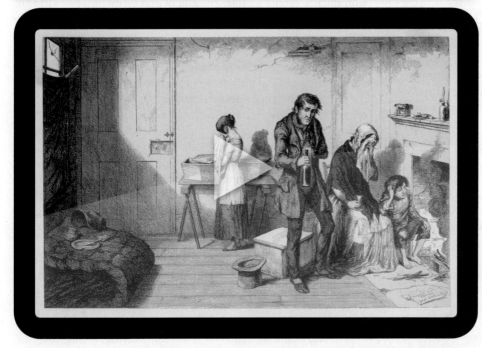

Drinking alcohol was a regular part of daily life in nineteenth-century America, at work, at home, and at social gatherings. But the anti-alcohol, or "temperance" movement gained steam in the 1830s, especially through portrayals of the negative effects of the "Demon Drink" on women and children, as seen above.

often contaminated). In some parts of the country, rum and brandy were also popular. Hard liquor was frequently consumed with food as a table beverage, even at breakfast, and children sometimes imbibed along with adults. Many evangelical reformers regarded intemperance as the greatest single obstacle to a republic of God-fearing, self-disciplined citizens. (For more on the temperance movement, see the Feature Essay "The War against Demon Drink," pp. 282–283.) Cooperating missionary and reform societies—collectively known as "the **benevolent empire**"—were a major force in American culture by the early 1830s. Efforts to modify American attitudes and institutions seemed to be bearing fruit. The middle class was embracing a new ethic of self-control and self-discipline, equipping individuals to confront a new world of economic growth and social mobility without losing their cultural and moral bearings.

Domesticity and Changes in the American Family

What was the doctrine of "separate spheres," and how did it change family life?

The evangelical culture of the 1820s and 1830s influenced the family as an institution and inspired new conceptions of its role in American society. Many parents viewed children's rearing as essential preparation for self-disciplined Christian life and performed their nurturing duties with great seriousness and self-consciousness. Women—regarded as particularly susceptible to religious and moral influences—were increasingly confined to the domestic circle, but they assumed a greater importance within it.

Marriage for Love

In the early nineteenth century, a new ideal of marriage for love arose among the American middle class. Many nineteenth-century Americans placed new value on ties of affection among family members, especially a married couple joined by romantic love. Parents now exercised even less control over their children's selection of mates than they had in the colonial period. The desire to protect family property and maintain social status remained strong, but mutual affection was now considered absolutely essential to a proper union. Beginning in the late eighteenth century, romantic novels popularized the idea that marriage should be based exclusively on love. It became easier for sons to marry while their fathers were still alive and for younger daughters to wed before their older sisters—trends that reflected a weakening of the traditional parental role.

Correspondence between spouses began to reflect this new "companionate" ideal. For the most part, eighteenth-century letters had been formal and distant in tone. The husband often assumed a patriarchal role, even using such salutations as "my dear child" and rarely confessing that he missed his wife or craved her company. Letters from women to their husbands were highly deferential and did not usually give advice or express disapproval.

By the early nineteenth century, first names, pet names, and terms of endearment such as "honey" or "darling" were increasingly used by both sexes, and absent husbands frequently confessed they felt lost without their mates. In their replies, wives assumed a more egalitarian tone and offered counsel on a wide range of subjects. One wrote to a husband who had admitted to flirting with pretty women that she was more than "a little jealous." She asked him angrily how he would feel if she made a similar confession: "Would it be more immoral in me than in you?"

The change in middle- and upper-class marriage should not be exaggerated or romanticized. In law, and in cases of conflict between spouses, the husband remained the unchallenged head of the household. True independence or equality for women was impossible at a time when men held exclusive legal authority over a couple's property and children. Divorce was difficult for everyone, but the double standard made it easier for husbands than wives to dissolve a marriage on grounds of adultery. Letters also reveal the strains spouses felt between their ideals of mutual love and the reality of very different gender roles and life paths—husbands away from home for long periods pursuing financial gain as "self-made men," while women stayed at home in the domestic sphere.

The Cult of Domesticity

The notion that women belonged in the home while the public sphere belonged to men has been called the ideology of "separate spheres." In particular, the view that women had a special role to play in the domestic sphere as guardians of virtue and spiritual heads of the home has been described as the **Cult of Domesticity** or the "Cult of True Womanhood." In the view of most men, a woman's place was in the home and on a pedestal. The ideal wife and mother was "an angel in the house," a model of piety and virtue who exerted a wholesome moral and religious influence over members of the coarser sex. A poem published in 1846 expressed a masculine view of the true woman:

> I would have her as pure as the snow on the mount—
> As true as the smile that to infancy's given—
> As pure as the wave of the crystalline fount,
> Yet as warm in the heart as the sunlight of heaven.

The sociological reality behind the Cult of True Womanhood was a growing division between the working lives of middle-class men and women. In the eighteenth century and earlier, most economic activity had been centered in and near the home, and husbands and wives often worked together in a common enterprise. By the early to mid-nineteenth century this way of life was declining, especially in

Read the Document   Catharine E. Beecher, from *A Treatise on Domestic Economy*

The sentiment on this sampler, stitched in 1820 by Ruth Titus, typifies beliefs about woman's proper role, according to the Cult of True Womanhood.

Source: Collection of The New-York Historical Society, negative number 1941.910.

the Northeast. In towns and cities, the rise of factories and counting-houses severed the home from the workplace. Men went forth every morning to work, leaving their wives at home to tend the house and the children. Married women were therefore increasingly deprived of a productive economic role. The cult of domesticity made a virtue of the fact that men were solely responsible for running the affairs of the world and building up the economy.

A new conception of gender roles justified and glorified this pattern. The doctrine of "separate spheres"—as set forth in novels, advice literature, and the new women's magazines—sentimentalized the woman who kept a spotless house, nurtured her children, and offered her husband a refuge from the heartless world of commerce and industry. From a modern point of view, it is easy to condemn the cult of domesticity as a rationalization for male dominance; to a considerable extent, it was. Yet the new norm of confinement to the home did not necessarily imply that women were inferior. By the standards of evangelical culture, women in the domestic sphere could be viewed as superior to men, since women were in a good position to cultivate the "feminine" virtues of love and self-sacrifice and thus act as official guardians of religious and moral values.

Furthermore, many women used domestic ideology to fashion a role for themselves in the public sphere. The evangelical movement encouraged women's role as the keepers of moral virtue. The revivals not only gave women a role in converting men but presented as the main object of worship a Christ with stereotypical feminine characteristics. A nurturing, loving, merciful savior, mediating between a stern father and his erring children, provided the model for woman's new role as spiritual head of the home. Membership in evangelical church-based associations inspired and prepared women for new roles as civilizers of men and guardians of domestic culture and morality. Female reform societies taught women the strict ethical code they were to instill in other family members; organized mothers' groups gave instruction in how to build character and encourage piety in children.

While many working-class women read about and aspired to the ideal of True Womanhood, domestic ideology only affected the daily lives of relatively affluent women. Working-class wives were not usually employed outside the home during this period, but they labored long and hard within the household. Besides cleaning, cooking, and taking care of large numbers of children, they often took in washing or piecework to supplement a meager family income. Life was especially hard for African American women. Most of those who were "free Negroes" rather than slaves did not have husbands who made enough to support them, and they were obliged to serve in white households or work long hours at home doing other people's washing and sewing.

In urban areas, unmarried working-class women often lived on their own and toiled as household servants, in the sweatshops of the garment industry, and in factories. Barely able to support themselves and at the mercy of male sexual predators, they were in no position to identify with the middle-class ideal of elevated, protected womanhood. For some of them, the relatively well-paid and gregarious life of the successful prostitute seemed to offer an attractive alternative to a life of loneliness and privation.

For middle-class women whose husbands or fathers earned a good income, freedom from industrial or farm labor offered some tangible benefits. They now had the leisure to read extensively the new literature directed primarily at housewives, to participate in female-dominated charitable activities, and to cultivate deep and lasting friendships with other women. The result was a distinctively feminine subculture emphasizing "sisterhood" or "sorority." This growing sense of solidarity with other women and of the importance of sexual identity could transcend the private home and even the barriers of social class. Beginning in the 1820s, urban women of the middle and upper classes organized societies for the relief and rehabilitation of poor or "fallen" women. The aim of the organizations was not economic and political equality with men but the elevation of all women to true womanhood.

For some women, the domestic ideal even sanctioned efforts to extend their sphere until it conquered the masculine world outside the home. This domestic feminism was reflected in women's involvement in crusades to stamp out such masculine sins as intemperance, gambling, and sexual vice.

In the benevolent societies and reform movements of the Jacksonian era, especially those designated as women's organizations, women handled money, organized meetings and public appeals, made contracts, and sometimes even gave orders to male subordinates they could not usually perform in their own households. The desire to extend the feminine sphere was the motivating force behind Catharine Beecher's campaign to make school teaching a woman's occupation. A prolific and influential writer on the theory and practice of domesticity, this unmarried daughter of Lyman Beecher saw the spinster-teacher as equivalent to a mother. By instilling in young males the virtues that only women could teach, the schoolmarm could help liberate America from corruption and materialism.

But Beecher and other domestic feminists continued to emphasize the role of married women who stayed home and did their part simply by being wives and mothers. Reforming husbands was difficult: They were away much of the time and tended to be preoccupied with business. But this very fact gave women primary responsibility for the rearing of children—an activity to which nineteenth-century Americans attached almost cosmic significance. Since women were considered particularly well qualified to transmit piety and morality to future citizens of the republic, the cult of domesticity exalted motherhood and encouraged a new concern with childhood as the time of life when "character" was formed.

The Discovery of Childhood

The nineteenth century has been called "the century of the child." More than before, childhood was seen as a distinct stage of life requiring the special and sustained attention of adults, at least until the age of thirteen or fourteen. The middle-class family now became "child centered," which meant that the care, nurture, and rearing of children was viewed as the family's main function. In earlier times, adults treated children in a more casual way, often sending them away from home for education or apprenticeship at a very early age. Among the well to do, children spent more time with servants or tutors than with their parents.

By the early decades of the nineteenth century, however, children were staying at home longer and receiving much more attention from parents, especially mothers. Much less common was the colonial custom—nearly inconceivable today—of naming a child after a sibling who had died in infancy. Each child was now looked on as a unique and irreplaceable individual.

New customs and fashions heralded the "discovery" of childhood. Books aimed specifically at juveniles began to roll off the presses. Parents became more self-conscious about their responsibilities and sought help from a new literature providing expert advice on child rearing. One early nineteenth-century mother wrote, "There is scarcely any subject concerning which I feel more anxiety than the proper education of my children. It is a difficult and delicate subject, the more I feel how much is to be learnt by myself."

The new concern for children resulted in more intimate relations between parents and children. The ideal family described in the advice manuals and sentimental literature was bound together by affection rather than authority. Firm discipline remained at the core of "family government," but there was a change in the preferred method of enforcing good behavior. Corporal punishment declined, partially displaced by shaming or withholding of affection. Disobedient middle-class children were now more likely to be confined to their rooms to reflect on their sins than to receive a good thrashing. Discipline could no longer be justified as the constant application of physical force over naturally wayward beings. In an age of moral **perfectionism**, the role of discipline was to induce repentance and change basic attitudes. The intended result was often described as "self-government"; to achieve it, parents used guilt, rather than fear, as their main source of leverage. A mother's sorrow or a father's stern and prolonged silence was deemed more effective in forming character than were blows or angry words.

Some shared realities of childhood cut across class and ethnic lines. For example, there was a high rate of mortality for infants and young children throughout the nineteenth century. Even wealthy families could expect to lose one child out of five or six before the age of five. But class and region made a big difference to children's lives. Farm children tended livestock, milked cows, churned butter, scrubbed laundry, harvested crops, and hauled water; working-class urban children did "outwork" in textiles, worked in street markets, and scavenged.

One important explanation for the growing focus on childhood is the smaller size of families. For reasons that are still not completely understood, the average number of children born to each woman during her fertile years dropped from 7.04 in 1800 to 5.42 in 1850. As a result, the average number of children per family declined about 25 percent, beginning a long-range trend lasting to the present day.

The practice of various forms of birth control undoubtedly contributed to this demographic revolution. Ancestors of the modern condom and diaphragm were openly advertised and sold during the pre–Civil War period, but it is likely that most couples controlled family size by practicing the withdrawal method or limiting the frequency of intercourse. Abortion was also surprisingly common and was on the rise. One historian has estimated that by 1850 there was one abortion for every five or six live births.

Parents seemed to understand that having fewer children meant they could provide their offspring with a better start in life. Such attitudes were appropriate in a society that was beginning to shift from agriculture to commerce and industry. For rural households short of labor, large families were an economic asset. For urban couples who hoped to send their children into a competitive world that demanded special talents and training, they were a financial liability.

Institutional Reform

How did Horace Mann change ideas about public schooling in America?

The family could not carry the whole burden of socializing and reforming individuals. Children needed schooling as well as parental nurturing, and many were thought to lack a proper home environment. Some adults, too, seemed to require special kinds of attention and treatment. Seeking to extend the advantages of "family government" beyond the domestic circle, reformers worked to establish or improve public institutions that were designed to shape individual character and instill a capacity for self-discipline.

The Extension of Education

The period from 1820 to 1850 saw an enormous expansion of free public schools. The new resolve to put more children in school for longer periods reflected many of the same values that exalted the child-centered family. Up to a certain age, children could be effectively nurtured and educated in the home. But after that they needed formal training at a character-molding institution that would prepare them to make a living and bear the burdens of republican citizenship. Intellectual training at school was regarded as less important than moral indoctrination.

Sometimes the school served as a substitute for the family. Educational reformers were alarmed at the masses of poor and immigrant children who allegedly failed to get proper nurturing at home. It was up to schools to make up for this disadvantage. Otherwise, the republic would be in danger from masses of people "incapable of self-government."

Before the 1820s, schooling in the United States was a haphazard affair. The wealthy sent their children to private schools, and some of the poor sent their children to charity or "pauper" schools that were usually financed in part by local governments. Public education was most highly developed in the New England states, where towns were required by law to support elementary schools. It was weakest in the South, where almost all education was private.

Agitation for expanded public education began in the 1820s and early 1830s as a central demand of the workingmen's movements in eastern cities. These hard-pressed artisans viewed free schools open to all as a way of countering the growing gap between rich and poor. Initially, strong opposition came from more affluent taxpayers who did not see why they should pay for the education of other people's children. But middle-class reformers soon seized the initiative, shaped educational reform to their own end of social discipline, and provided the momentum needed for legislative success.

The most influential supporter of the common school movement was Horace Mann of Massachusetts. As a lawyer and member of the state legislature, Mann worked tirelessly to establish a state board of education and adequate tax support for local schools. In 1837, he persuaded the legislature to enact his proposals, and

he subsequently resigned his seat to become the first secretary of the new board, an office he held with great distinction until 1848. He believed children were clay in the hands of teachers and school officials and could be molded to a state of perfection. Like advocates of child rearing through moral influence rather than physical force, he discouraged corporal punishment except as a last resort. His position on this issue led to a bitter controversy with Boston schoolmasters who retained a Calvinist sense of original sin and favored a freer use of the rod.

Against those who argued that school taxes violated property rights, Mann contended that private property was actually held in trust for the good of the community. "The property of this commonwealth," he wrote, "is pledged for the education of all its youth up to such a point as will save them from poverty and vice, and prepare them for the adequate performance of their social and civil duties." Mann's conception of public education as a means of social discipline converted the middle and upper classes to the cause. By teaching middle-class morality and respect for order, the schools could turn potential rowdies and revolutionaries into law-abiding citizens. They could also encourage social mobility by opening doors for lower-class children who were determined to do better than their parents.

In practice, new or improved public schools often alienated working-class pupils and their families rather than reforming them. Compulsory attendance laws in Massachusetts and other states deprived poor families of needed wage earners without guaranteeing new occupational opportunities for those with an elementary education. As the laboring class became increasingly immigrant and Catholic in the 1840s and 1850s, dissatisfaction arose over the evangelical Protestant tone of "moral instruction" in the schools. Quite consciously, Mann and his disciples were trying to impose a uniform culture on people who valued differing traditions.

In addition to the "three Rs" ("reading, 'riting, and 'rithmetic"), the public schools of the mid-nineteenth century taught the "Protestant ethic"—industry, punctuality, sobriety, and frugality. These were the virtues emphasized in the famous *McGuffey's Eclectic Readers*, which first appeared in 1836. Millions of children learned to read by digesting McGuffey's parables about the terrible fate of those who gave in to sloth, drunkenness, or wastefulness. Such moral indoctrination helped produce generations of Americans with personalities and beliefs adapted to the needs of an industrializing society—people who could be depended on to adjust to the precise and regular routines of the factory or the office. But as an education for self-government—in the sense of learning to think for oneself—it left much to be desired.

Fortunately, however, education was not limited to the schools nor devoted solely to children. Every city and almost every town or village had a lyceum, debating society, or mechanics' institute where adults of all social classes could broaden their intellectual horizons. Lyceums featured discourses on such subjects as "self-reliance" or "the conduct of life" by creative thinkers such as Ralph Waldo Emerson, explanations and demonstrations of the latest scientific discoveries, and debates among members on controversial issues.

Young Abraham Lincoln, who had received less than two years of formal schooling as a child in backwoods Indiana, sharpened his intellect in the early 1830s as a member of the New Salem (Illinois) debating society. In 1838, after moving to Springfield, he set forth

Watch the Video Who Was Horace Mann and Why are So Many Schools Named After Him?

Horace Mann has been called the father of American public education. He saw schools creating citizens for the new Democratic society in the United States.

his political principles when he spoke at the local lyceum on "The Perpetuation of Our Political Institutions." More than the public schools, the lyceums and debating societies fostered independent thought and encouraged new ideas.

Discovering the Asylum

Some segments of the population were obviously beyond the reach of family government and character training provided in homes and schools. In the 1820s and 1830s, reformers became acutely aware of the danger to society posed by an apparently increasing number of criminals, lunatics, and paupers. Their answer was to establish special institutions to house those deemed incapable of self-discipline. Their goals were humanitarian; they believed reform and rehabilitation were possible in a carefully controlled environment.

In earlier times, the existence of paupers, lawbreakers, and insane persons had been taken for granted. Their presence was viewed as the consequence of divine judgment or original sin. For the most part, these people were not isolated from local communities. The insane were allowed to wander about if harmless and were confined at home if they were dangerous; the poor were supported by private charity or the dole provided by towns or counties; convicted criminals were whipped, held for limited periods in local jails, or—in the case of very serious offenses—executed.

By the early nineteenth century, these traditional methods had come to seem both inadequate and inhumane. Dealing with deviants in a neighborly way broke down as economic development and urbanization made communities less cohesive. At the same time, reformers were concluding that all defects of mind and character were correctable—the insane could be cured, criminals reformed, and paupers taught to pull themselves out of destitution. The result was what historian David Rothman termed "the discovery of the asylum"—the invention and establishment of special institutions for the confinement and reformation of deviants.

The 1820s and 1830s saw the emergence of state-supported prisons, insane asylums, and poorhouses. New York and Pennsylvania led the way in prison reform. Institutions at Auburn, New York, and Philadelphia attracted international attention as model penitentiaries, mainly because of their experiments in isolating inmates from one another. Solitary confinement was viewed as a humanitarian and therapeutic policy because it gave inmates a chance to reflect on their sins, free from the corrupting influence of other convicts. In theory, prisons and asylums substituted for the family. Custodians were meant to act as parents, providing moral advice and training.

In practice, the institutions were far different from the affectionate families idealized by the cult of domesticity. Most accommodated only a single sex or maintained a strict segregation of male and female inmates. Their most prominent feature was the imposition of a rigid daily routine. The early superintendents and wardens believed the enforcement of a rigorous set of rules and procedures would encourage self-discipline. The French observers Alexis de Tocqueville and Gustave de Beaumont summed up these practical expectations after a tour of American prisons in 1831 and 1832: "The habits or order to which the prisoner is subjected for several years … the obedience of every moment to inflexible rules, the regularity of a uniform life … are calculated to produce a deep impression upon his mind. Perhaps, leaving the prison he is not an honest man, but he has contracted honest habits."

Prisons, asylums, and poorhouses did not achieve the aims of their founders. Public support was inadequate to meet the needs of a growing inmate population, and the personnel of the institutions often lacked the training needed to help the incarcerated. The results were overcrowding and the use of brutality to keep order. For the most part, prisons failed to reform hardened criminals, and the primitive psychotherapy known as "moral treatment" failed to cure most asylum patients. Poorhouses rapidly degenerated into sinkholes of despair. A combination of naive theories and poor performance doomed the institutions to a custodial rather than a reformatory role.

Conditions would have been even worse had it not been for Dorothea Dix. Between 1838 and the Civil War, this remarkable woman devoted her energies and skills to publicizing the inhumane treatment prevailing in prisons, almshouses, and insane asylums and to lobbying for corrective action. As a direct result of her activities, fifteen states opened new hospitals for the insane and others improved their supervision of penitentiaries, asylums, and poorhouses. Dix ranks as one of the most practical and effective of all the reformers of the pre–Civil War era.

Reform Turns Radical

What were some of the major antebellum reform movements?

During the 1830s, internal dissension split the great reform movement spawned by the Second Great Awakening. Efforts to promote evangelical piety, improve personal and public morality, and shape character through familial or institutional discipline continued and even flourished. But bolder spirits went beyond such goals and set their sights on the total liberation and perfection of the individual.

Divisions in the Benevolent Empire

Early nineteenth-century reformers were, for the most part, committed to changing existing attitudes and practices gradually and in ways that would not invite conflict or disrupt society. But by the mid-1830s, a new mood of impatience and perfectionism surfaced within the benevolent societies. In 1836, for example, the Temperance Society split over two issues—whether the abstinence pledge should be extended to include beer and wine and whether pressure should be applied to producers and sellers of alcoholic beverages as well as to consumers. Radicals insisted on a total commitment to "cold water" and were prepared to clash head-on with an important economic interest. Moderates held back from such goals and tactics because they wanted to avoid hostility from prominent citizens who drank wine or had money invested in the liquor industry.

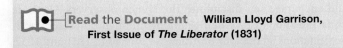

Read the Document   William Lloyd Garrison, First Issue of *The Liberator* (1831)

In the inaugural issue of his antislavery weekly, *The Liberator*, William Lloyd Garrison announced that he was launching a militant battle against the evil and sin of slavery. The stirring words that appeared in that first issue are repeated on *The Liberator's* banner.

A similar rift occurred in the American Peace Society, an antiwar organization founded in 1828 by clergymen seeking to promote Christian concern for world peace. Most of the founders admitted the propriety of "defensive wars" and were shocked when some members of the society began to denounce all use of force as a violation of the Sermon on the Mount. Dissidents, who called themselves "nonresistants," withdrew from the organization in 1838. Led by Henry C. Wright, they formed the New England Non-Resistance Society to promote an absolute pacifism, which denied the right of self-defense to nations or individuals and repudiated all forms of government coercion.

The new perfectionism realized its most dramatic and important success within the antislavery movement. Before the 1830s, most people who expressed religious and moral concern over slavery were affiliated with the American Colonization Society, a benevolent organization founded in 1817. Most colonizationists admitted that slavery was an evil, but they also viewed it as a deeply rooted social and economic institution that could be eliminated only very gradually and with the cooperation of slaveholders. Reflecting the power of racial prejudice, they proposed to provide transportation to Africa for free blacks who chose to go, or were emancipated for the purpose, as a way of relieving southern fears that a race war would erupt if slaves were simply released from bondage and allowed to remain in America. In 1821, the society established the colony of Liberia in West Africa, and during the next decade a few thousand African Americans were settled there.

Colonization proved to be grossly inadequate as a step toward the elimination of slavery. Many of the blacks transported to Africa were already free, and those liberated by masters influenced by the movement represented only a tiny percentage of the natural increase of the southern slave population. Northern blacks denounced the enterprise because it denied the prospect of racial equality in America. Black opposition to colonizationism helped persuade William Lloyd Garrison and other white abolitionists to repudiate the Colonization Society and support immediate emancipation without emigration.

Garrison launched a new and more radical antislavery movement in 1831 in Boston, when he began to publish a journal called *The Liberator*. Besides calling for immediate and unconditional emancipation, Garrison denounced colonization as a slaveholder's plot to remove troublesome free blacks and as an ignoble surrender to un-Christian prejudices. His rhetoric was as severe as his proposals were radical. As he wrote in the first issue of *The Liberator*, "I will be as harsh as truth and as uncompromising as justice.... I am in earnest—I will not equivocate—I will not excuse—I will not retreat a single inch—And I WILL BE HEARD!" Heard he was. In 1833, Garrison and other abolitionists founded the American Anti-Slavery Society. "We shall send forth agents to lift up the voice of remonstrance, of warning, of entreaty, and of rebuke," its Declaration of Sentiments proclaimed. The colonization movement was placed on the defensive, and during the 1830s, many of its most active northern supporters became abolitionists.

The Abolitionist Enterprise

The **abolitionist movement**, like the temperance crusade, was a direct outgrowth of the Second Great Awakening. Many leading abolitionists had undergone conversion experiences in the 1820s and were already committed to a life of Christian activism before they dedicated themselves to freeing the slaves. Several were ministers or divinity students seeking a mission in life that would fulfill spiritual and professional ambitions.

The career of Theodore Dwight Weld exemplified the connection between revivalism and abolitionism. Weld came from a long line of New England ministers. After dropping out of divinity school, he migrated to western New York. There he fell under the influence of Charles G. Finney and, after a long struggle, underwent a conversion experience in 1826. He then became an itinerant lecturer for various reform causes. By the early 1830s, he focused his attention on the moral issues raised by the institution of slavery. After a brief flirtation with the colonization movement, Weld was converted to abolitionism in 1832, recognizing that colonizationists did not really accept blacks as equals or "brothers-in-Christ." In 1834, he instigated what amounted to a series of abolitionist revivals at Lane Theological Seminary in Cincinnati. When the trustees of the seminary attempted to suppress further discussion of the case for immediate emancipation, Weld led a mass walkout of most students. The "Lane rebels" subsequently founded Oberlin College as a center for abolitionist activity.

In 1835 and 1836, Weld toured Ohio and western New York preaching abolitionism. He also supervised and trained other agents and orators as part of a campaign to convert the entire region to immediate emancipation. The tried-and-true methods of the revival—fervent preaching, protracted meetings, and the call for individuals to come forth and announce their redemption—were put at the service of the antislavery movement. Weld and his associates often had to face angry mobs, but they left behind them tens of thousands of new abolitionists and hundreds of local antislavery societies. As a result of their efforts, northern Ohio and western New York became hotbeds of abolitionist sentiment.

Antislavery orators and organizers tended to have their greatest successes in the small- to medium-sized towns of the upper North. The typical convert came from an upwardly mobile family engaged in small business, the skilled trades, or market farming. In larger towns and cities, or when they ventured close to the Mason-Dixon line, abolitionists were more likely to encounter fierce and effective opposition. In 1835, Garrison was mobbed in the streets of Boston and almost lynched. In New York City, the Tappan brothers—Lewis and Arthur—were frequent objects of threats and violence. These two successful merchants were key figures in the movement because they used their substantial wealth to finance antislavery activities. In 1835–1836, they supported a massive effort to print antislavery pamphlets and distribute them through the U.S. mail. But they made relatively few converts in their own city; most New Yorkers regarded them as dangerous radicals.

Abolitionists who thought of taking their message to the fringes of the South had reason to pause, given the fate of the antislavery editor Elijah Lovejoy. In 1837, while attempting to defend himself and his printing press from a mob in Alton, Illinois, just across the Mississippi River from slaveholding Missouri, Lovejoy was shot and killed.

Racism was a major cause of antiabolitionist violence in the North. Rumors that abolitionists advocated or practiced interracial marriage could easily incite an urban crowd. If it could not find white abolitionists, the mob was likely to turn on local blacks. Working-class whites tended to fear that economic and social competition with blacks would increase if abolitionists succeeded in freeing slaves and making them citizens. But a striking feature of many of the mobs was that they were dominated by "gentlemen of property and standing." Solid citizens resorted to violence, it would appear, because abolitionism threatened their conservative notions of social order and hierarchy.

By the end of the 1830s, the abolitionist movement was under great stress. Besides the burden of external repression, there was dissension within the movement. Becoming an abolitionist required an exacting conscience and an unwillingness to compromise on matters of principle. These character traits also made it difficult for abolitionists to work together and maintain a united front. During the late 1830s, Garrison, the most visible proponent of the cause, began to adopt positions that some other abolitionists found extreme and divisive. He embraced the nonresistant or "no-government" philosophy of Henry C. Wright and urged abolitionists to abstain from voting or otherwise participating in a corrupt political system. He also attacked the clergy and the churches for refusing to take a strong antislavery stand and encouraged his followers to "come out" of the established denominations rather than continuing to work within them.

These positions alienated those members of the Anti-Slavery Society who continued to hope that organized religion and the existing political system could be influenced or even taken over by abolitionists. But it was Garrison's stand on women's rights that led to an open break at the national convention of the American Anti-Slavery Society in 1840. Following their leader's principle that women should be equal partners in the crusade, a Garrison-led majority elected a woman abolitionist to the society's executive committee. A minority, led by Lewis Tappan, then withdrew to form a competing organization—the American and Foreign Anti-Slavery Society.

The new organization never amounted to much, but the schism did weaken Garrison's influence within the movement. When he later repudiated the U.S. Constitution as a proslavery document and called for northern secession from the Union, few antislavery people in the Middle Atlantic or midwestern states went along. Outside New England, most abolitionists worked within the churches and avoided controversial side issues such as women's rights and nonresistant pacifism. Some antislavery advocates chose the path of political action. The Liberty Party, organized in 1840, was their first attempt to enter the electoral arena under their own banner; it signaled a new effort to turn antislavery sentiment into political power.

Black Abolitionists

From the beginning the abolitionist movement depended heavily on the support of the northern free black community. Most of the early subscribers to Garrison's *Liberator* were African Americans. Black orators, especially escaped slaves such as Frederick Douglass, made northern audiences aware of the realities of bondage. But relations between white and black abolitionists were often tense and uneasy. Blacks protested that they did not have their fair share of leadership positions or influence over policy. Eventually a black antislavery movement emerged that was largely independent of the white-led crusade. In addition to Douglass, prominent black male abolitionists were Charles Remond, William Wells Brown, Robert Purvis, and Henry Highland Garnet. Outspoken women such as Sojourner Truth, Maria Stewart, and Frances Harper also played a significant role in black antislavery activity. The Negro Convention movement, which sponsored national meetings of black leaders beginning in 1830, provided an important forum for independent black expression. Their most eloquent statement came in 1854, when black leaders met in Cleveland to declare their faith in a separate identity, proclaiming, "We pledge our integrity to use all honorable means, to unite us, as one people, on this continent."

Black newspapers, such as *Freedom's Journal*, first published in 1827, and the *North Star*, founded by Douglass in 1847, gave black writers a chance to preach their gospel of liberation to black readers. African American authors also produced a stream of books and pamphlets attacking slavery, refuting racism, and advocating various forms of resistance. One of the most influential publications was David Walker's *Appeal … to the Colored Citizens of the World*, which appeared in 1829. Walker denounced slavery in the most vigorous language possible and called for a black revolt against white tyranny.

Free blacks in the North did more than make verbal protests against racial injustice. They were also the main conductors on the fabled Underground Railroad that opened a path for fugitives from slavery. It has been supposed that benevolent whites were primarily responsible for organized efforts to guide and assist fugitive slaves,

Read the Document   **David Walker, A Black Abolitionist Speaks**

David Walker was a free African American who operated a second-hand clothing shop in Boston and spoke out on abolition. Unlike many abolitionists, Walker advocated violent action, the rebellion of slaves, and the killing of masters.

but modern research has shown that the Underground Railroad was largely a black-operated enterprise. Courageous ex-slaves such as Harriet Tubman and Josiah Henson made regular forays into the slave states to lead other blacks to freedom, and many of the "stations" along the way were run by free blacks. In northern towns and cities, free blacks organized "vigilance committees" to protect fugitives and thwart the slave catchers. Groups of blacks even used force to rescue recaptured fugitives from the authorities. In Boston in 1851, one such group seized a slave named Shadrack from a U.S. marshal who was in the process of returning him to bondage. In deeds as well as words, free blacks showed their unyielding hostility to slavery and racism.

Historians have debated the question of whether the abolitionist movement of the 1830s and early 1840s was a success or a failure. It obviously failed to convert a majority of Americans to its position that slavery was a sinful institution that should be abolished immediately. This position implied that blacks should be granted equality as American citizens, so it ran up against the powerful commitment to white supremacy prevailing in all parts of the country. In the South, abolitionism caused a strong counteraction and helped inspire a more militant and uncompromising defense of slavery. The belief that peaceful agitation, or what abolitionists called "moral suasion," would convert slaveholders and their northern sympathizers to abolition was obviously unrealistic.

But in another sense the crusade was successful. It brought the slavery issue to the forefront of public consciousness and convinced a substantial and growing segment of the northern population that the South's peculiar institution was morally wrong and potentially dangerous to the American way of life. The South helped the antislavery cause in the North by responding hysterically and repressively to abolitionist agitation. In 1836, Southerners in Congress forced adoption of a "gag rule" requiring that abolitionist petitions be tabled without being read; at about the same time, the post office refused to carry antislavery literature into the slave states. Prominent Northerners who had not been moved to action by abolitionist depictions of slave suffering became more responsive to the movement when it appeared their own civil liberties might be threatened. The politicians who later mobilized the North against the expansion of slavery into the territories drew strength from the antislavery and antisouthern sentiments that abolitionists had already called forth.

From Abolitionism to Women's Rights

Abolitionism also served as a catalyst for the women's rights movement. From the beginning, women were active participants in the abolitionist crusade. Between 1835 and 1838, the American Anti-Slavery Society bombarded Congress with petitions, mostly calling for abolition of slavery in the District of Columbia. More than half of the thousands of antislavery petitions sent to Washington had women's signatures on them.

Some antislavery women went further and defied conventional ideas of their proper sphere by becoming public speakers and demanding an equal role in the leadership of antislavery societies. The most famous of these were the Grimké sisters, Sarah and Angelina, who attracted enormous attention being the rebellious daughters of a South Carolina slaveholder. When some male abolitionists objected to their speaking in public to mixed audiences of men and women, Garrison came to their defense and helped forge a link between blacks' and women's struggles for equality.

The battle to participate equally in the antislavery crusade made a number of women abolitionists acutely aware of male dominance and oppression. For them, the same principles that justified the liberation of the slaves also applied to the emancipation of women from all restrictions on their rights as citizens. In 1840, Garrison's American followers withdrew from the first World's Anti-Slavery Convention in London because the sponsors refused to seat the women in their delegation. Among the women thus excluded were Lucretia Mott and Elizabeth Cady Stanton.

Wounded by men's reluctance to extend the cause of emancipation to include women, Stanton and Mott began discussing plans for a women's rights convention. They returned to New York, where a campaign was already under way to reform the state's laws limiting the rights of married women, spearheaded by a young Jewish activist, Ernestine Rose, and Judge Thomas Herttell, the political radical and freethinker who had introduced the first bill to reform the state's marriage laws to the New York state legislature. (See the Law and Society essay "The Legal Rights of Married Women: Reforming the Law of Coverture," pp. 286–289.) The campaign for women's rights came to a head at the famous **Seneca Falls Convention** that Stanton and Mott organized in upstate New York in 1848. The Declaration of Sentiments issued by this first national gathering of feminists charged that "the history of mankind is a history of repeated injuries and usurpations on the part of man toward woman, having in direct object the establishment of an absolute tyranny over her." It went on to demand that all women be given the right to vote and that married women be freed from unjust laws giving husbands control of their property, persons, and children. Rejecting the cult of domesticity with its doctrine of separate spheres, these women and their male supporters launched the modern movement for gender equality.

Radical Ideas and Experiments

Hopes for individual or social perfection were not limited to reformers inspired by evangelicalism. Between the 1820s and 1850s, a great variety of schemes for human redemption came from those who had rejected orthodox Protestantism. Some were secular humanists carrying on the freethinking tradition of the Enlightenment, but most were seekers of new paths to spiritual or religious fulfillment. A movement that achieved remarkable success or notoriety was spiritualism—the belief that one could communicate with the dead. These philosophical and religious radicals attacked established institutions, prescribed new modes of living, and founded utopian communities to put their ideas into practice.

A radical movement of foreign origin that gained a toehold in Jacksonian America was utopian socialism. In 1825–1826, the British manufacturer and reformer Robert Owen visited the United States and founded a community based on common and equal ownership of property at New Harmony, Indiana. About the same time, Owen's associate Frances Wright gathered a

group of slaves at Nashoba, Tennessee, and set them to work earning their freedom in an atmosphere of "rational cooperation." The rapid demise of both of these model communities suggested that utopian socialism did not easily take root in American soil.

But the impulse survived. In the 1840s, a number of Americans, including the prominent editor Horace Greeley, became interested in the ideas of the French utopian theorist Charles Fourier. Fourier called for cooperative communities in which everyone did a fair share of the work and tasks were allotted to make use of the natural abilities and instincts of the members. Between 1842 and 1852, about thirty Fourierist "phalanxes" were established in the northeastern and midwestern states, and approximately a hundred thousand people lived for a time in these communities or otherwise supported the movement. The phalanxes were not purely socialistic; in fact, they were organized as joint-stock companies. But they did give the members an opportunity to live and work in a communal atmosphere. Like the Owenite communities, they were short-lived, surviving

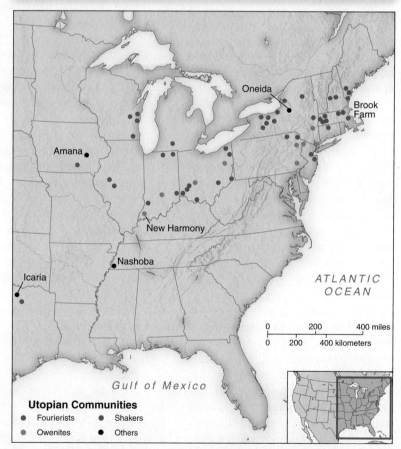

UTOPIAN COMMUNITIES BEFORE THE CIVIL WAR The search for new paths to spiritual or religious fulfillment attracted many to utopian communitarian societies. By far the largest of these societies during the period before the Civil War was the Shakers, who by the 1830s had established twenty settlements in seven states with a combined membership of approximately six thousand. Their rule of celibacy meant that Shaker communities gained members through adoption and conversion, rather than by natural reproduction.

Feature Essay

The War Against "Demon Drink"

'Mid charnels and pest houses though we may roam,
Be it ever so frightful, there's no plague like Rum!
A charm from below seems to lead to the snare,
And leaves us in darkness, and gloom, and despair.
Rum, Rum, curst, curst Rum,
There's no plague like Rum, there's no plague like Rum.

Tunes like this one rang from the windows of American homes in the mid-nineteenth century, signaling the rise of one of the longest lasting social revolutions in American history—the Temperance Movement. The rise of this movement was especially astonishing because drinking was so widespread in early America.

Americans in the new republic loved to drink. They drank at weddings, funerals, and civic celebrations. They drank at work during the day, and at home at night. Not only did they enjoy wine and beer, but rum, whiskey, and rye. By 1830, the average American drank nearly ten gallons of distilled spirits per year—nearly twice the average per person in 1790, and almost four times what Americans drink today.

While drinking was not limited to men, it was an important aspect of male-bonding culture, at work and in the tavern. Drinking together offered an opportunity for sociability across class lines in the early republic. Artisans drank in the workplace, and during the Revolution, toasting was both a social and political ritual in workingmen's Revolutionary committees. When George Washington's presidential home was built in 1792–1793, the laborers and craftsmen were treated to a drink when the cornerstone had been set, again when each of three floors was completed, and when they began work on the roof rafters.

In Philadelphia paper mills, it was customary for journeymen to receive a half-pint of spirits at eleven o'clock each morning, and again in the afternoon. Because many journeymen and apprentices boarded in the master's home, drinking together carried over into the household sphere as well.

In the 1820s, household commodity production began to decline, with masters separating their workshops from their homes. As historian Paul Johnson explains, "By 1830, the doorway to a middle-class home separated radically different kinds of space: drunkenness and promiscuous sociability on the outside, privacy and icy sobriety indoors." Master artisans who now headed growing manufactories began to realize that the new market values of efficiency and productivity were at odds with the sociability—and drinking—of the old workplace. They were primed and ready for the message of evangelical temperance reformers.

The temperance reformers viewed indulgence in alcohol as a threat to public morality. Drunkenness was seen as a loss of self-control and moral responsibility that spawned crime, vice, and disorder. Above all, it threatened the family. The main target of temperance propaganda was the husband and father who abused, neglected, or abandoned his wife and children because he was a slave to the bottle. Women played a vital role in the movement and were instrumental in making it a crusade for the protection of the home. The drinking habits of the poor or laboring classes also aroused great concern. Particularly in urban areas, the "respectable" and propertied elements lived in fear that lower-class mobs, crazed with drink, would attack private property and create social chaos.

In 1826, a group of clergymen previously active in mission work organized the American Temperance Society to coordinate and extend the work already begun by local churches and moral reform societies. The original aim was to encourage abstinence from "ardent spirits" or hard liquor; there was no agreement on the evils of beer and wine. The society sent out lecturers, issued a flood of literature, and sponsored essay contests. Its agents organized revival meetings and called on those in attendance to sign a pledge promising abstinence from spirits. The campaign was enormously effective. By 1834, there were five thousand local branches with more than a million members.

Some workingmen defiantly insisted on their right to drink, and built their own autonomous social life, in grog halls and taverns, with heavy drinking an important part of it. As one working-class letter-writer angrily asked, "Who are the most temperate men of modern times? Those who quaff the juice of the grape with their friends, with the greatest good nature, after the manner of the ancient patriarchs, without any malice

TREE of TEMPERANCE
BY A.D. FILLMORE

TREE of INTEMPERANCE
BY A.D. FILLMORE

A pair of prints issued by A.D. Fillmore in 1855 extolling the social and moral benefits of temperance and condemning the evils of alcohol. On the Tree of Temperance, the fruits are labeled with the names of virtues, including "Industry," "Philanthropy," "Goodwill," and "Charity." On either side, the church and the schoolhouse represent the twin ideals of religion and education that were believed to flourish in a temperance regime. The Tree of Intemperance demonstrates the evils of drink using religious imagery of a serpent with an apple in its mouth, and branches labeled with social and moral evils such as "Ignorance," "Vice," and "Crime," as well as anarchy, counterfeiting, and dueling. The men attempting to chop down the tree are temperance reformers, celebrating the 1851 Maine Prohibition Law.

in their hearts, or the cold-water, pale-faced, money-making men, who make the necessities of their neighbors their opportunity for grinding the face of the poor?"

But others joined temperance societies of their own. The first Washingtonian Society was born in 1840 when four Baltimore craftsmen attended a temperance lecture, intending to mock the speaker, but instead were converted to the cause. They persuaded their friends to swear off liquor, and quickly touched off a wave of temperance activity among journeymen, apprentices, and other members of the working class.

Unlike middle-class evangelicals, who reserved their gospel for the sober, Washingtonian societies sought out the confirmed drunkard and offered him salvation. They also offered more concrete mutual benefits, such as soup kitchens for the poor. The Washingtonians held weekly experience meetings to testify and confess their own experiences with "Demon Drink" and to swear off the

bottle. The societies also tried to recreate the enjoyable community aspects of tavern life with temperance songs, poems, and theatrical shows. T. S. Arthur's "Ten Nights in a Bar-Room and What I Saw There," penned in 1854, was a huge best-seller, and the stage adaptation was one of the longest-running and most popular plays of the antebellum era, entertaining large crowds of teetotalers.

Washingtonian societies spread like wildfire; anyone could start one, including women, children, and African Americans. In Utica, New York, alone, there was a Martha Washington Union, an Irish Hibernian Association, a Workingmen's Temperance Union, youth clubs, and even a black women's temperance association. While most Washingtonian societies presented themselves as "young men's associations," the average age of the men involved was between thirty and thirty-five—and the majority of members may have been women.

Beginning in the 1840s, the temperance movement, like other reform movements of the period, turned from evangelical hope in individual redemption to a drive for legal regulation. It won some success in the 1850s: Maine enacted dry laws in 1851, followed by twelve more states by 1855. Beginning in the 1850s, as new waves of immigration from Ireland and Germany brought a surge of beer and whiskey consumption, temperance became entangled with the politics of nativism—and, like other reform efforts, it was soon overshadowed by the sectional conflict over slavery.

But the mass movement of the "Cold Water Army" did achieve some significant goals. Although it may be doubted whether huge numbers of confirmed drunkards were cured, the movement did succeed in altering the drinking habits of middle-class American males by making temperance a mark of respectability. Per capita consumption of hard liquor declined more than 50 percent during the 1830s, and by 1850 was down to one-third of what it had been in 1830. And the antebellum temperance movement set the stage for national Prohibition—one of the few major social reforms to take place by constitutional amendment, on January 29, 1920, when the Eighteenth Amendment outlawing the "manufacture, sale, and transportation" of liquor in the United States took effect. With the enactment of national Prohibition, temperance at last became embedded, temporarily, in the law of the nation.

QUESTIONS FOR DISCUSSION

1. Why was heavy drinking so prevalent in America in the early nineteenth century?

2. Why did the temperance movement become so active in the 1820s and 1830s?

3. How did the temperance movement change the drinking habits of middle-class American males?

for an average of only two years. The common complaint of the founders was that Americans were too individualistic to cooperate in the ways that Fourier's theories required.

Two of the most successful and long-lived manifestations of pre–Civil War utopianism were the Shakers and the Oneida community. The Shakers—officially known as the Millennial Church or the United Society of Believers—began as a religious movement in England. In 1774, a Shaker leader, Mother Ann Lee, brought their radical beliefs to the United States. Lee believed herself to be the feminine incarnation of Christ and advocated a new theology based squarely on the principle of sexual equality. The Shakers, named for their expressions of religious fervor through vigorous dancelike movements, believed in communal ownership and strict celibacy. They lived simply and minimized their contact with the outside world because they expected Christ's Second Coming to occur momentarily. The Oneida community was established in 1848

> **▶ Read the Document**   Ralph Waldo Emerson, "Self Reliance" (1841)

Ralph Waldo Emerson, who was born in Boston in 1803, was a famous essayist, lecturer, and poet. He is perhaps best known as the leader of the Transcendentalist movement.

at Oneida, New York, and was inspired by an unorthodox brand of Christian perfectionism. Its founder, John Humphrey Noyes, believed the Second Coming of Christ had already occurred; hence human beings were no longer obliged to follow the moral rules that their previously fallen state had required. At Oneida, traditional marriage was outlawed, and a carefully regulated form of "free love" was put into practice.

It was the literary and philosophical movement known as transcendentalism that inspired the era's most memorable experiments in thinking and living on a higher plane. The main idea was that the individual could transcend material reality and ordinary understanding, attaining through a higher form of reason—or intuition—a oneness with the universe as a whole and with the spiritual forces that lay behind it. Transcendentalism was the major American version of the romantic and idealist thought that emerged in the early nineteenth century. Throughout the Western world, and especially in Germany, romanticism was challenging the rationalism and materialism of the Enlightenment in the name of exalted feeling and cosmic spirituality. Most American transcendentalists were Unitarians or ex-Unitarians who were dissatisfied with the sober rationalism of their denomination and sought a more intense kind of spiritual experience. Unable to embrace evangelical Christianity because of intellectual resistance to its doctrines, they sought inspiration from a philosophical and literary idealism of German origin.

Their prophet was Ralph Waldo Emerson, a brilliant essayist and lecturer who preached that each individual could commune directly with a benign spiritual force that animated nature and the universe, which he called the "oversoul." Emerson was a radical individualist committed to "self-culture" and "the sufficiency of the private man." He carefully avoided all involvement in organized movements or associations because he believed they limited the freedom of the individual to develop inner resources and find a personal path to spiritual illumination. In the vicinity of Emerson's home in Concord, Massachusetts, a group of like-minded seekers of truth and spiritual fulfillment gathered during the 1830s and 1840s. Among them for a time was Margaret Fuller, the leading woman intellectual of the age. In *Woman in the Nineteenth Century* (1845), she made a strong claim for the spiritual and artistic equality of women.

One group of transcendentalists, led by the Reverend George Ripley, rejected Emerson's radical individualism and founded a cooperative community at Brook Farm, near Roxbury, Massachusetts, in 1841. For the next four years, group members worked the land in common, conducted an excellent school on the principle that spontaneity rather than discipline was the key to education, and allowed ample time for conversation, meditation, communion with nature, and artistic activity of all kinds. Visitors and guest lecturers included such luminaries as Emerson, Margaret Fuller, and Theodore Parker, the Unitarian theologian and radical reformer. In 1845, Brook Farm was reconstituted as a Fourierist phalanx, but some of the original spirit persisted until its dissolution in 1849.

Another experiment in transcendental living adhered more closely to the individualistic spirit of the movement. Between 1845 and 1847, Henry David Thoreau, a young disciple of Emerson, lived by himself in the woods along the shore of Walden Pond and carefully recorded his thoughts and impressions. In a sense, he pushed the ideal of self-culture to its logical outcome—a utopia of one. The result was *Walden* (published in 1854), one of the greatest achievements in American literature.

Conclusion: Counterpoint on Reform

One great American writer observed at close quarters the perfectionist ferment of the age but held himself aloof, suggesting in his novels and tales that pursuit of the ideal led to a distorted view of human nature and possibilities. Nathaniel Hawthorne lived in Concord, knew Emerson and Margaret Fuller, and even spent time at Brook Farm. But his sense of human frailty made him skeptical about the claims of transcendentalism and utopianism. He satirized transcendentalism as unworldly and overoptimistic in his allegorical tale "The Celestial Railroad" and gently lampooned the denizens of Brook Farm in his novel *The Blithedale Romance* (1852). His view of the dangers of pursuing perfection too avidly came out in his tale of a father who kills his beautiful daughter by trying to remove her one blemish, a birthmark. His greatest novels, *The Scarlet Letter* (1850) and *The House of the Seven Gables* (1851), imaginatively probed New England's Puritan past and the shadows it cast on the present. By dwelling on original sin as a psychological reality, Hawthorne told his contemporaries that their efforts to escape from guilt and evil were futile. One simply had to accept the world as an imperfect place. Although he did not engage in polemics against humanitarian reformers and cosmic optimists, Hawthorne wrote parables and allegories that implicitly questioned the fundamental assumptions of pre–Civil War reform.

One does not have to agree with Hawthorne's antiprogressive view of the human condition to acknowledge that the dreams of perfectionist reformers promised more than they could possibly deliver. Revivals could not make all men like Christ; temperance could not solve all social problems; abolitionist agitation could not bring a peaceful end to slavery; and transcendentalism (as Emerson himself sometimes conceded) could not fully emancipate people from the limitations and frustrations of daily life. The consequences of perfectionist efforts were often far different from what their proponents expected. In defense of the reformers, however, one could argue that Hawthorne's skepticism and fatalism were a prescription for doing nothing in the face of intolerable evils. If the reform impulse was long on inspirational rhetoric but somewhat short on durable, practical achievements, it did at least disturb the complacent and opportunistic surface of American life and open the way to necessary changes.

Law and Society | The Legal Rights of Married Women
Reforming the Law of Coverture

By the common law in effect in the United States in the early nineteenth century, women lost their legal personality when they married. The system of coverture governed the union of husband and wife; married women were under the "wing, protection, or cover" of their husbands.

Coverture was based on the English medieval feudal system in which lords and vassals owed allegiance to the king, and commoners to lords and vassals. Under the common law of England, husband and wife were referred to as "baron" and "feme." William Blackstone, the English jurist, professor of common law, and author of *Commentaries on the Law of England*, explained, "the word baron, or lord, attributes to the husband not a very courteous superiority ... if the baron kills his feme, it is the same as if he had killed a stranger, or any other person; but if the feme kills her baron, it is regarded by the laws as a much more atrocious crime; as she not only breaks through the restraints of humanity and conjugal affection, but throws off all subjection to the authority of her husband. And therefore the law denominates her crime, a species of treason, and condemns her to the same punishment as if she had killed the king." As Blackstone explained, "By marriage, the husband and wife are one person in the law."

Coverture denied married women their rights to own and manage property, to form contracts, to sue and be sued, and to exercise legal control over children. Upon marriage, all of a wife's personal property became her husband's, which he could give or will to someone else if he chose. The husband could not sell his wife's real estate, but he could control and manage it, and any profits derived from the property belonged to him.

Coverture had a few benefits for women. Husbands took legal responsibility for any crimes their wives committed, and sometimes wives could avoid responsibility for unwise financial transactions because they had had no legal right to enter into them. A widow had a right to one-third of her husband's property (her "dower"), if he died without a will. And a husband had a limited obligation to provide for his wife's "necessaries." Blackstone concluded his chapter on husband and wife with the observation that "even the disabilities, which the wife lies under, are for the most part intended for her protection and benefit. So great a favourite is the female sex of the laws of England."

In practice, some women, especially wealthy women, were able to get around some of the laws of coverture by taking advantage of loopholes in the law. First of all, women could go to courts of "equity" or "chancery," in which a chancellor, rather than a jury, could decide the fair or just outcome based on the facts of the individual case, rather than applying rules of law. (These two court systems of law and equity are merged into one in most states today.) An equity court had the power not only to assign money damages but to require a contract to be carried out. For example, a couple might specify in a prenuptial contract—made before the marriage was entered into—that the wife could keep her own property from before the

Women's rights activist Ernestine Rose began petitioning for married women's property rights in New York in 1836.

marriage in a "separate estate." It was also possible for a husband to assign some of his property to his wife after the marriage in a "marriage settlement." And often they arranged for the wife's separate estate to be held in "trust" and managed by a third-party trustee, usually a man.

It was the legal arrangement of coverture into which Harriet Douglas, a rich New York heiress, resisted entering. Harriet Douglas had very definite ideas about what she wanted in a husband. If she married, she intended to keep control over all of her property, "in obedience to, and conformity with the opinions and precepts of her parents," and she wanted her husband to renounce his own name, his home, and his profession, to devote himself to her and her family property. As historian Hendrik Hartog observed, according to the norms of early America, Harriet Douglas effectively wanted "her husband [to] become her wife." Henry Cruger, a young lawyer who came to New York from South Carolina and who courted Harriet Douglas, at first chafed at the restrictions she proposed for a marriage arrangement. Henry argued that "the husband ought always to possess an absolute control over the wife's property." But a few years later, Henry rethought his position, writing to Harriet in 1829 that he would accept her terms, "however derogatory to proper pride…and self-respect." After extensive negotiations, they finally married in 1833. Henry took "D" for his middle initial without changing his last name, and Harriet was to be known as "Mrs. Douglas Cruger." Harriet agreed to sign a property settlement agreement after rather than before the marriage ceremony, because Henry claimed that a pre-marital contract would become part of an embarrassing public record.

Harriet's and Henry's marriage fell almost immediately on hard times, largely over money matters. Henry repeatedly threatened to return to legal practice if Harriet did not give him more freedom to control their property, urging her, "Take away this poignard of ice from between us…I desire no interests separate from yours, for I love you, and we are married." On several occasions, Harriet drew up new "agency" agreements, giving Henry more control of her estate as her "agent." Her friends all urged her to "relieve" Henry "from a state of dependence" that could only be galling to a "man of honor." After years of Henry's haranguing and lobbying, in 1841 Harriet signed an order guaranteeing him one-half of her income for life. That same year, their marriage fell apart completely.

It took eight more years in New York courts to work out Henry's and Harriet's rights to her property. Henry argued that their marriage settlement was invalid because it came after rather than before the marriage.

Harriet claimed the original settlement should be enforced, but the 1841 gift was invalid because Henry and his friends had coerced her into signing it. In 1848, the case ended up in the New York Supreme Court, where Judge Selah Strong decreed that the original marriage settlement was valid, giving Harriet control over her own property, but that the 1841 order was enforceable as well, giving control over half of it to Henry. Years later, Strong wrote, "She was mad and he was bad, and the legal muddle they brought about between them was very deep and formidable."

At the end of their legal muddle, Henry emerged victorious with control over half of Harriet's separate estate. Despite her strenuous efforts to be an independent married woman, she had failed. In disgust, she "had her marriage bed cut in two, transforming it into two 'slightly peculiar' sofas."

The New York Supreme Court made its final decision in *Cruger* v. *Cruger*, just one year after the New York legislature passed its first Married Women's Property Act, allowing women for the first time to maintain ownership and control over property they had inherited before they married. Over the course of the middle decades of the nineteenth century, an increasingly vocal minority of women chafed against the laws of husband and wife that restricted the independence of women like Harriet Cruger. They demanded the reform of the laws of coverture, first through Married Women's Property Acts, and then through Earnings Laws. Nowhere were they more vocal and successful than in New York.

At first, women's rights reformers concentrated on changing people's hearts and minds, as had temperance reformers, abolitionists, and others who were part of the great wave of reform in the United States in the early nineteenth century. In their private writings, women's rights reformers were often more frank than in public discussion, about how marriage kept women subjugated to their husbands. They often compared the married woman to a slave—with no right to own property, sign a contract, sue another, or even keep her own name.

After 1840, as in so many of the reform movements sparked by the religious fervor of the Second Great Awakening, women's rights reformers began to turn to legal solutions. The first group of advocates for women's rights took particular aim at the laws of marriage and divorce. They also organized women's rights activity on a large scale for the first time. On July 19–20, 1848, the first women's rights convention in the world took place at Seneca Falls, New York. Elizabeth Cady Stanton, a women's rights activist and an organizer of the convention, delivered the "Declaration of Sentiments," modeled on the Declaration of Independence: "We hold these truths to be self-evident: that all men and women are created equal …" Stanton declared further that "The history of mankind is a history of repeated injuries and usurpations on the part of man toward woman, having in direct object the establishment of an absolute tyranny over her."

The declaration listed a series of wrongs, followed by twelve resolutions. While winning the right to vote was part of the women's aim, their chief focus was reforming the laws of marriage. Eleven resolutions passed unanimously; the twelfth, calling for the extension of the vote to women, passed narrowly only after abolitionist and former slave Frederick Douglass made a rousing speech in its favor. The Declaration of Sentiments quickly became famous around the world, sparking women's rights reform movements in England and across Europe.

New York's first Married Women's Property Act, passed in 1848, the same year as the Seneca Falls convention, was the product of a number of factors. The persistent petition campaigns of feminist reformers had some influence on the legislators, but several other forces were at work as well. There was a strong movement in New York to "codify" the common law into written codes, accessible to everyone, thereby minimizing the power of judges and lawyers to shape decisions as they pleased. The leaders of that movement especially took aim at equity courts, which they saw as undemocratic institutions whose individually tailored settlements benefited only the propertied elite. For these politicians, reform of the laws governing married women's property was a way to democratize property law, making available to everyone the "separate estates" that wealthy families had been able to arrange through equity courts. Finally, wealthy Dutch landowners in the Hudson Valley saw the acts as a way to protect family property. Thus, the Married Women's Property Acts, in New York and elsewhere, were a good example of the way that legal reform comes about as a result of reformers' efforts coming together with other circumstances and constituencies.

The 1848 act pronounced that "the real and personal property of any female who may hereafter marry, and which she shall own at the time of the marriage, and the rents, issues and profits thereof, shall not be subject to the disposal of her husband, nor be liable for his debts, and shall continue her sole and separate property, as if she were a single female." It also provided that gifts to married women could remain their separate property, and that marriage settlements and prenuptial agreements would be enforced. The second act, in 1849, made it possible for women to sell or transfer their separate property under certain conditions, and for the trustees of their separate estates to deed property to them if a judge found them capable of managing it.

Despite the Married Women's Property Acts, women who did not have substantial property to inherit from their families still suffered severe legal constraints, most importantly because they still did not control their earnings. New Yorker Ernestine Rose, an early activist for women's rights,

observed, "Here is some provision for the favored few; but for the laboring many, there is none. The mass of people commence life with no other capital than the union of heads, hearts and hands. To the benefit of this best of capital, the wife has no right. If they are unsuccessful in married life, who suffers more the bitter consequences of poverty than the wife? But if successful, she can not call a dollar her own."

In the summer of 1854, Elizabeth Cady Stanton rose to address the Joint Judiciary Committee of the New York State Legislature, the first time a woman had ever spoken before that body. She began: "The thinking minds of all nations call for change. There is a deep-lying struggle in the whole fabric of society; a boundless grinding collision of the New with the Old." Stanton asked the legislators to consider the "legal disabilities under which [women] labor."

On behalf of women, Stanton demanded the right to vote, the right to sit on juries, and the reform of the law of coverture. "Look at the position of woman as wife," she demanded. "The wife who inherits no property holds about the same legal position that does the slave on the Southern plantation. She can own nothing, sell nothing. She has no right even to the wages she earns; her person, her time, her services are the property of another.... But the wife who is so fortunate as to have inherited property, has, by the new law in this State, been redeemed from her lost condition." Stanton told the legislators that she spoke on behalf of the "daughters of the revolutionary heroes of '76," and exhorted them to be true to the goals of the Revolution, mocking their claims to republicanism: "How like feudal barons you freemen hold your women." At the same time that Stanton spoke before the legislature, she presented more than six thousand petitions from women across the state.

Six years later, in 1860, New York passed the first Earnings Act in the nation, providing that a married woman could "carry on any trade or business, and perform any labor or services on

her sole and separate account, and the earnings of any married woman, from her trade, business, labor or services, shall be her sole and separate property, and may be used or invested by her in her own name." By the 1870s, most states had passed some version of married women's property acts, and many northern states passed Earning Acts as well.

By and large, courts interpreted Earnings Acts narrowly. For example, in one 1876 case, the New York Supreme Court ruled that a wife who kept a boardinghouse and nursed a very ill man for several years could not control her earnings because work done in the home was considered to be on the "family account," rather than her "sole and separate account," and was therefore the property of the husband. Repeatedly, courts held that women's labor in the household belonged to the husband, so that only wages earned outside the home—although a minor part of most women's earnings—were covered by the act.

In the Iowa case of *Miller* v. *Miller*, a husband and wife attempted to create their own marriage contract, in which both spouses promised to "refrain from scolding, faultfinding and anger." Mr. Miller promised to provide for family necessaries as well as a sum of $16.66 per month for Mrs. Miller's individual use, and she promised to "keep her home and family in a comfortable and reasonably good condition." When Mrs. Miller sued her husband to enforce this contract, she was turned away by the court because she had promised to do only what she was already obligated to do, but he had promised far more than marriage required from a husband, which was only to provide "necessaries."

New York's 1860 Earnings Act was a limited victory for reformers—they won a change in the law, but courts limited its reach through narrow interpretation. Had courts interpreted the act more broadly to cover all forms of women's earnings, it would have gone a long way to making women independent legally and economically.

Although the 1860 Earnings Act gained some legal rights for women, it failed to resolve completely the inequities that women faced. In the later nineteenth century, women's rights advocates became convinced that political power was the way to secure civil rights, and they began to focus more specifically on winning the right to vote. Achieving that goal would take another sixty years.

QUESTIONS FOR DISCUSSION

1. What was the system of "coverture"? How could couples avoid some of the legal disabilities of coverture? Could they avoid all of them?

2. What were the chief concerns of women's rights advocates in the mid-nineteenth century? How did their aims and tactics resemble those of other reform movements during this period?

3. How did the Married Women's Property Acts and Earnings Acts improve the legal status of married women, and in what ways did they fall short of reformers' aims? Why do you think these acts were passed?

Study Resources

 Take the **Study Plan** for **Chapter 12** *The Pursuit of Perfection* on **MyHistoryLab**

TIME LINE

1801 Massive revival held at Cane Ridge, Kentucky

1826 American Temperance Society organized

1830–1831 Charles G. Finney evangelizes Rochester, New York

1831 William Lloyd Garrison publishes first issue of *The Liberator*

1833 Abolitionists found American Anti-Slavery Society

1835–1836 Theodore Weld advocates abolition in Ohio and upstate New York

1836 American Temperance Society splits into factions

1837 Massachusetts establishes a state board of education; Abolitionist editor Elijah Lovejoy killed by a proslavery mob

1840 American Anti-Slavery Society splits over women's rights and other issues

1841 Transcendentalists organize a model community at Brook Farm

1848 Feminists gather at Seneca Falls, New York, and found the women's rights movement

1854 Henry David Thoreau's *Walden* published

CHAPTER REVIEW

The Rise of Evangelicalism

 How did the evangelical revivalism of the early nineteenth century spur reform movements?

Evangelical revivalists preached the perfectibility of individual moral agents, encouraging each person to choose his or her own moral and political destiny. This perfectionism led evangelical Christians to organize voluntary associations and benevolent societies that would teach people moral and social values. The most important of these reform efforts was the temperance movement. (p.269)

Domesticity and Changes in the American Family

 What was the doctrine of "separate spheres," and how did it change family life?

The doctrine of "separate spheres" glorified women's role in caring for the home and family, guarding religious and moral values while men went into the public sphere to earn money and participate in politics. Smaller families and more leisure time for middle-class families also emphasized children's development, including new public schools open to all. (p. 273)

Institutional Reform

 How did Horace Mann change ideas about public schooling in America?

In 1837, Horace Mann persuaded the Massachusetts legislature to establish a state board of education and allocate taxes to support free local public schools open to all. Mann believed that by teaching middle-class morality and respect for order, schools could produce law-abiding citizens and encourage social mobility by enabling lower-class children to do better than their parents. (p. 276)

Reform Turns Radical

 What were some of the major antebellum reform movements?

Religious revivalism inspired movements for temperance, abolition of slavery, and women's rights. These movements grew more radical over time, turning to the political sphere in the 1840s as they lost confidence that changing men's hearts could transform society. The abolitionists organized the Liberty Party in 1840, and feminists held their first convention at Seneca Falls in 1848. (p. 278)

KEY TERMS AND DEFINITIONS

Second Great Awakening Evangelical Protestant revivals that swept over America in the early nineteenth century. p. 270

Temperance movement Temperance—moderation or abstention in the consumption of alcoholic beverages—attracted many advocates in the early nineteenth century. p. 272

Benevolent empire Collection of missionary and reform societies that sought to stamp out social evils in American society in the 1820s and 1830s. p. 273

Cult of Domesticity   Term used to characterize the dominant gender role for white women in the antebellum period. It stressed the virtue of women as guardians of the home, which was considered their proper sphere. p. 274

Perfectionism   The doctrine that a state of freedom from sin is attainable on earth. p. 275

Abolitionist movement   Reform movement dedicated to the immediate and unconditional end of slavery in the United States. p. 278

Seneca Falls Convention   An 1848 gathering of women's rights advocates that culminated in the adoption of a Declaration of Sentiments demanding voting and property rights for women. p. 281

CRITICAL THINKING QUESTIONS

1. Do you think it was healthy for American politics that religion played such a strong role in antebellum political movements?

2. In your view, were women helped or harmed by the doctrine of "separate spheres," and why?

3. Why do you think so many antebellum reform movements turned to politics in the 1840s?

4. What is the connection between women's influence in the public sphere, and the influence of evangelical religion on society?

MyHistoryLab Media Assignments

Find these resources in the Media Assignments folder for Chapter 12 on MyHistoryLab

The Rise of Evangelicalism

■ **View** the **Closer Look**   *Methodist Camp Meeting, 1819 p. 271*

■ **Read** the **Document**   *Lyman Beecher, "Six Sermons on Intemperance" (1828) p. 272*

Watch the **Video**   *Drinking and the Temperance Movement in Nineteenth-Century America p. 273*

Domesticity and Changes in the American Family

Read the **Document**   *Catharine E. Beecher, from A Treatise on Domestic Economy p. 274*

Institutional Reform

■ **Watch** the **Video**   *Who Was Horace Mann and Why Are So Many Schools Named After Him? p. 277*

Reform Turns Radical

■ **Read** the **Document**   *William Lloyd Garrison, First Issue of* The Liberator *(1831) p. 278*

Read the **Document**   *David Walker, A Black Abolitionist Speaks p. 280*

View the **Map**   *Utopian Communities Before the Civil War p. 281*

■ **Complete** the **Assignment**   *The War Against "Demon Drink" p. 282*

Read the **Document**   *Ralph Waldo Emerson, "Self Reliance" (1841) p. 284*

Complete the **Assignment**   *The Legal Rights of Married Women: Reforming the Law of Coverture p. 286*

■ *Indicates Study Plan Media Assignment*

13 An Age of Expansionism

Contents and Learning Objectives

((●— Listen to the **Audio File** on **myhistorylab**   **Chapter 13** *An Age of Expansionism*

The Spirit of Young America

In the 1840s and early 1850s, politicians, writers, and entrepreneurs frequently proclaimed themselves champions of **Young America**. One of the first to use the phrase was the famous author and lecturer Ralph Waldo Emerson, who told an audience of merchants and manufacturers in 1844 that the nation was entering a new era of commercial development, technological progress, and territorial expansion. Emerson suggested that a progressive new generation—the Young Americans—would lead this surge of physical development. More than a slogan and less than an organized movement, Young America stood for a positive attitude toward the market economy and industrial growth, a more aggressive and belligerent foreign policy, and a celebration of America's unique strengths and virtues.

Young Americans favored enlarging the national market by acquiring new territory. They called for the annexation of Texas, asserted an American claim to all of Oregon, and urged the appropriation of vast new territories from Mexico. They also celebrated the technological advances that would knit this new empire together, especially the telegraph and the railroad. Telegraphs, according to one writer, would "flash sensation and volition . . . to and from towns and provinces as if they were organs and limbs of a single organism"; railroads would provide "a vast system of iron muscles which, as it were, move the limbs of the mighty organism."

Young America was a cultural and intellectual movement as well as an economic and political one.

In 1845, a Washington journal hailed the election of the 49-year-old James K. Polk, at that time the youngest man to have been elected president, as a sign that youth will "dare to take antiquity by the beard, and tear the cloak from hoary-headed hypocrisy. Too young to be corrupt . . . it is Young America, awakened to a sense of her own intellectual greatness by her soaring spirit. It stands in strength, the voice of the majority." During the Polk administration, Young American writers and critics—mostly based in New York City—called for a new and distinctive national literature, free of subservience to European themes or models and expressive of the democratic spirit. Their organ was the Literary World, founded in 1847, and its ideals influenced two of the greatest writers America has produced: Walt Whitman and Herman Melville.

Whitman captured much of the exuberance and expansionism of Young America in his "Song of the Open Road":

> From this hour I ordain myself loos'd of limits and imaginary lines,
> Going where I list, my own master total and absolute,
>
> . . . .
>
> I inhale great draughts of space,
> The east and the west are mine, and the north and the south are mine.
> I am larger, better than I thought.

other things—the dangers facing a nation that was overreaching itself by indulging its pride and exalted sense of destiny with too little concern for the moral and practical consequences.

The Young American ideal—the idea of a young country led by young men into new paths of prosperity and greatness—appealed to many people and found support across political party lines. But the attitude came to be identified primarily with young Democrats who wanted to move their party away from its traditional fear of the expansion of commerce and industry. Unlike old-line Jeffersonians and Jacksonians, Young Americans had no qualms about the market economy and the speculative, materialistic spirit it called forth.

Before 1848, the Young American impulse focused mainly on the great expanse of western lands that lay just beyond the nation's borders. After the Mexican-American War, when territorial gains extended the nation's boundaries from the Atlantic to the Pacific, attention shifted to internal development. New discoveries of gold in the nation's western territories fostered economic growth, technological advances spurred industrialization, and increased immigration brought more people to populate the lands newly acquired—by agreement or by force.

Movement to the Far West

What were some of the reasons for which Americans headed into the Western territories, and what were some of the consequences of expansion?

In the 1830s and 1840s, pioneers pursued fertile land and economic opportunity beyond the existing boundaries of the United States and thus helped set the stage for the annexations and international crises of the 1840s. Some went for material gain, others went for adventure, and a significant minority sought freedom from religious persecution.

Borderlands of the 1830s

Since the birth of the republic, there had been a major dispute over the boundary between Maine and the Canadian province of New Brunswick. In 1839, fighting broke out between Canadian lumberjacks and the Maine militia. In 1842, Secretary of State Daniel Webster concluded an agreement with the British government,

Walt Whitman in the "carpenter portrait" that appeared in the first edition of his great work, *Leaves of Grass*, in 1855. The poet's rough clothes and slouch hat signify his identification with the common people.

In *Moby-Dick*, Herman Melville produced a novel sufficiently original in form and conception to more than fulfill the demand of Young Americans for "a New Literature to fit the New Man in the New Age." But Melville was too deep a thinker not to see the perils that underlay the soaring ambition and aggressiveness of the new age. The whaling captain Ahab, who brings destruction to himself and his ship by his relentless pursuit of the white whale, symbolized—among

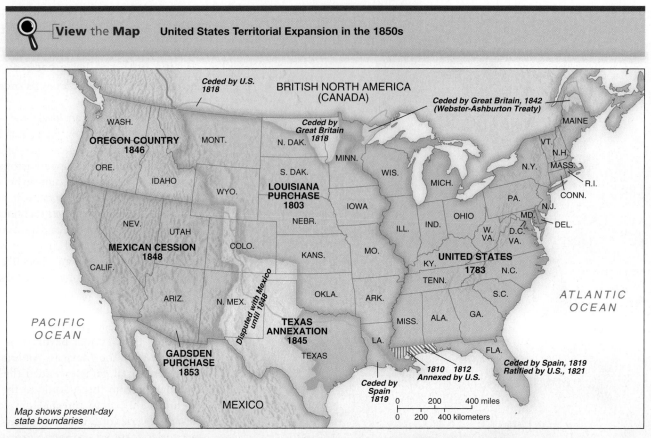

TERRITORIAL EXPANSION BY THE MID-NINETEENTH CENTURY Fervent nationalists identified the growth of America through territorial expansion as the divinely ordained "Manifest Destiny" of a chosen people.

represented by Lord Ashburton. The Webster-Ashburton Treaty gave over half of the disputed territory to the United States and established a definite northeastern boundary with Canada.

On the other side of the continent, the United States and Britain both laid claim to Oregon, a vast area that lay between the Rockies and the Pacific from the 42nd parallel (the northern boundary of California) to the latitude of 54°0′ (the southern boundary of Alaska). In 1818, the two nations agreed to joint occupation for ten years, an agreement that was renewed indefinitely in 1827. Meanwhile, the Americans had strengthened their claim by acquiring Spain's rights to the Pacific Northwest in the Adams-Onís Treaty (see Chapter 9), and the British had gained effective control of the northern portion of the Oregon Country through the activities of the Hudson's Bay Company, a well-financed fur-trading concern. Blocking an equitable division was the reluctance on both sides to surrender access to the Columbia River basin and the adjacent territory extending north to the 49th parallel (the future northern border of the state of Washington).

The Oregon Country was scarcely populated before 1840. The same could not be said of the Mexican borderlands that lay directly west of Jacksonian America. Spanish settlements in present-day New Mexico date from the late sixteenth century. By 1820, about forty thousand people of Spanish descent populated this province, engaging mainly in sheep raising and mining. In 1821, Spain granted independence to Mexico, which then embraced areas that currently make up the states of Texas, New Mexico, Arizona, California, Nevada, Utah, and much of Colorado. The Republic of Mexico opted for a more open trade policy than its predecessor and in 1821 informed its northern neighbors of the changed laws encouraging trade.

California was the other major northward extension of Mexico. Spanish missionaries and soldiers had taken control of the region in the late eighteenth century. In the 1820s and 1830s, this land of huge estates and enormous cattle herds was far less populous than New Mexico—only about four thousand Mexicans of Spanish origin lived in California in 1827. Of the region's thirty thousand Indians, many were forced to work on vast land tracts owned by Spanish missions. At the beginning of the 1830s, a chain of twenty-one mission stations, stretching from San Diego to Sonoma, north of San Francisco, controlled most of the province's land and wealth. The Indian population may seem large, yet the number represented only a small fraction of the original indigenous population; there had been a catastrophic decline in Indian population during the previous sixty years of Spanish rule. The stresses and strains of forced labor and exposure to European diseases had taken an enormous toll.

In 1833, the Mexican Congress's "secularization act" emancipated the Indians from church control and opened the mission lands to settlement. The government awarded immense tracts of the mission land to Mexican citizens and left the Indians landless.

A new class of large landowners, or *rancheros*, replaced the *padres* as rulers of Old California and masters of the province's indigenous population. Seven hundred grantees took possession of *ranchos* ranging up to nearly 50,000 acres and proceeded to subject the Indians to a new and even harsher form of servitude. During the fifteen years they held sway, the rancheros created an American legend and aroused American envy through their lavish hospitality, extravagant dress, superb horsemanship, and taste for violent and dangerous sports. The Americans who saw California in the 1830s were mostly merchants and sailors involved in the oceanic trade between Boston and California ports. New England clipper ships sailed around Cape Horn at the southern tip of South America to barter manufactured goods for cowhides. By the mid-1830s, several Yankee merchants had taken up permanent residence in towns such as Monterey and San Diego in order to conduct the California end of the business.

The Texas Revolution

At the same time as some Americans were trading with California, others were taking possession of Texas. In the early 1820s, Mexican officials encouraged settlers from the United States to settle in Texas. Newly independent Mexico granted Stephen F. Austin, son of a one-time Spanish citizen, a huge piece of land in hopes he would help attract and settle new colonists from the United States. Some fifteen other Anglo-American *empresarios* received land grants in the 1820s. In 1823, three hundred American families were settled on the Austin grant, and within a year, the colony's population had swelled to 2021.

Friction soon developed between the Mexican government and the Anglo-American colonists over the status of slavery and the authority of the Catholic Church. At its core, the dispute centered on the unwillingness of Anglo-American settlers to become Mexicans. Under the terms of settlement, all people living in Texas had to become Mexican citizens and adopt the Roman Catholic faith. Slavery presented another problem, for in 1829 Mexico freed all slaves under its jurisdiction. Slaveholders in Texas were given a special exemption that allowed them to emancipate their slaves and then force them to sign lifelong contracts as indentured servants, but many refused to limit their ownership rights in any way. Settlers either converted to Catholicism only superficially or ignored the requirement entirely.

A Mexican government commission reported in 1829 that Americans were the great majority of the Texas population and were flagrantly violating Mexican law. The following year, the Mexican Congress prohibited further American immigration and importation of slaves to Texas.

Enforcement of the new law was feeble, and the flow of settlers, slaves, and smuggled goods continued virtually unabated. A long-standing complaint of the Texans was the failure of the Mexican constitution to grant them local self-government. Under the Mexican federal system, Texas was joined to the state of Coahuila, and Texan representatives were outnumbered three to one in the state legislature. In 1832, the colonists showed their displeasure with Mexican rule by rioting in protest against the arrest of several Anglo-Americans by a Mexican commander.

Battle of San Jacinto by H.A. McArdle. In this panorama of the Texas Revolution's decisive battle at San Jacinto, Sam Houston leads the charge against Santa Anna's forces.

In 1834, General Antonio López de Santa Anna made himself dictator of Mexico and abolished the federal system of government. News of these developments reached Texas late in the year, accompanied by rumors of the impending disfranchisement and even expulsion of American immigrants, threatening Texans' status as "tolerated guests."

In 1835, some Texans revolted against Mexico's central government. While the insurrectionists claimed they were fighting for freedom from oppression, Mexican rule had not been harsh; the worst that can be said was that it was inefficient, inconsistent, and sometimes corrupt. Furthermore, the Texans' devotion to "liberty" did not prevent them from defending slavery against Mexico's attempt to abolish it. The rebels, aroused by the rumors of what the new Mexican government had in store for them, prepared to resist Santa Anna's effort to enforce tariff regulations by military force.

When he learned that Texans were resisting customs collections, Santa Anna sent reinforcements. The settlers first engaged Mexican troops at Gonzales in October and forced the retreat of a cavalry detachment. Shortly thereafter, Austin laid siege to San Antonio with a force of five hundred men and after six weeks forced its surrender, thereby capturing most of the Mexican troops then in Texas.

After entering Texas to quell the unrest, Santa Anna issued his "Message to the Inhabitants of Texas." Santa Anna promised that his troops would respect the "persons and property" of those who were not "implicated in such iniquitous rebellion." But such a message really wasn't intended for *all* of the "Inhabitants" of Texas. Even before Texas had won its independence, Santa Anna recognized the driving presence of the United States in the territory's Anglo-American inhabitants, and the difficulty of assimilating that population into Mexico. Santa Anna declared the root of the rebellion to be "adventurers, maliciously protected by some inhabitants of a neighboring republic" who had planned to attack Mexico City. It was remarkable foreshadowing of the Mexican-American War that would begin 10 years later.

The Republic of Texas

Meanwhile, delegates from the American communities in Texas convened and after some hesitation voted overwhelmingly to declare their independence on March 2, 1836. A constitution, based closely on that of the United States, was adopted for the new Republic of Texas, and a temporary government was installed to carry on the military struggle. Although the ensuing conflict was largely one of Americans against Mexicans, some Texas Mexicans, or *Tejanos*, sided with the Anglo rebels. They too wanted to be free of Santa Anna's heavy-handed rule, though, they would later become victims of the same anti-Mexican prejudice that spurred the revolt. Tejano leader Juan Seguin, who served as a captain in the Texas army and became a hero of the independence struggle, was driven off his land by Anglo-Texans in 1841.

Within days after Texas declared itself a republic, rebels and Mexican troops in San Antonio fought the famous battle of the **Alamo**. Myths about that battle have magnified the Anglo rebels' valor at the Mexicans' expense. The folklore is based on fact—only

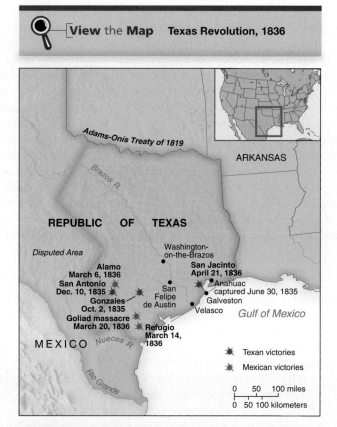

TEXAS REVOLUTION Major battles of the Texas Revolution. The Texans suffered severe losses at the Alamo and Goliad, but they scored a stunning victory at San Jacinto.

187 rebels fought off a far larger number of Mexican soldiers for more than a week before eventually capitulating—but it is not true that all rebels, including the folk hero Davy Crockett, fought to the death. Crockett and seven other survivors were captured and then executed. Nevertheless, a tale that combined actual and mythical bravery inside the Alamo gave the insurrection new inspiration, moral sanction, outside support, and the rallying cry "Remember the Alamo."

The revolt ended with an exchange of slaughters. A few days after the Alamo battle, another Texas detachment was surrounded and captured in an open plain near the San Antonio River and was marched to the town of Goliad, where most of its three hundred and fifty members were executed. The next month, on April 21, 1836, the main Texas army, under General Sam Houston, assaulted Santa Anna's troops at an encampment near the San Jacinto River during the siesta hour. The final count showed that six hundred and thirty Mexicans and only a handful of Texans had been killed. Santa Anna was captured and marched to Velasco, the meeting place of the Texas government, where he was forced to sign treaties recognizing the independence of Texas and its claim to territory all the way to the Rio Grande. The Mexican Congress failed to repudiate the treaty; although a strip of land between the Nueces River and the Rio Grande would be disputed during the next decade, Mexico failed to impose its authority on the victorious Texas rebels.

Sam Houston, the hero of San Jacinto, became the first president of Texas. His platform sought annexation to the United States, and one of his first acts in office was to send an emissary to Washington to test the waters. Houston's agent found much sympathy for Texas independence but was told by Andrew Jackson and others that domestic politics and fear of a war with Mexico made immediate annexation impossible. The most that he could win from Congress and the Jackson administration was formal recognition of Texas sovereignty.

In its ten-year existence as the Lone Star Republic, Texas drew settlers from the United States at an accelerating rate, the population growing from 30,000 to 142,000. The Panic of 1837 impelled many debt-ridden and land-hungry farmers to take advantage of the free grants of 1280 acres that Texas offered to immigrating heads of white families. Most of the newcomers assumed, as did the old settlers, that they would soon be annexed and restored to American citizenship.

Trails of Trade and Settlement

After New Mexico opened its trade to American merchants, a thriving commerce developed between Missouri and Santa Fe. The first of the merchants to reach the New Mexican capital was William Becknell, who arrived with his train of goods late in 1821. Others followed rapidly. For protection from hostile Indians, traders traveled in large caravans, one or two of which would arrive in Santa Fe every summer. The federal government assisted them by providing troops when necessary and by appropriating money to purchase rights of passage from various tribes. But profits from the exchange of textiles and other manufactured goods for furs, mules, and precious metals were substantial enough to make the risky trip worth taking.

Relations between the United States and Mexico soured following the Texas revolution and further Anglo-American aggressions, both having devastating effects on the Santa Fe trade. An expedition of Texas businessmen and soldiers to Santa Fe in 1841 alarmed the Mexican authorities, who arrested its members. In retaliation, a volunteer force of Texas avengers attacked Mexican troops along the Santa Fe Trail. The Mexican government then moved to curtail the Santa Fe trade. In April 1842, it passed a new tariff banning the importation of many of the goods sold by American merchants and prohibiting the export of gold and silver. Further restrictions in 1843 denied American traders full access to the Santa Fe market.

The famous Oregon Trail was the great overland route that brought the wagon trains of American migrants to the West Coast during the 1840s. Extending for two thousand miles, across the northern Great Plains and the mountains beyond, it crossed the Rockies at South Pass and then forked; the main northern route led to the Willamette Valley of Oregon, but alternative trails were opened during the decade for overlanders heading for California. The journey from Missouri to the West Coast took about six months.

After small groups had made their way to both Oregon and California in 1841 and 1842, a mass migration—mostly to Oregon—began in 1843. Within two years, five thousand Americans, living in the Willamette Valley south of the Columbia River, were demanding the extension of full American sovereignty over the Oregon Country.

The Mormon Trek

An important and distinctive group of pioneers followed the Oregon Trail as far as South Pass and then veered southwestward to establish a thriving colony in the region of the Great Salt Lake. These were Mormons, members of the largest religious denomination founded on American soil—the Church of Jesus Christ of Latter-day Saints.

The background of the Mormon trek was a history of persecution in the eastern states. Joseph Smith of Palmyra, New York, the founder of Mormonism, revealed in 1830 that he had received over many years a series of revelations that called upon him to establish Christ's pure church on Earth. As the prophet of this faith, he published the Book of Mormon, a new scripture that he claimed to have discovered and translated with the aid of an angel. It was the record of a community of pious Jews who left the Holy Land six centuries before the birth of Christ and sailed to the American continent. After his crucifixion and resurrection, Christ appeared to this community and proclaimed the Gospel. Four hundred years later, a fratricidal war annihilated the believing Christians but not all of the descendents of the original Jewish migrants. Mormons held that the survivors had contributed to the ancestry of the American Indians. Smith and those he converted to his new faith were committed to restoring the pure religion that had once thrived on American soil by founding a western Zion where they could practice their faith unmolested and carry out their special mission to convert the Native Americans.

In the 1830s, the Mormons established communities in Ohio and Missouri, but the former went bankrupt in the Panic of 1837 and the latter was the target of angry mobs and vigilante violence. After the Mormons lost the "war" they fought against the Missourians in 1839, Smith led his followers back across the Mississippi to Illinois, where he received a liberal charter from the state legislature to found a town at Nauvoo. Here the Mormons had a temporary measure of security and self-government, but Smith soon reported new revelations that engendered dissension among his followers and hostility from neighboring "gentiles." Most controversial was his authorization of polygamy, or plural marriage. In 1844, Smith was killed by a mob while being held in jail in Carthage, Illinois, on a charge stemming from his quarrels with dissident Mormons who objected to his new policies.

The death of Smith confirmed the growing conviction of the Mormon leadership that they needed to move beyond the borders of the United States to establish their Zion in the wilderness. In late 1845, Smith's successor, Brigham Young, decided to send a party of fifteen hundred men to assess the chances of a colony in the vicinity of the Great Salt Lake (then part of Mexico). Nauvoo was quickly depopulated as twelve thousand Mormons took to the trail in 1846. The following year, Young himself arrived in Utah and sent back word to the thousands encamped along the trail that he had found the promised land.

The Mormon community that Young established in Utah is one of the great success stories of western settlement. In contrast to the rugged individualism and disorder that often characterized mining camps and other new communities, "the state of Deseret" (the name the Mormons originally applied to Utah) was a model of discipline and cooperation. Because of its communitarian form of social organization, its centralized government, and the

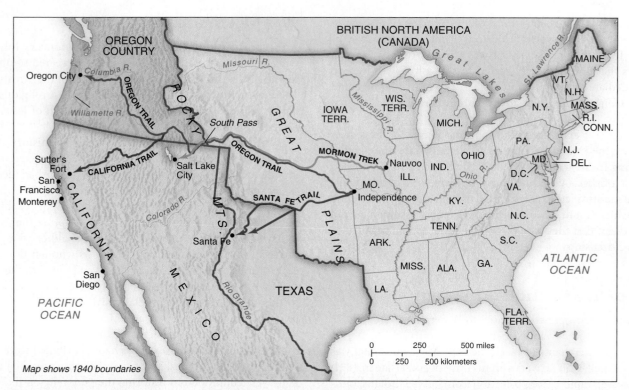

WESTERN TRAILS Among the greatest hazards faced by those migrating to the West was the rough and unfamiliar terrain over which their wagon trains traveled.

religious dedication of its inhabitants, this frontier society was able to expand settlement in a planned and efficient way and develop a system of irrigation that "made the desert bloom."

Utah's main problem was the determination of its political status. When the Mormons first arrived, they were encroaching illegally into Mexican territory. After Utah came under American sovereignty in 1848, the state of Deseret fought to maintain its autonomy and its custom of polygamy against the efforts of the federal government to extend American law and set up the usual type of territorial administration. In 1857, President Buchanan sent a military force to bring Utah to heel, and the Mormons prepared to repel this "invasion." But after a heavy snow prevented the army from crossing the Rockies, Buchanan offered an olive branch in the form of a general pardon for Mormons who had violated federal law but agreed to cooperate with U.S. authorities in the future. The Mormons accepted, and in return, Brigham Young called off his plan to resist the army by force and accepted the nominal authority of an appointed territorial governor.

Manifest Destiny and the Mexican-American War

Why did the U.S. annex Texas and the Southwest?

The rush of settlers beyond the nation's borders in the 1830s and 1840s inspired politicians and propagandists to call for annexation of those areas occupied by migrants. Some went further and proclaimed it was the **Manifest Destiny** of the United States to expand until it had absorbed all of North America, including Canada and Mexico. Such ambitions led to a major diplomatic confrontation with Great Britain and a war with Mexico.

Tyler and Texas

President John Tyler initiated the politics of Manifest Destiny. He was vice president when William Henry Harrison died in office in 1841 after serving scarcely a month. The first of America's "accidental presidents," Tyler was a states' rights, proslavery Virginian who had been picked as Harrison's running mate to broaden the appeal of the Whig ticket. Profoundly out of sympathy with the mainstream of his own party, he soon broke with the Whigs in Congress, who had united behind the latest version of Henry Clay's "American System." Although Tyler lacked a base in either of the major parties, he hoped to be elected president in his own right in 1844. To accomplish this difficult feat, he needed a new issue around which he could build a following that would cut across established party lines.

In 1843, Tyler decided to put the full weight of his administration behind the annexation of Texas. He anticipated that its incorporation would be a popular move, especially in the South where it would feed the appetite for additional slave states. With the South solidly behind him, Tyler expected to have a good chance in the election of 1844.

To achieve his objective, Tyler enlisted the support of John C. Calhoun, the leading political defender of slavery and state sovereignty. Calhoun saw the annexation issue as a way of uniting the South and taking the offensive against the abolitionists. Success or failure in this effort would constitute a decisive test of whether the North was willing to give the southern states a fair share of national power and adequate assurances for the future of their way of life. If antislavery sentiment succeeded in blocking the acquisition of Texas, the Southerners would at least know where they stood and could begin to "calculate the value of the union."

To prepare the public for annexation, the Tyler administration launched a propaganda campaign in the summer of 1843 based on

THE LIBERTY PARTY SWINGS AN ELECTION

Candidate	Party	Actual Vote in New York	National Electoral Vote	If Liberty Voters Had Voted Whig	Projected Electoral Vote
Polk	Democratic	237,588	170	237,588	134
Clay	Whig	232,482	105	248,294	141
Birney	Liberty	15,812	0	—	—

reports of British designs on Texas. It is doubtful the British had such intentions, but the stories were believed and used to give urgency to the annexation cause.

Secretary of State Abel Upshur, a proslavery Virginian and protégé of Calhoun, began negotiating an annexation treaty. After Upshur was killed in an accident, Calhoun replaced him and carried the negotiations to a successful conclusion. When the treaty was brought before the Senate in 1844, Calhoun denounced the British for attempting to subvert the South's essential system of labor and racial control by using Texas as a base for abolitionist operations. According to the supporters of Tyler and Calhoun, the South's security and well-being—and by extension that of the nation—required the immediate incorporation of Texas into the Union.

The strategy of linking annexation explicitly to the interests of the South and slavery led northern antislavery Whigs to charge that the whole scheme was a proslavery plot to advance the interest of the South. The Senate rejected the treaty by a decisive vote of 35 to 16 in June 1844. Though Tyler then attempted to bring Texas into the Union through a joint resolution of both houses of Congress admitting it as a state, Congress adjourned before the issue came to a vote, and the whole question hung fire in anticipation of the election of 1844.

The Triumph of Polk and Annexation

Tyler's initiative made the future of Texas the central issue in the 1844 campaign. But party lines held firm, and the president himself was unable to capitalize on the issue because his stand was not in line with the views of either party. Tyler tried to run as an independent, but his failure to gain significant support eventually forced him to withdraw from the race.

If the Democratic party convention had been held in 1843—as it was originally scheduled—ex-President Martin Van Buren would have won the nomination. But postponement of the Democratic conclave until May 1844 weakened his chances. In the meantime, the annexation question came to the fore, and Van Buren was forced to take a stand on it. He persisted in the view he had held as president—that incorporation of Texas would risk war with Mexico, arouse sectional strife, and destroy the unity of the Democratic party. Fears of sectional and

party division seemed confirmed in 1844 when the dominant party faction in Van Buren's home state of New York came out against Tyler's Texas policy. In an effort to keep the issue out of the campaign, Van Buren struck a gentleman's agreement with Henry Clay, the overwhelming favorite for the Whig nomination, that both of them would publicly oppose immediate annexation.

Van Buren's letter opposing annexation appeared shortly before the Democratic convention, costing him the nomination. Angry southern delegates, who secured a rule requiring approval by a two-thirds vote, blocked Van Buren's nomination. After several ballots, a dark horse candidate—James K. Polk of Tennessee—emerged triumphant. Polk, a protégé of Andrew Jackson, had been speaker of the House of Representatives and governor of Tennessee.

An avowed expansionist, Polk ran on a platform calling for the simultaneous annexation of Texas and assertion of American claims to all of Oregon. He identified himself and his party with the popular cause of turning the United States into a continental nation, an aspiration that attracted support from all parts of the country. His was

Watch the Video   The Annexation of Texas

Texans voted in favor of annexation to the United States in the first election following independence in 1836. However, throughout the Republic period (1836-1845) no treaty of annexation negotiated between the Republic and the United States was ratified by both nations.

a much more astute political strategy than the overtly prosouthern expansionism advocated by Tyler and Calhoun. The Whig nominee, Henry Clay, was basically antiexpansionist, but his sense of the growing popularity of Texas annexation among southern Whigs caused him to waffle on the issue during the campaign. This vacillation in turn cost Clay the support of a small but crucial group of northern anti-slavery Whigs, who defected to the abolitionist Liberty party.

Polk won the fall election by a relatively narrow popular margin. His triumph in the electoral college—170 votes to 105—was secured by victories in New York and Michigan, where the Liberty party candidate, James G. Birney, had taken away enough votes from Clay to affect the outcome. The closeness of the election meant the Democrats had something less than a clear mandate to implement their expansionist policies, but this did not prevent them from claiming that the people backed border expansion.

After the election, Congress reconvened to consider the annexation of Texas. The mood had changed as a result of Polk's victory, and some leading senators from both parties who had initially opposed Tyler's scheme for annexation by joint resolution of Congress now changed their position. As a result, annexation was approved a few days before Polk took office.

Read the Document   John O'Sullivan, "The Great Nation of Futurity" (1845)

John O'Sullivan was editor of the *United States Magazine and Democratic Review*. He advocated the view that the United States was destined to expand. In the process, he coined the phrase "Manifest Destiny." His vision caught the imagination of the immigrant nation searching for its identity and meaning as well as a definition of success.

THE ELECTION OF 1844

Candidate	Party	Popular Vote	Electoral Vote
Polk	Democratic	1,338,464	170
Clay	Whig	1,300,097	105
Birney	Liberty	62,300	—

The Doctrine of Manifest Destiny

The expansionist mood that accompanied Polk's election and the annexation of Texas was given a name and a rationale in the summer of 1845. John L. O'Sullivan, a proponent of the Young America movement and editor of the influential *United States Magazine and Democratic Review,* charged that foreign governments were conspiring to block the annexation of Texas in an effort to thwart "the fulfillment of our manifest destiny to overspread the continent allotted by providence for the free development of our yearly multiplying millions."

Besides coining the phrase Manifest Destiny, O'Sullivan pointed to the three main ideas that lay behind it. One was that God was on the side of American expansionism. This notion came naturally out of the tradition, going back to the New England Puritans, that identified the growth of America with the divinely ordained success of a chosen people. A second idea,

implied in the phrase free development, was that the spread of American rule meant what other propagandists for expansion described as "extending the area of freedom." Democratic institutions and local self-government would follow the flag if areas claimed by autocratic foreign governments were annexed to the United States. O'Sullivan's third premise was that population growth required the outlet that territorial acquisitions would provide. Behind this notion lurked a fear that growing numbers would lead to diminished opportunity and a European-type polarization of social classes if the restless and the ambitious were not given new lands to settle and exploit.

In its most extreme form, the doctrine of Manifest Destiny meant that the United States would someday occupy the entire North American continent. "Make way, I say, for the young American Buffalo," bellowed a Democratic orator in 1844, "—he has not yet got land enough . . . . I tell you we will give him Oregon for his summer shade, and the region of Texas as his winter pasture. (Applause) Like all of his race, he wants salt, too. Well, he shall have the use of two oceans—the mighty Pacific and the turbulent Atlantic . . . . He shall not stop his career until he slakes his thirst in the frozen ocean. (Cheers)"

Polk and the Oregon Question

In 1845 and 1846, the United States came closer to armed conflict with Great Britain than at any time since the War of 1812. The willingness of some Americans to go to war over

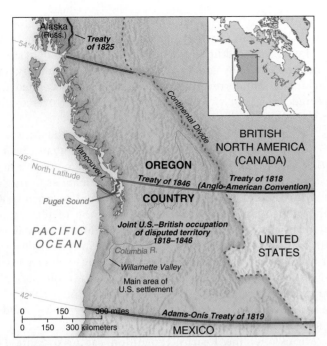

NORTHWEST BOUNDARY DISPUTE President Polk's policy of bluff and bluster nearly involved the United States in a war with Great Britain over the disputed boundary in Oregon.

Oregon was expressed in the rallying cry "Fifty-four forty or fight" (referring to the latitude of the northern boundary of the desired territory). This slogan was actually coined by Whigs seeking to ridicule Democratic expansionists, but Democrats later took it over as a vivid expression of their demand for what is now British Columbia. Polk fed this expansionist fever by laying claim in his inaugural address to all of the Oregon Country, then jointly occupied by Britain and the United States. Privately, he was willing to accept the 49th parallel as a dividing line. What made the situation so tense was that Polk was dedicated to an aggressive diplomacy of bluff and bluster, convinced that his foreign adversaries would only respond to a hard-line approach.

In July 1845, Polk authorized Secretary of State James Buchanan to reply to the latest British request for terms by offering a boundary along the 49th parallel. When the British ambassador rejected this proposal, Polk angrily withdrew it and refused to renew it when the British sought to reopen negotiations. In April 1846, Congress terminated the agreement for joint occupation of the Pacific Northwest at Polk's request The British government then took the initiative, submitting a new treaty proposal and dispatching warships at the same time. When the draft treaty was received in June, Polk refused either to endorse or reject it and took the unusual step of submitting it directly to the Senate for advice, which recommended its acceptance almost without change. It was ratified on June 15.

Polk was prompted to settle the Oregon question because he now had a war with Mexico on his hands. American policy makers got what they wanted from the Oregon treaty, namely Puget Sound, a splendid natural harbor and the first U.S. deep-water port on the Pacific. Polk's initial demand for all of Oregon was made partly for domestic political consumption and partly

to bluff the British into making more concessions. It was a dangerous game on both fronts. When Polk finally agreed to the solution, he alienated expansionist advocates in the Old Northwest who had supported his call for "all of Oregon."

For many Northerners, the promise of new acquisitions in the Pacific Northwest was the only thing that made annexation of Texas palatable. They hoped new free states could be created to counterbalance the admission of slaveholding Texas to the Union. As this prospect receded, the charge of antislavery advocates that Texas annexation was a southern plot became more believable; to Northerners, Polk began to look more and more like a president concerned mainly with furthering the interests of his native region.

War with Mexico

While the United States was avoiding a war with Great Britain, it was getting into one with Mexico. Although the Mexicans had recognized Texas independence in 1845, they rejected the Lone Star Republic's dubious claim to the unsettled territory between the Nueces River and the Rio Grande. When the United States annexed Texas and assumed its claim to the disputed area, Mexico broke off diplomatic relations and prepared for armed conflict.

This 1846 cartoon titled "This Is the House That Polk Built" shows President Polk sitting forlornly in a house of cards, which represents the delicately balanced issues facing him.

Polk responded by placing troops in Louisiana on the alert and by dispatching John Slidell as an emissary to Mexico City in the hope he could resolve the boundary dispute and also persuade the Mexicans to sell New Mexico and California to the United States. The Mexican government refused to receive Slidell because the nature of his appointment ignored the fact that regular diplomatic relations were suspended. While Slidell was cooling his heels in Mexico City in January 1846, Polk ordered General Zachary Taylor, commander of American forces in the Southwest, to advance well beyond the Nueces and proceed toward the Rio Grande, thus encroaching on territory claimed by both sides.

By April, Taylor had taken up a position near Matamoros on the Rio Grande. On the opposite bank of the river, Mexican forces had assembled and erected a fort. On April 24, sixteen hundred Mexican soldiers crossed the river and the following day met and attacked a small American detachment, killing eleven and capturing the rest. After learning of the incident, Taylor sent word to the president: "Hostilities," he reported, "may now be considered as commenced."

The news was neither unexpected nor unwelcome. Polk in fact was already preparing his war message to Congress when he learned of the fighting on the Rio Grande. A short and decisive war, he had concluded, would force the cession of California and New Mexico to the United States. When Congress declared war on May 13, American agents and an "exploring expedition" under John C. Frémont were already in California stirring up dissension against Mexican rule, and ships of the U.S. Navy lay waiting expectantly off the shore. Two days later, Polk ordered a force under Colonel Stephen Kearny to march to Santa Fe and take possession of New Mexico.

The war was fought almost entirely by volunteers, including a number of recent immigrants from Europe, especially Irish escaping the Potato Famine. Thousands of Irish had joined the army by 1845, where they encountered significant prejudice. Some were punished for refusing to participate in Protestant services. They also witnessed the purposeful destruction of Catholic churches and monuments during the invasion of Mexico. This led some of the immigrant soldiers to switch sides, including the famous "Batallion of San Patricio," a group of Irish deserters who fought for the Mexican Army. In 1847, the U.S. Army hanged 16 surviving members of the San Patricios as traitors. They are still considered heroes in Mexico.

The **Mexican-American War** lasted much longer than expected because the Mexicans refused to make peace despite a succession of military defeats. In the first major campaign of the conflict, Taylor followed up his victory in two battles fought north of the Rio Grande by crossing the river, taking Matamoros, and marching on Monterrey. In September, his forces assaulted and captured this major city of northern Mexico after overcoming fierce resistance.

Taylor's controversial decision to allow the Mexican garrison to go free and his unwillingness or inability to advance farther into Mexico angered Polk and led him to adopt a new strategy for winning the war and a new commander to implement it. General Winfield Scott was ordered to prepare an amphibious attack on Veracruz with the aim of placing an American army within striking distance of Mexico City itself. With half his forces detached for the new invasion, Taylor was left to hold his position in northern Mexico. At Buena Vista, in February 1847, he claimed victory over a sizable Mexican army sent northward to dislodge him. Though unpopular with the administration, Taylor was hailed as a national hero and a possible candidate for president.

Meanwhile, the Kearny expedition captured Santa Fe, proclaimed the annexation of New Mexico by the United States, and set off for California. There they found that American settlers,

Handkerchief depicting Major General Zachary Taylor in battle scenes from the Mexican War. When the popular hero displeased President Polk with his actions in the capture of Monterrey, Winfield Scott was appointed to carry out Polk's plan for the attack on the port city of Veracruz, which led to the capture of Mexico City.

Source: Collection of The New-York Historical Society, 1941.129.

in cooperation with John C. Frémont's exploring expedition, had revolted against Mexican authorities and declared their independence as the Bear Flag Republic. The navy had also captured the port of Monterey. With the addition of Kearny's troops, a relatively small number of Americans were able to take possession of California in early 1847 against scattered and disorganized Mexican opposition.

The decisive Veracruz campaign was slow to develop because of the massive and careful preparations required. But in March 1847, the main American army under General Scott finally landed near that crucial port city and laid siege to it. Veracruz fell after eighteen days, and then Scott began his advance on Mexico City. In the most important single battle of the war, Scott met forces under General Santa Anna at Cerro Gordo on April 17 and 18. The Mexicans occupied an apparently impregnable position on high ground blocking the way to Mexico City. A daring flanking maneuver that required soldiers to scramble up the mountainsides enabled Scott to win the decisive victory that opened the road to the Mexican capital. By August, American troops were drawn up in front of Mexico City. After a temporary armistice, a brief respite that the Mexicans used to regroup and improve their defenses, Scott ordered the massive assault that captured the city on September 14.

Settlement of the Mexican-American War

Accompanying Scott's army was a diplomat, Nicholas P. Trist, who was authorized to negotiate a peace treaty whenever the Mexicans decided they had had enough. Despite a sequence of American victories and the imminent fall of Mexico City, Trist made little progress. No Mexican leader was willing to invite the wrath of an intensely proud and patriotic citizenry by agreeing to the kind of terms that Polk wanted to impose. Even after the United States had achieved an overwhelming military victory, Trist found it difficult to exact an acceptable treaty from the Mexican government. In November, Polk ordered Trist to return to Washington. Radical adherents of Manifest Destiny were now clamoring for the annexation of all Mexico, and Polk himself may have been momentarily tempted by the chance to move from military occupation to outright annexation.

Trist ignored Polk's instructions and lingered in Mexico City. On February 2, 1848, he signed a treaty that gained all the concessions he had been commissioned to obtain. The **Treaty of Guadalupe Hidalgo** ceded New Mexico and California to the United States for $15 million, established the Rio Grande as the border between Texas and Mexico, and promised that the U.S. government would assume the substantial claims of American citizens against Mexico. The treaty also provided that the Mexican residents of the new territories would become U.S. citizens. When the agreement reached Washington, Polk censured Trist for disobeying orders but approved most of his treaty, which he sent to the Senate for ratification. Senate approval by a vote of 38 to 14 came on March 10.

The United States gained 500,000 square miles of territory from Mexico. The treaty of 1848 enlarged the size of the nation by about 20 percent, adding to its domain the present states of

Richard Caton Woodville's *War News from Mexico* suggests the role of the newspaper in keeping the public informed of developments in the expanding nation's quest for new territory.

Source: *War News from Mexico* by Richard Caton Woodville, 1848. Board of Trustees, National Gallery of Art, Washington, DC.

California, Utah, New Mexico, Nevada, Arizona, and parts of Colorado and Wyoming. Soon those interested in a southern route for a transcontinental railroad pressed for even more territory along the southern border of the cession. That pressure led in 1853 to the Gadsden Purchase of the southernmost parts of present-day Arizona and New Mexico. But one intriguing question remains. Why, given the expansionist spirit of the age, did the campaign to acquire all of Mexico fail?

According to historian Frederick Merk, a major factor was the peculiar combination of racism and anticolonialism that dominated American opinion. It was one thing to acquire thinly populated areas that could be settled by "Anglo-Saxon" pioneers. It was something else again to incorporate a large population that was mainly of mixed Spanish and Indian origin. These "mongrels," charged racist opponents of the "All Mexico" movement, could never be fit citizens of a self-governing republic. They would have to be ruled in the way the British governed India, and the possession of colonial dependencies was contrary to American ideals and traditions.

View the Map   Mexican-American War, 1846–1848

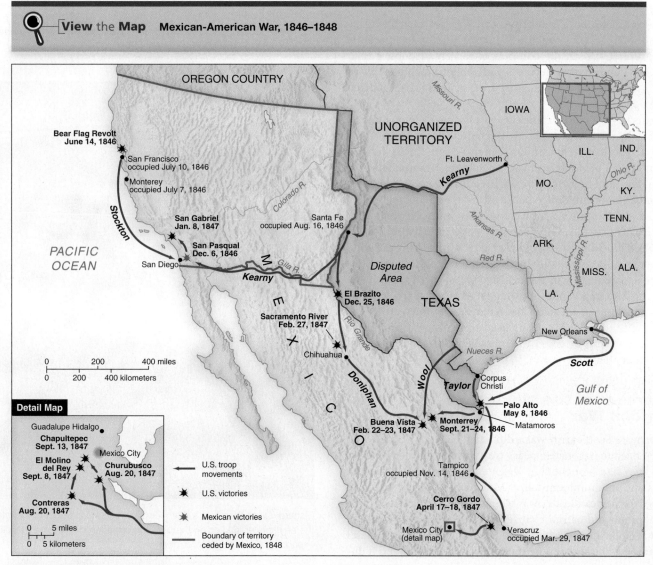

THE MEXICAN-AMERICAN WAR   The Mexican-American War added half a million square miles of territory to the United States, but the cost was high: $100 million and thirteen thousand lives.

Merk's thesis sheds light on why the general public had little appetite for swallowing all of Mexico, but those actually making policy had more mundane and practical reasons for being satisfied with what was obtained at Guadalupe Hidalgo. What they had really wanted all along, historian Norman Graebner contended, were the great California harbors of San Francisco and San Diego. From these ports, Americans could trade directly with the Orient and dominate the commerce of the Pacific. Once acquisition of California had been assured, policy makers had little incentive to press for more Mexican territory.

The war with Mexico divided the American public and provoked political dissension. A majority of the Whig party opposed the war in principle, arguing that the United States had no valid claims to the area south of the Nueces. Whig congressmen voted for military appropriations while the conflict was going on, but they constantly criticized the president for starting it. More ominous was the charge of some Northerners from both parties that the real purpose of the war was to spread the institution of

slavery and increase the political power of the southern states. While battles were being fought in Mexico, Congress debated the Wilmot Proviso, a proposal to prohibit slavery in any territories that might be acquired from Mexico. The Mexican-American War left a legacy of a bitter sectional quarrel over the status of slavery in new areas (see Chapter 14).

The domestic controversies aroused by the war and the propaganda of Manifest Destiny revealed the limits of mid-nineteenth-century American expansionism and put a damper on additional efforts to extend the nation's boundaries. Concerns about slavery and race impeded acquisition of new territory in Latin America and the Caribbean. Resolution of the Oregon dispute clearly indicated that the United States was not willing to go to war with a powerful adversary to obtain large chunks of British North America, and the old ambition of incorporating Canada faded. From 1848 until the revival of expansionism in the late nineteenth century, American growth usually took the form of populating and developing the vast territory already acquired. Although the rights of former inhabitants of Mexico were supposedly guaranteed by treaty, they in effect became second-class citizens of the United States. (See the Feature Essay, "Hispanic America After 1848," pp. 308–309.)

Internal Expansionism

How did developments in transportation foster industrialization and encourage immigration?

Young American expansionists saw a clear link between acquisition of new territory and other forms of material growth and development. In 1844, Samuel F. B. Morse perfected and demonstrated his electric telegraph, a device that would make it possible to communicate rapidly over the expanse of a continental nation. Simultaneously, the railroad was becoming increasingly important as a means of moving people and goods over the same great distances. Improvements in manufacturing and agricultural methods led to an upsurge in the volume and range of internal trade, and the beginnings of mass immigration were providing human resources for the exploitation of new areas and economic opportunities.

After gold was discovered in California in 1848, a flood of emigrants from the East and several foreign nations arrived by ship or wagon train, their appetites whetted by the thought of striking it rich. The gold they unearthed spurred the national economy, and the rapid growth of population centers on the Pacific Coast inspired projects for transcontinental telegraph lines and railroad tracks.

Despite the best efforts of the Young Americans, the spirit of Manifest Destiny and the thirst for acquiring new territory waned after the Mexican-American War. The expansionist impulse was channeled instead into internal development. Although the nation ceased to grow in size, the technological advances and population increase of the 1840s continued during the 1850s, resulting in an acceleration of economic growth, a substantial increase in industrialization and urbanization, and the emergence of a new American working class.

The Triumph of the Railroad

More than anything else, the rise of the railroad transformed the American economy during the 1840s and 1850s. In 1830 and 1831, two American railroads began commercial operation—the Charleston and Hamburg in South Carolina and the Baltimore and Ohio in Maryland. After these pioneer lines had shown that steam locomotion was practical and profitable, several other railroads were built and began to carry passengers and freight during the 1830s.

By 1840, railroads had 2,818 miles of track—a figure almost equal to the combined length of all canals—but the latter still carried a much larger volume of goods. Passengers might prefer the speed of trains, but the lower unit cost of transporting freight on the canal boats prevented most shippers from changing their habits. Furthermore, states such as New York and Pennsylvania had invested heavily in canals and resisted chartering a competitive form of transportation. Most of the early railroads reached out from port cities, such as Boston and Baltimore, that did not have good canal routes to the interior. Steam locomotion provided them a chance to cut into the enormous commerce that flowed along the Erie Canal and gave New York an advantage in the scramble for western trade.

 **Read the Document** Senate Report on the Railroads (1852)

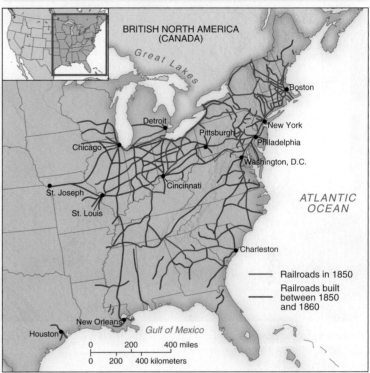

RAILROADS, 1850 AND 1860 During the 1840s and 1850s, railroad lines moved rapidly westward. By 1860, more than 30,000 miles of track had been laid.

During the 1840s, rails extended beyond the northeastern and Middle Atlantic states, and mileage increased more than threefold, reaching a total of more than 9,000 miles by 1850. Expansion, fueled by massive European investment, was even greater in the following decade, when about 20,000 miles of additional track were laid. By 1860, all the states east of the Mississippi had rail service, and a traveler could go by train from New York to Chicago and return by way of Memphis. Throughout the 1840s and 1850s, railroads cut deeply into the freight business of the canals and succeeded in driving many of them out of business. The cost of hauling goods by rail decreased dramatically because of improved track construction and the introduction of powerful locomotives that could haul more cars. New York and Pennsylvania were slow to encourage rail transportation because of their early commitment to canals, but by the 1850s, both states had accepted the inevitable and were promoting massive railroad building.

The development of railroads had an enormous effect on the economy as a whole. Although the burgeoning demand for iron rails was initially met mainly by importation from England, it eventually spurred development of the domestic iron industry. Since railroads required an enormous outlay of capital, their promoters pioneered new methods for financing business enterprise. At a time when most manufacturing and mercantile concerns were still owned by families or partnerships, the railroad companies sold stock to the general public and helped to set the pattern for the separation

Watch the **Video**   Mastering Time and Space: How the Railroads Changed America

Railroads began to spread across the United States in the early 1830s, slowly at first and then more rapidly, growing from zero in 1830 to three thousand miles in 1840, to nine thousand miles of railroad track in 1850.

of ownership and control that characterizes the modern corporation. They also developed new types of securities, such as "preferred stock" (with no voting rights but the assurance of a fixed rate of return) and long-term bonds at a set rate of interest.

The gathering and control of private capital did not fully meet the desires of the early railroad barons. State and local governments, convinced that railroads were the key to their future prosperity, loaned the railroads money, bought their stock, and guaranteed their bonds. The federal government helped the railroads by surveying the routes of projected lines, by devolving significant powers of eminent domain onto the railroads to allow them to take lands that had been in private hands, and by providing land grants. In 1850, for example, several million acres of public land were granted to the Illinois Central. In all, forty companies received such aid before 1860, setting a precedent for the massive land grants of the post–Civil War era.

The Industrial Revolution Takes Off

While railroads were initiating a revolution in transportation, American industry was entering a new phase of rapid and sustained growth. The factory mode of production, which had originated before 1840 in the cotton mills of New England, was extended to a variety of other products (see Chapter 9). The weaving and processing of wool, instead of being carried on in different locations, was concentrated in single production units beginning in the 1830s, and by 1860 some of the largest textile mills in the country were producing wool cloth. In the coal and iron regions of eastern

Pennsylvania, iron was being forged and rolled in factories by 1850. Among the other industries that adopted the factory system during this period were those producing firearms, clocks, and sewing machines. While small workshops continued to predominate in most industries, and some relatively large factories were not yet mechanized, mass production was clearly the wave of the future.

The essential features of the emerging mode of production were the gathering of a supervised workforce in a single place, the payment of cash wages to workers, the use of interchangeable parts, and manufacture by "continuous process." Within a factory setting, standardized parts, manufactured separately and in bulk, could be efficiently and rapidly assembled into a final product by an ordered sequence of continuously repeated operations. Mass production, which involved the division of labor into a series of relatively simple and repetitive tasks, contrasted sharply with the traditional craft mode of production, in which a single worker produced the entire product out of raw materials.

The transformation of a craft into a modern industry is well illustrated by the evolution of shoemaking. The independent cobbler producing shoes for order was first challenged by a putting-out system involving the assignment of various tasks to physically separated workers and then was virtually displaced by the great shoe factories that by the 1860s were operating in cities such as Lynn, Massachusetts.

New technology often played an important role in the transition to mass production. Elias Howe's invention of the sewing machine in 1846 laid the basis for the ready-to-wear clothing industry and also contributed to the mechanization of shoemaking. During the 1840s, iron manufacturers adopted the British practice of using coal rather than charcoal for smelting and thus produced a metal better suited to industrial needs. Charles Goodyear's discovery in 1839 of the process for the vulcanization of rubber made a new range of manufactured items available to the American consumer, most notably the overshoe. Perhaps the greatest triumph of American technology during the mid-nineteenth century was the development of the world's most sophisticated and reliable machine tools.

Yet the United States was still not an industrial society. Factory workers remained a small fraction of the workforce, and nearly 60 percent of the gainfully employed still worked on the land. But farming itself, at least in the North, was undergoing a technological revolution of its own. John Deere's steel plow, invented in 1837 and mass produced by the 1850s, enabled midwestern farmers to cultivate the tough prairie soils that had resisted cast-iron implements. The mechanical reaper, patented by Cyrus McCormick in 1834, offered an enormous saving in the labor required for harvesting grain; by 1851, McCormick was producing more than a thousand reapers a year in his Chicago plant. Other new farm implements that came into widespread use before 1860 included seed drills, cultivators, and threshing machines.

A dynamic interaction between advances in transportation, industry, and agriculture gave great strength and resiliency to the economy of the northern states during the 1850s. Railroads offered western farmers better access to eastern markets. After Chicago and New York were linked by rail in 1853, the flow of most midwestern farm commodities shifted from the north-south direction based on river-borne traffic, which had still predominated in the 1830s and 1840s, to an east-west pattern. The mechanization of agriculture provided an additional impetus to industrialization, and its laborsaving features released workers for other economic activities. The growth of industry and the modernization of agriculture can thus be seen as mutually reinforcing aspects of a single process of economic growth.

Mass Immigration Begins

The original incentive to mechanize northern industry and agriculture came in part from a shortage of cheap labor. Compared with that of industrializing nations of Europe, the economy of the United States in the early nineteenth century was labor-scarce.

Women and children made up a large percentage of the workers in the early textile mills, and commercial farmers had to rely heavily on the labor of their family members. In the face of such limited and uncertain labor supplies, producers were greatly tempted to experiment with laborsaving machinery. By the 1840s and 1850s, however, even the newly industrialized operations were ready to absorb a new influx of unskilled workers.

During the 1840s, what had been a substantial flow of European immigrants to the United States suddenly became a flood. No fewer than 4.2 million people crossed the Atlantic between 1840 and 1860, with 3 million arriving in the single decade between 1845 and 1855. This was the greatest influx in proportion to total population—then about 20 million—that the nation has ever experienced. The largest single source of the new mass immigration was Ireland, but Germany was not far behind. Smaller contingents came from Switzerland, Norway, Sweden, and the Netherlands.

The massive transatlantic movement had many causes. The great push factor that caused 1.5 million Irish to forsake the Emerald Isle between 1845 and 1854 was the great potato blight, which brought

THE AGE OF PRACTICAL INVENTION

Year*	Inventor	Contribution	Importance/Description
1787	John Fitch	Steamboat	First successful American steamboat
1793	Eli Whitney	Cotton gin	Simplified process of separating fiber from seeds; helped make cotton a profitable staple of southern agriculture
1798	Eli Whitney	Jig for guiding tools	Facilitated manufacture of interchangeable parts
1802	Oliver Evans	Steam engine	First American steam engine; led to manufacture of high-pressure engines used throughout eastern United States
1813	Richard B. Chenaworth	Cast-iron plow	First iron plow to be made in three separate pieces, thus making possible replacement of parts
1830	Peter Cooper	Railroad locomotive	First steam locomotive built in America
1831	Cyrus McCormick	Reaper	Mechanized harvesting; early model could cut six acres of grain a day
1836	Samuel Colt	Revolver	First successful repeating pistol
1837	John Deere	Steel plow	Steel surface kept soil from sticking; farming thus made easier on rich prairies of Midwest
1839	Charles Goodyear	Vulcanization of rubber	Made rubber much more useful by preventing it from sticking and melting in hot weather
1842	Crawford W. Long	First administered ether	Reduced pain and risk of shock during operations in surgery
1844	Samuel F. B. Morse	Telegraph	Made long-distance communication almost instantaneous
1846	Elias Howe	Sewing machine	First practical machine for automatic sewing
1846	Norbert Rillieux	Vacuum evaporator	Improved method of removing water from sugar cane; revolutionized sugar industry and was later applied to many other products
1847	Richard M. Hoe	Rotary printing press	Printed an entire sheet in one motion; vastly speeded up printing process
1851	William Kelly	"Air-boiling process"	Improved method of converting iron into steel (usually known as Bessemer process because English inventor Bessemer had more advantageous patent and financial arrangements)
1853	Elisha G. Otis	Passenger elevator	Improved movement in buildings; when later electrified, stimulated development of skyscrapers
1859	Edwin L. Drake	First American oil well	Initiated oil industry in the United States
1859	George M. Pullman	Pullman passenger car	First railroad sleeping car suitable for long-distance travel

*Dates refer to patent or first successful use.

Source: From *Freedom and Crisis: An American History*, 3rd ed., by Allen Weinstein and Frank Otto Gatell. Copyright © 1974, 1978, 1981 by Random House, Inc. Reprinted by permission of Random House, Inc.

Feature Essay

Hispanic America After 1848
A Case Study in Majority Rule

With the discovery of gold in 1848, more than one thousand Californians of Mexican ancestry joined the frenetic rush to the Sierras. Among them was Don Antonio Franco Coronel, a Los Angeles schoolteacher, who led a group of fellow *Californios* into the rich goldfields. Just months before the expedition, the United States and Mexico had concluded the Treaty of Guadalupe Hidalgo, which transformed Coronel and his companions from Mexicans to Americans. At the insistence of the Mexican government, the treaty stipulated that Mexicans living in the newly acquired territories would be granted "all the rights of citizens of the United States . . . according to the principles of the Constitution." Coronel's gold-seeking enterprise would put that promise to the test.

Upon arriving in gold country, Coronel and his men immediately hit pay dirt. In the first day alone, Coronel pulled 45 ounces of gold from the ground; within eight days, one of his associates had amassed a pile of gold weighing a staggering 52 pounds. The Californios seemed to have a head start in the race for gold. They understood the terrain, cooperated among themselves, and were familiar with the best mining techniques. Not surprisingly, their dramatic successes stirred the envy of their Anglo-American competitors.

After a year of relatively peaceful competition, Anglo miners began to express their resentments. Lumping Californios with all other "foreigners," they unleashed a barrage of physical and political attacks against their competitors. Lynch mobs, camp riots, and legal harassment were common forms of Yankee intimidation. Despite their entitlements to the rights of citizenship, the Californios were badgered and bullied into retreat. Fearing for his life, Coronel returned to Southern California, where Hispanics still outnumbered the newcomers. Earning prestige and prosperity in Los Angeles, Coronel went on to become mayor and state treasurer. But to the end of his life, he still painfully remembered his experiences in Northern California, where his rights as a U.S. citizen were so easily disregarded by his fellow Americans.

Coronel's experiences exemplify two truths about the effect U.S. expansion had on the lives of Mexicans who suddenly found themselves in American territory. First, in areas where Anglo-American settlement grew rapidly—such as Northern California—the Hispanic community typically faced discrimination, intimidation, and a denial of the very civil rights that Guadalupe Hidalgo had supposedly guaranteed. Second, in areas where the Hispanic population remained a majority—such as Southern California—Spanish-speaking Americans were able to exercise the rights of republican citizenship, often wielding considerable political influence. Coronel had a taste of both experiences, going from intimidated miner to powerful politician. However, as Anglo settlers began to stream into Southern California, even that region ceased to be a safe haven for Hispanic rights.

By the mid-1840s, Hispanics living in Texas, known as Tejanos, were outnumbered by Anglos at a ratio of twenty to one. True to the pattern described above, this decided minority faced intense prejudice. Among the most notable victims of this prejudice was Juan Seguin, a hero of the Texas war for independence (see p. 296). Perhaps no Tejano family fell further or faster than the posterity of Don Martin de Leon. The scion of an aristocratic family, de Leon had spearheaded Spanish efforts to colonize Texas and continued to organize settlements after Mexican independence. Establishing extensive cattle ranches, the de Leons enjoyed prominence and wealth on their holdings. As with most Tejanos, they fervently supported the struggle for Texan independence, fighting shoulder to shoulder with their Anglo neighbors. But when the war ended, the de Leon estate fell under siege from the surging wave of new settlers. Relying on the intricacies of Anglo-American law and the power of an electoral majority, the newcomers quickly encroached on de Leon's lands. With frightening rapidity, the de Leon family was reduced from its preeminent position to abject poverty.

The de Leons were not alone. A contemporary observed that many Anglo settlers worked "dark intrigues against the native families, whose only crime was that they owned large tracts of land and desirable property." Even after U.S. annexation of the Lone Star Republic, Hispanics continued to be pushed off their land. In 1856, a Texas newspaper reported that "The people of Matagorda county have held a meeting and ordered every Mexican to leave the county. To strangers this may seem wrong, but we hold it to be perfectly right and highly necessary." For many Mexican Americans, life on U.S. soil taught the cruelest lesson in white man's democracy.

Yet majority rule actually worked to the favor of Hispanics living in New Mexico, where they enjoyed numerical dominance. When U.S. troops entered

Blessing of the Enrequita Mine, 1860, by Alexander Edouart. Spaniards and Mexicans, men and women, surround the makeshift altar where the priest is saying the blessing to dedicate the Enrequita Mine in northern California. The idyllic scene does not hint at the violent and rough treatment Hispanic miners experienced during the California gold rush days.

Santa Fe in 1846, Albino Chacón, a prominent city judge, controlled his own future. Although he had been loyal to the Mexican government throughout the war, the U.S. Army offered him the opportunity to retain his judgeship. Given similar offers, other New Mexicans who had initially opposed the U.S. invasion accepted positions of prominence, such as Donanciano Vigil, who served as interim governor of the territory. But Chacón lived by a strict code of honor and could not switch loyalties so easily. Opting for exile,

Chacón moved out of Santa Fe, left the practice of law, and took up farming. Aside from such self-imposed changes, however, American rule actually had little impact on most New Mexicans' lives. Hispanics still formed the demographic and political backbone of the territory and often served their new nation with distinction. Chacón's own son, Rafael, served as a Union officer during the Civil War, winning acclaim in defending New Mexico against a Confederate invasion from Texas, and was eventually elected as

territorial senator. Rafael's son studied law at Notre Dame and held several important positions in the Department of Justice. Majority status afforded New Mexican Hispanics opportunities in the American system that were denied their compatriots living in Anglo-dominated regions.

As settlement increased throughout the century, such Hispanic-controlled communities dwindled. The rise of the railroad acted as a funnel through which Anglo-Americans poured into western territories, and remaining pockets of Hispanic dominance rapidly disappeared. American majoritarianism and racism combined to place Hispanics in positions subordinate to those of the Anglo newcomers. Throughout the region the story was sadly similar: As Hispanic Americans lost their majority status, they also lost many of their basic rights.

QUESTIONS FOR DISCUSSION

1. How did the American citizenship granted them under the Treaty of Guadalupe Hidalgo benefit persons of Mexican ancestry in California and the Southwest?

2. How did Anglo prejudice and discrimination deny these benefits in subsequent years?

IMMIGRATION TO THE UNITED STATES, 1820–1860

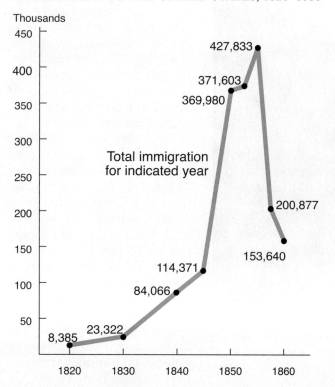

famine to a population that subsisted on this single crop. Escape to America was made possible by the low fares then prevailing on sailing ships bound from England to North America. Ships involved in the timber trade carried their bulky cargoes from Boston or Halifax to Liverpool; as an alternative to returning to America partly in ballast, they packed Irish immigrants into their holds. The squalor and misery in these steerage accommodations were almost beyond belief.

Because of the ports involved in the lumber trade—Boston, Halifax, Saint John's, and Saint Andrews—the Irish usually arrived in Canada or the northeastern states. Immobilized by poverty and a lack of the skills required for pioneering in the West, most of them remained in Northeastern cities. Forced to subsist on low-paid menial labor and crowded into festering urban slums, they were looked down on by most native-born Americans. Their devotion to Catholicism aroused Protestant resentment and mob violence. Some race-conscious people even doubted that the Irish were "white" like other northern Europeans. (See Chapter 14 for a discussion of the growth of nativism and anti-Catholicism.)

The million or so Germans who also came in the late 1840s and early 1850s were somewhat more fortunate. Most of them were also peasants, but they had fled hard times rather than outright catastrophe. Changes in German landholding patterns and a fluctuating market for grain crops put pressure on small operators. Unlike the Irish, they often escaped with a small amount of capital with which to make a fresh start in the New World.

Many German immigrants were artisans and sought to ply their trades in cities such as New York, St. Louis, Cincinnati, and Milwaukee. But a large portion of those with peasant backgrounds went back to the land. The possession of diversified agricultural skills and small amounts of capital enabled many Germans to become successful midwestern farmers. In general, they encountered less prejudice and discrimination than the Irish. For Germans who were Protestant, religious affinity with their American neighbors made

for relative tolerance. But even Germans who were Catholic normally escaped the virulent scorn heaped on the Irish, perhaps because they were not so poverty stricken and did not carry the added burden of being members of an ethnic group Anglo-Americans had learned to despise from their English ancestors and cousins.

What attracted most of the Irish, German, and other European immigrants to America was the promise of economic opportunity. A minority, like some of the German revolutionaries of 1848, chose the United States because they admired its democratic political system. But most immigrants were more interested in the chance to make a decent living than in voting or running for office. The arrival of large numbers of immigrants exacerbated the already serious problems of America's rapidly growing cities. The old "walking city" in which rich and poor lived in close proximity near the center of town was changing to a more segregated environment. The advent of railroads and horse-drawn streetcars enabled the affluent to move to the first American suburbs, while areas nearer commercial and industrial centers became the congested abode of newcomers from Europe. Emerging slums, such as the notorious Five Points district in New York City, were characterized by overcrowding, poverty, disease, and crime. Recognizing that these conditions created potential dangers for the entire urban population, middle-class reformers worked for the professionalization of police forces, introduction of sanitary water and sewage disposal systems, and the upgrading of housing standards.

They made some progress in these endeavors in the period before the Civil War, but the lot of the urban poor, mainly immigrants, was not dramatically improved. Except to the extent that their own communal activities—especially those sponsored by churches and mutual aid societies—provided a sense of security and solidarity, the existence of most urban immigrants remained unsafe, unhealthy, and unpleasant.

Despite the increasing segregation of the city into ethnic neighborhoods, the urban experience also produced a unifying effect on its mixed population. Individuals of all classes, occupations, and ethnicities met on the crowded streets and in the public squares of cities. Often, the entire population—or at least wide cross sections—came together in colorful parades, public celebrations, and political contests. Many city residents met other citizens as members of political parties, religious groups, and civic organizations. A single individual may have voted as a Democrat, worshiped as a Baptist, and served as a member of a volunteer fire department. These different affiliations created relationships that existed outside of ethnic identity. Antebellum cities showed the dark side of urbanization in their crowded slums and growing poverty, but they also became cauldrons of democracy in which different elements of nineteenth-century America met face to face to create a wider definition of what it meant to be an American.

The New Working Class

A majority of immigrants ended up as wage workers in factories, mines, and construction camps or as casual day laborers doing the many unskilled tasks required for urban and commercial growth. During the 1850s, factory production in Boston and other port cities previously devoted to commerce grew—partly because thousands of recent Irish immigrants worked for the kind of low wages that almost guaranteed large profits for entrepreneurs.

In established industries and older mill towns of the Northeast, immigrants added to, or in some cases displaced, the

📖 ●┤**Read** the **Document**   **Samuel Morse, Foreign Immigration (1835)**

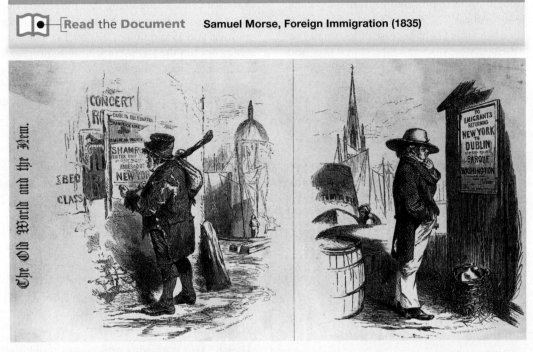

This 1854 cartoon titled "The Old World and the New" shows a shabbily dressed man in Ireland examining posters for trips to New York (left). At right, he is shown later, in America, wearing finer clothes and looking at posters advertising trips for emigrants returning to Dublin. As was the case for many immigrants seeking economic opportunities in the "New World," his situation has apparently changed for the better.

native-born workers who had predominated in the 1830s and 1840s. The changing workforce of the textile mills in Lowell, Massachusetts, provided a striking example of this process. In 1836, only 3.7 percent of the workers in one Lowell mill were foreign born; most members of the labor force at that time were young unmarried women from New England farms. By 1860, immigrants constituted 61.7 percent of the workforce. Women still formed the majority, but there had been a great proportional increase in the number of men who tended machines in textile factories. Irish males, employers found, were willing to perform tasks that native-born men had generally regarded as women's work.

This trend reveals much about the changing character of the American working class. In the 1830s, most male workers were artisans, and factory work was still largely the province of native-born American women and children. In the 1840s, the proportion of men engaged in factory work increased, and work conditions in many mills deteriorated. Workdays of twelve to fourteen hours were not new, but a more impersonal and cost-conscious form of management replaced paternalism and cooperation. During the depression that followed the Panic of 1837, bosses attempted to reduce expenses and increase productivity by cutting wages, increasing the speed of machinery, and "stretching out"—giving each worker more machinery to operate.

The result was a new upsurge of labor militancy involving female as well as male factory workers. Mill girls in Lowell, for example, formed a union of their own—the Female Labor Reform Association—and agitated for shorter working hours. On a broader front, workers' organizations petitioned state legislatures to pass laws limiting the workday to ten hours. The laws that were actually passed turned out to be ineffective because employers could still require a prospective worker to sign a special contract agreeing to longer hours.

The employment of immigrants in increasing numbers between the mid-1840s and the late 1850s made it more difficult to organize industrial workers. Impoverished fugitives from the Irish potato famine tended to have lower economic expectations and more conservative social attitudes than did native-born workers. Consequently, the Irish immigrants were initially willing to work for less and were not so prone to protest bad working conditions. By contrast, some German immigrants brought labor radicalism with them from their native land, and became leaders of union organization.

Conclusion: The Costs of Expansion

By 1860, industrial expansion and immigration had created a working class of men and women who seemed destined for a life of low-paid wage labor. This reality stood in contrast to America's self-image as a land of opportunity and upward mobility. Wage labor was popularly viewed as a temporary condition from which workers were supposed to extricate themselves by hard work and frugality. According to Abraham Lincoln, speaking in 1859 of the North's "free-labor" society, "there is no such thing as a freeman being fatally fixed for life, in the condition of a hired laborer." This ideal still had some validity in rapidly developing regions of the western states, but it was mostly myth when applied to the increasingly foreign-born industrial workers of the Northeast.

Both internal and external expansion had come at a heavy cost. Tensions associated with class and ethnic rivalries were only one part of the price of rapid economic development. The acquisition of new territories became politically divisive and would soon lead to a catastrophic sectional controversy. The Young America wing of the Democratic party fought vainly to prevent this from happening. Its leader in the late 1840s and early 1850s was Senator Stephen A. Douglas of Illinois, called the Little Giant because of his small stature and large public presence. More than anyone else of this period, he sought political power for himself and his party by combining an expansionist foreign policy with the encouragement of economic development within the territories already acquired. His youthful dynamism made him seem the very embodiment of the Young

America ideal. Recognizing that the slavery question was the main obstacle to his program, he sought to neutralize it through compromise and evasion (see Chapter 14). His failure to win the presidency or even the Democratic nomination before 1860 showed that the Young Americans' dream of a patriotic consensus supporting headlong expansion and economic development could not withstand the tensions and divisions that expansionist policies created or brought to light.

Study Resources

 Take the **Study Plan** for **Chapter 13** *An Age of Expansionism* on MyHistoryLab

TIME LINE

1822 Santa Fe opened to American traders

1823 Earliest American settlers arrive in Texas

1830 Mexico attempts to halt American migration to Texas

1831 American railroads begin commercial operation

1834 Cyrus McCormick patents mechanical reaper

1835 Revolution breaks out in Texas

1836 Texas becomes independent republic

1837 John Deere invents steel plow

1841 President John Tyler inaugurated

1842 Webster-Ashburton Treaty fixes border between Maine and New Brunswick

1843 Mass migration to Oregon begins; Mexico closes Santa Fe trade to Americans

1844 Samuel F. B. Morse demonstrates electric telegraph; James K. Polk elected president on platform of expansionism

1845 Mass immigration from Europe begins; United States annexes Texas; John L. O'Sullivan coins slogan "Manifest Destiny"

1846 War with Mexico breaks out; United States and Great Britain resolve diplomatic crisis over Oregon

1847 American conquest of California completed; Mormons settle Utah; American forces under Zachary Taylor defeat Mexicans at Buena Vista; Winfield Scott's army captures Veracruz and defeats Mexicans at Cerro Gordo; Mexico City falls to American invaders

1848 Treaty of Guadalupe Hidalgo consigns California and New Mexico to United States; Gold discovered in California

1849 "Forty-niners" rush to California to dig for gold

1858 War between Utah Mormons and U.S. forces averted

CHAPTER REVIEW

Movement to the Far West

 What were some of the reasons for which Americans headed into the Western territories, and what were some of the consequences of expansion?

In the 1820s and 1830s, pioneers pursued fertile land in the West beyond the borders of the United States and thus helped set the stage for the annexations and international crises of the 1840s. Some went for adventure, others for material gain or to escape religious persecution. (p. 293)

Manifest Destiny and the Mexican-American War

 Why did the U.S. annex Texas and the Southwest?

The annexation of Texas and the Southwest had several causes. Early settlers of Texas grew dissatisfied with the Catholic, antislavery Mexican administration. Many

Americans believed that it was America's "Manifest Destiny" to expand across the continent. This ideology was a useful rallying cry for politicians willing to go to war with Mexico to gain new territory. (p. 298)

Internal Expansionism

 How did developments in transportation foster industrialization and encourage immigration?

Rail transportation allowed the swift movement of people and goods. Other advances in technology permitted the new "mass production." The new industries drew many immigrants from Ireland and Germany, who were fleeing famine and persecution. Immigration made labor more plentiful and thus cheaper, so working conditions declined. (p. 305)

KEY TERMS AND DEFINITIONS

Young America   In the 1840s and early 1850s, many public figures—especially younger members of the Democratic party—used this term to describe their program of territorial expansion and industrial growth. p. 292

Alamo   In 1835, Americans living in Mexican-ruled Texas fomented a revolution. Mexico lost the resulting conflict, but not before its troops defeated and killed a group of American rebels at the Alamo, a fortified mission in San Antonio. p. 296

Manifest Destiny   Coined in 1845, this term referred to a doctrine in support of territorial expansion based on the belief that the United States should expand to encompass all of North America. p. 298

Mexican-American War   Conflict (1846–1848) between the United States and Mexico after the U.S. annexation of Texas. As victor, the United States acquired vast new territories from Mexico. p. 302

Treaty of Guadalupe Hidalgo   Signed in 1848, this treaty ended the Mexican-American War. Mexico relinquished its claims to Texas and ceded an additional 500,000 square miles to the United States for $15 million. p. 303

CRITICAL THINKING QUESTIONS

1. Why do you think Americans turned from expansion beyond U.S. borders to internal expansion after the Mexican-American War?

2. What do you think was the most important force driving change in American life during the 1840s and 1850s: Technology, politics, or international movements of people? Why?

3. Once again in this period, economic and material changes greatly influenced the makeup of American society. What lessons can you draw from the ongoing interplay of social and material changes in U.S. history?

MyHistoryLab Media Assignments

Find these resources in the Media Assignments folder for Chapter 13 on MyHistoryLab

Movement to the Far West

■ **View** the **Map**   *United States Territorial Expansion in the 1850s p. 294*

View the **Map**   *Texas Revolution, 1836 p. 296*

Manifest Destiny and the Mexican-American War

Watch the **Video**   *The Annexation of Texas p. 299*

Read the **Document**   *John O'Sullivan, "The Great Nation of Futurity" (1845) p. 300*

Read the **Document**   *Thomas Corwin, "Against the Mexican War" (1847) p. 303*

■ **View** the **Map**   *Mexican-American War, 1846–1848 p. 304*

Internal Expansionism

Read the **Document**   *Senate Report on the Railroads (1852) p. 305*

■ **Watch** the **Video**   *Mastering Time and Space: How the Railroads Changed America p. 306*

■ **Complete** the **Assignment**   *Hispanic America After 1848: A Case Study in Majority Rule p. 308*

■ **Read** the **Document**   *Samuel Morse, Foreign Immigration (1835) p. 311*

■ *Indicates Study Plan Media Assignment*

14 The Sectional Crisis

Contents and Learning Objectives

((•●—[**Listen** to the **Audio File** on **myhistorylab**   Chapter 14 *The Sectional Crisis*

Brooks Assaults Sumner in Congress

On May 22, 1856, Representative Preston Brooks of South Carolina erupted onto the floor of the Senate with a cane in his hand. He approached Charles Sumner, the antislavery senator from Massachusetts who had recently given a fiery oration condemning the South for plotting to extend slavery to the Kansas Territory. What was worse, the speech had included insulting references to Senator Andrew Butler of South Carolina, a kinsman of Brooks. When Brooks found Sumner seated at his desk, Brooks proceeded to batter him over the head. Amazed and stunned, Sumner made a desperate effort to rise and ripped his bolted desk from the floor. He then collapsed under a continued torrent of blows.

Sumner was so badly injured by the assault that he did not return to the Senate for three years. But his home state reelected him in 1857 and kept his seat vacant as testimony against southern brutality and "barbarism." In parts of the North that were up in arms against the expansion of slavery, Sumner was hailed as a martyr to the cause of "free soil." Brooks, denounced in the North as a bully, was lionized by his fellow Southerners. When he resigned from the House after a vote of censure had narrowly failed because of solid southern opposition, his constituents reelected him unanimously.

These contrasting reactions show how bitter sectional antagonism had become by 1856. Sumner spoke for the radical wing of the new Republican Party, which was making a bid for national power by mobilizing the North against the alleged aggressions of "the slave power." Southerners viewed the very existence of this party as an insult to their section of the country and a threat to its vital interests. Sumner came closer to being an abolitionist than any other member of Congress, and nothing created greater fear and anxiety among Southerners than their belief that antislavery forces were plotting against their way of life. To many Northerners, "bully Brooks" stood for all the arrogant and violent slaveholders who were allegedly conspiring to extend their barbaric labor system. By 1856, therefore, the sectional cleavage that would lead to the Civil War had already undermined the foundations of national unity.

The crisis of the mid-1850s came only a few years after the elaborate compromise of 1850 had seemingly resolved the dispute over the future of slavery in the territories acquired as a result of the Mexican War. The Kansas-Nebraska Act of 1854 set in motion the renewed agitation over the extension of slavery that led to Brooks' attack on Sumner. This legislation revived the sectional conflict and led to the emergence of the Republican Party. From that point on, a dramatic series of events increased sectional

SOUTHERN CHIVALRY — ARGUMENT VERSUS CLUB'S.

After his constituents learned of Preston Brooks' caning of Senator Sumner, they sent Brooks a gold-handled cowhide whip to use on other antislavery advocates.

confrontation and destroyed the prospects for a new compromise. The caning of Charles Sumner was one of these events, and violence on the Senate floor foreshadowed violence on the battlefield.

less tangible features of sectionalism—emotion and ideology—were not as divisive as they would later become. Hence a fragile compromise was achieved through a kind of give-and-take that would not be possible in the changed environment of the mid-1850s.

The Compromise of 1850

How did territorial expansion intensify the conflict over slavery?

The "irrepressible conflict" over slavery in the territories began in the late 1840s. The positions taken on this issue between 1846 and 1850 established the range of options that would reemerge after 1854. But during this earlier phase of the sectional controversy, the leaders of two strong national parties, each with substantial followings in both the North and the South, had a vested interest in resolving the crisis. Efforts to create uncompromising sectional parties failed to disrupt what historians call the second party system—the vigorous competition between Whigs and Democrats that had characterized elections since the 1830s. Furthermore, the

The Problem of Slavery in the Mexican Cession

As the price of union between states committed to slavery and those in the process of abolishing it, the Founders had attempted to limit the role of the slavery issue in national politics. The Constitution gave the federal government the right to abolish the international slave trade but no definite authority to regulate or destroy the institution where it existed under state law. Although many of the Founders hoped for the eventual demise of slavery, they provided no direct means to achieve this end except voluntary state action. These ground rules limited the effect of northern attacks on the South's peculiar institution. It was easy to condemn slavery in principle but very difficult to develop a practical program to eliminate it without defying the Constitution.

Radical abolitionists saw this problem clearly and resolved it by rejecting the law of the land in favor of a "higher law" prohibiting human bondage. In 1844, William Lloyd Garrison publicly burned the Constitution, condemning it as "a Covenant with Death, an Agreement with Hell." But Garrison spoke for a small minority dedicated to freeing the North, at whatever cost, from the sin of condoning slavery.

During the 1840s, the majority of Northerners showed that while they disliked slavery, they were not abolitionists. They were inclined to view slavery as a backward and unwholesome institution, much inferior to their own free-labor system, and could be persuaded that slaveholders were power-hungry aristocrats seeking more than their share of national political influence. But they regarded the Constitution as a binding contract between slave and free states and were likely to be prejudiced against blacks and reluctant to accept large numbers of them as free citizens. Consequently, they saw no legal or desirable way to bring about emancipation within the southern states.

But the Constitution had not predetermined the status of slavery in *future* states. Since Congress had the power to admit new states to the Union under any conditions it wished to impose, a majority arguably could require the abolition of slavery as the price of admission. An effort to use this power had led to the Missouri crisis of 1819–1820 (see Chapter 9). The resulting compromise was designed to decide future cases by drawing a line between slave and free states and extending it westward through the unsettled portions of what was then American soil. When specific territories were settled, organized, and prepared for statehood, slavery would be permitted south of the line and prohibited north of it.

The tradition of providing both the free North and the slave South with opportunities for expansion and the creation of new states broke down when new territories were wrested from Mexico in the 1840s. When Texas was admitted as a slave state, northern expansionists could still look forward to the admission of Oregon as a counterbalancing free state. But the Mexican War raised the prospect that California and New Mexico, both south of the Missouri Compromise line, would also be acquired. Since it was generally assumed in the North that Congress had the power to prohibit slavery in new territories, a movement developed in Congress to do just that.

The Wilmot Proviso Launches the Free-Soil Movement

The Free-Soil crusade began in August 1846, only three months after the start of the Mexican-American War, when Congressman David Wilmot, a Pennsylvania Democrat, proposed an amendment to the military appropriations bill that would ban slavery in any territory acquired from Mexico.

Wilmot spoke for the large number of northern Democrats who felt neglected and betrayed by the party's choice of Polk over Van Buren in 1844 and by the "prosouthern" policies of the Polk administration, including a low tariff and lack of federal funding for internal improvements. Democratic expansionists also felt betrayed that Polk had gone back on his pledge to obtain "all of Oregon" right before waging a war to win all of Texas and the Southwest. Like David Wilmot, they were "jealous of the power of the South."

The pioneer Free-Soilers had a genuine interest in the issue actually at hand—the question of who would control and settle the new territories. Combining an appeal to racial prejudice with opposition to slavery as an institution, Wilmot defined his cause as involving the "rights of white freemen" to go to areas where they could live "without the disgrace which association with negro slavery brings on white labor." Wilmot proposed that slavery as well as settlement by free African Americans be prohibited in the territory obtained in the Mexican cession, thus enhancing the opportunities of the North's common folk by preventing job competition from slaves and free blacks. By linking racism with resistance to the spread of slavery, Wilmot appealed to a broad spectrum of northern opinion.

Northern Whigs backed the proviso because they shared Wilmot's concern about the outcome of an unregulated competition between slave and free labor in the territories. Furthermore, voting for the measure provided a good outlet for their frustration at being unable to halt the annexation of Texas and the Mexican-American War. The preferred position of some Whig leaders was no expansion at all, but when expansion could not be avoided, the northern wing of the party endorsed the view that acquisition of Mexican territory should not be used to increase the power of the slave states.

In the first House vote on the **Wilmot Proviso**, party lines crumbled and were replaced by a sharp sectional cleavage. Every northern congressman with the exception of two Democrats voted for the amendment, and every Southerner except two Whigs went on record against it. After passing the House, the proviso was blocked in the Senate by a combination of southern influence and Democratic loyalty to the administration. When the appropriations bill went back to the House without the proviso, the administration's arm-twisting succeeded in changing enough northern Democratic votes to pass the bill and thus send the proviso down to defeat.

The end of the Mexican-American War, the formal acquisition of New Mexico and California, and the approaching election of 1848 gave new urgency to a search for politically feasible solutions. The extreme alternatives—the proviso policy of free soil and the radical southern response that slavery could be extended to any territory—threatened to destroy the national parties because there was no bisectional support for either of them.

Squatter Sovereignty and the Election of 1848

After a futile attempt was made to extend the Missouri Compromise line to the Pacific—a proposal that was unacceptable to Northerners because most of the Mexican cession lay south of the line—a new approach was devised that appealed especially to Democrats. Its main proponent was Senator Lewis Cass of Michigan, an aspirant for the party's presidential nomination. Cass, who described his formula as "squatter sovereignty," would leave the determination of the status of slavery in a territory to the actual settlers. From the beginning, this proposal contained an ambiguity that allowed it to be interpreted differently in the North and the South. For northern Democrats, squatter sovereignty—or **popular sovereignty** as it was later called—meant the settlers could vote slavery up or down at the first meeting of a territorial legislature. For the southern wing of the party, it meant a decision would be made only at the time a convention drew up a constitution and applied for statehood. It was in the interest of national Democratic leaders to leave this ambiguity unresolved for as long as possible.

THE ELECTION OF 1848

Candidate	Party	Popular Vote	Electoral Vote
Taylor	Whig	1,360,967	163
Cass	Democratic	1,222,342	127
Van Buren	Free-Soil	291,263	—

Congress failed to resolve the future of slavery in the Mexican cession in time for the election of 1848, and the issue entered the arena of presidential politics. The Democrats nominated Cass on a platform of squatter sovereignty. The Whigs evaded the question by running General Zachary Taylor—the hero of the battle of Buena Vista—without a platform. Taylor refused to commit himself on the status of slavery in the territories, but northern Whigs favoring restriction took heart from the general's promise not to veto any territorial legislation passed by Congress. Southern Whigs went along with Taylor mainly because he was a Southerner who owned slaves and would presumably defend the interests of his native region.

Northerners who strongly supported the Wilmot Proviso—and felt betrayed that neither the Whigs nor the Democrats were supporting it—were attracted by a third-party movement. In August, a tumultuous convention in Buffalo nominated former-President Van Buren to carry the banner of the Free-Soil Party. Support for the Free-Soilers came from antislavery Whigs dismayed by their party's nomination of a slaveholder and its evasiveness on the territorial issue, disgruntled Democrats who had backed the proviso and resented southern influence in their party, and some of the former adherents of the abolitionist Liberty Party. Van Buren himself was motivated less by antislavery zeal than by bitterness at being denied the Democratic nomination in 1844 because of southern obstructionism. The founding of the Free-Soil Party was the first significant effort to create a broadly based sectional party addressing itself to voters' concerns about the extension of slavery.

After a noisy and confusing campaign, Taylor came out on top, winning a majority of the electoral votes in both the North and the South and a total of 1,360,967 popular votes to 1,222,342 for Cass and 291,263 for Van Buren. The Free-Soilers failed to carry a single state but did quite well in the North, coming in second behind Taylor in New York, Massachusetts, and Vermont.

Taylor Takes Charge

Once in office, Taylor devised a bold plan to decide the fate of slavery in the Mexican cession. A brusque military man who disdained political give-and-take, he tried to engineer the immediate admission of California and New Mexico to the Union as states, thus bypassing the territorial stage entirely and avoiding a congressional debate on the status of slavery in the federal domain. Under the administration's urging, California, which was filling up rapidly with settlers drawn by the lust for gold, convened a constitutional convention and applied for admission to the Union as a free state.

Instead of resolving the crisis, President Taylor's initiative only worsened it. Once it was clear that California was going to be a free state, the administration's plan aroused intense opposition in the South. Fearing that New Mexico would also be free because

In this cartoon, Democrats Lewis Cass and John C. Calhoun and antislavery radicals Horace Greeley, William Lloyd Garrison, and Abby Folsom look on as Martin Van Buren, the Free-Soil Party candidate in the election of 1848, attempts to bridge the chasm between the Democratic platform and that of the antislavery Whigs. The Free-Soil influence was decisive in the election; it split the New York Democratic vote, thus allowing Whig candidate Zachary Taylor to win New York and the presidency.

Mexican law had prohibited slavery there, Southerners of both parties accused the president of trying to impose the Wilmot Proviso in a new form. The prospect that only free states would emerge from the entire Mexican cession inspired serious talk of secession.

In Congress, Senator John C. Calhoun of South Carolina saw a chance to achieve his long-standing goal of creating a southern voting bloc that would cut across regular party lines. State legislatures and conventions throughout the South denounced "northern aggression" against the rights of the slave states. As signs of southern fury increased, Calhoun rejoiced that the South had never been so "united . . . bold, and decided." In the fall and winter of 1849–1850, several southern states agreed to participate in a convention, to be held in Nashville in June, where grievances could be aired and demands made. For an increasing number of southern political leaders, the survival of the Union would depend on the North's response to the demands of the southern rights movement.

Forging a Compromise

When it became clear that the president would not abandon or modify his plan in order to appease the South, independent efforts began in Congress to arrange a compromise. Hoping that he could again play the role of "great pacificator" as he had in the Missouri

Compromise of 1820, Senator Henry Clay of Kentucky offered a series of resolutions meant to restore sectional harmony. He hoped to reduce tension by providing mutual concessions. On the critical territorial question, his solution was to admit California as a free state and organize the rest of the Mexican cession with no explicit prohibition of slavery—in other words, without the Wilmot Proviso. Noting that Mexican law had already abolished slavery there, he also pointed to the arid climate of the New Mexico region, which made it unsuitable for cotton culture and slavery. He also sought to resolve a major boundary dispute between New Mexico and Texas by granting the disputed region to New Mexico while compensating Texas through federal assumption of its state debt. As a concession to the North on another issue—the existence of slavery in the District of Columbia—he recommended prohibiting the buying and selling of slaves at auction and permitting the abolition of slavery itself with the consent of the District's white inhabitants. He also called for a more effective Fugitive Slave Law.

These proposals provided the basis for the **Compromise of 1850**. Proposed in February 1850, it took several months for the compromise to get through Congress. One obstacle was President Taylor's firm resistance to the proposal; another was the difficulty of getting congressmen to vote for it in the form of a single package or "omnibus bill." Few politicians from either section

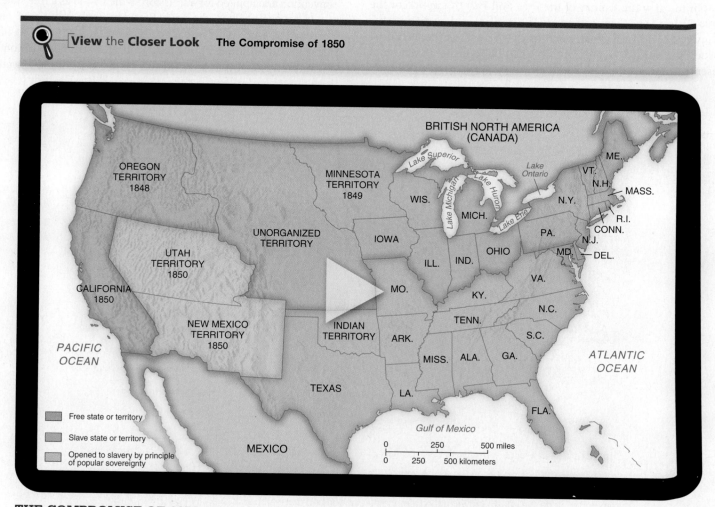

View the Closer Look   The Compromise of 1850

THE COMPROMISE OF 1850 The "compromise" was actually a series of resolutions granting some concessions to the North—especially admission of California as a free state—and some to the South, such as a stricter Fugitive Slave Law.

were willing to go on record as supporting the key concessions to the *other* section. The logjam was broken in July by two crucial developments: President Taylor died and was succeeded by Millard Fillmore, who favored the compromise, and a decision was made to abandon the omnibus strategy in favor of a series of measures that could be voted on separately. After the breakup of the omnibus bill, Democrats replaced the original Whig sponsors as leaders of the compromise movement, and some of Clay's proposals were modified to make them more acceptable to the South and the Democrats. Senator Stephen A. Douglas, a Democrat from Illinois, was particularly influential.

As the price of Democratic support, the popular sovereignty principle was included in the bills organizing New Mexico and Utah. Territorial legislatures in the Mexican cession were explicitly granted power over "all rightful subjects of legislation." Abolition of slave auctions and depots in the District of Columbia and a new **Fugitive Slave Law** were also enacted. The latter was a particularly outrageous piece of legislation: Suspected fugitives were now denied a jury trial, the right to testify in their own behalf, and other basic constitutional rights. As a result, there were no effective safeguards against falsely identifying fugitives or kidnapping free blacks.

The compromise passed because its key measures were supported by northern Democrats, southern Whigs, and representatives of both parties from the border states. No single bill was backed by a majority of the congressmen from both sections, and few senators or representatives actually voted for the entire package.

> **Read the Document**   **The Fugitive Slave Act (1850)**

Effects of the Fugitive-Slave-Law.

Southerners had long objected to northern states' attitudes toward runaway slaves. In fact, many northern states had passed personal liberty laws in an effort to protect free black people from kidnapping and to shield runway slaves from capture by making it more difficult, as well as more expensive, for slaveholders to recover their property. Nevertheless, for the thousands of northerners who wanted to remain neutral, passage of the Fugitive Slave Act quashed their comfortable middle ground.

Both sides doubted the value and workability of a "compromise" that was really more like an armistice or a cease-fire.

Yet the Compromise of 1850 did serve for a short time as a basis for sectional peace. Probably the greatest challenges to the stability of the compromise came from a few sensational rescues or attempted rescues of fugitive slaves by free blacks in the North. In Boston in 1854, an antislavery mob led by armed abolitionists tried to free fugitive Anthony Burns from the court house where his extradition hearing was to take place. One of the men guarding Burns was killed, but the fugitive himself could not be reached. After the hearing had declared Burns an escaped slave, he was escorted by units of the U.S. Army through a hissing and groaning crowd of twenty thousand to a waiting ship. After this event few efforts were made to apprehend escaped slaves in those parts of the North where antislavery sentiment was deeply rooted.

Political Upheaval, 1852–1856

How did the two-party system change during this period?

The second party system—Democrats versus Whigs—survived the crisis over slavery in the Mexican cession, but in the long run the Compromise of 1850 may have weakened it. Although both national parties had been careful during the 1840s not to take stands on the slavery issue that would alienate their supporters in either section of the country, they had in fact offered voters alternative ways of dealing with the question. Democrats had endorsed headlong territorial expansion with the promise of a fair division of the spoils between slave and free states. Whigs had generally opposed annexations or acquisitions, because they were likely to bring the slavery question to the fore and threaten sectional harmony. With some shifts of emphasis and interpretation, each strategy could be presented as either a protection or containment of slavery.

Yet the stability of the situation was fragile. When the Democrats sought to revive the Manifest Destiny issue in 1854, they reopened the explosive issue of slavery in the territories. The Whigs were too weak and divided to respond with a policy of their own, and a purely sectional Free-Soil Party—the Republicans—gained prominence. Without strong national parties to contain sectionalism, the divisions between North and South intensified.

The Party System in Crisis

The presidential campaign of 1852 was singularly devoid of major issues. With the slavery question under wraps, some Whigs tried to revive interest in the nationalistic economic policies that were the traditional hallmarks of their party. But convincing arguments in favor of a protective tariff, a national bank, and internal improvements were hard to make in a period of sustained prosperity.

Another tempting issue was immigration. Many evangelical Protestant Whigs were upset by the massive influx of Catholics from Europe, who voted overwhelmingly for their Democratic opponents. While some Whig leaders called for restrictions on immigrant voting rights, others wanted to compete with the Democrats for the immigrant vote, including the Whig nominee for President, General Winfield Scott. The fact that Scott's

THE ELECTION OF 1852

Candidate	Party	Popular Vote	Electoral Vote
Pierce	Democratic	1,601,117	254
Scott	Whig	1,385,453	42
Hale	Free-Soil	155,825	—

daughters were being raised as Catholics was publicized to demonstrate his good intentions toward immigrant communities. This strategy backfired. For the most part, Catholic immigrants retained their Democratic allegiance, and some nativist Whigs apparently sat out the election to protest their party's disregard of their cultural prejudices.

But the main cause for Scott's crushing defeat was the support he lost in the South when he allied himself with the dominant northern antislavery wing of the party, led by Senator William Seward of New York. The Democratic candidate, Franklin Pierce of New Hampshire, was a colorless nonentity compared to his rival, but he ran up huge majorities in the Deep South, where Whigs stayed home in massive numbers. He also edged out Scott in most of the free states. In the most one-sided election since 1820,

Pierce received 254 electoral votes from 27 states while Scott carried only 4 states with 42 electoral votes. This outcome revealed that the Whig Party was in deep trouble because it lacked a program that would distinguish it from the Democrats and would appeal to voters in both sections of the country.

Despite their overwhelming victory in 1852, the Democrats had reasons for anxiety about the loyalty of their supporters. Because the major parties had ceased to offer clear-cut alternatives to the electorate, voter apathy or alienation was a growing trend in the early 1850s.

The Kansas-Nebraska Act Raises a Storm

In January 1854, Senator Stephen A. Douglas of Illinois proposed a bill to organize the territory west of Missouri and Iowa. Since this region fell within the area where slavery had been banned by the Missouri Compromise, Douglas anticipated objections from Southerners concerned about the creation of more free states. To head off this opposition and keep the Democratic Party united, Douglas disregarded the compromise line and sought to set up the territorial government in Kansas and Nebraska on the basis of popular sovereignty, relying on the alleged precedent set in the Compromise of 1850.

View the Map   The Compromise of 1850 and the Kansas-Nebraska Act

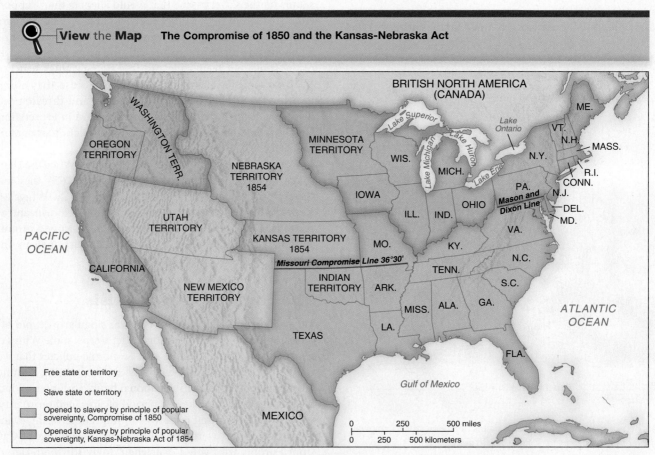

THE KANSAS-NEBRASKA ACT OF 1854 The Kansas Nebraska Act applied the principle of popular sovereignty to voters in the Kansas and Nebraska territories, allowing them to decide for themselves whether to permit slavery in their territories. The act repudiated the Missouri Compromise of 1820, which had prohibited slavery in the territory of the Louisiana Purchase north of 36°30' latitude.

Douglas wanted to organize the Kansas-Nebraska area quickly. Along with other midwestern promoters of the economic development of the frontier, he hoped a railroad would soon be built from Chicago to the Pacific and did not want controversy over the status of slavery in the new territory to slow down the building of the railroad. Douglas also hoped his Kansas-Nebraska bill would revive the spirit of Manifest Destiny that had given the Democratic Party cohesion and electoral success in the mid-1840s (see Chapter 13). The price of southern support, Douglas soon discovered, was the addition of an amendment explicitly repealing the Missouri Compromise. Although he realized this would "raise a hell of a storm," he reluctantly agreed. In this more provocative form, the bill made its way through Congress, passing the Senate by a large margin and the House by a narrow one. The vote in the House showed that Douglas had split his party rather than uniting it; exactly half of the northern Democrats voted against the legislation.

The Democrats who broke ranks created the storm that Douglas had predicted but underestimated. A manifesto of "independent Democrats" denounced the bill as "a gross violation of a sacred pledge." A memorial from three thousand New England ministers described it as a craven and sinful surrender to the slave power. For many Northerners, probably a majority, the **Kansas-Nebraska Act**

was an abomination because it permitted the possibility of slavery in an area where it had previously been prohibited. Southerners who had not pushed for such legislation or even shown much interest in it now felt obligated to support it, lending fuel to Northern fears of a conspiracy to extend slavery.

Douglas's bill had a catastrophic effect on sectional harmony. It repudiated a compromise that many in the North regarded as a binding sectional compact, almost as sacred and necessary to the survival of the Union as the Constitution itself. In defiance of the whole compromise tradition, it made a concession to the South on the issue of slavery extension without providing an equivalent concession to the North. From then on, northern sectionalists would be fighting to regain what they had lost, while Southerners would battle to maintain rights already conceded.

The act also destroyed what was left of the second party system. The already weakened and tottering Whig Party totally disintegrated when its congressional representation split cleanly along sectional lines on the Kansas-Nebraska issue. The Democratic Party survived, but now firmly under southern control, without the ability to act as a unifying national force.

The congressional elections of 1854 revealed the political chaos Douglas had created. In the North, "anti-Nebraska" coalitions of Whigs, dissident Democrats, and Free-Soilers swept regular

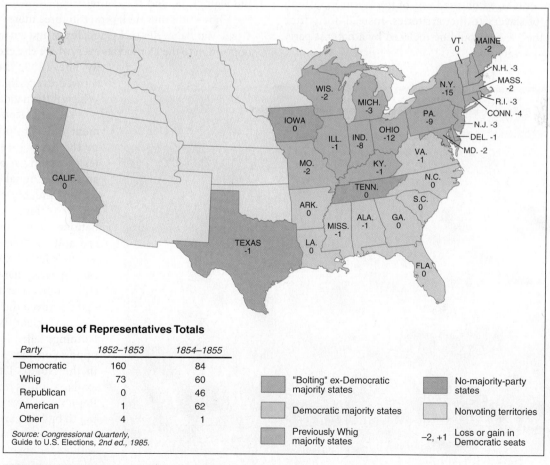

House of Representatives Totals

Party	1852–1853	1854–1855
Democratic	160	84
Whig	73	60
Republican	0	46
American	1	62
Other	4	1

Source: Congressional Quarterly, Guide to U.S. Elections, 2nd ed., 1985.

"Bolting" ex-Democratic majority states

Democratic majority states

Previously Whig majority states

No-majority-party states

Nonvoting territories

−2, +1 Loss or gain in Democratic seats

CONGRESSIONAL ELECTION OF 1854 The impact of the Kansas-Nebraska Act was immediately felt in the election of 1854. "Anti-Nebraska" coalitions and the fledgling Republican Party made gains in the North; the Democrats remained dominant in the South.

Democrats out of office. In some states, these anti-Democratic coalitions would evolve directly into a new and stronger Free-Soil Party—the Republicans. In the Deep South, however, the Democrats routed the remaining Whigs and came close to ending two-party competition on the state level.

The furor over Kansas-Nebraska also doomed the efforts of the Pierce administration to revive an expansionist foreign policy by acquiring Cuba from Spain. In October 1854, the American ministers to England, France, and Spain met in Ostend, Belgium, and drew up a memorandum for the administration urging acquisition of Cuba by any means necessary—including force—if Spain refused to sell the island.

The **Ostend Manifesto** became public in the midst of the controversy resulting from the Kansas-Nebraska Act. Northerners who were convinced that the administration was trying to extend slavery to the Great Plains were enraged to discover it was also scheming to fulfill the southern expansionist dream of a "Caribbean slave empire." The resulting storm of protest forced Pierce and his cohorts to abandon their scheme.

An Appeal to Nativism: The Know-Nothing Episode

The collapse of the Whigs created the opening for a new political party. The anti-Nebraska coalitions of 1854 suggested that such a party might be organized on the basis of northern opposition to the extension of slavery to the territories. Instead, for a time it appeared that the Whigs would be replaced by a nativist party rather than an antislavery one.

Native-born and even some immigrant Protestants looked with suspicion on the mostly Catholic Irish and Germans (see Chapter 13), who clustered in separate communities or neighborhoods in American cities. Nativists expressed their hatred in bloody anti-Catholic riots, in church and convent burnings, and in a barrage of propaganda and lurid literature trumpeting the menace of "popery" to the American way of life. In 1849, a secret fraternal organization, the Order of the Star-Spangled Banner, was founded in New York as a vehicle for anti-immigrant attitudes. When members were asked about the organization, they were instructed to reply, "I know nothing." The order grew rapidly in size, by 1854 reaching a membership of between 800,000 and 1,500,000. The political objective of the American Party, or Know-Nothing Party, as it became known, was to extend the period of naturalization in order to undercut immigrant voting strength and to keep aliens in their place. Much of the party's backing came from Whigs looking for a new home, but the party also attracted some ex-Democrats. In the North, Know-Nothing candidates generally opposed the Kansas-Nebraska Act, and some of their support came from voters who were as anxious about the expansion of slavery as they were about the evils of immigration.

The success of the new party was so dramatic that it was compared to a hurricane. In 1854, it won complete control in Massachusetts, capturing the governorship, most of the seats in the legislature, and the entire congressional delegation. In 1855, the Know-Nothings took power in three more New England states; swept Maryland, Kentucky, and Texas; and emerged as the principal opposition to the Democrats everywhere else except in the Midwest.

By late 1855, the Know-Nothings showed every sign of displacing the Whigs as the nation's second party.

Yet, the Know-Nothing movement quickly collapsed. Its demise in 1856 is one of the great mysteries of American political history. As an intersectional party, its failure is understandable enough. When the Know-Nothings attempted to hold a national convention in 1856, northern and southern delegates split on the question of slavery in the territories, showing that former Whigs were still at odds over the same issue that had destroyed their old party.

Less clear is why the Know-Nothings failed to become the major opposition party to the Democrats in the North. The most persuasive explanation is that their Free-Soil Republican rivals, who were seeking to build a party committed to the containment of slavery, had an issue with wider appeal. In 1855 and 1856, the rate of immigration declined noticeably, and the conflict in Kansas heightened the concern about slavery.

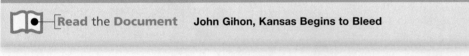

Read the Document   John Gihon, *Kansas Begins to Bleed*

The bitter contest over popular sovereignty in Kansas erupted into violence between proslavery and antislavery groups. The skirmishes, including the one at Hickory Point, near Leavenworth, depicted here, resulted in two hundred deaths and heavy property destruction before federal troops were brought in to restore order.

Consequently, voters who opposed both the expansion of slavery and unrestricted immigration were inclined to give priority to the former threat.

Kansas and the Rise of the Republicans

The new Republican Party was an outgrowth of the anti-Nebraska coalition of 1854. The Republican name was first used in midwestern states such as Wisconsin and Michigan where Know-Nothingism failed to win a mass following. A new political label was required because Free-Soil Democrats—who were an especially important element in the midwestern coalitions—refused to march under the Whig banner or even support any candidate for high office who called himself a Whig.

When the Know-Nothing Party split over the Kansas-Nebraska issue in 1856, most of the northern nativists became Republicans. The Republican argument that the "slave-power conspiracy" was a greater threat to American liberty and equality than an alleged "popish plot" proved to be persuasive. Although Republican leaders generally avoided taking anti-immigrant positions—some out of strong principle and others with an eye to the votes of the foreign born—the party showed a clear commitment to the values of native-born evangelical Protestants. On the local level, Republicans generally supported causes that reflected an anti-immigrant or anti-Catholic bias—such as prohibition of the sale of alcoholic beverages, observance of the Sabbath, defense of Protestant Bible reading in schools, and opposition to state aid for parochial education.

Unlike the Know-Nothings, the Republican Party was led by seasoned professional politicians who had earlier been prominent Whigs or Democrats. Adept at organizing the grass roots, building coalitions, and employing all the techniques of popular campaigning, they built up an effective party apparatus in an amazingly short time. By late 1855, the party had won over two-thirds of the anti-Nebraska congressmen elected in 1854. By early 1856, the new party was well established throughout the North and was preparing to make a serious bid for the presidency.

The Republican Party's position on slavery in the territories had a strong and growing appeal. Republicans viewed the unsettled West as a land of opportunities, a place to which the ambitious and hardworking could migrate in the hope of improving their social and economic position. Free soil would serve as a guarantee of free competition or "the right to rise." But if slavery was permitted to expand, the rights of "free labor" would be denied. Slaveholders would monopolize the best land, use their slaves to compete unfairly with free white workers, and block efforts at commercial and industrial development. They could also use their political control of new western states to dominate the federal government in the interest of the "slave power." Some Republicans also pandered to racial prejudice: They presented their policy as a way to keep African Americans out of the territories, thus preserving the new lands for exclusive white occupancy.

The turmoil associated with attempts to implement popular sovereignty in Kansas kept the territorial issue alive and enabled the Republicans to increase their following throughout the North. When Kansas was organized in the fall of 1854, a bitter contest began for control of the territorial government. New Englanders founded an Immigrant Aid Society to encourage antislavery settlement in Kansas, but the earliest arrivals came from the neighboring slaveholding state of Missouri. In the first territorial elections, proslavery settlers were joined at the polls by thousands of Missouri residents who crossed the border to vote illegally. The result was a decisive victory for the slave-state forces. The legislature then proceeded to pass laws that not only legalized slavery but made it a crime to speak or act against it.

Settlers favoring free soil were already a majority of the actual residents of the territory when the fraudulently elected legislature denied them the right to agitate against slavery. To defend themselves and their convictions, they took up arms and established a rival territorial government under a constitution that outlawed slavery. The Pierce administration and its appointed local agents refused to recognize this "free-state" initiative, but Republicans in Congress defended it.

A small-scale civil war then broke out between the rival regimes, culminating in May 1856 when proslavery adherents raided the free-state capital at Lawrence. Portrayed in Republican propaganda as "the sack of Lawrence," this incursion resulted in substantial property damage but no deaths. More bloody was the reprisal carried out by the antislavery zealot John Brown. Upon hearing of the attack on Lawrence, Brown and a few followers murdered five proslavery settlers in cold blood. During the next few months—until a truce was arranged by an effective territorial governor in the fall of 1856—a hit-and-run guerrilla war raged between free-state and slave-state factions. Since the "sack of Lawrence" occurred at about

"BLEEDING KANSAS" One result of the Kansas-Nebraska Act of 1854 was the border war that erupted between proslavery and antislavery forces in "bleeding" Kansas.

the same time that Preston Brooks assaulted Charles Sumner on the Senate floor (see pp. 314–315), the Republicans launched their 1856 campaign under twin slogans "Bleeding Kansas" and "Bleeding Sumner." The image of an evil and aggressive "slave power," using violence to deny constitutional rights to its opponents, was a potent device for gaining northern sympathies and votes.

Sectional Division in the Election of 1856

The Republican nominating convention revealed the strictly sectional nature of the new party. Only a handful of the delegates from the slave states attended, and all of these were from the upper South. The platform called for liberation of Kansas from the slave power and for congressional prohibition of slavery in all territories. The nominee was John C. Frémont, explorer of the West and participant in the conquest of California during the Mexican-American War.

The Democratic convention dumped the ineffectual Pierce, passed over Stephen A. Douglas, and nominated James Buchanan of Pennsylvania, who had a long career in public service. The Democrats' platform endorsed popular sovereignty in the territories. The American Party, a Know-Nothing remnant that survived mainly as the rallying point for anti-Democratic conservatives in the border states and parts of the South, chose ex-President Millard Fillmore as its standard-bearer and received the backing of those northern Whigs who refused to become Republicans and hoped to revive the tradition of sectional compromise.

The election was really two separate races—one in the North between Frémont and Buchanan, and the other in the South, between Fillmore and Buchanan. The Pennsylvania Democrat emerged victorious because he outpolled Fillmore in all but one of the slave states (Maryland) and edged out Frémont in Pennsylvania, New Jersey, Indiana, and Illinois. But the Republicans did remarkably well for a party that was scarcely more than a year old. Frémont won eleven of the sixteen free states, sweeping the upper North with substantial majorities and winning a larger proportion of the northern popular vote than either of his opponents. Since the free states had a substantial majority in the Electoral College, a future Republican candidate could win the presidency simply by overcoming a slim Democratic edge in the lower North.

THE ELECTION OF 1856

Candidate	Party	Popular Vote	Electoral Vote
Buchanan	Democratic	1,832,955	174
Frémont	Republican	1,339,932	114
Fillmore	American (Know-Nothing)	871,731	8

In the South, where the possibility of a Frémont victory had revived talk of secession, the results of the election brought momentary relief tinged with deep anxiety about the future. The very existence of a sectional party committed to restricting the expansion of slavery constituted an insult to the Southerners' way of life. That such a party was genuinely popular in the North was profoundly

alarming and raised grave doubts about the security of slavery within the Union. The continued success of a unified Democratic Party under southern control was widely viewed as the last hope for the maintenance of sectional balance and "southern rights."

The House Divided, 1857–1860

How did the institution of slavery go beyond political and economic debates?

The sectional quarrel deepened and became virtually "irreconcilable" in the years between Buchanan's election in 1856 and Lincoln's victory in 1860. A series of incidents provoked one side or the other, heightened the tension, and ultimately brought the crisis to a head. Behind the panicky reaction to public events lay a growing sense that the North and South were so culturally different and so opposed in basic interests that they could no longer coexist.

President Buchanan did little to halt the downward spiral. A series of scandals emerged in the second half of his presidency, and Buchanan's unwillingness to deal with them revealed his

Watch the **Video** **Harriet Beecher Stowe and the Making of *Uncle Tom's Cabin***

Harriet Beecher Stowe's best known novel, *Uncle Tom's Cabin* (1852), changed forever how Americans viewed slavery, the system that treated people as property.

weakness. For example, Secretary of War John Floyd sold land containing an Army fort in Minnesota for a suspiciously low price, while at the same time overpaying contractors for munitions. Buchanan rebuffed Congressional investigators in part because getting rid of Floyd, a fellow Southern Democrat, would have damaged his fragile political support. Buchanan hoped to keep the South in the Union by "maintaining the status quo," according to his biographer, and hoped that the sectional crisis could be resolved by Congress or the Supreme Court, without his having to take action. But his passivity only hastened the descent into conflict.

Cultural Sectionalism

Signs of cultural and intellectual cleavage had appeared well before the triumph of sectional politics. In the mid-1840s, a number of churches split into northern and southern denominations, officially as well as informally, because of differing attitudes toward slaveholding. Increasingly, northern preachers and congregations denounced slaveholding as a sin, while most southern church leaders rallied to a biblical defense of the peculiar institution and became influential apologists for the southern way of life. Prominent religious leaders were in the forefront of sectional mobilization. As men of God, they helped to turn political questions into moral issues and reduced the prospects for a compromise.

American literature also became sectionalized during the 1840s and 1850s. Southern men of letters, including such notable figures as novelist William Gilmore Simms and Edgar Allan Poe, wrote proslavery polemics. Popular novelists produced a flood of "plantation romances" that seemed to glorify southern civilization and sneer at that of the North. The notion that planter "cavaliers" were superior to money-grubbing Yankees was the message that most Southerners derived from this homegrown literature. In the North, prominent men of letters—Emerson, Thoreau, James Russell Lowell, and Herman Melville—expressed strong antislavery sentiments in prose and poetry, particularly after the outbreak of the Mexican-American War.

Literary abolitionism reached a climax in 1852 when Harriet Beecher Stowe published *Uncle Tom's Cabin*, an enormously successful novel (it sold more than 300,000 copies in a single year) that fixed in the northern mind the image of the slaveholder as a brutal Simon Legree. Much of its emotional impact came from the book's portrayal of slavery as a threat to the family and the cult of domesticity. When the saintly Uncle Tom was sold away from his adoring wife and children, Northerners shuddered with horror and some Southerners felt a painful twinge of conscience.

Southern defensiveness gradually hardened into cultural and economic nationalism. Northern textbooks were banished from southern schools in favor of those with a prosouthern slant; young men of the planter class were induced to stay in the South for higher education rather than going North (as had been the custom), and a movement developed to encourage southern industry and commerce as a way of reducing dependence on the North. Almost without exception, prominent southern educators and intellectuals of the late 1850s rallied behind southern sectionalism, and many even endorsed the idea of an independent southern nation.

The Dred Scott Case

When James Buchanan was inaugurated on March 4, 1857, the dispute over the legal status of slavery in the territories allowed sectional fears and hatreds to enter the political arena. Buchanan hoped to close that door by encouraging the Supreme Court to resolve the constitutional issue once and for all.

The Court was then about to render its decision in the case of *Dred Scott* v. *Sandford*. (See the Law and Society essay, "The Case of Dred and Harriet Scott," pp. 334–337.) The plaintiff in the case was a Missouri slave who sued for his freedom on the grounds that he had lived for many years in an area where slavery had been outlawed by the Missouri Compromise. The Supreme Court could have decided the issue on the narrow ground that a slave was not a citizen and therefore had no right to sue in federal courts. But President-elect Buchanan, in the days just before the inauguration, encouraged the Court to render a broader decision that would settle the slavery issue.

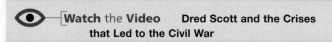

👁 **Watch** the **Video**   **Dred Scott and the Crises that Led to the Civil War**

Dred Scott's legal battle to gain his freedom traveled all the way to the U.S. Supreme Court, where Justice Taney's effort to settle once and for all the constitutional questions regarding slavery in a sweeping decision instead incited Northerners to vote for the Republican Party and hastened the coming of the Civil War.

On March 6, Chief Justice Roger B. Taney announced that the majority had ruled against Scott. Taney argued that no African American—slave or free—could be a citizen of the United States. But the real bombshell in the decision was the ruling that Dred Scott would not have won his case even if he had been a legal plaintiff. His residence in the Wisconsin Territory established no right to freedom because Congress had no power to prohibit slavery there. The Missouri Compromise was thus declared unconstitutional and so, implicitly, was the plank in the Republican platform that called for the exclusion of slavery from all federal territories.

In the North, and especially among Republicans, the Court's verdict was viewed as the latest diabolical act of the "slave-power conspiracy." The charge that the decision was a political maneuver rather than a disinterested interpretation of the Constitution was supported by strong circumstantial evidence. Five of the six judges who voted in the majority were proslavery Southerners, and their resolution of the territorial issue was close to the extreme southern rights position long advocated by John C. Calhoun.

Republicans denounced the decision as "a wicked and false judgment" and as "the greatest crime in the annals of the republic," but they stopped short of openly defying the Court's authority. The decision actually helped the Republicans build support; it lent credence to their claim that an aggressive slave power was dominating all branches of the federal government and attempting to use the Constitution to achieve its own ends.

The Lecompton Controversy

While the Dred Scott case was being decided, leaders of the proslavery faction in Kansas concluded that the time was ripe to draft a constitution and seek admission to the Union as a slave state. Since settlers with free-state views were now an overwhelming majority in the territory, supporters of slavery tried to rig the election for convention delegates. When it became clear the election was fixed, the free-staters boycotted it , and the proslavery forces won complete control. The resulting constitution, drawn up at Lecompton, was certain to be voted down if submitted to the voters in a fair election and sure to be rejected by Congress if no referendum of any kind was held.

To resolve the dilemma, supporters of the Lecompton Constitution decided to permit a vote on the slavery provision alone, giving the electorate the narrow choice of allowing or forbidding the future importation of slaves. Since there was no way to vote for total abolition, the free-state majority again resorted to a boycott, thus allowing ratification of a constitution that protected existing slave property and did not restrict importations. Meanwhile, however, the free-staters had finally gained control of the territorial legislature, and they authorized a second referendum on the constitution as a whole. This time, the proslavery party boycotted the election, and the Lecompton Constitution was overwhelmingly rejected.

The Lecompton Constitution was such an obvious perversion of popular sovereignty that Stephen A. Douglas spoke out against it. But the Buchanan administration, bowing to southern pressure, tried to push it through Congress in early 1858, despite overwhelming evidence that the people of Kansas did not want to enter the Union as a slave state. While Buchanan scored a victory in the Senate, a

Stephen Douglas, the "Little Giant" from Illinois, won election to Congress when he was just thirty years old. Four years later, he was elected to the Senate.

Source: Collection of The New-York Historical Society, neg. number 38219.

coalition of Republicans and Douglas Democrats defeated the bill in the House. A face-saving compromise allowed resubmission of the constitution to the Kansas voters on the pretext that a change in the provisions for a federal land grant was required. Finally, in August 1858, the people of Kansas killed the Lecompton Constitution when they voted it down by a margin of 6 to 1.

The Lecompton controversy aggravated the sectional quarrel and made it truly "irreconcilable." For Republicans, the administration's frantic efforts to admit Kansas as a slave state exposed southern dominance of the Democratic Party and the lengths to which proslavery conspirators would go to achieve their ends. Among Democrats, the affair opened a deep rift between the followers of Douglas and the backers of the Buchanan administration. Because of his anti-Lecompton stand, Douglas gained popularity in the North, and some Republicans even flirted with the idea of joining forces with him against the "doughfaces"—prosouthern Democrats—who stood with Buchanan.

For Douglas himself, however, the affair was a disaster; it destroyed his hopes of uniting the Democratic Party and defusing the slavery issue through the application of popular sovereignty. What had happened in Kansas suggested that popular sovereignty in practice was an invitation to civil war. For his stand against Lecompton, Douglas was denounced as a traitor in the South, and his hopes of being elected president were seriously diminished.

Debating the Morality of Slavery

Douglas's more immediate problem was to win reelection to the Senate from Illinois in 1858. Here he faced surprisingly tough opposition from a Republican candidate who, in defiance of precedent, was nominated by a party convention. (At this time, senators were elected by state legislatures.) Douglas's rival, former Whig Congressman Abraham Lincoln, set out to convince the voters that Douglas could not be relied on to oppose the extension of slavery, even though he had opposed the admission of Kansas under a proslavery constitution.

In the famous speech that opened his campaign, Lincoln tried to distance himself from his opponent by taking a more radical position. He argued that the nation had reached the crisis point in the struggle between slavery and freedom: "'A house divided against itself cannot stand.' I believe this government cannot endure, permanently half *slave* and half *free*." Lincoln then described the chain of events between the Kansas-Nebraska Act and the Dred Scott decision as evidence of a plot to extend and nationalize slavery. He called for defensive actions to stop the spread of slavery and place it "where the public mind shall rest in the belief that it is in the course of ultimate extinction." He tried to link Douglas to this proslavery conspiracy by pointing to his rival's unwillingness to take a stand on the morality of slavery and to his professed indifference about whether slavery was voted up or down in the territories. For Lincoln, the only security against the triumph of slavery and the slave power was moral opposition to human bondage. Neutrality on the moral issue would lull the public into accepting the expansion of slavery until it was legal everywhere.

In the subsequent series of debates that focused national attention on the Illinois senatorial contest, Lincoln hammered away at the theme that Douglas was a covert defender of slavery because he was not a principled opponent of it. Douglas responded by accusing Lincoln of endangering the Union by his talk of putting slavery on the path to extinction. Denying that he was an abolitionist, Lincoln made a distinction between tolerating slavery in the South, where it was protected by the Constitution, and allowing it to expand to places where it could legally be prohibited. Restriction of slavery, he argued, had been the policy of the Founders, and it was Douglas and the Democrats who had departed from the great tradition of containing an evil that could not be immediately eliminated.

In the debate at Freeport, Illinois, Lincoln questioned Douglas on how he could reconcile popular sovereignty with the Dred Scott decision. The Little Giant, as Douglas was called by his admirers, responded that slavery could not exist without supportive

Read the Document   Abraham Lincoln, Debate at Galesburg, Illinois (1858)

Abraham Lincoln, shown here in his first full-length portrait. Although Lincoln lost the contest for the Senate seat in 1858, the Lincoln–Douglas debates established his reputation as a rising star of the Republican Party.

legislation to sustain it and that territorial legislatures could simply refrain from passing a slave code. Douglas's most effective tactic was to charge that Lincoln's moral opposition to slavery implied a belief in racial equality. Lincoln, facing an intensely racist electorate, vigorously denied this charge and affirmed his commitment to

Feature Essay

The Enigma of John Brown

On December 2, 1859, an old man with a thick white beard, who might have stepped out of the pages of the Old Testament, stood on a scaffold in Virginia awaiting execution for attempting to start a slave insurrection. He was unrepentant and without fear. Defiantly facing the assembled militiamen and other onlookers, he handed one of his attendants a prophetic message claiming that he had acted under divine inspiration and that it was God's will that "the crimes of this *guilty*, land: *will* never be purged *away*; but with Blood." His abortive raid on the federal arsenal at Harpers Ferry, Virginia, had sent a wave of fear through the slaveholding South, but the manner of his death and his strong antislavery sentiments made him a hero to many in the North. No single man did more to heighten the sectional crisis of the late 1850s and increase the probability of civil war.

But who was this man and how did he come to play such an important role in the sectional drama? Controversy surrounded him during his lifetime and has continued to do so ever since. Many African Americans have revered him as the rare example of a white man willing to give his life for black freedom. Unlike most white Americans, he seems to have been totally free of racial prejudice and at times identified with blacks so completely that he—and they—could almost forget that he was not one of them. But the means that he used to pursue his ends—his willingness to resort to violence, even to terrorism—has troubled many of those who find his objectives praiseworthy.

The obvious impracticality of the plan for a massive slave uprising that he tried to put into effect at Harpers Ferry also has raised questions about his soundness of mind.

John Brown was born in Connecticut in 1800, the descendent of an old New England family that may have been represented on the *Mayflower*. He received little formal education and followed in his father's occupation as a tanner of leather. Lured westward like so many New Englanders of the time, he pursued the tanning business first in western Pennsylvania and then in Ohio. But unsuccessful land speculations and the hard times following the Panic of 1837 drove him into bankruptcy in 1842. He then became a wool dealer but faced ruin again in 1849 when his attempt to cut out the usual middlemen and make a direct sale of 200,000 pounds of American wool to buyers in England resulted in a huge loss. Such risk taking and the resulting ups and downs were normal experiences for the businessmen of the time. Brown may have been unluckier than some others, but the notion that his antislavery zeal was somehow a compensation for business failure makes little sense.

As early as 1834, at a time when his tannery was doing well, Brown proposed to raise a black boy in his own family as an experiment to show slaveholders that race was no obstacle to the building of character. He also considered opening a school for black children. By 1847, however, Brown had given up on the idea that education and example could end slavery. While still a successful wool merchant in Springfield, Massachusetts, he confided to the black abolitionist Frederick Douglass the germ of the

plan he later tried to put into effect at Harpers Ferry: instigation of guerrilla war against slavery based in the mountains of the South. In 1851, Brown organized Springfield's blacks into a secret militia to resist enforcement of the Fugitive Slave Act of 1850. In 1854, he retired from the wool business with the intention of devoting the rest of his life to the cause of black freedom and equality. From a farm in North Elba, New York, he acted as patron of a struggling black agricultural colony and also served as a conductor on the Underground Railroad when fugitives heading for Canada came his way.

By the fall of 1855 the front line of the struggle against slavery was in Kansas (see p. 323). Following in the wake of his five sons, Brown went west to join the fray in September. After proslavery ruffians sacked the Free State capital of Lawrence in the spring of 1856, Brown led a retaliatory raid on proslavery settlers living along Pottawatamie Creek. In what can only be described as an act of terrorism, Brown and his men executed five defenseless men who had been rousted from their beds. His apparent objective was to instill fear and panic among the proslavery forces, possibly driving them to commit outrages of their own and thus further polarize the nation on the slavery question. Perhaps Brown already had concluded that a civil war, or something like it, was the only way to end slavery, and he appeared committed to bringing it about by any means necessary. For the next two years Brown operated as a guerrilla fighter in Kansas, raising money from eastern supporters who were unaware of his role in the Pottawatamie massacre.

This painting, *The Last Moments of John Brown*, celebrates the passionate abolitionist as a hero and martyr to the antislavery cause. On his way to the gallows, he pauses to greet a slave mother and her child.

Source: Detail from *The Last Moments of John Brown*. Gift of Mr. and Mrs. Carl Stoeckel, 1897. The Metropolitan Museum of Art, New York, NY, U.S.A. Image copyright © The Metropolitan Museum of Art/Art Resource, NY.

In May 1858, when the threat of the admission of Kansas to the Union as a slave state had been averted, Brown started organizing his raid on Harpers Ferry. He began by assembling a convention of black fugitives and abolitionists in Canada to draw up the constitution for the independent black state that he hoped to establish in the southern mountains as the base for a guerrilla war against the slaveholders. He then sought financial support from northern abolitionists and gathered a racially integrated force of twenty-two volunteers, eighteen of whom raided the federal arsenal. The plan was to seize the arms and distribute them to rebellious slaves. The raid turned into a debacle when the local militia trapped Brown and his men in a fire-engine house. Ten of Brown's men, including two of his sons, died as a result of the shooting that ensued. The survivors, including Brown himself, were captured by a force of U.S. Marines sent from Washington and commanded by Colonel Robert E. Lee. Local slaves did not, as Brown had hoped, rise up spontaneously in rebellion once the violence had commenced.

If Brown was certain that his attempt to ignite a slave uprising and a guerrilla war would succeed, he was clearly deluded and possibly deranged. Frederick Douglass, whom Brown had invited to join the raiders, decided that the plan had no reasonable chance of success and refused to participate. But the fact that Brown seemed to welcome his martyrdom, almost rejoicing in it, raises another intriguing possibility. Brown may have realized that the odds were against him and that he would probably fail. But he may also have calculated, quite correctly as it turned out, that the panic that even an abortive raid would evoke from the South and the sympathy that the punishment of its perpetrators might arouse in the North would push the nation closer to the civil war that he had come to believe was the only way to end slavery. If the voice he heard in his head was indeed that of an angry God ready to punish the nation for the sin of slavery, his logic was irrefutable.

QUESTIONS FOR DISCUSSION

1. Why was John Brown's attitude toward black people so unusual in antebellum America?

2. What did Brown hope to achieve by raiding Harper's Ferry?

3. Why did the raid push the nation closer to civil war?

white supremacy. He would grant blacks the right to the fruits of their own labor while denying them the "privileges" of full citizenship. This was an inherently contradictory position, and Douglas made the most of it.

Although Republican candidates for the state legislature won a majority of the popular votes, the Democrats carried enough counties to send Douglas back to the Senate. Lincoln lost an office, but he won respect in Republican circles. By emphasizing the moral dimension of the slavery question and undercutting any possibility of fusion between Republicans and Douglas Democrats, he sharpened his party's ideological focus and stiffened its backbone against any temptation to compromise its Free-Soil position.

The South's Crisis of Fear

After Kansas became a free territory in August 1858, the issue of slavery in the territories lost some of its immediacy. The remaining unorganized areas in the Rockies and northern Great Plains were unlikely to attract slaveholding settlers. Southern expansionists still dreamed of annexations in the Caribbean and Central America but had little hope of winning congressional approval. Nevertheless, Southerners continued to demand the "right" to take their slaves into the territories, and Republicans persisted in denying it to them. Although the Republicans repeatedly promised they would not interfere with slavery where it already existed, Southerners refused to believe them and interpreted their unyielding stand against the extension of slavery as a threat to southern rights and security.

Events in late 1859 and early 1860 turned southern anxiety about northern attitudes and policies into a "crisis of fear." The events alarmed slaveholders because they appeared to threaten their safety and dominance in a new and direct way.

The first of these incidents was John Brown's raid on Harpers Ferry, Virginia, in October 1859. (See the Feature Essay, "The Enigma of John Brown," pp. 328–329.) Brown, who had the appearance and manner of an Old Testament prophet, thought of himself as God's chosen instrument "to purge this land with blood" and eradicate the sin of slaveholding. On October 16, he led eighteen men from his band of twenty-two (which included five free blacks) across the Potomac River from his base in Maryland and seized the federal arsenal and armory in Harpers Ferry.

While Brown hoped his revolt would spread, the neighboring slaves did not rise up to join him. Brown's raiders were either killed or captured and put on trial for treason against the state of Virginia.

The subsequent investigation produced evidence that several prominent northern abolitionists had approved of Brown's plan—to the extent they understood it—and had raised money for his preparations. This seemed to confirm southern fears that abolitionists were actively engaged in fomenting slave insurrection.

After Brown was sentenced to be hanged, Southerners were further stunned by the outpouring of sympathy and admiration that his impending fate aroused in the North. As Ralph Waldo Emerson expressed it, Brown "would make the gallows as glorious as the cross." His actual execution on December 2 completed Brown's elevation to the status of a martyred saint of the antislavery cause. The day of his death was marked in parts of the North

by the tolling of bells, the firing of cannons, and the holding of memorial services.

Although Republican politicians were quick to denounce John Brown for his violent methods, Southerners interpreted the wave of northern sympathy as an expression of the majority opinion and the Republicans' "real" attitude. According to historian James McPherson, "They identified Brown with the abolitionists, the abolitionists with Republicans, and Republicans with the whole North." Within the South, the raid and its aftermath incited fear, repression, and mobilization. Witch hunts searched for the agents of a vast imagined conspiracy to stir up slave rebellion; vigilance committees were organized in many localities to resist subversion and ensure control of slaves, and orators pointed increasingly to secession as the only way to protect southern interests.

Brown was scarcely in his grave when another set of events put southern nerves on edge again. Next to abolitionist-abetted rebellions, the slaveholding South's greatest fear was that the non-slaveholding majority would turn against the master class and the solidarity of southern whites behind the peculiar institution would crumble. Hinton R. Helper, a white Southerner, published *The Impending Crisis of the South* in 1859, calling on lower-class whites to resist planter dominance and abolish slavery in their own interest. Slaveholders regarded the book as even more seditious than *Uncle Tom's Cabin*, and they feared the spread of "Helperism" among poor whites almost as much as they feared the effect of "John Brownism" on the slaves.

Southern suspicion of the Republicans grew even more heated when the Republican candidate for Speaker of the House of Representatives, John Sherman of Ohio, used Helper's book as a campaign manifesto. Southern congressmen threatened secession if Sherman was elected, and feelings became so heated that some representatives began to carry weapons on the floor of the House. It became clear that Sherman could not be elected, and his name was withdrawn in favor of a moderate Republican who had refrained from endorsing Helper's book. The contest helped persuade Southerners that the Republicans were committed to stirring up class conflict among southern whites. Anxiety about the future allegiance of nonslaveholding whites had been growing during the 1850s because of changes in the pattern of slave ownership. A dramatic rise in the price of slaves meant that fewer whites could own slaves—slave ownership was down from 30 to 25 percent of all white households across the South and from 50 to 40 percent in the cotton belt of the lower South. Perceiving in this trend the seeds of class conflict, some proslavery extremists had called for the reopening of the Atlantic slave trade as a way to reduce the price of slaves and make them more widely available (others wanted to preserve the appreciated value of their human property). Either way, many planters became convinced that a Republican victory in the presidential election of 1860 would be intolerable.

The Election of 1860

The Republicans, sniffing victory and generally insensitive to the depth of southern feeling against them, met in Chicago on May 16 to nominate a presidential candidate. The initial front-runner,

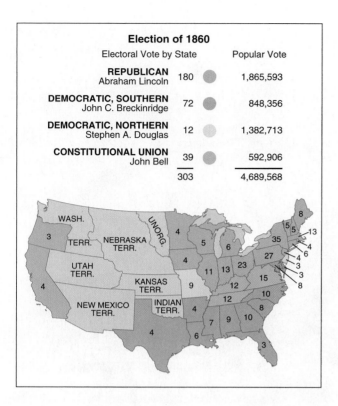

Election of 1860

	Electoral Vote by State		Popular Vote
REPUBLICAN Abraham Lincoln	180		1,865,593
DEMOCRATIC, SOUTHERN John C. Breckinridge	72		848,356
DEMOCRATIC, NORTHERN Stephen A. Douglas	12		1,382,713
CONSTITUTIONAL UNION John Bell	39		592,906
	303		4,689,568

southern opposition. He did succeed in getting the convention to endorse popular sovereignty as its slavery platform, but the price was a walkout by Deep South delegates who favored a federal slave code for the territories.

Unable to agree on a nominee, the convention adjourned to reconvene in Baltimore in June. The next time around, a fight developed over whether to seat newly selected pro-Douglas delegations from some Deep South states in place of the bolters from the first convention. When the Douglas forces won most of the contested seats, another and more massive southern walkout took place. The result was a fracture of the Democratic Party. The delegates who remained nominated Douglas and reaffirmed the party's commitment to popular sovereignty, while the bolters convened elsewhere to nominate John Breckinridge of Kentucky on a platform of federal protection for slavery in the territories.

By the time the campaign was under way, four parties were running presidential candidates: the Republicans, the Douglas Democrats, the "Southern Rights" Democrats, and a remnant of conservative Whigs and Know-Nothings known as the Constitutional Union Party. Taking no explicit stand on the issue of slavery in the territories, the Constitutional Unionists tried to represent the spirit of sectional accommodation that had led to compromise in 1820 and 1850. In effect, the race became a separate two-party contest in each section: In the North, the real choice was between Lincoln and Douglas; in the South, the only candidates with a fighting chance were Breckinridge and John Bell, the Constitutional Union candidate. Douglas alone tried to carry on a national campaign, gaining some support in every state, but actually winning only in Missouri.

When the results came in, the Republicans had achieved a stunning victory. By gaining the electoral votes of all the free states, except those from three districts of New Jersey that voted for Douglas, Lincoln won a decisive majority—180 to 123 over his combined opponents. In the North, his 54 percent of the popular vote annihilated Douglas. In the South, where Lincoln was not even on the ballot, Breckinridge triumphed everywhere except in Virginia, Kentucky, and Tennessee, which went for Bell and the Constitutional Unionists. The Republican strategy of seeking power by trying to win decisively in the majority section was brilliantly successful. Although less than 40 percent of those who went to the polls throughout the nation actually voted for Lincoln, his support in the North was so solid that he would have won in the electoral college even if his opponents had been unified behind a single candidate.

Most Southerners saw the result of the election as a catastrophe. A candidate and a party with no support in their own section had won the presidency on a platform viewed as insulting to southern honor and hostile to vital southern interests. Since the birth of the republic, Southerners had either sat in the White House or exerted considerable influence over those who did. Those days might now be gone forever. Rather than accepting permanent minority status in American politics and facing the resulting dangers to black slavery and white "liberty," the political leaders of the lower South launched a movement for immediate secession from the Union.

Senator William H. Seward of New York, had two strikes against him: he had a reputation for radicalism and a record of strong opposition to the nativist movement. The majority of the delegates wanted a less controversial nominee who could win two or three of the northern states that had been in the Democratic column in 1856. Abraham Lincoln met their specifications: He was from Illinois, a state the Republicans needed to win; he had a more moderate image than Seward, and he had kept his personal distaste for Know-Nothingism to himself. In addition, he was a self-made man, whose rise from frontier poverty to legal and political prominence embodied the Republican ideal of equal opportunity for all. After trailing Seward by a large margin on the first ballot, Lincoln picked up enough strength on the second to pull virtually even and was nominated on the third.

The platform, like the nominee, was meant to broaden the party's appeal in the North. Although a commitment to halt the expansion of slavery remained, economic matters received more attention than they had in 1856. With an eye on Pennsylvania, the delegates called for a high protective tariff; other planks included endorsement of free homesteads, which was popular in the Midwest and among working people, and federal aid for internal improvements, especially a transcontinental railroad. The platform was cleverly designed to bring most ex-Whigs into the Republican camp while also accommodating enough renegade Democrats to give the party a solid majority in the northern states.

The Democrats failed to present a united front. When the party first met in the sweltering heat of Charleston in late April, Douglas commanded a majority of the delegates but was unable to win the two-thirds required for nomination due to unyielding

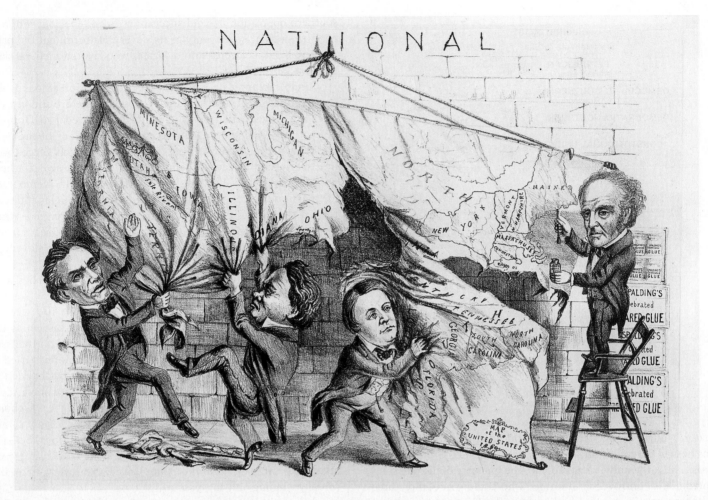

In this cartoon from the 1860 election, candidates Lincoln and Douglas struggle for control of the country, while Breckinridge tears away the South. John Bell of the Constitutional Union Party futilely attempts to repair the damage to the torn nation.

Conclusion: Explaining the Crisis

Generations of historians have searched for the underlying causes of the crisis leading to disruption of the Union but have failed to agree on exactly what they were. Some emphasize the clash of economic interests between agrarian and industrializing regions. But this interpretation does not reflect the way people at the time expressed their concerns. The main issues in the sectional debates of the 1850s were whether slavery was right or wrong and whether it should be extended or contained. Disagreements over protective tariffs and other economic measures benefiting one section or the other were clearly secondary. Furthermore, it has never been clear why the interests of northern industry and those of the South's commercial agriculture were irreconcilable. Economically, there was no necessity for producers of raw materials to go to war with those who marketed or processed those raw materials.

Another group of historians blame the crisis on "irresponsible" politicians and agitators on both sides of the Mason-Dixon line. Public opinion, they argue, was whipped into a frenzy over issues that competent statesmen could have resolved. But this viewpoint has been sharply criticized for failing to acknowledge the depths of feeling that could be aroused by the slavery question and for underestimating the obstacles to a peaceful solution.

The predominating view is that the crisis was rooted in profound ideological differences over the morality and utility of slavery as an institution. Most interpreters now agree that the roots of the conflict lay in the fact that the South was a slave society and determined to stay that way, while the North was equally committed to a free-labor system. No other differences divided the regions in this decisive way, and it is hard to imagine that secessionism would have developed if the South had followed the North's example and abolished slavery earlier.

Nevertheless, slavery will not explain why the crisis came when it did and in the way that it did. Why did the conflict become "irreconcilable" in the 1850s and not earlier or later? Why did it take the form of a political struggle over the future of slavery in the territories? Adequate answers to both questions require an understanding of political developments that were not directly caused by tensions over slavery.

By the 1850s, the established Whig and Democratic parties were in trouble partly because they no longer offered the voters clear-cut alternatives on economic issues that had been the bread and butter of politics during the second party system's heyday. This situation created an opening for new parties and issues. After the Know-Nothings failed to use attitudes toward immigrants as the basis for a political realignment, the Republicans used the issue of slavery in the territories to build the first successful sectional party in American history. They were not abolitionists, calling for "free soil" rather than freedom for blacks. Indeed, the majority of Northerners were committed to white supremacy and to the original constitutional compromise establishing a hands-off policy toward slavery in the southern states. For Southerners, the Republican Party now became the main issue, and they fought against it from within the Democratic Party until it ceased to function as a national organization in 1860.

Why did the slavery extension issue arouse such strong feelings in the two sections during the 1850s? The same issue had arisen earlier and had proved adjustable, even in 1820 when the second party system—with its vested interest in compromise—had not yet emerged. If the expansion of slavery had been as vital and emotional a question in 1820 as it was in the 1850s, the declining Federalist Party presumably would have revived in the form of a northern sectional Party adamantly opposed to the admission of slave states to the Union.

Ultimately, therefore, the crisis of the 1850s must be understood as having a deep social and cultural dimension as well as a purely political one. In *Uncle Tom's Cabin*, Harriet Beecher Stowe personified the cultural conflict in her depiction of two brothers with similar personalities, one of whom settled in Vermont "to rule over rocks and stones" and the other in Louisiana "to rule over men and women." The first became a deacon in the church, a member of the local abolition society, and, despite his natural authoritarianism, the adherent of "a democratic theory." The second became indifferent to religion, openly aristocratic, a staunch defender of slavery, and an extreme racist—"he considered the negro, through all possible gradations of color, as the intermediate link between man and animals." Stowe's comparison may have been biased, but she showed a good understanding of how the contrasting environments of slavery and freedom could lead very similar men to have sharply conflicting world views.

This divergence in basic beliefs and values had widened and become less manageable between the 1820s and the 1850s. Both sections continued to profess allegiance to the traditional "republican" ideals of individual liberty and independence, and both were strongly influenced by evangelical religion. But differences in the economic and social development of each region transformed a common culture into two conflicting cultures. In the North, a rising middle class adapted to the new market economy with the help of an evangelical Christianity that sanctioned self-discipline and social reform (see Chapter 12). The South, on the other hand, embraced slavery as a foundation for the liberty and independence of whites. Its evangelicalism encouraged personal piety but not social reform and gave only limited attention to building the kind of personal character that made for commercial success. The notion that white liberty and equality depended on resistance to social and economic change and—to get to the heart of the matter—on continuing to have enslaved blacks to do menial labor became more deeply entrenched.

When politicians appealed to sectionalism during the 1850s, therefore, they could evoke conflicting views of what constituted the good society. The South—with its allegedly idle masters, degraded unfree workers, and shiftless poor whites—seemed to a majority of Northerners to be in flagrant violation of the Protestant work ethic and the ideal of open competition in "the race of life." From the dominant southern point of view, the North was a land of hypocritical money-grubbers who denied the obvious fact that the virtue, independence, and liberty of free citizens was possible only when dependent laboring classes—especially racially inferior ones—were kept under the kind of rigid control that only slavery could provide. According to the ideology of northern Republicans, the freedom of the individual depended on equality of opportunity for everyone; in the minds of southern sectionalists, it required that part of the population be enslaved. Once these contrary views of the world had become the main themes of political discourse, sectional compromise was no longer possible.

Law and Society

The Case of Dred and Harriet Scott
Blurring the Borders of Politics and Justice

In 1856, a violent civil war in Kansas over the right to bring slaves into the territory, along with Preston Brooks' near-fatal caning of abolitionist Senator Charles Sumner on the floor of the Senate, convinced free-soil Northerners that the "slave power" had grown impossibly aggressive. Likewise, Southerners had come to believe that the abolitionists' tentacles were everywhere. It was in this overheated atmosphere that the Supreme Court decided the case of Dred Scott in 1857. Chief Justice Roger Taney apparently hoped that his opinion might settle the roiling constitutional controversies over the status of slavery in the territories, of fugitive slaves in free states, and of Congress's power to regulate slavery. Instead, he probably hastened the resort to armed conflict.

To understand the *Dred Scott* case, we must go back to the fall of 1832. With the Black Hawk War raging, a young physician named John Emerson accepted a temporary assignment as surgeon at Jefferson Barracks, an army post in Missouri, where he acquired his sole slave, Dred Scott. As the war drew to a close, he sought and secured a full-time commission at Fort Armstrong, Illinois, and headed north with Scott.

After arriving in Illinois, Scott continued to attend to Emerson's personal needs and performed most of the work on Emerson's land claims. For two years, Scott functioned as a contradiction in terms—a slave laboring in a free state. Scott's status grew even more complicated with Emerson's

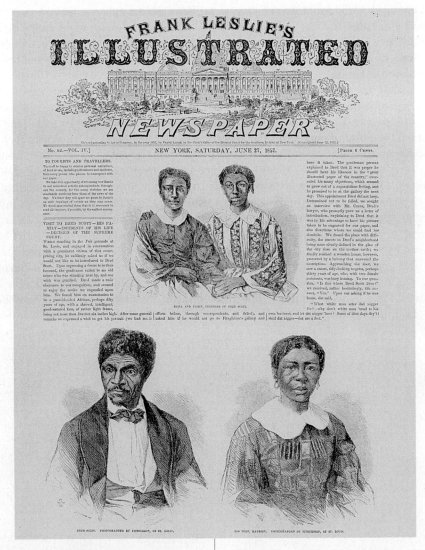

next transfer, which took the two men farther north. The pair traveled to Fort Snelling, in what was then Wisconsin Territory—an area where the Missouri Compromise explicitly forbade the practice of slavery. While in Wisconsin Territory, Scott met and married another transported slave, Harriet Robinson. Their union would last for the remainder of Dred Scott's

life and produce four children, two of whom died in infancy.

When John Emerson died in December 1843, Dred and Harriet Scott found themselves back in Missouri and under the authority of Emerson's wife, Irene Sanford Emerson. Dred Scott attempted to purchase his family's freedom, but Mrs. Emerson refused his offer. Then, in the spring of 1846, the Scotts took Mrs. Emerson to court, claiming Dr. Emerson had forfeited all rights of ownership a decade earlier when he transported them into free territory. This relatively common maneuver by the Scotts initiated a series of legal struggles that would eventually reach the Supreme Court of the United States.

To avoid any direct challenge to the logic or legality of slavery, legal doctrine in Missouri required Dred and Harriet Scott to file a convoluted claim, which accused Mrs. Emerson of assault and false imprisonment. Such a claim did not directly argue the case for freedom, but in fact forced the court to decide on that very issue. If the Scotts were rightfully the slaves of Mrs. Emerson, her abusive behavior toward them would have been perfectly legitimate. If they were not her slaves, the claim of assault and false imprisonment would have been valid. Therefore, in order to consider the petitions of the Scotts, the court would first have to determine whether the Scotts were still slaves or whether their lengthy sojourn into free territory had automatically set them free.

Suits such as that filed by the Scotts were quite commonplace in the 1840s, and the typical outcome was freedom for the slave. Missouri courts had repeatedly held that slaves transported into free territory were thereby emancipated. A decade before the Scotts' suit came to trial, a Missouri court had ruled in the slaves' favor in a case involving the specific issue of an army transfer. Given such precedents, the Scotts seemed to have a very strong case.

The Scotts also had the misfortune, however, of bringing their case to court at a time when public opinion in Missouri was experiencing a profound shift. As slavery came under increasing attack from the North and slaveholding became a fundamental element of Missourians' identity, judicial decisions grew steadily more hostile to the petitions of slaves. Missouri's precarious position as a border state intensified its preoccupation with any threat to the institution of slavery.

As the premier student of the Scotts' case has commented, "the Scotts as suitors for freedom would become casualties of the sectional conflict."

When the trial finally began in June 1846, the Scotts' attorney brought a series of witnesses before the jury, all of whom testified that Dred Scott had indeed been at Forts Armstrong and Snelling. All that remained to secure the Scotts' freedom was the relatively simple task of proving what everyone already knew, that they were held as slaves by Mrs. Emerson. In a surprising legal move, Mrs. Emerson's lawyers raised doubts as to whether Mrs. Emerson, her brother, or her father actually claimed ownership of the Scotts. With bizarre logic, the jury returned the Scotts to Mrs. Emerson because the trial had failed to establish her as their rightful owner. The peculiar institution required a peculiar brand of law.

Undeterred, the Scotts moved for a retrial. After a series of complicated moves by both legal teams, the case came before the Missouri Supreme Court. The court handed down its decision in 1852, six years after the Scotts originally filed their petitions. During those six years, the slavery issue had reached a boiling point and no state felt its effects more than Missouri. Disputes over slavery had divided the state into two hostile factions.

Relying heavily on a doctrine of states' rights, the court held that laws prohibiting slavery in Wisconsin Territory had no binding effect on the State of Missouri. Therefore, the court determined, the Scotts remained slaves. The decision explicitly referred to the deteriorating political climate, arguing that, "Times are not now as they were when the former decisions on this subject were made. Since then . . . States have been possessed with a dark and fell spirit in relation to slavery . . . . Under such circumstances it does not behoove the state of Missouri to show the least countenance to any measure which might gratify this spirit . . . ." Always closely related, law and politics had become indistinguishable in the *Scott* case.

Despite the ruling, neither the Scotts nor their supporters were

prepared to give up the fight. The next step was to appeal to the nation's highest court, but such a move did not seem very promising. Not only did the United States Supreme Court have a majority of justices from slave states, but one year earlier it had refused to hear a similar suit. In dismissing that case, Chief Justice Roger Taney followed the same logic that the Missouri Supreme Court had used in rejecting the Scotts' claims. Laws of federal territories, he reasoned, could have no effect on the policies of any state. Fearful of appealing to the court that had so recently issued an unfavorable ruling, the Scotts stalled.

Looking for a solution to the dilemma, the Scotts dropped the case of *Scott* v. *Emerson* and filed a new suit, *Scott* v. *Sandford*. John Sanford, the widow Emerson's brother, agreed to bring a "collusive" suit in federal court. (In a misprint, the official court docket rendered his name as *Sandford*.) The terms of the new case would transform the Scotts' initially modest petition for freedom into a test case on the citizenship status of free African Americans and on the extent of federal prerogative in limiting the expansion of slavery. *Scott* v. *Sandford* was tried in the small back room of a St. Louis store that served as the site of the United States Circuit Court for the District of Missouri. Neither side introduced new evidence or called witnesses; the case would be decided on the basis of evidence that had already been well established. The one new wrinkle was that a federal court could only have jurisdiction of the case if there were "diversity of citizenship" between the litigants—in other words, if the plaintiff and defendants were citizens of different states. But that raised a controversial question that had yet to be resolved in American law: To what extent were free blacks entitled to the rights of citizens? While some Northern states, such as Massachusetts, had gone so far as to grant men of color the right to vote, some Southern state courts had in the previous decade decided cases explicitly holding that even free blacks were not citizens. In May 1854, with the debate over the Kansas-Nebraska bill reaching a fevered pitch, the federal district court ratified the earlier Missouri decision, on relatively narrow grounds. With no other recourse, the Scotts' attorney promptly made preparations to take their case to the U.S. Supreme Court.

Both sides pulled out the big guns for this final battle. Friends of the Scotts hired Montgomery Blair, a former U.S. solicitor general and a prominent figure in Washington society. Yet even a character as illustrious as Blair was outshone by Sanford's attorneys, among whom was Reverdy Johnson, a former U.S. attorney general, perhaps "the most respected constitutional lawyer in the country," and—even more importantly—the close personal friend of Chief Justice Taney. Both legal teams pursued arguments that promoted their larger political objectives at the expense of their clients. Blair focused on the question of citizenship, which had already been *de facto* decided in Scott's favor by the lower court and could have been left alone. Instead of employing the proven strategy of claiming that territorial laws could not affect the policies of a given state, Sanford's attorneys used the more controversial but more consequential argument that federal antislavery laws were fundamentally unconstitutional.

After four days of such arguments, the Court surprisingly postponed the remainder of the trial until the next term, seven months away. During the lengthy recess, tensions in the country continued to rise at a frightening rate. In November, James Buchanan won a tight and acrimonious presidential race in which the extension of slavery had emerged as the preeminent political issue. The following month, with the nation still reeling from the bitter campaign, the trial resumed. The case was now more politicized than ever, and the lawyers did not try to hide their respective agendas. Sanford's attorneys, in particular, frequently indulged in extensive defenses of the southern way of life. Not surprisingly, the debate grew hostile. The Supreme

Court had become the showcase for a nation coming apart at the seams.

Following the closing arguments, the justices gathered in early February to consider the *Scott* case. In addition to the specific question of the Scotts' freedom, the court debated the two weighty questions that had arisen from the trial: Were free African Americans citizens? Did Congress have the authority to prohibit slavery in the federal territories? The justices considered options that would have allowed them to decide on the Scotts' fate and still avoid the controversial issues, but there was immense public and political pressure for the Court to answer the broader questions once and for all. Chief Justice Taney was determined to do just that.

Roger Taney's presence on the bench loomed as the greatest single obstacle to the Scotts' freedom. In his late seventies when the *Scott* case was heard, Taney was a sickly man described by a colleague as "exceedingly feeble and broken." He had a stark courtroom demeanor and, despite his age and ill health, presided over the court with firmness. Taney spent most of his life in Maryland, and his views on slavery—and on just about everything else—were shaped by his experiences in that border state. A staunch Democrat and an unapologetic Southerner, Taney doggedly defended states' rights against all federal encroachments. As the friction between North and South grew, the aged chief justice had become personally and emotionally embroiled in the issue. By the time the *Scott* case came before the Court, Taney was a "bitter sectionalist," anxious to put an end to "Northern insult and aggression."

On March 6, 1857, Taney addressed the packed courtroom and read the Court's official opinion, which he himself had composed. From start to finish, Taney read for two full hours. As his tired voice concluded, the Scotts had lost their fight for freedom.

In rejecting the Scotts' claims, Taney tackled the issue of citizenship head on. The chief justice argued that the

Constitution failed to afford blacks, slave or free, the rights of citizenship. Taney insisted that the framers of the Constitution considered people of African descent as a "subordinate and inferior class of beings, who had been subjugated by the dominant race, and, whether emancipated or not, yet remained subject to their authority, and had no rights or privileges but such as those who held the power . . . might choose to grant them." Emancipation, therefore, did not confer the rights of citizenship on blacks. Their race constituted a permanent mark of civil inferiority. In making the claim, Taney conspicuously failed to note that four New England states had already offered African Americans basic citizenship rights. Yet, despite this omission, the chief justice had actually been fairly accurate in gauging the era's prevailing mood. While Taney's racial doctrine seems extreme and even obscene by today's standards, it was representative of social attitudes of the time, even among many who opposed the institution of slavery. It would take a war of unprecedented carnage before the nation was prepared to accept the citizenship of black Americans.

Having established that free blacks did not hold the rights of U.S. citizenship, Taney should have stopped. If Dred Scott was not entitled to bring a suit in federal court, the case was closed. But Taney was determined to issue an opinion on the second major question of the case, congressional authority to prohibit slavery in the territories. The second half of Taney's ruling denied such congressional authority and declared the Missouri Compromise unconstitutional. Taney relied on two highly questionable arguments to support this position: first, that the Constitution allowed Congress to legislate only on issues relating to the disposal of land, not on those affecting the legal status of the people living on that land, and second, that Congress only held such authority for land already claimed when the Constitution was drafted, excluding all territory acquired after 1787. Such arguments contradicted years of policy and precedent, including some of Taney's own rulings.

The Supreme Court's decision had four immediate effects. It outraged committed abolitionists, delighted apprehensive Southerners, invalidated the principal plank of the new Republican Party, and relieved worried moderates who believed the decision would lay the national controversy to rest. But despite the tremendous emotion the ruling evoked, many of its predicted effects proved illusory. It invited slavery to expand into the territories, but that never actually happened. It denied the Scotts their freedom, but they were shortly emancipated by new owners. And it claimed to answer fundamental questions of national importance, but those same questions continued to be debated until ultimately resolved by powder and shot.

The ruling's actual effects were quite different from those Taney expected. The emerging Republican Party, for instance, used the decision as a rallying point, decrying the slave power conspiracy that clearly controlled the highest court in the land. The party realized that it could overturn the decision only by changing the composition of the court and set its sights even more firmly on winning the presidency in 1860. By sparking intense political reactions and giving the Republican Party a needed boost, the decision catalyzed sectional tensions, speeding the nation along the path to war.

Long after the Civil War had faded into history, *Scott* v. *Sandford* continued to leave its imprint on American law. The decision marked the first time the Supreme Court had actually struck down a major piece of federal legislation, paving the way for more aggressive judicial review in the future. It also signaled the development of a defining characteristic of American governance, a reliance on the courts to settle controversies that the normal processes of democracy cannot resolve. Ironically, *Scott* v. *Sandford* may have served as precedent for *Brown* v. *Board of Education*.

Although the legacy of the decision lives to this day, the major figures of this story did not long survive the momentous events. John Sanford died in an asylum two months after the Court handed down its decision. Dred and Harriet Scott remained in St. Louis after their emancipation where they worked as a hotel porter and a laundress; both died shortly before the onset of the Civil War. Roger Taney continued to serve as chief justice during the war, but he faced bitter animosity from the northern public, who considered him a traitor to the very government he claimed to serve. Taney died in 1864, not living to see the conclusion of the conflict he had helped start. As one contemporary noted, "The Hon. Old Roger B. Taney has earned the gratitude of his country by dying at last. Better late than never."

QUESTIONS FOR DISCUSSION

1. What made the *Dred Scott* decision so important in American history?

2. What does the decision tell us about the status of African Americans in the United States on the eve of the Civil War?

Study Resources

 Take the **Study Plan** for **Chapter 14** *The Sectional Crisis* on **MyHistoryLab**

TIME LINE

1846 David Wilmot introduces proviso banning slavery in the Mexican cession

1848 Free-Soil Party is founded; Zachary Taylor (Whig) elected president, defeating Lewis Cass (Democrat) and Martin Van Buren (Free-Soil)

1849 California seeks admission to the Union as a free state

1850 Congress debates sectional issues and enacts Compromise of 1850

1852 Harriet Beecher Stowe publishes *Uncle Tom's Cabin*; Franklin Pierce (Democrat) elected president by a large majority over Winfield Scott (Whig)

1854 Congress passes Kansas-Nebraska Act, repealing Missouri Compromise; Republican Party founded in several northern states; Anti-Nebraska coalitions score victories in congressional elections in the North

1854–1855 Know-Nothing Party achieves stunning successes in state politics

1854–1856 Free-state and slave-state forces struggle for control of Kansas Territory

1856 Preston Brooks assaults Charles Sumner on Senate floor; James Buchanan wins presidency despite strong challenge in the North from John C. Frémont

1857 Supreme Court decides *Dred Scott* case and legalizes slavery in all territories

1858 Congress refuses to admit Kansas to Union under the proslavery Lecompton constitution; Lincoln and Douglas debate slavery issue in Illinois

1859 John Brown raids Harpers Ferry, is captured and executed

1859–1860 Fierce struggle takes place over election of a Republican as speaker of the House (December–February)

1860 Republicans nominate Abraham Lincoln for presidency (May); Democratic Party splits into northern and southern factions with separate candidates and platforms (June); Lincoln wins the presidency over Douglas, Breckinridge, and Bell

CHAPTER REVIEW

The Compromise of 1850

 How did territorial expansion intensify the conflict over slavery?

Manifest Destiny raised questions about states' rights. The Constitution did not permit the federal government to override state slavery laws, but the Wilmot Proviso attempted and failed to ban slavery in the Mexican cession. Despite that defeat, California was admitted as a free state under the Compromise of 1850, while the Fugitive Slave Law appeased the South. (p. 315)

Political Upheaval, 1852–1856

 How did the two-party system change during this period?

The Whig candidate lost in 1852 for supporting the antislavery cause, while the Kansas-Nebraska Act sought to repeal the Missouri Compromise—a move most northerners and some southerners considered abominable. This gave rise to Republicanism, which adhered to native Protestant values while supporting development in the West and opposing slavery. The 1856 election was largely a choice between rivals, one northern and one southern. (p. 319)

The House Divided, 1857–1860

 How did the institution of slavery go beyond political and economic debates?

Slavery divided American society culturally, legally, and morally. Religious congregations broke up, while literature expressed increasingly the sentiments surrounding slaveholding. The *Dred Scott* decision stripped American blacks—free and slave alike—of most legal rights. Finally, Lincoln chose to oppose slavery on moral grounds, making freedom a human (and not simply legal) right. (p. 324)

KEY TERMS AND DEFINITIONS

Wilmot Proviso In 1846, shortly after outbreak of the Mexican-American War, Congressman David Wilmot of Pennsylvania introduced this amendment banning slavery in any lands won from Mexico. p. 316

Popular sovereignty The concept that the settlers of a newly organized territory had the right to decide (through voting) whether to accept slavery. p. 318

Compromise of 1850 Five federal laws that temporarily calmed the sectional crisis. The compromise made California a free state, ended the slave trade in the District of Columbia, and strengthened the Fugitive Slave Law. p. 318

Fugitive Slave Law Passed in 1850, this federal law made it easier for slaveowners to recapture runaway slaves; it also made it easier for kidnappers to take free blacks. The law became an object of hatred in the North. p. 319

Kansas-Nebraska Act This 1854 act repealed the Missouri Compromise, split the Louisiana Purchase into two territories, and allowed its settlers to accept or reject slavery by popular sovereignty. p. 321

Ostend Manifesto Written by American diplomats in 1854, this secret memorandum urged acquiring Cuba by any means necessary. When it became public, northerners claimed it was a plot to extend slavery, and the manifesto was disavowed. p. 322

CRITICAL THINKING QUESTIONS

1. How did "popular sovereignty" reemerge as a definitive concept in the debates on slavery in new and existing states?

2. Which qualities did the Whig and Republican parties share? Which did they not?

3. How did cultural divisions affect the political compromises made over slavery?

MyHistoryLab Media Assignments

Find these resources in the Media Assignments folder for Chapter 14 on MyHistoryLab

The Compromise of 1850

■ **View** the **Closer Look** *The Compromise of 1850 p. 318*

■ **Read** the **Document** *The Fugitive Slave Act (1850) p. 319*

Political Upheaval, 1852–1856

View the **Map** *The Compromise of 1850 and the Kansas-Nebraska Act p. 320*

Read the **Document** *John Gihon, Kansas Begins to Bleed p. 322*

The House Divided, 1857–1860

■ **Watch** the **Video** *Harriet Beecher Stowe and the Making of Uncle Tom's Cabin p. 324*

■ **Watch** the **Video** *Dred Scott and the Crises that Lead to the Civil War p. 325*

Read the **Document** *Stephen A. Douglas, Debate at Galesburg, Illinois (1858) p. 326*

Read the **Document** *Abraham Lincoln, Debate at Galesburg, Illinois (1858) p. 327*

■ **Complete** the **Assignment** *The Enigma of John Brown p. 328*

Read the **Document** *John Brown's Address Before Sentencing p. 329*

Complete the **Assignment** *The Case of Dred and Harriet Scott: Blurring the Borders of Politics and Justice p. 334*

■ *Indicates Study Plan Media Assignment*

15 Secession and the Civil War

Contents and Learning Objectives

((•—[Listen to the **Audio File** on **myhistorylab**   **Chapter 15** *Secession and the Civil War*

The Emergence of Lincoln

The man elected to the White House in 1860 was striking in appearance—he was 6 feet, 4 inches, but seemed even taller because of his disproportionately long legs and his habit of wearing a high silk "stovepipe" hat. But Abraham Lincoln's previous career provided no guarantee he would tower over most of the other presidents in his legacy. When Lincoln sketched the main events of his life for a campaign biographer in June 1860, he was modest almost to the point of self-deprecation. Especially regretting his "want of education," he assured the biographer that "he does what he can to supply the want."

Born to poor, illiterate parents on the Kentucky frontier in 1809, Lincoln received a few months of formal schooling in Indiana after the family moved there in 1816. But mostly he educated himself, reading and rereading a few treasured books by firelight. In 1831, when the family migrated to Illinois, he left home to make a living for himself in the struggling settlement of New Salem, where he worked as a surveyor, shopkeeper, and local postmaster. His brief career as a merchant was disastrous: He went bankrupt and was saddled with debt for years to come. But he eventually found a path to success in law and politics. While studying law on his own in New Salem, he managed to get elected to the state legislature. In 1837, he moved to Springfield, a growing town that offered bright prospects for a young lawyer-politician. Lincoln combined exceptional political and legal skills with a

down-to-earth, humorous way of addressing jurors and voters. Consequently, he became a leader of the Whig party in Illinois and one of the most sought after lawyers riding the central Illinois judicial circuit.

The high point of his political career as a Whig was one term in Congress (1847–1849). Lincoln would have faced certain defeat had he sought reelection. His strong stance against the Mexican-American War alienated much of his constituency, and the voters expressed their disaffection in 1848 by electing a Democrat over the Whig who tried to succeed Lincoln. In 1849, President Zachary Taylor, for whom Lincoln had campaigned vigorously and effectively, failed to appoint him to a patronage job he coveted. Having been repudiated by the electorate and ignored by the national leadership of a party he had served loyally and well, Lincoln concentrated on building his law practice.

The Kansas–Nebraska Act of 1854, with its advocacy of popular sovereignty, provided Lincoln with a heaven-sent opportunity to return to politics with a stronger base of support. For the first time, his driving ambition for political success and his personal convictions about what was best for the country were easy to reconcile. Lincoln had long believed slavery was an unjust institution that should be tolerated only to the extent the Constitution and the tradition of sectional compromise required. He attacked Douglas's plan of popular sovereignty because it broke with precedents for

On February 27, 1860, Abraham Lincoln gave his famous "Right Makes Might" speech at Cooper Union. That same day, he went over to famed photographer Mathew Brady's studio at Broadway and Bleecker Street where he sat for an official campaign portrait. Lincoln would later credit the speech and the photo with making him president.

federal containment or control of the growth of slavery. After trying in vain to rally Free-Soilers around the Whig standard, Lincoln threw his lot in with the Republicans, assumed leadership of the new party in Illinois, attracted national attention in his bid for Douglas's Senate seat in 1858, and was the Republican presidential nominee in 1860. After Lincoln's election provoked southern secession and plunged the nation into the greatest crisis in its history, there was understandable skepticism about him in many quarters: Was the former rail-splitter from Illinois up to the responsibilities he faced? Lincoln had less experience relevant to a wartime presidency than any previous or future chief executive; he had never been a governor, senator, cabinet officer, vice president, or high-ranking military officer. But some of his training as a prairie politician would prove extremely useful.

Lincoln was also effective because he identified wholeheartedly with the northern cause and could inspire others to make sacrifices for it. To him, the issue in the conflict was nothing less than the survival of the kind of political system that gave men like himself a chance for high office. In addressing a special session of Congress in 1861, Lincoln provided a powerful statement of what the war was all about:

> And this issue embraces more than the fate of these United States. It presents to the whole family of man, the question of whether a constitutional republic, or a democracy—a government of the people by the same people—can, or cannot, maintain its territorial integrity against its own domestic foes.

The Civil War put on trial the very principle of democracy at a time when most European nations had rejected political liberalism and accepted the conservative view that popular government would inevitably collapse into anarchy. It also showed the shortcomings of a purely white man's democracy and brought the first hesitant steps toward black citizenship. As Lincoln put it in the Gettysburg Address, the only cause great enough to justify the enormous sacrifice of life on the battlefields was the struggle to preserve and extend the democratic ideal, or to ensure that "government of the people, by the people, for the people, shall not perish from the Earth."

As he prepared to take office in 1861, Lincoln could scarcely anticipate the challenges he would face. The immediate problem was how to respond to the secession of the Deep South. But secession was just an expression of the larger question: Did the authority of the federal government outweigh the power of the individual states? No less important were questions about slavery: Was it morally acceptable for one person to "own" another? Could the Union continue to exist half-slave and half-free?

The sectionalism that had already led to a number of violent incidents—bloody fighting in Kansas, the assault on Charles Sumner, John Brown's raid on Harpers Ferry, his conviction on charges of treason against Virginia, and his eventual execution—continued to mount. Finally, irreconcilable differences erupted into "total war" that left no part of society—North or South—untouched.

The Storm Gathers

What developments and events drew the Union toward Civil War?

Lincoln's election provoked the secession of seven states of the Deep South but did not lead immediately to armed conflict. Before the sectional quarrel would turn from a cold war into a hot one, two things had to happen: A final effort to defuse the conflict by compromise and conciliation had to fail, and the North needed to develop a firm resolve to maintain the Union by military action. Both of these developments may seem inevitable in

◉ Watch the Video   What Caused the Civil War?

There really should not be a great debate over what caused the Civil War. Imagine if you will an America before the Civil War without slavery.

retrospect, but for most of those living at the time, it was not clear until the guns blazed at Fort Sumter that the sectional crisis would have to be resolved on the battlefield.

The Deep South Secedes

South Carolina, which had long been in the forefront of southern rights and proslavery agitation, was the first state to secede. On December 20, 1860, a convention meeting in Charleston declared unanimously that "the union now subsisting between South Carolina and other states, under the name of the 'United States of America,'

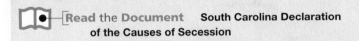

Read the Document   **South Carolina Declaration of the Causes of Secession**

CHARLESTON

MERCURY

EXTRA:

Passed unanimously at 1.15 o'clock, P. M., December 20th, 1860.

AN ORDINANCE

To dissolve the Union between the State of South Carolina and other States united with her under the compact entitled " The Constitution of the United States of America."

We, the People of the State of South Carolina, in Convention assembled, do declare and ordain, and it is hereby declared and ordained,

That the Ordinance adopted by us in Convention, on the twenty-third day of May, in the year of our Lord one thousand seven hundred and eighty-eight, whereby the Constitution of the United States of America was ratified, and also, all Acts and parts of Acts of the General Assembly of this State, ratifying amendments of the said Constitution, are hereby repealed; and that the union now subsisting between South Carolina and other States, under the name of "The United States of America," is hereby dissolved.

THE

UNION

IS

DISSOLVED!

A South Carolina newspaper announces the dissolution of the Union. South Carolina's secession was celebrated in the South with bonfires, parades, and fireworks.

is hereby dissolved." The constitutional theory behind secession was that the Union was a "compact" among sovereign states, each of which could withdraw from the Union by the vote of a convention similar to the one that had initially ratified the Constitution. The South Carolinians justified seceding at that time by charging that "a sectional party" had elected a president "whose opinions and purposes are hostile to slavery."

In other states of the Cotton Kingdom, there was similar outrage at Lincoln's election but less certainty about how to respond to it. Those who advocated immediate secession by each state individually were opposed by the **cooperationists**, who believed the slave states should act as a unit. If the cooperationists had triumphed, secession would have been delayed until a southern convention had agreed on it. Some of these moderates hoped a delay would provide time to extort major concessions from the North, removing the need for secession. But South Carolina's unilateral action set a precedent that weakened the cooperationists' cause.

Elections for delegates to secession conventions in six other Deep South states were hotly contested. Cooperationists did especially well in Georgia, Louisiana, and Texas. But nowhere did they stop secessionists from winning a majority. By February 1, seven states had removed themselves from the Union—South Carolina, Alabama, Mississippi, Florida, Georgia, Louisiana, and Texas. In the upper South, however, a moderate Unionist element, deriving mainly from the old Whig party, had maintained its strength and cohesion. Economic diversification had increased the importance of free labor and ties to the northern economy. Consequently, leaders in the border slave states were more willing than those in the lower South to seek a sectional compromise.

Without waiting for their sister slave states to the north, delegates from the Deep South met in Montgomery, Alabama, on February 4 to establish the Confederate States of America. The convention acted as a provisional government while at the same time drafting a permanent constitution. Relatively moderate leaders dominated the proceedings and defeated or modified some of the pet schemes of a radical faction composed of extreme southern nationalists. The resulting constitution was surprisingly similar to that of the United States. Most of the differences merely spelled out traditional southern interpretations of the federal charter: The central government was denied the authority to impose protective tariffs, subsidize internal improvements, or interfere with slavery in the states and was required to pass laws protecting slavery in the territories. As provisional president and vice president, the convention chose Jefferson Davis of Mississippi and Alexander Stephens of Georgia, men who had resisted secessionist agitation. Stephens, in fact, had led the cooperationist forces in his home state. Radical "fire eaters" such as William Yancey of Alabama and Robert Barnwell Rhett of South Carolina were denied positions of authority.

The moderation shown in Montgomery resulted in part from a desire to win support for the cause of secessionism in the reluctant states of the upper South, where such radical measures as reopening the slave trade were unpopular. But it also revealed something important about the nature of the separatist impulse. Proslavery reactionaries, who were totally lacking in reverence for the Union and wanted to found an aristocratic nation very different from the democratic United States, had never succeeded in getting a majority behind them. Most Southerners opposed dissolving the Union for so long as slavery was safe from northern interference.

[View the Map] Secession

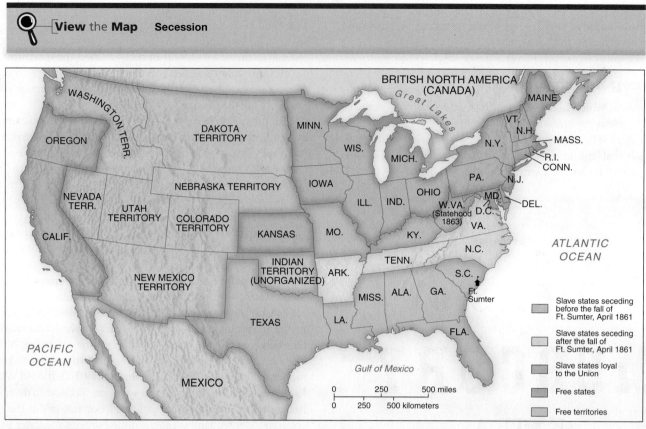

SECESSION The fall of Fort Sumter was a watershed for the secessionist movement. With no room left for compromise, slave states of the upper South chose to join the Confederacy.

The Montgomery convention did not try to establish a slaveholder's reactionary utopia but just aimed to re-create the Union as it had been before the rise of the new Republican party. The decision to allow free states to join the Confederacy reflected a hope that much of the old Union could be reconstituted under southern direction. Some optimists even predicted that all of the North except New England would eventually transfer its loyalty to the new government.

Secession and the formation of the Confederacy thus amounted to a very conservative and defensive kind of "revolution." The only justification for southern independence on which a majority could agree was the need for greater security for the "peculiar institution." Vice President Stephens spoke for all the founders of the Confederacy when he described the cornerstone of the new government as "the great truth that the negro is not equal to the white man—that slavery—subordination to the superior race—is his natural condition."

The Failure of Compromise

While the Deep South was opting for independence, moderates in the North and border slave states were trying to devise a compromise that would stem the secessionist tide before it could engulf the entire South. When the lame-duck Congress reconvened in December 1860, strong sentiment existed, even among some Republicans, to seek an adjustment of sectional differences. Senator John Crittenden of Kentucky presented a plan that served as the focus for discussion. The proposed

Crittenden Compromise, which resembled Henry Clay's earlier compromises, advocated extending the Missouri Compromise line to the Pacific to guarantee the protection of slavery in the southwestern territories and in any territories south of the line that might later be acquired. It also recommended federal compensation to the owners of escaped slaves and a constitutional amendment that would forever prohibit the federal government from abolishing or regulating slavery.

Initially, congressional Republicans showed some willingness to take the proposals seriously. At one point, William Seward of New York, the leading Republican in the Senate, leaned toward supporting a version of the Crittenden plan. Republicans in Congress turned for guidance to the president-elect, who had remained in Springfield and was refusing to make public statements on the secession crisis. An emissary brought back word that Lincoln was adamantly opposed to the compromise. Congressional Republicans therefore voted against compromise, as did the remaining senators and congressmen of the seceding states, who had vowed in advance to support no compromise unless the majority of Republicans also endorsed it. Their purpose in taking this stand was to obtain guarantees that the northern sectional party would end its attacks on "southern rights." The Republicans did in the end agree to support Crittenden's "un-amendable" amendment guaranteeing that slavery would be immune from future federal action. This action was not really a concession to the South, because Republicans had always acknowledged that the federal government had no constitutional authority to meddle with slavery in the states.

Some historians have blamed Lincoln and the Republicans for causing an unnecessary war by rejecting a compromise that would have appeased southern pride without providing any immediate practical opportunities for the expansion of slavery. But it is questionable whether approval of the compromise would have halted secession of the Deep South. The Republicans also believed that extending the Missouri Compromise line of 36°30′ to the Pacific would not halt agitation for extending slavery to new areas such as Cuba and Central America. The only way to resolve the crisis over the future of slavery and to reunite "the house divided" was to remove any chance that slaveholders could enlarge their domain.

Lincoln was also convinced that backing down in the face of secessionist threats would fatally undermine the democratic principle of majority rule. In his inaugural address of March 4, 1861, he recalled that during the winter, many "patriotic men" had urged him to accept a compromise that would "shift the ground" on which he had been elected. But to do so would have signified that a victorious presidential candidate "cannot be inaugurated till he betrays those who elected him by breaking his pledges, and surrendering to those who tried and failed to defeat him at the polls." Making such a concession would mean that "this government and all popular government is already at an end."

And the War Came

By the time of Lincoln's inauguration, seven states had seceded, formed an independent confederacy, and seized most federal forts and other installations in the Deep South without firing a shot.

Some Northerners thought it would be best to let the Confederate states "depart in peace," whether because they wanted to maintain commercial links with the cotton-producing South, or because they opposed a bloody war.

The collapse of compromise efforts narrowed the choices to peaceful separation or war between the sections. By early March, the tide of public opinion, even in the business community, was beginning to shift in favor of coercive measures to preserve the Union.

In his inaugural address, Lincoln called for a cautious and limited use of force. He would defend federal forts and installations not yet in Confederate hands but would not attempt to recapture the ones already taken. He thus tried to shift the burden for beginning hostilities to the Confederacy, which would have to attack before it would be attacked.

As Lincoln spoke, only four military installations within the seceded states were still held by U.S. forces. One of these was Fort Sumter in Charleston Harbor, which was under pressure from the Confederacy, and running low on food. Against the advice of some of his cabinet, Lincoln decided to send a ship to resupply the fort. Before the expedition arrived, the Confederate army attacked the fort. After two days of heavy bombardment, the Union forces surrendered, and the Confederate flag was raised over Fort Sumter. The South had won a victory, without a single death on either side.

On April 15, Lincoln proclaimed that an insurrection against federal authority existed in the Deep South and called on the militia of the loyal states to provide seventy-five thousand troops for short-term service to put it down. Two days later, a sitting Virginia convention, which had earlier rejected secession, reversed itself

This contemporary Currier and Ives lithograph depicts the bombardment of Fort Sumter on April 12–13, 1861. The soldiers are firing from Fort Moultrie in Charleston Harbor, which the Union garrison had evacuated the previous December in order to strengthen Fort Sumter.

and voted to join the Confederacy. Within the next five weeks, Arkansas, Tennessee, and North Carolina followed suit. These slave states of the upper South had been unwilling to secede just because Lincoln was elected, but when he called on them to provide troops to "coerce" other southern states, they had to choose sides.

In the North, the firing on Sumter evoked strong feelings of patriotism and dedication to the Union. "It seems as if we were never alive till now; never had a country till now," wrote a New Yorker; and a Bostonian noted, "I never before knew what a popular excitement can be." Stephen A. Douglas, Lincoln's former political rival, pledged his full support for the crusade against secession and literally worked himself to death rallying midwestern Democrats. By firing on the flag, the Confederacy united the North. Everyone assumed the war would be short and not very bloody. It remained to be seen whether Unionist fervor could be sustained through a prolonged struggle.

The entire Confederacy, which now moved its capital from Montgomery to Richmond, Virginia, contained only eleven of the fifteen states in which slavery was lawful. In the border slave states of Maryland, Delaware, Kentucky, and Missouri, a combination of local Unionism and federal intervention thwarted secession. Kentucky, the most crucial of these states, greeted the outbreak of war by proclaiming its neutrality. Kentucky eventually sided with the Union, mainly because Lincoln, who was careful to respect this tenuous neutrality, provoked the South into violating it first by sending regular troops into the state. Maryland, which surrounded the nation's capital and provided it with access to the free states, was kept in the Union by more ruthless methods, which included the use of martial law to suppress Confederate sympathizers. In Missouri, the presence of regular troops, aided significantly by a staunchly pro-Union German immigrant population, stymied the secession movement. But pro-Union forces failed to establish order in this deeply divided frontier state. Brutal guerrilla fighting made wartime Missouri an unsafe and bloody place.

Hence the Civil War was not, strictly speaking, a struggle between slave and free states. Nor did it simply pit states that could not tolerate Lincoln's election against those that could. More than anything else, conflicting views on the right of secession determined the ultimate division of states and the choices of individuals in areas where sentiment was divided. General Robert E. Lee, for example, was neither a defender of slavery nor a southern nationalist. But he followed Virginia out of the Union because he was the loyal son of a "sovereign state." General George Thomas, another Virginian, chose the Union because he believed it was indissoluble. Although concern about the future of slavery had driven the Deep South to secede in the first place, the actual lineup of states and supporters meant the two sides would initially define the war less as a struggle over slavery than as a contest to determine whether the Union was indivisible.

Adjusting to Total War

What challenges did "total war" bring for each side?

The Civil War was a "total war." It involved every aspect of society because the North could achieve its aim of restoring the Union only by defeating the South so thoroughly that its separatist government would be overthrown. Total war is a test of societies, economies, and political systems, as well as a battle of wits between generals and military strategists—and the Civil War was no exception.

Prospects, Plans, and Expectations

If the war was to be decided by sheer physical strength, then the North had an enormous edge in population, industrial capacity, and railroad mileage. Nevertheless, the South had some advantages that went a long way toward counterbalancing the North's demographic and industrial superiority. The South could do more with less because its armies faced an easier task. To achieve its aim of independence, the Confederacy needed only to defend its own territory successfully. The North, on the other hand, had to invade and conquer the South. Consequently, the Confederacy faced a less serious supply problem, had a greater capacity to choose the time and place of combat, and could take advantage of familiar terrain and a sympathetic civilian population.

The nature of the war meant southern leaders could define their cause as defense of their homeland against an alien invader and thus appeal to the fervid patriotism of a white population that viewed Yankee domination as a form of slavery. The northern cause, however, was not nearly as clear-cut as that of the South. It seemed doubtful in 1861 that Northerners would be willing to give equally fervent support to a war fought for the seemingly abstract principle that the Union was sacred and perpetual.

Confederate optimism on the eve of the war was also fed by other—and more dubious—calculations. It was widely assumed that Southerners would make better fighting men than Yankees. Farm boys accustomed to riding and shooting could allegedly whip several times their number among the clerks and factory workers (many of them immigrants) who, it was anticipated, would make up a large part of the Union army. (Actually, a majority of northern soldiers would also be farm boys.) When most of the large proportion of high-ranking officers in the U.S. Army who were of southern origin resigned to accept Confederate commands, Southerners confidently expected that their armies would be better led. If external help was needed, major foreign powers such as England and France might aid the Confederacy because the industrial economies of those European nations depended on the importation of southern cotton.

As they thought about strategy after Fort Sumter, the leaders of both sides tried to find the best way to capitalize on their advantages and compensate for their limitations. Although the Confederates' primary strategic orientation was defensive, it was an "offensive defense" that southern commanders enacted, acting aggressively against exposed Northern forces within the South.

Northern military planners had greater difficulty in working out a basic strategy, and it took a good deal of trial and error before there was a clear sense of what had to be done. Quite early it became evident that the optimistic hope of a quick and easy war was unrealistic. Aware of the costs of invading the South at points where its forces were concentrated, the aged General Winfield Scott—who commanded the Union army during the early months of the war—recommended an anaconda policy. Like a great boa constrictor, the North would squeeze the South

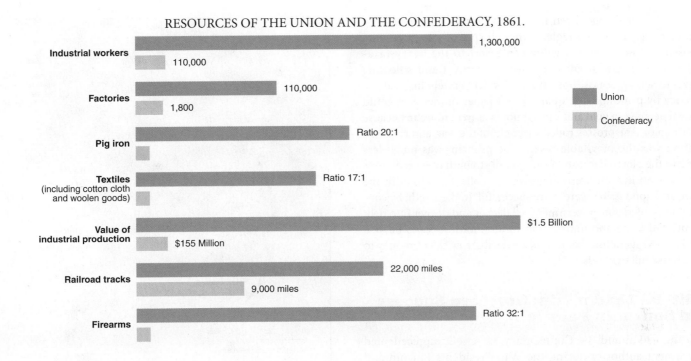

RESOURCES OF THE UNION AND THE CONFEDERACY, 1861.

Industrial workers: Union 1,300,000; Confederacy 110,000

Factories: Union 110,000; Confederacy 1,800

Pig iron: Ratio 20:1

Textiles (including cotton cloth and woolen goods): Ratio 17:1

Value of industrial production: Union $1.5 Billion; Confederacy $155 Million

Railroad tracks: Union 22,000 miles; Confederacy 9,000 miles

Firearms: Ratio 32:1

Union / Confederacy

into submission by blockading the southern coasts, seizing control of the Mississippi, and cutting off supplies of food and other essential commodities. This plan pointed to the West as the main locus of military operations.

Eventually Lincoln decided on a two-front war. He would keep the pressure on Virginia in the hope a breakthrough would occur there, while at the same time, he would authorize an advance down the Mississippi Valley with the aim of isolating Texas, Arkansas, and Louisiana. Lincoln also attached great importance to the coastal blockade and expected naval operations to seize the ports through which goods entered and left the Confederacy. His basic plan of applying pressure and probing for weaknesses at several points simultaneously was a good one because it took maximum advantage of the North's superiority in manpower and *matériel*. But it required better military leadership than the North possessed at the beginning of the war and took a painfully long time to put into effect.

Mobilizing the Home Fronts

The North and South faced similar problems in trying to create the vast support systems needed by armies in the field. At the beginning of the conflict, both sides had more volunteers than could be armed and outfitted. The South was forced to reject about two hundred thousand men in the first year of the war, and the North could commit only a fraction of its forces to battle. Further confusion resulted from the fact that recruiting was done primarily by the states, which were reluctant to surrender control of their forces. Both Lincoln and Davis had to deal with governors who resisted centralized military direction.

As it became clear that hopes for a short and easy war were false, the pool of volunteers began to dry up. Many of the early recruits, who had been enrolled for short terms, showed a reluctance to reenlist. To resolve this problem, the Confederacy passed a conscription law in April 1862, and the Union edged toward a draft in July. (See the Feature Essay, "Soldiering in the Civil War," pp. 350–351.)

To produce the materials of war, both governments relied mainly on private industry. While there was some inefficiency in its private contracting system, the North's economy was strong at the core, and by 1863 its factories and farms were producing more than enough to provision the troops without significantly lowering the living standards of the civilian population.

The southern economy was much less adaptable. Because of the weakness of its industrial base, the South of 1861 depended on the outside world for most of its manufactured goods. As the Union blockade became more effective, the Confederacy had to rely increasingly on a government-sponsored crash program to produce war materials. Astonishingly, the Confederates succeeded in producing or procuring sufficient armaments to keep southern armies well supplied.

Southern agriculture, however, failed to meet the challenge. Planters were reluctant to shift from staples that could no longer be readily exported to foodstuffs that were urgently needed. But more significant was the inadequacy of the South's internal transportation system. New railroad construction during the war did not resolve the problem; most of the new lines were aimed at facilitating the movement of troops rather than the distribution of food.

When northern forces penetrated parts of the South, they created new gaps in the system. As a result, much of the corn or livestock that was raised could not reach the people who needed it. Although well armed, Confederate soldiers were increasingly undernourished, and by 1863 civilians in urban areas were rioting to protest shortages of food. To supply the troops, the Confederate commissary resorted to the impressment of available agricultural produce at below the market price, a policy resisted so vigorously by farmers and local politicians that it eventually had to be abandoned.

Another challenge faced by both sides was how to finance an enormously costly struggle. Although special war taxes were imposed, neither side was willing to resort to the heavy taxation that was needed to maintain fiscal integrity. Besides floating loans and selling bonds, both treasuries deliberately inflated the currency by printing large quantities of paper money that could not be redeemed in gold and silver, known as **greenbacks** because of their color. The presses rolled throughout the war, and runaway inflation was the inevitable result. The problem was much less severe in the North because of the overall strength of its economy. War taxes on income were more readily collectable than in the South, and bond issues were more successful. In the South, by contrast, the Confederate government fell deeper and deeper into debt and printed more and more paper money, until it could be said with little exaggeration that it took a wheelbarrow full of money to buy a purse full of goods.

Political Leadership: Northern Success and Southern Failure

Both the Union and the Confederacy exercised unprecedented government authority during the War. Presidents Lincoln and Davis took actions that would have been regarded as arbitrary or even tyrannical in peacetime. Nevertheless, "politics as usual"—in the form of free elections, public political controversy, and the maneuverings of parties, factions, and interest groups—persisted to a surprising degree.

Lincoln was especially bold in assuming new executive powers, even interfering with civil liberties to an extent that may have been unconstitutional. He expanded the regular army and advanced public money to private individuals without authorization by Congress. On April 27, 1861, he declared martial law, which enabled the military to arrest civilians suspected of aiding the enemy, and suspended the writ of habeas corpus in the area between Philadelphia and Washington, an action deemed necessary because of mob attacks on Union troops passing through Baltimore. Suspension of the writ enabled the government to arrest Confederate sympathizers and hold them without trial, and in September 1862 Lincoln extended this authority to all parts of the United States where "disloyal" elements were active.

Lincoln argued that "necessity" justified a flexible interpretation of his war powers. For critics of suspension, he had a question: "Are all the laws, *but one*, to go unexecuted, and the government itself to go to pieces, lest that one be violated?" In fact, however, most of the thousands of civilians arrested by military authorities were not exercising their right to criticize the government but were suspected deserters and draft dodgers, refugees, smugglers, or people who were simply found wandering in areas under military control.

For the most part, the Lincoln administration showed restraint and tolerated a broad spectrum of political dissent. Although the government closed down a few newspapers for brief periods when they allegedly published false information or military secrets, anti-administration journals were allowed to criticize the president and his party. A few politicians, including an Ohio Congressman, were arrested for pro-Confederate activity, but a large number of "Peace Democrats"—who called for restoration of the Union by negotiation

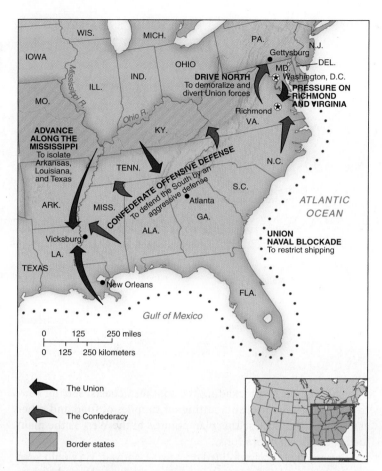

OVERVIEW OF CIVIL WAR STRATEGY Confederate military leaders were convinced the South could not be defended unless they took the initiative to determine where critical battles would be fought.

rather than force—ran for office and sat in Congress and in state legislatures, where they were able to present their views to the public. In fact, the persistence of vigorous two-party competition in the North during the Civil War strengthened Lincoln's hand. Since his war policies were also the platform of his party, he could usually rely on unified partisan backing for the most controversial of his decisions.

Lincoln was singularly adept at the art of party leadership, accommodating disagreement and encouraging unity and dedication to the cause. When a majority of the Republican party came around to the view that freeing the slaves was necessary to the war effort, Lincoln found a way to comply with their wishes while minimizing the disenchantment of the conservative minority. Republican cohesiveness was essential to Lincoln's success in unifying the nation by force.

Jefferson Davis, most historians agree, was a less effective war leader than Lincoln. He assumed personal direction of the armed forces but left policy making for the mobilization and control of the civilian population primarily to the Confederate Congress. He stumbled as commander in chief when he passed over able generals in favor of the incompetent but personal favorite Braxton E. Bragg.

Davis also ignored the problems of the homefront, especially the deteriorating economic situation that was sapping Confederate morale. Although the South had a much more serious problem of internal division and disloyalty than the North, he refrained from declaring martial law on his own authority, and the Confederate Congress allowed it to be applied only in limited areas and for short periods.

As the war dragged on, Davis's political and popular support eroded. He was opposed and obstructed by state governors who resisted conscription and other Confederate policies that violated the tradition of states' rights. The Confederate Congress served as a forum for bitter attacks on the administration's conduct of the war, and by 1863 a majority of southern newspapers were taking an anti-Davis stand. Even if he had been a more able and inspiring leader, Davis would have had difficulty maintaining his authority because he did not have an organized party behind him to mobilize popular support for his policies.

Early Campaigns and Battles

The war's first major battle was a disaster for northern arms. Against his better judgment, General Winfield Scott ordered poorly trained Union troops to advance against the Confederate forces gathered at Manassas Junction, Virginia. They attacked the enemy position near Bull Run Creek on July 21, 1861, and seemed on their way to victory until nine thousand Confederate reinforcements arrived. After Confederate General Thomas J. Jackson had earned the nickname "Stonewall" for holding the line against the northern assault, the augmented southern army counterattacked and routed the invading force. As they retreated toward Washington, the raw Union troops gave in to panic and broke ranks in their stampede to safety.

The humiliating defeat at Bull Run led to a shake-up of the northern high command. The man of the hour was George McClellan, who first became commander of troops in the Washington area and then became general in chief when Scott retired. A cautious disciplinarian, McClellan spent the fall and winter drilling his troops and whipping them into shape. President Lincoln, who could not understand why McClellan was taking so long to go into the field, became increasingly impatient and finally tried to order the army into action.

Before McClellan made his move, Union forces in the West won important victories. In February 1862, a joint military–naval operation commanded by General Ulysses S. Grant captured Fort Henry on the Tennessee River and Fort Donelson on the Cumberland. Fourteen thousand prisoners were taken at Donelson, and the Confederate army was forced to withdraw from Kentucky and middle Tennessee. Southern forces in the West then massed at Corinth, Mississippi, just across the border from Tennessee. When a slow-moving Union army arrived just north of the Mississippi state line, the South launched a surprise attack on April 6. In the battle of Shiloh, one of the bloodiest of the war, only the timely arrival of reinforcements prevented the annihilation of Union troops backed up against the Tennessee River. After a second day of fierce fighting, the Confederates retreated to Corinth, leaving the enemy forces battered and exhausted.

Although the Union's military effort to seize control of the Mississippi Valley was temporarily halted at Shiloh, the Union navy soon contributed dramatically to the pursuit of that objective. On April 26, a fleet under Flag Officer David Farragut, coming up from the Gulf, captured the Port of New Orleans after boldly running past the forts below the city. The occupation of New Orleans, besides securing the mouth of the Mississippi, climaxed a series of naval and amphibious operations around the edges of the Confederacy that had already succeeded in capturing South Carolina's Sea Islands and North Carolina's Roanoke Island. Strategically located bases were thus available to enforce a blockade of the southern coast. The last serious challenge to the North's naval supremacy ended on March 9, 1862, when the Confederate ironclad vessel *Virginia* (originally the USS *Merrimac*)—which had demolished wooden-hulled northern ships in the vicinity of Hampton Roads, Virginia—was repulsed by the *Monitor*, an armored and turreted Union gunship.

Successes around the edges of the Confederacy did not relieve northern frustration at the inactivity or failure of Union forces on the eastern front. Only after Lincoln had relieved him of supreme command and ordered him to take the offensive at the head of the Army of the Potomac did McClellan start campaigning. He moved his forces by water to the peninsula southeast of Richmond, and began moving up the peninsula in early April 1862. For a month he was bogged down before Yorktown, which he chose to besiege rather than assault directly. After Yorktown fell on May 4, he pushed ahead to a point twenty miles from Richmond, where he awaited the additional troops that he expected Lincoln to send.

The reinforcements were not forthcoming. While McClellan was inching his way up the peninsula, a relatively small southern force under Stonewall Jackson was on the rampage in the Shenandoah Valley, where it succeeded in pinning down a much larger Union army and defeating its detached units in a series of lightning moves. When it appeared by late May that Jackson might be poised to march east and attack the Union capital, Lincoln decided to withhold troops from McClellan so they would be available to defend Washington.

If McClellan had moved more boldly and decisively, he probably could have captured Richmond with the forces he had. But a combination of faulty intelligence reports and his own natural caution led him to falter in the face of what he wrongly believed to be superior numbers. At the end of May, the Confederates under Joseph E. Johnston took the offensive. During the battle, General Johnston was severely wounded; succeeding him in command of the Confederate Army of Northern Virginia was native Virginian and West Point graduate Robert E. Lee.

Toward the end of June, Lee began an all-out effort to expel McClellan from the outskirts of Richmond. In a series of battles that lasted for seven days, the two armies clawed at each other indecisively. Although McClellan repulsed Lee's final assaults at Malvern Hill, the Union general decided to retreat down the peninsula to a more secure base. This backward step convinced Lincoln that the peninsula campaign was an exercise in futility.

On July 11, Lincoln appointed General Henry W. Halleck, who had been in overall command in the western theater, to be the new general in chief and through Halleck ordered McClellan to withdraw his troops from the peninsula and send reinforcements to an army under General John Pope that was preparing to move on Richmond by the overland route. At the end of August, in the second battle fought near Bull Run, Lee established his reputation for brilliant generalship; he sent Stonewall Jackson to Pope's rear, provoked

Feature Essay | Soldiering in the Civil War

Youthful idealism is still evident on the faces of these young Civil War soldiers who had not yet learned General Sherman's message that "war is hell."

Early in the Civil War, William Tecumseh Sherman told an audience of fresh-faced recruits, "There's many a boy here today who looks on war as all glory, but, boys, it is all hell." Letters from Civil War soldiers reveal that Sherman's lesson was painfully learned by young men in both armies over the four years of conflict. At the outset, the firing on Fort Sumter infected both North and South with war fever. What later became a national nightmare began as a glorious defense of home and country. Young men rushed to join up in great numbers, taxing the ability of the authorities to process enlistments.

In contrast to the typical soldier of modern warfare, many of the early Civil War volunteers had well-developed ideas of what the war was about. On both sides, such troops formed a core of stalwart soldiers who were committed to the ideological and political implications of the struggle. In the democratic atmosphere of the nineteenth century, when governments had little power to coerce citizen-soldiers, neither army could have sustained four years of brutal fighting if significant numbers of their troops did not genuinely believe in their side's cause. The ideologically motivated troops may have accounted for about half of the fighting force.

The other half was another matter. As with any large military force, the Union and Confederate armies struggled to motivate and discipline men who cared little for the principles at the root of the conflict. Such soldiers, who were typically drafted, cajoled, or bribed into service, found numerous ways to avoid the dangers of combat. Known as skulkers and sneaks, these reluctant troops could avoid combat by feigning sickness, hiding, hanging back, asking for "bomb-proof" assignments, or simply deserting in droves. The bad blood between such soldiers and those who fervently believed in the war effort could be intense.

But the skulker and the ideologue shared one thing in common: Neither was fully prepared for the rigors of war.

Early Union defeats and a strategic stalemate not only ended talk in both the North and the South of a "short engagement filled with glory" but also revealed how undisciplined the troops were. Of the more than three million Civil War servicemen, two-thirds were younger than twenty-three years of age and came from rural areas. They were not accustomed to the regimentation necessary to military life; as a young recruit from Illinois put it, "It comes rather hard at first to be deprived of liberty." Inadequate leadership, as well as the beginnings of war weariness and the arrival of letters from home pleading for help with the harvest, led to a degree of military anarchy. The early battles were contests among armed mobs that might break and run with little provocation. Moreover, the long casualty lists from the early battles discouraged new waves of enlistments.

Both governments hit on similar methods of recruiting and disciplining troops. Enlistment and reenlistment bounties were instituted, and the nation's first conscription laws were passed. The dual aim was to maintain the ranks of the original volunteers while at the same time stimulating more enlistments. Terms of service were lengthened, in most cases to three years, and all nonenlisted men of military age were registered and called on to either volunteer or be faced with the disgrace of being drafted. Although some Southerners were exempted to oversee their large numbers of slaves, and Northerners could escape military duty by paying a $300 fee, the laws did spur enlistments. Between 1861 and 1865, more than half of the nation's 5.5 million men of military age were mustered into service.

The solution to the problem of training the troops was the army training camp. With its "50,000 pup tents and wigwams," the camp was the volunteer's way station between home and battlefield. It was the place the raw recruit received his first bitter taste of the tedium, hardship, and deprivation of soldiering. "A soldier is not his own man," a Louisiana recruit wrote, astonished at how markedly camp routines differed from civilian life. "He has given up all claim on himself . . . . I will give you a little information concerning every day business. consider yourself a private soldier and in camp . . . the drum beats for drill. you fall in and start. you here feel youre inferirority.

even the Sargeants is hollering at you close up; Ketch step. dress to the right, and sutch like."

Professional noncommissioned officers from the peacetime army were used, more effectively by the Union, to turn men into soldiers who could fire a rifle and understand simple commands. The liberal use of the court-martial and the board of review enabled the professional soldiers to rid the army of its most incompetent officer-politicians and instill discipline in the ranks. Many recruits spent their entire terms of service within the tent cities, forming a reserve on which field commanders could call to replace casualties.

The camps were themselves the sites of hundreds of thousands of Civil War casualties. Fewer men died of battle wounds than of dysentery, typhoid fever, and other waterborne diseases contracted in the camps, which were often located on swampy land without adequate fresh water. The army food was always the butt of soldier humor— one soldier complained the beef issued to him must have been carved from a bull "too old for the conscript law"—but it was also the source of its own set of diseases, particularly scurvy. Men in the field were condemned to a diet of "hardtack and half-cooked beans," and no soldier could expect to receive fresh fruit or vegetables. But food became steadily more plentiful in the Union camps, and doctors, officers, and agents of the U.S. Sanitary Commission teamed up to improve camp cleanliness. "Johnny Reb," however, had to survive under steadily worsening conditions. The Confederate supply system did not improve significantly during the course of the war and grew worse wherever the North invaded or blockaded. Nevertheless, the battlefield performance of fighting men on the two sides remained roughly on a par throughout the war.

Camp lessons were often forgotten in the heat of battle, particularly by green troops who "saw the elephant" (went into battle for the first time) and ran from it like the youth in Stephen Crane's *The Red Badge of Courage*. A Mississippian anxiously admitted after his first fight that "though i did not run i mite have if i had thought of it in time." The Union's ability to call more new men into service may have guaranteed ultimate victory, but it meant that battle-hardened Confederate veterans faced large numbers of raw northern recruits in every major battle. Since experience often counted for more than basic training and equipment, southern troops could expect to engage the enemy on fairly equal terms.

The Civil War was the most costly and brutal struggle in which American soldiers have ever been engaged. More American servicemen died in that war (618,000) than in the two world wars and Korea combined and was not surpassed until well into the Vietnam War. Contests were decided by deadly charges in which muskets were exploded at such close range as to sear the faces of the contestants. The survivors, in their letters home, attempted to describe the inhuman events, but, as a Maine soldier wrote to his parents after the battle of Gettysburg, "You can form no idea of a battlefield . . . . no pen can describe it. No tongue can tell its horror[.] I hope none of my brothers will ever have to go into a fight."

QUESTIONS FOR DISCUSSION

1. What did the "stalwart soldiers" on each side believe they were fighting for?

2. How did the experience of war change how the typical soldier thought and acted after the war was over?

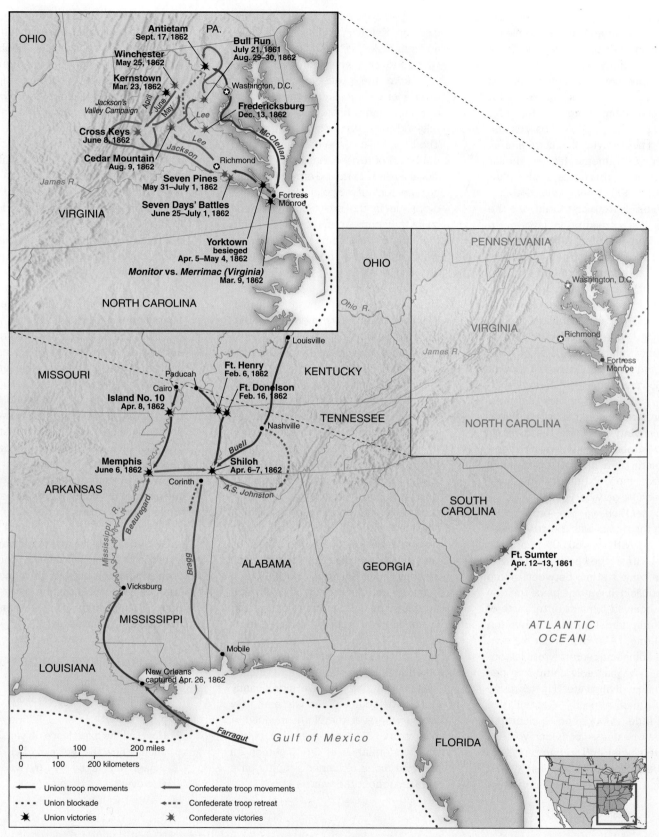

CIVIL WAR, 1861–1862 Defeats on the battlefield forced a change in the Union's initial military campaign of capturing Richmond, the Confederate capital. The Union's targets in the West were the key cities of Vicksburg and New Orleans.

the rash Union general to attack Jackson with full force, and then threw the main Confederate army against the Union's flank. Badly beaten, Pope retreated to the defenses of Washington, where he was stripped of command. Out of sheer desperation, Lincoln reappointed McClellan to head the Army of the Potomac.

Lee proceeded to lead his exuberant troops on an invasion of Maryland, in the hope of isolating Washington from the rest of the North. McClellan caught up with him near Sharpsburg, and the bloodiest one-day battle of the war ensued. When the smoke cleared at Antietam on September 17, almost five thousand men had been killed on the two sides and more than eighteen thousand wounded. The result was a draw, but Lee was forced to fall back south of the Potomac to protect his dangerously extended supply lines. McClellan was slow in pursuit, and Lincoln blamed him for letting the enemy escape.

Convinced that McClellan was fatally infected with "the slows," Lincoln once again sought a more aggressive general and put Ambrose E. Burnside in command of the Army of the Potomac. Burnside was aggressive enough, but he was also rather dense. His limitations were disastrously revealed at the Battle of Fredericksburg, Virginia, on December 13, 1862, when he launched a direct assault to try to capture an entrenched and elevated position. Throughout the Civil War, such uphill charges almost invariably failed because of the range and deadly accuracy of small-arms fire when concentrated on exposed troops. The debacle at Fredericksburg, where Union forces suffered more than twice as many casualties as their opponents, ended a year of bitter failure for the North on the eastern front.

The Diplomatic Struggle

The critical period of Civil War diplomacy was 1861 to 1862, when the South was making every effort to induce major foreign powers to recognize its independence and break the Union blockade. The hope that England and France could be persuaded to intervene on the Confederate side stemmed from the fact that these nations depended on the South for three-quarters of their cotton supply.

The Confederate commissioners sent to England and France in May 1861 succeeded in gaining recognition of southern "belligerency," which meant the new government could claim some international rights of a nation at war. The main advantage of belligerent status was that it permitted the South to purchase and outfit privateers in neutral ports. As a result, Confederate raiders built and armed in British shipyards devastated northern shipping to such an extent that insurance costs eventually forced most of the American merchant marine off the high seas for the duration of the war.

In the fall of 1861, the Confederate government dispatched James M. Mason and John Slidell to be its permanent envoys to England and France, respectively. A U.S. warship stopped and boarded the British steamer *Trent*, on which they were traveling, and Mason and Slidell were taken into U.S. custody. This flagrant violation of its maritime rights almost led England to declare war on the United States. After a few weeks of ferocious posturing by both sides, Lincoln and Secretary of State Seward made the prudent decision to release Mason and Slidell.

These envoys may as well have stayed at home; they failed in their mission to obtain full recognition of the Confederacy from either England or France. The anticipated cotton shortage was slow to develop, for the bumper crop of 1860 had created a large surplus in British and French warehouses. While Napoleon III, the emperor of France, personally favored the southern cause, he was unwilling to risk war with the United States without British support. Although sympathetic to the South, the British feared the consequences of recognition or support for the Confederacy. In September 1862, the British cabinet debated mediation and recognition as serious possibilities. But they hesitated to intervene unless the South won decisively on the battlefield.

The cotton famine finally hit in late 1862, causing massive unemployment in the British textile industry. But, contrary to southern hopes, public opinion did not compel the government to abandon its neutrality and use force to break the Union blockade. Influential interest groups actually benefited from the famine, including owners of large cotton mills, who had made extravagant profits on their existing stocks and were happy to see weaker competitors go under while they awaited new sources of supply. By early 1863, cotton from Egypt and India put the industry back on the track toward full production.

By early 1863, when it was clear that "King Cotton diplomacy" had failed, the Confederacy broke off formal relations with Great Britain. Its hopes for foreign intervention came to nothing because the European powers acted out of self-interest and calculated that the advantages of getting involved were not worth the risk of a long and costly war with the United States. Only a decisive military victory would have gained recognition for southern independence, and if the Confederacy had actually won such a victory, it would not have needed foreign backing.

Fight to the Finish

How did the Union finally attain victory, and what role did emancipation play in it?

The last two and a half years of the struggle saw the implementation of more radical war measures. The most dramatic and important of these was the North's effort to follow through on Lincoln's decision to free the slaves and bring the black population into the war on the Union side. The tide of battle turned in the summer of 1863, but the South continued to resist valiantly for two more years, until it was finally overcome by the sheer weight of the North's advantages in manpower and resources.

The Coming of Emancipation

At the beginning of the war, when the North still hoped for a quick and easy victory, only dedicated abolitionists favored turning the struggle for the Union into a crusade against slavery. In the summer of 1861, Congress voted almost unanimously for a resolution affirming that the war was being fought only to preserve the Union and not to change the domestic institutions of any state. But as it became clear how hard it was going to be to subdue the "rebels," sentiment developed for striking a blow at the South's economic and social system by freeing its slaves. In a tentative move toward emancipation, Congress in July 1862 authorized the government to confiscate the slaves of masters who supported the Confederacy.

By this time, the actions of the slaves themselves were influencing policy making. They were voting for freedom with their feet by deserting their plantations in areas where the Union forces were close enough to offer a haven. In this way, they put pressure on the government to determine their status and, in effect, offered themselves as a source of manpower to the Union on the condition that they be made free.

Although Lincoln favored freedom for blacks as an ultimate goal, he was reluctant to commit his administration to a policy of immediate emancipation. In the fall of 1861 and again in the spring of 1862, he disallowed the orders of field commanders who sought to free slaves in areas occupied by their forces, thus angering abolitionists and the strongly antislavery Republicans known as Radicals. Lincoln's caution stemmed from a fear of alienating Unionist elements in the border slave states and from his own preference for a gradual, compensated form of emancipation. He hoped that such a plan could be put into effect in loyal slaveholding areas and then extended to the rebellious states as the basis for a voluntary restoration of the Union.

Lincoln was also aware of the strong racial prejudice of most whites in both the North and the South. Although personally more tolerant than most white Americans, Lincoln was pessimistic about prospects of equality for blacks in the United States. He therefore coupled a proposal for gradual emancipation with a plea for government subsidies to support the voluntary "colonization" of freed blacks outside of the United States.

But the slaveholding states that remained loyal to the Union refused to endorse Lincoln's gradual plan, and the failure of Union arms in the spring and summer of 1862 increased the public clamor for striking directly at the South's peculiar institution. The Lincoln administration also realized that emancipation would win sympathy for the Union cause in England and France and thus might counter the growing threat that these nations would come to the aid of the Confederacy. In July, Lincoln drafted an emancipation proclamation and read it to his cabinet, but he was persuaded by Secretary of State Seward not to issue it until the North had won a victory and could not be accused of acting out of desperation. Later in the summer, Lincoln responded publicly to critics of his cautious policy, indicating that he would take any action in regard to slavery that would further the Union cause.

Finally, on September 22, 1862, Lincoln issued his preliminary **Emancipation Proclamation**. McClellan's success in stopping Lee at Antietam provided the occasion, but the president was also responding to growing political pressures. Most Republican politicians were now firmly committed to an emancipation policy, and many were on the verge of repudiating the administration for its inaction. Had Lincoln failed to act, his party would have been badly split, and he would have been in the minority faction. The proclamation gave the Confederate states one hundred days to give up the struggle without losing their slaves. There was little chance they would do so, but in offering them the chance, Lincoln left the door open for a more conservative and peaceful way of ending slavery than sudden emancipation at the point of a gun. In December, Lincoln proposed to Congress that it approve a series of constitutional amendments providing for gradual, compensated emancipation and subsidized colonization.

Since there was no response from the South and little enthusiasm in Congress for Lincoln's gradual plan, the president

▶ Read the Document   The Emancipation Proclamation (1863)

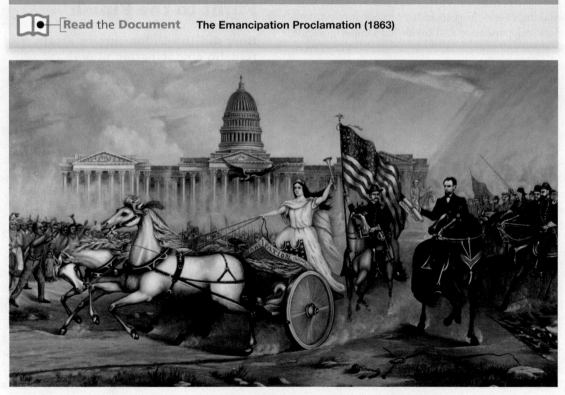

In this allegorical painting, President Lincoln extends a copy of his proclamation to the goddess of liberty who is driving her chariot, Emancipation.

went ahead on January 1, 1863, and declared that all slaves in those areas under Confederate control "shall be . . . thenceforward, and forever free." He justified the final proclamation as an act of "military necessity" sanctioned by the war powers of the president, and he authorized the enlistment of freed slaves in the Union army. The language and tone of the document—one historian has described it as having "all the moral grandeur of a bill of lading"—made it clear that blacks were being freed for reasons of state and not out of humanitarian conviction.

The proclamation did not extend to slave states loyal to the Union or to occupied areas and thus did not immediately free a single slave. However, it did commit the Union to the abolition of slavery as a war aim. It also accelerated the breakdown of slavery as a labor system, a process that was already well under way by early 1863. The blacks who had remained in captured areas or deserted their masters to cross Union lines before 1863 had been kept in a kind of way station between slavery and freedom, in accordance with the theory that they were "contraband of war." As word spread among the slaves that emancipation was now official policy, larger numbers of them were inspired to run off and seek the protection of approaching northern armies. One slave who crossed the Union lines summed up their motives: "I wants to be free. I came in from the plantation and don't want to go back; . . . I don't want to be a slave again." Approximately one-quarter of the slave population gained freedom during the war under the terms of the Emancipation Proclamation and thus deprived the South of an important part of its agricultural workforce.

African Americans and the War

Almost two hundred thousand African Americans, most of them newly freed slaves, eventually served in the Union armed forces and made a vital contribution to the North's victory. Without

 View the **Closer Look**   **Black Union Soldiers**

This lithograph depicts the 54th Massachusetts Volunteer Regiment engaged in the assault on Fort Wagner, South Carolina on July 18, 1863. The regiment was one of the first official black units of the Union Army during the Civil War and saw extensive service during the war.

them it is doubtful that the Union could have been preserved. Although they were enrolled in segregated units under white officers, were initially paid less than their white counterparts, and were used disproportionately for garrison duty or heavy labor behind the lines, "blacks in blue" fought heroically in several major battles during the last two years of the war. One of the most celebrated was the unsuccessful but heroic assault on Fort Wagner in the harbor of Charleston, South Carolina, in July 1863. The casualty rate for the 54th Massachusetts Colored Regiment exceeded 50 percent. Among the dead was the young white commander, Robert Gould Shaw, who became an abolitionist martyr. The assistant secretary of war observed blacks in action at Millikin's Bend on the Mississippi in June 1863 and reported that "the bravery of blacks in the battle . . . completely revolutionized the sentiment of the army with regard to the employment of Negro troops."

Those freed during the war who did not serve in the military were often conscripted to serve as contract wage laborers on cotton plantations owned or leased by "loyal" white planters within the occupied areas of the Deep South. Abolitionists protested that the coercion used by military authorities to get blacks back into the cotton fields amounted to slavery in a new form, but those in power argued that the necessities of war and the northern economy required such "temporary" arrangements. To some extent, regimentation of the freedmen within the South was a way of assuring racially prejudiced Northerners, especially in the Midwest, that emancipation would not result in a massive migration of black refugees to their region of the country.

The heroic performance of African American troops and the easing of northern fears of being swamped by black migrants led to a deepening commitment to emancipation as a permanent and comprehensive policy. Realizing that his proclamation had a shaky constitutional foundation and might apply only to slaves actually freed while the war was going on, Lincoln sought to organize and recognize loyal state governments in southern areas under Union control on the condition that they abolish slavery in their constitutions. He also encouraged local campaigns to emancipate the slaves in the border states and saw these programs triumph in Maryland and Missouri in 1864.

Finally, Lincoln pressed for an amendment to the federal constitution outlawing involuntary servitude. After supporting its inclusion as a central plank in the Republican platform of 1864, Lincoln used all his influence to win congressional approval for the new Thirteenth Amendment. On January 31, 1865, the House narrowly approved the amendment. There was an explosion of joy on the floor and in the galleries, and then the House voted to adjourn for the rest of the day "in honor of this immortal and sublime event." The cause of freedom for blacks and the cause of the Union had at last become one and the same. Lincoln, despite his earlier hesitations and misgivings, had earned the right to go down in history as the Great Emancipator.

The Tide Turns

By early 1863, the Confederate economy was in shambles and its diplomacy had collapsed. The social order of the South was also severely strained. Masters were losing control of their slaves,

and nonslaveholding whites were becoming disillusioned with the hardships of a war that some of them described as "a rich man's war and a poor man's fight." As slaves fled from the plantations, increasing numbers of lower-class whites deserted the army or refused to be drafted in the first place. Whole counties in the southern backcountry became "deserter havens," which Confederate officials could enter only at the risk of their lives. Appalachian mountaineers, who had remained loyal to the Union, resisted the Confederacy more directly by enlisting in the Union army or joining guerrilla units operating behind southern lines.

Yet the North was slow to capitalize on the South's internal weaknesses because it had its own serious morale problems. The long series of defeats on the eastern front had engendered war weariness, and the new policies that "military necessity" forced the government to adopt encountered fierce opposition.

Although popular with Republicans, emancipation was viewed by most Democrats as a betrayal of northern war aims. Racism was a main ingredient in their opposition to freeing blacks. According to one Democratic senator, "We mean that the United States . . . shall be the white man's home . . . and the nigger shall never be his equal." Riding a backlash against the preliminary proclamation, Democrats made significant gains in the congressional elections of 1862, especially in the Midwest, where they also captured several state legislatures.

The Enrollment Act of March 1863, which provided for outright conscription of white males but permitted men of wealth to hire substitutes or pay a fee to avoid military service, provoked a violent response from those unable to buy their way out of service and unwilling to "fight for the niggers." A series of antidraft riots broke out, culminating in one of the bloodiest domestic disorders in American history—the New York Riot of July 1863. The New York mob, composed mainly of Irish-American laborers, burned the draft offices, the homes of leading Republicans, and an orphanage for black children. They also lynched more than a dozen defenseless blacks. At least 120 people died before federal troops restored order. Besides racial prejudice, the draft riots also reflected working-class anger at the wartime privileges and prosperity of the middle and upper classes; they exposed deep divisions in the North on the administration's conduct of the war.

To fight dissension and "disloyalty," the government used its martial law authority to arrest a few alleged ringleaders, including one prominent Democratic congressman—Clement Vallandigham of Ohio. Private patriotic organizations also issued a barrage of propaganda aimed at what they believed was a vast secret conspiracy to undermine the northern war effort. Historians disagree about the real extent of covert and illegal antiwar activity. No vast conspiracy existed, but militant advocates of "peace at any price"—popularly known as **Copperheads**—were certainly active in some areas, especially among the immigrant working classes of large cities and in southern Ohio, Indiana, and Illinois. Many Copperheads presented themselves as Jeffersonian believers in limited government who feared a war-induced growth of federal power. But it was opposition to emancipation on racial grounds rather than anxiety about big government that gave the movement most of its emotional force.

Read the **Document** "If it were not for my trust in Christ," Testimony from the New York Draft Riots (1863)

THE RIOTS IN NEW YORK: THE MOB LYNCHING A NEGRO IN CLARKSON-STREET.—SEE PAGE 142.

An 1863 draft call in New York provoked violence against African Americans, viewed by the rioters as the cause of an unnecessary war, and rage against the rich men who had been able to buy exemptions from the draft. This 1863 illustration from *Harper's Weekly* depicts a mob lynching a black man on Clarkson Street in New York City.

Source: Collection of The New-York Historical Society.

The only effective way to overcome the disillusionment that fed the peace movement was to start winning battles and thus convince the northern public that victory was assured. Before this could happen, the North suffered one more humiliating defeat on the eastern front. In early May 1863, Union forces under General Joseph Hooker were routed at Chancellorsville, Virginia, by a Confederate army less than half its size. Once again, Robert E. Lee demonstrated his superior generalship, this time by dividing his forces and sending Stonewall Jackson to make a devastating surprise attack on the Union right. The Confederacy prevailed, but it did suffer one major loss: Jackson himself died as a result of wounds he received in the battle.

In the West, however, a major Union triumph was taking shape. For more than a year, General Ulysses S. Grant had been trying to put his forces in position to capture Vicksburg, Mississippi, the almost inaccessible Confederate bastion that stood between the North and control of the Mississippi River. Finally, in late March 1863, he crossed to the west bank north of the city and moved his forces to a point south of it, where he joined up with naval forces that had run the Confederate batteries mounted on Vicksburg's high bluffs. In one of the boldest campaigns of the war, Grant crossed the river, deliberately cutting himself off from his sources of supply, and marched into the interior of Mississippi. Living off the land and out of communication with an anxious and perplexed Lincoln, his troops won a series of victories over two separate Confederate armies and advanced on Vicksburg from the east. After unsuccessfully assaulting the city's defenses, Grant settled down for a siege on May 22.

The Confederate government considered and rejected proposals to mount a major offensive into Tennessee and Kentucky in the hope of drawing Grant away from Vicksburg. Instead, President Davis approved Robert E. Lee's plan for an all-out invasion of the Northeast. Although this option provided no hope for relieving Vicksburg, it might lead to a dramatic victory that would more than compensate for the probable loss of the Mississippi stronghold. Lee's army crossed the Potomac in June and kept going until it reached Gettysburg, Pennsylvania. There Lee confronted a Union army that had taken up strong defensive positions on Cemetery Ridge and Culp's Hill. This was one of the few occasions in the war when the North could capitalize on the tactical advantage of choosing its ground and then defending it against an enemy whose supply lines were extended.

On July 2, a series of Confederate attacks failed to dislodge Union troops from the high ground they occupied. The following day, Lee faced the choice of retreating to protect his lines of communication or launching a final, desperate assault. With more boldness than wisdom, he chose to make a direct attack on the strongest part of the Union line. The resulting charge on Cemetery Ridge was disastrous; advancing Confederate soldiers dropped like flies under the barrage of Union artillery and rifle fire. Only a few made it to the top of the ridge, and they were killed or captured.

Retreat was now inevitable, and Lee withdrew his battered troops to the Potomac, only to find that the river was at flood stage and could not be crossed for several days. But Meade failed to follow up his victory with a vigorous pursuit, and Lee was allowed to escape a predicament that could have resulted in his annihilation. Vicksburg fell to Grant on July 4, the same day Lee began his withdrawal, and Northerners rejoiced at the simultaneous Independence Day victories that turned the tide of the war. The Union had secured control of the Mississippi and had at last won a major battle in the East. But Lincoln's joy turned to frustration when he learned his generals had missed the chance to capture Lee's army and bring a quick end to the war.

Last Stages of the Conflict

Grant's victories in the West earned him promotion to general-in-chief of all the Union armies. After assuming that position in March 1864, he ordered a multipronged offensive to finish off the Confederacy. The offensive's main movements were a march on Richmond under Grant's personal command and a thrust by the western armies, now led by General William Tecumseh Sherman, toward Atlanta and the heart of Georgia.

In May and early June, Grant and Lee fought a series of bloody battles in northern Virginia that tended to follow a set pattern. Lee would take up an entrenched position in the path of the invading force, and Grant would attack it, sustaining heavy losses but also inflicting Confederate casualties. When his direct assault had failed, Grant would move to his left, hoping in vain to maneuver Lee into a less defensible position. In the battles of the Wilderness, Spotsylvania, and Cold Harbor, the Union lost about sixty thousand men—more than twice the number of Confederate casualties—without defeating Lee or opening the road to Richmond. Grant decided to change his tactics, moving his army to the south of Richmond and settling down for a siege.

The siege of Petersburg was a long, drawn-out affair, and the resulting stalemate in the East caused northern morale to plummet during the summer of 1864. Lincoln was facing reelection, and his failure to end the war dimmed his prospects. Lincoln confronted growing opposition within his own party, especially from Radicals who disagreed with his apparently lenient approach to the future restoration of seceded states to the Union. After Lincoln vetoed a Radical-supported congressional reconstruction plan in July, some Radicals began to call for a new convention to nominate another candidate.

The Democrats seemed to be in a good position to capitalize on Republican divisions and make a strong bid for the White House. Their platform appealed to war weariness by calling for a cease-fire followed by negotiations to reestablish the Union. The party's nominee, General George McClellan, announced he would not be bound by the peace plank and would pursue the war. But he promised to end the conflict sooner than Lincoln could because he would not insist on emancipation as a condition for reconstruction. By late summer, Lincoln confessed privately that he would probably be defeated.

But northern military successes changed the political outlook. Sherman's invasion of Georgia went well; between May and September, he employed a series of skillful flanking movements to force the Confederates to retreat to the outskirts of Atlanta. On September 2, the city fell, and northern forces occupied the hub of the Deep South. The news unified the Republican party behind Lincoln and improved his chances for defeating McClellan in November. The election itself was almost an anticlimax: Lincoln won 212 of a possible 233 electoral votes and 55 percent of the popular vote. The Republican cause of "liberty and Union" was secure.

THE ELECTION OF 1864

Candidate	Party	Popular Vote	Electoral Vote
Lincoln	Republican	2,213,655	212
McClellan	Democratic	1,805,237	21

*Out of a total of 233 electoral votes. The eleven secessionist states— Alabama, Arkansas, Florida, Georgia, Louisiana, Mississippi, North Carolina, South Carolina, Tennessee, Texas, and Virginia—did not vote.

The concluding military operations revealed the futility of further southern resistance. Cutting himself off from his supply lines and living off the land, Sherman marched unopposed through Georgia to the sea, destroying almost everything of possible military or economic value in a corridor three hundred miles long and sixty miles wide. The Confederate army that had opposed him at Atlanta, now under the command of General John B. Hood, moved northward into Tennessee, where it was defeated and almost destroyed by Union forces under General George Thomas at Nashville in mid-December. Sherman captured Savannah on December 22 and presented the city to Lincoln as a Christmas present. He then turned north and carried his scorched-earth policy into South Carolina with the aim of continuing through North Carolina and eventually joining up with Grant at Petersburg near Richmond.

While Sherman was bringing the war to the Carolinas, Grant finally ended the stalemate at Petersburg. When Lee's starving and exhausted army tried to break through the Union lines, Grant renewed his attack and forced the Confederates to abandon Petersburg and Richmond on April 2, 1865. He then pursued them westward for a hundred miles, placing his forces in position to cut off their line of retreat to the South. Recognizing the hopelessness of further resistance, Lee surrendered his army at Appomattox Courthouse on April 9.

But the joy of the victorious North turned to sorrow and anger when John Wilkes Booth, a pro-Confederate actor, assassinated Abraham Lincoln as the president watched a play at Ford's Theater in Washington on April 14. Although Booth had a few

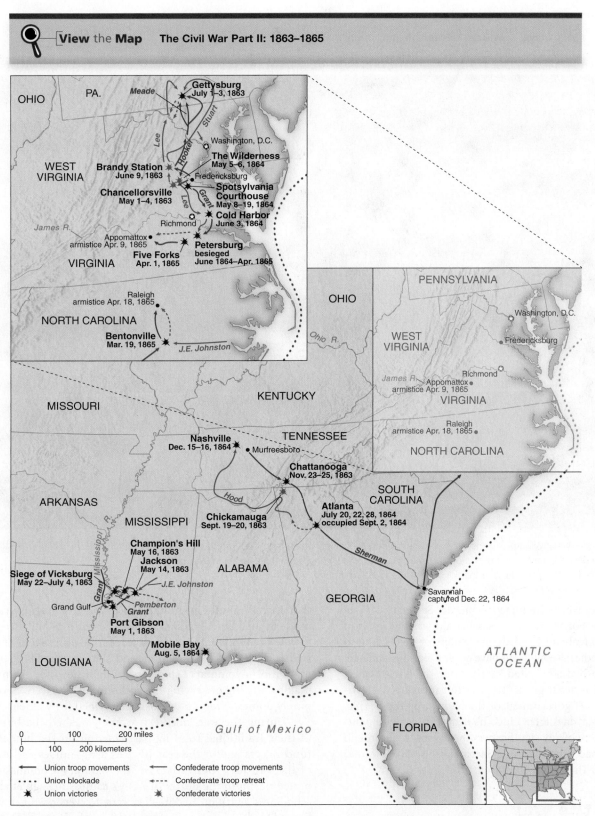

View the Map   The Civil War Part II: 1863–1865

CIVIL WAR, 1863–1865 In the western theater of war, Grant's victories at Port Gibson, Jackson, and Champion's Hill cleared the way for his siege of Vicksburg. In the east, after the hard-won Union victory at Gettysburg, the South never again invaded the North. In 1864 and 1865, Union armies gradually closed in on Lee's Confederate forces in Virginia. Leaving Atlanta in flames, Sherman marched to the Georgia coast, took Savannah, then moved his troops north through the Carolinas. Grant's army, though suffering enormous losses, moved on toward Richmond, marching into the Confederate capital on April 3, 1865, and forcing surrender.

Read the Document   William T. Sherman, the March Through Georgia

This illustration depicts General William Tecumseh Sherman's successful Union Army march through Georgia from May 1864 to December 1864. Sherman's destruction of almost all valuable military and economic assets in Georgia and later in the Carolinas during this period broke the will of continued resistance by Southern forces.

accomplices—one of whom attempted to murder Secretary of State Seward—popular theories that the assassination was the result of a vast conspiracy involving Confederate leaders or (according to another version) Radical Republicans have never been substantiated.

The man who had advocated sacrifice for the Union cause at Gettysburg had himself given "the last full measure of devotion" to the cause of "government of the people, by the people, for the people." Four days after Lincoln's death, the only remaining Confederate force of any significance (the troops under Joseph E. Johnston, who had been opposing Sherman in North Carolina) laid down its arms. The Union was saved.

Effects of the War

How did the outcome of the war affect America socially and politically?

The nation that emerged from four years of total war was not the same America that had split apart in 1861. Over 618,000 young men were in their graves, victims of enemy fire or the diseases that spread rapidly in military encampments in this era before modern medicine and sanitation. The widows and sweethearts they left behind temporarily increased the proportion of unmarried women in the population, and some members of this generation of involuntary "spinsters" sought new opportunities for making a living or serving the community that went beyond the purely domestic roles previously prescribed for women.

During the war, northern women pushed the boundaries of their traditional roles by participating on the homefront as fund-raisers and in the rear lines as army nurses and members of the **Sanitary Commission**. The Sanitary Commission promoted health in the northern army's camps through attention to cleanliness, nutrition, and medical care. However, women were not limited to playing roles as nurses and "angels of mercy." Throughout the war, they also filled key positions in the administration and organization of patriotic organizations. Women in the North simultaneously utilized their traditional position as nurturers to participate in the war effort while they advanced new ideas about their role in society. The large number who had served as nurses or volunteer workers during the war were especially responsive to

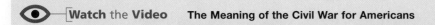

Watch the **Video**   The Meaning of the Civil War for Americans

Over the past 150 years, Americans have given many different meanings to the Civil War. For some in the South, it was the "Lost Cause," a romantic contest of fallen heroes. Even some Northerners came to accept this view of the conflict in the decades afterward. Today, we celebrate the end of slavery but mourn the terrible loss of life in that bloody war.

calls for broadening "the woman's sphere." Some of the northern women who were prominent in wartime service organizations—such as Louise Lee Schuyler, Josephine Shaw Lowell, and Mary Livermore—became leaders of postwar philanthropic and reform movements. The war did not destroy the barriers to sexual equality that had long existed in American society, but the efforts of women during the Civil War broadened beliefs about what women could accomplish outside of the home.

The effect on white women in the Confederacy was different from the effect of the war on women in the victorious North. Southern women had always been intimately involved in the administration of

the farms and plantations of the South, but the coming of the war forced them to shoulder even greater burdens. This was true for wealthy plantation mistresses, who took over the administration and maintenance of huge plantations without the benefit of extensive training or the assistance of male relatives. The wives of small farmers found it hard to survive at all, especially at harvest time when they often had to do all the work themselves. The loss of fathers and brothers, the constant advance of Union troops, and the difficulty of controlling a slave labor force destroyed many southern women's allegiance to the Confederate cause. At the close of the conflict, southern women faced the challenge of rebuilding a society that had been

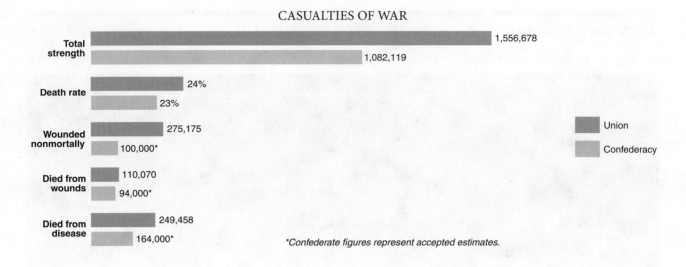

CASUALTIES OF WAR

	Union	Confederacy
Total strength	1,556,678	1,082,119
Death rate	24%	23%
Wounded nonmortally	275,175	100,000*
Died from wounds	110,070	94,000*
Died from disease	249,458	164,000*

Confederate figures represent accepted estimates.

permanently transformed by the experience of war. As in the North, the Civil War changed the situation of women in society. The devastation of the southern economy forced many women to play a more conspicuous public and economic role. These women responded by forming associations to assist returning soldiers, entering the workforce as educators, and establishing numerous benevolent and reform societies or temperance organizations. Although these changes created a more visible presence of southern women in public, the South remained more conservative in its views about women's "proper place" than did the North.

At enormous human and economic cost, the nation had emancipated four million African Americans from slavery, but it had not yet resolved that they would be equal citizens. At the time of Lincoln's assassination, most northern states still denied blacks equality under the law and the right to vote. Whether the North would extend more rights to southern freedmen than it had granted to "free Negroes" was an open question.

The impact of the war on white working people was also unclear. Those in the industrializing parts of the North had suffered and lost ground economically because prices had risen much faster than wages during the conflict. But Republican rhetoric emphasizing "equal opportunity" and the "dignity of labor" raised hopes that the crusade against slavery could be broadened into a movement to improve the lot of working people in general. Foreign-born workers had additional reason to be optimistic; the fact that so many immigrants had fought and died for the Union cause had—for the moment—weakened nativist sentiment and encouraged ethnic tolerance.

What the war definitely decided was that the federal government was supreme over the states and had a broad grant of constitutional authority to act on matters affecting "the general welfare." The southern principle of state sovereignty and strict construction died at Appomattox, and the United States was on its way to becoming a true nation-state with an effective central government. But it retained a federal structure; although states could no longer claim the right to secede or nullify federal law, they still had primary responsibility for most functions of government. Everyone agreed that the Constitution placed limits on what the national government could do, and questions would continue to arise about where federal authority ended and states' rights began.

A broadened definition of federal powers had its greatest impact in the realm of economic policy. During the war, the Republican-dominated Congresses passed a rash of legislation designed to give stimulus and direction to the nation's economic development. Taking advantage of the absence of southern opposition, Republicans rejected the pre–Civil War tradition of virtual laissez-faire and enacted a Whiggish program of active support for business and agriculture. In 1862, Congress passed a high protective tariff, approved a homestead act intended to encourage settlement of the West by providing free land to settlers, granted huge tracts of public land to railroad companies to support the building of a transcontinental railroad, and gave the states land for the establishment of agricultural colleges. The following year, Congress set up a national banking system that required member banks to keep adequate reserves and invest one-third of their capital in government securities. The notes the national banks issued became the country's first standardized and reliable circulating paper currency.

These wartime achievements added up to a decisive shift in the relationship between the federal government and private enterprise. The Republicans took a limited government that did little more than seek to protect the marketplace from the threat of monopoly and changed it into an activist state that promoted and subsidized the efforts of the economically ambitious and industrious.

Conclusion: An Organizational Revolution

The most pervasive effect of the war on northern society was to encourage an "organizational revolution." Aided by government policies, venturesome businessmen took advantage of the new national market created by military procurement to build larger firms that could operate across state lines; some of the huge corporate enterprises of the postwar era began to take shape. Philanthropists also developed more effective national associations; the most notable of these were the Sanitary and Christian Commissions that ministered to the physical and spiritual needs of the troops. Efforts to care for the wounded influenced the development of the modern hospital and the rise of nursing as a female profession. Both the men who served in the army and those men and women who supported them on the homefront or behind the lines became accustomed to working in large, bureaucratic organizations of a kind that had scarcely existed before the war.

Ralph Waldo Emerson, the era's most prominent man of letters, revealed in his Civil War writings that the conflict encouraged a dramatic shift in American thought about the relationship between the individual and society. Before the war, Emerson had generally championed "the transcendent individual," who stood apart from institutions and organizations and sought fulfillment in an inner world of imagination and cosmic intuition. During the conflict, he began to exalt the claims of organization, government, and "civilization" over the endeavors of "the private man" to find fulfillment through "self-culture." He even extolled military discipline and became an official visitor to West Point. In 1837, he had said of young men who aspired to political office, "Wake them up and they shall quit the false good and leap to the true, and leave governments to clerks and desks." Now he affirmed almost the opposite: "Government must not be a parish clerk, a justice of the peace. It has, of necessity, in any crisis of the state, the absolute powers of a dictator." In purging his thoughts of extreme individualism and hailing the need to accept social discipline and participate in organized, cooperative activity, Emerson epitomized the way the war affected American thought and patterns of behavior.

The North won the war mainly because it had shown a greater capacity than the South to organize, innovate, and "modernize." Its victory meant the nation as a whole would now be ready to embrace the conception of progress that the North had affirmed in its war effort—not only its advances in science and technology, but also its success in bringing together and managing large numbers of men and women for economic and social goals. The Civil War was thus a catalyst for the great transformation of American society from an individualistic society of small producers into the more highly organized and "incorporated" America of the late nineteenth century.

Study Resources

 Take the **Study Plan** for **Chapter 15** *Secession and the Civil War* on **MyHistoryLab**

TIME LINE

1860 South Carolina secedes from the Union (December)

1861 Rest of Deep South secedes: Confederacy is founded (January–February); Fort Sumter is fired upon and surrenders to Confederate forces (April); Upper South secedes (April–May); South wins first battle of Bull Run (July)

1862 Grant captures Forts Henry and Donelson (February); Farragut captures New Orleans for the Union (April); McClellan leads unsuccessful campaign on the peninsula southeast of Richmond (March–July); South wins second battle of Bull Run (August); McClellan stops Lee at battle of Antietam (September); Lincoln issues preliminary Emancipation Proclamation (September); Lee defeats Union army at Fredericksburg (December)

1863 Lincoln issues final Emancipation Proclamation (January); Lee is victorious at Chancellorsville (May); North gains major victories at Gettysburg and Vicksburg (July); Grant defeats Confederate forces at Chattanooga (November)

1864 Grant and Lee battle in northern Virginia (May–June); Atlanta falls to Sherman (September); Lincoln is reelected president, defeating McClellan (November); Sherman marches through Georgia (November–December)

1865 Congress passes Thirteenth Amendment abolishing slavery (January); Grant captures Petersburg and Richmond; Lee surrenders at Appomattox (April); Lincoln assassinated by John Wilkes Booth (April); Remaining Confederate forces surrender (April–May)

CHAPTER REVIEW

The Storm Gathers

 What developments and events drew the Union toward Civil War?

Lincoln's election prompted the secession of seven states. In South Carolina, "cooperationism" was defeated, sparking other states to follow. Republicans rejected compromise on the question of slavery in new states, and Lincoln resolved to use force should the South strike first. At Fort Sumter in 1861, it did. (p. 342)

Adjusting to Total War

 What challenges did "total war" bring for each side?

Total war meant no cease-fire until the southern separatists were defeated. The North, with its large population, heavy industry, and agriculture, was better suited for the long conflict. The South struggled to feed itself and lacked wealth, yet put up a strong fight. Meanwhile, Lincoln maintained northern unity (p. 346)

Fight to the Finish

 How did the Union finally attain victory, and what role did emancipation play in it?

Lincoln was skeptical of emancipation, although he favored it morally. Later he saw the strategic benefit of opposing slavery, so he declared the freedom of slaves in unoccupied areas in the January 1863 Emancipation Proclamation. Many African Americans escaped slavery and joined the Union army, helping to turn the tide of the war. Union victories helped reelect Lincoln in 1864. (p. 352)

Effects of the War

 How did the outcome of the war affect America socially and politically?

The Civil War changed the status of many social groups, including women, who took on new social roles after the death of male family members, and blacks, who were adjusting to free status in a white society. New national institutions, including benevolent organizations and banks, contributed to an "organizational revolution." The federal government grew stronger than ever. (p. 360)

KEY TERMS AND DEFINITIONS

Cooperationists   Southerners in 1860 who advocated secession by the South as a whole rather than unilateral secession by each state. p. 343

Crittenden Compromise   Introduced by Kentucky Senator John Crittenden in 1861 in an attempt to prevent secession and civil war, it would have extended the Missouri Compromise line west to the Pacific. p. 344

Greenbacks   Paper currency issued by the Union during the Civil War. p. 348

Emancipation Proclamation   On January 1, 1863, President Abraham Lincoln proclaimed that the slaves of the Confederacy were free. Since the

South had not yet been defeated, the proclamation did not immediately free anyone, but it made emancipation an explicit war aim of the North. p. 354

Copperheads   Northern Democrats suspected of being indifferent or hostile to the Union cause in the Civil War. p. 356

Sanitary Commission   An association chartered by the government during the Civil War to promote health in the northern army's camps through cleanliness, nutrition, and medical care. p. 360

CRITICAL THINKING QUESTIONS

1. Given your knowledge of society and economy in the South and public policy in the North, do you think the Union could have been preserved through means other than outright warfare?

2. How did Lincoln's personal character affect the morale of the North and the outcome of the war?

3. What were the pros and cons of emancipation for someone like Lincoln who supported it personally?

4. During the course of the war, did the American people shape the fate of government or did government shape the lives of its people?

MyHistoryLab Media Assignments

Find these resources in the Media Assignments folder for Chapter 15 on MyHistoryLab

The Storm Gathers

■ ◉─┤Watch the **Video**   *What Caused the Civil War? p. 342*

📖─┤Read the **Document**   *South Carolina Declaration of the Causes of Secession p. 343*

🔍─┤View the **Map**   *Secession p. 344*

Adjusting to Total War

■ 📖─┤Complete the **Assignment**   *Soldiering in the Civil War p. 350*

Fight to the Finish

■ 📖─┤Read the **Document**   *The Emancipation Proclamation p. 354*

■ 🔍─┤View the **Closer Look**   *Black Union Soldiers p. 355*

📖─┤Read the **Document**   *"If it were not for my trust in Christ," Testimony from the New York Draft Riots (1863) p. 357*

■ 🔍─┤View the **Map**   *The Civil War Part II: 1863–1865 p. 359*

■ 📖─┤Read the **Document**   *William T. Sherman, the March Through Georgia p. 360*

Effects of the War

◉─┤Watch the **Video**   *The Meaning of the Civil War for Americans p. 361*

■ Indicates Study Plan Media Assignment

Contents and Learning Objectives

((•●—[Listen to the **Audio File** on **myhistorylab**   Chapter 16 *The Agony of Reconstruction*

Robert Smalls and Black Politicians During Reconstruction

During the Reconstruction period immediately following the Civil War, African Americans struggled to become equal citizens of a democratic republic. They produced a number of remarkable leaders who showed that blacks were as capable as other Americans of voting, holding office, and legislating for a complex and rapidly changing society. Among these leaders was Robert Smalls of South Carolina. Although virtually forgotten by the time of his death in 1915, Smalls was perhaps the most famous and widely respected southern black leader of the Civil War and Reconstruction era. His career reveals some of the main features of the African American experience during that crucial period.

Born a slave in 1839, Smalls had a white father whose identity has never been clearly established. But his white ancestry apparently gained him some advantages, and as a young man he was allowed to live and work independently, hiring his own time from a master who may have been his half brother. Smalls worked as a sailor and trained himself to be a pilot in Charleston Harbor.

When the Union navy blockaded Charleston in 1862, Smalls, who was then working on a Confederate steamship called the *Planter*, saw a chance to win his freedom in a particularly dramatic way. At three o'clock in the morning on May 13, 1862, when the white officers of the *Planter* were ashore, he took command of the vessel and its slave crew, sailed it out of the heavily fortified harbor, and surrendered it to the Union navy.

Smalls immediately became a hero to those antislavery Northerners who were seeking evidence that the slaves were willing and able to serve the Union. The *Planter* was turned into a Union army transport, and Smalls was made its captain after being commissioned as an officer. During the remainder of the war, he rendered conspicuous and gallant service as captain and pilot of Union vessels off the coast of South Carolina.

Like a number of other African Americans who had fought valiantly for the Union, Smalls went on to a distinguished political career during Reconstruction, serving in the South Carolina constitutional convention, in the state legislature, and for several terms in the U.S. Congress. He was also a shrewd businessman and became the owner of extensive properties in Beaufort, South Carolina, and its vicinity. (His first purchase was the house of his former master, where he had spent his early years as a slave.) As the leading citizen of Beaufort during Reconstruction and for some years thereafter, he acted like many successful white Americans, combining the acquisition of wealth with the exercise of political power.

The electoral organization Smalls established resembled in some ways the well-oiled "machines" being established in northern towns and cities. It was so effective that he was able to control local government and get himself elected to Congress even after the election of 1876 had placed the state under the

With the help of several black crewmen, Robert Smalls—then twenty-three years old—commandeered the *Planter*, a Confederate steamship used to transport guns and ammunition, and surrendered it to the Union vessel, USS *Onward*. Smalls provided distinguished service to the Union during the Civil War and after the war went on to become a successful politician and businessman.

control of white conservatives bent on depriving blacks of political power. Organized mob violence defeated him in 1878, but he bounced back to win by decision of Congress a contested congressional election in 1880. He did not leave the House of Representatives for good until 1886, when he lost another contested election that had to be decided by Congress. It revealed the changing mood of the country that his white challenger was seated despite evidence of violence and intimidation against black voters.

In their efforts to defeat him, Smalls' white opponents frequently charged that he had a hand in the corruption that was allegedly rampant in South Carolina during Reconstruction. But careful historical investigation shows that he was, by the standards of the time, an honest and responsible public servant. In the South Carolina convention of 1868 and later in the state legislature, he was a conspicuous champion of free and compulsory public education. In Congress, he fought for the enactment and enforcement of federal civil rights laws. Not especially radical on social questions, he sometimes bent over backward to accommodate what he regarded as the legitimate interests and sensibilities of South Carolina whites. Like other middle-class black political leaders in Reconstruction-era South Carolina, he can perhaps be faulted in hindsight for not doing more to help poor blacks gain access to land of their own. But in 1875, he sponsored congressional legislation that opened for purchase at low prices the land in his own district that had been confiscated by the federal government during the war. As a result, blacks were able to buy most of it, and they soon owned three-fourths of the land in Beaufort and its vicinity.

Robert Smalls spent the later years of his life as U.S. collector of customs for the port of Beaufort, a beneficiary of the patronage that the Republican party continued to provide for a few loyal southern blacks. But the loss of real political clout for Smalls and men like him was one of the tragic consequences of the fall of Reconstruction.

For a brief period of years, black politicians such as Robert Smalls exercised more power in the South than they would for another century. A series of political developments on the national and regional stage made Reconstruction "an unfinished revolution," promising but not delivering true equality for newly freed African Americans. National party politics, shifting priorities among Northern Republicans, white Southerners' commitment to white supremacy, backed by legal restrictions, as well as massive extralegal violence against blacks, all combined to stifle the promise of Reconstruction.

Yet the Reconstruction Era also saw major transformations in American society in the wake of the Civil War—new ways of organizing labor and family life, new institutions within and outside of the government, and new ideologies regarding the role of institutions and government in social and economic life. Many of the changes begun during Reconstruction laid the groundwork for later revolutions in American life.

The President vs. Congress

What conflicts arose among Lincoln, Johnson, and Congress during Reconstruction?

The problem of how to reconstruct the Union in the wake of the South's military defeat was one of the most difficult and perplexing challenges ever faced by American policy makers. The Constitution provided no firm guidelines, for the framers had not anticipated a division of the country into warring sections. After emancipation became a northern war aim, the problem was compounded by a new issue: How far should the federal government go to secure freedom and civil rights for four million former slaves?

The debate that evolved led to a major political crisis. Advocates of a minimal Reconstruction policy favored quick restoration of the Union with no protection for the freed slaves beyond the prohibition of slavery. Proponents of a more radical policy wanted readmission of the southern states to be dependent on guarantees that "loyal" men would displace the Confederate elite in positions of power and that blacks would acquire basic rights of American citizenship. The White House favored the minimal approach, whereas Congress came to endorse the more radical and thoroughgoing form of Reconstruction. The resulting struggle between Congress and the chief executive was the most serious clash between two branches of government in the nation's history.

Wartime Reconstruction

Tension between the president and Congress over how to reconstruct the Union began during the war. Occupied mainly with achieving victory, Lincoln never set forth a final and comprehensive plan for bringing rebellious states back into the fold. But he did take initiatives that indicated he favored a lenient and conciliatory policy toward Southerners who would give up the struggle and repudiate slavery. In December 1863, he issued a Proclamation of Amnesty and Reconstruction, which offered a full pardon to all Southerners (with the exception of certain classes of Confederate leaders) who would take an oath of allegiance to the Union and acknowledge the legality of emancipation. This **Ten Percent Plan** provided that once 10 percent or more of the voting population of any occupied state had taken the oath, they were authorized to set up a loyal government. By 1864, Louisiana and Arkansas, states that were wholly or partially occupied by Union troops, had established Unionist governments. Lincoln's policy was meant to shorten the war. First, he hoped to weaken the southern cause by making it easy for disillusioned or lukewarm Confederates to switch sides. Second, he hoped to further his emancipation policy by insisting that the new governments abolish slavery.

Congress was unhappy with the president's Reconstruction experiments and in 1864 refused to seat the Unionists elected to the House and Senate from Louisiana and Arkansas. A minority of congressional Republicans—the strongly antislavery **Radical Republicans**—favored protection for black rights (especially black male suffrage) as a precondition for the readmission of southern states. But a larger group of congressional moderates opposed Lincoln's plan, not on the basis of black rights but because they did not trust the repentant Confederates who would play a major role in the new governments. They feared that the old ruling class would return to power and cheat the North of the full fruits of its impending victory.

Congress also believed the president was exceeding his authority by using executive powers to restore the Union. Lincoln operated on the theory that secession, being illegal, did not place the Confederate states outside the Union in a constitutional sense. Since individuals and not states had defied federal authority, the president could use his pardoning power to certify a loyal electorate, which could then function as the legitimate state government.

The dominant view in Congress, however, was that the southern states had forfeited their place in the Union and that it was up to Congress to decide when and how they would be readmitted. The most popular justification for congressional responsibility was based on the clause of the Constitution providing that "the United States shall guarantee to every State in this Union a Republican Form of Government." By seceding, Radicals argued, the Confederate states had ceased to be republican, and Congress had to set the conditions to be met before they could be readmitted.

After refusing to recognize Lincoln's 10 percent governments, Congress passed a Reconstruction bill of its own in July 1864. Known as the **Wade-Davis Bill**, this legislation required that 50 percent of the voters take an oath of future loyalty before the restoration process could begin. Once this had occurred, those who could swear they had never willingly supported the Confederacy could vote in an election for delegates to a constitutional convention. The bill in its final form did not require black suffrage, but it did give federal courts the power to enforce emancipation. Faced with this attempt to nullify his own program, Lincoln exercised a pocket veto by refusing to sign the bill before Congress adjourned. He justified his action by announcing that he did not want to be committed to any single Reconstruction plan. The sponsors of the bill responded with an angry manifesto, and Lincoln's relations with Congress reached their low.

Congress and the president remained stalemated on the Reconstruction issue for the rest of the war. During his last months in office, however, Lincoln showed some willingness to compromise. He persisted in his efforts to obtain full recognition for the governments he had nurtured in Louisiana and Arkansas but seemed receptive to the setting of other conditions—perhaps including black suffrage—for readmission of those states where wartime conditions had prevented execution of his plan. However, he died without clarifying his intentions, leaving historians to speculate whether his

quarrel with Congress would have worsened or been resolved. Given Lincoln's past record of political flexibility, the best bet is that he would have come to terms with the majority of his party.

Andrew Johnson at the Helm

Andrew Johnson, the man suddenly made president by an assassin's bullet, attempted to put the Union back together on his own authority in 1865. But his policies eventually set him at odds with Congress and the Republican party and provoked the most serious crisis in the history of relations between the executive and legislative branches of the federal government.

Johnson's background shaped his approach to Reconstruction. Born in dire poverty in North Carolina, he migrated as a young

Read the Document   Thirteenth, Fourteenth, and Fifteenth Amendments (1865, 1868, 1870)

In this cartoon, President Andrew Johnson (left) and Thaddeus Stevens, the Radical Republican Congressman from Pennsylvania, are depicted as train engineers in a deadlock on the tracks. Indeed, neither Johnson nor Stevens would give way on his plans for Reconstruction.

▭● Read the Document   The Mississippi Black Code (1865)

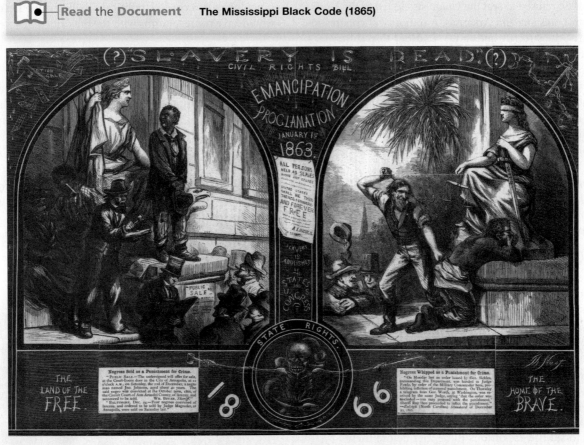

"Slavery Is Dead?" asks this 1866 cartoon by Thomas Nast. To the cartoonist, the Emancipation Proclamation of 1863 and the North's victory in the Civil War meant little difference to the treatment of the freed slaves in the South. Freed slaves convicted of crimes often endured the same punishments as had slaves—sale, as depicted in the left panel of the cartoon, or beatings, as shown on the right.

man to eastern Tennessee, where he made his living as a tailor. Lacking formal schooling, he did not learn to read and write until adult life. Entering politics as a Jacksonian Democrat, he became known as an effective stump speaker. His railing against the planter aristocracy made him the spokesman for Tennessee's nonslaveholding whites and the most successful politician in the state. He advanced from state legislator to congressman to governor and in 1857 was elected to the U.S. Senate.

When Tennessee seceded in 1861, Johnson was the only senator from a Confederate state who remained loyal to the Union and continued to serve in Washington. But his Unionism and defense of the common people did not include antislavery sentiments. Nor was he friendly to blacks. While campaigning in Tennessee, he had objected only to the fact that slaveholding was the privilege of a wealthy minority. He revealed his attitude when he wished that "every head of family in the United States had one slave to take the drudgery and menial service off his family."

During the war, while acting as military governor of Tennessee, Johnson endorsed Lincoln's emancipation policy and carried it into effect. But he viewed it primarily as a means of destroying the power of the hated planter class rather than as a recognition of black humanity. He was chosen as Lincoln's running mate in 1864 because it was thought that a proadministration Democrat, who was a southern Unionist in the bargain, would strengthen the ticket.

No one expected Johnson to succeed to the presidency; it is one of the strange accidents of American history that a southern Democrat, a fervent white supremacist, came to preside over a Republican administration immediately after the Civil War.

Some Radical Republicans initially welcomed Johnson's ascent to the nation's highest office. Their hopes make sense in the light of Johnson's record of fierce loyalty to the Union and his apparent agreement with the Radicals that ex-Confederates should be severely treated. More than Lincoln, who had spoken of "malice toward none and charity for all," Johnson seemed likely to punish southern "traitors" and prevent them from regaining political influence. Only gradually did the deep disagreement between the president and the Republican Congressional majority become evident.

The Reconstruction policy that Johnson initiated on May 29, 1865, created some uneasiness among the Radicals, but most Republicans were willing to give it a chance. Johnson placed North Carolina and eventually other states under appointed provisional governors chosen mostly from among prominent southern politicians who had opposed the secession movement and had rendered no conspicuous service to the Confederacy. The governors were responsible for calling constitutional conventions and ensuring that only "loyal" whites were permitted to vote for delegates. Participation required taking the oath of allegiance that Lincoln had prescribed earlier. Once again, Confederate leaders and former officeholders who had participated in the rebellion were excluded. To regain their political and property rights, those in the exempted categories had to apply for individual presidential pardons. Johnson made one significant addition to the list of the excluded: all those possessing taxable property exceeding $20,000 in value. In this fashion, he sought to prevent his longtime adversaries—the wealthy planters—from participating in the Reconstruction of southern state governments.

Once the conventions met, Johnson urged them to do three things: Declare the ordinances of secession illegal, repudiate the Confederate debt, and ratify the **Thirteenth Amendment** abolishing slavery. After governments had been reestablished under constitutions meeting these conditions, the president assumed that the Reconstruction process would be complete and that the ex-Confederate states could regain their full rights under the Constitution.

The results of the conventions, which were dominated by prewar Unionists and representatives of backcountry yeoman farmers, were satisfactory to the president but troubling to many congressional Republicans. Rather than quickly accepting Johnson's recommendations, delegates in several states approved them begrudgingly or with qualifications. Furthermore, all the resulting constitutions limited suffrage to whites, disappointing the large number of Northerners who hoped, as Lincoln had, that at least some African Americans—perhaps those who were educated or had served in the Union army—would be given the right to vote. Johnson on the whole seemed eager to give southern white majorities a free hand in determining the civil and political status of the freed slaves.

Republican uneasiness turned to disillusionment and anger when the state legislatures elected under the new constitutions proceeded to pass **Black Codes** subjecting former slaves to a variety of special regulations and restrictions on their freedom. (For more on the Black Codes, see p. 376.) To Radicals, the Black Codes looked suspiciously like slavery under a new guise. More upsetting to northern public opinion in general, a number of prominent ex-Confederate leaders were elected to Congress in the fall of 1865.

Johnson himself was partly responsible for this turn of events. Despite his lifelong feud with the planter class, he was generous in granting pardons to members of the old elite who came to him, hat in hand, and asked for them. When former Confederate vice president Alexander Stephens and other proscribed ex-rebels were elected to Congress although they had not been pardoned, Johnson granted them special amnesty so they could serve.

The growing rift between the president and Congress came into the open in December, when the House and Senate refused to seat the recently elected southern delegation. Instead of endorsing Johnson's work and recognizing the state governments he had called into being, Congress established a joint committee, chaired by Senator William Pitt Fessenden of Maine, to review Reconstruction policy and set further conditions for readmission of the seceded states.

Congress Takes the Initiative

The struggle over how to reconstruct the Union ended with Congress doing the job of setting policy all over again. The clash between Johnson and Congress was a matter of principle and could not be reconciled. President Johnson, an heir of the Democratic states' rights tradition, wanted to restore the prewar federal system as quickly as possible and without change except that states would not have the right to legalize slavery or to secede.

Most Republicans wanted firm guarantees that the old southern ruling class would not regain regional power and national influence by devising new ways to subjugate blacks. They favored a Reconstruction policy that would give the federal government authority to limit the political role of ex-Confederates and provide some protection for black citizenship.

Republican leaders—with the exception of a few extreme Radicals such as Charles Sumner—lacked any firm conviction that blacks were inherently equal to whites. They did believe, however, that in a modern democratic state, all citizens must have the same basic rights and opportunities, regardless of natural abilities. Principle coincided easily with political expediency; southern blacks, whatever their alleged shortcomings, were likely to be loyal to the Republican party that had emancipated them. They could be used, if necessary, to counteract the influence of resurgent ex-Confederates, thus preventing the Democrats from returning to national dominance through control of the South.

The disagreement between the president and Congress became irreconcilable in early 1866, when Johnson vetoed two bills that had passed with overwhelming Republican support. The first extended the life of the **Freedmen's Bureau**—a temporary agency set up to aid the former slaves by providing relief, education, legal help, and assistance in obtaining land or employment. The second was a civil rights bill meant to nullify the Black Codes and guarantee to freedmen "full and equal benefit of all laws and proceedings for the security of person and property as is enjoyed by white citizens."

Johnson's vetoes shocked moderate Republicans who had expected the president to accept the relatively modest measures as a way of heading off more radical proposals, such as black suffrage and a prolonged denial of political rights to ex-Confederates. Presidential opposition to policies that represented the bare minimum of Republican demands on the South alienated moderates in the party and ensured a wide opposition to Johnson's plan of Reconstruction. Johnson succeeded in blocking the Freedmen's Bureau bill, although a modified version later passed. But the Civil Rights Act won the two-thirds majority necessary to override his veto, signifying that the president was now hopelessly at odds with most of the congressmen from what was supposed to be his own party. Never before had Congress overridden a presidential veto.

Johnson soon revealed that he intended to abandon the Republicans and place himself at the head of a new conservative party uniting the small minority of Republicans who supported him with a reviving Democratic party that was rallying behind his Reconstruction policy. In preparation for the elections of 1866, Johnson helped found the National Union movement to promote his plan to readmit the southern states to the Union without further qualifications. A National Union convention meeting in Philadelphia in August 1866 called for the election to Congress of men who endorsed the presidential plan for Reconstruction.

Meanwhile, the Republican majority on Capitol Hill, fearing that Johnson would not enforce civil rights legislation or that the courts would declare such federal laws unconstitutional, passed the **Fourteenth Amendment**. This, perhaps the most important of all the constitutional amendments, gave the federal government responsibility for guaranteeing equal rights under the law to all Americans. Section 1 defined national citizenship for the first time as extending to "all persons born or naturalized in the United States." The states were prohibited from abridging the rights of American citizens and could not "deprive any person of life, liberty, or property, without due process of law; nor deny to any person . . . equal protection of the laws."

The other sections of the amendment were important in the context of the time but had fewer long-term implications. Section 2 sought to penalize the South for denying voting rights to black men by reducing the congressional representation of any state that formally deprived a portion of its male citizens of the right to vote. Section 3 denied federal office to those who had taken an oath of office to support the U.S. Constitution and then had supported the Confederacy, and Section 4 repudiated the Confederate debt. The amendment was sent to the states with the understanding that Southerners would have no chance of being readmitted to Congress unless their states ratified it.

The congressional elections of 1866 served as a referendum on the Fourteenth Amendment. Johnson opposed the amendment on the grounds that it created a "centralized" government and denied states the right to manage their own affairs; he also counseled southern state legislatures to reject it, and all except Tennessee followed his advice. But the president's case for state autonomy was weakened by the publicity resulting from bloody race riots in New Orleans and Memphis. These and other reported atrocities against blacks made it clear that the existing southern state governments were failing abysmally to protect the "life, liberty, or property" of ex-slaves.

Johnson further weakened his cause by campaigning for candidates who supported his policies. In his notorious "swing around the circle," he toured the nation, slandering his opponents in crude language and engaging in undignified exchanges with hecklers. Enraged by southern inflexibility and the antics of a president who acted as if he were still campaigning in the backwoods of Tennessee, northern voters repudiated the administration. The Republican majority in Congress increased to a solid two-thirds in both houses, and the Radical wing of the party gained strength at the expense of moderates and conservatives.

Congressional Reconstruction Plan Enacted

Congress was now in a position to implement its own plan of Reconstruction. In 1867 and 1868, it passed a series of acts that nullified the president's initiatives and reorganized the South on a new

basis. Generally referred to as **Radical Reconstruction**, the measures actually represented a compromise between genuine Radicals and more moderate Republicans.

Consistent Radicals such as Senator Charles Sumner of Massachusetts and Congressmen Thaddeus Stevens of Pennsylvania and George Julian of Indiana wanted to reshape southern society before readmitting ex-Confederates to the Union. Their program of "regeneration before Reconstruction" required an extended period of military rule, confiscation and redistribution of large landholdings among the freedmen, and federal aid for schools to educate blacks and whites for citizenship. But the majority of Republican congressmen found such a program unacceptable because it broke too sharply with American traditions of federalism and regard for property rights and might mean that decades would pass before the Union was back in working order.

The First Reconstruction Act, passed over Johnson's veto on March 2, 1867, placed the South under the rule of the army by reorganizing the region into five military districts. But military rule would last for only a short time. Subsequent acts of 1867 and 1868 opened the way for the quick readmission of any state that framed and ratified a new constitution providing for black suffrage. Ex-Confederates disqualified from holding federal office under the Fourteenth Amendment were prohibited from voting for delegates to the constitutional conventions or in the elections to ratify the conventions' work. Since blacks were allowed to participate in this process, Republicans thought they had found a way to ensure that "loyal" men would dominate the new governments. Radical Reconstruction was based on the dubious assumption that once blacks had the vote, they would have the power to protect themselves against white supremacists' efforts to deny them their rights. The Reconstruction Acts thus signaled a retreat from the true Radical position that a sustained use of federal authority was needed to complete the transition from slavery to freedom and prevent the resurgence of the South's old ruling class. (Troops were used in the South after 1868, but only in a very limited and sporadic way.) The majority of Republicans were unwilling to embrace centralized government and an extended period of military rule over civilians, and even Radicals such as Thaddeus Stevens supported the compromise as the best that could be achieved. Yet a genuine spirit of democratic idealism did give legitimacy and fervor to the cause of black male suffrage. Enabling people who were so poor and

RECONSTRUCTION AMENDMENTS, 1865–1870

Amendment	Main Provisions	Congressional Passage (2/3 majority in each house required)	Ratification Process (3/4 of all states required, including ex-Confederate states)
13	Slavery prohibited in United States	January 1865	December 1865 (27 states, including 8 southern states)
14	National citizenship; state representation in Congress reduced proportionally to number of voters disfranchised; former Confederates denied right to hold office; Confederate debt repudiated	June 1866	Rejected by 12 southern and border states, February 1867; Radicals make readmission of southern states hinge on ratification; ratified July 1868
15	Denial of franchise because of race, color, or past servitude explicitly prohibited	February 1869	Ratification required for readmission of Virginia, Texas, Mississippi, Georgia; ratified March 1870

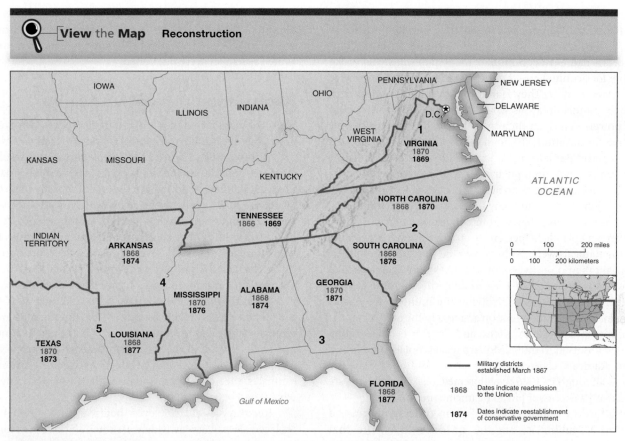

View the Map   Reconstruction

RECONSTRUCTION   During the Reconstruction era, the southern state governments passed through three phases: control by white ex-Confederates; domination by Republican legislators, both white and black; and, finally, the regain of control by conservative white Democrats.

downtrodden to have access to the ballot box was a bold and innovative application of the principle of government by the consent of the governed. The problem was finding a way to enforce equal suffrage under conditions then existing in the postwar South.

The Impeachment Crisis

The first obstacle to enforcement of congressional Reconstruction was resistance from the White House. Johnson thoroughly disapproved of the new policy and sought to thwart the will of Congress by administering the plan in his own obstructive fashion. He immediately began to dismiss officeholders who sympathized with Radical Reconstruction, and he countermanded the orders of generals in charge of southern military districts who were zealous in their enforcement of the new legislation. Some Radical generals were transferred and replaced by conservative Democrats. Congress responded by passing laws designed to limit presidential authority over Reconstruction matters. One of the measures was the Tenure of Office Act, requiring Senate approval for the removal of cabinet officers and other officials whose appointment had needed the consent of the Senate. Another measure—a rider to an army appropriations bill—sought to limit Johnson's authority to issue orders to military commanders.

Johnson objected vigorously to the restrictions on the grounds that they violated the constitutional doctrine of the separation of powers. When it became clear that the president was resolute in fighting for his powers and using them to resist the establishment

of Radical regimes in the southern states, some congressmen began to call for his impeachment. A preliminary effort foundered in 1867, but when Johnson tried to discharge Secretary of War Edwin Stanton—the only Radical in the cabinet—and persisted in his efforts despite the disapproval of the Senate, the proimpeachment forces gained in strength.

In January 1868, Johnson ordered General Grant, who already commanded the army, to replace Stanton as head of the War Department. But Grant had his eye on the Republican presidential nomination and refused to defy Congress. Johnson subsequently appointed General Lorenzo Thomas, who agreed to serve. Faced with this apparent violation of the Tenure of Office Act, the House voted overwhelmingly to impeach the president on February 24, and he was placed on trial before the Senate.

Because seven Republican senators broke with the party leadership and voted for acquittal, the effort to convict Johnson and remove him from office fell one vote short of the necessary two-thirds. This outcome resulted in part from a skillful defense. Attorneys for the president argued for a narrow interpretation of the constitutional provision that a president could be impeached only for "high crimes and misdemeanors," asserting that this referred only to indictable offenses. Responding to the charge that Johnson had deliberately violated the Tenure of Office Act, the defense contended that the law did not apply to the removal of Stanton because he had been appointed by Lincoln, not Johnson.

The prosecution countered with a different interpretation of the Tenure of Office Act, but the core of their case was that Johnson had abused the powers of his office in an effort to sabotage the congressional Reconstruction policy. Obstructing the will of the legislative branch, they claimed, was sufficient grounds for conviction even if no crime had been committed. The Republicans who broke ranks to vote for acquittal could not endorse such a broad view of the impeachment power. They feared that removal of a president for essentially political reasons would threaten the constitutional balance of powers and open the way to legislative supremacy over the executive. In addition, the man who would have succeeded Johnson—Senator Benjamin Wade of Ohio, the president pro tem of the Senate—was unpopular with conservative Republicans because of his radical position on labor and currency questions.

Although Johnson's acquittal by the narrowest of margins protected the American presidency from congressional domination, the impeachment episode helped create an impression in the public mind that the Radicals were ready to turn the Constitution to their own use to gain their objectives. Conservatives were again alarmed when Congress took action in 1868 to deny the Supreme Court's appellate jurisdiction in cases involving the military arrest and imprisonment of anti-Reconstruction activists in the South. But the evidence of congressional ruthlessness and illegality is not as strong as most historians used to think. Modern legal scholars have found merit in the Radicals' claim that their actions did not violate the Constitution, although in 1926 the Supreme Court held the Tenure of Office Act and a successor law to be unconstitutional.

Their failure to remove Johnson from office embarrassed congressional Republicans, but the episode did ensure that Reconstruction in the South would proceed as the majority in Congress intended. During the trial, Johnson helped influence the verdict by pledging to enforce the Reconstruction Acts, and he held to this promise during his remaining months in office. Unable to depose the president, the Radicals had at least succeeded in neutralizing his opposition to their program.

Reconstructing Southern Society

What problems did southern society face during Reconstruction?

The Civil War left the South devastated, demoralized, and destitute. Slavery was dead, but what this meant for future relationships between whites and blacks was still in doubt. The overwhelming majority of southern whites wanted to keep blacks adrift between slavery and freedom—without rights, in a status resembling that of the "free Negroes" of the Old South. Blacks sought independence from their former masters and viewed the acquisition of land, education, and the vote as the best means of achieving this goal. The thousands of Northerners who went south after the war for materialistic or humanitarian reasons hoped to extend Yankee "civilization" to what they viewed as an unenlightened and barbarous region. For most of them, this reformation required the aid of the freedmen; not enough southern whites were willing to accept the new order and embrace northern middle-class values.

The struggle of these groups to achieve their conflicting goals bred chaos, violence, and instability. Unsettled conditions created many opportunities for corruption, crime, and terrorism. This was scarcely an ideal setting for an experiment in interracial democracy, but one was attempted nonetheless. Its success depended on massive and sustained support from the federal government. To the extent that this was forthcoming, progressive reform could be achieved. When federal support faltered, the forces of reaction and white supremacy were unleashed.

Reorganizing Land and Labor

The Civil War scarred the southern landscape and wrecked its economy. One devastated area—central South Carolina—looked to an 1865 observer "like a broad black streak of ruin and desolation—the fences are gone; lonesome smokestacks, surrounded by dark heaps of ashes and cinders, marking the spots where human habitations had stood; the fields all along the roads widely overgrown with weeds, with here and there a sickly patch of cotton or corn cultivated by negro squatters." Other areas through which the armies had passed were similarly ravaged. Several major cities—including Atlanta, Columbia, and Richmond—were gutted by fire. Most factories were dismantled or destroyed, and long stretches of railroad were torn up.

Physical ruin would not have been so disastrous if investment capital had been available for rebuilding. But the substantial wealth represented by Confederate currency and bonds had melted away, and emancipation of the slaves had divested the propertied classes of their most valuable and productive assets. According to some estimates, the South's per capita wealth in 1865 was only about half what it had been in 1860.

Recovery could not even begin until a new labor system replaced slavery. It was widely assumed in both the North and the South that southern prosperity would continue to depend on cotton and that the plantation was the most efficient unit for producing the crop. Hindering efforts to rebuild the plantation economy were lack of capital, the deep-rooted belief of southern whites that blacks would work only under compulsion, and the freedmen's resistance to labor conditions that recalled slavery.

Blacks strongly preferred to determine their own economic relationships, and for a time they had reason to hope the federal government would support their ambitions. The freed slaves were placed in a precarious position and were, in effect, fighting a two-front war. Although they were grateful for the federal aid in ending slavery, freed slaves often had ideas about freedom that contradicted the plans of their northern allies. Many ex-slaves wanted to hold on to the family-based communal work methods that they utilized during slavery. Freed slaves in areas of South Carolina, for example, attempted to maintain the family task system rather than adopting the individual piecework system pushed by northern capitalists. Many ex-slaves opposed plans to turn them into wage laborers who produced exclusively for a market. Finally, freed slaves often wanted to stay on the land their families had spent generations farming rather than move elsewhere to assume plots of land as individual farmers.

While not guaranteeing all of the freed slaves' hopes for economic self-determination, the northern military attempted to establish a new economic base for the freed men and women. General Sherman, hampered by the huge numbers of black fugitives that followed his army on its famous march, issued an order in January 1865 that set aside the islands and coastal areas of Georgia and South Carolina for exclusive black occupancy on 40-acre plots. Furthermore, the Freedmen's Bureau, as one of its many responsibilities, was given control of hundreds of thousands of acres of

📖—⎡Read the **Document**   A Sharecrop Contract (1882)

The Civil War brought emancipation to slaves, but the sharecropping system kept many of them economically bound to their employers. At the end of a year the sharecropper tenants might owe most—or all—of what they had made to their landlord. Here, a sharecropping family poses in front of their cabin. Ex-slaves often built their living quarters near woods in order to have a ready supply of fuel for heating and cooking. The cabin's chimney lists away from the house so that it can be easily pushed away from the living quarters should it catch fire.
Source: Collection of the New-York Historical Society—Negative number 50475.

giving them something they allegedly had not earned, and the desire to restore cotton production as quickly as possible to increase agricultural exports and stabilize the economy. Consequently, most blacks in physical possession of small farms failed to acquire title, and the mass of freedmen were left with little or no prospect of becoming landowners. Recalling the plight of southern blacks in 1865, an ex-slave later wrote that "they were set free without a dollar, without a foot of land, and without the wherewithal to get the next meal even."

Despite their poverty and landlessness, ex-slaves were reluctant to settle down and commit themselves to wage labor for their former masters. Many took to the road, hoping to find something better. Some were still expecting grants of land, but others were simply trying to increase their bargaining power. One freedman later recalled that an important part of being free was that, "we could move around [and] change bosses." As the end of 1865 approached, many freedmen had still not signed up for the coming season; anxious planters feared that blacks were plotting to seize land by force. Within a few weeks, however, most holdouts signed for the best terms they could get.

One common form of agricultural employment in 1866 was a contract labor system. Under this system, workers committed themselves for a year in return for fixed wages, a substantial portion of which was withheld until after the harvest. Since many planters were inclined to drive hard bargains, abuse their workers, or cheat them at the end of the year, the Freedmen's Bureau assumed the role of reviewing the contracts and enforcing them. But bureau officials had differing notions of what it meant to protect African Americans from exploitation. Some stood up strongly for the rights of the freedmen; others served as allies of the planters, rounding up available workers, coercing them to sign contracts for low wages, and then helping keep them in line.

abandoned or confiscated land and was authorized to make 40-acre grants to black settlers for three-year periods, after which they would have the option to buy at low prices. By June 1865, forty thousand black farmers were at work on 300,000 acres of what they thought would be their own land. (For more on this, see the Feature Essay, "Forty Acres and A Mule," pp. 384–385.)

But for most of them the dream of "forty acres and a mule," or some other arrangement that would give them control of their land and labor, was not to be realized. President Johnson pardoned the owners of most of the land consigned to the ex-slaves by Sherman and the Freedmen's Bureau, and proposals for an effective program of land confiscation and redistribution failed to get through Congress. Among the considerations prompting most congressmen to oppose land reform were a tenderness for property rights, fear of sapping the freedmen's initiative by

The bureau's influence waned after 1867 (it was phased out completely by 1869), and the experiment with contract wage labor was abandoned. Growing up alongside the contract system and eventually displacing it was an alternative capital-labor relationship—**sharecropping**. First in small groups known as "squads" and later as individual families, blacks worked a piece of land independently for a fixed share of the crop, usually one-half. The advantage of this arrangement for credit-starved landlords was that it did not require much expenditure in advance of the harvest. The system also forced the tenant to share the risks of crop failure or a fall in cotton prices. These considerations loomed larger after disastrous harvests in 1866 and 1867.

African Americans initially viewed sharecropping as a step up from wage labor in the direction of landownership. But during the 1870s, this form of tenancy evolved into a new kind of servitude.

Croppers had to live on credit until their cotton was sold, and planters or merchants seized the chance to "provision" them at high prices and exorbitant rates of interest. Creditors were entitled to deduct what was owed to them out of the tenant's share of the crop, and this left most sharecroppers with no net profit at the end of the year—more often than not with a debt that had to be worked off in subsequent years. Various methods, legal and extralegal, were eventually devised in an effort to bind indebted tenants to a single landlord for extended periods, but considerable movement was still possible.

Black Codes: A New Name for Slavery?

While landless African Americans in the countryside were being reduced to economic dependence, those in towns and cities found themselves living in an increasingly segregated society. The Black Codes of 1865 attempted to require separation of the races in public places and facilities; when most of the codes were overturned by federal authorities as violations of the Civil Rights Act of 1866, the same end was often achieved through private initiative and community pressure. In some cities, blacks successfully resisted being consigned to separate streetcars by appealing to the military during the period when it exercised authority or by organizing boycotts. But they found it almost impossible to gain admittance to most hotels, restaurants, and other privately owned establishments catering to whites. Although separate black, or "Jim Crow," cars were not yet the rule on railroads, African Americans were often denied first-class accommodations. After 1868, black-supported Republican governments passed civil rights acts requiring equal access to public facilities, but little effort was made to enforce the legislation.

The Black Codes had other onerous provisions meant to control African Americans and return them to quasi-slavery. Most codes even made black unemployment a crime, which meant blacks had to make long-term contracts with white employers or be arrested for vagrancy. Others limited the rights of African Americans to own property or engage in occupations other than those of servant or laborer. The codes were set aside by the actions of Congress, the military, and the Freedmen's Bureau, but vagrancy laws remained in force across the South.

Furthermore, private violence and discrimination against blacks continued on a massive scale unchecked by state authorities. Hundreds, perhaps thousands, of blacks were murdered by whites in 1865–1866, and few of the perpetrators were brought to justice. The imposition of military rule in 1867 was designed in part to protect former slaves from such violence and intimidation, but the task was beyond the capacity of the few thousand troops stationed in the South. When new constitutions were approved and states readmitted to the Union under the congressional plan in 1868, the problem became more severe. White opponents of Radical Reconstruction adopted systematic terrorism and organized mob violence to keep blacks away from the polls.

The freed slaves, in the face of opposition from both their Democratic enemies and some of their Republican allies, tried to defend themselves by organizing their own militia groups for protection and to assert their political rights. However, the militia groups were not powerful enough to overcome the growing power of the anti-Republican forces. Also, the military presence was progressively reduced, leaving the new Republican regimes to fight a losing battle against armed white supremacists. In the words of historian William Gillette, "there was simply no federal force large enough to give heart to black Republicans or to bridle southern white violence."

Republican Rule in the South

Hastily organized in 1867, the southern Republican party dominated the constitution making of 1868 and the regimes that came out of it. The party was an attempted coalition of three social groups (which varied in their relative strength from state to state). One was the same class that was becoming the backbone of the Republican party in the North—businessmen with an interest in enlisting government aid for private enterprise. Many Republicans of this stripe were recent arrivals from the North—the so-called carpetbaggers—but some were scalawags, former Whig planters or merchants who were born in the South or had immigrated to the region before the war and now saw a chance to realize their dreams for commercial and industrial development.

Poor white farmers, especially those from upland areas where Unionist sentiment had been strong during the Civil War, were a second element in the original coalition. These owners of small farms expected the party to favor their interests at the expense of the wealthy landowners and to come to their aid with special legislation when—as was often the case in this period of economic upheaval—they faced the loss of their homesteads to creditors. Newly enfranchised blacks were the third group to which the Republicans appealed. Blacks formed the vast majority of the Republican rank and file in most states and were concerned mainly with education, civil rights, and landownership.

Under the best of conditions, these coalitions would have been difficult to maintain. Each group had its own distinct goals and did not fully support the aims of the other segments. White yeomen, for example, had a deeply rooted resistance to black equality. And for how long could one expect essentially conservative businessmen to support costly measures for the elevation or relief of the lower classes of either race? In some states, astute Democratic politicians exploited these divisions by appealing to disaffected white Republicans.

But during the relatively brief period when they were in power in the South—varying from one to nine years depending on the state—the Republicans made some notable achievements. They established (on paper at least) the South's first adequate systems of public education, democratized state and local government, and appropriated funds for an enormous expansion of public services and responsibilities.

As important as these social and political reforms were, they took second place to the Republicans' major effort—to foster economic development and restore southern prosperity by subsidizing the construction of railroads and other internal improvements. But the policy of aiding railroads turned out to be disastrous, even though it addressed the region's real economic needs and was initially very popular. Extravagance, corruption, and routes laid out in response to local political pressure rather than on sound economic grounds made for an increasing burden of public debt and taxation.

The policy did not produce the promised payoff of efficient, cheap transportation. Subsidized railroads frequently went bankrupt, leaving the taxpayers holding the bag. When the Panic of 1873 brought many southern state governments to the verge of bankruptcy, and railroad building came to an end, it was clear the Republicans' "gospel of prosperity" through state aid to private enterprise had failed miserably. Their political opponents, many of whom had originally favored such policies, now saw an opportunity to take advantage of the situation by charging that Republicans had ruined the southern economy.

In general, the Radical regimes failed to conduct public business honestly and efficiently. Embezzlement of public funds and bribery of state lawmakers or officials were common occurrences. State debts and tax burdens rose enormously, mainly because governments had undertaken heavy new responsibilities, but partly because of waste and graft. The situation varied from state to state; ruling cliques in Louisiana and South Carolina were guilty of much wrongdoing, yet Mississippi had a relatively honest and frugal regime.

Furthermore, southern corruption was not exceptional, nor was it a special result of the extension of suffrage to uneducated African Americans, as critics of Radical Reconstruction have claimed. It was part of a national pattern during an era when private interests considered buying government favors to be a part of the cost of doing business, and many politicians expected to profit by obliging them.

Blacks bore only a limited responsibility for the dishonesty of the Radical governments. Although sixteen African Americans served in Congress—two in the Senate—between 1869 and 1880, only in South Carolina did blacks constitute a majority of even one house of the state legislature. Furthermore, no black governors were elected during Reconstruction (although Pinkney B. S. Pinchback served for a time as acting governor of Louisiana). The biggest grafters were opportunistic whites. Some of the most notorious were carpetbaggers, but others were native Southerners. Businessmen offering bribes included members of the prewar gentry who were staunch opponents of Radical programs. Some black legislators went with the tide and accepted "loans" from those railroad lobbyists who would pay most for their votes, but the same men could usually be depended on to vote the will of their constituents on civil rights or educational issues.

If blacks served or supported corrupt and wasteful regimes, it was because the alternative was dire. Although the Democrats, or Conservatives as they called themselves in some states, made sporadic efforts to attract African American voters, it was clear that if they won control, they would attempt to strip blacks of their civil and political rights. But opponents of Radical Reconstruction were able to capitalize on racial prejudice and persuade many Americans that "good government" was synonymous with white supremacy.

Contrary to myth, the small number of African Americans elected to state or national office during Reconstruction demonstrated on the average more integrity and competence than their white counterparts. Most were fairly well educated, having been free or unusually privileged slaves before the war. Among the most capable were Robert Smalls (whose career was described earlier); Blanche K. Bruce of Mississippi, elected to the U.S. Senate in 1874 after rising to deserved prominence in the Republican party of his home state; Congressman Robert Brown Elliott of South Carolina, an adroit politician who was also a consistent champion of civil rights; and Congressman James T. Rapier of Alabama, who stirred Congress and the nation in 1873 with his eloquent appeals for federal aid to southern education and new laws to enforce equal rights for African Americans.

Claiming Public and Private Rights

As important as party politics to the changing political culture of the Reconstruction South were the ways that freed slaves claimed rights for themselves. They did so not only in negotiations with employers and in public meetings and convention halls, but also through the institutions they created and perhaps most important, the households they formed.

As one black corporal in the Union Army told an audience of ex-slaves, "The Marriage covenant is at the foundation of all our rights. In slavery we could not have *legalized* marriage: *now* we have it . . . and we shall be established as a people." Through marriage, historian Laura Edwards tells us, African Americans claimed citizenship. Freedmen hoped that marriage would allow them to take on the rights that accrued to the independent head of a household, not only political rights, but the right to control the labor of wives and children for the first time.

While they were in effect in 1865–1866, many states' Black Codes included apprenticeship provisions, providing for freed children to be apprenticed by courts to some white person (with preference given to former masters) if their parents were paupers, unemployed, of "bad character," or even simply if it were found to be "better for the habits and comfort of a child." Ex-slaves struggled to win their children back from what often amounted to reenslavement. Freedpeople challenged the apprenticeship system in county courts, and through the Freedmen's Bureau. As one group of petitioners from Maryland asserted, "Our homes are invaded and our little ones seized at the family fireside."

While many former slaves lined up eagerly to formalize their marriages, many also retained their own definitions of marriage and defied the efforts of the Freedmen's Bureau to use the marriage relation as a disciplinary tool. Perhaps as many as 50 percent of ex-slaves chose not to marry legally, and whites criticized them heavily for it. African American leaders worried about this refusal to follow white norms. The army corporal who had described marriage as "the foundation of all our rights" urged his audience: "Let us conduct ourselves worthy of such a blessing—and all the people will respect us." Yet many poor blacks continued to recognize as husband and wife people who cared for and supported one another without benefit of legal sanction. The new legal system punished couples who deviated from the legal norm through laws against bastardy, adultery, and fornication. Furthermore, the Freedmen's Bureau made the marriage of freedpeople a priority because, as historian Noralee Frankel explained, "The agency's overriding concern was keeping blacks from depending on the federal government for economic assistance." Once married, the husband became legally responsible for his family's support.

Some ex-slaves used institutions formerly closed to them like the courts to assert rights against white people as well as other blacks, suing over domestic violence, child support, assault, and debt. Freed women sued their husbands for desertion and alimony in order to enlist the Freedmen's Bureau to help them claim property from men. Other ex-slaves mobilized kin networks and other community resources to make claims on property and family.

⦿ ⌐Watch the Video   The Schools that the Civil War and Reconstruction Created

A Freedmen's school, one of the more successful endeavors supported by the Freedmen's Bureau. The bureau, working with teachers from northern abolitionist and missionary societies, founded thousands of schools for freed slaves and poor whites.

Immediately after the war, freed people flocked to create institutions that had been denied to them under slavery: churches, fraternal and benevolent associations, political organizations, and schools. Many joined all-black denominations such as the African Methodist Episcopal Church, which provided freedom from white dominance and a more congenial style of worship. Black women formed all-black chapters of organizations such as the Women's Christian Temperance Union, and their own women's clubs to oppose lynching and work for "uplift" in the black community.

The freed slaves were thirsty for education. It is estimated that in 1865, less than two percent of black school-age children in the South attended school and only five percent could read. According to Charlotte Forten, a black teacher from Philadelphia, "I never before saw children so eager to learn . . . The majority learn with wonderful rapidity. Many of the grown people are desirous of learning to read. It is wonderful how a people who have been so long crushed to the earth, so embruted as these have been . . . can have so great a desire for knowledge and such a capability of sustaining it."

The first schools for freed people were all-black institutions established by the Freedmen's Bureau and various northern missionary societies. The teachers included both black and white Northerners and educated Southern blacks who were free before emancipation. At the time, having been denied all education during the antebellum period, most blacks viewed separate schooling as an opportunity rather than as a form of discrimination. However, these schools were precursors to the segregated public school systems first instituted by Republican governments. By 1870, the Freedmen's Bureau was sponsoring 4,239 schools and employing 9,300 teachers to teach 247,000 pupils in these all-black schools. Only in city schools of New Orleans and at the University of South Carolina were there serious attempts during Reconstruction to bring white and black students together in the same classrooms. Both the Freedmen's Bureau and the Northern Missionary Society also established Black colleges, which faced many struggles. The nondenominational private schools stressed industrial training but those supported by black churches emphasized a liberal arts education.

In a variety of ways, African American men and women during Reconstruction asserted freedom in the "private" realm as well as the public sphere, by claiming rights to their own families and building their own institutions. They did so despite the vigorous efforts of their former masters as well as the new government agencies to control their private lives and shape their new identities as husbands, wives, and citizens.

Retreat from Reconstruction

Why did Reconstruction end?

The era of Reconstruction began coming to an end almost before it got started. Although it was only a scant three years from the end of the Civil War, the impeachment crisis of 1868 represented the high point of popular interest in Reconstruction issues. That year, Ulysses S. Grant was elected president. Many historians blame Grant for the corruption of his administration and for the inconsistency and failure of his southern policy. He had neither the vision nor the sense of duty to tackle the difficult challenges the nation faced. From 1868 on, political issues other than southern Reconstruction moved to the forefront of national politics, and the plight of African Americans in the South receded in white consciousness.

Rise of the Money Question

In the years immediately following the Civil War, another issue already competing for public attention was the money question: whether to allow "greenbacks"—paper money issued during the war—to continue to circulate or to return to "sound" or "hard" money, meaning gold or silver. Supporters of paper money, known as greenbackers, were strongest in the credit-hungry West and among expansion-minded manufacturers. Defenders of hard money were mostly the commercial and financial interests in the East; they received crucial support from intellectuals who regarded government-sponsored inflation as immoral or contrary to the natural laws of classical economics.

In 1868, the money question surged briefly to the forefront of national politics. Faced with a business recession blamed on the Johnson administration's policy of contracting the currency, Congress voted to stop the retirement of greenbacks. The Democratic Party, responding to Midwestern pressure, included in its platform for the 1868 national election a plan calling for the redemption of much of the Civil War debt in greenbacks rather than gold. Yet they nominated for president a sound-money supporter, so that the greenback question never became an issue in the 1868 presidential campaign. Grant, already a popular general, won the election handily with the help of the Republican-dominated southern states.

In 1869 and 1870, a Republican-controlled Congress passed laws that assured payment in gold to most bondholders but eased the burden of the huge Civil War debt by exchanging bonds that were soon coming due for those that would not be payable for ten, fifteen, or thirty years. In this way, the public credit was protected.

Still unresolved, however, was the problem of what to do about the $356 million in greenbacks that remained in circulation. Hard-money proponents wanted to retire them quickly; inflationists thought more should be issued to stimulate the economy. The Grant administration followed the middle course of allowing the greenbacks to float until economic expansion would bring them to a par with gold, thus permitting a painless return to specie payments. But the Panic of 1873, which brought much of the economy to its knees, led to a revival of agitation to inflate the currency. Debt-ridden farmers, who would be the backbone of the greenback movement for years to come, now joined the soft-money clamor for the first time.

Responding to the money and credit crunch, Congress moved in 1874 to authorize a modest issue of new greenbacks. But Grant, influenced by the opinions of hard-money financiers, vetoed the bill. In 1875, Congress, led by Senator John Sherman of Ohio, enacted the Specie Resumption Act, which provided for a limited reduction of greenbacks leading to full resumption of specie payments by January 1, 1879. Its action was widely interpreted as deflation in the midst of depression. Farmers and workers, who were already suffering acutely from deflation, reacted with dismay and anger.

The Democratic Party could not capitalize adequately on these sentiments because of the influence of its own hard-money faction, and in 1876 an independent Greenback Party entered the national political arena. The party's nominee for president, Peter Cooper, received an insignificant number of votes, but in 1878 the Greenback Labor Party polled more than a million votes and elected fourteen congressmen. The Greenbackers were able to keep the money issue alive into the following decade.

THE ELECTION OF 1868

Candidate	Party	Popular Vote	Electoral Vote*
Grant	Republican	3,012,833	214
Seymour	Democratic	2,703,249	80
Not voted*		23	

*Unreconstructed states did not participate in the election.

Final Efforts of Reconstruction

The Republican effort to make equal rights for blacks the law of the land culminated in the **Fifteenth Amendment**. Passed by Congress in 1869 and ratified by the states in 1870, the amendment prohibited any state from denying a male citizen the right to vote because of race, color, or previous condition of servitude. A more radical version, requiring universal manhood suffrage, was rejected partly because it departed too sharply from traditional views of federal–state relations. States, therefore, could still limit the suffrage by imposing literacy tests, property qualifications, or poll taxes allegedly applying to all racial groups; such devices would eventually be used to strip southern blacks of the right to vote. But the makers of the amendment did not foresee this result. They believed their action would prevent future Congresses or southern constitutional conventions from repealing or nullifying the provisions for black male suffrage included in the Reconstruction acts. A secondary aim was to enfranchise African Americans in those northern states that still denied them the vote.

Many feminists were bitterly disappointed that the amendment did not also extend the vote to women as well as freedmen. A militant wing of the women's rights movement, led by Elizabeth Cady Stanton and Susan B. Anthony, was so angered that the Constitution was being amended in a way that, in effect, made gender a qualification for voting, that they campaigned against ratification of the Fifteenth Amendment. Another group of feminists led by Lucy Stone supported the amendment on the grounds that

View the **Closer Look** The First Vote

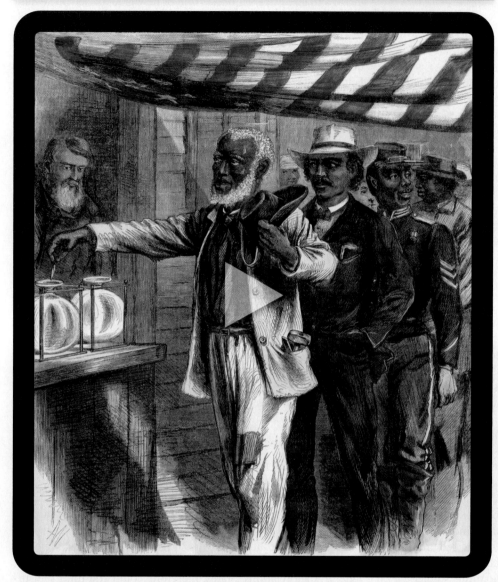

The First Vote, drawn by A. H. Ward for *Harper's Weekly*, November 16, 1867.

sought to exercise their political rights. First organized in Tennessee in 1866, the Klan spread rapidly to other states, adopting increasingly lawless and brutal tactics. A grassroots vigilante movement and not a centralized conspiracy, the Klan thrived on local initiative and gained support from whites of all social classes. Its secrecy, decentralization, popular support, and utter ruthlessness made it very difficult to suppress. As soon as blacks had been granted the right to vote, hooded "night riders" began to visit the cabins of those who were known to be active Republicans; some victims were only threatened, but others were whipped or even murdered. One black Georgian related a typical incident: "They broke my door open, took me out of bed, took me to the woods and whipped me three hours or more and left me for dead. They said to me, 'Do you think you will vote for another damned radical ticket?'"

Such methods were first used effectively in the presidential election of 1868. Grant lost in Louisiana and Georgia mainly because the Klan—or the Knights of the White Camellia, as the Louisiana variant was called—launched a reign of terror to prevent prospective black voters from exercising their rights. In Louisiana, political violence claimed more than a thousand lives, and in Arkansas, which Grant managed to carry, more than two hundred Republicans, including a congressman, were assassinated.

Thereafter, Klan terrorism was directed mainly at Republican state governments. Virtual insurrections broke out in Arkansas, Tennessee, North Carolina, and parts of South Carolina. Republican governors called out the state militia to fight the Klan, but only the Arkansas militia succeeded in bringing it to heel. In Tennessee, North Carolina, and Georgia, Klan activities helped undermine Republican control, thus allowing the Democrats to come to power in all of these states by 1870.

this was "the Negro's hour" and that women could afford to wait a few years for the vote. This disagreement divided the woman suffrage movement for a generation to come.

The Grant administration was charged with enforcing the amendment and protecting black men's voting rights in the reconstructed states. Since survival of the Republican regimes depended on African American support, political partisanship dictated federal action, even though the North's emotional and ideological commitment to black citizenship was waning.

A Reign of Terror Against Blacks

Between 1868 and 1872, the main threat to southern Republican regimes came from the **Ku Klux Klan** and other secret societies bent on restoring white supremacy by intimidating blacks who

Faced with the violent overthrow of the southern Republican party, Congress and the Grant administration were forced to act. A series of laws passed in 1870–1871 sought to enforce the Fifteenth Amendment by providing federal protection for black suffrage and authorizing use of the army against the Klan. The **Force acts**, also known as the Ku Klux Klan acts, made interference with voting rights a federal crime and established provisions for government supervision of elections. In addition, the legislation empowered the president to call out troops and suspend the writ of habeas corpus to quell insurrection. In 1871–1872, thousands of suspected Klansmen were arrested by the military or U.S. marshals, and the writ was suspended in nine counties of South Carolina that had been virtually taken over by the secret order. Although most of the

Read the **Document**   **Hannah Irwin Describes Ku Klux Klan Ride**

This 1868 photograph shows typical regalia of members of the Ku Klux Klan, a secret white supremacist organization. Before elections, hooded Klansmen terrorized African Americans to discourage them from voting.

accused Klansmen were never brought to trial, were acquitted, or received suspended sentences, the enforcement effort was vigorous enough to put a damper on hooded terrorism and ensure relatively fair and peaceful elections in 1872.

A heavy black turnout in these elections enabled the Republicans to hold on to power in most states of the Deep South, despite efforts of the Democratic-Conservative opposition to cut into the Republican vote by taking moderate positions on racial and economic issues. This setback prompted the Democratic-Conservatives to make a significant change in their strategy and ideology. No longer did they try to take votes away from the Republicans by proclaiming support for black suffrage and government aid to business. Instead they began to appeal openly to white supremacy and to the traditional Democratic and agrarian hostility to government promotion of economic development. Consequently, they were able to bring back to the polls a portion of the white electorate, mostly small farmers, who had not been turning out because they were alienated by the leadership's apparent concessions to Yankee ideas.

This new and more effective electoral strategy dovetailed with a resurgence of violence meant to reduce Republican, especially black Republican, voting. The new reign of terror differed from the previously discussed Klan episode; its agents no longer wore masks but acted quite openly. They were effective because the northern public was increasingly disenchanted with federal intervention on behalf of what were widely viewed as corrupt and tottering Republican regimes. Grant used force in the South for the last time in 1874 when an overt paramilitary organization in Louisiana, known as the White League, tried to overthrow a Republican government accused of stealing an election. When another unofficial militia in Mississippi instigated a series of bloody race riots prior to the state elections of 1875, Grant refused the governor's request for federal troops. As a result, black voters were successfully intimidated—one county registered only seven Republican votes where there had been a black majority of two thousand—and Mississippi fell to the Democratic-Conservatives. According to one account, Grant decided to withhold troops because he had been warned that intervention might cost the Republicans the crucial state of Ohio in the same off-year elections.

By 1876, Republicans held on to only three southern states: South Carolina, Louisiana, and Florida. Partly because of Grant's hesitant and inconsistent use of presidential power, but mainly because the northern electorate would no longer tolerate military action to sustain Republican governments and black voting rights, Radical Reconstruction was falling into total eclipse.

Spoilsmen vs. Reformers

One reason Grant found it increasingly difficult to take strong action to protect southern Republicans was the bad odor surrounding his stewardship of the federal government and the Republican party. Reformers charged that a corrupt national administration was propping up bad governments in the South for personal and partisan advantage. When Grant intervened in Louisiana in 1872 on behalf of a Republican faction headed by his wife's brother-in-law, who controlled federal patronage as collector of customs in New Orleans, it created the appearance of corruption, although Grant justified it on the ground that the opposing faction was blocking civil rights legislation for blacks.

The Republican party in the Grant era was losing the idealism and high purpose associated with the crusade against slavery. By the beginning of the 1870s, the men who had been the conscience of the party—old-line radicals such as Thaddeus Stevens, Charles Sumner, and Benjamin Wade—were either dead, out of office, or at odds with the administration. New leaders of a different stamp, whom historians have dubbed "spoilsmen" or "politicos," were taking their place. When he made common cause with hard-boiled manipulators such as senators Roscoe Conkling of New York and James G. Blaine of Maine, Grant lost credibility with reform-minded Republicans.

During Grant's first administration, an aura of scandal surrounded the White House but did not directly implicate the president. In 1869, the financial buccaneer Jay Gould enlisted the aid of a brother-in-law of Grant to further his fantastic scheme to corner the gold market. Gould failed in the attempt, but he did manage to save himself and come away with a huge profit.

Grant's first-term vice president, Schuyler Colfax of Indiana, was directly involved in the notorious Crédit Mobilier scandal. Crédit Mobilier was a construction company that actually served as a fraudulent device for siphoning off profits that should have gone to the stockholders of the Union Pacific Railroad, which was the beneficiary of massive federal land grants. To forestall government inquiry into this arrangement, Crédit Mobilier stock was distributed to influential congressmen, including Colfax (who was speaker of the House before he was elected vice president). The whole business came to light just before the campaign of 1872.

THE ELECTION OF 1872

Candidate	Party	Popular Vote	Electoral Vote*
Grant	Republican	3,597,132	286
Greeley	Democratic and Liberal Republican	2,834,125	Greeley died before the electoral college voted.

*Out of a total of 366 electoral votes. Greeley's votes were divided among the four minor candidates.

Republicans who could not tolerate such corruption or had other grievances against the administration broke with Grant in 1872 and formed a third party committed to "honest government" and "reconciliation" between the North and the South. Led initially by high-minded reformers such as Senator Carl Schurz of Missouri, the Liberal Republicans endorsed reform of the civil service to curb the corruption-breeding patronage system and advocated laissez-faire economic policies—which meant low tariffs, an end to government subsidies for railroads, and hard money. Despite their rhetoric of idealism and reform, the Liberal Republicans were extremely conservative in their notions of what government should do to assure justice for blacks and other underprivileged Americans.

The Liberal Republicans' national convention nominated Horace Greeley, editor of the respected *New York Tribune*. This was a curious and divisive choice, since Greeley was at odds with the founders of the movement on the tariff question and was indifferent to civil service reform. The Democrats also nominated Greeley, mainly because he promised to end Radical Reconstruction by restoring "self-government" to the South.

But the journalist turned out to be a poor campaigner who failed to inspire enthusiasm from lifelong supporters of either party. Most Republicans stuck with Grant, despite the corruption issue, because they still could not stomach the idea of ex-rebels returning to power in the South. Many Democrats, recalling Greeley's previous record as a staunch Republican, simply stayed away from the polls. The result was a decisive victory for Grant, whose 56 percent of the popular vote was the highest percentage won by any candidate between Andrew Jackson and Theodore Roosevelt.

Grant's second administration seemed to bear out the reformers' worst suspicions about corruption in high places.

In 1875, the public learned that federal revenue officials had conspired with distillers to defraud the government of millions of dollars in liquor taxes. Grant's private secretary, Orville E. Babcock, was indicted as a member of the "Whiskey Ring" and was saved from conviction only by the president's personal intercession. The next year, Grant's secretary of war, William W. Belknap, was impeached by the House after an investigation revealed he had taken bribes for the sale of Indian trading posts. He avoided conviction in the Senate only by resigning from office before his trial. Grant fought hard to protect Belknap, to the point of participating in what a later generation might call a cover-up.

There is no evidence that Grant profited personally from any of the misdeeds of his subordinates. Yet he is not entirely without blame for the corruption in his administration. He failed to take firm action against the malefactors, and, even after their guilt had been clearly established, he sometimes tried to shield them from justice. Ulysses S. Grant was the only president between Jackson and Wilson to serve two full and consecutive terms. But unlike other chief executives so favored by the electorate, Grant is commonly regarded as a failure. Although the problems he faced would have challenged any president, the shame of Grant's administration was that he made loyalty to old friends a higher priority than civil rights or sound economic principles.

Reunion and the New South

Who benefited and who suffered from the reconciliation of the North and South?

Congressional Reconstruction prolonged the sense of sectional division and conflict for a dozen years after the guns had fallen silent. Its final liquidation in 1877 opened the way to a reconciliation of North and South. But the costs of reunion were high for less privileged groups in the South. The civil and political rights of African Americans, left unprotected, were progressively and relentlessly stripped away by white supremacist regimes. Lower-class whites saw their interests sacrificed to those of capitalists and landlords. Despite the rhetoric hailing a prosperous "New South," the region remained poor and open to exploitation by northern business interests.

The Compromise of 1877

The election of 1876 pitted Rutherford B. Hayes of Ohio, a Republican governor untainted by the scandals of the Grant era, against Governor Samuel J. Tilden of New York, a Democratic reformer who had battled against Tammany Hall and the Tweed Ring. Honest government was apparently the electorate's highest priority. When the returns came in, Tilden had clearly won the popular vote and seemed likely to win a narrow victory in the electoral college. But the result was placed in doubt when the returns from the three southern states still controlled by the Republicans—South Carolina, Florida, and Louisiana—were contested. If Hayes were to be awarded these three states, plus one contested electoral vote in Oregon, Republican strategists realized, he would triumph in the electoral college by a single vote.

The outcome of the election remained undecided for months, plunging the nation into a major political crisis. To resolve the

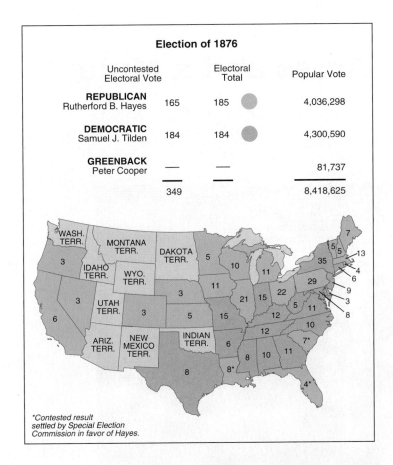

Election of 1876

	Uncontested Electoral Vote	Electoral Total		Popular Vote
REPUBLICAN Rutherford B. Hayes	165	185		4,036,298
DEMOCRATIC Samuel J. Tilden	184	184		4,300,590
GREENBACK Peter Cooper	—	—		81,737
		349		8,418,625

Contested result settled by Special Election Commission in favor of Hayes.

impasse, Congress appointed a special electoral commission of fifteen members to determine who would receive the votes of the disputed states. Originally composed of seven Democrats, seven Republicans, and an independent, the commission fell under Republican control when the independent member resigned to run for the Senate and a Republican was appointed to take his place. The commission split along party lines and voted eight to seven to award Hayes all of the disputed votes. But this decision still had to be ratified by both houses of Congress. The Republican-dominated Senate readily approved it, but the Democrats in the House planned a filibuster to delay the final counting of the electoral votes until after inauguration day. If the filibuster succeeded, neither candidate would have a majority and, as provided in the Constitution, the election would be decided by the House, where the Democrats controlled enough states to elect Tilden.

To ensure Hayes's election, Republican leaders negotiated secretly with conservative southern Democrats, some of whom seemed willing to abandon the filibuster if the last troops were withdrawn and home rule restored to the South. Eventually an informal bargain was struck, which historians have dubbed the **Compromise of 1877**. What precisely was agreed to and by whom remains a matter of dispute, but one thing at least was understood by both sides: Hayes would be president and southern blacks would be abandoned to their fate. In a sense, Hayes did not concede anything, because he had already decided to end federal support for the crumbling Radical regimes. But southern negotiators were heartened by firm assurances that this would indeed be the policy. Some also were influenced by vaguer promises involving federal support for southern railroads and internal improvements.

With southern Democratic acquiescence, the filibuster was broken, and Hayes took the oath of office. He immediately ordered the army not to resist a Democratic takeover of state governments in South Carolina and Louisiana. Thus fell the last of the Radical governments, and the entire South was firmly under the control of white Democrats. The trauma of the war and Reconstruction had destroyed the chances for a renewal of two-party competition among white Southerners.

Northern Republicans soon reverted to denouncing the South for its suppression of black suffrage. But this "waving of the bloody shirt," which also served as a reminder of the war and northern casualties, quickly degenerated into a campaign ritual aimed at northern voters who could still be moved by sectional antagonism.

"Redeeming" a New South

The men who came to power after Radical Reconstruction fell in one southern state after another are usually referred to as the **Redeemers**. They had differing backgrounds and previous loyalties. Some were members of the Old South's ruling planter class who had warmly supported secession and now sought to reestablish the old order with as few changes as possible. Others, of middle-class origin or outlook, favored commercial and industrial interests over agrarian groups and called for a New South committed to diversified economic development. A third group was professional politicians bending with the prevailing winds, such as Joseph E. Brown of Georgia, who had been a secessionist, a wartime governor, and a leading scalawag Republican before becoming a Democratic Redeemer.

Although historians have tried to assign the Redeemers a single coherent ideology or view of the world and have debated whether it was Old South agrarianism or New South industrialism they endorsed, these leaders can perhaps best be understood as power brokers mediating among the dominant interest groups of the South in ways that served their own political advantage. In many ways, the "rings" that they established on the state and county level were analogous to the political machines developing at the same time in northern cities. Redeemers did, however, agree on and endorse two basic principles: laissez-faire and white supremacy. Laissez-faire—the notion that government should be limited and should not intervene openly and directly in the economy—could unite planters, frustrated at seeing direct state support going to businessmen, and capitalist promoters who had come to realize that low taxes and freedom from government regulation were even more advantageous than state subsidies. It soon became clear that the Redeemers responded only to privileged and entrenched interest groups, especially landlords, merchants, and industrialists, and offered little or nothing to tenants, small farmers, and working people. As industrialization began to gather steam in the 1880s, Democratic regimes became increasingly accommodating to manufacturing interests and hospitable to agents of northern capital who were gaining control of the South's transportation system and its extractive industries.

White supremacy was the principal rallying cry that brought the Redeemers to power in the first place. Once in office, they found they could stay there by charging that opponents of ruling Democratic cliques were trying to divide "the white man's party" and open the way for a return to "black domination." Appeals to racism could also deflect attention from the economic grievances of groups without political clout.

Feature Essay | "Forty Acres and a Mule"

Serving as a kind of dress rehearsal for Reconstruction, the Port Royal Experiment provides a glimpse of what might have occurred had the freed slaves actually been given "forty acres and a mule."

Few dreams have died harder than the desire of the freed slaves to own the land on which they labored. The hope of "forty acres and a mule" for every freedman was raised by General William Tecumseh Sherman's Special Field Order 15, in January 1865, which decreed that 40-acre plots of "abandoned and confiscated" land would be set aside for ex-slaves. Yet the order was in effect for less than a year, and few slaves realized the dream of land ownership after emancipation.

Even before Sherman's order, however, there were experiments across the South with free black labor on plantations formerly held by slaveholders. Two of these so-called "rehearsals for Reconstruction," at Port Royal, South Carolina, and Davis Bend, Mississippi, show how Reconstruction might have developed had true land reform been implemented.

The efforts to resettle freed people on abandoned plantations began out of the Army's practical concern to rid itself of the many runaways who were following it and crowding its camps.

In November 1861, General Benjamin F. Butler, in a novel interpretation of international law, declared runaway slaves to be "contraband of war," whom the Union Army could rightfully seize from their rebel owners.

The "Port Royal Experiment" began as a solution to the problem of what to do with the contrabands. When the U.S. Navy occupied the Sea Islands of South Carolina and Georgia in November 1861, the whites fled, leaving behind 10,000 slaves who already organized their own labor according to the task system, often with black drivers rather than white overseers. The abandoned slaves sacked the plantation houses and cotton gins but had little inclination to return to the fields and plant cotton.

To get the black laborers back to the fields as soon as possible, Treasury Secretary Salmon Chase recruited Edward L. Pierce to administer Port Royal and show the world that free labor could produce as much cotton as slave labor. A motley crew of military officers, Treasury agents, investors, and idealistic teachers and missionaries, known as "Gideon's Band," followed Pierce south.

Tension soon arose among these groups. For example, Edward Atkinson, agent for six Boston cotton manufacturers, was motivated by both anti-slavery sentiments and profit. He wrote the pamphlet "Cheap Cotton by Free Labor" to prove that free labor would be more profitable than slavery. By contrast, Gideon's Band were young men "fresh from Harvard, Yale, and Brown" (and twelve women) and included, "clerks, doctors, divinity-students; professors and teachers, underground railway agents and socialist . . . Unitarians, free-thinkers, Methodists, straitlaced, and the other Evangelical sects." All were motivated by abolitionism and idealism about free labor; none knew anything about cotton production, which led to conflicts with plantation superintendents like Atkinson and Edward Philbrick.

The freed slaves believed they had a right to the land on which they had lived and worked for so long without compensation. They celebrated freedom from white overseers and sang:

No more peck o' corn for me;
    No more, no more; . . .
No more driver's lash for me . . .
No more pint o' salt for me . . .
No more hundred lash for me . . .
No more mistress' call for me,
    No more, no more, . . .
Many thousands go.

Despite the conflicts between the idealists and the capitalists, and the ex-slaves' preference for raising food crops rather than cotton, the Port Royal Experiment was a qualified success even for the cotton agents. Although cotton yields were lower than in the 1850s because of the wartime loss of fine seed and competition from cotton in Egypt, profits were high, and free labor was nearly as productive as slave labor. Philbrick made an $80,000 profit on a $40,000 investment. Even the philanthropic Gideonities earned $6,000-$7,000 each.

Another site of black self-sufficiency was Davis Bend, the Mississippi plantation belonging to Confederate President Jefferson Davis's brother Joseph. Joseph Davis had administered it as a "model" plantation, with limited self-government by slaves, including a slave jury for criminal offenses, and unusual material comforts. By 1850, one slave, Benjamin Montgomery, was running the plantation store, managing its cotton gin, and keeping the profits.

After whites fled southern Mississippi in 1863, General Ulysses S. Grant decided that Davis Bend should become a "Negro paradise," and the land was leased directly to former slaves, who paid only for tools, mules, and rations. They set up an even more comprehensive self-government that included an elected sheriff and judges. Davis Bend was an impressive success. By 1865, laborers there had produced nearly 2,000 bales of cotton and earned a profit of $160,000. During Reconstruction, Davis Bend also produced several elected black officials.

On January 12, 1865, Secretary of War Edwin Stanton and General Sherman met with twenty black leaders to hear the concerns of the freed people. The next day, Sherman issued Special Field Order 15, designating the whole Sea Island region "for exclusive Negro settlement." Yet the experiment on "Sherman land" ended almost before it began. President Andrew Johnson rescinded Sherman's order in the summer of 1865 and restored the land to its former owners. While the Port Royal Experiment did lead to limited black land ownership, education, and strong communities, it was not a "rehearsal for Reconstruction" for the South as a whole. Instead, the Reconstruction South followed the model of the occupied Deep South during the war, which had maintained large white-owned plantations with the freed people working in gangs under coercive one-year contracts.

When General Oliver O. Howard told the freed people on the Sea Islands that the land was to be restored to its white owners, they were bitter: "we want Homesteads, we were promised Homesteads . . . if the government . . . now takes away from them all right to the soil they stand upon save such as they can get by again working for *your* late and their *all time* enemies . . . we are left in a more unpleasant condition than our former one . . . this is not the condition of really freemen." Some did not leave without a struggle. Black squatters told Edisto Island owners who returned in February 1866: "You have better go back to Charleston, and go to work there, and if you can do nothing else, you can pick oysters and earn your living as the loyal people have done – by the sweat of their brows."

Even Davis Bend was restored to Joseph Davis, although he sold it on long-term credit to Ben Montgomery and his two sons. Davis was a lenient creditor, and Montgomery had a measure of prosperity through the mid-1870s, until economic reversals led him to bankruptcy in 1879. By then, Joseph Davis had died, and his heirs were less generous: the plantation was sold at foreclosure auction, and the dream of large-scale black self-sufficiency in Mississippi ended for generations.

QUESTIONS FOR DISCUSSION

1. How were the attempts to give land to the freed slaves in the South related to the Union war effort?

2. Why did land reform under the Port Royal Experiment and at Davis Bend ultimately fail?

The new governments were more economical than those of Reconstruction, mainly because they cut back drastically on appropriations for schools and other needed public services. But they were scarcely more honest—embezzlement of funds and bribery of officials continued to occur to an alarming extent. Louisiana, for example, suffered for decades from the flagrant corruption associated with a state-chartered lottery.

The Redeemer regimes of the late 1870s and 1880s badly neglected the interests of small white farmers. Whites and blacks were suffering from the notorious crop lien system that gave local merchants who advanced credit at high rates of interest during the growing season the right to take possession of the harvested crop on terms that buried farmers deeper and deeper in debt. As a result, increasing numbers of whites lost title to their homesteads and were reduced to tenancy. When a depression of world cotton prices added to the burden of a ruinous credit system, agrarian protesters began to challenge the ruling elite, first through the Southern Farmers' Alliance of the late 1880s and then by supporting its political descendant—the Populist Party of the 1890s (see Chapter 20).

The Rise of Jim Crow

African Americans bore the greatest hardships imposed by the new order. From 1876 through the first decade of the twentieth century, southern states imposed a series of restrictions on black civil rights known as **Jim Crow laws**. The term "Jim Crow" came from an antebellum minstrel show figure first popularized by Thomas "Daddy" Rice, who blackened his face and sang a song called "Jump Jim Crow." By the 1850s, Jim Crow was a familiar figure in minstrel shows, and had become a synonym for black or Negro person in popular white speech. It was a short step to referring to segregated railroad cars for black people as Jim Crow cars. While segregation and disfranchisement began as informal arrangements in the immediate aftermath of the Civil War, they culminated in a legal regime of separation and exclusion that took firm hold in the 1890s.

The rise of Jim Crow in the political arena was especially bitter for southern blacks who realized that only political power could ensure other rights. The Redeemers promised, as part of the understanding that led to the end of federal intervention in 1877, that they would respect the rights of blacks as set forth in the Fourteenth and Fifteenth Amendments. Governor Wade Hampton of South Carolina was especially vocal in pledging that African Americans would not be reduced to second-class citizenship by the new regimes. But when blacks tried to vote Republican in the "redeemed" states, they encountered renewed violence and intimidation. "Bulldozing" African American voters remained common practice in state elections during the late 1870s and early 1880s; those blacks who withstood the threat of losing their jobs or being evicted from tenant farms if they voted for the party of Lincoln were visited at night and literally whipped into line. The message was clear: Vote Democratic, or vote not at all.

Black and white men serve on a jury together during Reconstruction but they segregate themselves.

Furthermore, white Democrats now controlled the electoral machinery and were able to manipulate the black vote by stuffing ballot boxes, discarding unwanted votes, or reporting fraudulent totals. Some states also imposed complicated new voting requirements to discourage black participation. Full-scale disfranchisement did not occur until literacy tests and other legalized obstacles to voting were imposed in the period from 1890 to 1910, but by that time, less formal and comprehensive methods had already made a mockery of the Fifteenth Amendment.

Nevertheless, blacks continued to vote freely in some localities until the 1890s; a few districts, like the one Robert Smalls represented, even elected black Republicans to Congress during the immediate post-Reconstruction period. The last of these, Representative George H. White of North Carolina, served until 1901. His farewell address eloquently conveyed the agony of southern blacks in the era of Jim Crow (strict segregation):

> These parting words are in behalf of an outraged, heart-broken, bruised, and bleeding but God-fearing people, faithful, industrious, loyal people—rising people, full of potential force . . . . The only apology that I have to make for the earnestness with which I have spoken is that I am pleading for the life, the liberty, the future happiness, and manhood suffrage of one-eighth of the entire population of the United States.

Conclusion: Henry McNeal Turner and the "Unfinished Revolution"

The career of Henry McNeal Turner sums up the bitter side of the black experience in the South during and after Reconstruction. Born free in South Carolina in 1834, Turner became a minister of the African Methodist Episcopal (AME) Church just before the outbreak of the Civil War. During the war, he recruited African Americans for the Union army and later served as chaplain for black troops. After the fighting was over, he went to Georgia to work for the Freedmen's Bureau but encountered racial discrimination from white Bureau officers and left government service for church work and Reconstruction politics. Elected to the 1867 Georgia constitutional convention and to the state legislature in 1868, he was one of a number of black clergymen who assumed leadership roles among the freedmen. But whites won control of the Georgia legislature and expelled all the black members. Turner's reaction was an angry speech in which he proclaimed that white men were never to be trusted. As the inhabitant of a state in which blacks never gained the degree of power that they achieved in some other parts of the South, Turner was one of the first black leaders to see the failure of Reconstruction as the betrayal of African American hopes for citizenship.

Becoming a bishop of the AME Church in 1880, Turner emerged as the late nineteenth century's leading proponent of black emigration to Africa. Because he believed that white Americans were so deeply prejudiced against blacks that they would never grant them equal rights, Turner became an early advocate of black nationalism and a total separation of the races. Emigration became a popular movement among southern blacks, who were

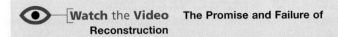

Watch the Video   The Promise and Failure of Reconstruction

In January of 1865, General Sherman's Field Order 15 set aside 400,000 acres for use by former slaves. With help from Gideon's Band, a ragtag group of Northern teachers and missionaries, as many as 40,000 ex-slaves achieved some success at cotton planting until the new President Johnson returned the land to its former owners.

especially hard hit by terror and oppression just after the end of Reconstruction. Still, a majority of blacks in the nation as a whole and even in Turner's own church refused to give up on the hope of eventual equality in America. But Bishop Turner's anger and despair were the understandable responses of a proud man to the way that he and his fellow African Americans had been treated in the post–Civil War period.

By the late 1880s, the wounds of the Civil War were healing, and white Americans were seized by the spirit of sectional reconciliation. Union and Confederate veterans were tenting together and celebrating their common Americanism. "Reunion" was becoming a cultural as well as political reality. But whites could come back together only because Northerners had tacitly agreed to give Southerners a free hand in their efforts to reduce blacks to a new form of servitude. The "outraged, heart-broken, bruised, and bleeding" African Americans of the South paid the heaviest price for sectional reunion. Reconstruction remained an "unfinished revolution." It would be another century before African Americans rose up once more to demand full civil and political rights.

Study Resources

 Take the **Study Plan** for **Chapter 16** *The Agony of Reconstruction* on **MyHistoryLab**

TIME LINE

1863 Lincoln sets forth 10 percent Reconstruction plan

1864 Wade-Davis Bill passes Congress but is pocket-vetoed by Lincoln

1865 Johnson moves to reconstruct the South on his own initiative; Congress refuses to seat representatives and senators elected from states reestablished under presidential plan (December)

1866 Johnson vetoes Freedmen's Bureau Bill (February); Johnson vetoes Civil Rights Act; it passes over his veto (April); Congress passes Fourteenth Amendment (June); Republicans increase their congressional majority in the fall elections

1867 First Reconstruction Act is passed over Johnson's veto (March)

1868 Johnson is impeached; he avoids conviction by one vote (February–May); Southern blacks vote and serve in constitutional conventions; Grant wins presidential election, defeating Horatio Seymour

1869 Congress passes Fifteenth Amendment, granting African Americans the right to vote

1870-1871 Congress passes Ku Klux Klan Acts to protect black voting rights in the South

1872 Grant reelected president, defeating Horace Greeley, candidate of Liberal Republicans and Democrats

1873 Financial panic plunges nation into depression

1875 Congress passes Specie Resumption Act; "Whiskey Ring" scandal exposed

1876-1877 Disputed presidential election resolved in favor of Republican Hayes over Democrat Tilden

1877 Compromise of 1877 ends military intervention in the South and causes fall of the last Radical governments

CHAPTER REVIEW

The President Versus Congress

 What conflicts arose among Lincoln, Johnson, and Congress during Reconstruction?

Both Lincoln and Johnson had their own notions of how Reconstruction should be governed. Radical Republicans who sought more protection for black rights challenged Lincoln's Ten Percent Plan. Later, when Johnson hesitated to renew the Freedmen's Bureau and fight the Black Codes, Congress passed the Fourteenth Amendment to ensure equal rights to all Americans. (p. 368)

Reconstructing Southern Society

 What problems did southern society face during Reconstruction?

The immediate problems facing the South were economic and physical devastation, and providing for the mass of freed slaves. While former slaveholders hoped to reduce ex-slaves to conditions not unlike slavery, northern Republicans wanted to reorganize southern land and labor on a northern free-labor model. Freedmen's Bureau agents emphasized that ex-slaves had to sign contracts and work for wages. The freed slaves hoped instead to own land. Sharecropping was a compromise. (p. 374)

Retreat from Reconstruction

 Why did Reconstruction end?

Although intended to protect civil rights, the Fifteenth Amendment allowed states to limit local suffrage through difficult voting prerequisites. Further, the Ku Klux Klan intimidated black voters and representation. By 1876, these tactics had defeated the Republicans in most southern states and Reconstruction was nearly dead. (p. 379)

Reunion and the New South

 Who benefited and who suffered from the reconciliation of North and South?

Reunion came at the expense of African Americans. The Compromise of 1877 restored autonomous government in the South to resolve the 1876 election. The North would no longer enforce unpopular civil rights, allowing the Redeemers to bring back laissez-faire economics and restore white supremacy through the Jim Crow laws. (p. 382)

KEY TERMS AND DEFINITIONS

Ten Percent Plan Reconstruction plan proposed by President Abraham Lincoln as a quick way to readmit the former Confederate States. It called for pardon of all southerners except Confederate leaders, and readmission to the Union for any state after 10 percent of its voters signed a loyalty oath and the state abolished slavery. p. 368

Radical Republicans Congressional Republicans who insisted on black suffrage and federal protection of civil rights of African Americans. p. 369

Wade–Davis Bill In 1864, Congress passed the Wade-Davis bill to counter Lincoln's Ten Percent Plan for Reconstruction. The bill required that a majority of a former Confederate state's white male population take a loyalty oath and guarantee equality for African Americans. President Lincoln pocket-vetoed the bill. p. 369

Thirteenth Amendment   Ratified in 1865, it prohibits slavery and involuntary servitude. p. 371

Black Codes   Laws passed by southern states immediately after the Civil War to maintain white supremacy by restricting the rights of the newly freed slaves. p. 371

Freedmen's Bureau   Agency established by Congress in March 1865 to provide freedmen with shelter, food, and medical aid and to help them establish schools and find employment. The Bureau was dissolved in 1872. p. 371

Fourteenth Amendment   Ratified in 1868, it provided citizenship to ex-slaves after the Civil War and constitutionally protected equal rights under the law for all citizens. Radical Republicans used it to enact a congressional Reconstruction policy in the former Confederate states. p. 371

Radical Reconstruction   The Reconstruction Acts of 1867 divided the South into five military districts. They required the states to guarantee black male suffrage and to ratify the Fourteenth Amendment as a condition of their readmission to the Union. p. 372

Sharecropping   After the Civil War, the southern states adopted a sharecropping system as a compromise between former slaves who wanted land of their own and former slave owners who needed labor. The landowners provided land, tools, and seed to a farming family, who in turn provided labor. The resulting crop was divided between them, with the farmers receiving a "share" of one-third to one-half of the crop. p. 375

Fifteenth Amendment   Ratified in 1870, it prohibits the denial or abridgment of the right to vote by the federal or state governments on the basis of race, color, or prior condition as a slave. It was intended to guarantee African Americans the right to vote in the South. p. 379

Ku Klux Klan   A secret terrorist society first organized in Tennessee in 1866. The original Klan's goals were to disfranchise African Americans, stop Reconstruction, and restore the prewar social order of the South. The Ku Klux Klan re-formed in the twentieth century to promote white supremacy and combat aliens, Catholics, and Jews. p. 380

Force acts   Designed to protect black voters in the South from the Ku Klux Klan in 1870–1871, these laws placed state elections under federal jurisdiction and imposed fines and punished those guilty of interfering with any citizen exercising his right to vote. p. 380

Compromise of 1877   Compromise struck during the contested presidential election of 1876, in which Democrats accepted the election of Rutherford B. Hayes (Republican) in exchange for the withdrawal of federal troops from the South and the end of Reconstruction. p. 383

Redeemers   A loose coalition of prewar Democrats, Confederate veterans, and Whigs who took over southern state governments in the 1870s, supposedly "redeeming" them from the corruption of Reconstruction. p. 383

Jim Crow laws   Segregation laws enacted by southern states after Reconstruction. p. 386

CRITICAL THINKING QUESTIONS

1. Do you think Reconstruction may have turned out differently had Lincoln not been assassinated?

2. Why was it difficult to enforce social and cultural changes using military force?

3. What role did local, grassroots efforts play in reserving federal government policy? How did people retain that much autonomy even under a strong federal government?

4. Do you think the "Redemption" of southern government was an inevitable backlash to Reconstruction? How could things have turned out differently?

MyHistoryLab Media Assignments

Find these resources in the Media Assignments folder for Chapter 16 on MyHistoryLab

The President Vs. Congress

- Read the Document   *Pearson Profiles, Robert Smalls* p. 367

- Read the Document   *Thirteenth, Fourteenth, and Fifteenth Amendment (1865, 1868, 1870)* p. 369

- ■ Read the Document   *The Mississippi Black Code (1865)* p. 370

- ■ View the Map   *Reconstruction* p. 373

Reconstructing Southern Society

- Read the Document   *A Sharecrop Contract (1882)* p. 375

- ■ Watch the Video   *The Schools that the Civil War and Reconstruction Created* p. 378

Retreat From Reconstruction

- ■ View the Closer Look   *The First Vote* p. 380

- Read the Document   *Hannah Irwin Describes Ku Klux Klan Ride* p. 381

Reunion and the New South

- ■ Complete the Assignment   *"Forty Acres and a Mule"* p. 384

- Watch the Video   *The Promise and Failure of Reconstruction* p. 387

■ Indicates Study Plan Media Assignment

17 The West: Exploiting an Empire

Contents and Learning Objectives

((•—[Listen to the **Audio File** on **myhistorylab**   Chapter 17 *The West: Exploiting an Empire*

Lean Bear's Changing West

In 1863, federal Indian agents took a delegation of Cheyenne, Arapaho, Comanche, Kiowa, and Plains Apache to visit the eastern United States, hoping to impress them with the power of the white man. The visitors were, in fact, impressed. In New York City, they stared at the tall buildings and crowded streets, so different from the wide-open plains with which they were accustomed. They visited the museum of the great showman Phineas T. Barnum, who in turn put them on display.

In Washington, they met with President Abraham Lincoln. Lean Bear, a Cheyenne chief, assured Lincoln that Indians wanted peace but worried about the numbers of white people who were pouring into their country. Lincoln swore friendship, said the Indians would be better off if they began to farm, and promised he would do his best to keep the peace. But, he said, smiling at Lean Bear, "You know it is not always possible for any father to have his children do precisely as he wishes them to do."

Lean Bear, who had children of his own, understood what Lincoln had had to say in Washington, at least in a way. Just a year later, back on his own lands, he watched as federal troops, Lincoln's "children," approached his camp. Wearing a peace medal that Lincoln had given him, Lean Bear rode slowly toward the troops to once again offer his friendship. When he was twenty yards away, they opened fire, then rode closer and fired again and again into his fallen body.

As Lean Bear had feared, in the last three decades of the nineteenth century, a flood of settlers ventured into the vast lands across the Mississippi River. Prospectors searched for "pay dirt," railroads crisscrossed the continent, eastern and foreign capitalists invested in cattle and land bonanzas, and farmers took up the promise of free western lands. In 1867, Horace Greeley, editor of the New York *Tribune*, told New York City's unemployed: "If you strike off into the broad, free West, and make yourself a farm from Uncle Sam's generous domain, you will crowd nobody, starve nobody, and neither you nor your children need evermore beg for something to do."

With the end of the Civil War, white Americans again claimed a special destiny to expand across the continent. In the process, they crushed the culture of the Native Americans and ignored the contributions of people of other races, such as the Chinese miners and laborers and the Mexican herdsmen. As millions moved west, the states of Colorado, Washington, Montana, the Dakotas, Idaho, Wyoming, and Utah were carved out of the lands across the Mississippi. At the turn of the century, only Arizona, New Mexico, and Oklahoma remained as territories.

The West became a great colonial empire, harnessed to eastern capital and tied increasingly to national and international markets. Its raw materials, sent east by wagon, train, and ship, helped fuel eastern factories. Western economies relied heavily on the federal government, which subsidized their railroads, distributed their land, and spent millions of dollars for the upkeep of soldiers and Indians.

By the 1890s, the lands beyond the Mississippi had undergone substantial change. In place of buffalo and unfenced vistas,

Kicking Bear recorded the Battle of the Little Bighorn in this pictograph.

there were cities and towns, health resorts, homesteads, sheep ranches, and, in the arid regions, the beginnings of the irrigated agriculture that would reshape the West in the twentieth century. Ghost towns, abandoned farms, and the scars in the earth left by miners and farmers spoke to the less favorable side of settlement. As the new century dawned, the West had become a place of conquest and exploitation, as well as a mythic land of cowboys and quick fortunes.

Beyond the Frontier

What were the challenges of settling the country west of the Mississippi?

The line of white settlement had reached the edge of the Missouri timber country by 1840. Beyond lay an enormous land of rolling prairies, parched deserts, and rugged, majestic mountains. Emerging from the timber country, travelers first encountered the Great Plains—treeless, nearly flat, an endless "sea of grassy hillocks" extending from the Mississippi River to the Rocky Mountains. To the west of the Great Plains were the High Plains, rough, semiarid, rising gently to the foothills of the Rocky Mountains.

Running from Alaska to central New Mexico, the Rockies presented a formidable barrier. There were valuable beaver in the streams and gold near Pikes Peak. But most travelers hurried through the northern passes, emerging in the desolate basin of present-day southern Idaho and Utah. Native Americans lived there—the Ute, Paiute, Bannock, and Shoshone tribes—surviving in the harsh environment by digging for roots and gathering seeds and berries. In the west, the lofty Coast Ranges—the Cascades and Sierra Nevada—held back rainfall; beyond were the temperate lands of the Pacific coast.

Early explorers such as Zebulon Pike thought the country beyond the Mississippi was uninhabitable, fit only, Pike said, for "wandering and uncivilized aborigines." Mapmakers agreed; between 1825 and 1860, American maps showed this land as "The Great American Desert." As a result, settlement paused on

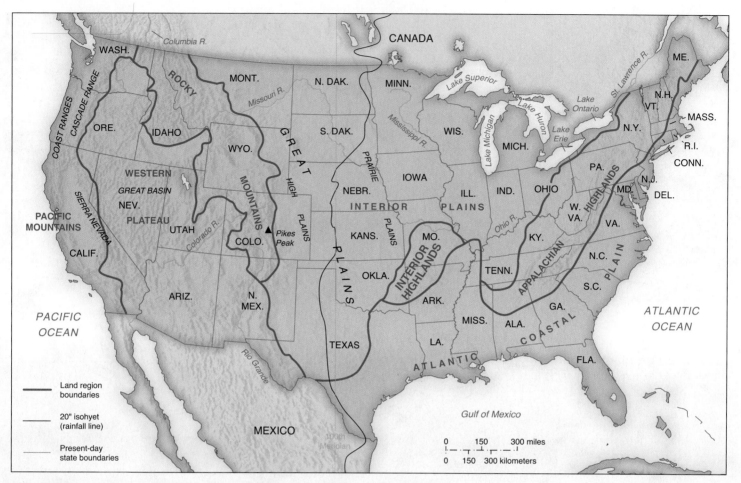

PHYSIOGRAPHIC MAP OF THE UNITED STATES In the Great Plains and Rocky Mountains, the topography, altitudes, crops, and climate—especially the lack of rain west of the rainfall line shown here—led to changes in a mode of settlement that had been essentially uniform from the Atlantic coast through Kentucky, Ohio, and Missouri. The rectangular land surveys and quarter-section lots that were traditional before could not accommodate Great Plains conditions.

the edge of the Plains, and most early settlers headed directly for California and Oregon.

Few rivers cut through the plains; those that did raged in the winter and trickled in the summer. Rainfall usually did not reach fifteen inches a year, not enough to support extensive agriculture. There was little lumber for homes and fences, and the tools of eastern settlement—the cast-iron plow, the boat, and the ax—were virtually useless on the tough and treeless plains soil. "East of the Mississippi," historian Walter Prescott Webb noted, "civilization stood on three legs—land, water, and timber; west of the Mississippi not one but two of these legs were withdrawn—water and timber—and civilization was left on one leg—land."

Hot winds seared the plains in summer, and northers, blizzards, and hailstorms froze them in winter. Wildlife roamed in profusion. The American bison, better known as the buffalo, grazed in enormous herds from Mexico to Canada. In 1865, perhaps fifteen million buffalo lived on the plains, so many they seemed like "leaves in a forest" to an early observer. A single herd sighted in 1871 had four million head.

Crushing the Native Americans

How did white Americans crush the culture of the Native Americans as they moved west?

When Greeley urged New Yorkers to move West and "crowd nobody," he—like almost all white Americans—ignored the fact that large numbers of people already lived there. At the close of the Civil War, Native Americans inhabited nearly half the United States. By 1880, they had been driven onto smaller and smaller reservations and were no longer an independent people. A decade later, even their culture had crumbled under the impact of white domination.

In 1865, nearly a quarter million Native Americans lived in the western half of the country. Tribes such as the Winnebago, Menominee, Cherokee, and Chippewa were resettled there, forced out of their eastern lands by advancing white settlement. Other tribes were native to the region. In the Southwest there were the Pueblo groups, including the Hopi, Zuni, and Rio Grande Pueblos.

Peaceful farmers and herders, they had built up complex traditions around a settled way of life.

The Pueblo groups were cultivators of corn. They lived on the subdesert plateau of present-day western New Mexico and eastern Arizona. Harassed by powerful neighboring tribes, they built communal houses of adobe brick on high mesas or in cracks in the cliffs. More nomadic were the Camp Dwellers, the Jicarilla Apache and Navajo who roamed eastern New Mexico and western Texas. Blending elements of the Plains and Plateau environments, they lived in tepees or mud huts, grew some crops to supplement their hunting, and moved readily from place to place. The Navajo herded sheep and produced beautiful ornamental silver, baskets, and blankets. Fierce fighters, Apache horsemen were feared by whites and fellow Indians across the southwestern plains.

Farther west were the tribes that inhabited present-day California. Divided into many small bands, they eked out a difficult existence living on roots, grubs, berries, acorns, and small game. In the Pacific Northwest, where fish and forest animals made life easier, the Klamath, Chinook, Yurok, and Shasta tribes developed a rich civilization. They built plank houses and canoes, worked extensively in wood, and evolved a complex social and political organization. Settled and determined, they resisted the invasion of the whites.

By the 1870s, most of these tribes had been destroyed or beaten into submission. The powerful Ute, crushed in 1855, ceded most of their Utah lands to the United States and settled on a small reservation near Great Salt Lake. The Navajo and Apache fought back fiercely, but between 1865 and 1873 they too were confined to reservations. The Native Americans of California succumbed to the contagious diseases carried by whites during the Gold Rush of 1849. Miners burned their villages, and by 1880, fewer than twenty thousand Indians lived in California.

Life of the Plains Indians

In the mid-nineteenth century, nearly two-thirds of the Native Americans lived on the Great Plains. The Plains tribes included the Sioux of present-day Minnesota and the Dakotas; the Blackfoot of Idaho and Montana; the Cheyenne, Crow, and Arapaho of the central plains; the Pawnee of western Nebraska; and the Kiowa, Apache, and Comanche of present-day Texas and New Mexico.

Nomadic and warlike, the Plains Indians depended on the buffalo and horse. The modern horse, first brought by Spanish explorers in the 1500s, spread north from Mexico onto the plains, and by the 1700s the Plains Indians' way of life had changed. The Plains tribes gave up farming almost entirely and hunted the buffalo, ranging widely over the rolling plains. The men became superb warriors and horsemen, among the best light cavalry in the world.

Equipped with stout wooden bows three feet or less in length, Plains Indians were fierce warriors. Hiding their bodies behind their racing ponies, they drove deadly arrows clear through buffalo. Against white troops or settlers, the skillful Comanche rode three hundred yards and shot twenty arrows in the time it took a soldier to load his firearm once. The introduction of the new Colt six-shooters during the 1850s gave government troops a rapid-fire weapon but did not entirely offset the Indians' advantage.

Migratory in culture, the Plains Indians formed tribes of several thousand people but lived in smaller bands of three to five hundred. The Comanche, who numbered perhaps seven thousand, had thirteen bands with such names as Burnt Meat, Making Bags While Moving, and Those Who Move Often. Each band was governed by a chief and a council of elder men, and Indians of the same tribe transferred freely from band to band. Bands acted independently, making it difficult for the U.S. government to deal with the fragmented tribes.

The Comanche dominated most of the Plains through their exploitation of the horse, their use of violence, and the timely cooperation among their bands. Over the course of two centuries, they crushed the feared Apache, harassed the Spanish and Mexicans, and tormented American immigrants who wanted to establish trading posts in Taos and Santa Fe. Although official maps showed Spanish ownership of the southern and western Plains, the Comanche actually controlled it, their domain known as the Comancheria, or the Comanche empire. Their last important chief, Quanah Parker, the son of a Comanche brave and a captive Anglo-Texan, died in 1911.

Whether Comanche or other tribes, all native Americans on the Plains followed and lived off the buffalo. Buffalo provided food, clothing, and shelter; the Indians, unlike later white hunters, used every part of the animal. The meat was dried or "jerked" in the hot plains air. The skins made tepees, blankets, and robes. Buffalo bones became knives; tendons were made into bowstrings; horns and hooves were boiled into glue. Buffalo "chips"—dried manure—were burned as fuel. All in all, the buffalo was "a galloping department store."

Warfare among tribes usually took the form of brief raids and skirmishes. Plains Indians fought few prolonged wars and rarely coveted territory. Most conflicts involved only a few warriors intent on stealing horses or "counting coup"—touching an enemy body with the hand or a special stick. Tribes developed a fierce and trained warrior class, recognized for achievements in battle. Speaking different languages, Native Americans of various tribes were nevertheless able to communicate with one another through a highly developed sign language.

The Plains tribes divided labor tasks according to gender. Men hunted, traded, supervised ceremonial activities, and cleared ground for planting. They usually held the positions of authority, such as chief or medicine man. Women were responsible for child rearing and artistic activity. They also performed the camp work, grew vegetables, prepared buffalo meat and hides, and gathered berries and roots. In most tribes, women played an important role in political, economic, and religious activities. Among the Navajo and Zuni, kinship descended from the mother's side, and Navajo women were in charge of most of the family's property. In tribes such as the Sioux, there was little difference in status. Men were respected for hunting and war, women for their artistic skills with quill and paint.

"As Long as Waters Run": Searching for an Indian Policy

Before the Civil War, Americans used the land west of the Mississippi as "one big reservation." The government named the area "Indian Country," moved eastern tribes there with firm treaty guarantees, and in 1834 passed the Indian Intercourse Act, which prohibited any white person from entering Indian country without a license.

The situation changed in the 1850s. Wagon trains wound their way to California and Oregon, miners pushed into western goldfields, and there was talk of a transcontinental railroad. To clear the way for settlement, the federal government in 1851 abandoned "One Big Reservation" in favor of a new policy of concentration. For the first time, it assigned definite boundaries to each tribe. The Sioux, for example, were given the Dakota country north of the Platte River, the Crow a large area near the Powder River, and the Cheyenne and Arapaho the Colorado foothills between the North Platte and Arkansas Rivers for "as long as waters run and the grass shall grow."

The concentration policy lasted only a few years. Accustomed to hunting widely for buffalo, many Native Americans refused to stay within their assigned areas. White settlers poured into Indian lands, then called on the government to protect them. Indians were pushed out of Kansas and Nebraska in the 1850s, even as white reformers fought to hold those territories open for free blacks. In 1859, gold miners moved into the Pikes Peak country, touching off warfare with the Cheyenne and Arapaho.

In 1864, tired of the fighting, the two tribes asked for peace. Certain that the war was over, Chief Black Kettle led his seven hundred followers to camp on Sand Creek in southeastern Colorado. Early on the morning of November 29, 1864, a group of Colorado militia led by Colonel John M. Chivington attacked the sleeping group. "Kill and scalp all, big and little," Chivington told his men. "Nits make lice." Black Kettle tried to stop the ambush,

View the Map   Native Americans, 1850–1896

NATIVE AMERICANS IN THE WEST: MAJOR BATTLES AND RESERVATIONS "They made us many promises, more than I remember, but they never kept but one; they promised to take our land, and they took it." So said Red Cloud of the Oglala Sioux, summarizing Native American–white relations in the 1870s.

Read the **Document** Chief Red Cloud's Speech

Red Cloud was chief of the Oglala Teton Sioux. He was an important leader who opposed white incursions into Native American lives and territory, although he openly advocated peace whenever possible and did not support the more violent actions of Crazy Horse and his followers.

raising first an American flag and then a white flag. Neither worked. The Native American men, women, and children were clubbed, stabbed, and scalped.

The Chivington massacre set off angry protests in Colorado and the East. Congress appointed an investigating committee, and the government concluded a treaty with the Cheyenne and Arapaho, condemning "the gross and wanton outrages." Still, the two tribes were forced to surrender their Sand Creek reservation in exchange for lands elsewhere. The Kiowa and Comanche were also ousted from areas they had been granted "forever" only a few years before. As the Sioux chief Spotted Tail said, "Why does not the Great Father put his red children on wheels so that he can move them as he will?"

Before long, the powerful Sioux were on the warpath in the great Sioux War of 1865–1867. Once again, an invasion of gold miners touched off the war, which flared even more intensely when the federal government announced plans to connect the various mining towns by building the Bozeman Trail through the heart of the Sioux hunting grounds in Montana. Red Cloud, the Sioux chief, determined to stop the trail. In December 1866, pursued by an army column under Captain William J. Fetterman, he lured the incautious Fetterman deep into the wilderness, ambushed him, and wiped out all eighty-two soldiers in his command.

The Fetterman massacre, coming so soon after the Chivington massacre, sparked a public debate over the nation's Indian policy. Like the policy itself, the debate reflected differing white views of the Native Americans. In the East, some reform, humanitarian, and church groups wanted a humane peace policy, directed toward educating and "civilizing" the tribes. Many white people, in the East and West, questioned this approach, convinced that Native Americans were savages unfit for civilization. Westerners, of course, had some reason to fear Indian attacks, and the fears often fed on wild rumors of scalped settlers and besieged forts. As a result, Westerners in general favored firm control over the Native Americans, including swift punishment of any who rebelled.

In 1867, the peace advocates won the debate. Halting construction on the Bozeman Trail, Congress created a Peace Commission of four civilians and three generals to end the Sioux War and eliminate permanently the causes of Indian wars. Setting out for the West, the Peace Commissioners agreed that only one policy offered a permanent solution: a policy of "small reservations" to isolate the Native Americans on distant lands, teach them to farm, and gradually "civilize" them.

The commissioners chose two areas to hold all the Plains Indians. Fifty-four thousand Native Americans on the northern plains would be moved north of the Black Hills in Dakota Territory, far from prospective white settlement. On the southern plains, eighty-six thousand Native Americans would be moved into present-day Oklahoma, a region also considered difficult to farm and unattractive to whites. In both areas, tribes would be assigned specific reservations where government agents could supervise them.

The Kiowa, Comanche, Cheyenne, and Arapaho agreed to the plan in 1867, the Sioux in 1868. The policy was extended beyond the plains, and the Ute, Shoshone, Bannock, Navajo, and Apache tribes also accepted small reservations. "We have now selected and provided reservations for all, off the great road," an army commander wrote. "All who cling to their old hunting-grounds are hostile and will remain so till killed off."

Final Battles on the Plains

Few Native Americans settled peacefully into life on the new reservations. The reservation system not only changed their age-old customs; it chained them in a situation of poverty and isolation. Soon, young warriors and minor chiefs denounced the treaties and drifted back to the open countryside. In late 1868, warfare broke out again, and it took more than a decade of violence

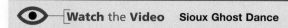
Watch the Video **Sioux Ghost Dance**

This wood engraving from 1891 depicts a group of Sioux dancers performing, most likely, one of their last ghost dances before the arrest of the warrior chief Sitting Bull.

to beat the Indians into submission. The Kiowa and Comanche rampaged through the Texas Panhandle, looting and killing, until the U.S. Army—including the feared "buffalo soldiers," African American cavalrymen on the western frontier—crushed them in the Red River War of 1874–1875 and ended warfare in the Southwest. (See the Feature Essay, "Blacks in Blue: The Buffalo Soldiers in the West," pp. 398–399.)

On the northern plains, fighting resulted from the Black Hills Gold Rush of 1875. As prospectors tramped across Native American hunting grounds, the Sioux gathered to stop them. They were led by Rain-in-the-Face, the great war chief Crazy Horse, and the famous medicine man Sitting Bull. The army sent several columns of troops after the Indians, but one, under flamboyant Lieutenant Colonel George Armstrong Custer, pushed recklessly ahead, eager to claim the victory. On the morning of June 25, 1876, thinking he had a small band of Native Americans surrounded in their village on the banks of the Little Bighorn River in Montana, Custer divided his column and took 265 men toward it. Instead of finding a small band, he discovered he had stumbled on the main Sioux camp with 2,500 warriors. It was the largest Native American army ever assembled in the United States.

By midafternoon it was over; Custer and his men were dead. Custer was largely responsible for the loss, but "Custer's Last Stand," set in blazing headlines across the country, set off

a nationwide demand for revenge. Within a few months, the Sioux were surrounded and beaten, three thousand of them surrendering in October 1876. Sitting Bull and a few followers who had fled to Canada gave up in 1881.

The Sioux War ended the major Indian warfare in the West, but occasional outbreaks occurred for several years thereafter. In 1877, the Nez Percé tribe of Oregon, a people who had warmly welcomed Lewis and Clark in 1805, rebelled against government policy. Hoping to reach Canada, Chief Joseph led the tribe on a courageous flight lasting 75 days and covering 1,321 miles. They defeated the pursuing army at every turn but then ran out of food, horses, and ammunition. Surrendering, they were sent to barren lands in the Indian Country of Oklahoma, and there, most of them died from disease.

In 1890, the Teton Sioux of South Dakota, bitter and starving, became restless. Many of them turned to the **Ghost Dances**, a set of dances and rites that grew from a vision of a Paiute messiah named Wovoka. Performance of the dances, Wovoka said, would bring back Native American lands and would cause the whites to disappear. All Native Americans would reunite, the earth would be covered with dust, and a new Earth would come upon the old. The vanished buffalo would return in great herds.

The army intervened to stop the dancing, touching off violence that killed Sitting Bull and a number of other warriors. Frightened Native Americans fled southwest to join other Ghost Dancers under the aging chief Big Foot. Moving quickly, troops of the Seventh Cavalry, Custer's old regiment, caught up with Big Foot's band and took them to the army camp on Wounded Knee Creek in South Dakota. A Native American, it is thought, fired the first shot, returned by the army's new machine guns. Firing a shell a second, they shredded tepees and people. In the infamous **Wounded Knee Massacre**, about two hundred men, women, and children were killed in the snow.

The End of Tribal Life

The final step in Indian policy came in the 1870s and 1880s. Some reformers had long argued against segregating the Native Americans on reservations, urging instead that the nation assimilate them individually into white culture. These "assimilationists" wanted to use education, land policy, and federal law to eradicate tribal society.

[Read the Document   **Accounts of the Wounded Knee Massacre**

In late 1890 troops of the Seventh Cavalry killed more than 200 Native American men, women, and children at a reservation located along Wounded Knee Creek in South Dakota. A number of longstanding issues on the reservation contributed to the tension prior to the massacre.

Congress began to adopt the policy in 1871 when it ended the practice of treaty making with Native American tribes. Since tribes were no longer separate nations, they lost many of their political and judicial functions, and the power of the chiefs was weakened. In 1882, Congress created a Court of Indian Offenses to try Native Americans who broke government rules, and soon thereafter it made them answerable in regular courts for certain crimes.

While Congress worked to break down the tribes, educators trained young Native Americans to adjust to white culture. In 1879, fifty Pawnee, Kiowa, and Cheyenne youths were brought east to the new Carlisle Indian School in Carlisle, Pennsylvania. Other Native American schools soon opened, including the Haskell Institute in Kansas and numerous day schools on the western reservations. The schools taught students to fix machines and farm; they forced young Indians to trim their long hair and made them speak English, banned the wearing of tribal paint or clothes, and forbade tribal ceremonies and dances. "Kill the Indian and save the man," said Richard H. Pratt, the army officer who founded the Carlisle School.

Land ownership was the final and most important link in the new policy. Native Americans who owned land, it was thought, would become responsible, self-reliant citizens. Deciding to give each Native American a farm, Congress in 1887 passed the **Dawes Severalty Act**, the most important legal development in Indian–white relations in more than three centuries.

Aiming to end tribal life, the Dawes Act divided tribal lands into small plots for distribution among members of the tribe. Each family head received 160 acres, single adults 80 acres, and children 40 acres. Once the land was distributed, any surplus was sold to white settlers, with the profits going to Native American schools.

To keep the Indians' land from falling into the hands of speculators, the federal government held it in trust for twenty-five years. Finally, American citizenship was granted to Native Americans who accepted their land, lived apart from the tribe, and "adopted the habits of civilized life."

Through the Dawes Act, 47 million acres of land were distributed to Native Americans and their families. There were another 90 million acres in the reservations, and these lands, often the most fertile, were sold to white settlers. Speculators evaded the twenty-five-year rule, leasing rather than purchasing the land from the Native Americans. Many Native Americans knew little about farming. Their tools were rudimentary, and in the culture of the Plains Indians, men had not ordinarily participated in farming. In 1934, the government returned to the idea of tribal land ownership, but by then 138 million acres of Indian land had shrunk to 48 million acres, half of which was barren.

The final blow to tribal life came not in the Dawes Act but in the virtual extermination of the buffalo, the Plains Indians' chief resource and the basis for their unique way of life. The killing began in the 1860s as the transcontinental railroads pushed west, and it stepped up as settlers found they could harm the Indians by harming the buffalo. "Kill every buffalo you can," an army officer said. "Every buffalo dead is an Indian gone." Then, in 1871, a Pennsylvania tannery discovered that buffalo hides made valuable leather. Professional hunters such as William F. "Buffalo Bill" Cody swarmed across the plains, killing millions of the beasts.

Between 1872 and 1874, professional hunters slaughtered three million buffalo a year. In a frontier form of a factory system, riflemen, skinners, and transport wagons pushed through the vast herds, which shrank steadily behind them.

By 1883, the buffalo were almost gone. When the government set out to produce the famous "buffalo nickel," the designer had to go to the Bronx Zoo in New York City to find a buffalo.

By 1900, there were only 250,000 Native Americans in the country. (There were 600,000 within the limits of the present-day United States in 1800, and more than 5 million in 1492, when Columbus first set foot in the New World.) Most of the Indians lived on reservations. Many lived in poverty. Alcoholism and unemployment were growing problems, and Native Americans, no longer able to live off the buffalo, became wards of the state. They lost their cultural distinctiveness. Once possessors of the entire continent, they had been crowded into smaller and smaller areas, overwhelmed by the demand to become settled, literate, and English-speaking. "Except for the internment of the West Coast Japanese during World War II," said historian Roger L. Nichols, "Indian removal is the only example of large-scale government-enforced migration in American history. For the Japanese, the move was temporary; for the Indians it was not."

Feature Essay

Blacks in Blue
The Buffalo Soldiers in the West

Although they were not, in fact, treated as well as the white soldiers in their regiments, many African American cavalrymen such as those pictured here were probably drawn into service by hard-sell recruitment posters such as the one shown on the facing page.

On Saturday afternoons, youngsters used to sit in darkened movie theaters and cheer the victories of the U.S. Cavalry over the Indians. Typically, the Indians were about to capture a wagon train when army bugles suddenly sounded. Then the blue-coated cavalry charged over the hill. Few in the theaters cheered for the Indians; fewer still noticed the absence of black faces among the charging cavalry. But in fact, more than two thousand African American cavalrymen served on the western frontier between 1867 and 1890. Known as the buffalo soldiers, they made up one-fifth of the U.S. Cavalry.

Black troops were first used on a large scale during the Civil War. Organized in segregated units, with white officers, they fought with distinction. Nearly 180,000 blacks served in the Union army; 34,000 of them died. When the war ended in 1865, Congress for the first time authorized black troops to serve in the regular peacetime army. In addition to infantry, it created two cavalry regiments—the Ninth and Tenth, which became known as the famous buffalo soldiers.

Like other black regiments, the Ninth and Tenth Cavalry had white officers who took special examinations before they could serve. The chaplains were assigned not only to preach but to teach reading, writing, and arithmetic. The food was poor; racism was widespread. The army stocked the first black units with worn-out horses, a serious matter to men whose lives depended on the speed and stamina of their mounts. "Since our first mount in 1867 this regiment has received nothing but broken down horses and repaired equipment," an officer said in 1870.

Many white officers refused to serve with black troops. George Armstrong Custer, the handsome "boy general," turned down a position in the Ninth and joined the new Seventh Cavalry, headed for disaster at Little

Bighorn. The *Army and Navy Journal* carried ads that told a similar story:

A FIRST LIEUTENANT
OF INFANTRY
(white)
Stationed at a
very desirable post
in the Department of the South
desires a transfer with
an officer of the same grade
on equal terms
if in a white regiment
but if in a colored regiment
a reasonable bonus
would be expected.

There was no shortage of black troops for the officers to lead. Blacks enlisted because the army offered some advancement in a closed society. It also paid $13 a month, plus room and board.

In 1867, the Ninth and Tenth Cavalry were posted to the West, where they remained for two decades. Under Colonel Benjamin H. Grierson, a Civil War hero, the Tenth went to Fort Riley, Kansas; the regiment arrived in the midst of a great Indian war. The Kiowa, Comanche, Cheyenne, Arapaho, and Sioux were on the warpath. Troopers of the Tenth defended farms, stages, trains, and work crews building railroad tracks to the West. Cornered by a band of Cheyenne, they beat back the attack and won a new name. They had been known as the "brunettes" or "Africans," but the Cheyenne now called them the buffalo soldiers, a name that soon applied to all African American soldiers in the West.

From 1868 to 1874, the Tenth served on the Kansas frontier. The dull winter days were filled with drills and scouting parties outside the post. In spring and summer, the good weather brought forth new forays. Indian bands raided farms and ranches and stampeded cattle herds on the way north from Texas. They struck and then melted back into the reservations.

The Ninth Cavalry also had a difficult job. Commanded by Colonel Edward Hatch, who had served with Grierson in the Civil War, it was stationed in West Texas and along the Rio Grande. The summers were so hot that men collapsed with sunstroke, the winters so cold that water froze in canteens. Native Americans from outside the area frequently raided it. From the north, Kiowa and Comanche warriors rode down the Great Comanche War Trail; Kickapoo crossed the Rio Grande from Mexico. Gangs of Mexican bandits and restless Civil War veterans roamed and plundered at will.

From 1874 to 1875, the Ninth fought in the great Red River War, in which the Kiowa and Comanche, fed up with conditions on the reservations, revolted against Grant's peace policy. Marching, fighting, then marching again, the soldiers harried and wore out the Indians, who finally surrendered in the spring of 1875. Herded into a new and desolate reservation, the Mescalero Apache of New Mexico took to the warpath in 1877 and again in 1879. Each time, it took a year of grueling warfare to effect their surrender. In 1886, black cavalrymen surrounded and captured the famous Apache chief Geronimo. In that and other campaigns, several buffalo soldiers won the Congressional Medal of Honor.

Black troops hunted Big Foot and his band before the slaughter at Wounded Knee in 1890 (see p. 396), and they served in many of the West's most famous Indian battles. While one-third of all army recruits deserted between 1865 and 1890, the Ninth and Tenth Cavalry had few desertions. In 1880, the Tenth had the fewest desertions of any regiment in the country.

It was ironic that in the West, black men fought red men to benefit white men. Once the Indian wars ended, the buffalo soldiers worked to keep illegal settlers out of Indian or government land—much of which was later opened to settlement. Both regiments saw action in the Spanish-American War, the Ninth at San Juan Hill, the Tenth in the fighting around Santiago. Unlike white veterans of the same campaigns, the old buffalo soldiers were forgotten in retirement, although some of them had the satisfaction of settling on the western lands they had done so much to pacify.

QUESTIONS FOR DISCUSSION

1. Why did many African American men join the military during this era?

2. Why did so few of these "buffalo soldiers" desert at a time when so many other U.S. soldiers did?

View the **Closer Look** Railroad and Buffalo

In 1872, the Northern Pacific Railroad began to build a route that would violate Sioux territory. The government sent an army to protect the surveyors.

Even as the Native Americans lost their identity, they entered the romantic folklore of the West. Dime novels, snapped up by readers young and old, told tales of Indian fighting on the plains. "Buffalo Bill" Cody turned it all into a profitable business. Beginning in 1883, his Wild West Show ran for more than three decades, playing to millions of viewers in the United States, Canada, and Europe. It featured Plains Indians chasing buffalo, performing a war dance, and attacking a settler's cabin. In 1885, Sitting Bull himself, victor over Custer at the battle of Little Bighorn, performed in the show.

Settlement of the West

Why did Americans and others move to the West?

Between 1870 and 1900, white—and some African, Hispanic, and Asian—Americans settled the enormous total of 430 million acres west of the Mississippi; they took over more land than had been occupied by Americans in all the years before 1870.

People moved West for many reasons. Some sought adventure; others wanted to escape the drab routine of factory or city life.

Many moved to California for their health. The Mormons settled Utah to escape religious persecution. Others followed the mining camps, the advancing railroads, and the farming and cattle frontier.

Whatever the specific reason, most people moved West to better their lot. On the whole, their timing was good, for as the nation's population grew, so did demand for the livestock and the agricultural, mineral, and lumber products of the expanding West. Contrary to older historical views, the West did not act as a major "safety valve," an outlet for social and economic tensions. The poor and unemployed did not have the means to move there and establish farms. "Moreover," as Douglass C. North, an economic historian, said, "most people moved West in good times . . . in periods of rising prices, of expanding demand, when the prospects for making money from this new land looked brightest; and this aspect characterized the whole pattern of settlement."

Men and Women on the Overland Trail

The first movement west aimed not for the nearby plains but for California and Oregon on the continent's far shore. It started in the **Gold Rush of 1849** to California, and in the next three decades perhaps as many as half a million individuals made the long journey over the **Overland Trail** leading west. Some walked; others rode horses alone or in small groups. About half joined great caravans, numbering 150 wagons or more, that inched across the two thousand miles between the Missouri River and the Pacific coast.

More often than not, men made the decision to make the crossing, but, except for the stampedes to the mines, migration usually turned out to be a family affair. Wives were consulted, though in some cases they had little real choice. They could either go along or live alone at home. While many women regretted leaving family and friends, they agreed to the trip, sometimes as eagerly as the men. "I would not be left behind," said Luzena Wilson, whose husband ached to join the Gold Rush to California. "I thought where he could go I could, and where I went I could take my two little toddling babies." Like the Wilsons, the majority of people traveled in family groups, including in-laws, grandchildren, aunts, and uncles. As one historian said, "The quest for something new would take place in the context of the very familiar."

Individuals and wagon trains set out from various points along the Missouri River. Leaving in the spring and traveling through the summer, they hoped to reach their destination before the first snowfall. During April, travelers gradually assembled in spring camp just across the Missouri River, waiting for the new grass to ripen into forage. They packed and repacked the wagons and elected the trains' leaders, who would set the line of march, look for water and campsites, and impose discipline. Some trains adopted detailed rules, fearing a lapse into savagery in the wild lands across the Missouri. "Every man to carry with him a Bible and other religious books, as we hope not to degenerate into a state of barbarism," one agreement said.

Setting out in early May, travelers divided the enormous route into manageable portions. The first leg of the journey followed the Platte River west to Fort Kearney in central Nebraska Territory, a distance of about three hundred miles. The land was even, with good supplies of wood, grass, and water. From a distance, the white-topped wagons seemed driven by a common force, but, in fact, internal discipline broke down almost immediately. Arguments erupted over the pace of the march, the choice of campsites, the number of guards to post, whether to rest or push on. Elected leaders quit; new ones were chosen. Every train was filled with individualists, and as the son of one train captain said, "If you think it's any snap to run a wagon train of sixty-six wagons with every man in the train having a different idea of what is the best thing to do, all I can say is that some day you ought to try it."

Men, women, and children had different tasks on the trail. Men concerned themselves almost entirely with hunting buffalo and antelope, guard duty, and transportation. They rose at 4 A.M. to hitch the wagons, and after breakfast began the day's march. At noon, they stopped and set the teams to graze. After the midday meal, the march continued until sunset. Then, while the men relaxed, the women fixed dinner and the next day's lunch, and the children kindled the fires, brought water to camp, and searched for wood or other fuel. Walking fifteen miles a day, in searing heat and mountain cold, travelers were exhausted by late afternoon.

For women, the trail was lonely, and they worked to exhaustion. Before long, some adjusted their clothing to the harsh conditions, adopting the new bloomer pants, shortening their skirts, or wearing regular "wash dresses"—so called because they had shorter hemlines that did not drag on the wet ground on washday. Other women continued to wear their long dresses, thinking bloomers "indecent." Both men and women carried firearms in case of Indian attacks, but most emigrants saw few Indians en route.

What they often did see was trash, miles of it, for the wagon trains were an early example of the impact of migration and settlement on the western environment. On the Oregon and other trails, travelers sidestepped mounds of garbage, tin cans, furniture, cooking stoves, kegs, tools, and clothing, all discarded by people who had passed through before. Along a 40-mile trail in the Nevada desert, a migrant tallied two thousand abandoned wagons. On some trails, animals and people stirred up so much dust that drivers wore goggles to protect their eyes.

The first stage of the journey was deceptively easy, and travelers usually reached Fort Kearney by late May. The second leg led another 300 miles up the Platte River to Fort Laramie on the eastern edge of Wyoming Territory. The heat of June had dried the grass, and there was no wood. Anxious to beat the early snowfalls, travelers rested a day or two at the fort, then hurried on to South Pass, 280 miles to the west, the best route through the forbidding Rockies.

Beyond South Pass, some emigrants turned south to the Mormon settlements on the Great Salt Lake, but most headed 340 miles north to Fort Hall on the Snake River in Idaho. It took another three months to cover the remaining 800 miles. California-bound travelers followed the Humboldt River through the summer heat of Nevada.

Under the best of conditions the trip took six months, sixteen hours a day, dawn to dusk, of hard, grueling labor. Walking halfway across the continent was no easy task, and it provided a never-to-be-forgotten experience for those who did it. The wagon trains, carrying the dreams of thousands of individuals, reproduced society in small focus: individualistic, hopeful, mobile, divided by age and gender roles, apprehensive, yet willing to strike out for the distant and new.

Land for the Taking

As railroads pushed west in the 1870s and 1880s, locomotive trains replaced wagon trains, but the shift was gradual, and until the end of the century, emigrants often combined both modes of travel. Into the 1890s, travelers could be seen making their way across the West by any available means. Early railroad transportation was expensive, and the average farm family could not afford to buy tickets and ship supplies. Many Europeans traveled by rail to designated outfitting places and then proceeded west with wagons and oxen.

Traffic flowed in all directions, belying the image of a simple "westward" movement. Many people did go west, of course, but others, such as migrants from Mexico, became westerners by moving north, and Asian Americans moved eastward from the Pacific coast. Whatever their route, they all ended up in the meeting ground of cultures that formed the modern West.

Why did they come? "The motive that induced us to part with the pleasant associations and the dear friends of our childhood days," explained Phoebe Judson, an early emigrant, "was to obtain from the government of the United States a grant of land that 'Uncle

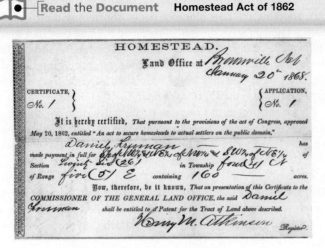

Read the Document   Homestead Act of 1862

Between 1862 and 1890, the government gave away 48 million acres under the Homestead Act of 1862. A law of great significance, it gave 160 acres of land to anyone who would pay 10% registration fee and pledge to live on the land, cultivating it for five years.

Sam' had promised to give to the head of each family who settled in this new country." A popular camp song reflected the same motive:

Come along, come along—don't be alarmed,
Uncle Sam is rich enough to give us all a farm.

Uncle Sam owned about one billion acres of land in the 1860s, much of it mountain and desert land unsuited for agriculture. By 1900, the various land laws had distributed half of it. Between 1862 and 1890, the government gave away 48 million acres under the **Homestead Act of 1862**, sold about 100 million acres to private citizens and corporations, granted 128 million acres to railroad companies to tempt them to build across the unsettled West, and sold huge tracts to the states.

The Homestead Act of 1862, a law of great significance, gave 160 acres of land to anyone who would pay a $10 registration fee and pledge to live on it and cultivate it for five years. The offer set off a mass migration of land-hungry Europeans, dazzled by a country that gave its land away. Americans also seized on the act's provisions, and between 1862 and 1900, nearly 600,000 families claimed free homesteads under it.

Yet the Homestead Act did not work as Congress had hoped. Few farmers and laborers had the cash to move to the frontier, buy farm equipment, and wait out the year or two before the farm became self-supporting. Tailored to the timber and water conditions of the East, the act did not work as well in the semiarid West. In the fertile valleys of the Mississippi, 160 acres provided a generous farm. A farmer on the Great Plains needed either a larger farm for dry farming or a smaller one for irrigation.

The Timber Culture Act of 1873 attempted to adjust the Homestead Act to western conditions. It allowed homesteaders to claim an additional 160 acres if they planted trees on a quarter of it within four years. A moderately successful act, it distributed 10 million acres of land, encouraged needed forestation, and enabled homesteaders to expand their farms to a workable size. Cattle ranchers lobbied for another law, the Desert Land Act of 1877, which allowed individuals to obtain 640 acres in the arid states for $1.25 an acre, provided they irrigated part of it within three years. The act invited fraud. More than 2.6 million acres of land were distributed, much of it fraudulently.

The Timber and Stone Act of 1878 applied only to lands "unfit for cultivation" and valuable chiefly for timber or stone. It permitted anyone in California, Nevada, Oregon, and Washington to buy up to 160 acres of forest land for $2.50 an acre. Like ranchers, lumber companies used employees to file false claims. By 1900, 3.6 million acres of rich forest land had been claimed under the measure.

Speculators made ingenious use of the land laws. Sending agents in advance of settlement, they moved along choice river bottoms or irrigable areas, accumulating large holdings to be held for high prices. In the arid West, where control of water meant control of the surrounding land, shrewd ranchers plotted their holdings accordingly. In Colorado, one cattleman, John F. Iliff, owned only 105 small parcels of land, but by placing them around the few water holes, he effectively dominated an empire stretching over 6,000 square miles.

Water, in fact, became a dominant western issue, since aside from the Pacific Northwest, northern California, parts of the Rocky Mountain West, and the eastern half of the Great Plains, much of the trans-Mississippi West was arid, receiving less than twenty inches of rainfall annually. People speculated in water as if it were gold and planned great irrigation systems in Utah, eastern Colorado, and California's Central Valley to "make the desert bloom." A sign in Modesto, California, read "Water, Wealth, Contentment, Health."

Irrigators received a major boost in 1902 when the **National Reclamation Act (Newlands Act)** set aside most of the proceeds from the sale of public lands in sixteen western states to finance irrigation projects in the arid states. Over the next decades, dams, canals, and irrigation systems channeled water into dry areas, creating a "hydraulic" society that was rich in crops and cities (such as Los Angeles and Phoenix), but ever thirstier and in danger of outrunning the precious water on which it all depended.

As beneficiaries of the government's policy of land grants for railway construction, the railroad companies were the West's largest landowners. Eager to have immigrants settle on the land they owned near the railroad right-of-way, and eager to boost their freight and passenger business, the companies sent agents to the East and Europe. Attractive brochures touted life in the West.

Railroad lines set up land departments and bureaus of immigration. The land departments priced the land, arranged credit terms, and even gave free farming courses to immigrants. The bureaus of immigration employed agents in Europe, met immigrants at eastern seaports, and ran special cars for land seekers heading west.

Half a billion acres of western land were given or sold to speculators and corporations. At the same time, only 600,000 homestead patents were issued, covering 80 million acres. Thus, only one acre in every nine initially went to individual pioneers, the intended beneficiaries of the nation's largesse. Two-thirds of all homestead claimants before 1890 failed in their efforts to farm their new land.

Territorial Government

As new areas of the West opened, they were organized as territories under the control of Congress and the president. The territorial system started with the famous Northwest Ordinance of 1787, which established the rules by which territories became states. Washington ran the territories like "a passive group of colonial mandates." The president appointed the governor and judges in each territory; Congress detailed their duties, set their budgets, and oversaw their activities. Territorial officials had almost absolute power over the territories.

Until they obtained statehood, then, the territories depended on the federal government for their existence. The national political parties, especially the Republicans, funneled government funds into the territorial economies, and in areas such as Wyoming and the Dakotas, where resources were scarce, economic growth depended on this money. Many early settlers held patronage jobs or hoped for them, traded with government-supported Native Americans, sold supplies to army troops, and speculated in government lands.

In a large portion of the trans-Mississippi West, a generation grew up under territorial rule. Inevitably, these citizens developed distinct ideas about politics, government, and the economy.

The Spanish-Speaking Southwest

In the nineteenth century, almost all Spanish-speaking people in the United States lived in California, Arizona, New Mexico, Texas, and Colorado. Their numbers were small—California had only 8,086 Mexican residents in 1900—but the influence of their culture and institutions was large. In some respects, the southwestern frontier was more Spanish American than Anglo-American.

Pushing northward from Mexico, the Spanish gradually established the present-day economic structure of the Southwest. They brought with them techniques of mining, stock raising, and irrigated farming. After winning independence in the 1820s, the Mexicans brought new laws and ranching methods as well as chaps and the burro. Both Spanish and Mexicans created the legal framework for distributing land and water, a precious resource in the Southwest. They gave large grants of land to communities for grazing, to individuals as rewards for service, and to the various Native American pueblos.

In Southern California, the Californios, descendants of the original colonizers, began after the 1860s to lose their once vast landholdings to drought and mortgages. Some turned to crime and became feared bandidos; others, such as José María Amador, lived in poverty and remembered better days:

> When I was but a little boy I drained the
>   chocolate pot,
> But now I am a poor man and am condemned
>   to slop.

In 1875, Romualdo Pacheco, an aristocratic native son, served as governor of California and then went on to Congress. But as the Californios died out, Mexican Americans continued the Spanish–Mexican influence. In 1880, one-fourth of the residents of Los Angeles County were Spanish speaking.

In New Mexico, Spanish-speaking citizens remained the majority ethnic group until the 1940s, and the Spanish Mexican culture dominated the territory. Contests over land grants became New Mexico's largest industry; lawyers who dealt in them amassed huge holdings. After 1888, *Las Gorras Blancas* ("The White Caps"), a secret organization of Spanish Americans, attacked the movement of Anglo ranchers into the Las Vegas community land grant.

Armed and hooded, they cut down fences and scattered the stock of those they viewed as intruders.

Throughout the Southwest, the Spanish Mexican heritage gave a distinctive shape to society. Men headed the families and dominated economic life. Women had substantial economic rights (though few political ones), and they enjoyed a status their English American counterparts did not have. Wives kept full control of property acquired before their marriage; they also held half title to all property in a marriage, which later caused many southwestern states to pass community property laws.

In addition, the Spanish Mexican heritage fostered a modified economic caste system, a strong Roman Catholic influence, and the primary use of the Spanish language. Continuous immigration from Mexico kept language and cultural ties strong. Spanish names and customs spread, even among Anglos. David Starr Jordan, arriving from Indiana to become the first president of Stanford University in California, bestowed Spanish names on streets, houses, and a Stanford dormitory. Spanish was the region's first or second language. Confronted by Sheriff Pat Garrett in a darkened room, New Mexico's famous outlaw Billy the Kid died asking, "Quién es? Quién es?" ("Who is it? Who is it?").

The Bonanza West

Why was the West a bonanza of dreams and get-rich-quick schemes?

Between 1850 and 1900, wave after wave of newcomers swept across the trans-Mississippi West. There were riches for the taking, hidden in gold-washed streams, spread lushly over grass-covered prairies, or available in the gullible minds of greedy newcomers. The nineteenth-century West took shape in the search for mining, cattle, and land bonanzas that drew eager settlers from the East and around the world.

As with all bonanzas, the consequences in the West were uneven growth, boom-and-bust economic cycles, and wasted resources. Society seemed constantly in the making. People moved here and there, following river bottoms, gold strikes, railroad tracks, and other opportunities. "Instant cities" arose. San Francisco, Salt Lake City, and Denver were the most spectacular examples, but every cow town and mining camp witnessed similar phenomena of growth. Boston needed more than two centuries to attract one-third of a million people; San Francisco did the same in a little more than twenty years.

Many Westerners had left home to get rich quickly, and they adopted institutions that reflected that goal. The West was an idea as well as a region, and the idea molded them as much as they molded it.

The Mining Bonanza

Mining was the first important magnet to attract people to the West. Many hoped to "strike it rich" in gold and silver, but at least half the newcomers had no intention of working in the mines. Instead, they provided food, clothing, and services to the thousands of miners. Leland Stanford and Collis P. Huntington, who later built the Central Pacific Railroad, set up a general store in Sacramento where they sold shovels and supplies. Stephen J. Field, later a prominent justice of the U.S. Supreme Court, followed the Gold Rush to California to practice law.

Read the Document   John Lester, "Hydraulic Mining"

This photograph from the mid-1800s shows gold miners on the American River in California pausing for a lunch break. Although significantly outnumbered by men, women on the mining frontier took a variety of jobs, including working claims.

The California Gold Rush of 1849 began the mining boom and set the pattern for subsequent strikes in other regions. Individual prospectors made the first strikes, discovering pockets of gold along streams flowing westward from the Sierra Nevada. To get the gold, they used a simple process called **placer mining**, which required little skill, technology, or capital. A placer miner needed only a shovel, a washing pan, and a good claim. As the placers gave out, a great deal of gold remained, but it was locked in quartz or buried deep in the earth. Mining became an expensive business, far beyond the reach of the average miner.

Large corporations moved in to dig the deep shafts and finance costly equipment. Quartz mining required heavy rock crushers, mercury vats to dissolve the gold, and large retorts to recapture it. Eastern and European financiers assumed control, labor became unionized, and mining towns took on some of the characteristics of the industrial city. Individual prospectors meanwhile dashed on to the next find. Unlike other frontiers, the mining frontier moved from west to east, as the original California miners—the "yonder-siders," they were called—hurried eastward in search of the big strike.

In 1859, fresh strikes were made near Pikes Peak in Colorado and in the Carson River Valley of Nevada. News of both discoveries set off wild migrations—one hundred thousand miners were in Pikes Peak country by June 1859. The gold there quickly played out, but the Nevada find uncovered a thick bluish black ore that was almost pure silver and gold. A quick-witted drifter named Henry T. P. Comstock talked his way into partnership in the claim, and word of the **Comstock Lode**—with ore worth $3,876 a ton—flashed over the mountains.

Thousands of miners climbed the Sierra Nevada that summer. On the rough slopes of Davidson Mountain, they created Virginia City, the prototype of the tumultuous western mining town.

The biggest strike was yet to come. In 1873, John W. Mackay and three partners formed a company to dig deep into the mountain, and at 1,167 feet they hit the Big Bonanza, a seam of gold and silver more than 54 feet wide. It was the richest discovery in the history of mining. Between 1859 and 1879, the Comstock Lode produced gold and silver worth $306 million. Most of it went to financiers and corporations. Mackay himself became the richest person in the world, earning (according to a European newspaper) $25 a minute, $5 a minute more than Czar Alexander II of Russia.

In the 1860s and 1870s, important strikes were made in Washington, Idaho, Nevada, Colorado, Montana, Arizona, and Dakota. Extremely mobile, miners flocked from strike to strike, and new camps and mining towns sprang up overnight. "The miners of Idaho were like quicksilver," said Hubert Howe Bancroft, an early historian. "A mass of them dropped in any locality, broke up into individual globules, and ran off after any atom of gold in their vicinity. They stayed nowhere longer than the gold attracted them."

The final fling came in the Black Hills rush of 1874 to 1876. The army had tried to keep miners out of the area, the heart of the Sioux hunting grounds, and even sent a scientific party under Colonel George Armstrong Custer to disprove the rumors of gold and stop the miners' invasion. Instead, Custer found gold all over the hills, and the rush was on. Miners, gamblers, desperadoes, and prostitutes flocked to Deadwood, the most lawless of all the mining camps. There, Martha Jane Canary—a crack shot who, as Calamity Jane, won fame as a scout and teamster—fell in love with "Wild Bill" Hickok. Hickok himself—a western legend who had tamed Kansas cow towns, killed an unknown number of men, and toured in Buffalo Bill's Wild West Show—died in Deadwood, shot in the back of the head. Hickok was thirty-nine years old.

Towns such as Deadwood, in the Dakota Territory; Virginia City, Nevada; Leadville, Colorado; and Tombstone, Arizona, demonstrated a new development process in the frontier experience. The farming frontier had developed naturally in a rural setting. On the mining frontier, the germ of a city—the camp—appeared almost simultaneously with the first "strike." Periodicals, the latest fashions, theaters, schools, literary clubs, and lending libraries came quickly to the camps, providing civilized refinements not available on other frontiers. Urbanization also created the need for municipal government, sanitation, and law enforcement.

Mining camps were governed by a simple democracy. Soon after a strike, the miners in the area met to organize a mining "district" and adopted rules governing behavior in it. Rules regulated the size and boundaries of claims, established procedures for settling disputes, and set penalties for crimes. Petty criminals were banished from the district; serious offenders were hanged. In the case of a major dispute, the whole camp gathered, chose legal counsel for both sides, and heard the evidence. If all else failed, miners

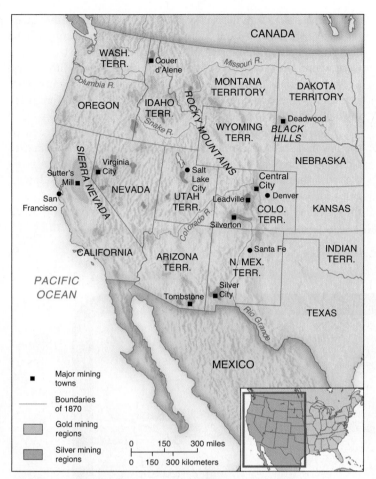

MINING REGIONS OF THE WEST Gold and silver mines dotted the West, drawing settlers and encouraging political organization in many areas.

formed secret vigilance committees to hang a few offenders as a lesson to the rest. Early visitors to the mining country were struck by the way miners, solitary and competitive, joined together, founded a camp, and created a society.

In 1870, men outnumbered women in the mining districts by more than two to one; there were few children. Prostitutes followed the camps around the West, and a "respectable" woman was an object of curiosity. Four arrived in Nevada City in 1853, and one observed, "The men stand and gaze at us with mouth and eyes wide open, every time we go out." Some women worked claims, but more often they took jobs as cooks, housekeepers, and seamstresses—for wages considerably higher than in the East.

In most camps, between one-quarter and one-half of the population was foreign born. The lure of gold drew large numbers of Chinese, Chileans, Peruvians, Mexicans, French, Germans, and English. Experienced miners, the Latin Americans brought valuable mining techniques. At least six thousand Mexicans joined the California rush of 1849, and by 1852, there were twenty-five thousand Chinese in California. Painstakingly, the Chinese profitably worked claims others had abandoned. In the 1860s, almost one-third of the miners in the West were Chinese.

Hostility often surfaced against foreign miners, particularly the French, Latin Americans, and Chinese. In 1850, California passed a Foreign Miners' Tax that charged foreign miners a $20 monthly licensing fee. As intended, it drove out Mexicans and other foreigners. Riots against Chinese laborers occurred in the 1870s and 1880s in Los Angeles, San Francisco, Seattle, Reno, and Denver. Responding to pressure, Congress passed the **Chinese Exclusion Act of 1882**, which suspended immigration of Chinese laborers for ten years. The number of Chinese in the United States fell drastically.

By the 1890s, the early mining bonanza was over. All told, the western mines contributed billions of dollars to the economy. They had helped finance the Civil War and provided needed capital for industrialization. The vast boost in silver production from the Comstock Lode changed the relative value of gold and silver, the base of American currency. Bitter disputes over the currency affected politics and led to the famous "battle of the standards" in the presidential election of 1896 (see Chapter 20).

The mining frontier populated portions of the West and sped its process of political organization. Nevada, Idaho, and Montana were granted early statehood because of mining. Merchants, editors, lawyers, and ministers moved with the advancing frontier, establishing permanent settlements. Women in the mining camps helped to foster family life and raised the moral tone by campaigning against drinking, gambling, and prostitution. But not all the effects of the mining boom were positive. The industry also left behind painful scars in the form of invaded Indian reservations, pitted hills, and lonely ghost towns.

Gold from the Roots Up: The Cattle Bonanza

"There's gold from the grass roots down," said California Joe, a guide in the gold districts of Dakota in the 1870s, "but there's more gold from the grass roots up." Ranchers began to recognize the potential of the vast grasslands of the West. The plains were covered with buffalo or grama grass, a wiry variety with short, hard stems. Cattle thrived on it.

For twenty years after 1865, cattle ranching dominated the "open range," a vast fenceless area extending from the Texas Panhandle north into Canada. The techniques of the business came from Mexico. Long before American cowboys moved herds north, their Mexican counterparts, the *vaqueros*, developed the essential techniques of branding, roundups, and roping. The cattle themselves, the famous Texas longhorns, also came from Mexico. Spreading over the grasslands of southern Texas, the longhorns multiplied rapidly. Although their meat was coarse and stringy, they fed a nation hungry for beef at the end of the Civil War.

The problem was getting the beef to eastern markets, and Joseph G. McCoy, a livestock shipper from Illinois, solved it. Looking for a way to market Texas beef, McCoy conceived the idea of taking the cattle to railheads in Kansas. He talked first with the president of the Missouri Pacific, who ordered him out of his office, and then with the head of the Kansas Pacific, who laughed at the idea. The persistent McCoy finally signed a contract in 1867 with the Hannibal and St. Joseph Railroad. Searching for an appropriate rail junction, he settled on the sleepy Kansas town of Abilene, "a very small, dead place," he remembered, with about a dozen log huts and one nearly bankrupt saloon.

In September 1867, McCoy shipped the first train of twenty cars of longhorn cattle. By the end of the year, a thousand carloads had followed, all headed for Chicago markets. In 1870, three hundred thousand head of Texas cattle reached Abilene, followed the next year—the peak year—by seven hundred thousand head. The Alamo Saloon, crowded with tired cowboys at the end of the drive, now employed seventy-five bartenders, working three 8-hour shifts.

The profits were enormous. Drivers bought cheap Texas steers for $4 a head and sold them for $30 or $40 a head at the northern railhead. The most famous trail was the Chisholm, running from southern Texas through Oklahoma Territory to Ellsworth and Abilene, Kansas, on the Kansas Pacific Railroad. Dodge City, Kansas, became the prime shipping center between 1875 and 1879.

Cowboys pushed steers northward in herds of two to three thousand. Novels and films have portrayed the cowboys as white,

but at least a quarter of them were black, and possibly another quarter were Mexicans. A typical crew on the trail north might have eight men, half of them black or Mexican. Most of the trail bosses were white; they earned about $125 a month. James "Jim" Perry, a renowned black cowboy who worked for more than twenty years as a rider, roper, and cook for the XIT ranch, said, "If it weren't for my damned old black face, I'd have been a boss long ago."

Like miners, cattlemen lived beyond the formal reach of the law and so established their own. Before each drive, Charles Goodnight drew up rules governing behavior on the trail. A cowboy who shot another was hanged on the spot. Ranchers adopted rules for cattle ownership, branding, roundups, and drives, and they formed associations to enforce them. The Wyoming Stock

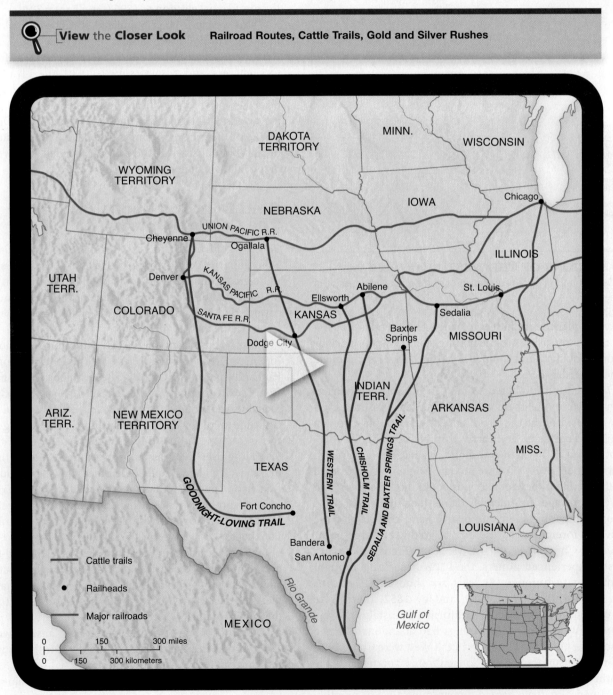

🔍 **View the Closer Look**   **Railroad Routes, Cattle Trails, Gold and Silver Rushes**

CATTLE TRAILS Cattle raised in Texas were driven along the cattle trails to the northern railheads, and trains carried them to market.

Growers' Association, the largest and most formidable, had four hundred members owning two million cattle; its reach extended well beyond Wyoming into Colorado, Nebraska, Montana, and the Dakotas. Throughout this vast territory, the "laws" of the association were often the law of the land.

By 1880, more than six million cattle had been driven to northern markets. But the era of the great cattle drive was ending. Farmers were planting wheat on the old buffalo ranges; barbed wire, a recent invention, cut across the trails and divided up the big ranches. Mechanical improvements in slaughtering, refrigerated transportation, and cold storage modernized the industry. Ranchers bred the Texas longhorns with heavier Hereford and Angus bulls, and as the new breeds proved profitable, more and more ranches opened on the northern ranges.

By the mid-1880s, some 4.5 million cattle grazed the High Plains, reminding people of the once great herds of buffalo. Stories of vast profits circulated, attracting outside capital. Large investments transformed ranching into big business, often controlled by absentee owners and subject to new problems.

By 1885, experienced cattle ranchers were growing alarmed. A presidential order that year forced them out of the Indian Territory in Oklahoma, adding two hundred thousand cattle to the overcrowded northern ranges. The winter of 1885 to 1886 was cold, and the following summer was one of the hottest on record. Water holes dried up; the grass turned brown. Beef prices fell.

The winter of 1886–1887 was one of the worst in western history. Temperatures dropped to 45 degrees below zero, and cattle that once would have saved themselves by drifting ahead of the storms came up against the new barbed wire fences. Herds jammed together, pawing the frozen ground or stripping bark from trees in search of food. Cattle died by the tens of thousands. In the spring of 1887, when the snows thawed, ranchers found stacks of carcasses piled up against the fences.

The melting snows did, however, produce a lush crop of grass for the survivors. The cattle business recovered, but it took different directions. Outside capital, so plentiful in the boom years, dried up. Ranchers began fencing their lands, reducing their herds, and growing hay for winter food. To the dismay of cowboys, mowing machines and hay rakes became as important as chuck wagons and branding irons. "I tell you times have changed," one cowboy said sadly.

The last roundup on the northern ranges took place in 1905. Ranches grew smaller, and some ranchers, at first in the scrub country of the Southwest, then on the plains themselves, switched to raising sheep. By 1900, there were nearly thirty-eight million sheep west of the Missouri River, far more than there were cattle. In Montana, there were six or seven sheep for each cow, and even Wyoming, the great center of the northern ranches, had more sheep than cows.

Ranchers and sheepherders fought bitterly to control the grazing lands, but they had one problem in common: the troubles ahead. Homesteaders, armed with barbed wire and new strains of wheat, were pushing onto the plains, and the day of the open range was over.

Sodbusters on the Plains: The Farming Bonanza

Like miners and cattle ranchers, millions of farmers moved into the West in the decades after 1870 to seek crop bonanzas and new ways of life. Some realized their dreams; many fought just to survive.

Said a folksong from Greer County, Oklahoma,

Hurrah for Greer County! The land of the free,
The land of the bedbug, grasshopper, and flea;
I'll sing of its praises, I'll tell of its fame,
While starving to death on my government claim.

Between 1870 and 1900, farmers cultivated more land than ever before in American history. They peopled the plains from Dakota to Texas, pushed the Indians out of their last sanctuary in Oklahoma, and poured into the basins and foothills of the Rockies. By 1900, the western half of the nation contained almost 30 percent of the population, compared to less than 1 percent just a half century earlier.

Unlike mining, farm settlement often followed predictable patterns, taking population from states east of the settlement line and moving gradually westward. Crossing the Mississippi, farmers settled first in western Iowa, Minnesota, Nebraska, Kansas, Texas, and South Dakota. The movement slumped during the depression of the 1870s, but then a new wave of optimism carried thousands more west. Several years of above average rainfall convinced farmers that the Dakotas, western Nebraska and Kansas, and eastern Colorado were the "rain belt of the plains." Between 1870 and 1900, the population on the plains tripled.

In some areas, the newcomers were blacks who had fled the South, fed up with beatings and murders, crop liens, and the Black Codes that institutionalized their subordinate status. In 1879, about six thousand African Americans known as the **Exodusters** left their homes in Louisiana, Mississippi, and Texas to establish new and freer lives in Kansas, the home of John Brown and the Free-Soil campaigns of the 1850s. Once there, they farmed or worked as laborers; women worked in the fields alongside the men or cleaned houses and took in washing to make ends meet. All told, the Exodusters homesteaded 20,000 acres of land, and though they met prejudice, it was not as extreme as they had known at home. "I asked my wife did she know the ground she stands on," said John Solomon Lewis, a Louisianan, soon after arriving. "She said, 'No!' I said it is free ground; and she cried like a child for joy."

Other African Americans moved to Oklahoma, thinking they might establish the first African American state. Whether headed for Oklahoma or Kansas, they picked up and moved in sizable groups that were based on family units; they took with them the customs they had known, and in their new homes they were able, for the first time, to have some measure of self-government.

For blacks and whites alike, farming on the plains presented new problems. There was little surface water, and wells ranged between 50 and 500 feet deep. Well drillers charged up to $2 a foot. Taking advantage of the steady plains winds, windmills brought the water to the surface, but they too were expensive, and until 1900, many farmers could not afford them. Lumber for homes and fences was also scarce.

Unable to afford wood, farmers often started out in dreary sod houses. Cut into 3-foot sections, the thick prairie sod was laid like brick, with space left for two windows and a door. Since glass was scarce, cloth hung over the windows; a blanket was hung from the ceiling to make two rooms. Sod houses were small, provided little light and air, and were impossible to keep

Disappointed with the failures of Reconstruction and fearful of the violence that surrounded them, many southern blacks migrated to Kansas in the 1870s and 1880s. Comparing their trek to the biblical story of the Israelites' exodus from Egypt, they became known as Exodusters.

clean. When it rained, water seeped through the roof. Yet a sod house cost only $2.78 to build.

Outside, the plains environment sorely tested the men and women who moved there. Neighbors were distant; the land stretched on as far as the eye could see. Always the wind blew. "As long as I live I'll never see such a lonely country," a woman said of the Texas plains; a Nebraska woman said, "These unbounded prairies have such an air of desolation—and the stillness is very oppressive."

In the winters, savage storms swept the open grasslands. Ice caked on the cattle until their heads were too heavy to hold up. Summertime temperatures stayed near 110 degrees for weeks at a time. Fearsome rainstorms, building in the summer's heat, beat down the young corn and wheat. The summers also brought grasshoppers, arriving without warning, flying in clouds so huge they shut out the sun. The grasshoppers ate everything in sight: crops, clothing, mosquito netting, tree bark, even plow handles. In the summer of 1874, they devastated the whole plains from Texas to the Dakotas, eating everything "but the mortgage," as one farmer said.

New Farming Methods

Farmers adopted new techniques to meet conditions on the plains. For one thing, they needed cheap and effective fencing material, and in 1874, Joseph F. Glidden, a farmer from De Kalb, Illinois, provided it with the invention of barbed wire. By 1883, his factory was turning out six hundred miles of barbed wire every day, and farmers were buying it faster than it could be produced.

Dry farming, a new technique, helped compensate for the lack of rainfall. By plowing furrows twelve to fourteen inches deep and creating a dust mulch to fill the furrow, farmers loosened the soil and slowed evaporation. Wheat farmers imported European varieties of plants that could withstand the harsh plains winters. Hard-kerneled varieties such as Turkey red wheat from Russia required new milling methods, developed during the 1870s. By 1881, Minneapolis, St. Louis, and Kansas City had become milling centers for the rich "new process" flour.

Farm technology changed long before the Civil War, but later developments improved it. In 1877, James Oliver of Indiana patented a chilled-iron plow with a smooth-surfaced moldboard that did not clog in the thick prairie soils. The spring-tooth harrow (1869) sped soil preparation; the grain drill (1874) opened furrows and scientifically fed seed into the ground. The lister (1880) dug a deep furrow, planted corn at the bottom, and covered the seed—all in one operation.

The first baling press was built in 1866, and the hay loader was patented in 1876. The first successful harvester, the cord binder (1878), cut and tied bundles of grain, enabling two men and a team of horses to harvest 20 acres of wheat a day. Invented earlier, threshers grew larger; employing as many as nine men and ten horses, one machine could thresh 300 bushels of grain a day.

In 1890, more than nine hundred corporations manufactured farm machinery. Scientific agriculture flourished under new discoveries linking soil minerals and plant growth. Samuel Johnson of Yale University published *How Crops Grow* (1868) and *How Crops Feed* (1870), and one of his students pioneered work on nitrogen, the base of many modern fertilizers. The Hatch Act, passed in 1887, supported agricultural experiment stations that spread the discoveries among farmers. Four years later, the stations employed more than 450 persons and distributed more than 300 published reports annually to some 350,000 readers.

In the late 1870s, huge **bonanza farms** rose, run by the new machinery and financed with outside capital. Oliver Dalrymple, the most famous of the bonanza farmers, headed an experiment in North Dakota's Red River Valley in 1875, then moved on to manage the Grandin Bonanza of 61,000 acres, five times the size of Manhattan Island. Dalrymple hired armies of workers, bought machinery by the carload, and planted on a scale that dazzled the West.

The bonanza farms—thanks to their size and machinery—captured the country's imagination. Using 200 pairs of harrows, 155 binders, and 16 threshers, Dalrymple produced 600,000 bushels of wheat in 1881. He and other bonanza managers profited from the economies of scale, buying materials at wholesale prices and receiving rebates from the railroads. Then a period of drought began. Rainfall dropped between 1885 and 1890, and the large-scale growers found it hard to compete with smaller farmers who diversified their crops and cultivated more intensively. Many of the large bonanzas slowly disintegrated, and Dalrymple himself went bankrupt in 1896.

Discontent on the Farm

Touring the South in the 1860s, Oliver H. Kelley, a clerk in the Department of Agriculture, was struck by the drabness of rural life. In 1867, he founded the **National Grange of the Patrons of Husbandry**, known simply as the Grange. The Grange provided social, cultural, and educational activities for its members. Its constitution banned involvement in politics, but Grangers often ignored the rules and supported railroad regulation and other measures.

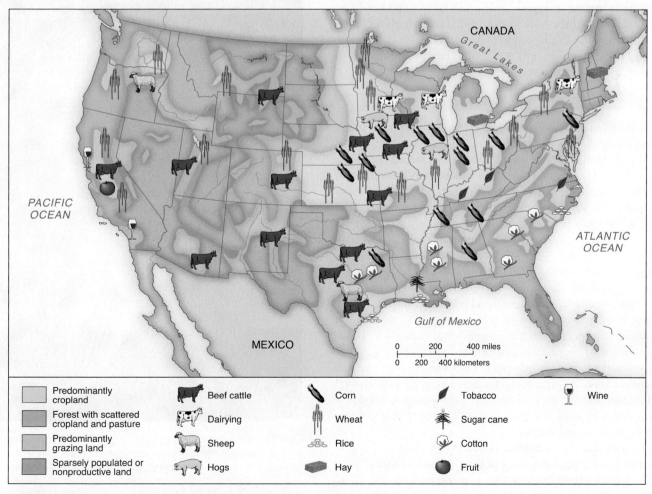

AGRICULTURAL LAND USE IN THE 1880S New farming technology and new crops enabled more and more land to be put to productive use.

The Grange grew rapidly during the depression of the 1870s, and by 1875, it had more than eight hundred thousand members in twenty thousand local Granges. Most were in the Midwest and South. The Granges set up cooperative stores, grain elevators, warehouses, insurance companies, and farm machinery factories. Many failed, but in the meantime the organization made its mark. Picking up where the Grange left off, farm-oriented groups such as the Farmers' Alliance, with branches in both South and West, began to attract followers.

Like the cattle boom, the farming boom ended sharply after 1887. A severe drought that year cut harvests, and other droughts followed in 1889 and 1894. Thousands of new farmers were wiped out on the western plains. Between 1888 and 1892, more than half the population of western Kansas left. Farmers grew angry and restless. They complained about declining crop prices, rising railroad rates, and heavy mortgages.

Although many farmers were unhappy, the peopling of the West in those years transformed American agriculture. The states beyond the Mississippi became the garden land of the nation. California sent fruit, wine, and wheat to eastern markets. Under the Mormons, Utah flourished with irrigation. Texas beef stocked the country's tables, and vast wheat fields, stretching to the horizon, covered Minnesota, the Dakotas, Montana, and eastern Colorado. All produced more than Americans could consume. By 1890, American farmers were exporting large amounts of wheat and other crops.

Farmers became more commercial and scientific. They needed to know more and work harder. Mail-order houses and rural free delivery diminished their isolation and tied them ever closer to the national future. "This is a new age to the farmer," said a statistician in the Department of Agriculture in 1889. "He is now, more than ever before, a citizen of the world."

The Final Fling

As the West filled in with people, pressure mounted on the president and Congress to open the last Indian territory, Oklahoma, to settlers. In March 1889, Congress acted and forced the Creek and Seminole tribes, which had been moved into Oklahoma in the 1820s, to surrender their rights to the land. With arrangements complete, President Benjamin Harrison announced the opening of the Oklahoma District as of noon, April 22, 1889.

Preparations were feverish all along the frontier. "From all the West," historian Ray Allen Billington noted, "the homeless, the speculators, the adventurers, flocked to the still forbidden land." On the morning of April 22, nearly a hundred thousand people lined the Oklahoma borders; "for miles on end horsemen, wagons, hacks, carriages, bicycles, and a host of vehicles beggaring description stood wheel to wheel awaiting the signal." Fifteen Santa Fe trains were jammed with people from platform to roof.

At noon, the starting flag dropped. Bugles and cannon signaled the opening of the "last" territory. Horsemen lunged forward; overloaded wagons collided and overturned. The trains steamed slowly forward, forced by army troops to keep a pace that would not give their passengers an undue advantage.

By sunset that day, settlers claimed twelve thousand homesteads, and the 1.92 million acres of the Oklahoma District were officially settled. Homesteaders threw up shelters for the night. By evening, Oklahoma City, that morning merely a spot on the prairie with cottonwoods and grass, had ten thousand people;

Guthrie to the north had fifteen thousand. Speculators swiftly erected pay toilets, and drinking water cost as much as a beer.

The "Boomers" (those who waited for the signal) and "Sooners" (those who had jumped the gun) reflected the speed of western settlement. "Creation!" a character in Edna Ferber's novel *Cimarron* declared. "Hell! That took six days. This was done in one. It was History made in an hour—and I helped make it."

Conclusion: The Meaning of the West

Between the Civil War and 1900, the West witnessed one of the greatest migrations in history. With the Native Americans driven into smaller and smaller areas, farms, ranches, mines, and cities took over the vast lands from the Mississippi to the Pacific.

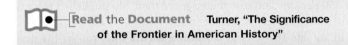

Read the Document   Turner, "The Significance of the Frontier in American History"

During a gathering of historians at the World's Columbian Exhibition in Chicago in 1893, Frederick Jackson Turner presented an essay titled "The Significance of the Frontier in American History." Turner's article, also known as the Frontier Thesis, argued that the settlement of the frontier made the American nation unique. Turner credited the frontier's settlement as the primary force in shaping the nation's democratic institutions.

The 1890 census noted that for the first time in the country's history, "there can hardly be said to be a frontier line." Picking up the theme, Frederick Jackson Turner, a young history instructor at the University of Wisconsin, examined its importance in an influential 1893 paper, "The Significance of the Frontier in American History."

"The existence of an area of free land," Turner wrote, "its continuous recession, and the advance of American settlement westward, explain American development." It shaped customs and character; gave rise to independence, self-confidence, and individualism; and fostered invention and adaptation. Historians have substantially modified **Turner's thesis** by pointing to frontier conservatism and imitativeness, the influence of varying racial groups, and the persistence of European ideas and institutions. Most recently, they have shown that family and community loomed as large as individualism on the frontier; men, women, and children played very much the same roles as they had back home.

Rejecting Turner almost completely, a group of "new Western historians" has advanced a different and complex view of the West, and one with few heroes and heroines. Emphasizing the region's racial and ethnic diversity, these historians emphasize the role of women as well as men, trace struggles between economic interests instead of fights between gunslingers, and question the impact of development on the environment. White English-speaking Americans, they suggest, could be said to have conquered the West rather than settled it.

The West, in this view, was not settled by a wave of white migrants moving west across the continent (Turner's "frontier") but by a set of waves—Anglo, Mexican American, African American, Asian American, and others—moving in many directions and interacting with each other and with Native American cultures to produce the modern West. Nor did western history end in 1890 as Turner would have it. Instead, migration, development, and economic exploitation continued into the twentieth century, illustrated in the fact that the number of people who moved to the West after 1900 far exceeded those who had moved there before.

In both the nineteenth and twentieth centuries, there can be no doubt that the image of the frontier and the West influenced American development. Western lands attracted European, Latin American, and Asian immigrants, adding to the society's talent and diversity. The mines, forests, and farms of the West fueled the economy, sent raw materials to eastern factories, and fed the growing cities. Though defeated in warfare, the Native Americans and Mexicans influenced art, architecture, law, and western folklore. The West was the first American empire, and it had a profound impact on the American mind and imagination.

Study Resources

 Take the **Study Plan** for **Chapter 17** *The West: Exploiting an Empire* on **MyHistoryLab**

TIME LINE

1849 Gold Rush to California

1859 More gold and silver discoveries in Colorado and Nevada

1862 Congress passes Homestead Act encouraging western settlement

1864 Nevada admitted to the Union; Colonel John Chivington leads massacre of Indians at Sand Creek, Colorado

1865–1867 Sioux War against white miners and U.S. Army

1866 "Long drive" of cattle touches off cattle bonanzas

1867 Horace Greeley urges Easterners to "Go West, young man"; National Grange of the Patrons of Husbandry (the Grange) founded to enrich farmers' lives

1867–1868 Policy of "small reservations" for Indians adopted

1873 Congress passes Timber Culture Act; Big bonanza discovered on the Comstock Lode in Nevada

1874 Joseph F. Glidden invents barbed wire; Discovery of gold in Dakota Territory sets off Black Hills Gold Rush

1876 Colorado admitted to the Union; Custer and his men defeated and killed by the Sioux at battle of the Little Bighorn (June)

1883 Museum expedition discovers fewer than two hundred buffalo in the West

1886–1887 Severe drought and winter damage cattle and farming bonanzas

1887 Congress passes Dawes Severalty Act, making Indians individual landowners; Hatch Act provides funds for establishment of agricultural experiment stations

1889 Washington, Montana, and the Dakotas admitted to the Union; Oklahoma Territory opened to settlement

1890 Idaho and Wyoming admitted to the Union; Teton Sioux massacred at battle of Wounded Knee, South Dakota (December)

1893 Young historian Frederick Jackson Turner analyzes closing of the frontier

1902 Congress passes National Reclamation Act (the Newlands Act)

CHAPTER REVIEW

Beyond the Frontier

What were the challenges of settling the country west of the Mississippi?

West of the Mississippi River, settlers encountered new conditions, including vast treeless plains and towering mountain ranges. Above all, they left behind the water and timber on which they had depended in the East, forcing them to devise new ways to deal with the different challenges. (p. 391)

Crushing the Native Americans

How did white Americans crush the culture of the Native Americans as they moved west?

Native Americans had a complex culture suited to the various environments in which they lived. The United States government and white settlers employed various methods—political, military, legal, and cultural—to oust the Indians from their lands, "civilize" them, and contain and control them. (p. 392)

Settlement of the West

Why did Americans and others move to the West?

Americans moved west for many reasons, including a desire to get rich, seek religious freedom, and improve health. The federal government helped out with generous land laws and laws favoring irrigation in the arid West. In the Southwest a proud culture took shape around Spanish laws and customs, involving water, the rights of women, and the sale, ownership, and use of land. (p. 400)

The Bonanza West

Why was the West a bonanza of dreams and get-rich-quick schemes?

The West attracted many people seeking a better economic life. Many failed, but others found bonanzas in mining, cattle ranching, and farming. In many of these areas, western development paralleled trends in the rest of the nation: larger and larger businesses, new uses for technology, and the employment of outside capital. (p. 403)

KEY TERMS AND DEFINITIONS

Ghost Dances A religious movement that arose in the late nineteenth century under the prophet Wavoka, a Paiute Indian. Its followers believed that dances and rites would cause white men to disappear and restore lands to the Native Americans. The U.S. government outlawed the Ghost Dances, and army intervention to stop them led to the Wounded Knee Massacre. p. 396

Wounded Knee Massacre In December 1890, troopers of the Seventh Cavalry, under orders to stop the Ghost Dance religion among the Sioux, took Chief Big Foot and his followers to a camp on Wounded Knee Creek in South Dakota. It is uncertain who fired the first shot, but two hundred Native Americans were killed. p. 396

Dawes Severalty Act Legislation passed by Congress in 1887 that aimed to break up traditional Indian life by promoting individual land ownership. It divided tribal lands into small plots that were distributed among members of each tribe. Provisions were made for education and eventual citizenship. The law led to corruption and exploitation and weakened tribal culture. p. 397

Gold Rush of 1849 Prospectors made the first gold strikes along the Sierra Nevada Mountains in California in 1849, touching off a mining boom that set the pattern for subsequent strikes in other regions. p. 401

Overland Trail The route from the Mississippi Valley to the Pacific Coast in the last half of the nineteenth century. p. 401

Homestead Act of 1862 Legislation granting 160 acres to anyone who paid a $10 fee and pledged to live on and cultivate the land for five years. Between 1862 and 1900, nearly 600,000 families claimed homesteads under its provisions. p. 402

National Reclamation Act (Newlands Act) Passed in 1902, this legislation set aside most of the proceeds from the sale of public land in sixteen western states to fund irrigation projects. p. 402

Placer mining Mining that included using a shovel and washing pan to separate gold from the ore in streams and riverbeds. Placer miners worked as individuals or in small groups. p. 404

Comstock Lode Discovered in 1859 near Virginia City, Nevada, this ore deposit was the richest discovery in the history of mining. Named after T. P. Comstock, the deposit produced silver and gold worth more than $306 million. p. 404

Chinese Exclusion Act of 1882 Legislation passed in 1882 that excluded Chinese immigrants for ten years and denied U.S. citizenship to Chinese nationals. It was the first U.S. exclusionary law aimed at a specific racial group. p. 405

Exodusters A group of about 6,000 African Americans who left Louisiana, Mississippi, and Texas in 1879, for freer lives as farmers or laborers in Kansas. p. 406

Dry farming A farming technique developed to allow farming in the more arid parts of the West where settlers had to deal with far less rainfall than they had east of the Mississippi. Furrows were plowed approximately a foot deep and filled with a dust mulch to loosen soil and slow evaporation. p. 408

Bonanza farms Huge farms covering thousands of acres on the Great Plains. In relying on large size and new machinery, they represented a development in agriculture similar to that taking place in industry. p. 409

National Grange of the Patrons of Husbandry Founded by Oliver H. Kelly in 1867, the Grange sought to relieve the drabness of farm life by providing a social, educational, and cultural outlet for its members. It also set up grain elevators, cooperative stores, warehouses, insurance companies, and farm machinery factories. p. 409

Turner's thesis Put forth by historian Frederick Jackson Turner in 1893, this thesis asserted that the existence of a frontier and its settlement had shaped American character; given rise to individualism, independence, and self-confidence; and fostered the American spirit of invention and adaptation. Later historians modified the thesis by pointing out the environmental and other consequences of frontier settlement, the federal government's role in peopling the West, and the clash of races and cultures that took place on the frontier. p. 411

CRITICAL THINKING QUESTIONS

1. What kinds of conditions did settlers find as they moved into lands west of the Mississippi River, and how had the peoples who already lived there dealt with these conditions?

2. What was the nature of Indian culture on the Plains, and how did it deal with the hordes of settlers moving into the area?

3. By what methods did settlers move west and adjust to the "bonanzas" they found in the West and Southwest?

4. What were the three bonanzas that drew settlers into the West, and in what ways did they lead to the destruction of Native American culture and shape the growth of the area?

MyHistoryLab Media Assignments

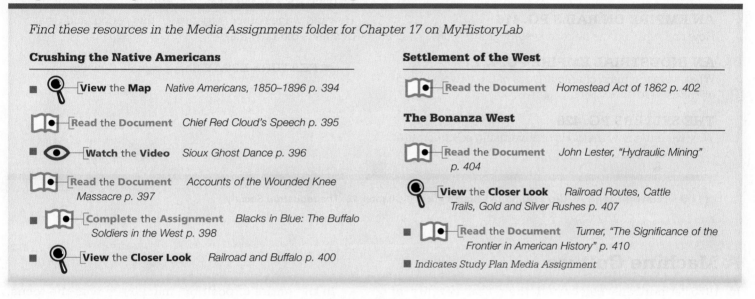

Find these resources in the Media Assignments folder for Chapter 17 on MyHistoryLab

Crushing the Native Americans

- **View** the **Map**   Native Americans, 1850–1896 p. 394

- **Read** the **Document**   Chief Red Cloud's Speech p. 395

- **Watch** the **Video**   Sioux Ghost Dance p. 396

- **Read** the **Document**   Accounts of the Wounded Knee Massacre p. 397

- **Complete** the **Assignment**   Blacks in Blue: The Buffalo Soldiers in the West p. 398

- **View** the **Closer Look**   Railroad and Buffalo p. 400

Settlement of the West

- **Read** the **Document**   Homestead Act of 1862 p. 402

The Bonanza West

- **Read** the **Document**   John Lester, "Hydraulic Mining" p. 404

- **View** the **Closer Look**   Railroad Routes, Cattle Trails, Gold and Silver Rushes p. 407

- **Read** the **Document**   Turner, "The Significance of the Frontier in American History" p. 410

■ Indicates Study Plan Media Assignment

18 The Industrial Society

Contents and Learning Objectives

((•—Listen to the **Audio File** on **myhistorylab**   Chapter 18 *The Industrial Society*

A Machine Culture

In 1876, Americans celebrated their first century of independence. Survivors of a recent civil war, they observed the centenary proudly and rather self-consciously, in song and speech, and above all in the grand Centennial Exposition held in Philadelphia, Pennsylvania.

Spread over several hundred acres, the exposition occupied 180 buildings and attracted nine million visitors, about one-fifth of the country's population at the time. Significantly, it focused more on the present than the past. Fairgoers strolled through exhibits of life in colonial times, then hurried off to see the main attractions: machines, inventions, and products of the new industrial era. They saw linoleum, a new, easy-to-clean floor covering. For the first time, they tasted root beer, supplied by a young druggist named Charles Hires, and the exotic banana, wrapped in foil and selling for a dime. They saw their first bicycle, an awkward high-wheeled contraption with solid tires.

A Japanese pavilion generated widespread interest in the culture of Japan. There was also a women's building, the first ever in a major exposition. Inside were displayed paintings and sculpture by women artists, along with rows of textile machinery staffed by female operators.

In the entire exposition, machinery was the focus, and Machinery Hall was the most popular building. Here were the products of an ever-improving civilization. Long lines of the curious waited to see the telephone, Alexander Graham Bell's new device. ("My God, it talks!" the emperor of Brazil exclaimed.) Thomas A. Edison displayed several recent inventions, while nearby, whirring machines turned out bricks, chewing tobacco, and other products. Fairgoers saw the first public display of the typewriter, Elisha Otis's new elevator, and the Westinghouse railroad air brake.

But above all, they crowded around the mighty Corliss engine, the focal point of the exposition. A giant steam engine, it dwarfed everything else in Machinery Hall, its twin vertical cylinders towering almost four stories in the air. Alone, it supplied power for the eight thousand other machines, large and small, on the exposition grounds. Poorly designed, the Corliss was soon obsolete, but for the moment it captured the nation's imagination. It symbolized swift movement toward an industrial and urban society. John Greenleaf Whittier, the aging rural poet, likened it to the snake in the Garden of Eden and refused to see it.

The Corliss engine, a "mechanical marvel" at the Centennial Exposition, was a prime example of the giantism so admired by the public.

As Whittier feared, the United States was fast becoming an industrial society. Developments earlier in the century laid the basis, but the most spectacular advances in industrialization came during the three decades after the Civil War. At the start of the war, the country lagged well behind industrializing nations such as Great Britain, France, and Germany. By 1900, it had vaulted far into the lead, with a manufacturing output that exceeded the *combined* output of its three European rivals. Over the same years, cities grew, technology advanced, and farm production rose. Developments in manufacturing, mining, agriculture, transportation, and communications changed society.

In this change, railroads, steel, oil, and other industries, all shaped by the hands of labor, played a leading role. Many Americans eagerly welcomed the new directions. William Dean Howells, a leading novelist, visited the Centennial Exposition and stood in awe before the Corliss. Comparing it to the paintings and sculpture on display, Howells preferred the machine: "It is in these things of iron and steel," he said, "that the national genius most freely speaks."

Industrial Development

What enabled the United States to build an industrial economy?

American industry owed its remarkable growth to several considerations. It fed on an abundance of natural resources: coal, iron, timber, petroleum, and waterpower. An iron manufacturer likened the nation to "a gigantic bowl filled with treasure." Labor was also abundant, drawn from American farm families and the hosts of European immigrants who flocked to American mines, cities, and factories. Nearly eight million immigrants arrived in the 1870s and 1880s; another fifteen million came between 1890 and 1914—large figures for a nation whose total population in 1900 was about seventy-six million people.

The burgeoning population led to expanded markets, which new devices such as the telegraph and telephone helped to exploit. The swiftly growing urban populations devoured goods, and the railroads, spreading pell-mell across the land, linked the cities together and opened a national market. Within its boundaries, the United States had the largest free trade market in the world, while tariff barriers partially protected its producers from outside competition.

Expansive market and labor conditions buoyed the confidence of investors, European and American, who provided large amounts of capital. Technological progress, so remarkable in these years, doomed some older industries (tallow, for example) but increased productivity in others, such as the kerosene industry, and created entirely new industries as well. Through inventions such as the harvester and the combine, it also helped foster a firm agricultural base, on which industrialization depended.

Eager to promote economic growth, government at all levels—federal, state, and local—gave manufacturers money, land, and other resources. Other benefits, too, flowed from the American system of government: stability, commitment to the concept of private property, and, initially at least, a reluctance to regulate industrial activity. Unlike their European counterparts, American manufacturers faced few legal or social barriers, and

their main domestic rivals, the southern planters, had lost political power in the Civil War.

In this atmosphere, entrepreneurs flourished. Taking steps crucial for industrialization, they organized, managed, and assumed the financial risks of the new enterprises. Admirers called them captains of industry; foes labeled them robber barons. To some degree, they were both—creative *and* acquisitive. If sometimes they seemed larger than life, it was because they dealt in concepts, distances, and quantities often unknown to earlier generations.

Industrial growth, it must be remembered, was neither a simple nor steady nor inevitable process. It involved human decisions and brought with it large social benefits and costs. Growth varied from industry to industry and from year to year. It was concentrated in the Northeast, where in 1890, more than 85 percent of America's manufactured goods originated. The more sparsely settled West provided raw materials, while the South, although making major gains in iron, textiles, and tobacco, had to rebuild after wartime devastation. In 1890, the industrial production of the entire South amounted in value to about half that of the state of New York.

Still, industrial development proceeded at an extraordinary pace. Between 1865 and 1914, the real gross national product—the total monetary value of all goods and services produced in a year, with prices held stable—grew at a rate of more than 4 percent a year, increasing about eightfold overall. As Robert Higgs, an economic historian, noted, "Never before had such rapid growth continued for so long."

An Empire on Rails

How and why did the railroad system grow?

Genuine revolutions happen rarely, but a major one occurred in the nineteenth century: a revolution in transportation and communications. When the nineteenth century began, people traveled and communicated much as they had for centuries before; when it ended, the railroad, the telegraph, the telephone, and the oceangoing steamship had wrought enormous changes.

The steamship sliced in half the time of the Atlantic crossing and, not dependent on wind and tide, introduced new regularity in the movement of goods and passengers. The telegraph, flashing messages almost instantaneously along miles of wire (four hundred thousand miles of it in the early 1880s), transformed communications, as did the telephone a little later. But the railroad worked the largest changes of all. Along with Bessemer steel, it was the most significant technical innovation of the century.

"Emblem of Motion and Power"

The railroad dramatically affected economic and social life. Economic growth would have occurred without it, of course; canals, inland steamboats, and the country's superb system of interior waterways already provided the outlines of an effective transportation network. But the railroad added significantly to the network and contributed advantages all its own.

Those advantages included more direct routes, greater speed, greater safety and comfort than other modes of land travel, more dependable schedules, a larger volume of traffic, and year-round service. A day's land travel on stagecoach or horseback might cover fifty miles. The railroad covered fifty miles in about an hour, seven hundred miles in a day. It went where canals and rivers did not go—directly to the loading platforms of great factories or across the arid West. As construction crews pushed tracks onward, vast areas of the continent opened for settlement.

Consequently, American railroads differed from European ones. In Europe, railroads were usually built between cities and towns that already existed; they carried mostly the same goods that earlier forms of transportation had. In the United States, they did that and more: They often created the very towns they then served, and they ended up carrying cattle from Texas, fruit from Florida, and other goods that had never been carried before.

Linking widely separated cities and villages, the railroad ended the relative isolation and self-sufficiency of the country's "island communities." It tied people together, brought in outside products, fostered greater interdependence, and encouraged economic specialization. Under its stimulus, Chicago supplied meat to the nation, Minneapolis supplied grain, and St. Louis, beer. For these and other communities, the railroad made possible a national market and in so doing pointed the way toward mass production and mass consumption, two of the hallmarks of twentieth-century society.

It also pointed the way toward later business development. The railroad, as Alfred D. Chandler, a historian of business, has written, was "the nation's first big business"; it worked out "the modern ways of finance, management, labor relations, competition, and government regulation."

A railroad corporation, far-flung and complex, was a new kind of business. It stretched over thousands of miles, employed thousands of people, dealt with countless customers, and required a scale of organization and decision making unknown in earlier business. Railroad managers never met most customers or even many employees; thus arose new problems in marketing and labor relations. Year by year, railroad companies consumed large quantities of iron, steel, coal, lumber, and glass, stimulating growth and employment in numerous industries.

No wonder, then, that the railroad captured so completely the country's imagination. Walt Whitman, a poet who celebrated American achievement, chanted the locomotive's praises:

> Thy black cylindric body, golden brass and silvery steel,
> . . . .
> Thy great protruding head-light fix'd in front,
> Thy knitted frame, thy springs and valves, the tremulous twinkle of thy wheels,
> Type of the modern—emblem of motion and power—pulse of the continent,
> . . . .
> Fierce-throated beauty!

◉—Watch the Video **Railroads and Expansion**

Like no form of transportation before it, the railroad could meet the challenge presented by the varied topography of the land west of the Mississippi River—from the Great Plains to the vast deserts, from the deep gorges to the Rocky Mountains.

For nearly a hundred years—the railroad era lasted through the 1940s—children gathered at depots, paused in the fields to wave as the fast express flashed by, listened at night to far-off whistles, and wondered what lay down the tracks. They lived in a world grown smaller.

Building the Empire

When Lee surrendered at Appomattox in 1865, the country already had thirty-five thousand miles of track, and much of the railroad system east of the Mississippi River was in place. Farther west, the rail network stood poised on the edge of settlement. Although southern railroads were in shambles from the war, the United States had nearly as much railroad track as the rest of the world.

After the Civil War, rail construction increased by leaps and bounds. From 35,000 miles in 1865, the network expanded to 93,000 miles in 1880; 166,000 in 1890; and 193,000 in 1900—more than in all Europe, including Russia. Mileage peaked at 254,037 miles in 1916, just before the industry began its long decline into the mid-twentieth century.

To build such an empire took vast amounts of capital—more than $4.5 billion by 1880, before even half of it was complete. American and European investors provided some of the money; government supplied the rest. In all, local governments gave railroad companies about $300 million, and state governments added $228 million more. The federal government loaned nearly $65 million to a half dozen western railroads and donated millions of acres of the public domain. Between 1850 and 1871, some eighty railroads received more than 170 million acres of land.

Almost 90 percent of the federal land grants lay in twenty states west of the Mississippi River. Federal land grants helped build 18,738 miles of track, less than 8 percent of the system. The land was frequently distant and difficult to market. Railroad companies sometimes sold it to raise cash, but more often they used it as security for bonds or loans.

Beyond doubt, the grants of cash and land promoted waste and corruption. The companies built fast and wastefully, eager to collect the subsidies that went with each mile of track. Wanting quick profits, some owners formed separate construction companies to which they awarded lavish contracts. In this way, the notorious Crédit Mobilier, a construction company controlled by an inner ring on the Union Pacific, enriched its owners in the 1860s, while the Contract and Finance Company did the same on the Central Pacific. The Crédit Mobilier bribed congressmen and state legislators to avoid investigation of its activities. The grants also enabled railroads to build into territories that were pledged to the Indians, thus contributing to the wanton destruction of Indian life.

Yet, on balance, the grants probably worked more benefits than evils. As Congress had hoped, the grants were the lure for railroad building across the rugged, unsettled West, where it would be years before the railroads' revenues would repay their construction. Farmers, ranchers, and merchants poured into the newly opened areas, settling the country and boosting the value of government and private land nearby. The grants seemed necessary in a nation which, unlike Europe, expected private enterprise to build the railroads. In return for government aid, Congress required the railroads to carry government freight, troops, and

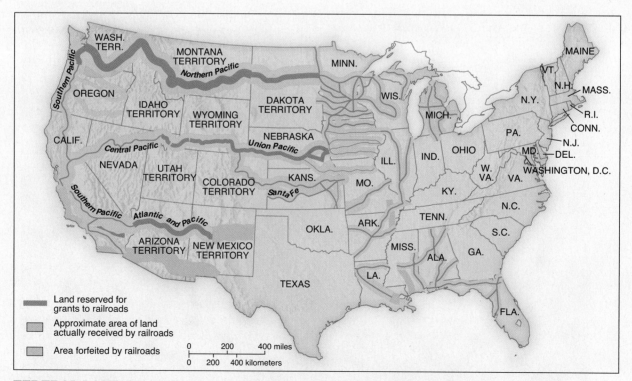

FEDERAL LAND GRANTS TO RAILROADS AS OF 1871 Besides land, the government provided loans of $16,000 for each mile built on level ground, $32,000 for each mile built on hilly terrain, and $48,000 for each mile in high mountain country.

RAILROAD CONSTRUCTION, 1830–1920

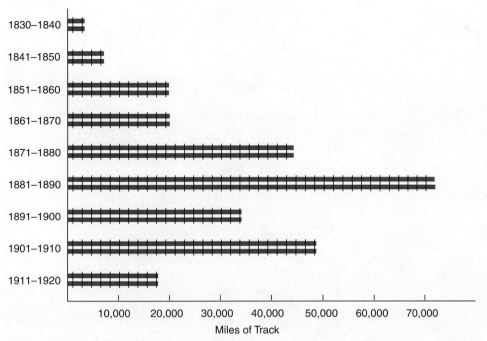

Source: U.S. *Bureau of the Census, Historical Statistics of the United States, Colonial Times to 1970*, Bicentennial Edition, Washington, DC, 1975.

mail at substantially reduced rates—resulting in savings to the government of almost $1 billion between 1850 and 1945. In no other cases of federal subsidies to carriers—canals, highways, and airlines—did Congress exact specific benefits in return.

Linking the Nation via Trunk Lines

The early railroads may seem to have linked different regions, but in fact they did not. Built with little regard for through traffic, they were designed more to protect local interests than to tap outside markets. Many extended less than fifty miles. To avoid cooperating with other lines, they adopted conflicting schedules, built separate depots, and above all, used different gauges. Gauges, the distance between the rails, ranged from 4 feet 8½ inches, which became the standard gauge, to 6 feet. Without special equipment, trains of one gauge could not run on tracks of another.

The Civil War showed the value of fast long-distance transportation, and after 1865, railroad managers worked to provide it. In a burst of consolidation, the large companies swallowed the small; integrated rail networks became a reality. Railroads also adopted standard schedules, signals, and equipment and finally, in 1886, the standard gauge. In 1866, in a dramatic innovation to speed traffic, railroad companies introduced fast freight lines that pooled cars for service between cities.

In the Northeast, four great **trunk lines** took shape, all intended to link eastern seaports with the rich traffic of the Great Lakes and western rivers. Like a massive river system, trunk lines drew traffic from dozens of tributaries (feeder lines) and carried it to major markets. The Baltimore and Ohio (B & O), which reached Chicago in 1874, was one; the Erie Railroad, which ran from New York to Chicago, was another. The Erie competed bitterly with the New York Central Railroad, the third trunk line,

and its owner, Cornelius Vanderbilt—the "Commodore"—a crusty old multimillionaire from the shipping business.

Nearly seventy years old when he first entered railroading, Vanderbilt wasted no time. In 1867, he took over the New York Central and merged it with other lines to provide a track from New York City to Buffalo and Chicago. When he died in 1877, his Central operated more than 4,500 miles of track.

J. Edgar Thomson and Thomas A. Scott built the fourth trunk line, the Pennsylvania Railroad, which initially ran from Philadelphia to Pittsburgh. Restless and energetic, they dreamed of a rail empire stretching through the South and West. An aggressive business leader, Scott expanded the Pennsylvania system to Cincinnati, Indianapolis, St. Louis, and Chicago in 1869; New York City in 1871; and Baltimore and Washington soon thereafter.

In the war-damaged South, consolidation took longer. As Reconstruction waned, northern and European capital rebuilt and integrated the southern lines, especially during the 1880s, when rail construction in the South led the nation. By 1900, the South had five large systems linking its major cities and farming and industrial regions. Four decades after the secession crisis, these systems tied the South into a national transportation network.

Over that rail system, passengers and freight moved in relative speed, comfort, and safety. Automatic couplers (1867), air brakes (1869), refrigerator cars (1867), dining cars, heated cars, electric switches, and stronger locomotives transformed railroad service. George Pullman's lavish sleeping cars became popular. Handsome depots, such as New York's Grand Central and Washington's Union Station, were erected at major terminals. Passenger miles per year increased from five billion in 1870 to sixteen billion in 1900.

In November 1883, the railroads even changed time. Ending the crazy quilt jumble of local times that caused scheduling difficulties, the American Railway Association divided the country into four time zones and adopted the modern system of standard time. Congress took thirty-five years longer; it adopted standard time in 1918, in the midst of World War I.

Rails Across the Continent

The dream of a transcontinental railroad, linking the Atlantic and Pacific Oceans, stretched back many years but had always been lost to sectional quarrels over the route. In 1862 and 1864, with the South out of the picture, Congress moved to build the first transcontinental railroad. It chartered the Union Pacific Railroad Company to build westward from Nebraska and the Central Pacific Railroad Company to build eastward from the Pacific coast. For each mile built, the two companies received from Congress 20 square miles of land in alternate sections along the track. For each mile, they also received a thirty-year loan of $16,000, $32,000, or $48,000, depending on the difficulty of the terrain over which they built.

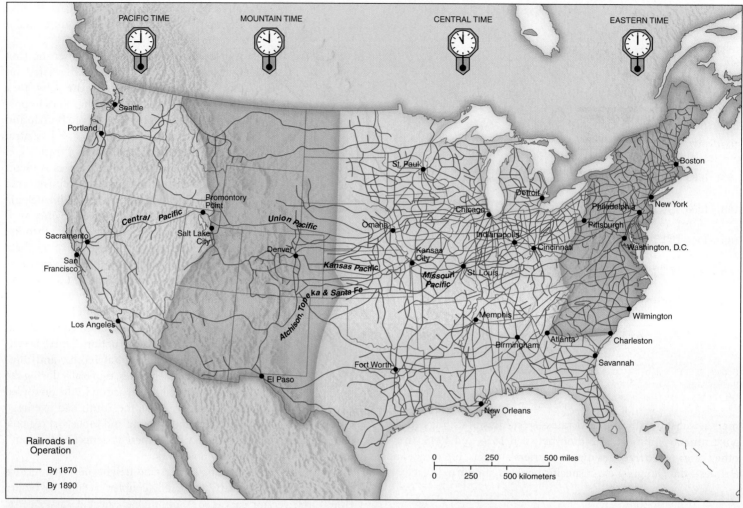

RAILROADS, 1870 AND 1890 In the last quarter of the nineteenth century, railroads expanded into Texas, the far Southwest, and the Northwest, carrying settlers, businesses, and government to the far-flung areas.

Construction began simultaneously at Omaha and Sacramento in 1863, lagged during the war, and moved vigorously ahead after 1865. It became a race, each company vying for land, loans, and potential markets. General Grenville M. Dodge, a tough Union army veteran, served as construction chief for the Union Pacific, while Charles Crocker, a former Sacramento dry goods merchant, led the Central Pacific crews. Dodge organized an army of ten thousand workers, many of them ex-soldiers and Irish immigrants. Pushing rapidly westward, he encountered frequent attacks from Native Americans defending their lands, but he had the advantage of building over flat prairie.

Crocker faced more trying conditions in the high Sierra Nevada along California's eastern border. After several experiments, he decided that Chinese laborers worked best, and he hired six thousand of them, most brought directly from China. "I built the Central Pacific," Crocker enjoyed boasting, but the Chinese crews in fact did the awesome work. Under the most difficult conditions, they dug, blasted, and pushed their way slowly east.

On May 10, 1869, the two lines met at Promontory, Utah, near the northern tip of the Great Salt Lake. Dodge's crews had built 1,086 miles of track, Crocker's 689. The Union Pacific and Central

Pacific presidents hammered in a golden spike (both missed it on the first try), and the dreamed-of connection was made. The telegraph flashed the news east and west, setting off wild celebrations. A photograph was taken, but it included none of the Chinese who had worked so hard to build the road; they were all asked to step aside.

The transcontinental railroad symbolized American unity and progress. Along with the Suez Canal, completed the same year, it helped knit the world together. Three more railroads reached the coast in 1883: the Northern Pacific, running from Minnesota to Oregon; the Atchison, Topeka, and Santa Fe, connecting Kansas City and Los Angeles; and the powerful Southern Pacific, running from San Francisco and Los Angeles to New Orleans. Ten years later, James J. Hill's superbly built Great Northern Railway extended from Minneapolis–St. Paul to Seattle, Washington.

Problems of Growth

Overbuilding during the 1870s and 1880s caused serious problems for the railroads. Lines paralleled each other, and where they did not, speculators such as Jay Gould often laid one down to force a rival line to buy it at inflated prices. While many managers worked to improve service, Gould and others bought and sold railroads like toys, watered their stock, and milked their assets. By 1885, almost one-third of railroad stock represented "water," that is, stock distributed in excess of the real value of the assets.

Competition was severe, and managers fought desperately for traffic. They offered special rates and favors: free passes for large shippers; low rates on bulk freight, carload lots, and long hauls; and, above all, rebates—secret, privately negotiated reductions below published rates. Fierce rate wars broke out frequently, convincing managers that ruthless competition helped no one. Rebates made more enemies than friends.

Managers such as Albert Fink, the brilliant vice president of the Louisville & Nashville, tried first to arrange pooling agreements, a way to control competition by sharing traffic. Fink directed the Eastern Trunk Line Association (1877), which divided westbound traffic among the four trunk lines. Similar associations pooled traffic in the South and West, but none survived the intense pressures of competition. Legally unenforceable, pools were handshake agreements among individuals who did not always keep their word. Customers grew adept at bargaining for rebates and other privileges, and railroads rarely felt able to refuse them.

Failing to cooperate, railroad owners next tried to consolidate. Through purchase, lease, and merger, they gobbled up competitors and built "self-sustaining systems" that dominated entire regions. But many of the systems, expensive and unwieldy, collapsed in the Panic of 1893. By mid-1894, a quarter of the railroads were bankrupt. The victims of the panic included such legendary names as the Erie, B & O, Santa Fe, Northern Pacific, and Union Pacific.

Needing money, railroads turned naturally to bankers, who finally imposed order on the industry. J. Pierpont Morgan, head of the New York investment house of J. P. Morgan and Company, took the lead. Massively built, with eyes so piercing they seemed like the headlights of an onrushing train, Morgan was the most powerful figure in American finance. He liked efficiency, combination, and order. He disliked "wasteful" competition. In 1885, during a bruising rate war between the New York Central and the Pennsylvania, Morgan invited the combatants to a conference aboard his palatial steam yacht, *Corsair*. Cruising on Long Island Sound, he arranged a traffic-sharing agreement and collected a million-dollar fee. Bringing peace to an industry could be profitable. It also satisfied Morgan's passion for stability.

After 1893, Morgan and a few other bankers refinanced ailing railroads, and in the process they took control of the industry. Their methods were direct: Fixed costs and debt were ruthlessly cut, new stock was issued to provide capital, rates were stabilized, rebates and competition were eliminated, and control was vested in a "voting trust" of handpicked trustees. Between 1894 and 1898, Morgan reorganized—critics said "Morganized"—the Southern Railway, the Erie, the Northern Pacific, and the B & O. In addition, he took over a half dozen other important railroads. By 1900, he was a dominant figure in American railroading.

As the new century began, the railroads had pioneered the patterns followed by most other industries. Seven giant systems controlled nearly two-thirds of the mileage, and they in turn answered to a few investment banking firms such as the House of Morgan. For good and ill, a national transportation network, centralized and relatively efficient, was now in place.

An Industrial Empire

What were the main characteristics of the new steel and oil industries?

The new industrial empire was based on a number of dramatic innovations, including steel, oil, and inventions of all kinds that transformed ordinary life. In this process, steel was as important as the railroads. Harder and more durable than other kinds of iron, steel wrought changes in manufacturing, agriculture, transportation, and architecture. It permitted construction of longer bridges, taller buildings, stronger railroad track, deadlier weapons, better plows, heavier machinery, and faster ships. Made in great furnaces by strong men, it symbolized the tough, often brutal nature of industrial society. From the 1870s onward, steel output became the worldwide accepted measure of industrial progress, and nations around the globe vied for leadership.

The Bessemer process, developed in the late 1850s by Henry Bessemer in England and independently by William Kelly in the United States, made increased steel production possible. Both Bessemer and Kelly discovered that a blast of air forced through molten iron burned off carbon and other impurities, resulting in steel of a more uniform and durable quality. The discovery transformed the industry. While earlier methods produced amounts a person could lift, a Bessemer converter handled 5 tons of molten metal at a time. The mass production of steel was now possible.

Carnegie and Steel

Bessemer plants demanded extensive capital investment, abundant raw materials, and sophisticated production techniques. Using chemical and other processes, the plants required research

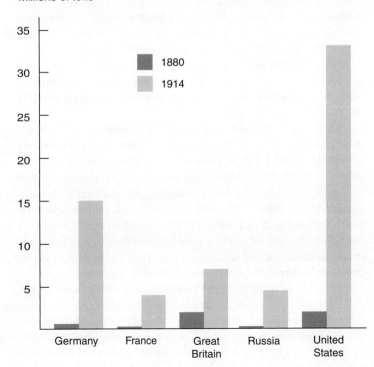

INTERNATIONAL STEEL PRODUCTION, 1880–1914

Millions of tons

departments, which became critical components of later American industries. Costly to build, they limited entry into the industry to the handful who could afford them.

Great steel districts arose in Pennsylvania, Ohio, and Alabama—in each case around large coal deposits that fueled the huge furnaces. Pittsburgh became the center of the industry, its giant mills employing thousands of workers. Output shot up. In 1874, the United States produced less than half the amount of pig iron produced in Great Britain. By 1890, it took the lead, and in 1900, it produced four times as much as Britain.

Iron ore abounded in the fabulous deposits near Lake Superior, the greatest deposits in the world. In the mines of the Mesabi Range in Minnesota, giant steam shovels loaded ore onto railroad cars for transport to ships on the Great Lakes. Powered lifts, self-loading devices, and other innovations sped the process. "By the turn of the century," historian Peter Temin noted, "the transport of Lake ores had become an intricate ballet of large and complex machines."

Like the railroads, steel companies grew larger and larger. In 1880, only nine companies could produce more than 100,000 tons a year. By the early 1890s, several companies exceeded 250,000 tons, and two—including the great Carnegie Steel Company—produced more than one million tons a year. As operations expanded, managers needed more complex skills. Product development, marketing, and consumer preferences became important. Competition was fierce, and steel companies, like the railroads, tried secret agreements, pools, and consolidation. During the 1880s and 1890s, they moved toward vertical integration, a type of organization in which a single company owns and controls the entire process from the unearthing of the raw materials to the manufacture and sale of the finished product. Such companies combined coal and iron mines, transportation companies, blast furnaces, and rolling mills into integrated networks.

Andrew Carnegie emerged as the undisputed master of the industry. Born in Scotland, he came to the United States in 1848 at the age of twelve. Settling near Pittsburgh, he went to work as a bobbin boy in a cotton mill, earning $1.20 a week. He soon took a job in a telegraph office, where in 1852 his hard work and skill caught the eye of Thomas A. Scott of the Pennsylvania Railroad. Starting as Scott's personal telegrapher, Carnegie spent a total of twelve years on the Pennsylvania, a training ground for company managers. By 1859, he had become a divisional superintendent. He was twenty-four years old.

Soon rich from shrewd investments, Carnegie plunged into the steel industry in 1872. On the Monongahela River south of Pittsburgh, he built the giant J. Edgar Thomson Steel Works, named after the president of the Pennsylvania Railroad, his biggest customer. With his warmth and salesmanship, he attracted able partners and subordinates such as Henry Clay Frick and Charles M. Schwab, whom he drove hard and paid well. Although he had written magazine articles defending the rights of workers, Carnegie kept the wages of the laborers in his mills low and disliked unions. With the help of Frick, he crushed a violent strike at his Homestead works in 1892 (see p. 434).

In 1878, he won the steel contract for the Brooklyn Bridge. During the next decade, as city building boomed, he converted the huge Homestead works near Pittsburgh to the manufacture of structural beams and angles, which went into the New York City elevated railway, the first skyscrapers, and the Washington

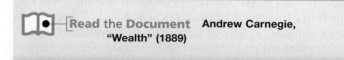
Read the Document   Andrew Carnegie, "Wealth" (1889)

The machinery dwarfs the workers in this colored engraving of steel making using the Bessemer process at Andrew Carnegie's Pittsburgh steel works. Men worked twelve hours a day in the blazing heat and deafening roar of the machines.

Monument. Carnegie profits mounted: from $2 million in 1888 to $40 million in 1900. That year, Carnegie Steel alone produced more steel than Great Britain. Employing twenty thousand people, it was the largest industrial company in the world.

In 1901, Carnegie sold it. Believing that wealth brought social obligations, he wanted to devote his full time to philanthropy. He found a buyer in J. Pierpont Morgan, who in the late 1890s had put together several steel companies, including Federal Steel, Carnegie's chief rival. Carnegie Steel had blocked Morgan's well-known desire for control, and in mid-1900, when a war loomed between the two interests, Morgan decided to buy Carnegie out. In early January 1901, Morgan told Charles M. Schwab, "Go and find his price." Schwab cornered Carnegie on the golf course; Carnegie listened, and the next day he handed Schwab a note, scribbled in blunt pencil, asking almost a half billion dollars. Morgan glanced at it and said, "I accept this price."

Drawing other companies into the combination, on March 3, 1901, Morgan announced the creation of the United States Steel Corporation. The new firm was capitalized at $1.4 billion, the first billion-dollar company. It absorbed more than 200 other companies, employed 168,000 people, and produced 9 million tons of iron and steel a year. It controlled three-fifths of the country's steel business. Soon there were other giants, including Bethlehem Steel, Republic Steel, and National Steel. As the nineteenth century ended, steel products—rare just thirty years before—had altered the landscape. Huge firms, investment bankers, and professional managers dominated the industry.

Rockefeller and Oil

Petroleum worked comparable changes in the economic and social landscape, although mostly after 1900. Distilled into oil, it lubricated the machinery of the industrial age. There seemed little use for gasoline (the internal combustion engine had only just been developed), but kerosene, another major distillate, brought inexpensive illumination into almost every home. Whale oil, cottonseed oil, and even tallow candles were expensive to burn; consequently, many people went to bed at nightfall. Kerosene lamps opened the evenings to activity, altering the patterns of life.

Like other changes in these years, the oil boom happened with surprising speed. In the mid-1850s, petroleum was a bothersome, smelly fluid that occasionally rose to the surface of springs and streams. Clever entrepreneurs bottled it in patent medicines; a few scooped up enough to burn. Other entrepreneurs soon found that drilling reached pockets of oil beneath the earth. In 1859, Edwin L. Drake drilled the first oil well near Titusville in northwest Pennsylvania, and the "black gold" fever struck. Chemists soon discovered ways to transform petroleum into lubricating oil, grease, paint, wax, varnish, naphtha, and paraffin. Within a few years, there was a world market in oil.

At first, growth of the oil industry was chaotic. Early drillers and refiners produced for local markets, and since drilling wells and even erecting refineries cost little, competition flourished. Output fluctuated dramatically; prices rose and fell, with devastating effect. Refineries—usually a collection of wooden shacks and tanks—were centered in Cleveland and Pittsburgh, near the original oil-producing regions.

A young merchant from Cleveland named John D. Rockefeller imposed order on the industry. "I had an ambition to build," he later recalled, and beginning in 1863 at the age of twenty-four, he built the Standard Oil Company, soon to become one of the titans of corporate business. Like Morgan, Rockefeller considered competition wasteful, small-scale enterprise inefficient, and consolidation the path of the future. Consolidation "revolutionized the way of doing business all over the world," he said. "The time was ripe for it. It had to come, though all we saw at the moment was the need to save ourselves from wasteful conditions."

Methodically, Rockefeller absorbed or destroyed competitors in Cleveland and elsewhere. As ruthless in his methods as Carnegie, he lacked the steel master's spontaneous charm. He was distant and taciturn, a man of deep religious beliefs who taught Bible classes at Cleveland's Erie Street Baptist Church. Like Carnegie, he demanded efficiency, relentless cost cutting, and the

latest technology. He attracted exceptional lieutenants—although, as one said, he could see farther ahead than any of them, "and then see around the corner."

"Nothing in haste, nothing ill-done," Rockefeller often said to himself. "Your future hangs on every day that passes." Paying careful attention to detail, he counted the stoppers in barrels, shortened barrel hoops to save metal, and, in one famous incident, reduced the number of drops of solder on kerosene cans from forty to thirty-nine. In large-scale production, Rockefeller realized, even small reductions meant huge savings. Research uncovered other ways of lowering costs and improving products, and Herman Frasch, a brilliant Standard Oil chemist, solved problem after problem in the refining of oil.

In the end, Rockefeller triumphed over his competitors by marketing products of high quality at the lowest unit cost. But he employed other, less savory methods as well. He threatened rivals and bribed politicians. He employed spies to harass the customers of competing refiners. Above all, he extorted railroad rebates that lowered his transportation costs and undercut competitors. By 1879, he controlled 90 percent of the country's entire oil-refining capacity.

Vertically integrated, Standard Oil owned wells, timberlands, barrel and chemical plants, refineries, warehouses, pipelines, and fleets of tankers and oil cars. Its marketing organization served as the model for the industry. Standard exported oil to Asia, Africa, and South America; its five-gallon kerosene tin, like Coca-Cola bottles and cans of a later era, was a familiar sight in the most distant parts of the world.

To manage it all, the company developed a new plan of business organization, the **trust**, which had profound significance for American business. In 1881, Samuel C. T. Dodd, Standard's attorney, set up the Standard Oil Trust, with a board of nine trustees empowered "to hold, control, and manage" all Standard's properties. Stockholders exchanged their stock for trust certificates, on which dividends were paid. On January 2, 1882, the first of the modern trusts was born. As Dodd intended, it immediately centralized control of Standard's far-flung empire.

Competition almost disappeared; profits soared. A trust movement swept the country as industries with similar problems—whiskey, lead, and sugar, among others—followed Standard's example. The word *trust* became synonymous with monopoly, amid vehement protests from the public. *Antitrust* became a watchword for a generation of reformers from the 1880s through the era of Woodrow Wilson. But Rockefeller's purpose had been *management* of a monopoly, not monopoly itself, which he had already achieved.

During the 1890s, Rockefeller helped pioneer another form of industrial consolidation, the holding company. Taking advantage of an 1889 New Jersey law that allowed companies to purchase other companies, he moved Standard Oil to New Jersey and bought up his own subsidiaries to form a holding company. The trust, he had learned, was somewhat cumbersome, and it was under attack in Congress and the courts. Holding companies offered the next step in industrial management. They were simply large-scale mergers, in which a central corporate organization purchased the stock of the member companies and established direct formal control.

Other companies followed suit, including American Sugar Refining, the Northern Securities Company, and the National Biscuit Company. Merger followed merger. By 1900, 1 percent of the nation's companies controlled more than one-third of its industrial production. A decade later, a congressional investigation showed that two individuals, Rockefeller and Morgan, between them controlled businesses worth more than $22 billion.

In 1897, Rockefeller retired with a fortune of nearly $900 million, but for Standard Oil and petroleum in general, the most expansive period was yet to come. The great oil pools of Texas and Oklahoma had not yet been discovered. Plastics and other oil-based synthetics were several decades in the future. There were only four usable automobiles in the country, and the day of the gasoline engine, automobile, and airplane lay just ahead.

The Business of Invention

"America has become known the world around as the home of invention," boasted the commissioner of patents in 1892. It had not always been so; until the last third of the nineteenth century, the country had imported most of its technology. Then an extraordinary group of inventors and tinkerers—"specialists in invention," Thomas A. Edison called them—began to study the world around them. Some of their inventions gave rise to new industries; a few actually changed the quality of life.

In the very act of inventing, Edison and others drew on a deeper "invention," a realization that people could mold nature to their own ends. They could create out of "first nature," as one environmental historian has noted, a "second nature," shaped as they wished.

The number of patents issued to inventors reflected the trend. During the 1850s, fewer than 2,000 patents were issued each year. By the 1880s and 1890s, the figure reached more than 20,000 a year. Between 1790 and 1860, the U.S. Patent Office issued just 36,000 patents; in the decade of the 1890s alone, it issued more than 200,000.

Some of the inventions transformed communications. In 1866, Cyrus W. Field improved the transatlantic cable linking the telegraph networks of Europe and the United States. By the early 1870s, land and submarine cables ran to Brazil, Japan, and the China coast; in the next two decades, they reached Africa and spread across South America. Diplomats and business leaders could now "talk" to their counterparts in Berlin or Hong Kong. Even before the telephone, the cables quickened the pace of foreign affairs, revolutionized journalism, and allowed businesses to expand and centralize.

The typewriter (1867), stock ticker (1867), cash register (1879), calculating machine (1887), and adding machine (1888) helped business transactions. High-speed spindles, automatic looms, and electric sewing machines transformed the clothing industry, which for the first time in history turned out ready-made clothes for the masses. In 1890, the Census Bureau first used machines to sort and tabulate data on punched cards, a portent of a new era of information storage and processing.

In 1879, George Eastman patented a process for coating gelatin on photographic dry plates, which led to celluloid film and motion pictures. By 1888, he was marketing the Kodak camera, which weighed 35 ounces, took 100 exposures, and cost $25. Even though early Kodaks had to be returned to the factory, camera and all, for film developing, they revolutionized photography. Now almost anyone could snap a picture.

Other innovations changed the diet. There were new processes for flour, canned meat, vegetables, condensed milk, and even beer (from an offshoot of Louis Pasteur's discoveries about bacteria). Packaged cereals appeared on breakfast tables. Refrigerated railroad cars, ice-cooled, brought fresh fruit from Florida and California to all parts of the country. In the 1870s, Gustavus F. Swift, a Chicago meat packer, hit on the idea of using the cars to distribute meat nationwide. Setting up "disassembly" factories to butcher meat (Henry Ford later copied them for his famous "assembly" lines), he started an "era of cheap beef," as a newspaper said.

No innovation, however, rivaled the importance of the telephone and the use of electricity for light and power. The telephone was the work of Alexander Graham Bell, a shrewd and genial Scot who settled in Boston in 1871. Interested in the problems of the deaf, Bell experimented with ways to transmit speech electrically, and after several years he had developed electrified metal disks that, much like the human ear, converted sound waves to electrical impulses and back again. On March 10, 1876, he transmitted the first sentence over a telephone: "Mr. Watson, come here; I want you." Later that year, he exhibited the new device to excited crowds at the Centennial Exposition in Philadelphia.

In 1878—the year a telephone was installed in the White House—the first telephone exchange opened in New Haven, Connecticut. Fighting off competitors who challenged the patent, the young Bell Telephone Company dominated the growing industry. By 1895, there were about 310,000 phones; a decade later, there were ten million—about one for every ten people. American Telephone and Telegraph Company, formed by the Bell interests in

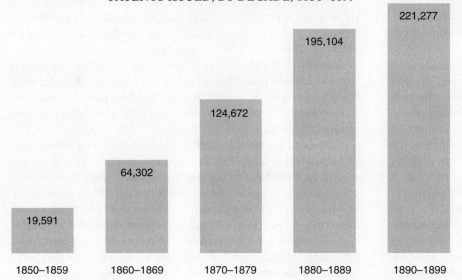

PATENTS ISSUED, BY DECADE, 1850–1899

19,591	64,302	124,672	195,104	221,277
1850–1859	1860–1869	1870–1879	1880–1889	1890–1899

Source: U.S. Bureau of the Census, *Historical Statistics of the United States, Colonial Times to 1970*, Bicentennial Edition, Washington, DC, 1975.

📖—[Read the Document   Thomas Edison, "The Success of the Electric Light"

In the late 1870's the electric light and power transfer were only at inventive stages, having been explored unsuccessfully by a number of inventors. At that time Thomas Edison, with his ideas and proven analytical abilities, undertook the problem. It was Edison's interest in technological systems that led him to a general system of incandescent lighting in the fall of 1878.

1885, became another of the vast holding companies, consolidating more than a hundred local systems.

If the telephone dissolved communication barriers as old as the human race, Thomas Alva Edison, the "Wizard of Menlo Park," invented processes and products of comparable significance. Born in 1847, Edison had little formal education, although he was an avid reader. Like Carnegie, he went into the new field of telegraphy. Tinkering in his spare time, he made several important improvements, including a telegraph capable of sending four messages over a single wire. Gathering teams of specialists to work on specific problems, Edison built the first modern research laboratory at Menlo Park, New Jersey. It may have been his most important invention.

The laboratory, Edison promised, would turn out "a minor invention every ten days and a big thing every six months or so." In 1877, it turned out a big thing. Worried about a telephone's high cost, Edison set out to invent a "telephone repeater," which became the phonograph. Those unable to afford a phone, he thought, could record their voices for replay from a central telephone station. Using tin foil wrapped around a grooved, rotating cylinder, he shouted the verses of "Mary Had a Little Lamb" and then listened in awe as the machine played them back. "I was never so taken aback in all my life," he later said. "Everybody was astonished. I was always afraid of things that worked the first time."

In 1896, records made of hard rubber and shellac appeared on the market; the following year, a phonograph sold for $20. In 1904, someone had the idea of recording on both sides of the disk, and the phonograph record in its modern form was born. For the first time in history, people could listen again and again to a favorite symphony or piano solo. The phonograph made human experience repeatable in a way never before possible.

In 1879 came an even larger triumph, the incandescent lamp. Sir Joseph William Swan, an English inventor, had already experimented with the carbon filament, but Edison's task involved more than finding a durable filament. He set out to do nothing less than change light. A trial-and-error inventor, Edison tested sixteen hundred materials before producing, late in 1879, the carbon filament he wanted. Then he had to devise a complex system of conductors, meters, and generators by which electricity could be divided and distributed to homes and businesses.

With the financial backing of J. P. Morgan, he organized the Edison Illuminating Company and built the Pearl Street power station in New York City, the testing ground of the new apparatus. On September 4, 1882, as Morgan and others watched, Edison threw a switch and lit the House of Morgan, the stock exchange, the *New York Times*, and a number of other buildings. Amazed, a *Times* reporter marveled that writing stories in the office at night "seemed almost like writing in daylight." Power stations soon opened in Boston, Philadelphia, and Chicago. By 1900, there were 2,774 stations, lighting some two million electric lights around the country. In a nation alive with light, the habits of centuries changed. A flick of the switch lit homes and factories at any hour of the day or night.

In a rare blunder, Edison based his system on low-voltage direct current, which could be transmitted only about two miles. George Westinghouse, the inventor of the railroad air brake, demonstrated the advantages of high-voltage alternating current for transmission over great distances. In 1886, he formed the Westinghouse Electric Company and with the inventor Nikola Tesla, a Hungarian immigrant, developed an alternating-current motor that could convert electricity into mechanical power. Electricity could light a lamp or illuminate a skyscraper, pull a streetcar or drive an entire railroad, run a sewing machine or power a mammoth assembly line. Transmitted easily over long distances, it freed factories and cities from location near water or coal. Electricity, in short, brought a revolution.

Buried under pavement or strung from pole to pole, wires of every description—trolley, telephone, and power—marked the birth of the modern city.

Feature Essay | Shopping in a New Society

Macy's was founded by Rowland Hussey Macy, who between 1843 and 1855 opened four retail dry goods stores, including the original Macy's store in downtown Haverhill, Massachusetts, established in 1851 to serve the mill industry employees of the area.

Of all the innovations that changed the way people lived between the 1870s and 1920s, one of the most important was the rise and development of the department store, those sprawling urban empires of goods and services that fueled the mass consumption of the new society.

A significant invention in itself, the department store took advantage of myriad other changes in American and European society, especially the industrial transformation that led to the mass production of consumer goods in varieties and amounts never seen before.

That industrial revolution in turn drew on breakthroughs in transportation, including a vast railroad network that linked cities and villages and ended the relative isolation and self-sufficiency of the nation's "island communities." The railroads tied people together, brought in products from outside, fostered greater interdependence, and encouraged economic specialization.

In the cities, new streetcar systems, another revolution in transportation, carried shoppers directly to stores, workplaces, and other destinations, regardless of the weather. As a New York City department store suggested one winter, "Ladies, if walking is too bad, just take the cars." The advice took hold. The word "commuter" first entered the language in the 1870s.

As machines turned out a plethora of new products, it became vital to sell them, and a "new science of marketing" spread. *Printer's Ink*, the first major advertising journal, began publishing in 1881. The rotary press, invented in 1875, initiated a new era in newspaper advertising. Woodcuts, halftones, and photo-engraving added illustrations to catch the consumer's eye.

Liking the results, businesses spent more on advertising every year. In 1870, they spent about $50 million; in 1900, about $95 million; in 1920, over $500 million. (By the 1970s, it was $22.4 billion.) Ads and billboards sprouted up everywhere, touting cigarettes, cars, perfumes, and cosmetics. Advertising agents, using new statistical sampling techniques, developed modern concepts of market testing and research. "When people see your name constantly in the paper," *Printer's Ink* argued, "they begin to believe they know you and it is but a short step from advertising to patronage."

Reflecting common values, department stores flourished in Europe as well as in America, particularly in Paris. Emile Zola, the famed French novelist, said the department store democratized luxury, offering the public for the first time in history free admission to displays of material goods. "Shop," he and others pointed out, had become a verb.

In the United States, R. H. Macy in New York City, John Wanamaker in Philadelphia, and Marshall Field in Chicago turned the department store into a national institution. There, people learned to "browse," a relatively new concept, and to buy. Innovations in pricing, display, and advertising helped customers develop wants they had not known they had. In 1870, Wanamaker took out the first full-page newspaper ad, and by 1891, Macy, too, had turned to full-page advertisements, often placed on pages next to an article of special interest to women.

The ads were hard to resist:

Follow the crowd [an 1885 ad in a
    New York newspaper said] and
    it will always take
you to
R. H. MACY & CO.
What better evidence do you wish
    that ours is
The All Around Store
of New York City? Ride our
    bicycles,
read our books, cook in our
    saucepans,
dine off our china, wear our silks,
get under our blankets, smoke our
    cigars,
drink our wines
– Shop at Macy's –
and life will
Cost You Less and Yield You More
Than You Dreamed Possible.

Even the surroundings often evoked a dream. Cash registers, a new invention, rang up every sale, and by the 1880s, electric lights highlighted the goods. Electric elevators and escalators carried shoppers to new heights. Plate-glass windows, a product of discoveries in the technology of glassmaking, flooded the stores with daylight. Windows on the street levels became "show windows," a term developed in the United States. "Window-shopping," another new word, became popular.

Looking through those windows, store owners soon noted, were women, hundreds of them, and it was around women that they built their businesses. "Woman is a shopper," as an industry journal noted. "Out of that fact has come the modern department store."

In these years, growing numbers of women worked in factories, telephone exchanges, and business offices, and they could spend their wages on items they desired. By 1880, 2.6 million women were in the work force; in 1890, 4 million. In 1900, more than 5 million women—one fifth of all adult women—worked outside the home.

Within limits, of course, that meant money in women's pockets, and the new department stores tailored their advertising and wares to appeal to women. They also did everything they could to make their stores safe, clean, and appealing. In 1892, Macy's built a new ladies' waiting room, calling it the "most luxurious and beautiful department devoted to the comfort of ladies to be found in a mercantile establishment in the city." Soon there were ladies' lunch rooms; dressing rooms specially lit to show off evening gowns in broad daylight; and shelves of hats, glass, and china with monograms and other special designs. It was not unusual for a department store to stock 1,300 types of women's shoes.

The department store, along with advertising, brand names, and other innovations, brought Americans of all backgrounds into a national market. Even as the country itself grew, a homogeneity of goods bound it together, touching cities and farms, East and West, rich and poor. A common language of consumption turned Americans into a community of consumers, who were surrounded by goods unavailable just decades before and able to purchase them. They had learned to make, want, and buy.

These are lessons not forgotten. The department store even today accounts for more than one-tenth of all annual commercial sales in the United States.

The spread of the World Wide Web has added, like transportation and communication innovations in an earlier era, another route for consumers to buy the alluring products of the department stores. The so-called "Cyber-Monday" of the 2011 Christmas season enticed those who preferred to shop and spend their money buying goods online. According to the *New York Times*, on "Cyber-Monday" shoppers bought $1.25 billion worth of goods over the Internet. Somehow, one suspects, this would not have surprised Macy, Wanamaker, and their nineteenth-century colleagues.

QUESTIONS FOR DISCUSSION

1. What conditions between the 1870s and 1920s led to the rise of the department store?

2. What changes did department stores bring in people's lives?

The Sellers

Why were the new methods of advertising so important?

The increased output of the industrial age alone was not enough to ensure huge profits. The products still had to be sold, and that gave rise to the new "science" of marketing. Some business leaders—such as Swift in meatpacking, James B. Duke in tobacco, and Rockefeller in oil—built extensive marketing organizations of their own. Others relied on retailers, merchandising techniques, and advertising, developing a host of methods to convince consumers to buy.

In 1867, businesses spent about $50 million on advertising; in 1900, they spent more than $500 million, and the figure was increasing rapidly. The first advertising agency, N. W. Ayer and Son, of Philadelphia, began to service businesses in the mid-1870s, and it was followed by numerous imitators. The rotary press (1875) churned out newspapers and introduced a new era in newspaper advertising. Woodcuts, halftones, and photoengraving added illustrations to catch the consumer's eye.

Bringing producer and consumer together, nationwide advertising was the final link in the national market. From roadside signs to newspaper ads, it pervaded American life.

R. H. Macy in New York, John Wanamaker in Philadelphia, and Marshall Field in Chicago turned the department store into a national institution. There people could browse (a relatively new concept) and buy. Innovations in pricing, display, and advertising helped customers develop wants they did not know they had. In 1870, Wanamaker took out the first full-page newspaper ad, and Macy, an aggressive advertiser, touted "goods suitable for the millionaire at prices in reach of the millions."

The "chain store"—an American term—spread across the country. The A & P grocery stores, begun in 1859, numbered sixty-seven by 1876, all marked by a familiar red-and-gold facade. By 1915, there were a thousand of them. In 1880, F. W. Woolworth, bored with the family farm, opened the first "Five and Ten Cent Store" in Utica, New York. He had fifty-nine stores in 1900, the year he adopted the bright red storefront and heaping counters to lure customers in and persuade them to buy.

In similar fashion, Sears, Roebuck and Montgomery Ward sold to rural customers through mail-order catalogs—a means of selling that depended on effective transportation and a high level of customer literacy.

As a traveler for a dry goods firm, Aaron Montgomery Ward had seen an unfulfilled need of people in the rural West. He started the mail-order trend in 1872, with a one-sheet price list offered from a Chicago loft. By 1884, he offered almost ten thousand items in a catalog of 240 pages.

Richard W. Sears also saw the possibilities in the mail-order business. Starting with watches and jewelry, he gradually expanded his list. In the early 1880s, he moved to Chicago and with Alvah C. Roebuck founded Sears, Roebuck and Company. Sears sold anything and everything, prospering in a business that relied on mutual faith between unseen customers and distant distributors. Sears catalogs, soon more than five hundred pages long, exploited four-color illustration and other new techniques. By the early 1900s, Sears distributed six million catalogs annually.

Advertising, brand names, chain stores, and mail-order houses brought Americans of all varieties into a national market. Even as the country grew, a certain homogeneity of goods bound it together, touching cities and farms, East and West, rich and poor. There was a common language of consumption.

The market, some contemporaries thought, also bridged ethnic and other differences. A prominent English economist wrote in 1919, "Widely as the Scandinavians are separated from the Italians, and the native Americans from the Poles, in sentiment, in modes of living, and even in occupations, they are yet purchasers of nearly the same goods. . . . They buy similar clothes, furniture, and implements."

The theory had severe limits; ethnic and racial differences remained entrenched in the society. But Americans *had* become a community of consumers, surrounded by goods unavailable just a few decades before, and able to purchase them. They had learned to make, want, and buy. (See Feature Essay, "Shopping in a New Society" on pp 426-427).

The Wage Earners

Who were the wage earners in the new economy?

Although entrepreneurs were important, it was the labor of millions of men and women that built the new industrial society. In their individual stories, nearly all unrecorded, lay much of the achievement, drama, and pain of these years.

In a number of respects, their lot improved during the last quarter of the nineteenth century. Real wages rose, working conditions improved, and the workers' influence in national affairs increased. Between 1880 and 1914, wages of the average worker rose about $7 a year. Like others, workers also benefited from expanding health and educational services.

Working Men, Working Women, Working Children

Still, life for workers was not easy. Before 1900, most wage earners worked at least ten hours a day, six days a week. If skilled, they earned about 20 cents an hour; if unskilled, just half that. On average, workers earned between $400 and $500 a year. It took about $600 for a family of four to live decently. Construction workers, machinists, government employees, printers, clerical workers, and western miners made more than the average. Eastern coal miners, agricultural workers, garment workers, and unskilled factory hands made considerably less.

There were few holidays or vacations, and there was little respite from the grueling routine. Skilled workers could turn the system to their own ends—New York City cigar makers, for example, paid someone to read to them while they worked—but the unskilled seldom had such luxury. They were too easily replaced. "A bit of advice to you," said a guidebook for immigrant Jews in the 1890s: "do not take a moment's rest. Run, do, work, and keep your own good in mind."

Work was not only grueling; it was very dangerous. Safety standards were low, and accidents were common, more common in fact than in any other industrial nation in the world at that time.

On the railroads, 1 in every 26 workers was injured and 1 in every 399 was killed each year. Thousands suffered from chronic illness, unknowing victims of dust, chemicals, and other pollutants. In the early 1900s, physician Alice Hamilton established a link between jobs and disease, but meanwhile, illness weakened or struck down many a breadwinner.

The breadwinner might be a woman or a child; both worked in increasing numbers. In 1870, about 15 percent of women over the age of 16 were employed for wages; in 1900, 20 percent (5.3 million women) were. Of 303 occupations listed in the 1900 census, women were represented in 296.

The textile industry was their largest single employer. Between 1870 and 1900, the number of working children rose nearly 130 percent to 1.8 million. In 1900, 1 out of every 10 girls and 1 out of every 5 boys between the ages of 10 and 15 held jobs. In Paterson, New Jersey, an important industrial city, about half of all boys and girls aged 11 to 14 had jobs.

There were so many children in the labor force that when people spoke of child labor, they often meant boys and girls under the age of fourteen. Boys were paid little enough, but girls made even less. Girls, it was argued, were headed for marriage; those who worked were just doing so in order to help out their families. "We try to employ girls who are members of

families," a box manufacturer said, "for we don't pay the girls a living wage in this trade."

Most working women were young and single. Many began working at sixteen or seventeen, worked a half dozen years or so, married, and quit. In 1900, only 5 percent of all married women were employed outside the home, although African American women were an important exception.

Among them, 25 percent of married women worked in 1900, usually on southern farms or as low-paid laundresses or domestic servants. As clerical work expanded, women learned new skills such as typing and stenography. Moving into formerly male occupations, they became secretaries, bookkeepers, typists, telephone operators, and clerks in the new department stores.

A few women—very few—became ministers, lawyers, and doctors. Arabella Mansfield, admitted to the Iowa bar in 1869, was the first woman lawyer in the country. But change was slow, and in the 1880s, some law schools still were refusing to admit women because they "had not the mentality to study law." Among women entering the professions, the overwhelming majority became nurses, schoolteachers, and librarians. In such professions, a process of "feminization" occurred: Women became a majority of the workers, a small number of men took the management roles, and most men left for other jobs, lowering the profession's status.

In most jobs, status and pay were divided unequally between men and women. Many of both sexes thought a woman's place was in the home, "queen of a little house—no matter how humble—where there are children rolling on the floor." When employed in factories, women tended to occupy jobs that were viewed as natural extensions of household activity. They made clothes and textiles, processed food, and made cigars, tobacco, and shoes. In the women's garment industry, which employed large numbers of women, they were the sewers and finishers, doing jobs that paid less; men were the higher-paid cutters and pressers.

In *The Long Day: The Story of a New York Working Girl as Told by Herself* (1906), the "working girl," a young schoolteacher, earned $2.50 a week, paid $1.00 for her room, and had $1.50 for food, clothes, transportation, and any social life. For breakfast, she had bread, butter, and coffee; for lunch, bread and butter; for dinner, potato soup, bread, and butter. In Pittsburgh, a worker in a pickle factory said of her day: "I have stood ten hours; I have fitted 1,300 corks; I have hauled and loaded 4,000 jars of pickles. My pay is seventy cents." Exhausted, such workers fell into bed at night and crawled out again at dawn to begin another "long day."

In general, adults earned more than children, the skilled more than the unskilled, native born more than foreign born,

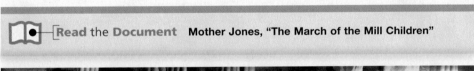

Read the Document   Mother Jones, "The March of the Mill Children"

Many children in the late nineteenth century grew up in the nation's factories, working long hours for low wages in often dangerous conditions. These girls bundling brooms at an Indiana manufacturing plant were photographed by Lewis Hine.

◨◧—Read the Document   Massachusetts Bureau of Statistics of Labor (1884)

This report documents the poor working and living conditions of women workers in Massachusetts. Of special concern in the report, and to reformers of the time, were the unsanitary conditions in which many of the women lived. The forthcoming economic depression of the 1890s would force even more women into such working conditions.

Protestants more than Catholics or Jews, and whites more than blacks and Asians. On average, women made a little more than half as much as men, according to contemporary estimates. In some cases, employers defended the differences—the foreign born, for example, might not speak English—but most simply reflected bias against race, creed, or gender. In the industrial society, white, native-born Protestant men—the bulk of the male population— reaped the greatest rewards.

Blacks labored on the fringes, usually in menial occupations. The last hired and first fired, they earned less than other workers at almost every level of skill. On the Pacific coast, the Chinese—and later the Japanese—lived in enclaves and suffered periodic attacks of discrimination. In 1879, the Workingmen's party of California got a provision in the state constitution forbidding corporations to employ Chinese, and in 1882, Congress passed the Chinese Exclusion Act, prohibiting the immigration of Chinese workers for ten years.

Culture of Work

How did wage earners organize in this period, and what demands did they make?

Among almost all groups, industrialization shattered age-old patterns, including work habits and the culture of work, as Herbert G. Gutman, a social historian, noted. It made people adapt "older work routines to new necessities and strained those wedded to premodern patterns of labor." Adaptation was difficult and often demeaning. Virtually everyone went through it, and newcomers repeated the experiences of those who came before.

Men and women fresh from farms were not accustomed to the factory's disciplines. Now they worked indoors rather than out, paced themselves to the clock rather than the movements of the sun, and followed the needs of the market rather than the natural rhythms of the seasons. They had supervisors and hierarchies and strict rules.

As industries grew larger, work became more impersonal. Machines displaced skilled artisans, and the unskilled tended the machines for employers they never saw. Workers picked up and left their jobs with startling frequency, and factories drew on a churning, highly mobile labor supply. Historian Stephan Thernstrom, who carefully studied the census records, found that only about half the people recorded in any census still lived in the same community ten years later. "The country had an enormous reservoir of restless and footloose men, who could be lured to new destinations when opportunity beckoned."

Thernstrom and others have also found substantial economic and social mobility. The rags-to-riches stories of Horatio Alger had always said so, and careers of men such as Andrew Carnegie—the impoverished immigrant boy who made good—seemed to confirm it. The actual record was considerably more limited. Most business leaders in the period came from well-to-do or middle-class families of old American stock. Of 360 iron and steel barons in Pittsburgh, Carnegie's own city, only five fit the Carnegie characteristics, and one of those was Carnegie himself. Still, if few workers became steel magnates, many workers made major progress during their lifetimes. Thernstrom discovered that a quarter of the manual laborers rose to middle-class positions, and working-class children were even more likely to move up the ladder. In Boston, about half the Jewish immigrants rose from manual to middle-class jobs, and English, Irish, and Italian immigrants were not far behind.

The chance for advancement played a vital role in American industrial development. It gave workers hope, wedded them to the system, and tempered their response to the appeal of labor unions and working-class agitation. Very few workers rose from rags to riches, but a great many rose to better jobs and higher status.

Labor Unions

Weak throughout the nineteenth century, labor unions never included more than 2 percent of the total labor force or more than 10 percent of industrial workers. To many workers, unions seemed "foreign," radical, and out of step with the American tradition of individual advancement. Craft, ethnic, and other differences fragmented the labor force, and its extraordinary mobility made organization difficult. Employers opposed unions. "I have always had one rule," said an executive of U.S. Steel. "If a worker sticks up his head, hit it."

As the national economy emerged, however, national labor unions gradually took shape. The early unions often represented skilled workers in local areas, but in 1866, William H. Sylvis, a Pennsylvania iron molder, united several unions into a single national organization, the National Labor Union. Like many of the era's labor leaders, Sylvis sought long-range humanitarian reforms, such as the establishment of workers' cooperatives, rather than specific bread-and-butter goals. A talented propagandist, he attracted many members—some 640,000 by 1868—but he died in 1869, and the organization did not long survive him.

The year Sylvis died, Uriah S. Stephens and a group of Philadelphia garment workers founded a far more successful organization, the Noble and Holy Order of the Knights of Labor, known simply as the **Knights of Labor**. A secret fraternal order, it grew slowly through the 1870s, until Terence V. Powderly, the new Grand Master Workman elected in 1879, ended the secrecy and embarked on an aggressive recruitment program. Wanting to unite all labor, the Knights welcomed everyone who "toiled," regardless of skill, creed, sex, or color. Unlike most unions, it organized women workers, and at its peak, it had sixty thousand black members.

Harking back to the Jacksonians, the Knights set the "producers" against monopoly and special privilege. As members they excluded only "nonproducers"—bankers, lawyers, liquor dealers, and gamblers. Since employers were "producers," they could join; and since workers and employers had common interests, the Knights maintained that workers should not strike. The order's platform included the eight-hour day and the abolition of child labor, but more often it focused on uplifting, utopian reform. Powderly, the eloquent and idealistic leader, spun dreams of a new era of harmony and cooperation. He wanted to sweep away trusts and end drunkenness. Workers should pool their resources, establish worker-run factories, railroads, and mines, and escape from the wage system. "The aim of the Knights of Labor—properly understood—is to make each man his own employer," Powderly said.

Membership grew steadily—from 42,000 in 1882 to 110,000 in 1885. In March 1885, ignoring Powderly's dislike of strikes, local Knights in St. Louis, Kansas City, and other cities won a victory against Jay Gould's Missouri Pacific Railroad, and membership soared. It soon reached almost 730,000, but neither Powderly nor the union's loose structure could handle the growth. In 1886, the wily Gould struck back, crushing the Knights on the Texas and Pacific Railroad. The defeat punctured the union's growth and revealed the ineffectiveness of its national leaders. Tens of thousands of unskilled laborers, who had recently rushed to join, deserted the ranks. The Haymarket Riot turned public sympathy against unions like the Knights. By 1890, the order had shrunk to 100,000 members, and a few years later, it was virtually defunct.

Even as the Knights waxed and waned, another organization emerged that was to endure. Founded in 1886, the **American Federation of Labor (AFL)** was a loose alliance of national craft unions. It organized only skilled workers along craft lines, avoided politics, and worked for specific practical objectives. "I have my own philosophy and my own dreams," said Samuel Gompers, the founder and longtime president, "but first and foremost I want to increase the workingman's welfare year by year."

Born in a London tenement in 1850, Gompers was a child of the union movement. Settling in New York, he worked as a cigar maker, took an active hand in union activities, and experimented for a time with socialism and working-class politics. As leader of the AFL, he adopted a pragmatic approach to labor's needs. Gompers accepted capitalism and did not argue for fundamental changes in it. For labor he wanted simply a recognized place within the system and a greater share of the rewards.

Unlike Powderly, Gompers and the AFL assumed that most workers would remain workers throughout their lives. The task, then, lay in improving lives in "practical" ways: higher wages, shorter hours, and better working conditions. The AFL offered some attractive assurances to employers. As a trade union, the AFL would use the strike and boycott, but only to achieve limited gains;

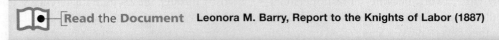

Read the **Document**   Leonora M. Barry, Report to the Knights of Labor (1887)

Women delegates at a national meeting of the Knights of Labor in 1886. Women belonged to separate associations affiliated with local all-male unions.

if treated fairly, the organization would provide a stable labor force. The AFL would not oppose monopolies and trusts, as Gompers said, "so long as we obtain fair wages."

By the 1890s, the AFL was the most important labor group in the country, and Gompers, the guiding spirit, was its president, except for one year, until his death in 1924. Membership expanded from 140,000 in 1886, past 250,000 in 1892, to more than one million by 1901. The AFL then included almost one-third of the country's skilled workers. By 1914, it had more than two million members. The great majority of workers—skilled and unskilled— remained unorganized, but Gompers and the AFL had become a significant force in national life.

Few unions allowed women to join. The Knights of Labor had a Department of Woman's Work headed by Leonora M. Barry, a shrewd, enthusiastic organizer who established a dozen women's locals and investigated the condition of women's labor. The Knights welcomed housewives because they were "producers." The AFL either ignored or opposed women workers. Only two of its national affiliates—the Cigar Makers' Union and the Typographical Union— accepted women as members; others prohibited them outright, and Gompers himself often complained that women workers undercut the pay scales for men. Working conditions improved after 1900, but even then, unions were largely a man's world. In 1910, when

there were 6.3 million women at work, only 125,000 of them were in unions.

The AFL did not expressly forbid black workers from joining, but member unions used high initiation fees, technical examinations, and other means to discourage black membership. The AFL's informal exclusion practices were, all in all, a sorry record, but Gompers defended his policy toward blacks, women, and the unskilled by pointing to the dangers that unions faced. Only by restricting membership, he argued, could the union succeed.

Labor Unrest

Workers used various means to adjust to the factory age. To the dismay of managers and "efficiency" experts, the employees often dictated the pace and quality of their work and set the tone of the workplace. Friends and relatives of newly arrived immigrants found jobs for them, taught them how to deal with factory conditions, and humanized the workplace.

Workers also formed their own institutions to deal with their jobs. Overcoming differences of race or ethnic origin, they often banded together to help each other. They joined social or fraternal organizations, and their unions did more than argue

🔍 **View** the **Map**   Organizing American Labor in the Late Nineteenth Century

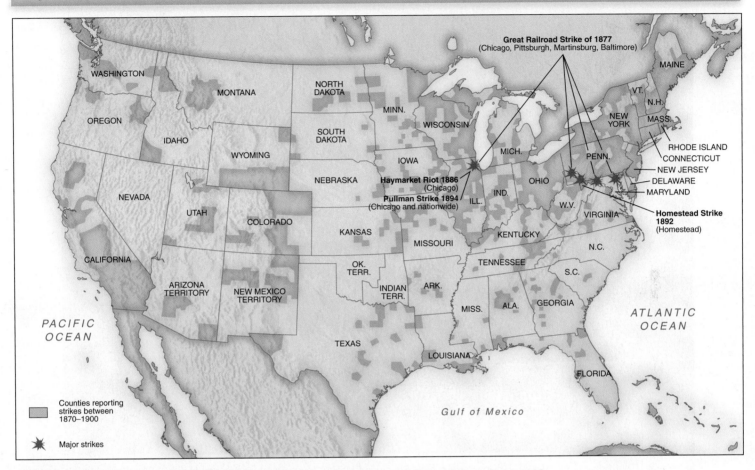

LABOR STRIKES, 1870–1900 More than fourteen thousand strikes occurred in the 1880s and early 1890s, involving millions of workers.

for higher wages. Unions offered companionship, news of job openings, and much needed insurance plans for sickness, accident, or death. Workers went to the union hall to play cards or pool, sing union songs, and hear older workers tell of past labor struggles. Unions provided food for sick members, and there were dances, picnics, and parades. "The night I joined the Cattle Butchers' Union," a young Lithuanian said, "I was led into the room by a negro member. With me were Bohemians, Germans and Poles . . . . We swore to be loyal to our union above everything else except the country, the city and the State—to be faithful to each other—to protect the women workers—to do our best to understand the history of the labor movement, and to do all we could to help it on."

Many employers believed in an "iron law of wages" in which supply and demand, not the welfare of their workers, dictated wages. "If I wanted boiler iron," a steelmaker said, "I would go out on the market and buy where I could get it the cheapest, and if I wanted to employ men I would do the same thing." Wanting a docile labor force, employers fired union members, hired scabs to replace strikers, and used a new weapon, the court injunction, to quell strikes.

The injunction, which forbade workers to interfere with their employers' business, was used to break the great Pullman Strike of 1894, and the Supreme Court upheld use of the injunction in *In re Debs* (1895). Court decisions also affected the legal protection offered to workers. In *Holden* v. *Hardy* (1898), the Court upheld a law limiting working hours for miners because their work was dangerous and long hours might increase injuries. In *Lochner* v. *New York* (1905), however, it struck down a law limiting bakery workers to a sixty-hour week and ten-hour day. Because baking was safer than mining, the Court saw no need to interfere with the right of bakers to sell their labor freely.

As employers' attitudes hardened, strikes and violence broke out. The United States had the greatest number of violent confrontations between capital and labor in the industrial world. Between 1880 and 1900, there were more than 23,000 strikes involving 6.6 million workers.

The worst incident took place at Haymarket Square in Chicago, where workers had been campaigning for an eight-hour workday. In early May 1886, police, intervening in a strike at the McCormick Harvester works, shot and killed two workers. The next evening, May 4, labor leaders called a protest meeting at Haymarket Square near downtown Chicago. The meeting was peaceful, even a bit dull. About three thousand people were there; police ordered them to disperse, and someone threw a dynamite

Read the **Document** **George Engel, Address by a Haymarket Anarchist**

In the rioting that followed the bomb explosion in Haymarket Square in Chicago, seven police officers and four workers died and more than seventy officers were wounded, many of them by fellow police. August Spies, one of the anarchists convicted of murder and sent to the gallows, said at his trial, "Let the world know that in A.D. 1886, in the state of Illinois, eight men were sentenced to death because they believed in a better future; because they had not lost their faith in the ultimate victory of liberty and justice!" (Actually, seven of the agitators were sentenced to death, the eighth to imprisonment.)

bomb that instantly killed one policeman and fatally wounded six others. Police fired into the crowd and killed four people.

The authorities never discovered who threw the bomb, but many Americans—not just business leaders—immediately labeled the incident the Haymarket Riot and demanded action against labor "radicalism." Cities strengthened their police forces and armories. In Chicago, donors helped to establish nearby Fort Sheridan and the Great Lakes Naval Training Station to curb social turmoil. Uncertain who threw the bomb, Chicago police rounded up eight anarchists, who were convicted of murder. Although there was no evidence of their guilt, four were hanged, one committed suicide, and three remained in jail until pardoned by the governor in 1893. Linking labor and anarchism in the public mind, the Haymarket Riot weakened the national labor movement.

Violence again broke out in the unsettled conditions of the 1890s. In 1892, federal troops crushed a strike of silver miners in the Coeur d'Alene district of Idaho. That same year, Carnegie and

Henry Clay Frick, Carnegie's partner and manager, cut wages nearly 20 percent at the Homestead steel plant. The Amalgamated Iron and Steel Workers, an AFL affiliate, struck, and Frick responded by locking the workers out of the plant. The workers surrounded it, and Frick, furious, hired a small private army of Pinkerton detectives to drive them off. But alert workers spotted the detectives, pinned them down with gunfire, and forced them to surrender. Three detectives and ten workers died in the battle.

A few days later, the Pennsylvania governor ordered the state militia to impose peace at Homestead. On July 23, an anarchist named Alexander Berkman, who was not one of the strikers, walked into Frick's office and shot him twice, then stabbed him several times. Incredibly, Frick survived, watched the police take Berkman away, called in a doctor to bandage his wounds, and stayed in the office until closing time. "I do not think I shall die," he told reporters. "But if I do or not, the company will pursue the same policy and it will win." In late July, the Homestead works reopened under military guard, and in November the strikers gave up.

Events like the **Homestead Strike** troubled many Americans who wondered whether industrialization, for all its benefits, might carry a heavy price in social upheaval, class tensions, and even outright warfare. Most workers did not share in the immense profits of the industrial age, and as the nineteenth century came to a close, there were some who rebelled against the inequity.

Conclusion: Industrialization's Benefits and Costs

In the half century after the Civil War, the United States became an industrial nation—the leading one, in fact, in the world. On one hand, industrialization meant "progress," growth, world power, and in some sense, fulfillment of the American promise of abundance. National wealth grew from $16 billion in 1860 to $88 billion in 1900; wealth per capita more than doubled. For the bulk of the population, the standard of living—a particularly American concept—rose.

But industrialization also meant rapid change, social instability, exploitation of labor, and growing disparity in income between rich and poor. Industry flourished, but control rested in fewer and fewer hands. Maturing quickly, the young system became a new corporate capitalism: giant businesses, interlocking in ownership, managed by a new professional class, and selling an expanding variety of goods in an increasingly controlled market. As goods spread through the society, so did a sharpened, aggressive materialism. Workers felt the strains of the shift to a new social order.

In 1902, a well-to-do New Yorker named Bessie Van Vorst decided to see what it was like to work for a living in a factory. Disguising herself in coarse woolen clothes, a shabby felt hat, a cheap piece of fur, and an old shawl and gloves, she went to Pittsburgh and got a job in a canning factory. She worked ten hours a day, six days a week, including four hours on Saturday afternoons when she and the other women, on their hands and knees, scrubbed the tables, stands, and entire factory floor. For that she earned $4.20 a week, $3 of which went for food alone. "My hands are stiff," she said, "my thumbs almost blistered . . . . Cases are emptied and refilled; bottles are labeled, stamped and rolled

Watch the **Video**   The Gilded Age: The Rise of Capitalism, Industrialism, andPoverty

The Gilded Age is associated with an enormous expansion of American industry, American manufacturing, and the growth of the factory system. It's also the moment when it's increasingly clear that large numbers of Americans are going to be doing wage labor for all their life.

away . . . and still there are more cases, more jars, more bottles. Oh! the monotony of it!" The noise around her was deafening; her head grew dazed and weary.

Van Vorst was lucky—when she tired of the life, she could go back to her home in New York. The working men and women around her were not so fortunate. They stayed on the factory floor and, by dint of their labor, created the new industrial society.

Study Resources

 Take the **Study Plan** for **Chapter 18** *The Industrial Society* on **MyHistoryLab**

TIME LINE

1859 First oil well drilled near Titusville, Pennsylvania

1866 William Sylvis establishes National Labor Union

1869 Transcontinental railroad completed at Promontory, Utah; Knights of Labor organize

1876 Alexander Graham Bell invents the telephone; Centennial Exposition held in Philadelphia

1877 Railroads cut workers' wages, leading to bloody and violent strike

1879 Thomas A. Edison invents the incandescent lamp

1882 Rockefeller's Standard Oil Company becomes nation's first trust; Edison opens first electric generating station in New York

1883 Railroads introduce standard time zones

1886 Samuel Gompers founds American Federation of Labor (AFL); Labor protest erupts in violence in Haymarket Riot in Chicago; Railroads adopt standard gauge

1892 Workers strike at Homestead steel plant in Pennsylvania

1893 Economic depression begins

1901 J. P. Morgan announces formation of U.S. Steel Corporation, nation's first billion-dollar company

CHAPTER REVIEW

Industrial Development

 What enabled the United States to build an industrial economy?

The United States had an abundance of natural resources, plentiful labor from Europe and American farms, numerous inventions, a national market, plentiful capital, favorable government policies, and entrepreneurs who saw the possibilities in developing a national economy. (p. 416)

An Empire on Rails

 How and why did the railroad system grow?

Through the infusion of foreign and domestic capital, and the help of local, state, and federal government, a railroad system grew that dwarfed those in other countries. It changed the economic, political, and social landscape, creating a different nation from the country that had come before. (p. 416)

An Industrial Empire

 What were the main characteristics of the new steel and oil industries?

In the late nineteenth century, an industrial empire took shape, centered around steel and oil, leading to the importance of the automobile in the twentieth century. The result was larger and more complex business organizations and greater concentrations of wealth, capital, and control by a relatively few individuals and companies. (p. 421)

The Sellers

 Why were the new methods of advertising so important?

Advertising, a relatively new industry, helped to sell the goods of the new industrial economy. Americans learned to buy goods they did not even know they wanted. When bored or troubled, they went to a store—today's mall—to shop. (p. 428)

The Wage Earners

 Who were the wage earners in the new economy?

The hard work of millions of men and women built the new factory society. Their work was grueling and often dangerous. Men, women, and children often worked for low wages in unsafe conditions. (p. 428)

Culture of Work

 How did wage earners organize in this period, and what demands did they make?

Laborers faced many challenges in the new economy, including work that followed the clock, bigger industries, machines, and wages. Unions formed, including the American Federation of Labor (AFL), which still exists. Labor unrest for better wages and safer working conditions took peaceful forms, but also resulted in violence that disturbed other Americans. (p. 430)

KEY TERMS AND DEFINITIONS

trunk lines   Four major railroad networks that emerged after the Civil War to connect the eastern seaports to the Great Lakes and western rivers. They reflected the growing integration of transportation across the country that helped spur large-scale industrialization. p. 419

Trust   A device to centralize and make more efficient the management of diverse and far-flung business operations. It allowed stockholders to exchange their stock certificates for trust certificates, on which dividends were paid. John D. Rockefeller organized the first major trust, the Standard Oil Trust, in 1882. p. 423

Knights of Labor   Founded in 1869, this labor organization pursued broad-gauged reform and practical issues such as improved wages and hours. The Knights welcomed all laborers regardless of race, gender, or skill. p. 431

American Federation of Labor (AFL)   Founded by Samuel Gompers in 1886, the AFL organized skilled workers by craft and worked for specific practical objectives, such as higher wages, shorter hours, and better working conditions. The AFL avoided politics, and while it did not expressly forbid blacks and women from joining, it used exclusionary practices to keep them out. p. 431

Homestead Strike   In July 1892, wage-cutting at Andrew Carnegie's Homestead Steel Plant in Pittsburgh provoked a violent strike in which three company-hired detectives and ten workers died. Using ruthless force and strikebreakers, company officials broke the strike and destroyed the union. p. 435

CRITICAL THINKING QUESTIONS

1. What were eight advantages the United States possessed that helped spur industrial development, and in what ways did these advantages lead to the growth of specific industries?

2. In what ways did the revolution in transportation and communications also spur industrial development?

3. Drawing on the conditions leading to the growth of industry, how did the huge steel and oil industries grow?

4. What role did the culture of work and advances in areas like advertising play in shaping economic growth?

5. In what ways did the hard work of men, women, and children contribute to the growth of industry?

6. How did American workers respond to the demands of industrial growth, and what did their various responses indicate about the dangerous effects of industrialization?

MyHistoryLab Media Assignments

Find these resources in the Media Assignments folder for Chapter 18 on MyHistoryLab

An Empire On Rails

Watch the **Video**   *Railroads and Expansion p. 417*

An Industrial Empire

Read the **Document**   *Andrew Carnegie, "Wealth" (1889) p. 422*

■ **Read** the **Document**   *Thomas Edison, The Success of the Electric Light p. 425*

The Sellers

■ **Complete** the **Assignment**   *Shopping in a New Society p. 426*

The Wage Earners

Read the **Document**   *Mother Jones, "The March of the Mill Children" p. 429*

Read the **Document**   *Massachusetts Bureau of Statistics of Labor (1884) p. 430*

Culture of Work

Read the **Document**   *Leonora M. Barry, Report to the Knights of Labor (1887) p. 432*

■ **View** the **Map**   *Organizing American Labor in the Late Nineteenth Century p. 433*

■ **Read** the **Document**   *George Engel, Address by a Haymarket Anarchist p. 434*

■ **Watch** the **Video**   *The Gilded Age: The Rise of Capitalism, Industrialism, and Poverty p. 435*

■ *Indicates Study Plan Media Assignment*

19 Toward an Urban Society, 1877–1900

Contents and Learning Objectives

((•─ **Listen** to the **Audio File** on **myhistorylab**   Chapter 19 *Toward an Urban Society, 1877–1900*

The Overcrowded City

One day around 1900, Harriet Vittum, a settlement house worker in Chicago, went to the aid of a young Polish girl who lived in a nearby slum. The girl, aged 15, had discovered she was pregnant and had taken poison. An ambulance was on the way, and Vittum, told of the poisoning, rushed over to do what she could.

Quickly, she raced up the three flights of stairs to the floor where the girl and her family lived. Pushing open the door, she found the father, several male boarders, and two or three small boys asleep on the kitchen floor. In the next room, the mother was on the floor among several women boarders and one or two small children. Glancing out the window, Vittum saw the wall of another building so close she could reach out and touch it.

There was a third room; in it lay the 15-year-old girl, along with two more small children who were asleep. Looking at the scene, Vittum thought about the girl's life in the crowded tenement. Should she try to save her? Vittum asked herself. Should she even try to bring the girl back "to the misery and hopelessness of the life she was living in that awful place"?

The young girl died, and in later years, Vittum often told her story. It was easy to see why. The girl's life in the slum, the children on the floor, the need to take in boarders to make ends meet, the way the mother and father collapsed at the end of a workday that began long before sunup—all reflected the experiences of millions of people living in the nation's cities.

Vittum and people like her were attempting to respond to the overwhelming challenges of the nation's burgeoning cities. People poured into cities in the last part of the nineteenth century, lured by glitter and excitement, by friends and relatives who were already there, and, above all, by the greater opportunities for jobs and higher wages. Between 1860 and 1910, the rural population of the United States almost doubled; the number of people living in cities increased sevenfold.

Little of the increase came from natural growth, since urban families had high rates of infant mortality, a declining fertility rate, and a high death rate from injury and disease. Many of the newcomers came from rural America, and many more came from Europe, Latin America, and Asia. In one of the most significant migrations in American history, thousands of African Americans began in the 1880s to move from the rural South to northern cities. By 1900, there were large black communities in New York, Baltimore, Chicago, Washington, D.C., and other cities. Yet to come was the even greater black migration during World War I.

Two major forces reshaped American society between 1870 and 1920. One was industrialization; the other was urbanization, the headlong rush of people from their rural roots into the modern urban environment. In these years, cities grew upward and outward,

The kitchen of a tenement apartment was often a multipurpose room. Here the tenement dwellers prepared and ate their meals; the room might also serve as a workroom, and it might be used as sleeping quarters for one or more members of the family.
Source: © The Museum of the City of New York, The Byron Collection.

attracting millions of newcomers and influencing politics, education, entertainment, and family life. By 1920, they had become the center of American economic, social, and cultural life.

The Lure of the City

Why did cities in the United States grow between 1880 and 1900?

Between 1870 and 1900, the city—like the factory—became a symbol of a new America. Drawn from farms, small towns, and foreign lands, newcomers swelled the population of older

cities and created new ones almost overnight. At the beginning of the Civil War, only one-sixth of the American people lived in cities of eight thousand people or more. By 1900, one-third did; by 1920, one-half. "We live in the age of great cities," wrote the Reverend Samuel Lane Loomis in 1887. "Each successive year finds a stronger and more irresistible current sweeping in towards the centers of life."

The current brought growth of an explosive sort. Thousands of years of history had produced only a handful of cities with more than a half million in population. In 1900, the United States had six such cities, including three—New York, Chicago, and Philadelphia—with populations greater than one million.

The Wainwright Building (1890) in St. Louis Missouri was designed by Chicago architect Louis Sullivan. The 10-story red brick office building was one of the first skyscrapers in the world and had many of the modern design features found in Sullivan's buildings of this period.

Skyscrapers and Suburbs

Like so many things in these years, the city was transformed by a revolution in technology. Beginning in the 1880s, the age of steel and glass produced the skyscraper; the streetcar produced the suburbs and new residential patterns.

On the eve of the change, American cities were a crowded jumble of small buildings. Church steeples stood out on the skyline, clearly visible above the roofs of factories and office buildings. Buildings were usually made of masonry, and since the massive walls had to support their own weight, they could be no taller than a dozen or so stories. Steel frames and girders ended that limitation and allowed buildings to soar higher and higher. "Curtain walls,"

which concealed the steel framework, were no longer load bearing; they were pierced by many windows that let in fresh air and light. Completed in 1885, the Home Insurance Building in Chicago was the country's first metal-frame structure.

To a group of talented Chicago architects, the new trends served as a springboard for innovative forms. The leaders of the movement were John Root and Louis H. Sullivan, both of whom were attracted by the chance to rebuild Chicago after the great fire of 1871. Noting that the fire had fed on fancy exterior ornamentation, Root developed a plain, stripped-down style, bold in mass and form—the keynotes of modern architecture. He had another important insight, too. In an age of business, Root thought, the office tower, more than a church or a government building, symbolized the society, and he designed office buildings that carried out, as he said, "the ideas of modern business life: simplicity, stability, breadth, dignity."

Sullivan had studied at the Massachusetts Institute of Technology (MIT) and in Paris before settling in Chicago. In 1886, at the age of thirty, he began work on the Chicago Auditorium, one of the last great masonry buildings. "Then came the flash of imagination which saw the single thing," he later said. "The trick was turned; and there swiftly came into being something new under the sun." Sullivan's skyscrapers, that "flash of imagination," changed the urban skyline.

In the Wainwright Building in St. Louis (1890), the Schiller Building (1892) and the Carson, Pirie, and Scott department store (1899) in Chicago, and the Prudential Building in Buffalo (1895), Sullivan developed the new forms. Architects must discard "books, rules, precedents," he announced; responding to the new, they should design for a building's function. "Form follows function," Sullivan believed, and he passed the idea on to a talented disciple, Frank Lloyd Wright. The modern city should stretch to the sky.

Electric elevators, first used in 1871, carried passengers upward in the new skyscrapers. During the same years, streetcars, another innovation, carried the people outward to expanded boundaries that transformed urban life.

Cities were no longer largely "walking cities," confined to a radius of two or three miles, the distance an individual might walk. Streetcar systems extended the radius and changed the urban map. Cable lines, electric surface lines, and elevated rapid transit brought shoppers and workers into central business districts and sped them home again. Offering a modest five-cent fare with a free transfer, the mass transit systems fostered commuting and widely separated business and residential districts sprang up. The middle class moved farther and farther out to the leafy greenness of the suburbs.

As the middle class moved out of the cities, the immigrants and working class poured in. They took over the older brownstones, row houses, and workers' cottages, turning them, under the sheer weight of numbers, into the slums of the central city. In the cities of the past, classes and occupations had been thrown together; without streetcars and subways, there was no other choice. The streetcar city, sprawling and specialized, became a more fragmented and stratified society with middle-class residential rings surrounding a business and working-class core.

Tenements and the Problems of Overcrowding

In the shadow of the skyscrapers, grimy rows of tenements filled the central city. Tenement houses on small city lots crowded people into cramped apartments. In the late 1870s, architect James E. Ware won a competition for tenement design with the "dumbbell tenement." Rising seven or eight stories in height, the dumbbell tenement packed about thirty four-room apartments on a lot only 25 by 100 feet. Between four and sixteen families lived on a floor; two toilets in the hall of each floor served their needs. Narrowed at the middle, the tenement resembled a giant dumbbell in shape. The indented middle created an air shaft between adjoining buildings that provided a little light and ventilation. In case of fire, it also carried flames from one story to the next, making the buildings notorious firetraps. In 1890, nearly half the dwellings in New York City were tenements.

That year, more than 1.4 million people lived on Manhattan Island, one of whose wards had a population density of 334,000 people per square mile. Many people lived in alleys and basements so dark they could not be photographed until flashlight photography was invented in 1887. Exploring the city, William Dean Howells, the prominent author, inhaled "the stenches of the neglected street . . . [and] the yet fouler and dreadfuller poverty smell which breathes from the open doorways."

Howells smelled more than poverty. In the 1870s and 1880s, cities stank. One problem was horse manure, hundreds of tons of it a day in every city. Another was the privy, "a single one of which," said a leading authority on public health, "may render life in a whole neighborhood almost unendurable in the summer."

Said one New York City resident, "The stench is something terrible." Another wrote that "the stink is enough to knock you down." In 1880, the Chicago *Times* said that a "solid stink" pervaded the city. "No other word expresses it so well as stink. A stench means something finite. Stink reaches the infinite and becomes sublime in the magnitude of odiousness." In 1892, one neighborhood of Chicago, covering one-third of a square mile, had only three bathtubs.

Cities dumped their wastes into the nearest body of water, then drew drinking water from the same site. Many built modern purified waterworks but could not keep pace with spiraling growth. In 1900, fewer than one in ten city dwellers drank filtered water. Factories, the pride of the era, polluted the urban air. At night, Pittsburgh looked and sounded like "Hell with the lid off," according to contemporary observers. Smoke poured from seventy-three

glass factories, forty-one iron and steel mills, and twenty-nine oil refineries. The choking air helped prevent lung diseases and malaria—or so the city's advertising claimed.

Crime was another growing problem. The nation's homicide rate nearly tripled in the 1880s, much of the increase coming in the cities. After remaining constant for many decades, the suicide rate rose steadily between 1870 and 1900, according to a study of Philadelphia. Alcoholism also rose, especially among men, though recent studies have shown that for working-class men, the urban saloon was as much a gathering spot as it was a place to drink. Nonetheless, a 1905 survey of Chicago counted as many saloons as grocery stores, meat markets, and dry goods stores combined.

Strangers in a New Land

While some of the new city dwellers came from farms and small towns, many more came from abroad. Most came from Europe, where unemployment, food shortages, and increasing threats of war sent millions fleeing across the Atlantic to make a fresh start. Often they knew someone already in the United States, a friend or relative who had written them about prospects for jobs and freer lives in a new land. Italians first came in large numbers to escape an 1887 cholera epidemic in southern Italy; tens of thousands of Jews sought refuge from the anti-Semitic massacres that swept Russia and czarist-ruled Poland after 1880.

View the **Closer Look**   Group of Emigrants (Women and Children) from Eastern Europe on Deck of the S.S. *Amsterdam*

Francis Eastman Johnston, the photographer of Group Emigrants (Women and Children) from Eastern Europe on Deck of the S.S. *Amsterdam* (1899), was one of the earliest female photographers and photojournalists. Her photograph above captures the productive promise of Eastern European immigrants coming to the United States during this era seeking economic opportunity, religious freedom, and an escape from deadly epidemics in Europe.

Feature Essay

Ellis Island
Isle of Hope, Isle of Tears

👁— Watch the Video   Ellis Island Immigrants

From 1892 to 1924, Ellis Island in New York Harbor was America's largest and most active immigration station, where over 12 million immigrants, mostly from Europe, were processed. The review process included a personal health inspection and proof of minimal funds. In exceptional cases, an immigrant would be sent home if he or she failed the inspection and could not be treated in the hospital for any medical problems.

Ten years after he left Selo, his small Bulgarian village, for the United States, Michael Gurkin returned to tell of the wonders he had seen, including "buildings that scratched the sky," rooms in them that moved up and down, buttons that, pushed, lit a house or a street. Stoyan Christowe, thirteen, listened intently, caught up in the "Americamania," as he called it, that swept through his village. Soon he was on his way to the new

land, his pockets stuffed with walnuts because he was too young to drink the farewell toast.

Unknowingly, he had joined a flood of people who were making their way to the United States. Between 1880 and 1920, a period of just forty years, the remarkable total of 23.5 million immigrants arrived in the country. They came from around the world, though mostly from Europe, driven from their homelands by economic, religious, or other troubles, lured across the ocean by the chance for a

better life. They entered the country through several ports, but by far the most—about seven out of every ten—landed in the city of New York.

Until 1892, they landed at a depot known as Castle Garden, a sprawling building on the tip of Manhattan Island. When it could no longer handle the flow, the entry site was moved to Ellis Island, close to the Statue of Liberty. Contractors erected a wooden structure, which opened in 1892 and burned down five years later. They then put up the current edifice, an imposing red brick building

442

with triple-arch entrances and corner steeples. A small city, it had dormitories, a hospital, a post office, and showers that could bathe eight thousand people a day. It opened in 1900.

The change to Ellis Island represented more than just a shift in site. Entrance at Castle Garden had been fairly informal, since control over immigration still rested largely in the hands of the states. Officials merely registered newcomers, a process that took about thirty seconds.

In 1891, worried about the growing numbers of people who wanted in, Congress acted to bring immigration under federal control. Ellis Island was given tasks Castle Garden had never had, including mandates to keep out people some Americans considered undesirable. It became, one observer said, "the nearest earthly likeness to the Final Day of Judgement, when we have to prove our fitness to enter Heaven."

Many of those who sailed into the harbor, it should be remembered, never passed through the island at all. Arriving in first or second class, they had a fast on-board examination and went ashore, monied enough, it was assumed, not to become wards of the state. But those in third class—"steerage," as it was known—had a very different experience, and they faced it chock full of fear they would fail some test and be sent back home.

The day they docked, in 1910, Christowe and others washed thoroughly, hoping to look clean enough to pass inspection. Crowding the ship's rails, they gazed in wonder at the statue in the harbor, its arm lifted in the air. It was a saint, some guessed; Christopher Columbus, others said. It was a monument to freedom, Christowe was told, with Emma Lazarus's inviting poem at its base, "Give me your tired, your poor, Your huddled masses yearning to breathe free."

Once on the island, those huddled masses were under scrutiny from the moment they landed. Officials watched them climb the stairs, looking for heart problems or lameness. Physicians administered the "six-second exam," checking quickly for disabilities or contagious diseases. If anything seemed out of sort, they put a chalk mark on the immigrant's coat calling for closer examination.

The next exam was the most feared: a doctor using a tailor's buttonhook to pull back eyelids to look for signs of diseases such as trachoma, a highly contagious bacterial eye infection that could lead to blindness. Most immigrants had never heard of trachoma, nor even knew they had the disease, but it alone could strand them in the island's hospital or put them on a boat back home.

No one who went through the exam ever forgot it, as an immigrant poet wrote:

A stranger receives us
Harshly and asks: "And your health?"
He examines us. His look
Assesses us like dogs.
He studies in depth
Eyes and mouth. No doubt
That if he'd probed our hearts
He would have seen the wound.

Immigrants with chalk marks were herded to the left, while most went to the right, filing by a matron who searched the faces of women for evidence of "loose character." With so many languages among the arrivals, there were few written signs, and officials used metal barricades to guide people along, "like puppets on conveyor belts," Christowe later recalled.

Last there were the inspectors, seated behind desks, asking name, age, occupation, among dozens of other questions. On a busy day, the inspectors had two minutes to decide the fate of a newcomer. Those who "failed" went before a feared Board of Special Inquiry for final decision. For most immigrants the whole process took less than five hours; many others, held for proof of funds or further examination, spent days in the dormitories or hospital. Despite the harsh rumors, no more than 3 percent in a given year were turned away.

Still, it was becoming harder to get in. People who feared the effect of immigrants on the nation clamored to keep them out. Some worried about the numbers of people who were arriving, others about disease or "radical" political views. Some did not like the shift in immigration after 1890 from largely Protestant northern and western Europe to Catholics, Jews, and others from southern and eastern Europe.

Reflecting such concerns, Congress passed laws to keep certain types of people out. In 1875, it prohibited the entrance of criminals and prostitutes. In 1882, it barred convicts and lunatics and excluded laborers from China, the first measure aimed directly at a racial group. In 1885, it banned the entry of laborers under contract, imported by industries to work at low wages; in 1891, polygamists and people with "loathsome" diseases; in 1903, anarchists. In 1917, it passed, over Woodrow Wilson's veto, a literacy test that required immigrants to read a passage in their native tongue.

The great burst of immigration, halted during World War I, ended with the adoption of restrictive legislation in the 1920s. Ellis Island became a detention center for "radicals" and other people awaiting deportation. Once the gateway to the United States, the famous island had become an exit.

Ellis Island closed in 1954 and in 1965, recognizing its historic importance, the government made it a national monument. It reopened in 1990 as a museum of American immigration, attracting more than two million tourists a year, many of whom retrace the footsteps of their ancestors who had landed there. Stoyan Christowe's name is in the records. Starting with a miserable job in a railroad yard in St. Louis, he went to college, served in military intelligence during World War II, wrote several books, and became a member of the Vermont legislature.

His experience on Ellis Island blended into the nation's experience. More than one hundred million Americans—about four in every ten—trace their ancestry to those who found a new home through its gates.

QUESTIONS FOR DISCUSSION

1. What arguments did Americans use to justify limiting immigration during this era?

2. How did the experience on arrival in the U.S. of those who traveled in first or second class differ from that of steerage passengers?

443

View the Map   Immigration, 1880–1920

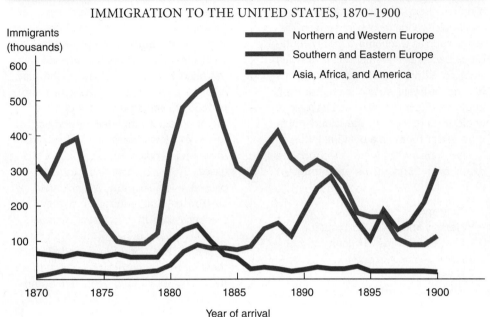

IMMIGRATION TO THE UNITED STATES, 1870–1900

Note: For purposes of classification, "Northern and Western Europe" includes Great Britain, Ireland, Scandinavia, the Netherlands, Belgium, Luxembourg, Switzerland, France, and Germany. "Southern and Eastern Europe" includes Poland, Austria-Hungary, Russia and the Baltic States, Romania, Bulgaria, European Turkey, Italy, Spain, Portugal, and Greece. "Asia, Africa, and America" includes Asian Turkey, China, Japan, India, Canada, the Caribbean, Latin America, and all of Africa.

Source: U.S. Bureau of the Census, *Historical Statistics of the United States*, *Colonial Times to 1970*, Bicentennial Edition, Washington, DC, 1975.

All told, the immigration figures were staggering. Between 1877 and 1890, more than 6.3 million people entered the United States. In one year alone, 1882, almost 789,000 people came. By 1890, about 15 percent of the population, nine million people, were foreign born.

Most newcomers were job seekers. Nearly two-thirds were males, and the majority were between the ages of fifteen and forty. Most were unskilled laborers. Most settled on the eastern seaboard. In 1901, the Industrial Relocation Office was established to relieve overcrowding in the eastern cities; opening Galveston, Texas, as a port of entry, it attracted many Russian Jews to Texas and the Southwest. But most immigrants preferred the shorter, more familiar journey to New York. Entering through Ellis Island in New York harbor, as four in every ten immigrants did, most tended to crowd into northern and eastern cities, settling in areas where others of their nationality or religion lived. (See the Feature Essay, "Ellis Island: Isle of Hope, Isle of Tears," pp. 442–443.)

They were often dazzled by what they saw. They stared at electric lights, indoor plumbing, soda fountains, streetcars, plush train seats for all classes, ice cream, lemons, and bananas. Relatives whisked them off to buy new "American" clothes and showed them the teeming markets, department stores, and Woolworth's new five-and-ten stores. "It seemed quite advanced compared with our home in Khelm," said a Polish girl. "There was a sense of safety and hope that we had never felt in Poland."

Cities had increasingly large foreign-born populations. In 1900, four-fifths of Chicago's population was foreign born or of foreign-born parentage, two-thirds of Boston's, and one-half of Philadelphia's. New York City, where most immigrants arrived and many stayed, had more Italians than lived in Naples, more Germans than lived in Hamburg, and twice as many Irish as lived in Dublin. Four out of five New York City residents in 1890 were of foreign birth or foreign parentage.

Beginning in the 1880s, the sources of immigration shifted dramatically away from northern and western Europe, the chief source of immigration for more than two centuries. More and more immigrants came from southern and eastern Europe: Italy, Greece, Austria-Hungary, Poland, and Russia. Between 1880 and 1910, approximately 8.4 million people came from these lands. The **new immigrants** tended to be Catholics or Jews rather than Protestants. Like their predecessors, most were unskilled rather than skilled, and they often spoke "strange" languages. Most were poor and uneducated; sticking together in close-knit communities, they clung to their native customs, languages, and religions.

More than any previous group, the so-called new immigrants troubled the mainstream society. Could they be assimilated? Did they share "American" values? Such questions preoccupied such groups as the American Protective Association, a midwestern anti-Catholic organization that expanded in the 1890s and worked to limit or end immigration. Sneering epithets became part of the national vocabulary: "wop" and "dago" for Italians; "bohunk" for Bohemians, Hungarians, and other Slavs; "greaseball" for Greeks; and "kike" for Jews. "You don't call . . . an Italian a white man?" a congressman asked a railroad construction boss in 1890. "No, sir," the boss replied. "An Italian is a Dago."

Anti-Catholicism and anti-Semitism flared up again, as they had in the 1850s. The Immigration Restriction League, founded in 1894, demanded a literacy test for immigrants from southern and eastern Europe. Congress passed such a law in 1896, but President Cleveland vetoed it.

Immigrants and the City

Industrial capitalism—the world of factories and foremen and grimy machines—tested the immigrants and placed an enormous strain on their families. Many immigrants came from peasant societies where life proceeded according to outdoor routine and age-old tradition. In their new city homes, they found both new freedoms and new confinements, a different language, and a novel set of customs and expectations. Historians have only recently begun to discover the remarkable ways in which they learned to adjust.

Like native-born families, most immigrant families were nuclear in structure—they consisted of two parents and their children. Though variations occurred from group to group, men and women occupied roles similar to those in native families: Men were wage earners, women were housekeepers and mothers.

FOREIGN-BORN POPULATION, 1890 Immigrants tended to settle in regions where jobs were relatively plentiful or conditions were similar to those they had left in their homelands. Cities of the Northeast, Midwest, and West offered job opportunities, while land available for cultivation drew immigrant farmers to the plains and prairies of the nation's midsection.

Percent of Total Population

- 34 or more
- 10–34
- 1–10
- 1 or less
- Not reported

Margaret Byington, who studied steelworkers' homes in Homestead in the early 1900s, learned that the father played a relatively small role in child rearing or managing the family's finances. "His part of the problem is to earn and hers to spend." In Chicago, social reformer Jane Addams discovered that immigrant women made it "a standard of domestic virtue that a man must not touch his pay envelope, but bring it home unopened to his wife."

Although patterns varied among ethnic groups, and between economic classes within ethnic groups, immigrants tended to marry within the group more than did the native born. Immigrants also tended to marry at a later age than natives, and they tended to have more children, a fact that worried nativists opposed to immigration.

Immigrants shaped the city as much as it shaped them. Most of them tried to retain their traditional culture for themselves and their children while at the same time adapting to life in their new country. To do this, they spoke their native language, practiced their religious faith, read their own newspapers, and established special parochial or other schools. They observed traditional holidays and formed a myriad of social organizations to maintain ties among members of the group.

Immigrant associations—there were many of them in every city—offered fellowship in a strange land. They helped newcomers find jobs and homes; they provided important services such as

unemployment insurance and health insurance. In a Massachusetts textile town, the Irish Benevolent Society said, "We visit our sick, and bury our dead." Some groups were no larger than a neighborhood; others spread nationwide. In 1914, the Deutsch-Amerikanischer Nationalbund, the largest of the associations, had more than two million members in dozens of cities and towns. Many women belonged to and participated in the work of the immigrant associations; in addition, there were groups exclusively for women, such as the Polish Women's Alliance, the Jednota Ceskyck Dam (Society of Czech Women), and the National Council of Jewish Women.

The Polish National Alliance (PNA), a typical immigrant association, was founded in 1880. Like other organizations, it helped new immigrants on their arrival, offered insurance plans, established libraries and museums, sponsored youth programs, fielded baseball teams, and organized trips back to Poland. Each year, the PNA published a sought-after calendar filled with Polish holidays, information, and proverbs. Extolling Poles' contributions to their new country, it erected monuments to distinguished Americans of Polish descent.

Every major city had dozens of foreign language newspapers, with circulations large and small. The first newspaper published in the Lithuanian language appeared in the United States, not in Lithuania. Eagerly read, the papers not only carried news of events in the homeland but also reported on local ethnic leaders, told readers how to vote and become citizens, and gave practical tips on adjusting to life in the United States. The Swedes, Poles, Czechs, and Germans established ethnic theaters that performed national plays and music. The most famous of these, the Yiddish (Jewish) Theater, started in the 1880s in New York City and lasted more than fifty years.

The church and the school were the most important institutions in every immigrant community. Eastern European Jews established synagogues and religious schools wherever they settled; they taught the Hebrew language and raised their children in a heritage they did not want to leave behind. Among such groups as the Irish and the Poles, the Roman Catholic church provided spiritual and educational guidance. In the parish schools, Polish priests and nuns taught Polish American children about Polish as well as American culture in the Polish language.

Church, school, and fraternal societies shaped the way in which immigrants adjusted to life in America. By preserving language, religion, and heritage, they also shaped the country itself.

The House That Tweed Built

Closely connected with explosive urban growth was the emergence of the powerful city political machine. As cities grew, lines of responsibility in city governments became hopelessly confused, increasing the opportunity for corruption and greed. Burgeoning populations required streets, buildings, and public services; immigrants needed even more services. In this situation, political party machines played an important role.

The machines traded services for votes. Loosely knit, they were headed by a strong, influential leader—the "boss"—who tied together a network of ward and precinct captains, each of whom looked after his local constituents. In New York, "Honest" John Kelly, Richard Croker, and Charles F. Murphy led Tammany Hall, the famous Democratic party organization that dominated city politics from the 1850s to the 1930s. Other bosses included "Hinky Dink" Kenna and "Bathhouse John" Coughlin in Chicago, James McManes in Philadelphia, and Christopher A. Buckley—the notorious "Blind Boss," who used an exceptional memory for voices to make up for failing eyesight—in San Francisco.

Watch the Video Democracy and Corruption: The Rise of Political Machines

"THAT'S WHAT'S THE MATTER."

BOSS TWEED. "As long as I count the Votes, what are you going to do about it? say?"

This political cartoon skewers the success of political bosses, such as the depicted Boss (William) Tweed of New York, to manipulate the political process and use patronage to enrich themselves and retain political power in various cities during this period.

William M. Tweed, head of the famed Tweed Ring in New York, provided the model for them all. Nearly six feet tall, weighing almost three hundred pounds, Tweed rose through the ranks of Tammany Hall. He served in turn as city alderman, member of Congress, and New York State assemblyman. A man of culture and warmth, he moved easily between the rough back alleys of New York and the parlors and clubs of the city's elite. Behind the scenes, he headed a ring that plundered New York for tens of millions of dollars.

The New York County Courthouse—"the house that Tweed built"—was his masterpiece. Nestled in City Hall Park in downtown Manhattan, the three-story structure was designed to cost $250,000, but the bills ran a bit higher. Andrew Garvey, the "prince of plasterers," charged $500,000 for plasterwork, and then $1 million to repair the same work. His total bill came to

$2,870,464.06. (The *New York Times* suggested that the six cents be donated to charity.) In the end, the building cost more than $13 million—and in 1872, when Tweed fell, it was still not finished.

The role of the political bosses can be overemphasized. Power structures in the turn-of-the-century city were complex, involving a host of people and institutions. Banks, real estate investors, insurance companies, architects, and engineers, among others, played roles in governing the city. Viewed in retrospect, many city governments were remarkably successful. With populations that in some cases doubled every decade, city governments provided water and sewer lines, built parks and playgrounds, and paved streets. When it was over, Boston had the world's largest public library and New York City had the Brooklyn Bridge and Central Park, two of the finest achievements in city planning and architecture of any era. By the 1890s, New York also had 660 miles of water lines, 464 miles of sewers, and 1,800 miles of paved streets, far more than comparable cities in Europe.

Bosses, moreover, differed from city to city. Buckley stayed in power in San Francisco by keeping city tax rates low. "Honest" John Kelly earned his nickname serving as a watchdog over the New York City treasury. Tweed was one of the early backers of the Brooklyn Bridge. Some bosses were plainly corrupt; others believed in *honest graft*, a term Tammany's George Washington Plunkitt coined to describe "legitimate" profits made from advance knowledge of city projects.

Why did voters keep the bosses in power? The answers are complex, but two reasons were skillful political organization and the fact that immigrants and others made up the bosses' constituency. Most immigrants had little experience with democratic government and proved easy prey for well-oiled machines. For the most part, however, the bosses stayed in power because they paid attention to the needs of the least privileged city voters. They offered valued services in an era when neither government nor business lent a hand.

If an immigrant, tired and bewildered after the long crossing, came looking for a job, bosses like Tweed, Plunkitt, or Buckley found him one in city offices or local businesses. If a family's breadwinner died or was injured, the bosses donated food and clothing and saw to it that the family made it through the crisis. If the winter was particularly cold, they provided free coal to heat tenement apartments. They ran picnics for slum children on hot summer days and contributed to hospitals, orphanages, and dozens of worthy neighborhood causes.

Most bosses became wealthy; they were not Robin Hoods who took from the rich to give to the poor. They took for themselves as well. Reformers occasionally ousted them. Tweed fell from power in 1872, "Blind Boss" Buckley in 1891, Croker in 1894. But the reformers rarely stayed in power long. Drawn mainly from the middle and upper classes, they had little understanding of the needs of the poor. Before long, they returned to private concerns, and the bosses, who had known that they would all along, cheerily took power again.

"What tells in holdin' your grip on your district," the engaging Plunkitt once said, "is to go right down among the poor families and help them in the different ways they need help. . . . It's philanthropy, but it's politics, too—mighty good politics . . . . The poor are the most grateful people in the world."

Social and Cultural Change, 1877–1900

How did the growth of American cities affect social, cultural, and political life?

The rise of cities and industry between 1877 and the 1890s affected all aspects of American life. Mores changed; family ties loosened. Factories turned out consumer goods, and the newly invented cash register rang up record sales. Public and private educational systems burgeoned, illiteracy declined, life expectancy increased. While many people worked harder and harder just to survive, others found they had a greater amount of leisure time. The roles of women and children changed in a number of ways, and the family took on functions it had not had before. Thanks to advancing technology, news flashed quickly across the oceans, and for the first time in history, people read of the day's events in distant lands when they opened their daily newspapers.

"We are in a period," President Rutherford B. Hayes said in 1878, "when old questions are settled, and the new ones are not yet brought forward." Old questions—questions of racial, social and economic justice, and of federal-state relations—were not settled, but people wanted new directions. Political issues lost the sharp focus of the Civil War and Reconstruction. For men and women of middle age in 1877, the issues of the Union and slavery had been the overriding public concerns throughout their adult lives. Now, with the end of Reconstruction, it seemed time for new concerns.

In 1877, the country had 47 million people. In 1900, it had nearly 76 million. Nine-tenths of the population was white; just under one-tenth was black. There were 66,000 American Indians, 108,000 Chinese, and 148 Japanese. The bulk of the white population,

URBAN AND RURAL POPULATION, 1870–1900 (IN MILLIONS)

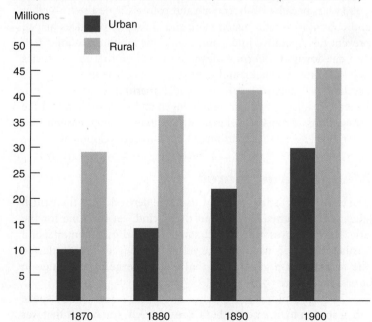

Source: U.S. Bureau of the Census, *Historical Statistics of the United States, Colonial Times to 1970*, Bicentennial Edition, Washington, DC, 1975.

most of whom were Protestant, came from the so-called Anglo-Saxon countries of northern Europe. WASPs—white Anglo-Saxon Protestants—were the dominant members of American society.

Though the rush to the cities was about to begin, most people of 1877 still lived on farms or in small towns. Their lives revolved around the farm, the church, and the general store. In 1880, nearly 75 percent of the population lived in communities of fewer than 2,500 people. In 1900, in the midst of city growth, 60 percent still did. The average family in 1880 had three children, dramatically fewer than at the beginning of the century, and life expectancy was about 43 years. By 1900, it had risen to 47 years, a result of improved health care. For blacks and other minorities, who often lived in unsanitary rural areas, life expectancy was substantially lower: 33 years.

Meals tended to be heavy, and so did people. Even breakfast had several courses and could include steak, eggs, fish, potatoes, toast, and coffee. Food prices were low. Families ate fresh homegrown produce in the summer and "put up" their fruits and vegetables for the long winters. Toward the end of the century, eating habits changed. New packaged breakfast cereals became popular; fresh fruit and vegetables came in on fast trains from Florida and California, and commercially canned food became safer and cheaper. The newfangled icebox, cooled by blocks of ice, kept food fresher and added new treats such as ice cream.

Medical science was in the midst of a major revolution. Louis Pasteur's recent discovery that germs cause infection and disease created the new science of microbiology and led the way to the development of vaccines and other preventive measures. But tuberculosis, typhoid, diphtheria, and pneumonia—all now curable—were still the leading causes of death. Infant mortality declined between 1877 and 1900, but the decline was gradual; a great drop did not come until after 1920.

There were few hospitals and no hospital insurance. Most patients stayed at home, although medical practice, especially surgery, expanded rapidly. Once brutal and dangerous, surgery in these years became relatively safe and painless. Anesthetics—ether and chloroform—eliminated pain, and antiseptic practices helped prevent postoperative infections. Antiseptic practices at childbirth also cut down on puerperal fever, an infection that for centuries had killed many women and newborn infants. The new science of psychology began to explore the mind, hitherto uncharted. William James, a leading American psychologist and philosopher, laid the foundations of modern behavioral psychology, which emphasized the importance of the environment on human development.

Manners and Mores

The code of Victorian morality, its name derived from the British queen who reigned throughout the period, set the tone for the era. The code prescribed strict standards of dress, manners, and sexual behavior. It was both obeyed and disobeyed, and it reflected the tensions of a generation that was undergoing a change in moral standards.

In 1877, children were to be seen and not heard. They spoke when spoken to, listened rather than chattered—or at least that was the rule. Older boys and girls were often chaperoned, although they could always find moments alone. They played post office and spin the bottle; they puffed cigarettes behind the barn. Counterbalancing such youthful exuberance was strong pride in virtue and self-control. "Thank heaven I am absolutely pure," Theodore Roosevelt, the future president, wrote in 1880 after proposing to Alice Lee. "I can tell Alice everything I have ever done."

Gentlemen of the middle class dressed in heavy black suits, derby hats, and white shirts with paper collars. Women wore tight corsets, long dark dresses, and black shoes reaching well above the ankles. As with so many things, styles changed dramatically toward the end of the century, spurred in part by new sporting fads such as golf, tennis, and bicycling, which required looser clothing. By the 1890s, a middle-class woman wore a tailored suit or a dark skirt and a blouse, called a shirtwaist, modeled after men's shirts. Her skirts still draped about the ankles, but more and more she removed or loosened the corset, the dread device that squeezed skin and internal organs into fashionable 18-inch waistlines.

Religious and patriotic values were strong. A center of community life, the church often set the tenor for family and social relationships. In the 1880s, eight out of ten church members were Protestants; most of the rest were Roman Catholics. Evangelists such as Dwight L. Moody (a former Chicago shoe salesman) and Ira B. Sankey (an organist and singer) conducted mass revival meetings across the country. Enormously successful, Moody preached to millions and sparked a spiritual awakening on American college campuses.

With slavery abolished, reformers turned their attention to new moral and political issues. One group, known as the **Mugwumps**, worked to end corruption in politics. Drawn mostly from the educated and upper class, they included Thomas Nast, the famous political cartoonist; George William Curtis, editor of *Harper's Weekly*; and E. L. Godkin, editor of the influential *Nation*. Other zealous reformers campaigned for prohibition of the sale of intoxicating liquors, hoping to end the social evils that stemmed from drunkenness. In 1874, women who advocated total abstinence from alcoholic beverages formed the **Women's Christian Temperance Union (WCTU)**. Their leader, Frances E. Willard, served as president of the group from 1879 until her death in 1898. By then, the WCTU had ten thousand branches and five hundred thousand members.

In New York City, Anthony Comstock formed the Society for the Suppression of Vice, which supervised public morality. At his request, Congress passed the Comstock Law (1873) prohibiting the mailing or transporting of "obscene, lewd or lascivious" articles. The law was not successful; within a few years, Comstock reported finding 64,094 "articles for immoral use," 700 pounds of "lead moulds for making obscene matter," 202,679 obscene photographs, and 26 "obscene pictures, framed on walls of saloons."

Leisure and Entertainment

In the 1870s, people tended to rise early. On getting up, they washed from the pitcher and bowl in the bedroom, first breaking the layer of ice if it was winter. After dressing and eating, they went off to work and school. Without large refrigerators, housewives marketed almost daily. In the evening, families gathered in the "second parlor" or living room, where the children did their lessons, played games, sang around the piano, and listened to that day's verse from the Bible.

Popular games included cards, dominoes, backgammon, chess, and checkers. Many homes had a packet of "author cards" that required knowledge of books, authors, and noted quotations. The latest fad was the stereopticon or "magic lantern," which brought three-dimensional life to art, history, and nature. Like author cards and other games, it was instructional as well as entertaining.

Sentimental ballads such as "Silver Threads Among the Gold" (1873) remained the most popular musical form, but the insistent syncopated rhythms of ragtime were being heard, reflecting the influence of the new urban culture. By the time the strains of Scott Joplin's "Maple Leaf Rag" (1899) popularized ragtime, critics complained that "a wave of vulgar, filthy and suggestive music has inundated the land." Classical music flourished. The New England Conservatory (1867), the Cincinnati College of Music (1878), and the Metropolitan Opera (1883) were new sources of civic pride; New York, Boston, and Chicago launched first-rate symphony orchestras between 1878 and 1891.

In the hamlets and small towns of America, traveling circuses were enormously popular. Hamlin Garland, an author who grew up in small Iowa villages, recalled how the circus came "trailing clouds of glorified dust and filling our minds with the color of romance . . . . It brought to our ears the latest band pieces and taught us the popular songs. It furnished us with jokes. It relieved our dullness. It gave us something to talk about." Larger circuses, run by entrepreneurs such as P. T. Barnum and James A. Bailey, played the cities, but every town attracted its own smaller version.

Fairs, horse races, balloon ascensions, bicycle tournaments, and football and baseball contests attracted avid fans. The years between 1870 and 1900 saw the rise of organized spectator sports, a trend reflecting both the rise of the city and the new uses of leisure. Baseball's first professional team, the Cincinnati Red Stockings, appeared in 1869, and baseball soon became the preeminent national sport. Fans sang songs about it ("Take Me Out to the Ballgame"), wrote poems about it ("Casey at the Bat"), and made up riddles about it ("What has eighteen feet and catches flies?"). Modern rules were adopted. Umpires were designated to call balls and strikes; catchers wore masks and chest protectors and moved closer to the plate instead of staying back to catch the ball on the bounce. Fielders had to catch the ball on the fly rather than on one bounce in their caps. By 1890, professional baseball teams were drawing crowds of sixty thousand daily. In 1901, the American League was organized, and two years later the Boston Red Sox beat the Pittsburgh Pirates in the first modern World Series.

In 1869, Princeton and Rutgers played the first intercollegiate football game. Soon, other schools picked up the sport, and by the early 1890s, crowds of fifty thousand or more attended the most popular contests. Basketball, invented in 1891, gained a large following. Boxing, a popular topic of conversation in saloons and schoolyards, was outlawed in most states. For a time, championship prizefights were held in secret, with news of the result spread rapidly by word of mouth. Matches were long and bloody, fought with bare knuckles until the invention in the 1880s of the 5-ounce boxing glove. John L. Sullivan, the "Boston Strong Boy" and the era's most popular champion, won the heavyweight title in 1889 in a brutal 75-round victory over the stubborn Jake Kilrain.

As gas and electric lights brightened the night, and streetcars crisscrossed city streets, leisure habits changed. Delighted with the new technology, people took advantage of an increasing variety of things to do. They stayed home less often. New York City's first electric sign—"Manhattan Beach Swept by Ocean Breezes"— appeared in 1881, and people went out at night filling the streets on their way to the theater, vaudeville shows, and dance halls or just out for an evening stroll.

Changes in Family Life

Under the impact of industrialization and urbanization, family relationships were changing. On the farm, parents and children worked more or less together, and the family was a producing unit. In factories and offices, family members rarely worked together. In working-class families, mothers, fathers, and children separated at dawn and returned, ready for sleep, at dark. Morris Rosenfeld, a clothing presser lamenting that he was unable to spend more time with his son, wrote a poem titled "My Boy":

> I have a little boy at home,
> A pretty little son;
> I think sometimes the world is mine
> In him, my only one. . . .
>
> 'Ere dawn my labor drives me forth;
> Tis night when I am free;
> A stranger am I to my child;
> And stranger my child to me.

Working-class families of the late nineteenth century, like the family of the young Polish girl that Harriet Vittum saw, often lived in complex household units—taking in relatives and boarders to pay the rent. As many as one-third of all households contained people who were not members of the immediate family. Although driven apart by the daily routine, family ties among the working class tended to remain strong, cemented by the need to join forces in order to survive in the industrial economy.

The middle-class wife and children, however, became increasingly isolated from the world of work. Turning inward, the middle-class family became more self-contained. Older children spent more time in adolescence, and periods of formal schooling were lengthier. Families took in fewer apprentices and boarders. By the end of the century, most middle-class offspring continued to live with their parents into their late teens and their twenties, a larger proportion than today.

Fewer middle-class wives participated directly in their husbands' work. As a result, they and their children occupied what contemporaries called a "separate sphere of domesticity," set apart from the masculine sphere of income-producing work. The family home became a "walled garden," a place to retreat from the crass materialism of the outside world. Middle-class fathers began to move their families out of the city to the suburbs, commuting to work on the new streetcars and leaving wives and children at home and school.

The middle-class family had once functioned in part to transmit a craft or skill, arrange marriages, and offer care for dependent kin. Now, as these functions declined, the family took on new emotional and ideological responsibilities. In a society that worried about the weakening hold of other institutions, the family became more and more important as a means of social control. It also placed new burdens on wives.

"In the old days," said a woman in 1907, "a married woman was supposed to be a frump and a bore and a physical wreck. Now you are supposed to keep up intellectually, to look young and well and be fresh and bright and entertaining." Magazines such as the *Ladies' Home Journal*, which started in 1889, glorified motherhood and the home, but its articles and ads featured women as homebound, child-oriented consumers. While society's leaders spoke fondly of the value of home-making, the status of housewives declined under the factory system, which emphasized money rewards and devalued household labor.

Underlying all these changes was one of the modern world's most important trends, a major decline in fertility rates that lasted from 1800 to 1939. Though blacks, immigrants, and rural dwellers continued to have more children than white native-born city dwellers, the trend affected all classes and races; among white women, the birthrate fell from seven in 1800 to just over four in 1880 to about three in 1900. People everywhere tended to marry later and have fewer children.

Since contraceptive devices were not yet widely used, the decline reflected abstinence and a conscious decision to postpone or limit families. Some women decided to devote greater attention to a smaller number of children, others to pursue their own careers. There was a marked increase in the number of young unmarried women working for wages or attending school, an increase in the number of women delaying marriage or not marrying at all, and a gradual decline in rates of illegitimacy and premarital pregnancy.

In large part, the decline in fertility stemmed from people's responses to the social and economic forces around them, the rise of cities and industry. In a host of individual decisions, they decided to have fewer children, and the result reshaped some of the fundamental attitudes and institutions of American society.

Changing Views: A Growing Assertiveness among Women

In and out of the family, there was growing recognition of self-sufficient working women, employed in factory, telephone exchange, or business office, who were entering the workforce in increasing numbers. In 1880, 2.6 million women were gainfully employed; in 1890, 4 million. In 1882, the Census Bureau took the first census of working women; most were single and worked out of necessity rather than choice.

Many regarded this "new woman" as a corruption of the ideal vision of the American woman, in which man worshiped "a diviner self than his own," innocent, helpless, and good. Women were to be better than the world around them. They were brought up, said Ida Tarbell, a leading political reformer, "as if wrongdoing were impossible to them."

Views changed, albeit slowly. One important change occurred in the legal codes pertaining to women, particularly in the common law doctrine of *femme couverte*. Under that doctrine, wives were chattel of their husbands; they could not legally control their own earnings, property, or children unless they had drawn up a specific contract before marriage. By 1890, many states had substantially revised the doctrine to allow wives control of their earnings and inherited property. (See "The Legal Rights of Married Women: Reforming the Law of Coverture," pp. 286–289.) In cases of divorce, the new laws also recognized women's rights to custody or joint custody of their children. Although divorce was

still far from being socially acceptable, divorce rates more than doubled during the last third of the century. By 1905, one in twelve marriages was ending in divorce.

In the 1870s and 1880s, a growing number of women were asserting their own humanness. They fought for the vote, lobbied for equal pay, and sought self-fulfillment. The new interest in psychology and medicine strengthened their causes. Charlotte Perkins Gilman, author of *Women and Economics* (1898), joined other women in questioning the ideal of womanly "innocence," which, she argued, actually meant ignorance. In medical and popular literature, menstruation, sexual intercourse, and childbirth were becoming viewed as natural functions instead of taboo topics.

Edward Bliss Foote's *Plain Home Talk of Love, Marriage, and Parentage*, a best-seller that went through many editions between the 1880s and 1900, challenged Victorian notions that sexual intercourse was unhealthy and intended solely to produce children. In *Plain Facts for Old and Young* (1881), Dr. John H. Kellogg urged parents to recognize the early awakening of sexual feelings in their children. Still, such matters were avoided in many American homes. Rheta Childe Dorr, a journalist, remembered that when a girl reached the age of fourteen, new rules were introduced, "and when you asked for an explanation you met only embarrassed silence."

Women espoused causes with new fervor. Susan B. Anthony, a veteran of many reform campaigns, tried to vote in the 1872 presidential election and was fined $100, which she refused to pay. In 1890, she helped form the **National American Woman Suffrage Association** to work for the enfranchisement of women. On New York's Lower East Side, the Ladies Anti–Beef Trust Association, which formed to protest increases in the price of meat, established a boycott of butcher shops. When their demands were ignored, the women invaded the shops, poured kerosene on the meat, and set fire to it. "We don't riot," Rebecca Ablowitz told the judge. "But if all we did was to weep at home, nobody would notice it; so we have to do something to help ourselves."

Educating the Masses

Continuing a trend that stretched back a hundred years, childhood was becoming an even more distinct time of life. There was still only a vague concept of adolescence—the special nature of the teenage years—but the role of children was changing. Less and less were children perceived as "little adults," valued for the additional financial gain they might bring into the family. Now children were to grow and learn and be nurtured rather than rushed into adulthood.

As a result, schooling became more important, and American children came closer than ever before to universal education. By 1900, thirty-one states and territories (out of fifty-one) had enacted laws making school attendance compulsory, though most required attendance only until the age of fourteen. In 1870, there were only 160 public high schools; in 1900, there were 6,000. In the same years, public school budgets rose from $63 million to $253 million; illiteracy declined from 20 percent to just over 10 percent of the population. Still, even as late as 1900, the average adult had only five years of schooling.

Educators saw the school as the primary means to train people for life and work in an industrializing society. Hence teachers focused on basic skills—reading and mathematics—and on values—obedience and attentiveness to the clock. Most schools had a highly structured curriculum, built around discipline and routine. In 1892, Joseph Rice, a pediatrician, toured twelve hundred classrooms in thirty-six cities. In a typical classroom, he reported, the atmosphere was "damp and chilly," the teacher strict. "The unkindly spirit of the teacher is strikingly apparent; the pupils being completely subjugated to her will, are silent and motionless." One teacher asked her pupils, "How can you learn anything with your knees and toes out of order?"

Many children dropped out of school early, and not just to earn money. Helen Todd, a factory inspector in Chicago, found a group of young girls working in a hot, stuffy attic. When she asked why they were not in school, Tillie Isakowsky, who was 14, said, "School! School is de fiercest t'ing youse kin come up against. Factories ain't no cinch, but schools is worst." A few blocks away, Todd stumbled on a 13-year-old boy hiding in a basement. He cried when she said he would have to go to school, blurting that "they hits ye if yer don't learn, and they hits ye if ye whisper, and they hits ye if ye have string in yer pocket, and they hits ye if yer seat squeaks, and they hits ye if ye don't stan' up in time, and they hits ye if yer late, and they hits ye if ye ferget the page." Curious, Todd asked 500 children whether they would go to school or work in a factory if their families did not need the money—412 preferred the factory.

School began early; boys attended all day, but girls often stayed home after lunch, since it was thought they needed less in the way of learning. On the teacher's command, students stood and recited from *Webster's Spellers* and *McGuffey's Eclectic Readers*, the period's most popular textbooks. The work of William Holmes McGuffey, a professor of languages at Miami University in Ohio, *McGuffey's Eclectic Readers* had been in use since 1836; 100 million copies were sold in the last half of the nineteenth century. Nearly every child read them; they taught not only reading but also ethics, values, and religion. In the *Readers,* boys grew up to be heroes, girls to be mothers, and hard work always meant success:

> Shall birds, and bees, and ants, be wise,
> While I my moments waste?
> O let me with the morning rise,
> And to my duty haste.

The South lagged far behind in education. The average family size there was about twice as large as in the North, and a greater proportion of the population lived in isolated rural areas. State and local authorities mandated fewer weeks in the average school year, and many southern states refused to adopt compulsory education laws. Even more important was the effect of southern Jim Crow laws, passed in the 1890s and after to keep African Americans from voting, serving on juries, and participating in other aspects of southern life. Southerners used these laws to maintain separate school systems to segregate the races. Supported by the U.S. Supreme Court decision of 1896 in **Plessy v. Ferguson** (see *Plessy* v. *Ferguson*: "The Shaping of Jim Crow," pp. 460–463), segregated schooling added a devastating financial burden to education in the South.

North Carolina and Alabama mandated segregated schools in 1876, South Carolina and Louisiana in 1877, Mississippi in 1878, and Virginia in 1882. A series of Supreme Court decisions in the 1880s and 1890s upheld the concept of segregation. In the

Civil Rights Cases (1883), the Court ruled that the Fourteenth Amendment barred state governments from discriminating on account of race but did not prevent private individuals or organizations from doing so. *Plessy* v. *Ferguson* (1896) established the doctrine of "separate but equal" and upheld a Louisiana law requiring different railroad cars for whites and blacks. The Court applied the doctrine directly to schools in *Cumming* v. *County Board of Education* (1899), which approved the creation of separate schools for whites, even if there were no comparable schools for blacks.

Southern school laws often implied that the schools would be "separate but equal," and they were often separate but rarely equal. Black schools were usually dilapidated, and black teachers were paid considerably less than white teachers. In 1890, only 35 percent of black children attended school in the South; 55 percent of white children did. That year nearly two-thirds of the country's black population was illiterate.

Educational techniques changed after the 1870s. Educators paid more attention to early elementary education, a trend that placed young children in school and helped the growing number of mothers who worked outside the home. The kindergarten movement, started in St. Louis in 1873, spread across the country. In kindergartens, four- to six-year-old children learned by playing, not by keeping their knees and toes in order. For older children, social reformers advocated "practical" courses in manual training and homemaking. "We are impatient with the schools which lay all stress on reading and writing," Jane Addams said, for "they fail to give the child any clew to the life about him."

For the first time, education became a field of university study. European theorists such as Johann Friedrich Herbart, a German educator, argued that learning occurred best in an atmosphere of freedom and confidence between teachers and pupils. Teacher training became increasingly professional. Only ten normal schools, or teacher training institutions, existed in the United States before the Civil War. By 1900, there were 345, and one in every five elementary teachers had graduated from a professional school.

Higher Education

Nearly one hundred fifty new colleges and universities opened in the twenty years between 1880 and 1900. The Morrill Land Grant Act of 1862 gave large grants of land to the states for the establishment of colleges to teach "agriculture and the mechanic arts." The act fostered sixty-nine "land-grant" institutions, including the great state universities of Wisconsin, California, Minnesota, and Illinois.

Private philanthropy, born of the large fortunes of the industrial age, also spurred growth in higher education. Leland Stanford gave $24 million to endow Stanford University on his California ranch, and John D. Rockefeller, founder of the Standard Oil Company, gave $34 million to found the University of Chicago. Other industrialists established Cornell (1865), Vanderbilt (1873), and Tulane (1884).

As colleges expanded, their function changed and their curriculum broadened. No longer did they exist primarily to train young men for the ministry. They moved away from the classical curriculum of rhetoric, mathematics, Latin, and Greek toward "reality and practicality," as President David Starr Jordan of Stanford University said. The Massachusetts Institute of Technology (MIT), founded in 1861, focused on science and engineering.

📖● Read the Document   The Morrill Act (1862)

Eng⁴ by G.E. Perine N.York.

HON. JUSTIN S. MORRILL.

The Morrill Land Grant Act of 1862 gave large grants of land to the states for the establishment of colleges to teach "agriculture and the mechanic arts." The act, sponsored by U.S. Representative Justin Smith Morrill of Vermont, facilitated the creation of sixty-nine "land-grant" institutions, including the state universities of Wisconsin, California, Minnesota, Massachusetts, and Illinois.

Influenced by the new German universities, which emphasized specialized research, Johns Hopkins University in Baltimore opened the nation's first separate graduate school in 1876. Under President Daniel Coit Gilman, Johns Hopkins stressed the seminar and laboratory as teaching tools, bringing together student and teacher in close association.

Charles W. Eliot, who became president of Harvard in 1869 at the age of thirty-five, moved to end, as an admirer said, the "old fogyism" that marked the institution. Revising the curriculum, Eliot set up the elective system, in which students chose their own courses rather than following a rigidly prescribed curriculum. Lectures and discussions replaced rote recitation, and courses in the natural and social sciences, fine arts, and modern languages multiplied. In the 1890s, Eliot's Harvard moved to the forefront of educational innovation.

Women still had to fight for educational opportunities. Some formed study clubs, an important movement that spread rapidly between 1870 and 1900. Groups such as the Decatur (Illinois) Art Class, the Boston History Class, and the Barnesville (Georgia) Shakespeare Club aimed "to enlarge the mental horizon as well as the knowledge of our members." Club members read Virgil and Chaucer, studied history and architecture, and discussed women's rights.

Clubs sprang up almost everywhere there were women: in Caribou, Maine; Tyler, Texas; and Leadville, Colorado—as well as San Francisco, New York, and Boston. Although they were usually small, study clubs sparked a greater interest in education among women and their daughters and contributed to a rapid rise in the number of women entering college in the early 1900s.

Before the Civil War, only three private colleges admitted women to study with men. After the war, educational opportunities increased for women. A number of women's colleges opened, including Vassar (1865), Wellesley (1875), Smith (1875), Bryn Mawr (1885), Barnard (1889), and Radcliffe (1893). The land-grant colleges of the Midwest, open to women from the outset, spurred a nationwide trend toward coeducation, although some physicians, such as Harvard Medical School's Dr. Edward H. Clarke in his popular *Sex in Education* (1873), continued to argue that the strain of learning made women sterile. By 1900, women made up about 40 percent of college students, and four out of five colleges admitted them.

Fewer opportunities existed for African Americans and other minorities. Jane Stanford encouraged the Chinese who had worked on her husband's Central Pacific Railroad to apply to Stanford University, but her policy was unusual. Most colleges did not accept minority students, and only a few applied. W. E. B. Du Bois, the brilliant African American sociologist and civil rights leader, attended Harvard in the late 1880s but found the society of Harvard Yard closed against him. Disdained and disdainful, he "asked no fellowship of my fellow students." Chosen as one of the commencement speakers, Du Bois picked as his topic "Jefferson Davis," treating it, said an onlooker, with "an almost contemptuous fairness."

Black students turned to black colleges such as the Hampton Normal and Industrial Institute in Virginia and the Tuskegee Institute in Alabama. These colleges were often supported by whites who favored manual training for blacks. Booker T. Washington, an ex-slave, put into practice his educational ideas at Tuskegee, which opened in 1881. Washington began Tuskegee with limited funds, four run-down buildings, and only thirty students; by 1900, it was a model industrial and agricultural school. Spread over forty-six buildings, it offered instruction in thirty trades to fourteen hundred students.

Washington emphasized patience, manual training, and hard work. "The wisest among my race understand," he said in a widely acclaimed speech at the Atlanta Exposition in 1895, "that the agitation of questions of social equality is the extremest folly." Blacks should focus on economic gains; they should go to school, learn skills, and work their way up the ladder. "No race," he said at Atlanta, "can prosper till it learns that there is as much dignity in tilling a field as in writing a poem. It is at the bottom of life we must begin, and not at the top." Southern whites should help out because they would then have "the most patient, faithful, law-abiding, and unresentful people that the world has seen."

Outlined most forcefully in Washington's speech in Atlanta, the philosophy became known as the Atlanta Compromise, and many whites and some blacks welcomed it. Acknowledging white domination, it called for slow progress through self-improvement, not through lawsuits or agitation. Rather than fighting for equal rights, blacks should acquire property and show they were worthy of their rights. But Washington did believe in black equality. Often secretive in his methods, he worked behind the scenes to organize black voters and lobby against harmful laws. In his own way, he bespoke a racial pride that contributed to the rise of black nationalism in the twentieth century.

Du Bois wanted a more aggressive strategy. Born in Massachusetts in 1868, the son of poor parents, he studied at Fisk University in Tennessee and the University of Berlin before he went to Harvard. Unable to find a teaching job in a white college, he took a low-paying research position at the University of Pennsylvania. He had no office but did not need one. Du Bois used the new discipline of sociology, which emphasized factual observation in the field, to study the condition of blacks.

Notebook in hand, he set out to examine crime in Philadelphia's black seventh ward. He interviewed five thousand people, mapped and classified neighborhoods, and produced *The Philadelphia Negro* (1898). The first study of the effect of urban life on blacks, it cited a wealth of statistics, all suggesting that crime in the ward stemmed not from inborn degeneracy but from the environment in which blacks lived. Change the environment, and people would change, too; education was a good way to go about it.

In *The Souls of Black Folk* (1903), Du Bois openly attacked Booker T. Washington and the philosophy of the Atlanta Compromise. He urged African Americans to aspire to professional careers, to fight for the restoration of their civil rights, and, wherever possible, to get a college education. Calling for integrated schools with equal opportunity for all, Du Bois urged blacks to educate their "talented tenth," a highly trained intellectual elite, to lead them.

Du Bois was not alone in promoting careers in the professions. Throughout higher education there was increased emphasis on professional training, particularly in medicine, dentistry, and law. Enrollments swelled, even as standards of admission tightened. The number of medical schools in the country rose from 75 in 1870 to 160 in 1900, and the number of medical students—including more and more women—almost tripled. Schools of nursing grew from

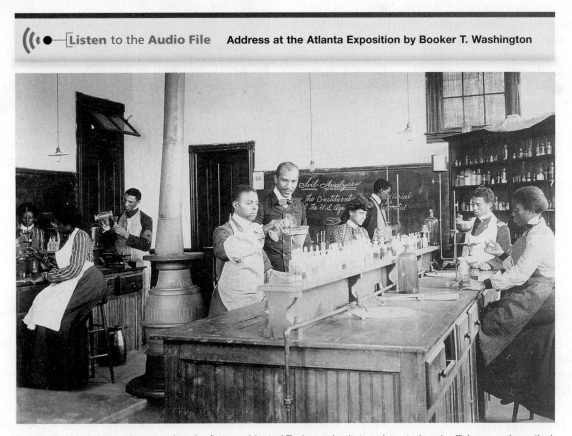

((•●— Listen to the **Audio File**   **Address at the Atlanta Exposition by Booker T. Washington**

Booker T. Washington, who served as the first president of Tuskegee Institute, advocated work efficiency and practical skills as keys to advancement for African Americans. Students like these at Tuskegee studied academic subjects and received training in trades and professions.

only 15 in 1880 to 432 in 1900. Doctors, lawyers, and others became part of a growing middle class that shaped the concerns of the Progressive Era of the early twentieth century.

Although less than 5 percent of the college-age population attended college during the 1877–1890 period, the new trends had great impact. A generation of men and women encountered new ideas that changed their views of themselves and society. Courses never before offered, such as Philosophy II at Harvard, "The Ethics of Social Reform," which students called "drainage, drunkenness, and divorce," heightened interest in social problems and the need for reform. Some graduating students burned with a desire to cure society's ills. "My life began . . . at Johns Hopkins University," Frederic C. Howe, an influential reformer, recalled. "I came alive, I felt a sense of responsibility to the world, I wanted to change things."

The Spread of Jim Crow

Why did Jim Crow laws spread across the South after the end of Reconstruction?

Though Washington and Du Bois differed widely in their views, both of them fought the growing restrictions on black civil rights known as Jim Crow laws (see Chapter 16). While segregation and disfranchisement began as informal arrangements in the immediate aftermath of the Civil War, they soon culminated in a legal regime of separation and exclusion that took firm hold in the 1890s.

Throughout the South, the new measures lent the sanction of law to a racial ostracism that included voting booths, churches, schools, housing, and jobs. Touching virtually all parts of life, they affected public transportation, hospitals, prisons, and asylums— even funeral homes and cemeteries.

A number of influences lay behind their rapid growth. By the 1870s, many northerners had lost interest in guarding the rights of blacks. Weariness with Civil War issues played a role in this trend, as did beliefs in Anglo-Saxon superiority and, after the Spanish-American War of 1898, the acquisition of colonial subjects—called, revealingly, "the white man's burden"—in Hawaii, Guam, Puerto Rico, and the Philippines.

As a result, the North and the federal government did little to stem the tide. Supreme Court decisions between 1878 and 1898 gutted the Reconstruction amendments and the legislation passed to enforce them, leaving blacks virtually defenseless against political and social discrimination. (See Table 19.1.)

Most visible in areas like voting, Jim Crow laws soon penetrated nearly every aspect of Southern life. In 1915, a South Carolina code banned textile factories from allowing laborers of different races to work together in the same room or to use the same entrances, exits, toilets, and drinking water. That year, Oklahoma required telephone companies to maintain separate phone booths for whites and blacks. North Carolina and Florida ordered separate textbooks for black and white children. Florida even required that the books be segregated while they were in storage. A New Orleans ordinance placed black and white prostitutes in separate districts of the city. There were Jim Crow Bibles for African American witnesses in Atlanta courts and Jim Crow elevators in Atlanta buildings.

Perhaps no event better expresses the cruel and barbaric nature of the racism and white supremacy that swept the South after Reconstruction than lynching. Although lynchings were not confined to the South, most occurred there, and African American men were the most frequent victims. Here, two men lean out of a barn window above a black man who is about to be hanged. Others below prepare to set on fire the pile of hay at the victim's feet. Lynchings were often public events, drawing huge crowds to watch the victim's agonizing death.

Jim Crow laws expanded during the 1920s and 1930s. Mississippi segregated white and black patients in hospitals and mandated that nurses could tend only the sick of their own race. City ordinances required Jim Crow taxis in Jacksonville, Florida, in 1929; Birmingham, Alabama, in 1930; and Atlanta, Georgia, in 1940. In 1930, a Birmingham ordinance forbade blacks and whites from playing each other at dominoes or checkers.

Lynchings also spread. Between 1889 and 1899, an average of 187 blacks were lynched every year for alleged offenses against white supremacy. Many blacks (and whites) convicted of petty crimes were leased out to private contractors whose brutality rivaled that of the most sadistic slaveholders. The convict-lease system enabled entrepreneurs, such as mine owners and lumber companies, to rent prisoners

SUPREME COURT DECISIONS AFFECTING BLACK CIVIL RIGHTS, 1875–1900

Case	Effects of Court's Decisions
Hall v. *DeCuir* (1878)	Struck down Louisiana law prohibiting racial discrimination by "common carriers" (railroads, steamboats, buses). Declared the law a "burden" on interstate commerce, over which states had no authority.
United States v. *Harris* (1882)	Declared federal laws to punish crimes such as murder and assault unconstitutional. Declared such crimes to be the sole concern of local government. Ignored the frequent racial motivation behind such crimes in the South.
Civil Rights Cases (1883)	Struck down Civil Rights Act of 1875. Declared that Congress may not legislate on civil rights unless a state passes a discriminatory law. Declared the Fourteenth Amendment silent on racial discrimination by private citizens.
Plessy v. *Ferguson* (1896)	Upheld Louisiana statute requiring "separate but equal" accommodations on railroads. Declared that segregation is *not* necessarily discrimination.
Williams v. *Mississippi* (1898)	Upheld state law requiring a literacy test to qualify for voting. Refused to find any implication of racial discrimination in the law, although it permitted illiterate whites to vote if they "understood" the Constitution. Using such laws, southern states rapidly disfranchised blacks.

from the state and treat them as they saw fit. Unlike slaveowners, they suffered no loss when a forced laborer died from overwork.

Racism, of course, was not limited to the South, as race riots in East St. Louis, Illinois, (1917) and Chicago (1919), among other events, attested. In 1903, the New York public school system banned *Uncle Tom's Cabin* from its reading lists, saying that Harriet Beecher Stowe's depiction of antebellum slavery "does not belong to today but to an unhappy period of our country's history, the memory of which it is not well to revive in our children." Encountering the racism of the North—far less brutal but racism nonetheless—blacks who had migrated there called it James Crow.

The Stirrings of Reform

How did life in the growing cities lead to ideas of reform?

When Henry George, one of the era's leading reformers, asked a friend what could be done about the problem of political corruption in American cities, his friend replied, "Nothing! You and I can do nothing at all. . . . We can only wait for evolution. Perhaps in four or five thousand years evolution may have carried men beyond this state of things."

This emphasis on the slow pace of change reflected the doctrine of **Social Darwinism**, based on the writings of English social philosopher Herbert Spencer. In several influential books, Spencer took the evolutionary theories of Charles Darwin and applied Darwinian principles of natural selection to society, combining biology and sociology in a theory of "social selection" that tried to explain human progress. Like animals, society evolved, slowly, by adapting to the environment. The "survival of the fittest"—a term that Spencer, not Darwin, invented—preserved the strong and weeded out the weak. "If they are sufficiently complete to live, they do live, and it is well they should live. If they are not sufficiently complete to live, they die, and it is best they should die."

Social Darwinism had a number of influential followers in the United States, including William Graham Sumner, a professor of political and social science at Yale University. One of the country's best known academic figures, Sumner was forceful and eloquent. In writings such as *What Social Classes Owe to Each Other* (1883) and "The Absurd Effort to Make the World Over" (1894), he argued that government action on behalf of the poor or weak interfered with evolution and sapped the species. Reform tampered with the laws of nature. "It is the greatest folly of which a man can be capable to sit down with a slate and pencil to plan out a new social world," Sumner said.

The influence of Social Darwinism on American thinking has been exaggerated, but in the powerful hands of Sumner and others it did influence some journalists, ministers, and policy makers. Between 1877 and the 1890s, however, it came under increasing attack. In fields such as religion, economics, politics, literature, and law, thoughtful people raised questions about established conditions and suggested the need for reform.

Progress and Poverty

Read and reread, passed from hand to hand, Henry George's nationwide best-seller *Progress and Poverty* (1879) led the way to a more critical appraisal of American society in the 1880s and beyond. The book jolted traditional thought. "It was responsible," one historian has said, "for starting along new lines of thinking an amazing number of the men and women" who became leaders of reform.

Born in 1839, the child of a poor Philadelphia family, George had little formal schooling. As a boy he went to sea; he also worked as a prospector, printer, and journalist. Self-educated as an economist, he moved to San Francisco in the late 1850s and began to study "the fierce struggle of our civilized life." Disturbed by the depression of the 1870s and labor upheavals such as the great railroad strikes of 1877, George saw modern society—rich, complex, with material goods hitherto unknown—as sadly flawed.

"The present century," he wrote, "has been marked by a prodigious increase in wealth-producing power. . . . It was natural to expect, and it was expected, that . . . real poverty [would become] a thing of the past." Instead, he argued,

> it becomes no easier for the masses of our people to make a living. On the contrary, it is becoming harder. The wealthy class is becoming more wealthy; but the poorer class is becoming more dependent. The gulf between the employed and the employer is growing wider; social contrasts are becoming sharper; as liveried carriages appear, so do barefooted children.

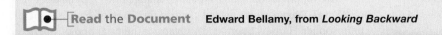

Read the **Document**   Edward Bellamy, from *Looking Backward*

Edward Bellamy was the author in 1887 of *Looking Backward, 2000–1887*. The book envisioned a nation cured of its social problems through the creation of a socialist utopia including the elimination of private competition and government ownership of industry.

solution, simplistic and unappealing, had much less impact than his analysis of the problem itself. He raised questions a generation of readers set out to answer.

New Currents in Social Thought

George's emphasis on deprivation in the environment excited a young country lawyer in Ashtabula, Ohio—Clarence Darrow. Unlike the Social Darwinists, Darrow was sure that criminals were made and not born. They grew out of "the unjust condition of human life." In the mid-1880s, he left for Chicago and a forty-year career working to convince people that poverty lay at the root of crime. "There is no such thing as crime as the word is generally understood," he told a group of startled prisoners in the Cook County jail. "If every man, woman and child in the world had a chance to make a decent, fair, honest living there would be no jails and no lawyers and no courts."

As Darrow rejected the implications of social Darwinism, in similar fashion Richard T. Ely and a group of young economists poked holes in traditional economic thought. Fresh from graduate study in Germany, Ely in 1884 attacked classical economics for its dogmatism, simple faith in laissez-faire, and reliance on self-interest as a guide for human conduct. The "younger" economics, he said, must no longer be "a tool in the hands of the greedy and the avaricious for keeping down and oppressing the laboring classes. It does not acknowledge laissez-faire as an excuse for doing nothing while people starve."

Accepting a post at Johns Hopkins University, Ely assigned graduate students to study labor conditions in Baltimore and other cities; one of them, John R. Commons, went on to publish a massive four-volume study, *History of Labour in the United States*. In 1885, Ely led a small band of rebels in founding the American Economic Association, which linked economics to social problems and urged government intervention in economic affairs. Social critic Thorstein Veblen saw economic laws as a mask for human greed. In *The Theory of the Leisure Class* (1899), Veblen analyzed the "predatory wealth" and "conspicuous consumption" of the business class.

George proposed a simple solution. Land, he thought, formed the basis of wealth, and a few people could grow wealthy just because the price of their land rose. Since the rise in price did not result from any effort on their part, it represented an "unearned increment," which, George argued, should be taxed for the good of society. A "single tax" on the increment, replacing all other taxes, would help equalize wealth and raise revenue to aid the poor. "Single-tax" clubs sprang up around the country, but George's

Edward Bellamy dreamed of a cooperative society in which poverty, greed, and crime no longer existed. A lawyer from western Massachusetts, Bellamy published *Looking Backward, 2000–1887*, in 1887 and became a national reform figure virtually overnight. The novel's protagonist, Julian West, falls asleep in 1887 and awakes in the year 2000. Wide-eyed, he finds himself in a socialist utopia: The government owns the means of production, and citizens share the material rewards. Cooperation, rather than competition, is the watchword.

The world of *Looking Backward* had limits; it was regimented, paternalistic, and filled with the gadgets and material concerns of Bellamy's own day. But it had a dramatic effect on many readers. The book sold at the rate of ten thousand copies a week, and its followers formed Nationalist Clubs to work for its objectives. By 1890, there were such clubs in twenty-seven states, all calling for the nationalization of public utilities and a wider distribution of wealth.

Walter Rauschenbusch, a young Baptist minister, read widely from the writings of Bellamy and George, along with the works of other social reformers. When he took his first church post in Hell's Kitchen, a blighted area of New York City, he soon discovered the weight of the slum environment. "One could hear," he said, "human virtue cracking and crushing all around." In the 1890s, Rauschenbusch became a professor at the Rochester Theological Seminary, and he began to expound on the responsibility of organized religion to advance social justice.

Some Protestant sects emphasized individual salvation and a better life in the next world, not in this one. Poverty was evidence of sinfulness; the poor had only themselves to blame. "God has intended the great to be great and the little to be little," said Henry Ward Beecher, the country's best known pastor. Wealth and destitution, suburbs and slums—all formed part of God's plan.

Challenging those traditional doctrines, a number of churches in the 1880s began establishing missions in the city slums. William Dwight Porter Bliss, an Episcopal clergyman, founded the Church of the Carpenter in a working-class district of Boston. Lewis M. Pease worked in the grim Five Points area of New York; Alexander Irvine, a Jewish missionary, lived in a flophouse in the Bowery. Irvine walked his skid row neighborhood every afternoon to lend a hand to those in need. Living among the poor and homeless, the urban missionaries grew impatient with religious doctrines that endorsed the status quo.

Many of the new trends were reflected in an emerging religious philosophy known as the **Social Gospel**. As the name suggests, the Social Gospel focused on society as well as individuals, on improving living conditions as well as saving souls. Sermons in Social Gospel churches called on church members to fulfill their social obligations, and adults met before and after the regular service to discuss social and economic problems. Children were excused from sermons, organized into age groups, and encouraged to make the church a center for social as well as religious activity. Soon churches included dining halls, gymnasiums, and even theaters.

The most active Social Gospel leader was Washington Gladden, a Congregational minister and prolific writer. Linking Christianity to the social and economic environment, Gladden spent a lifetime working for "social salvation." He saw Christianity as a fellowship of love and the church as a social agency. In *Applied Christianity* (1886) and other writings, he denounced competition, urged an "industrial partnership" between employers and employees, and called for efforts to help the poor.

The Settlement Houses

A growing number of social reformers living in the urban slums shared Gladden's concern. Like Tweed and Plunkitt, they appreciated the dependency of the poor; unlike them, they wanted to eradicate the conditions that underlay it. To do so, they formed **settlement houses** in the slums and went to live in them to experience the problems they were trying to solve.

Youthful, idealistic, and mostly middle class, these social workers took as their model Toynbee Hall, founded in 1884 in the slums of East London to provide community services. Stanton Coit, a moody and poetic graduate of Amherst College, was the first American to borrow the settlement house idea; in 1886, he opened the Neighborhood Guild on the Lower East Side of New York. The idea spread swiftly. By 1900, there were more than a hundred settlements in the country; five years later, there were more than two hundred, and by 1910, more than four hundred.

The settlements included Jane Addams's famous Hull House in Chicago (1889), Robert A. Woods's South End House in Boston (1892), and Lillian Wald's Henry Street Settlement in New York (1893). The reformers wanted to bridge the socioeconomic gap between rich and poor and to bring education, culture, and hope to the slums. They sought to create in the heart of the city the values and sense of community of small-town America. Of settlement workers, Wald said in *The House on Henry Street* (1915), "We were to live in a neighborhood . . . identify ourselves with it socially, and, in brief, contribute to it our citizenship."

Many of the settlement workers were women, some of them college graduates, who found that society had little use for their talents and energy. Jane Addams, a graduate of Rockford College in Illinois, opened Hull House on South Halsted Street in the heart of the Chicago slums. Twenty-nine years old, endowed with a forceful and winning personality, she intended "to share the lives of the poor" and humanize the industrial city. "American ideals," she said, "crumbled under the overpowering poverty of the overcrowded city."

Occupying an old, rundown house, Hull House focused on education, offering classes in elementary English and Shakespeare, lectures on ethics and the history of art, and courses in cooking, sewing, and manual skills. A pragmatist, Addams believed in investigating a problem and then doing something to solve it. Noting the lack of medical care in the area, she established an infant welfare clinic and free medical dispensary. Because the tenements lacked bathtubs, she installed showers in the basement of the house and built a bathhouse for the neighbors. Because there was no local library, she opened a reading room. Gradually, Hull House expanded to occupy a dozen buildings sprawling over more than a city block.

Like settlement workers in other cities, Addams and her colleagues studied the immigrants in nearby tenements. Laboriously, they identified the background of every family in a one-third-square-mile area around Hull House. Finding people of eighteen different nationalities, they taught them American history and the English language, yet Addams also encouraged them—through folk festivals and art—to preserve their own heritage.

In Boston, Robert Woods of South End House focused on the problem of school dropouts. He offered manual training, formed clubs to get young people off the streets, and established a cheap restaurant where the hungry could eat. Lillian Wald, the daughter of a middle-class family and herself a graduate nurse, concentrated on providing health care for the poor. In 1898, the first Catholic-run settlement house opened in New York, and in 1900, Bronson House opened in Los Angeles to work in the Mexican American community.

Florence Kelley, an energetic graduate of Cornell University, taught night school one winter in Chicago. Watching children

📖 **Read the Document**   **Jane Addams, from** *Twenty Years at Hull House (1910)*

OPENING OF

HULL=HOUSE
PLAY GROUND

Polk Street, Near Halsted

Saturday, May 1st, 1897,
AT 3 O'CLOCK, P. M.

"The air is warm, the skies are clear,
Birds and blossoms all are here,
Come old and young with spirits gay,
To welcome back the charming May."

MUSIC BY THE BRASS BAND

...Kindergarten Games---May Pole Dance...

ALL KINDS OF RACES

Jane Addams founded Chicago's Hull House in 1889. The settlement house provided recreational and day-care facilities; offered extension classes in academic, vocational, and artistic subjects; and, above all, sought to bring hope to poverty-stricken slum dwellers.

break under the burden of poverty, she devoted her life to the problem of child labor. Convinced of the need for political activism, she worked with Addams and others to push through the Illinois Factory Act of 1893, which mandated an eight-hour day for women in factories and for children under the age of fourteen.

The settlement house movement had its limits. Hull House, one of the best, attracted two thousand visitors a week, still just a fraction of the seventy thousand people who lived within six blocks. Immigrants sometimes resented the middle-class "strangers" who told them how to live. Dressed always in a brown suit and dark stockings, Harriet Vittum, the head resident of Chicago's Northwestern University Settlement (who told the story of the suicide victim at the beginning of this chapter), was known in the neighborhood as "the police lady in brown." She once stopped a dance because it was too wild, and then watched in disgust as the boys responded by "making vulgar sounds with their lips." Though her attempts to help were sincere, in private Vittum called the people she was

trying to help "ignorant foreigners, who live in an atmosphere of low morals ... surrounded by anarchy and crime."

Although Addams tried to offer a few programs for blacks, most white reformers did not, and after 1900, a number of black reformers opened their own settlements. Like the whites, they offered employment information, medical care, and recreational facilities, along with concerts, lectures, and other educational events. White and black, the settlement workers made important contributions to urban life.

Crisis in Social Welfare

The depression of 1893 jarred the young settlement workers, many of whom had just begun their work. Addams and the Hull House workers helped form the Chicago Bureau of Charities to coordinate emergency relief. Kelley, recently appointed the chief factory inspector of Illinois, worked even harder to end child labor, and in

1899, she moved to New York City to head the National Consumers League, which marshaled the buying power of women to encourage employers to provide better working conditions.

In cities and towns across the country, traditional methods of helping the needy foundered in the crisis. Churches, charity organization societies, and community chests did what they could, but their resources were limited, and they functioned on traditional lines. Many of them still tried to change rather than aid individual families, and people were often reluctant to call on them for help.

Gradually, a new class of professional social workers arose to fill the need. Unlike the church and charity volunteers, these social workers wanted not only to feed the poor but to study their condition and alleviate it. Revealingly, they called themselves "case workers" and daily collected data on the income, housing, jobs, health, and habits of the poor. Prowling tenement districts, they gathered information about the number of rooms, number of occupants, ventilation, and sanitation of the buildings, putting together a fund of useful data.

Studies of the poor popped up everywhere. Walter Wyckoff, a graduate of Princeton University, embarked in 1891 on what he called "an experiment in reality." For eighteen months, he worked as an unskilled laborer in jobs from Connecticut to California. "I am vastly ignorant of the labor problems and am trying to learn by experience," he said as he set out. After working as a ditchdigger, farmhand, and logger, Wyckoff summarized his findings in *The Workers* (1897), a book immediately hailed as a major contribution to sociology.

So many others followed Wyckoff's example that sometimes it seemed the observers outnumbered those being observed. W. E. B. Du Bois did his pioneering study of urban blacks; Lillian Pettengill took a job as a domestic servant to see "the ups and downs of this particular dog-life from the dog's end of the chain." Others became street beggars, miners, lumberjacks, and factory laborers. Bessie and Marie Van Vorst's *The Woman Who Toils: Being the Experiences of Two Gentlewomen as Factory Girls* (1903) studied female workers, as did Helen Campbell's *Women Wage-Earners: Their Past, Their Present and Their Future* (1893), which suggested that the conditions of factory employment prepared women mainly "for the hospital, the workhouse, and the prison."

William T. Stead, a prominent British editor, visited the Chicago World's Fair in 1893 and stayed to examine the city. He roamed the flophouses and tenements and dropped in at Hull House to drink hot chocolate and talk over conditions with Jane Addams. Later he wrote an influential book, *If Christ Came to Chicago* (1894), and in a series of mass meetings during 1893, he called for a civic revival. In response, Chicagoans formed the Civic Federation, a group of forty leaders who aimed to make Chicago "the best governed, the healthiest city in this country." Setting up task forces for philanthropy, moral improvement,

and legislation, the new group helped spawn the National Civic Federation (1900), a nationwide organization devoted to the reform of urban life.

Conclusion: The Pluralistic Society

"The United States was born in the country and moved to the city," historian Richard Hofstadter said. Much of that movement occurred during the nineteenth century when the United States was the most rapidly urbanizing nation in the Western world. American cities bustled with energy; they absorbed millions of migrants who came from Europe and other distant and not-so-distant parts of the world. That migration, and the urban growth that accompanied it, reshaped American politics and culture.

By 1920, the census showed that, for the first time, most Americans lived in cities. By then, too, almost half the population was descended from people who had arrived after the American Revolution. As European, African, and Asian cultures met in the American city, a culturally pluralistic society emerged. Dozens of nationalities produced a culture whose members considered themselves Polish Americans, African Americans, and Irish Americans. The melting pot sometimes softened distinctions between the various groups, but it only partially blended them into a unified society.

"Ah, Vera," said a character in Israel Zangwill's popular play *The Melting Pot* (1908), "what is the glory of Rome and Jerusalem where all nations and races come to worship and look back, compared with the glory of America, where all races and nations come to labour and look forward!" Critics scorned the play as "romantic claptrap," and indeed it was. But the metaphor of the melting pot clearly depicted a new national image. In the decades after the 1870s a jumble of ethnic and racial groups struggled for a place in society.

That society, it is clear, experienced a crisis between 1870 and 1900. Together, the growth of cities and the rise of industrial capitalism brought jarring change: the exploitation of labor, ethnic and racial tensions, poverty—and, for a few, wealth beyond the imagination. At Homestead, Pullman, and a host of other places, there was open warfare between capital and labor. As reformers struggled to mediate the situation, they turned more and more to state and federal government to look after human welfare, a tendency the Supreme Court stoutly resisted. In the midst of the crisis, the depression of the 1890s struck, adding to the turmoil and straining American institutions. Tracing the changes wrought by waves of urbanization and industrialization, Henry George described the country as "the House of Have and the House of Want," almost in paraphrase of Lincoln's earlier metaphor of the "house divided." The question was, could this house, unlike that one, stand?

Law and Society

Plessy v. Ferguson

The Shaping of Jim Crow

In a nation of laws, the interpretation of law can profoundly change people's lives. *Plessy* v. *Ferguson* (1896), one of the most important cases ever to reach the Supreme Court, changed the lives of millions of black and white Americans. Interpreting law in a way that lasted for more than a half century, it permitted the segregation of blacks in public facilities throughout the land.

Given the significance of the case, we know surprisingly little about Homer A. Plessy, the man who figured in it. He was young—we know that—and apparently worked as a carpenter in Louisiana. According to the court records, he was "seven-eighths Caucasian," which perhaps was a reason he was chosen to test the constitutionality of a Louisiana law requiring railroad companies to segregate whites and blacks on trains in the state. It seemed a good law to test. Louisiana's own constitution forbade such discrimination; so did the federal Civil Rights Act of 1875, which guaranteed blacks "full and equal enjoyment" of public conveyances.

Whatever the details of his life, Plessy lived in a post–Reconstruction South in which racism was widespread but segregation was not. Where segregation did exist, it usually was not enacted into law. During the 1870s and 1880s, blacks and whites often ate together, rode together, and worked together. "I can ride in first-class cars on the railroads and in the streets," a delighted black visitor wrote home from South Carolina in 1885. "I can stop in and drink a glass of soda and be more politely waited upon than in some parts of New England."

That situation changed near the end of the century. The courts often reflect trends in the society, and whites in both North and South in the 1890s had little enthusiasm for civil rights or racial equality. In addition, economic depression heightened racial tensions, and the spread of colonial imperialism in Africa and Asia led to talk about "inferior" people, both at home and abroad. Beginning in the 1870s, the Supreme Court handed down a series of decisions that overturned much Reconstruction legislation, limited federal protection for blacks, and encouraged racial segregation.

In the *Slaughterhouse Cases* of 1873, the Supreme Court narrowed the scope of the Fourteenth Amendment protecting blacks; a decade later, in the *Civil Rights Cases* (1883), it said that Congress could not punish private individuals for acts of racial discrimination. Emboldened by such decisions, southern states passed many segregation laws, including laws requiring railroad companies to separate white and black riders. In the summer of 1890, Louisiana passed "An Act to promote the comfort of passengers" that made railroads in the state provide "equal but separate" cars "for the white and colored races."

Segregationists were delighted. "The Southern whites," a New Orleans newspaper said, had passed the law "in no spirit of hostility to the negroes," but to make sure that "the two races shall live separate and distinct from each other in all things, with separate schools, separate hotels, and separate cars."

New Orleans, more than most southern cities, had a group of talented African American leaders, educated, aggressive, and experienced in politics and the judicial system. Outraged by the new law, they thought first of boycotting the railroads that obeyed it but then decided to contest it in the courts. Led by Louis A. Martinet, a well-known lawyer and physician, and Rodolphe L. Desdunes, an important Reconstruction Republican, they formed the Citizens' Committee to Test the Constitutionality of the Separate Car Law, raised money for the cause, and enlisted the aid of Albion W. Tourgée of New York, a prominent white lawyer, novelist, and longtime crusader for African American rights.

Tourgée did not hesitate to join in the fight, for which he charged no fee. "Submission to such outrages," he angrily wrote his New Orleans friends, tends "only to their multiplication and exaggeration. It is by constant resistance to oppression that the race must ultimately win equality of right."

As a first step, Citizens' Committee members went to various railroad officials to ask for aid in establishing a case that could test the law. Disliking the cost of the extra cars the law forced them to buy, the officials were sympathetic but reluctant. One railroad already refused to enforce the law; officials on two other railroads said it was "a bad and mean one; they would like to get rid of it," but were afraid of public opinion. At last, the East Louisiana Railway agreed to help.

And so on June 7, 1892, to test the law, Homer A. Plessy boarded

an East Louisiana Railway train in New Orleans for the 30-mile trip to Covington. He took a seat in the car reserved for whites, refused to move when a conductor asked him to, and was arrested by a detective who was standing by for the occasion. John H. Ferguson, a local judge, ruled against Plessy's argument that the law violated his rights, and Plessy appealed to the State Supreme Court, arguing that the law violated the "equal protection" clause of the Fourteenth Amendment to the Constitution. That Court, too, promptly ruled against him.

Delighted, Louisiana segregationists hoped, as one of their newspapers said, that the two decisions would knock some sense into "the silly negroes who are trying to fight this law. The sooner they drop their so-called 'crusade' against the 'Jim Crow Car,' and stop wasting their money in combating so well-established a

principle—the right to separate the races in cars and elsewhere—the better for them."

It took three more years before the United States Supreme Court heard the case. Tourgée himself was pleased with the delay, hoping that time might improve racial feelings in the country and bring popular support to his cause. Those hopes did not bear out, nor did his arguments before the Court.

In an unusual approach, Tourgée began by arguing that Homer A. Plessy, who was light-skinned in color, had been deprived of property without due process of law, contrary to the Fourteenth Amendment. Able to pass for white, he had been identified by the railroad conductor as black. He had been robbed, therefore, of his "property," Tourgée said, the sense of being white, and thus barred from association with white people, who in the United States controlled the avenues to advancement.

"Probably most white persons if given a choice," Tourgée argued, "would prefer death to life in the United States *as colored persons*. Under these conditions, is it possible to conclude that the *reputation of being white* is not property? Indeed, is it not the most valuable sort of property, being the master-key that unlocks the golden door of opportunity?"

The remainder of Tourgée's brief was straightforward, emphasizing the incompatibility of the separate car law with the intent of the Thirteenth and Fourteenth Amendments, the inequities it fostered, and its basis in claims of white superiority. Unless the Court stopped it now, enforced segregation would soon spread everywhere through life. "Why may [a law] not require all red-headed people to ride in a separate car? Why not require all colored people to walk on one side of the street and the whites on the other?" Why not houses of different color, or clothes, or carriages? Laws might make blacks and whites (or Protestants and Catholics, natives and foreign-born, or anyone else, for that matter) sit on opposite sides of a courtroom or use different playgrounds.

Deciding the case was simple, Tourgée concluded: "Suppose you, the members of the Court, were suddenly ordered into a Jim Crow car of your own. What humiliation, once owned slaves. But accepting what rage would then fill the judicial mind!"

Finally, on May 18, 1896, the Court handed down its decision in *Plessy* v. *Ferguson*. By a vote of 7 to 1, it decided against Plessy. Upholding the doctrine of "separate but equal," it held that the Louisiana law did not violate Plessy's rights. It did not violate them, the Court said, because the law was "reasonable"; it had been passed "with reference to the established usages, customs, and traditions of the people."

It was precisely those usages and customs—race prejudice, in short—that Tourgée had argued against. They were contrary to the Reconstruction amendments to the Constitution, he had argued, but the majority of the Court would have none of it. The authors of those amendments, they said, could not have meant to do away with racial distinctions or institute social equality; that simply could not be done. Laws did not create race prejudice, and they could not change it. Enforced segregation did not label anyone as inferior. "We consider," the Court said, "the underlying fallacy of the plaintiff's argument to consist in the assumption that the enforced separation of the two races stamps the colored race with a badge of inferiority. If this be so, it is not by reason of anything found in the act, but solely because the colored race chooses to put that construction upon it."

There was irony in the Court's vote. Justice Henry Billings Brown, a son of Massachusetts and Michigan, wrote the opinion for the majority, a measure of changing opinion in the North. The single dissenter in the case, Justice John Marshall Harlan of Kentucky, on the other hand, was not only from the South, he had once owned slaves. But accepting the changed requirements of the Reconstruction amendments, he became the "Great Dissenter" in a Court—and a country—fast fleeing its important responsibilities.

Dissenting in *Plessy*, he scoffed at the majority's reasoning. The Louisiana law, he said, was clearly prejudicial, designed to keep blacks from railroad cars occupied by whites, and as such was in clear conflict with both the Thirteenth and Fourteenth Amendments. It was "a badge of servitude," inconsistent with "the equality before the law established by the Constitution. It cannot be justified upon any legal grounds."

"Our Constitution is color-blind, and neither knows nor tolerates classes among citizens. In respect of civil rights, all citizens are equal before the law. The humblest is the peer of the most powerful. The law regards man as man, and takes no account of his surroundings or of his color when his civil rights as guaranteed by the supreme law of the land are involved."

"In my opinion," Harlan concluded, "the judgment this day rendered will, in time, prove to be quite as pernicious as the decision made by this tribunal in the *Dred Scott case*."

It was.

After *Plessy*, Jim Crow laws spread swiftly through the South. More and more public conveyances, schools, and restaurants were segregated. Signs saying "Whites only" or "Colored" appeared on entrances and exits, restrooms and water fountains, waiting rooms, and even elevators. In 1905, Georgia passed the first law requiring separate public parks. In 1909, Mobile, Alabama, enacted a curfew requiring blacks to be off the streets by 10 P.M. In 1915, South Carolina forbade blacks and whites to work in the same rooms in textile factories. The Oklahoma legislature required separate telephone booths; New Orleans segregated white and black prostitutes. Atlanta had separate Bibles for black witnesses in the city courts.

Harlan had, in general terms, predicted it all, in words still worth reading today: "The destinies of the two races, in this country, are indissolubly linked together, and the interests of both require that the common government of all shall not permit the seeds of race hate to be planted under the sanction of law. What can more certainly arouse race hate, what more certainly create and perpetuate a feeling of distrust between these races, than state enactments, which, in fact, proceed on the ground that colored citizens are so inferior and degraded that they cannot be allowed to sit in public coaches occupied by white citizens? That, as all will admit, is the real meaning of such legislation as was enacted in Louisiana."

Plessy v. *Ferguson* set a pattern of court-supported segregation that lasted sixty years. Generations of blacks and whites, children and adults alike, were deeply affected—sometimes traumatized—by it. The practice became a major focus of grievance in the growing movement for civil rights during the 1930s and 1940s.

"Justice," Tourgée had written in his original brief, "is pictured blind and her daughter, the Law, ought at least to be color-blind." Harlan had used the same word, "color-blind," a welcome concept to those fighting for civil rights in the 1890s. But history takes interesting and different turns, as does the law, and the word would come up again decades later, in arguments against affirmative action programs that helped African Americans get into colleges and professional schools. (See discussion of *Bakke* v. *Regents of the University of California*, p. 792.)

Plessy, by then, was no more. At last, exactly fifty-eight years after the decision had been announced, on May 17, 1954, in the case of *Brown* v. *Board of Education of Topeka* (see Chapter 29), the Supreme Court reversed itself and overturned *Plessy*. Ruling that segregated schools are inherently unequal, the Court's stand toppled segregation of many kinds and changed lives once again.

QUESTIONS FOR DISCUSSION

1. What did the majority of the Supreme Court give as its reasons in deciding *Plessy* v. *Ferguson*? What do you think of these reasons? How do you think the majority reflected the climate of their times? What changes in public opinion have occurred since?

2. Do you think Tourgée established an effective defense in arguing that the light-skinned Plessy had been deprived of his valuable property, "*the reputation of being white*"? Why or why not?

3. What are some of the factors that contributed to increased segregation in the South and North, after 1890?

Study Resources

 Take the **Study Plan** for **Chapter 19** *Toward an Urban Society, 1877–1900* on **MyHistoryLab**

TIME LINE

1862 Morrill Land Grant gives land to states for establishment of colleges

1869 Rutgers and Princeton play in nation's first intercollegiate football game; Cincinnati Red Stockings, baseball's first professional team, organized

1873 Comstock Law bans obscene articles from U.S. mail; Nation's first kindergarten opens in St. Louis, Missouri

1874 Women's Christian Temperance Union formed to crusade against evils of liquor

1876 Johns Hopkins University opens first separate graduate school

1879 Henry George analyzes problems of urbanizing America in *Progress and Poverty*; Salvation Army arrives in United States

1880 Polish National Alliance formed to help Polish immigrants adjust to life in America

1881 Booker T. Washington opens Tuskegee Institute in Alabama; Dr. John H. Kellogg advises parents to teach their children about sex in *Plain Facts for Old and Young*

1883 Metropolitan Opera opens in New York

1885 Home Insurance Building, country's first metal-frame structure, erected in Chicago; American Economic Association formed to advocate government intervention in economic affairs

1887 Edward Bellamy promotes idea of socialist utopia in *Looking Backward, 2000–1887*

1889 Jane Addams opens Hull House in Chicago

1890 National Woman Suffrage Association and the American Woman Suffrage Association, both formed in 1869, merge to consolidate the woman suffrage movement

1894 Immigration Restriction League formed to limit immigration from southern and eastern Europe

1896 Supreme Court decision in *Plessy* v. *Ferguson* establishes constitutionality of "separate but equal" facilities; John Dewey's Laboratory School for testing and practice of new educational theory opens at University of Chicago

CHAPTER REVIEW

The Lure of the City

 Why did cities expand in the United States between 1880 and 1900?

American cities grew by leaps and bounds between 1880 and 1900. Among the reasons for the growth were the needs of an industrializing society; technological change in the form of electricity, elevators, steel beams, and other advances; and the arrival of millions of immigrants. Politically, city bosses retained power by responding to the needs of immigrants and other urban voters. (p. 439)

Social and Cultural Change, 1877–1900

 How did the growth of American cities affect social, cultural, and political life?

The rapid growth of cities changed how Americans thought and acted. Cities opened up new areas of entertainment, employment, and behavior. They reshaped the family, brought more women into the workforce, and emphasized education. (p. 447)

The Spread of Jim Crow

 Why did Jim Crow laws spread across the South after end of the Reconstruction?

After Reconstruction ended in 1877, northern weariness with Civil War issues, a series of Supreme Court decisions, and growing racism led the federal government to stop trying to uphold civil rights legislation in the South. This enabled Southern states and cities to pass and enforce Jim Crow laws that mandated rigid separation between blacks and whites. (p. 454)

The Stirrings of Reform

 How did life in the growing cities lead to ideas of reform?

Urban life, which forced many people close together, made social problems unprecedentedly visible. The city could not hide the contrasts between rich and poor, the dirtiness and dangers of factory life, and the woeful lot of millions of immigrants. Reformers argued for change. Some of them, like Jane Addams, opened urban settlement houses where they lived among the poor. (p. 455)

KEY TERMS AND DEFINITIONS

New immigrants Starting in the 1880s, immigration into the United States began to shift from northern and western Europe to southern and eastern Europe. These new immigrants were mostly poor, non-Protestant, and unskilled; they tended to stay in close-knit communities and retain their language, customs, and religions. Between 1880 and 1910, approximately 8.4 million of these so-called new immigrants came to the United States. p. 444

Mugwumps Educated and upper-class reformers who crusaded for lower tariffs, limited federal government, and civil service reform. They were best known for helping elect Grover Cleveland president in 1884. p. 448

Women's Christian Temperance Union (WCTU) This organization campaigned to end drunkenness and the social ills that accompanied it. By 1898, it had 10,000 branches and 500,000 members. The WCTU illustrated the role women played in politics and reform long before they won the right to vote. p. 448

National American Woman Suffrage Association Founded by Susan B. Anthony in 1890, this organization worked to secure women the right to vote. It stressed careful organization and peaceful lobbying. p. 450

Plessy v. Ferguson A Supreme Court case in 1896 that established the doctrine of "separate but equal." The Court applied it to schools in *Cumming* v. *County Board of Education* (1899). The doctrine was finally overturned in 1954, in *Brown* v. *Board of Education of Topeka*. p. 451

Civil Rights Cases A group of cases in 1883 in which the Supreme Court ruled that the Fourteenth Amendment barred state governments from discriminating on the basis of race but did not prevent private individuals or organizations from doing so. The ruling dealt a major blow to efforts to protect African Americans. p. 451

Social Darwinism Adapted by English social philosopher Herbert Spencer from Charles Darwin's theory of evolution, this theory held that the "laws" of evolution applied to human life, that change or reform therefore took centuries, and that the "fittest" would succeed in business and social relationships. It promoted competition and individualism, saw government intervention into human affair as futile, and was used by the economic and social elite to oppose reform. p. 455

Social Gospel Preached by urban Protestant ministers, the Social Gospel focused as much on improving the conditions of life on earth as on saving souls for the hereafter. Its adherents worked for child-labor laws and measures to alleviate poverty. p. 457

Settlement houses Located in poor districts, these community centers tried to soften the impact of urban life for immigrant and other families. Often run by young, educated women, they provided social services and a political voice for their neighborhoods. Chicago's Hull House, founded by Jane Addams in 1889, was the most famous of them. p. 457

CRITICAL THINKING QUESTIONS

1. What were the main economic, social, and political characteristics of the new urban society?

2. In what ways did the social and cultural changes of urban society affect fundamental outlooks on the family, the role of women, and education, and lead to demands for reform?

3. How did reform-minded critics try to meet the challenges of urban growth?

MyHistoryLab Media Assignments

Find these resources in the Media Assignments folder for Chapter 19 on MyHistoryLab

The Lure of the City

Read the **Document** Charles Loring Brace, "The Life of the Street Rats" (1872) p. 439

View the **Closer Look** Group of Emigrants (Women and Children) from Eastern Europe on Deck of the S.S. Amsterdam p. 441

Watch the **Video** Ellis Island Immigrants (1903) p. 442

View the **Map** Immigration, 1880–1920 p. 444

Complete the **Assignment** Ellis Island: Isle of Hope, Isle of Tears p. 442

Watch the **Video** Democracy and Corruption: The Rise of Political Machines p. 446

Social and Cultural Change, 1877–1900

Read the **Document** The Morrill Act (1862) p. 452

Listen to the **Audio File** Address at the Atlanta Exposition by Booker T. Washington p. 453

The Stirrings of Reform

Read the **Document** Edward Bellamy, from Looking Backward p. 456

Read the **Document** Jane Addams, from Twenty Years at Hull House (1910) p. 458

Complete the **Assignment** Plessy v. Ferguson: The Shaping of Jim Crow p. 460

■ Indicates Study Plan Media Assignment

20 Political Realignments in the 1890s

Contents and Learning Objectives

((•●─ **Listen** to the **Audio File** on **myhistorylab**   Chapter 20 *Political Realignments in the 1890s*

Hardship and Heartache

In June 1894, Susan Orcutt, a young farm woman from western Kansas, sat down to write the governor of her state a letter. She was desperate. The nation was in the midst of a devastating economic depression, and, like thousands of other people, she had no money and nothing to eat. "I take my Pen In hand to let you know that we are Starving to death," she wrote. Hail had ruined the Orcutts' crops, and none of the household could find work. "My Husband went away to find work and came home last night and told me that we would have to Starve. [H]e has bin in ten countys and did not Get no work....I havent had nothing to Eat today and It is three oclock[.]"

As bad as conditions were on the farms, they were no better in the cities. "There are thousands of homeless and starving men in the streets," reported a journalist in Chicago in the winter of 1893. "I have seen more misery in this last week than I ever saw in my life before." Charity societies and churches tried to help, but they could not handle the huge numbers of people who were

in need. The records of the Massachusetts state medical examiner told a grim story:

K.R., 29 Suicide by drowning
Boston October 2, 1896
Out of work and despondent for a long while. Body found floating in the Charles [River].
F.S., 29 Suicide by arsenic
Boston January 1, 1896

Much depressed for several weeks. Loss of employment. At 7:50 A.M. Jan. 1, she called her father and told him she had taken poison and wished to die.

R.N., 23 Suicide by bullet wound of brain
Boston June 22, 1896
Out of work. Mentally depressed. About 3 P.M. June 21 shot himself in right temple....Left a letter explaining that he killed himself to save others the trouble of caring for him.

Homesteading on the Plains.

Lasting until 1897, the depression was the decisive event of the decade. At its height, three million people were unemployed—fully 20 percent of the workforce. The human costs were enormous, even among the well-to-do. "They were for me years of simple Hell," shattering "my whole scheme of life," said Charles Francis Adams, Jr., the descendant of two American presidents. "I was sixty-three years old and a tired man when at last the effects of the 1893 convulsion wore themselves out."

Like the Great Depression of the 1930s that gave rise to the New Deal, the depression of the 1890s had profound and lasting effects. Bringing to a head many of the tensions that had been building in the society, it increased rural hostility toward the cities, brought about a bitter fight over the currency, and changed people's thinking about government, unemployment, and reform. There were outbreaks of warfare between capital and labor; farmers demanded a fairer share of economic and social benefits; the new immigrants came under fresh attack. The depression of the 1890s changed the course of American history, as did another event of that decade: the war with Spain in 1898.

Under the cruel impact of the depression, ideas changed in many areas, including a stronger impulse toward reform, a larger role for the presidency, and a call for help from many farmers and laborers. One of the most important of these areas was politics. A realignment of the American political system, which had been developing since the end of Reconstruction, finally reached its fruition in the 1890s, establishing new patterns that gave rise to the Progressive Era and lasted well into the twentieth century.

Politics of Stalemate

Why was there a stalemate between Republicans and Democrats until the mid-1890s?

Politics was a major fascination of the late nineteenth century, its mass entertainment and favorite sport. Political campaigns were events that involved the whole community, even though in most states only men could vote. During the weeks leading up to an election, there were rallies, parades, picnics, and torchlight processions. Millions of Americans read party newspapers, listened to three-hour speeches by party leaders, and in elections turned out in enormous numbers to vote. In the six presidential elections from 1876 to 1896, an average of almost 79 percent of the electorate voted, a higher percentage than voted before or after.

White males made up the bulk of the electorate; until after the turn of the century, women could vote in national elections only in Wyoming, Utah, Idaho, and Colorado. The National Woman Suffrage Association sued early for the vote, but in 1875, the Supreme Court (*Minor* v. *Happersett*) upheld the power of the states to deny this right to women. On several occasions, Congress refused to pass a constitutional amendment for woman suffrage, and between 1870 and 1910, nearly a dozen states defeated referenda to grant women the vote.

Black men were another group kept from the polls. In 1877, Georgia adopted the poll tax to make voters pay an annual tax for the right to vote. The technique, aimed at impoverished blacks, was quickly copied across the South. In 1882, South Carolina adopted the "eight box" law, soon copied elsewhere, that required ballots for separate offices to be placed in separate boxes, a difficult task for illiterate voters.

In 1890, Mississippi required voters to be able to read and interpret the federal Constitution to the satisfaction of registration officials, all of them white. Such literacy tests, which the Supreme Court upheld in the case of *Williams* v. *Mississippi* (1898), excluded poor white voters as well as blacks. In 1898, Louisiana avoided the problem by adopting the famous "grandfather clause," which used a literacy test to disqualify black voters but permitted men who had failed the test to vote anyway if their fathers and grandfathers had voted before 1867—a time, of course, when no blacks could vote. The number of black voters decreased dramatically. In 1896, there were 130,334 registered black voters in Louisiana; in 1904, there were 1,342.

The Party Deadlock

The 1870s and 1880s were still dominated by the Civil War generation, the unusual group of people who rose to power in the turbulent 1850s. In both the North and South, they had ruled longer than most generations, with a consciousness that the war experience had set them apart. Five of the six presidents elected between 1865 and 1900 had served in the war, as had many civic, business, and religious leaders. In 1890, well over one million veterans of the Union army were still alive, and Confederate veterans numbered in the hundreds of thousands.

Party loyalties—rooted in Civil War traditions, ethnic and religious differences, and perhaps class distinctions—were remarkably strong. Voters clung to their old parties, shifts were infrequent, and there were relatively few "independent" voters. Although linked to the defeated Confederacy, the Democrats revived quickly after the war. In 1874, they gained control of the House of Representatives, which they maintained for all but four of the succeeding twenty years. The Democrats rested on a less sectional base than the Republicans. Identification with civil rights and military rule cut Republican strength in the South, but the Democratic party's principles of states' rights, decentralization, and limited government won supporters everywhere.

While Democrats wanted to keep government local and small, the Republicans pursued policies for the nation as a whole, in which government was an instrument to promote moral progress and material wealth. The Republicans passed the Homestead Act (1862), granted subsidies to the transcontinental railroads, and pushed other measures to encourage economic growth. They enacted legislation and constitutional amendments to protect civil rights. They advocated a high protective tariff as a tool of economic policy to keep out foreign products while "infant industries" grew.

In national elections, sixteen states, mostly in New England and the North, consistently voted Republican; fourteen states, mostly in the South, consistently voted Democratic. Elections, therefore, depended on a handful of "doubtful" states, which could swing elections either way. These states—New York, New Jersey, Connecticut, Ohio, Indiana, and Illinois—received special attention at election time. Politicians lavished money and time on them; presidential candidates usually came from them. From 1868 to 1912, eight of the nine Republican presidential candidates and six of the seven Democratic candidates came from the "doubtful" states, especially New York and Ohio.

The two parties were evenly matched, and elections were closely fought. In three of the five presidential elections from 1876 to 1892, the victor won by less than 1 percent of the vote; in 1876 and 1888, the losing candidates actually had more popular votes than the winners but lost in the electoral college. Knowing that small mistakes could lose elections, politicians became extremely cautious. Only twice during these years did one party control both the presidency and the two houses of Congress—the Republicans in 1888 and the Democrats in 1892.

Historians once believed that political leaders accomplished little between 1877 and 1900, but those who saw few achievements were looking in the wrong location. With the impeachment of Andrew Johnson, the authority of the presidency dwindled in relation to congressional strength. For the first time in many years, attention shifted away from Washington itself. North and South, people who were weary of the centralization brought on by war and Reconstruction looked first to state and local governments to deal with the problems of an urban-industrial society.

Experiments in the States

Across the country, state bureaus and commissions were established to regulate the new industrial society. Many of the early commissions were formed to oversee the railroads, at the time the nation's largest businesses. People who shipped goods over the railroads, especially farmers and merchants, wanted to end the policies of rate discrimination and other harmful practices. In 1869, Massachusetts

which created the Interstate Commerce Commission (ICC) to investigate and oversee railroad activities. The act outlawed rebates and pooling agreements, and the ICC became the prototype of the federal commissions that today regulate many parts of the economy.

Read the Document   The Interstate Commerce Act (1887)

The Interstate Commerce Act of 1887 was a federal law crafted to regulate the railroad industry and its anti-competitive practices. The Act created a regulatory agency, the Interstate Commerce Commission, which was empowered to investigate and oversee railroad activities.

established the first commission to regulate the railroads; by 1900, twenty-eight states had taken such action.

Most of the early commissions were advisory in nature. They collected statistics and published reports on rates and practices—serving, one commissioner said, "as a sort of lens" to focus public attention. Impatient with the results, legislatures in the Midwest and on the Pacific coast established commissions with greater power to fix rates, outlaw rebates, and investigate rate discrimination. These commissions, experimental in nature, served as models for later policy at the federal level.

Illinois had one of the most thoroughgoing provisions. Responding to local merchants who were upset with existing railroad rate policies, the Illinois state constitution of 1870 declared railroads to be public highways and authorized the legislature to pass laws establishing maximum rates and preventing rate discrimination. In the important case of *Munn v. Illinois* (1877), the Supreme Court upheld the Illinois legislation, declaring that private property "affected with the public interest ... must submit to being controlled by the public for the common good."

But the Court soon weakened that judgment. In the *Wabash* case of 1886 (*Wabash, St. Louis, & Pacific Railway Co. v. Illinois*), it narrowed the Munn ruling and held that states could not regulate commerce extending beyond their borders. Only Congress could. The *Wabash* decision turned people's attention back to the federal government. It spurred Congress to pass the Interstate Commerce Act (1887),

Reestablishing Presidential Power

Johnson's impeachment, the scandals of the Grant administrations, and the controversy surrounding the 1876 election weakened the presidency. During the last two decades of the nineteenth century, presidents fought to reassert their authority, and by 1900, under William McKinley, they had succeeded to a remarkable degree. The late 1890s, in fact, marked the birth of the modern powerful presidency.

Rutherford B. Hayes entered the White House with his title clouded by the disputed election of 1876. Opponents called him "His Fraudulency" and "Rutherfraud B. Hayes," but soon he began to reassert the authority of the presidency. Hayes worked for reform in the civil service, placed well-known reformers in high offices, and, ordering the last troops out of South Carolina and Louisiana, ended military Reconstruction. Committed to the gold standard—the only basis, Hayes thought, of a sound currency—in 1878 he vetoed a bill that called for the partial coinage of silver, but Congress passed this **Bland-Allison Silver Purchase Act** over his veto.

James A. Garfield, a Union army hero and longtime member of Congress, succeeded Hayes. Winning by a handful of votes in 1880, he took office energetically, determined to unite the Republican party (which had been split by personality differences and disagreement over policy toward the tariff and the South), lower the tariff to cut taxes, and assert American economic and strategic interests in Latin America. Ambitious and eloquent, Garfield had looked forward to the presidency, yet within a few weeks he said to friends, "My God! What is there in this place that a man should ever want to get into it?"

Office seekers, hordes of them, evoked Garfield's anguish. Each one wanted a government job, and each one thought nothing of cornering the president on every occasion. The problem of government jobs also provoked a bitter fight with the powerful senator from New York, Roscoe Conkling, who resented some of Garfield's choices. On the verge of victory over Conkling, Garfield planned to leave Washington on July 2, 1881, for a vacation in New England. Walking toward his train, he was shot in the back by Charles J. Guiteau, a deranged lawyer and disappointed office seeker. Suffering through the summer, Garfield died on September 19, 1881, and Vice President Chester A. Arthur—an ally of Senator Conkling—became president.

THE ELECTION OF 1880

Candidate	Party	Popular Vote	Electoral Vote
Garfield	Republican	4,454,416	214
Hancock	Democrat	4,444,952	155
Weaver	Greenback	308,578	0

Arthur was a better president than many had expected. Deftly, he established his independence of Conkling. Conservative in outlook, he reversed Garfield's foreign policy initiatives in

Latin America, but he approved the construction of the modern American navy. Arthur worked to lower the tariff, and in 1883, with his backing, Congress passed the **Pendleton Act** to reform the civil service. In part a reaction to Garfield's assassination, the act created a bipartisan Civil Service Commission to administer competitive examinations and appoint officeholders on the basis of merit. Initially, the act affected only about fourteen thousand of some one hundred thousand government offices, but it laid the basis for the later expansion of the civil service.

In the election of 1884, Grover Cleveland, the Democratic governor of New York, narrowly defeated Republican nominee, James G. Blaine, largely because of the continuing divisions in the Republican party. The first Democratic president since 1861, Cleveland was slow and ponderous, known for his honesty, stubbornness, and hard work. His term in the White House from 1885 to 1889 reflected the Democratic party's desire to curtail federal activities. Cleveland vetoed more than two-thirds of the bills presented to him, more than all his predecessors combined.

Forthright and sincere, he brought a new respectability to a Democratic party still tainted by its link with secession. Working long into the night, he reviewed veterans' pensions and civil service appointments. He continued Arthur's naval construction program and forced railroad, lumber, and cattle companies to surrender millions of acres of fraudulently occupied public domain. Late in 1887, he devoted his annual message to an attack on the tariff, "the vicious, inequitable, and illogical source of unnecessary taxation," and committed himself and the Democratic party to lowering the tariff.

The Republicans accused him of undermining American industries, and in 1888, they nominated for the presidency Benjamin Harrison, a defender of the tariff. Cleveland garnered ninety thousand more popular votes than Harrison but won the electoral votes of only two northern states and the South. Harrison won the rest of the North, most of the "doubtful" states, and the election.

THE ELECTION OF 1884

Candidate	Party	Popular Vote	Electoral Vote
Cleveland	Democrat	4,874,986	219
Blaine	Republican	4,851,981	182
Butler	Greenback	175,370	0
St. John	Prohibition	150,369	0

Republicans in Power: The Billion-Dollar Congress

How did the Republican party's vision shape the "Billion-Dollar Congress"?

Despite Harrison's narrow margin, the election of 1888 was the most sweeping victory for either party in almost twenty years; it gave the Republicans the presidency and both houses of Congress. The Republicans, it seemed, had broken the party stalemate and become the majority party in the country.

Democratic leaders hoped not, and, eager to embarrass the Republicans and block Republican-sponsored laws, the Democrats

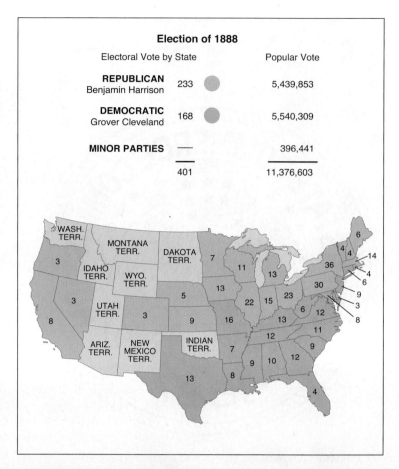

Election of 1888

	Electoral Vote by State		Popular Vote
REPUBLICAN Benjamin Harrison	233		5,439,853
DEMOCRATIC Grover Cleveland	168		5,540,309
MINOR PARTIES	—		396,441
	401		11,376,603

in Congress used minority tactics, especially the "disappearing quorum" rule, which let members of the House of Representatives join in debate but then refuse to answer the roll call to determine whether a quorum was present.

For two months, the Democrats used the rule to bring Congress to a halt. The Republicans grew angry and impatient. On January 29, 1890, they fell two votes short of a quorum, and Speaker of the House Thomas B. Reed, a crusty veteran of Maine politics, made congressional history. "The Chair," he said, "directs the Clerk to record the following names of members present and refusing to vote." Democrats shouted "Czar! Czar!", a title that stuck to Reed for the rest of his life. Tumult continued for days, but in mid-February 1890, the Republicans adopted the Reed rules and proceeded to enact the party's program.

Tariffs, Trusts, and Silver

As if a dam had burst, law after law poured out of the Republican Congress during 1890. The Republicans passed the McKinley Tariff Act, which raised tariff duties about 4 percent, higher than ever before; it also included a novel reciprocity provision that allowed the president to lower duties if other countries did the same. In addition, the act used duties to promote new industries, such as tinplate for packaging the new "canned" foods appearing on grocery store shelves. A Dependent Pensions Act granted pensions to Union army veterans and their widows and children. The pensions were modest—$6 to $12 a month—but the number of pensioners doubled by 1893, when nearly one million individuals received about $160 million in pensions.

📖 **Read** the **Document**   **Workingman's Amalgamated Sherman Anti-Trust (1893)**

THE BOSSES OF THE SENATE.

Congress passed the Sherman Anti-Trust Act in 1890, which authorized federal action against any "combination in the form of trusts or otherwise, or conspiracy, in restraint of trade." Though the act was envisioned as a way to control big business, its wording was sufficiently vague as to allow the federal government to use this law against labor unions, which many people considered to be combinations.

With little debate, the Republicans and Democrats joined in passing the **Sherman Antitrust Act**, the first federal attempt to regulate big business. As the initial attempt to deal with the problem of trusts and industrial growth, the act shaped all later antitrust policy. It declared illegal "every contract, combination in the form of trust or otherwise, or conspiracy, in restraint of trade or commerce." Penalties for violation were stiff, including fines and imprisonment and the dissolution of guilty trusts. Experimental in nature, the act's terms were often vague and left precise interpretation to later experience and the courts.

One of the most important laws Congress passed, the Sherman Antitrust Act made the United States virtually the only industrial nation to regulate business combinations. It tried to harness big business without harming it. Many members of Congress did not expect the new law to have much effect on businesses, and for a decade, in fact, it did not. The Justice Department rarely filed suit under it, and in the *United States v. E. C. Knight Co.* decision (1895), the first judicial interpretation of the law, the Supreme Court severely crippled it. Though the E. C. Knight Co. controlled 98 percent of all sugar refining in the country, the Court drew a sharp distinction between commerce and manufacturing, holding that the company, as a

manufacturer, was not subject to the law. But judicial interpretations changed after the turn of the century, and the Sherman Antitrust Act gained fresh power.

Another measure, the **Sherman Silver Purchase Act**, tried to end the troublesome problem presented by silver. As one of the two most commonly used precious metals, silver had once played a large role in currencies around the world, but by the mid-1800s, it had slipped into disuse. With the discovery of the great bonanza mines in Nevada, American silver production quadrupled between 1870 and 1890, glutting the world market, lowering the price of silver, and persuading many European nations to demonetize silver in favor of the scarcer metal, gold. The United States kept a limited form of silver coinage with congressional passage of the Bland-Allison Act in 1878.

Support for silver coinage was especially strong in the South and West, where people thought it might inflate the currency, raise wages and crop prices, and challenge the power of the gold-oriented Northeast. Eager to avert the free coinage of silver, which would require the coinage of all silver presented at the U.S. mints, President Harrison and other Republican leaders pressed for a compromise that took shape in the Sherman Silver Purchase Act of 1890.

The act directed the Treasury to purchase 4.5 million ounces of silver a month and to issue legal tender in the form of Treasury notes in payment for it. The act was a compromise; it satisfied both sides. Opponents of silver were pleased that it did not include free coinage. Silverites, on the other hand, were delighted that the monthly purchases would buy up most of the country's silver production. The Treasury notes, moreover, could be cashed for either gold or silver at the bank, a gesture toward a true bimetallic system based on silver and gold.

As a final measure, Republicans in the House courageously passed a federal elections bill to protect the voting rights of blacks in the South. Although restrained in language and intent, it set off a storm of denunciation among the Democrats, who called it a "force bill" that would station army troops in the South. Because of the outcry, the bill failed in the Senate; it was the last major effort until the 1950s to enforce the Fifteenth Amendment to the Constitution.

The 1890 Elections

The Republican Congress of 1890 was one of the most important Congresses in American history. It passed a record number of significant laws that helped shape later policy and asserted the authority of the federal government to a degree the country would not then accept. Sensing the public reaction, the Democrats labeled it the "Billion-Dollar Congress" for spending that much in appropriations and grants.

"This is a billion-dollar country," Speaker Reed replied, but the voters disagreed. The 1890 elections crushed the Republicans, who lost an extraordinary seventy-eight seats in the House. The elections also crushed Republicans in the Midwest, where, again enlarging government authority, they had passed state laws prohibiting the sale of alcoholic beverages, requiring the closing of businesses on Sunday, and mandating the use of English in the public and parochial schools. Roman Catholics, German Lutherans, and other groups resented such laws, which they saw as a direct attack on their religion and personal freedoms, and they angrily deserted the Republicans.

Political veterans went down to defeat, and new leaders vaulted into sudden prominence. Nebraska elected a Democratic governor for the first time in its history. The state of Iowa, once so staunchly Republican that a local leader had predicted that "Iowa will go Democratic when Hell goes Methodist," went Democratic in 1890.

The Rise of the Populist Movement

What factors led to the formation and growth of the Farmers' Alliance and People's party?

The elections of 1890 drew attention to a fast-growing movement among farmers that soon came to be known far and wide as populism. The movement had begun rather quietly, in places distant from normal centers of attention, and for a time it went almost unnoticed in the press. But during the summer of 1890, wagonloads of farm families in the South and West converged on campgrounds and picnic areas to socialize and discuss common problems. They came by the thousands, weary of drought, mortgages, and low crop prices. At the campgrounds, they picnicked, talked, and listened to recruiters from an organization called the **National Farmers' Alliance and Industrial Union**, which promised unified action to solve agricultural problems.

Farmers were joining the Alliance at the rate of 1,000 a week; the Kansas Alliance alone claimed 130,000 members in 1890. The summer of 1890 became "that wonderful picnicking, speech-making Alliance summer," a time of fellowship and spirit long remembered by farmers.

The Farm Problem

Farm discontent was a worldwide phenomenon between 1870 and 1900. With the new means of transportation and communication, farmers everywhere were caught up in a complex international market they neither controlled nor entirely understood.

American farmers complained bitterly about declining prices for their products, rising railroad rates for shipping them, and burdensome mortgages. Some of their grievances were valid. Farm profits were certainly low; agriculture in general tends to produce low profits because of the ease of entry into the industry. The prices of farm commodities fell between 1865 and 1890—corn sold at sixty-three cents a bushel in 1881 and twenty-eight cents in 1890—but they did not fall as low as did other commodity prices. Despite the fact that farmers received less for their crops, their purchasing power actually increased.

Neither was the farmers' second grievance—rising railroad rates—entirely justified. Railroad rates actually fell during these years, benefiting shippers of all products. Farm mortgages, the farmers' third grievance, were common because many farmers mortgaged their property to expand their holdings or buy new farm machinery. While certainly burdensome, most mortgages did not bring hardship. They were often short, with a term of four years or less, after which farmers could renegotiate at new rates, and the new machinery the farmers bought enabled them to triple their output and increase their income.

The terms of the farm problem varied from area to area and year to year. New England farmers suffered from overworked land; farmers in western Kansas and Nebraska went broke in a severe drought that followed a period of unusual rainfall. Many southern farmers were trapped in the crop lien system that kept them in debt. They called it the "anaconda" system because of the way it coiled slowly and tightly around them.

Some farmers did have valid grievances, though many understandably tended to exaggerate them. More important, many farmers were sure their condition had declined, and this perception—as bitterly real as any actual fact—sparked a growing anger. Equally upsetting, everyone in the 1870s and 1880s seemed excited about factories, not farms. Farmers had become "hayseeds," a word that first appeared in 1889, and they watched their offspring leave for city lights and new careers. A literature of disillusionment emerged, most notably Hamlin Garland's *Son of the Middle Border* (1890) and *Main-Travelled Roads* (1891), which described the drabness of farm life.

SELECTED COMMODITY PRICES

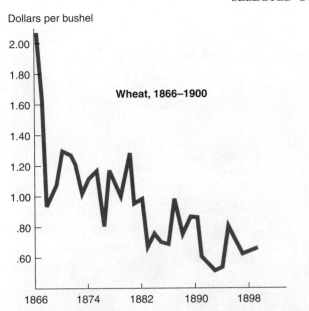

Dollars per bushel

Wheat, 1866–1900

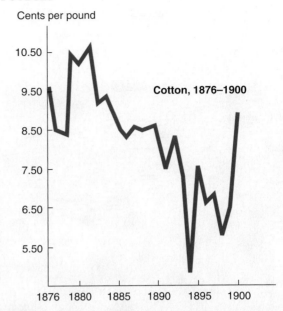

Cents per pound

Cotton, 1876–1900

Source: U.S. Bureau of the Census, *Historical Statistics of the United States, Colonial Times to 1970*, Bicentennial Edition, Washington, DC, 1975.

The Fast-Growing Farmers' Alliance

Originally a social organization for farmers, the Grange lost many of its members as it turned more and more toward politics in the late 1870s. In its place, a multitude of farm societies sprang into existence. By the end of the 1880s, they had formed into two major organizations: the National Farmers' Alliance, located on the plains west of the Mississippi and known as the Northwestern Alliance, and the Farmers' Alliance and Industrial Union, based in the South and known as the Southern Alliance.

The Southern Alliance began in Texas in 1875 but did not assume major proportions until Dr. Charles W. Macune, an energetic and farsighted person, took over the leadership in 1886. Rapidly expanding, the Alliance absorbed other agricultural societies. Its agents spread across the South, where farmers were fed up with crop liens, depleted lands, and sharecropping. They "seem like unto ripe fruit," an Alliance organizer said; "you can garner them by a gentle shake of the bush." In 1890, the Southern Alliance claimed more than a million members. It welcomed to membership the farmers' "natural friends"—country doctors, schoolteachers, preachers, and mechanics. It excluded lawyers, bankers, cotton merchants, and warehouse operators.

An effective organization, the Southern Alliance published a newspaper and distributed Alliance material to hundreds of local newspapers, and in five years it sent lecturers to forty-three states and territories where they spoke to two million farm families. It was "the most massive organizing drive by any citizen institution of nineteenth-century America." Like the Grange, the Alliance also established cooperative grain elevators, marketing associations, and retail stores—all designed to bring farmers together to make greater profits. Most of the projects were short-lived, but for a time, between 1886 and 1892, cooperative enterprises blossomed in the South.

Loosely affiliated with the Southern Alliance, a separate Colored Farmers' National Alliance and Cooperative Union enlisted black farmers in the South. Claiming more than one million members, it probably had closer to 250,000, but even that figure was sizable in an era when "uppity" blacks faced not merely defeat, but death. In 1891, black cotton pickers struck for higher wages near Memphis, Tennessee. Led by Ben Patterson, a 30-year-old picker, they walked off several plantations, but a posse hunted them down and, following violence on both sides, lynched fifteen strikers, including Patterson. The abortive strike ended the Colored Farmers' Alliance.

On the plains, the Northwestern Alliance, a smaller organization, was formed in 1880. Its objectives were similar to those of the Southern Alliance, but it disagreed with the Southerners' emphasis on secrecy, centralized control, and separate organizations for blacks. In 1889, the Southern Alliance changed its name to the National Farmers' Alliance and Industrial Union and persuaded the three strongest state alliances on the plains—those in North Dakota, South Dakota, and Kansas—to join. Thereafter, the renamed organization dominated the Alliance movement.

The Alliance mainly sponsored social and economic programs, but it turned early to politics. In the West, its leaders rejected both the Republicans and Democrats and organized their own party; in June 1890, Kansas Alliance members formed the first major People's party. The Southern Alliance resisted the idea of a new party for fear it might divide the white vote, thus undercutting white supremacy.

Thomas E. Watson and Leonidas L. Polk, two politically minded Southerners, reflected the high quality of Alliance leadership. Georgia born, Watson was a talented orator and organizer; he urged Georgia farmers, black and white, to unite against their oppressors.

Read the Document **Proceedings of Grange Session (1879)**

The Alliance movement grew quickly in the late 1800s among discontented farmers. This photograph shows Southern Alliance members meeting at the cabin that was the site of their first formal meeting in 1877 in Lampasas County, Texas. The cabin was later uprooted and exhibited at the World's Columbian Exposition in Chicago in 1893.

The president of the National Farmers' Alliance, Polk believed in scientific farming and cooperative action. Jeremiah Simpson of Kansas, probably the most able of the western leaders, was reflective and well read. A follower of reformer Henry George, he pushed for major social and economic change. Also from Kansas, Mary E. Lease helped head a movement remarkably open to female leadership. A captivating speaker, she made 160 speeches during the summer of 1890, calling on farmers to rise against Wall Street and the industrial East.

Meeting in Ocala, Florida, in 1890, the Alliance adopted the **Ocala Demands**, the platform the organization pushed as long as it existed. First and foremost, the demands called for the creation of a "sub-treasury system," which would allow farmers to store their crops in government warehouses. In return, they could claim Treasury notes for up to 80 percent of the local market value of the crop, a loan to be repaid when the crops were sold. Farmers could thus hold their crops for the best price. The Ocala Demands also urged the free coinage of silver, an end to protective tariffs and national banks, a federal income tax, the direct election of senators by voters instead of state legislatures, and tighter regulation of railroad companies.

The Alliance strategy worked well in the elections of 1890. In Kansas, the Alliance-related People's party, organized just a few months before, elected four congressmen and a U.S. senator. Across the South, the Alliance won victories based on the "Alliance yardstick," a demand that Democratic party candidates pledge support for Alliance measures. Alliance leaders claimed thirty-eight Alliance supporters elected to Congress, with at least a dozen more pledged to Alliance principles.

The People's Party

After the 1890 elections, Northern Alliance leaders urged the formation of a national third party to promote reform, although the Southerners remained reluctant, still hopeful of capturing control of the Democratic party. Plans for a new party were discussed at Alliance conventions in 1891 and the following year. In July 1892, a convention in Omaha, Nebraska, formed the new **People's (or Populist) party**. Southern Alliance leaders joined in, convinced now that there was no reason to cooperate with

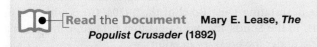
Read the **Document**　Mary E. Lease, *The Populist Crusader* (1892)

Populist Mary E. Lease advised farmers to "raise less corn and more hell." She also said, "If one man has not enough to eat three times a day and another man has $25 million, that last man has something that belongs to the first."

Source: Kansas State Historical Society.

the Democrats who exploited Alliance popularity but failed to adopt its reforms.

In the South, some Populists had worked to unite black and white farmers. "They are in the ditch just like we are," a white Texas Populist said. Blacks and whites served on Populist election committees; they spoke from the same platforms, and they ran on the same tickets. Populist sheriffs called blacks for jury duty, an unheard-of practice in the close-of-the-century South. In 1892, a black Populist was threatened with lynching; he took refuge with Tom Watson, and two thousand white farmers, some of whom rode all night to get there, guarded Watson's house until the threat passed.

Many of the delegates at the Omaha convention had planned to nominate Leonidas L. Polk for president, but he died suddenly in June, and the convention turned instead to James B. Weaver of Iowa, a former congressman, Union army general, and third-party candidate for president in 1880 (on the Greenback-Labor party ticket). As its platform, the People's party adopted many of the Ocala Demands.

Weaver waged an active campaign but with mixed results. He won 1,027,329 votes, the first third-party presidential candidate ever

to attract more than a million. He carried Kansas, Idaho, Nevada, and Colorado, along with portions of North Dakota and Oregon, for a total of twenty-two electoral votes, a measure of agrarian unrest. The Populists elected governors in Kansas and North Dakota, ten congressmen, five senators, and about fifteen hundred members of state legislatures.

Despite the Populists' victories, the election brought disappointment. Southern Democrats used intimidation, fraud, and manipulation to hold down Populist votes. Weaver was held to less than a quarter of the vote in every southern state except Alabama. In most of the country, he lost heavily in urban areas, with the exception of some mining towns in the Far West. He also failed to win over most farmers. In no midwestern state except Kansas and North Dakota did he win as much as 5 percent of the vote.

In the election of 1892, many voters switched parties, but they tended to realign with the Democrats rather than the Populists, whose platform on silver and other issues had relatively little appeal among city dwellers or factory workers. Although the Populists did run candidates in the next three presidential elections, they had reached their peak in 1892. That year, Farmers' Alliance membership dropped for the second year in a row, and the organization, which was once the breeding ground of the People's party, was broken.

While it lived, the Alliance was one of the most powerful protest movements in American history. Catalyzing the feelings of hundreds of thousands of farmers, it attempted to solve specific economic problems while at the same time advancing a larger

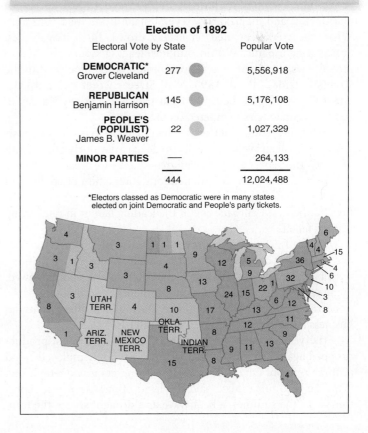
Read the **Document**　Ocala Platform 1890

Election of 1892

	Electoral Vote by State		Popular Vote
DEMOCRATIC* Grover Cleveland	277	●	5,556,918
REPUBLICAN Benjamin Harrison	145	●	5,176,108
PEOPLE'S (POPULIST) James B. Weaver	22	●	1,027,329
MINOR PARTIES	—		264,133
	444		12,024,488

*Electors classed as Democratic were in many states elected on joint Democratic and People's party tickets.

vision of harmony and community, in which people who cared about each other were rewarded for what they produced.

The Crisis of the Depression

What were the main political and labor effects of the panic and depression of the 1890s?

It was economic crisis, however, not harmony and community, that dominated the last decade of the century. Responding to the heady forces of industrialization, the American economy had expanded too rapidly in the 1870s and 1880s. Railroads had overbuilt, gambling on future growth. Companies had grown beyond their markets; farms and businesses had borrowed heavily for expansion.

The Panic of 1893

The mood changed early in 1893. In mid-February, panic suddenly hit the New York stock market. In one day, investors dumped one million shares of a leading company, the Philadelphia and Reading Railroad, and it went bankrupt. Business investment dropped sharply in the railroad and construction industries, touching off the worst economic downturn to that point in the country's history.

Frightened, people hurriedly sold stocks and other assets to buy gold. The overwhelming demand depleted the gold reserve of the U.S. Treasury. Eroding almost daily, in March 1893, the Treasury's reserve slumped toward the $100 million mark, an amount that stood for the government's commitment to maintain the gold standard. On April 22, for the first time since the 1870s, the reserve fell below $100 million.

The news shattered business confidence—the stock market broke. On Wednesday, May 3, railroad and industrial stocks plummeted, and the next day, several major firms went bankrupt. When the market opened on Friday, crowds filled its galleries, anticipating a panic. Within minutes, leading stocks plunged to record lows, and there was pandemonium on the floor and in the streets outside. May 5, 1893, Wall Street's worst day until the Great Crash of 1929, became "Industrial Black Friday," "a day of terrible strain long remembered on the market."

Afterward, banks cut back on loans. Unable to get capital, businesses failed at an average rate of two dozen a day during the month of May. "The papers are full of failures—banks are breaking all over the country, and there is a tremendous contraction of credits and hoarding of money going on everywhere," an observer noted. On July 26, the Erie Railroad, one of the leading names in railroading history, failed.

August 1893 was the worst month. Across the country, factories and mines shut down. On August 15, the Northern Pacific Railroad went bankrupt; the Union Pacific and the Santa Fe soon followed. Some economists estimated unemployment at two million people, or nearly 15 percent of the labor force. During 1893, fifteen thousand business firms and more than six hundred banks closed.

The year 1894 was even worse. The gross national product dropped again, and by midyear the number of unemployed stood at three million. One out of every five workers was unemployed. "Famine is in our midst," said the head of one city's relief committee. In the summer, a heat wave and drought struck the farm belt west of the Mississippi River, creating conditions unmatched until the devastating Dust Bowl of the 1930s. Corn withered in the fields. In the South, the price of cotton fell below five cents a pound, far under the break-even point.

People became restless and angry. As one newspaper said in 1896: "On every corner stands a man whose fortune in these dull times has made him an ugly critic of everything and everybody." There was even talk of revolution and bloodshed. "Everyone scolds," Henry Adams, the historian, wrote a British friend. "Everyone also knows what ought to be done. Everyone reviles everyone who does not agree with him, and everyone differs, or agrees only in contempt for everyone else. As far as I can see, everyone is right."

Coxey's Army and the Pullman Strike

Some of the unemployed wandered across the country—singly, in small groups, and in small armies. During 1894, there were some fourteen hundred strikes involving more than a half million workers.

On Easter Sunday 1894, an unusual "army" of perhaps three hundred people left Massillon, Ohio. At its head rode "General" Jacob S. Coxey, a mild-looking middle-aged businessman who wanted to put the nation's jobless to work building roads. Coxey wanted Congress to pass the Coxey Good Roads bill, which would authorize the printing of $500 million in paper money to finance road construction. His march to Washington—"a petition in boots," he called it—drew nationwide attention.

Other armies sprang up around the country, and all headed for Washington to persuade the government to provide jobs on irrigation, road construction, or other projects. In the West, they commandeered freight trains and headed east. Coxey himself reached Washington on May 1, 1894, after a difficult, tiring march. Police were everywhere, lining the streets and blocking the approaches to the Capitol. Coxey made it to the foot of the Capitol steps, but before he could do anything, the police were on him. He and a companion were clubbed, then arrested for trespassing. A week later, Coxey was sentenced to twenty days in jail.

The armies melted away, but discontent did not. The great **Pullman strike**—one of the largest strikes in the country's history—began just a few days after Coxey's arrest when the employees of the Pullman Palace Car Company, living in a company town just outside Chicago (a town in which everything was owned and meted out by the company), struck to protest wage cuts, continuing high rents, and layoffs. On June 26, 1894, the American Railway Union (ARU) under Eugene V. Debs joined the strike by refusing to handle trains that carried Pullman sleeping cars.

Within hours, the strike paralyzed the western half of the nation. Grain and livestock could not reach markets. Factories shut down for lack of coal. The strike extended into twenty-seven states and territories, tying up the economy and renewing talk of class warfare. In Washington, President Grover Cleveland, who had been reelected to the presidency in 1892, decided to break the strike on the grounds that it obstructed delivery of the mail.

On July 2, he secured a court injunction against the ARU, and he ordered troops to Chicago. When they arrived on the morning of Independence Day, the city was peaceful. Before long, however, violence broke out, and mobs, composed mostly of nonstrikers,

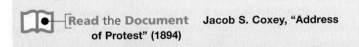 **Read the Document**   Jacob S. Coxey, "Address of Protest" (1894)

Coxey's army is shown here entering Washington, D.C. Jacob Coxey was arrested for trespassing on the lawn surrounding the U.S. Capitol. On the fiftieth anniversary of his march to Washington, Coxey was permitted to finish the speech that had been interrupted by his arrest in 1894.

overturned freight cars, looted, and burned. Restoring order, the army occupied railroad yards in Illinois, California, and other places. By late July, the strike was over; Debs was jailed for violating the injunction. Many people applauded Cleveland's action, "nominally for the expedition of the mails," a newspaper said, but "really for the preservation of society."

The Pullman strike had far-reaching consequences for the development of the labor movement. Working people resented Cleveland's actions in the strike, particularly as it became apparent that he sided with the railroads. Upholding Debs's sentence in *In re Debs* (1895), the Supreme Court endorsed the use of the injunction in labor disputes, thus giving business and government an effective antilabor weapon that hindered union growth in the 1890s. The strike's failure catapulted Debs into prominence. During his time in jail, he turned to socialism, and after his release, he worked to build the Socialist Party of America, which experienced some success after 1900.

The Miners of the Midwest

The plight of coal miners in the Midwest illustrated the personal and social impact of the depression. Even in the best of times, mining was a dirty and dangerous business. One miner in twelve died underground; one in three suffered injury. Mines routinely closed for as long as six months a year, and wages fell with the depression.

Midwestern mining was often a family occupation, passed down from father to son. It demanded delicate judgments about when to blast, where to follow a seam, and how to avoid rockfalls. Until 1890, English and Irish immigrants dominated the business. They migrated from mine to mine, and they nearly always lived in flimsy shacks owned by the company. Time and again the miners struck for higher wages—between 1887 and 1894, there were 116 major coal strikes in Illinois, 111 in Ohio.

After 1890, immigration from southern and eastern Europe, hitherto a trickle, became a flood. Italians, Lithuanians, Poles, Slovaks, Magyars, Russians, Bohemians, and Croatians came to the mines to find work. In three years, nearly one thousand Italians settled in Coal City, Illinois; they comprised more than one-third of the population. In other mining towns, Italian and Polish miners soon made up almost half the population.

As the depression deepened, tensions grew between miners and their employers and between "old" miners and the "new." Many new miners spoke no English, and often they were "birds of passage," transients who had come to the United States to make money to take back home. Lacking the skills handed down by the old miners, they were often blamed for accidents, and they worked longer hours for less pay. At many a tavern after work, old miners grumbled about the different-looking newcomers and considered ways to get rid of them.

In April 1894, a wave of wage reductions sparked an explosion of labor unrest in the mines. The United Mine Workers, a struggling union formed just four years earlier, called for a strike of bituminous coal miners, and on April 21, virtually all midwestern and Pennsylvania miners—some 170,000 in all—quit working. The flow of crucial coal slackened; cities faced blackouts; factories closed.

The violence that soon broke out followed a significant pattern. Over the years, the English and Irish miners had built up a set of unspoken understandings with their employers. The new miners had not, and they were more prone to violent action to win a strike. The depression hit them especially hard, frustrating their plans to earn money and return home. In many areas, anger and frustration turned the 1894 strikes into outright war.

For nearly two weeks in June 1894, fighting rocked the Illinois, Ohio, and Indiana coalfields. Mobs ignited mine shafts, dynamited coal trains, and defied state militias. While miners of all backgrounds participated in the violence, it often divided old miners and new. In Spring Valley, Illinois, exiled Italian anarchists took over the strike leadership and incited rioting despite the opposition of the old miners. Elsewhere, a mine fired by arsonists burned because the new miners prevented the old ones from extinguishing the blaze.

Shocked by the violence, public opinion shifted against the strikers. The strike ended in a matter of weeks, but its effects lingered. English and Irish miners moved out into other jobs or up into supervisory positions. Jokes and songs poked cruel fun at the new immigrants, and the Pennsylvania and Illinois legislatures adopted laws to keep them out of the mines. Thousands of old miners voted Populist in 1894—the Populist platform called for restrictions on immigration—in one of the Populists' few successes that year. The United Mine Workers, dominated by the older miners, began in 1896 to urge Congress to stop the "demoralizing effects" of immigration.

Occurring at the same time, the Pullman strike pulled attention away from the crisis in the coalfields, yet the miners' strike involved three times as many workers and provided a revealing glimpse of the tensions within American society. The miners of the Midwest were the first large group of skilled workers seriously affected by the flood of immigrants from southern and eastern Europe. Buffeted by depression, they reflected the social and economic discord that permeated every industry.

A Beleaguered President

Building on the Democratic party's sweeping triumph in the midterm elections of 1890, Grover Cleveland decisively defeated the Populist candidate, James B. Weaver, and the incumbent president, Benjamin Harrison, in 1892. He won by nearly four hundred thousand votes, a large margin by the standards of the era, and the Democrats increased their strength in the cities and among working-class voters. For the first time since the 1850s, they controlled the White House and both branches of Congress.

The Democrats, it now seemed, had broken the party stalemate, but unfortunately for Cleveland, the Panic of 1893 struck almost as he took office. He was sure that he knew its cause. The Sherman Silver Purchase Act of 1890, he believed, had damaged business confidence, drained the Treasury's gold reserve, and caused the panic. The solution to the depression was equally simple: repeal the act.

In June 1893, Cleveland summoned Congress into special session. India had just closed its mints to silver, and Mexico was now the only country in the world with free silver coinage. The silverites were on the defensive, although they pleaded for a compromise. Rejecting the pleas, Cleveland pushed the repeal bill through Congress, and on November 1, 1893, he signed it into law. Always sure of himself, he had staked everything on a single measure—a winning strategy if he succeeded, a devastating one if he did not.

Repeal of the Sherman Silver Purchase Act was probably a necessary action. It responded to the realities of international finance, reduced the flight of gold out of the country, and, over the long run, boosted business confidence. Unfortunately, it contracted the currency at a time when inflation might have helped. It did not bring economic revival. The stock market remained listless, businesses continued to close, unemployment spread, and farm prices dropped. "We are hourly expecting the arrival of the benevolent man who is to pay ten cents a pound for cotton," a Virginia newspaper said.

The repeal battle of 1893, discrediting the conservative Cleveland Democrats who had dominated the party since the 1860s, reshaped the politics of the country. It confined the Democratic party largely to the South, helped the Republicans become the majority party in 1894, and strengthened the position of the silver Democrats in their bid for the presidency in 1896. It also focused national attention on the silver issue and thus intensified the silver sentiment Cleveland had intended to dampen. In the end, repeal did not even solve the Treasury's gold problem. By January 1894, the reserve had fallen to $65 million. A year later, it fell to $44.5 million.

In January 1894, Cleveland desperately resorted to a sale of $50 million in gold bonds to replenish the gold reserve. The following November, he again sold bonds, and in February 1895, arousing outrage among many, he agreed to a third bond sale that allowed financier J. Pierpont Morgan and other bankers to reap large profits. A fourth bond sale in January 1896 also failed to stop the drain on the reserve, although it further sharpened the silverites' hatred of President Cleveland.

Still another blow to the morale of the Democrats came in 1894, when they tried to fulfill their long-standing promise to reduce the tariff. Despite all their efforts, the Wilson-Gorman Tariff Act, passed by Congress in August 1894, contained only modest reductions in duties. It reduced the tariff on coal, iron ore, wool, and sugar, ended the McKinley Tariff Act's popular reciprocity agreements with other countries, and moved some duties higher than ever before. It also imposed a small income tax, a provision the Supreme Court overturned in 1895 (*Pollock* v. *Farmer's Loan and Trust Co.*). Very few Democrats, including Cleveland, were pleased with the measure, and the president let it become law without his signature.

Breaking the Party Deadlock

The Democrats were buried in the elections of 1894. Suffering the greatest defeat in congressional history, they lost 113 House seats, while the Republicans gained 117. In twenty-four states, not a single Democrat was elected to Congress. Only one Democrat (Boston's John F. Fitzgerald, the grandfather of President John F. Kennedy) came from all of New England. The Democrats even lost some of the "solid South," and in the Midwest, a crucial battleground of the 1890s, the party was virtually destroyed.

Wooing labor and the unemployed, the Populists made striking inroads in parts of the South and West, yet their progress was far from enough. In a year in which thousands of voters switched parties, the People's party elected only four senators and four congressmen. Southern Democrats again used fraud and violence to keep the Populists' totals down. In the Midwest, the Populists won double the number of votes they had received in 1892, yet still attracted less than 7 percent of the vote. Across the country, the discontented tended to vote for the Republicans, not the Populists, a discouraging sign for the Populist party.

For millions of people, Grover Cleveland became a scapegoat for the country's economic ills. The Democratic party split, and southern and western Democrats deserted him in droves. At Democratic conventions, Cleveland's name evoked jeers. "He is an old bag of beef," Democratic Congressman "Pitchfork" Ben Tillman told a South Carolina audience, "and I am going to go to Washington with a pitchfork and prod him in his old fat ribs."

The elections of 1894 marked the end of the party deadlock that had existed since the 1870s. The Democrats lost, the Populists gained somewhat, and the Republicans became the majority party in the country. In the midst of the depression, the Republican doctrines of activism and national authority, which voters had repudiated in the elections of 1890, became more attractive. This was a development of great significance, because as Americans became more accepting of the use of government power to regulate the economy and safeguard individual welfare, the way lay open to the reforms of the Progressive Era, the New Deal, and beyond.

Changing Attitudes

What changes in outlook did the panic and depression of the 1890s bring about?

The depression, brutal and far reaching, did more than shift political alignments. Across the country, it undermined traditional views and caused people to rethink older ideas about government, the economy, and society. As men and women concluded that established ideas had failed to deal with the depression, they looked for new ones. There was, the president of the University of Wisconsin said, "a general, all-pervasive, restless discontent with the results of current political and economic thought."

In prosperous times, Americans had thought of unemployment as the result of personal failure, affecting primarily the lazy and immoral. "Let us remember," a leading Protestant minister once said, "that there is not a poor person in the United States who was not made poor by his own shortcomings." In the midst of depression, such views were harder to maintain, since everyone knew people who were both worthy and unemployed. Next door, a respected neighbor might be laid off; down the block, an entire factory might be shut down.

People debated issues they had long taken for granted. New and reinvigorated local institutions—discussion clubs, women's clubs, reform societies, university extension centers, church groups, farmers' societies—gave people a place to discuss alternatives to the existing order. Pressures for reform increased, and demand grew for government intervention to help the poor and unemployed.

"Everybody Works But Father"

Women and children had been entering the labor force for years, and the depression accelerated the trend. As husbands and fathers lost their jobs, more and more women and children went to work. Even as late as 1901, well after the depression had ended, a study of working-class families showed that more than half the principal breadwinners were out of work. So many women and children worked that in 1905 there was a popular song titled "Everybody Works But Father."

During the 1890s, the number of working women rose from 4 million to 5.3 million. Trying to make ends meet, they took in boarders and found jobs as laundresses, cleaners, or domestics. Where possible, they worked in offices and factories. Far more black urban women than white worked to supplement their husbands' meager earnings. In New York City in 1900, nearly 60 percent of all black women worked, compared to 27 percent of the foreign-born and 24 percent of native-born white women. Men still dominated business offices, but during the 1890s, more

 Read the Document "Everybody Works But Father" (1905)

Tiny children peddling newspapers and women domestics serving the rich—their meager earnings were desperately needed.

and more employers noted the relative cheapness of female labor. Women telegraph and telephone operators nearly tripled in number during the decade. Women worked as clerks in the new five-and-tens and department stores, and as nurses; in 1900, a half million were teachers. They increasingly entered office work as stenographers and typists, occupations in which they earned between $6.00 and $15.00 a week, compared to factory wages of $1.50 to $8.00 a week.

The depression also caused an increasing number of children to work. During the 1890s, the number of children employed in southern textile mills jumped more than 160 percent, and boys and girls under sixteen years of age made up nearly one-third of the labor force of the mills. Youngsters of eight and nine years worked twelve hours a day for pitiful wages. In most cases, however, children worked not in factories but in farming and city street trades such as peddling and shoe shining. In 1900, the South had more than half the child laborers in the nation.

Concerned about child labor, middle-class women in 1896 formed the League for the Protection of the Family, which called for compulsory education to get children out of factories and into classrooms. The Mothers Congress of 1896 gave rise to the National Congress of Parents and Teachers, the spawning ground of thousands of local Parent-Teacher Associations. The National Council of Women and the General Federation of Women's Clubs took up similar issues. By the end of the 1890s, the Federation had 150,000 members who worked for various civic reforms in the fields of child welfare, education, and sanitation.

Changing Themes in Literature

The depression also gave point to a growing movement in literature toward realism and naturalism. In the years after the Civil War, literature often reflected the mood of romanticism—sentimental and unrealistic. Walt Whitman called it "ornamental confectionary" and "copious dribble," but it remained popular through the end of the century.

The novels of Horatio Alger, which provided simple lessons about how to get ahead in business and life, continued to attract large numbers of readers. A failed New York minister, Alger published some 130 novels—with titles such as *Sink or Swim*, *Work and Win*, and *Struggling Upward*—which sold more than 20 million copies. They told of poor youngsters who made their way to the top through hard work, thrift, honesty, and luck. Louisa May Alcott's *Little Women* (1868–1869) related the daily lives of four girls in a New England family, Anna Sewell's *Black Beauty* (1877) charmed readers with the story of an abused horse that found a happy home, and Lew Wallace's *Ben Hur* (1880), one of the era's best-selling books, offered a sweeping epic of life in the Roman empire.

After the 1870s, however, a number of talented authors began to reject romanticism and escapism, turning instead to realism. Determined to portray life as it was, they studied local dialects, wrote regional stories, and emphasized the "true" relationships between people. In doing so, they reflected broader trends in the society, such as industrialism; evolutionary theory, which emphasized the effect of the environment on humans; and the new philosophy of pragmatism, which emphasized the relativity of values.

Regionalist authors such as Joel Chandler Harris and George Washington Cable depicted life in the South. Hamlin Garland described the grimness of life on the Great Plains, and Sarah Orne Jewett wrote about everyday life in rural New England. Another regionalist, Bret Harte, achieved fame with stories that portrayed the local color of the California mining camps, particularly in his popular tale "The Outcasts of Poker Flat."

Harte was joined by a more talented writer, Mark Twain, who became the country's most outstanding realist author. Growing up along the Mississippi River in Hannibal County, Missouri, the young Samuel Langhorne Clemens observed life around him with a humorous and skeptical eye. Adopting a pen name from the river term "mark twain" (two fathoms), he wrote a number of important works that drew on his own experiences. *Life on the Mississippi* (1883) described his career as a steamboat pilot. *The Adventures of Tom Sawyer* (1876) and *The Adventures of Huckleberry Finn* (1884) gained international prominence. In these books, Twain used dialect and common speech instead of literary language, touching off a major change in American prose style.

William Dean Howells—after Twain, the country's most famous author—came more slowly to the realist approach. At first, he wrote about the happier sides of life, but then he grew worried about the impact of industrialization. *A Traveler from Altruria* (1894), a utopian novel, described an industrial society that consumed lives. The poem "Society" (1895), written in the midst of the depression, compared society to a splendid ball in which men and women danced on flowers covering the bodies of the poor:

> And now and then from out the dreadful floor
> An arm or brow was lifted from the rest,
> As if to strike in madness, or implore
> For mercy; and anon some suffering breast
> Heaved from the mass and sank; and as before
> The revellers above them thronged and prest.

Other writers, the naturalists, became impatient even with realism. Pushing Darwinian theory to its limits, they wrote of a world in which a cruel and merciless environment determined human fate. Often focusing on economic hardship, naturalist writers studied the poor, the lower classes, and the criminal mind; they brought to their writing the social worker's passion for direct and honest experience.

Stephen Crane spent a night in a seven-cent lodging house on the Bowery and in "An Experiment in Misery" captured the smells and sounds of the poor. Crane depicted the carnage of war in *The Red Badge of Courage* (1895) and the impact of poverty in *Maggie: A Girl of the Streets* (1893).

Frank Norris assailed the power of big business in two dramatic novels, *The Octopus* (1901) and *The Pit* (1903), both the story of individual futility in the face of the heartless corporations. Norris's *McTeague* (1899) studied the disintegration of character under economic pressure. Jack London, another naturalist author, traced the power of nature over civilized society in novels such as *The Sea Wolf* (1904) and *The Call of the Wild* (1903), his classic tale of a sled dog that preferred the difficult life of the wilderness to the world of human beings.

Theodore Dreiser, the foremost naturalist writer, grimly portrayed a dark world in which human beings were tossed about by forces beyond their understanding or control. "My own ambition," Dreiser said, "is to represent my world, to conform to the large, truthful lines of life." In his great novel *Sister Carrie* (1901), he followed a young farm girl who took a job in a Chicago shoe factory. He described the exhausting nature of factory work: "Her hands began to ache at the wrists and then in the fingers, and towards the last she seemed one mass of dull, complaining muscle, fixed in an eternal position, and performing a single mechanical movement."

Like other naturalists, Dreiser focused on environment and character. He thought writers should tell the truth about human affairs, not fabricate romance, and *Sister Carrie*, he said, was "not intended as a piece of literary craftsmanship, but was a picture of conditions."

The Presidential Election of 1896

Why was the presidential election of 1896 so important?

The election of 1896 was known as the "battle of the standards" because it focused primarily on the gold and silver standards of money. As an election, it was exciting and decisive. New voting patterns replaced old, a new majority party confirmed its control of the country, and national policy shifted to suit new realities.

The Mystique of Silver

Sentiment for free silver coinage grew swiftly after 1894, dominating the South and West, appearing even in the farming regions of New York and New England. Pro-silver literature flooded the country. (See the Feature Essay, "The Wonderful Wizard of Oz," pp. 482–483.) Pamphlets issued by the millions argued silver's virtues.

People wanted quick solutions to the economic crisis. During 1896, unemployment shot up and farm income and prices fell to the lowest point in the decade. "I can remember back as far as 1858," an Iowa hardware dealer said in February 1896, "and I have never seen such hard times as these are." The silverites offered a solution, simple but compelling: the free and independent coinage of silver at the ratio of 16 ounces of silver to every ounce of gold. Free coinage meant that the U.S. mints would coin all the silver offered to them. Independent coinage meant that the country would coin silver regardless of the policies of other nations, nearly all of which were on the gold standard.

It is difficult now to understand the kind of faith the silverites placed in silver as a cure for the depression. But faith it was, and of a sort that some observers compared to religious fervor. Underlying it all was a belief in a quantity theory of money: The silverites believed the amount of money in circulation determined the level of activity in the economy. If money was short, that meant there was a limit on economic activity and ultimately a depression. If the government coined silver as well as gold, that meant more money in circulation, more business for everyone, and thus prosperity. Farm prices would rise; laborers would go back to work.

By 1896, silver was also a symbol. It had moral and patriotic dimensions—by going to a silver standard, the United States could assert its independence in the world—and it stood for a wide range of popular grievances. For many, it reflected rural values rather than urban ones, suggested a shift of power away from the Northeast, and spoke for the downtrodden instead of the well-to-do. Silver represented the common people, as the vast literature of the movement showed.

William H. Harvey's *Coin's Financial School* (1894), the most popular of all silver pamphlets, had the eloquent Coin, a wise but unknown youth, tutoring famous people on the currency. Bankers, lawyers, and scholars came to argue for gold, but they left shaken, leaning toward silver. *Coin's Financial School* sold five thousand copies a day at its peak in 1895, with tens of thousands of copies distributed free by silver organizations. It "is being sold on every railroad train by the newsboys and at every cigar store," a Mississippi congressman said. "It is being read by almost everybody."

Silver was more than just a political or economic issue. It was a social movement, one of the largest in American history, but its life span turned out to be brief. As a mass phenomenon, it flourished between 1894 and 1896, then succumbed to electoral defeat, the return of prosperity, and the onset of fresh concerns. But in its time, the silver movement bespoke a national mood and won millions of followers.

The Republicans and Gold

Sensing victory over the discredited Democrats, numerous Republicans fought for the party's presidential nomination, including "Czar" Thomas B. Reed of the Billion-Dollar Congress. Reed picked up early support but suffered from his reputation for biting wit. William McKinley of Ohio, his chief rival, soon passed him in the race for the nomination.

Able, calm, and affable, McKinley had served in the Union army during the Civil War. In 1876, he won a seat in Congress, where he became the chief sponsor of the tariff act named for him. In the months before the 1896 national convention, Marcus A. Hanna, his campaign manager and trusted friend, built a powerful national organization that featured McKinley as "the advance agent of prosperity," an alluring slogan in a country beset with depression. When the convention met in June, McKinley had the nomination in hand, and he backed a platform that favored the gold standard against the free coinage of silver.

Republicans favoring silver proposed a prosilver platform, but the convention overwhelmingly defeated it. Twenty-three silverite Republicans, far fewer than prosilver forces had hoped, marched out of the convention hall. The remaining delegates waved handkerchiefs and flags and shouted "Good-bye" and

Feature Essay | The Wonderful Wizard of Oz

A restless dreamer, Frank Baum tried his hand at several careers before he gained fame and fortune as a writer of children's literature. From 1888 to 1891, he ran a store and newspaper in South Dakota, where he experienced the desolation and grayness that accompanied agrarian discontent. An avid supporter of William Jennings Bryan in the "battle of the standards," Baum wrote what many interpret as an enduring allegory of the silver movement, *The Wonderful Wizard of Oz*. Published in April 1900, it was an immediate success.

The book opens with a grim description of Kansas, the drab environment in which Dorothy grew up:

When Dorothy stood in the doorway and looked around, she could see nothing but the great gray prairie on every side. Not a tree nor a house broke the broad sweep of flat country that reached the edge of the sky in all directions. The sun had baked the plowed land into a gray mass, with little cracks running through it. Even the grass was not green, for the sun had burned the tops of the long blades until they were the same gray color to be seen everywhere. Once the house had been painted, but the sun blistered the paint and the rains washed it away, and now the house was as dull and gray as everything else.

Kansas had not always seemed that way. After 1854, when the Kansas–Nebraska Act opened to settlement its 50 million acres of grassland, people poured into the state to stake their claims. Many came from the hilly timbered country to the east, and breaking onto the prairie, they saw "a new world, reaching to the far horizon without break of trees or chimney stack; just sky and grass and grass and sky....The hush was so loud.... The heavens seemed nearer than ever before and awe and beauty and majesty over all."

In later years, railroads crisscrossed the state, and advertisements touted the fertile soil. Land was plentiful, rainfall somehow seemed to increase each year, crop prices held at levels high enough to pay, new farming implements yielded larger crops, and property values increased.

Yet life on the prairie was never an easy matter. Flat, lonely, and windswept, the land affected people in ways that were hard to describe to the folks back East. When Aunt Em, Dorothy's aunt, came to Kansas to live, she was young and pretty, but the sun and wind soon changed her. "They had taken the sparkle from her eyes and left them a sober gray; they had taken the red from her cheeks and lips, and they were gray also." Like Aunt Em, Uncle Henry never laughed. "He worked hard from morning till night and did not know what joy was."

After 1887, the environment of the Great Plains family changed dramatically. A series of droughts struck Kansas, and as many as three out of four farms were mortgaged in some Kansas counties. Thousands of settlers like Aunt Em and Uncle Henry gave up and retraced their steps East; others trusted in the Farmers' Alliance and pinned their hopes on the free coinage of silver. While gold as a standard of currency symbolized the idle rich of the industrial Northeast, silver stood

The Wicked Witch of the West.

for the common folk. Added to the currency in the form of silver dollars, it meant more money, higher crop prices, and a return of prosperity.

Or so the supporters of silver coinage believed. In *The Wonderful Wizard of Oz*, read as an allegory, Dorothy (every person) is carried by a cyclone (a victory of the silver forces at the polls) from drought-stricken Kansas to a marvelous land of riches and witches. Unlike dry, gray Kansas, Oz is beautiful, with rippling brooks, stately trees, colorful flowers, and bright-feathered birds. On arrival, Dorothy disposes of one witch, the Wicked Witch of the East (the eastern money power and those favoring gold), and frees the Munchkins (the common people) from servitude. To return to Kansas, she must first go to the Emerald City (the greenback-colored national capital).

Dorothy wears magical silver slippers and follows the yellow brick road, thus achieving a proper relationship between the precious metals, silver and gold. Like many of her countrymen, she does not at first recognize the power of the silver slippers, but a kiss from the Good Witch of the North (Northern voters) protects her on the road. Dorothy meets the Scarecrow (the farmer), who has been told he has no brain but actually possesses great common sense (no "hick" or "hayseed," he); the Tin Woodman (the industrial worker), who fears he has become heartless but discovers the spirit of love and cooperation; and the Cowardly Lion (reformers, particularly William Jennings Bryan), who turns out not to be very cowardly at all.

When the four companions reach the Emerald City, they meet the "Great and Terrible" Wizard, who tells them that, to gain his help, they must destroy the Wicked Witch of the West (mortgage companies, heartless nature, and other things opposing progress there). Courageously, they set forth. Dorothy dissolves the witch with a bucket of water (what else for drought-ridden farmers?), but when they return to the Emerald City, they find that the great and powerful Wizard (the money power) is only a charlatan, a manipulator, whose power rests on myth and illusion. "'I thought Oz was a great Head,' said Dorothy.... 'And I thought Oz was a terrible Beast,' said the Tin Woodman. 'And I thought Oz was a Ball of Fire,' exclaimed the Lion. 'No; you are all wrong,' said the little man meekly. 'I have been making believe.'"

Dorothy unmasks the wizard, and with the help of Glinda, the Good Witch of the South (support for silver was strong in the South), uses the silver slippers to return home to Kansas. Sadly, the shoes are lost in flight. Back in Oz, the Scarecrow rules the Emerald City (the triumph of the farmers), and the Tin Woodman reigns in the West (industrialism moves West). *Oz* was a familiar abbreviation to those involved in the fight over the ratio of silver to gold—16 ounces to 1.

Baum wanted to write American fairy tales to "bear the stamp of our times and depict the progressive fairies of today." The land of Oz reflected his belief in the American values of freedom and independence, love of family, self-reliance, individualism, and sympathy for the underdog. *Oz*, he said in the original introduction, "aspires to being a modernized fairy tale, in which the wonderment and joy are retained and the heartaches and nightmares are left out."

The *Oz* stories have remained popular, and they still rest on many children's bookshelves. A 1939 film starring Judy Garland as Dorothy, with Ray Bolger as the Scarecrow, Jack Haley as the Tin Woodman, Bert Lahr as the Cowardly Lion, and Frank Morgan as the Wizard, was spectacularly successful. Released in the midst of another depression, the film included songs designed to escape hardship, as Dorothy once had, "somewhere over the rainbow."

QUESTIONS FOR DISCUSSION

1. Why was *The Wizard of Oz* so popular as a book in the 1890s and a film during the Great Depression in the 1930s?

2. How do Baum's characters symbolize the values and social forces he was trying to address?

3. If Baum were writing today, what social forces and issues might he address?

"Put them out." Hanna stood on a chair screaming "Go! Go! Go!" William Jennings Bryan, who was there as a special correspondent for a Nebraska newspaper, climbed on a desk to get a better view.

The Democrats and Silver

Silver, meanwhile, had captured large segments of the Democratic party in the South and West. Despite President Cleveland's opposition, more than twenty Democratic state platforms came out for free silver in 1894. Power in the party shifted to the South, where it remained for decades. The party's base narrowed; its outlook increasingly reflected southern views on silver, race, and other issues. In effect, the Democrats became a sectional—no longer a national—party.

> **Read the Document**   William Jennings Bryan, "Cross of Gold" Speech (1896)

William Jennings Bryan was well known for his dramatic speeches. During the Democratic Convention of 1896, Bryan delivered his best-known speech, which attacked the gold standard. His stirring rhetoric captivated his audience and won him the Democratic presidential nomination for the election of 1896.

The anti-Cleveland Democrats had their issue, but they lacked a leader. Out in Nebraska, Bryan saw the opportunity to take on that role. He was barely thirty-six years old and had relatively little political experience. But he had spent months wooing support, and he was a captivating public speaker—tall, slender, and handsome, with a resounding voice that, in an era without microphones, projected easily into every corner of an auditorium.

From the outset of the 1896 Democratic convention, the silver Democrats were in charge, and they put together a platform that stunned the Cleveland wing of the party. It demanded the free coinage of silver, attacked Cleveland's actions in the Pullman strike, and censured his sales of gold bonds. On July 9, as delegates debated the platform, Bryan's moment came. Striding to the stage, he stood for an instant, a hand raised for silence, waiting for the applause to die down. He would not contend with the previous speakers, he began, for "this is not a contest between persons. The humblest citizen in all the land, when clad in the armor of a righteous cause, is stronger than all the hosts of error. I come to speak to you in defense of a cause as holy as the cause of liberty—the cause of humanity."

The delegates were captivated. Like a trained choir, they rose, cheered each point, and sat back to listen for more. Easterners, Bryan said, liked to praise businessmen but forgot that plain people—laborers, miners, and farmers—were businessmen, too. Shouts rang through the hall, and delegates pounded on chairs. Savoring each cheer, Bryan defended silver. Then came the famous closing: "Having behind us the producing masses of this nation and the world . . . we will answer their demand for a gold standard by saying to them: 'You shall not press down upon the brow of labor this crown of thorns, you shall not crucify mankind upon a cross of gold.'"

Bryan moved his fingers down his temples, suggesting blood trickling from his wounds. He ended with his arms outstretched as on a cross. Letting the silence hang, he dropped his arms, stepped back, then started to his seat. Suddenly, there was pandemonium. Delegates shouted and cheered. When the tumult subsided, they adopted the anti-Cleveland platform, and the next day, Bryan won the presidential nomination.

Campaign and Election

The Democratic convention presented the Populists with a dilemma. The People's party had staked everything on the assumption that neither major party would endorse silver. Now it faced a painful choice: Nominate an independent ticket and risk splitting the silverite forces, or nominate Bryan and give up its separate identity as a party.

The choice was unpleasant, and it shattered the People's party. Meeting late in July, the party's national convention nominated Bryan, but rather than accept the Democratic candidate for vice president, it named Tom Watson instead. The Populists' endorsement probably hurt Bryan as much as it helped. It won him relatively few votes, since many Populists would have voted for him anyway. It also identified him as a Populist, which he was not, allowing the Republicans to accuse him of heading a ragtag army of malcontents. The squabble over Watson seemed

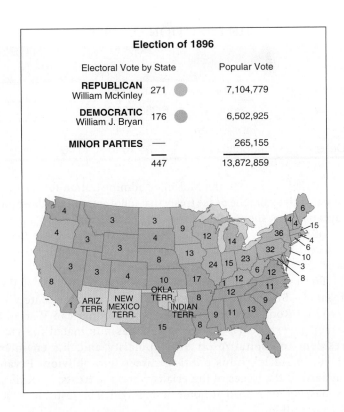

Election of 1896

	Electoral Vote by State		Popular Vote
REPUBLICAN William McKinley	271		7,104,779
DEMOCRATIC William J. Bryan	176		6,502,925
MINOR PARTIES	—		265,155
	447		13,872,859

to prove that the Democratic-Populist alliance could never stay together long enough to govern.

In August 1896, Bryan set off on a campaign that became an American legend. Much of the conservative Democratic eastern press had deserted him, and he took his campaign directly to the voters, the first presidential candidate in history to do so in a systematic way. By his own count, Bryan traveled 18,009 miles, visited 27 states, and spoke 600 times to a total of some 3 million people. He built skillfully on a new "merchandising" style of campaign in which he worked to educate and persuade voters.

Bryan summoned voters to an older America: a land where farms were as important as factories, where the virtues of rural and religious life outweighed the doubtful lure of the city, where common people still ruled and opportunity existed for all. He drew on the Jeffersonian tradition of rural virtue, distrust of central authority, and abiding faith in the powers of human reason.

Urged to take the stump against Bryan, McKinley replied, "I might just as well put up a trapeze on my front lawn and compete with some professional athlete as go out speaking against Bryan." The Republican candidate let voters come to him. Railroads brought them by the thousands into McKinley's hometown of Canton, Ohio, and he spoke to them from his front porch. Through use of the press, he reached fully as many people as Bryan's more strenuous effort. Appealing to labor, immigrants, well-to-do farmers, businessmen, and the middle class, McKinley defended economic nationalism and the advancing urban-industrial society.

On election day, voter turnout was extraordinarily high, a measure of the intense interest. By nightfall, the outcome was clear: McKinley won 50 percent of the vote to Bryan's 46 percent. He won

the Northeast and Midwest and carried four border states. In the cities, McKinley crushed Bryan.

The election struck down the Populists, whose totals sagged nearly everywhere. Many Populist proposals were later adopted under different leadership. The graduated income tax, crop loans to farmers, the secret ballot, and direct election of U.S. senators all were early Populist ideas. But the People's party never could win over a majority of the voters, and failing that, it vanished after 1896.

The McKinley Administration

What did McKinley accomplish that placed the results of the 1896 election on a solid basis?

The election of 1896 cemented the voter realignment of 1894 and initiated a generation of Republican rule. For more than three decades after 1896, with only a brief Democratic resurgence under Woodrow Wilson, the Republicans remained the country's majority party.

McKinley took office in 1897 under favorable circumstances. To everyone's relief, the economy had begun to revive. The stock market rose, factories once again churned out goods, and farmers prospered. Farm prices climbed sharply during 1897 on bumper crops of wheat, cotton, and corn. Discoveries of gold in Australia and Alaska—together with the development of a new cyanide process for extracting gold from ore—enlarged the world's gold supply, decreased its price, and inflated the currency as the silverites had hoped. For the first time since 1890, the 1897 Treasury statements showed a comfortable gold reserve.

McKinley and the Republicans basked in the glow. They became the party of progress and prosperity, an image that helped them win victories until another depression hit in the 1930s. McKinley's popularity soared. Open and accessible, in contrast to Cleveland's isolation, he rode the Washington streetcars, walked the streets, and enjoyed looking in department store windows. McKinley became the first president to ride in an automobile, reaching the speed of 18 miles an hour.

An activist president, he set the policies of the administration. Conscious of the limits of power, he maintained close ties with Congress and worked hard to educate the public on national choices and priorities. McKinley struck new relations with the press and traveled far more than previous presidents. In some ways, he began the modern presidency.

Shortly after taking office, he summoned Congress into special session to revise the tariff. In July 1897, the Dingley Tariff passed the House and Senate. It raised average tariff duties to a record level, and as the final burst of nineteenth-century protectionism, it caused trouble for the Republican party. By the end of the 1890s, consumers, critics, and the Republicans themselves were wondering if the tariff had outlived its usefulness in the maturing American economy.

From the 1860s to the 1890s, the Republicans had built their party on a pledge to *promote* economic growth through the use of state and national power. By 1900, with the industrial system

View the Closer Look   Republican Campaign Poster of 1896, William McKinley

This Republican campaign poster of 1896 depicts candidate William McKinley as the champion of commerce and civilization. The sun rising behind the flag McKinley is holding suggests that a new day will dawn with a Republican administration.

firmly in place, the focus had shifted. The need to *regulate*, to control the effects of industrialism, became a central public concern of the new century. McKinley prodded the Republicans to meet that shift, but he died before his plans matured.

McKinley toyed with the idea of lowering the tariff, but one obstacle always stood in the way: The government needed revenue, and tariff duties were one of the few taxes the public would support. The Spanish-American War of 1898 persuaded people to accept greater federal power and, with it, new forms of taxation. In 1899, McKinley spoke of lowering tariff barriers in a world that technology had made smaller. "God and man have linked the nations together," he said in his last speech at Buffalo, New York, in 1901. "Isolation is no longer possible or desirable."

THE ELECTION OF 1900

Candidate	Party	Popular Vote	Electoral Vote
McKinley	Republican	7,207,923	292
Bryan	Democrat	6,358,133	155
Woolley	Prohibition	209,004	0
Debs	Socialist	94,768	0

In 1898 and 1899, the McKinley administration focused on the war with Spain, the peace treaty that followed, and the dawning realization that the war had thrust the United States into a position of world power. In March 1900, Congress passed the **Gold Standard Act**, which declared gold the standard of currency and ended the silver controversy that had dominated the 1890s.

The presidential campaign of 1900 was a replay of the McKinley–Bryan fight of 1896. McKinley's running mate was Theodore Roosevelt, hero of the Spanish-American War and former governor of New York, who was nominated for vice president to capitalize on his popularity and, his enemies hoped, to sidetrack his political career into oblivion. Bryan emphasized the issues of imperialism and the trusts; McKinley emphasized his record at home and abroad. The result in 1900 was a landslide.

On September 6, 1901, a few months after his second inauguration, McKinley stood in a receiving line at the Pan-American Exposition in Buffalo. Leon Czolgosz, a 28-year-old unemployed laborer and anarchist, moved through the line and, reaching the president, shot him. Surgeons probed the wound but could find nothing. A recent discovery called the X ray was on display at the exposition, but it was not used. On September 14, McKinley died, and Vice President Theodore Roosevelt became president. A new century had begun.

Conclusion: A Decade's Dramatic Changes

As the funeral train carried McKinley's body back to Ohio, Mark Hanna, McKinley's old friend and ally, sat slumped in his parlor car. "I told William McKinley it was a mistake to nominate that wild man at Philadelphia," he mourned. "I asked him if he realized what would happen if he should die. Now look, that damned cowboy is president of the United States!"

Hanna's world had changed, and so had the nation's—not so much because "that damned cowboy" was suddenly president, but because events of the 1890s had had powerful effects. In the course of that decade, political patterns shifted, the presidency acquired fresh power, and massive unrest prompted social change. The war with Spain brought a new empire and worldwide responsibilities. Economic hardship posed questions of the most difficult sort about industrialization, urbanization, and the quality of American life. Worried, people embraced new ideas and causes. Reform movements begun in the 1890s flowered in the Progressive Era after 1900.

Technology continued to alter the way Americans lived. In 1896, Henry Ford produced a two-cylinder, four-horsepower car, the first of the famous line that bore his name. In 1899, the first automobile salesroom opened in New York, and some innovative thinkers were already imagining a network of service stations to keep the new cars running. At Kitty Hawk, North Carolina, Wilbur and Orville Wright, two bicycle manufacturers, neared the birth of powered flight.

The realignments that reached their peak in the 1890s seem distant, yet they are not. Important decisions in those years shaped nearly everything that came after them. In character and influence, the 1890s were as much a part of the twentieth century as of the nineteenth and continue to have repercussions into the twenty-first century.

Study Resources

 Take the **Study Plan** for **Chapter 20** *Political Realignments in the 1890s* on **MyHistoryLab**

TIME LINE

1876 Mark Twain publishes *The Adventures of Tom Sawyer*

1877 Disputed election of 1876 results in awarding of presidency to Republican Rutherford B. Hayes

1880 Republican James A. Garfield elected president

1881 Garfield assassinated; Vice President Chester A. Arthur becomes president

1884 Democrat Grover Cleveland elected president, defeating Republican James G. Blaine

1887 Cleveland calls for lowering of tariff duties

1888 Republican Benjamin Harrison wins presidential election

1889 National Farmers' Alliance and Industrial Union formed to address problems of farmers

1890 Republican-dominated "Billion-Dollar" Congress enacts McKinley Tariff Act, Sherman Antitrust Act, and Sherman Silver Purchase Act; Farmers' Alliance adopts the Ocala Demands

1892 Democrat Cleveland defeats Republican Harrison for presidency; People's party formed

1893 Financial panic touches off depression lasting until 1897; Sherman Silver Purchase Act repealed; World Columbian Exposition opens in Chicago

1894 Coxey's army marches on Washington; Pullman employees strike

1896 Republican McKinley defeats William Jennings Bryan, Democratic and Populist candidate, in "battle of the standards"

1897 Gold discovered in Alaska; Dingley Tariff Act raises tariff duties

1900 McKinley reelected, again defeating Bryan; Gold Standard Act establishes gold as standard of currency

1901 McKinley assassinated; Vice President Theodore Roosevelt assumes presidency; Naturalist writer Theodore Dreiser publishes *Sister Carrie*

CHAPTER REVIEW

Politics of Stalemate

Why was there a stalemate between Republicans and Democrats until the mid-1890s?

For more than two decades after Reconstruction, there was a stalemate, in which the Democrats and Republicans fought for votes and focused on a handful of "doubtful" states. In general, Democrats dominated the South, and Republicans controlled crucial sections of the North. Presidents reestablished the authority of their office. (p. 468)

Republicans in Power: The Billion-Dollar Congress

How did the Republican party's vision shape the "Billion-Dollar Congress"?

In control of both the presidency and Congress after 1888, Republicans enacted their activist policies, only to discover that voters were not ready for them. The congressional elections of 1890 restored the Democrats to power. (p. 470)

The Rise of the Populist Movement

What factors led to the formation and growth of the Farmers' Alliance and People's party?

In the late 1880s and early 1890s, farmers in the South and West joined the Farmers' Alliance, and later the People's party. The People's party failed, as voters turned to the Democrats in the presidential election of 1892. (p. 472)

The Crisis of the Depression

What were the main political and labor effects of the panic and depression of the 1890s?

The depression encouraged people to rethink their views on the causes of poverty and unemployment. It discredited President Cleveland and crushed the Democrats in the midterm elections of 1894, giving the Republican party a long-term lease on power. (p. 476)

Changing Attitudes

What changes in outlook did the panic and depression of the 1890s bring about?

The depression led people to reconsider the roles of the government, the economy, and society. They had once thought that people lost their jobs because of their own failings; now they knew that economic forces were at fault. People joined organizations like women's clubs, church groups, and farm societies to discuss cures for the situation. More women and children worked. Realism and naturalism dominated American literature. (p. 479)

The Presidential Election of 1896

Why was the presidential election of 1896 so important?

The election of 1896 brought to a head the fight between supporters of silver and gold, established the Republicans as the majority party, and shaped the nation's politics until 1932. (p. 481)

The McKinley Administration

What did McKinley accomplish that placed the results of the 1896 election on a solid basis?

The McKinley administration profited from economic recovery. It enacted the gold standard, passed a new tariff, and defeated Spain. How to *regulate* big business instead of simply promoting it became a new challenge. (p. 485)

KEY TERMS AND DEFINITIONS

Bland–Allison Silver Purchase Act This 1878 act called for the partial coinage of silver. Those favoring silver coinage argued that it would increase the money supply and help farmers and workers repay their debts. Opponents advocated a restricted money supply based solely on gold and pointed out that few other major countries accepted silver coinage. Congress passed the bill over President Rutherford B. Hayes's veto. p. 469

Pendleton Act This 1883 law created a bipartisan Civil Service Commission to administer competitive exams for civil service jobs and appoint officeholders based on merit. It also outlawed compulsory political contributions from appointed officials. p. 470

Sherman Antitrust Act This 1890 act was the first major U.S. attempt to deal with the problem of the increasing size of business. It declared illegal "every contract, combination in the form of trust or otherwise, or conspiracy, in restraint of trade or commerce." p. 471

Sherman Silver Purchase Act An 1890 act that attempted to resolve the controversy over silver coinage by requiring the Treasury to purchase 4.5 million ounces of silver each month and issue legal tender (in the form of Treasury notes) for it. The act pleased opponents of silver because it did not call for free coinage; it pleased proponents of silver because it bought up most of the nation's silver production. p. 471

National Farmers' Alliance and Industrial Union   The Alliance sought to organize farmers in the South and West to fight for reforms that would improve their lot, including measures to overcome low crop prices, burdensome mortgages, and high railroad rates. The Alliance ultimately organized the People's (Populist) party. p. 472

Ocala Demands   Adopted by the Farmers' Alliance in 1890 in Ocala, Florida, these demands became the organization's main platform. They called for a sub-treasury system to allow farmers to store their crops until they could get the best price, the free coinage of silver, an end to protective tariffs and national banks, a federal income tax, the direct election of senators by voters, and tighter regulation of railroads. (See **People's party**.) p. 474

People's (or Populist) party   This political party was organized in 1892 by farm, labor, and reform leaders, mainly from the Farmers' Alliance. It offered a broad-based reform platform reflecting the Ocala Demands.

After 1896, it became identified as a one-issue party focused on free silver and gradually died away. p. 474

Pullman strike   Beginning in May 1894, this strike at the Pullman Palace Car Company near Chicago was one of the largest strikes in American history. Workers struck to protest wage cuts, high rents for company housing, and layoffs. The American Railway Union, led by Eugene v. Debs, joined the strike in June. Extending into 27 states and territories, it paralyzed the western half of the nation. President Grover Cleveland secured an injunction to break the strike on the grounds that it obstructed the mail, and sent federal troops to enforce it. p. 476

Gold Standard Act   Passed by Congress in 1900, this law made all currency redeemable in gold. The United States remained on the gold standard until 1933. p. 486

CRITICAL THINKING QUESTIONS

1. What effect did the rise of the People's party have on American politics?

2. How did the depression give rise to conditions that made the election of 1896 important?

3. How would events have been different if William Jennings Bryan and the Democrats won the election of 1896?

4. Why did McKinley and the Republican party demonstrate about the changes in popular attitudes since 1890?

MyHistoryLab Media Assignments

Find these resources in the Media Assignments folder for Chapter 20 on MyHistoryLab

Politics of Stalemate

Read the **Document**   *The Interstate Commerce Act (1887) p. 469*

Republicans in Power: The Billion-Dollar Congress

Read the **Document**   *Workingman's Amalgamated Sherman Anti-Trust (1893) p. 471*

The Rise of the Populist Movement

■ **Read** the **Document**   *Proceedings of Grange Session, 1879 p. 474*

Read the **Document**   *Mary E. Lease, The Populist Crusader (1892) p. 475*

■ **Read** the **Document**   *Ocala Platform, 1890 p. 475*

The Crisis of the Depression

Read the **Document**   *Jacob S. Coxey, "Address of Protest" (1894) p. 477*

Changing Attitudes

Read the **Document**   *"Everybody Works But Father" (1905) p. 479*

The Presidential Election of 1896

■ **Complete** the **Assignment**   *The Wonderful Wizard of Oz p. 482*

■ **Read** the **Document**   *William Jennings Bryan, "Cross of Gold" Speech (1896) p. 484*

The McKinley Administration

■ **View** the **Closer Look**   *Republican Campaign Poster of 1896, William McKinley p. 486*

■ *Indicates Study Plan Media Assignment*

21 Toward Empire

Contents and Learning Objectives

((•●—[Listen to the **Audio File** on **myhistorylab**   Chapter 21 *Toward Empire*

Roosevelt and the Rough Riders

Many Americans regretted the start of the war with Spain that began in April 1898, but many others welcomed it. Many highly respected people believed that nations must fight every now and then to prove their power and test the national spirit.

Theodore Roosevelt, 39 years old in 1898, was one of them. Nations needed to fight in order to survive, he thought. For months, Roosevelt argued strenuously for war with Spain for three reasons: first, on grounds of freeing Cuba and expelling Spain from the hemisphere; second, because of "the benefit done to our people by giving them something to think of which isn't material gain"; and third, because the army and navy needed the practice.

In April 1898, Roosevelt was serving in the important post of assistant secretary of the navy. When war broke out, he quickly resigned to join the army, rejecting the advice of the secretary of the navy, who warned he would only "ride a horse and brush mosquitoes from his neck in the Florida sands." The secretary was wrong—dead wrong—and later had the grace to admit it. "Roosevelt was right," he said. "His going into the Army led straight to the Presidency."

In 1898, officers supplied their own uniforms, and Roosevelt, the son of well-to-do parents, wanted his to be stylish. He wired Brooks Brothers, the expensive New York clothier, for a "regular Lieutenant-Colonel's uniform without yellow on the collar and with leggings," to be ready in a week. Joining a friend, he chose to enlist his own regiment, and after a few telephone calls

to friends, and telegrams to the governors of Arizona, New Mexico, and Oklahoma asking for "good shots and good riders," he had more than enough men. The First United States Volunteer Cavalry, an intriguing mixture of Ivy League athletes and western frontiersmen, was born.

Known as the Rough Riders, it included men from the Harvard, Yale, and Princeton clubs of New York City, the Somerset Club of Boston, and New York's exclusive Knickerbocker Club. Former college athletes—football players, tennis players, and track stars—enlisted. Woodbury Kane, a wealthy yachtsman, signed up and promptly volunteered for kitchen duty.

Other volunteers came from the West—natural soldiers, Roosevelt called them, "tall and sinewy, with resolute, weather-beaten faces, and eyes that looked a man straight in the face without flinching." Among the cowboys, hunters, and prospectors, there were Bucky O'Neill, a legendary Arizona sheriff and Indian fighter; a half dozen other sheriffs and Texas Rangers; a large number of Indians; a famous broncobuster; and an ex-marshal of Dodge City, Kansas.

Eager for war, the men trained hard, played harder, and rarely passed up a chance for an intellectual discussion—if Roosevelt's memoir of the war is to be believed. Once, he overheard Bucky O'Neill and a Princeton graduate "discussing Aryan word-roots together, and then sliding off into a review of the novels of Balzac, and a discussion as to how far Balzac could be said to be the founder of the modern realistic school of

This lithograph depicts Lieutenant Colonel Teddy Roosevelt and his Rough Rider regiment charging up San Juan Hill on July 1, 1898. The Battle of San Juan Hill was considered the bloodiest of the war and the greatest victory by the Rough Riders.

fiction." Roosevelt himself spent his spare time reading *Superiorité des Anglo-Saxons*, a French work that strove to prove the superiority of English-speaking peoples. In such a camp, discipline was lax, and enlisted men got on easily with the officers.

The troops howled with joy when orders came to join the invasion army for Cuba. They won their first victories in Florida, fighting off other regiments to capture a train to take them to the wharf and then seizing the only available troopship to Cuba. The

Rough Riders set sail on June 14, 1898, and Lieutenant Colonel Roosevelt, who had performed a war dance for the troops the night before, caught their mood: "We knew not whither we were bound, nor what we were to do; but we believed that the nearing future held for us many chances of death and hardship, of honor and renown. If we failed, we would share the fate of all who fail; but we were sure that we would win, that we should score the first great triumph in a mighty world-movement."

That "world-movement," Roosevelt was sure, would establish the United States as a world power, whose commerce and influence would extend around the globe, particularly in Latin America and Asia. As he hoped, the nation in the 1890s underwent dramatic expansion, building on the foreign policy approaches of administrations from Lincoln to William McKinley. Policy makers fostered business interests abroad, strengthened the navy, and extended American influence into Latin America and the Pacific. Differences over Cuba resulted in a war with Spain that brought new colonies and colonial subjects, establishing for the first time an American overseas empire.

America Looks Outward

Why did Americans look outward in the last half of the nineteenth century?

The overseas expansion of the 1890s differed in several important respects from earlier expansionist moves of the United States. From its beginning, the American republic had been expanding. After the first landings in Jamestown and Plymouth, settlers pushed westward into the trans-Appalachian region, the Louisiana Territory, Florida, Texas, California, Arizona, and New Mexico. Most of these lands were contiguous with existing territories of the United States, and most were intended for settlement, usually agricultural.

The expansion of the 1890s was different. It sought to gain island possessions, the bulk of them already thickly populated. The new territories were intended less for settlement than for use as naval bases, trading outposts, or commercial centers on major trade routes. More often than not, they were viewed as colonies, not as states in the making.

Historian Samuel F. Bemis described the overseas expansion of the 1890s as "the great aberration," a time when the country adopted expansionist policies that did not fit with prior experience. Other historians, pointing to expansionist tendencies in thought and foreign policy that surfaced during the last half of the nineteenth century, have found a developing pattern that led naturally to the overseas adventures of the 1890s. In the view of Walter LaFeber, "The United States did not set out on an expansionist path in the late 1890s in a sudden, spur-of-the-moment fashion. The overseas empire that Americans controlled in 1900 was not a break in their history, but a natural culmination."

Catching the Spirit of Empire

Most people in most times in history tend to look at domestic concerns, and Americans in the years following the Civil War were no exception. Among other things, they focused on Reconstruction, the movement westward, and simply making a living. They took seriously the well-remembered advice of George Washington's farewell address to "steer clear" of foreign entanglements. Throughout the nineteenth century, Americans enjoyed "free security" without fully appreciating it. Sheltered by two oceans and the British navy, they could enunciate bold policies such as the Monroe Doctrine,

which instructed European nations to stay out of the affairs of the Western Hemisphere, while remaining virtually impregnable to foreign attack.

In those circumstances a sense of **isolationism** spread, fostering a desire to stay out of foreign entanglements. Some people even urged abolition of the foreign service, considering it an unnecessary expenditure, a dangerous profession that might lead to involvement in the struggles of the world's great powers.

In the 1870s and after, however, Americans began to take an increasing interest in events abroad. There was a growing sense of internationalism, which stemmed in part from the telegraphs, telephones, and undersea cables that kept people better informed about political and economic developments in distant lands. Many Americans continued to be interested in expansion of the country's borders; relatively few were interested in **imperialism**. Expansion meant the kind of growth that had brought California and Oregon into the American system. Imperialism meant the imposition of control over other peoples through annexation, military conquest, or economic domination.

Reasons for Expansion

Several developments in these years combined to shift attention outward across the seas. The end of the frontier, announced officially in the census report of 1890, sparked fears about diminishing opportunities at home. Further growth, it seemed to some, must take place abroad, as John A. Kasson, an able and experienced diplomat, said in the *North American Review*: "We are rapidly utilizing the whole of our continental territory. We must turn our eyes abroad, or they will soon look inward upon discontent."

Factories and farms multiplied, producing more goods than the domestic market could consume. Both farmers and industrialists looked for new overseas markets, and the growing volume of exports—including more and more manufactured goods—changed the nature of American trade relations with the world. American exports of merchandise amounted to $393 million in 1870, $858 million in 1890, and $1.4 billion in 1900. In 1898, the United States exported more than it imported, beginning a trend that lasted through the 1960s.

Political leaders such as James G. Blaine began to argue for the vital importance of foreign markets to continued economic growth. Blaine, secretary of state under Garfield and again under Harrison, aggressively sought wider markets in Latin America, Asia, and Africa, using tariff reciprocity agreements and other measures. To some extent, he and others were also caught up in a worldwide scramble for empire. In the last third of the century, Great Britain, France, and Germany divided up Africa and looked covetously at Asia. The idea of imperialistic expansion was in the air, and the great powers measured their greatness by the colonies they acquired. Inevitably, some Americans—certain business interests and foreign policy strategists, for example—caught the spirit and wanted to enter the international hunt for territory.

Intellectual currents that supported expansion drew on Charles Darwin's theories of evolution. Adherents pointed, for example, to *The Origin of Species*, which mentioned in its subtitle *The Preservation of Favoured Races in the Struggle for Life*.

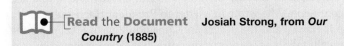**Read the Document** Josiah Strong, from *Our Country* (1885)

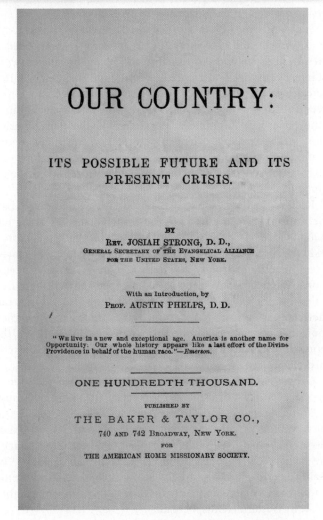

Josiah Strong (1847–1916) was a Protestant minister who advocated in his works and speeches the responsibility of the Anglo-Saxons to civilize and Christianize "inferior" races around the world. Strong's opinions influenced support among American Protestants, by the 1890s, for the development of an expansionist and imperialist foreign policy.

Applied to human and social development, biological concepts seemed to call for the triumph of the fit and the elimination of the unfit. "In this world," said Theodore Roosevelt, who thought of himself as one of the fit, "the nation that has trained itself to a career of unwarlike and isolated ease is bound, in the end, to go down before other nations which have not lost the manly and adventurous qualities."

The "biogenetic law" formulated by German biologist Ernst Haeckel suggested that the development of the race paralleled the development of the individual. Primitive peoples thus were in the arrested stages of childhood or adolescence; they needed supervision and protection. In a similar vein, John Fiske, a popular writer and lecturer, argued for Anglo-Saxon racial superiority, as a result of the process of natural selection. The English and Americans, Fiske said, would occupy every land on the globe that was not already "civilized," bringing the advances of commerce and democratic institutions.

Such views were widespread among the lettered and unlettered alike. In Cuba, one of the Rough Riders ushered a visiting Russian prince around the trenches, informing him with ill-considered enthusiasm: "You see, Prince, the great result of this war is that it has united the two branches of Anglo-Saxon people; and now that they are together they can whip the world, Prince! They can whip the world!" Eminent scholars such as John W. Burgess, a professor of political science at Columbia University, argued in similar though more dignified fashion that people of English origin were destined to impose their political institutions on the world.

The career of Josiah Strong, a Congregational minister and fervent expansionist, suggested the strength of the developing ideas. A champion of overseas missionary work, Strong traveled extensively through the West for the Home Missionary Society, and in 1885, drawing on his experiences, he published a book titled *Our Country: Its Possible Future and Its Present Crisis*. An immediate best seller, the book called on foreign missions to civilize the world under the Anglo-Saxon races. Strong became a national celebrity.

Our Country argued for expanding American trade and dominion. Trade was important, it said, because the desire for material things was one of the hallmarks of civilized people. So was the Christian religion, and by exporting both trade and religion, Americans could civilize and Christianize "inferior" races around the world. As Anglo-Saxons, they were members of a God-favored race destined to lead the world. Anglo-Saxons already owned one-third of the Earth, Strong said, and in a famous passage he concluded that they would take more. In "the final competition of races," they would win and "move down upon Mexico, down upon Central and South America, out upon the islands of the sea, over upon Africa and beyond."

Taken together, these developments in social, political, and economic thought prepared Americans for a larger role in the world. The change was gradual, and there was never a day when people awoke with a sudden realization of their interests overseas. But change there was, and by the 1890s, Americans were ready to reach out into the world in a more determined and deliberate fashion than ever before. For almost the first time, they felt the need for a foreign "policy."

Foreign Policy Approaches, 1867–1900

Rarely consistent, American foreign policy in the last half of the nineteenth century took different approaches to different areas of the world. In relation to Europe, seat of the dominant world powers, policy makers promoted trade and tried to avoid diplomatic entanglements. In North and South America, they based policy on the Monroe Doctrine, a recurrent dream of annexing Canada or Mexico, a hope for extensive trade, and Pan-American unity against the nations of the Old World. In the Pacific, they coveted Hawaii and other outposts on the sea-lanes to China.

Secretary of State William Henry Seward, who served from 1861 to 1869, aggressively pushed an expansive foreign policy.

"Give me . . . ; fifty, forty, thirty more years of life," he told a Boston audience in 1867, "and I will give you possession of the American continent and control of the world." Seward, it turned out, had only five more years of life, but he developed a vision of an American empire stretching south into Latin America and west to the shores of Asia. His vision included Canada and Mexico; islands in the Caribbean as strategic bases to protect a canal across the isthmus; and Hawaii and other islands as stepping-stones to Asia, which Seward and many others considered a virtually bottomless outlet for farm and manufactured goods.

Seward tried unsuccessfully to negotiate a commercial treaty with Hawaii in 1867, and the same year he annexed the Midway Islands, a small atoll group twelve hundred miles northwest of Hawaii. In 1867, he concluded a treaty with Russia for the purchase of Alaska (which was promptly labeled "Seward's Folly") partly to sandwich western Canada between American territory and lead to its annexation. As the American empire spread, Seward thought, Mexico City would become its capital.

Secretary of State Hamilton Fish, an urbane New Yorker, followed Seward in 1869, serving under President Ulysses S. Grant. An avid expansionist, Grant wanted to extend American influence in the Caribbean and Pacific, though the more conservative Fish often restrained him. They moved first to repair relations with Great Britain. The first business was settlement of the *Alabama* claims—demands that Britain pay the United States for damages to Union ships caused by Confederate vessels which, like the *Alabama*, had been built and outfitted in British shipyards. Negotiating patiently, Fish signed the Treaty of Washington in 1871, providing for arbitration of the *Alabama* issue and other nettlesome controversies. The treaty, one of the landmarks in the peaceful settlement of international disputes, marked a significant step in cementing Anglo-American relations.

Grant and Fish looked most eagerly to Latin America. In 1870, Grant became the first president to proclaim the nontransfer principle—"hereafter no territory on this continent shall be regarded as subject to transfer to a European power." Fish also promoted the independence of Cuba, restive under Spanish rule, while holding off the annexation desired by the more eager Grant. Influenced by speculators, Grant tried to annex Santo Domingo in 1869 but was thwarted by powerful Republicans in the Senate who disliked foreign involvement and feared a subsequent attempt to annex Haiti.

James G. Blaine served briefly as secretary of state under President James Garfield and laid extensive plans to establish closer commercial relations with Latin America. Blaine's successor, Frederick T. Frelinghuysen, changed Blaine's approach but not his strategy. Like Blaine, Frelinghuysen wanted to find Caribbean markets for American goods; he negotiated separate reciprocity treaties with Mexico, Cuba and Puerto Rico, the British West Indies, Santo Domingo, and Colombia. Using these treaties, Frelinghuysen hoped not only to obtain markets for American goods but to bind these countries to American interests.

When Blaine returned to the State Department in 1889 under President Benjamin Harrison, he moved again to expand markets in Latin America. Drawing on earlier ideas, he envisaged a hemispheric system of peaceful intercourse, arbitration of disputes, and expanded trade. He also wanted to annex Hawaii. "I think there are only three places that are of value and not already taken, that are not continental," he wrote in a letter to President Harrison in 1891. "One is Hawaii and the others are Cuba and Puerto Rico." The last two might take a generation to acquire, but "Hawaii may come up for decision at any unexpected hour and I hope we shall be prepared to decide it in the affirmative."

Harrison and Blaine toyed with naval acquisitions in the Caribbean and elsewhere, but in general they focused on Pan-Americanism and tariff reciprocity. Blaine presided over the first Inter-American Conference in Washington on October 2, 1889, where delegates from nineteen American nations negotiated several agreements to promote trade and created the International Bureau of the American Republics, later renamed the Pan-American Union, for the exchange of general information, including political, scientific, and cultural knowledge. The conference, a major step in hemispheric relations, led to later meetings promoting trade and other agreements.

Reciprocity, Harrison and Blaine hoped, would divert Latin American trade from Europe to the United States. Working hard to sell the idea in Congress, Blaine lobbied for a reciprocity provision in the McKinley Tariff Act of 1890, and once that was enacted, he negotiated reciprocity treaties with most Latin American nations. The treaties failed to foster the hoped-for trade because of the depression of the 1890s; nevertheless, they resulted in greater American exports of flour, grain, meat, iron, and machinery. Exports to Cuba jumped by one-third between 1891 and 1893, then dropped precipitously when the 1894 Wilson-Gorman Tariff Act ended reciprocity.

Grover Cleveland, Harrison's successor, also pursued an aggressive policy toward Latin America. In 1895, he brought the United States precariously close to war with Great Britain over a boundary dispute between Venezuela and British Guiana. Cleveland sympathized with Venezuela, and he and Secretary of State Richard Olney urged Britain to arbitrate the dispute. When Britain failed to act, Olney drafted a stiff diplomatic note affirming the Monroe Doctrine and denying European nations the right to meddle in Western Hemisphere affairs.

Four months passed before Lord Salisbury, the British foreign secretary, replied. Rejecting Olney's arguments, he sent two letters, the first bluntly repudiating the Monroe Doctrine as international law. The second letter, carefully reasoned and sometimes sarcastic, rejected Olney's arguments for the Venezuelan boundary. Enraged, Cleveland defended the Monroe Doctrine, and he asked Congress for authority to appoint a commission to decide the boundary and enforce its decision. "I am fully alive to the responsibility incurred and keenly realize all the consequences that may follow," he told Congress, plainly implying war.

Preoccupied with larger diplomatic problems in Africa and Europe, Britain changed its position. In November 1896, the two countries signed a treaty of arbitration, under which Great Britain and Venezuela divided the disputed territory. Though Cleveland's approach was clumsy—throughout the crisis, for example, he rarely consulted Venezuela—the Venezuelan incident demonstrated a growing determination to exert American power in the Western Hemisphere. Cleveland and Olney had persuaded Great Britain to recognize the dominance of the United States, and they had increased American influence in Latin America.

The Monroe Doctrine assumed new importance. In averting war, an era of Anglo-American friendship was begun.

The Lure of Hawaii and Samoa

The islands of Hawaii offered a tempting way station to Asian markets. In the early 1800s, they were already called the "Crossroads of the Pacific," and trading ships of many nations stopped there. In 1820, the first American missionaries arrived to convert the islanders to Christianity. Like missionaries elsewhere, they advertised Hawaii's economic and other benefits and attracted new settlers. Their children later came to dominate Hawaiian political and economic life and played an important role in annexation.

After the Civil War, the United States tightened its connections with the islands. The reciprocity treaty of 1875 allowed Hawaiian sugar to enter the United States free of duty and bound the Hawaiian monarchy to make no territorial or economic concessions to other powers. The treaty increased Hawaiian economic dependence on the United States; its political clauses effectively made Hawaii an American protectorate. In 1887, a new treaty reaffirmed these arrangements and granted the United States exclusive use of Pearl Harbor, a magnificent harbor that had early caught the eye of naval strategists.

Following the 1875 treaty, white Hawaiians became more and more influential in the islands' political life. The McKinley Tariff Act of 1890 ended the special status given Hawaiian sugar and at the same time awarded American producers a bounty of two cents a pound. Hawaiian sugar production dropped dramatically, unemployment rose, and property values fell. The following year, the weak King Kalakaua died, bringing to power a strong-willed nationalist, Queen Liliuokalani. Resentful of white minority rule, she decreed a new constitution that gave greater power to native Hawaiians.

Read the **Document**   Liliuokalani, *Hawaii's Story*

The first step toward American annexation of Hawaii came in 1893 when Queen Liliuokalani was removed from the throne. Hawaii was annexed to the United States as a possession in 1898 and became a U.S. territory in 1900.

Unhappy, the American residents revolted in early 1893 and called on the United States for help. John L. Stevens, the American minister in Honolulu, sent 150 marines ashore from the cruiser *Boston*, and within three days, the bloodless revolution was over. Queen Liliuokalani surrendered "to the superior force of the United States," and the victorious rebels set up a provisional government. Stevens urged annexation, telling Washington that the "Hawaiian pear is now fully ripe, and this is the golden hour for the United States to pluck it." On February 14, 1893, Harrison's secretary of state, John W. Foster, and delegates of the new government signed a treaty annexing Hawaii to the United States.

But only two weeks remained in Harrison's term, and the Senate refused to ratify the agreement. Five days after taking office, Cleveland withdrew the treaty; he then sent a representative to investigate the cause of the rebellion. The investigation revealed that the Americans' role in it had been improper, and Cleveland

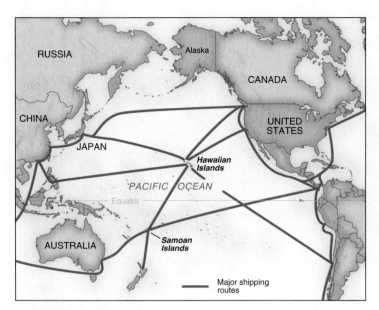

HAWAIIAN ISLANDS The Hawaiian Islands provided the United States with both a convenient stopping point on the way to Asian markets and a strategic naval station in the Pacific.

decided to restore the queen to her throne. He made the demand, but the provisional government in Hawaii politely refused and instead established the Republic of Hawaii, which the embarrassed Cleveland, unable to do otherwise, recognized.

The debate over Hawaiian annexation, continuing through the 1890s, foreshadowed the later debate over the treaty to end the Spanish-American War. People in favor of annexation pointed to Hawaii's strategic location, argued that Japan or other powers might seize the islands if the United States did not, and suggested that Americans had a responsibility to civilize and Christianize the native Hawaiians. Opponents warned that annexation might lead to a colonial army and colonial problems, the inclusion of a "mongrel" population in the United States, and rule over an area not destined for statehood.

Annexation came swiftly in July 1898 in the midst of excitement over victories in the Spanish-American War. The year before, President William McKinley had sent a treaty of annexation to the Senate, but opposition quickly arose, and the treaty stalled. Japan protested against it, pointing out that Japanese made up a quarter of the Hawaiian population. Japan dispatched a cruiser to Honolulu; the Navy Department sent the battleship *Oregon* and ordered naval forces to take Hawaii if the Japanese made threatening moves.

In 1898, annexationists redoubled arguments about Hawaii's commercial and military importance. McKinley and congressional leaders switched strategies to seek a joint resolution, rather than a treaty, for annexation. A joint resolution required only a majority of both houses, while a treaty needed a two-thirds vote in the Senate. Bolstered by the new strategy, the annexation measure moved quickly through Congress, and McKinley signed it on July 7, 1898. His signature, giving the United States a naval and commercial base in the mid-Pacific, realized a goal held by policy makers since the 1860s.

While annexation of Hawaii represented a step toward China, the Samoan Islands, three thousand miles to the south, offered a strategic location astride the sea-lanes of the South Pacific. Americans showed early interest in Samoa, and in 1872, a naval officer negotiated a treaty granting the United States the use of Pago Pago, a splendid harbor on one of its islands. The Senate rejected the treaty but six years later approved a similar agreement providing for a naval station there. The agreement bound the United States to use its good offices to adjust any disputes between the Samoan chiefs and foreign governments. Great Britain and Germany also secured treaty rights in Samoa, and thereafter the three nations jockeyed for position.

The situation grew tense in 1889, when warships from all three countries gathered in a Samoan harbor. But a sudden typhoon damaged the fleets, and tensions eased. A month later, delegates from Britain, Germany, and the United States met in Berlin to negotiate the problem. Britain and Germany wanted to divide up the islands; Secretary of State Blaine held out for some degree of authority by the indigenous population, with American control over Pago Pago.

The agreement, an uneasy one, ended in 1899 when the United States and Germany divided Samoa and compensated Britain with lands elsewhere in the Pacific. Germany claimed the two larger islands in the chain; the United States kept the harbor at Pago Pago.

The New Navy

Large navies were vital in the scramble for colonies, and in the 1870s the United States had almost no naval power. One of the most powerful fleets in the world during the Civil War, the American navy had fallen into rapid decline. By 1880, there were fewer than two thousand vessels, only forty-eight of which could fire a gun. Ships rotted, and many officers left the service.

Conditions changed during the 1880s. A group of rising young officers, steeped in a new naval philosophy, argued for an expanded navy equipped with fast, aggressive fleets capable of fighting battles across the seas. This group had its greatest influence in a special Naval Advisory Board, formed by the secretary of the navy in 1881. Big-navy proponents pointed to the growing fleets of Great Britain, France, and Germany, arguing that the United States needed greater fleet strength to protect its economic and other interests in the Caribbean and Pacific.

In 1883, Congress authorized construction of four steel ships, marking the beginning of the new navy. Experts also worked to improve naval management and the quality of fleet personnel, and between 1885 and 1889, Congress budgeted funds for thirty additional ships. The initial building program focused on lightly armored fast cruisers for raiding enemy merchant ships and protecting American shores, but after 1890, the program shifted to the construction of a seagoing offensive battleship navy capable of challenging the strongest fleets of Europe.

Alfred Thayer Mahan and Benjamin F. Tracy were two of the main forces behind the new navy. Austere and scholarly, Mahan was the era's most influential naval strategist. After graduating from the Naval Academy in 1859, he devoted a lifetime to studying the influence of sea power in history; for more than two decades, he headed the Newport Naval War College, where officers imbibed the latest in strategic thinking. A clear, logical writer, Mahan summarized his beliefs in several major books, including *The Influence of Sea Power upon History, 1660–1783* (1890), and *The Interest of America in Sea Power* (1897).

Mahan's reasoning was simple and, to that generation, persuasive. Industrialism, he argued, produced vast surpluses of agricultural and manufactured goods, for which markets must be found. Markets involved distant ports; reaching them required a large merchant marine and a powerful navy to protect it. Navies, in turn, needed coaling stations and repair yards. Coaling stations meant colonies, and colonies became strategic

bases, the foundation of a nation's wealth and power. The bases might serve as markets themselves, but they were more important as stepping-stones to other objectives, such as the markets of Latin America and Asia.

Mahan called attention to the worldwide race for power, a race, he warned, the United States could not afford to lose. "All around us now is strife; 'the struggle of life,' 'the race of life' are phrases so familiar that we do not feel their significance till we stop to think about them. Everywhere nation is arrayed against nation; our own no less than others." To compete in the struggle, Mahan argued, the United States must expand. It needed strategic bases, a powerful oceangoing navy, a canal across the isthmus to link the East Coast with the Pacific, and Hawaii as a way station on the route to Asia.

Mahan influenced a generation of policy makers in the United States and Europe; one of them, Benjamin F. Tracy, became Harrison's secretary of the navy in 1889. Tracy organized the Bureau of Construction and Repair to design and build new ships, established the naval reserve in 1891, and ordered construction of the first American submarine in 1893. He also adopted the first heavy rapid-fire guns, smokeless powder, torpedoes, and heavy armor. Above all, Tracy joined with big-navy advocates in Congress to push for a far-ranging battleship fleet capable of attacking distant enemies. He wanted two fleets of battle ships, eight ships in the Pacific and twelve in the Atlantic. He got four first-class battleships.

In 1889, when Tracy entered office, the United States ranked twelfth among world navies; in 1893, when he left, it ranked seventh and was climbing rapidly. "The sea," he predicted in 1891, "will be the future seat of empires. And we shall rule it as certainly as the sun doth rise." By the end of the decade, the navy had seventeen steel battleships, six armored cruisers, and many smaller craft. It ranked third in the world.

War with Spain

What were the causes and results of the war with Spain?

The war with Spain in 1898 built a mood of national confidence; altered older, more insular patterns of thought; and reshaped the way Americans saw themselves and the world. Its outcome pleased some people but troubled others who raised questions about war itself, colonies, and subject peoples. The war left a lingering strain of isolationism and antiwar feeling that affected later policy. It also left an American empire, small by European standards, but quite new to the American experience by virtue of its overseas location. When the war ended, American possessions stretched into the Caribbean and deep into the Pacific. American influence went further still, and the United States was recognized as a "world power."

The Spanish-American War established the United States as a dominant force for the twentieth century. It brought America colonies and millions of colonial subjects; it brought the responsibilities of governing an empire and protecting it. For better

Read the **Document**   Alfred Thayer Mahan, *The Interest of America in Sea Power*

This 1881 cartoon depicted "our top heavy navy," a decrepit vessel sinking with idle officers.

or worse, it involved the country in other nations' arguments and affairs. The war strengthened the office of the presidency, swept the nation together in a tide of emotion, and confirmed the long-standing belief in the superiority of the New World over the Old. When it was over, Americans looked outward as never before, touched, they were sure, with a special destiny.

A War for Principle

By the 1890s, Cuba and the nearby island of Puerto Rico comprised nearly all that remained of Spain's once vast empire in the New World. Several times, Cuban insurgents had rebelled against Spanish rule, including a decade-long rebellion from 1868 to 1878 (the Ten Years' War) that failed to settle the conflict. The depression of 1893 damaged the Cuban economy, and the Wilson-Gorman Tariff of 1894 prostrated it. Duties on sugar, Cuba's lifeblood, were raised 40 percent. With the island's sugar market in ruins, discontent with Spanish rule heightened, and in late February 1895, revolt again broke out.

Recognizing the importance of the nearby United States, Cuban insurgents established a junta in New York City to raise money, buy weapons, and wage a propaganda war to sway American public opinion. Conditions in Cuba were grim. The insurgents pursued a hit-and-run scorched-earth policy to force the Spanish to leave. Spain committed more than two hundred thousand soldiers; the Spanish commander, who had won with similar tactics in 1878, tried to pin the insurgents in the eastern part of the island where they could be cornered and destroyed.

When this strategy failed, Spain, in January 1896, sent a new commander, General Valeriano Weyler y Nicolau. Relentless and brutal, Weyler gave the rebels ten days to lay down their arms. He then put into effect a "reconcentration" policy designed to move the native population into camps and destroy the rebellion's popular base. Herded into fortified areas, Cubans died by the thousands, victims of unsanitary conditions, overcrowding, and disease.

Stories in American newspapers spurred a wave of sympathy for the insurgents. Two brash newspaper publishers in New York City, William Randolph Hearst of the *New York Journal*, and Joseph Pulitzer of the *New York World*, hoped to use the situation in Cuba to increase sales of their newspapers. To do so they published accounts of lurid Spanish atrocities, rebel victories, and of innocent Cuban women harassed by Spanish troops. Because of the yellow color of the comic strips in both papers, the tactic became known as **yellow journalism**, and some blamed it for causing the war.

In actual fact, it did not. The conflict stemmed from larger disputes in policies and perceptions between Spain and the United States. Grover Cleveland, under whose administration the rebellion began, preferred Spanish rule to the kind of turmoil that might invite foreign intervention. Opposed to the annexation of Cuba, he issued a proclamation of neutrality and tried to restrain public opinion. In 1896, Congress passed a resolution favoring recognition of Cuban belligerence, but Cleveland ignored it. Instead, he offered to mediate the struggle, an offer Spain declined.

Taking office in March 1897, President McKinley also urged neutrality but leaned slightly toward the insurgents. He immediately sent a trusted aide on a fact-finding mission to Cuba; the aide reported in mid-1897 that Weyler's policy had wrapped Cuba "in the stillness of death and the silence of desolation." The report in hand, McKinley offered to mediate the struggle, but, concerned over the suffering, he protested against Spain's "uncivilized and inhuman" conduct. The United States, he made clear, did not contest Spain's right to fight the rebellion but insisted it be done within humane limits.

Late in 1897, a change in government in Madrid brought a temporary lull in the crisis. The new government recalled Weyler and agreed to offer the Cubans some form of autonomy. It also declared an amnesty for political prisoners and released Americans from Cuban jails. The new initiatives pleased McKinley, though he again warned Spain that it must find a humane end to the rebellion. Then, in January 1898, Spanish army officers led riots in Havana against the new autonomy policy, shaking the president's confidence in Madrid's control over conditions in Cuba.

McKinley ordered the battleship *Maine* to Havana to demonstrate strength and protect American citizens if necessary. On February 9, 1898, the *New York Journal*, a leader of the yellow press, published a letter stolen from Enrique Dupuy de Lôme, the Spanish ambassador in Washington. In the letter, which was private correspondence to a friend, de Lôme called McKinley "weak," "a would-be politician," and "a bidder for the admiration of the crowd." Many Americans were angered by the insult; McKinley himself was more worried about other sections of the letter that revealed Spanish insincerity in the negotiations. De Lôme immediately resigned and went home, but the damage was done.

A few days later, at 9:40 in the evening of February 15, an explosion tore through the hull of the *Maine*, riding at anchor in Havana harbor. The ship, a trim symbol of the new steel navy, sank quickly; 266 lives were lost. McKinley cautioned patience and promised an immediate investigation. Crowds gathered quietly on Capitol Hill and outside the White House, mourning the lost men. Soon there was a new slogan: "Remember the *Maine* and to Hell with Spain!"

The most recent study of the *Maine* incident blames the sinking on an accidental internal explosion, caused perhaps by spontaneous combustion in poorly ventilated coal bunkers. In 1898, Americans blamed it on Spain. Spaniards were hanged in effigy in many communities. Roosevelt, William Jennings Bryan, and others urged war, but McKinley delayed, hopeful that Spain might yet agree to an armistice and perhaps Cuban independence. In early March 1898, wanting to be ready for war if it came, McKinley asked Congress for $50 million in emergency defense appropriations, a request Congress promptly approved. The unanimous vote stunned Spain; allowing the president a latitude that was highly unusual for the era, it appropriated the money "for the National defense and for each and every purpose connected therewith to be expended at the discretion of the President." In late March, the report of the investigating board blamed the sinking of the *Maine* on an external (and thus presumably Spanish) explosion. Pressures for war increased.

On March 27, McKinley cabled Spain his final terms. He asked Spain to declare an armistice, end the reconcentration

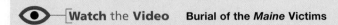

This photo of the burial procession of victims of the *Maine* was taken at Key West, FL, on March 27, 1898. Two hundred sixty-six sailors and marines were killed in the explosion in Havana harbor.

policy, and—implicitly—move toward Cuban independence. When the Spanish answer came, it conceded some things, but not, in McKinley's judgment, the important ones. Spain offered a suspension of hostilities (but not an armistice) and left the Spanish commander in Cuba to set the length and terms of the suspension. It also revoked the reconcentration policy. But the Spanish response made no mention of a true armistice, McKinley's offer to mediate, or Cuba's independence.

Reluctantly McKinley prepared his war message. Congress heard it on April 11, 1898. On April 19, Congress passed a joint resolution declaring Cuba independent and authorizing the president to use the army and navy to expel the Spanish from it. The **Teller Amendment**, offered by Colorado senator Henry M. Teller, pledged that the United States had no intention of annexing the island.

On April 21, Spain severed diplomatic relations. The following day, McKinley proclaimed a blockade of Cuba and called for 125,000 volunteers. On Monday, April 25, Congress passed a declaration of war. Late that afternoon, McKinley signed it.

Some historians have suggested that in leading the country toward war, McKinley was weak and indecisive, a victim of war hysteria in the Congress and the country; others have called him a wily manipulator for war and imperial gains. In truth, he was neither. Throughout the Spanish crisis, McKinley pursued a moderate middle course that sought to end the suffering in Cuba, promote Cuba's independence, and allow Spain time to adjust to the loss of the remnant of empire. He also wanted peace, as did Spain, but in the end, the conflicting national interests of the two countries brought them to war.

"A Splendid Little War"

Ten weeks after the declaration of war, the fighting was over. For Americans, they were ten glorious, dizzying weeks, with victories to fill every headline and slogans to suit every taste. No war can be a happy occasion for those who fight it, but the Spanish-American War came closer than most. Declared in April, it ended in August. Relatively few Americans died, and the quick victory seemed to verify burgeoning American power, though Sherwood Anderson, the author, suggested that fighting a weakened Spain was "like robbing an old gypsy woman in a vacant lot at night after a fair." John Hay, soon to be McKinley's secretary of state, called it "a splendid little war."

At the outset, the United States was militarily unprepared. Unlike the navy, the army had not been rebuilt or modernized, and it had shrunk drastically since the day thirty-three years before when Grant's great Civil War army marched sixty abreast, two hundred thousand strong, down Washington's Pennsylvania Avenue. In 1898, the regular army consisted of only twenty-eight thousand officers and men, most of them more experienced in quelling Indian uprisings than fighting large-scale battles.

When McKinley called for 125,000 volunteers, as many as one million young Americans responded. Ohio alone had 100,000 volunteers. Keeping the regular army units intact, War Department officials enlisted the volunteers in National Guard units that were then integrated into the national army. Men clamored to join. The secretary of war feared "there is going to be more trouble to satisfy those who are not going than to find those who are willing to go."

In an army inundated with men, problems of equipment and supply quickly appeared. The regulars had the new .30-caliber Krag-Jorgensen rifles, but National Guard units carried Civil War Springfield rifles that used old black-powder cartridges. The cartridges gave off a puff of smoke when fired, neatly marking the troops' position. Spanish troops were better equipped; they had modern Mausers with smokeless powder, which they used to devastating effect. Food was also a problem, as was sickness. The War Department fell behind in supplies and received many complaints about the canned beef it offered the men. Tropical disease felled many soldiers. Scores took ill after landing in Cuba and the Philippines, and it was not uncommon for half a regiment to be unable to answer the bugle call.

Americans then believed that "a foreign war should be fought by the hometown military unit acting as an extension of their community." Soldiers identified with their hometowns, dressed in the local fashion, and thought of themselves as members of a town unit in a national army. The poet Carl Sandburg, twenty years old in 1898, rushed to join the army and called his unit a "living part" of his hometown of Galesburg, Illinois. And the citizens of Galesburg, for their part, took a special interest in Sandburg's unit, in a fashion repeated in countless towns across the country.

Not surprisingly, then, National Guard units mirrored the social patterns of their communities. Since everyone knew each other, there was an easygoing familiarity, tempered by the deference

Charge of the 24th and 25th Colored Infantry and Rescue of the Rough Riders at San Juan Hill, July 2, 1898, colored lithograph by Kurz and Allison, 1899 (above). The Twenty-fourth and Twenty-fifth Colored Infantry regiments served with exceptional gallantry in the Spanish-American War. Charles Young (right), an 1889 graduate of West Point, was the only African American officer in the army during the Spanish-American War except for a few chaplains.

Q │View the Map   The Spanish-American War

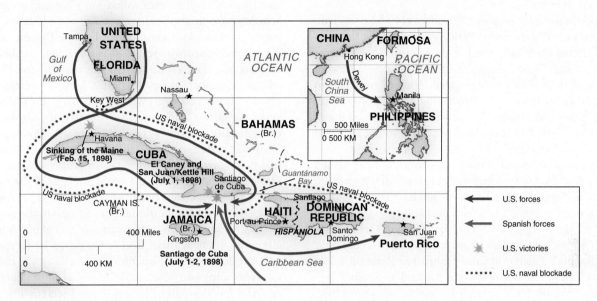

Disputes regarding Cuba and the sinking of the battleship *U.S.S. Maine* prompted the United States to declare war on Spain in 1898. The two nations dueled over another Spanish possession, the Philippines. The Treaty Of Paris of 1898 that ended the war granted Cuba its independence (although it remained an American protectorate until 1934) and established U.S. control over Puerto Rico, Guam, and the Philippines.

that went with hometown wealth, occupation, education, and length of residence. Enlisted men resented officers who grabbed too much authority, and they expected officers and men to call each other by their first names. Sandburg knew most of the privates in his unit, had worked for his corporal, and had gone to school with the first lieutenant. "Officers and men of the Guard mingle on a plane of beautiful equality," said a visitor to one volunteer camp. "Privates invade the tents of their officers at will, and yell at them half the length of the street."

Each community thought of the hometown unit as its own unit, an extension of itself. In later wars, the government censored news and dominated press relations; there was little censorship in the war with Spain, and the freshest news arrived in the latest letter home. Small-town newspapers printed news of the men, and townswomen knit special red or white bellybands of stitched flannel, thought to ward off tropical fevers. Towns sent food, clothing, and occasionally even local doctors to the front. At the close of the war, the Clyde (Ohio) Ladies Society collected funds to provide each member of the town's company a medal struck on behalf of the town.

"Smoked Yankees"

When the invasion force sailed for Cuba, nearly one-fourth of it was African American. In 1898, the regular army included four regiments of African American soldiers, the Twenty-fourth and

Twenty-fifth Infantry and the Ninth and Tenth Cavalry. Black regiments had served with distinction in campaigns against the Indians in the West. Most African American troops in fact were posted in the West; no eastern community would accept them. A troop of the Ninth Cavalry was stationed in Virginia in 1891, but whites protested and the troop was ordered back to the West.

When the war broke out, the War Department called for five black volunteer regiments. The army needed men, and military authorities were sure that black men had a natural immunity to the climate and diseases of the tropics. But most state governors refused to accept black volunteers. Only Alabama, Ohio, and Massachusetts mustered in black units in response to McKinley's first call for volunteers. Company L of the Sixth Massachusetts Regiment took part in the invasion of Puerto Rico in July 1898, the only one of the black volunteer units to see action in the Caribbean. African American leaders, among them P. B. S. Pinchback, former acting governor of Louisiana, and George White of North Carolina, the lone African American member of Congress, protested the discrimination. The McKinley administration intervened, and in the end, the volunteer army included more than ten thousand black troops.

Orders quickly went out to the four black regular army regiments in the West to move to camps in the South to prepare for the invasion of Cuba. Crowds and cheers followed the troop trains across the plains, but as they crossed into Kentucky and Tennessee, the cheering stopped. Welcoming crowds were kept away from the trains, and the troops were hustled onward. Station restaurants refused to serve them; all waiting rooms were segregated. "It mattered not if we were soldiers of the United States, and going to fight for the honor of our country," Sergeant Frank W. Pullen of the Twenty-fourth Infantry wrote; "we were 'niggers' as they called us and treated us with contempt."

Many soldiers were not prepared to put up with the treatment. Those stationed near Chickamauga Park, Tennessee, shot "at some whites who insulted them" and forcibly desegregated the railroad cars on the line into Chattanooga. Troops training near Macon, Georgia, refused to ride in the segregated "trailers" attached to the trolleys, and fights broke out. Discovering a Macon park with a sign saying "Dogs and niggers not allowed," they invaded it and removed the sign. They also chopped down a tree in the park that had been used for lynchings.

More than four thousand black troops training near Tampa and Lakeland, Florida, found segregated saloons, cafes, and drugstores. "Here the Negro is not allowed to purchase over the same counter in some stores as the white man purchases over," Chaplain George W. Prioleau charged. "Why sir, the Negro of this country is a freeman and yet a slave. Talk about fighting and freeing poor Cuba and of Spain's brutality; of Cuba's murdered thousands, and starving reconcentradoes. Is America any better than Spain?"

When the invasion force sailed a few days later, segregation continued on some of the troopships. Blacks were assigned to the lowest decks, or whites and blacks were placed on different sides of the ship. But the confusion of war often ended the problem, if only temporarily. Blacks took command as white officers died, and Spanish troops soon came to fear the "smoked Yankees," as they called them. Black soldiers played a major role in the Cuban campaign and probably staved off defeat for the Rough Riders at San Juan Hill. In Cuba, they won twenty-six Certificates of Merit and five Congressional Medals of Honor.

The Course of the War

Mahan's Naval War College had begun studying strategy for a war with Spain in 1895. By 1898, it had a detailed plan for operations in the Caribbean and Pacific. Naval strategy was simple: Destroy the Spanish fleet, damage Spain's merchant marine, and harry the colonies or the coast of Spain. Planners were excited; two steam-powered armored fleets had yet to meet in battle anywhere in the world. The army's task was more difficult. It had to defend the United States, invade Cuba and probably Puerto Rico, and undertake possible action in far-flung places such as the Philippines or Spain.

Even before war was declared, the secretary of war arranged joint planning between the army and navy. Military intelligence was plentiful, and planners knew the numbers and locations of the Spanish troops. Earlier they had rejected a proposal to send an officer in disguise to map Cuban harbors; such things, they said, were simply not done in peacetime. Still, the War Department's new Military Information Division, a sign of the increasing professionalization of the army, had detailed diagrams of Spanish fortifications in Havana and other points. On the afternoon of April 20, 1898, McKinley summoned the strategists to the White House; to the dismay of those who wanted a more aggressive policy, they decided on the limited strategy of blockading Cuba, sending arms to the insurgents, and annoying the Spanish with small thrusts by the army.

Victories soon changed the strategy. In case of war, long-standing naval plans had called for a holding action against the Spanish base in the Philippines. On May 1, 1898, with the war barely a week old, Commodore George Dewey, commander of the Asiatic Squadron located at Hong Kong, crushed the Spanish fleet in Manila Bay. Suddenly, Manila and the Philippines lay within American grasp. At home, Dewey portraits, songs, and poems blossomed everywhere, and his calm order to the flagship's captain—"You may fire when ready, Gridley"—hung on every tongue. Dewey had two modern cruisers, a gunboat, and a Civil War paddle steamer. He sank eight Spanish warships. Dewey had no troops to attack the Spanish army in Manila, but the War Department, stunned by the speed and size of the victory, quickly raised an expeditionary force. On August 13, 1898, the troops accepted the surrender of Manila, and with it, the Philippines.

McKinley and his aides were worried about Admiral Pascual Cervera's main Spanish fleet, thought to be headed across the Atlantic for an attack on Florida. On May 13, the navy found Cervera's ships near Martinique in the Caribbean but then lost them again. A few days later, Cervera slipped secretly into the harbor of Santiago de Cuba, a city on the island's southern coast. But a spy in the Havana telegraph office alerted the Americans, and on May 28, a superior American force under Admiral William T. Sampson bottled Cervera up.

In early June, a small force of Marines seized Guantánamo Bay, the great harbor on the south of the island. They established depots for the navy to refuel and pinned down Spanish troops in the area. On June 14, an invasion force of about seventeen thousand men set sail from Tampa. Seven days later, they landed at Daiquiri on Cuba's southeastern coast. All was confusion, but the Spanish offered no resistance. Helped by Cuban insurgents, the Americans immediately pushed west toward Santiago, which they hoped to surround and capture. At first, the advance through the lush tropical countryside was peaceful.

The first battle broke out at Las Guasimas, a crossroads on the Santiago road. After a sharp fight, the Spanish fell back. On July 1, the Rough Riders, troops from the four black regiments, and the other regulars reached the strong fortifications at El Caney and San Juan Hill. Black soldiers of the Twenty-fifth Infantry charged the El Caney blockhouses, surprising the Spanish defenders with Comanche yells. For the better part of a day, the defenders fought stubbornly and held back the army's elite corps. In the confusion of battle, Roosevelt rallied an assortment of infantry and cavalry to take Kettle Hill, adjacent to San Juan Hill.

They charged directly into the Spanish guns, Roosevelt at their head, mounted on a horse, a blue polka-dot handkerchief floating from the brim of his sombrero. "I waved my hat and we went up the hill with a rush," he recalled in his autobiography. Actually, it was not quite so easy. Losses were heavy; eighty-nine Rough Riders were killed or wounded in the attack. Dense foliage concealed the enemy and smokeless powder gave no clue to their position. At nightfall, the surviving Spanish defenders withdrew, and the Americans prepared for the counterattack.

American troops now occupied the ridges overlooking Santiago. They were weakened by sickness, a fact unknown to the Spanish, who decided the city was lost. The Spanish command in Havana ordered Cervera to run for the open sea, although he knew the attempt to escape was hopeless. On the morning of July 3, Cervera's squadron steamed down the bay and out through the harbor's narrow channel, but the waiting American fleet closed in, and in a few hours every Spanish vessel was destroyed. Two weeks later, Santiago surrendered.

Soon thereafter, army troops, meeting little resistance, occupied Puerto Rico. Cervera had commanded Spain's only battle fleet, and when it sank, Spain was helpless against attacks on the colonies or even its own shores. The war was over. Lasting 113 days, it took relatively few lives, most of them the result of accident, yellow fever, malaria, and typhoid in Cuba. Of the 5,500 Americans who died in the war, only 379 were killed in battle. The navy lost one man in the battle at Santiago Bay, and only one to heatstroke in the stunning victory in Manila Bay.

Acquisition of Empire

What were the various viewpoints about the acquisition of empire after the war with Spain?

Late in the afternoon of August 12, 1898, representatives of Spain and the United States met in McKinley's White House office to sign the preliminary instrument of peace. Secretary of State William R. Day beckoned a presidential aide over to a large globe, remarking, "Let's see what we get by this."

View the Closer Look   **American Empire**

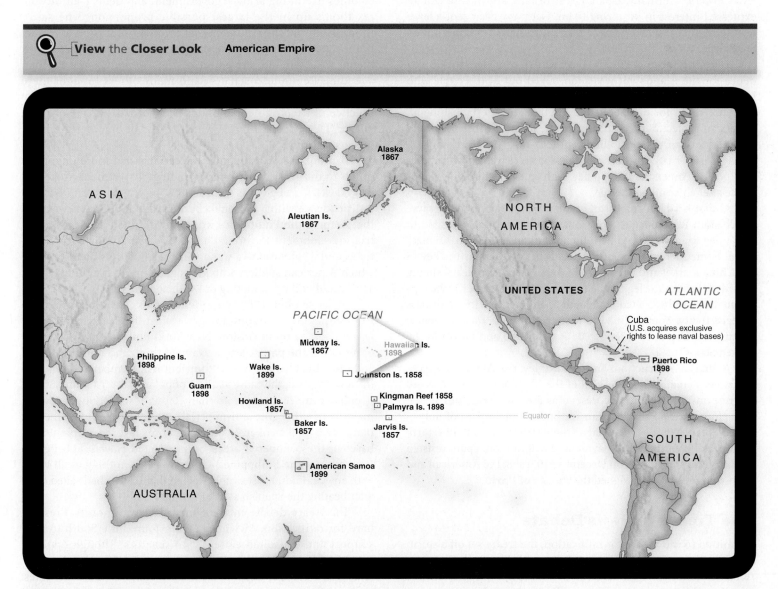

AMERICAN EMPIRE, 1900   With the Treaty of Paris, the United States gained an expanded colonial empire stretching from the Caribbean to the far Pacific. It embraced Puerto Rico, Alaska, Hawaii, part of Samoa, Guam, the Philippines, and a chain of Pacific islands. The dates on the map refer to the date of U.S. acquisition.

What the United States got was an expansion of its territory and an even larger expansion of its responsibilities. According to the preliminary agreement, Spain granted independence to Cuba, ceded Puerto Rico and the Pacific island of Guam to the United States, and allowed Americans to occupy Manila until the two countries reached final agreement on the Philippines. To McKinley, the Philippines were the problem. Puerto Rico was close to the mainland, and it appealed even to many of the opponents of expansion. Guam was small and unknown; it escaped attention. The Philippines, on the other hand, were huge, sprawling, and thousands of miles from America.

McKinley weighed a number of alternatives for the Philippines, but he liked none of them. He believed he could not give the islands back to Spain; public opinion would not allow it. He might turn them over to another nation, but then they would fall, as he later said, "a golden apple of discord, among the rival powers." Germany, Japan, Great Britain, and Russia had all expressed interest in acquiring them. Germany even sent a large fleet to Manila and laid plans to take the Philippines if the United States let them go.

Rejecting those alternatives, McKinley considered independence for the islands but was soon talked out of it. People who had been there, reflecting the era's racism, told him the Filipinos were not ready for independence. He thought of establishing an American protectorate but discarded the idea, convinced it would bring American responsibilities without full American control. Sifting the alternatives, McKinley decided there was only one practical policy: Annex the Philippines, with an eye to future independence after a period of tutelage.

At first hesitant, American opinion was swinging to the same conclusion. Religious and missionary organizations appealed to McKinley to hold on to the Philippines in order to "Christianize" them. Some merchants and industrialists saw them as the key to the China market and the wealth of Asia. Many Americans simply regarded them as the legitimate fruits of war. In October 1898, representatives of the United States and Spain met in Paris to discuss a peace treaty. Spain agreed to recognize Cuba's independence, assume the Cuban debt, and cede Puerto Rico and Guam to the United States.

Acting on instructions from McKinley, the American representatives demanded the cession of the Philippines. "Grave as are the responsibilities and unforeseen as are the difficulties which are before us, the President can see but one plain path of duty—the acceptance of the archipelago," the instructions said. In return, the United States offered a payment of $20 million. Spain resisted but had little choice, and on December 10, 1898, the American and Spanish representatives signed the **Treaty of Paris**.

The Treaty of Paris Debate

Submitted to the Senate for ratification, the treaty set off a storm of debate throughout the country. Industrialist Andrew Carnegie, reformer Jane Addams, labor leader Samuel Gompers, prominent Republicans such as Thomas B. Reed and John Sherman, Mark Twain, William Dean Howells, and a host of others argued forcefully against annexing the Philippines. Annexation of the Philippines, the anti-imperialists protested over and over again,

violated the very principles of independence and self-determination on which the United States was founded.

Some labor leaders feared the importation of cheap labor from new Pacific colonies. Gompers warned about the "half-breeds and semi-barbaric people" who might undercut wages and the union movement. Other anti-imperialists argued against assimilation of different races, "Spanish-Americans," as one said, "with all the mixture of Indian and negro blood, and Malays and other unspeakable Asiatics, by the tens of millions!" Such racial views were also common among those favoring expansion, and the anti-imperialists usually focused on different arguments. If the United States established a tyranny abroad, they were sure, there would soon be tyranny at home. "This nation," declared William Jennings Bryan, "cannot endure half republic and half colony—half free and half vassal."

Charles Francis Adams, Jr., warned that the possession of colonies meant big armies, government, and debts ("an income tax looms up in the largest possible proportions," he said). Bryan scoffed at the argument that colonies were good for trade, pointing out, "It is not necessary to own people to trade with them." E. L. Godkin, the editor of *The Nation*; George F. Hoar, a leading Republican senator; and many others thought there was no way to reconcile the country's republican ideals with the practice of keeping people under heel abroad. As one of them put it, "Dewey took Manila with the loss of one man—and all our institutions."

To Booker T. Washington, the country had more important things to think about at home, including its treatment of Indians and blacks. Carnegie was so upset that he offered to buy Filipino independence with a personal check for $20 million. He was sure that keeping the Philippines would divert attention from industrial development to foreign adventure, would glorify physical force, and would lead to a war against the Filipinos themselves, in which American soldiers who had signed up "to fight the oppressor" would end up "shooting down the oppressed."

In November 1898, opponents of expansion formed the **Anti-Imperialist League** to fight against the peace treaty. Local leagues sprang up in Boston, New York, Philadelphia, and many other cities; the parent league claimed thirty thousand members and more than half a million "contributors." Membership centered in New England; the cause was less popular in the West and South. It enlisted more Democrats than Republicans, though never a majority of either. The anti-imperialists were weakened by the fact that they lacked a coherent program. Some favored keeping naval bases in the conquered areas. Some wanted Hawaii and Puerto Rico but not the Philippines. Others wanted nothing at all to do with any colonies. Most simply wished that Dewey had sailed away after beating the Spanish at Manila Bay.

The treaty debate in the Senate lasted a month. Pressing hard for ratification, McKinley earlier toured the South to rally support and consulted closely with senators. Though opposed to taking the Philippines, Bryan supported ratification in order to end the war; his support influenced some Democratic votes. Still, on the final weekend before the vote, the treaty was two votes short. That Saturday night, news reached Washington that fighting had broken out between American troops and Filipino insurgents who demanded immediate independence. The news

**Read** the **Document** Carl Schurz, Platform of the American Anti-Imperialist League

Carl Schurz and other anti-imperialists of the American Anti-Imperialists League lobbied President McKinley not to annex the Philippines after the Spanish American War in 1898. These anti-imperialists argued that annexation of the Philippines would violate republican principles.

increased pressure to ratify the treaty, which the Senate did on February 6, 1899, with two votes to spare. An amendment promising independence as soon as the Filipinos established a stable government lost by one vote. The United States had a colonial empire.

Guerrilla Warfare in the Philippines

Historians rarely write of the **Philippine-American War**, but it was an important event in American history. The war with Spain was over a few months after it began, but war with the Filipinos lasted more than three years. Four times as many American soldiers fought in the Philippines as in Cuba. For the first time, Americans fought men of a different color in an Asian guerrilla war. The Philippine-American War of 1898–1902 took a heavy toll: 4,300 American lives and untold thousands of Filipino lives (estimates range from 50,000 to 200,000).

Emilio Aguinaldo, the Filipino leader, was twenty-nine years old in 1898. An early organizer of the anti-Spanish resistance, he

had gone into exile in Hong Kong; from there he welcomed the outbreak of the Spanish-American War. Certain the United States would grant independence, he worked for an American victory. Filipino insurgents helped guide Dewey into Manila Bay, and Dewey himself sent a ship to Hong Kong to bring back Aguinaldo to lead a native uprising against the Spanish. On June 12, 1898, the insurgents proclaimed their independence.

Cooperating with the Americans, they drove the Spanish out of many areas of the islands. In the liberated regions, Aguinaldo established local governments with appointed provincial governors. He waited impatiently for American recognition, but McKinley and others had concluded that the Filipinos were not ready. Soon, warfare broke out between the Filipinos and Americans over the question of Filipino independence.

By late 1899, the American army had defeated and dispersed the organized Filipino army, but claims of victory proved premature. Aguinaldo and his advisers shifted to guerrilla tactics, striking suddenly and then melting into the jungle or friendly native villages. In many areas, the Americans ruled the day, the guerrillas the night. There were terrible atrocities on both sides. The Americans found themselves using brutal, Weyler-like tactics. After any attack on an American patrol, the Americans burned all the houses in the nearest district. They tortured people and executed prisoners. They established protected "zones" and herded Filipinos into them. Seizing or destroying all food outside the zones, they starved many guerrillas into submission.

Bryan tried to turn the election of 1900 into a debate over imperialism, but the attempt failed. For one thing, he himself refused to give up the silver issue, which cost him some support among anti-imperialists in the Northeast who were for gold. McKinley, moreover, was able to take advantage of the surging economy, and he could defend expansion as an accomplished fact. "It is no longer a question of expansion with us," he told one audience. "If there is any question at all it is a question of contraction; and who is going to contract?" Riding a wave of patriotism and prosperity, McKinley won the election handily—by an even larger margin than he had in 1896.

In 1900, McKinley sent a special Philippine Commission to the islands under William Howard Taft, a prominent Ohio judge. Directed to establish a civil government, the commission organized municipal administrations and, in stages, created a government for the Philippines. In March 1901, five American soldiers tricked their way into Aguinaldo's camp deep in the mountains and took him prisoner. Back in Manila, he signed a proclamation urging his people to end the fighting. Some guerrillas held out for another year, but to no avail. On July 4, 1901, authority was transferred from the army to Taft, who was named civilian governor of the islands, and his civilian commission. McKinley reaffirmed his purpose to grant the Filipinos self-government as soon as they were deemed ready for it.

Given broad powers, the Taft Commission introduced many changes. New schools provided education and vocational training for Filipinos of all social classes. The Americans built roads and bridges, reformed the judiciary, restructured the tax system, and introduced sanitation and vaccination programs. They established local governments built on Filipino traditions and hierarchies.

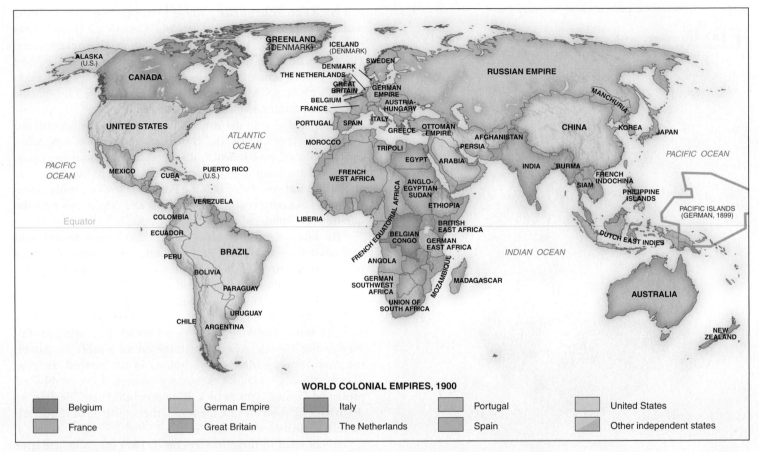

WORLD COLONIAL EMPIRES, 1900

Belgium	German Empire	Italy	Portugal	United States
France	Great Britain	The Netherlands	Spain	Other independent states

WORLD COLONIAL EMPIRES, 1900   Events of the nineteenth century increased European hegemony over the world. By 1900, most independent African nations had disappeared and the major European nations had divided the continent among themselves. In the East, the European powers and Japan took advantage of China's internal weakness to gain both trading ports and economic concessions.

Taft encouraged Filipino participation in government. During the following decades, other measures broadened Filipino rights. Independence finally came on July 4, 1946, nearly fifty years after Aguinaldo proclaimed it.

Governing the Empire

Ruling the colonies raised new and perplexing questions. How could—and how should—the distant dependencies be governed? Did their inhabitants have the rights of American citizens? Some people contended that acquisition did not automatically incorporate the new possessions into the United States and endow them with constitutional privileges. Others argued that "the Constitution followed the flag," meaning that acquisition made the possessions part of the nation and thus entitled them to all constitutional guarantees. A third group suggested that only "fundamental" constitutional guarantees—citizenship, the right to vote, and the right to trial by jury—not "formal" privileges—the right to use American currency, the right to be taxed, and the right to run for the presidency—were applicable to the new empire.

In a series of cases between 1901 and 1904 (*De Lima* v. *Bidwell, Dooley* v. *U.S.,* and *Downes* v. *Bidwell*), the Supreme Court asserted

the principle that the Constitution did not automatically and immediately apply to the people of an annexed territory and did not confer upon them all the privileges of U.S. citizenship. Instead, Congress could specifically extend such constitutional provisions as it saw fit. "Ye-es," the secretary of war said of the Court's ambiguous rulings, "as near as I can make out the Constitution follows the flag—but doesn't quite catch up with it."

Four dependencies—Hawaii, Alaska, Guam, and Puerto Rico—were organized quickly. In 1900, Congress granted territorial status to Hawaii, gave American citizenship to all citizens of the Hawaiian republic, authorized an elective legislature, and provided for a governor appointed from Washington. A similar measure made Alaska a territory in 1912. Guam and American Samoa were simply placed under the control of naval officers.

Unlike the Filipinos, Puerto Ricans readily accepted the war's outcome, and McKinley early withdrew troops from the island. The Foraker Act of 1900 established civil government in Puerto Rico. It organized the island as a territory, made its residents citizens of Puerto Rico (U.S. citizenship was extended to them in 1917), and empowered the president to appoint a governor general and a council to serve as the upper house of the legislature. A lower house of delegates was to be elected.

View the **Image**   Emilio Aguinaldo

Emilio Aguinaldo in the Philippines, 1896. Aguinaldo's forces helped the Americans drive Spain out of the Philippines, expecting that the United States would recognize Filipino independence. When the United States failed to do so, Aguinaldo led his forces in warfare against the Americans.

Cuba proved a trickier matter. McKinley asserted the authority of the United States over conquered territory and promised to govern the island until the Cubans had established a firm and stable government of their own. "I want you to go down there to get the people ready for a republican form of government," he instructed General Leonard Wood, commander of the army in Cuba until 1902. "I leave the details of procedure to you. Give them a good school system, try to straighten out their ports, and put them on their feet as best you can. We want to do all we can for them and to get out of the island as soon as we safely can."

Wood moved quickly to implement the instructions. Early in 1900, he completed a census of the Cuban population, conducted municipal elections, and arranged the election of delegates to a constitutional convention. The convention adopted a constitution modeled on the U.S. Constitution and, at Wood's prodding, included provisions for future relations with the United States. Known as the Platt Amendment to the new Cuban Constitution, the provisions stipulated that Cuba should make no treaties with other powers that might impair its independence, acquire no debts it could not pay, and lease naval bases such as Guantánamo Bay to the United States. Most important, the amendment empowered the United States to intervene in Cuba to maintain orderly government.

Between 1898 and 1902, the American military government worked hard for the economic and political revival of the island, though it often demonstrated a paternalistic attitude toward the Cubans themselves. It repaired the damage of the civil war, built roads and schools, and established order in rural areas. A public health campaign headed by Dr. Walter Reed, an army surgeon, wiped out yellow fever. Most troops withdrew at the end of 1899, but a small American occupation force remained until May 1902. When it sailed for home, the Cubans at last had a form of independence, but they were still under the clear domination of their neighbor to the north.

The Open Door

Poised in the Philippines, the United States had become an Asian power on the doorstep of China. Weakened by years of warfare, China in 1898 and 1899 was unable to resist foreign influence. Japan, England, France, Germany, and Russia eyed it covetously, dividing parts of the country into "spheres of influence." They forced China to grant "concessions" that allowed them exclusive rights to develop particular areas and threatened American hopes for extensive trade with the country.

McKinley first outlined a new China policy in September 1898 when he said that Americans sought more trade, "but we seek no advantages in the Orient which are not common to all. Asking only the open door for ourselves, we are ready to accord the open door to others." In September 1899, Secretary of State John Hay addressed identical diplomatic notes to England, Germany, and Russia, and later to France, Japan, and Italy, asking them to join the United States in establishing the **Open Door policy**. This policy urged three agreements: Nations possessing a sphere of influence would respect the rights and privileges of other nations in that sphere; the Chinese government would continue to collect tariff duties in all spheres; and nations would not discriminate against other nations in levying port dues and railroad rates within their respective spheres of influence.

Under the Open Door policy, the United States would retain many commercial advantages it might lose if China was partitioned into spheres of influence. McKinley and Hay also attempted to preserve for the Chinese some semblance of national authority. Great Britain most nearly accepted the principle of the Open Door. Russia declined to approve it, and the other powers, sending evasive replies, stated they would agree only if all the other nations did. Hay turned the situation to American advantage by boldly announcing in March 1900 that all the powers had accepted the Open Door policy. (See the Feature Essay, "The 400 Million Customers of China," pp. 508–510, for more on U.S. trade in China.)

The policy's first test came just three months later with the outbreak of the Boxer Rebellion in Peking (now Beijing). In June 1900, a secret, intensely nationalistic Chinese society called the Boxers tried to oust all foreigners from their country. Overrunning Peking, they drove foreigners into their legations and penned them up for nearly two months. In the end, the United States joined Britain, Germany, and other powers in sending troops to lift the siege.

Fearing that the rebellion gave some nations, especially Germany and Russia, an excuse to expand their spheres of influence, Hay took quick action to emphasize American policy. In July, he sent off another round of Open Door notes affirming

Feature Essay | The 400 Million Customers of China

Duke's Cameo Cigarettes card depicting the ruler, flag, and coat of arms of China. The W. Duke & Sons Company merged with other tobacco manufacturers in 1890 to form the American Tobacco Company, which began selling cigarettes in China that same year.

The issue of American trade with China, so much in the news today, has been a concern of the United States for more than two centuries. Many of the things Americans now buy and wear carry the label, "Made in China." The United States had long hoped that the Chinese would be buying goods "Made in the U.S.A.," but it has not worked out entirely that way.

For a time it seemed it would. When the United States won independence from Great Britain, it opened up markets the British had monopolized, such as China, whose huge population of 400 million people fascinated American business leaders throughout the nineteenth century. "Let me say to the businessmen of America,"

a member of Congress exclaimed in 1898, "Look to the land of the setting sun, look to the Pacific! There are teeming millions there who will ere long want to be fed and clothed the same as we are."

Step-by-step, Americans in the 1800s moved closer to those teeming millions, by actions including Secretary of State William H. Seward's 1867 purchase of Alaska and the later decisions to acquire Hawaii and construct a canal across the Isthmus of Panama. President William McKinley offered several reasons for retaining the Philippine Islands after the Spanish-American War, but one of them was their nearness to China.

Adding a sense of urgency, business and political leaders during the

1880s and 1890s became increasingly concerned that the avalanche of goods pouring out of the nation's farms and factories outpaced the purchasing power of customers at home. Presidents from McKinley to Woodrow Wilson pointed out that businesses must find new markets abroad or face collapse. "[O]ur industries have expanded to such a point," Wilson argued in 1912, "that they will burst their jackets if they cannot find a free outlet to the markets of the world."

But doing that was not easy in China, whose great distances, different language, and restrictive laws stymied even some of America's most legendary business leaders. Both J. P. Morgan, the famed financier who bought up railroads everywhere and created the gigantic U.S. Steel Company, and E. H. Harriman, a railroad magnate who dreamed of China as part of a transportation system that circled the globe, tried and failed.

Others, who took account of Chinese customs and conditions, succeeded. "Bring me the atlas," James B. Duke, head of the American Tobacco Company, said to an aide soon after he founded the company. Turning the pages, he quickly scanned population figures until he came to one he liked: "Pop.: 430,000,000." "That," he said, "is where we are going to sell cigarettes."

And that place, of course, was China. American Tobacco shipped its first cigarettes to China in 1890 and watched sales rise dramatically, from 1.25 billion cigarettes in 1902 to 9.75 billion in 1912 and 12 billion in 1916. It built large plants in two Chinese cities, established key distribution centers, and advertised widely. The company employed some native Chinese to market its cigarettes but also hired teams of Westerners, usually bachelors under the age of 25 who could accept the risks of living and working in China. Urging them to learn colloquial Chinese, the company held language exams every six months and awarded a $500 bonus to anyone who passed. Before long, American Tobacco produced nearly two-thirds of the cigarettes consumed in China.

Other businesses adopted similar strategies, among them John D. Rockefeller's Standard Oil Company, which by 1910 marketed more than half the kerosene sold in China. Standard's famous red kerosene tin, flattened to make roofs and walls of houses around the world, became a symbol of America's economic reach.

Significantly, Americans in the Progressive period exported not only oil and tobacco but also major social reforms, reflecting a certainty, so common in our history, that the Chinese could not do it for themselves. "The pigtails, the old pinched shoes, the parasols and banners," a leading reform magazine said in 1915, "must give way to parks, and sewers, and filtered water, and war on rats and mosquitoes."

American agencies and universities eagerly took up "the Far Eastern question," as Lillian Wald, a prominent female reformer, put it. The Rockefeller Foundation worked to encourage cultivation of arable land; the *Suffragist* magazine campaigned to give Chinese women the vote; Americans in China tried to improve the postal service and introduce the wireless radio; the American Red Cross employed engineers to eliminate floods on Chinese rivers and open up new farmland.

Before long, the Young Men's Christian Association extended its mission to China, aiming to improve schools, form settlement houses in major cities, and reform the sanitation of China's prisons, parks, and businesses. Drawing on its staff of young, dedicated college graduates, it held literacy campaigns, worked for better public health, paid for social surveys, and tried to provide recreation and residences for some of China's poor. Students from Princeton University established a settlement house soon known as Princeton-in-Peking. In 1906, Yale University students founded the Yale-in-China Medical College at Changsha, to function, as one of the founders said, as a center for the "uplifting of leading Chinese young men toward civilization."

Heady ideas, they were typical of the United States in the Progressive period, a conviction that changing the environment would change people, a desire to expand business growth and progressive reform, and export both to other countries. Business leaders, eager to acquire more and more of the vast China market, were among those who urged the McKinley administration to establish the famed Open Door.

The Great Depression and World War II diverted American attention from the China market, but once the war ended, business leaders again flocked there, only to find that the victory in 1949 of Mao Tse-tung and his Communist People's Liberation Army had closed the door to trade. China emptied of Americans. The last American diplomats left in the spring of 1950, followed soon after by business figures and missionaries.

It took two decades to begin a thaw, even longer to begin the serious business of trading once again. President Richard M. Nixon visited China in 1972 in a historic trip that signaled a new direction in relations between the two countries. Six years later, President Jimmy Carter restored diplomatic relations. Sounding very much like his nineteenth-century predecessors, President Bill Clinton noted in 2000 that "China, with more than a billion people, is home to the largest potential market in the world." Backed by the United States, China entered the World Trade Organization in 2001, with much of American business, still hopeful of capturing the China trade, in favor.

And the Chinese did buy American goods as those businesses hoped, $35 billion worth in the year 2000, making China America's fifth largest market in the world. American tobacco companies continue to sell millions of cigarettes in China; companies dealing in aircraft engines, power plant equipment, soybeans, cotton, and fruit also do well. But the old dream proves elusive still. Americans buy from China far more than the Chinese buy from the United States, about six times more, in fact. By the end of 2005, the U.S. deficit with China reached $202 billion, "the largest trade deficit in the history of the world," the U.S. trade representative said in a recent speech in Beijing.

That deficit continues to grow. With many American name brands now made in China, the Chinese have begun to wonder what a "Made in the U.S.A." label really means.

QUESTIONS FOR DISCUSSION

1. Why did American business in the late nineteenth century want to tap the China market?

2. What social reforms did Americans in the Progressive Era want to export to China?

509

An American cartoon of 1900 showing Uncle Sam opening China to free trade with the key of American diplomacy while economic competitors England and Russia look on.

U.S. commitment to equal commercial opportunity and respect for China's independence. While the first Open Door notes had implied recognition of China's continued independence, the second notes explicitly stated the need to preserve it. Together, the two notes composed the Open Door policy, which became a central element in American policy in the Far East.

To some degree, the policy tried to help China, but it also led to further American meddling in the affairs of another country. Moreover, by committing itself to a policy that Americans were not prepared to defend militarily, the McKinley administration left the opportunity for later controversy with Japan and other expansion-minded powers in the Pacific.

Conclusion: Outcome of the War with Spain

The war with Spain over, Roosevelt and the Rough Riders sailed for home in mid-August 1898. They sauntered through the streets of New York, the heroes of the city. A few weeks later, Roosevelt bade them farewell. They presented him with a reproduction of Frederick Remington's famed bronze *The Bronco-Buster*, and, close to tears, he told them, "I am proud of this regiment beyond measure." Roosevelt later wrote an account of the war in which he played so central a role that Mr. Dooley suggested, "If I was him, I'd call th' book 'Alone in

Cubia.'" By then, Roosevelt was already governor of New York and on his way to the White House.

Other soldiers were also glad to be home, although they were sometimes resentful of the reception they found. "The war is over now," said Winslow Hobson, a black trooper from the Ninth Ohio, "and Roosevelt . . . ; and others (white of course) have all there is to be gotten out of it." Bravery in Cuba and the Philippines won some recognition for black soldiers, but the war itself set back the cause of civil rights. It spurred talk about "inferior" races, at home and abroad, and united whites in the North and South. "The Negro might as well know it now as later," a black editor said, "the closer the North and South get together by this war, the harder he will have to fight to maintain a footing."

A fresh outburst of segregation and lynching occurred during the decade after the war.

McKinley and the Republican party soared to new heights of popularity. Firmly established, the Republican majority dominated politics until 1932. Scandals arose about the canned beef and the conduct of the War Department, but there was none of the sharp sense of deception and betrayal that was to mark the years after World War I. In a little more than a century, the United States had grown from thirteen states stretched along a thin Atlantic coastline into a world power that reached from the Caribbean to the Pacific. As Seward and others had hoped, the nation now dominated its own hemisphere, dealt with European powers on more equal terms, and was a major power in Asia.

Study Resources

 Take the **Study Plan** for **Chapter 21** *Toward Empire* on **MyHistoryLab**

TIME LINE

1867 United States purchases Alaska from Russia; Midway Islands are annexed

1871 Treaty of Washington between United States and Great Britain sets precedent for peaceful settlement of international disputes

1875 Reciprocity treaty with Hawaii binds Hawaii economically and politically to United States

1878 United States acquires naval base in Samoa

1883 Congress approves funds for construction of first modern steel ships; beginning of modern navy

1887 New treaty with Hawaii gives United States exclusive use of Pearl Harbor

1889 First Inter-American Conference meets in Washington, D.C.

1893 American settlers in Hawaii overthrow Queen Liliuokalani; provisional government established

1895 Cuban insurgents rebel against Spanish rule

1898 Battleship *Maine* explodes in Havana harbor (February); Congress declares war against Spain (April); Commodore Dewey defeats Spanish fleet at Manila Bay (May); United States annexes Hawaii (July); Americans defeat Spanish at El Caney, San Juan Hill (actually Kettle Hill), and Santiago (July); Spain sues for peace (August); Treaty of Paris ends Spanish-American War (December)

1899 Congress ratifies Treaty of Paris; United States sends Open Door notes to Britain, Germany, Russia, France, Japan, and Italy; Philippine-American War erupts

1900 Foraker Act establishes civil government in Puerto Rico

1901 Platt Amendment authorizes American intervention in Cuba

1902 Philippine-American War ends with American victory

CHAPTER REVIEW

America Looks Outward

 Why did Americans look outward in the last half of the nineteenth century?

In the late nineteenth century, Americans increasingly looked overseas, influenced by the example of other nations and confidence in what their country could offer other peoples, including Christianity, commerce, and American values. Policy makers were sure that the nation needed a navy, colonial outposts, foreign markets, and a new foreign policy. (p. 492)

War with Spain

 What were the causes and results of the war with Spain?

In 1898, the United States fought a war with Spain, which resulted in a quick victory and enormous changes for American society, including a larger military, an increased role for the federal government in American life, the acquisition of colonies, and increased power for the presidency. (p. 497)

Acquisition of Empire

 What were the various viewpoints about the acquisition of empire after the war with Spain?

In the peace treaty ending the war with Spain, the United States acquired a new empire, including Puerto Rico, Guam, and the Philippines. For the first time, the United States owned territories overseas, to which it did not intend to grant statehood. That, together with historical, racial, and other arguments, caused an angry debate between those in favor and those opposing the new colonies. Adding to the furor was the outbreak of warfare between American troops and Filipino insurgents in the Philippines. (p. 503)

KEY TERMS AND DEFINITIONS

Isolationism A belief that the United States should avoid entanglements with other nations. p. 492

Imperialism The policy of extending a nation's power over other areas through military conquest, economic domination, or annexation. p. 492

Yellow journalism To sell newspapers before and during the Spanish-American War, publishers William Randolph Hearst and Joseph Pulitzer engaged in blatant sensationalization of the news, which became known as "yellow journalism." Although it did not cause the war, it helped turn U.S. public opinion against Spain. p. 498

Teller Amendment In this amendment to the declaration of war on Spain in 1898, the United States pledged that it did not intend to annex Cuba and that it would recognize Cuban independence after the Spanish-American War. p. 499

Treaty of Paris Treaty in December 1898 ending the Spanish-American War. Under its terms, Spain recognized Cuba's independence, assumed the Cuban debt, and ceded Puerto Rico, Guam, and the Philippines to the United States. p. 504

Anti-Imperialist League An organization formed in 1898 to fight the Treaty of Paris ending the Spanish-American War. Members opposed acquiring overseas colonies, believing it would subvert American ideals and institutions. Membership centered in New England; the cause was less popular in the South and West. p. 504

Philippine-American War A war fought from 1899 to 1903 to quell Filipino resistance to U.S. control of the Philippine Islands. p. 505

Open Door policy This policy established free trade between the United States and China in 1900 and attempted to induce European nations and Japan to recognize the territorial integrity of China. It marked a departure from the American tradition of isolationism and signaled the country's growing involvement in the world. p. 507

CRITICAL THINKING QUESTIONS

1. What were the key developments in leading the United States to look abroad between the 1870s and the 1890s, and how did these developments ultimately lead to the war with Spain in 1898?

2. Why did the important causes and events of the Spanish-American War lead to the crucial decision to acquire and overseas empire?

3. What were the most important effects of the end of the war and the acquisition of empire?

MyHistoryLab Media Assignments

Find these resources in the Media Assignments folder for Chapter 21 on MyHistoryLab

America Looks Outward

■ **Watch** the **Video** *Roosevelt's Rough Riders p. 491*

■ **Read** the **Document** *Josiah Strong, from Our Country (1885) p. 493*

Read the **Document** *Liliuokalani, Hawaii's Story p. 495*

■ **Read** the **Document** *Alfred Thayer Mahan, The Interest of America in Sea Power p. 497*

War with Spain

Watch the **Video** *Burial of the Maine Victims p. 499*

View the **Map** *The Spanish-American War p. 501*

Acquisition of Empire

■ **View** the **Closer Look** *American Empire p. 503*

Read the **Document** *Carl Schurz, Platform of the American Anti-Imperialist League p. 505*

View the **Image** *Emilio Aguinaldo p. 507*

■ **Complete** the **Assignment** *The 400 Million Customers of China p. 508*

■ *Indicates Study Plan Media Assignment*

22 The Progressive Era

Contents and Learning Objectives

((•—Listen to the **Audio File** on **myhistorylab**   Chapter 22 *The Progressive Era*

Muckrakers Call for Reform

In 1902, Samuel S. McClure, the shrewd owner of *McClure's Magazine*, sensed something astir in the country that his reporters were not covering. Like *Life*, *Munsey's*, the *Ladies' Home Journal*, and *Cosmopolitan*, *McClure's* was reaching more and more people—more than a quarter million readers a month. Americans were snapping up the new popular magazines filled with eye-catching illustrations and up-to-date fiction. Advances in photoengraving during the 1890s dramatically reduced the cost of illustrations; at the same time, income from advertisements rose sharply. By the turn of the century, some magazines earned as much as $60,000 an issue from advertising alone, and publishers could price them as low as 10 cents a copy.

McClure was always chasing new ideas and readers, and in 1902, certain that something was happening in the public mood, he told one of his editors, 36-year-old Lincoln Steffens, a former Wall Street reporter, to find out what it was. "Get out of here, travel, go—somewhere," he said to Steffens. "Buy a railroad ticket, get on a train, and there, where it lands you, there you will learn to edit a magazine."

McClure's, it turned out, had an unpaid bill from the Lackawanna Railroad, and Steffens traveled west. In St. Louis, he came across a young district attorney named Joseph W. Folk who had found a trail of corruption linking politics and some of the city's respected business leaders. Eager for help, Folk did not mind naming names to the visiting editor from New York. "It is good business men that are corrupting our bad politicians," he emphasized again and again. "It is the leading citizens that are battening on our city." Steffens's story, "Tweed Days in St. Louis," appeared in the October 1902 issue of *McClure's*.

The November *McClure's* carried the first installment of Ida Tarbell's scathing "History of the Standard Oil Company," and in January 1903, Steffens was back with "The Shame of Minneapolis," another tale of corrupt partnership between business and politics. McClure had what he wanted, and in the January issue he printed an editorial, "Concerning Three Articles in This Number of *McClure's*, and a Coincidence That May Set Us Thinking." Steffens on Minneapolis, Tarbell on Standard Oil, and an article on abuses in labor unions—all, McClure said, on different topics but actually on the same theme: corruption in American life. "Capitalists, workingmen, politicians, citizens—all breaking the law, or letting it be broken."

Readers were enthralled, and articles and books by other **muckrakers**—Theodore Roosevelt coined the term in 1906 to describe the writers who made a practice of exposing the corruption of public and

MC CLURE'S MAGAZINE

NOVEMBER

PUBLISHED MONTHLY BY THE S. S. McCLURE CO., 141-155 E. 25th ST., NEW YORK CITY

At the beginning of the twentieth century, magazines enjoyed increasing popularity. *McClure's Magazine* pioneered investigative journalism. The November 1902 edition featured the first installment of Ida Tarbell's two-year series on Standard Oil that exposed the corrupt practices and deals that had helped create the company.

prominent figures—spread swiftly. *Collier's* had articles on questionable stock market practices, patent medicines, and the beef trust. Novelist Upton Sinclair tackled the meatpackers in *The Jungle* (1906). In 1904, Steffens collected his McClure's articles in *The Shame of the Cities*, with an introduction expressing confidence that reform was possible, "that our shamelessness is superficial, that beneath it lies a pride which, being real, may save us yet."

Muckraking flourished from 1903 to 1909, and while it did, good writers and bad investigated almost every corner of American life: government, labor unions, big business, Wall Street, health care, the food industry, child labor, women's rights, prostitution, ghetto living, and life insurance.

As McClure had hoped, Steffens *had* found something astir in the country, something so important and pervasive that it altered the course of American history in the twentieth century. The muckrakers were a journalistic voice of this larger movement in American society. Called **progressivism**, it lasted from the mid-1890s through World War I. Like muckraking itself, progressivism reflected worry about the state of society, the effects of industrialization and urbanization, social disorder, political corruption, and a host of other issues. With concerns so large, progressivism often had a sense of crisis and urgency, although it was rooted in a spirit of hopefulness and confidence in human progress. For varying reasons, thousands of people became concerned about their society, and, separately and together, they set out to cure some of the ills they saw around them. The efforts of the so-called progressives changed the nation and gave the era its name.

The Changing Face of Industrialism

How did industrialism change after 1900?

"Life in the States," an English visitor said in 1900, "is one perpetual whirl of telephones, telegrams, phonographs, electric bells, motors, lifts, and automatic instruments." If not quite as automated as the visitor described, conditions in America were better than just a few years before. Farms and factories were once again prosperous; in 1901, for the first time in years, the economy reached full capacity. Farm prices rose almost 50 percent between 1900 and 1910. Unemployment dropped. "In the United States of today," a Boston newspaper said in 1904, "everyone is middle class. The resort to force, the wild talk of the nineties are over. Everyone is busily, happily getting ahead."

Everyone, of course, was not middle class, nor was everyone getting ahead. "Wild talk" persisted. Many of the problems that had angered people in the 1890s continued into the new century, and millions of Americans still suffered from poverty and disease. Racism sat even more heavily on African Americans in both South and North, and there was increasing hostility against immigrants from southern and eastern Europe and from Mexico and Asia. Yet to some degree the Boston newspaper was right: Economic conditions were better for many people, and as a result, prosperity became one of the keys to understanding the era and the nature of progressive reform.

The start of the new century was another key as well, for it influenced people to take a fresh look at themselves and their times. Excited about beginning the twentieth century, people believed technology and enterprise would shape a better life. Savoring the word *new*, they talked of the new poetry, new cinema, new history, new democracy, new woman, new art, new immigration, new morality, and new city. Magazines picked up the word; there were the *New Republic* and the *New Statesman*. Presidents Theodore Roosevelt and Woodrow Wilson called their political programs the New Nationalism and the New Freedom.

The word *mass* also cropped up frequently. Victors in the recent war with Spain, Americans took pride in teeming cities, burgeoning corporations, and other marks of the mass society. They enjoyed the fruits of mass production, read mass circulation newspapers and magazines, and took mass transit from the growing spiral of suburbs into the central cities.

Behind mass production lay significant changes in the nation's industrial system. Businesses grew at a rapid rate. They were large in the three decades after the Civil War, but in the years between 1895 and 1915, industries became mammoth, employing thousands of workers and equipped with assembly lines to turn out huge quantities of the company's product. Inevitably, changes in management attitudes, business organization, and worker roles influenced the entire society. Inevitably, too, the growth of giant businesses gave rise to a widespread fear of "trusts" and a desire among many progressive reformers to break them up or regulate them.

The Innovative Model T

In the movement toward large-scale business and mass production, the automobile industry was one of those that led the way. In 1895, there were only four cars on the nation's roads; in 1917, there were nearly five million, and the automobile had already helped work a small revolution in industrial methods and social mores.

Mass production of automobiles began in the first years of the century. Using an assembly-line system that foreshadowed later techniques, Ransom E. Olds turned out five thousand Olds runabouts in 1904. But Olds's days of leadership were numbered. In 1903, Henry Ford and a small group of associates formed the Ford Motor Company, the firm that transformed the business.

Ford was forty years old. He had tried farming and hated it. During the 1890s, he worked as an engineer for Detroit's Edison Company but spent his spare time designing internal combustion engines and automobiles. At first, like many others in the industry, he concentrated on building luxury and racing cars. Racing his own cars, Ford became the "speed demon" of Detroit; in 1904, he set the world's land speed record—more than ninety miles per hour—in the 999, a large red racer that shot flames from the motor.

In 1903, Ford sold the first Ford car. The price was high, and in 1905, Ford raised prices still higher. Sales plummeted. In 1907,

 Watch the **Video** **The Rise and Fall of the Automobile Economy**

The twentieth century was the century of the expansive automobile industry. It remade American culture. In the Model T Era of 1908 to 1927, automobiles transitioned from being toys to being household necessities.

he lowered the price; sales and revenues rose. Ford learned an important lesson of the modern economy: A smaller unit profit on a large number of sales meant enormous revenues. Early in 1908, he introduced the Model T, a four-cylinder, 20-horsepower "Tin Lizzie," costing $850, and available only in black. Eleven thousand were sold the first year.

"I am going to democratize the automobile," Ford proclaimed. "When I'm through everybody will be able to afford one, and about everyone will have one." The key was mass production, and after many experiments, Ford copied the techniques of meat-packers who moved animal carcasses along overhead trolleys from station to station. Adapting the process to automobile assembly, Ford in 1913 set up moving assembly lines in his plant in Highland Park, Michigan, that dramatically reduced the time and cost of producing cars. Emphasizing continuous movement, he strove for a nonstop flow from raw material to finished product. In 1914, he sold 248,000 Model T cars.

That year, Ford workers assembled a car in ninety-three minutes, one-tenth the time it had taken just eight months before. On a single day in 1925, Ford set a record by turning out 9109 Model Ts, a new car for every ten seconds of the workday.

While Ford was putting more and more cars on the road, the 1916 Federal Aid Roads Act, a little noticed measure, set the framework for road building in the twentieth century. Removing control from county governments, it required every state desiring federal funds to establish a highway department to plan routes, oversee construction, and maintain roads. In states that had such departments, the federal government paid half the cost of building the roads. Providing for a planned highway system, the act produced a national network of two-lane all-weather intercity roads.

The Burgeoning Trusts

As businesses like Ford's grew, capital and organization became increasingly important, and the result was the formation of a growing number of trusts. Standard Oil started the trend in 1882, but the greatest momentum came two decades later. Between 1898 and 1903, a series of mergers and consolidations swept the economy. Many smaller firms disappeared, swallowed up in giant corporations. By 1904, large-scale combinations of one form or another controlled nearly two-fifths of the capital in manufacturing in the country.

The result was not monopoly but oligopoly—control of a commodity or service by a small number of large, powerful companies. Six great financial groups dominated the railroad industry; a handful of holding companies controlled utilities and steel. Rockefeller's Standard Oil owned about 85 percent of the oil business. Large companies such as Standard Oil and American Tobacco had weathered the depression of the 1890s, and after 1898, financiers and industrialists followed their example and formed the Amalgamated Copper Company, Consolidated Tobacco, U.S. Rubber, and a host of others.

By 1909, just 1 percent of the industrial firms were producing nearly half of all manufactured goods. Giant businesses reached abroad for raw materials and new markets. United Fruit, an empire of plantations and steamships in the Caribbean, exploited opportunities created by victory in the war with Spain. U.S. Steel worked with overseas companies to fix the price of steel rails, an unattainable

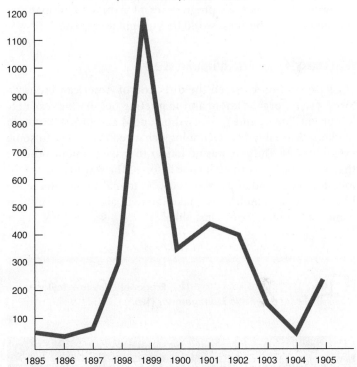

BUSINESS CONSOLIDATIONS
(MERGERS), 1895–1905

dream just a few years before. For decades, competition had sent rail prices up and down; now they stayed at $28 a ton, and through the famous "Gary dinners" in which Elbert H. Gary of U.S. Steel brought steel executives from "competing" firms together to set prices, market conditions were fixed for wide areas of the industry.

Though the trend has been overstated, finance capitalists such as J. P. Morgan tended to replace the industrial capitalists of an earlier era. Able to finance the mergers and reorganizations, investment bankers played a greater and greater role in the economy. A multibillion-dollar financial house, J. P. Morgan and Company operated a network of control that ran from New York City to every industrial and financial center in the nation. Like other investment firms, it held directorships in many corporations, creating "interlocking directorates" that allowed it to control many businesses. In 1913, two banking groups—Morgan's and Rockefeller's—held 341 directorships in 112 corporations with an aggregate capital of more than $22 billion.

Massive business growth set off a decade-long debate over what government should do about the trusts. Some critics who believed that the giant companies were responsible for stifling individual opportunity and raising prices wanted to break them up into small competitive units. Others argued that large-scale business was a mark of the times, and that it produced more goods and better lives.

The debate over the trusts was one of the issues that shaped the Progressive Era, but it was never a simple contest between high-minded reformers and greedy business titans. Some progressives favored big business; others wanted it broken up. Business leaders themselves were divided in their viewpoints, and some welcomed reform-led assaults on giant competitors. As a rule, both progressives and business leaders drew on similar visions of the country: complex, expansive, hopeful, managerially minded, and oriented toward results and efficiency. They both believed in private property and the importance of economic progress. In fact, in working for reform, the progressives often drew on the managerial methods of a business world they sought to regulate.

Managing the Machines

Mass production changed the direction of American industry. Size, system, organization, and marketing became increasingly important. Management focused on speed and product, not on workers. Assembly-line technology changed tasks and, to some extent, values. The goal was no longer to make a unique product that would be better than the one before. "The way to make automobiles," Ford said as early as 1903, "is to make one automobile like another automobile, to make them all alike, to make them come through the factory just alike."

Read the Document   **Frederick Winslow Taylor,**
***Scientific Management* (1911)**

In 1911, Frederick Winslow Taylor published his book *The Principles of Scientific Management*. In this work, Taylor proposed two major reforms. First, management must take responsibility for job-related knowledge and classify it into rules. Second, management should control the workplace through standardization of methods.

In a development that rivaled assembly lines in importance, businesses established industrial research laboratories where scientists and engineers developed new products. General Electric founded the first one in 1900, housed in a barn. It soon attracted experts who designed improvements in light bulbs, invented the cathode-ray tube, worked on early radio, and even tinkered with atomic theory. Du Pont opened its labs in 1911, Eastman Kodak in 1912, and Standard Oil in 1919. As the source of new ideas and technology, the labs altered life in the twentieth century.

Through all this, business became large-scale, mechanized, and managed. While many shops still employed fewer than a dozen workers, the proportion of such shops shrank. By 1920, close to one-half of all industrial workers toiled in factories employing more than 250 people. More than one-third worked in factories that were part of multiplant companies.

Industries that processed materials—iron and steel, paper, cement, and chemicals—were increasingly automated and operated continuously. In the glass industry, machines ended the domination of highly skilled and well-paid craftspeople. In 1908, Irving W. Colburn invented a machine to manufacture plate glass; the Libbey-Owens-Ford Company bought the patent; and Ford soon had a glassmaking machine from which emerged every day for two years a 3½-mile ribbon of automobile window glass. Eventually, the plant produced almost two thousand miles of glass.

Workers tending such ribbons could not fall behind. Foremen still managed the laborers on the factory floor, but more and more, the rules came down from a central office where trained professional managers supervised production flow. Systematic record keeping, cost accounting, and inventory and production controls became widespread. Workers lost control of the work pace. "If you need to turn out a little more," a manager at Swift and Company said, "you speed up the conveyor a little and the men speed up to keep pace." It worked. For that and other reasons, in the automobile industry, output per worker-hour multiplied an extraordinary four times between 1909 and 1919.

Folkways of the workplace—workers passing job-related knowledge to each other, performing their tasks with little supervision, setting their own pace, and in effect running the shop—began to give way to "scientific" labor management. More than anyone else, Frederick Winslow Taylor, an inventive mechanical engineer, strove to extract maximum efficiency from each worker. "In the past," he believed, "the man has been first; in the future the system must be first."

In his book *The Principles of Scientific Management* (1911), Taylor proposed two major reforms. First, management must take responsibility for job-related knowledge and classify it into "rules, laws, and formulae." Second, management should control the workplace "through *enforced* standardization of methods, *enforced* adoption of the best implements and working conditions, and *enforced* cooperation." Although few factories wholly adopted Taylor's principles, he had great influence, and the doctrines of scientific management spread through American industry.

Workers caught up in the changing industrial system experienced the benefits of efficiency and productivity; in some industries, they earned more. But they suffered important losses as well.

Performing repetitive tasks, they seemed part of the machinery, moving to the pace and needs of their mechanical pacesetters. Bored, they might easily lose pride of workmanship, though many workers, it is clear, did not. Efficiency engineers experimented with tools and methods, a process many workers found unsettling. Yet the goal was to establish routine—to work out, as someone said of a garment worker, "one single precise motion each second, 3,600 in one hour, and all exactly the same." Praising that worker, the manager said, "She is a sure machine."

Jobs became not only monotonous but dangerous. As machines and assembly lines sped up, boredom or miscalculation could bring disaster. Meat cutters sliced fingers and hands. Illinois steel mills, a magazine said, were "Making Steel and Killing Men"; one mill had forty-six deaths in 1906 alone. Injuries were part of many jobs. "The machines go like mad all day," a garment worker said, "because the faster you work the more money you get. Sometimes in my haste I get my finger caught and the needle goes right through it . . . I bind the finger up with a piece of cotton and go on working."

Society's Masses

How did mass production affect women, children, immigrants, and African Americans?

Spreading consumer goods through society, mass production not only improved people's lives but sometimes cost lives, too. Tending the machines took hard, painful labor, often under dangerous conditions. As businesses expanded, they required more and more people, and the labor force increased tremendously to keep up with the demand for workers in the factories, mines, and forests. Women, African Americans, Asian Americans, and Mexican Americans played larger and larger roles. Immigration soared. Between 1901 and 1910, nearly 8.8 million immigrants entered the United States; between 1911 and 1920, another 5.7 million came.

For many of these people, life was harsh, spent in crowded slums and long hours on the job. Fortunately, the massive unemployment of the 1890s was over, and in many skilled trades, such as cigar making, there was plenty of work to go around. Though the economic recovery helped nearly everyone, the less skilled continued to be the less fortunate. Migrant workers, lumberjacks, ore shovelers, and others struggled to find jobs that paid decently.

Under such circumstances, many people fought to make a living, and many, too, fought to improve their lot. Their efforts, along with the efforts of the reform-minded people who came to their aid, became another important hallmark of the Progressive Era.

Better Times on the Farm

While people continued to flee the farms—by 1920, fewer than one-third of all Americans lived on farms, and fewer than one-half lived in rural areas—farmers themselves prospered, the beneficiaries of greater production and expanding urban markets. Rural free delivery, begun in 1896, helped diminish the farmers' sense of isolation and changed farm life. The delivery

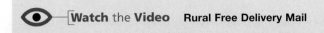

Watch the Video Rural Free Delivery Mail

The West Virginia experiment with rural free delivery was launched in relative obscurity and in an atmosphere of hostility. Critics of the plan claimed it was impractical and too expensive to have a postal carrier trudge over rutted roads and through forests trying to deliver mail in all kinds of weather.

of mail to the farm door opened that door to a wider world; it exposed farmers to urban thinking, national advertising, and political events. In 1911, more than one billion newspapers and magazines were delivered over RFD routes.

Parcel post (1913) permitted the sending of packages through the U.S. mail. Mail-order houses flourished; rural merchants suffered. Packages went both ways—President Woodrow Wilson's first parcel-post delivery held 8 pounds of New Jersey apples—and within a year, 300 million packages were being mailed annually. While telephones and electricity did not reach most rural areas for decades, better roads, mail-order catalogs, and other innovations knit farmers into the larger society. Early in the new century, Mary E. Lease—who in her Populist days had urged Kansas farmers to raise less corn and more hell—moved to Brooklyn.

Farmers still had problems. Land prices rose with crop prices, and farm tenancy increased, especially in the South. Tenancy grew from one-quarter of all farms in 1880 to more than one-third in 1910. In South Carolina, Georgia, Alabama, and Mississippi, nearly two-thirds of the farms were run by tenant farmers. Many southern tenant farmers were African Americans, and they suffered from farm-bred diseases. In one of the reforms of the Progressive Era, in 1909, the Rockefeller Sanitary Commission, acting on recent scientific discoveries, began a sanitation campaign that eventually wiped out the hookworm disease, and in 1912, the U.S. Public Health Service began work on rural malaria.

In the arid West, irrigation transformed the land as the federal government and private landholders joined to import water from mountain watersheds. The dry lands bloomed, and so did a rural

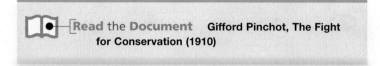
Read the Document   Gifford Pinchot, The Fight for Conservation (1910)

IRRIGATION AND CONSERVATION IN THE WEST TO 1917
To make the arid lands of the western states productive, the state and federal governments regulated the water supply through irrigation projects and the creation of water reservoirs. The federal government also created land reserves.

class structure that sharply separated owners from workers. Under the Newlands Act of 1902, the secretary of the interior formed the U.S. Reclamation Service, which gathered a staff of thousands of engineers and technicians, "the largest bureaucracy ever assembled in irrigation history."

Dams and canals channeled water into places such as California's Imperial Valley, and as the water streamed in, cotton, cantaloupes, oranges, tomatoes, lettuce, and a host of other crops streamed out to national markets. By 1920, Idaho, Montana, Utah, Wyoming, Colorado, and Oregon had extensive irrigation systems, all drawing on scarce water supplies; California, the foremost importer of water, had 4.2 million acres under irrigation, many of them picked by migrant workers from Mexico, China, and Japan. The work was backbreaking—and poorly paid. A worker from

India called picking asparagus a "ghastly" job, paid at the rate of ten cents a box:

> They gave us miles and miles of asparagus rows. As soon as I had knelt down with my knife and cut out one head and put it in the box, there would be another one sprouting before me. Then I would have to stoop again, and it was continuous picking and stooping that made it a terrible form of exercise. It is walk and bend, bend and walk, from half past four [in the morning] or thereabouts, until seven in the evening.

Women and Children at Work

Women worked in larger and larger numbers. In 1900, more than five million worked—one-fifth of all adult women—and among those aged fourteen to twenty-four, the employment rate was almost one-third. Of those employed, single women outnumbered married women by seven to one, yet more than one-third of married women worked. Most women held service jobs. Only a small number held higher-paying jobs as professionals or managers.

In the 1890s, women made up more than one-quarter of medical school graduates. Using a variety of techniques, men gradually squeezed them out, and by the 1920s, only about 5 percent of the graduates were women. Few women taught in colleges and universities, and those who did were expected to resign if they married. In 1906, Harriet Brooks, a promising physicist at Barnard College in New York, became engaged and refused to resign; the dean told her icily that Barnard expected a married woman to "dignify her home-making into a profession, and not assume that she can carry on two full professions at a time."

More women than men graduated from high school, and with such professions as medicine and science largely closed to them, women often turned to the new "business schools" that offered training in stenography, typing, and bookkeeping. In 1920, more than one-quarter of all employed women held clerical jobs. Many others taught school.

In 1907 and 1908, investigators studied twenty-two thousand women workers in Pittsburgh; 60 percent of them earned less than $7 a week, a minimum for "decent living." Fewer than 1 percent held skilled jobs; most tended machines, wrapped and labeled, or did handwork that required no particular skill. In New York, many women toiled six days a week as garment workers from eight in the morning to six in the evening, with an extra hour off on Saturdays. They earned $7 to $12 a week, nothing at all during slack season. They had to buy their own needles and thread and pay for electricity and chairs to sit on.

Black women had always worked, and in far larger numbers than their white counterparts. The reason was usually economic; an African American man or woman alone could rarely earn enough to support a family. Unlike many white women, black women tended to remain in the labor force after marriage or the start of a family. They also had less opportunity for job advancement, and in 1920, between one-third and one-half of all African American women who were working were restricted to personal and domestic service jobs.

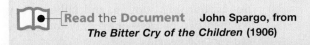
Read the **Document** John Spargo, from *The Bitter Cry of the Children* (1906)

Breaker boys, who picked out pieces of slate from the coal as it rushed past, often became bent-backed and suffered respiratory diseases such as bronchitis and tuberculosis after years of working fourteen hours a day in the coal mines. Accidents—and deaths—were common in the mines.

Critics charged that women's employment endangered the home, threatened their reproductive functions, and even, as one man said, stripped them of "that modest demeanor that lends a charm to their kind." Adding to these fears, the birthrate continued to drop between 1900 and 1920, and the divorce rate soared, in part because working-class men took advantage of the newer moral freedom and deserted their families in growing numbers. By 1916, there was one divorce for every nine marriages as compared to one for twenty-one in 1880.

Many children also worked. In 1900, about three million children—nearly 20 percent of those between the ages of 5 and 15—held full-time or almost full-time jobs. Twenty-five thousand boys under 16 worked in mining; twenty thousand children under 12, mainly girls, worked in southern cotton mills. Gradually, as public indignation grew, the use of child labor shrank.

Determined to do something about the situation, the Women's Trade Union League lobbied the federal Bureau of Labor to investigate the conditions under which women and children worked. Begun in 1907, the investigation took four years and produced nineteen volumes of data, some of it shocking, all of it factual. In 1911,

spurred by the data, the Children's Bureau was formed within the U.S. Bureau of Labor, with Grace Abbott, a social worker, at its head. It immediately began its own investigations, showing among other things the need for greater protection of maternal and infant health. In 1921, Congress passed the Sheppard-Towner Maternity and Infancy Protection Act, which helped fund maternity and pediatric clinics. Providing a precedent for the Social Security Act of 1935, it demonstrated the increasing effectiveness of women reformers in the Progressive Era.

Numerous middle-class women became involved in the fight for reform, while many others, reflecting the ongoing changes in the family, took increasing pride in homemaking and motherhood. Mother's Day, the national holiday, was formally established in 1913. Women who preferred smaller numbers of children turned increasingly to birth control, which became a more acceptable practice. Margaret Sanger, a nurse and outspoken social reformer, led a campaign to give physicians broad discretion in prescribing contraceptives. When Sanger became involved in the birth control movement, the federal Comstock Law banned the interstate transport of contraceptive devices and information.

The Niagara Movement and the NAACP

At the turn of the century, eight of every ten African Americans still lived in rural areas, mainly in the South. Most were poor sharecroppers. Jim Crow laws segregated many schools, railroad cars, hotels, and hospitals. Poll taxes and other devices disfranchised blacks and many poor whites. Violence was common; from 1900 to 1914, white mobs murdered more than a thousand black people.

Two murders occurred near Vicksburg, Mississippi, in 1904, and they revealed a great deal about the kind of violence African Americans faced. Looking for the killer of a white planter, a mob captured a black man and woman, their guilt or innocence unknown. They were tied to trees, and their fingers and ears were cut off as souvenirs. "The most excruciating form of punishment consisted in the use of a large corkscrew in the hands of some of the mob. This instrument was bored into the flesh of the man and the woman, in the arms, legs and body, and then pulled out, the spirals tearing out big pieces of raw, quivering flesh every time it was withdrawn." Finally, both people were thrown on a fire and burned to death, "a relief," a witness said, "to the maimed and suffering victims."

Many African Americans labored on the cotton farms and in the railroad camps, sawmills, and mines of the South under conditions of peonage. Peons traded their lives and labor for food and shelter. Often illiterate, they were forced to sign contracts allowing the planter "to use such force as he or his agents may deem necessary to require me to remain on his farm and perform good and satisfactory services." Armed guards patrolled the camps and whipped those trying to escape. "In the woods," a peon said, "they can do anything they please, and no one can see them but God."

Few blacks belonged to labor unions, and blacks almost always earned less than whites in the same job. In Atlanta, white electricians earned $5.00 a day, blacks $3.50. Black songs such as "I've Got a White Man Workin' for Me" (1901) voiced more hope than reality. The illiteracy rate among African Americans dropped from 45 percent in 1900 to 30 percent in 1910, but nowhere were

👁 Watch the Video   The Conflict Between Booker T. Washington and W.E.B. DuBois

The differences between Booker T. Washington and W.E.B. DuBois were differences of personality, differences of leadership, and, quite frankly, differences over who was going to exercise power—a southern former slave or a northern African American intellectual.

they given equal school facilities, teachers' salaries, or educational materials. In 1910, scarcely eight thousand African American youths were attending high schools in all the states of the Southeast. South Carolina spent $13.98 annually for the education of each white child, $1.13 for each black child.

African American leaders grew increasingly impatient with this kind of treatment, and in 1905 a group of them, led by sociologist W. E. B. DuBois, met near Niagara Falls, New York (they met on the Canadian side of the Falls, since no hotel on the American side would take them). There they pledged action in the matters of voting, equal access to economic opportunity, integration, and equality before the law. Rejecting Booker T. Washington's gradualist approach, the **Niagara Movement** claimed for African Americans "every single right that belongs to a freeborn American, political, civil and social; and until we get these rights we will never cease to protest."

The Niagara Movement focused on equal rights and the education of African American youth, of whom it said, "They have a right to know, to think, to aspire." Keeping alive a program of militant action, it spawned later civil rights movements. Du Bois was its inspiration. In *The Souls of Black Folk* (1903) and other works, he called eloquently for justice and equality. "By every civilized and peaceful method," he said, "we must strive for the right which the world accords to man."

Peace was sometimes hard to come by. Race riots broke out in Atlanta, Georgia, in 1906 and in Springfield, Illinois, in 1908, the latter the home of Abraham Lincoln. Unlike the riots of the 1960s, white mobs invaded black neighborhoods, burning, looting, and killing. They lynched two blacks—one eighty-four years old—in Springfield.

Outrage was voiced by William E. Walling, a wealthy southerner and settlement house worker; Mary Ovington, a white anthropology student; and Oswald Garrison Villard, grandson of the famous abolitionist William Lloyd Garrison. Along with other reformers, white and black (among them Jane Addams and John Dewey), they issued a call for the conference that organized the **National Association for the Advancement of Colored People (NAACP)**, which swiftly became the most important civil rights organization in the country. Created in 1909, within five years the NAACP grew to fifty branches and more than six thousand members. Walling headed it, and Du Bois, the only African American among the top officers, directed publicity and edited *The Crisis*, the voice of the organization.

Joined by the National Urban League, which was created in 1911, the NAACP pressured employers, labor unions, and the government on behalf of African Americans. It had some victories. In *Guinn* v. *United States* (1915), the Supreme Court overturned a "grandfather clause" that kept African Americans from voting in Oklahoma, and in *Buchanan* v. *Worley* (1917), it struck down a law in Louisville, Kentucky, that required residential segregation. In 1918, in the midst of World War I, the NAACP and the National Urban League persuaded the federal government to form a special Bureau of Negro Economics within the Labor Department to look after the interests of African American wage earners.

Despite these gains, African Americans continued to experience disfranchisement, poor job opportunities, and segregation. As Booker T. Washington said in 1913, "I have never seen the colored people so discouraged and so bitter as they are at the present time."

"I Hear the Whistle": Immigrants in the Labor Force

While women and African Americans worked in growing numbers, much of the huge increase in the labor force in these years came from outside the country, particularly from Europe and Mexico. Between 1901 and 1920, the extraordinarily high total of 14.5 million immigrants entered the country, more than in any previous twenty-year period. Continuing the trend begun in the 1880s, many came from southern and eastern Europe. Still called the "new" immigrants, they met hostility from "older" immigrants of northern European stock who questioned their values, religion (often Catholic or Jewish), traditions, and appearance.

Labor agents—called *padroni* among the Italians, Greeks, and Syrians—recruited immigrant workers, found them jobs, and deducted a fee from their wages. Headquartered in Salt Lake City, Leonidas G. Skliris, the "czar of the Greeks," provided workers for the Utah Copper Company and the Western Pacific Railroad. In Chicago at the turn of the century, padroni employed more than one-fifth of all Italians; in New York City, they controlled two-thirds of the entire labor force.

Immigrant patterns often departed from traditional stereotypes. Immigrants, for example, moved both to and from their homelands. Fifty percent or more of the members of some groups returned home, although the proportion varied. Jews and Czechs often brought their families to resettle in America; Serbs and Poles tended to come singly, intent on earning enough money to make a fresh start at home. Some migrants—Italian men, in particular—virtually commuted, returning home every slack season. These temporary migrants became known as **birds of passage**. The outbreak of World War I interrupted the practice and trapped thousands of Italians and others who had planned to return to Europe.

Older residents lumped the newcomers together, ignoring geographic, religious, and other differences. Preserving important regional distinctions, Italians tended to settle as Calabreses, Venetians, Abruzzis, and Sicilians. Old-stock Americans viewed them all simply as Italians. Henry Ford and other employers tried to erase the differences through English classes and deliberate "Americanization" programs.

The Ford Motor Company ran a school where immigrant employees were first taught to say, "I am a good American." At the graduation ceremony, the pupils acted out a gigantic pantomime in which, clad in their old-country dress, they filed into a large "melting pot." When they emerged, they were wearing identical American-made clothes, and each was waving a little American flag.

In similar fashion, the International Harvester Corporation taught Polish laborers to speak English, but it had other lessons in view as well. According to Lesson One, drilled into the Polish "pupils":

I hear the whistle. I must hurry.
I hear the five minute whistle.
It is time to go into the shop.
I take my check from the gate board and hang it on the department board.
I change my clothes and get ready to work.
The starting whistle blows.
I eat my lunch.
It is forbidden to eat until then.
The whistle blows at five minutes of starting time.
I get ready to go to work.
I work until the whistle blows to quit.
I leave my place nice and clean.
I put all my clothes in the locker.
I must go home.

Labor groups soon learned to counter these techniques. The **Women's Trade Union League (WTUL)** urged workers to ignore business-sponsored English lessons because they did not "tell the girl worker the things she really wants to know. They do not suggest that $5 a week is not a living wage. They tell her to be respectful to her employer." Designing its own educational

program, the WTUL in 1912 published "New World Lessons for Old World Peoples," which provided quite a different kind of English lesson:

A Union girl takes me into the Union.
The Union girls are glad to see me.
They call me sister.
I will work hard for our Union.
I will come to all the Union meetings.

In another significant development at the beginning of the twentieth century, Mexicans for the first time immigrated in large numbers, especially after a revolution in Mexico in 1910 forced many to flee across the northern border into Texas, New Mexico, Arizona, and California. Their exact numbers were unknown. American officials did not count border crossings until 1907, and even then, many migrants avoided the official immigration stations. Almost all came from the Mexican lower class, eager to escape

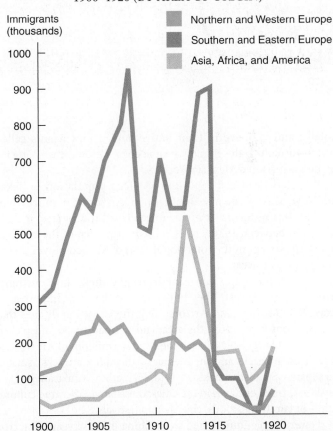

IMMIGRATION TO THE UNITED STATES, 1900–1920 (BY AREA OF ORIGIN)

- Northern and Western Europe
- Southern and Eastern Europe
- Asia, Africa, and America

Note: For purposes of classification, "Northern and Western Europe" includes Great Britain, Ireland, Scandinavia, the Netherlands, Belgium, Luxembourg, Switzerland, France, and Germany. "Southern and Eastern Europe" includes Poland, Austria-Hungary, Russia and the Baltic States, Romania, Bulgaria, European Turkey, Italy, Spain, Portugal, and Greece. "Asia, Africa, and America" includes Asian Turkey, China, Japan, India, Canada, the Caribbean, Latin America, and all of Africa.

Source: U.S. Bureau of the Census, Historical *Statistics of the United States, Colonial Times to 1970*, Bicentennial Edition, Washington, DC, 1975.

MEXICAN IMMIGRATION TO THE
UNITED STATES, 1900–1920

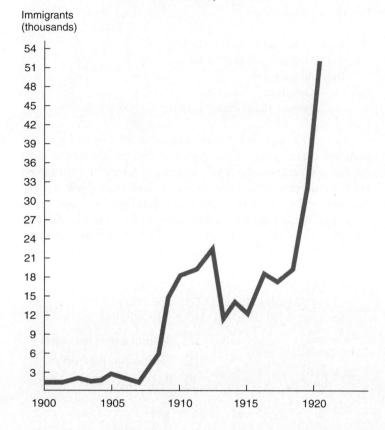

men outnumbered women by ten to one in the Chinese American population, and with a male median age of 42, their communities were generally dominated by the elderly.

The Chinese American population differed in another respect as well. Unlike other immigrant groups, whose numbers tended to grow, the number of Chinese Americans shrank in these years—from about 125,000 in the early 1880s to just over 60,000 in 1920. After 1910, the U.S. government set up a special immigration facility at Angel Island in San Francisco Bay, but unlike European immigrants who landed at Ellis Island in New York and were quickly sent on, Chinese immigrants were kept for weeks and months, examined and reexamined, before being allowed to cross the narrow band of water to San Francisco. Angel Island remained open until 1940, and a poem carved into the wall of Building 317 showed the feelings of some of those who waited:

> There are tens of thousands of poems composed on these walls,
> They are all cries of complaint and sadness.
> The day I am rid of this prison and attain success,
> I must remember that this prison once existed.
> In my daily needs I must be frugal.
> Needless extravagance leads youth to ruin.
> All my compatriots please be mindful.
> Once you have some small gains, return home early.
> By One from Xiangshan

Many Japanese also arrived at Angel Island, and though at first fewer in numbers than the Chinese, they developed communities along the Pacific coast, where they settled mainly on farms. The number of Japanese Americans grew. In 1907, the heaviest year of immigration from Japan, nearly 31,000 Japanese entered the United States; by 1920, there were 111,000 Japanese in the country, nearly three-quarters of them in California.

As the newcomers arrived from Asia, Europe, and Mexico, nativist sentiment, which had criticized earlier waves of immigrants, intensified. Old-stock Americans sneered at their dress and language. Racial theories emphasized the superiority of northern Europeans, and the new "science" of eugenics suggested the need to control the population growth of "inferior" peoples. Hostility toward Catholics and Jews was common but touched other groups as well.

In 1902, Congress enacted a law prohibiting immigration from China. Statutes requiring literacy tests designed to curtail immigration from southern and eastern Europe were vetoed by William Howard Taft in 1913 and by Woodrow Wilson in 1915 and 1917. In 1917, such a measure passed despite Wilson's veto. Other measures tried to limit immigration from Mexico and Japan.

peonage and violence in their native land. Labor agents called *coyotes*—usually in the employ of large corporations or working for ranchers—recruited Mexican workers.

Between 1900 and 1910, the Mexican population of Texas and New Mexico nearly doubled; in Arizona, it more than doubled; in California, it quadrupled. In all four states, it doubled again between 1910 and 1920. After the turn of the century, almost 10 percent of the total population of Mexico moved to the American Southwest.

In time, these Mexican Americans and their children transformed the Southwest. They built most of the early highways in Texas, New Mexico, and Arizona; dug the irrigation ditches that watered crops throughout the area; laid railroad track; and picked the cotton and vegetables that clothed and fed millions of Americans. Many lived in shacks and shanties along the railroad tracks, isolated in a separate Spanish-speaking world. Like other immigrant groups, they also formed enclaves in the cities; these *barrios* became cultural islands of family life, foods, church, and festivals.

Fewer people immigrated from China in these years, deterred in part by anti-Chinese laws and hostility. Like many other immigrants, most Chinese who came did not intend to remain. Wanting to make money and return home, they mined, farmed, and worked as common laborers. In their willingness to work hard for low wages, their desire to preserve clan and family associations from China, and their maintenance of strong ties with their home villages, Chinese Americans resembled other immigrant groups, but they differed in two important respects. As late as 1920,

Conflict in the Workplace

Why were there so many strikes in this period?

Assembly lines, speedups, long hours, and low pay produced a dramatic increase in American industrial output (and profits) after 1900; they also gave rise to numerous strikes and other kinds of labor unrest. Sometimes strikes took place through the

Japanese picture brides arrive at Angel Island and are lined up for passport inspection before meeting their new husbands.

action of unions; sometimes workers just decided they had had enough and walked off the job. Whatever the cause, strikes were frequent. In one industry, in one city—the meatpacking industry in Chicago—there were 251 strikes in 1903 alone.

Strikes and absenteeism increased after 1910; labor productivity dropped 10 percent between 1915 and 1918, the first such decline in memory. In many industries, labor turnover became a serious problem; workers changed jobs in droves. Union membership grew. In 1900, only about a million workers—less than 4 percent of the workforce—belonged to unions. By 1920, five million workers belonged, increasing the unionized portion of the workforce to about 13 percent.

As tensions grew between capital and labor, some people in the middle class became fearful that, unless something was done to improve the workers' situation, there might be violence or even revolution. This fear motivated some of the labor-oriented reforms of the Progressive Era. While some reform supporters genuinely wanted to improve labor's lot, others embraced reform because they were afraid of something else.

Organizing Labor

Samuel Gompers's American Federation of Labor increased from 250,000 members in 1897 to 1.7 million in 1904. By far the largest union organization, it remained devoted to the interests of skilled craftspeople. While it aimed partly at better wages and working conditions, it also sought to limit entry into the crafts and protect worker prerogatives. Within limits, the AFL found acceptance among giant business corporations eager for conservative policies and labor stability.

Of the eight million female workers in 1910, only 125,000 belonged to unions. Gompers continued to resist organizing them, saying they were too emotional and, as union organizers, "had a way of making serious mistakes." Margaret Dreier Robins, an organizer of proven skill, scoffed at that. "These men died twenty years ago and are just walking around dead!" she protested.

Robins helped found the Women's Trade Union League in 1903. The WTUL led the effort to organize women into trade unions, to lobby for legislation protecting female workers, and to educate the

📖—|Read the Document   **Samuel Gompers, The American Labor Movement (1914)**

Samuel Gompers (second from bottom left) co-founded the American Federation of Labor in 1886 and served as its president in 1914 when its membership approached two million skilled workers. Gompers's trade union philosophy focused on the economic ends of skilled workers including achieving higher wages, the eight-hour day, and safe working conditions through collective bargaining with employers.

public on the problems and needs of working women. It took in all working women who would join, regardless of skill (although not, at first, African American women), and it won crucial financial support from well-to-do women such as Anne Morgan, daughter of the feared financier J. P. Morgan. Robins's close friend Jane Addams belonged, as did Mary McDowell, the "Angel of the Stockyards," who worked with slaughterhouse workers in Chicago; Julia Lathrop, who tried to improve the lot of wage-earning children; and Dr. Alice Hamilton, a pioneer in American research on the causes of industrial disease.

The WTUL never had many members—a few thousand at most—but its influence extended far beyond its membership. In 1909, it supported the "Uprising of the 20,000," a strike of shirt-waist workers in New York City. When female employees of the

Triangle Shirtwaist Company tried to form a union, the company fired them, and they walked out; twenty thousand men and women in five hundred other shops followed. Strike meetings were conducted in three languages—English, Yiddish, and Italian—and before being forced to go back to work, the strikers won a shorter workweek and a few other gains. Sadly, the Triangle women lost out on another important demand—for unlocked shop doors and safe fire escapes. Their loss proved lethal in the famous Triangle Shirtwaist Company fire of 1911 (see the Feature Essay, "The Triangle Fire," pp. 528–529).

The WTUL also backed a strike in 1910 against Hart, Schaffner and Marx, Chicago's largest manufacturer of men's clothing. One day, Annie Shapiro, the 18-year-old daughter of Russian immigrants, was told her wages were being cut from

$7 a week to $6.20. That was a large cut, and along with sixteen other young women, Shapiro refused to accept it and walked out. "We had to be recognized as people," she said later. Soon other women walked out, and the revolt spread. Managers quickly promised to restore the cuts, but as one woman said, "just then there was big noise outside and we all rushed to the windows and there we saw the police beating the strikers on our account, and when we saw that we went out."

In a matter of days, some forty thousand garment workers were on strike, about half of them women. Manufacturers hurried to negotiate, and the result was the important Hart, Schaffner agreement, which created an arbitration committee composed of management and labor to handle grievances and settle disputes. The first successful experiment in collective bargaining, the Hart, Schaffner agreement became the model for the kind of agreements that govern industrial relations today.

Another union, the **Industrial Workers of the World (IWW)**, attracted by far the greatest attention (and the most fears) in these years. Unlike the WTUL, it welcomed everyone regardless of gender or race. Unlike the AFL, it tried to organize the unskilled and foreign-born laborers who worked in the mass production industries. Founded in Chicago in 1905, it aimed to unite the American working class into a mammoth union to promote labor's interests. Its motto— "An injury to one is an injury to all"—emphasized labor solidarity, as had the earlier Knights of Labor. But unlike the Knights, the IWW, or Wobblies as they were often known, urged social revolution.

"It is our purpose to overthrow the capitalist system by forcible means if necessary," William D. "Big Bill" Haywood, one of its founders, said; and he went on in his speeches to say he knew of nothing a worker could do that "will bring as much anguish to the boss as a little sabotage in the right place." Joe Hill, the IWW's legendary folk poet, reminded labor of its potential strength:

> If the workers took a notion
> They could stop all speeding trains;
> Every ship upon the ocean
> They can tie with mighty chains.
> Every wheel in the creation
> Every mine and every mill;
> Fleets and armies of the nation,
> Will at their command stand still.

IWW leaders included Mary Harris ("Mother") Jones, a famous veteran of battles in the Illinois coalfields; Elizabeth Gurley Flynn, a fiery young radical who joined as a teenager; and Big Bill Haywood himself, the strapping one-eyed founder of the Western Federation of Miners.

The IWW led a number of major strikes. Strikes in Lawrence, Massachusetts (1912), and Paterson, New Jersey (1912), attracted national attention: in Lawrence, when the strikers sent their children, ill-clad and hungry, out of the city to stay with sympathetic families; in Paterson, when they rented New York's Madison Square Garden for a massive labor pageant. IWW leaders welcomed the revolutionary tumult sweeping Russia and other countries. In the United States, they thought, a series of local strikes would bring about capitalist repression, then a general strike, and eventually a workers' commonwealth.

The IWW fell short of these objectives, but during its lifetime— from 1905 to the mid-1920s—it made major gains among immigrant workers in the Northeast, migrant farm laborers on the Plains, and loggers and miners in the South and Far West. In factories like Ford's, it recruited workers resentful of the speedups on the assembly lines. Although IWW membership probably amounted to no more than one hundred thousand at any one time, workers came and left so often that its total membership may have reached as high as one million.

Working with Workers

Concerned about labor unrest, some business leaders used violence and police action to keep workers in line, but others turned to the new fields of applied psychology and personnel management. A school of industrial psychology emerged. As had Taylor, industrial psychologists studied workers' routines, and, further, they showed that output was also affected by job satisfaction. While most businesses pushed ahead with efficiency campaigns, a few did establish industrial relations departments, hire public relations firms to improve their corporate image, and link productivity to job safety and worker happiness.

Ivy L. Lee, a pioneer in the field of corporate public relations, advised clients such as the Pennsylvania Railroad and Standard Oil on how to improve relations with labor and the public. Calling himself a "physician to corporate bodies," Lee urged complete openness on the company's part. To please employees, companies printed newsletters and organized softball teams; they awarded prizes and celebrated retirements. Ford created a "sociology department" staffed by 150 experts who showed workers how to budget their incomes and care for their health. They even taught them how to shop for meat.

LABOR UNION MEMBERSHIP, 1897–1920

Millions

Source: U.S. Bureau of the Census, *Statistical Abstract of the United States: 1982–1983*, 103rd ed., Washington, DC, 1982.

Feature Essay | The Triangle Fire

Women's fashion changed rather dramatically in the 1890s and early 1900s, reflecting in part the desires of women for greater freedom in many parts of their lives. Confining corsets began to disappear, as women turned to looser, more casual designs. The "shirtwaist," or blouse, became especially popular, flattering to the figure and tapered to a fitted waistline, usually worn with a tailored skirt.

That trend brought business, a great deal of it, to the Triangle Waist Company of New York City, which employed more than 500 people and was the largest maker of blouses in the city. It produced 2,000 of them a day, a million dollars' worth a year.

At Triangle, as at similar companies, immigrants from Eastern Europe provided much of the labor. The Triangle Company did not pay well—none of the companies did—but to many immigrants it was a good place to work because, unlike many competitors, it offered jobs all year round.

Triangle also reflected an important factory movement, characteristic of these years, in which the garment industry changed from the traditional piece-work system to large, efficient, and mass-production factories. Under the old system, each worker had pushed a treadle, usually in her own apartment, to power her machine; now, electricity powered long drive shafts that connected machine after machine.

Triangle Company employees worked hard, five nine-hour days a week, plus a shorter seven-hour day on Saturdays. Saturday was also payday. That was why people were at work on Saturday, March 25, 1911.

At 4:45 P.M. that day, floor leader Annah Gullo rang the closing bell and shut off the power to the drive shafts; the machines fell silent. Chairs pushed back on the wooden floors as workers made their way to the exits to pick up their pay and get their coats for home.

Then suddenly, a worker came running across the floor, shouting, "Fire!" Workers grabbed the fire pails from a ledge above the tables and poured water on the fire, but to no avail. Other workers were already lined up at wooden partitions near the exits, which channeled them through one at a time so that watchmen could look in their handbags for stolen lace or blouses.

Smoke pouring from the eighth floor windows soon attracted a crowd of bystanders outside. When a large, dark bundle fell from one of the windows, an onlooker said, "He's trying to save his best cloth." When another bundle hit the ground, people realized that this was not cloth; it was a human being. "I learned a new sound," a reporter said that day, "a more horrible sound than description can picture. It was the thud of a speeding, living body on a stone sidewalk."

The first person jumped at about 4:50 P.M., deciding not to die in the raging fire. But it was hard to survive the jump, too; the street was nearly 100 feet below, and in March 1911, ladders on fire trucks could reach no higher than the sixth floor. Inside, people screamed as they searched for the exits, eyes blinded by the shifting smoke. As they crowded onto the flimsy fire escape, it twisted and fell, the victim of its own poor design.

Adding to the tragedy, workers at Triangle had gone on strike in 1909, two years before, in the famous Uprising of the 20,000, "the largest strike ever organized by working women anywhere in the world," as one journalist has noted. Some garment workers had won, but the Triangle women had not. They had asked for adequate fire escapes and unblocked exits; they got neither.

"I remembered their great strike . . ., in which these girls demanded more sanitary workrooms, and *more safety precautions* in the shops," a reporter wrote after the fire. "These dead bodies told the result."

In the days following the fire, protest meetings were held across the city. "I would be a traitor to those poor burned bodies if I were to come here to talk good fellowship," Rose Schneiderman, a dynamic 29-year-old organizer for the Women's Trade Union League, told one rally. "We have tried you good people of the public—and we have found you wanting . . . . This is not the first time girls have been burned alive in this city. Every week I must learn of the untimely death of one of my sister workers. Every year thousands of us are maimed. The life of men and women is so cheap and property is so sacred!"

One hundred forty-six people, nearly all young women, died in the fire.

The fire galvanized reformers interested in factory safety, and there were many of them in this Progressive Era. Frances Perkins, later secretary of labor under Franklin D. Roosevelt, the first female cabinet member in the country's history, was visiting friends near the Triangle factory on the day of the fire. They heard the fire engines and rushed out to see what was happening. "We got there just as they started to jump," Perkins recalled. "I shall never forget the frozen horror which came over us as we stood with our hands on our throats, watching that horrible sight, knowing that there was no help."

528

Crowds of young women who made it out onto the fire escape perished when it gave way under their weight.

On April 5, signaling public protest, eighty thousand people marched silently in the rain in a funeral procession up Fifth Avenue. A quarter-million people lined the route.

In response to the outcry, New York State authorities created a Factory Investigating Commission that sent examiners into factories across the state. In all, the tragedy spurred passage of thirty-six new labor laws, a new Industrial Code for the State of New York, and higher national standards for factory safety. New laws required automatic fire sprinklers in high-rise buildings, mandatory fire drills, and unlocked doors at factory exits.

Frances Perkins, who had advised the Commission, thought the events at Triangle had lasting consequences. "The Triangle fire," she later said, "was the first day of the New Deal."

QUESTIONS FOR DISCUSSION

1. What changes in American society and industry lay behind the circumstances of the Triangle Fire?

2. Why were so many women killed in the Triangle Fire?

3. Why did Frances Perkins say that the Triangle Fire was "the first day of the New Deal"?

529

On January 5, 1914, Ford took another significant step. He announced the five-dollar day, "the greatest revolution," he said, "in the matter of rewards for workers ever known to the industrial world." With a stroke, he doubled the wage rate for common labor, reduced the working day from nine hours to eight, and established a personnel department to place workers in appropriate jobs. The next day, ten thousand applicants stood outside the gates.

As a result, Ford had the pick of the labor force. Turnover declined; absenteeism, previously as much as one-tenth of all Ford workers every day, fell to 0.3 percent. Output increased; the IWW at Ford collapsed. The plan increased wages, but it also gave the company greater control over a more stable labor force. Workers had to meet a behavior code in order to qualify for the five-dollar day. At first scornful of the "utopian" plan, business leaders across the country soon copied it, and on January 2, 1919, Ford announced the six-dollar day.

Amoskeag

In size, system, and worker relations, the record of the Amoskeag Company textile mills was revealing. Located beside the Merrimack River in Manchester, New Hampshire, the mills—an enormous complex of factories, warehouses, canals, and machinery—had been built in the 1830s. By the turn of the century, they were producing nearly fifty miles of cloth an hour, more cloth each day than any other set of mills in the entire world.

The face of the mills, an almost solid wall of red brick, stretched nearly a mile. Archways and bridges pierced the facade. Amoskeag resembled a walled medieval city within which workers found "a total institution, a closed and almost self-contained world." At first the mills employed young women for labor, but by 1900, more and more immigrant males staffed the machines. French Canadians, Irish, Poles, and Greeks—seventeen thousand in all—worked there, and their experiences revealed a great deal about factory work and life at the turn of the century.

The company hired and fired at will, and it demanded relentless output from the spindles and spinning frames. Yet it also viewed employees as its "children" and looked for total loyalty in return, an expectation often realized. Workers identified with Amoskeag and, decades later, still called themselves Amoskeag men and women. "We were all like a family," one said.

Most Amoskeag workers preferred the industrial world of the mills to the farms they had left behind. They did not feel displaced; they knew the pains of industrial life, and they adapted in ways that fit their own needs and traditions. Families played a large role. They neither disintegrated nor lost their relationships. French Canadians and others often came in family units. One or two family members left the farm for the mills, maintained close ties with those back home, and then sent for others, creating a form of "chain migration."

Once in Manchester, families often toiled in the same workrooms. Looking after each other, they asked for transfers and promotions for relatives; they taught their children technical skills and how to get along with bosses and fellow workers. Although low paid, Amoskeag employees took pride in their work, and for many of them, a well-turned-out product provided dignity and self-esteem.

As part of its paternal interest in employee welfare, in 1910 the company inaugurated a welfare and efficiency program, which aimed to increase productivity, accustom immigrants to industrial work, instill company loyalty, and curb labor unrest. Playgrounds and visiting nurses, home-buying plans, a cooking school, and dental service were part of the plan. The Amoskeag Textile Club held employee dinners and picnics, organized shooting clubs and a baseball team, sponsored Christmas parties for the children, and published the *Amoskeag Bulletin*, a monthly magazine of employee news.

From 1885 to 1919, no strike touched the mills. Thereafter, however, labor unrest increased. Overproduction and foreign competition took their toll, and Amoskeag closed in 1935.

A New Urban Culture

What happened to art and culture in these years so filled with change?

For many Americans, the quality of life improved significantly between 1900 and 1920. Jobs were relatively plentiful, and, in a development of great importance, more and more people were entering the professions as doctors, lawyers, teachers, and engineers. With comfortable incomes, a growing middle class could take advantage of new lifestyles, inventions, and forms of entertainment. Mass production could not have worked without mass consumption, and Americans in these years increasingly became a nation of consumers.

Production and Consumption

In 1900, business firms spent about $95 million on advertising; twenty years later, they spent more than $500 million. Ads and billboards touted cigarettes, cars, perfumes, and cosmetics. Advertising agencies boomed. Using new sampling techniques, they developed modern concepts of market testing and research. Sampling customer preferences affected business indirectly as well, making it more responsive to public opinion on social and political issues.

Mass production swept the clothing industry and dressed more Americans better than any people ever before. Using lessons learned in making uniforms during the Civil War, manufacturers for the first time developed standard clothing and shoe sizes that fit most bodies. Clothing prices dropped; the availability of inexpensive "off-the-rack" clothes lessened distinctions between rich and poor. By 1900, nine of every ten men and boys wore the new "ready-to-wear" clothes.

In 1900, people employed in manufacturing earned on average $418 a year. Two decades later, they earned $1,342 a year, though inflation took much of the increase. While the middle class expanded, the rich also grew richer. In 1920, the new income tax showed the first accurate tabulation of income, and it confirmed what many had suspected all along. Five percent of the population received almost one-fourth of all income.

Living and Dying in an Urban Nation

In 1920, the median age of the population was only 25. (It is now 35.) Immigration accounted for part of the population's youthfulness, since most immigrants were young. Thanks to medical advances and better living conditions, the death rate dropped in the early years of the century; the average life span increased. Between 1900 and 1920, life expectancy rose from 49 to 56 years for white women and from 47 to 54 years for white men. It rose from 33 to 45 years for blacks and other racial minorities.

Despite the increase in life expectancy, infant mortality remained high; nearly 10 percent of white babies and 20 percent of minority babies died in the first year of life. In comparison to today, fewer babies on average survived to adolescence, and fewer people survived beyond middle age. In 1900, the death rate among people between 45 and 65 was more than twice the modern rate. As a result, there were relatively fewer older people—in 1900, only 4 percent of the population was older than 65 compared to nearly 13 percent today. Fewer children than today knew their grandparents. Still, improvements in health care helped people live longer, and as a result, the incidence of cancer and heart disease increased.

Cities grew, and by any earlier standards, they grew on a colossal scale. Downtowns became a central hive of skyscrapers, department stores, warehouses, and hotels. Strips of factories radiated from the center. As street railways spread, cities took on a systematic pattern of socioeconomic segregation, usually in rings. The innermost ring filled with immigrants, circled by a belt of working-class housing. The remaining rings marked areas of rising affluence outward toward wealthy suburbs, which themselves formed around shopping strips and grid patterns of streets that restricted social interaction.

The giants were New York, Chicago, and Philadelphia, industrial cities that turned out every kind of product from textiles to structural steel. Smaller cities such as Rochester, New York, or Cleveland, Ohio, specialized in manufacturing a specific line of goods or processing regional products for the national market. Railroads instead of highways tied things together; in 1916, the rail network, the largest in the world, reached its peak—254,000 miles of track that carried more than three-fourths of all intercity freight tonnage.

Step by step, cities adopted their twentieth-century forms. Between 1909 and 1915, Los Angeles, a city of three hundred thousand people, passed a series of ordinances that gave rise to modern urban zoning. For the first time, the ordinances divided a city into three districts of specified use: a residential area, an industrial area, and an area open to residence and a limited list of industries. Other cities followed. Combining several features, the New York zoning law of 1916 became the model for the nation; within a decade, 591 cities copied it.

Zoning ordered city development, keeping skyscrapers out of factory districts, factories out of the suburbs. It also had powerful social repercussions. In the South, zoning became a tool to extend racial segregation; in northern cities, it acted against ethnic minorities. Jews in New York, Italians in Boston, Poles in Detroit, African Americans in Chicago—zoning laws held them all at arm's length. Like other migrants, African Americans often preferred to settle together, but zoning also helped put them there. By 1920, ten districts in Chicago were more than three-quarters black. In Los Angeles, Cleveland, Detroit, and Washington, D.C., most blacks lived in only two or three wards.

Popular Pastimes

Thanks to changing work rules and mechanization, many Americans enjoyed more leisure time. The average workweek for manufacturing laborers fell from 60 hours in 1890 to 51 in 1920. By the early 1900s, white-collar workers might spend only 8 to 10 hours a day at work and a half day on weekends. Greater leisure time gave more people more opportunity for play, and people flocked to places of entertainment. Baseball entrenched itself as the national pastime. Automobiles and streetcars carried growing numbers of fans to ballparks; attendance at major league games doubled between 1903 and 1920. Football also drew fans, although critics attacked the sport's violence and the use of "tramp athletes," nonstudents whom colleges paid to play. In 1905, the worst year, 18 players were killed and 150 seriously injured.

Alarmed, President Theodore Roosevelt—who had once said, "I am the father of three boys [and] if I thought any one of them would weigh a possible broken bone against the glory of being chosen to play on Harvard's football team I would disinherit him"—called a White House conference to clean up college sports. The conference founded the Intercollegiate Athletic Association, which in 1910 became the National Collegiate Athletic Association (NCAA).

Movie theaters opened everywhere. By 1910, there were ten thousand of them, drawing a weekly audience of ten million people. Admission was usually five cents, and movies full of laughter and pathos appealed to a mass market. In 1915, D. W. Griffith, a talented and creative director—as well as a racist—produced the first movie spectacular: *Birth of a Nation*. Griffith adopted new film techniques, including close-ups, fade-outs, and artistic camera angles, and he staged dramatic battle scenes.

Phonographs brought ready-made entertainment into the home. By 1901, phonograph and record companies included the Victor Talking Machine Company, the Edison Speaking Machine Company, and Columbia Records. Ornate mahogany Victrolas became standard fixtures in middle-class parlors. Early records were usually of vaudeville skits; orchestral recordings began in 1906. In 1919, 2.25 million phonographs were produced; two years later, more than 100 million records were sold.

As record sales grew, families sang less and listened more. Music became a business. In 1909, Congress enacted a copyright law that provided a two-cent royalty on each piece of music on phonograph records or piano rolls. The royalty, small as it was, offered welcome income to composers and publishers, and in 1914, composer Victor Herbert and others formed the American Society of Composers, Authors, and Publishers (ASCAP) to protect musical rights and royalties.

The faster rhythms of syncopated ragtime became the rage, especially after 1911, when Irving Berlin, a Russian immigrant, wrote "Alexander's Ragtime Band." Ragtime set off a nationwide dance craze. Secretaries danced on their lunch hour, the first nightclubs opened, and restaurants and hotels introduced dance floors. Waltzes and polkas gave way to a host of new dances, many with

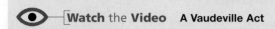

Watch the Video **A Vaudeville Act**

Consisting of a wide variety, vaudeville was probably the most popular mass entertainment in the early 1900s. With the addition of jugglers, pantomimists, magicians, and others, the number of vaudeville theaters increased exponentially.

animal names: the fox-trot, bunny hop, turkey trot, snake, and kangaroo dip. Partners were not permitted to dance too close; bouncers tapped them on the shoulder if they got closer than nine inches. The aging John D. Rockefeller hired a private instructor to teach him the tango; Yale University, however, banned that dance at its 1914 junior prom.

Vaudeville, increasingly popular after 1900, reached maturity around 1915. Drawing on the immigrant experience, it voiced the variety of city life and included skits, songs, comics, acrobats, and magicians. Dances and jokes showed an earthiness new to mass audiences. By 1914, stage runways extended into the crowd; women performers had bared their legs and were beginning to show glimpses of the midriff. Fanny Brice; Ann Pennington, the "shimmy" queen; and Eva Tanguay, who sang "It's All Been Done Before But Not the Way I Do It," starred in Florenz Ziegfeld's Follies, the peak of vaudeville.

In such songs as "St. Louis Blues" (1914), W. C. Handy took the black southern folk music of the blues to northern cities. Gertrude "Ma" Rainey, the daughter of minstrels, sang in black vaudeville for nearly thirty-five years. Performing in Chattanooga, Tennessee, about 1910, she came across a twelve-year-old orphan, Bessie Smith, who became the "Empress of the Blues." Smith's voice was huge and sweeping. Recording for the Race division of Columbia Records, she made more than eighty records that together sold nearly ten million copies.

Another musical innovation came north from New Orleans. Charles (Buddy) Bolden, a cornetist; Ferdinand "Jelly Roll" Morton, a pianist; and a youngster named Louis Armstrong played an improvisational music that had no formal name. Reaching Chicago, it became "jas," then "jass," and finally "jazz." Jazz jumped, and jazz musicians relied on feeling and mood. A restaurant owner once asked Jelly Roll Morton to play a waltz. "Waltz?" Morton exclaimed. "Man, these people want to dance! And you talking about waltz. This is the Roll you're talking to."

Popular fiction reflected changing interests. Kate Douglas Wiggins's *Rebecca of Sunnybrook Farm* (1903) and Lucy M. Montgomery's *Anne of Green Gables* (1908) showed the continuing popularity of rural themes. Westerns also sold well, but readers turned more and more to detective thrillers with hard-bitten city detectives and science fiction featuring the latest dream in technology. The Tom Swift series, begun in 1910, looked ahead to spaceships, ray guns, and gravity nullifiers.

Edward L. Stratemeyer, the mind behind Tom Swift, brought the techniques of mass production to book writing. In 1906, he formed the Stratemeyer Literary Syndicate, which employed a stable of writers to turn out hundreds of Tom Swift, Rover Boys, and Bobbsey Twins stories for young readers. Burt Standish, another prolific author, took the pen name Gilbert Patten and created the character of Frank Merriwell, wholesome college athlete. As Patten said, "I took the three qualities I most wanted him to represent—frank and merry in nature, well in body and mind—and made the name Frank Merriwell." The Merriwell books sold twenty-five million copies.

Experimentation in the Arts

"There is a state of unrest all over the world in art as in all other things," the director of New York's Metropolitan Museum said in 1908. "It is the same in literature, as in music, in painting, and in sculpture."

Isadora Duncan and Ruth St. Denis transformed the dance. Departing from traditional ballet steps, both women emphasized improvisation, emotion, and the human form. "Listen to the music with your soul," Duncan told her students. "Unless your dancing springs from an inner emotion and expresses an idea, it will be meaningless." Draped in flowing robes, she revealed more of her legs than some thought tasteful, and she proclaimed that the "noblest art is the nude." After a triumphant performance with the New York Symphony in 1908, her ideas and techniques swept the country. Duncan died tragically in 1927, her neck broken when her long red scarf caught in the wheel of a racing car.

The lofts and apartments of New York's Greenwich Village attracted artists, writers, and poets interested in experimentation and change. To these artists, the city was the focus of national life and the sign of a new culture. Robert Henri and the realist painters—known to their critics as the **Ashcan School**—relished the city's excitement. They wanted, a friend said, "to paint truth and to paint it with strength and fearlessness and individuality."

To the realists, a painting carried into the future the look of life as it happened. Their paintings depicted street scenes, colorful crowds, and slum children swimming in the river. In paintings such as the *Cliff Dwellers*, George W. Bellows captured the color and excitement of the tenements; John Sloan, one of Henri's most talented students, painted the vitality of ordinary people and familiar scenes.

In 1913, a show at the New York Armory presented sixteen hundred modernist paintings, prints, and sculptures. The work of Picasso, Cézanne, Matisse, Brancusi, Van Gogh, and Gauguin dazed and dazzled American observers. Critics attacked the show as worthless and depraved; a Chicago official wanted it banned from the city because the "idea that people can gaze at this sort of thing without [it] hurting them is all bosh."

The postimpressionists changed the direction of twentieth-century art and influenced adventuresome American painters. John Marin, Max Weber, Georgia O'Keeffe, Arthur Dove, and other modernists experimented in ways foreign to Henri's realists. Defiantly avant-garde, they shook off convention and experimented with new forms. Using bold colors and abstract patterns, they worked to capture the energy of urban life. "I see great forces at work, great movements," Marin said, "the large buildings and the small buildings, the warring of the great and the small. . . . I can hear the sound of their strife, and there is a great music being played."

There was an extraordinary outburst of poetry. In 1912, Harriet Monroe started the magazine *Poetry* in Chicago, the hotbed of the new poetry; Ezra Pound and Vachel Lindsay, both daring experimenters with ideas and verse, published in the first issue. T. S. Eliot published the classic "Love Song of J. Alfred Prufrock" in *Poetry* in 1915. Attacked bitterly by conservative critics, the poem established Eliot's leadership among a group of poets, many of them living and writing in London, who rejected traditional meter and rhyme as artificial constraints. Eliot, Pound, and Amy Lowell, among others, believed the poet's task was to capture fleeting images in verse.

Others experimenting with new techniques in poetry included Robert Frost (*North of Boston*, 1914), Edgar Lee Masters (*Spoon River Anthology*, 1915), and Carl Sandburg (*Chicago Poems*, 1916). Sandburg's poem "Chicago" celebrated the vitality of the city:

> Come and show me another city with lifted head
>   singing so proud to be
>   alive and coarse and strong and cunning.
> . . . .

> Fierce as a dog with tongue lapping for action,
>   cunning as a savage
>   pitted against the wilderness,
>   Bareheaded,
>   Shoveling,
>   Wrecking,
>   Planning,
>   Building, breaking, rebuilding,
> . . . .
> Bragging and laughing that under his wrist is the
>   pulse, and under his
>   ribs the heart of the people,
>   Laughing!
> Laughing the stormy, husky, brawling laughter of
>   Youth, half-naked,
>   sweating, proud to be Hog Butcher, Tool
>   Maker, Stacker of Wheat,
>   Player with Railroads and Freight Handler to
>   the Nation.

Conclusion: A Ferment of Discovery and Reform

Manners and morals change slowly, and many Americans overlooked the importance of the first two decades of the twentieth century. Yet sweeping change was under way; anyone who doubted it could visit a gallery, see a film, listen to music, or read one of the new literary magazines. Garrets and galleries were filled with a breathtaking sense of change. "There was life in all these new things," Marsden Hartley, a modernist painter, recalled. "There was excitement, there was healthy revolt, investigation, discovery, and an utterly new world out of it all."

The ferment of progressivism in city, state, and nation reshaped the country. In a burst of reform, people built playgrounds, restructured taxes, regulated business, won the vote for women, shortened working hours, altered political systems, opened kindergartens, and improved factory safety. They tried to fulfill the national promise of dignity and liberty.

Marsden Hartley, it turned out, had voiced a mood that went well beyond painters and poets. Across society, people in many walks of life were experiencing a similar sense of excitement and discovery. Racism, repression, and labor conflict were present, to be sure, but there was also talk of hope, progress, and change. In politics, science, journalism, education, and a host of other fields, people believed for a time that they could make a difference, and in trying to do so, they became part of the progressive generation.

Study Resources

 Take the **Study Plan** for **Chapter 22** *The Progressive Era* on **MyHistoryLab**

TIME LINE

1898 Mergers and consolidations begin to sweep the business world, leading to fear of trusts

1903 Ford Motor Company formed; W. E. B. DuBois calls for justice and equality for African Americans in *The Souls of Black Folk*; Women's Trade Union League (WTUL) formed to organize women workers

1905 Industrial Workers of the World (IWW) established; African American leaders inaugurate the Niagara Movement, advocating integration and equal opportunity for African Americans

1909 Shirtwaist workers in New York City strike in the Uprising of the 20,000; Campaign by Rockefeller Sanitary Commission wipes out hookworm disease

1910 NAACP founded; Strike at Hart, Schaffner and Marx leads to pioneering collective bargaining agreement; National Collegiate Athletic Association (NCAA) formed

1911 Fire at the Triangle Shirtwaist Company kills 146 people; Irving Berlin popularizes rhythm of ragtime with "Alexander's Ragtime Band";

Frederick Winslow Taylor publishes *The Principles of Scientific Management*

1912 Harriet Monroe begins publishing magazine *Poetry*; IWW leads strikes in Massachusetts and New Jersey

1913 Ford introduces the moving assembly line in Highland Park, Michigan, plant; Mother's Day becomes national holiday

1915 D. W. Griffith produces the first movie spectacular, *Birth of a Nation*; T. S. Eliot publishes "The Love Song of J. Alfred Prufrock"

1916 Margaret Sanger forms New York Birth Control League; Federal Aid Roads Act creates national road network; New York zoning law sets the pattern for zoning laws across the nation

1917 Congress passes law requiring literacy test for all immigrants

1921 Congress passes the Sheppard-Towner Act to help protect maternal and infant health

CHAPTER REVIEW

The Changing Face of Industrialism

 How did industrialism change after 1900?

As prosperity returned after the late 1890s, the American industrial system underwent important changes. Mass production, spurred by the spread of the moving assembly line, turned out more and more products for American and foreign consumers. New management methods organized workers on the factory floor. Jobs became both routine and more dangerous. Trusts grew. (p. 515)

Society's Masses

 How did mass production affect women, children, immigrants, and African Americans?

While life improved for many people in the post-1900 industrial society, many others faced challenges: women and children in the workforce, and laborers in their efforts to organize. Between 1901 and 1920, some 14.8 million immigrants entered the country and began the difficult process of adjusting to life in their new home. All of these people faced difficult challenges due to low wages, dangerous working conditions, and the steady demands of the factory system. (p. 519)

Conflict in the Workplace

 Why were there so many strikes in this period?

Low wages, speeded-up assembly lines, and dangerous conditions in the workplace brought about numerous attempts to organize workers for their own defense. The Women's Trade Union League had many successes. The International Workers of the World, a radical union, wanted to place workers in control. In the end, Samuel Gompers and the American Federation of Labor won the allegiance of most workers. (p. 524)

A New Urban Culture

 What happened to art and culture in these years so filled with change?

In the dozen years after 1900, American culture changed in important ways. Cities took on their modern form. Suburbs flourished. Sports became increasingly popular, reflecting people's increased leisure time. Experimentation occurred in literature, poetry, painting, and the arts. (p. 530)

KEY TERMS AND DEFINITIONS

Muckrakers Writers who made a practice between 1903 and 1909 of exposing the wrongdoings of public figures and corporations and highlighting social and political problems. p. 514

Progressivism Movement for social change between the late 1890s and World War I. Its orgins lay in a fear of big business and corrupt government and a desire to improve living conditions. Progressives set out to cure the social ills brought about by industrialization and urbanization, social disorder, and corruption. p. 515

Niagara Movement A movement, led by W. E. B. DuBois, that focused on equal rights for and the education of African American youth. Rejecting the gradualist approach of Booker T. Washington, it favored militant action and claimed for African Americans all the rights afforded to other Americans. p. 522

National Association for the Advancement of Colored People (NAACP) Created in 1909, this organization became the most important civil rights organization in the country. p. 522

Birds of passage Immigrants who came to the United States to work and save money and then returned to their native countries during the slack season. p. 523

Women's Trade Union League (WTUL) Founded in 1903, this group worked to organize women into trade unions. It also lobbied for laws to safeguard female workers and backed strikes, especially in the garment industry. While it never attracted many members, its leaders were influential enough to give the union considerable power. p. 523

Industrial Workers of the World (IWW) Founded in 1905, this radical union, also known as the Wobblies, aimed to unite the American working class into one union. It organized unskilled and foreign-born laborers, advocated social revolution, and led strikes. p. 527

Ashcan School Early twentieth-century realist painters who portrayed the slums and streets of the nation's cities and the lives of ordinary urban dwellers. They often advocated political and social reform. p. 533

CRITICAL THINKING QUESTIONS

1. How did the changing nature of industrialism after the 1890s influence the beginnings of a Progressive Era?

2. In what specific ways did workers, African Americans, and immigrants respond to the changing nature of industrial society and in the process help bring about the Progressive Era?

3. How did workers organize to try to improve their lot in the cities and factories of the advancing industrial society?

4. How did changes in popular culture mold attitudes in the new Progressive Era?

MyHistoryLab Media Assignments

Find these resources in the Media Assignments folder for Chapter 22 on MyHistoryLab

The Changing Face of Industrialism

- **Watch** the **Video** *The Rise and Fall of the Automobile Economy* p. 516

- ■ **Read** the **Document** *Frederick Winslow Taylor, Scientific Management (1911)* p. 518

Society's Masses

- **Watch** the **Video** *Rural Free Delivery Mail* p. 519

- **Read** the **Document** *Gifford Pinchot, The Fight for Conservation (1910)* p. 520

- **Read** the **Document** *John Spargo, The Bitter Cry of the Children (1906)* p. 521

- ■ **Watch** the **Video** *The Conflict Between Booker T. Washington and W.E.B. DuBois* p. 522

Conflict in the Workplace

- ■ **Read** the **Document** *Samuel Gompers: The American Labor Movement (1914)* p. 526

- ■ **Complete** the **Assignment** *The Triangle Fire* p. 528

- ■ **View** the **Closer Look** *Triangle Fire, March 25, 1911* p. 529

A New Urban Culture

- **Watch** the **Video** *A Vaudeville Act* p. 532

■ *Indicates Study Plan Media Assignment*

23 From Roosevelt to Wilson in the Age of Progressivism

Contents and Learning Objectives

((•●─┤Listen to the Audio File on myhistorylab   Chapter 23 *From Roosevelt to Wilson in the Age of Progressivism*

The Republicans Split

On a sunny spring morning in 1909, Theodore Roosevelt, wearing the greatcoat of a colonel of the Rough Riders, left New York for a safari in Africa. An ex-president at the age of 50, he had turned over the White House to his chosen successor, William Howard Taft, and was now off for "the joy of wandering through lonely lands, the joy of hunting the mighty and terrible lords" of Africa, "where death broods in the dark and silent depths."

Some of Roosevelt's enemies hoped he would not return. "I trust some lion will do its duty," Wall Street magnate J. P. Morgan said. Always prepared, Roosevelt took nine extra pairs of eyeglasses, and, just in case, several expert hunters accompanied him. When the near-sighted Roosevelt took aim, three others aimed at the same moment. "Mr. Roosevelt had a fairly good idea of the general direction," the safari leader said, "but we couldn't take chances with the life of a former president." Though he had built a reputation as an ardent conservationist, Roosevelt shot nine lions, five elephants, thirteen rhinoceroses, seven hippopotamuses, and assorted other game—acquiring nearly three hundred trophies in all.

It was all good fun, and afterward Roosevelt set off on a tour of Europe. He attended the funeral of the king of England with the crowned heads of Europe, dined with the king and queen of Italy—an experience he likened to "a Jewish wedding on the East Side of New York"—and happily spent five hours reviewing troops of the German empire. Less happily, he followed events back home where, in the judgment of many friends, Taft was not working out as president. Gifford Pinchot, Roosevelt's close companion in the conservation movement, came to Italy to complain personally about Taft, and at almost every stop there were letters waiting for him from other disappointed Republicans.

For his part, Taft was puzzled by it all. Honest and warmhearted, he had intended to continue Roosevelt's policies, even writing Roosevelt that he would "see to it that your judgment in selecting me as your successor and bringing about that succession shall be vindicated." But events turned out differently. The conservative and progressive wings of the Republican party split, and Taft often sided with the conservatives. Among progressive Republicans, Taft's troubles stirred talk of a Roosevelt "back from Elba" movement, akin to Napoleon's return from exile.

Thousands gathered to greet Roosevelt on his return from Europe. He sailed into New York harbor on June 18, 1910, to the sound of naval guns and loud cheers.

A 1910 Puck cartoon shows Taft snarled in the intricacies of office as his disappointed mentor looks on.

In characteristic fashion, he had helped make the arrangements: "If there is to be a great crowd, do arrange it so that the whole crowd has a chance to see me and that there is as little disappointment as possible." Greeting Pinchot, one of Taft's leading opponents, with a hearty "Hello, Gifford," Roosevelt slipped away to his home in Oyster Bay, New York, where other friends awaited him.

He carried with him a touching letter from Taft, received just before he left Europe. "I have had a hard time—I do not know that I have had harder luck than other Presidents, but I do know that thus far I have succeeded far less than have others. I have been conscientiously trying to carry out your policies but my method of doing so has not worked smoothly." Taft invited Teddy to spend a night or two at the White House, but Roosevelt declined, saying that ex-presidents should not visit Washington. Relations between the two friends cooled. "It is hard, very hard," Taft said in 1911, "to see a devoted friendship going to pieces like a rope of sand."

A year later, there was no longer thought of friendship, only a desperate fight between Taft and Roosevelt for the Republican presidential nomination. Taft won the nomination, but, angry and ambitious, Roosevelt bolted and helped form a new party, the **Progressive (or "Bull Moose") party**, to unseat Taft and capture the White House. With Taft, Roosevelt, Woodrow Wilson (the Democratic party's candidate), and Socialist party candidate Eugene V. Debs all in the race, the election of 1912 became one of the most exciting in American history.

It was also one of the most important. People were worried about the social and economic effects of urban-industrial growth. The election of 1912 provided a forum for those worries, and, to a degree unusual in American politics, it pitted deeply opposed candidates against one another and outlined differing views of the nation's future. In the spirited battle between Roosevelt and Wilson, it also brought to the forefront some of the currents of progressive reform.

Those currents built on a number of important developments, including the rise of a new professional class, reform movements designed to cure problems in the cities and states, and the activist, achievement-oriented administrations of Roosevelt and Wilson. Together they produced the age of progressivism.

The Spirit of Progressivism

What were the six major characteristics of progressivism?

In one way or another, progressivism touched all aspects of society. Politically, it fostered a reform movement that sought cures for the problems of city, state, and nation. Intellectually, it drew on the expertise of the new social sciences and reflected a shift from older absolutes such as religion to newer schools of thought that emphasized relativism and the role of the environment in human development. Culturally, it inspired fresh modes of expression in dance, film, painting, literature, and architecture. Touching individuals in different ways, progressivism became a set of attitudes as well as a definable movement.

Though broad and diverse, progressivism as a whole had a half dozen characteristics that gave it definition. First, the progressives acted out of concern about the effects of industrialization and the conditions of industrial life. While their viewpoints varied, they did not, as a rule, set out to harm big business, but instead sought to humanize and regulate it.

In pursuing these objectives, the progressives displayed a second characteristic: a fundamental optimism about human nature, the possibilities of progress, and the capacity of people to recognize problems and take action to solve them. Progressives believed they could "investigate, educate, and legislate"—learn about a problem, inform people about it, and, with the help of an informed public, find and enforce a solution.

Third, more than many earlier reformers, the progressives were willing to intervene in people's lives, confident that it was their right to do so. They knew best, some of them thought, and as a result, there was an element of coercion in a number of their ideas. Fourth, while progressives preferred if possible to use voluntary means to achieve reform, they tended to turn more and more to the authority of the state and government at all levels in order to put into effect the reforms they wanted.

As a fifth characteristic, many progressives drew on a combination of evangelical Protestantism (which gave them the desire— and, they thought, the duty—to purge the world of sins such as prostitution and drunkenness) and the natural and social sciences (whose theories made them confident that they could understand and control the environment in which people lived). Progressives tended to view the environment as a key to reform, thinking—in the way some economists, sociologists, and other social scientists were suggesting—that if they could change the environment, they could change the individual.

Finally, progressivism was distinctive because it touched virtually the whole nation. Not everyone, of course, was a progressive, and there were many who opposed or ignored the ideas of the movement. There were also those who were untouched by progressive reforms and those whom the movement overlooked. But in one way or another, a remarkable number of people were caught up in it, giving progressivism a national reach and a mass base.

That was one of the features, in fact, that set it off from populism, which had grown mostly in the rural South and West. Progressivism drew support from across society. "The thing that constantly amazed me," said William Allen White, a leading progressive journalist, "was how many people were with us." Progressivism appealed to the expanding middle class, prosperous farmers, and skilled laborers; it also attracted significant support in the business community.

The progressives believed in progress and disliked waste. No single issue or concern united them all. Some progressives wanted to clean up city governments, others to clean up city streets. Some wanted to purify politics or control corporate abuses, others to eradicate poverty or prostitution. Some demanded social justice in the form of women's rights, child labor laws, temperance, and factory safety. They were Democrats, Republicans, Socialists, and independents.

Read the **Document** Lincoln Steffens, from *The Shame of the Cities* (1904)

Lincoln Steffens was among the best known of the muckraking journalists. His famous book *The Shame of the Cities was* a collection of articles on municipal corruption that he wrote for *McClure's Magazine* in 1902 and 1903. In his articles, he reflected the disgust that reformers felt for political machines and their methods.

Progressives believed in a better world and in the ability of people to achieve it. They paid to people, as a friend said of social reformer Florence Kelley, "the high compliment of believing that, once they knew the truth, they would act upon it." Progress depended on knowledge. The progressives emphasized individual morality and collective action, the scientific method, and the value of expert opinion. Like contemporary business leaders, they valued system, planning, management, and predictability. They wanted not only reform but efficiency. In the introduction to *The Shame of the Cities*, Steffens said that the cure for American ills lay in "good conduct in the individual, simple honesty, courage, and efficiency."

Historians once viewed progressivism as the triumph of one group in society over another. In this view, farmers took on the hated and powerful railroads; upstart reformers challenged the city bosses; business interests fought for favorable legislation; youthful professionals carved out their place in society. Now, historians emphasize the way progressivism brought people together rather than drove them apart. Disparate groups united in an effort to improve the well-being of many groups in society.

The Rise of the Professions

Progressivism fed on an organizational impulse that encouraged people to join forces, share information, and solve problems. Between 1890 and 1920, a host of national societies and associations took shape—nearly four hundred of them in just three decades. Groups such as the National Child Labor Committee, which lobbied for legislation to regulate the employment and working conditions of children, were formed to attack specific issues. Other groups reflected one of the most significant developments in American society at the turn of the century—the rise of the professions.

Growing rapidly in these years, the professions—law, medicine, religion, business, teaching, and social work—were the source of much of the leadership of the progressive movement. The professions attracted young, educated men and women, who in turn were part of a larger trend: a dramatic increase in the number of individuals working in administrative and professional jobs. In businesses, these people were managers, architects, technicians, and accountants. In city governments, they were experts in everything from education to sanitation. They organized and ran the urban-industrial society.

These professionals formed part of a new middle class whose members did not derive their status from birth or inherited wealth, as had many members of the older middle class. Instead, they moved ahead through education and personal accomplishment and worked to become doctors, lawyers, ministers, and teachers. Proud of their skills, they were ambitious and self-confident, and they thought of themselves as experts who could use their knowledge for the benefit of society. (See the Feature Essay, "Madam C. J. Walker: African American Business Pioneer," pp. 556–557.)

As a way of asserting their status, they formed professional societies to look after their interests and govern entry into their professions. Just a few years before, for example, a doctor had become a doctor simply by stocking up on patent medicines and hanging out a sign. Now doctors began to insist they were part of a medical profession, and they wanted to set educational requirements and minimum standards for practice. In 1901, they reorganized the American Medical Association (AMA) and made it into a modern national professional society. The AMA had 8,400 members that year. A decade later, it had more than 70,000, and by 1920, nearly two-thirds of all doctors belonged.

Other groups and professions showed the same pattern. Lawyers formed bar associations, created examining boards, and lobbied for regulations restricting entry into the profession. Teachers organized the National Education Association (1905) and pressed for teacher certification and compulsory education laws. Social workers formed the National Federation of Settlements (1911); business leaders created the National Association of Manufacturers (1895) and the U.S. Chamber of Commerce (1912); and farmers joined the National Farm Bureau Federation to spread information about farming and to try to improve their lot.

Working both as individuals and groups, members of the professions had a major effect on the era, as the career of one of them, Dr. Alice Hamilton, illustrated. Hamilton early decided to devote her life to helping the less fortunate. Choosing medicine, she went to the University of Michigan Medical School, one of a shrinking number of medical schools that admitted women, and then settled in Chicago, where she met Jane Addams and took a room in Hull House. Soon thereafter, she traced a local typhoid epidemic to flies carrying germs from open privies. The study won national acclaim, but Hamilton had already turned her attention to the work-related illnesses she found everywhere around Hull House.

Combining field study with meticulous laboratory techniques, she pioneered research into the causes of lead poisoning and other industrial disease. In 1908, the governor of Illinois appointed her to a commission on occupational diseases; two years later, she headed a statewide survey of industrial poisons. Thanks to her work, in 1911, Illinois passed the first state law providing compensation for industrial disease caused by poisonous fumes and dust. By the end of the 1930s, all the major industrial states had such laws.

One of the new professionals, Hamilton had used her education and skill to broaden knowledge of her subject, change industrial practices, and improve the lives of countless workers. "For me," she said later in a comment characteristic of the progressives, "the satisfaction is that things are better now, and I had some part in it."

The Social-Justice Movement

As Alice Hamilton's career exemplified, progressivism began in the cities during the 1890s. It first took form around settlement workers and others interested in freeing individuals from the crushing impact of cities and factories.

Ministers, intellectuals, social workers, and lawyers joined in a social-justice movement that focused national attention on the need for tenement house laws, more stringent child labor legislation, and better working conditions for women. They brought pressure on municipal agencies for more and better parks, playgrounds, day nurseries, schools, and community services. Blending private and public action, settlement leaders turned increasingly to government aid. "Private beneficence," Jane Addams said, "is totally inadequate to deal with the vast numbers of the city's disinherited."

Social-justice reformers were more interested in social cures than individual charity. Unlike earlier reformers, they saw problems as endless and interrelated; individuals became part of a city's larger patterns. With that insight, social-service casework shifted from a focus on an individual's well-being to a scientific analysis of neighborhoods, occupations, and classes.

In the spring of 1900, the Charity Organization Society of New York held a tenement house exhibition that graphically presented the new kind of sociological data. Put together by Lawrence Veiller, a young social worker, the exhibition included more than a thousand photographs, detailed maps of slum districts, statistical tables and charts, and graphic cardboard depictions of tenement blocks. Never before had so much information been pulled together in one place. Veiller correlated data on poverty and disease with housing conditions, and he pointed out that new slums were springing up in more areas of the city. Stirred by the public outcry, Governor Theodore Roosevelt appointed the New York State Tenement House Commission to do something about the problem.

With Veiller's success as a model, study after study analyzed the condition of the poor. Books and pamphlets such as *The Standard of Living Among Working Men's Families in New York City* (1909) contained pages of data on family budgets, women's wages and working conditions, child labor, and other matters. Between 1910 and 1913, the U.S. Commissioner of Labor issued a massive nineteen-volume report on *Conditions of Women and Children Wage-Earners in the United States.*

Social-justice reformers, banding together to work for change, formed the National Conference of Charities and Corrections, which in 1915 became the National Conference of Social Work. Controlled by social workers, the conference reflected the growing professional-ization of reform. Through it, social workers discovered each other's efforts, shared methodology, and tried to establish themselves as a separate field within the social sciences. Once content with infor-mal training sessions in a settlement house living room, they now founded complete professional schools at Chicago, Harvard, and other universities. After 1909, they had their own professional mag-azine, the *Survey*, and instead of piecemeal reforms, they aimed at a comprehensive program of minimum wages, maximum hours, workers' compensation, and widows' pensions.

The Purity Crusade

Working in city neighborhoods, social-justice reformers were often struck by the degree to which alcohol affected the lives of the people they were trying to help. Workers drank away their wages; some men spent more time at the saloon than at home. Drunkenness caused violence, and it angered employers who did not want intoxi-cated workers on the job. In countless ways, alcohol wasted human resources, the reformers believed, and along with business leaders, ministers, and others, they launched a crusade to remove the evils of drink from American life.

At the head of the crusade was the Women's Christian Temperance Union (WCTU), which had continued to grow since it was founded in the 1870s. By 1911, the WCTU had nearly a quarter of a million members; it was the largest organization of women in American history to that time. In 1893, it was joined by the Anti-Saloon League, and together the groups pressed to abolish alcohol and the places where it was consumed. By 1916, they had succeeded in nineteen states, but as drinking continued elsewhere, they pushed for a nationwide law. In the midst of the moral fervor of World War I, they succeeded, and the Eighteenth Amendment to the Constitution, prohibiting the manufacture, sale, and transportation of intoxicating liquors, took effect in January 1920.

The amendment encountered troubles later in the 1920s as the social atmosphere changed, but at the time it passed, progressives thought Prohibition was a major step toward eliminating social instability and moral wrong. In a similar fashion, some progressive reformers also worked to get rid of prostitution, convinced that pov-erty and ignorance drove women to the trade. By 1915, nearly every state had banned brothels, and in 1910, Congress passed the Mann Act, which prohibited the interstate transportation of women for immoral purposes. Like the campaign against liquor, the campaign against prostitution reflected the era's desire to purify and elevate, often through the instrument of government action.

Woman Suffrage, Women's Rights

Women played a large role in the social-justice movement. Feminists were particularly active, especially in the political sphere, between 1890 and 1914—feminists were more active then, in fact,

than at any other time until the 1960s. Some working-class women pushed for higher wages and better working conditions. College-educated women—five thousand a year graduated after 1900—took up careers in the professions, from which some of them supported reform. From 1890 to 1910, the work of a number of national women's organizations, including the National Council of Jewish Women, the National Congress of Mothers, and the Women's Trade Union League, furthered the aims of the progressive movement.

Excluded from most of these organizations, African American women formed their own groups. The National Association of

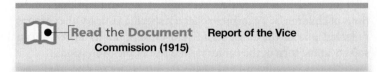

Read the Document Report of the Vice Commission (1915)

During the first two decades of the twentieth century, Progressive reformers set out to improve society. One strategy they employed was eradicating vice. Termed vice crusaders, these reformers attempted to stamp out prostitution, especially in large cities, as well as homosexuality. The pinnacle of the anti-vice movement was the passage of the Mann Act of 1910, which made it illegal to transport women across state lines for "immoral purposes."

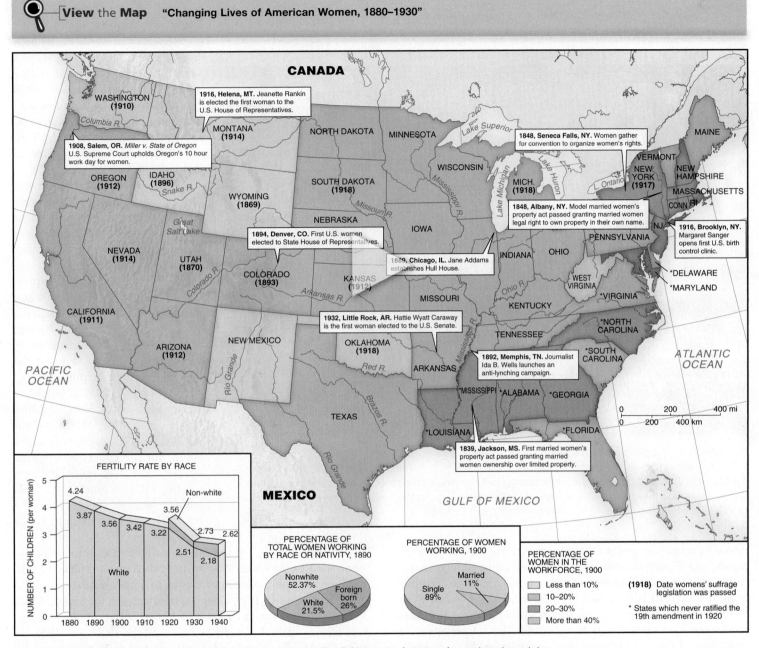

View the **Map**   "Changing Lives of American Women, 1880–1930"

FERTILITY RATE BY RACE

PERCENTAGE OF TOTAL WOMEN WORKING BY RACE OR NATIVITY, 1890

Nonwhite 52.37%
Foreign born 26%
White 21.5%

PERCENTAGE OF WOMEN WORKING, 1900

Married 11%
Single 89%

PERCENTAGE OF WOMEN IN THE WORKFORCE, 1900

Less than 10%
10–20%
20–30%
More than 40%

(1918) Date womens' suffrage legislation was passed

* States which never ratified the 19th amendment in 1920

Wyoming was the first of several western states to grant women the right to vote; however, in most eastern states women's suffrage came only with the passage of the Nineteenth Amendment in 1920. The number of women in the workforce grew steadily to 18 percent by 1900, a figure that reflects an emphasis on industrial workers and ignores workers more informally employed in agricultural and domestic occupations.

Colored Women was founded in 1895, fourteen years before the better known male-oriented National Association for the Advancement of Colored People (NAACP). Aimed at social welfare, the women's organization was the first African American social-service agency in the country. At the local level, African American women's clubs established kindergartens, day nurseries, playgrounds, and retirement homes.

From two hundred thousand members in 1900, the General Federation of Women's Clubs grew to more than one million by 1912. The clubs met, as they had before, for coffee and literary conversation, but they also began to look closely at conditions around them. Forming an Industrial Section and a Committee on

Legislation for Women and Children, the federation supported reforms to safeguard child and women workers, improve schools, ensure pure food, and beautify the community.

Reluctant at first, the federation finally lent support in 1914 to woman suffrage, a cause that dated back to the first women's rights convention in Seneca Falls, New York, in 1848. Divided over tactics since the Civil War, the suffrage movement suffered from disunity, male opposition, indecision over whether to seek action at the state or at the national level, resistance from the Catholic Church, and opposition from liquor interests, who linked the cause to Prohibition.

Women in the social-justice movement needed to influence elected officials—most of them men, whom they could not reach

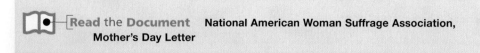

Read the Document National American Woman Suffrage Association, Mother's Day Letter

The National American Woman Suffrage Association (NAWSA) was formed in 1890 from the merger of two organizations founded by Elizabeth Cady Stanton and Susan B. Anthony, respectively, in 1869. Under the leadership of Carrie Chapman Catt, membership in the organization rose to 2 million. Catt's organization was relatively mainstream, especially in contrast to the militant National Woman's Party, which adopted radical tactics including hunger strikes, demonstrations, and pickets.

through the vote. Because politics was an avenue for reform, growing numbers of women activists became involved in the suffrage movement. After years of disagreement, the two major suffrage organizations, the National Woman Suffrage Association and the American Woman Suffrage Association, merged in 1890 to form the **National American Woman Suffrage Association**. The merger opened a new phase of the suffrage movement, characterized by unity and a tightly controlled national organization.

In 1900, Carrie Chapman Catt, a superb organizer, became president of the National American Woman Suffrage Association, which by 1920 had nearly two million members. Catt and Anna Howard Shaw, who became the association's head in 1904, believed in organization and peaceful lobbying to win the vote. Alice Paul and Lucy Burns, founders of the Congressional Union, were more militant; they interrupted public meetings, focused on Congress rather than the states, and in 1917 picketed the White House.

Significantly, Catt, Paul, and others made a major change in the argument for woman suffrage. When the campaign began in the nineteenth century, suffragists had claimed the vote as a natural right, owed to women as much as men. Now, they emphasized a pragmatic argument: Since women were more sensitive to moral issues than men, they would use their votes to help create a better society. They would support temperance, clean government,

laws to protect workers, and other reforms. This argument attracted many progressives who believed the women's vote would purify politics. In 1918, the House passed a constitutional amendment stating simply that the right to vote shall not be denied "on account of sex." The Senate and enough states followed, and, after three generations of suffragist efforts, the Nineteenth Amendment took effect in 1920.

The social justice movement had the most success in passing state laws limiting the working hours of women. By 1913, thirty-nine states set maximum working hours for women or banned the employment of women at night. Illinois had a ten-hour law; California and Washington had eight-hour laws. Wisconsin, Oregon, and Kansas allowed expert commissions to set different hours depending on the degree of strain in various occupations. As early as 1900, thanks to groups such as the National Child Labor Committee, twenty-eight states had laws regulating child labor. But the courts often ruled against such laws, and families—needing extra income—sometimes ignored them. Parents sent children off to jobs with orders to lie about their ages.

In 1916, President Woodrow Wilson backed a law to limit child labor, the Keating-Owen Act, but in *Hammer* v. *Dagenhart* (1918), the Supreme Court overturned it as an improper regulation of local labor conditions. In 1919, Congress tried again in the Second Child Labor Act, but in *Bailey* v. *Drexel Furniture Company* (1922) the legislation was again struck down. Not until the 1930s did Congress succeed in passing a court-supported national child labor law.

A Ferment of Ideas: Challenging the Status Quo

A dramatic shift in ideas became one of the most important forces behind progressive reform. Most of the ideas focused on the role of the environment in shaping human behavior. Progressive reformers accepted society's growing complexity, called for factual treatment of piecemeal problems, allowed room for new theories, and, above all, rejected age-encrusted divine or natural "laws" in favor of thoughts and actions that worked.

A new doctrine called **pragmatism** emerged in this ferment of ideas. It came from William James, a brilliant Harvard psychologist who became the key figure in American thought from the 1890s to World War I. A warm, tolerant person, James was impatient with theories that regarded truth as abstract. Truth, he believed, should

Read the Document   Eugene V. Debs, from "The Outlook for Socialism in America" (1900)

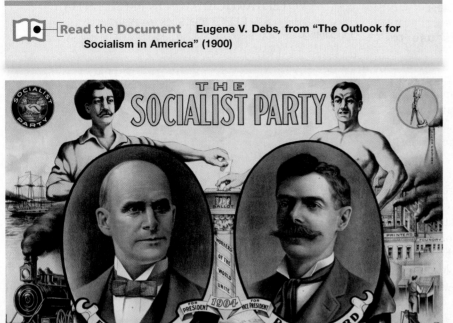

Presidential campaign poster for Eugene V. Debs on the Socialist party of America ticket in 1904. The poster's imagery appeals to industrial workers, miners, and farmers, and its slogan, "Workers of the world unite," was a key call to action of the party to challenge the injustices of capitalism.

work for the individual, and it worked best not in abstraction, but in action. "True ideas are those we can assimilate, validate, corroborate, and verify. False ideas are those we cannot."

People, James thought, not only were shaped by their environment; they shaped it. In *Pragmatism* (1907), he praised "tough-minded" individuals who could live effectively in a world with no easy answers. The tough-minded accepted change; they knew how to pick manageable problems, gather facts, discard ideas that did not work, and act on those that did. Ideas that worked became truth. "What is the 'cash value' of a thought, idea, or belief?" James asked. Does it work? Does it make a difference to the individual who experiences it? "The ultimate test for us of what a truth means," said James, "is the conduct it dictates."

The most influential educator of the Progressive Era, John Dewey, applied pragmatism to educational reform. A friend and disciple of William James, he argued that thought evolves in relation to the environment and that education is directly related to experience. In 1896, Dewey founded a separate School of Pedagogy at the University of Chicago, with a laboratory in which educational theory based on the newer philosophical and psychological studies could be tested and practiced.

Dewey introduced an educational revolution that emphasized children's needs and capabilities. He described his beliefs and methods in a number of books, notably *School and Society* (1899) and *Democracy and Education* (1916). New ideas in education, he said, are "as much a product of the changed social situation, and as much an effort to meet the needs of the society that is forming, as are changes in modes of industry and commerce." He opposed memorization, rote learning, and dogmatic, authoritarian teaching methods; he emphasized personal growth, free inquiry, and creativity.

Rejecting the older view of the law as universal and unchanging, lawyers and legal theorists instead viewed it as a reflection of the environment—an instrument for social change. Law reflected the environment that shaped it. A movement grew among judges for "sociological jurisprudence" that related the law to social reform instead of only to legal precedent, a shift most evident in the famed Brandeis brief, presented in the case of *Muller* v. *Oregon* that came before the Supreme Court in 1908.

In Denver, Colorado, after Judge Ben Lindsey sentenced a boy to reform school for stealing coal, the boy's mother rushed forward and, grief stricken, beat her head against the wall. Lindsey investigated the case and found that the father was a smelting worker dying of lead poisoning; the family needed coal for heat. From such experiences, Lindsey concluded that children were not born with a genetic tendency to crime; they were made good or bad by the environment in which they grew. Lindsey "sentenced" youthful offenders to education and good care. He worked for playgrounds, slum clearance, public baths, and technical schools. Known as the "Kids' Judge," he attracted visitors from as far away as Japan, who wanted to study and copy his methods.

Socialism, a reformist political philosophy, grew dramatically before World War I. Socialist political parties, composed of followers of Karl Marx, first appeared in New York, Chicago, Milwaukee, and other cities after the Civil War. They urged workers to join a worldwide revolution to overthrow capitalism. Such public appeals, however, drew little support. Leaders of a new Socialist Labor Party, founded in 1877, tried in secret to gain control of important labor unions. That strategy also failed.

Daniel De Leon, a brilliant tactician, took over leadership of the Socialist Labor Party during the 1890s, but he too lacked mass support. Arguing for a more moderate form of socialism, Eugene V. Debs, president of the American Railway Union, in 1896 formed a rival organization, the Social Democratic Party. Gentle and reflective, not at all the popular image of the wild-eyed radical, Debs was thrust into prominence by the Pullman strike. In 1901, persuading opponents of De Leon to join him, he formed the Socialist party of America. Neither Debs nor the party ever developed a cohesive platform, nor was Debs an effective organizer. But he was eloquent, passionate, and visionary. An excellent speaker, he captivated audiences, attacking the injustices of capitalism and urging a workers' republic.

The Socialist Party of America enlisted some intellectuals, factory workers, disillusioned Populists, tenant farmers, miners, and lumberjacks. By 1911, there were Socialist mayors in thirty-two cities, including Berkeley, California; Butte, Montana; and Flint, Michigan. Although its doctrines were aimed at an urban proletariat, the Socialist Party drew support in rural Texas, Missouri, Arkansas, Idaho, and Washington. In Oklahoma, it attracted as much as one-third of the vote.

Although torn by factions, the Socialist Party doubled in membership between 1904 and 1908, then tripled in the four years after that. Running for president, Debs garnered 100,000 votes in 1900; 400,000 in 1904; and 900,000 in 1912, the party's peak year.

Reform in the Cities and States

What methods did progressive reformers use to attack problems in the cities and states?

Progressive reformers realized government could be a crucial agent in accomplishing their goals. They wanted to curb the influence of "special interests" and, through such measures of political reform as the direct primary and the direct election of senators, make government follow the public will. Once it did, they welcomed government action at whatever level was appropriate.

As a result of this thinking, the use of federal power increased, as did the power and prestige of the presidency. Progressives not only lobbied for government-sponsored reform but also worked actively in their home neighborhoods, cities, and states; much of the significant change occurred in local settings, outside the national limelight. Most important, the progressives believed in the ability of experts to solve problems. At every level—local, state, and federal—thousands of commissions and agencies took form. Staffed by trained experts, they oversaw a multitude of matters ranging from railroad rates to public health.

Interest Groups and the Decline of Popular Politics

Placing government in the hands of experts was one way to get it out of the hands of politicians and political parties. The direct primary, which allowed voters rather than parties to choose candidates for office, was another way. These initiatives and others like them were part of a fundamental change in the way Americans viewed their political system.

As one sign of the change, fewer and fewer people were going to the polls. Voter turnout dropped dramatically after 1900, when the intense partisanship of the decades after the Civil War gave way to media-oriented political campaigns based largely on the personalities of the candidates. From 1876 to 1900, the average turnout in presidential elections was 77 percent. From 1900 to 1916, it was 65 percent, and in the 1920s, it dropped to 52 percent, close to the average today. Turnout was lowest among young people, immigrants, the poor, and, ironically, the newly enfranchised women.

It was particularly low in the South where conservative whites used restrictive election laws to keep blacks and others from the polls. Turnout in the South fell sharply, from an average of 64 percent in the presidential elections of the 1880s to just 20 percent in 1920 and 1924. Although the decline in the North was less sharp, the reasons for it were more complex. By the 1920s, as many as one-quarter of all eligible northern voters never cast a ballot.

There were numerous causes for the falloff, but among the most important was the fact that people had found another way to achieve some of the objectives they had once assigned to political parties. They had found the "interest group," a means of action that assumed importance in this era and became a major feature of politics ever after. Professional societies, trade associations, labor organizations, farm lobbies, and scores of other interest groups worked outside the party system to pressure government for things their members wanted. Social workers, women's clubs, reform groups, and others learned to apply pressure in similar ways, and the result was much of the significant legislation of the Progressive Era.

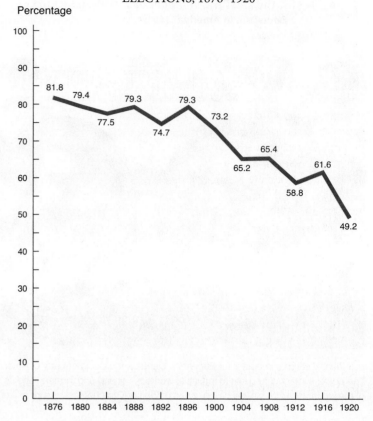

VOTER PARTICIPATION IN PRESIDENTIAL ELECTIONS, 1876–1920

Reform in the Cities

During the early years of the twentieth century, urban reform movements, many of them born in the depression of the 1890s, spread across the nation. In 1894, the National Municipal League was organized, and it became the forum for debate over civic reform, changes in the tax laws, and municipal ownership of public utilities. Within a few years, nearly every city had a variety of clubs and organizations directed at improving the quality of city life.

In the 1880s, reformers would call an evening conference, pass resolutions, and then go home; after 1900, they formed associations, adopted long-range policies, and hired a staff to achieve them. In the mid-1890s, only Chicago had an urban reform league with a full-time paid executive; within a decade, there were such leagues in every major city.

In city after city, reformers reordered municipal government. Tightening controls on corporate activities, they broadened the scope of utility regulation and restricted city franchises. They updated tax assessments, often skewed in favor of corporations, and tried to clean up the electoral machinery. Devoted to efficiency, they developed a trained civil service to oversee planning and operations. The generation of the 1880s also had believed in civil service, but the goal then was mostly negative: to get spoilsmen out and "good" people in. Now the goal was efficiency and, above all, results.

In constructing their model governments, urban reformers often turned to recent advances in business management and organization. They emphasized continuity and expertise, a system in which professional experts staffed a government overseen by elected officials. At the top, the elected leader surveyed the breadth of city, state, or national affairs and defined directions. Below, a corps of experts—trained in the various disciplines of the new society—funneled the definition into specific, scientifically based policies.

Reformers created a growing number of regulatory commissions and municipal departments. They hired engineers to oversee utility and water systems, physicians and nurses to improve municipal health, and city planners to oversee park and highway development. They created specialized "academies" to train police and firefighters. Imitated by the state and federal governments, the proliferation of experts and commissions widened the gap between voters and decision makers but dramatically improved the efficiency of government.

As cities exploded in size, they freed themselves from the tight controls of state legislatures and began to experiment with their own governments. Struggling to recover from a devastating hurricane in 1900, Galveston, Texas, pioneered the commission form of government: a form of municipal government in which commissions of appointed experts, rather than elected officials, ran the city. Wanting nonpartisan expertise, Staunton, Virginia, was the first to hire a city manager. Other cities followed, and by 1910 more than one hundred cities were using either the commission or manager type of government.

In the race for reform, a number of city mayors won national reputations—among them Seth Low in New York City and Hazen S. Pingree in Detroit—working to modernize taxes, clean up politics, lower utility rates, and control the awarding of valuable city franchises. In Toledo, Ohio, Mayor Samuel M. ("Golden Rule") Jones, a wealthy manufacturer, took billy clubs away from the police; established free kindergartens, playgrounds, and night schools; and improved wages for city workers.

In Cleveland, Ohio, Tom L. Johnson demonstrated an innovative approach to city government. A millionaire who had made his fortune manipulating city franchises, Johnson one day read Henry George's *Progress and Poverty* and turned to reform. Elected mayor of Cleveland, he served from 1901 to 1909 and collected a group of aggressive and talented young advisers. Frederic C. Howe, Newton D. Baker, and Edward Bemis—all of whom later won national reputations—shaped Johnson's ideas on taxes, prison reform, utility regulation, and other issues facing the city.

Johnson combined shrewdness and showmanship. Believing in an informed citizenry, he held outdoor meetings in huge tents. He used colorful charts to give Cleveland residents a course in utilities and taxation. He cut down on corruption, cut off special privilege, updated taxes, and gave Cleveland a reputation as the country's best governed city.

Finding it difficult to regulate powerful city utilities and keep their costs down, Johnson and mayors in other cities turned more and more to public ownership of gas, electricity, water, and transportation. The idea of "gas and water socialism"—in which cities owned their own gas, electricity, water, and other utilities—spread swiftly. In 1896, fewer than half of American cities owned their own waterworks; by 1915, almost two-thirds did.

Action in the States

Reformers soon discovered, however, that many problems lay beyond a city's boundaries, and they turned for action to the state governments. From the 1890s to 1920, reformers worked to stiffen state laws regulating the labor of women and children, to create

and strengthen commissions to regulate railroads and utilities, to impose corporate and inheritance taxes, to improve mental and penal institutions, and to allocate more funds for state universities, which were viewed as the training ground for the experts and educated citizenry needed for the new society.

Maryland passed the first workers' compensation law in 1902; soon most industrial states had such legislation. After 1900, many states adopted factory inspection laws, and by 1916, almost two-thirds of the states mandated insurance for the victims of factory accidents. By 1914, twenty-five states had enacted employers' liability laws.

To regulate business, virtually every state created regulatory commissions empowered to examine corporate books and hold public hearings. Building on earlier experience, state commissions after 1900 were given new power to initiate actions, rather than await complaints, and in some cases to set maximum prices and rates. Dictating company practices, they pioneered regulatory methods later adopted in federal legislation of 1906 and 1910. Some business leaders supported the federal laws in order to get rid of "the intolerable supervision" of dozens of separate state commissions.

Historians have long praised the regulation movement, but the commissions did not always act wisely or even in the public interest. Elective commissions often produced commissioners who had little knowledge of corporate affairs. In addition, to win an election, some promised specific rates or reforms, obligations that might bias the commission's investigative functions. Appointive commissions sometimes fared better, but they too had to oversee extraordinarily complex businesses such as the railroads. Shaping everything from wages to train schedules, the regulatory commissions affected railroad profits and growth negatively and, in the end, damaged the railroad industry.

To the progressives, commissions offered a way to end the corrupt alliance between business and politics. There was another way, too, and that was to "democratize" government by reducing the power of politicians and increasing the influence of the electorate. To do that, progressives backed three measures to make office holders responsive to popular will: the initiative, which allowed voters to propose new laws; the referendum, which allowed them to accept or reject a law at the ballot box; and the recall, which gave them a way to remove an elected official from office.

Oregon adopted the initiative and referendum in 1902; by 1912, twelve states had them. That year Congress added the Seventeenth Amendment to the Constitution to provide for the direct election of U.S. senators. By 1916, all but three states had direct primaries, which allowed the people, rather than nominating conventions, to choose candidates for office.

As attention shifted from the cities to the states, reform governors throughout the country earned greater visibility. Joseph Folk, Steffens's hero in St. Louis, became the governor of Missouri in 1904. Hiram Johnson won fame in California for his shrewd and forceful campaign against the Southern Pacific Railroad. In the East, the cause of reform was upheld by Charles Evans Hughes in New York and Woodrow Wilson, the former president of Princeton University, in New Jersey.

Robert M. La Follette became the most famous reform governor. A graduate of the University of Wisconsin, La Follette served three terms in Congress during the late 1880s. A staunch Republican, he supported the tariff and other Republican doctrines, but the Democratic landslide of 1890 turned him out of office. Moving to state politics, he became interested in reform, spurred in part, as so many were, by the depression of the 1890s. In 1901, he became governor of Wisconsin. Then forty-five years old, La Follette was talented, aggressive, and a superb stump speaker.

In the following six years, he put together the "Wisconsin Idea," one of the most important reform programs in the history of state government. He established an industrial commission, the first in the country, to regulate factory safety and sanitation. He improved education, workers' compensation, public utility controls, and resource conservation. He lowered railroad rates and raised railroad taxes. Under La Follette's prodding, Wisconsin became the first state to adopt a direct primary for all political nominations. It also became the first to adopt a state income tax.

Like other progressives, La Follette drew on expert advice and relied on academic figures such as Richard Ely and Edward Ross at the University of Wisconsin. La Follette supporters established the first Legislative Reference Bureau in the university's library; the bureau stocked the governor and his allies with facts and figures to support the measures they wanted. Theodore Roosevelt called La Follette's Wisconsin "the laboratory of democracy," and the Wisconsin Idea soon spread to many other states, including New York, California, Michigan, Iowa, and Texas.

After 1905, the progressives looked more and more to Washington. For one thing, Teddy Roosevelt was there with his zest for publicity and his alluring grin. Progressives also had a growing sense that many concerns—corporations and conservation, factory safety and child labor—crossed state lines. Federal action seemed desirable; specific reforms fit into a larger plan perhaps best seen from the nation's center. Within a few years, La Follette and Hiram Johnson became senators, and while reform went on back home, the focus of progressivism shifted to Washington.

The Republican Roosevelt

How would you describe the personality and programs of Theodore Roosevelt?

When President William McKinley died of gunshot wounds in September 1901, Vice President Theodore Roosevelt succeeded him in the White House. The new president initially vowed to carry on McKinley's policies. He continued some, developed others of his own, and in the end brought to them all the particular exuberance of his own personality.

At age forty-two, Roosevelt was then the youngest president in American history. In contrast to the dignified McKinley, he was open, aggressive, and high spirited. At his desk by 8:30 every morning, he worked through the day, usually with visitors for breakfast, lunch, and dinner. Politicians, labor leaders, industrialists, poets, artists, and writers paraded through the White House.

If McKinley cut down on presidential isolation, Roosevelt virtually ended it. The presidency, he thought, was the "bully pulpit," a forum of ideas and leadership for the nation. The president was "a steward of the people bound actively and affirmatively to do all he could for the people." Self-confident, Roosevelt enlisted talented associates, including Elihu Root, secretary of war and later secretary of state; William Howard Taft, secretary of war; Gifford Pinchot, the nation's chief forester and leading conservationist; and Oliver Wendell Holmes, Jr., whom he named to the Supreme Court.

> **Read** the **Document**   **Theodore Roosevelt, from *The Strenuous Life* (1900)**

This photograph of TR (Theodore Roosevelt) captures key parts of his personality: exuberant, jovial, expansive, self-confident, personally warm, outgoing, aggressive, spirited, and friendly. These characteristics, among others, are important because they shaped his presidency between 1901 and 1909.

In 1901, Roosevelt invited Booker T. Washington, the prominent African American educator, to dinner at the White House. Many southerners protested—"a crime equal to treason," a newspaper said—and they protested again when Roosevelt appointed several African Americans to important federal offices in South Carolina and Mississippi. At first, Roosevelt considered building a biracial "black-and-tan" southern Republican party, thinking it would foster racial progress and his own renomination in 1904. He denounced lynching and ordered the Justice Department to act against peonage.

But Roosevelt soon retreated. In some areas of the South, he supported "lily-white" Republican organizations, and his policies often reflected his own belief in African American inferiority. He said nothing when a race riot broke out in Atlanta in 1906, although twelve persons died. He joined others in blaming African American soldiers stationed near Brownsville, Texas, after a night of violence there in August 1906. Acting quickly and on little evidence, he discharged "without honor" three companies of African American troops. Six of the soldiers who were discharged held the Congressional Medal of Honor.

Busting the Trusts

"There is a widespread conviction in the minds of the American people that the great corporations known as trusts are in certain of their features and tendencies hurtful to the general welfare," Roosevelt reported to Congress in 1901. Like most people, however, the president wavered on the trusts. Large-scale production and industrial growth, he believed, were natural and beneficial; they needed only to be controlled. Still, he distrusted the trusts' impact on local enterprise and individual opportunity. Distinguishing between "good" and "bad" trusts, he pledged to protect the former while controlling the latter.

At first, Roosevelt hoped the combination of investigative journalism and public opinion would be enough to uncover and correct business evils, and in public he both praised and attacked the trusts. Mr. Dooley poked fun at his wavering: "'Th' trusts,' says he, 'are heejous monsthers built up be th' enlightened intherprise iv th' men that have done so much to advance progress in our beloved country,' he says. 'On wan hand I wud stamp thim undher fut; on th' other hand not so fast.'"

In 1903, Roosevelt asked Congress to create a Department of Commerce and Labor, with a Bureau of Corporations empowered to investigate corporations engaged in interstate commerce. Congress balked; Roosevelt called in reporters and, in an off-the-record interview, charged that John D. Rockefeller had organized the opposition to the measure. The press spread the word, and in the outcry that followed, the proposal passed easily in a matter of weeks. Roosevelt was delighted. With the new Bureau of Corporations publicizing its findings, he thought, the glare of publicity would eliminate most corporate abuses.

Roosevelt also undertook direct legal action. On February 18, 1902, he instructed the Justice Department to bring suit against the Northern Securities Company for violation of the Sherman Antitrust Act. It was a shrewd move. A mammoth holding company, Northern Securities controlled the massive rail networks of the Northern Pacific, Great Northern, and Chicago, Burlington & Quincy railroads. Some of the most prominent names in business were behind the giant company—J. P. Morgan and Company; the Rockefeller interests; Kuhn, Loeb and Company; and railroad operators James J. Hill and Edward H. Harriman.

Shocked by Roosevelt's action, Morgan charged that the president had not acted like a "gentleman," and Hill talked glumly of having "to fight for our lives against the political adventurers who have never done anything but pose and draw a salary." Morgan rushed to Washington to complain and to ask whether there were plans to "attack my other interests," notably U.S. Steel. "No," Roosevelt replied, "unless we find out they have done something that we regard as wrong."

In 1904, the Supreme Court, in a 5 to 4 decision, upheld the suit against Northern Securities and ordered the company dissolved. Roosevelt was jubilant, and he followed up the victory with several other antitrust suits. In 1902, he had moved against the beef trust, an action applauded by western farmers and urban consumers alike. After a lull, he initiated suits in 1906 and 1907 against the American Tobacco Company, the Du Pont Corporation, the New Haven Railroad, and Standard Oil.

But Roosevelt's policies were not always clear, nor his actions always consistent. He invited Morgan to the White House to confer with him and allowed the president of National City Bank to preview a draft of the president's third annual message to Congress.

Roosevelt also asked for (and received) business support in his bid for reelection in 1904. Large donations came in from industrial leaders, and Morgan himself later testified that he gave $150,000 to Roosevelt's campaign. In 1907, acting in part to avert a threatened financial panic, the president permitted Morgan's U.S. Steel to absorb the Tennessee Coal and Iron Company, an important competitor.

Roosevelt, in truth, was not a trustbuster, although he was frequently called that. William Howard Taft, his successor in the White House, initiated forty-three antitrust indictments in four years—nearly twice as many as the twenty-five Roosevelt initiated in the seven years of his presidency. Instead, Roosevelt used antitrust threats to keep businesses within bounds. Regulation, he believed, was a better way to control large-scale enterprise.

"Square Deal" in the Coalfields

A few months after announcing the Northern Securities suit, Roosevelt intervened in a major labor dispute involving the anthracite coal miners of northeastern Pennsylvania. Led by John Mitchell, a moderate labor leader, the United Mine Workers demanded wage increases, an eight-hour workday, and company recognition of the union. The coal companies refused, and in May 1902, one hundred forty thousand miners walked off the job. The mines closed.

As the months passed and the strike continued, coal prices rose. With winter coming on, schools, hospitals, and factories ran short of coal. Public opinion turned against the companies. Morgan and other industrial leaders privately urged them to settle, but George F. Baer, head of one of the largest companies, refused: "The rights and interests of the laboring man," Baer said, "will be protected and cared for—not by the labor agitators, but by the Christian men to whom God in his infinite wisdom has given the control of the property interests of this country."

Roosevelt was furious. Complaining of the companies' arrogance, he invited both sides in the dispute to an October 1902 conference at the White House. There, Mitchell took a moderate tone and offered to submit the issues to arbitration, but the companies again refused to budge. Roosevelt ordered the army to prepare to seize the mines and then leaked word of his intent to Wall Street leaders.

Alarmed, Morgan and others again urged settlement of the dispute, and at last the companies retreated. They agreed to accept the recommendations of an independent commission the president would appoint. In late October, the strikers returned to work, and in March 1903, the commission awarded them a 10 percent wage increase and a cut in working hours. It recommended, however, against union recognition. The coal companies, in turn, were encouraged to raise prices to offset the wage increase.

More and more, Roosevelt saw the federal government as an honest and impartial "broker" between powerful elements in society. Rather than leaning toward labor, he pursued a middle way to curb corporate and labor abuses, abolish privilege, and enlarge individual opportunity. Conservative by temperament, he sometimes backed reforms in part to head off more radical measures.

During the 1904 campaign, Roosevelt called his actions in the coal miners' strike a "square deal" for both labor and capital, a term that stuck to his administration. Roosevelt was not the first president to take a stand for labor, but he was the first to bring opposing sides in a labor dispute to the White House to settle it.

He was the first to threaten to seize a major industry, and he was the first to appoint an arbitration commission whose decision both sides agreed to accept.

Roosevelt Progressivism at its Height

What were the major measures of Theodore Roosevelt's term from 1905 to 1909?

In the election of 1904, the popular Roosevelt soundly drubbed his Democratic opponent, Alton B. Parker of New York, and the Socialist party candidate, Eugene V. Debs of Indiana. Roosevelt attracted a large campaign chest and won votes everywhere. In a landslide victory, he received 57 percent of the vote to Parker's 38 percent, and on election night, he savored the public's confidence. Overjoyed, he pledged that "under no circumstances will I be a candidate for or accept another nomination," a statement he later regretted.

THE ELECTION OF 1904

Candidate	Party	Popular Vote	Electoral Vote
T. Roosevelt	Republican	7,623,486	336
Parker	Democrat	5,077,911	140
Debs	Socialist	402,400	0
Swallow	Prohibition	258,596	0

Regulating the Railroads

Following his election, Roosevelt, in late 1904, laid out a reform program that included railroad regulation, employers' liability for federal employees, greater federal control over corporations, and laws regulating child labor, factory inspection, and slum clearance in the District of Columbia. He turned first to railroad regulation. In 1903, he had worked with Congress to pass the Elkins Act to prohibit railroad rebates and increase the powers of the Interstate Commerce Commission (ICC). The Elkins Act, a moderate law, was framed with the consent of railroad leaders. In 1904 and 1905, the president wanted much more, and he urged Congress to empower the ICC to set reasonable and nondiscriminatory rates and prevent inequitable practices.

Widespread demand for railroad regulation strengthened Roosevelt's hand. In the Midwest and farther west, the issue was a popular one, and reform governors La Follette in Wisconsin and Albert B. Cummins in Iowa urged federal action. Roosevelt maneuvered cannily. As the legislative battle opened, he released figures showing that Standard Oil had reaped $750,000 a year from railroad rebates. He also skillfully traded congressional support for a strong railroad measure in return for his promise to postpone a reduction of the tariff, a stratagem that came back to plague President Taft.

Triumph came with passage of the **Hepburn Act** of 1906. A significant achievement, the act strengthened the rate-making power of the Interstate Commerce Commission. It increased membership on the ICC from five to seven, empowered it to fix reasonable maximum railroad rates, and broadened its jurisdiction to include oil pipeline, express, and sleeping car companies. ICC orders were binding, pending any court appeals, thus placing the burden of proof of injustice on the companies. Delighted, Roosevelt viewed the Hepburn Act as a major step in his plan for continuous expert federal control over industry.

Cleaning up Food and Drugs

Soon Roosevelt was dealing with two other important bills, these aimed at regulating the food and drug industries. Muckraking articles had touched frequently on filthy conditions in meatpacking houses, but Upton Sinclair's *The Jungle* (1906) set off a storm of

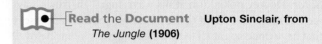

▶ **Read** the **Document**   Upton Sinclair, from *The Jungle* (1906)

A poster for the movie version of Upton Sinclair's *The Jungle* promises a "wonderful story of the beef packing industry." The conditions that Sinclair described in the book brought to public attention the scandals of the meatpacking industry knowingly selling diseased meat and the filthy, disease-ridden, dangerous conditions in which the workers toiled for their subsistence wages.

indignation. Ironically, Sinclair had set out to write a novel about the packinghouse workers, the "wage slaves of the Beef Trust," hoping to do for wage slavery what Harriet Beecher Stowe had done for chattel slavery. But readers largely ignored his story of the workers and seized instead on the graphic descriptions of the things that went into their meat:

> There would be meat stored in great piles in rooms; and the water from leaky roofs would drip over it, and thousands of rats would race about on it. It was too dark in these storage places to see well, but a man could run his hand over these piles of meat and sweep off handfuls of the dried dung of rats. These rats were nuisances, and the packers would put poisoned bread out for them; they would die, and then rats, bread, and meat would go into the hoppers together.

Sinclair was disappointed at the reaction. "I aimed at the public's heart," he later said, "and by accident I hit it in the stomach." He had, indeed. After reading *The Jungle*, Roosevelt ordered an investigation. The result, he said, was "hideous," and he threatened to publish the entire "sickening report" if Congress did not act. Meat sales plummeted in the United States and Europe. Demand for reform grew. Alarmed, the meat packers themselves supported a reform law, which they hoped would be just strong enough to still the clamor. The Meat Inspection Act of 1906, stronger than the packers wanted, set rules for sanitary meatpacking and government inspection of meat products.

A second measure, the Pure Food and Drug Act, passed more easily. Samuel Hopkins Adams, a muckraker, exposed the dangers of patent medicines in several sensational articles in *Collier's*. Patent medicines, Adams pointed out, contained mostly alcohol, drugs, and "undiluted fraud." Dr. Harvey W. Wiley, the chief chemist in the Department of Agriculture, led a "poison squad" of young assistants who experimented with the medicines. With evidence in hand, Wiley pushed for regulation; Roosevelt and the recently reorganized American Medical Association joined the fight, and the act passed on June 30, 1906. Requiring manufacturers to list certain ingredients on the label, it represented a pioneering effort to ban the manufacture and sale of adulterated, misbranded, or unsanitary food or drugs.

Conserving the Land

An expert on birds, Roosevelt loved nature and the wilderness, and some of his most enduring accomplishments came in the field of **conservation**. Working closely with Gifford Pinchot, chief of the Forest Service, he established the first comprehensive national conservation policy. To Roosevelt, conservation meant the wise use of natural resources, not locking them away, so those who thought the wilderness should be preserved rather than developed generally opposed his policies.

Using experts in the federal government, Roosevelt undertook a major reclamation program, created the federal Reclamation Service, and strengthened the forest preserve program in the Department of Agriculture. Broadening the concept of conservation, he placed power sites, coal lands, and oil reserves as well as national forest in the public domain.

When Roosevelt took office in 1901, there were 45 million acres in government preserves. In 1908, there were almost

NATIONAL PARKS AND FORESTS During the presidency of Theodore Roosevelt, who considered conservation his most important domestic achievement, millions of acres of land were set aside for national parks and forests.

195 million. That year, he called a National Conservation Congress attended by forty-four governors and hundreds of experts. Roosevelt formed the National Commission on the Conservation of Natural Resources to look after waters, forests, lands, and minerals. With Pinchot as head, it drew up an inventory of the nation's natural resources.

As 1908 approached, Roosevelt became increasingly strident in his demand for sweeping reforms. He attacked "malefactors of great wealth," urged greater federal regulatory powers, criticized the conservatism of the federal courts, and called for laws protecting factory workers. Many business leaders blamed him for a severe financial panic in the autumn of 1907, and conservatives in Congress stiffened their opposition. Divisions between Republican conservatives and progressives grew.

Immensely popular, Roosevelt prepared in 1908 to turn over the White House to William Howard Taft, his close friend and colleague. "The Roosevelt policies will not go out with the Roosevelt administration," a party leader said. "If Taft weakens, he will annihilate himself." As expected, Taft soundly defeated the Democratic standard-bearer William Jennings Bryan, who was making his third try for the presidency. The Republicans retained control of Congress. Taft prepared to move into the White House, ready and willing to carry on the Roosevelt legacy.

The Ordeal of William Howard Taft

Why was the presidency of William Howard Taft so difficult for him?

The Republican national convention that nominated Taft had not satisfied either Roosevelt or Taft. True, Taft won the presidential nomination as planned, but conservative Republicans beat back the attempts of progressive Republicans to influence the convention. They named a conservative, James S. Sherman, for vice president and built a platform that reflected conservative views on labor, the courts, and other issues. Taft wanted a pledge to lower the tariff but got only a promise of revision, which might lower—or raise—it. La Follette, Cummins, Jonathan P. Dolliver of Iowa, Albert J. Beveridge of Indiana, and other progressive Republicans were openly disappointed.

Taking office in 1909, Taft felt "just a bit like a fish out of water." The son of a distinguished Ohio family and a graduate of Yale Law School, he became an Ohio judge, solicitor general of the United States, and a judge of the federal circuit court. In 1900, McKinley asked him to head the Philippine Commission, charged with the difficult and challenging task of forming a civil government in the Philippines. Later Taft was named the first governor general of the Philippines. In 1904, Roosevelt appointed him secretary of war. In all these positions, Taft made his mark as a skillful administrator. He worked quietly behind the scenes, avoided controversy, and shared none of Roosevelt's zest for politics. A good-natured man, Taft had personal charm and infectious humor. He fled from fights rather than seeking them out, and he disliked political maneuvering, preferring instead quiet solitude. "I don't like politics," he said. "I don't like the limelight."

THE ELECTION OF 1908

Candidate	Party	Popular Vote	Electoral Vote
Taft	Republican	7,678,908	321
Bryan	Democrat	6,409,104	162
Debs	Socialist	402,820	0
Chafin	Prohibition	252,821	0

Weighing close to three hundred pounds, Taft enjoyed conversation, golf and bridge, good food, and plenty of rest. Compared to the hardworking Roosevelt and Wilson, he was lazy. He was also honest, kindly, and amiable, and in his own way he knew how to get things done. Reflective, he preferred the life of a judge, but his wife, Helen H. Taft, who enjoyed politics, prodded him toward the White House. When a Supreme Court appointment opened in 1906, Taft reluctantly turned it down. "Ma wants him to wait and be president," his youngest son said.

Taft's years as president were not happy. Mrs. Taft's health soon collapsed, and as it turned out, Taft presided over a Republican party torn with tensions that Roosevelt had either brushed aside or concealed. The tariff, business regulation, and other issues split conservatives and progressives, and Taft often wavered or sided with the conservatives. Taft revered the past and distrusted change; although an ardent supporter of Roosevelt, he never had Roosevelt's faith in the ability of government to impose reform and alter individual behavior. He named five corporation attorneys to his cabinet, leaned more to business than to labor, and spoke of a desire to "clean out the unions."

At that time and later, Taft's reputation suffered by comparison to the flair of Roosevelt and the moral majesty of Woodrow Wilson. He deserved better. Taft was an honest and sincere president, who—sometimes firm, sometimes befuddled—faced a series of important and troublesome problems during his term of office.

Party Insurgency

Taft started his term with an attempt to curb the powerful Republican speaker of the House, Joseph "Uncle Joe" Cannon of Illinois. Using the powers of his position, Cannon had been setting House procedures, appointing committees, and virtually dictating legislation. Straightforward and crusty, he often opposed reform. In March 1909, thirty Republican congressmen joined Taft's effort to curb Cannon's power, and the president sensed success. But Cannon retaliated and, threatening to block all tariff bills, forced a compromise. Taft stopped the anti-Cannon campaign in return for Cannon's pledge to help with tariff cuts.

Republicans were divided over the tariff, and there was a growing party insurgency against high rates. The House quickly passed a bill providing for lower rates, but in the Senate, protectionists raised them. Senate leader Nelson W. Aldrich of Rhode Island introduced a revised bill that added more than eight hundred amendments to the rates approved in the House.

Angry, La Follette and other Republicans attacked the bill as the child of special interests. In speeches on the Senate floor they called themselves "progressives," invoked Roosevelt's name, and urged Taft to defeat the high-tariff proposal. Caught between protectionists and progressives, Taft wavered, then tried to compromise. In the end, he backed Aldrich. The Payne-Aldrich Act, passed in November 1909, called for higher rates than the original House bill, though it lowered them from the Dingley Tariff of 1897. An unpopular law, Payne-Aldrich helped discredit Taft and revealed the tensions in the Republican party.

Republican progressives and conservatives drifted apart. Thin-skinned, Taft resented the persistent pinpricks of the progressives who criticized him for virtually everything he did. He tried to find middle ground but leaned more and more toward the conservatives. During a nationwide speaking tour in the autumn of 1909, he praised Aldrich, scolded the low-tariff insurgents, and called the Payne-Aldrich Act "the best bill that the Republican party ever passed." Traveling through the Midwest, he pointedly ignored La Follette, Cummins, and other progressive Republicans.

By early 1910, progressive Republicans in Congress no longer looked to Taft for leadership. As before, they challenged Cannon's power, and Taft wavered. In an outcome embarrassing to the president, the progressives won, managing to curtail Cannon's authority to dictate committee assignments and schedule debate. In progressive circles there was growing talk of a Roosevelt return to the White House.

The Ballinger-Pinchot Affair

The conservation issue dealt another blow to relations between Roosevelt and President Taft. In 1909, Richard A. Ballinger, Taft's secretary of the interior, offered for sale a million acres of public land that Pinchot, who had stayed on as Taft's chief forester, had withdrawn from sale. Pinchot, fearing that Ballinger would hurt conservation programs, protested and, seizing on a report that Ballinger had helped sell valuable Alaskan coal lands to a syndicate that included J. P. Morgan, asked Taft to intervene. After investigating, Taft supported Ballinger on every count, although he asked Pinchot to remain in office.

Pinchot refused to drop the matter. Behind the scenes, he provided material for two anti-Ballinger magazine articles, and he wrote a critical public letter that Senator Dolliver of Iowa read to the Senate. Taft had had enough. He fired the insubordinate Pinchot, an action which, though appropriate, again lost support for Taft. Newspapers followed the controversy for months, and muckrakers assailed the administration's "surrender" to Morgan and other "despoilers of the national heritage."

The Ballinger-Pinchot controversy obscured Taft's important contributions to conservation. He won from Congress the power to remove lands from sale, and he used it to conserve more land than Roosevelt did. Still, the controversy tarred Taft, and it upset his old friend Roosevelt. Pinchot hurried to Italy where Roosevelt was on tour; he talked again with Roosevelt within days of the ex-president's arrival home in June 1910.

Taft Alienates the Progressives

Interested in railroad regulation, Taft backed a bill in 1910 to empower the ICC to fix maximum railroad rates. Progressive Republicans favored that plan but attacked Taft's suggestion of

a special Commerce Court to hear appeals from ICC decisions because most judges were traditionally conservative in outlook and usually rejected attempts to regulate railroad rates. They also thought the railroads had been consulted too closely in drawing up the bill. Democratic and Republican progressives tried to amend the bill to strengthen it; Taft made support of it a test of party loyalty.

The Mann-Elkins Act of 1910 gave something to everyone. It gave the ICC power to set rates, stiffened long- and short-haul regulations, and placed telephone and telegraph companies under ICC jurisdiction. These provisions delighted progressives. The act also created a Commerce Court, pleasing conservatives. In a trade-off, conservative Republican Senate leaders pledged their support for a statehood bill for Arizona and New Mexico, which were both predicted to be Democratic. In return, enough Democratic senators promised to vote for the Commerce Court provision to pass the bill. While pleased with the act, Taft and the Republican party lost further ground. In votes on key provisions of the Mann-Elkins Act, Taft raised the issue of party regularity, and progressive Republicans defied him.

Taft attempted to defeat the progressive Republicans in the 1910 elections. He helped form antiprogressive organizations, and he campaigned against progressive Republican candidates for the Senate. In California, he opposed Hiram Johnson, the progressive Republican champion; in Wisconsin, the home of La Follette, he sent Vice President James S. Sherman to take control of the state convention. Progressive Republicans retaliated

According to this 1913 cartoon, the new income tax legislation distributed the tax burden more evenly, so that contributions from the wealthy eased some of the burden on the working class.

by organizing a nationwide network of anti-Taft Progressive Republican Clubs.

The 1910 election results were a major setback for Taft and the Republicans—especially conservative Republicans. A key issue in the election, the high cost of living, gave an edge to the progressive wings in both major parties, lending support to their attack on the tariff and the trusts. In party primaries, progressive Republicans overwhelmed most Taft candidates, and in the general election, they tended to fare better than the conservatives, which increased progressive influence in the Republican Party.

For Republicans of all persuasions, however, it was a difficult election. The Democrats swept the urban-industrial states from New York to Illinois. New York, New Jersey, Indiana, and even Taft's Ohio elected Democratic governors. For the first time since 1894, Republicans lost control of both the House and the Senate. In all, they lost fifty-eight seats in the House and ten in the Senate. Disappointed, Taft called it "not only a landslide, but a tidal wave and holocaust all rolled into one general cataclysm."

Despite the defeat, Taft pushed through several important measures before his term ended. With the help of the new Democratic House, he backed laws to regulate safety in mines and on railroads, create a Children's Bureau in the federal government, establish employers' liability for all work done on government contracts, and mandate an eight-hour workday for government workers.

In 1909, Congress initiated a constitutional amendment authorizing an income tax, which, along with woman suffrage, was one of the most significant legislative measures of the twentieth century. The Sixteenth Amendment took effect early in 1913. A few months later, an important progressive goal was realized when the direct election of senators was ratified as the Seventeenth Amendment to the Constitution.

An ardent supporter of competition, Taft relentlessly pressed a campaign against trusts. The Sherman Antitrust Act, he said in 1911, "is a good law that ought to be enforced, and I propose to enforce it." That year, the Supreme Court in cases against Standard Oil and American Tobacco established the "rule of reason," which allowed the Court to determine whether a business presented "reasonable" restraint on trade. Taft thought the decisions gave the Court too much discretion, and he pushed ahead with the antitrust effort.

In October 1911, he sued U.S. Steel for its acquisition of the Tennessee Coal and Iron Company in 1907. Roosevelt had approved the acquisition (see p. 547), and the suit seemed designed to impugn his action. Enraged, he attacked Taft, and Taft, for once, fought back. He accused Roosevelt of undermining the conservative tradition in the country and began working to undercut the influence of the progressive Republicans. Increasingly

now, Roosevelt listened to anti-Taft Republicans who urged him to run for president in 1912. In February 1912, he announced, "My hat is in the ring."

Differing Philosophies in the Election of 1912

Delighted Democrats looked on as Taft and Roosevelt fought for the Republican nomination. As the incumbent president, Taft controlled the party machinery, and when the Republican convention met in June 1912, he took the nomination. In early July, the Democrats met in Baltimore and, confident of victory for the first time in two decades, struggled through forty-six ballots before finally nominating Woodrow Wilson, the reform-minded governor of New Jersey.

A month later, some of the anti-Taft and progressive Republicans—now calling themselves the Progressive Party—whooped it up in Chicago. Roosevelt was there to give a stirring "Confession of Faith" and listen to the delegates sing:

> Thou wilt not cower in the dust,
> Roosevelt, O Roosevelt!
> Thy gleaming sword shall never rust,
> Roosevelt, O Roosevelt!

 Watch the Video   **Bull Moose Campaign Speech**

Theodore Roosevelt campaigns for President in 1912. Roosevelt champions national health insurance and tries to ride his progressive Bull Moose Party back to the White House. It's an idea ahead of its time; health insurance is a rarity and medical fees are relatively low because doctors cannot do much for most patients. But medical breakthroughs are beginning to revolutionize hospitals and drive up costs.

Naming Roosevelt for president at its convention, the Progressive Party—soon known as the Bull Moose Party—set the stage for the first important three-cornered presidential contest since 1860.

Taft was out of the running before the campaign even began. "I think I might as well give up so far as being a candidate is concerned," he said in July. "There are so many people in the country who don't like me." Taft stayed at home and made no speeches before the election. Roosevelt campaigned strenuously, even completing one speech after being shot in the chest by an anti-third-term fanatic. "I have a message to deliver," he said, "and will deliver it as long as there is life in my body."

Roosevelt's message involved a program he called the **New Nationalism**. An important phase in the shaping of twentieth-century American political thought, it demanded a national approach to the country's affairs and a strong president to deal with them. The New Nationalism called for efficiency in government and society. It exalted the executive and the expert; urged social-justice reforms to protect workers, women, and children; and accepted "good" trusts. The New Nationalism encouraged large concentrations of labor and capital, serving the nation's interests under a forceful federal executive.

For the first time in the history of a major political party, the Progressive campaign enlisted women in its organization. Jane Addams, the well-known settlement worker, seconded

Roosevelt's nomination at Chicago, and she and other women played a leading role in his campaign. Some labor leaders, who saw potential for union growth, and some business leaders, who saw relief from destructive competition and labor strife, supported the new party.

Wilson, in contrast, set forth a program called the **New Freedom** that emphasized business competition and small government. A states' rights Democrat, he wanted to rein in federal authority, using it only to sweep away special privilege, release individual energies, and restore competition. Drawing on the thinking of Louis D. Brandeis, the brilliant shaper of reform-minded law, he echoed the Progressive party's social-justice objectives, while continuing to attack Roosevelt's planned state. For Wilson, the vital issue was not a planned economy but a free one. "The history of liberty is the history of the limitation of governmental power," he said in October 1912. "If America is not to have free enterprise, then she can have freedom of no sort whatever."

In the New Nationalism and New Freedom, the election of 1912 offered competing philosophies of government. Both Roosevelt and Wilson saw the central problem of the American nation as economic growth and its effect on individuals and society. Both focused on the government's relation to business, both believed in bureaucratic reform, and both wanted to use government to protect the ordinary citizen. But Roosevelt welcomed federal power, national planning, and business growth; Wilson distrusted them all.

On election day, Wilson won 6.3 million votes to 4.1 million for Roosevelt (who had recovered quickly from his wound) and 900,000 for Eugene V. Debs, the Socialist Party candidate. Taft, the incumbent president, finished third with 3.5 million votes; he carried only Vermont and Utah for 8 electoral votes. The Democrats also won outright control of both houses.

Woodrow Wilson's New Freedom

What were the central principles of Woodrow Wilson's New Freedom?

If under Roosevelt social reform took on the excitement of a circus, "under Wilson it acquired the dedication of a sunrise service." Born in Virginia in 1856 and raised in the South, Wilson was the son of a Presbyterian minister. As a young man, he wanted a career in public service, and he trained himself carefully in history and oratory. A moralist, he reached judgments easily. Once reached, almost nothing shook them. Opponents called him stubborn and smug. "He gives me the creeps," a Maryland ward boss said. "The time I met him, he said something to me, and I didn't know whether God or him was talking."

After graduating from Princeton University and the University of Virginia Law School, Wilson found that practicing law bored him. Shifting to history, from 1890 to 1902 he served as professor of jurisprudence and political economy at Princeton. In 1902, he became president of the university. Eight years later, he was governor of New Jersey, where he led a campaign to reform election procedures, abolish corrupt practices, and strengthen railroad regulation.

Wilson's rise was rapid, and he knew relatively little about national issues and personalities. But he learned fast, and in some

Read the Document Woodrow Wilson, from *The New Freedom* (1913)

Election of 1912

	Electoral Vote by State	Popular Vote
DEMOCRATIC Woodrow Wilson	435	6,293,454
PROGRESSIVE (BULL MOOSE) Theodore Roosevelt	88	4,119,538
REPUBLICAN William H. Taft	8	3,484,980
MINOR PARTIES	—	1,135,697
	531	15,033,939

ways the lack of experience served him well. He had few political debts to repay, and he brought fresh perspectives to older issues. Ideas intrigued Wilson; details bored him. Although he was outgoing at times, he could also be cold and aloof, and aides soon learned that he preferred loyalty and flattery to candid criticism.

Prone to self-righteousness, Wilson often turned differences of opinion into bitter personal quarrels. Like Roosevelt, he believed in strong presidential leadership. A scholar of the party system, he cooperated closely with Democrats in Congress, and his legislative record placed him among the most effective presidents in terms of passing bills that he supported. Forbidding in individual conversation, Wilson could move crowds with graceful oratory. Unlike Taft, and to a greater degree than Roosevelt, he could inspire.

His inaugural address was eloquent. "The Nation," he said, "has been deeply stirred, stirred by a solemn passion, stirred by the knowledge of wrong, of ideals lost, of government too often debauched and made an instrument of evil. The feelings with which we face this new age of right and opportunity sweep across our heartstrings like some air out of God's own presence."

The New Freedom in Action

On the day of his inauguration, Wilson called Congress into special session to lower the tariff. When the session opened on April 8, 1913, Wilson himself was there, the first president since John Adams in 1801 to appear personally before Congress. In forceful language, he urged Congress to reduce tariff rates.

As the bill moved through Congress, Wilson showed exceptional skill. He worked closely with congressional leaders, and when lobbyists threatened the bill in the Senate, he appealed for popular support. The result was a triumph for Wilson and the Democratic party. The **Underwood Tariff Act** passed in 1913. It lowered tariff rates about 15 percent and removed duties from sugar, wool, and several other consumer goods.

To make up for lost revenue, the act also levied a modest graduated income tax, authorized under the just ratified Sixteenth Amendment. Marking a significant shift in the American tax structure, it imposed a 1 percent tax on individuals and corporations earning more than $4,000 annually and an additional 1 percent tax on incomes more than $20,000. Above all, the act reflected a new unity within the Democratic party, which had worked together to pass a difficult tariff law.

Wilson himself emerged as an able leader. "At a single stage," a foreign editor said, "[he went] from the man of promise to the man of achievement." Encouraged by his success, Wilson decided to keep Congress in session through the hot Washington summer. Now he focused on banking reform, and the result in December 1913 was the **Federal Reserve Act**, the most important domestic law of his administration.

Meant to provide the United States with a sound yet flexible currency, the act established the country's first efficient banking system since Andrew Jackson killed the second Bank of the United States in 1832. It created twelve regional banks, each to serve the banks of its district. The regional banks answered to a Federal Reserve Board, appointed by the president, which governed the nationwide system.

A compromise law, the act blended public and private control of the banking system. Private bankers owned the federal reserve banks but answered to the presidentially appointed Federal Reserve Board. The reserve banks were authorized to issue currency, and through the discount rate—the interest rate at which they loaned money to member banks—they could raise or lower the amount of money in circulation. Monetary affairs no longer depended solely on the price of gold. Within a year, nearly half the nation's banking resources were in the Federal Reserve System.

The **Clayton Antitrust Act** (1914) completed Wilson's initial legislative program. Like previous antitrust measures, it reflected confusion over how to discipline a growing economy without putting a brake on output. In part it was a response to the revelations of the Pujo Committee of the House, publicized by Brandeis in a disquieting series of articles, "Other People's Money." In its investigation of Wall Street, the committee discovered a pyramid of money and power capped by the Morgan-Rockefeller empire that, through "interlocking directorates," controlled companies worth $22 billion, more than one-tenth of the national wealth.

The Clayton Act outlawed such directorates and prohibited unfair trade practices. It forbade pricing policies that created monopoly, and it made corporate officers personally responsible for antitrust violations. Delighting Samuel Gompers and the labor movement, the act declared that unions were not conspiracies in restraint of trade, outlawed the use of injunctions in labor disputes unless necessary to protect property, and approved lawful strikes and picketing. To Gompers's dismay, the courts continued to rule against union activity.

A related law established a powerful Federal Trade Commission to oversee business methods. Composed of five members, the commission could demand special and annual reports, investigate complaints, and order corporate compliance, subject to court review. At first, Wilson opposed the commission concept, which was an approach more suitable to Roosevelt's New Nationalism, but he changed his mind and, along with Brandeis, called it the cornerstone of his antitrust plan. To reassure business leaders, he appointed a number of conservatives to the new commission and to the Federal Reserve Board.

In November 1914, Wilson proudly announced the completion of his New Freedom program. Tariff, banking, and antitrust laws promised a brighter future, he said, and it was now "a time of healing because a time of just dealing." Many progressives were aghast. That Wilson could think society's ills were so easily cured, the *New Republic* said, "casts suspicion either upon his own sincerity or upon his grasp of the realities of modern social and industrial life."

Wilson Moves Toward the New Nationalism

Distracted by the start of war in Europe, Wilson gave less attention to domestic issues for more than a year. When he returned to concern with reform, he adopted more and more of Roosevelt's New Nationalism and blended it with the New Freedom to set it off from his earlier policies.

One of Wilson's problems was the Congress. To his dismay, the Republicans gained substantially in the 1914 elections. Reducing the Democratic majority in the House, they swept key industrial and farm states. At the same time, a recession struck the economy, which had been hurt by the outbreak of the European war in August 1914. Some business leaders blamed the tariff and other New Freedom laws. On the defensive, Wilson soothed business sentiment and invited bankers and industrialists to the White House. He allowed companies fearful of antitrust actions to seek advice from the Justice Department.

Preoccupied with such problems, Wilson blocked significant action in Congress through most of 1915. He refused to support a bill providing minimum wages for women workers, sidetracked a child labor bill on the ground that it was unconstitutional, and opposed a bill to establish long-term credits for farmers. He also refused to endorse woman suffrage, arguing that the right to vote was a state matter, not a federal one.

Wilson's record on race disappointed African Americans and many progressives. He had appealed to African American voters during the 1912 election, and a number of African American leaders campaigned for him. Soon after the inauguration, Oswald Garrison Villard, a leader of the NAACP, proposed a National Race Commission to study the problem of race relations. Initially sympathetic, Wilson rejected the idea because he feared he might lose southern Democratic votes in Congress. A Virginian himself, he appointed many Southerners to high office, and for the first time since the Civil War, southern views on race dominated the nation's capital.

At one of Wilson's first cabinet meetings, the postmaster general proposed the segregation of all African Americans in the federal service. No one dissented, including Wilson. Several government bureaus promptly began to segregate workers in offices, shops, rest rooms, and restaurants. Employees who objected were fired. African American leaders protested, and they were joined by progressive leaders and clergymen. Surprised at the protest, Wilson backed quietly away from the policy, although he continued to insist that segregation benefited African Americans.

As the year 1916 began, Wilson made a dramatic switch in focus and again pushed for substantial reforms. The result was a virtual river of reform laws, which was significant because it began the second, more national-minded phase of the New Freedom. With scarcely a glance over his shoulder, Wilson embraced important portions of Roosevelt's New Nationalism campaign.

In part, he was motivated by the approaching presidential election. A minority president, Wilson owed his victory in 1912 to the split in the Republican party, now almost healed. Roosevelt was moving back into Republican ranks, and there were issues connected with the war in Europe that he might use against Wilson. Moreover, many progressives were voicing disappointment with Wilson's limited reforms and his failure to support more advanced reform legislation on matters such as farm credits, child labor, and woman suffrage.

Moving quickly to patch up the problem, Wilson named Brandeis to the Supreme Court in January 1916. Popular among progressives, Brandeis was also the first person of Jewish faith to serve on the Court. When conservatives in the Senate tried to defeat the nomination, Wilson stood firm and won, earning further praise from progressives, Jews, and others. In May,

he reversed his stand on farm loans and accepted a rural credits bill to establish farm-loan banks backed by federal funds. The Federal Farm Loan Act of 1916 created a Federal Farm Loan Board to give farmers credit similar to the Federal Reserve's benefits for trade and industry.

Wilson was already popular within the labor movement. Going beyond Roosevelt's policies, which had sought a balance between business and labor, he defended union recognition and collective bargaining. In 1913, he appointed William B. Wilson, a respected leader of the United Mine Workers, as the first head of the Labor Department, and he strengthened the department's Division of Conciliation. In 1914, in Ludlow, Colorado, state militia and mine guards fired machine guns into a tent colony of coal strikers, killing twenty-one men, women, and children. Outraged, Wilson stepped in and used federal troops to end the violence while negotiations to end the strike went on.

In August 1916, a threatened railroad strike again revealed Wilson's sympathies with labor. Like Roosevelt, he invited the two sides to the White House, where he urged the railroad companies to grant an eight-hour day and labor leaders to abandon the demand for overtime pay. Labor leaders accepted the proposal; railroad leaders did not. "I pray God to forgive you, I never can," Wilson said as he left the room. Soon he signed the Adamson Act (1916) that imposed the eight-hour day on interstate railways and established a federal commission to study the railroad problem. Ending the threat of a strike, the act marked a milestone in the expansion of the federal government's authority to regulate industry.

With Wilson leading the way, the flow of reform legislation continued until the election. The Federal Workmen's Compensation Act established workers' compensation for government employees. The Keating-Owen Act, the first federal child labor law, prohibited the shipment in interstate commerce of products manufactured by children under the age of fourteen. It too expanded the authority of the federal government, though it was soon struck down by the Supreme Court. The Warehouse Act authorized licensed warehouses to issue negotiable receipts for farm products deposited with them.

In September, Wilson signed the Tariff Commission Act creating an expert commission to recommend tariff rates. The same month, the Revenue Act of 1916 boosted income taxes and furthered tax reform. Four thousand members of the National American Woman Suffrage Association cheered when Wilson finally came out in support of woman suffrage. Two weeks later he endorsed the eight-hour day for all the nation's workers.

The 1916 presidential election was close, but Wilson won it on the issues of peace and progressivism. By the end of 1916, he and the Democratic party had enacted most of the important parts of Roosevelt's Progressive party platform of 1912. To do it, Wilson abandoned portions of the New Freedom and accepted much of the New Nationalism, including greater federal power and commissions governing trade and tariffs. In mixing the two programs, he blended some of the competing doctrines of the Progressive Era, established the primacy of the federal government, and foreshadowed the pragmatic outlook of Franklin D. Roosevelt's New Deal of the 1930s.

Feature Essay

Madam C. J. Walker
African American Business Pioneer

At the 1912 convention of the National Negro Business League, a group devoted to promoting African American businesses, a 45-year-old woman, Madam C. J. Walker, tried to catch the eye of Booker T. Washington, the League's founder and head. But Washington ignored her until finally, her patience gone, she sprang to her feet and said, "Surely you are not going to shut the door in my face. I feel that I am in a business that is a credit to the womanhood of our race."

"I . . . came from the cotton fields of the South," she went on. "I was promoted from there to the washtub; then I was promoted to the cook kitchen, and from there *I promoted myself* into the business of manufacturing hair goods and preparations . . . I have built my own factory on my own ground."

Had Washington listened, Madam Walker had a remarkable story to tell. She was born Sarah Breedlove in 1867 on a plantation in Delta, Louisiana, the first in her sharecropper family born free. Orphaned at age seven, she married at fourteen to escape a cruel brother-in-law and find a home. Her husband died when she was twenty, leaving her with a young daughter and a back already aching from years of picking cotton and doing laundry. Looking for a better life, she moved to St. Louis and then to Denver, working as a cook and laundress. In Denver, she married Charles J. Walker and began calling herself "Madam," a title that lent prestige to a new business she had just begun.

For years, Walker had had trouble with her hair. It came out in bunches, partly because of the painful "wrap and twist" method that was popular

Madam Walker before and after her wonderful discovery.

Photographs of Madam C. J. Walker before and after using her hair care formula. Madam Walker was the first black woman millionaire and a pioneer in the development and manufacture of beauty products for African American women.

for styling African American hair. After trying various remedies, she developed her own formula that she said came to her in a dream. "I tried it on my friends," she said. "It helped them. I made up my mind to begin to sell it." Filling jars of the mixture in the attic of her home, she sold it door to door.

Madam Walker began promoting her system of hair care in 1905. The Walker system called for women first to wash their hair with Madam Walker's Vegetable Shampoo, then apply her Wonderful Hair Grower, add a light oil called Glossine, and finally press and relax the hair with a wide-toothed "hot comb."

As her business grew, Walker opened schools to teach her system, hired thousands of African American women as sales agents, and in 1910 moved her factory to Indianapolis for its central location. Knowing that white

stores would not stock her products, she relied on churches and women's clubs, two key institutions of the black community. Sales soon extended throughout the United States, Central America, and the Caribbean; Josephine Baker, the famous dancer, used Walker's products in Paris.

Dressed in white shirts and long black skirts, Walker agents became a familiar sight in African American neighborhoods everywhere. There were twenty thousand agents by 1916, most of them former maids, laundresses, and farm workers. "I have made it possible for many colored women to abandon the washtub for more pleasant and profitable occupation," she said.

As her income grew, Walker gave generously to various causes, including the YMCA, Mary McLeod Bethune's Educational and Industrial Institute for Negro Girls (now Bethune-Cookman

College), the Tuskegee Institute, and the NAACP. "Lady Bountiful," she was called, and she encouraged her agents to contribute to charity, too. "I love to use a part of what I make in trying to help others," she said.

When the country entered World War I, Walker helped sell war bonds and joined the many black leaders who encouraged African Americans to aid in the war effort, hoping that contributions to victory abroad would improve race relations at home. But she grew impatient as lynchings and other racial incidents continued. Angered by a race riot in East St. Louis, Illinois, in 1917, she supported the Negro Silent Protest Parade, in which ten thousand black New Yorkers marched in silence down Fifth Avenue while another twenty thousand African Americans looked on.

Walker went to Washington to ask President Woodrow Wilson to support legislation making lynching a federal crime, but Wilson was too "busy" to see her. Refusing to give up, Walker donated $5,000 to the NAACP's anti-lynching campaign and defended the rights of returning war veterans.

In 1918, Walker built Villa Lewaro, a mansion overlooking the Hudson River above New York City, near the estate of John D. Rockefeller. Walker called her home a symbol, to show "young Negroes what a lone woman accomplished and to inspire them to do big things." Madam Walker died at the villa in 1919, aged fifty-one. At her death, *The Crisis*, the journal of the NAACP, said she had "revolutionized the personal habits and appearance of millions of human beings."

According to the *Guinness Book of World Records*, Madam Walker was the first self-made woman millionaire. What she did, said Ida B. Wells-Barnett, the militant black leader, "made me take pride anew in Negro womanhood." Mary McLeod Bethune, the black educator, said, "She has gone, but her work still lives and shall live as an inspiration to not only her race but to the world." Walker bequeathed her company to her daughter—asking that a woman always serve at the head—but it began to fail during the Great Depression. Housed in the Walker Building, a National Historic Landmark, the Madam Walker Theatre Center today serves as a cultural center for the performing arts in downtown Indianapolis.

Even at the height of Madam Walker's business, "hot combs" and hair straighteners were controversial. Some black leaders (Booker T. Washington among them) denounced them as attempts to imitate whites, but many African American women straightened their hair anyway. Walker herself argued that she had no interest in straightening hair, only in boosting confidence and personal hygiene.

Walker's business dwindled, but the debate over hair continued, carrying important economic as well as social dimensions. In recent years, African Americans spent three times more per person than other consumer groups on hair-care products, cosmetics, toiletries, and other grooming aids.

Famous African American singers, actresses, and television personalities, including Oprah Winfrey, relax their hair. Others object. Alice Walker, an African American and one of the nation's foremost authors, calls hair straightening a form of oppression, a "ceiling on the brain" that keeps people from fulfillment. Hip-hop music reinforces the message, taking hair, as one music magazine has said, "back to its African roots. From dreads, cornrows, and braids to twists, coils to 'fros, hip hop is keeping it real . . . natural. For many, hair is more than just a style—it's a statement."

Madam Walker would have agreed. Hair care, she believed, involved more than hair; it meant pride, better health, and new opportunities for black women everywhere. When she returned to the Negro Business League convention in 1913, she talked about economic independence for African American women. "The girls and women of our race," she said, "must not be afraid to take hold of business endeavor . . . wring success out of a number of business opportunities that lie at their very doors. . . . I want to say to every Negro woman present, don't sit down and wait for the opportunities to come. . . . Get up and make them!"

QUESTIONS FOR DISCUSSION

1. Why was Madam C.J. Walker's business so successful?

2. Why did some black people oppose using her products?

3. How did Walker try to empower black women and win more rights for black Americans?

Conclusion: The Fruits of Progressivism

The election of 1916 showed how deeply progressivism had reached into American society. "We have in four years," Wilson said that fall, "come very near to carrying out the platform of the Progressive Party as well as our own; for we are also progressives."

In retrospect, however, 1916 also marked the beginning of progressivism's decline. At most, the years of progressive reform lasted from the 1890s to 1921, and in large measure they were compressed into a single decade between 1906 and American entry into World War I in 1917. Many problems the progressives addressed but did not solve; and some important ones, such as race, they did not even tackle. Yet their regulatory commissions, direct primaries, city improvements, and child labor laws marked an era of important and measured reform.

The institution of the presidency expanded. From the White House radiated executive departments that guided a host of activities. Independent commissions, operating within flexible laws, supplemented executive authority.

These developments owed a great deal to both Roosevelt and Wilson. To manage a complex society, Roosevelt developed a simple formula: expert advice; growth-minded policies; a balancing of business, labor, and other interests; the use of publicity to gather support; and stern but often permissive oversight of the economy. Roosevelt strengthened the executive office, and he called on the newer group of professional, educated, public-minded citizens to help him. "I believe in a strong executive," he said; "I believe in power."

At first, Wilson had different ideas, wanting to dismantle much of Roosevelt's governing apparatus. But driven by outside forces and changes in his own thinking, Wilson soon moved in directions similar to those Roosevelt had championed. Starting out to disperse power, he eventually consolidated it.

Through such movements, government at all levels accepted responsibility for the welfare of various elements in the social order. A reform-minded and bureaucratic society took shape, in which men and women, labor and capital, political parties and social classes competed for shares in the expansive framework of twentieth-century life. But there were limits to reform. As both Roosevelt and Wilson found, the new government agencies, understaffed and underfinanced, depended on the responsiveness of those they sought to regulate.

Soon there was a far darker cloud on the horizon. The spirit of progressivism rested on a belief in human potential, peace, and progress. After Napoleon's defeat in 1815, a century of peace began in western Europe, and as the decades passed, war seemed a dying institution. "It looks as though this were going to be the age of treaties rather than the age of wars," an American said in 1912, "the century of reason rather than the century of force." It was not to be. Two years later, the most devastating of wars broke out in Europe, and in 1917, Americans were fighting on the battlefields of France.

Study Resources

 Take the **Study Plan** for **Chapter 23** *From Roosevelt to Wilson in the Age of Progressivism* on **MyHistoryLab**

TIME LINE

1894 National Municipal League formed to work for reform in cities

1900 Galveston, Texas, is first city to try commission form of government

1901 Theodore Roosevelt becomes president; Robert M. La Follette elected reform governor of Wisconsin; Doctors reorganize the American Medical Association; Socialist party of America organized

1902 Roosevelt sues Northern Securities Company for violation of Antitrust Act; Coal miners in northeastern Pennsylvania strike; Maryland is first state to pass workers' compensation law; Oregon adopts the initiative and referendum

1904 Roosevelt elected president

1906 Hepburn Act strengthens Interstate Commerce Commission (ICC); Upton Sinclair attacks meatpacking industry in *The Jungle*; Congress passes Meat Inspection Act and Pure Food and Drug Act

1908 Taft elected president; Supreme Court upholds Oregon law limiting working hours for women in *Muller* v. *Oregon*

1909 Payne-Aldrich Tariff Act divides Republican party

1910 Mann-Elkins Act passed to regulate railroads; Taft fires Gifford Pinchot, head of U.S. Forest Service; Democrats sweep midterm elections

1912 Progressive party formed; nominates Roosevelt for president; Woodrow Wilson elected president

1913 Underwood Tariff Act lowers rates; Federal Reserve Act reforms U.S. banking system; Sixteenth Amendment authorizes Congress to collect taxes on incomes

1914 Clayton Act strengthens antitrust legislation

1916 Wilson wins reelection

1918 Supreme Court strikes down federal law limiting child labor in *Hammer* v. *Dagenhart*

1920 Nineteenth Amendment gives women the right to vote

CHAPTER REVIEW

The Spirit of Progressivism

What were the six major characteristics of progressivism?

Progressivism sought cures for social and economic problems and was defined by six major characteristics: (1) a desire not to harm big business but to humanize and regulate it; (2) optimism about human nature; (3) a willingness to intervene in people's lives; (4) a tendency to stress the authority of the state and the government; (5) belief in the environment as a key to reform; and (6) a nationwide base. p. 537

Reform in the Cities and States

What methods did progressive reformers use to attack problems in the cities and states?

Progressive reformers turned increasingly to the government to carry out their measures. At the same time, ironically, fewer people tended to vote. Reformers focused on life in the growing cities. Robert M. La Follette of Wisconsin personified the movement. His focus was on improving factory safety, regulating the railroads, and adopting political reforms. p. 544

The Republican Roosevelt

How would you describe the personality and programs of Theodore Roosevelt?

Roosevelt attacked some trusts and, through the courts, broke up a railroad holding company. His intervention in the coal strike of 1902 reflected his active, energetic personality and represented an advance in presidential power. p. 546

Roosevelt Progressivism at its Height

What were the major measures of Theodore Roosevelt's term from 1905 to 1909?

Winning easy election in 1904, Roosevelt persuaded Congress to improve railroad regulation, backed pure food and drug laws, and enlarged national parks. In all these actions, he reflected the values of the progressive generation: a reliance on experts, a faith in government power to initiate reform, and a desire to tame big business. p. 548

The Ordeal of William Howard Taft

Why was the presidency of William Howard Taft so difficult for him?

Roosevelt had left Taft a variety of difficult problems, including the tariff and a widening split between progressive and conservative Republicans. Taft increasingly alienated the progressives and Roosevelt. In the election of 1912, Taft finished third behind Woodrow Wilson and Roosevelt. p. 550

Woodrow Wilson's New Freedom

What were the central principles of Woodrow Wilson's New Freedom?

Victorious in 1912, Wilson set out to put into effect the central principles of his New Freedom program, including tariff reform, an antitrust law, and the Federal Reserve Act, a measure that still guides our economy today. By 1916, however, Wilson found greater value in Roosevelt's New Nationalism, which had emphasized government intervention and measures to protect women, labor, and other groups. p. 553

KEY TERMS AND DEFINITIONS

Progressive (or "Bull Moose") Party This political party was formed by Theodore Roosevelt to advance progressive ideas and unseat President William Howard Taft in 1912. p. 537

National American Woman Suffrage Association Founded by Susan B. Anthony in 1890, this organization worked to secure women the right to vote. It stressed careful organization and peaceful lobbying. p. 541

Pragmatism An early twentieth-century doctrine, based n the ideas of William James. Pragmatists were impatient with the concept of truth as an abstract reality. They believed that truth should work for the individual and that people were not only shaped by their environment but also helped to shape it. If an idea worked, it became truth. p. 542

Hepburn Act A 1906 law that strengthened the power of the Interstate Commerce Commission (ICC) to regulate the railroads. p. 548

Conservation President Theodore Roosevelt made this principle one of his administration's top goals. Conservation in his view aimed at protecting the nation's natural resources, but called for the wise use of them rather than locking them away. p. 549

New Nationalism President Theodore Roosevelt's program calling for a national approach to the country's affairs and a strong president to deal with them; efficiency in government and society; and protection of children, women, and workers. It accepted "good" trusts; and exalted the expert and the executive. It also encouraged large concentrations of capital and labor. p. 553

New Freedom President Woodrow Wilson's program, which emphasized business competition and small government. It sought to rein in federal authority, release individual energy, and restore competition. It achieved many of the progressive social-justice objectives while pushing for a free economy rather than a planned one. p. 553

Underwood Tariff Act This 1913 law reduced tariff rates and levied a graduated income tax to make up for the lost revenue. p. 554

Federal Reserve Act This 1913 act created a central banking system, consisting of 12 regional banks governed by the Federal Reserve Board. It was an attempt to provide the United States with a sound yet flexible currency. p. 554

Clayton Antitrust Act This law outlawed interlocking directorates (in which the same people served as directors for several competing companies), forbade policies that created monopolies, and made corporate officers responsible for antitrust violations. It also declared that unions were not conspiracies in restraint of trade and outlawed the use of injunctions in labor disputes unless they were necessary to protect property. p. 554

CRITICAL THINKING QUESTIONS

1. How might American history have changed if the Progressive Era had not occurred?

2. How did the major measures of Roosevelt's second term continue the progressive approaches on his first term?

3. How did the differences of opinion during the Progressive Era affect the Taft administration?

4. How did the Wilson administration draw on the characteristics of the Progressive Era?

MyHistoryLab Media Assignments

Find these resources in the Media Assignments folder for Chapter 23 on MyHistoryLab

The Spirit of Progressivism

Read the **Document**   *Lincoln Steffens, from* The Shame of the Cities *p. 538*

■ **Read** the **Document**   *Report of the Vice Commission (1915) p. 540*

■ **View** the **Map**   *Changing Lives of American Women, 1880–1930 p. 541*

Read the **Document**   *National Woman Suffrage Association, Mother's Day Letter p. 542*

Read the **Document**   *Eugene V. Debs, from "The Outlook for Socialism in America" p. 543*

The Republican Roosevelt

Read the **Document**   *Theodore Roosevelt, from* The Strenuous Life *(1900) p. 546*

Roosevelt Progressivism at its Height

Read the **Document**   *Upton Sinclair, from* The Jungle *(1906) p. 548*

The Ordeal of William Howard Taft

■ **Watch** the **Video**   *Bull Moose Campaign Speech p. 552*

■ **Read** the **Document**   *Woodrow Wilson, from* The New Feedom *p. 553*

Woodrow Wilson's New Freedom

■ **Complete** the **Assignment**   *Madam C. J. Walker: African American Business Pioneer p. 556*

■ *Indicates Study Plan Media Assignment*

24 The Nation at War

Contents and Learning Objectives

((•—[Listen to the **Audio File** on **myhistorylab**   Chapter 24 *The Nation at War*

The Sinking of the *Lusitania*

On the morning of May 1, 1915, the German government took out the following important advertisement in the *New York World* as a warning to Americans and other voyagers setting sail for England:

NOTICE—

Travellers intending to embark on the Atlantic voyage are reminded that a state of war exists between Germany and her allies and Great Britain and her allies; that the zone of war includes the waters adjacent to the British Isles; that, in accordance with formal notice given by the Imperial German Government, vessels flying the flag of Great Britain, or of any of her allies, are liable to destruction in those waters and that travelers sailing in the war zone on ships of Great Britain or her allies do so at their own risk.

At 12:30 that afternoon, the British steamship *Lusitania* set sail from New York to Liverpool. Secretly, it carried a load of ammunition as well as passengers.

The steamer was two hours late in leaving, but it held several speed records and could easily make up the time. The passenger list of 1,257 was the largest since the outbreak of war in Europe in 1914. Alfred G. Vanderbilt, the millionaire sportsman, was aboard; so were Charles Frohman, a famous New York theatrical producer, and Elbert Hubbard, a popular writer who jested that a submarine attack might help sell his new book. While some passengers chose the *Lusitania* for speed, others liked the modern staterooms, more comfortable than the older ships of the competing American Line.

Six days later, the *Lusitania*, back on schedule, reached the coast of Ireland. German U-boats were known to patrol the dangerous waters. When the war began, Great Britain imposed a naval blockade of Germany. In return, Germany in February 1915 declared the area around the British Isles a war zone; all enemy vessels, armed or unarmed, were at risk. Germany had only a handful of U-boats, but the submarines were a new and frightening weapon. On behalf of the United States, President Woodrow Wilson protested the German action, and on February 10, he warned Germany of its "strict accountability" for any American losses resulting from U-boat attacks.

Off Ireland, the passengers lounged on the deck of the *Lusitania*. As if it were peacetime, the ship sailed

"All the News That's Fit to Print."

The New York Times.

EXTRA
5:30 A.M.

Weather Today and Sunday: Fair.

VOL. LXIV...NO. 20,923. *****   NEW YORK, SATURDAY, MAY 8, 1915.—TWENTY-FOUR PAGES.   ONE CENT In Greater New York, Jersey City and Newark. | Elsewhere TWO CENTS.

LUSITANIA SUNK BY A SUBMARINE, PROBABLY 1,260 DEAD;
TWICE TORPEDOED OFF IRISH COAST; SINKS IN 15 MINUTES;
CAPT. TURNER SAVED, FROHMAN AND VANDERBILT MISSING;
WASHINGTON BELIEVES THAT A GRAVE CRISIS IS AT HAND

SHOCKS THE PRESIDENT

Washington Deeply Stirred by the Loss of American Lives.

BULLETINS AT WHITE HOUSE

Wilson Reads Them Closely, but Is Silent on the Nation's Course.

HINTS OF CONGRESS CALL

Loss of Lusitania Recalls Firm Tone of Our First Warning to Germany.

CAPITAL FULL OF RUMORS

Reports That Liner Was to be Sunk Were Heard Before Actual News Came.

Special to The New York Times.

WASHINGTON, May 7.— Never since that April day, three years ago, when word came that the Titanic had gone down, has Washington been so stirred as it is tonight over the sinking of the Lusitania. The early reports told that there had been no loss of life, but the belief that these advices caused gave way to apprehension and concern this evening when it became known that there had been many deaths. Although they are profoundly reticent, officials realize that this tragedy, involving the loss of American citizens, is likely to bring about a crisis in the international relations of this United States.

The Lost Cunard Steamship Lusitania
X Where the First Torpedo Struck.   XX Where the Second Torpedo Struck.

SOME DEAD TAKEN ASHORE

Several Hundred Survivors at Queenstown and Kinsale.

STEWARD TELLS OF DISASTER

One Torpedo Crashes Into the Doomed Liner's Bow, Another Into the Engine Room.

SHIP LISTS OVER TO PORT

Makes It Impossible to Lower Many Boats, So Hundreds Must Have Gone Down.

ATTACKED IN BROAD DAY

Passengers at Luncheon—Warning Had Been Given by Germans Before the Ship Left New York.

Only 650 Were Saved, Few Cabin Passengers

QUEENSTOWN, Saturday, May 8, 4:28 A. M.— Survivors of the Lusitania who have arrived here estimate that only about 650 of those aboard the steamer were saved, and say only a small proportion of those rescued were saloon passengers.

Official Confirmation

WASHINGTON, May 8.—A dispatch to the State Department early today from American Consul Lauriet at Queenstown stated that the total number of survivors of the Lusitania was about 700.

LONDON, Saturday, May 8.—The Cunard liner Lusitania, which sailed out of New York last Saturday with 1,918 souls aboard, lies at the bottom of the ocean off the Irish coast.

She was sunk by a German submarine, which sent two torpedoes crashing into her side at 2:30 o'clock yesterday afternoon while the passengers, seemingly confident that the great, swift vessel could elude the German underwater craft, were having luncheon.

The great inrush of water caused the liner to list heavily to port, so that she could not launch many of her lifeboats.

About 1,260 of those on board the great ship, including many Americans, apparently went down with her, as a statement issued late this morning by the Admiralty says the total number of survivors is only 658.

There were 1,253 passengers on board the steamship, including 200 who were transferred to her from the steamer Cameronia. The Americans totaled 188. The crew numbered 665.

It is believed that only a few first class passengers were saved as they thought the ship would remain afloat, and made little effort to escape.

There appears to be a large proportion of the ship's crew among the survivors landed at Queenstown. Only a few offi-

Cunard Office Here Besieged for News; Fate of 1,918 on Lusitania Long in Doubt

Nothing Heard from the Well-Known Passengers on Board—Story of Disaster Long Unconfirmed While Anxious Crowds Seek Details.

Official news of the sinking of the Lusitania yesterday reached New York in fragmentary reports, and several hours elapsed between the first unverified rumor of the disaster and the cable messages that told at night of the saving of some of the passengers and gave meagre details of the most sensational incident of its kind in the war.

The early accounts that indicated all on board had been saved reassured hundreds of friends and relatives of passengers. Later, it was made known that lives had been lost and probably many persons had been injured.

Among the prominent passengers rescued was George A. Kessler. The list of those of whom no word was received included A. G. Vanderbilt, Charles Frohman, Justus Miles Forman, and Elbert Hubbard, besides persons widely known in society.

A cablegram sent to Farley Hopkins of The Yale News staff at New Haven, by his father, who was aboard the Lusitania, stated that the vessel was sunk, not beached, that three hundred persons had been already landed, and that the rest in small boats were making for shore. Several bulletins reached New York at 8:15 o'clock and were signed " Los Higginson & Co., London."

Word of the safety of Charles J. Lauriat, Jr., of Boston, Mass., a member of the firm of Charles E. Lauriat & Co., booksellers, who was a first-cabin passenger, reached relatives there in a cablegram early this morning. The message, dated at Queenstown, 2:20 A. M., read simply:

" Charles E. Lauriat, Jr., safe and well. "

For more than half a century it was the boast of the Cunard Line that it never had lost a life. The record was sunk in collision near Fire Island in 1886, but no lives were lost until five passengers were swept off the Campania's forward deck by a wave on Oct. 5, 1905. The sinking of the Lusitania is the first big disaster of the Cunard Line has had.

List of Saved Includes Capt. Turner; Vanderbilt and Frohman Reported Lost

LONDON, Saturday, May 8—5:30 A. M.—The Press Bureau 'as received from the British Admiralty at Queenstown a report that all the torpedo boats and tugs and armed trawlers, except the Heron, which went out from Queenstown to the relief of the Lusitania have returned.

These vessels have landed 395 survivors and forty dead. Fifty-two more survivors are reported aboard a steamer, while eleven others and five bodies have been landed at Kinsale, making the total number of survivors 658, besides forty-five dead. The numbers will be verified later, and it is considered possible Kinsale fishing boats may have rescued a few more.

Among the survivors is the Captain of the Lusitania, William T. Turner. Some of the survivors at Queenstown say that Alfred Gwynne Vanderbilt was drowned. Every effort to find Mr. Vanderbilt and Charles Frohman, the theatrical manager, among the survivors has failed.

The Central News says that the number of the Lusitania's passengers who died of injuries while being taken to Queenstown will reach 100.

QUEENSTOWN Saturday, May 8, 4:45 A. M.—The list of the Lusitania's survivors, as far as compiled, follows:

TURNER, Captain.	LAURIAT, CHARLES E., Jr., Boston.
MATHEWS, A. T., Montreal.	PAYNTER, Miss IRENE, Liverpool, England.
BRASOWITZ, S.	
LANE, G. H.	KINSALE, Ireland, May 8.—
MEYERS, W. G. E.	Eleven survivors of the Lusitania
TRIMMINS, J. T.	have been landed here, together
WITHERBEE, Mrs. A. F.	with the bodies of five persons who
MACKWORTH, Lady.	were dead. Among the survivors
ADAMS, Mrs. HENRY, Boston.	are:
RANKIN, ROBERT, New York.	SMITH, J. RESTON, New York.
SHARP, SAMUEL.	BRITTOMLEY, FREDERICK
BYRNE, M. B., New York.	BOYLE, N. L.
DAVIE, EMILY.	HOTCHKISS, CHARLES.
WALKER, ANNIE.	HARRIMAN, CORNELIUS.
HOUSNELL, S.	LIVERMORE, VERNAR.
CROSS, A. E.	SULLIVAN, Mrs. P.
YOUNG, PHILIP, Montreal.	
VASSAR, W. A. F., London.	Consul's List of Saved.
STEELE, GEORGE.	WASHINGTON, May 8.—Consul
CROSLEY, CYRUS.	Lauriat at Queenstown sent this
PARKER, JAMES.	report:
COLEBROOK, the Rev. R.	"Total saved of all nationalities,
MORRIS, H. C. B.	700. The following are Americans
FISH, Mrs., and children.	survivors of Lusitania. Other
MARTIN, Miss H.	names will follow:
GAUTLETT, F. J., New York.	CRAB, O. S.
MAYCOCK, Miss MAT.	PEARL, Major and Mrs., and two
HENDERSON, VIOLET.	children.
MARDERUD, UNO.	SMITH, Mrs. JESSIE TAFT.
LUND, THOMAS D.	HARDWICK, CHARLES C.
THOMAS, D. A. Cardiff, Wales.	EARL, STUART D.
EVANS, T. J. M.	PEARL, AMY.
CLARKE, A. F.	STANLEY, Mrs.
BURGESS, W. G.	LINES, L. B.
CHARLES, J. H. and daughter,	RANKIN, ROBERT.
Toronto.	DOHERTY, Mrs. WILLIAM and
JONES, Miss New York.	infant.
HORRIS, JOHN.	PHILLIPS, THOMAS.
BRANDELL, Miss JOSEPHINE,	McADAMS, WILLIAM.
New York.	HOUGHTON, J. H.
PERRY, F. K. A.	SWEENEY, JOHN M.
CRAB, O. H.	HAMMOND, GADEN H.
MOSLEY, G. G., New York.	BROOKS, J. H.
BROOKS, J. H., New York.	JEFFEY, CHARLES T.
JEFFRY, A. M.	LUND, Mrs. C. H.
CAIRNS, M.	SHEPPERSON, ARTHUR.
HAMMOND, G. H., New York.	MOORE, Dr. D. V.
MASLEY, A.	BERNARD, CLINTON.
NEATH, H.	LIGHT, HERBERT.
NORTH, Mrs.	LINNSON, J. Jr.
WINTER, Miss.	WILLIAMS, EDITH.
WINTER, Miss.	LEARY, JAMES J.
DUGITD, GEORGE.	SLIDELL, THOMAS.
MOORE, DANIEL.	WOLFENDEN, Mrs. JOHN.
McCONNELL, JOHN W., Memphis, Tenn.	HOLLAND, Mrs. NINA.
SHARPE, Miss.	MESH, Mrs. THOMAS.
CONNER, Miss.	KESSLER, GEORGE A.
DALY, H. M.	McMURRAY, L.
CLIFFE, PATRICK.	KAY, ROBERT.
BOHAN, JAMES, Toronto.	LACKHART, R. R.
CROSLEY, Mrs. CYRUS.	CANNON, OWEN.
BRETHERTON, Mrs. CYRIL H.	HARRIS, DURIGHT C.
MESH, Mrs. THOMAS, Los Angeles.	JUDSON, FRED S.
— Cal.	COLLIE, ED M.
HOPKINS, A. L., New York.	WRIGHT, B. C.
LASSETTER, Mrs. H. B., of Sydney, Australia, wife of General Lassetter.	GAUNTLEY, F. J.
LASSETTER, Master P.	KNOX, S. N.
	O'DONNELL, PATRICK.

Saw the Submarine 100 Yards Off and Watched Torpedo as It Struck Ship

Ernest Cowper, a Toronto Newspaper Man, Describes Attack, Seen from Ship's Rail—Poison Gas Used in Torpedoes, Say Other Passengers.

Queenstown, Saturday, May 8, 3:18 A. M.

A sharp lookout for submarines was kept aboard the Lusitania as she approached the Irish coast, according to Ernest Cowper, a Toronto newspaper man, who was among the survivors landed at Queenstown.

He said that after the ship was torpedoed there was no panic among the crew, but that they went about the work of getting passengers into the boats in a prompt and efficient manner.

" As we neared the coast of Ireland," said Mr. Cowper, " we all joined in the lookout, for a possible attack by a submarine was the sole topic of conversation.

" I was chatting with a friend at the rail about 2 o'clock when suddenly I caught a glimpse of the conning tower of a submarine about a thousand yards distant. I immediately called my friend's attention to it. Immediately we both saw the track of a torpedo followed almost instantly by an explosion. Portions of splintered hull were sent flying into the air, and then another torpedo struck. The ship began to list to starboard.

" The crew at once proceeded to get the passengers into boats.

Poison Fumes from Torpedoes.

From interviews with passengers it appears that when the torpedoes burst they sent forth suffocating fumes which had their effect on the passengers, causing some of them to lose consciousness.

Two stokers, Byrne and Hussey of Liverpool, gave a few details. They said the submarine gave no notice and fired two torpedoes, one hitting No. 1 stoke hole and the second the engine room. The first torpedo was discharged at 2 o'clock. In twenty-five minutes the great liner disappeared.

Signals from the vessel had been received at Queenstown that an armed trawler, believed to be the Heron, and two fishing trawlers are bringing in 100 more bodies.

The Cunard Line agent states that the total number of persons aboard the Lusitania was 2,160.

Loss of the Lusitania Fills London With Horror and Utter Amazement

Special Cable to The New York Times.

LONDON, Saturday, May 8.—Stupefaction is the word which best describes the first impression created by the news of the sinking of the Lusitania. People seemed unable to realize that at this stage of the world's progress such a straight ahead, with no zigzag maneuvers to throw off pursuit. But the submarine U-20 was there, and its commander, seeing a large ship, fired a single torpedo. Seconds after it hit, a boiler exploded and blew a hole in the *Lusitania*'s side. The ship listed immediately, hindering the launching of lifeboats, and in eighteen minutes it sank. Nearly 1,200 people died, including 128 Americans. As the ship's bow lifted and went under, the U-20 commander for the first time read the name: *Lusitania*.

The sinking, the worst since the *Titanic* went down with 1,500 people in 1912, horrified Americans. Theodore Roosevelt called it "an act of piracy" and demanded war. Most Americans, however, wanted to stay out of war; like Wilson, they hoped negotiations could solve the problem. "There is such a thing," Wilson said a few days after the sinking, "as a man being too proud to fight. There is such a thing as a nation being so right that it does not need to convince others by force."

In a series of diplomatic notes, Wilson demanded a change in German policy. The first *Lusitania* note (May 13, 1915) called on Germany to abandon unrestricted submarine warfare, disavow the sinking, and compensate for lost American lives. Germany sent an evasive reply, and Wilson drafted a second *Lusitania* note (June 9) insisting on specific pledges. Fearful the demand would lead to war, Secretary of State William Jennings Bryan resigned rather than sign the note. Wilson sent it anyway and followed with a third note (July 21)—almost an ultimatum—warning Germany that the United States would view similar sinkings as "deliberately unfriendly."

Unbeknownst to Wilson, Germany had already ordered U-boat commanders not to sink passenger liners without warning. In August 1915, a U-boat mistakenly torpedoed the British liner *Arabic*, killing two Americans. Wilson protested, and Germany, eager to keep the United States out of the war, backed down. The *Arabic* pledge (September 1) promised that U-boats would stop and warn liners, unless they tried to resist or escape. Germany also apologized for American deaths on the *Arabic*, and for the rest of 1915, U-boats hunted freighters, not passenger liners.

Although Wilson's diplomacy had achieved his immediate goal, the *Lusitania* and *Arabic* crises contained the elements that led to war. Trade and travel tied the world together, and Americans no longer hid behind safe ocean barriers. New weapons, such as the submarine, strained old rules of international law. But while Americans sifted the conflicting claims of Great Britain and Germany, they hoped for peace. A generation of progressives, inspired with confidence in human progress, did not easily accept war.

Wilson also hated war, but he found himself caught up in a worldwide crisis that demanded the best in American will and diplomacy. In the end, diplomacy failed, and in April 1917, the United States entered a war that changed the nation's history. Building on several major trends in American foreign policy since the 1890s, the years around World War I firmly established the United States as a world power, confirmed the country's dominance in Latin America, and ended with a war with Germany and her allies that had far-reaching results, including establishing the United States as one of the world's foremost economic powers.

A New World Power

What were the main events that showed the United States was becoming a world power?

As they had in the late nineteenth century, Americans after 1900 continued to pay relatively little attention to foreign affairs. Newspapers and magazines ran stories every day about events abroad, but people paid closer attention to what was going on at home. Walter Lippmann, one of the twentieth century's most outstanding political commentators, once said, "I cannot remember taking any interest whatever in foreign affairs until after the outbreak of the First World War."

For Americans at the time, foreign policy was something to be left to the president in office, an attitude the presidents themselves favored. Foreign affairs became an arena in which they could exert a free hand largely unchallenged by Congress or the courts, and Roosevelt, Taft, and Wilson all took advantage of the opportunity to do so.

The foreign policy they pursued from 1901 to 1920 was aggressive and nationalistic. During these years, the United States intervened in Europe, the Far East, and Latin America. It dominated the Caribbean.

In 1898, the United States left the peace table possessing the Philippines, Puerto Rico, and Guam. Holding distant possessions required a colonial policy; it also required a change in foreign policy, reflecting an outward approach. From the Caribbean to the Pacific, policy makers paid attention to issues and countries they had earlier ignored. Like other nations in these years, the United States built a large navy, protected its colonial empire, and became increasingly involved in international affairs.

The nation also became more and more involved in economic ventures abroad. Turning out goods from textiles to steel, mass production industries sold products overseas, and financiers invested in Asia, Africa, Latin America, and Europe. During the years between the Spanish-American War and World War I, investments abroad rose from $445 million to $2.5 billion. While investments and trade never wholly dictated American foreign policy, they fostered greater involvement in foreign lands.

"I Took the Canal Zone"

Convinced the United States should take a more active international role, Theodore Roosevelt spent his presidency preparing the nation for world power. Working with Secretary of War Elihu Root, he modernized the army, using lessons learned from the war with Spain. Roosevelt and Root established the Army War College,

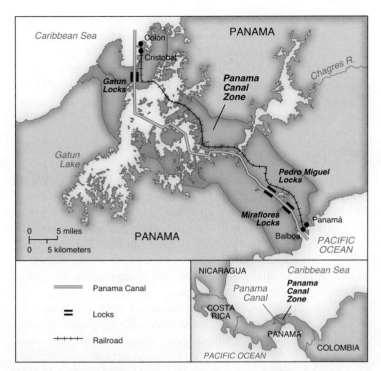

THE PANAMA CANAL ZONE Construction of the canal began in 1904, and despite landslides, steamy weather, and yellow fever, work was completed in 1914.

imposed stiff tests for the promotion of officers, and in 1903 created a general staff to oversee military planning and mobilization. Determined to end dependence on the British fleet, Roosevelt doubled the strength of the navy during his term in office.

Stretching his authority to the limits, Roosevelt took steps to consolidate the country's new position in the Caribbean and Central America. European powers, which had long resisted American initiatives there, now accepted American supremacy. Preoccupied with problems in Europe and Africa, Great Britain agreed to U.S. plans for an Isthmian canal in Central America and withdrew much of its military force from the area.

Roosevelt wanted a canal to link the Atlantic and Pacific oceans across the isthmus connecting North and South America. When the war with Spain started in 1898, the battleship *Oregon* took seventy-one days to sail from San Francisco around Cape Horn to its battle station in the Atlantic; years later, naval experts still shuddered at the memory. Secretary of State John Hay negotiated with Britain the Hay-Pauncefote Treaty of 1901 that permitted the United States to construct and control an Isthmian canal, providing it would be free and open to ships of all nations.

Delighted, Roosevelt began selecting the route. One route, fifty miles long, wandered through the rough, swampy terrain of the Panama region of Colombia. A French company had recently tried and failed to dig a canal there. To the northwest, another route ran through mountainous Nicaragua. Although two hundred miles in length, it followed natural water ways, a factor that would make construction easier.

An Isthmian Canal Commission investigated both routes in 1899 and recommended the shorter route through Panama. Roosevelt backed the idea, and he authorized Hay to negotiate an agreement with the Colombian chargé d'affaires, Thomas Herrán.

The Hay-Herrán Convention (1903) gave the United States a 99-year lease, with option for renewal, on a canal zone six miles in width. In exchange, the United States agreed to pay Colombia a one-time fee of $10 million and an annual rental of $250,000.

To Roosevelt's dismay, the Colombian Senate rejected the treaty, in part because it infringed on Colombian sovereignty. The Colombians also wanted more money. Calling them "jack rabbits" and "contemptible little creatures," Roosevelt considered seizing Panama, then hinted he would welcome a Panamanian revolt from Colombia. In November 1903, the Panamanians took the hint, and Roosevelt moved quickly to support them. Sending the cruiser *Nashville* to prevent Colombian troops from putting down the revolt, he promptly recognized the new Republic of Panama.

Two weeks later, the **Hay-Bunau-Varilla Treaty** with Panama granted the United States control of a canal zone ten miles wide across the isthmus of Panama. In return, the United States guaranteed the independence of Panama and agreed to pay the same fees offered Colombia. Using giant steam shovels and thousands of laborers from Jamaica, engineers cut their way across the isthmus. On August 15, 1914, the first ocean steamer sailed through the completed canal, which had cost $375 million to build.

Roosevelt's actions angered many Latin Americans. Trying to soothe feelings, Wilson agreed in 1914 to pay Colombia $25 million in cash, give it preferential treatment in using the canal, and express "sincere regret" over American actions. Roosevelt was furious, and his friends in the Senate blocked the agreement. Colombian–American relations remained strained until 1921, when the two countries signed a treaty that included Wilson's first two provisions but omitted the apology.

For his part, Roosevelt took great pride in the canal, calling it "by far the most important action in foreign affairs." Defending his methods, he said in 1911, "If I had followed traditional conservative methods, I would have submitted a dignified state paper of two hundred pages to Congress and the debate on it would have been going on yet; but I took the Canal Zone and let Congress debate; and while the debate goes on the Canal does also."

The Roosevelt Corollary

With interests in Puerto Rico, Cuba, and the canal, the United States developed a Caribbean policy to ensure its dominance in the region. It established protectorates over some countries and subsidized others to keep them dependent. When necessary, the United States purchased islands to keep them out of the hands of other powers, as in the case of the Danish West Indies (now the Virgin Islands), bought in 1917 to prevent the Germans from acquiring them.

From 1903 to 1920, the United States intervened often in Latin America to protect the canal, promote regional stability, and exclude foreign influence. One problem worrying American policy makers was the scale of Latin American debts to European powers. Many countries in the Western Hemisphere owed money to European governments and banks, and often these nations were poor, prone to revolution, and unable to pay. The situation invited European intervention. In 1902, Venezuela defaulted on debts; England, Germany, and Italy sent Venezuela an ultimatum and blockaded its ports. American pressure forced a settlement of the issue, but the general problem remained.

Roosevelt was concerned about it, and in 1904, when the Dominican Republic defaulted on its debts, he was ready with a major announcement. Known as the **Roosevelt Corollary** of the Monroe Doctrine, the policy warned Latin American nations to keep their affairs in order or face American intervention.

Applying the new policy immediately, Roosevelt in 1905 took charge of the Dominican Republic's revenue system. American officials collected customs and saw to the payment of debt. Within two years, Roosevelt also established protectorates in Cuba and Panama. In 1912, the U.S. Senate added the Lodge Corollary, which warned foreign corporations not to purchase harbors and other sites of military significance in Latin America. Continued by Taft, Wilson, and other presidents, the Roosevelt Corollary guided American policy in Latin America until the 1930s, when Franklin D. Roosevelt's Good Neighbor policy replaced it.

Ventures in the Far East

The Open Door policy toward China and possession of the Philippine Islands shaped American actions in the Far East. Congress refused to arm the Philippines, and the islands were vulnerable to the growing power of Japan. Roosevelt wanted to balance Russian and Japanese power, and he was not unhappy at first when war broke out between them in 1904. As Japan won victory after victory, however, Roosevelt grew worried. Acting on a request from Japan, he offered to mediate the conflict, and both Russia and Japan accepted: Russia because it was losing, and Japan because it was financially drained.

In August 1905, Roosevelt convened a peace conference at Portsmouth, New Hampshire. The conference ended the war, but Japan emerged as the dominant force in the Far East. Adjusting policy, Roosevelt sent Secretary of War Taft to Tokyo to negotiate the Taft-Katsura Agreement (1905), which recognized Japan's dominance over Korea in return for its promise not to invade the Philippines. Giving Japan a free hand in Korea violated the Open Door policy, but Roosevelt argued that he had little choice.

Relations between Japan and the United States were again strained in 1906 when the San Francisco school board ordered the segregation of Japanese, Chinese, and Korean children into a separate Oriental school. A year later, the California legislature considered a bill limiting the immigration of Japanese laborers into the state. As resentment mounted in Japan, Roosevelt intervened to persuade the school board to rescind its order, while at the same time he obtained from Japan the "Gentlemen's Agreement" (1907) promising to stop the flow of Japanese agricultural laborers into the United States.

In case Japan viewed his policy as a sign of weakness, Roosevelt sent sixteen battleships of the new American fleet around the world, including a stop in Tokyo in October 1908. Critics at home predicted dire consequences, and European naval experts felt certain Japan would attack the fleet. Instead, the Japanese welcomed it, even posting ads to sell the sailors Mitsukoshi washing powder to "rid yourselves of the seven blemishes on the way home." For the moment, Japanese-American relations improved, and in 1908 the two nations, in an exchange of diplomatic notes, reached the comprehensive Root-Takahira Agreement in which they promised to maintain the status quo in the Pacific, uphold the Open Door, and support Chinese independence.

In later years, tensions again grew in the Far East. Anger mounted in Japan in 1913 when the California legislature prohibited Japanese residents from owning property in the state. At the start of World War I, Japan seized some German colonies, and in 1915 it issued the Twenty-One Demands insisting on authority over China. Coveting an Asian empire, Japan eyed American possessions in the Pacific.

Taft and Dollar Diplomacy

In foreign as well as domestic affairs, President Taft tried to continue Roosevelt's policies. For secretary of state he chose Philander C. Knox, Roosevelt's attorney general, and together they pursued a policy of "**dollar diplomacy**" to promote American financial and business interests abroad. The policy had profit-seeking motives, but it also aimed to substitute economic ties for military alliances with the idea of increasing American influence and bringing lasting peace.

Intent, like Roosevelt, on supremacy in the Caribbean, Taft worked to replace European loans with American ones, thereby reducing the danger of outside meddling. In 1909, he asked American bankers to assume the Honduran debt in order to fend off English bondholders. A year later, he persuaded them to take over the assets of the National Bank of Haiti, and in 1911 he helped Nicaragua secure a large loan in return for American control of Nicaragua's National Bank. When Nicaraguans revolted against the agreement, Taft sent marines to put them down. A marine detachment was stationed in the country intermittently until the 1930s.

In the Far East, Knox worked closely with Willard Straight, an agent of American bankers, who argued that dollar diplomacy was the financial arm of the Open Door. Straight had close ties to Edward H. Harriman, the railroad magnate, who wanted to build railroads in Manchuria in northern China. Roosevelt had tacitly promised Japan he would keep American investors out of the area, and Knox's plan reversed the policy. Trying to organize an international syndicate to loan China money to purchase the Manchurian railroads, Knox approached England, Japan, and Russia. In January 1910, all three turned him down.

The outcome was a blow to American policy and prestige in Asia. Russia and Japan found reasons to cooperate with each other and staked out spheres of influence in violation of the Open Door. Japan resented Taft's initiatives in Manchuria, and China's distrust of the United States deepened. Instead of cultivating friendship, as Roosevelt had envisioned, Taft had started an intense rivalry with Japan for commercial advantage in China.

Foreign Policy Under Wilson

What did Woodrow Wilson mean by "moral diplomacy"?

When he took office in 1913, Woodrow Wilson knew little about foreign policy. As a Princeton professor, he had studied Congress and the presidency, but his books made only passing reference to foreign issues, and during the 1912 campaign he mentioned foreign policy only when it affected domestic concerns. "It would be the irony of fate if my administration had to deal chiefly with foreign affairs," he said to a friend before becoming president. And so it was. During his two terms, Wilson faced crisis after crisis in foreign affairs, including the outbreak of World War I.

The idealistic Wilson believed in a principled, ethical world in which militarism, colonialism, and war were brought under control. He emphasized moral purposes over material interests and said during one crisis, "The force of America is the force of moral principle." Rejecting the policy of dollar diplomacy, Wilson initially chose a course of **moral diplomacy**, designed to bring right to the world, preserve peace, and extend to other peoples the blessings of democracy.

Conducting Moral Diplomacy

William Jennings Bryan, whom Wilson appointed as secretary of state, was also an amateur in foreign relations. Trusting in the common people, Bryan was skeptical of experts in the State Department. To key posts abroad he appointed "deserving Democrats," believing they could do the job as well as career diplomats. Bryan was a fervent pacifist, and like Wilson, he believed in the American duty to "help" less favored nations.

In 1913 and 1914, he embarked on an idealistic campaign to negotiate treaties of arbitration throughout the world. Known as "cooling-off" treaties, they provided for submitting all international disputes to permanent commissions of investigation. Neither party could declare war or increase armaments until the

investigation ended, usually within one year. The idea drew on the era's confidence in commissions and the sense that human reason, given time for emotions to fade, could settle problems without war. Bryan negotiated cooling-off treaties with thirty nations, including Great Britain, France, and Italy. Germany refused to sign one. Based on a generous idea, the treaties were naive, and they did not work.

Wilson and Bryan promised a dramatic new approach in Latin America, concerned not with the "pursuit of material interest" but with "human rights" and "national integrity." Signaling the change, in 1913 they negotiated the treaty with Colombia apologizing for Roosevelt's Panamanian policy. Yet in the end, Wilson, distracted by other problems and impatient with the results of his idealistic approach, continued the Roosevelt–Taft policies. He defended the Monroe Doctrine, gave unspoken support to the Roosevelt Corollary, and intervened in Latin America more than had either Roosevelt or Taft.

In 1914, Wilson negotiated a treaty with Nicaragua to grant the United States exclusive rights to build a canal and lease sites for naval bases. This treaty made Nicaragua an American satellite. In 1915, he sent marines into Haiti to quell a revolution; they stayed until 1934. In 1916, he occupied the Dominican Republic, establishing a protectorate that lasted until 1924. By 1917, American troops "protected" Nicaragua, Haiti, the Dominican Republic, and Cuba—four nations that were U.S. dependencies in all but name.

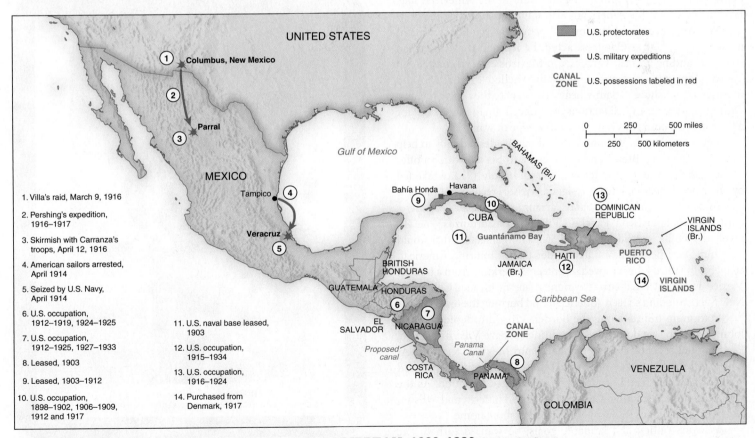

ACTIVITIES OF THE UNITED STATES IN THE CARIBBEAN, 1898–1930 During the first three decades of the twentieth century, the United States policed the Caribbean, claiming the right to take action when it judged Latin American countries were doing a bad job of running their affairs.

Troubles Across the Border

Wilson's moral diplomacy encountered one of its greatest challenges across the border in Mexico. Porfirio Dáaz, president of Mexico for thirty-seven years, was overthrown in 1911. Dáaz had encouraged foreign investments in Mexican mines, railroads, oil, and land; by 1913, Americans had invested more than $1 billion. But most Mexicans remained poor and uneducated, and Dáaz's overthrow led to a decade of violence that tested Wilson's policies and brought the United States close to war with Mexico.

A liberal reformer, Francisco I. Madero, followed Dáaz as president in 1911. But Madero could not keep order in the troubled country, and opponents of his reforms undermined him. With support from wealthy landowners, the army, and the Catholic Church, General Victoriano Huerta ousted Madero in 1913, threw him in jail, and arranged his murder. Most European nations immediately recognized Huerta, but Wilson, calling him a "butcher," refused to do so. Instead, he announced a new policy toward revolutionary regimes in Latin America. To win American recognition, they must not only exercise power but reflect "a just government based upon law, not upon arbitrary or irregular force."

On that basis, Wilson withheld recognition from Huerta and maneuvered to oust him. Early in 1914, he stationed naval units off Mexico's ports to cut off arms shipments to the Huerta regime. The action produced trouble. On April 9, 1914, several American sailors, who had gone ashore in Tampico to purchase supplies, were arrested. They were promptly released, but the American admiral demanded an apology and a 21-gun salute to the American flag. Huerta agreed—if the Americans also saluted the Mexican flag.

Wilson asked Congress for authority to use military force if needed; then, just as Congress acted, he learned that a German ship was landing arms at Veracruz on Mexico's eastern coast. With Wilson's approval, American warships shelled the harbor, and marines went ashore. Against heavy resistance, they took the city. Outraged, Mexicans of all factions denounced the invasion, and for a time the two countries hovered on the edge of war.

Retreating hastily, Wilson explained that he desired only to help Mexico. Argentina, Brazil, and Chile came to his aid with an offer to mediate the dispute, and tensions eased. In July 1914, weakened by an armed rebellion, Huerta resigned. Wilson recognized the new government, headed by Venustiano Carranza, an associate of Madero. Early in 1916, Francisco ("Pancho") Villa, one of Carranza's generals, revolted. Hoping to goad the United States into an action that would help him seize power, he raided border towns, injuring American civilians. In January, he removed seventeen Americans from a train in Mexico and murdered them. Two months later he invaded Columbus, New Mexico, killing sixteen Americans and burning the town.

Stationing militia along the border, Wilson ordered General John J. Pershing on a punitive expedition to seize Villa in Mexico. Pershing led six thousand troops deep into Mexican territory. At first, Carranza agreed to the drive, but as the Americans pushed farther and farther into his country, he changed his mind. As the wily Villa eluded Pershing, Carranza protested bitterly, and Wilson, worried about events in Europe, ordered Pershing home.

Wilson's policy had laudable goals; he wanted to help the Mexicans achieve political and agrarian reform. But his motives and methods were condescending. Wilson tried to impose gradual progressive reform on a society sharply divided along class

and other lines. With little forethought, he interfered in the affairs of another country, and in doing so he revealed the themes—moralism, combined with pragmatic self-interest and a desire for peace—that also shaped his policies in Europe.

Toward War

What were the reasons behind and dangers of Wilson's neutrality policy?

In May 1914, Colonel Edward M. House, Wilson's close friend and adviser, sailed to Europe on a fact-finding mission. Tensions there were rising. "The situation is extraordinary," he reported to Wilson. "It is jingoism [extreme nationalism] run stark mad. ... There is too much hatred, too many jealousies."

Large armies dominated the European continent. A web of alliances entangled nations, maximizing the risk that a local conflict could produce a wider war. In Germany, the ambitious Kaiser Wilhelm II coveted a world empire to match those of Britain and France. Germany had military treaties with Turkey and Austria-Hungary, a sprawling central European country of many

> 👁 **Watch the Video**   The Outbreak of World War I

HIS ROYAL HIGHNESS
THE GRAND DUKE FERDINAND OF AUSTRIA.

Franz Ferdinand (1863–1914) was born in Graz, Austria. As the heir to the Austro-Hungarian empire, his assassination on June 28, 1914 sparked the First World War.

nationalities. Linked in another alliance, England, France, and Russia agreed to aid each other in case of attack.

On June 28, 1914, a Bosnian assassin linked to Serbia murdered Archduke Franz Ferdinand, heir to the Austro-Hungarian throne. Within weeks, Germany, Turkey, and Austria-Hungary (the Central Powers) were at war with England, France, and Russia (the Allied Powers). Americans were shocked at the events. "I had a feeling that the end of things had come," one of Wilson's cabinet members said. "I stopped in my tracks, dazed and horror-stricken." Wilson immediately proclaimed neutrality and asked Americans to remain "impartial in thought as well as in action."

The war, he said, was one "with which we have nothing to do, whose causes cannot touch us." In private, Wilson was stunned. A man who loved peace, he had long admired the British parliamentary system, and he respected the leaders of the British Liberal party, who supported social programs akin to his own. "Everything I love most in the world," he said, "is at stake."

The Neutrality Policy

In general, Americans accepted neutrality. They saw no need to enter the conflict, especially after the Allies in September 1914 halted the first German drive toward Paris. America resisted involvement in other countries' problems, with the notable exception of Latin America, and had a tradition of freedom from foreign entanglements.

Many of the nation's large number of progressives saw additional reasons to resist. War, they thought, violated the very spirit of progressive reform. Why demand safer factories in which people could work and then kill them by the millions in war? To many progressives, moreover, England represented international finance, an institution they detested. Germany, on the other hand, had pioneered some of their favorite social reforms.

Furthermore, progressives and others tended to put the blame for war on the greed of "munition manufacturers, stockbrokers, and bond dealers" eager for wartime profits. "Do you want to know the cause of the war?" Henry Ford, who was no progressive, asked. "It is capitalism, greed, the dirty hunger for dollars." Above all, progressives were sure that war would end reform. It consumed money and attention; it inflamed emotions.

As a result, Jane Addams, Florence Kelley, Frederic C. Howe, Lillian Wald, and other progressives fought to keep the United States out of war. In late 1915, they formed the American Union Against Militarism, to throw, they said, "a monkey wrench into the machinery" of war. Throughout 1915 and 1916, *La Follette's Magazine*, the voice of the progressive leader, railed against the Morgans, Rockefellers, Du Ponts, and "the thirty-eight corporations most benefited by war orders."

The war's outbreak also tugged at the emotions of millions of immigrant Americans. Those who came from the British Isles tended to support the Allies; those from Ireland tended to support Germany, hoping Britain's wartime troubles might free their homeland from British domination. The large population of German Americans often sympathized with the Central Powers. But many people thought that, in a nation of immigrants, a policy of neutrality would be wise from a domestic point of view as well as from the viewpoint of foreign policy.

At the deepest level, a majority in the country, bound by common language and institutions, sympathized with the Allies and blamed Germany for the war. Like Wilson, many Americans admired English literature, customs, and law; they remembered Lafayette and the times when France had helped the United States in its early years. Germany, on the other hand, seemed arrogant and militaristic. When the war began, it invaded Belgium to strike at France and violated a treaty that the German chancellor called "just a scrap of paper." Many Americans resented the violation, and they liked it even less when German troops executed Belgian civilians who resisted.

Both sides sought to sway American opinion, and fierce propaganda campaigns flourished. The German Literary Defense Committee distributed more than a million pamphlets during the first year of the war. German propaganda tended to emphasize strength and will; Allied propaganda called on historical ties and took advantage of German atrocities, both real and alleged. In the end, the propaganda probably made little difference. Ties of heritage and the course of the war, not propaganda, decided the American position. At the outset, no matter which side they cheered for, Americans of all persuasions preferred simply to remain at peace.

Freedom of the Seas

The demands of trade tested American neutrality and confronted Wilson with difficult choices. Under international law, neutral countries were permitted to trade in nonmilitary goods with all belligerent countries. But Great Britain controlled the seas, and it intended to cut off shipments of war materials to the Central Powers.

As soon as war broke out, Britain blockaded German ports and limited the goods Americans could sell to Germany. American ships had to carry cargoes to neutral ports from which, after examination, they could be carried to Germany. As time passed, Britain stepped up the economic sanctions by forbidding the shipment to Germany of all foodstuffs and most raw materials, seizing and censoring mail, and "blacklisting" American firms that dealt directly with the Central Powers. British ships often stopped American ships and confiscated cargoes.

Again and again, Wilson protested against such infringements on neutral rights. Sometimes Britain complied, sometimes not, and Wilson often grew angry. But needing American support and supplies, Britain pursued a careful strategy to disrupt German–American trade without disrupting Anglo–American relations. After forbidding cotton shipments to Germany in 1915, it agreed to buy enough cotton to make up for the losses. When necessary, it also promised to reimburse American businesses after the war's end.

Other than the German U-boats, there were no constraints on trade with the Allies, and a flood of Allied war orders fueled the American economy. England and France bought huge amounts of arms, grain, cotton, and clothing. To finance the purchases, the Allies turned to American bankers for loans. By 1917, loans to Allied governments exceeded $2 billion; loans to Germany came to only $27 million.

In a development that influenced Wilson's policy, the war produced the greatest economic boom in the nation's history. Loans and trade drew the United States ever closer to the Allied cause. And even though Wilson often protested English maritime policy, the protests involved American goods and money, whereas Germany's submarine policy threatened American lives.

The U-Boat Threat

A relatively new weapon, the *Unterseeboot*, or submarine, strained the guidelines of international law. Traditional law required a submarine to surface, warn the target to stop, send a boarding party to check papers and cargo, then allow time for passengers and crew to board lifeboats before sinking the vessel. Flimsy and slow, submarines could ill afford to surface while the prey radioed for help. If they did surface, they might be rammed or blown up by deck guns.

When Germany announced the submarine campaign in February 1915, Wilson protested sharply, calling the sinking of merchant ships without checking cargo "a wanton act." The Germans promised not to sink American ships—an agreement that lasted until 1917—and thereafter the issue became the right of Americans to sail on the ships of belligerent nations. In March, an American citizen aboard the British liner *Falaba* perished when the ship was torpedoed off the Irish coast. Bryan urged Wilson to forbid Americans to travel in the war zones, but the president, determined to stand by the principles of international law, refused.

Wilson reacted more harshly in May and August of 1915 when U-boats sank the *Lusitania* and the *Arabic*. He demanded that the Germans protect passenger vessels and pay for American losses. At odds with Wilson's understanding of neutrality, Bryan resigned as secretary of state and was replaced by Robert Lansing, a lawyer and counselor in the State Department. Lansing brought a very different spirit to the job. He favored the Allies and believed that democracy was threatened in a world dominated by Germany. He urged strong stands against German violations of American neutrality.

In February 1916, Germany declared unrestricted submarine warfare against all armed ships. Lansing protested and told Germany it would be held strictly accountable for American losses. A month later, a U-boat torpedoed the unarmed French channel steamer *Sussex* without warning, injuring several Americans. Arguing that the sinking violated the *Arabic* pledge, Lansing urged Wilson to break relations with Germany. Wilson rejected the advice, but on April 18 he sent an ultimatum to Germany, stating that unless the Germans immediately called off attacks on cargo and passenger ships, the United States would sever relations.

The kaiser, convinced he did not yet have enough submarines to risk war, yielded. In the *Sussex* pledge of May 4, 1916, he agreed to Wilson's demands and promised to shoot on sight only ships of the enemy's navy. But he attached the condition that the United States compel the Allies to end their blockade and comply with international law. Wilson accepted the pledge but turned down the condition.

The *Sussex* pledge marked the beginning of a short period of friendly relations between Germany and the United States. The agreement applied not only to passenger liners but to all merchant ships, belligerent or not. There was one problem: Wilson had taken such a strong position that if Germany renewed submarine warfare on merchant shipping, war was likely. Most Americans, however, viewed the agreement as a diplomatic stroke for peace by Wilson, and the issues of peace and preparedness dominated the presidential election of 1916.

"He Kept Us Out of War"

The "preparedness" issue pitted antiwar groups against those who wanted to prepare for war. Bellicose as always, Teddy Roosevelt led the preparedness campaign. He called Wilson "yellow" for not pressing Germany harder and scoffed at the popular song "I Didn't Raise My Boy to Be a Soldier," which he

▷ Read the Document — Adolf K. G. E. von Spiegel, U-boat 202 (1919)

Adolf K.G.E. von Spiegel commanded a German U-boat during World War I. He published his memoirs in 1919.

compared to singing "I Didn't Raise My Girl to Be a Mother." Defending the military's state of readiness, Wilson refused to be stampeded just because "some amongst us are nervous and excited." In fact, when government revenue dropped in 1915, he cut military appropriations.

Wilson's position was attacked from both sides as preparedness advocates charged cowardice, while pacifists denounced any attempt at military readiness. The difficulty of his situation, plus the growing U-boat crisis, soon changed Wilson's mind. In mid-1915, he asked the War Department to increase military planning, and he quietly notified congressional leaders of a switch in policy. Later that year, Wilson approved large increases in the army and navy, a move that upset many peace-minded progressives. In January 1916, he toured the country to promote preparedness, and in June, with an American flag draped over his shoulder, he marched in a giant preparedness parade in Washington.

For their standard-bearer in the presidential election of 1916, the Republicans nominated Charles Evans Hughes, a moderate justice of the Supreme Court. Hughes seemed to have all the qualifications for victory. A former reform governor of New York, he could lure back the Roosevelt progressives while at the same time appealing to the Republican conservatives. To woo the Roosevelt wing, Hughes called for a tougher line against Germany, thus allowing the Democrats to label him the "war" candidate. Even so, Roosevelt and others considered Hughes a "bearded iceberg," a dull campaigner who wavered on important issues.

The Democrats renominated Wilson in a convention marked by spontaneous demonstrations for peace. Determined to outdo Republican patriotism, Wilson himself had ordered the convention's theme to be "Americanism." The delegates were to sing "America" and "The Star-Spangled Banner" and to cheer any mention of America and the flag. They did it all dutifully but then broke into spontaneous applause at the mention of Wilson's careful diplomatic moves. As the keynote speaker reviewed them, the delegates shouted, "What did we do? What did we do?" The speaker shouted back, "We didn't go to war! We didn't go to war!"

Picking up the theme, perhaps with reservations, Wilson said in October, "I am not expecting this country to get into war." The campaign slogan "He kept us out of war" was repeated again and again, and just before the election, the Democrats took full-page ads in leading newspapers:

> You Are Working—Not Fighting!
> Alive and Happy—Not Cannon Fodder!
> Wilson and Peace with Honor?
> or
> Hughes with Roosevelt and War?

On election night, Hughes had swept most of the East, and Wilson retired at 10 P.M. thinking he had lost. During the night, the results came in from California, New Mexico, and North Dakota; all supported Wilson—California by a mere 3773 votes. Wilson won with 9.1 million votes against 8.5 million for Hughes. Holding the Democratic South, he carried key states in the Midwest and West and took large portions of the labor and progressive vote. Women—who were then allowed to vote in presidential elections in twelve states—also voted heavily for Wilson.

The Final Months of Peace

Just before election day, Great Britain further limited neutral trade, and there were reports from Germany of a renewal of unrestricted submarine warfare. Fresh from his victory, Wilson redoubled his efforts for peace. Aware that time was running out, he hoped to start negotiations to end the bloodshed and create a peaceful postwar world.

In December 1916, he sent messages to both sides asking them to state their war aims. Should they do so, he pledged the "whole force" of the United States to end the war. The Allies refused, although they promised privately to negotiate if the German terms were reasonable. The Germans replied evasively and in January 1917 revealed their real objectives. Close to forcing Russia out of the war, Germany sensed victory and wanted territory in eastern Europe, Africa, Belgium, and France.

On January 22, in an eloquent speech before the Senate, Wilson called for a "peace without victory." Outlining his own ambitious aims, he urged respect for all nations, freedom of the seas, arms limitations, and a League of Nations to keep the peace. "Only a peace between equals can last, only a peace the very principle of which is equality and a common participation in a common benefit." The speech made a great impression on many Europeans, but it was too late. The Germans had decided a few weeks before

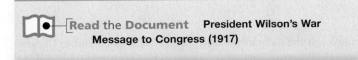

Read the Document President Wilson's War Message to Congress (1917)

Wilson's re-election in 1916 owed a great deal to the campaign slogan, "He kept us out of war." But the resumption of unrestricted submarine warfare by Germany in 1917 significantly changed the international situation. Several U.S. merchant ships were sunk in March by German U-boats. That April, Wilson called Congress into extraordinary session to ask for a declaration of war against Germany.

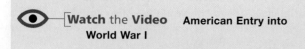

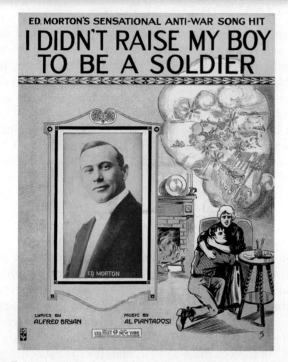

In 1914, Europe explodes into war, and Woodrow Wilson has to make a decision about what America is going to do. And his decision is to ask the American public to remain neutral in word as well as deed.

to unleash the submarines and gamble on a quick end to the war. Even as Wilson spoke, U-boats were in the Atlantic west of Ireland, preparing to attack.

On January 31, the German ambassador in Washington informed Lansing that beginning February 1, U-boats would sink on sight all ships—passenger or merchant, neutral or belligerent, armed or unarmed—in the waters around England and France. Staking everything on a last effort, the Germans calculated that if they could sink 600,000 tons of shipping a month, they could defeat England in six months. As he had pledged in 1916, Wilson broke off relations with Germany, although he still hoped for peace.

On February 25, the British government privately gave Wilson a telegram intercepted from Arthur Zimmermann, the German foreign minister, to the German ambassador in Mexico. A day later, Wilson asked Congress for authority to arm merchant ships to deter U-boat attacks. When La Follette and a handful of others threatened to filibuster, Wilson divulged the contents of the Zimmermann telegram. It proposed an alliance with Mexico in case of war with the United States, offering financial support and recovery of Mexico's "lost territory" in New Mexico, Texas, and Arizona.

Spurred by a wave of public indignation toward the Germans, the House passed Wilson's measure, but La Follette and others still blocked action in the Senate. On March 9, 1917, Wilson ordered

merchant ships armed on his own authority. Three days later, he announced the arming, and on March 13, the navy instructed all vessels to fire on submarines. Between March 12 and March 21, U-boats sank five American ships, and Wilson decided to wait no longer.

He called Congress into special session and at 8:30 in the evening on April 2, 1917, asked for a declaration of war. "It is a fearful thing to lead this great peaceful people into war, into the most terrible and disastrous of all wars, civilization itself seeming to be in the balance. But the right is more precious than peace, and we shall fight for the things which we have always carried nearest our hearts—for democracy, … for the rights and liberties of small nations, for a universal dominion of right by such a concert of free peoples as shall bring peace and safety to all nations and make the world itself at last free."

Congressmen broke into applause and crowded the aisles to congratulate Wilson. "My message today was a message of death for our young men," he said afterward. "How strange it seems to applaud that."

Pacifists in Congress continued to hold out, and for four days they managed to postpone action. Finally, on April 6, the declaration of war passed, with fifty members of the House and six senators voting against it. Even then, the country was divided over entry into the war.

Over There

How did the United States' entry affect the course of World War I?

With a burst of patriotism, the United States entered a war its new allies were in danger of losing. That same month, the Germans sank 881,000 tons of Allied shipping, the highest amount for any one month during the war. There were mutinies in the French army; a costly British drive in Flanders stalled. In November, the Bolsheviks seized power in Russia, and, led by V. I. Lenin, they soon signed a separate peace treaty with Germany, freeing German troops to fight in the West. German and Austrian forces routed the Italian army on the southern flank, and the Allies braced for a spring 1918 offensive.

Mobilization

The United States was not prepared for war. Some Americans hoped the declaration of war itself might daunt the Germans; there were those who thought that naval escorts of Allied shipping would be enough. Others hoped money and arms supplied to the Allies would be sufficient to produce victory without sending troops.

Bypassing older generals, Wilson named John J. ("Black Jack") Pershing, leader of the Mexican campaign, to head the American Expeditionary Force (AEF). Pershing inherited an army unready for war. In April 1917, it had 200,000 officers and men, equipped with 300,000 old rifles, 1500 machine guns, 55 out-of-date airplanes, and 2 field radio sets. Its most recent battle experience had been chasing Pancho Villa around northern Mexico. It had not caught him.

((•○—[Listen to the **Audio File**   *"Over There"*

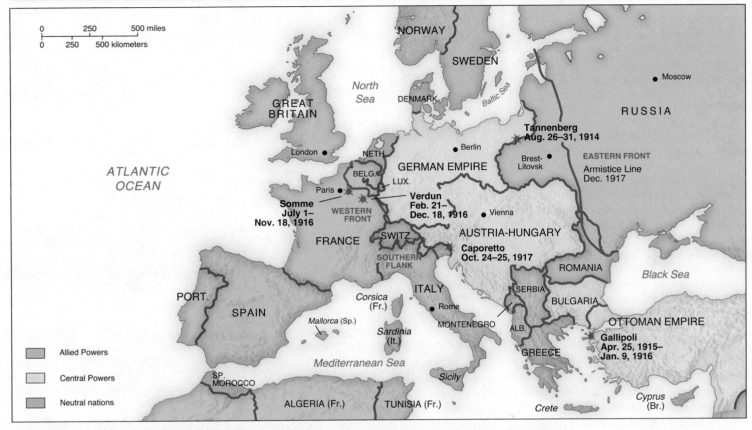

EUROPEAN ALLIANCES AND BATTLEFRONTS, 1914–1917 Allied forces suffered early defeats on the eastern front (Tannenberg) and in the Dardanelles (Gallipoli). In 1917, the Allies were routed on the southern flank (Caporetto); the western front then became the critical theater of the war.

U.S. LOSSES TO THE GERMAN SUBMARINE CAMPAIGN, 1916–1918

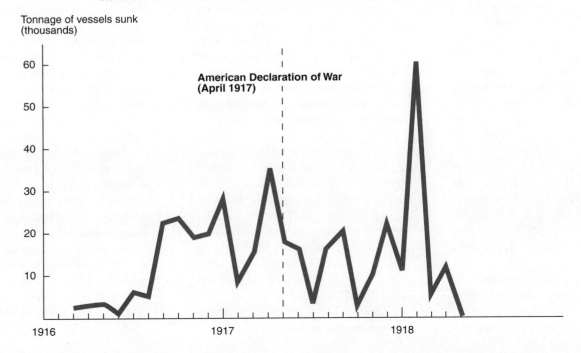

Feature Essay | Measuring the Mind

From 1870 to 1920, scientists and physicians explored new ideas about the mind. In Europe, the Viennese psychiatrist Sigmund Freud studied the unconscious, which, he thought, shaped human behavior. Russia's Ivan Pavlov tested the conditioned reflex in mental activity (Pavlov's dogs), and in the United States William James, the psychologist and philosopher, examined emotions and linked psychology to everyday problems.

As one way of understanding the mind, psychologists studied the mental processes of a great many minds, a task to which the relatively new science of statistics lent a hand. Testing large samples of subjects, they developed the concept of the "normal" and "average," helpful boundaries used to determine an individual's place in the population. In 1890, the psychologist James McKeen Cattell tested one hundred first-year students at the University of Pennsylvania for vision and hearing, sensitivity to pain, reaction time, and memory. He called these examinations by a new name—mental tests—and the idea spread. In 1895, the American Psychological Association (APA) set up a special committee to promote the nationwide collection of mental statistics.

Work was under way on both sides of the ocean, and in 1905 Alfred Binet and Theodore Simon, two French psychologists, devised a metric intelligence scale. Seizing on the idea that intelligence increases with age until maturity, they tested children to find an average level of performance for different ages. Once they had determined the average, they could compare any child's test performance to

it and thus distinguish between the child's "mental age" and chronological age. In 1912, William Stein, a German psychologist, introduced the "intelligence quotient," found by dividing a person's mental age by the chronological age. In 1916, Lewis M. Terman of Stanford University improved Binet's test, and the term *IQ* became part of the American vocabulary.

Employers and educators, however, remained skeptical of measuring intelligence. Thus, when the United States entered World War I, psychologists at once saw the opportunity to overcome the doubts and prove their theories. Huge numbers of men needed to be recruited, classified, and assigned to units quickly. Why not use the new mental tests? APA leaders formed twelve committees, including one on the Psychological Examination of Recruits, to explore the military uses of psychology.

Preferring to issue promotions on the basis of seniority, the army resisted the "mental meddlers," but the APA persuaded the War Department to use the tests. In early 1918, psychological examiners were posted at all training camps to administer the Alpha Test to literates and the Beta Test (with instructions given in pantomime) to illiterates and recruits who did not understand English. At the start of each Alpha Test, the examiners put the men at ease by explaining that the army was "not looking for crazy people. The aim is to help find out what we are best fitted to do." On the Beta Test, which was made up largely of pictures, the examiners were reminded that Beta men "sometimes sulk and refuse to work."

On the basis of the tests, the examiners classified recruits as "superior,"

Questions from one portion of the U.S. Army Intelligence Alpha Test.

"average," or "inferior." From the "superior" category, they selected men for officer training, a helpful winnowing process in an army that expanded quickly from nine thousand officers to two hundred thousand. They then distributed the remaining "superior," "average," and "inferior" men among each military unit. In all, the examiners tested 1.7 million men—by far the largest testing program in human history to that time. To some degree, the tests served their purpose, but they also seemed to raise questions about the education and mental ability of many American men.

For one thing, there was the extent of illiteracy—nearly one-quarter of the draft-age men in 1918 could neither read nor write. (One-third, incidentally, were physically unfit for service.) There was also the limited schooling of the recruits, most of whom had left school between the fifth and seventh grades. More alarming, according to the test results, 47 percent of the white draftees and 89 percent of the black draftees had a "mental age" of twelve years or under, which classified them as "feebleminded." Did that mean half or more of the American population was feebleminded?

The tests also turned up racial and national distinctions—or so some of the examiners concluded. Men of "native" backgrounds and "old" immigrant stock (from northern Europe and the British Isles) tended to score well and fell in the "superior" category; "new" immigrants (from central and southern Europe) tended to score less well and were ranked as "inferior." Among Russian, Polish, and Italian draftees, more than half were classified as "inferior." Such results came as no surprise to those who had long doubted the intelligence of the "new" immigrants, nor did the fact that 80 percent of the African American men taking the Alpha Test scored in the "inferior" range.

Some observers, however, wondered what the tests really measured.

The APA examiners claimed they measured "native intelligence," but questions about Edgar Allan Poe's poem "The Raven" or the paintings of Rosa Bonheur, a French artist of the mid-nineteenth century, required answers that native intelligence alone could not supply. When blacks and whites scored comparably on the early Beta Test, the examiners decided that something must be wrong with the test, so they changed the questions until the scores showed the expected racial differences. Most of those taking the Beta Test had never taken a written test before; many had probably never held a pencil.

Still skeptical, the army discontinued the tests the moment the war ended, but what the army rejected, the nation adopted. Businesses, government, and above all, educational institutions found more and more uses for intelligence testing. In 1926, the College Entrance Examination Board (CEEB) administered the first Scholastic Aptitude Test (SAT), designed to test "intelligence" and predict performance in college. In 1935, it established scoring ranges from 200 to 800, with the average score set at 500. During World War II, SAT tests were widely used. In 1947, the CEEB became part of a new Educational Testing Service that spurred an educational revolution by making "intelligence" instead of social or economic standing the main criterion of college admissions.

Before long, intelligence testing—the measuring of minds—touched every aspect of American life. Shaping lives and careers, it pushed some people forward and held others back, in the military, industry, the civil service, and higher education. "Intelligence tests . . . ," an expert said in 1971, "have more and more become society's instrument for the selection of human resources."

QUESTIONS FOR DISCUSSION

1. What arguments did advocates and opponents of intelligence testing use to support and attack these tests?

2. Why were the intelligence tests the army administered during World War I so problematic?

3. What were the positive and negative results of intelligence tests?

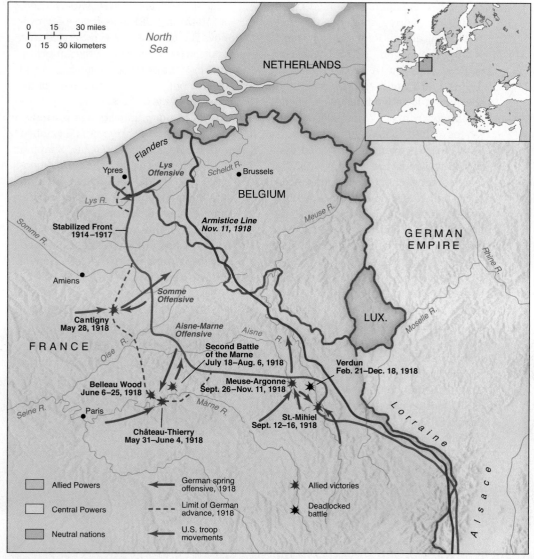

0 15 30 miles
0 15 30 kilometers

North Sea

NETHERLANDS

Flanders

Ypres
Lys Offensive
Scheldt R.
Brussels

BELGIUM

Lys R.

Armistice Line
Nov. 11, 1918

Meuse R.

GERMAN
EMPIRE

Stabilized Front
1914–1917

Somme R.

Rhine R.

Amiens

Somme Offensive

LUX.

Moselle R.

Cantigny
May 28, 1918

Aisne-Marne
Offensive

Aisne R.

Verdun
Feb. 21–Dec. 18, 1918

FRANCE

Oise R.

Second Battle
of the Marne
July 18–Aug. 6, 1918

Meuse-Argonne
Sept. 26–Nov. 11, 1918

Belleau Wood
June 6–25, 1918

Marne R.

St.-Mihiel
Sept. 12–16, 1918

Lorraine

Seine R.

Paris

Château-Thierry
May 31–June 4, 1918

	Allied Powers	→ German spring offensive, 1918	✳ Allied victories
	Central Powers	--- Limit of German advance, 1918	✶ Deadlocked battle
	Neutral nations	← U.S. troop movements	

Alsace

THE WESTERN FRONT: U.S. PARTICIPATION, 1918 The turning point of the war came in July, when the German advance was halted at the Marne. The "Yanks," now a fighting force, were thrown into the breach. They played a dramatic role in stemming the tide and mounting the counteroffensives that ended the war.

War in the Trenches

World War I may have been the most terrible war of all time, more terrible even than World War II and its vast devastation. After the early offensives, the European armies dug themselves into trenches only hundreds of yards apart in places. Artillery, poison gas, hand grenades, and a new weapon—rapid-fire machine guns—kept them pinned down.

Even in moments of respite, the mud, rats, cold, fear, and disease took a heavy toll. Deafening bombardments shook the earth, and there was a high incidence of shell shock. From time to time, troops went "over the top" of the trenches in an effort to break through the enemy's lines, but the costs were enormous. The German offensive at Verdun in 1916 killed six hundred thousand men; the British lost twenty thousand on the first day of an offensive on the Somme.

The first American soldiers reached France in June 1917. By March of the following year, three hundred thousand Americans were there, and by war's end, two million men had crossed the Atlantic. No troop ships were sunk, a credit to the British and American navies. In the summer of 1917, Admiral William S. Sims, a brilliant American strategist, pushed through a convoy plan that used Allied destroyers to escort merchant vessels across the ocean. At first resisted by English captains who liked to sail alone, the plan soon cut shipping losses in half.

As expected, on March 21, 1918, the Germans launched a massive assault in western Europe. Troops from the Russian front added to the force, and by May they had driven Allied forces back to the Marne River, just fifty miles from Paris. There, the Americans saw their first action. The American forces blocked the Germans at the town of Château-Thierry and four weeks later forced them out of Belleau Wood, a crucial stronghold. On July 15, the Germans threw everything into a last drive for Paris, but they were halted at the Marne, and in three days of battle they were finished. "On the 18th," the German chancellor said, "even the most optimistic among us knew that all was lost. The history of the world was played out in three days."

With the German drive stalled, the Allies counterattacked along the entire front. On September 12, 1918, a half million Americans and a smaller contingent of French drove the Germans from the St. Mihiel salient, twelve miles south of Verdun. Two weeks later, 896,000 American soldiers attacked between the Meuse River and the Argonne Forest. Focusing their efforts on a main

Although some in Congress preferred a voluntary army of the kind that had fought in the Spanish-American War, Wilson turned to conscription, which he believed was both efficient and democratic. In May 1917, Congress passed the **Selective Service Act**, providing for the registration of all men between the ages of 21 and 30 (later changed to 18 and 45). Early in June, 9.5 million men registered for the draft. By the end of the war, the act had registered 24.2 million men, about 2.8 million of whom were inducted into the army. Defending the draft, Wilson said it was not really a draft at all, but a "selection from a nation which has volunteered in mass." Newly devised intelligence tests became part of the selection process. (See the Feature Essay, "Measuring the Mind," pp. 574–575.)

The draft included black men as well as white, and four African American regiments were among the first sent into action. Despite their contributions, however, no black soldiers were allowed to march in the victory celebrations that eventually took place in Paris. Nor were they included in a French mural of the different races in the war, even though black servicemen from English and French colonies were represented.

railroad supply line for the German army in the West, American troops broke through in early November, cut the line, and drove the Germans back along the whole front.

The German high command knew that the war was lost. On October 6, 1918, Germany appealed to Wilson for an armistice, and by the end of the month, Turkey, Bulgaria, and Austria-Hungary were out of the war. At 4 A.M. on November 11, Germany signed the armistice. The AEF lost 48,909 dead and 230,000 wounded; losses to disease brought the total of dead to more than 112,000.

The American contribution, although small in comparison to the enormous costs to European nations, was vital. Fresh, enthusiastic American troops raised Allied morale; they helped turn the tide at a crucial point in the war.

Over Here

What programs and changes did World War I bring at home?

Victory at the front depended on economic and emotional mobilization at home. Consolidating federal authority, Wilson moved quickly in 1917 and 1918 to organize war production and distribution. An idealist who knew how to sway public opinion, he also recognized the need to enlist American emotions. To him, the war for people's minds, the "conquest of their convictions," was as vital as events on the battlefield.

The Conquest of Convictions

A week after war was declared, Wilson formed the **Committee on Public Information (CPI)** and asked George Creel, an outspoken progressive journalist, to head it. Creel hired progressives such as Ida Tarbell and Ray Stannard Baker and recruited thousands of people in the arts, advertising, and film industries to publicize the war. He worked out a system of voluntary censorship with the press, plastered walls with colorful posters, and issued more than seventy-five million pamphlets.

Creel also enlisted seventy-five thousand "four-minute men" to give quick speeches at public gatherings and places of entertainment on "Why We Are Fighting" and "The Meaning of America." At first, they were instructed to emphasize facts and stay away from emotions, particularly hatred, but by the beginning of 1918, the instructions shifted; the Germans were to be depicted as bloodthirsty Huns bent on world conquest. Exploiting a new medium,

▶ **Read the Document**   Espionage Act (1917)

Anti-German sentiment spread in America during World War I, escalating dramatically after the United States entered the war in April 1917. A wave of verbal and physical attacks on German Americans was accompanied by a campaign to repress German culture. In this photograph from 1917, a group of children stand in front of an anti-German sign posted in the Edison Park community of Chicago, Illinois. As the sign suggests, some Americans questioned the loyalty of their German American neighbors.

the CPI promoted films such as *The Prussian Cur* and *The Kaiser, the Beast of Berlin.*

Helped along by the propaganda campaign, anti-German sentiment spread rapidly. Many schools stopped offering instruction in the German language—California's state education board called it a language "of autocracy, brutality, and hatred." Sauerkraut became "liberty cabbage"; saloonkeepers removed pretzels from the bar. Orchestral works by Bach, Beethoven, and Brahms vanished from some symphonic programs, and the New York Philharmonic agreed not to perform the music of living German composers. Government agents harassed Karl Muck, the German conductor of the Boston Symphony, imprisoned him for more than a year, and then, after the war ended, deported him. German Americans and antiwar figures were badgered, beaten, and in some cases killed.

Vigilantism, sparked often by superpatriotism of a ruthless sort, flourished. Frequently, it focused on radical antiwar figures such as Frank Little, an official of the Industrial Workers of the World (IWW) in Butte, Montana, who was taken from his boardinghouse in August 1917, tied to the rear of an automobile, and dragged through the streets until his kneecaps were scraped off. Little was then hanged from a railroad trestle. In April 1918, a Missouri mob seized Robert Prager, a young man whose sole crime was being born in Germany. They bound him with an American flag, paraded him through town, and then lynched him. A jury acquitted the mob's members—who wore red, white, and blue ribbons to court—as one juror shouted, "Well, I guess nobody can say we aren't loyal now."

Rather than curbing the repression, Wilson encouraged it. "Woe be to the man or group of men that seeks to stand in our way," he told peace advocates soon after the war began. At his request, Congress passed the **Espionage Act** of 1917, which imposed sentences of up to twenty years in prison for persons found guilty of aiding the enemy, obstructing recruitment of soldiers, or encouraging disloyalty. It allowed the postmaster general to remove from the mails materials that incited treason or insurrection. The Trading-with-the-Enemy Act of 1917 authorized the government to censor the foreign language press.

In 1918, Congress passed the **Sedition Act**, imposing harsh penalties on anyone using "disloyal, profane, scurrilous, or abusive language" about the government, flag, or armed forces uniforms. In all, more than fifteen hundred persons were arrested under the new laws. People indicted or imprisoned included a Californian who laughed at rookies drilling at an army camp, a woman who greeted a Red Cross solicitor in a "hostile" way, and an editor who printed this sentence: "We must make the world safe for democracy even if we have to 'bean' the Goddess of Liberty to do it."

The sedition laws clearly went beyond any clear or present danger. There were, to be sure, German spies in the country, Germans who wanted to encourage strikes in American arms factories. Moreover, the U.S. government and other national leaders were painfully aware of how divided Americans had been about entering the war. They set out to promote unity—by force, if necessary—in order to convince Germany that the nation was united behind the war.

But none of these matters warranted a nationwide program of repression. Conservatives took advantage of wartime feelings to try to stamp out American socialists, who in fact were vulnerable because, unlike their European counterparts, they continued to oppose the war even after their country had entered it. Using the sedition laws, conservatives harried the Socialist party and another favorite target,

the Industrial Workers of the World. In 1921, ill and facing imprisonment, "Big Bill" Haywood, one of the IWW's best known members, fled to the Soviet Union, where he died a few years later.

Wilson's postmaster general banned from the mails more than a dozen socialist publications, including the *Appeal to Reason*, which went to more than half a million people weekly. In 1918, Eugene V. Debs, the Socialist party leader, delivered a speech denouncing capitalism and the war. He was convicted for violation of the Espionage Act and spent the war in a penitentiary in Atlanta. Nominated as the Socialist party candidate in the presidential election of 1920, Debs—prisoner 9653—won nearly a million votes, but the Socialist movement never fully recovered from the repression of the war.

In fostering hostility toward anything that smacked of dissent, the war also gave rise to the great "Red Scare" that began in 1919. Pleased at first with the Russian revolution, Americans in general turned quickly against it, especially after Lenin and the Bolsheviks seized control late in 1917. The Americans feared Lenin's anticapitalist program, and they denounced his decision in early 1918 to make peace with Germany because it freed German troops to fight in France.

Once again, Wilson himself played a prominent role in the development of anti-Bolshevik sentiment. In the summer of 1918, he sent fifteen thousand American troops into the Soviet Union, where they joined other Allied soldiers. Ostensibly, the troops were there to protect Allied supplies from the Germans and to rescue a large number of Czechs who wanted to return home to fight Germany. But the underlying reason for their presence was that Wilson and others hoped to bring down the fledgling Bolshevik government, fearful it would spread revolution around the world.

Besides sending troops, Wilson joined in an economic blockade of Russia, sent weapons to anti-Bolshevik insurgents, and refused to recognize Lenin's government. He also blocked Russian participation in the peace conference that ended the war. American troops remained in Russia until April 1920, and on the whole, American willingness to interfere soured Russian–American relations for decades to come.

A Bureaucratic War

Quick, effective action was needed to win the war. To meet the need, Wilson and Congress set up an array of new federal agencies, nearly five thousand in all. Staffed largely by businessmen, the agencies drew on funds and powers of a hitherto unknown scope. At night, the secretary of the treasury sat in bed, a yellow pad on his knees, adding up the money needed to finance the war. "The noughts attached to the many millions were so boisterous and prolific," he later said, "that, at times, they would run clear over the edge of the paper."

By the time the war was over, the "noughts" had boisterously added up to $32 billion in direct war expense—in an era when the entire federal budget rarely exceeded $1 billion. To raise the money, the administration sold about $23 billion in "Liberty Bonds," and, using the new Sixteenth Amendment, boosted taxes on corporations and personal incomes. The taxes brought in another $10 billion to help pay for the war.

At first, Wilson tried to organize the wartime economy along decentralized lines, almost in the fashion of his early New

View the **Closer Look**   Mobilizing the Home Front

FOOD WILL WIN THE WAR
You came here seeking Freedom
You must now help to preserve it
WHEAT is needed for the allies
Waste nothing

UNITED STATES FOOD ADMINISTRATION

Many Americans identified with the Allies. British propaganda bolstered those sympathies with exaggerated stories of German atrocities.

the number of stops on elevators. Working closely with business, Baruch for a time acted as the dictator of the American economy.

Herbert Hoover, the hero of a campaign to feed starving Belgians, headed a new **Food Administration**, and he set out with customary energy to supply food to the armies overseas. Appealing to the "spirit of self-sacrifice," Hoover convinced people to save food by observing "meatless" and "wheatless" days. He fixed prices to boost production, bought and distributed wheat, and encouraged people to plant "victory gardens" behind homes, churches, and schools. He sent a half million campaigners door to door to get housewives to sign cards pledging their cooperation. One householder—Wilson—set an example by grazing sheep on the White House lawn.

At another new agency, the Fuel Administration, Harry A. Garfield, the president of Williams College, introduced daylight saving time, rationed coal and oil, and imposed gasless days when motorists could not drive. To save coal, he shut down nonessential factories one day a week, and in January 1918, he closed all factories east of the Mississippi for four days to divert coal to munitions ships stranded in New York harbor. A fourth agency, the Railroad Administration, dictated rail traffic over nearly four hundred thousand miles of track—standardizing rates, limiting passenger travel, and speeding arms shipments. The War Shipping Board coordinated shipping, the Emergency Fleet Corporation supervised shipbuilding, and the War Trade Board oversaw foreign trade.

As never before, the government intervened in American life. When strikes threatened the telephone and telegraph companies, the government simply seized and ran them. Businessmen, paid a nominal dollar a year, flocked to Washington to run the new agencies, and the partnership between government and business grew closer. As government expanded, business expanded as well, responding to wartime contracts. Industries such as steel, aluminum, and cigarettes boomed, and corporate profits increased threefold between 1914 and 1919.

Freedom thinking. But that proved unworkable, and he moved instead to a series of highly centralized planning boards, each with broad authority over a specific area of the economy. There were boards to control virtually every aspect of transportation, agriculture, and manufacturing. Though only a few of them were as effective as Wilson had hoped, they did coordinate the war effort to some degree.

The **War Industries Board (WIB)**, one of the most powerful of the new agencies, oversaw the production of all American factories. Headed by millionaire Bernard M. Baruch, a Wall Street broker and speculator, it determined priorities, allocated raw materials, and fixed prices. It told manufacturers what they could and could not make. The WIB set the output of steel and regulated

Labor in the War

The war also brought organized labor into the partnership with government, although the results were more limited than in the business-government alliance. Samuel Gompers, president of the AFL, served on Wilson's Council of National Defense, an advisory group formed to unify business, labor, and government. Gompers hoped to trade labor peace for labor advances, and he formed a War Committee on Labor to enlist workers' support for the war. With the blessing of the Wilson administration, membership in the AFL and other unions grew from about 2.7 million in 1916 to more than 4 million in 1919.

Hoping to encourage production and avoid strikes, Wilson adopted many of the objectives of the social-justice reformers.

He supported an eight-hour day in war-related industries and improved wages and working conditions. In May 1918, he named Felix Frankfurter, a brilliant young law professor, to head a new War Labor Board (WLB). The agency standardized wages and hours, and at Wilson's direction, it protected the right of labor to organize and bargain collectively. Although it did not forbid strikes, it used various tactics to discourage them. It enforced decisions in well-publicized cases; when the Smith and Wesson arms factory in Massachusetts and the Western Union telegraph company disobeyed the WLB's union rules, the agency took them over.

The WLB also ordered that women be paid equal wages for equal work in war industries. In 1914, the flow of European immigrants suddenly stopped because of the war, and in 1917, the draft began to take large numbers of American men. The result was a labor shortage, filled by women, African Americans, and Mexican Americans. One million women worked in war industries. Some of them took jobs previously held by men, but for the most part, they moved from one set of "women's jobs" into another. From the beginning of the war to the end, the number of women in the workforce held steady at about eight million, and unlike the experience in World War II, large numbers of housewives did not leave the home for machine shops and arms plants.

Still, there were some new opportunities and in some cases higher pay. In food, airplane, and electrical plants, women made up one-fifth or more of the workforce. As their wages increased, so did

their expectations; some became more militant, and conflict grew between them and male co-workers. To set standards for female employment, a Women's Bureau was established in the Department of Labor, but the government's influence varied. In the federally run railroad industry, women often made wages equal to those of men; in the federally run telephone industry, they did not.

Looking for more people to fill wartime jobs, corporations found another major source among southern blacks. Beginning in 1916, northern labor agents traveled across the South, promising jobs, high wages, and free transportation. Soon the word spread, and the movement northward became a flood. Between 1916 and 1918, more than 450,000 African Americans left the Old South for the booming industrial cities of St. Louis, Chicago, Detroit, and Cleveland. In the decade before 1920, Detroit's black population grew by more than 600 percent, Cleveland's by more than 300 percent, and Chicago's by 150 percent.

Most of the newcomers were young, unmarried, and skilled or semiskilled. The men found jobs in factories, railroad yards, steel mills, packinghouses, and coal mines; black women worked in textile factories, department stores, and restaurants. In their new homes, African Americans found greater racial freedom but also different living conditions. If the South was often hostile, the North could be impersonal and lonely. Accustomed to the pace of the farm—ruled by the seasons and the sun—those blacks who were able to enter the industrial sector now worked for hourly wages in

AFRICAN AMERICAN MIGRATION NORTHWARD, 1910–1920 The massive migration of African Americans from the South to the North during World War I changed the dynamics of race relations in the United States.

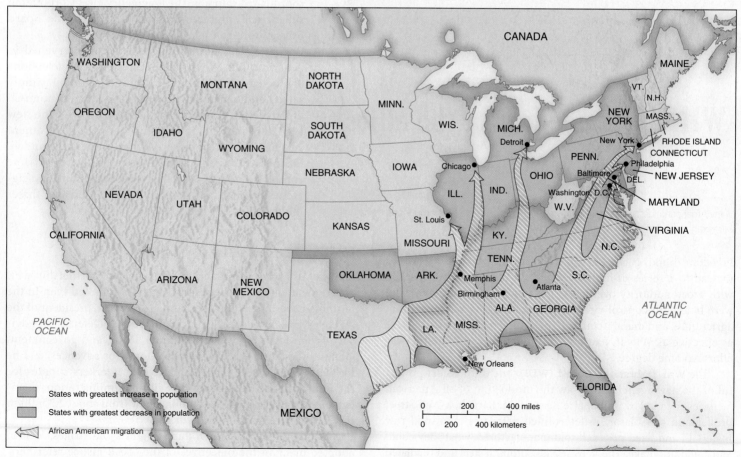

mass production industries, where time clocks and line supervisors dictated the daily routine.

Racial tensions increased, resulting in part from growing competition for housing and jobs. In mid-1917, a race war in East St. Louis, Illinois, killed nine whites and about forty blacks. In July 1919, the month President Wilson returned from the peace conference in Paris, a race riot in Washington, D.C., killed six people. Riots in Chicago that month killed thirty-eight—fifteen whites and twenty-three blacks—and there were later outbreaks in New York City and Omaha. Lynch mobs killed forty-eight blacks in 1917, sixty-three in 1918, and seventy-eight in 1919. Ten of the victims in 1919 were war veterans, several still in uniform.

Blacks were more and more inclined to fight back. Two hundred thousand blacks served in France—forty-two thousand as combat troops. Returning home, they expected better treatment. "I'm glad I went," a black veteran said. "I done my part, and I'm going to fight right here till Uncle Sam does his." Roscoe Jameson, Claude McKay, and other black poets wrote biting poetry, some of it—such as Fenton Johnson's "The New Day"—drawn from the war experience:

For we have been with thee in No Man's Land,
Through lake of fire and down to Hell itself;
And now we ask of thee our liberty,
Our freedom in the land of Stars and Stripes.

"Lift Ev'ry Voice and Sing," composed in 1900, became known as the "Negro National Anthem." Parents bought black dolls for their children, and W. E. B. Du Bois spoke of a "New Negro," proud and more militant: "We return. We return from fighting. We return fighting."

Eager for cheap labor, farmers and ranchers in the Southwest persuaded the federal government to relax immigration restrictions, and between 1917 and 1920, more than 100,000 Mexicans migrated into Texas, Arizona, New Mexico, and California. The Mexican American population grew from 385,000 in 1910 to 740,000 in 1920. Tens of thousands of Mexican Americans moved to Chicago, St. Louis, Omaha, and other northern cities to take wartime jobs. Often scorned and insecure, they created urban barrios similar to the Chinatowns and Little Italys around them.

Like most wars, World War I affected patterns at home as much as abroad. Business profits grew, factories expanded, and industries

◉—[Watch the Video   The Great Migration

The Great Migration, over a series of decades, witnessed the relocation of approximately 1.5 million African Americans from their southern homes to northern metropolises. It took a long time for that many people to move. But it was the single most dramatic, most powerful example or evidence of an African American agency in the twentieth century because this was not an organized movement.

turned out huge amounts of war goods. Government authority swelled, and people came to expect different things of their government. Labor made some gains, as did women and blacks. Society assimilated some of the shifts, but social and economic tensions grew, and when the war ended, they spilled over in the strikes and violence of the Red Scare that followed.

The United States emerged from the war the strongest economic power in the world. In 1914, it was a debtor nation, and American citizens owed foreign investors about $3 billion. Five years later, the United States had become a creditor nation. Foreign governments owed more than $10 billion, and foreign citizens owed American investors nearly $3 billion. The war marked a shift in economic power rarely equaled in history.

The Treaty of Versailles

What mistakes did Wilson make in negotiating the Treaty of Versailles?

Long before the fighting ended, Wilson began to formulate plans for the peace. Like many others, he was disconcerted when the new Bolshevik government in Russia began revealing the terms of secret agreements among Britain, France, and czarist Russia to divide up Germany's colonies. To try to place the war on a higher plane, he appeared before Congress on January 8, 1918, and outlined terms for a far-reaching, nonpunitive settlement. Wilson's **Fourteen Points** were generous and farsighted, but they failed to satisfy wartime emotions that sought vindication.

England and France distrusted Wilsonian idealism as the basis for peace. They wanted Germany disarmed and crippled; they wanted its colonies; and they were skeptical of the principle of self-determination. As the end of the war neared, the Allies, who had in fact made secret commitments with one another, balked at making the Fourteen Points the basis of peace. When Wilson threatened to negotiate a separate treaty with Germany, however, they accepted.

Wilson had won an important victory, but difficulties lay ahead. As Georges Clemenceau, the 78-year-old French premier, said, "God gave us the Ten Commandments, and we broke them. Wilson gives us the Fourteen Points. We shall see."

A Peace at Paris

Unfortunately, Wilson made a grave error just before the peace conference began. He appealed to voters to elect a Democratic Congress in the November 1918 elections, saying that any other result would be "interpreted on the other side of the water as a repudiation

📖 **Read the Document**   **President Wilson's Fourteen Points**

On January 8, 1918, U.S. President Woodrow Wilson, speaking before a joint session of Congress, put forth his Fourteen Points proposal for ending the war. In this speech, he established the basis of a peace treaty and the foundation of a League of Nations.

of my leadership." Many Republicans were furious, especially those who had supported the Fourteen Points; Wilson's problems deepened when the Democrats went on to lose both the House and Senate.

Wilson's opponents immediately announced that voters had rejected his policies, as he had suggested they could. In fact, the Democratic losses stemmed largely from domestic problems, such as the price of wheat and cotton. But they hurt Wilson, who had alienated some important Republican party leaders. Soon, he would be negotiating with European leaders buoyed by rousing victories at their own polls.

Two weeks after the elections, Wilson announced he would attend the peace conference. This was a dramatic break from tradition, and his personal involvement drew attacks from Republicans. They renewed criticism when he named the rest of the delegation: Secretary of State Lansing; Colonel House; General Tasker H. Bliss, a military expert; and Henry White, a career diplomat. Wilson named no member of the Senate, and the only Republican in the group was White.

In selecting the delegation, Wilson passed over Henry Cabot Lodge, the powerful Republican senator from Massachusetts who opposed the Fourteen Points and who would soon head the Senate Foreign Relations Committee. He also decided not to appoint Elihu Root or ex-President Taft, both of them enthusiastic internationalists. Never good at accepting criticism or delegating authority, Wilson wanted a delegation he could control—an advantage at the peace table but not in any battle over the treaty at home.

Upon his arrival, Wilson received a tumultuous welcome in England, France, and Italy. Never before had such crowds acclaimed a democratic political figure. In Paris, two million people lined the Champs-Elysées, threw flowers at him, and shouted, "Wilson le Juste [the just]" as his carriage drove by. Overwhelmed, Wilson was sure that the people of Europe shared his goals and would force their leaders to accept his peace. He was wrong. Like their leaders,

many people on the Allied side hated Germany and wanted victory unmistakably reflected in the peace.

Opening in January 1919, the Peace Conference at Paris continued until May. Although twenty-seven nations were represented, the "Big Four" dominated it: Wilson; Clemenceau of France, tired and stubborn, determined to end the German threat forever; David Lloyd George, the crafty British prime minister who had pledged to squeeze Germany "until the pips squeak"; and the Italian prime minister, Vittorio Orlando. A clever negotiator, Wilson traded various "small" concessions for his major goals—national self-determination, a reduction in tensions, and a League of Nations to enforce the peace.

Wilson had to surrender some important principles. Departing from the Fourteen Points by violating the principle of self-determination, the treaty created two new independent nations—Poland and Czechoslovakia—with large German-speaking populations. It divided up the German colonies in Asia and Africa. Instead of a peace without victory, it made Germany accept responsibility for the war and demanded enormous reparations—which eventually totaled $33 billion. It made no mention of disarmament, free trade, or freedom of the seas. Instead of an open covenant openly arrived at, the treaty was drafted behind closed doors.

But Wilson deflected some of the most extreme Allied demands, and he won his coveted Point 14, a League of Nations, designed "to achieve international peace and security." The League included a general assembly; a smaller council composed of the United States, Great Britain, France, Italy, Japan, and four nations to be elected by the assembly; and a court of international justice. League members pledged to submit to arbitration every dispute threatening peace and to enjoin military and economic sanctions against nations resorting to war. Article X, for Wilson the heart of the League, obliged members to look out for one another's independence and territorial integrity.

WOODROW WILSON'S FOURTEEN POINTS, 1918: SUCCESS AND FAILURE IN IMPLEMENTATION

1.	Open covenants of peace openly arrived at	Not fulfilled
2.	Absolute freedom of navigation on the seas in peace and war	Not fulfilled
3.	Removal of all economic barriers to the equality of trade among nations	Not fulfilled
4.	Reduction of armaments to the level needed only for domestic safety	Not fulfilled
5.	Impartial adjustments of colonial claims	Not fulfilled
6.	Evacuation of all Russian territory; Russia to be welcomed into the society of free nations	Not fulfilled
7.	Evacuation and restoration of Belgium	**Fulfilled**
8.	Evacuation and restoration of all French lands; return of Alsace-Lorraine to France	**Fulfilled**
9.	Readjustment of Italy's frontiers along lines of Italian nationality	Compromised
10.	Self-determination for the former subjects of the Austro-Hungarian Empire	Compromised
11.	Evacuation of Romania, Serbia, and Montenegro; free access to the sea for Serbia	Compromised
12.	Self-determination for the former subjects of the Ottoman Empire; secure sovereignty for Turkish portion	Compromised
13.	Establishment of an independent Poland, with free and secure access to the sea	**Fulfilled**
14.	Establishment of a League of Nations affording mutual guarantees of independence and territorial integrity	Not fulfilled

Sources: Data from G. M. Gathorne-Hardy, *The Fourteen Points and the Treaty of Versailles* (Oxford Pamphlets on World Affairs, no. 6, 1939), pp. 8–34; Thomas G. Paterson et al., *American Foreign Policy: A History Since 1900*, 2nd ed., vol. 2, pp. 282–293.

EUROPE AFTER THE TREATY OF VERSAILLES, 1919
The treaty changed the map of Europe, creating a number of new and reconstituted nations. (Note the boundary changes from the map on p. 573.)

The draft treaty in hand, Wilson returned home in February 1919 to discuss it with Congress and the people. Most Americans, the polls showed, favored the League; thirty-three governors endorsed it. But over dinner with the Senate and House Foreign Relations Committees, Wilson learned of the strength of congressional opposition to it. On March 3, Senator Lodge produced a "round robin" signed by thirty-seven senators declaring they would not vote for the treaty without amendment. Should the numbers hold, Lodge had enough votes to defeat it.

Returning to Paris, Wilson attacked his critics, while he worked privately for changes to improve the chances of Senate approval. In return for major concessions, the Allies amended the League draft treaty, agreeing that domestic affairs remained outside League jurisdiction (exempting the Monroe Doctrine) and allowing nations to withdraw after two years' notice. On June 28, 1919, they signed the treaty in the Hall of Mirrors at Versailles, and Wilson started home for his most difficult fight.

Rejection in the Senate

There were ninety-six senators in 1919, forty-nine of them Republicans. Fourteen Republicans, led by William E. Borah of Idaho, were the "irreconcilables" who opposed the League on any grounds. "If the Savior of man," Borah said, "would revisit the earth and declare for a League of Nations, I would be opposed to it."

Frank B. Kellogg of Minnesota led a group of twelve "mild reservationists" who accepted the treaty but wanted to insert several reservations that would not greatly weaken it. Finally, there were the Lodge-led "strong reservationists," twenty-three of them in all, who wanted major changes that the Allies would have to approve.

With only four Democratic senators opposed to the treaty, the Democrats and Republicans willing to compromise had enough votes to ratify it, once a few reservations were inserted. Bidding for time to allow public opposition to grow, Lodge scheduled lengthy hearings and spent two weeks reading the 268-page treaty aloud. Democratic leaders urged Wilson to appeal to the Republican "mild reservationists," but he refused: "Anyone who opposes me in that I'll crush!"

Fed up with Lodge's tactics, Wilson set out in early September to take the case directly to the people. Crossing the Midwest, his speeches aroused little emotion, but on the Pacific Coast he won ovations, which heartened him. On his way back to Washington, he stopped in Pueblo, Colorado, where he delivered one of the most eloquent speeches of his career. People wept as he talked of Americans who died in battle and the hope that they would never fight again in foreign lands. That night Wilson felt ill, returned to Washington, and on October 2, Mrs. Wilson found him lying unconscious on the floor of the White House, the victim of a stroke that paralyzed his left side.

After the stroke, Wilson could not work more than an hour or two at a time. No one was allowed to see him except family members, his secretary, and his physician. For more than seven months, he did not meet with the cabinet. Secretary of State Lansing convened cabinet meetings, but when Wilson learned of them, he ordered Lansing to stop and then cruelly forced Lansing to resign. Focusing his remaining energy on the fight over the treaty, Wilson lost touch with other issues, and critics charged that his wife, Edith Bolling Wilson, ran the government.

On November 6, 1919, while Wilson convalesced, Lodge finally reported the treaty out of committee, along with "Fourteen Reservations," one for each of Wilson's points. The most important reservation stipulated that implementation of Article X, Wilson's key article, required the action of Congress before any American intervention abroad.

The next day, the president's floor leader in the Senate told him that the Democrats could not pass the treaty without reservations. "Is it possible?" Wilson asked sadly. "It might be wise to compromise," the senator said. "Let Lodge compromise!" Wilson replied. When Mrs. Wilson urged her husband to accept the Lodge reservations, he said, "Better a thousand times to go down fighting than to dip your colors to dishonorable compromise."

On November 19, the treaty—with the Lodge reservations—failed, 39 to 55. Following Wilson's instructions, the Democrats voted against it. A motion to approve without the reservations lost 38 to 53, with only one Republican voting in favor. The defeat brought pleas for compromise, but neither Wilson nor Lodge would back down. When the treaty with reservations again came up for vote on March 19, 1920, Wilson ordered the Democrats to hold firm against it. Although twenty-one of them defied him, enough obeyed his orders to defeat it, 49 to 35, seven votes short of the necessary two-thirds majority.

To Wilson, walking now with the help of a cane, one chance remained: the presidential election of 1920. For a time, he thought of running for a third term himself, but his party shunted him aside. The Democrats nominated Governor James M. Cox of Ohio, along with the young and popular Franklin D. Roosevelt, assistant secretary of the navy, for vice president. Wilson called for "a great and solemn referendum" on the treaty. The Democratic platform endorsed the treaty but agreed to accept reservations that clarified the American role in the League.

THE ELECTION OF 1920

Candidate	Party	Popular Vote	Electoral Vote
Harding	Republican	16,152,200	404
Cox	Democrat	9,147,353	127
Debs	Socialist	917,799	0

On the Republican side, Senator Warren G. Harding of Ohio, who had nominated Taft in 1912, won the presidential nomination. Harding waffled on the treaty, but that issue made little difference. Voters wanted a change. Harding won in a landslide, taking 61 percent of the vote and beating Cox by seven million votes. Without a peace treaty, the United States remained technically at war, and it was not until July 1921, almost three years after the last shot was fired, that Congress passed a joint resolution ending the war.

Conclusion: Postwar Disillusionment

After 1919, there was disillusionment. World War I was feared before it started, popular while it lasted, and hated when it ended. To a whole generation that followed, it appeared futile, killing without cause, sacrificing without benefit. Books, plays, and movies—Hemingway's *A Farewell to Arms* (1929), John Dos Passos's *Three Soldiers* (1921), Laurence Stallings and Maxwell Anderson's *What Price Glory?* (1924), among others—showed it as waste, horror, and death.

The war and its aftermath damaged the humanitarian, progressive spirit of the early years of the century. It killed "something precious and perhaps irretrievable in the hearts of thinking men and women." Progressivism survived well into the 1920s and the New Deal, but it no longer had the old conviction and broad popular support. Bruising fights over the war and the League drained people's energy and enthusiasm.

Confined to bed, Woodrow Wilson died in Washington in 1924, three years after Harding, the new president, promised "not heroics but healing; not nostrums but normalcy; not revolution but restoration." Nonetheless, the "war to end all wars" and the spirit of Woodrow Wilson left an indelible imprint on the country.

Study Resources

 Take the **Study Plan** for **Chapter 24** *The Nation at War* on **MyHistoryLab**

TIME LINE

1901 Hay-Pauncefote Treaty with Great Britain empowers United States to build Isthmian canal

1904 Theodore Roosevelt introduces corollary to Monroe Doctrine

1904–1905 Russo-Japanese War

1905 Taft-Katsura Agreement recognizes Japanese power in Korea

1908 Root-Takahira Agreement vows to maintain status quo in the Pacific; Roosevelt sends the fleet around the world

1911 Revolution begins in Mexico

1913–1914 Bryan negotiates "cooling-off" treaties to end war

1914 World War I begins; U.S. Marines take Veracruz; Panama Canal completed

1915 Japan issues Twenty-one Demands to China (January); Germany declares water around British Isles a war zone (February); *Lusitania* torpedoed (May); Bryan resigns; Robert Lansing becomes secretary of state (June); *Arabic* pledge restricts submarine warfare (September)

1916 Germany issues *Sussex* pledge (March); General John J. Pershing leads unsuccessful punitive expedition into Mexico to seize Pancho Villa (April); Wilson wins reelection

1917 Wilson calls for "peace without victory" (January); Germany resumes unrestricted U-boat warfare (February); United States enters World War I (April); Congress passes Selective Service Act (May); First American troops reach France (June); War Industries Board established (July)

1918 Wilson outlines Fourteen Points for peace (January); Germany asks for peace (October); Armistice ends the war (November)

1919 Peace negotiations in Paris (January); Treaty of Versailles defeated in Senate

1920 Warren G. Harding elected president

CHAPTER REVIEW

A New World Power

What were the main events that showed the United States was becoming a world power?

After winning the Spanish-American War, American presidents began to exert more influence in the world. Roosevelt took extraordinary steps to build the Panama Canal. He enlarged the country's role in the Western Hemisphere and tried to deal with the growing power of Japan. Taft focused on protecting American economic interests abroad. (p. 564)

Foreign Policy Under Wilson

What did Woodrow Wilson mean by "moral diplomacy"?

Wilson hoped to focus on domestic affairs but was soon involved in crises abroad. He first tried what he called "moral diplomacy," asking the United States and other countries to treat each other in a moral manner, especially in Europe and Mexico. In Mexico, he had praiseworthy aims but misjudged the country. (p. 566)

Toward War

What were the reasons behind and dangers of Wilson's neutrality policy?

With the outbreak of war in Europe in 1914, Wilson proclaimed neutrality, which was difficult to maintain. Neutrality, he hoped, would favor neither side and keep the United States out of war. Progressives knew that war would distract attention from reform. Submarine warfare offered new threats, which Wilson tried to control but could not. On April 6, 1917, the United States joined the war. (p. 568)

Over There

How did the United States' entry affect World War I?

The United States entered the war at a crucial time for the Allies. American troops helped stop the last German offensive in 1918. Entry into the war gave the United States a stake in the peace treaty. (p. 572)

Over Here

What programs and changes did World War I bring at home?

American participation in World War I drew on many of the techniques of progressive reformers, including using people with expertise and exploiting bureaucracy. The War Industries Board oversaw the production of all American factories; the Food Administration Board looked after food for the armies overseas. The government played a larger role in American life than ever before. (p. 577)

The Treaty of Versailles

What mistakes did Wilson make in negotiating the Treaty of Versailles?

Wilson's Fourteen Points sought to reduce armaments, lower trade barriers, provide for self determination, and establish a League of Nations to prevent further wars. He was forced to compromise at Versailles, but the Senate refused to ratify the peace treaty when he would not compromise on issues such as the League of Nations. (p. 582)

KEY TERMS AND DEFINITIONS

Hay–Bunau–Varilla Treaty This 1903 treaty with Panama granted the United States control over a canal zone ten miles wide across the Isthmus of Panama. p. 565

Roosevelt Corollary A corollary to the Monroe Doctrine, which asserted that the United States would intervene in Latin American affairs if those countries could not keep their affairs in order. p. 566

"Dollar diplomacy" The Taft administration's policy in the early 1900s to promote U.S. financial and business interests abroad, especially in Latin America. p. 566

"Moral diplomacy" Policy of President Woodrow Wilson that rejected "dollar diplomacy." Rather than focusing mainly on economic ties with other nations, Wilson sought to practice morality in international relations, preserve peace, and extend to other peoples the blessings of democracy. p. 567

Selective Service Act: This 1917 law required all American men between the ages of 21 and 30 to register for a military draft. The age limits were later changed to 18 and 45. p. 576

Committee on Public Information (CPI) Created in 1917 by President Wilson and headed by progressive journalist George Creel, this organization rallied support for American involvement in World War I through art, advertising, and film.

Creel worked out a system of voluntary censorship with the press and distributed posters and pamphlets. p. 577

Espionage Act of 1917 This law, passed after the United States entered World War I, imposed sentences of up to 20 years on anyone found guilty of aiding the enemy, obstructing recruitment of soldiers, or encouraging disloyalty. It allowed the postmaster general to remove from the mail any materials that incited treason or insurrection. p. 578

Sedition Act A World War I law that imposed harsh penalties on anyone using "disloyal, profane, scurrilous, or abusive language about the U.S. government, flag, or armed forces." p. 578

War Industries Board (WIB) This government agency oversaw the production of American factories during World War I. p. 579

Food Administration A government agency that encouraged Americans to save food during World War I. p. 579

Fourteen Points In January 1918, President Woodrow Wilson presented these terms for a far-reaching, nonpunitive settlement of World War I and the establishment of a League of Nations. While generous and optimistic, the Points did not satisfy wartime hunger for revenge and were largely rejected by European nations. p. 582

CRITICAL THINKING QUESTIONS

1. What role did the United States' becoming a world power play in shaping the foreign policy of Roosevelt and Wilson?

2. What events and influences led the United States toward entry into World War I?

3. What were the main events of America's involvement in the war in Europe, and how did these events affect the treaty ending the war?

4. How might Wilson have handled the Versailles treaty negotiations differently?

MyHistoryLab Media Assignments

Find these resources in the Media Assignments folder for Chapter 24 on MyHistoryLab

Toward War

- **Watch** the **Video**   *The Outbreak of World War I p. 568*

- **Read** the **Document**   *Adolf K.G.E. von Spiegel, U-boat 202 (1919) p. 570*

- **Read** the **Document**   *President Wilson's War Message to Congress (1917) p. 571*

- **Watch** the **Video**   *American Entry into World War I p. 572*

Over There

- **Listen** to the **Audio File**   *"Over There" p. 573*

- **Complete** the **Assignment**   *Measuring the Mind p. 574*

Over Here

- **Read** the **Document**   *Espionage Act (1917) p. 577*

- **View** the **Closer Look**   *Mobilizing the Home Front p. 579*

- **Watch** the **Video**   *The Great Migration p. 581*

The Treaty of Versailles

- **Read** the **Document**   *President Wilson's Fourteen Points p. 582*

■ *Indicates Study Plan Media Assignment*

25 Transition to Modern America

Contents and Learning Objectives

((¦●—[Listen to the **Audio File** on **myhistorylab**   **Chapter 25** *Transition to Modern America*

Wheels for the Millions

The moving assembly line that Henry Ford perfected in 1913 for manufacture of the Model T marked only the first step toward full mass production and the beginning of America's worldwide industrial supremacy. A year later, Ford began buying large plots of land along the Rouge River southeast of Detroit, Michigan. He already had a vision of a vast industrial tract where machines, moving through a sequence of carefully arranged manufacturing operations, would transform raw materials into finished cars, trucks, and tractors. The key would be control over the flow of goods at each step along the way—from lake steamers and railroad cars bringing in the coal and iron ore, to overhead conveyor belts and huge turning tables carrying the moving parts past the stationary workers on the assembly line. "Everything must move," Ford commanded, and by the mid-1920s at River Rouge, as the plant became known, it did.

Ford began fulfilling his industrial dream in 1919 when he built a blast furnace and foundry to make engine blocks for both the Model T and his tractors. By 1924, more than forty thousand workers were turning out nearly all the metal parts used in making Ford vehicles. One tractor factory was so efficient that it took just over twenty-eight hours to convert raw ore into a new farm implement.

Visitors from all over the world came to marvel at River Rouge. Some were disturbed by the jumble of machines (by 1926, there were forty-three thousand in operation) and the apparent congestion on the plant floor, but industrial experts recognized that the arrangement led to incredible productivity because "the work moves and the men stand still." A trained engineer summed it up best when he wrote that a visitor to the plant "sees each unit as a carefully designed gear which meshes with other gears and operates in synchronism with them, the whole forming one huge, perfectly-timed, smoothly-operating industrial machine of almost unbelievable efficiency."

In May 1927, after producing more than fifteen million Model Ts, Ford closed the assembly line at Highland Park. For the next six months, his engineers worked on designing a more compact and efficient assembly line at River Rouge for the Model A, which went into production in November. By then, River Rouge had more than justified Ford's vision. "Ford had brought together everything at a single site and on a scale no one else had ever attempted," concluded historian Geoffrey Perrett. "The Rouge plant became to a generation of engineers far more than a factory. It was a monument."

Mass production, born in Highland Park in 1913 and perfected at River Rouge in the 1920s, became the hallmark of American industry. Other car makers copied Ford's methods, and soon his emphasis on the flow of parts moving past stationary workers became the standard in nearly every American factory. The moving assembly line—with its emphasis on uniformity, speed, precision,

The development of the efficient and compact automobile assembly line by engineers at the Ford Motor Company in the late 1920s enabled the cost-efficient mass production of automobiles.

and coordination—took away the last vestiges of crafts-manship and turned workers into near robots. It led to amazing efficiency that produced both high profits for man-ufacturers and low prices for buyers. By the mid-1920s, the cost of the Model T had dropped from $950 to $290.

Most important, mass production contributed to a consumer goods revolution. American factories turned out a flood of automobiles, electrical appliances, and other items that made life easier and more pleasant for most Americans. The result was the cre-ation of a distinctively modern America, one marked by the material abundance that has characterized American society ever since.

But the abundance came at a price. The 1920s have been por-trayed as a decade of escape and frivolity, and for many Americans they were just that. But those years also were an era of transition: a time when the old America of individualistic rural values gave way to a new America of conformist urban values. The transition was often wrenching, and many Americans clung desperately to the old ways. Modernity finally won, but not without a struggle.

The Second Industrial Revolution

What was new about the American economy in the 1920s?

The first Industrial Revolution in the late nineteenth century had catapulted the United States into the forefront among the world's richest and most highly developed nations. With the advent of the new consumer goods industries, the American people by the 1920s enjoyed the highest standard of living of any nation on earth. After a brief postwar depression, 1922 saw the beginning of a great boom that peaked in 1927 and lasted until 1929. In this brief period, American industrial output nearly doubled, and the gross national product rose by 40 percent. Most of this explosive growth took place in industries producing con-sumer goods—automobiles, appliances, furniture, and clothing. Equally important, the national per capita income increased by 30 percent to $681 in 1929. American workers became the highest paid in history. Combined with the expansion of install-ment credit programs that allowed customers to buy now and pay later, this income growth allowed a purchasing spree like nothing the nation had ever experienced.

The key to the new affluence lay in technology. The moving assembly line pioneered by Ford became a standard feature in nearly all American plants. Electric motors replaced steam engines as the basic source of energy in factories; by 1929, 70 percent of all industrial power came from electricity. Efficiency experts broke down the industrial process into minute parts, using time and motion studies, and then showed managers and workers how to maximize the output of their labor. Production per worker-hour increased an amazing 75 percent over the decade; in 1929, a workforce no larger than that of 1919 was producing almost twice as many goods.

The Automobile Industry

The nature of the consumer goods revolution can best be seen in the automobile industry, which became the nation's largest in the 1920s. Rapid growth was its hallmark. In 1920, there were ten million cars in the nation; by the end of the decade, twenty-six million were on the road. Production jumped from fewer than two million units a year to more than five million by 1929.

The automobile boom, at its peak from 1922 to 1927, depended on the apparently insatiable appetite of the American people for cars. But as the decade continued, the market became saturated as more and more of those who could afford the new luxury had become car owners. Marketing became as crucial as production. Automobile makers began to rely heavily on advertising and annual model changes, seeking to make customers dissatisfied with their old vehicles and eager to order new ones. Despite these efforts, sales slumped in 1927 when Ford stopped making the Model T, picked up again the next year with the new Model A, but began to slide again in 1929. The new industry revealed a basic weakness in the consumer goods economy; once people had bought an item with a long life, they would be out of the market for a few years.

In the affluent 1920s, few noticed the emerging economic instability. Instead, contemporary observers focused on the stimulating effect the automobile had on the rest of the economy. The mass production of cars required huge quantities of steel; entire new rolling mills had to be built to supply sheet steel for car bodies. Rubber factories boomed with the demand for tires, and paint and glass suppliers had more business than ever before. The auto changed the pattern of city life, leading to a suburban explosion. Real estate developers, no longer dependent on streetcars and railway lines, could now build houses in ever wider concentric circles around the central cities.

The automobile had a profound effect on all aspects of American life in the 1920s. Filling stations appeared on the main streets, replacing the smithies and stables of the past. In Kansas City, Jess D. Nichols built the first shopping center, Country Club Plaza, and thus set an example quickly followed by other suburban developers.

Even in smaller communities, the car ruled. In Muncie, Indiana, site of a famous sociological survey in the 1920s, one elder replied when asked what was taking place, "I can tell you what's happening in just four letters: A-U-T-O!" A nation that had always revered symbols of movement, from the *Mayflower* to the covered wagon, now had a new icon to worship.

Patterns of Economic Growth

Automobiles were the most conspicuous of the consumer products that flourished in the 1920s, but certainly not the only ones. The electrical industry grew almost as quickly. Central power stations, where massive steam generators converted coal into electricity, brought current into the homes of city and town dwellers. Two-thirds of all American families enjoyed electricity by the end of the decade, and they spent vast sums on washing machines, vacuum cleaners, refrigerators, and ranges. The new appliances eased the burdens of housework and ushered in an age of leisure.

Radio broadcasting and motion picture production also boomed in the 1920s. The early success of KDKA in Pittsburgh stimulated the growth of more than eight hundred independent radio stations, and by 1929, NBC had formed the first successful radio network. Five nights a week, *Amos 'n Andy*, a comic serial featuring two "blackface" vaudevillians, held the attention of millions of Americans. The film industry thrived in Hollywood, reaching its maturity in the mid-1920s when in every large city there were huge theaters seating as many as four thousand people. With the advent of the "talkies" by 1929, average weekly movie attendance climbed to nearly one hundred million.

Other industries prospered as well. Production of light metals such as aluminum and magnesium grew into a major business. Chemical engineering came of age with the invention of synthetics, ranging from rayon for clothing to cellophane for packaging. Americans found a whole new spectrum of products to buy—cigarette lighters, wristwatches, heat-resistant glass cooking dishes, and rayon stockings, to name just a few.

The corporation continued to be the dominant economic unit in the 1920s. Growing corporations now had hundreds of thousands of stockholders; and one individual or family rarely held more than 5 percent of the stock. The enormous profits generated by the corporations enabled their managers to finance growth and expansion internally, thus freeing companies from their earlier dependence on investment bankers like J. P. Morgan. Voicing a belief in social responsibility and enlightened capitalism, the new professional class operated independently, free from outside restraint. In the final analysis, the corporate managers were accountable only to other managers.

Another wave of mergers accompanied the growth of corporations during the 1920s. From 1920 to 1928, some eight thousand mergers took place as more and more small firms proved unable to compete effectively with the new giants. By the end of the decade, the two hundred largest nonfinancial corporations owned almost half of the country's corporate wealth. The automobile industry set the example for other areas. The greatest abuses took place in public utilities; promoters such as Samuel Insull built vast paper empires by gaining control of power companies and then draining them of their assets.

The most distinctive feature of the new consumer-oriented economy was the emphasis on marketing. Advertising earnings rose from $1.3 billion in 1915 to $3.4 billion in 1926. Skillful practitioners such as Edward Bernays and Bruce Barton sought to control public taste and consumer spending by identifying the good life with the possession of the latest product of American industry, whether it be a car, a refrigerator, or a brand of cigarettes. Chain stores advanced rapidly at the expense of small retail shops.

View the **Closer Look**   *The Great White Way – Times Square*

Howard Thain's painting, *The Great White Way—Times Square*, captures the bright lights and excitement of New York's entertainment center in the Roaring Twenties.

Source: Collection of The New-York Historical Society, accession number 1963.150.

A&P dominated the retail food industry, growing from 400 stores in 1912 to 15,500 by 1932. Woolworth's "five-and-tens" spread almost as rapidly, while such drugstore chains as Rexall and Liggetts—both owned by one huge holding company—opened outlets in nearly every town and city in the land.

Uniformity and standardization, the characteristics of mass production, now prevailed. The farmer in Kansas bought the same kind of car, the same groceries, and the same pills as the factory worker in Pennsylvania. Sectional differences in dress, food, and furniture began to disappear. Even the regional accents that distinguished Americans in different parts of the country were threatened with extinction by the advent of radio and films, which promoted a standard national dialect devoid of any local flavor.

Economic Weaknesses

The New Era, as business leaders labeled the decade, was not as prosperous as it first appeared. The revolution in consumer goods disguised the decline of many traditional industries in the 1920s. Railroads, overcapitalized and poorly managed, suffered from internal woes and from competition with the growing trucking industry. The coal industry was also troubled, with petroleum and natural gas beginning to replace coal as a fuel. The use of cotton textiles declined with the development of rayon and other synthetic fibers. The New England mills moved south in search of cheap labor, leaving behind thousands of unemployed workers and virtual ghost towns in the nation's oldest industrial center.

Hardest hit of all was agriculture. American farmers had expanded production to meet the demands of World War I, when they fed their own nation and most of Europe as well. A sharp cutback of exports in 1919 caused a rapid decline in prices. By 1921, farm exports had fallen by more than $2 billion. Throughout the 1920s, the farmers' share of the national income dropped, until by 1929, the per capita farm income was only $273, compared to the national average of $681.

Urban workers were better off than farmers in the 1920s, but they did not share fully in the decade's affluence. The industrial labor force remained remarkably steady during this period of economic growth; technical innovations meant the same number of workers could produce far more than before. Most new jobs appeared in the lower-paying service industry. During the decade, factory wage rates rose only a modest 11 percent; in 1929, nearly half of all American families had an income of less than $1,500. At the same time, however, conditions of life improved. Prices remained stable, even dropping somewhat in the early 1920s, so workers enjoyed a gain in real wages.

Organized labor proved unable to advance the interests of workers in the 1920s. Conservative leadership in the AFL neglected the task of organizing the vast number of unskilled laborers in the mass production industries. Aggressive management weakened the appeal of unions by portraying them as radical organizations after a series of strikes in 1919. Many businesses used injunctions and "yellow-dog contracts"—which forbade employees to join unions—to establish open shops and deny workers the benefits of collective bargaining. Other employers wooed their workers away from unions using techniques of welfare capitalism—spending money to improve plant conditions and winning employee loyalty with pensions, paid vacations, and company cafeterias. The net result was a decline in union membership from a postwar high of five million to less than three million by 1929.

Black workers remained on the bottom, both economically and socially. Nearly half a million African Americans had migrated northward from the rural South during World War I. Some found jobs in northern industries, but many more worked in menial service areas collecting garbage, washing dishes, and sweeping floors. Yet even these jobs offered them a better life than they found on the depressed southern farms where millions of African Americans still lived in poverty, and so the migration continued. The black ghettos in northern cities grew rapidly in the 1920s; Chicago's African American population doubled during the decade while New York's rose from 152,467 to 327,706 with most African Americans living in Harlem.

Middle- and upper-class Americans were the groups who thrived in the 1920s. The rewards of this second Industrial Revolution went to the managers—the engineers, bankers, and executives—who directed the new industrial economy. Corporate profits nearly doubled in ten years, and income from dividends rose 65 percent,

nearly six times the rate of increase in workers' wages. Bank accounts, reflecting the accumulated savings of the upper-middle and wealthy classes, rose from $41.1 billion to $57.9 billion. These were the people who bought the fine new houses in the suburbs and who could afford more than one car. Their conspicuous consumption helped fuel the prosperity of the 1920s, but their disposable income eventually became greater than their material wants. The result was speculation, as those with idle money began to invest heavily in the stock market to reap the gains from industrial growth.

The economic trends of the decade had both positive and negative implications for the future. On one hand, there was the solid growth of new consumer-based industries. Automobiles and appliances were not passing fancies; their production and use became a part of the modern American way of life, creating a high standard of living that roused the envy of the rest of the world. The future pattern of American culture—cars and suburbs, shopping centers and skyscrapers—was determined by the end of the 1920s.

But at the same time, there were ominous signs of danger. The unequal distribution of wealth, the growth of consumer debt, the saturation of the market for cars and appliances, and the rampant speculation all contributed to economic instability. The boom of the 1920s would end in a great crash; yet the achievements of the decade would survive even that dire experience to shape the future of American life.

City Life in the Jazz Age

How did life in the cities change after World War I?

The city replaced the countryside as the focal point of American life in the 1920s. The 1920 census revealed that, for the first time, slightly more than half of the population lived in cities (defined broadly to include all places of more than 2,500 people). During the decade, the metropolitan areas grew rapidly as both whites and blacks from rural areas came seeking jobs in the new consumer industries. Between 1920 and 1930, cities with populations of 250,000 or more had added some eight million people to their ranks. New York City grew by nearly 25 percent, while Detroit more than doubled its population during the decade.

The skyscraper soon became the most visible feature of the city. Faced with inflated land prices, builders turned upward—developing a distinctively American architectural style in the process. New York led the way with the ornate Woolworth Building in 1913. The sleek 102-story Empire State Building, completed in 1931, was for years the tallest building in the world. Other cities erected their own jagged skylines. By 1929, there were 377 buildings more than 20 stories tall across the nation. Most significantly, the skyscraper came to symbolize the new mass culture. "The New York skyscrapers are the most striking manifestation of the triumph of numbers," wrote one French observer. "One cannot understand or like them without first having tasted and enjoyed the thrill of counting or adding up enormous totals and of living in a gigantic, compact and brilliant world."

In the metropolis, life was different. The old community ties of home, church, and school were absent, but there were important gains to replace them—new ideas, new creativity, new perspectives. Some city dwellers became lost and lonely without the old institutions; others thrived in the urban environment.

Women and the Family

The urban culture of the 1920s witnessed important changes in the American family. This vital institution began to break down under the impact of economic and social change. A new freedom for women and children seemed to be emerging in its wake.

Although World War I accelerated the process of women leaving the home for work, the postwar decade witnessed a return to the slower pace of the prewar years. During the 1920s, there was no permanent gain in the number of working women. Two million more women were employed in 1930 than in 1920, but this represented an increase of only 1 percent. Most women workers, moreover, had low-paying jobs, ranging from stenographers to maids. The number of women doctors actually decreased, and even though women earned nearly one-third of all graduate degrees, only 4 percent of full professors were female. For the most part, the professions were reserved for men, with women relegated to such fields as teaching and nursing.

Women had won the right to vote in 1920, but the Nineteenth Amendment proved to have less impact than its proponents had hoped. Adoption of the amendment robbed women of a unifying cause, and the exercise of the franchise itself did little to change prevailing sex roles. Men remained the principal breadwinners in the family; women cooked, cleaned, and reared the children. "The creation and fulfillment of a successful home," a *Ladies Home Journal* writer advised women, "is a bit of craftsmanship that compares favorably with building a beautiful cathedral."

The feminist movement, however, still showed signs of vitality in the 1920s. Social feminists pushing for humanitarian reform won enactment of the Sheppard-Towner Act of 1921, which provided for federal aid to establish state programs for maternal and infant health care. Although the failure to enact a child labor amendment in 1925 marked the beginning of a decline in humanitarian reform, for the rest of the decade, women's groups continued to work for good-government measures, for the inclusion of women on juries, and for consumer legislation.

One group of activists, led by Alice Paul's National Woman's Party (NWP), lobbied for full equality for women under the law. In 1923, the NWP succeeded in having an Equal Rights Amendment introduced in Congress. The amendment stated simply, "Men and women shall have equal rights throughout the United States and every place subject to its jurisdiction." Most other women's organizations, notably the League of Women Voters, opposed the amendment because it threatened gender-specific legislation such as the Sheppard-Towner Act that women had fought so hard to enact. The drive for the ERA in the 1920s failed.

Growing assertiveness had a profound impact on feminism in the 1920s. Instead of crusading for social progress, young women concentrated on individual self-expression by rebelling against Victorian restraints. In the larger cities, some quickly adopted what critic H. L. Mencken called the flapper image, portrayed most strikingly by artist John Held, Jr. Cutting their hair short, raising their skirts above the knee, and binding their breasts, "flappers" set out

to compete on equal terms with men on the golf course and in the speakeasy. Young women delighted in shocking their elders—they rouged their cheeks and danced the Charleston. Women smoked cigarettes and drank alcohol in public more freely than before. The flappers assaulted the traditional double standard in sex, demanding that equality with men should include sexual fulfillment before and during marriage. New and more liberal laws led to a sharp rise in the divorce rate; by 1928, there were 166 divorces for every 1,000 marriages, compared to only 81 in 1900.

The sense of woman's emancipation was heightened by a continuing drop in the birthrate and by the abundance of consumer goods. With fewer children to care for and with washing machines and vacuum cleaners to ease their household labor, it seemed that women of the 1920s would have more leisure time. Yet appearances were deceptive. Advertisers eagerly sought out women as buyers of labor-saving consumer products, but wives exercised purchasing power only as delegated by their husbands. In addition, many women were not in the position to put the new devices to use—one-fourth of the homes in Cleveland lacked running water in the 1920s, and three-quarters of the nation's families did not have washing machines. The typical childless woman spent between forty-three and fifty hours a week on household duties; for mothers, the average workweek was fifty-six hours, far longer than that of their husbands. And despite the talk of the "new woman," the flappers fell victim to the sex-role conditioning of their parents. Boys continued to play with guns and grew up to head their families; girls played with dolls and looked forward to careers as wives and mothers. "In the 1920s, as in the 1790s," concluded historian June Sochen, "marriage was the only approved state for women."

The family, however, did change. It became smaller as easier access to effective birth control methods enabled couples to limit the number of their offspring. More and more married women took jobs outside the home, bringing in an income and gaining a measure of independence (although their rate of pay was always lower than that for men). Young people, who had once joined the labor force when they entered their teens, now discovered adolescence as a stage of life. A high school education was no longer uncommon, and college attendance increased.

Prolonged adolescence led to new strains on the family in the form of youthful revolt. Freed of the traditional burden of earning a living at an early age, many young people in the 1920s went on a spree. Heavy drinking, casual sexual encounters, and a constant search for excitement became the hallmarks of the upper-class youth immortalized by F. Scott Fitzgerald. "I have been kissed by dozens of men," one of his characters commented. "I suppose I'll kiss dozens more." The theme of rebellion against parental authority, which runs through all aspects of the 1920s, was at the heart of the youth movement.

The Roaring Twenties

Excitement ran high in the cities as both crime waves and highly publicized sports events flourished. Prohibition ushered in such distinctive features of the decade as speakeasies, bootleggers, and bathtub gin. Crime rose sharply as middle- and upper-class Americans willingly broke the law to gain access to alcoholic beverages. City streets became the scene of violent shoot-outs between rival bootleggers; by 1929, Chicago had witnessed more than five hundred gangland murders. Underworld czars controlled illicit empires; Al Capone's produced revenue of $60 million a year.

Sports became a national mania in the 1920s as people found more leisure time. Golf boomed, with some two million men and women playing on nearly five thousand courses across the country. Spectator sports attracted even more attention. Boxing drew huge crowds to see fighters such as Jack Dempsey and Gene Tunney. Baseball attendance soared. More than twenty million fans attended games in 1927, the year Babe Ruth became a national idol by hitting sixty home runs. On college campuses, football became more popular than ever. Universities vied with each other in building massive stadiums, seating upward of seventy thousand people.

In what Frederick Lewis Allen called "the ballyhoo years," the popular yearning for excitement led people to seek vicarious thrills in all kinds of ways—applauding Charles Lindbergh's solo flight across the Atlantic, cheering Gertrude Ederle's swim across the English Channel, and flocking to such bizarre events as six-day bicycle races, dance marathons, and flagpole sittings. It was a time of pure pleasure seeking, when people sought to escape from the increasingly drab world of the assembly line by worshiping heroic individuals.

Sex became another popular topic in the 1920s as Victorian standards began to crumble. Sophisticated city dwellers seemed to be intent on exploring a new freedom in sexual expression. Plays and novels focused on adultery, and the new urban tabloids—led by the *New York Daily News*—delighted in telling their readers about love nests and kept women. The popular songs of the decade, such as "Hot Lips" and "Burning Kisses," were less romantic and more explicit than those of years before. Hollywood exploited the obsession with sex by producing movies with such provocative titles as *Up in Mabel's Room*, *A Shocking Night*, and *Women and Lovers*. Theda Bara and Clara Bow, the "vamp" and the "It" girl, set the model for feminine seductiveness while Rudolph Valentino became the heartthrob of millions of American women. Young people embraced the new

📖 **Read** the **Document**   Elanor Rowland Wembridge, "Petting and the Campus" (1925)

Sheik with Sheba is the title of this John Held, Jr., drawing, which appeared on a 1925 cover of *Judge* magazine. Held's drawings define the image of the "flapper" era—the young woman with rolled-down stockings and rouged knees and the young man with cigarette and pocket flask at the wheel of his car.

permissiveness joyfully, with the automobile giving couples an easy way to escape parental supervision.

There is considerable debate, however, over the extent of the sexual revolution in the 1920s. Later studies by Dr. Alfred C. Kinsey showed that premarital intercourse was twice as common among women born after 1900 than for those born before the turn of the century. But a contemporary survey of more than two thousand middle-class women by Katherine B. Davis found that only 7 percent of those who were married had had sexual relations before marriage and that only 14 percent of the single women had engaged in intercourse. Actual changes in sexual behavior are beyond the historian's reach, hidden in the privacy of the bedroom, but the old Victorian prudishness was a clear casualty of the 1920s. Sex was no longer a taboo subject, at least in urban areas; men and women now could discuss it openly, and many of them did.

The Flowering of the Arts

The greatest cultural advance of the 1920s was visible in the outpouring of literature. The city gave rise to a new class of intellectuals—writers who commented on the new industrial society. Many had been uprooted by World War I. They were bewildered by the rapidly changing social patterns of the 1920s and appalled by the materialism of American culture. Some fled to Europe to live as expatriates, congregating in Paris cafés to bemoan the loss of American innocence and purity. Others stayed at home, observing and condemning the excesses of a business civilization. All shared a sense of disillusionment and wrote pessimistically of the flawed promise of American life. Yet, ironically, their body of writing revealed a profound creativity that suggested America was coming of age intellectually.

The exiles included the poets T. S. Eliot and Ezra Pound and the novelist Ernest Hemingway. Pound discarded rhyme and meter in a search for clear, cold images that conveyed reality. Like many of the writers of the 1920s, he reacted against World War I, expressing a deep regret for the tragic waste of a whole generation in defense of a "botched civilization."

Eliot, who was born in Missouri but became a British subject, displayed even more profound despair. In *The Waste Land*, which appeared in 1922, he evoked images of fragmentation and sterility that had a powerful impact on the other disillusioned writers of the decade. He reached the depths in *The Hollow Men* (1925), a biting description of the emptiness of modern man.

Ernest Hemingway sought redemption from the modern plight in the romantic individualism of his heroes. Preoccupied with violence, he wrote of men alienated from society who found a sense of identity in their own courage and quest for personal honor. His own experiences, ranging from driving an ambulance in the war to stalking lions in Africa, made him a legendary figure; his greatest effect on other writers, however, came from his sparse, direct, and clean prose style.

The writers who stayed home were equally disdainful of contemporary American life. F. Scott Fitzgerald chronicled American youth in *This Side of Paradise* (1920) and *The Great Gatsby* (1925), writing in bittersweet prose about "the beautiful and the damned." Amid the glitter of life among the wealthy on Long Island's North Shore came the haunting realization of emptiness and lack of human concern.

Sinclair Lewis became the most popular of the critical novelists. *Main Street*, published in 1920, satirized the values of small-town America as dull, complacent, and narrow-minded; *Babbitt*, which appeared two years later, poked fun at the commercialism of the 1920s, portraying George Babbitt as the stereotype of the lazy, smug middle-class businessman who hailed the decade as a New Era.

Most savage of all was H. L. Mencken, the Baltimore newspaperman and literary critic who founded *American Mercury* magazine in 1923. Declaring war on "Homo boobiens," Mencken mocked everything he found distasteful in America, from the Rotary Club to the Ku Klux Klan. "From Boy Scouts, and from Home Cooking, from Odd Fellows' funerals, from socialists, from Christians—Good Lord, deliver us," he pleaded. It was not difficult to discover Mencken's dislikes (including Jews, as his published diary makes clear); the hard part was finding out what he affirmed, other than wit and a clever turn of phrase. A born cynic, he served as a zealous guardian of public rationality in an era of excessive boosterism.

The cultural explosion of the 1920s was surprisingly broad. It included novelists such as Sherwood Anderson and John Dos Passos, who described the way the new machine age undermined such traditional American values as craftsmanship and a sense of community, and playwrights such as Eugene O'Neill, Maxwell Anderson, and Elmer Rice, who added greatly to the stature of American theater. Women writers were particularly effective in dealing with regional themes. Edith Wharton continued to write penetratingly about eastern aristocrats in books such as *The House of Mirth* (1905) and *The Age of Innocence* (1921); Willa Cather and Ellen Glasgow focused on the plight of women in the Midwest and the South, respectively, in their short stories and novels. These writers portrayed their heroines in the traditional roles of wives and mothers; playwright Zona Gale, on the other hand (who won the Pulitzer Prize for drama in 1920 for *Miss Lulu Bett*), used her title character to depict the dilemmas facing an unmarried woman in American society.

Art and especially music made significant advances as well. Edward Hopper and Charles Burchfield captured the ugliness of city life and the loneliness of its inhabitants in their realistic paintings. Aaron Copland and George Gershwin added a new vitality to American music. But African Americans migrating northward brought the most significant contribution: the spread of jazz—first to St. Louis, Kansas City, and Chicago, and finally to New York. The form of jazz known as the blues, so expressive of the suffering of African Americans, became an authentic national folk music, and performers such as Louis Armstrong enjoyed popularity around the world.

The cultural growth of the 1920s was the work of blacks as well as whites. W. E. B. Du Bois, the editor of the newspaper *Crisis*, became the intellectual voice of the black community developing in New York City's Harlem. In 1917, James Weldon Johnson, who had been a professor of literature at Fisk University, published *Fifty Years and Other Poems*, in which the title poem commented on the half century of suffering that had followed the Emancipation Proclamation, and called for the promise of that period to be redeemed:

> Think you that John Brown's spirit stops?
> That Lovejoy was but idly slain?
> Or do you think those precious drops
> From Lincoln's heart were shed in vain?

As other African American writers gathered around them, Du Bois and Johnson became the leaders of the **Harlem Renaissance**. The NAACP moved its headquarters to Harlem, and in 1923, the Urban League began publishing *Opportunity*, a magazine devoted to scholarly studies of racial issues, including black nationalism and emigration to Africa. (See the Feature Essay, "Marcus Garvey: Racial Redemption and Black Nationalism," pp. 596–597.)

African American literature blossomed rapidly. In 1922, critics hailed the appearance of Claude McKay's book of verses, *White Shadows*. In stark images, McKay expressed both his resentment against racial injustice and his pride in blackness.

Complete the Assignment **Marcus Garvey: Racial Redemption and Black Nationalism** on **myhistorylab**

Feature Essay

Marcus Garvey
Racial Redemption and Black Nationalism

Read the Document **Pearson Profiles, Marcus Garvey**

Marcus Garvey's advocacy of black nationalism and independent black entrepreneurship were, in part, discredited by his trial and conviction for mail fraud. He is shown here in custody on the way to Atlanta federal prison in 1925.

"In a world of wolves one should go armed," wrote Marcus Garvey in 1919, "and one of the most powerful defensive weapons within the reach of Negroes is the practice of race first in all parts of the world." This emphasis on black solidarity reflected Garvey's belief that racial oppression and exploitation lay at the heart of most of the world's societies. Negro equality, he insisted, would come not through integration or civil rights legislation, but only by transforming black heritage from a mark of inferiority into the basis of a program of pride and liberation. "The world has made being black a crime," he declared, "and instead of making it a crime I hope to make it a virtue."

Nowhere did these ideas find a more enthusiastic reception than in the United States. World War I brought American blacks to northern cities in unprecedented numbers, but the postwar economic slump aggravated already existing racial tensions. Urban slums, job discrimination, disfranchisement, and segregation gave powerful reinforcement to black disillusionment with white America, and to Garvey's message of black nationalism and racial redemption.

Garvey's upbringing in Jamaica, under the color-based caste system of the British-ruled West Indies, convinced him that only black solidarity could lead his race out of subjugation. Dreaming of an independent black Africa, he embraced black nationalism and economic self-help, and in 1914 he molded these ideas into a vision of the Negro race redeemed through his new organization, the United

Negro Improvement Association (UNIA). In 1916, Garvey toured the United States, and American blacks responded so strongly to his message that he moved UNIA headquarters to Harlem. With a new weekly, the *Negro World*, Garvey advanced his crusade for racial redemption and separatism. The paper extolled the beauty of black skin color and African features, and his editorials demanded economic self-reliance and collective black action. "Up, you mighty race," he exhorted. "You can accomplish what you will."

Garvey put his principles into practice in 1919 when he launched the Black Star Line (BSL), a steamship corporation that he believed would demonstrate black competence in business, enhance racial pride, and strengthen the bonds among blacks worldwide. A company brochure offered every black investor the promise of easy dividends and an opportunity to climb the ladder of success for only $5 per share. In November 1919, the BSL launched its first of three ships and stock sales soared. Spirits were equally high at UNIA's first international convention, held in New York in 1920, which brought together several thousand delegates from all forty-eight states and more than twenty countries. After leading the opening day parade, which stretched for several miles through the streets of Harlem, Garvey delivered the keynote address before a crowd of twenty-five thousand:

We are the descendents of a suffering people. We are the descendents of a people determined to suffer no longer. We shall now organize the 400,000,000 Negroes of the world into a vast organization to plant the banner of freedom on the great continent of Africa....If Europe is for Europeans, then Africa shall be for the black peoples of the world.

Others echoed his sentiments. UNIA delegates meeting in Harlem approved the Declaration of Rights of the Negro Peoples of the World, which declared that the black man had "an inherent right...to possess himself of Africa." The convention also urged the teaching of black history in schools, demanded an end to lynching and segregation, and elected Garvey as the provisional president of Africa.

Garvey's vision began to unravel with his Liberian Rehabilitation project. The black African republic welcomed his offer of financial and technical assistance through the UNIA, and in late 1920 he began to raise money for a reconstruction loan. In subsequent months, however, he diverted much of the proceeds to keep the ailing BSL afloat. With large capital outlays, poor management, and high operating costs, Garvey's dream of a maritime empire verged on financial collapse. The "establishment" black press accused Garvey of adventurism, opportunism, and diversion from the real path of progress. His views on the Ku Klux Klan made him even more controversial. While deploring Klan terror and violence, Garvey voiced appreciation of Klan candor on race relations:

I regard the Klan, the Anglo-Saxon Clubs, and White American societies as better friends of the race than all other groups of hypocritical whites put together. I like honesty and fair play. You may call me a Klansman if you will, but potentially every white man is a Klansman, as far as the Negro in competition with whites socially, economically, and politically is concerned ...

So stark a statement of racial separatism and suspicion of whites appalled other black leaders. W. E. B. Du Bois described him as "the most dangerous enemy of the Negro race," and a black newspaper promised to "drive Garvey and Garveyism in all its sinister viciousness from the American soil." Yet Marcus Garvey and his message endured; by 1921, the UNIA had more than eight hundred official and unofficial branches.

Garvey's battle with black leaders was but one of his challenges. In May 1923, he and three associates went on trial for mail fraud in the sale of BSL stock. The evidence suggested that while BSL's leaders made poor business decisions, neither Garvey nor his executives drew large salaries or lived lavishly at company expense. The BSL may have been ill-advised and badly managed, but it does not appear to have been fraudulent. The jury, however, found Garvey guilty (despite acquitting his codefendants), and the judge sentenced him to the maximum five-year term.

On February 8, 1925, Garvey entered the federal penitentiary at Atlanta. Ironically, once he was behind bars, he gained the support of many of his erstwhile detractors who protested the severity of white justice. Under mounting pressure, President Coolidge commuted Garvey's sentence in 1927. Immediate deportation followed, as required by U.S. immigration law. On December 10, 1927, Garvey returned to Jamaica, where one of the largest crowds in the island's history greeted him with a hero's welcome.

Garvey tried in vain to revitalize the UNIA in Jamaica, but with the onset of the Great Depression, American blacks concentrated more on survival than on racial nationalism. Garvey slipped into obscurity and died in 1940 at the age of fifty-two. Despite this end, however, his movement had inspired many blacks who were disgusted by the hypocrisy of American democracy and frustrated by the failure of gradualism to improve their lot. His appeals offered them an alternative to the legalistic approach of the more conservative black establishment, and an emphasis on pride in their heritage that influenced many black Americans in succeeding generations.

QUESTIONS FOR DISCUSSION

1. Why did W. E. B. Du Bois and other black leaders find Marcus Garvey so threatening?

2. Why did Garvey embrace the Ku Klux Klan?

Archibald Motley, *Barbecue*. Motley, one of the artists of the Harlem Renaissance, combined the traditions of his native New Orleans with the energy and rhythms of 1920s Harlem.

Countee Cullen and Langston Hughes won critical acclaim for the beauty of their poems and the eloquence in their portrayals of the black tragedy.

Art and music also flourished during Harlem's golden age. Plays and concerts at the 135th Street YMCA; floor shows at Happy Rhone's nightclub (attended by many white celebrities); rent parties where jazz musicians played to raise money to help writers, artists, and neighbors pay their bills—all were part of the ferment that made Harlem "the Negro Capital of the World" in the 1920s. "Almost everything seemed possible above 125th Street in the early twenties for these Americans who were determined to thrive separately to better proclaim the ideals of integration," commented historian David Lewis. "You could be black and proud, politically assertive and economically independent, creative, and disciplined—or so it seemed."

Although its most famous writers were identified with New York's Harlem, the new African American cultural awareness spread to other cities in the form of poetry circles and theater groups. The number of African Americans graduating from college rose from 391 in 1920 to 1,903 by 1929. Although blacks were still an oppressed minority in the America of the 1920s, they had taken major strides toward achieving cultural and intellectual fulfillment.

In retrospect, there is a striking paradox about the literary flowering of the 1920s. Nearly all the writers, black as well as white, cried out against the conformity and materialism of the contemporary scene. They were critical of mass production and reliance on the machine; they wrote wistfully of the disappearance of the artisan and of a more relaxed way of life. Few took any interest in politics or in social reform. They retreated instead into individualism, seeking an escape into their art from the prevailing business civilization. Whether they went abroad or stayed home, the writers of the 1920s turned inward to avoid being swept up in the consumer goods revolution. Yet despite their withdrawal, and perhaps because of it, they produced an astonishingly rich and varied body of work. American writing had a greater intensity and depth than in the past; American writers, despite their alienation, had placed their country in the forefront of world literature.

The Rural Counterattack

How did conservatives resist the changes of the decade?

The shift of population from the countryside to the city led to heightened social tensions in the 1920s. Intent on preserving traditional social values, rural Americans saw in the city all that was evil in contemporary life. Saloons, whorehouses, little Italys and little Polands, communist cells, free love, and atheism—all were identified with the city. Accordingly, the countryside struck back at the newly dominant urban areas, aiming to restore the primacy of the Anglo-Saxon and predominantly Protestant culture they revered. This counterattack won considerable support in the cities from those so recently uprooted from their rural backgrounds.

Other factors contributed to the intensity of the counterattack. The war had unleashed a nationalistic spirit that craved unity and conformity. In a nation where one-third of the people were foreign born, the attack on immigrants and the call for 100 percent Americanism took on a frightening zeal. When the war was over, groups such as the American Legion tried to root out "un-American" behavior and insisted on cultural as well as political conformity. The prewar progressive reform spirit added to the social tension. Stripped of much of its former idealism, progressivism focused on such social problems as drinking and illiteracy to justify repressive measures such as prohibition and immigration restriction. The result was tragic. Amid the emergence of a new urban culture, the movements aimed at preserving the values of an earlier America succeeded only in complicating life in an already difficult period of cultural transition.

The Fear of Radicalism

The first and most intense outbreak of national alarm, the **Red Scare**, came in 1919. The heightened nationalism of World War I, aimed at achieving unity at the expense of ethnic diversity, found a new target in bolshevism. The Russian Revolution and the triumph of Marxism frightened many Americans. A growing turn to communism among American radicals (especially the foreign born) accelerated these fears. Although the numbers involved were tiny—at most there were sixty thousand communists in the United States in 1919—they were highly visible. Located in the cities, their influence appeared to be magnified with the outbreak of widespread labor unrest.

A general strike in Seattle, a police strike in Boston, and a violent strike in the iron and steel industry thoroughly alarmed the American people in the spring and summer of 1919. A series of bombings led to panic. First the mayor of strikebound Seattle received a small brown package containing a homemade bomb; then an alert New York postal employee detected sixteen bombs addressed to a variety of famous citizens (including John D. Rockefeller); and finally, on June 2, a bomb shattered the front of Attorney General A. Mitchell Palmer's home. Although the man who delivered it was blown to pieces, authorities quickly identified him as an Italian anarchist from Philadelphia.

In the ensuing public outcry, Attorney General Palmer led the attack on the alien threat. A Quaker and progressive, Palmer abandoned his earlier liberalism to launch a massive roundup of foreign-born radicals. In a series of raids that began

📖●─ Read the Document   A. Mitchell Palmer on the Menace of Communism (1920)

United States Attorney General A. Mitchell Palmer organized and implemented law enforcement raids against suspected communists and other radicals in 1919 and 1920. The Palmer raids, part of a nationwide Red Scare, involved the arrest of over three thousand persons and the deportation of over five hundred resident aliens.

on November 7, federal agents seized suspected anarchists and communists and held them for deportation with no regard for due process of law. In December, 249 aliens—including such well-known radical leaders as Emma Goldman and Alexander Berkman—were sent to Russia aboard the *Buford*, dubbed the "Soviet Ark" by the press. Nearly all were innocent of the charges against them. A month later, Palmer rounded up nearly four thousand suspected communists in a single evening. Federal agents broke into homes, meeting halls, and union offices without search warrants. Many native-born Americans were caught in the dragnet and spent several days in jail before being released; aliens rounded up were deported without hearings or trials.

For a time, it seemed that the Red Scare reflected the prevailing views of the American people. Instead of condemning their government's action, citizens voiced their approval and even urged more drastic steps. One patriot said his solution to the alien problem was simple: "S.O.S.—ship or shoot." General Leonard Wood, the former army chief of staff, favored placing Bolsheviks on "ships of stone with sails of lead," while evangelist Billy Sunday preferred to take "these ornery, wild-eyed socialists" and "stand them up before a firing squad and save space on our ships." Inflamed by public statements like these, a group of legionnaires in Centralia, Washington, dragged a radical from the town jail, castrated him, and hanged him from a railway bridge. The coroner's report blandly stated that the victim "jumped off with a rope around his neck and then shot himself full of holes."

The very extremism of the Red Scare led to its rapid demise. In early 1920, courageous government officials from the Department of Labor insisted on due process and full hearings before anyone else was deported. Prominent public leaders began to speak out against the acts of terror. Charles Evans Hughes, the defeated GOP candidate in 1916, offered to defend six socialists expelled from the New York legislature; Ohio Senator Warren G. Harding, the embodiment of middle-class values, expressed his opinion that "too much has been said about Bolshevism in America." Finally, Palmer himself, with evident presidential ambition, went too far. In April 1920, he warned of a vast revolution to occur on May 1; the entire New York City police force, some eleven thousand strong, was placed on duty to prepare for imminent disaster. When no bombings or violence took place on May Day, the public began to react against Palmer's hysteria. Despite a violent explosion on Wall Street in September that killed thirty-three people, the Red Scare died out by the end of 1920. Palmer passed into obscurity, the tiny Communist party became torn with factionalism, and the American people tried hard to forget their loss of balance.

Yet the Red Scare exerted a continuing influence on American society in the 1920s. The foreign-born lived in the uneasy realization that they were viewed with hostility and suspicion. Two Italian aliens in Massachusetts, Nicola Sacco and Bartolomeo Vanzetti, were arrested in May 1920 for a payroll robbery and murder. They faced a prosecutor and jury who condemned them more for their ideas than for any evidence of criminal conduct and a judge who referred to them as "those anarchist bastards." Despite a worldwide effort that became the chief liberal cause of the 1920s, the courts rejected all appeals. Sacco, a shoemaker, and Vanzetti, a fish peddler, died in the electric chair on August 23, 1927. Their fate symbolized the bigotry and intolerance that lasted through the 1920s and made that decade one of the least attractive in American history.

Prohibition

In December 1917, Congress passed the Eighteenth Amendment, prohibiting the manufacture and sale of alcoholic beverages, and sent the amendment to the states for ratification. A little over a year later, in January 1919, Nebraska was the necessary thirty-sixth state to ratify, and **Prohibition** became the law of the land.

Effective January 16, 1920, the Volstead Act, which implemented Prohibition, banned most commercial production and distribution of beverages containing more than one-half of 1 percent of alcohol by volume. (Exceptions were made for medicinal and religious uses of wine and spirits. Production for one's own private use was also allowed.) Prohibition was the result of both a rural effort of the Anti-Saloon League, backed by Methodist and Baptist clergy men, and the urban progressive concern over the social disease of drunkenness, especially among industrial workers. The moral issue had already led to the enactment of prohibition laws in twenty-six states by 1920; the real tragedy would occur in the effort to extend this "noble experiment" to the growing cities, where it was deeply resented by ethnic groups such as the Germans and the Irish and was almost totally disregarded by the well-to-do and the sophisticated.

Prohibition did in fact lead to a decline in drinking. Americans consumed much less alcohol in the 1920s than in the prewar years. Rural areas became totally dry, and in the cities, the consumption of alcoholic beverages dropped sharply among the lower classes, who could not afford the high prices for bootleg liquor. Among the middle class and the wealthy, however, drinking became fashionable. Bootleggers supplied whiskey, which quickly replaced lighter spirits such as wine and beer. The alcohol was either smuggled from abroad (a $40 million a year business by 1924) or illicitly manufactured in America. Exotic products such as Jackass Brandy, Soda Pop Moon, and Yack Yack Bourbon were common—and all could be fatal. Despite the risk of illness or death from extraordinarily high alcohol content or poorly controlled distillation, Americans consumed some 150 million quarts of liquor a year in the 1920s. Bootleggers took in nearly $2 billion annually, about 2 percent of the gross national product.

Urban resistance to Prohibition finally led to its repeal in 1933. But in the intervening years, it damaged American society by breeding a profound disrespect for the law. The flamboyant excesses of bootleggers were only the more obvious evils spawned by prohibition. In city after city, police openly tolerated the traffic in liquor, and judges and prosecutors agreed to let bootleggers pay merely token fines, creating almost a system of licenses. Prohibition satisfied the countryside's desire for vindication, yet rural and urban America alike suffered from this overzealous attempt to legislate morals.

The Ku Klux Klan

The most ominous expression of protest against the new urban culture was the rebirth of the Ku Klux Klan. On Thanksgiving night in 1915, on Stone Mountain in Georgia, Colonel William J.

📖 **Read** the **Document**   **Court Statements from Sacco and Vanzetti**

Italian immigrants Nicola Sacco and Bartolomeo Vanzetti were accused of killing a paymaster and stealing about $16,000 in 1920. Many believed they were convicted and executed in 1927 because of their anarchistic beliefs.

Simmons and thirty-four followers founded the modern Klan. Only "native born, white, gentile Americans" were permitted to join "the Invisible Empire, Knights of the Ku Klux Klan." Membership grew slowly during World War I, but after 1920, fueled by postwar fears and shrewd promotional techniques, the Klan mushroomed. In villages, towns, and small cities across the nation—no longer simply in the South—Anglo-Saxon Protestant men flocked into the newly formed chapters, seeking to relieve their anxiety over a changing society by embracing the Klan's unusual rituals and by demonstrating their hatred against those they considered a threat to American values.

The Klan of the 1920s, unlike the night riders of the post–Civil War era, was not just antiblack; the threat to American culture, as Klansmen perceived it, came also from immigrants, Jews, and Catholics. They attributed much of the tension and conflict in society to the prewar flood of immigrants, foreigners who spoke different languages, worshiped in strange churches, and lived in distant, threatening cities. The Klansmen struck back by coming together and enforcing their own values. They punished blacks who did not know their place, women who practiced the new morality, and aliens who refused to conform. Beating, flogging, burning with acid—even murder—were condoned. They also tried more peaceful methods of coercion, formulating codes of behavior and seeking community-wide support.

The Klan entered politics, at first hesitantly, then with growing confidence. The KKK gained control of the legislatures in Texas, Oklahoma, Oregon, and Indiana; in 1924, it blocked a resolution of censure at the Democratic national convention. With an estimated five million members by the mid-1920s, the Klan seemed to be fully established.

Much of its appeal lay in the sanctuary it offered to people anxious about the direction of American society. Protestant to the core, the Klan provided reassurance sometimes missing in members' churches. Members were beguiled by the titles, ranging from Imperial Wizard to Grand Dragon, and they gloried in the ritual that centered around the letter *K*. Thus each Klan had its own Klalendar, held its weekly Klonklave in the local Klavern, and followed the rules set forth in the Kloran. Members found a sense of identity in the group activities, whether they were peaceful picnics, ominous parades in white robes, or fiery cross burnings at night.

Although it was a men's organization, the Klan did not neglect the family. There was a Women's Order, a Junior Order for boys, and a Tri-K Klub for girls. Members had to be born in America, but foreign-born Protestants were allowed to join a special Krusaders affiliate. Only blacks, Catholics, Jews, and prostitutes were beyond redemption to these lonely and anxious men who came together to chant:

> United we stick
> Divided we're stuck.
> The better we stick
> The better we Klux!

The Klan fell even more quickly than it rose. Its more violent activities—which included kidnapping, lynching, setting fire to synagogues and Catholic churches, and, in one case, murdering a priest—began to offend the nation's conscience. Misuse of funds and sexual scandals among Klan leaders, notably in Indiana, repelled many of the rank and file; effective counterattacks by traditional politicians ousted the KKK from control in Texas and Oklahoma. Membership declined sharply after 1925; by the end of the decade, the Klan had virtually

📖 Read the Document   Creed of Klanswomen, 1924

A 1925 Ku Klux Klan demonstration in Cincinnati, Ohio, attended by nearly thirty thousand robed members and marked by the induction of eight thousand young boys in the Junior Order. Only native-born, white Americans "who believe in the tenets of the Christian religion" were admitted into the Klan. The original Klan, formed during the Reconstruction era to terrorize former slaves, disbanded in 1869. The Klan that formed in 1915 declined after the mid-1920s but did not officially disband until 1944. Two years later, a third Klan emerged, focusing on the civil rights movement and communism.

disappeared. But its spirit lived on, testimony to the recurring demons of **nativism** and hatred that have surfaced periodically throughout the American experience.

Immigration Restriction

The nativism that permeated the Klan found its most successful outlet in the immigration legislation of the 1920s. The sharp increase in immigration in the late nineteenth century had led to a broad-based movement, spearheaded by organized labor and by New England aristocrats such as Henry Cabot Lodge, to restrict the flow of people from Europe. In 1917, over Wilson's veto, Congress enacted a literacy test that reduced the number of immigrants allowed into the country. The war caused a much more drastic decline—from an average of 1 million a year between 1900 and 1914 to only 110,000 in 1918.

After the armistice, however, rumors began to spread of an impending flood of people seeking to escape war-ravaged Europe. Kenneth Roberts, a popular historical novelist, warned that all Europe was on the move, with only the limits of available steamship space likely to stem the flow. Worried congressmen spoke of a

"barbarian horde" and a "foreign tide" that would inundate the United States with "dangerous and deadly enemies of the country." Even though the actual number of immigrants, 810,000 in 1920 (fewer than the prewar yearly average), did not match these projections, Congress, in 1921, passed an emergency immigration act. The new quota system restricted immigration from Europe to 3 percent of the number of nationals from each country living in the United States in 1910.

The 1921 act failed to satisfy the nativists. The quotas still permitted more than five hundred thousand Europeans to come to the United States in 1923, nearly half of them from southern and eastern Europe. The declining percentage of Nordic immigrants alarmed writers such as Madison Grant, who warned the American people the Anglo-Saxon stock that had founded the nation was about to be overwhelmed by lesser breeds with inferior genes. "These immigrants adopt the language of the native American, they wear his clothes and are beginning to take his women, but they seldom adopt his religion or understand his ideals," Grant wrote.

Psychologists, relying on primitive IQ tests used by the army in World War I, confirmed this judgment. (See the Feature Essay in Chapter 24, "Measuring the Mind," pp. 574–575.) One senator claimed that all the nation's ills were due to an "intermingled and mongrelized people" as he demanded that racial purity replace the older reliance on the melting pot. In 1924, Congress adopted the **National Origins Quota Act**, which limited immigration from Europe to 150,000 a year; allocated most of the available slots to immigrants from Great Britain, Ireland, Germany, and Scandinavia; and banned all Asian immigrants. The measure passed Congress with overwhelming rural support.

The new restrictive legislation marked the most enduring achievement of the rural counterattack. Unlike the Red Scare, prohibition, and the Klan, the quota system would survive until the 1960s, enforcing a racist bias that excluded Asians and limited the immigration of Italians, Greeks, and Poles to a few thousand a year while permitting a steady stream of Irish, English, and Scandinavian immigrants. The large corporations, no longer dependent on armies of unskilled immigrant workers, did not object to the 1924 law; the machine had replaced the immigrant on the assembly line. Yet even here the victory was not complete. A growing tide of Mexican laborers, exempt from the quota act, flowed northward across the Rio Grande to fill the continuing need for unskilled workers on the farms and in the service trades. The Mexican immigrants, as many as one hundred thousand a year, marked the strengthening of an element in the national ethnic mosaic that would grow in size and influence until it became a major force in modern American society.

The Fundamentalist Challenge

The most significant—and, as it turned out, longest-lasting—challenge to the new urban culture was rooted in the traditional religious beliefs of millions of Americans who felt alienated from city life, from science, and from much of what modernization entailed. Sometimes this challenge was direct, as when Christian fundamentalists campaigned against the teaching of evolution in the public schools. Their success in Tennessee touched off a court battle, the **Scopes trial**, that drew the attention of the entire country to the small town of Dayton in the summer of 1925. (See the Law and Society essay, "The Scopes 'Monkey' Trial," pp. 608–611.)

Other aspects of the fundamentalist challenge were more subtle but no less important in countering the modernizing trend. As middle- and upper-class Americans drifted into a genteel Christianity that stressed good works and respectability, the Baptist and Methodist churches continued to hold on to the old faith. In addition, aggressive fundamentalist sects such as the Churches of Christ, the Pentecostals, and Jehovah's Witnesses grew rapidly. While church membership increased from 41.9 million in 1916 to 54.5 million in 1926, the number of churches actually declined during the decade. More and more rural dwellers drove their cars into town instead of going to the local crossroads chapel.

Many of those who came to the city in the 1920s brought their religious beliefs with them and found new outlets for their traditional ideas. Thus evangelist Aimee Semple McPherson enjoyed amazing success in Los Angeles with her Church of the Four-Square Gospel, building the Angelus Temple to seat more than five thousand worshipers. And in Fort Worth, the Reverend

J. Frank Norris erected a six thousand-seat sanctuary for the First Baptist Church, bathing it in spotlights so it could be seen for thirty miles across the North Texas prairie.

Far from dying out, as divinity professor Thomas G. Oden noted, biblical fundamentalism retained "remarkable grassroots strength among the organization men and the industrialized mass society of the 20th century." The rural counterattack, while challenged by the city, did enable some older American values to survive in the midst of the new mass production culture.

Politics of the 1920s

How did the politics of the 1920s reflect changes in the economy and in American society?

The tensions between the city and the countryside also shaped the course of politics in the 1920s. On the surface, it was a Republican decade. The GOP ("Grand Old Party") controlled the White House from 1921 to 1933 and had majorities in both houses of Congress from 1919 to 1931. The Republicans used their return to power after World War I to halt further reform legislation and to establish a friendly relationship between government and business. Important shifts were taking place, however, in the American electorate. The Democrats, although divided into competing urban and rural wings, were laying the groundwork for the future by winning over millions of new voters, especially among the ethnic groups in the cities. The rising tide of urban voters indicated a fundamental shift away from the Republicans toward a new Democratic majority.

Harding, Coolidge, and Hoover

The Republicans regained the White House in 1920 with the election of Warren G. Harding of Ohio. A dark-horse contender, Harding won the GOP nomination when the convention deadlocked and he became the compromise choice. Handsome and dignified, Harding reflected both the virtues and blemishes of small-town America. Originally a newspaper publisher in Marion, he had made many friends and few enemies throughout his career as a legislator, lieutenant governor, and finally, after 1914, U.S. senator. Conventional in outlook, Harding was a genial man who lacked the capacity to govern and who, as president, broadly delegated power.

He made some good cabinet choices, notably Charles Evans Hughes as secretary of state and Herbert C. Hoover as secretary of commerce, but two corrupt officials—Attorney General Harry Daugherty and Secretary of the Interior Albert Fall—sabotaged his administration. Daugherty became involved in a series of questionable deals that led ultimately to his forced resignation; Fall was the chief figure in the **Teapot Dome scandal**. Two oil promoters gave Fall nearly $400,000 in loans and bribes; in return, he helped them secure leases on naval oil reserves in Elk Hills, California, and Teapot Dome, Wyoming. The scandal came to light after Harding's death from a heart attack in 1923. Fall eventually served a year in jail, and the reputation of the Harding administration never recovered.

📖──│Read the **Document**   **Executive Orders and Senate Resolutions on Teapot Dome**

During the administration of William H. Taft, the U.S. government had set aside tracts of oil-rich land to be held in reserve for the U.S. Navy, to be used in case of national emergency. The land was under the control and discretion of the secretary of the Navy.

Vice President Calvin Coolidge assumed the presidency upon Harding's death, and his honesty and integrity quickly reassured the nation. Coolidge, born in Vermont of old Yankee stock, had first gained national attention in 1919 as governor of Massachusetts when he had dealt firmly with a Boston police strike by declaring, "There is no right to strike against the public safety by anybody, anywhere, any time." A reserved, reticent man, Coolidge became famous for his epigrams, which contemporaries mistook for wisdom. "The business of America is business," he proclaimed. "The man who builds a factory builds a temple; the man who works there worships there." Consistent with this philosophy, he believed his duty was simply to preside benignly, not govern the nation. "Four-fifths of all our troubles in this life would disappear," he said, "if we would just sit down and be still." Calvin Coolidge, one observer noted, "aspired to become the least President the country ever had; he attained his desire." Satisfied with the prosperity of the mid-1920s, the people responded favorably. Coolidge was elected to a full term by a wide margin in 1924.

When Coolidge announced in 1927 that he did not "choose to run," Herbert Hoover became the Republican choice to succeed him. By far the ablest GOP leader of the decade, Hoover epitomized the American myth of the self-made man. Orphaned as a boy, he had worked his way through Stanford University and had gained both wealth and fame as a mining engineer. During World War I, he had displayed admirable administrative skills in directing Wilson's food program at home and relief activities abroad. Sober, intelligent, and immensely hardworking, Hoover embodied the nation's faith in individualism and free enterprise.

As secretary of commerce under Harding and Coolidge, he had sought cooperation between government and business. He used his office to assist American manufacturers and exporters in expanding their overseas trade, and he strongly supported a trade association movement to encourage cooperation rather than cutthroat competition among smaller American companies. He did not view business and government as antagonists. Instead, he saw them as partners, working together to achieve efficiency and affluence for all Americans. His optimistic view of the future led him to declare in his speech accepting the Republican presidential nomination in 1928 that "we in America today are nearer to the final triumph over poverty than ever before in the history of any land."

Republican Policies

During the 1920 campaign, Warren Harding urged a return to "not heroism, but healing, not nostrums, but normalcy." Misreading his speechwriter's "normality," he coined a new word that became the theme for the Republican administrations of the 1920s. Aware that the public was tired of zealous reform-minded presidents such as Teddy Roosevelt and Woodrow Wilson, Harding and his successors sought a return to traditional Republican policies. In some areas they were successful, but in others the Republican leaders were forced to adjust to the new realities of a mass production society. The result was a mixture of traditional and innovative measures that was neither wholly reactionary nor entirely progressive.

The most obvious attempt to go back to the Republicanism of William McKinley came in tariff and tax policy. Fearful of a flood of postwar European imports, Congress passed an emergency tariff act in 1921 and followed it a year later with the protectionist Fordney-McCumber Tariff Act. The net effect was to raise the basic rates substantially over the moderate Underwood Tariff schedules of the Wilson period.

Secretary of the Treasury Andrew Mellon, a wealthy Pittsburgh banker and industrialist, worked hard to achieve a similar return to normalcy in taxation. Condemning the high wartime tax rates on businesses and wealthy individuals, Mellon pressed for repealing an excess profits tax on corporations and slashing personal rates on the very rich. Using the new budget system adopted by Congress in 1921, he reduced government spending from its World War I peak of $18 billion to just over $3 billion by 1925, thereby creating a slight surplus. Congress responded in 1926 by cutting the highest income tax bracket to a modest 20 percent.

The revenue acts of the 1920s greatly reduced the burden of taxation; by the end of the decade, the government was collecting one-third less than it had in 1921, and the number of people paying income taxes dropped from more than 6.5 million to 4 million. Yet the greatest relief went to the wealthy. The public was shocked to learn in the 1930s that J. P. Morgan, Jr. and his nineteen partners had paid no income tax at all during the depths of the Great Depression.

The growing crisis in American farming during the decade forced the Republican administrations to seek new solutions. The end of the European war led to a sharp decline in farm prices and a return to the problem of overproduction. Southern and western lawmakers formed a farm bloc in Congress to press for special legislation for American agriculture. The farm bloc supported the higher tariffs, which included protection for constituents' crops, and helped secure passage of legislation to create federal supervision over stockyards, packinghouses, and grain trading.

This special-interest legislation failed to get at the root of overproduction, however. Farmers then supported more controversial measures designed to raise domestic crop prices by having the government sell the surplus overseas at low world prices. Coolidge vetoed the legislation on grounds that it involved unwarranted government interference in the economy.

Yet the government's role in the economy increased rather than lessened in the 1920s. Republicans widened the scope of federal activity and nearly doubled the ranks of government employees. Herbert Hoover led the way in the Commerce Department, establishing new bureaus to help make American industry more efficient in housing, transportation, and mining. Under his leadership, the government encouraged corporations to develop welfare programs that undercut trade unions, and he tried to minimize labor disturbances by devising new federal machinery to mediate disputes. Instead of going back to the laissez-faire tradition of the nineteenth century, the Republican administrations of the 1920s were pioneering a close relationship between government and private business.

The Divided Democrats

While the Republicans ruled in the 1920s, the Democrats seemed bent on self-destruction. The Wilson coalition fell apart in 1920 as pent-up dissatisfaction stemming from the war enabled Harding to win by a landslide. The pace of the second Industrial Revolution and the growing urbanization split the party in two. One faction was centered in the rural South and West. Traditional Democrats who had supported Wilson stood for Prohibition, fundamentalism, the Klan, and other facets of the rural counterattack against the city. In contrast, a new breed of Democrat was emerging in the metropolitan areas of the North and Midwest. Immigrants and their descendants began to become active in the Democratic party. Catholic or Jewish in religion and strongly opposed to Prohibition, they had little in common with their rural counterparts.

The split within the party surfaced dramatically at the national convention in New York in 1924. Held in Madison Square Garden, a hall built in the 1890s and too small and cramped for the more than one thousand delegates, the convention soon degenerated into what one observer described as a "snarling, cursing, tenuous, suicidal, homicidal roughhouse." City slickers mocked the "rubes and hicks" from the "sticks"; populist orators struck back by denouncing the city as "wanting in national ideals, devoid of conscience ... rooted in corruption, directed by greed, and dominated by selfishness." An urban resolution to condemn the Ku Klux Klan led to a spirited response from the rural faction and its defeat by a single vote. Then for nine days, in the midst of a stifling heat wave, the delegates divided between Alfred E. Smith, the governor of New York, and William G. McAdoo of California, Wilson's secretary of the treasury. When it became clear that neither the city nor the rural candidate could win a majority, both men withdrew; on the 103rd ballot, the weary Democrats finally chose John W. Davis, a former West Virginia congressman and New York corporation lawyer, as their compromise nominee.

In the ensuing election, the conservative Davis had difficulty setting his views apart from those of Republican president Calvin Coolidge. For the discontented, Senator Robert La Follette of Wisconsin offered an alternative by running on an independent Progressive Party ticket. Coolidge won easily, receiving 15 million votes to 8 million for Davis and nearly 5 million for La Follette. Davis had made the poorest showing of any Democratic candidate in the twentieth century.

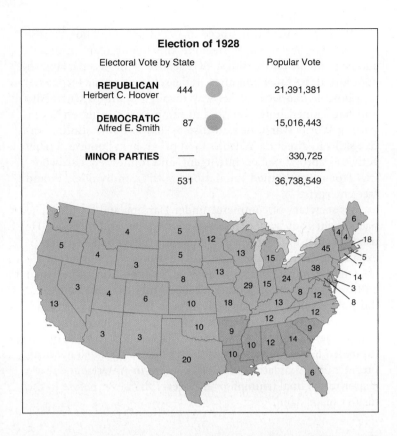

THE ELECTION OF 1924

Candidate	Party	Popular Vote	Electoral Vote
Coolidge	Republican	15,725,016	382
Davis	Democrat	8,386,503	136
La Follette	Progressive	4,822,856	13

Yet the Democrats were in far better shape than this setback indicated. Beginning in 1922, the party had made heavy inroads into the GOP majority in Congress. The Democrats took seventy-eight seats away from the Republicans in that election, many of them in the cities of the East and Midwest. In New York alone, they gained thirteen new congressmen, all but one in districts with heavy immigrant populations. Even in 1924, the Republican vote in large cities declined as many urban voters chose La Follette in the absence of an attractive Democratic candidate. In 1926, the Democrats came within one vote of controlling the Senate and picked up nine more seats in the House in metropolitan areas. The large cities were swinging clearly into the Democratic column; all the party needed was a charismatic leader who could fuse the older rural elements with the new urban voters.

The Election of 1928

The selection of Al Smith as the Democratic candidate in 1928 indicated the growing power of the city. Born on the Lower East Side of Manhattan of mixed Irish-German ancestry, Smith was the prototype of the urban Democrat. He was Catholic; he was associated with a big-city machine; he was a "wet" who wanted to end Prohibition. Starting out in the Fulton Fish Market as a boy, he had joined Tammany Hall and gradually climbed the political ladder, rising from subpoena server to state legislator to governor, a post he held with distinction for nearly a decade. Rejected by rural Democrats in 1924, he still had to prove he could unite the South and West behind his leadership. His lack of education, poor grammar, and distinctive New York accent all hurt him, as did his eastern provincialism. When reporters asked him about his appeal in the states west of the Mississippi, he replied, "What states are west of the Mississippi?"

The choice facing the American voter in 1928 seemed unusually clear-cut. Herbert Hoover was a Protestant, a dry, and an old-stock American, who stood for efficiency and individualism; Smith was a Catholic, a wet, and a descendant of immigrants, who was closely associated with big-city politics. Just as Smith appealed to new voters in the cities, so Hoover won the support of many old-line Democrats who feared the city, Tammany Hall, and the pope.

Yet beneath the surface, as Allan J. Lichtman points out, there were "striking similarities between Smith and Hoover." Both were self-made men who embodied the American belief in freedom of opportunity and upward mobility. Neither advocated any significant degree of economic change nor any redistribution of national wealth or power. Though religion proved to be the most important issue in the minds of the voters, hurting Smith far more than prohibition or his identification with the city, the Democratic candidate's failure to spotlight the growing cracks in prosperity or to offer alternative economic policies ensured his defeat.

The 1928 election was a dubious victory for the Republicans. Hoover won easily, defeating Smith by more than six million votes and carrying such traditionally Democratic states as Oklahoma, Texas, and Florida. But Smith succeeded for the first time in winning a majority of votes for the Democrats in the nation's twelve largest cities. A new Democratic electorate was emerging, consisting of Catholics and Jews, Irish and Italians, Poles and Greeks. Now the task was to unite the traditional Democrats of the South and West with the urban voters of the Northeast and Midwest.

Conclusion: The Old and the New

The election-night celebrations at Hoover campaign headquarters were muted by Prohibition and by the president-elect's natural reserve. Had Hoover known what lay just ahead for the country, and for his presidency, no doubt the party would have been even more somber.

During the 1920s, America struggled to enter the modern era. The economics of mass production and the politics of urbanization drove the country forward, but the persistent appeal of individualism and rural-based values held it back. Americans achieved greater prosperity than ever before, but the prosperity was unevenly distributed. Further, as the outbursts of nativism, ethnic and racial bigotry, and intolerance revealed, prosperity hardly guaranteed generosity or unity. Nor, for that matter, did it guarantee continued prosperity, even for those who benefited initially. As much as America changed during the 1920s, in one crucial respect the country remained as before. The American economy, for all its remarkable productive capacity, was astonishingly fragile. This was the message Hoover was soon to learn.

Watch the Video   Prosperity of the 1920s and the Great Depression

The development of mile-long breadlines in cities and towns throughout the country following the onset of the Great Depression in 1929 symbolized the crushing end of the prosperity of the 1920s.

Law and Society

The Scopes "Monkey" Trial
Contesting Cultural Differences

During the postwar 1920s, a "new" America emerged. Largely urban, secular, and focused on the future, the "modern" culture challenged the traditional values and familiar way of life of many Americans, especially those living in rural areas. Intense cultural conflict characterized the decade. Those who saw in modern culture numerous threats to the moral fabric of the nation increasingly turned to their faith for stability and comfort. The popularity of Protestant fundamentalism, which held to a literal interpretation of the Bible, increased dramatically during this period, particularly in the South. According to fundamentalists, one of the key modernist attacks on traditional religious beliefs came from the realm of science.

Advancements in science in the late nineteenth and early twentieth centuries fueled modernization, and Americans increasingly placed their faith in the authority of science and progress. There was growing acceptance of Charles Darwin's theory of evolution, which demonstrated that plants and animals—including humans—evolved from lower life forms by a process of natural selection. By the 1920s, discussion of evolution theory had entered public school classrooms. Though many Americans could reconcile a belief in evolution with their religious beliefs, fundamentalists thought the theory of evolution contradicted the Biblical story of creation and was therefore blasphemous—particularly the notion that humans evolved from a lower primate form. Fundamentalists led a charge against evolution, particularly against its teaching in the schools, and several southern states turned to

legislation to keep the scientific theory out of the classroom.

Such a law was introduced in Tennessee by John W. Butler, a state representative. The statute passed both houses of the Tennessee legislature by a large majority and was signed into law by the governor in March 1925. The Butler Act, as it became known, made it unlawful for a teacher in state-supported schools "to teach any theory that denies the story of Divine Creation of man as taught in the Bible, and to teach instead that man has descended from a lower order of animals." Violating the law was designated a misdemeanor punishable by a fine of $100 to $500 for each offense.

In response to the Butler Act, the American Civil Liberties Union (ACLU) advertised for teachers in Tennessee willing to challenge the new law in court. Civic boosters in Dayton, eager to draw attention to their small town in eastern Tennessee, persuaded John Scopes, a science teacher and assistant football coach in Dayton, to accept the ACLU offer. Scopes was a logical choice. He opposed the antievolution law on philosophical grounds, and he had little to lose personally, being twenty-four and single and with no particular desire to remain in Dayton. Furthermore, he was a likable young man, popular around town and with otherwise conventional views, and so wouldn't muddy the legal waters by provoking the judge or jury unnecessarily. Scopes admitted that anyone teaching from the state's approved biology textbook, Hunter's *Civic Biology*, which included sections on evolution of animals and humans, would be breaking the new law. Scopes had used the text as a substitute biology teacher. He agreed to be arrested to test the law in court.

From the start, *Tennessee* v. *John Thomas Scopes* was about far more than Scopes. Supporters and opponents of the antievolution law converged on Dayton from around the country. The law's supporters brought in the renowned orator William Jennings Bryan, a three-time Democratic nominee for president, former secretary of state, and fervent Christian fundamentalist, to assist the prosecution, headed by chief prosecutor A. Thomas Stewart, attorney general of Tennessee. Since the early 1920s Bryan had led the charge against the theories of Charles Darwin and the teaching of evolution in the schools; his syndicated newspaper column, "Weekly Bible Talks," frequently hammered Darwinism and what Bryan considered excessive faith in science.

The ACLU summoned counsel for the defense and Clarence Darrow, one of the most celebrated trial lawyers in America in the 1920s, volunteered his services as the chief defense attorney. He delighted in defending unpopular causes, including labor activists (he had defended socialist leader Eugene V. Debs in the Pullman strike of 1894), political radicals, and murder suspects. He was also an outspoken agnostic, doubting the existence of God, and a vocal critic of Christian fundamentalists, including Bryan.

A small army of reporters descended upon Dayton, including journalist H. L. Mencken, widely known for his biting wit and disdain for middle America, who was writing for the *Baltimore Sun* and the *American Mercury*. From all over America and from various foreign countries the journalists came, eager to convey to their readers every detail of "the Monkey trial," as the trial was dubbed. The new technology of radio supplemented the newspaper

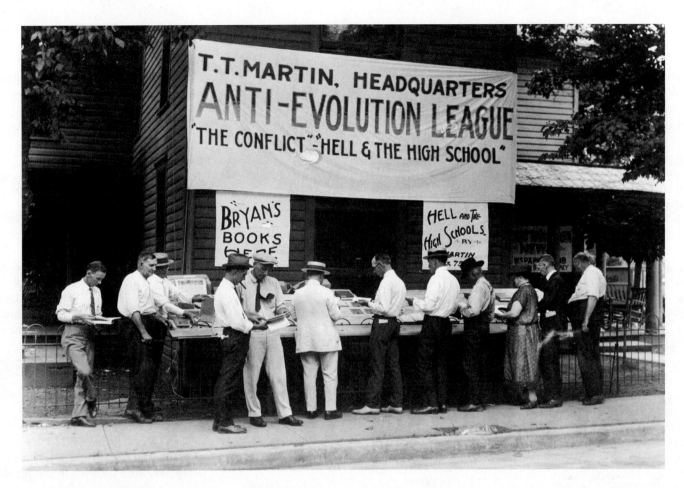

coverage, especially after Judge John Raulston agreed to allow microphones in the courtroom.

The proceedings opened on Friday, July 10. To the prosecution, the case was fairly simple. They held that the state had the constitutional right to set the curriculum in state-funded schools. The question to be decided was whether Scopes had violated the Butler Act by covering the theory of evolution in his classroom. Prosecution witnesses, including a school official and several of Scopes's students, testified that he had.

Darrow and the defense argued principally that the antievolution law violated several clauses of the Tennessee constitution as well as the guarantee of freedom of speech and provision for separation of church and state in the First Amendment of the U.S. Constitution. Contending that the law also violated the Fourteenth Amendment's declaration that no state was permitted to pass a law that abridged citizens' privileges, Darrow argued, "If today you can take a thing like evolution and make it a crime to teach it in the public school, tomorrow you can make it a crime to teach it in the private schools, and the next year you can make it a crime to teach it to the hustings or in the church."

Darrow and the defense team wanted to introduce scientific evidence supporting the theory of evolution by summoning a number of scientists from various fields as expert witnesses. The prosecution protested opening the case to this wider issue. "I say, bar the door and not allow science to enter," declared Stewart, the chief prosecutor. After hearing arguments from both sides and initial testimony from the defense's first witness, the court sided with Stewart and Tennessee. "The evidence of experts would shed no light on the issues," Judge Raulston ruled.

It was Bryan's speech for the prosecution that brought real excitement to the courtroom and the nationwide attention to Dayton that the city's supporters had hoped for. The Great Commoner, as Bryan was known, commenced softly, conveying an impression of calm reason. But as he warmed to his subject, his voice rose and his words became more intense. He denied that he or most of the citizens of Tennessee advocated teaching the Bible in schools. And even if they did advocate it, the Tennessee constitution prevented them. The question at hand was different, Bryan said.

The question is, can a minority in this state come in and compel a teacher to teach that the Bible is not true, and make the parents of these children pay the expenses of the teacher to tell their children what these people believe is false and dangerous? Has it come to a time when the minority can take charge of a state like Tennessee and compel the majority to pay their teachers while they take religion out of the heart of the children of the parents who pay the teachers?

Bryan was a master at working an audience, and the jurors and spectators in the courtroom—and a larger group listening in the yard outside the court—hung on his every word. They laughed as he lampooned the Darwinians; they nodded agreement as he affirmed the teachings of the Bible. They thundered their approval of his wry observation: "The Christian believes that man came from above, but the evolutionist believes he must have come from below." Following a loud "Amen!" from the audience, Darrow, who had been sitting silently through Bryan's long speech, interjected: "I hope the reporters got the amens in the record. I want somewhere, at some point, to find some court where a picture of this will be painted." Such information in the official record would ensure higher courts a more complete picture of the atmosphere in the courtroom.

Denied the opportunity to call on expert witnesses to provide support for the theory of evolution, Darrow found another opportunity after the defense made an unusual request to place Bryan on the witness stand. There was some question as to whether Bryan could or should testify, as he had no firsthand knowledge of what Scopes had or hadn't done, and was no expert on the constitutions of Tennessee or the United States. But the defense asked permission to question Bryan as an expert witness on the Bible. Bryan indicated willingness and Judge Raulston—who relished the publicity the case was generating—let the two celebrities go at each other. What resulted was one of the most dramatic courtroom scenes in American history.

Darrow asked Bryan whether he had given "considerable study to the Bible." Bryan responded, "I have studied the Bible for about fifty years, or some time more than that...."

Given that opening, Darrow went on to ask questions designed to undermine a strictly literal interpretation of the Bible.

Darrow: Do you claim that everything in the Bible should be literally interpreted?

Bryan: I believe everything in the Bible should be accepted as it is given there. Some of the Bible is given illustratively. For instance: "Ye are the salt of the earth." I would not insist that man was actually salt, or that he had flesh of salt, but it is used in the sense of salt as saving God's people.

Darrow pressed on. Did Bryan believe that a whale swallowed Jonah?

Bryan: When I read that a big fish swallowed Jonah—it does not say whale—

Darrow: Doesn't it? Are you sure?

Bryan: That is my recollection of it. A big fish, and I believe it, and I believe in a God who can make a whale and can make a man and make both do what He pleases.

Darrow continued his line of questioning, asking Bryan to interpret other passages of the Bible. Had Joshua really made the sun stand still?

Bryan: I believe what the Bible says.

Did that mean that the sun actually stood still, or that the Earth stopped spinning? For that matter, did Mr. Bryan believe that the Earth circled the sun, or vice versa?

Bryan assured Darrow and the court that he knew that the Earth orbited the sun. But he allowed that the author of the Joshua passage might not have. "I believe that the Bible is inspired, an inspired author. Whether one who wrote as he was directed to write understood the things he was writing about, I don't know." Darrow interrupted, but Bryan went on: "I believe it was inspired by the Almighty, and He may have used language that could be understood at that time—instead of using language that could not be understood until Darrow was born."

Listeners, siding with Bryan but squirming under Darrow's questioning, broke into loud applause here. When the applause recurred, Darrow said sarcastically, "Great applause from the bleachers."

Bryan: From those whom you call "yokels."

Darrow: I have never called them yokels.

The exchange grew nastier.

Bryan: Those are the people whom you insult.

Darrow: You insult every man of science and learning in the world because he does not believe in your fool religion.

Judge Raulston: I will not stand for that.

Darrow: For what he is doing?

Judge Raulston: I am talking to both of you.

Such dignity as the trial initially possessed had disappeared by now. After the exchange continued for some time, Darrow asked Bryan if he had ever wondered where Cain's wife came from. "No, sir," Bryan replied. "I leave the agnostics to hunt for her." Darrow asked Bryan if the six days of creation were twenty-four-hour days. Bryan allowed that they might have been longer.

Finally Tom Stewart broke into Darrow's questioning. "What is the purpose of this examination?" the chief prosecutor demanded.

"The purpose is to cast ridicule on everybody who believes in the Bible," Bryan asserted.

Darrow answered differently. "We have the purpose of preventing bigots and ignoramuses from controlling the education of the United States."

Darrow was allowed to continue his questioning about creation. Might it have lasted more than a modern week? Bryan granted that it could have. How much more? "It might have continued for millions of years."

Darrow's examination of Bryan lasted two hours. Before the end it was obvious that it had little to do with the case at hand—but everything to do with the larger issue joined by Darrow and Bryan. As a reporter for the *Nashville Banner* explained, "In reality, it was a debate between Darrow and Bryan on Biblical history, on agnosticism and belief in revealed religion."

Not surprisingly, judgments regarding the outcome of the debate depended on the source of those judgments. The *New York Times* thought Darrow scored a clear victory. "Mr. Bryan's complete lack of interest in many of the things closely connected with such religious questions as he had been supporting for many years was strikingly shown again and again by Mr. Darrow," the *Times* explained. The Memphis *Commercial Appeal* thought Bryan had held his own: "Darrow succeeded in showing that Bryan knows little about the science of the world. Bryan succeeded in bearing witness bravely to the faith which he believes transcends all the learning of men."

The reaction to the trial's verdict was similar. Scopes, to no one's surprise, was convicted of violating the law and Judge Raulston fined him $100. Even Darrow, intending to appeal the verdict to a higher court, recommended that the jury find Scopes guilty. Antievolutionists in Tennessee and elsewhere took the conviction as vindication of their beliefs. But to many Americans with more secular views, the conviction was simply further evidence of the wrongheadedness of Bryan and the Tennessee legislature. When Bryan died suddenly just five days after the trial ended, a southern journalist approached Darrow for comment. "People down here believe that Bryan died of a broken heart because of your questioning," the journalist said. Darrow, referring to Bryan's notoriously large appetite, reportedly responded, "Broken heart nothing. He died of a busted belly." H. L. Mencken remarked, "God aimed at Darrow, missed, and hit Bryan instead."

The Scopes trial settled nothing. The defense appealed the conviction to the Tennessee Supreme Court, where it was set aside on a technicality. But the antievolution law was left intact, and stood for another forty years, until the Tennessee legislature repealed it in 1967. In the immediate aftermath of the Scopes trial, both sides claimed moral victory, and the rift that gave rise to the case simply grew wider. Fundamentalism was discredited in large parts of urban America, but it sank roots in the rural regions of the country, becoming stronger than ever, if sometimes less visible. Several state legislatures considered antievolution bills in the latter half of the 1920s, but only Georgia and Mississippi actually passed laws restricting teaching of Darwin's theory. Concern over diminishing sales in the South and West, however, drove textbook publishers to revise coverage of evolution in many textbooks—deemphasizing the topic or eliminating it entirely. With or without legislation opposing its teaching, evolution did disappear from many classrooms.

In 1960, the liberal *New Republic* declared, "The Monkey Trial is now a historical curiosity"—a judgment that proved premature when evolution reemerged as a controversial issue. The constitutional question of whether the First Amendment permitted states to ban teaching of a theory that contradicted religious beliefs had not been resolved by the Scopes case. In the 1968 case *Epperson* v. *Arkansas*,

however, the U.S. Supreme Court ruled that such bans were unconstitutional. During the 1970s and 1980s various Sunbelt school districts mandated that "creationism"—essentially the Biblical version of life's origins, though typically without the explicit references to Genesis—be given equal time in the classroom with evolution. Arkansas and Louisiana passed such laws, but in 1987 the U.S. Supreme Court ruled in *Edwards* v. *Aguillard* that these laws were also unconstitutional. Still the issue refused to die. In 1999, the Kansas school board ordered that the theory of evolution should be deemphasized in the state's classrooms. The Kansas board eventually changed its mind, but in 2005 it reversed course again, directing teachers to point out the deficiencies in the theory of evolution, in the name of "intelligent design," the latest variant of creationism. Other states considered similar measures, demonstrating, if nothing else, that the Scopes trial was far more than a curiosity from the past.

QUESTIONS FOR DISCUSSION

1. Why did different observers interpret the outcome of the Scopes trial so differently?

2. Why does the issue of evolution in the public schools continue to resurface decades after laws banning its teaching were found unconstitutional?

Study Resources

TIME LINE

1919 U.S. agents arrest 1,700 in Red Scare raids; Eighteenth Amendment (Prohibition) ratified

1920 Nineteenth Amendment passed, granting women the right to vote

1922 Fordney-McCumber tariff becomes law; T. S. Eliot publishes *The Waste Land*

1923 Newspapers expose Ku Klux Klan graft, torture, and murder

1924 Senate probes Teapot Dome scandal; National Origins Quota Act restricts immigration from Europe and bans immigration from Asia

1925 John Scopes convicted of teaching theory of evolution in violation of Tennessee law (July)

1927 Charles Lindbergh completes first nonstop transatlantic flight from New York to Paris (May); Sacco and Vanzetti executed (August); Babe Ruth hits 60th home run (September)

1928 Hoover defeats Smith for president

CHAPTER REVIEW

The Second Industrial Revolution

What was new about the American economy in the 1920s?

The American economy in the 1920s underwent a second industrial revolution. Powered by electricity and featuring the mass production of automobiles and other consumer goods, the second industrial revolution lifted the American standard of living to new heights. (p. 589)

City life in the Jazz Age

How did life in the cities change after World War I?

During the 1920s, the focus of American life shifted to the cities, which for the first time contained most of the American population. Women found new opportunities to express themselves, and sports, music, literature, and the arts flourished as never before. (p. 592)

The Rural Counterattack

How did conservatives resist the changes of the decade?

The changes of the 1920s alarmed many conservatives, who tried to resist them. The police and courts cracked down on radicals; prohibition outlawed liquor; the Ku Klux Klan attacked immigrants and minorities; Congress restricted immigration; and fundamentalist Christians decried the changing code of morality and the teaching of evolution in the schools. (p. 598)

Politics in the 1920s

How did the politics of the 1920s reflect changes in the economy and in American society?

The 1920s were a decade of Republican politics. Presidents Harding, Coolidge, and Hoover favored business and the wealthy. In the election of 1928, voters had a clear choice between Hoover, the candidate of the countryside and conservatism, and Al Smith, the candidate of the cities and change, Hoover won in a landslide. (p. 603)

KEY TERMS AND DEFINITIONS

Harlem Renaissance An African American cultural, literary, and artistic movement centered in Harlem, in New York City, in the 1920s. Harlem, the largest black community in the world outside of Africa, was considered the cultural capital of African Americans. p. 595

Red Scare A wave of anticommunist, antiforeign, and antilabor hysteria that swept over America in 1919. It resulted in the deportation of many alien residents and violated the civil liberties of many of its victims. p. 599

Prohibition The ban on the manufacture, sale, and transportation of alcoholic beverages in the United States. The Eighteenth Amendment, adopted in 1919, established prohibition. It was repealed by the Twenty-First Amendment in 1933. p. 600

Nativism Hostility to things foreign. p. 602

National Origins Quota Act This 1924 law established a quota system that restricted immigration from Asia and southern and Eastern Europe and reduced the annual total of immigrants. p. 603

Scopes Trial Also called the "monkey trial," the 1924 Scopes trial was a contest between modern liberalism and religious fundamentalism. John T. Scopes was prosecuted for teaching Darwinian evolution in defiance of Tennessee state law. He was found guilty and fined $100. Scopes's conviction was later set aside on a technicality. p. 603

Teapot Dome scandal A 1924 scandal in which Secretary of the Interior Albert Fall was convicted of accepting bribes in exchange for leasing government-owned oil lands in Wyoming (Teapot Dome) and California (Elks Hill) to private businessmen. p. 603

CRITICAL THINKING QUESTIONS

1. How did the automobile increase the independence of young people during the 1920s?

2. Why did the new opportunities for women upset conservatives?

3. What did the Red Scare and the desire for immigration reform have in common?

4. How did the presidential election of 1928 reflect the anxieties of the postwar era?

MyHistoryLab Media Assignments

Find these resources in the Media Assignments folder for Chapter 25 on MyHistoryLab

The Second Industrial Revolution

■ **View** the **Closer Look** The Great White Way – Times Square p. 591

City Life in the Jazz Age

■ **Read** the **Document** Elanor Rowland Wembridge, "Petting and the Campus" (1925) p. 594

■ **Complete** the **Assignment** Marcus Garvey: Racial Redemption and Black Nationalism p. 596

Read the **Document** Pearson Profiles, Marcus Garvey p. 594

■ **Watch** the **Video** Watch the Video: The Harlem Renaissance p. 598

The Rural Counterattack

Read the **Document** A. Mitchell Palmer on the Menace of Communism (1920) p. 599

Read the **Document** Court Statements from Sacco and Vanzetti p. 601

Read the **Document** Creed of Klanswomen (1924) p. 602

Politics of the 1920s

Read the **Document** Executive Orders and Senate Resolutions on Teapot Dome p. 604

■ **Watch** the **Video** Prosperity of the 1920s and the Great Depression p. 607

Complete the **Assignment** The Scopes "Monkey" Trial: Contesting Cultural Differences p. 608

■ Indicates Study Plan Media Assignment

26 Franklin D. Roosevelt and the New Deal

Contents and Learning Objectives Questions

((•●—[**Listen** to the **Audio File** on **myhistorylab**   Chapter 26 *Franklin D. Roosevelt and the New Deal*

The Struggle Against Despair

Oscar Heline never forgot the terrible waste of the Great Depression. "Grain was being burned," he told interviewer Studs Terkel. "It was cheaper than coal." Heline lived in Iowa, in the heart of the farm belt. "A county just east of here, they burned corn in their courthouse all winter.... You couldn't hardly buy groceries for corn." Farmers, desperate for higher prices, resorted to destruction. As Heline recalled, "People were determined to withhold produce from the market—livestock, cream, butter, eggs, what not. If they would dump the produce, they would force the market to a higher level. The farmers would man the highways, and cream cans were emptied in ditches and eggs dumped out. They burned the trestle bridge, so the trains wouldn't be able to haul grain."

Film critic Pauline Kael recounted a different memory of the 1930s. Kael was a college student in California during the Great Depression, and was struck by the number of students who were missing fathers. "They had wandered off in disgrace because they couldn't support their families. Other fathers had killed themselves, so the family could have the insurance. Families had totally broken down." Kael and many of her classmates struggled to stay in school. "There were kids who didn't have a place to sleep, huddling under bridges on the campus. I had a scholarship, but there were times when I didn't have any food. The meals were often three candy bars."

Howard Worthington resorted to trickery after losing his job in Chicago. One Easter Sunday during the depression, when his son was four years old, Worthington couldn't afford enough eggs for a proper egg hunt. So he devised a plan. "I hid a couple in the piano and all around. Tommy got his little Easter basket, and as he would find the eggs, I'd steal 'em out of the basket and rehide them.... He hunted Easter eggs for three hours and he never knew the difference."

N o American who lived through the Great Depression ever forgot the experience. As the stories of Heline, Kael, and Worthington show, the individual memories were of hard times, but also of determination, adaptation, and survival.

The depression decade had an equally profound effect on American institutions. To cope with the problems of poverty and dislocation, Americans looked to government as never before, and in doing so transformed American politics and public life. The agent of the transformation—the man America turned to in its moment of trial—was Franklin D. Roosevelt. His answer to the country's demands for action was an ambitious program of relief and reform called the **New Deal**.

The Great Depression

What were the causes and effects of the Great Depression?

The depression of the 1930s came as a shock to Americans who had grown used to the prosperity of the 1920s. The consumer revolution of that earlier decade had fostered a general confidence that the American way of life would continue to improve. But following the collapse of the stock market in late 1929, factories

During the Great Depression, market prices for produce were so low that farmers could scarcely afford to harvest their crops. Many resorted to destroying produce in an attempt to limit supplies and force prices higher, such as these striking dairy farmers in Illinois dumping cans of milk into the street.

closed, machines fell silent, and millions of Americans walked the streets looking for jobs that didn't exist.

The Great Crash

The consumer goods revolution contained the seeds of its own demise. The productive capacity of the automobile and appliance industries grew faster than the effective demand. Each year after 1924, the rate of increase in the sale of cars and refrigerators and ranges slowed, a natural consequence as more and more people already owned these durable goods. Production began to falter, and in 1927, the nation underwent a mild recession. The sale of durable goods declined, and construction of houses and buildings fell slightly. If corporate leaders had heeded these warning signs, they might have responded by raising wages or lowering prices, both effective ways to stimulate purchasing power and sustain the consumer goods revolution. Or if government officials had

recognized the danger signals and forced a halt in installment buying and slowed bank loans, the nation might have experienced a sharp but brief depression.

Neither government nor business leaders were so farsighted. The Federal Reserve Board lowered the discount rate, charging banks less for loans in an attempt to stimulate the economy. Much of this additional credit, however, went not into solid investment in factories and machinery but instead into the stock market, touching off a new wave of speculation that obscured the growing economic slowdown and ensured a far greater crash to come.

Individuals with excess cash began to invest heavily in the stock market, betting the already impressive rise in security prices would bring them even greater windfall profits. The market had advanced in spurts during the decade; the value of all stocks listed on the New York Stock Exchange rose from $27 billion in 1925 to $67 billion in early 1929. The strongest surge began in the spring of 1928, when investors ignored the declining production figures in

View the **Map** The Great Depression

U.S. UNEMPLOYMENT, 1929–1942

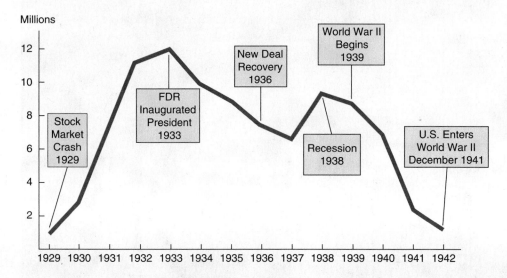

the belief they could make a killing in the market. People bet their savings on speculative stocks. Corporations used their large cash reserves to supply money to brokers who in turn loaned it to investors on margin; in 1929, for example, the Standard Oil Company of New Jersey loaned out $69 million a day in this fashion.

Investors could now play the market on credit, buying stock listed at $100 a share with $10 down and $90 on margin, the broker's loan for the balance. If the stock advanced to $150, the investor could sell and reap a gain of 500 percent on the $10 investment. And in the bull market climate of the 1920s, everyone was sure the market would go up.

By 1929, it seemed the whole nation was engaged in speculation. In city after city, brokers opened branch offices, each complete with a stock ticker and a huge board covered with the latest Wall Street quotations. People crowded into the customers' rooms in the offices, filling the seats and greeting the latest advances of their favorite stocks with shouts of approval. So great was the public's interest in the stock market that newspapers carried the stock averages on their front pages.

In reality, though, more people were spectators than speculators; fewer than three million Americans owned stocks in 1929, and only about a half million were active buyers and sellers. But the bull market became a national obsession, assuring everyone that the economy was healthy and preventing any serious analysis of its underlying flaws. When the market soared to more than $80 billion in total value by mid-summer, the *Wall Street Journal* discounted any possibility of a decline, proclaiming, "The outlook for the fall months seems brighter than at any time."

And then things changed, almost overnight. On October 24—later known as Black Thursday—the rise in stock prices faltered, and when it did investors nervously began to sell. Such leading stocks as RCA and Westinghouse plunged, losing nearly half their value in a single day. Speculators panicked as their creditors demanded new collateral, and the panic caused prices to plummet still further.

Within weeks the gains of the previous two years had vanished.

The great crash of the stock market soon spilled over into the larger economy. Banks and other financial institutions suffered heavy losses in the market and were forced to curtail lending for consumer purchases. As consumers came up short, factories cut back production, laying off some workers and reducing hours for others. The layoffs and cutbacks lowered purchasing power even further, so fewer people bought cars and appliances. More factory layoffs resulted, and some plants closed entirely, leading to the availability of even less money for the purchase of consumer goods.

This downward economic spiral continued for four years. By 1932, unemployment had swelled to 25 percent of the workforce. Steel production was down to 12 percent of capacity, and the vast assembly lines in Detroit produced only a trickle of cars each day. The gross national product fell to 67 percent of the 1929 level. The bright promise of mass production had ended in a nightmare.

The basic explanation for the Great Depression lies in the fact that U.S. factories produced more goods than the American people could consume. The problem was not that the market for such products was fully saturated. In 1929, there were still millions of Americans who did not own cars or radios or refrigerators, but many of them could not afford the new products. There were other contributing causes—unstable economic conditions in Europe, the agricultural decline since 1919, corporate mismanagement, and excessive speculation—but it all came down to the fact that people did not have enough money to buy the consumer products coming off the assembly lines. Installment sales helped bridge the gap, but by 1929 the burden of debt was just too great.

The new economic system had failed to distribute wealth more broadly. Too much money had gone into profits, dividends, and industrial expansion, and not enough had gone into the hands of the workers, who were also consumers. Factory productivity had increased 43 percent during the decade, but the wages of industrial workers had gone up only 11 percent. If the billions that went into stock market speculation had been used instead to increase wages—which would then have increased consumer purchasing power—production and consumption could have been brought into balance. Yet it is too much to expect that the prophets of the new era could have foreseen this flaw and corrected it. They were pioneering a new industrial system, and only out of the bitter experience of the Great Depression would they discover the full dynamics of the consumer goods economy.

Effect of the Depression

It is difficult to measure the human cost of the Great Depression. The material hardships were bad enough. Men and women lived in lean-tos made of scrap wood and metal, and families went without meat and fresh vegetables for months, existing on a diet of soup and beans. The psychological burden was even greater: Americans suffered through year after year of grinding poverty with no letup in sight. The unemployed stood in line for hours waiting for relief checks; veterans sold apples or pencils on street corners, their manhood—once prized so highly by the nation—now in question. People left the city for the countryside but found no salvation on the farm. Crops rotted in the fields because prices were too low to make harvesting worthwhile; sheriffs fended off angry crowds as banks foreclosed long-overdue mortgages on once prosperous farms.

Few escaped the suffering. African Americans who had left the poverty of the rural South for factory jobs in the North were among the first to be laid off. Mexican immigrants, who had flowed in to replace European immigrants, met with competition from angry citizens now willing to do stoop labor in the fields and work as track layers on the railroads. Immigration officials used technicalities to halt the flow across the Rio Grande and even to reverse it; nearly a half million Mexicans were deported in the 1930s, including families with children born in the United States.

The poor—black, brown, and white—survived because they knew better than most Americans how to exist in poverty. They stayed in bed in cold weather, both to keep warm and to avoid unnecessary burning up of calories; they patched their shoes with pieces of rubber from discarded tires, heated only

 View the **Closer Look**   Homeless Shantytown, Seattle, 1937

Urban shantytowns, often called "Hoovervilles," named after President Herbert Hoover, were built by homeless men and women during the Great Depression. These settlements were composed of shacks and tents and often constructed on empty urban land near soup kitchens.

Read the **Document** **Women on the Breadlines**

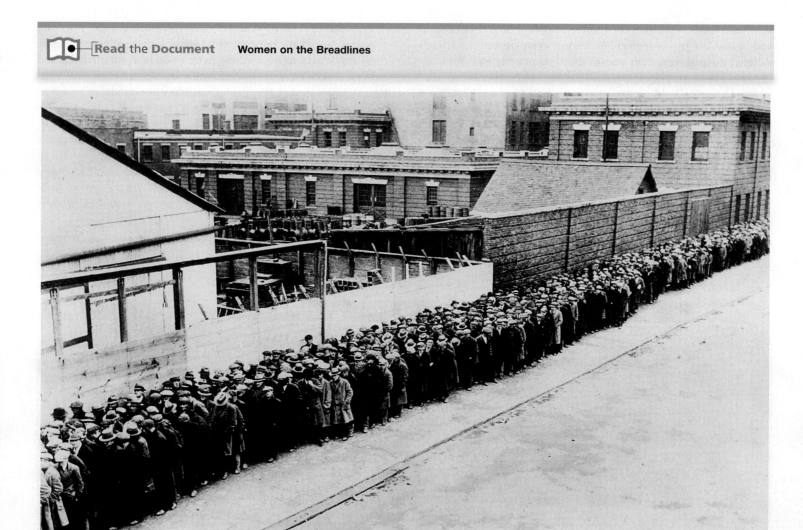

The Great Depression devastated millions who lost their jobs and often then the means to provide food and shelter for themselves and their families. Overwhelmed local and private charities could not keep up with the demands for assistance, and many looked to the federal government for direct relief from their suffering. Breadlines stretched as far as the eye could see as impoverished workers lined up in the hope of obtaining some meager rations for their hungry families.

the kitchens of their homes, and ate scraps of food that others would reject.

The middle class, which had always lived with high expectations, was hit hard. Professionals and white-collar workers refused to ask for charity even while their families went without food; one New York dentist and his wife turned on the gas and left a note saying, "We want to get out of the way before we are forced to accept relief money." People who fell behind in their mortgage payments lost their homes and then faced eviction when they could not pay the rent. Health care declined. Middle-class people stopped going to doctors and dentists regularly, unable to make the required cash payment in advance for services rendered.

Even the well-to-do were affected, giving up many of their former luxuries and weighed down with guilt as they watched former friends and business associates join the ranks of the impoverished. "My father lost everything in the depression" became an all-too-familiar refrain among young people who dropped out of college.

Many Americans sought escape in movement. Men, boys, and some women rode the rails in search of jobs, hopping freights to move south in the winter or west in the summer. On the Missouri Pacific alone, the number of vagrants increased from just over 13,000 in 1929 to nearly 200,000 in 1931. One town in the Southwest hired special police to keep vagrants from leaving the boxcars. Those who became tramps had to keep on the move, but they did find a sense of community in the hobo jungles that sprang up along the major railroad routes. Here the unfortunate could find a place to eat and sleep, and people with whom to share their misery. Louis Banks, a black veteran, told interviewer Studs Terkel what these informal camps were like:

Black and white, it didn't make any difference who you were, 'cause everybody was poor. All friendly, sleep in a jungle. We used to take a big pot and cook food, cabbage, meat and beans all together. We all set together, we made a tent. Twenty-five or thirty would be out on the side of the rail, white and colored: They didn't have no mothers or sisters, they didn't have no home, they were dirty, they had overalls on, they didn't have no food, they didn't have anything.

Fighting the Depression

How did Franklin Roosevelt fight the Depression?

The Great Depression presented an enormous challenge for American political leadership. The inability of the Republicans to overcome the economic catastrophe provided the Democrats with the chance to regain power. Although they failed to achieve full recovery before the outbreak of World War II, the Democrats did succeed in alleviating some of the suffering and establishing political dominance.

Hoover and Voluntarism

Herbert Hoover was the Great Depression's most prominent victim. When the economic downturn began in late 1929, he tried to rally the nation with bold forecasts of better days ahead. His repeated assertion that prosperity was just around the corner bred cynicism and mistrust. Expressing complete faith in the American economic system, Hoover blamed the depression on foreign causes, especially unstable European banks. The president rejected proposals for bold government action and relied instead on voluntary cooperation within business to halt the slide. He called the leaders of industry to the White House and secured their agreement to maintain prices and wages at high levels. Yet within a few months, employers were reducing wages and cutting prices in a desperate effort to survive.

Hoover also believed in voluntary efforts to relieve the human suffering brought about by the depression. He called on private charities and local governments to help feed and clothe those in need. But when these sources were exhausted, he rejected all requests for direct federal relief, asserting that such handouts would undermine the character of proud American citizens.

As the depression deepened, Hoover reluctantly began to move beyond voluntarism to undertake more sweeping government measures. A new Federal Farm Board loaned money to aid cooperatives and bought up surplus crops in the open market in a vain effort to raise farm prices. At Hoover's request, Congress cut taxes in an attempt to restore public confidence and adopted a few federal public works projects, such as Boulder (Hoover) Dam, to provide jobs for idle men.

To help imperiled banks and insurance companies, Hoover proposed the Reconstruction Finance Corporation (RFC), which Congress established in early 1932. The RFC loaned government money to financial institutions to save them from bankruptcy. Hoover's critics, however, pointed out that while he favored aid to business, he still opposed measures such as direct relief and massive public works that would help the millions of unemployed.

By 1932, Hoover's efforts to overcome the depression had clearly failed. The Democrats had gained control of the House of

Watch the Video   **Dorothea Lange and Migrant Mother**

Dorothea Lange was a documentary photographer whose work for the New Deal agencies, the Resettlement Administration (RA) and the Farm Security Administration (FSA), highlighted and sympathized with the plight of poor and displaced sharecroppers, farm families, and migrant worker families (above) during the Great Depression.

BANK FAILURES, 1929–1933

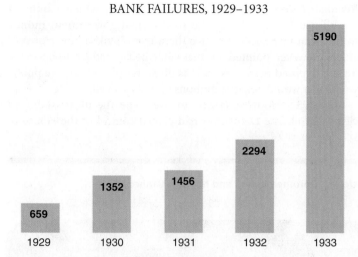

Source: Data compiled from C. D. Bremer, *American Bank Failures* (New York: Columbia University Press, 1935), p. 42.

Representatives in the 1930 elections and were pressing the president to take bolder action, but Hoover stubbornly resisted. His public image suffered its sharpest blow in the summer of 1932 when he ordered General Douglas MacArthur to clear out the **bonus army**. This ragged group of some twenty-two thousand World War I veterans had come to Washington in the summer of 1932 to lobby Congress to pay immediately a bonus for military service that was due them in 1945. After the Senate rejected the bonus bill, some of the veterans stayed in Washington, living in ramshackle huts in Anacostia Flats along the Potomac. Mounted troops drove the bonus army out of the capital, blinding the veterans with tear gas and burning their shacks.

Meanwhile, the nation's banking structure approached collapse. Bank failures rose steadily in 1931 and 1932 as customers responded to rumors of bankruptcy by rushing in to withdraw their deposits. The banking crisis completed the nation's disenchantment with Hoover; people were ready for a new leader in the White House.

The Emergence of Roosevelt

The man who came forward to meet this national need was Franklin D. Roosevelt. Born into the old Dutch colonial aristocracy of New York, FDR was a distant cousin of the Republican Teddy. He grew up with all the advantages of wealth: private tutors, his own sailboat and pony, frequent trips to Europe, and education at Groton and Harvard. His strong-willed mother smoothed all the obstacles in the path of her only child and gave him a priceless sense of inner security. After graduation from Harvard, he briefly attended law school but left to plunge into politics. He served in the New York legislature and then went to Washington as assistant secretary of the navy under Wilson, a post he filled capably during World War I. Defeated as the Democratic vice presidential candidate in 1920, Roosevelt had just begun a banking career when he suffered an attack of polio in the summer of 1921. Refusing to give in, he fought back bravely, and though he never again walked unaided, he reentered politics in the mid-1920s and was elected governor of New York in 1928.

Roosevelt's dominant trait was his ability to persuade and convince other people. He possessed a marvelous voice, deep and rich;

a winning smile; and a buoyant confidence he could easily transmit to others. Some believed he was too vain and superficial as a young man, but his bout with polio gave him both an understanding of human suffering and a broad political appeal as a man who had faced heavy odds and overcome them. He understood the give-and-take of politics, knew how to use flattery to win over doubters, and was especially effective in exploiting the media, whether in bantering with newspaper reporters or reaching out to the American people on the radio. Although his mind was quick and agile, he had little patience with philosophical nuances; he dealt with the appearance of issues, not their deeper substance, and he displayed a flexibility toward political principles that often dismayed even his warmest admirers.

Roosevelt took advantage of the opportunity offered by the Great Depression. With the Republicans discredited, he cultivated the two wings of the divided Democrats, appealing to both the traditionalists from the South and West and the new urban elements in the North. After winning the party's nomination in 1932, he broke with tradition by flying to Chicago and accepting in person, telling the cheering delegates, "I pledge you—I pledge myself to a new deal for the American people."

In the fall, he defeated Herbert Hoover in a near landslide for the Democrats. Roosevelt tallied 472 electoral votes as he swept the South and West and carried nearly all the large industrial states as well. Farmers and workers, Protestants and Catholics, immigrants and native born rallied behind the new leader who promised to restore prosperity. Roosevelt not only met the challenge of the depression but also solidified the shift to the Democratic Party and created an enduring coalition that would dominate American politics for a half century.

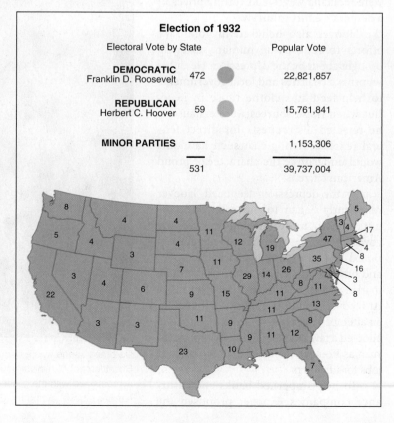

Election of 1932

	Electoral Vote by State		Popular Vote
DEMOCRATIC Franklin D. Roosevelt	472		22,821,857
REPUBLICAN Herbert C. Hoover	59		15,761,841
MINOR PARTIES	—		1,153,306
	531		39,737,004

PRESIDENTIAL VOTING IN CHICAGO BY ETHNIC GROUPS, 1924–1932 (PERCENTAGE DEMOCRATIC)

	1924	1928	1932
Czechoslovakians	40	73	83
Poles	35	71	80
Lithuanians	48	77	84
Yugoslavs	20	54	67
Italians	31	63	64
Germans	14	58	69
Jews	19	60	77

Source: John M. Allswang, *A House for All Peoples: Ethnic Politics in Chicago, 1890–1936* (Lexington: University of Kentucky Press, 1971).

The Hundred Days

When Franklin Roosevelt took the oath of office on March 4, 1933, the nation's economy was on the brink of collapse. Unemployment stood at nearly thirteen million, one-fourth of the labor force; banks were closed in thirty-eight states. On inauguration morning, the governors of New York and Illinois closed the banks in the nation's two largest cities, thus bringing the country's financial transactions to a halt. Speaking from the steps of the Capitol, FDR declared boldly, "First of all, let me assert my firm belief that the only thing we have to fear is fear itself—nameless, unreasoning, unjustified terror." Then he announced he would call Congress into special session and request "broad executive power to wage a war against the emergency, as great as the power that would be given to me if we were in fact invaded by a foreign foe."

Within the next ten days, Roosevelt won his first great New Deal victory by saving the nation's banks. On March 5, he issued a decree closing the banks and called Congress back into session. His aides drafted new banking legislation and presented it to Congress on March 9; a few hours later, both houses passed it, and FDR signed the new legislation that evening. The measure provided for government supervision and aid to the banks. Strong ones would be reopened with federal support, weak ones closed, and those in difficulty bolstered by government loans.

On March 12, FDR addressed the nation by radio in the first of his **fireside chats**. In conversational tones, he told the public what he had done. Some banks would begin to reopen the next day, with the government standing behind them. Other banks, once they became solvent, would open later, and the American

people could safely put their money back into these institutions. The next day, March 13, the nation's largest and strongest banks opened their doors; at the end of the day, customers had deposited more cash than they withdrew. The crisis was over; gradually, other banks opened, and the runs and failures ceased.

"Capitalism was saved in eight days," boasted one of Roosevelt's advisers. Most surprising was the conservative nature of FDR's action. Instead of nationalizing the banks, he had simply thrown the government's resources behind them and preserved private ownership. Though some other New Deal measures would be more radical, Roosevelt set a tone in the banking crisis. He was out to reform and restore the American economic system, not change it drastically. He drew on the progressive tradition and his experience with World War I mobilization to fashion a moderate program of government action.

For the next three months, until it adjourned in June, Congress responded to a series of presidential initiatives. During these "Hundred Days," Roosevelt sent fifteen major requests to Congress and received back fifteen pieces of legislation. A few created agencies that have become a part of American life. The **Tennessee Valley Authority (TVA)** was one of the most ambitious of Roosevelt's New Deal measures. This innovative effort at regional planning resulted in the building of a series of dams in seven states to control floods, ease navigation, and produce electricity.

Watch the Video   **FDR's Inauguration**

Franklin Roosevelt's presidential inaugural on March 4, 1933 marked the beginning of a frenzied and dramatic effort by the president and Congress to save the nation's economy and capitalism itself from complete collapse. President Roosevelt's inaugural speech offered a bold and optimistic confidence that Americans would recover from their desperate economic woes.

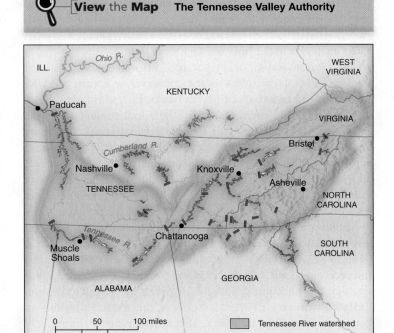

View the Map The Tennessee Valley Authority

THE TENNESSEE VALLEY AUTHORITY The Tennessee Valley Authority (TVA) served a seven-state region in the Southeast. Developing such a vast project required federal funding and management, both of which were provided through a federally owned corporation.

Although critics lamented the cost of the project and its impact on the environment and certain local communities, it went far toward bringing one of the most underdeveloped parts of the country into the modern era.

Other New Deal agencies were temporary in nature, designed to meet the specific economic problems of the depression. None were completely successful; the depression would continue for another six years, immune even to Roosevelt's magic. But psychologically, the nation turned the corner in the spring of 1933. Under FDR, the government seemed to be responding to the economic crisis, enabling people for the first time since 1929 to look to the future with hope.

Roosevelt and Recovery

Two major New Deal programs launched during the Hundred Days were aimed at industrial and agricultural recovery. The first was the **National Recovery Administration (NRA)**, FDR's attempt to achieve economic advance through planning and cooperation among government, business, and labor. In the midst of the depression, business owners were intent on stabilizing production and raising prices for their goods. Labor leaders were equally determined to spread work through maximum hours and to put a floor under workers' income with minimum wages.

The NRA hoped to achieve both goals by permitting companies in each major industry to cooperate in writing codes of fair competition that would set realistic limits on production, allocate percentages to individual producers, and set firm guidelines for prices. Section 7a of the enabling act mandated protection for labor in all the codes by establishing maximum

hours, minimum wages, and the guarantee of collective bargaining by unions. No company could be compelled to join, but the New Deal sought complete participation by appealing to patriotism. Each firm that took part could display a blue eagle and stamp the symbol on its products. With energetic Hugh Johnson in charge, the NRA quickly enrolled the nation's leading companies and unions. By the summer of 1933, more than five hundred industries had adopted codes that covered 2.5 million workers.

The NRA quickly bogged down in a huge bureaucratic morass. The codes proved to be too detailed to enforce easily. Written by the largest companies, the rules favored big business at the expense of smaller competitors. Labor quickly became disenchanted with Section 7a. The minimum wages were often near starvation level, while business avoided the requirement for collective bargaining by creating company unions that did not represent the real needs of workers. After a brief upsurge in the spring of 1933, industrial production began to sag as disillusionment with the NRA grew. By 1934, more and more business owners were complaining about the new agency, calling it the "National Run Around." When the Supreme Court finally invalidated the NRA in 1935 on constitutional grounds, few mourned its demise. The idea of trying to overcome the depression by relying on voluntary cooperation between competing businesses and labor leaders had collapsed in the face of individual self-interest and greed.

The New Deal's attempt at farm recovery fared a little better. Henry A. Wallace, FDR's secretary of agriculture, came up with an answer to the farmers' old dilemma of overproduction. The government would act as a clearinghouse for producers of major crops, arranging for them to set production limits for wheat, cotton, corn, and other leading crops. The **Agricultural Adjustment Administration (AAA)**, created by Congress in May 1933, would allocate acreage among individual farmers, encouraging them to take land out of production by paying them subsidies (raised by a tax on food processors). Unfortunately, Wallace preferred not to wait until the 1934 planting season to implement this program, and so farmers were paid in 1933 to plow under crops they had already planted and to kill livestock they were raising. Faced with the problem of hunger in the midst of plenty, the New Deal seemed to respond by destroying the plenty.

The AAA program worked better in 1934 and 1935 as land removed from production led to smaller harvests and rising farm prices. Farm income rose for the first time since World War I, increasing from $2 billion in 1933 to $5 billion by 1935. Severe weather, especially Dust Bowl conditions on the Great Plains, contributed to the crop-limitation program, but most of the gain in farm income came from the subsidy payments themselves rather than from higher market prices.

On the whole, large farmers benefited most from the program. Possessing the capital to buy machinery and fertilizer, they were able to farm more efficiently than before on fewer acres of land. Small farmers, tenants, and sharecroppers did not fare as well, receiving very little of the government payments and often being driven off the land as owners took the acreage previously cultivated by tenants and sharecroppers out of production. Some three million people left the land in the 1930s, crowding into the cities where they swelled the relief rolls. In the long run, the New Deal reforms improved the efficiency of American agriculture, but at a real human cost.

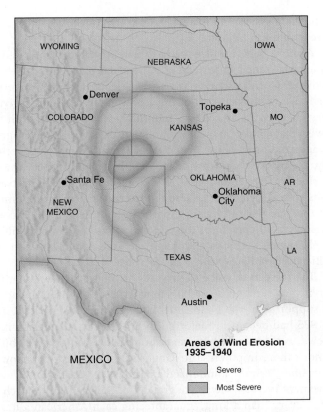

WYOMING

NEBRASKA

IOWA

• Denver

COLORADO

Topeka •

MO

KANSAS

• Santa Fe

OKLAHOMA

AR

NEW
MEXICO

Oklahoma
City •

TEXAS

LA

Austin •

**Areas of Wind Erosion
1935–1940**

Severe

Most Severe

MEXICO

THE DUST BOWL Drought and soil erosion brought on by overfarming turned the agricultural land of the Great Plains into a giant dust bowl during the 1930s. Especially hard hit were western Kansas and Oklahoma, eastern Colorado, and the Texas Panhandle. Giant dust storms forced many farmers to abandon their land.

The Supreme Court eventually found the AAA unconstitutional in 1936, but Congress reenacted it in modified form that year and again in 1938. The system of allotments, now financed directly by the government, became a standard feature of the farm economy. Other New Deal efforts to assist the rural poor, notably the Farm Security Administration (FSA), sought to loan money to tenants and sharecroppers so they could acquire land of their own, but the sums appropriated by Congress were too modest. The FSA was able to extend loans to fewer than 2 percent of the nation's tenant farmers. "Obviously," the FSA director informed Roosevelt, "this…program can be regarded as only an experimental approach to the farm tenancy problem." The result of the New Deal for American farming was to hasten its transformation into a business in which only the efficient and well capitalized would thrive.

Roosevelt and Relief

The New Deal was far more successful in meeting the most immediate problem of the 1930s—relief for the millions of unemployed and destitute citizens. Roosevelt never shared Hoover's distaste for direct federal support; on May 12, 1933, in response to FDR's March request, Congress authorized the RFC to distribute $500 million to the states to help individuals and families in need.

Roosevelt brought in Harry Hopkins to direct the relief program. A former social worker who seemed to live on black coffee and cigarettes, Hopkins set up a desk in the hallway of the RFC building and proceeded to spend more than $5 million in less than

two hours. By the end of 1933, Hopkins had cut through red tape to distribute money to nearly one-sixth of the American people. The relief payments were modest in size, but they enabled millions to avoid starvation and stay out of humiliating breadlines.

Another, more imaginative early effort was the **Civilian Conservation Corps (CCC)**, which was Roosevelt's own idea. The CCC enrolled young males from city families on relief and sent them to work on the nation's public lands, cutting trails, planting trees, building bridges, and paving roads. Ultimately, more than two million young people served in the CCC, contributing both to their families' incomes and to the nation's welfare.

Hopkins realized the need to do more than just keep people alive, and he soon became an advocate of work relief. Hopkins argued that the government should put the jobless to work, not just to encourage self-respect, but also to enable them to earn enough to purchase consumer goods and thus stimulate the entire economy. A Public Works Administration (PWA) headed by Secretary of the Interior Harold Ickes had been authorized in 1933, but Ickes, intent on the quality of the projects rather than human needs, failed to put many people to work. In the fall of 1933, Roosevelt created the Civil Works Administration (CWA) and charged Hopkins with getting people off the unemployment lines and relief rolls and back to work. Hopkins had more than four million men and women at work by January 1934, building roads, schools, playgrounds, and athletic fields. Many of the workers were unskilled, and some of the projects were shoddy, but the CWA at least enabled people to work and earn enough money to survive the winter. Roosevelt, appalled at the huge expenditures involved, shut down the CWA in 1934 and forced Hopkins to return to federal relief payments as the only source of aid to the jobless.

The final commitment to the idea of work relief came in 1935 when Roosevelt established the **Works Progress Administration (WPA)** to spend nearly $5 billion authorized by Congress for emergency relief. The WPA, under Hopkins, put the unemployed on the federal payroll so they could earn enough to meet their basic needs and help stimulate the stagnant economy. Conservatives complained that the WPA amounted to nothing more than hiring the jobless to do make-work tasks with no real value. But Hopkins cared less about what was accomplished than about helping those who had been unemployed for years to get off the dole and gain self-respect by working again.

In addition to funding the usual construction and conservation projects, the WPA tried to preserve the skills of American artists, actors, and writers. The Federal Theatre Project produced plays, circuses, and puppet shows that enabled entertainers to practice their crafts and to perform before people who often had never seen a professional production before. Similar projects for writers and artists led to a series of valuable state guidebooks and to murals that adorned public buildings across the land. A separate National Youth Administration (NYA) found part-time jobs for young people still in school and developed projects—ranging from automobile repairing in New York City to erecting tuberculosis isolation units in Arizona—for 2.5 million young adults.

The WPA helped ease the burden for the unemployed, but it failed to overcome the depression. Rather than spending too much, as his critics charged, Roosevelt's greatest failure was not spending enough. The WPA never employed at any one time more than three million of the ten million jobless. The wages, although larger than relief payments, were still pitifully low, averaging only $52 a month. Thus the WPA failed to prime the American economy by increasing consumer purchasing power. Factories remained closed and machinery idle because the American people still did not have the money, either from relief or the WPA, to buy cars, radios, appliances, and the other consumer goods that had been the basis for the prosperity of the 1920s. By responding to basic human needs, Roosevelt had made the depression bearable. The New Deal's failure, however, to go beyond relief to achieve prosperity led to a growing frustration and the appearance of more radical alternatives that challenged the conservative nature of the New Deal and forced FDR to shift to the left.

Roosevelt and Reform

How did the New Deal reform American life?

In 1935, the focus of the New Deal shifted from relief and recovery to reform. During his first two years in office, FDR had concentrated on fighting the Great Depression by shoring up the sagging American economy. Only a few new agencies, notably TVA, sought to make permanent changes in national life. Roosevelt was developing a "broker-state" concept of government, responding to pressures from organized elements such as corporations, labor unions, and farm groups while ignoring the needs and wants of the dispossessed who had no clear political voice. The early New Deal tried to assist bankers and industrialists, large farmers, and members of the labor unions, but it did little to help unskilled workers and sharecroppers.

The continuing depression and high unemployment began to build pressure for more sweeping changes. Roosevelt faced the choice of either providing more radical programs, ones designed to end historical inequities in American life, or deferring to others who put forth solutions to the nation's ills. Bolstered by an impressive Democratic victory in the 1934 congressional elections, Roosevelt responded by embracing a reform program that marked the climax of the New Deal.

Challenges to FDR

The signs of discontent were visible everywhere by 1935. In the upper Midwest, progressives and agrarian radicals, led by Minnesota governor Floyd Olson, were calling for government action to raise farm and labor income. "I am a radical in the sense that I want a definite change in the system," Olson declared. "I am not satisfied with patching." Upton Sinclair, the muckraking novelist, nearly won the governorship of California in 1934 running on the slogan "End poverty in California," while in the East a violent strike in the textile industry shut down plants in twenty states. The most serious challenge to Roosevelt's leadership, however, came from three demagogues who captured national attention in the mid-1930s.

The first was Father Charles Coughlin, a Roman Catholic priest from Detroit, who had originally supported FDR. Speaking to a rapt nationwide radio audience in his rich, melodious voice, Coughlin appealed to the discontented with a strange mixture of crank monetary schemes and anti-Semitism. He broke with the New Deal in late 1934, denouncing it as the "Pagan Deal," and founded his own National Union for Social Justice. Increasingly vitriolic, he called for monetary inflation and the nationalization of

the banking system in his weekly radio sermons to an audience of more than thirty million.

A more benign but equally threatening figure appeared in California. Francis Townsend, a 67-year-old physician, came forward in 1934 with a scheme to assist the elderly, who were suffering greatly during the depression. The Townsend Plan proposed giving everyone over the age of 60 a monthly pension of $200 with the proviso that it must be spent within thirty days. Although designed less as an old-age pension plan than as a way to stimulate the economy, the proposal understandably had its greatest appeal among the elderly. They embraced it as a holy cause, joining Townsend Clubs across the country. Despite the criticism from economists that the plan would transfer more than half the national income to less than 10 percent of the population, more than ten million people signed petitions endorsing the Townsend Plan, and few politicians dared oppose it.

The third new voice of protest was that of Huey Long, the flamboyant senator from Louisiana. Like Coughlin, an original supporter of the New Deal, Long turned against FDR and by 1935 had become a major political threat to the president. A shrewd, ruthless, yet witty man, Long had a remarkable ability to mock those in power. The Kingfish (a nickname he borrowed from *Amos 'n Andy*) announced a nationwide "Share the Wealth" movement in 1934. He spoke grandly of taking from the rich to make "every man a king," guaranteeing each American a home worth $5,000 and an annual income of $2,500. To finance the plan, Long advocated seizing all fortunes of more than $5 million and levying a tax of 100 percent on incomes greater than $1 million. By 1935, Long claimed to have founded twenty-seven thousand Share the Wealth clubs and had a mailing list of more than seven million people, including workers, farmers, college professors, and even bank presidents. Threatening to run as a third-party candidate in 1936, Long generated fear among Democratic leaders that he might attract three to four million votes, possibly enough to swing the election to the Republicans. Although an assassin killed Huey Long in Louisiana in late 1935, his popularity showed the need for the New Deal to do more to help those still in distress.

Social Security

When the new Congress met in January 1935, Roosevelt was ready to support a series of reform measures designed to take the edge off national dissent. The recent elections had increased Democratic congressional strength significantly, with the Republicans losing thirteen seats in the House and retaining less than one-third of the Senate. Many of the Democrats were to the left of Roosevelt, favoring increased spending and more sweeping federal programs. "Boys—this is our hour," exulted Harry Hopkins. "We got to get everything we want…now or never." Congress quickly appropriated $4.8 billion for the WPA and was prepared to enact virtually any proposal that Roosevelt offered.

The most significant reform enacted in 1935 was the **Social Security Act**. The Townsend movement had reminded Americans that the United States, alone among modern industrial nations, had never developed a welfare system to aid the aged, the disabled, and the unemployed. A cabinet committee began studying the

Federal work relief programs helped millions maintain their self-respect. Workers in the CCC (top) received $30 a month for planting trees and building parks and trails. As indicated on the map, the PWA hired workers to build schools, dig irrigation ditches, construct sewage treatment plants, and erect bridges across the country.

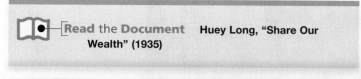

Read the **Document** Huey Long, "Share Our Wealth" (1935)

This political cartoon published in the *Chicago Tribune* in 1935 illustrates that conservatives and other opponents of the New Deal vehemently asserted that FDR's recovery and reform program represented a dangerous threat to Americans' economic liberties and the political freedoms secured by the Constitution of the United States.

problem in 1934, and President Roosevelt sent its recommendations to Congress the following January.

The proposed legislation had three major parts. First, it provided for old-age pensions financed equally by a tax on employers and workers, without government contributions. In addition, it gave states federal matching funds to provide modest pensions for the destitute elderly. Second, it set up a system of unemployment compensation on a federal-state basis, with employers paying a payroll tax and with each state setting benefit levels and administering the program locally. Finally, it provided for direct federal grants to the states, on a matching basis, for welfare payments to the blind, handicapped, needy elderly, and dependent children.

Although there was criticism from conservatives who mourned the passing of traditional American reliance on self-help and individualism, the chief objections came from those who argued that the administration's measure did not go far enough. Democratic leaders, however, defeated efforts to incorporate

Townsend's proposal for $200 monthly pensions and increases in unemployment benefits. Congress then passed the Social Security Act by overwhelming margins.

Critics began to point out its shortcomings, as they have ever since. The old-age pensions were paltry. Designed to begin in 1942, they ranged from $10 to $85 a month. Not everyone was covered; many of those who most needed protection in their old age, such as farmers and domestic servants, were not included. And all participants, regardless of income or economic status, paid in at the same rate, with no supplement from the general revenue. The trust fund also took out of circulation money that was desperately needed to stimulate the economy in the 1930s.

Other portions of the act were equally open to question. The cumbersome unemployment system offered no aid to those currently

Read the **Document** Frances Perkins and the Social Security Act (1935, 1960)

Despite the administration's boosterism, many believed that Social Security could not fulfill its promises.

out of work, only to people who would lose their jobs in the future, and the benefits (depending on the state) ranged from barely adequate to substandard. The outright grants to the handicapped and dependent children were minute in terms of the need; in New York City, for example, a blind person received only $5 a week in 1937.

The conservative nature of the legislation reflected Roosevelt's own fiscal orthodoxy, but even more it was a product of his political realism. Despite the severity of the depression, he realized that establishing a system of federal welfare went against deeply rooted American convictions. He insisted on a tax on participants to give those involved in the pension plan a vested interest in Social Security. He wanted them to feel they had earned their pensions and that in the future no one would dare take them away. "With those taxes in there," he explained privately, "no damned politician can ever scrap my social security program." Above all, FDR had succeeded in establishing the principle of government responsibility for the aged, the handicapped, and the unemployed. Whatever the defects of the legislation, Social Security stood as a landmark of the New Deal, creating a system to provide for the welfare of individuals in a complex industrial society.

Labor Legislation

The other major reform achievement in 1935 was passage of the National Labor Relations Act, or the **Wagner Act**, as it became known. Senator Robert Wagner of New York introduced legislation in 1934 to outlaw company unions and other unfair labor practices in order to ensure collective bargaining for unions. FDR, who had little knowledge of labor-management relations and apparently little interest in them, opposed the bill. In 1935, however, Wagner began to gather broad support for his measure, which passed the Senate in May with only twelve opposing votes, and the president, seeing passage as likely, gave it his approval. The bill moved quickly through the House, and Roosevelt signed it into law in July.

The Wagner Act created a National Labor Relations Board to preside over labor-management relations and enable unions to engage in collective bargaining with federal support. The act outlawed a variety of union-busting tactics and in its key provision decreed that whenever the majority of a company's workers voted for a union to represent them, management would be compelled to negotiate with the union on all matters of wages, hours, and working conditions. With this unprecedented government sanction, labor unions could now recruit the large number of unorganized workers throughout the country. The Wagner Act, the most far-reaching of all New Deal measures, led to the revitalization of the American labor movement and a permanent change in labor-management relations.

Three years later, Congress passed a second law that had a lasting impact on American workers—the Fair Labor Standards Act. A long-sought goal of the New Deal, this measure aimed to establish both minimum wages and maximum hours of work per week. Since labor unions usually were able to negotiate adequate levels of pay and work for their members, the act was aimed at unorganized workers and met with only grudging support from unions. Southern conservatives opposed it strongly, both on ideological grounds (it meant still greater government involvement in private enterprise) and because it threatened the low southern wages that had attracted northern industry since Reconstruction.

Roosevelt finally succeeded in winning passage of the Fair Labor Standards Act in 1938, but only at the cost of exempting many key industries from its coverage. The act provided for a minimum wage of 40 cents an hour by 1940 and a standard workweek of forty hours, with time and a half for overtime. Despite its loopholes, the legislation did lead to pay raises for the twelve million workers earning less than 40 cents an hour. More important, like Social Security it set up a system—however inadequate—that Congress could build on in the future to reach more generous and humane levels.

Other New Deal reform measures met with a mixed reception in Congress. Proposals to break up the huge public utility holding companies created by promoters in the 1920s and to levy a "soak the rich" tax on the wealthy stirred up bitter debate, and these bills were passed only in greatly weakened form. Roosevelt was more successful in passing a banking act that made important reforms in the Federal Reserve System. He also gained congressional approval of the Rural Electrification Administration (REA), which helped bring electricity to the 90 percent of American farms that still did not have it in the 1930s.

All in all, Roosevelt's record in reform was similar to that in relief and recovery—modest success but no sweeping victory. A cautious and pragmatic leader, FDR moved far enough to the left to overcome the challenges of Coughlin, Townsend, and Long without venturing too far from the mainstream. His reforms improved the quality of life in America significantly, but he made no effort to correct all the nation's social and economic wrongs.

Impact of the New Deal

What was the lasting impact of the New Deal?

The New Deal had a broad influence on the quality of life in the United States in the 1930s. Government programs reached into areas hitherto untouched. Many of them brought about long-overdue improvements, but others failed to make any significant dent in historic inequities. The most important advances came with the dramatic growth of labor unions; the conditions for working women and minorities in nonunionized industries showed no comparable advance.

Rise of Organized Labor

Trade unions were weak at the onset of the Great Depression, with a membership of fewer than three million workers. Most were in the American Federation of Labor (AFL), composed of craft unions that served the needs of skilled workers. The nation's basic industries, such as steel and automobiles, were unorganized; the great mass of unskilled workers thus fared poorly in terms of wages and working conditions. Section 7a of the NRA had led to some growth in AFL ranks, but the union's conservative leaders, eager to cooperate with business, failed to take full advantage of the opportunity to organize the mass production industries.

John L. Lewis, head of the United Mine Workers, took the lead in forming the Committee on Industrial Organization (CIO) in 1935. The son of a Welsh coal miner, Lewis was a dynamic and ruthless man. He had led the mine workers since 1919 and was determined to spread the benefits of unions throughout industry. Lewis first battled

👁 ◻ **Watch** the **Video** **Responding to the Great Depression: Whose New Deal?**

Mary McLeod Bethune was an African American educator and civil rights leader. She was one of several African American executive department administrators for President Franklin Roosevelt. McLeod was also a close friend of President Roosevelt's wife and confidant, Eleanor, and a key political supporter of the president in the African American community.

with the leadership of the AFL, and then—after being expelled—he renamed his group the Congress of Industrial Organizations and announced in 1936 that he would use the Wagner Act to extend collective bargaining to the nation's auto and steel industries.

Within five years, Lewis had scored a remarkable series of victories. Some came easily. The big steel companies, led by U.S. Steel, surrendered without a fight in 1937; management realized that federal support put the unions in a strong position. There was greater resistance in the automobile industry. When General Motors, the first target, resisted, the newly created United Automobile Workers (UAW) developed an effective strike technique. In late December 1936, GM workers in Flint, Michigan, simply sat down in the factory, refusing to leave until the company recognized their union, and threatening to destroy the valuable tools and machines if they were removed

forcibly. When the Michigan governor refused to call out the national guard to break the strike, General Motors conceded defeat and signed a contract with the UAW. Chrysler quickly followed suit, but Henry Ford refused to give in and fought the UAW, hiring strikebreakers and beating up organizers. In 1941, however, Ford finally recognized the UAW. Smaller steel companies, led by Republic Steel, engaged in even more violent resistance; in one incident in 1937, police shot ten strikers. The companies eventually reached a settlement with the steelworkers' union in 1941.

By the end of the 1930s, the CIO had some five million members, slightly more than the AFL. The successes were remarkable—in addition to the automaking and steel unions, organizers for the CIO and the AFL had been successful in the textile, rubber, electrical, and metal industries. For the first time, unskilled as well as skilled workers were unionized. Women and African Americans benefited from the creation of the CIO, not because the union followed enlightened policies, but simply because they made up a substantial proportion of the unskilled workforce that the CIO organized.

Yet despite these impressive gains, only 28 percent of all Americans (excluding farmworkers) belonged to unions by 1940. Millions in the restaurant, retail, and service trades remained unorganized, working long hours for very low wages. Employer resistance and traditional hostility to unions blocked further progress, as did the aloof attitude of President Roosevelt, who commented to labor and management, "A plague on both your houses" during the steel strike. The Wagner Act had helped open the way, but labor leaders such as Lewis, Philip Murray of the Steel Workers Organizing Committee, and Walter Reuther of the United Automobile Workers deserved most of the credit for union achievements.

The New Deal Record on Help to Minorities

The Roosevelt administration's attempts to aid the downtrodden were least effective with African Americans and other racial minorities. The Great Depression had hit blacks with special force. Share croppers and tenant farmers had seen the price of cotton drop from 18 to 6 cents a pound, far below the level needed to sustain a family on the land. In the cities, the saying "Last hired, first fired" proved all too true; by 1933, more than 50 percent of urban blacks were unemployed. Hard times sharpened racial prejudice. "No jobs for niggers until every white man has a job" became a rallying cry for many whites in Atlanta.

The New Deal helped African Americans survive the depression, but it never tried to confront squarely the racial injustice built into the federal relief programs. Although the programs served blacks as well as whites, in the South the weekly payments blacks received were much smaller. In the early days, NRA codes permitted lower wage scales for blacks, while the AAA led to the eviction of thousands of Negro tenants and sharecroppers. African American leaders referred to the NRA as standing for "Negro Robbed Again" and dismissed the AAA as "a continuation of the same old raw deal." Nor did later reform measures help very much. Neither the minimum wage nor Social Security covered those working as farmers or domestic servants, categories that comprised 65 percent of all African American workers. Thus an NAACP official commented that Social Security "looks like a sieve with the holes just large enough for the majority of Negroes to fall through."

Despite this bleak record, African Americans rallied behind Roosevelt's leadership, abandoning their historic ties to the Republican party. In 1936, more than 75 percent of those African Americans who voted supported FDR. In part, this switch came in response to Roosevelt's appointment of a number of prominent African Americans to high-ranking government positions, such as William H. Hastie in the Interior Department and Mary McLeod Bethune (founder and president of Bethune-Cookman College) in the National Youth Administration. Eleanor Roosevelt spoke out eloquently throughout the decade against racial discrimination, most notably in 1939 when the Daughters of the American Revolution refused to let African American contralto Marian Anderson sing in Constitution Hall. The first lady and Interior Secretary Harold Ickes arranged for the singer to perform at the Lincoln Memorial, where seventy-five thousand people gathered to hear her on Easter Sunday.

Perhaps the most influential factor in the African Americans' political switch was the color-blind policy of Harry Hopkins. He had more than one million blacks working for the WPA by 1939, many of them in teaching and artistic positions as well as in construction jobs. Overall, the New Deal provided assistance to 40 percent of the nation's blacks during the depression. Uneven as his record was, Roosevelt had still done more to aid this oppressed minority than any previous president since Lincoln. One African American newspaper commented that while "relief and WPA are not ideal, they are better than the Hoover bread lines and they'll have to do until the real thing comes along."

The New Deal did far less for Mexican Americans. Engaged primarily in agricultural labor, these people found their wages in California fields dropping from 35 to 14 cents an hour by 1933. The pool of unemployed migrant labor expanded rapidly with Dust Bowl conditions in the Great Plains and the subsequent flight of "Okies" and "Arkies" to the cotton fields of Arizona and the truck farms of California. The Roosevelt administration cut off any further influx from Mexico by barring entry of any immigrant likely to become a public charge; local authorities rounded up migrants and shipped them back to Mexico to reduce the welfare rolls.

The New Deal relief program did aid many thousands of Mexican Americans in the Southwest in the 1930s, although migrant workers had difficulty meeting state requirements. The WPA hired Mexican Americans for a variety of construction and cultural programs, but after 1937 such employment was denied to aliens. Overall, the pattern was one of great economic hardship and relatively little federal assistance for Mexican Americans.

Native Americans, after decades of neglect, fared slightly better under the New Deal. Roosevelt appointed John Collier, a social worker who championed Indian rights, to serve as commissioner of Indian affairs. In 1934, Congress passed the Indian Reorganization Act, a reform measure designed to emphasize tribal unity and autonomy instead of attempting (as previous policy had done) to transform Indians into self-sufficient farmers by granting them small plots of land. Collier employed more Native Americans in the Indian Bureau, supported educational programs on the reservations, and encouraged tribes to produce native handiwork such as blankets and jewelry. Despite modest gains however, the nation's one-third million Indians remained the most impoverished citizens in America.

Women at Work

The decade witnessed no significant gain in the status of American women. In the midst of the Great Depression, there was little concern expressed for protecting or extending their rights. The popular idea that women worked for "pin money" while men were the breadwinners for their families led employers to discriminate in favor of men when cutting the workforce. Working women "are holding jobs that rightfully belong to the God-intended providers of the household," declared a Chicago civic group. More than three-fourths of the nation's school boards refused to hire married women, and more than half of them fired women teachers who married. Federal regulations prohibited more than one member of a family from working in the civil service, and almost always it was the wife who had to defer to her husband. A Gallup poll revealed that 82 percent of the people disapproved of working wives, with 75 percent of the women polled agreeing.

Many of the working women in the 1930s were either single or the sole supporters of an entire family. Yet their wages remained lower than those for men, and their unemployment rate ran higher than 20 percent throughout the decade. Women over age 40 found it particularly hard to find or retain jobs during the depression. The New Deal offered little encouragement. NRA codes sanctioned lower wages for women, permitting laundries, for example, to pay them as little as 14 cents an hour. The minimum wage did help those women employed in industry, but too many worked as maids and waitresses—jobs not covered by the law—for the new law to have much overall effect on women's income. Despite these hardships, the number of married women and women between the ages of 25 and 40 in the labor force increased during the 1930s. Relatively few women worked in heavy industry, where unemployment was greatest; most were employed in the clerical and service sectors, areas of traditional female employment, in which jobs were more plentiful.

The one area of advance in the 1930s came in government. Eleanor Roosevelt set an example that encouraged millions of American women. Not content to be mistress of the White House, she traveled around the country, eager to uncover wrongs, bring them to the president's attention, and, if possible, rectify them. (See the Feature Essay, "Eleanor Roosevelt and the Quest for Social Justice," pp. 632–633.) Frances Perkins, the secretary of labor, became the first woman cabinet member, and FDR appointed women as ambassadors and federal judges for the first time.

Women also were elected to office in larger numbers in the 1930s. Hattie W. Caraway of Arkansas succeeded her husband in the Senate, winning a full term in 1934. That same year, voters elected six women to the House of Representatives. Public service, however, was one of the few professions open to women. The nation's leading medical and law schools discouraged women from applying, and the percentage of female faculty members in colleges and universities continued to decline in the 1930s. In sum, a decade that was grim for most Americans was especially hard on American women.

End of the New Deal

How and why did the New Deal end?

The New Deal reached its high point in 1936, when Roosevelt was overwhelmingly reelected, and the Democratic party strengthened its hold on Congress. This political triumph was deceptive. In the next two years, Roosevelt met with a series of defeats in Congress. Yet despite the setbacks, he remained a popular political leader who had restored American self-confidence as he strove to meet the challenges of the Great Depression.

The Election of 1936

Franklin Roosevelt enjoyed his finest political hour in 1936. A man who loved the give-and-take of politics, FDR faced challenges from both the left and the right as he sought reelection. Father Coughlin and Gerald L. K. Smith, who inherited Huey Long's following after the senator's assassination in 1935, organized a Union Party, with North Dakota Progressive Congressman William Lemke heading the ticket. At the other extreme, a group of wealthy industrialists formed the Liberty League to fight what they saw as the New Deal's assault on property rights. The Liberty League attracted prominent Democrats, including Al Smith, but in 1936 it endorsed the Republican presidential candidate, Governor Alfred M. Landon of Kansas. A moderate, colorless figure, Landon disappointed his backers by refusing to campaign for repeal of the popular New Deal reforms.

Roosevelt ignored Lemke and the Union Party, focusing attention instead on the assault from the right. Democratic spokesmen condemned the Liberty League as a "millionaire's union" and reminded the American people of how much Roosevelt had done for them in fighting unemployment and providing relief. In his speeches, FDR condemned the "economic royalists" who were "unanimous in their hatred for me." "I welcome their hatred," he declared, and promised that in his second term, these forces would meet "their master."

This frank appeal to class sympathies proved enormously successful. Roosevelt won easily, receiving five million more votes than he had in 1932 and outscoring Landon in the electoral college by 523 to 8. The Democrats did almost as well in Congress, piling up margins of 331 to 89 in the House and 76 to 16 in the Senate (with 4 not aligned with either major party).

Equally important, the election marked the stunning success of a new political coalition that would dominate American politics for the next three decades. FDR, building on the inroads into the

Republican majority that Al Smith had begun in 1928, carried urban areas by impressive margins, winning 3.6 million more votes than his opponents in the nation's twelve largest cities. He held on to the traditional Democratic votes in the South and West and added to them by appealing strongly to the diverse religious and ethnic groups in the northern cities—Catholics and Jews, Italians and Poles, Irish and Slavs. The strong support of labor, together with three-quarters of the black vote, indicated that the nation's new alignment followed economic as well as cultural lines. The poor and the oppressed, who in the depression years included many middle-class Americans, became attached to the Democratic party, leaving the GOP in a minority position, limited to the well-to-do and to rural and small-town Americans of native stock.

THE ELECTION OF 1936

Candidate	Party	Popular Vote	Electoral Vote
Roosevelt	Democratic	27,751,597	523
Landon	Republican	16,679,583	8

The Supreme Court Fight

FDR proved to be far more adept at winning electoral victories than in achieving his goals in Congress. In 1937, he attempted to use his recent success to overcome the one obstacle remaining in his path—the Supreme Court. During his first term, the Court had ruled several New Deal programs unconstitutional, most notably the NRA and the AAA. Only three of the nine justices were sympathetic to the need for emergency measures in the midst of the depression. Two others were unpredictable, sometimes approving New Deal measures and sometimes opposing them. Four justices were bent on using the Constitution to block Roosevelt's proposals. All were elderly men, and one, Willis Van Devanter, had planned to retire in 1932 but remained on the Court because he believed Roosevelt to be "unfitted and unsafe for the Presidency."

When Congress convened in 1937, the president offered a startling proposal to overcome the Court's threat to the New Deal. Instead of seeking a constitutional amendment either to limit the Court's power or to clarify the constitutional issues, FDR chose an oblique attack. Declaring the Court was falling behind schedule because of the age of its members, he asked Congress to appoint a new justice for each member of the Court over the age of 70, up to a maximum of six.

Although this **"court-packing" scheme**, as critics quickly dubbed it, was perfectly legal, it outraged not only conservatives but liberals as well, who realized it could set a dangerous precedent for the future. Republicans wisely kept silent, letting prominent Democrats such as Senator Burton Wheeler of Montana lead the fight against Roosevelt's plan. Despite all-out pressure from the White House, resistance in the Senate blocked early action on the proposal.

The Court defended itself well. Chief Justice Charles Evans Hughes testified tellingly to the Senate Judiciary Committee, pointing out that in fact the Court was up to date and not behind schedule as Roosevelt charged. The Court then surprised observers with a series of rulings approving such controversial New Deal measures as the Wagner Act and Social Security. In the midst of the struggle, Justice Van Devanter resigned, enabling FDR to make his first appointment to the Court since taking office in 1933. Believing he had proved his point, the president allowed his court-packing plan to die in the Senate.

During the next few years, four more vacancies occurred, and Roosevelt was able to appoint such distinguished jurists as Hugo Black, William O. Douglas, and Felix Frankfurter to the Supreme Court. Yet the price was high. The Court fight had badly weakened the president's relations with Congress, opening deep rifts with members of his own party. Many senators and representatives who had voted reluctantly for Roosevelt's measures during the depths of the Great Depression now felt free to oppose any further New Deal reforms.

The New Deal in Decline

The legislative record during Roosevelt's second term was meager. Aside from the minimum wage and a maximum-hour law passed in 1938, Congress did not extend the New Deal into any new areas. Attempts to institute national health insurance met with stubborn resistance, as did efforts by civil rights advocates to pass antilynching legislation. Disturbed by the growing congressional resistance, Roosevelt set out in the spring of 1938 to defeat a number of conservative Democratic congressmen and senators, primarily in the South. His targets gleefully charged the president with interference in local politics; only one of the men he sought to defeat lost in the primaries. The failure of this attempted purge further undermined Roosevelt's strained relations with Congress.

The worst blow came in the economic sector. The slow but steady improvement in the economy suddenly gave way to a sharp recession in the late summer of 1937. In the following ten months, industrial production fell by one-third, and nearly four million workers lost their jobs. Critics of the New Deal quickly labeled the downturn "the Roosevelt recession," and business executives claimed that it reflected a lack of confidence in FDR's leadership.

The criticism was overblown but not without basis. In an effort to reduce expanding budget deficits, Roosevelt had cut back sharply on WPA and other government programs after the election. Federal contributions to consumer purchasing power fell from $4.1 billion in 1936 to less than $1 billion in 1937. For several months, Roosevelt refused to heed calls from economists to restore heavy government spending. Finally, in April 1938, Roosevelt asked Congress for a $3.75 billion relief appropriation, and the economy began to revive. But FDR's premature attempt to balance the budget had meant two more years of hard times and had marred his reputation as the energetic foe of the depression.

The political result of the attempted purge and the recession was a strong Republican upsurge in the elections of 1938. The GOP won an impressive 81 seats in the House and 8 more in the Senate, as well as 13 governorships. The party many thought dead suddenly had new life. The Democrats still held a sizable majority in Congress, but their margin in the House was particularly deceptive. There were 262 Democratic representatives to 169 Republicans, but 93 southern Democrats held the balance of power.

More and more often after 1938, anti–New Deal Southerners voted with Republican conservatives to block social and economic reform measures. Thus not only was the New Deal over by the end of 1938, but a new bipartisan conservative coalition that would prevail for a quarter century had formed in Congress.

Conclusion: The New Deal and American Life

The New Deal lasted a brief five years, and most of its measures came in two legislative bursts in the spring of 1933 and the summer of 1935. Yet its impact on American life was enduring. Nearly every aspect of economic, social, and political development in the decades that followed bore the imprint of Roosevelt's leadership.

The least impressive achievement of the New Deal came in the economic realm. Whatever credit Roosevelt is given for relieving human suffering in the depths of the Great Depression must be balanced against his failure to achieve recovery in the 1930s. The moderate nature of his programs, especially the unwieldy NRA, led to slow and halting industrial recovery. Although much of the improvement that was made came as a result of government spending, FDR never embraced the concept of planned deficits, striving instead for a balanced budget. As a result, the nation had barely reached the 1929 level of production a decade later, and there were still nearly ten million men and women unemployed.

Equally important, Roosevelt refused to make any sweeping changes in the American economic system. Aside from the TVA, there were no broad experiments in regional planning and no attempts to alter free enterprise beyond imposing some limited forms of government regulation. The New Deal did nothing to alter the basic distribution of wealth and power in the nation. The outcome was the preservation of the traditional capitalist system with a thin overlay of federal control.

More significant change occurred in American society. With the adoption of Social Security, the government acknowledged for the first time its responsibility to provide for the welfare of those unable to care for themselves in an industrial society. The Wagner Act helped stimulate the growth of labor unions to balance corporate power, and the minimum wage law provided a much needed floor for many workers.

Yet the New Deal tended to help only the more vocal and organized groups, such as union members and commercial farmers. Those without effective voices or political clout—African Americans, Mexican Americans, women, sharecroppers, restaurant and laundry workers—received little help from the New Deal. For all the appealing rhetoric about the "forgotten man," Roosevelt did little more than Hoover in responding to the long-term needs of the dispossessed.

The most lasting impact of the Roosevelt leadership came in politics. Taking advantage of the emerging power of ethnic voters and capitalizing on the frustration growing out of the depression, FDR proved to be a genius at forging a new coalition. Overcoming the friction between rural and urban Democrats that had prolonged Republican supremacy in the 1920s, he attracted new groups to the Democratic Party, principally African Americans

Feature Essay | Eleanor Roosevelt and the Quest for Social Justice

During the Great Depression, Eleanor Roosevelt traveled thousands of miles each year to learn about conditions throughout the country. She is shown here in Des Moines, Iowa, in 1936, inspecting a WPA project to convert a city dump into a waterfront park.

In August 1933, Eleanor Roosevelt journeyed to Scotts Run, a poor mining community in West Virginia, to observe life in one of the nation's poorest and most desolate areas. The first lady toured the dilapidated homes and listened to the problems of the unemployed miners, some of whom had not worked in eight years. She also met with their wives and children, and visited with local African Americans. It was an experience few would forget; "Some of the Negroes," wrote a local newspaper editor to Eleanor's husband, President Franklin Delano Roosevelt, "think she is God." Millions of Americans held her in similar esteem. At the height of the Great Depression, ER's willingness to listen to, and act on

behalf of, those whose voices often went unheard made her one of the nation's leading symbols of hope and compassion.

Eleanor Roosevelt entered public life as a reformer long before she became first lady. Growing up shy and insecure in a prominent New York family (she was the niece of Theodore Roosevelt), she sought personal fulfillment through voluntary social work. Like many reformers of her day, she found her sense of social justice upset by the existence of poverty and inequality. Avoiding politics, which she then considered a "sinister affair," she limited her activities to nonpartisan reform and relief organizations, such as settlement houses and the Consumer's League. She curtailed her social work after her 1905 marriage to

Franklin Roosevelt, placing her responsibilities as wife and mother first, as she believed a woman should. FDR, as a New York state senator and later as assistant secretary of the Navy, carried the political torch for the family. However, her role changed in 1921 when Franklin was stricken with polio. Eleanor was determined to return him as soon as possible to political life, which she believed was the best antidote to his pain and depression. While working tirelessly to speed his recovery, she also struck out on her own to keep the Roosevelt name alive in New York politics, making speeches, writing magazine articles, and chairing the Women's Platform Committee at the Democratic National Convention in 1924. In the newly formed League of Women Voters and other activist organizations, she brought her reformer's impulse to politics by advocating measures such as a maximum hours law for working women. Through these efforts, she also formed the nucleus of a "woman's network" that she would employ extensively during the New Deal years.

Focusing on those whose needs were greatest, Eleanor became the administration's champion for the dispossessed. While her husband appealed to the "forgotten man," she concerned herself with the "forgotten woman." She worked with Harry Hopkins to achieve equity for women on relief and to create more jobs for women under the auspices of the CWA and the WPA. With Frances Perkins, she helped establish camps for unemployed girls patterned after the CCC, and worked with the Women's Trade Union League to guarantee women equal pay for equal work on federal projects. She saw to it that, whenever possible, women administrators were hired to supervise projects for women, and in her syndicated newspaper column, "My Day," she often dealt with the problems faced by women during the Great Depression. Her 1933 book, *It's Up to the Women*, urged American women to join her in a crusade for decency and fairness. "For more than a century," wrote one reviewer, "the Great White Father in the White House has been instructing his people in right conduct...But now the Great White Mother emerges as a personality in her own right and starts an independent course of instruction on her own account."

Eleanor worked hard for African Americans, whose position at the bottom of American society deeply offended her sense of fairness and decency; in the late 1930s, three-quarters of adult blacks in America had not finished high school, and almost 90 percent lived below the federal poverty standard. The first lady spoke out eloquently in favor of equal opportunity for blacks and sought their inclusion in New Deal programs. She worked with Hopkins to employ more African Americans in federal projects, and lobbied within the administration for the appointment of black men and women to administer programs designed specifically for them. Publicly, she endeavored to set an example by addressing black audiences throughout the country, presiding over a more egalitarian White House, and resigning her membership in the Daughters of the American Revolution over the Marian Anderson incident (see p. 629).

Her struggle against racial discrimination sometimes put Mrs. Roosevelt in conflict with her husband's efforts to keep the Democratic Party intact. Conservative southern Democrats castigated her as a radical; her more extreme critics called her a communist. Rumors of "Eleanor Clubs"—said to be secret associations of black maids pledged to boycott white households—circulated in every southern state. (The FBI investigated the rumors and found no factual basis for them.) Hate mail emphasized the criticism.

The attacks didn't deter Eleanor, but they caused Franklin Roosevelt to temporize on bills to ban lynching and abolish the poll tax; his wife's support of these measures, however, put the Roosevelt name behind them without the same damaging political consequences. In her efforts to advance the cause of civil rights, Eleanor arranged for White House meetings between FDR and African American leaders, supported interracial projects, and spoke out forcefully against racial discrimination. To ER, such change did not help just one element of society, but brought benefits to the entire country. "To deny any part of a population the opportunities for more enjoyment in life, for higher aspirations," she declared, "is a menace to the nation as a whole."

Like other first ladies, Eleanor Roosevelt had to strike a balance between capitalizing on her unique access to the president and intruding illegitimately into the affairs of the nation's elected officials. Her position was complicated, as well, by her own ambivalence on certain issues. Although she advocated greater rights for women, for example, she did not believe in full equality between men and women. She thought that women required protective legislation on account of their special roles as wives and mothers.

While Mrs. Roosevelt was instrumental in the few gains made by women and African Americans in the 1930s, her advocacy could not overcome the sexual and racial stereotypes that continued to limit their role in the workplace and society. Thus despite her efforts, the plight of these groups during the depression was only slightly relieved. However, this is not to minimize her achievements. As the self-appointed conscience of the Roosevelt administration, she exposed the areas where the New Deal had not been realized. Her courage and vitality in the pursuit of human rights and equality made her the embodiment of reform and social justice in the New Deal. Eleanor Roosevelt's goal was a simple one, concluded one biographer, "a life of dignity and decency for all."

QUESTIONS FOR DISCUSSION

1. Why did Eleanor Roosevelt's work with minorities upset some people?

2. What did Eleanor Roosevelt's advocacy for more rights for women, blacks, and other minorities actually accomplish?

MAJOR NEW DEAL LEGISLATION AND AGENCIES

Year Created	Act or Agency	Provisions
1933	Agricultural Adjustment Administration (AAA)	Attempted to regulate agricultural production through farm subsidies; reworked after the Supreme Court ruled its key regulatory provisions unconstitutional in 1936; coordinated agricultural production during World War II, after which it was disbanded.
	Banking Act of 1933 (Glass-Steagall Act)	Prohibited commercial banks from selling stock or financing corporations; created FDIC.
	Civilian Conservation Corps (CCC)	Young men between the ages of 18 and 25 volunteered to be placed in camps to work on regional environmental projects, mainly west of the Mississippi; they received $30 a month, of which $25 was sent home; disbanded during World War II.
	Civil Works Administration (CWA)	Emergency work relief program put more than four million people to work during the extremely cold winter of 1933–1934, after which it was disbanded.
	Federal Deposit Insurance Corporation (FDIC)	A federal guarantee of savings bank deposits initially of up to $2,500, raised to $5,000 in 1934, and frequently thereafter; continues today with a limit of $100,000.
	Federal Emergency Relief Administration (FERA)	Combined cash relief to needy families with work relief; superseded in early 1935 by the extensive work relief projects of the WPA and unemployment insurance established by Social Security.
	National Recovery Administration (NRA)	Attempted to combat the Great Depression through national economic planning by establishing and administering a system of industrial codes to control production, prices, labor relations, and trade practices among leading business interests; ruled unconstitutional by the Supreme Court in 1935.
	Public Works Administration (PWA)	Financed more than 34,000 federal and nonfederal construction projects at a cost of more than $6 billion; initiated the first federal public housing program, made the federal government the nation's leading producer of power, and advanced conservation of the nation's natural resources; discontinued in 1939 due to its effectiveness at reducing unemployment and promoting private investment.
	Tennessee Valley Authority (TVA)	An attempt at regional planning. Included provisions for environment and recreational design; architectural, educational, and health projects; and controversial public power projects; continues today to meet the Tennessee Valley's energy and flood-control needs.
1934	Federal Communications Commission (FCC)	Regulatory agency with wide discretionary powers established to oversee wired and wireless communication; reflected growing importance of radio in everyday lives of Americans during the Great Depression; continues to regulate television as well as radio.
	Federal Housing Administration (FHA)	Expanded private home ownership among moderate-income families through federal guarantees of private mortgages, the reduction of down payments from 30 to 10 percent, and the extension of repayment from 20 to 30 years; continues to function today.
	Securities and Exchange Commission (SEC)	Continues today to regulate trading practices in stocks and bonds according to federal laws.
1935	National Labor Relations Board (NLRB); established by Wagner Act	Greatly enhanced power of American labor by overseeing collective bargaining; continues to arbitrate labor-management disputes today.
	Social Security Act	Guaranteed retirement payments for enrolled workers beginning at age 65; set up federal-state system of unemployment insurance and care for dependent mothers and children, the handicapped, and public health; continues today.

Year Created	Act or Agency	Provisions
	National Youth Administration (NYA)	Established by the WPA to reduce competition for jobs by supporting education and training of youth; paid grants to more than 2 million high school and college students in return for work performed in their schools; also trained another 2.6 million out-of-school youths as skilled labor to prepare them for later employment in the private sector; disbanded during World War II.
	Works Progress Administration (WPA)	Massive work relief program funded projects ranging from construction to acting; disbanded by FDR during World War II.
	Farm Security Administration (FSA)	Granted loans to small farmers and tenants for rehabilitation and purchase of small-sized farms; Congress slashed its appropriations during World War II when many poor farmers entered the armed forces or migrated to urban areas.
1937	Rural Electrification Administration (REA)	Transformed American rural life by making electricity available at low rates to American farm families in areas that private power companies refused to service; closed the cultural gap between rural and urban everyday life by making modern amenities, such as radio, available in rural areas.
1938	Fair Labor Standards Act	Established a minimum wage of 40 cents an hour and a maximum workweek of 40 hours for businesses engaged in interstate commerce.

and organized labor. His political success led to a major realignment that lasted long after he left the scene.

His political achievement also reveals the true nature of Roosevelt's success. He was a brilliant politician who recognized the essence of leadership in a democracy—appealing directly to the people and giving them a sense of purpose. He succeeded in infusing them with the same indomitable courage and jaunty optimism that had marked his own battle with polio. Thus, despite his limitations as a reformer, Roosevelt proved to be the leader the American people needed in the 1930s—a president who provided the psychological lift that helped them endure and survive the Great Depression.

Study Resources

 Take the **Study Plan** for **Chapter 26** *Franklin D. Roosevelt and the New Deal* on **MyHistoryLab**

TIME LINE

1932 Franklin D. Roosevelt elected president

1933 Emergency Banking Relief Act passed in one day (March; Twenty-first Amendment repeals prohibition (December)

1934 Securities and Exchange Commission authorized (June)

1935 Works Progress Administration (WPA) hires unemployed (April); Wagner Act grants workers collective bargaining (July); Congress passes Social Security Act (August)

1936 FDR wins second term as president

1937 United Automobile Workers sit-down strike forces General Motors contract (February); FDR loses court-packing battle (July); "Roosevelt recession" begins (August)

1938 Congress sets minimum wage at 40 cents an hour (June)

CHAPTER REVIEW

The Great Depression

What were the causes and effects of the Great Depression?

The Great Depression resulted from imbalances in the American economy that developed during the 1920s. Wealth was unequally distributed, depriving millions of the purchasing power necessary to keep America's factories and farms operating at full capacity. The depression threw millions out of work, out of their homes, and into despair. (p. 614)

Fighting the Depression

How did Franklin Roosevelt fight the Depression?

Roosevelt persuaded Congress to pass relief, recovery, and reform measures known collectively as the New Deal. Begun during the Hundred Days, the New Deal stabilized the banks, reorganized American industry, assisted American agriculture, and put Americans to work conserving and restoring the nation's resources. (p. 619)

Roosevelt and Reform

How did the New Deal reform American life?

In responses to the challenges of Charles Coughlin, Francis Townsend, and Huey Long, Roosevelt persuaded Congress to approve sweeping measures to reform American life. The Social Security Act established old-age and disability pensions to alleviate poverty among the elderly and those unable to work. (p. 624)

The Impact of the New Deal

What was the lasting impact of the New Deal?

The New Deal encouraged the emergence of organized labor as a major force in American economic life. It modestly improved the lot of African Americans, although it failed to tackle the racial prejudice that was at the heart of much black poverty. It did little for Mexican Americans, and only a bit more for Native Americans. (p. 627)

End of the New Deal

How and why did the New Deal end?

After a high point in 1936, the New Deal declined as a result of Roosevelt's overreaching in the court-packing effort, growing resistance from conservatives, and a recession in 1937 that reminded the country that the New Deal had not ended the Great Depression. (p. 630)

KEY TERMS AND DEFINITIONS

New Deal President Franklin Delano Roosevelt's program to combat the Great Depression. p. 614

Bonus Army In June 1932, a group of 20,000 World War I veterans marched on Washington, D.C., to demand immediate payment of their "adjusted compensation" bonuses voted by Congress in 1924. Congress rejected their demands, and President Herbert Hoover had the Bonus Army forcibly dispersed. p. 620

Fireside chats Radio addresses by President Franklin D. Roosevelt from 1933 to 1944, in which he spoke to the American people about such issues as the banking crisis, Social Security, and World War II. The chats enhanced Roosevelt's popularity among ordinary Americans. p. 621

Tennessee Valley Authority A New Deal effort created in 1933 to build dams and power plants on the Tennessee River. Its programs helped raise the standard of living for millions in the Tennessee River valley. p. 621

Civilian Conservation Corps (CCC) One of the most popular New Deal programs, the CCC provided 300,000 young men between the ages of 18 and 25 with government jobs in reforestation and other conservation projects. p. 623

Works Progress Administration (WPA) New Deal agency to provide work relief for the unemployed. p. 623

National Recovery Administration (NRA) This New Deal agency was created in 1933 to promote economic recovery and revive industry during the Great Depression. It permitted manufacturers to establish industry wide codes of "fair business practices" setting prices and production levels. It also provided for minimum wages and maximum working hours for labor and guaranteed labor the right to organize and bargain collectively (Section 7a). The Supreme Court declared it unconstitutional in 1935. p. 622

Agricultural Adjustment Administration (AAA) Created by Congress in 1933 as part of the New Deal, this agency attempted to restrict agricultural production by paying farmers subsidies to take land out of production. The object was to raise farm prices, and it did, but the act did nothing for tenant farmers and sharecroppers. The Supreme Court declared it unconstitutional in 1936. p. 622

Social Security Act The 1935 Social Security Act established a system of old age, unemployment, and survivors' insurance funded by wage and payroll taxes. p. 624

Wagner Act The 1935 Wagner Act, formally known as the National Labor Relations Act, created the National Labor Relations Board to supervise union elections and designate winning unions as official bargaining agents. The board could also issue cease-and-desist orders to employers who dealt unfairly with their workers. p. 627

"court-packing" scheme Concerned that the conservative Supreme Court might declare all his New Deal programs unconstitutional, President Franklin D. Roosevelt asked Congress to allow him to appoint additional justices to the Court. Both Congress and the public rejected this "court-packing" scheme. p. 630

CRITICAL THINKING QUESTIONS

1. Could the Great Depression have been averted? What steps might the government have taken to prevent it?

2. Why did Americans respond so positively to Franklin Roosevelt?

3. How was the popularity of Francis Townsend and Huey Long like the popularity of Roosevelt? How was it different?

4. Why did minorities not fully share the benefits of New Deal reforms?

5. Why was Roosevelt's "court-packing" scheme so unpopular?

MyHistoryLab Media Assignments

Find these resources in the Media Assignments folder for Chapter 26 on MyHistoryLab

The Great Depression

View the **Map** *The Great Depression p. 616*

View the **Closer Look** *Homeless Shantytown, Seattle 1937 p. 617*

Read the **Document** *Women on the Breadlines p. 618*

Fighting the Depression

Watch the **Video** *Dorothea Lange and Migrant Mother p. 619*

Watch the **Video** *FDR'S Inauguration p. 621*

View the **Map** *The Tennessee Valley Authority p. 622*

Roosevelt and Reform

Read the **Document** *Huey Long, "Share Our Wealth" (1935) p. 626*

Read the **Document** *Frances Perkins and the Social Security Act (1935, 1960) p. 626*

The Impact of the New Deal

Watch the **Video** *Responding to the Great Depression: Whose New Deal? p. 628*

End of the New Deal

Complete the **Assignment** *Eleanor Roosevelt and the Quest for Social Justice p. 632*

■ *Indicates Study Plan Media Assignment*

27 America and the World, 1921–1945

Contents and Learning Objectives

((•●—[Listen to the Audio File on myhistorylab   Chapter 27 *America and the World, 1921–1945*

A Pact Without Power

On August 27, 1928, U.S. Secretary of State Frank B. Kellogg, French Foreign Minister Aristide Briand, and representatives of twelve other nations met in Paris to sign a treaty outlawing war. Several hundred spectators crowded into the ornate clock room of the Quai d'Orsay to watch the historic ceremony. Six huge klieg lights illuminated the scene so photographers could record the moment for a world eager for peace. Briand opened the ceremony with a speech in which he declared, "Peace is proclaimed," and then Kellogg signed the document with a foot-long gold pen given to him by the citizens of Le Havre as a token of Franco-American friendship. In the United States, a senator called the **Kellogg-Briand Pact** "the most telling action ever taken in human history to abolish war."

In reality, the Pact of Paris was the result of a determined American effort to avoid involvement in the European alliance system. In June 1927, Briand had sent a message to the American people inviting the United States to join with France in signing a treaty to outlaw war between the two nations. The invitation struck a sympathetic response, especially among pacifists who had advocated the outlawing of war throughout the 1920s, but the State Department feared correctly that Briand's true intention was to establish a close tie between France and the United States. The French had already created a network of alliances with the

smaller countries of eastern Europe; an antiwar treaty with the United States would at least ensure American sympathy, if not involvement, in case of another European war. Kellogg delayed several months and then outmaneuvered Briand by proposing the pledge against war not be confined just to France and the United States, but instead be extended to all nations. An unhappy Briand, who had wanted a bilateral treaty with the United States, had no choice but to agree, and so the diplomatic charade finally culminated in the elaborate signing ceremony in Paris.

Eventually the signers of the Kellogg-Briand Pact included nearly every nation in the world, but the effect was negligible. All promised to renounce war as an instrument of national policy, except of course, as the British made clear in a reservation, in matters of self-defense. Enforcement of the treaty relied solely on the moral force of world opinion. The Pact of Paris was, as one senator shrewdly commented, only "an international kiss."

Unfortunately, the Kellogg-Briand Pact was symbolic of American foreign policy in the years immediately following World War I. Instead of asserting the role of world leadership its resources and power commanded, the United States retreated from involvement with other nations. America went its own way, extending trade and economic dominance but refusing to take the lead in maintaining world order. This retreat from responsibility seemed unimportant in the 1920s when exhaustion from World War I ensured relative peace

Representatives of the United States, France, and twelve other nations gathered in Paris, France, in June 1927, to sign the Kellogg-Briand pact. The signatories promised to renounce war as a tool of national policy except in matters of self-defense.

and tranquility. But in the 1930s, when threats to world order arose in Europe and Asia, the American people retreated even deeper, searching for an isolationist policy that would spare them the agony of another great war.

There was no place to hide in the modern world. The Nazi onslaught in Europe and the Japanese expansion in Asia finally convinced America to reverse its isolationist stance and become involved in World War II in late 1941, at a time when the chances for an Allied victory seemed most remote. With incredible swiftness, the nation mobilized its military and industrial strength. American armies were soon fighting on three continents, the U.S. Navy controlled the world's oceans, and the nation's factories were sending a vast stream of war supplies to more than twenty Allied countries.

When the Allied victory came in 1945, the United States was by far the most powerful nation in the world. But instead of the

enduring peace that might have permitted a return to a less active foreign policy, the onset of the Cold War with the Soviet Union brought on a new era of tension and rivalry. This time the United States could not retreat from responsibility. World War II was a coming of age for American foreign policy.

Retreat, Reversal, and Rivalry

Why were the United States and Japan on a collision course in the years following World War I?

"The day of the armistice America stood on the hilltops of glory, proud in her strength, invincible in her ideals, acclaimed and loved by a world free of an ancient fear at last," wrote journalist George Creel in 1920. "Today we writhe in a pit of our own digging; despising ourselves and despised by the betrayed peoples of Earth." The bitter disillusionment Creel described ran through every aspect of American foreign policy in the 1920s. In contrast to diplomatic actions under Wilsonian idealism, American diplomats in the 1920s made loans, negotiated treaties and agreements, and pledged the nation's good faith, but they were careful not to make any binding commitments on behalf of world order. The result was neither isolation nor involvement but rather a cautious middle course that managed to alienate friends and encourage foes.

Retreat in Europe

The United States emerged from World War I as the richest nation on Earth, displacing England from its prewar position of economic primacy. The Allied governments owed the United States a staggering $10 billion in war debts, money they had borrowed during and immediately after the conflict. Each year of the 1920s saw the nation increase its economic lead as the balance of trade tipped heavily in America's favor. The war-ravaged countries of Europe borrowed enormous amounts from American bankers to rebuild their economies; Germany alone absorbed more than $3 billion in American investments during the decade. By 1929, American exports totaled more than $7 billion a year, three times the prewar level, and American overseas investment had risen to $17.2 billion.

The European nations could no longer compete on equal terms. The high American tariff, first imposed in 1922, was raised again with enactment of the Hawley-Smoot Tariff in 1930. The high tariff frustrated attempts by England, France, and a defeated Germany to earn the dollars necessary to meet their American financial obligations. The Allied partners in World War I asked Washington to cancel the $10 billion in war debts, particularly after they were forced to scale down their demands for German reparations payments. American leaders from Wilson to Hoover refused the request, claiming the ungrateful Allies were trying to repudiate their obligations.

Only a continuing flow of private American capital to Germany allowed the payment of reparations to the Allies and the partial repayment of the Allies' war debts in the 1920s. The financial crash of 1929 halted the flow of American dollars across the Atlantic and led to subsequent default on the debt payments, with accompanying bitterness on both sides of the ocean.

Political relations fared little better. The United States never joined the League of Nations, nor did it take part in the attempts by England and France to negotiate European security treaties. American observers attended League sessions and occasionally took part in economic and cultural missions in Geneva. But the Republican administrations of the 1920s refused to compromise American freedom of action by embracing collective security, the principle on which the League was founded. And FDR, always realistic, made no effort to renew Wilson's futile quest. Thus the United States remained aloof from the European balance of power and refused to stand behind the increasingly shaky Versailles settlement.

The U.S. government ignored the Soviet Union throughout the 1920s. American businesses, however, exported large quantities of heavy machinery to Russia as part of its rapid industrialization. When that trade began to slump after 1930, business leaders hoped to revive it by calling on Washington to extend diplomatic

recognition to the Bolshevik regime that had come to power in the Russian Revolution of 1917. In 1933, Franklin Roosevelt finally ended the long estrangement by signing an agreement opening up diplomatic relations between the two countries. The Soviets soon went back on promises to stop all subversive activity in the United States and to settle prerevolutionary debts, but even if they rarely understood one another, at least the two nations had opened a channel of communication.

Cooperation in Latin America

U.S. policy was both more active and more enlightened in the Western Hemisphere than in Europe. The State Department sought new ways in the 1920s to pursue traditional goals of political dominance and economic advantage in Latin America. The outcome of World War I lessened any fears of European threats to the area and thus enabled the United States to dismantle the interventions in the Caribbean carried out by Roosevelt, Taft, and Wilson. At the same time, both Republican and Democratic administrations worked hard to extend American trade and investment in the nations to the south.

Under Harding, Coolidge, and Hoover, American marines were withdrawn from Haiti and the Dominican Republic, and in 1924 the last detachment left Nicaragua, ending a twelve-year occupation. Renewed unrest there the next year, however, led to a second intervention in Nicaragua, which did not end until the early 1930s.

Showing a new sensitivity, the State Department released the Clark Memorandum in 1930, a policy statement repudiating the controversial Roosevelt Corollary to the Monroe Doctrine. Under the Monroe Doctrine, the United States had no right to intervene in neighboring states, declared Undersecretary of State J. Reuben Clark, although he asserted a traditional claim to protect American lives and property under international law.

When FDR took office in 1933, relations with Latin America were far better than they had been under Wilson, but American trade in the hemisphere had fallen drastically as the depression worsened. Roosevelt moved quickly to solidify the improved relations and gain economic benefits. With his usual flair for the dramatic, he proclaimed a Good Neighbor policy and then proceeded to win goodwill by renouncing the imperialism of the past.

In 1933, Secretary of State Cordell Hull signed a conditional pledge of nonintervention at the Pan-American Conference in Montevideo, Uruguay. A year later, the United States renounced the right to intervene in Cuban affairs it had asserted under the Platt Amendment and loosened its grip on Panama. By 1936, American troops were no longer occupying any Latin American nation. FDR personally cemented the new policy by traveling to Buenos Aires to sign an agreement that forbade intervention "directly or indirectly, and for whatever reason" in the internal affairs of a Central or South American state.

The United States had not changed its basic goal of political and economic dominance in the hemisphere; rather, the new policy of benevolence reflected Roosevelt's belief that cooperation and friendship were more effective tactics than threats and armed intervention. Mexico tried his patience in 1938 by nationalizing its oil resources; with admirable restraint, the president finally negotiated a settlement in 1941 on terms favorable to Mexico. Yet this economic loss was more than offset by the new trade opportunities opened up by the Good Neighbor policy. American commerce with Latin America increased fourfold in the 1930s, and investment rose substantially from its Great Depression low. Most important, FDR succeeded in forging a new policy of regional collective security. As the ominous events leading to World War II unfolded in Europe and Asia, the nations of the Western Hemisphere looked to the United States for protection against external danger.

Rivalry in Asia

In the years following World War I, the United States and Japan were on a collision course in the Pacific. The Japanese, lacking the raw materials to sustain their developing industrial economy, were determined to expand onto the Asian mainland. They had taken Korea by 1905 and during World War I had extended their control over the mines, harbors, and railroads of Manchuria, the industrial region of northeast China. The American Open Door policy remained the primary obstacle to complete Japanese dominion over China. The United States thus faced the clear-cut choice of either abandoning China or forcefully opposing Japan's expansion. American efforts to avoid making this painful decision postponed the eventual showdown but not the growing rivalry.

The first attempt at a solution came in 1921 when the United States convened the Washington Disarmament Conference, which included delegates from the United States, Japan, Great Britain, and six other nations. The major objective was a political settlement of the tense Asian situation, but the most pressing issue was a dangerous naval race between Japan and the United States. Both nations were engaged in extensive shipbuilding programs begun during the war. Great Britain was forced to compete in order to preserve its traditional control of the sea; even so, projected construction indicated that both the United States and Japan would overtake the British navy by the end of the decade. Japan, spending nearly one-third of its total budget on naval construction, was eager for an agreement; in the United States, growing congressional concern over appropriations suggested the need for slowing the naval buildup.

In his welcoming address at the Washington Conference, Secretary of State Charles Evans Hughes outlined a specific plan for naval disarmament, calling for the scrapping of sixty-six battleships—thirty American, nineteen British, and seventeen Japanese. Three months later, delegates signed the Five Power Treaty embodying the main elements of Hughes' proposal: limitation of capital ships (battleships and aircraft carriers) in a ratio of 5:5:3 for the United States, Britain, and Japan, respectively, and 1.67:1.67 for France and Italy. England reluctantly accepted equality with the United States, while Japan agreed to the lower ratio only in return for an American pledge not to fortify Pacific bases such as the Philippines and Guam. The treaty cooled off the naval race even though it did not include cruisers, destroyers, or submarines.

The Washington Conference produced two other major agreements: the Nine Power Treaty and the Four Power Treaty. The first simply pledged all the countries involved to uphold the Open Door policy, while the other compact replaced the old Anglo-Japanese alliance with a new Pacific security pact signed by the United States, Great Britain, Japan, and France. Neither document contained any enforcement provision beyond a promise to consult in case of a violation. In essence, the Washington treaties formed a parchment peace, a pious set of pledges that attempted to freeze the status quo in the Pacific.

This compromise lasted less than a decade. In September 1931, Japanese forces violated the Nine Power Treaty and the Kellogg-Briand Pact by overrunning Manchuria in a brutal act of aggression. The United States, paralyzed by the depression, responded feebly. Secretary of State Henry L. Stimson sent an observer to Geneva to assure cooperation with the League of Nations, which was content to investigate the "incident." In January 1932, Stimson fell back on moral force, issuing notes vowing the United States would not recognize the legality of the Japanese seizure of Manchuria. Despite concurrence by the League on nonrecognition, the Japanese ignored the American moral sanction and incorporated the former Chinese province, now renamed Manchukuo, into their rapidly expanding empire.

Aside from the Good Neighbor approach in the Western Hemisphere, American foreign policy faithfully reflected the prevailing disillusionment with world power that gripped the country after World War I. The United States avoided taking any constructive steps toward preserving world order, preferring instead the empty symbolism of the Washington treaties and the Kellogg-Briand Pact.

Isolationism

What was isolationism, and why was it so appealing to Americans in the 1920s and 1930s?

The retreat from an active world policy in the 1920s turned into a headlong flight back to isolationism in the 1930s. Two factors were responsible. First, the depression made foreign policy seem remote and unimportant to most Americans. As unemployment increased and the economic crisis intensified after 1929, many people grew apathetic about events abroad. Second, the danger of war abroad, when it did finally penetrate the American consciousness, served only to strengthen the desire to escape involvement.

Three powerful and discontented nations were on the march in the 1930s—Germany, Italy, and Japan. In Germany, Adolf Hitler came to power in 1933 as the head of a National Socialist, or Nazi, movement. A shrewd and charismatic leader, Hitler capitalized on both domestic discontent and bitterness over World War I. Blaming the Jews for all of Germany's ills and asserting the supremacy of the "Aryan" race of blond, blue-eyed Germans, he quickly imposed a totalitarian dictatorship in which the Nazi party ruled and the *Führer* was supreme. At first, his foreign policy seemed harmless, but as he consolidated his power, the ultimate threat to world peace became clearer. Hitler took Germany out of the League of Nations, reoccupied the Rhineland, and formally denounced the Treaty of Versailles. His boasts of uniting all Germans into a Greater Third Reich that would last a thousand years filled his European opponents with terror, blocking any effective challenge to his regime.

In Italy, another dictator, Benito Mussolini, had come to power in 1922. Emboldened by Hitler's success, he embarked on an aggressive foreign policy in 1935. His invasion of the independent African nation of Ethiopia led its emperor, Haile Selassie, to call on the

League of Nations for support. With England and France far more concerned about Hitler, the League's halfhearted measures utterly failed to halt Mussolini's conquest. "Fifty-two nations had combined to resist aggression," commented historian A. J. P. Taylor; "all they accomplished was that Haile Selassie lost all his country instead of only half." Collective security had failed its most important test.

Japan formed the third element in the threat to world peace. Militarists began to dominate the government in Tokyo by the mid-1930s, using tactics of fear and even assassination against their liberal opponents. By 1936, Japan had left the League of Nations and had repudiated the Washington treaties. A year later, its armies began an invasion of China that marked the beginning of the Pacific phase of World War II.

The resurgence of militarism in Germany, Italy, and Japan undermined the Versailles settlement and threatened to destroy the existing balance of power. England and France in Europe proved as powerless as China in Asia to stop the tide of aggression. In 1937, the three totalitarian nations signed an anti-Comintern pact completing a Berlin-Rome-Tokyo axis. The alliance of the **Axis Powers** ostensibly was aimed at the Soviet Union, but in fact it threatened the entire world. Only a determined American response could unite the other nations against the Axis threat. Unfortunately, the United States deliberately abstained from assuming this role of leadership until it was nearly too late.

The Lure of Pacifism and Neutrality

The growing danger of war abroad led to a rising American desire for peace and noninvolvement. Memories of World War I contributed heavily. Erich Maria Remarque's novel *All Quiet on the Western Front*, as well as the movie based on it, reminded people of the brutality of war. Historians began to treat the Great War as a mistake, criticizing Wilson for failing to preserve American neutrality and claiming the clever British had duped the United States into entering the war. Walter Millis advanced this thesis in *America's Road to War, 1914–1917*, published in 1935. It was hailed as a vivid description of the process by which "a peace-loving democracy, muddled but excited, misinformed and whipped to a frenzy, embarked upon its greatest foreign war."

American youth made clear their determination not to repeat the mistakes of their elders. Pacifism swept across college campuses. A Brown University poll indicated 72 percent of the students opposed military service in wartime. At Princeton, undergraduates formed the Veterans of Future Wars, a parody on veterans' groups, to demand a bonus of $1,000 apiece before they marched off to a foreign war. In April 1934, students and professors alike walked out of class to attend massive antiwar rallies, which became an annual rite of spring in the 1930s. Demonstrators carried signs reading "Abolish the R.O.T.C." and "Build Schools—Not Battleships," and pacifist orators urged students to sign a pledge not to support their country "in any war it might conduct."

The pacifist movement found a scapegoat in the munitions industry. The publication of several books exposing the unsavory business tactics of large arms dealers such as Krupp in Germany and Vickers in Britain led to a demand to curb these "merchants of death." Senator Gerald Nye of North Dakota headed a special Senate committee that spent two years investigating American munitions dealers. The committee revealed the enormous profits firms such as Du Pont reaped from World War I, but Nye went further, charging that bankers and munitions makers were responsible for American intervention in 1917. No proof was forthcoming, but the public—prepared to believe the worst of businessmen during the Great Depression—accepted the "merchants of death" thesis.

The Nye Committee's revelations culminated in neutrality legislation. In 1935, Senator Nye and another Senate colleague introduced measures to ban arms sales and loans to belligerents and to prevent Americans from traveling on belligerent ships. By outlawing the activities that led to World War I they hoped the United States could avoid involvement in the new conflict. This "never again" philosophy proved irresistible. In August 1935, Congress passed the first of three **Neutrality Acts**. The 1935 law banned the sale of arms to nations at war and warned American citizens not to sail on belligerent ships. In 1936, a second act added a ban on loans, and in 1937, a third Neutrality Act made these prohibitions permanent and required, on a two-year trial basis, that all trade other than munitions be conducted on a cash-and-carry basis.

President Roosevelt played a passive role in the adoption of the neutrality legislation. At first opposed to the arms embargo, he finally approved it for six months in 1935 in a compromise designed to save important New Deal legislation in Congress. Yet he also appeared to share the isolationist assumption that a European war would have no impact on vital national interests. He termed the first neutrality act "entirely satisfactory" when he signed it. Others in the administration criticized the mandatory nature of the new law, pointing out that it prevented the United States from distinguishing between aggressors and their victims. Privately, Roosevelt expressed some of the same reservations, but publicly he bowed to the prevailing isolationism. He signed the subsequent neutrality acts without protest, and during the 1936 election, he delivered an impassioned denunciation of war. "I hate war," he told an audience in Chautauqua, New York. "I have passed unnumbered hours, I shall pass unnumbered hours, thinking and planning how war may be kept from this nation."

Yet FDR did take a few steps to try to limit the nation's retreat into isolationism. His failure to invoke the Neutrality Act after the Japanese invasion of China in 1937 enabled the hard-pressed Chinese to continue buying arms from the United States. In January 1938, he used his influence to block a proposal by Indiana Congressman Louis Ludlow to require a nationwide referendum before Congress could declare war. FDR's strongest public statement came earlier, in Chicago in October 1937, when he denounced "the epidemic of world lawlessness" and called for an international effort to "quarantine" the disease. When reporters asked him if his call for "positive efforts to preserve peace" signaled a repeal of the neutrality acts, however, Roosevelt quickly reaffirmed this isolationist legislation. Whatever his private yearning for cooperation against aggressors, the president had no intention of challenging the prevailing public mood of the 1930s.

War in Europe

The neutrality legislation played directly into the hands of Adolf Hitler. Bent on the conquest of Europe, he could now proceed without worrying about American interference. In March 1938, he seized Austria in a bloodless coup. Six months later, he was demanding the Sudetenland, a province of Czechoslovakia with a large German population. When the British and French leaders agreed to meet with Hitler at Munich, FDR voiced his approval. Roosevelt carefully kept the United States aloof from the decision to surrender the Sudetenland in the hopes of appeasing Hitler's demand for land. At the same time, the president gave his tacit approval of the policy of appeasement by telling the British prime minister that he shared his "hope and belief that there exists today the greatest opportunity in years for the establishment of a new order based on justice and on law."

Six months after the meeting at Munich, Hitler violated his promises by seizing nearly all of Czechoslovakia. In the United States, Roosevelt permitted the State Department to press for neutrality revision. The administration proposal to repeal the arms embargo and place *all* trade with belligerents, including munitions, on a cash-and-carry basis soon met stubborn resistance from isolationists. They argued that cash-and-carry would favor England and France, who controlled the sea. The House rejected the measure by a narrow margin, and the Senate's Foreign Relations Committee voted 12 to 11 to postpone any action on neutrality revision.

In July 1939, Roosevelt finally abandoned his aloof position and met with Senate leaders to plead for reconsideration. Warnings of the imminence of war in Europe by both the president and the secretary of state failed to impress the isolationists.

Senator William Borah, who had led the fight against the League of Nations in 1919, responded that he believed the chances for war in Europe were remote. After canvassing the senators present, Vice President John Nance Garner bluntly told FDR that the neutrality revision was dead. "You haven't got the votes," Garner commented, "and that's all there is to it."

On September 1, 1939, Hitler began World War II by invading Poland. England and France responded two days later by declaring war, although there was no way they could prevent the German conquest of Poland. Russia had played a key role, refusing Western overtures for a common front against Germany and finally signing a nonaggression treaty with Hitler in late August. The Nazi-Soviet Pact enabled Germany to avoid a two-front war; the Russians were rewarded with a generous slice of eastern Poland.

President Roosevelt reacted to the outbreak of war by proclaiming American neutrality, but the successful aggression by Nazi Germany brought into question the isolationist assumption that American well-being did not depend on the European balance of power. Strategic as well as ideological considerations began to undermine the earlier belief that the United States could safely pursue a policy of neutrality and noninvolvement. The long retreat from responsibility was about to end as Americans came to realize that their own democracy and security were at stake in the European war.

 View the **Map**   **World War II in Europe**

Hitler sent his armies into Poland with tremendous force and firepower, devastating the country. Here German troops observe as the German Luftwaffe bombs Warsaw in September 1939, destroying the city and forcing its inhabitants to surrender.

The Road to War

How did the United States go from neutrality in the 1930s to war in 1941?

For two years, the United States tried to remain at peace while war raged in Europe and Asia. In contrast to the climate of the country while Wilson attempted to be impartial during most of World War I, however, the American people displayed an over-whelming sympathy for the Allies and total distaste for Germany and Japan. Roosevelt made no secret of his preference for an Allied victory, but a fear of isolationist criticism compelled him to move slowly, and often deviously, in adopting a policy of aid for England and France.

From Neutrality to Undeclared War

Two weeks after the outbreak of war in Europe, Roosevelt called Congress into special session to revise the neutrality legislation. He wanted to repeal the arms embargo in order to supply weapons to England and France, but he refused to state this aim openly. Instead he asked Congress to replace the arms embargo with cash-and-carry regulations. Belligerents would be able to purchase war supplies in the United States, but they would have to pay cash and transport the goods in their own ships. Public opinion strongly supported the president, and Congress passed the revised neutrality policy by heavy margins in early November 1939.

A series of dramatic German victories had a profound impact on American opinion. Quiet during the winter of 1939–1940, the Germans struck with lightning speed and devastating effect in the spring. In April, they seized Denmark and Norway, and on May 10, 1940, they unleashed the *blitzkrieg* (lightning war) on the western front. Using tanks, armored columns, and dive-bombers in close coordination, the German army cut deep into the Allied lines, dividing the British and French forces. Within three weeks, the British were driven off the continent. In another three weeks, France fell to Hitler's victorious armies.

Americans were stunned. Hitler had taken only six weeks to achieve what Germany had failed to do in four years of fighting in World War I. Suddenly they realized they did have a stake in the outcome; if England fell, Hitler might well gain control of the British navy. The Atlantic would no longer be a barrier; instead, it would be a highway for German penetration of the New World.

Roosevelt responded by invoking a policy of all-out aid to the Allies, short of war. In a speech at Charlottesville, Virginia, in June (just after Italy entered the war by invading France), he denounced Germany and Italy as representing "the gods of force and hate" and vowed, "The whole of our sympathies lies with those nations that are giving their life blood in combat against these forces." It was too late to help France, but in early September, FDR announced the transfer of fifty old destroyers to England in exchange for rights to build air and naval bases on eight British possessions in the Western Hemisphere. Giving warships to a belligerent nation was clearly a breach of neutrality, but Roosevelt emphasized the importance of guarding the Atlantic approaches, calling the destroyers-for-bases deal "the most important action in the reinforcement of our national defense that has been taken since the Louisiana Purchase."

Isolationists cried out against this departure from neutrality. A bold headline in the *St. Louis Post-Dispatch* read, "Dictator Roosevelt Commits Act of War." A group of Roosevelt's opponents in the Midwest formed the America First Committee to protest the drift toward war. Such diverse individuals as aviator-hero Charles Lindbergh, conservative Senator Robert A. Taft of Ohio, socialist leader Norman Thomas, and liberal educator Robert M. Hutchins condemned FDR for involving the United States in a foreign conflict. Voicing belief in a "Fortress America," they denied that Hitler threatened American security and claimed that the nation had the strength to defend itself regardless of what happened in Europe.

To support the administration's policies, opponents of the isolationists organized the Committee to Defend America by Aiding the Allies. Eastern Anglophiles, moderate New Dealers, and liberal Republicans made up the bulk of the membership, with Kansas newspaper editor William Allen White serving as chairman. The White Committee, as it became known, advocated unlimited assistance to England short of war, although some of its members privately favored entry into the conflict. Above all, the interventionists challenged the isolationist premise that events in Europe did not affect American security. "The future of Western civilization is being decided upon the battlefield of Europe," White declared.

In the ensuing debate, the American people gradually came to agree with the interventionists. The battle of Britain helped. "Every time Hitler bombed London, we got a couple of votes," noted one interventionist. Frightened by the events in Europe, Congress approved large sums for preparedness, increasing the defense budget from $2 billion to $10 billion during 1940. Roosevelt courageously asked for a peacetime draft, the first in American history, to build up the army; in September, Congress agreed.

The sense of crisis affected domestic politics. Roosevelt ran for an unprecedented third term in 1940 because of the European war; the Republicans nominated Wendell Willkie, a former Democratic businessman who shared FDR's commitment to aid for England. Both candidates made appeals to peace sentiment during the campaign, but Roosevelt's decisive victory made it clear that the nation supported his increasing departure from neutrality.

After the election, FDR took his boldest step. Responding to British Prime Minister Winston Churchill's warning that England was running out of money, the president asked Congress to approve a new program to lend and lease goods and weapons to countries fighting against aggressors. Roosevelt's call for America to become "the great arsenal of democracy" seemed straightforward enough, but he acted somewhat deviously by naming the program **Lend-Lease** and by comparing it to loaning a neighbor a garden hose to put out a fire.

Isolationists angrily denounced Lend-Lease as both unnecessary and untruthful. "Lending war equipment is a good deal like lending chewing gum," commented Senator Taft. "You don't want it back." In March 1941, however, Congress voted by substantial margins to authorize the president to "sell, transfer title to, exchange, lease, lend, or otherwise dispose of" war supplies to "any country the President deems vital to the defense of the United States." The accompanying $7 billion appropriation ended the "cash" part of cash-and-carry and ensured Britain full access to American war supplies.

The "carry" problem still remained. German submarines were sinking more than 500,000 tons of shipping a month. England desperately needed the help of the American navy in escorting

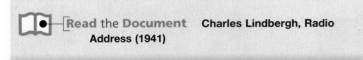

Read the **Document** Charles Lindbergh, Radio Address (1941)

The famous American aviator-hero Charles Lindbergh was one of several prominent isolationist Americans who joined a public campaign in 1939 and between 1940–1941 to preserve American neutrality as the military conflict in Europe began to rage.

convoys across the U-boat–infested waters of the North Atlantic. Roosevelt, fearful of isolationist reaction, responded with naval patrols in the western half of the ocean. Hitler placed his submarine commanders under strict restraints to avoid drawing America into the European war. Nevertheless, incidents were bound to occur. In September 1941, after a U-boat narrowly missed torpedoing an American destroyer tracking it, Roosevelt denounced the German submarines as the "rattlesnakes of the Atlantic" and issued orders for the navy to convey British ships halfway across the ocean.

Undeclared naval war quickly followed. On October 17, 1941, a German submarine damaged the U.S. destroyer *Kearney*; ten days later, another U-boat sank the *Reuben James*, killing more than one hundred American sailors. FDR issued orders for the destroyers to shoot U-boats on sight. He also asked Congress to repeal the "carry" section of the neutrality laws and permit American ships to deliver supplies to England. In mid-November, Congress approved these moves by slim margins. Now American merchant ships as well as destroyers would become targets for German attacks. By December, it seemed only a matter of

weeks—or months at most—until repeated sinkings would lead to a formal declaration of war against Germany.

THE ELECTION OF 1940

Candidate	Party	Popular Vote	Electoral Vote
Roosevelt	Democratic	27,244,160	449
Willkie	Republican	22,305,198	82

In leading the nation to the brink of war in Europe, Roosevelt opened himself to criticism from both sides in the domestic debate. Interventionists believed he had been too cautious in dealing with the danger to the nation from Nazi Germany. Isolationists were equally critical of the president, claiming he had misled the American people by professing peace while plotting for war. Roosevelt was certainly less than candid, relying on executive discretion to engage in highly provocative acts in the North Atlantic. He agreed with the interventionists that in the long run a German victory in Europe would threaten American security. But he also was aware that a poll taken in September 1941 showed nearly 80 percent of the American people wanted to stay out of World War II. Realizing that leading a divided nation into war would be disastrous, FDR played for time, inching the country toward war while waiting for the Axis nations to make the ultimate move. Japan finally obliged at Pearl Harbor.

Showdown in the Pacific

Japan had taken advantage of the war in Europe to expand farther in Asia. Although successful after 1937 in conquering the populous coastal areas of China, the Japanese had been unable to defeat Chiang Kai-shek, whose forces retreated into the vast interior of the country. The German defeat of France and the Netherlands in 1940, however, left their colonial possessions in the East Indies and Indochina vulnerable and defenseless. Japan now set out to incorporate these territories—rich in oil, tin, and rubber—into a Greater East Asia Co-Prosperity Sphere.

The Roosevelt administration countered with economic pressure. Japan depended heavily on the United States for petroleum and scrap metal. In July 1940, President Roosevelt signed an order setting up a licensing and quota system for the export of these crucial materials to Japan and banned the sale of aviation gasoline altogether. With Britain fighting for survival and France and the Netherlands occupied by Germany, the United States was now employing economic sanctions to defend Southeast Asia against Japanese expansion.

Tokyo appeared to be unimpressed. In early September, Japanese troops occupied strategic bases in the northern part of French Indochina. Later in the month, Japan signed the Tripartite Pact with Germany and Italy, a defensive treaty that confronted the United States with a possible two-ocean war. The new Axis alignment confirmed American suspicions that Japan was part of a worldwide totalitarian threat. Roosevelt and his advisers, however, saw Germany as the primary danger; thus they pursued a policy of all-out aid to England while hoping that economic measures alone would deter Japan.

View the **Closer Look** **The Japanese Raid on Pearl Harbor, December 7, 1941**

The early morning surprise Japanese attack on Pearl Harbor in Hawaii on December 7, 1941, brought America directly into World War II against the Axis powers. The attack devastated this major American naval base and resulted in the loss of twenty-four hundred American sailors, the sinking of eight battleships, and severe damage to another twenty-one U.S. naval ships.

The embargo on aviation gasoline, extended to include scrap iron and steel in late September 1940, was a burden Japan could bear, but a possible ban on all oil shipments was a different matter. Japan lacked petroleum reserves of its own and was entirely dependent on imports from the United States and the Dutch East Indies. In an attempt to ease the economic pressure through negotiation, Japan sent a new envoy to Washington in the spring of 1941. But the talks quickly broke down. Tokyo wanted nothing less than a free hand in China and an end to American sanctions, while the United States insisted on an eventual Japanese evacuation of all China.

In July 1941, Japan invaded southern Indochina, beginning the chain of events that led to war. Washington knew of this aggression before it occurred. Naval intelligence experts had broken the Japanese diplomatic code and were intercepting and reading all messages between Tokyo and the Japanese embassy in Washington. President Roosevelt responded on July 25, 1941, with an order freezing all Japanese assets in the United States. This step, initially intended only as a temporary warning to Japan, soon became a permanent embargo due to positive public reaction and State Department zeal. Trade with

Japan, including the vital oil shipments, came to a complete halt. When the Dutch government in exile took similar action, Japan faced a dilemma: To have oil shipments resumed, Tokyo would have to end its aggression; the alternative would be to seize the needed petroleum supplies in the Dutch East Indies, an action that would mean war.

After one final diplomatic effort failed, General Hideki Tojo, an army militant, became the new premier of Japan. To mask its war preparations, Tokyo sent yet another envoy to Washington with new peace proposals. Code breaking enabled American diplomats to learn that the Japanese terms were unacceptable even before they were formally presented. Army and navy leaders urged President Roosevelt to seek at least a temporary settlement with Japan to give them time to prepare American defenses in the Pacific. Secretary of State Cordell Hull, however, refused to allow any concession; on November 26, he sent a stiff ten-point reply to Tokyo that included a demand for Japanese withdrawal from China.

The Japanese response came two weeks later. On the evening of December 6, 1941, the first thirteen parts of the reply to Hull's note arrived in Washington, with the fourteenth part to follow the next morning. Naval intelligence actually decoded the message faster than the Japanese embassy clerks. A messenger delivered the text to President Roosevelt late that night; after glancing at it, he commented, "This means war." The next day, December 7, the fourteenth part arrived, revealing that Japan totally rejected the American position.

Officials in Washington immediately sent warning messages to American bases in the Pacific, but they failed to arrive in time. At 7:55 in the morning, just before 1 P.M. in Washington, squadrons of Japanese carrier-based planes caught the American fleet at Pearl Harbor totally by surprise. In little more than an hour, they crippled the American Pacific fleet and its major base, sinking eight battleships and killing more than twenty-four hundred American sailors.

In Washington, the Japanese envoys had requested a meeting with Secretary Hull at 1 P.M. Just before the meeting, news arrived of the attack on **Pearl Harbor**. An irate Cordell Hull read the note the Japanese handed him and then, unable to restrain himself any longer, burst out, "In all my fifty years of public service, I have never seen a document that was more crowded with infamous falsehoods and distortions—on a scale so huge that I never imagined until today that any government was capable of uttering them."

Speaking before Congress the next day, President Roosevelt termed December 7 "a date which will live in infamy" and asked for a declaration of war on Japan. With only one dissenting vote, both branches passed the measure. On December 11, Germany and Italy declared war against the United States; the nation was now fully involved in World War II.

The whole country united behind Roosevelt's leadership to seek revenge for Pearl Harbor and to defeat the Axis threat to American security. After the war, however, critics charged that FDR had entered the conflict by a back door, claiming the president had deliberately exposed the Pacific fleet to attack. Subsequent investigations uncovered negligence in both Hawaii and Washington but no evidence to support the conspiracy charge. Commanders in Hawaii, like most military experts, believed the Japanese would not launch an attack on a base four thousand miles from Japan. FDR, like too many Americans, had badly underestimated the daring and skill of the Japanese; he and the nation alike paid a heavy price for this cultural and racial prejudice. But there was no plot. Roosevelt could not have known that Hitler, so restrained in the Atlantic, would reverse his policy and foolishly declare war against the United States after Pearl Harbor. Perhaps the most frightening aspect of the whole episode is that it took the shock of the Japanese sneak attack to make the American people aware of the extent of the Axis threat to their well-being and lead them to end the long American retreat from responsibility.

Turning the Tide Against the Axis

How did America and its allies halt the advances of Germany and Japan?

In the first few months after the United States entered the war, the outlook for victory was bleak. In Europe, Hitler's armies controlled virtually the entire continent, from Norway in the north to Greece in the south. Despite the nonaggression pact, German armies had penetrated deep into Russia after an initial invasion in June 1941. Although they had failed to capture either Moscow or Leningrad, the Nazi forces had conquered the Ukraine and by the spring of 1942 were threatening to sweep across the Volga River and seize vital oil fields in the Caucasus. In North Africa, General Erwin Rommel's Afrika Korps had pushed the British back into Egypt and threatened the Suez Canal (see the map on p. 656).

The situation was no better in Asia. The Pearl Harbor attack had enabled the Japanese to move unopposed across Southeast Asia. Within three months, they had conquered Malaya and the Dutch East Indies, with its valuable oil fields, and were pressing the British back both in Burma and New Guinea. American forces under General Douglas MacArthur had tried vainly to block the Japanese conquest of the Philippines. MacArthur finally escaped by torpedo boat to Australia; the American garrison at Corregidor surrendered after a long siege, the survivors then enduring the cruel death march across the Bataan peninsula. With the American navy still recovering from the devastation at Pearl Harbor, Japan controlled the western half of the Pacific (see the map on p. 650).

Over the next two years, the United States and its allies would finally halt the German and Japanese offensives in Europe and Asia. But then they faced the difficult process of driving back the enemy, freeing the vast conquered areas, and finally defeating the Axis powers on their home territory. It would be a difficult and costly struggle that would require great sacrifice and heavy losses; World War II would test American will and resourcefulness to the utmost.

Wartime Partnerships

The greatest single advantage that the United States and its partners possessed was their willingness to form a genuine coalition to bring about the defeat of the Axis powers. Although there were many strains within the wartime alliance, it did permit a high degree of coordination. In striking contrast was the behavior of Germany and Japan, each fighting a separate war without any attempt at cooperation.

The United States and Britain achieved a complete wartime partnership. Prewar military talks led to the formation of a Combined Chiefs of Staff, headquartered in Washington, which directed Anglo-American military operations. The close cooperation between President Roosevelt and Prime Minister Churchill ensured a common strategy. The leaders decided at the outset that a German victory posed the greater danger and thus gave priority to the European theater in the conduct of the war. In a series of meetings in December 1941, Roosevelt and Churchill signed a Declaration of the United Nations, eventually subscribed to by twenty-six countries, that pledged them to fight together until the Axis powers were defeated.

Relations with the other members of the United Nations coalition in World War II were not quite so harmonious. The decision to defeat Germany first displeased the Chinese, who had been at war with Japan since 1937. Roosevelt tried to appease Chiang Kai-shek with a trickle of supplies, flown in at great risk by American airmen over the Himalayas from India. France posed a more delicate problem. FDR virtually ignored the Free French government in exile under General Charles de Gaulle. Roosevelt preferred to deal with the Vichy regime, despite its collaboration with Germany, because it still controlled the French fleet and retained France's overseas territories.

The greatest strain of all within the wartime coalition was with the Soviet Union. Although Roosevelt had ended the long period of nonrecognition in 1933, close ties had failed to develop. The Russian refusal to pay prerevolutionary debts, together with continued Soviet support of domestic communist activity in the United States in the 1930s, intensified American distaste for Stalin's regime. The great Russian purge trials and the temporary Nazi-Soviet alliance from 1939 to 1941, along with deep-seated cultural and ideological differences, made wartime cooperation difficult.

Ever the pragmatist, Roosevelt tried hard to break down the old hostility and establish a more cordial relationship with Russia during the war. Even before Pearl Harbor, he extended Lend-Lease aid to Russia, and after American entry into the war, this economic assistance grew rapidly, limited only by the difficulty of delivering the supplies. Eager to keep Russia in the war, the president promised a visiting Russian diplomat in May 1942 that the United States would create a second front in Europe by the end of that year—a pledge he could not fulfill. In January 1943, Roosevelt and Churchill met in Casablanca, Morocco, where they declared a policy of unconditional surrender, vowing that the Allies would fight until the Axis nations were completely defeated.

Despite these promises, the Soviet Union bore the brunt of battle against Hitler in the early years of the war, fighting alone against more than two hundred German divisions. The United States and England, grateful for the respite to build up their forces, could do little more than offer promises of future help and send Lend-Lease supplies. The result was a rift that never fully healed—one that did not prevent the defeat of Germany but did ensure future tensions and uncertainties between the Soviet Union and the Western nations.

Halting the German Blitz

From the outset, the United States favored an invasion across the English Channel. Army planners, led by Chief of Staff George C. Marshall and his protégé, Dwight D. Eisenhower, were convinced such a frontal assault would be the quickest way to win the war. Roosevelt concurred, in part because it fulfilled his second-front commitment to the Soviets.

The initial plan, drawn up by Eisenhower, called for a full-scale invasion of Europe in the spring of 1943, with provision for a temporary beachhead in France in the fall of 1942 if necessary to keep Russia in the war. Marshall surprised everyone by placing Eisenhower, until then a relatively junior general, in charge of implementing the plan.

But the British, remembering the heavy casualties of trench warfare in World War I, and hoping to protect the route to India, their most important colony, preferred a perimeter approach. Air and naval attacks around the edge of the continent, especially in the Mediterranean, would be a prelude to a final invasion of Germany. British strategists assented to the basic plan but strongly urged a preliminary invasion of North Africa in the fall of 1942. Roosevelt, too, wanted American troops engaged in combat against Germany before the end of 1942 to offset growing pressure at home to concentrate on the Pacific; hence, after he overruled objections from his military advisers, American and British troops landed on the Atlantic and Mediterranean coasts of Morocco and Algeria in November 1942.

The British launched an attack against Rommel at El Alamein in Egypt and soon forced the Afrika Korps to retreat across Libya to Tunisia. Eisenhower, delayed by poor roads and bad weather, was slow in bringing up his forces, and in their first encounter with Rommel at the Kasserine Pass in the desert south of Tunis, inexperienced American troops suffered a humiliating defeat. General George Patton quickly rallied the demoralized soldiers, and by May 1943, Germany had been driven from Africa, leaving behind nearly 300,000 troops.

During these same months, the Soviet Union's Red Army had broken the back of German military power in the battle of Stalingrad. Turned back at the critical bend in the Volga, Hitler had poured in division after division in what was ultimately a losing cause; never again would Germany be able to take the offensive in Europe.

At Churchill's insistence, FDR agreed to follow up the North African victory with the invasion first of Sicily and then Italy in the summer of 1943. Italy dropped out of the war when Mussolini fled to Germany, but the Italian campaign proved to be a strategic dead end. Germany sent in enough divisions to establish a strong defensive line in the mountains south of Rome; American and British troops were forced to fight their way slowly up the peninsula, suffering heavy casualties.

More important, these Mediterranean operations delayed the second front, postponing it eventually to the spring of 1944. Meanwhile, the Soviets began to push the Germans out of Russia and looked forward to the liberation of Poland, Hungary, and Romania, where they could establish "friendly" communist regimes. Having borne the brunt of the fighting against Nazi Germany, Russia was ready to claim its reward—the postwar domination of eastern Europe.

Checking Japan in the Pacific

Both the decision to defeat Germany first and the vast expanses of the Pacific dictated the nature of the war against Japan. The United States conducted amphibious island-hopping campaigns rather than attempting to reconquer the Dutch East Indies, Southeast Asia, and China. There would be two separate American operations. One, led by Douglas MacArthur based in Australia, would move from New Guinea back to the Philippines, while the other, commanded by Admiral Chester Nimitz from Hawaii, was directed at key Japanese islands in the Central Pacific. The original plan called for the two offensives to come together for the final invasion of the Japanese home islands.

Success in the Pacific depended above all else on control of the sea. The devastation at Pearl Harbor gave Japan the initial edge, but fortunately, the United States had not lost any of its four aircraft carriers. In the battle of the Coral Sea in May 1942, American naval forces blocked a Japanese thrust to outflank Australia. The turning point came one month later at Midway. A powerful Japanese task force threatened to seize this remote American outpost more than a thousand miles west of Pearl Harbor; Japan's real objective was the destruction of what remained of the American Pacific fleet. Superior American airpower enabled Nimitz's forces to engage the enemy at long range. Japanese fighters shot down thirty-five of forty-one attacking torpedo bombers, but a second wave of dive-bombers scored hits on three Japanese carriers. The battle of Midway ended with the loss of four Japanese aircraft carriers compared to just one American carrier. It was the first defeat the modern Japanese navy had ever suffered, and it left the United States in control of the Central Pacific.

Encouraged by the victory, American forces launched their first Pacific offensive in the Solomon Islands, east of New Guinea, in August 1942. Both sides suffered heavy losses, but six months later the last Japanese were driven from the key island of Guadalcanal. At the same time, MacArthur began the long, slow, and bloody job of driving the Japanese back along the north coast of New Guinea.

By early 1943, the defensive phase of the war with Japan was over. The enemy surge had been halted in both the central and the southwestern Pacific, and the United States was preparing to penetrate the Gilbert, Marshall, and Caroline Islands and recapture the Philippines. Just as Russia had broken German power in Europe, so the United States, fighting alone except for Australia and New Zealand, had halted the Japanese. And, like the USSR with its plans for eastern Europe, America expected to reap the rewards of victory by dominating the Pacific in the future.

The Home Front

How did American domestic life change during World War II?

World War II had a greater impact than the Great Depression on American life. While American soldiers and sailors fought abroad, the nation underwent sweeping social and economic changes at home. American industry worked to capacity to meet the need for war materials. Increased production in both industry and agriculture benefited workers and farmers alike. The expansion of war-related industries encouraged many people to move to where new jobs had sprung up. Women moved out of the home into the paid workforce; rural dwellers relocated to urban areas, and northerners and easterners sought new opportunities and new homes in the South and West. Another beneficiary of the return to prosperity brought on by the war was FDR, who had seen the nation through the dark days of the depression. The nation's economic recovery helped him win reelection to the presidency for a fourth term in 1944.

The Arsenal of Democracy

American industry made the nation's single most important contribution to victory. Even though more than fifteen million Americans served in the armed forces, it was the nearly sixty million who worked on farms and factories who achieved the miracle of production that ensured the defeat of Germany and Japan. The manufacturing plants that had run at half capacity through the 1930s now hummed with activity. In Detroit, automobile assembly lines were converted to produce tanks and airplanes; Henry Ford built the giant Willow Run factory, covering 67 acres, where forty-two thousand workers turned out a B-24 bomber every hour. Henry J. Kaiser, a California industrialist who constructed huge West Coast shipyards to meet the demand for cargo vessels and landing craft, operated on an equally large scale. His plant in Richmond, California, reduced the time to build a merchant ship from 105 to 14 days. In part, America won the battle of the Atlantic by building ships faster than German U-boats could sink them.

This vast industrial expansion, however, created many problems. In 1942, President Roosevelt appointed Donald Nelson, a Sears, Roebuck executive, to head a War Production Board (WPB). A jovial, easygoing man, Nelson soon was outmaneuvered by the army and the navy, which preferred to negotiate directly with large corporations. The WPB allowed business to claim rapid depreciation, and thus huge tax credits, for new plants, and it awarded lucrative cost-plus contracts for urgently needed goods. Shortages of critical materials such as steel, aluminum, and copper led to an allocation system based on military priorities. Rubber, cut off by the Japanese conquest of Southeast Asia, was particularly scarce; the administration finally began gasoline rationing in 1943 to curb pleasure driving and prolong tire life. The government itself built fifty-one synthetic-rubber plants, which by 1944 were producing nearly one million tons a year for the tires of American airplanes and military vehicles. All in all, the nation's factories turned out twice as many goods as did German and Japanese industry combined.

Roosevelt revealed the same tendency toward compromise in directing the economic mobilization as he did in shaping the New Deal. When the Office of Price Administration—which tried to curb inflation by controlling prices and rationing scarce goods such as sugar, canned food, and shoes—clashed with the WPB, FDR appointed James Byrnes to head an Office of Economic Stabilization. Byrnes, a former South Carolina senator and Supreme Court justice, used political judgment to settle disputes between agencies and keep all groups happy. The president was also forced to compromise with Congress, which pared down the administration's requests for large tax increases. Half the cost of the war was financed by borrowing; the other half came from revenues. A $7 billion revenue increase in 1942 included so many first-time taxpayers that in the following year the Treasury Department instituted a new practice—withholding income taxes from workers' wages.

A result of the wartime economic explosion was a growing affluence. Despite the federal incentives to business, heavy excess-profit taxes and a 94 percent tax rate for the very rich kept the wealthy from benefiting unduly. The huge increase in federal spending, from $9 billion in 1940 to $98 billion in 1944, spread through American society. A government agreement with labor unions in 1943 held wage rates to a 15 percent increase, but the long hours of overtime resulted in doubling and sometimes tripling the weekly paychecks of factory workers. Farmers shared in the new prosperity as their incomes quadrupled between 1940 and 1945. For the first time in the twentieth century, the lowest fifth of wage earners increased their share of the national income in relation to the more affluent; their income rose by 68 percent between 1941 and 1945, compared to a 20 percent increase for the well-to-do.

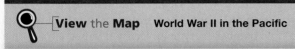

View the **Map**   World War II in the Pacific

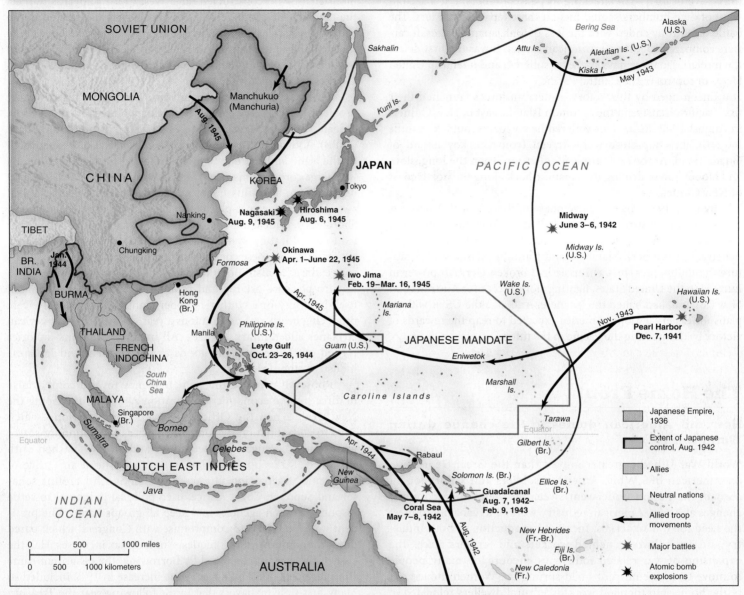

WORLD WAR II IN THE PACIFIC The tide of battle turned in the Pacific the same year as in Europe. The balance of sea power shifted back to the United States from Japan after the naval victories of 1942.

Most important, this rising income ensured postwar prosperity. Workers and farmers saved their money, channeling much of it into government war bonds, waiting for the day when they could buy the cars and home appliances they had done without during the long years of depression and war.

A Nation on the Move

The war led to a vast migration of the American population. Young men left their homes for training camps and then for service overseas. Defense workers and their families, some nine million people in all, moved to work in the new booming shipyards, munitions factories, and aircraft plants. Norfolk, Virginia; San Diego,

California; Mobile, Alabama; and other centers of defense production grew by more than 50 percent in just a year or two. Rural areas lost population while coastal regions, especially along the Pacific and the Gulf of Mexico, drew millions of people. The location of army camps in the South and West created boom conditions in the future Sunbelt, as did the concentration of aircraft factories and shipyards in this region. California had the greatest gains, adding nearly two million to its population in less than five years.

This movement of people caused severe social problems. Housing was in short supply. Migrating workers crowded into house trailers and boardinghouses, bringing unexpected windfalls to landlords. In one boomtown, a reporter described an old Victorian house that had five bedrooms on the second floor.

"Three of them," he wrote, "held two cots apiece, the two others held three cots." But the owner revealed that "the third floor is where we pick up the velvet.... We rent to workers in different shifts...three shifts a day...seven bucks a week apiece."

Family life suffered under these crowded living conditions. An increase in the number of marriages, as young people searched for something to hang on to in the midst of wartime turmoil, was offset by a rising divorce rate. The baby boom that would peak in the 1950s began during the war and brought its own set of problems. Only a few publicly funded day-care centers were available, and working mothers worried about their "latchkey children." Schools in the boom areas were unable to cope with the influx of new students; a teacher shortage, intensified by the lure of higher wages in war industries, compounded the education crisis.

Despite these problems, women found the war a time of economic opportunity. The demand for workers led to a dramatic rise in women's employment, from fourteen million working women in 1940 to nineteen million by 1945. Most of the new women workers were married and many were middle-aged, thus broadening the composition of the female workforce, which in the past had been composed primarily of young single women. Women entered industries once viewed as exclusively male; by the end of the war, they worked alongside men tending blast furnaces in steel mills and welding hulls in shipyards. Few challenged the traditional view of gender roles, yet the wartime experience helped temporarily undermine the concept that woman's only proper place was in the home. Women enjoyed the hefty weekly paychecks, which rose by 50 percent from 1941 to 1943, and they took pride in their contributions to the war effort. "To hell with the life I have had," commented a former fashion designer. "This war is too damn serious, and it is too damn important to win it."

African Americans shared in the wartime migration, but racial prejudice limited their social and economic gains. Nearly one million served in the armed forces, but relatively few saw combat. The army placed black soldiers in segregated units, usually led by white officers, and used them for service and construction tasks. The navy was even worse, relegating them to menial jobs until late in the war. African Americans were denied the chance to become petty officers, Secretary of the Navy Frank Knox explained, because experience had shown that "men of the colored race... cannot maintain discipline among men of the white race."

African American civilians fared a little better. In 1941, black labor leader A. Philip Randolph threatened a massive march on Washington to force President Roosevelt to end racial discrimination in defense industries and government employment and to integrate the armed forces. FDR compromised, persuading Randolph to call off the march and drop his integration demand in return for an executive order creating a Fair Employment Practices Committee (FEPC) to ban racial discrimination in war industries. As a result, African American employment by the federal government rose from sixty thousand in 1941 to two hundred thousand by the end of the war. The FEPC proved less successful in the private sector. Weak in funding and staff, the FEPC was able to act on only one-third of the eight thousand complaints it received. The nationwide shortage of labor was more influential than the FEPC in accounting for the rise in black employment during wartime. African Americans moved from the rural South

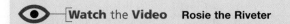 **Watch** the **Video** Rosie the Riveter

U.S. government publicity campaigns encouraged women to assume work in male dominated trades during World War II to replace men who were now in the military. Perhaps, the best known symbol of this industrial female worker was "Rosie the Riveter," a strong, efficient, and patriotic woman who also retained admirable feminine qualities.

to northern and western cities, finding jobs in the automobile, aircraft, and shipbuilding industries.

The movement of an estimated seven hundred thousand people helped transform black-white relations from a regional issue into a national concern that could no longer be ignored. The limited housing and recreational facilities for both black and white war workers created tensions that led to urban race riots. On a hot Sunday evening in June 1943, blacks and whites began exchanging insults and then blows near Belle Isle recreation park in Detroit. The next day, a full-scale riot broke out in which twenty-three blacks and nine whites died. The fighting raged for twenty-four hours until national guard troops were brought in to restore order. Later that summer, only personal intervention by New York Mayor Fiorello LaGuardia quelled a Harlem riot that took the lives of six blacks.

These outbursts of racial violence fueled the resentments that would grow into the postwar civil rights movement. For most African Americans, despite economic gains, World War II was a reminder of the inequality of American life. "Just carve on my tombstone,"

Read the Document   A. Philip Randolph, "Why Should We March" (1942)

A. Philip Randolph (1889–1979) was a prominent African American labor leader and civil rights leader. In 1941, FDR and Randolph reached a political compromise that averted a threatened march on Washington, D.C., demanding integration of the military and an end to racial discrimination in defense industries and government employment.

remarked one black soldier in the Pacific, "'Here lies a black man killed fighting a yellow man for the protection of a white man.'"

One-third of a million Mexican Americans served in the armed forces and shared some of the same experiences as African Americans. Although they were not as completely segregated, many served in the 88th Division, made up largely of Mexican American officers and troops, which earned the nickname "Blue Devils" in the Italian campaign. At home, Spanish-speaking people left the rural areas of Texas, New Mexico, and California for jobs in the cities, especially in aircraft plants and petroleum refineries. Despite low wages and union resistance, they improved their economic position substantially. But they still faced discrimination based both on skin color and language, most notably in the Los Angeles "zoot suit" riots in 1943 when white sailors attacked Mexican American youths

dressed in their distinctive outfits—long jackets worn with pants tightly pegged at the ankles. The racial prejudice heightened feelings of ethnic identity and led returning Mexican American veterans to form organizations such as the American G.I. Forum to press for equal rights in the future.

A tragic counterpoint to the voluntary movement of American workers in search of jobs was the forced relocation of 120,000 Japanese Americans from the West Coast. Responding to racial fears in California after Pearl Harbor, President Roosevelt approved an army order in February 1942 to move all Japanese Americans on the West Coast to concentration camps in the interior. More than two-thirds of those detained were *Nisei*, native-born Americans whose only crime was their Japanese ancestry. Forced to sell their farms and businesses at distress prices, the Japanese Americans lost not only their liberty but also most of their worldly goods. Herded into ten hastily built detention centers in seven western and southern states, they lived as prisoners in tar-papered barracks behind barbed wire, guarded by armed troops.

Appeals to the Supreme Court proved fruitless; in 1944, six justices upheld relocation on grounds of national security in wartime. Beginning in 1943, individual Nisei could win release by pledging their loyalty and finding a job away from the West Coast. Some thirty-five thousand left the camps during the next two years, including more than thirteen thousand who joined the armed forces. The all-Nisei 442nd Combat Team served gallantly in the European theater, losing more than five hundred men in battle and winning more than a thousand citations for bravery. One World War II veteran remembers that when his unit was in trouble, the commander would issue a familiar appeal: "Call in the Japs."

JAPANESE AMERICAN INTERNMENT CAMPS Following the attack on Pearl Harbor, President Roosevelt established the War Relocation Authority and charged the agency with the task of evacuating Japanese Americans from the West Coast and transporting them to internment camps.

📖—Read the Document Japanese Relocation Order

Family in Jerome Camp, by Japanese American painter Henry Sugimoto, depicts a family in their quarters at an internment camp in a southern Arkansas swampland. Like many Japanese Americans living on the West Coast, the Sugimotos were first ordered from their homes to large assembly centers such as the former fairgrounds at Fresno, California. There, whole families were assigned to individual horse stalls while they awaited relocation to one of the internment camps located in isolated areas of California, Arizona, Idaho, Utah, Colorado, Wyoming, and Arkansas. Conditions in the camps were equally dismal. Whole families lived in a single room furnished with little more than a few cots, some blankets, and a single light bulb.

For other Nisei, the experience was bitter. More than five thousand renounced their American citizenship and chose to live in Japan at the war's end. The government did not close down the last detention center until March 1946. Japanese Americans never experienced the torture and mass death of the German concentration camps, but their treatment was a disgrace to a nation fighting for freedom and democracy. Finally, in 1988, Congress voted an indemnity of $1.2 billion for the estimated sixty thousand surviving Japanese Americans detained during World War II. Susumi Emori, who had been moved with his wife

and four children from his farm in Stockton, California, to a camp in Arkansas, felt vindicated. "It was terrible," he said, with tears in his eyes, "but it was a time of war. Anything can happen. I didn't blame the United States for that."

Win-the-War Politics

Franklin Roosevelt used World War II to strengthen his leadership and maintain Democratic political dominance. As war brought about prosperity and removed the economic discontent that had sustained the New Deal, FDR announced that "Dr. New Deal" had given way to "Dr. Win-the-War." Congress, already controlled by a conservative coalition of southern Democrats and northern Republicans, had almost slipped into GOP hands in 1942. With a very low voter turnout, due in part to the large numbers of men in service and uprooted workers who failed to meet residency requirements for voting, the Republicans won forty-four new seats in the House and nine in the Senate and elected governors in New York and California as well.

In 1944, Roosevelt responded to the Democratic slippage by dropping Henry Wallace, his liberal and visionary vice president, for Harry Truman, a moderate and down-to-earth Missouri senator who was acceptable to all factions of the Democratic party. Equally important, FDR received increased political support from organized labor, which had grown in membership during the war from ten to fifteen million. The newly organized political action committee (PAC) of the CIO, headed by Sidney Hillman, conducted massive door-to-door drives to register millions of workers and their families.

THE ELECTION OF 1944

Candidate	Party	Popular Vote	Electoral Vote
Roosevelt	Democrat	25,602,504	432
Dewey	Republican	22,006,285	99

The Republicans nominated Thomas E. Dewey, who had been elected governor of New York after gaining fame as a prosecutor of organized crime. Dewey, moderate in his views, played down opposition to the New Deal and instead tried to make Roosevelt's age and health the primary issues, along with the charge that the Democrats were soft on communism.

Despite his abrasive campaign style, Dewey did not advocate a return to isolationism. The Republican Party was trying hard to shake the obstructionist image it had gained during the League of Nations fight in 1919; it went on record in 1943 as favoring American postwar cooperation for world peace. Indeed, Dewey pioneered a bipartisan approach to foreign policy. He accepted wartime planning for the future United Nations and kept the issue of an international organization out of the campaign.

Reacting to the issues of his age and health, especially after a long bout with influenza in the spring, FDR disregarded the advice of his doctors and took a five-hour drive in an open car through the rain-soaked streets of New York City just before the election. His vitality impressed the voters, and in November 1944 he swept back into office for a fourth term. The campaign, however, had taken its toll. The president, suffering from high blood pressure and congestive heart failure, had only a few months left to lead the nation.

Victory

How did the war end, and what were its consequences?

World War II ended with surprising swiftness. By 1943, the Axis tide had been turned in Europe and Asia, and it did not take long for Russia, the United States, and England to mount the offensives that drove Germany and Japan back across the vast areas they had conquered and set the stage for their final defeat.

The long-awaited second front finally came on June 6, 1944. For two years, the United States and England concentrated on building up an invasion force of nearly three million troops and a vast armada of ships and landing craft to carry them across the English Channel. Hoping to catch Hitler by surprise, Eisenhower chose the Normandy peninsula, where the absence of good harbors had led to lighter German fortifications. Allied aircraft bombed northern France for six weeks preceding the assault in order to block the movement of German reinforcements once the invasion began.

D-Day was originally set for June 5, but bad weather forced a delay. Relying on a forecasted break in the storm, Eisenhower gambled on going ahead on June 6. During the night, three divisions parachuted down behind the German defenses; at dawn, the British and American troops fought their way ashore at five points along a sixty-mile stretch of beach, encountering stiff German resistance at several points. By the end of the day, however, Eisenhower had won his beachhead; a week later, more than one-third of a million men were slowly pushing back the German forces through the hedgerows of Normandy. The breakthrough came on July 25 when General Omar Bradley decimated the enemy with a massive artillery and aerial bombardment at Saint-Lô, opening a gap for General George Patton's Third Army. American tanks raced across the French countryside, trapping thousands of Germans and liberating Paris by August 25. Allied troops reached the Rhine River by September, but a shortage of supplies, especially gasoline, forced a three-month halt.

Hitler took advantage of this breathing spell to deliver a daring counterattack. In mid-December, the remaining German armored divisions burst through a weak point in the Allied lines in the Ardennes Forest, planning a breakout to the coast that would have cut off nearly one-third of Eisenhower's forces. A combination of tactical surprise and bad weather, which prevented Allied air support, led to a huge bulge in the American lines. But an airborne division dug in at the key crossroads of Bastogne, in Belgium, and held off a much larger German force. Allied reinforcements and clearing weather then combined to end the attack. By committing nearly all his reserves to the Battle of the Bulge, Hitler had delayed Eisenhower's advance into Germany, but he also had fatally weakened German resistance in the west.

The end came quickly. A massive Russian offensive began in mid-January and swept across the Oder River toward Berlin. General Bradley's troops, finding a bridge left virtually intact by the retreating Germans, crossed the Rhine on March 7. Eisenhower overruled the British, who favored one concentrated drive on Berlin. Instead the Allied forces advanced on a broad front, capturing the industrial Ruhr basin and breaking the Nazi death grip on prisoner populations. (See the Feature Essay, "The Face of the Holocaust," pp. 658–659.) The Americans and British met the Russians at the Elbe in late April. With the Red Army already in the suburbs of Berlin, Adolf Hitler committed suicide on April 30. A week later, on May 7, 1945, Eisenhower accepted the unconditional surrender of all German forces. Just eleven months and a day after the landings

View the **Closer Look**   D-Day Landing, June 6, 1944

The D-Day Landing by American and British forces on June 6, 1944, actually represented two landings: an airborne assault of 24,000 Allied paratroopers shortly after midnight and an Allied amphibious landing by Allied armored and infantry divisions at 6:30 am off the coast of France in Normandy.

in Normandy, the Allied forces had brought the war in Europe to a successful conclusion.

War Aims and Wartime Diplomacy

The American contribution to Hitler's defeat was relatively minor compared to the damage inflicted by the Soviet Union. At the height of the German invasion of Russia, more than 300 Soviet divisions had been locked in battle with 250 German ones, a striking contrast to the 58 divisions the United States and Britain used in the Normandy invasion. As his armies overran Poland and the Balkan countries, Joseph Stalin was determined to retain control over this region, which had been the historic pathway for Western invasion into Russia. Delay in opening the second front and an innate distrust of the West convinced the Soviets that they should maximize their territorial gains by imposing communist regimes on eastern Europe.

American postwar goals were quite different. Now believing the failure to join the League of Nations in 1919 had led to the coming of World War II, the American people and their leaders vowed to put their faith in a new attempt at collective security. At Moscow in 1943, Secretary of State Cordell Hull had won Russian agreement to participate in a future world organization at the war's end. The first wartime Big Three conference brought together Roosevelt, Churchill, and Stalin at Teheran, Iran, in late 1943. Stalin reaffirmed this commitment and also indicated to President Roosevelt that Russia would enter the war against Japan once Germany was defeated.

By the time the Big Three met again in February 1945 at the **Yalta Conference**, the military situation favored the Russians. While British and American forces were still recovering from the Battle of the Bulge, the Red Army was advancing to within fifty miles of Berlin. Stalin drove a series of hard bargains. He refused to give up his plans for communist domination of Poland and the Balkans, although he did agree to Roosevelt's request for a Declaration of Liberated Europe, which called for free elections without providing for any method of enforcement or supervision. More important for the United States, Stalin promised to enter the Pacific war three months after Germany surrendered. In return, Roosevelt offered extensive concessions in Asia,

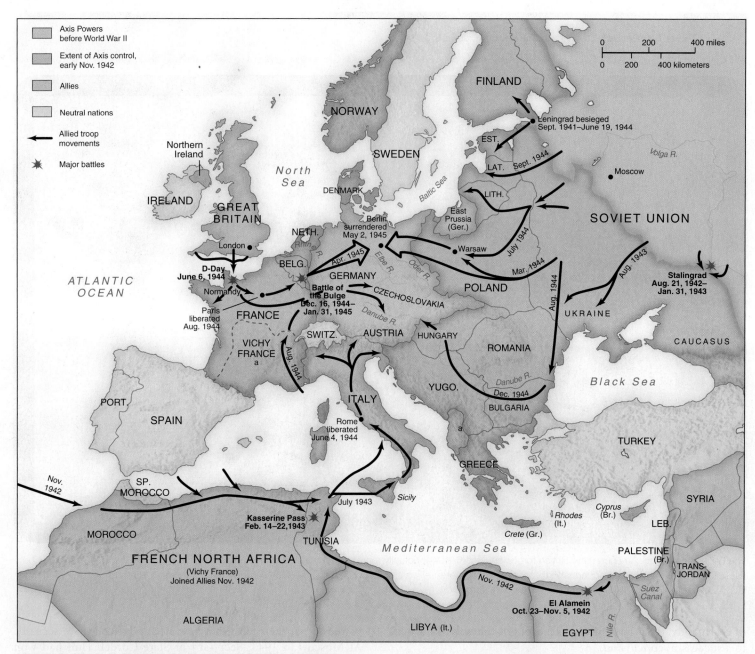

WORLD WAR II IN EUROPE AND NORTH AFRICA The tide of battle shifted in this theater during the winter of 1942–1943. The massive German assault on the eastern front was turned back by the Russians at Stalingrad, and the Allied forces recaptured North Africa.

including Russian control over Manchuria. While neither a sellout nor a betrayal, as some critics have charged, Yalta was a significant diplomatic victory for the Soviets—one that reflected Russia's major contribution to a victory in Europe.

For the president, the long journey to Yalta proved to be too much. His health continued to fail after his return to Washington. In early April, FDR left the capital for Warm Springs, Georgia, where he had always been able to relax. He was sitting for his portrait at midday on April 12, 1945, when he suddenly complained of a "terrific headache," then slumped forward and died.

The nation mourned a man who had gallantly met the challenge of depression and global war. Unfortunately, FDR had taken no steps to prepare his successor for the difficult problems that lay

ahead. The defeat of Nazi Germany dissolved the one strong bond between the United States and the Soviet Union. With very different histories, cultures, and ideologies, the two nations were bound to drift apart. It was now up to the inexperienced Harry Truman to manage the growing rivalry that was destined to develop into the future Cold War.

Triumph and Tragedy in the Pacific

The total defeat of Germany in May 1945 turned all eyes toward Japan. Although the combined chiefs of staff had originally estimated it would take eighteen months after Germany's surrender to conquer Japan, American forces moved with surprising speed.

British Prime Minister Winston Churchill (left) and Soviet Foreign Minister Vyacheslav Molotov (right) meet prior to the start of the Yalta Conference, February 4–11, 1945. The wartime conference, also attended by President Franklin Roosevelt and Soviet Premier Joseph Stalin, was organized mainly to discuss the postwar reorganization of European nations and Soviet entrance into the war against Japan.

Admiral Nimitz swept through the Gilbert, Caroline, and Marshall Islands in 1944, securing bases for further advances and building airfields for American B-29s to begin a deadly bombardment of the Japanese home islands. General MacArthur cleared New Guinea of the last Japanese defender in early 1944 and began planning his long-heralded return to the Philippines. American troops landed on the island of Leyte on October 20, 1944, and Manila fell in early February 1945. The Japanese navy, in a Pacific version of the Battle of the Bulge, launched a daring three-pronged attack on the American invasion fleet in Leyte Gulf. The U.S. Navy rallied to blunt all three Japanese thrusts, sinking four carriers and ending any further Japanese naval threat.

The defeat of Japan was now only a matter of time. The United States had three possible ways to proceed. The military favored a full-scale invasion, beginning on the southernmost island of Kyushu in November 1945 and culminating with an assault on Honshu (the main island of Japan) and a climactic battle for Tokyo in 1946; casualties were expected to run into the hundreds

of thousands. Diplomats suggested a negotiated peace, urging the United States to modify the unconditional surrender formula to permit Japan to retain the institution of the emperor.

The third possibility involved the highly secret **Manhattan Project**. Since 1939, the United States had spent $2 billion to develop an atomic bomb based on the fission of radioactive uranium and plutonium. Scientists, many of them refugees from Europe, worked to perfect this deadly new weapon at the University of Chicago; Oak Ridge, Tennessee; Hanford, Washington; and a remote laboratory in Los Alamos, New Mexico. In the New Mexico desert on July 16, 1945, they successfully tested the first atomic bomb, creating a fireball brighter than several suns and a telltale mushroom cloud that rose some 40,000 feet above an enormous crater in the desert floor.

Truman had been unaware of the existence of the Manhattan Project before he became president on April 12. Now he simply followed the recommendation of a committee headed by Secretary of War Henry L. Stimson to drop the bomb on a Japanese city. The committee discussed but rejected the possibility of inviting the

Feature Essay | The Face of the Holocaust

Thousands of piled shoes formerly belonging to Jewish and other European men, women, and children murdered at an unidentified Nazi death camp during World War II.

The liberation of the Nazi death camps near the end of World War II was not a priority objective; nor was it a planned operation. Since 1942, the U.S. government had known that the Nazis were murdering Jews en masse, but officials of the Roosevelt administration were divided on what to do about it. Some argued for air raids on the death camps, even if such raids were likely to kill large numbers of the Jewish inmates. Others contended that air raids alone would not stop the killing, that they would divert resources from the broader offensive against Germany, and that military victory was the surest path to the liberation of the camps. In part because no one in the United States comprehended the full enormity of Hitler's "Final Solution," Roosevelt sided with the latter group, and no special action was taken against the death camps. As a result, it was by chance that Allied forces first stumbled upon the camps, and the GIs who threw open the gates to that living hell were totally unprepared for what they found.

In November 1944 the U.S. Army discovered its first camp, Natzwiller-Struthof, which had been abandoned by the Germans months before. Viewing Natzwiller from a distance, Milton Bracker of the *New York Times* noted its deceptive similarity to an American Civilian Conservation Corps camp: "The sturdy green barracks buildings looked exactly like those that housed forestry trainees in the U.S. during the early New Deal."

As he toured the grounds, however, he faced a starker reality and slowly came to think the unthinkable. In the crematorium, he reported, "I cranked the elevator tray a few times and slid the furnace tray a few times, and even at that moment, I did not believe what I was doing was real."

"There were no prisoners," he wrote, "no screams, no burly guards, no taint of death in the air as on a battlefield." Bracker had to stretch his imagination to its limits to comprehend the camp's silent testimony to the Nazi attempt to exterminate the Jews of Europe. U.S. military personnel who toured Natzwiller shared this sense of the surreal. In their report to headquarters, they carefully qualified every observation. They described "what appeared to be a disinfection unit," a room "allegedly used as a lethal gas chamber," "a cellar room with a special type elevator," and "an incinerator room with equipment obviously intended for the burning of human bodies." They saw before them the evidence of German atrocities, but the truth was so horrible, they could not quite bring themselves to draw the obvious conclusions.

Inside the Vicious Heart, Robert Abzug's study of the liberation of the concentration camps, refers to this phenomenon as "double vision." Faced with a revelation so terrible, witnesses could not fully comprehend the evidence of the systematic murder of more than six million men, women, and children. But as the Allied armies advanced into Germany, the shocking evidence mounted. On April 4, 1945, the Fourth Armored Division of the Third Army unexpectedly discovered Ohrdruf, a relatively small concentration camp. Ohrdruf's liberation had a tremendous impact on American forces. It was the first camp discovered intact, with its grisly array of the dead and dying. Inside the compound, corpses were piled in heaps in the barracks. An infantryman recalled, "I guess the most vivid recollection of the whole camp is the pyre that was located on the edge of the camp. It was a big pit, where they stacked bodies—stacked bodies and wood and burned them."

On April 12, generals Eisenhower, Bradley, and Patton toured Ohrdruf. The generals, professional soldiers familiar with the devastation of battle, had never seen its like. Years later, Bradley recalled, "The smell of death overwhelmed us even before we passed through the stockade. More than 3200 naked, emaciated bodies had been flung into shallow graves. Others lay in the street where they had fallen."

Eisenhower ordered every available armed forces unit in the area to visit Ohrdruf. "We are told that the American soldier does not know what he is fighting for," said Eisenhower. "Now at least he will know what he is fighting against." He urged government officials and journalists to visit the camps and tell the world. In an official message Eisenhower summed it up:

We are constantly finding German camps in which they have placed political prisoners where unspeakable conditions exist. From my own personal observation, I can state unequivocally that all written statements up to now do not paint the full horrors.

On April 11, the Timberwolf Division of the Third Army uncovered Nordhausen. They found three thousand dead and only seven hundred survivors. The scene sickened battle-hardened veterans:

The odors, well there is no way to describe the odors.... Many of the boys I am talking about now—these were tough soldiers, there were combat men who had been all the way through the invasion—were ill and vomiting, throwing up, just at the sight of this.

For some, the liberation of Nordhausen changed the meaning of the war.

I must also say that my fellow GIs, most thought that any stories they had read in the paper... were either not true or at least exaggerated. And it did not sink in, what this was all about, until we got into Nordhausen.

If the experience at Nordhausen gave many GIs a new sense of mission in battle, it also forced them to distance themselves from the realities of the camps. Only by closing off their emotions could they go about the grim task of sorting out the living from the dead and tending to the survivors. Margaret Bourke-White, whose *Life* magazine photographs brought the horrors of the death camps to millions on the home front, recalled working "with a veil over my mind."

People often ask me how it is possible to photograph such atrocities. In photographing the murder camps, the protective veil was so tightly drawn that I hardly knew what I had taken until I saw prints of my own photographs.

By the end of 1945, most of the liberators had come home and returned to civilian life. Once home, their experiences produced no common moral responses. No particular pattern emerged in their occupational, political, and religious behavior, beyond a fear of the rise of postwar totalitarianism shared by most Americans. Few spoke publicly about their role in the liberation of the camps; most found that after a short period of grim fascination, their friends and families preferred to forget. Some had nightmares, but few reported being tormented by memories. For the liberators, the ordeal was over. For the survivors of the **Holocaust**, liberation was but the first step in the tortuous process of rebuilding broken bodies and shattered lives.

QUESTIONS FOR DISCUSSION

1. Why did American leaders during the war have such difficulty comprehending the scope of the Holocaust?

2. How did the discovery of the Holocaust confirm Americans' belief that the war was necessary and just?

The atomic bomb dropped on Nagasaki, a provincial capital and naval base in southern Japan, on August 9, 1945, virtually obliterated the city and killed about forty thousand people. Only buildings made with reinforced concrete remained standing after the blast.

Japanese to observe a demonstration shot at a remote Pacific site and even ruled out the idea of giving advance notice of the bomb's destructive power. Neither Truman nor Stimson had any qualms about the decision to drop the bomb without warning. They viewed it as a legitimate wartime measure, one designed to save the lives of hundreds of thousands of Americans—and Japanese—that would be lost in a full-scale invasion.

Weather conditions on the morning of August 6 dictated the choice of Hiroshima as the bomb's target. The explosion incinerated four square miles of the city, instantly killing more than sixty thousand. Two days later, Russia entered the war against Japan, and the next day, August 9, the United States dropped a second bomb on Nagasaki. There were no more atomic bombs available, but no more were needed. The emperor personally broke a deadlock in the Japanese cabinet and persuaded his ministers to surrender unconditionally on August 14, 1945. Three weeks later, Japan signed a formal capitulation agreement on the decks of the battleship *Missouri* in Tokyo Bay to bring World War II to its official close.

Many years later, scholars charged that Truman had more in mind than defeating Japan when he decided to use the atomic bomb. Citing air force and naval officers who claimed Japan could be defeated by a blockade or by conventional air attacks, these revisionists suggested the real reason for dropping the bomb was to impress the Soviet Union with the fact that the United States had exclusive possession of the ultimate weapon. The available evidence indicates that while Truman and his associates were aware of the possible effect on the Soviet Union, their primary motive was to end World War II as quickly and effortlessly as possible. The saving of American lives, along with a desire for revenge for Pearl Harbor, were uppermost in the decision to bomb Hiroshima and Nagasaki. Yet in using the atomic bomb to defeat Japan, the United States virtually guaranteed a postwar arms race with the Soviet Union.

Conclusion: The Transforming Power of War

The second great war of the twentieth century had a lasting impact on American life. For the first time, the nation's military potential had been reached. In 1945, the United States was unquestionably the strongest country on the earth, with eleven million men and women in uniform; a vast array of shipyards, aircraft plants, and munitions factories in full production; and a monopoly over the atomic bomb. For better or worse, the nation was now launched on a global career. In the future, the United States would be involved in all parts of the world, from western

Europe to remote jungles in Asia, from the nearby Caribbean to the distant Persian Gulf. And despite its enormous strength in 1945, the nation's new world role would encompass failure and frustration as well as power and dominion.

The legacy of war was equally strong at home. Four years of fighting brought about industrial recovery and unparalleled prosperity. The old pattern of unregulated free enterprise was as much a victim of the war as of the New Deal; big government and huge deficits had now become the norm as economic control passed from New York and Wall Street to Washington and Pennsylvania Avenue. The war led to far-reaching changes in American society that would become apparent only decades later. Such distinctive patterns of recent American life as the baby boom and the growth of the Sunbelt can be traced back to wartime origins. World War II was a watershed in twentieth-century America, ushering in a new age of global concerns and domestic upheaval.

Study Resources

 Take the **Study Plan** for **Chapter 27** *America and the World, 1921–1945* on **MyHistoryLab**

TIME LINE

1922 Washington Naval Conference limits tonnage

1928 Kellogg-Briand Pact outlaws war (August); Clark Memorandum repudiates Roosevelt Corollary (December)

1931 Japan occupies China's Manchurian province

1933 FDR extends diplomatic recognition to USSR

1936 Hitler's troops reoccupy Rhineland

1937 FDR signs permanent Neutrality Act (May); FDR urges quarantine of aggressor nations (October); Japanese planes sink USS *Panay* in China (December)

1938 Munich Conference appeases Hitler (September)

1939 Germany invades Poland; World War II begins

1941 Germany invades USSR; Japan attacks Pearl Harbor; United States enters World War II

1942 U.S. defeats Japanese at battle of Midway (June); Allies land in North Africa (November)

1943 Soviets smash Nazis at Stalingrad

1944 Allies land on Normandy beaches

1945 Big Three meet at Yalta (February); FDR dies, Harry Truman becomes president (April); Germany surrenders unconditionally (May); United States drops atomic bombs on Hiroshima and Nagasaki; Japan surrenders (August)

CHAPTER REVIEW

Retreat, Reversal, and Rivalry

Why were the United States and Japan on a collision course in the years following World War I?

To sustain its developing industrial economy after World War I, Japan sought to dominate China and exploit its resources. In response, the United States either had to abandon China or forcefully oppose Japan's expansion there. (p. 639)

Isolationism

What were isolationism, and why was it so appealing to Americans in the 1920s and 1930s?

Disillusionment with the outcome of World War I led to a policy of isolationism, by which Americans hoped to avoid responsibility for the peace of Europe and Asia, and to spare themselves the agony of war if peace failed. Isolationism had traditionally served Americans well, and many Americans expected that it would continue to do so. (p. 641)

The Road to War

How did the United States go from neutrality in the 1930s to war in 1941?

FDR gradually led the United States from neutrality in the 1930s to war in 1941, responding to German and Japanese aggression with careful political and diplomatic steps, including aid to Britain, an undeclared naval war against Germany, and economic pressure on Japan, which lashed out by attacking Pearl Harbor. (p. 644)

Turning the Tide Against the Axis

How did America and its allies halt the advances of Germany and Japan?

The United States formed an alliance with Britain and the Soviet Union against Germany and Japan. American and British forces fought the Germans in North Africa and Italy, while Soviet forces beat back the Germans in Russia. American ships and planes defeated Japanese forces at the Coral Sea and Midway. (p. 647)

The Home Front

How did American domestic life change during World War II?

During the war American industry churned out equipment at a rate unimagined before 1941. Record numbers of women and minorities entered the workforce. But 120,000 Japanese Americans were forced into concentration camps. (p. 649)

Victory

How did the war end, and what were its consequences?

The war in Europe ended in May 1945 after Allied and Soviet forces overran Germany. The war in the Pacific ended after the atomic bombing of Hiroshima and Nagasaki, and left the United States in undisputed control of Japan. (p. 654)

KEY TERMS AND DEFINITIONS

Kellogg–Briand Pact   Also called the Pact of Paris, this 1928 agreement was the brainchild of U.S. Secretary of State Frank B. Kellogg and French premier Aristide Briand. Its signatories, eventually including nearly all nations, pledged to shun war as an instrument of policy. It had little effect on the conduct of world affairs. p. 638

Axis Powers   During World War II, the alliance between Italy, Germany, and Japan was known as the "Rome–Berlin–Tokyo axis," and the three members were called the Axis Powers. They fought against the Allied Powers, led by the United States, Britain, and the Soviet Union. p. 642

Neutrality Acts   Laws in the 1930s that forbade selling munitions or lending money to belligerents. The 1937 act required that all other trade with countries at war be conducted on a cash-and-carry basis. p. 642

Lend-Lease   In 1941, Congress gave President Franklin D. Roosevelt the authority to sell, lend, lease, or transfer war materials to any country whose defense he declared vital to that of the United States. p. 644

Pearl Harbor   On December 7, 1941, Japanese warplanes attacked the U.S. fleet at Pearl Harbor, Hawaii. The attack marked America's entrance into World War II. p. 647

D-Day   June 6, 1944, the day Allied troops crossed the English Channel and opened a second front in western Europe during World War II. The "D" stands for "disembarkation": to leave a ship and go ashore. p. 654

Yalta Conference   A wartime conference in February 1945 in which the Allies agreed to final plans for the defeat of Germany and the terms of its occupation. The Soviets agreed to allow free elections in Poland, but they were never held. p. 655

Manhattan Project   The top-secret World War II program that produced the first atomic weapons. p. 657

Holocaust   The slaughter of six million Jews and other persons by Hitler's regime. p. 659

CRITICAL THINKING QUESTIONS

1. How did the memory of World War I affect the American approach to World War II?

2. How did Franklin Roosevelt aid Britain prior to American entry into World War II? Why did he have to be so careful in doing so?

3. What were some causes of tension within the American alliance during the war?

4. What happened to the civil rights movement during the war?

5. Was the atom bomb necessary to end the war? Why or why not?

MyHistoryLab Media Assignments

Find these resources in the Media Assignments folder for Chapter 27 on MyHistoryLab

Isolationism

View the **Map**   *World War II in Europe p. 643*

The Road to War

Read the **Document**   *Charles Lindbergh, Radio Address (1941) p. 645*

■ View the **Closer Look**   *The Japanese Raid on Pearl Harbor, December 7, 1941 p. 646*

The Home Front

View the **Map**   *World War II in the Pacific p. 650*

■ Watch the **Video**   *Rosie the Riveter p. 651*

Read the **Document**   *A. Philip Randolph, "Why Should We March" (1942) p. 652*

■ Read the **Document**   *Japanese Relocation Order p. 653*

Victory

■ View the **Closer Look**   *D-Day Landing, June 6, 1944 p. 655*

Watch the **Video**   *The Big Three—Yalta Conference p. 657*

■ Complete the **Assignment**   *The Face of the Holocaust p. 658*

■ *Indicates Study Plan Media Assignment*

Contents and Learning Objectives

((•●─[Listen to the **Audio File** on **myhistorylab**   **Chapter 28** *The Onset of the Cold War*

The Potsdam Summit

"I am getting ready to go see Stalin and Churchill," President Truman wrote to his mother in July 1945, "and it is a chore." On board the cruiser *Augusta*, the new president continued to complain about the upcoming **Potsdam Conference** in his diary. "How I hate this trip!" he confided. "But I have to make it win, lose, or draw, and we must win. I am giving nothing away except to save starving people, and even then I hope we can only help them to help themselves."

Halfway around the world, Joseph Stalin left Moscow a day late because of a slight heart attack. The Russian leader hated to fly, so he traveled by rail. Moreover, he ordered the heavily guarded train to detour around Poland for fear of an ambush, further delaying his arrival. When he made his entrance into Potsdam, a suburb of Berlin miraculously spared the total destruction that his forces had created in the German capital, he was ready to claim the spoils of war.

These two men, one the veteran revolutionary who had been in power for two decades, the other an untested leader in office for barely three months, symbolized the enormous differences that now separated the wartime allies. Stalin was above all a realist. Brutal in securing total control at home, he was more flexible in his foreign policy, bent on exploiting Russia's victory in World War II rather than aiming at world domination. Cunning and caution were the hallmarks of his diplomatic style.

Small in stature, ungainly in build, he radiated a catlike quality as he waited behind his unassuming façade, ready to dazzle an opponent with his "brilliant, terrifying tactical mastery." Truman, in contrast, personified traditional Wilsonian idealism. Lacking Roosevelt's guile, the new president placed his faith in international cooperation. Like many Americans, he believed implicitly in his country's innate goodness. Self-assured to the point of cockiness, he came to Potsdam clothed in the armor of self-righteousness.

Truman and Stalin met for the first time on July 17, 1945. "I told Stalin that I am no diplomat," the president recorded in his diary, "but usually said yes and no to questions after hearing all the argument." The Russian dictator's reaction to Truman remains a mystery, but Truman believed the first encounter went well. "I can deal with Stalin," he wrote. "He is honest—but smart as hell."

Together with Winston Churchill and his replacement, Clement Attlee, whose Labour party had just triumphed in British elections, Truman and Stalin clashed for the next ten days over such difficult issues as reparations, the Polish border, and the fate of eastern Europe. Truman presented the ideas and proposals formulated by his advisers; he saw his task as essentially procedural, and when he presided, he moved the agenda along in brisk fashion. After he

Churchill, Truman, and Stalin during the Potsdam Conference in July 1945. The conference revealed the growing divergence among the wartime allies that soon led to the onset of the Cold War.

had "banged through" three items one day, he commented, "I am not going to stay around this terrible place all summer, just to listen to speeches. I'll go home to the Senate for that." In an indirect, roundabout way, he informed Stalin of the existence of the atomic bomb, tested successfully in the New Mexico desert just before the conference began. Truman offered no details, and the impassive Stalin asked for none, commenting only that he hoped the United States would make "good use of it against the Japanese."

Reparations proved to be the crucial issue at Potsdam. The Russians wanted to rebuild their war-ravaged economy with German industry; the United States feared it would be saddled with the entire cost of caring for the defeated Germans. A compromise was finally reached. Each side would take reparations primarily from its own occupation zone, a solution that foreshadowed the future division of Germany. "Because they could not agree on how to govern Europe," wrote historian Daniel Yergin, "Truman and Stalin began to divide it." The other issues were referred to the newly created Council of Foreign Ministers, which would meet in the fall in London.

The Potsdam Conference thus ended on an apparent note of harmony; beneath the surface, however, the bitter antagonism of the Cold War was festering. A dozen years later, Truman reminisced to an old associate about Potsdam. "What a show that was!" Describing himself as "an innocent idealist" surrounded by wolves, he claimed that all the agreements reached there were "broken as soon as the unconscionable Russian Dictator returned to Moscow!" He added ruefully, "And I liked the little son of a bitch."

Potsdam marked the end of the wartime alliance. America and Russia, each distrustful of the other, began to engage in a long and bitter confrontation. For the next decade, the two superpowers would vie for control of postwar Europe, and later clash over the spread of communism to Asia. By the time Truman's and Stalin's successors met for the next summit conference at Geneva in 1955, the Cold War was at its height.

The Cold War Begins

How did the Cold War begin?

The conflict between the United States and the Soviet Union began gradually. For two years, the nations tried to adjust their differences over the division of Europe, postwar economic aid, and the atomic bomb through discussion and negotiation. The Council of Foreign Ministers provided the forum. Beginning in London during the fall of 1945 and meeting with their Russian counterparts in Paris, New York, and Moscow, American diplomats searched for a way to live in peace with a suspicious Soviet Union.

The Division of Europe

The fundamental disagreement was over who would control postwar Europe. In the east, the Red Army had swept over Poland and the Balkans, laying the basis for Soviet domination there. American and British forces had liberated western Europe from Scandinavia to Italy. The Russians, mindful of past invasions from the west across the plains of Poland, were intent on imposing communist governments loyal to Moscow in the Soviet sphere. The United States, on the other hand, upheld the principle of national self-determination, insisting the people in each country should freely choose their postwar rulers. The Soviets saw the demand for free elections as subversive, since they knew that popularly chosen regimes would be unfriendly to Russia. Suspecting American duplicity, Stalin brought down an **Iron Curtain** (Churchill's phrase) from the Baltic to the Adriatic as he created a series of satellite governments.

Germany was the key. The temporary zones of occupation gradually hardened into permanent lines of division. Ignoring the Potsdam Conference agreement that the country be treated as an economic unit, the United States and Great Britain were, by 1946, refusing to permit the Russians to take reparations from the industrial western zones. The initial harsh occupation policy gave way to more humane treatment of the German people and a slow but steady economic recovery. The United States and England merged their zones and championed the idea of the unification of all Germany. Russia, fearing a resurgence of German military power, responded by intensifying the communization of its zone, which included the jointly occupied city of Berlin. By 1947, England, France, and the United States were laying plans to transfer their authority to an independent West Germany.

The Soviet Union consolidated its grip on eastern Europe in 1946 and 1947. One by one, communist regimes replaced coalition governments in Poland, Hungary, Romania, and Bulgaria. Moving cautiously to avoid provoking the West, Stalin used communism as a means to dominate half of Europe, both to protect the security of the Soviet state and to advance its international power. The climax came in March 1948 when a coup in Czechoslovakia overthrew a democratic government and gave the Soviets a strategic foothold in central Europe.

The division of Europe was an inevitable aftereffect of World War II. Both sides were intent on imposing their values in the areas liberated by their troops. The Russians were no more likely to withdraw from eastern Europe than the United States and Britain were from Germany, France, and Italy. A frank recognition of competing spheres of influence might have avoided further escalation of tension. But the Western nations, remembering Hitler's aggression in the 1930s, began to see Stalin as an equally dangerous threat to their well-being. Instead of accepting him as a cautious leader bent on protecting Russian security, they perceived him as an aggressive dictator leading a communist drive for world domination.

Withholding Economic Aid

World War II had inflicted enormous damage on Russia. The brutal fighting had taken between fifteen and twenty million Russian lives, destroyed more than thirty thousand factories, and torn up forty thousand miles of railroad track. The industrialization

📖● Read the Document   Churchill's "Iron Curtain" Speech (March 5, 1946)

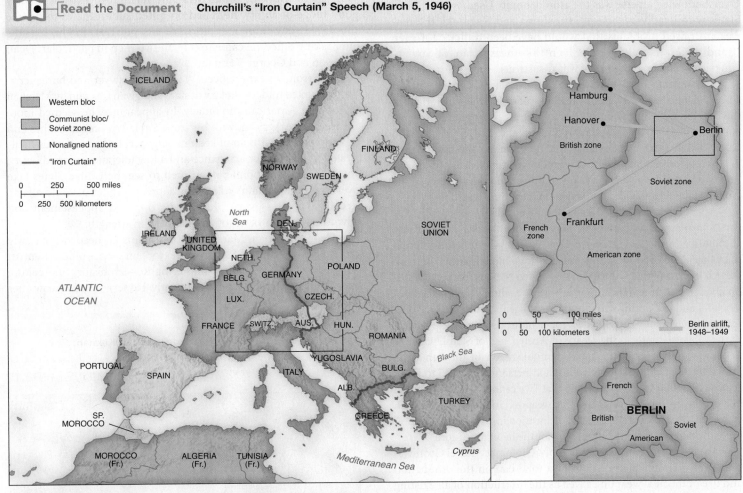

EUROPE AFTER WORLD WAR II The heavy red line splitting Germany shows in graphic form the division of Europe between the Western and Soviet spheres of influence. "From Stettin in the Baltic to Trieste in the Adriatic," said Winston Churchill in a speech at Fulton, Missouri, in 1946, "an iron curtain has descended across the continent."

that Stalin had achieved at such great sacrifice in the 1930s had been badly set back; even agricultural production had fallen by half during the war. Outside aid and assistance were vital for the reconstruction of the Soviet Union.

American leaders knew of Russia's plight and hoped to use it to good advantage. Wartime ambassador Averell Harriman wrote in 1944 that economic aid was "one of the most effective weapons at our disposal" in dealing with Russia. President Truman was convinced that economically "we held all the cards and the Russians had to come to us."

There were two possible forms of postwar assistance: loans and Lend-Lease. In January 1945, the Soviets requested a $6 billion loan to finance postwar reconstruction. Despite initial American encouragement, President Roosevelt deferred action on this request; as relations with Russia cooled, the chances for action dimmed. "Our experience," commented Harriman in April 1945, had "incontrovertibly proved it was not possible to bank goodwill in Moscow." By the war's end, the loan request, though never formally turned down, was dead.

Lend-Lease proved no more successful. In the spring of 1945, Congress instructed the administration not to use Lend-Lease for postwar reconstruction. President Truman went further, however, by signing an order on May 11, 1945, terminating all shipments to Russia, including those already at sea. The State Department saw the action as applying "leverage against the Soviet Union"; Stalin termed it "brutal." Heeding Russian protests, Truman resumed Lend-Lease shipments, but only until the war was over in August. After that, all Lend-Lease ended.

Deprived of American assistance, the Russians were forced to rebuild their economy through reparations. American and British resistance prevented them from taking reparations in western Germany, but the Soviets systematically removed factories and plants from other areas they controlled, including their zone of Germany, eastern Europe, and Manchuria. Slowly, the Russian economy recovered from the war, but the bitterness over the American refusal to extend aid convinced Stalin of Western hostility and thus deepened the growing antagonism between the Soviet Union and the United States.

The Atomic Dilemma

Overshadowing all else was the atomic bomb. Used by the United States with deadly success at Hiroshima and Nagasaki, the new weapon raised problems that would have been difficult for even friendly nations to resolve. Given the uneasy state of Soviet–American relations, the effect was disastrous.

The wartime policy followed by Roosevelt and Churchill ensured a postwar nuclear arms race. Instead of informing their major ally of the developing atomic bomb, they kept it a closely guarded secret. Stalin learned of the Manhattan Project through espionage and responded by starting a Soviet atomic program in 1943. By the time Truman informed Stalin of the weapon's existence at Potsdam, the Russians, aided by a steady stream of information from spies in the United States, were well on the way to making their own bomb.

After the war, the United States developed a disarmament plan that would turn control of fissionable material, then the processing plants, and ultimately the American stockpile of bombs over to an international agency. When President Truman appointed financier Bernard Baruch to present this proposal to the United Nations, Baruch insisted on changing it in several important ways, adding sanctions against violators and exempting the international agency from the UN veto. Ignoring scientists who pleaded for a more cooperative position, Baruch followed instead the advice of Army Chief of Staff Dwight D. Eisenhower, who cited the rapid demobilization of the American armed forces (from nearly twelve million personnel in 1945 to fewer than two million in 1947) to argue that "we cannot at this time limit our capability to produce or use this weapon." In effect, the **Baruch Plan**, with its multiple stages and emphasis on inspection, would preserve the American atomic monopoly for the indefinite future.

The Soviets responded predictably. Diplomat Andrei Gromyko presented a simple plan calling for a total ban on the production and use of the new weapon as well as the destruction of all existing bombs. The Russian proposal was founded on the same perception of national self-interest as the Baruch Plan. Although Russia had also demobilized rapidly, it still had nearly three million men under arms in 1947 and wanted to maximize its conventional strength by outlawing the atomic bomb.

No agreement was possible. Neither the United States nor the Soviet Union could abandon its position without surrendering a vital national interest. Wanting to preserve its monopoly, America stressed inspection and control; hoping to neutralize the U.S. advantage, Russia advocated immediate disarmament. The nuclear dilemma, inherent in the Soviet-American rivalry, blocked any negotiated settlement. Instead, the two superpowers agreed to disagree. Trusting neither each other nor any form of international cooperation, each concentrated on taking maximum advantage of its wartime gains. Thus the Russians exploited the territory they had conquered in Europe while the United States retained its economic and strategic advantages over the Soviet Union. The result was the Cold War.

Containment

What was containment, and why was it adopted?

A major departure in American foreign policy occurred in January 1947, when General George C. Marshall, the wartime army chief of staff, became secretary of state. Calm, mature, and orderly of mind, Marshall had the capability—honed in World War II—to think in broad strategic terms. An extraordinarily good judge of ability, he relied on gifted subordinates to handle the day-to-day implementation of his policies. In the months after taking office, he came to rely on two men in particular: Dean Acheson and George Kennan.

Acheson, an experienced Washington lawyer and bureaucrat, was appointed undersecretary of state and given free rein by Marshall to conduct American diplomacy. In appearance, he seemed more British than American, with his impeccable Ivy League clothes and bushy mustache. A man of keen intelligence, he had a carefully cultivated reputation for arrogance and a low tolerance for mediocrity. As an ardent Anglophile, he wanted to see the United States take over a faltering Britain's role as the supreme arbiter of world affairs. Recalling the lesson of Munich, he opposed appeasement and advocated a policy of negotiating only from strength.

George Kennan, Marshall's other mainstay, headed the newly created Policy Planning Staff. A career foreign service officer, Kennan had become a Soviet expert, mastering Russian history and culture as well as speaking the language fluently. He served in Moscow after

Read the Document   George F. Kennan, "The Long Telegram" (1946)

George F. Kennan (1904–2005) was an American political advisor, diplomat, political scientist, and historian. Kennan was instrumental in developing the policy of containment concerning the Soviet Union that dominated the immediate post–World War II era.

containment of Russian expansive tendencies." Such a policy of halting Soviet aggression would not lead to any immediate victory, Kennan warned. In the long run, however, he believed that the United States could force the Soviet Union to adopt more reasonable policies and live in peace with the West.

The Truman Doctrine

The initial step toward containment came in response to an urgent British request. Since March 1946, England had been supporting the Greek government in a bitter civil war against Communist guerrillas. On February 21, 1947, the British informed the United States that they could no longer afford to aid Greece or Turkey, the latter under heavy pressure from the Soviets for access to the Mediterranean. Believing the Russians responsible for the strife in Greece (in fact, they were not), Marshall, Acheson, and Kennan quickly decided the United States would have to assume Britain's role in the eastern Mediterranean.

Worried about congressional support, especially since the Republicans had gained control of Congress in 1946, Marshall called a meeting with the legislative leadership in late February. He outlined the problem; then Acheson took over to warn that "a highly possible Soviet breakthrough might open three continents to Soviet penetration." Comparing the situation in Greece to one rotten apple spoiling an entire barrel, Acheson warned that "the corruption of Greece would infect Iran and all to the east. It would also carry

Read the Document   George Marshall, The Marshall Plan (1947)

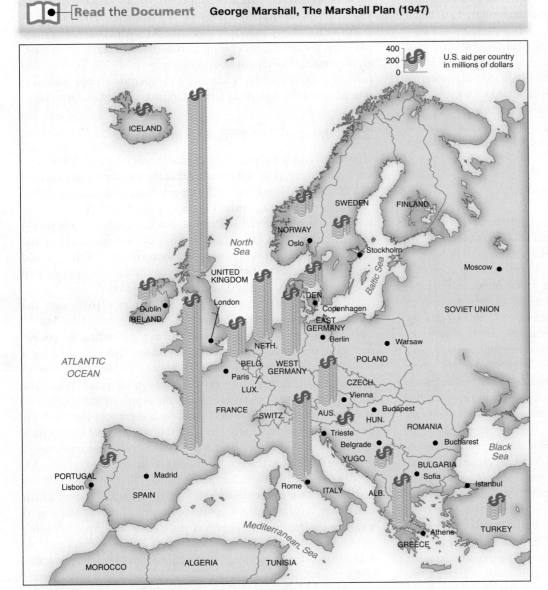

MARSHALL PLAN AID TO EUROPE, 1948–1952 The Marshall Plan, also known as the European Recovery Program, provided aid totaling $13 billion to European countries following World War II. Most went to former allies Great Britain and France but former enemies Italy and West Germany also received substantial aid. To receive the grants, countries pledged to control inflation and lower tariffs.

U.S. recognition in 1933 and again during World War II, developing there a profound distrust for the Soviet regime. In a crucial telegram in 1946, he warned that the Kremlin believed "that there can be no compromise with rival power" and advocated a policy of containment, arguing that only strong and sustained resistance could halt the outward flow of Russian power. As self-assured as Acheson, Kennan believed that neither Congress nor public opinion should interfere with the conduct of foreign policy by the experts.

In the spring of 1947, a sense of crisis impelled Marshall, Acheson, and Kennan to set out on a new course in American diplomacy. Dubbed **containment**, after an article by Kennan in *Foreign Affairs*, the new policy both consolidated the evolving postwar anticommunism and established guidelines that would shape America's role in the world for more than two decades. What Kennan proposed was "a long-term, patient but firm, and vigilant

infection to Africa through Asia Minor and Egypt, and to Europe through Italy and France." Claiming that the Soviets were "playing one of the greatest gambles in history," Acheson concluded that "we and we alone were in a position to break up the play."

The bipartisan group of congressional leaders was deeply impressed. Finally, Republican Senator Arthur M. Vandenberg spoke up, saying he would support the president, but adding that to ensure public backing, Truman would have to "scare hell" out of the American people.

The president followed the senator's advice. On March 12, 1947, he asked Congress for $400 million for military and economic assistance to Greece and Turkey. In stating what would become known as the **Truman Doctrine**, he made clear that more was involved than just these two countries—the stakes, in fact, were far higher. "It must be the policy of the United States," Truman told the Congress, "to support free peoples who are resisting attempted subjugation by armed minorities or by outside pressure." After a brief debate, both the House and the Senate approved the program by margins of better than three to one.

The Truman Doctrine marked an informal declaration of cold war against the Soviet Union. Truman used the crisis in Greece to secure congressional approval and build a national consensus for the policy of containment. In less than two years, the civil war in Greece ended, but the American commitment to oppose communist expansion, whether by internal subversion or external aggression, placed the United States on a collision course with the Soviet Union around the globe.

The Marshall Plan

Despite American interest in controlling Soviet expansion into Greece, western Europe was far more vital to U.S. interests than was the eastern Mediterranean. Yet by 1947, many Americans believed that western Europe was open to Soviet penetration. The problem was economic in nature. Despite $9 billion in piecemeal American loans, England, France, Italy, and the other European countries had great difficulty in recovering from World War II. Food was scarce, with millions existing on less than fifteen hundred calories a day; industrial machinery was broken down and obsolete; and workers were demoralized by years of depression and war. The cruel winter of 1947, the worst in fifty years, compounded the problem. Resentment and discontent led to growing communist voting strength, especially in Italy and France. If the United States could not reverse the process, it seemed as though all of Europe might drift into the communist orbit.

In the weeks following proclamation of the Truman Doctrine, American officials dealt with this problem. Secretary of State Marshall, returning from a frustrating Council of Foreign Ministers meeting in Moscow, warned that "the patient is sinking while the doctors deliberate." Acheson believed that it was time to extend American "economic power" in Europe, both "to call an effective halt to the Soviet Union's expansionism" and "to create a basis for political stability and economic well-being." The experts drew up a plan for the massive infusion of American capital to finance the economic recovery of Europe. Speaking at a Harvard commencement on June 5, 1947, Marshall presented the broad outline. He offered extensive economic aid to all the nations of Europe if they could reach agreement on ways to achieve "the revival of a working economy in the world so as to permit the emergence of political and social conditions in which free institutions can exist."

The fate of the **Marshall Plan** depended on the reaction of the Soviet Union and the U.S. Congress. Marshall had taken, in the words of one American diplomat, "a hell of a gamble" by including Russia in his offer of aid. At a meeting of the European nations in Paris in July 1947, the Soviet foreign minister ended the suspense by abruptly withdrawing. Neither the Soviet Union nor its satellites would take part, apparently because Moscow saw the Marshall Plan as an American attempt to weaken Soviet control over eastern Europe. The other European countries then made a formal request for $17 billion in assistance over the next four years.

Congress responded cautiously to the proposal, appointing a special joint committee to investigate. The administration lobbied vigorously, pointing out that the Marshall Plan would help the United States by stimulating trade with Europe as well as checking Soviet expansion. It was the latter argument, however, that proved decisive. When the Czech coup touched off a war scare in March 1948, Congress quickly approved the Marshall Plan by heavy majorities. Over the next four years, the huge American investment paid rich dividends, generating a broad industrial revival in western Europe that became self-sustaining by the 1950s. The threat of communist domination faded, and a prosperous Europe proved to be a bonanza for American farmers, miners, and manufacturers.

The Western Military Alliance

The third and final phase of containment came in 1949 with the establishment of the **North Atlantic Treaty Organization (NATO)**. NATO grew out of European fears of Russian military aggression. Recalling Hitler's tactics in the 1930s, the people of western Europe wanted assurance that the United States would protect them from attack as they began to achieve economic recovery. American diplomats were sympathetic. "People could not go ahead and make investments for the future," commented Averell Harriman, "without some sense of security."

England, France, and the Low Countries (Belgium, the Netherlands, and Luxembourg) began the process in March 1948 when they signed the Brussels Treaty, providing for collective self-defense. In January 1949, President Truman called for a broader defense pact including the United States; ten European nations, from Norway in the north to Italy in the south, joined the United States and Canada in signing the North Atlantic Treaty in Washington on April 4, 1949. This historic departure from the traditional policy of isolation—the United States had not signed such a treaty since the French alliance in the eighteenth century—caused extensive debate, but the Senate ratified it in July by a vote of 82 to 13.

There were two main features of NATO. First, the United States committed itself to the defense of Europe in the key clause, which stated that "an armed attack against one or more shall be considered an attack against them all." In effect, the United States was extending its atomic shield over Europe. The second feature was designed to reassure worried Europeans that the United States would honor this commitment. In late 1950, President Truman appointed General Dwight D. Eisenhower to the post of NATO supreme commander and authorized the stationing of four American divisions in Europe to serve as the nucleus of the NATO army. It was believed the threat of American troop involvement in any Russian assault would deter the Soviet Union from making such an attack.

The Western military alliance escalated the developing Cold War. Whatever its advantage in building a sense of security among worried Europeans, it represented an overreaction to the Soviet danger. Americans and Europeans alike were attempting to apply the lesson of Munich to the Cold War. But Stalin was not Hitler, and the Soviets were not the Nazis. There was no evidence of any Russian plan to invade western Europe, and in the face of the American atomic bomb, none was likely. NATO only intensified Russian fears of the West and thus increased the level of international tension.

The Berlin Blockade

The main Russian response to containment came in 1948 at the West's most vulnerable point. American, British, French, and Soviet troops each occupied a sector of Berlin, but the city was located more than a hundred miles within the Russian zone of Germany (see the map of postwar Europe on p. 669). Stalin decided to test his opponents' resolve by cutting off all rail and highway traffic to Berlin on June 20, 1948.

The timing was very awkward for Harry Truman. He had his hands full resisting efforts to force him off the Democratic ticket, and he faced a difficult reelection effort against a strong Republican candidate, Governor Thomas E. Dewey of New York. Immersed in election-year politics, Truman was caught unprepared by the Berlin blockade. The alternatives were not very appealing. The United States could withdraw its forces and lose not just a city, but the confidence of all Europe; it could try to send in reinforcements and fight for Berlin; or it could sit tight and attempt to find a diplomatic solution. Truman made the basic decision in characteristic fashion, telling the military that there would be no thought of pulling out. "We were going to stay, period," an aide reported Truman as saying.

In the next few weeks, the president and his advisers developed ways to implement the decision. Rejecting proposals for provoking a showdown by sending an armored column down the main highway, the administration adopted a two-phase policy. The first part was a massive airlift of food, fuel, and supplies for the ten thousand troops and the two million civilians in Berlin. A fleet of fifty-two C-54s and eighty C-47s began making two daily round-trip flights to Berlin, carrying 2,500 tons every twenty-four hours. Then, to guard against Soviet interruption of the **Berlin airlift**, Truman transferred sixty American B-29s, planes capable of delivering atomic bombs, to bases in England. The president was bluffing; the B-29s were not equipped with atomic bombs, but at the time, the threat was effective.

For a few weeks, the world teetered on the edge of war. Stalin did not attempt to disrupt the flights to Berlin, but he rejected all American diplomatic initiatives. Although at any time the Russians could have halted it by jamming radar or shooting down the defenseless cargo planes, the airlift gradually increased to more than 4,000 tons a day. Governor Dewey patriotically supported the president's policy, thus removing foreign policy from the presidential campaign. Yet for Truman, the tension was fierce. In early September, he asked his advisers to brief him "on bases, bombs, Moscow, Leningrad, etc." "I have a terrible feeling afterward that we are very close to war," he confided in his diary. "I hope not."

Slowly, the tension eased. The Russians did not shoot down any planes, and the daily airlift climbed to nearly 7,000 tons. Truman, a decided underdog, won a surprising second term in November over a complacent Dewey, in part because the Berlin crisis had rallied the nation behind his leadership. In early 1949, the Soviets gave in, ending the blockade in return for another meeting of the Council of Foreign Ministers on Germany—a conclave that proved as unproductive as all the earlier ones.

The Berlin crisis marked the end of the initial phase of the Cold War. The airlift had given the United States a striking political victory, showing the world the triumph of American ingenuity over Russian stubbornness. Yet it could not disguise the fact that the Cold War had cut Europe in two. Behind the Iron Curtain, the Russians had consolidated control over the areas won by their troops in the war, while the United States had used the Marshall Plan to revitalize western Europe. But a divided continent was a far cry from the wartime hopes for a peaceful world. And the rivalry that began in Europe would soon spread into a worldwide contest among the super powers.

The Cold War Expands

How did the Cold War expand from Europe to Asia?

The rivalry between the United States and the Soviet Union grew in the late 1940s and early 1950s. Both sides began to rebuild their military forces with new methods and new weapons. Equally significant, the diplomatic competition spread from Europe to Asia as each of the superpowers sought to enhance its influence in the Far East. By the time Truman left office in early 1953, the Cold War had taken on global proportions.

The Military Dimension

After World War II, American leaders were intent on reforming the nation's military system in light of their wartime experience. Two goals were uppermost. First, nearly everyone agreed in the aftermath of Pearl Harbor that the U.S. armed services should be unified into an integrated military system. The developing Cold War reinforced this decision. Without unification, declared George Marshall in 1945, "there can be little hope that we will be able to maintain through the years a military posture that will secure for us a lasting peace." Equally important, planners realized, was the need for new institutions to coordinate military and diplomatic strategy so the nation could cope effectively with threats to its security.

In 1947, Congress passed the **National Security Act**. It established a Department of Defense, headed by a civilian secretary of cabinet rank presiding over three separate services—the army, the navy, and the new air force. In addition, the act created the Central Intelligence Agency (CIA) to coordinate the intelligence-gathering activities of various government agencies. Finally, the act provided for a National Security Council (NSC)—composed of the service secretaries, the secretary of defense, and the secretary of state—to advise the president on all matters regarding the nation's security.

Despite the appearance of equality among the services, the air force quickly emerged as the dominant power in the atomic age, based on its capability both to deter an enemy from attacking and to wage war if deterrence failed. President Truman, intent on cutting back defense expenditures, favored the air force in his 1949 military budget, allotting this branch more than one-half the total sum. After the Czech coup and the resulting war scare, Congress granted an additional $3 billion to the military. The appropriation included funds for a new B-36 to replace the B-29 as the nation's primary strategic bomber.

American military planners received even greater support in the fall of 1949 when the Soviet Union exploded its first atomic bomb. President Truman appointed a high-level committee to explore mounting an all-out effort to build a hydrogen bomb to maintain American nuclear supremacy.

Some scientists had technical objections to the H-bomb, which was still far from being perfected, while others opposed the new weapon on moral grounds, claiming that its enormous destructive power (intended to be one thousand times greater than the atomic bomb) made it unthinkable. George Kennan suggested a new effort at international arms control with the Soviets, but Dean Acheson—who succeeded Marshall as secretary of state in early 1949—believed it was imperative that the United States develop the hydrogen bomb before the Soviet Union. When

The Berlin airlift (June 1948–May 1949) was organized by the Truman administration and the Western Allies to overcome the rail, roadways, and canals blockade of West Berlin instituted by the Soviet Union. Over two hundred thousand American and British air force flights over West Berlin delivered approximately nearly five thousand tons of food and other necessities to West Berliners in order to break successfully the Soviet blockade.

Acheson presented the committee's favorable report to the president in January 1950, Truman took only seven minutes to decide to go ahead with the awesome new weapon.

At the same time, Acheson ordered the Policy Planning Staff (headed by Paul Nitze after Kennan resigned in protest) to draw up a new statement of national defense policy. **NSC-68**, as the document eventually became known, was based on the premise that the Soviet Union sought "to impose its absolute authority over the rest of the world" and thus "mortally challenged" the United States. Rejecting such options as appeasement or a return to isolation, Nitze advocated a massive expansion of American military power so the United States could halt and overcome the Soviet threat. Contending the nation could afford to spend "upward of 50 percent of its gross national product" for security, NSC-68 proposed increasing defense spending from $13 to $45 billion annually. Approved in principle by the National Security Council in April 1950, NSC-68

stood as a symbol of the Truman administration's determination to win the Cold War regardless of cost.

The Cold War in Asia

The Soviet–American conflict developed more slowly in Asia. At Yalta, the two superpowers had agreed to a Far Eastern balance of power, with the Russians dominating Northeast Asia and the Americans in control of the Pacific, including both Japan and its former island empire.

The United States moved quickly to consolidate its sphere of influence. General Douglas MacArthur, in charge of Japanese occupation, denied the Soviet Union any role in the reconstruction of Japan. Instead, he supervised the transition of the Japanese government into a constitutional democracy, shaped along Western lines, in which Communists were barred from all government posts. The Japanese willingly renounced war in their new constitution, relying instead on American forces to protect their security. American policy was equally nationalistic in the Pacific. A trusteeship arrangement with the United Nations merely disguised the fact that the United States held full control over the Marshall, Mariana, and Caroline Islands. American scientists conducted atomic bomb tests at Bikini atoll in 1946, and by 1949, MacArthur was declaring that the entire Pacific "had become an Anglo-Saxon lake and our line of defense runs through the chain of islands fringing the coast of Asia."

As defined at Yalta, China lay between the Soviet and American spheres. When World War II ended, the country was torn between Chiang Kai-shek's Nationalists in the South and Mao Tse-tung's Communists in the North. Chiang had many advantages, including American political and economic backing and official Soviet recognition. But corruption was widespread among the Nationalist leaders, and a raging inflation that soon reached 100 percent a year devastated the Chinese middle classes and thus eroded Chiang's base of power. Mao used tight discipline and patriotic appeals to strengthen his hold on the peasantry and extend his influence. When the Soviets abruptly vacated Manchuria in 1946, after stripping it of virtually all the industrial machinery Japan had installed, Mao inherited control of this rich northern province. Ignoring American advice, Chiang rushed north to occupy Manchurian cities, overextending his supply lines and exposing his forces to Communist counterattack.

American policy sought to prevent a Chinese civil war. Before he became secretary of state, George Marshall undertook the difficult task of forming a coalition government between Chiang and Mao. For a few months in early 1946, Marshall appeared to have succeeded, but Chiang's attempts to gain control of Manchuria doomed the agreement. In reality, there was no basis for compromise. Chiang insisted he "was going to liquidate Communists," while Mao was trying to play the United States against Russia in his bid for power. By 1947, as China plunged into full-scale civil war, the Truman administration had given up any meaningful effort to influence the outcome. Political mediation had failed, military intervention was out of the question so soon after World War II, and a policy of continued American economic aid served only to appease domestic supporters of Chiang Kai-shek; 80 percent of the military supplies ended up in Communist hands.

The Chinese conflict climaxed at the end of the decade. Mao's forces drove the Nationalists out of Manchuria in late 1948 and advanced across the Yangtze by mid-1949. Acheson released a lengthy report justifying American policy in China on the grounds that the civil war there "was beyond the control of the government of the United States." An American military adviser concurred, telling Congress that the Nationalist defeat was due to "the world's worst leadership" and "a complete loss of will to fight." Republican senators, however, disagreed, blaming American diplomats for sabotaging the Nationalists and terming Acheson's report "a 1054-page white-wash of a wishful, do-nothing policy." While the domestic debate raged over responsibility for the loss of China, Chiang's forces fled the mainland for sanctuary on Formosa (Taiwan) in December 1949. Two months later, Mao and Stalin signed a Sino-Soviet treaty of mutual assistance that clearly placed China in the Russian orbit.

The American response to the Communist triumph in China was twofold. First, the State Department refused to recognize the legitimacy of the new regime in Beijing, maintaining instead formal diplomatic relations with the Nationalists on Formosa. Citing the Sino–Soviet alliance, Assistant Secretary of State Dean Rusk called

the Beijing regime "a colonial Russian government" and declared, "It is not the Government of China. It does not pass the first test. It is not Chinese." Then, to compensate for the loss of China, the United States focused on Japan as its main ally in Asia. The State Department encouraged the buildup of Japanese industry, and the Pentagon expanded American bases on the Japanese home islands and Okinawa. A Japanese-American security pact led to the end of American occupation by 1952. The Cold War had now split east Asia in two.

The Korean War

The showdown between the United States and the Soviet Union in Asia came in Korea. Traditionally the cockpit of international rivalry in Northeast Asia, Korea had been divided at the

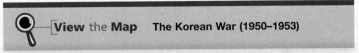

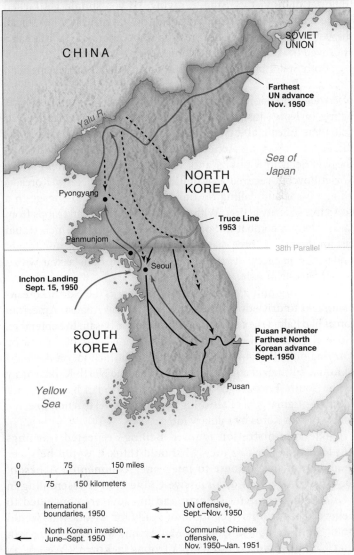

THE KOREAN WAR, 1950–1953 After a year of rapid movement up and down the Korean peninsula, the fighting stalled just north of the 38th parallel. The resulting truce line has divided North and South Korea since the July 1953 armistice.

38th parallel in 1945. The Russians occupied the industrial North, installing a communist government under the leadership of Kim Il-Sung. In the agrarian South, Syngman Rhee, a conservative nationalist, emerged as the American-sponsored ruler. Neither regime heeded a UN call for elections to unify the country. The two superpowers pulled out most of their occupation forces by 1949. The Russians, however, helped train a well-equipped army in the North, while the United States—fearful Rhee would seek unification through armed conquest—gave much more limited military assistance to South Korea.

On June 25, 1950, the North Korean army suddenly crossed the 38th parallel in great strength. Stalin had approved this act of aggression in advance. In January 1950, the Soviet leader had told Mao Tse-tung that he was ready to overthrow the Yalta settlement in the Far East ("and to hell with it," he exclaimed to Mao). In April, when Kim Il-Sung came to Moscow to gain approval for the assault on South Korea, Stalin gave it willingly, apparently in the belief that the United States was ready to abandon Syngman Rhee. But the ever-cautious Stalin warned Kim not to count on Soviet assistance, saying, "If you should get kicked in the teeth, I shall not lift a finger. You have to ask Mao for all the help." In May, despite expressing some reservations, Mao also approved the planned North Korean aggression.

Both Stalin and Mao had badly miscalculated the American response. President Truman saw the invasion as a clear-cut case of Soviet aggression reminiscent of the 1930s. "Communism was acting in Korea just as Hitler, Mussolini, and the Japanese had acted ten, fifteen, and twenty years earlier," he commented in his memoirs. Following Acheson's advice, the president convened the UN Security Council and, taking advantage of a temporary Soviet boycott, secured a resolution condemning North Korea as an aggressor and calling on the member nations to engage in a collective security action. Within a few days, American troops from Japan were in combat in South Korea. The conflict, which would last for more than three years, was technically a police action fought under UN auspices; in reality, the United States was at war with a Soviet satellite in Asia.

In the beginning, the fighting went badly as the North Koreans continued to drive down the peninsula. But by August, American forces had halted the communist advance near Pusan. In September, General MacArthur changed the whole complexion of the war by carrying out a brilliant amphibious assault at Inchon, on the waist of Korea, cutting off and destroying most of the North Korean army in the South. Encouraged by this victory, Truman began to shift from his original goal of restoring the 38th parallel to a new one: the unification of Korea by military force.

The administration ignored Beijing's repeated warnings not to invade North Korea. "I should think it would be sheer madness for the Chinese to intervene," commented Acheson. Despite CIA reports of a massive Chinese force assembling in Manchuria, President Truman and his advisers continued to believe that the Soviet Union, not ready for all-out war, would hold China in check. General MacArthur was equally certain that China would not attack his troops in Korea. "We are no longer fearful of their intervention," he told Truman in October, adding that if they crossed the Yalu into Korea, "there would be the greatest slaughter."

Rarely has an American president received worse advice. China was not a Soviet puppet. When UN forces crossed the 38th parallel and moved confidently toward the Yalu, the Chinese launched a devastating counterattack in late November which caught MacArthur by surprise and drove his armies out of North Korea by the end of the year. MacArthur finally stabilized the fighting near the 38th parallel, but when Truman decided to give up his attempt to unify Korea, the general protested to Congress, calling for a renewed offensive and proclaiming, "There is no substitute for victory."

Truman courageously relieved the popular hero of the Pacific of his command on April 11, 1951. At first, MacArthur seemed likely to force the president to back down. Huge crowds came forward to welcome him home and hear him call for victory over the Communists in Asia. At a special congressional hearing, the administration struck back effectively by warning that MacArthur's strategy would expose all Europe to Soviet attack. General Omar Bradley, Truman's chief military adviser, succinctly pointed out that a "showdown" with communism in Asia would be "the wrong war, at the wrong place, at the wrong time, and with the wrong enemy."

Congress and the American people came to accept MacArthur's recall. The Korean War settled into a stalemate near the 38th parallel as truce talks with the communists bogged down. The president had achieved his primary goal, defense of South Korea and the principle of collective security. Yet by taking the gamble to unify Korea by force, he had confused the American people and embarrassed the United States in the eyes of the world.

In the last analysis, the most significant result of the Korean conflict was the massive American rearmament it brought about. The war led to the implementation of NSC-68—the army expanded to 3.5 million troops, the defense budget increased to $50 billion a year by 1952, and the United States acquired distant military bases from Saudi Arabia to Morocco. America was now committed to waging a global contest against the Soviet Union with arms as well as words.

The Cold War at Home

How did the Cold War affect life in America?

The Cold War cast a long shadow over American life in the late 1940s and early 1950s. Truman tried to carry on the New Deal reform tradition he had inherited from FDR, but the American people were more concerned about events abroad. The Republican Party used both growing dissatisfaction with postwar economic adjustment and fears of communist penetration of the United States to revive its sagging fortunes and regain control of the White House in 1952 for the first time in twenty years.

Truman's Troubles

Matching his foreign policy successes with equal achievements at home was not easy for Harry S. Truman. As a loyal supporter of Franklin D. Roosevelt's New Deal programs during his Senate career, Truman had earned a reputation for being a hardworking, reliable, and intensely partisan legislator. But he was relatively unknown to the general public, and his background as a Missouri county official associated with Kansas City machine politics did little to inspire confidence in his ability to lead the nation. Surprisingly well-read—especially in history and biography—Truman possessed sound judgment, the ability to reach decisions quickly, and a fierce and uncompromising sense of right and wrong.

Two weaknesses marred his performance in the White House. One was a fondness for old friends, which resulted in the appointment of many Missouri and Senate cronies to high office. Men such as Attorney General Tom Clark, Secretary of the Treasury Charles Snyder, and White House military aide Harry Vaughn brought little credit to the Truman administration, while the loss of such effective public servants as Secretary of the Interior Harold Ickes and Labor Secretary Frances Perkins hurt it. The president's other serious limitation was his lack of political vision. Failing to pursue a coherent legislative program of his own, he tried to perpetuate FDR's New Deal and, as a result, engaged in a running battle with Congress.

The postwar mood was not conducive to an extension of New Deal reforms. Americans were weary of shortages and sacrifices; they wanted the chance to buy the consumer goods denied them under wartime conditions. But in the rush to convert industry from producing planes and tanks to cars and appliances, problems soon emerged. Prices and wages rose quickly as Congress voted to end wartime controls. With prices going up 25 percent in two years, workers demanded higher wages to offset the loss of overtime pay. A wave of labor unrest swept over the country in the spring of 1946, culminating in two critical strikes: a walkout by coal miners that threatened to close down much of American industry and a paralyzing strike by railroad workers.

President Truman was caught in the middle. Sensitive to union demands, he permitted businesses to negotiate large pay increases for their workers and then pass on the cost to consumers in the form of higher prices. He criticized Congress for weakening wartime price controls, but he failed to offer anything else to curb inflation. Homemakers blamed him for the rising price of food, while organized labor condemned Truman as the country's "No. 1 Strikebreaker" when he asked Congress for power to draft striking railway workers into the army.

In the face of this rising discontent, Truman's efforts to extend the New Deal met with little success. Congress ignored his September 1945 call for measures to ensure economic security and enacted only the Employment Act of 1946. This legislation created the Council of Economic Advisers to assist the president and asserted the principle that the government was responsible for the state of the economy, but it failed to address Truman's original goal of mandatory federal planning to achieve full employment.

The Republicans took advantage of increasing public dissatisfaction with postwar economic woes to attack the Democrats. "To err is Truman," the GOP proclaimed and then adopted a very effective two-word slogan for the 1946 congressional elections: "Had enough?" The American people, weary of inflation and labor unrest, responded by electing Republican majorities in both the House and Senate for the first time since 1930.

Truman Vindicated

The president's relations with Congress became even stormier after the 1946 elections. Truman successfully vetoed two GOP measures to give large tax cuts to the wealthy, but Congress

overrode his veto of the **Taft-Hartley Act** in 1947. Designed to undo the prolabor tilt of the Wagner Act, the Taft-Hartley Act outlawed specific labor union activities—including the closed shop and secondary boycotts—and it permitted the president to invoke an eighty-day cooling-off period to delay strikes that might endanger national health or safety. Despite Truman's claim that it was a "slave-labor" bill, unions were able to survive its provisions.

President Truman's political fortunes reached their lowest ebb in early 1948. Former Vice President Henry A. Wallace, claiming to represent the New Deal, announced his third-party (Progressive) candidacy in the presidential contest that year. Worried Democratic party leaders sought to persuade Truman to step aside and allow General Dwight D. Eisenhower to become the Democratic candidate. When Eisenhower turned down bids from both parties, the Democrats reluctantly nominated Truman. His prospects for victory in the fall, however, looked very dim—especially after disgruntled Southerners bolted from the Democratic party in protest over a progressive civil rights platform. The Dixiecrats, as they became known, nominated Strom Thurmond, the governor of South Carolina, on a States' Rights party ticket.

The defection of the Dixiecrats in the South and Wallace's liberal followers in the North led political experts to predict an almost certain Republican victory. Governor Thomas E. Dewey of New York, the GOP candidate, was so sure of winning that he waged a cautious and bland campaign designed to give him a free hand once he was in the White House. With nothing to lose, Truman

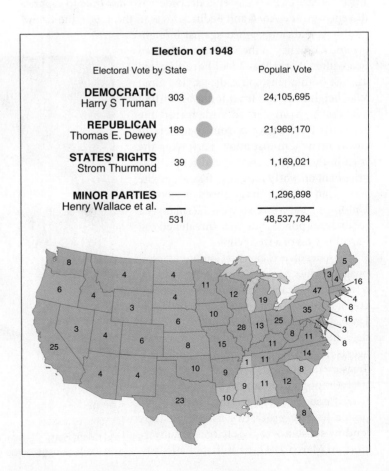

Election of 1948

	Electoral Vote by State		Popular Vote
DEMOCRATIC Harry S Truman	303		24,105,695
REPUBLICAN Thomas E. Dewey	189		21,969,170
STATES' RIGHTS Strom Thurmond	39		1,169,021
MINOR PARTIES Henry Wallace et al.	—		1,296,898
	531		48,537,784

barnstormed around the country denouncing the "do-nothing" Republican Eightieth Congress. The president's "give-'em hell" tactics reminded voters of how much they owed the Democrats for helping them survive the Great Depression. To the amazement of the pollsters, Truman won a narrow but decisive victory in November. The old Roosevelt coalition—farmers, organized labor, urban ethnic groups, and blacks—had held together, enabling Truman to remain in the White House and the Democrats to regain control of Congress.

There was one more reason for Truman's win in 1948. During this election, held at the height of the Berlin crisis, the GOP failed to challenge Truman's conduct of the Cold War. Locked in a tense rivalry with the Soviet Union, the American people saw no reason to reject a president who had countered aggression overseas with the Truman Doctrine and the Marshall Plan. The Republicans, committed to support the bipartisan policy of containment, had allowed the Democrats to preempt the foreign policy issue. Until they found a way to challenge Truman's Cold War policies, GOP leaders had little chance to regain the White House.

The Loyalty Issue

Despite Truman's surprising victory in 1948, there was one area on which the Democrats were vulnerable. The fear of communism abroad that had led to the bipartisan containment policy could be used against them at home by politicians who were more willing to exploit the public's deep-seated anxiety.

Fear of radicalism had been a recurrent feature of American life since the early days of the republic. Federalists had tried to suppress dissent with the Alien and Sedition Acts in the 1790s; the Know-Nothings had campaigned against foreigners and Catholics in the 1850s; and the Red Scare after World War I had been directed against both aliens and radicals. The Cold War heightened the traditional belief that subversion from abroad endangered the republic. Bold rhetoric from members of the Truman administration, portraying the men in the Kremlin as inspired revolutionaries bent on world conquest, frightened the American people. They viewed the Soviet Union as a successor to Nazi Germany—a totalitarian police state that threatened the basic liberties of a free people.

A series of revelations of Communist espionage activities reinforced these fears, sparking a second Red Scare. Canadian officials uncovered a Soviet spy ring in 1946, and the House Un-American Activities Committee (HUAC) held hearings indicating that Communist agents had flourished in the Agriculture and Treasury Departments in the 1930s.

Although Truman tried to dismiss the loyalty issue as a "red herring," he felt compelled to take protective measures, thus lending substance to the charges of subversion. In March 1947, he initiated a loyalty program, ordering security checks of government employees in order to root out Communists. Originally intended to remove subversives for whom "reasonable grounds exist for belief that the person involved is disloyal," within four years the Loyalty Review Board was dismissing workers as security risks if there was "reasonable doubt" of their loyalty. Thousands of government workers lost their jobs, charged with guilt by association with radicals or with membership in left-wing organizations. Often those who were charged had no chance to face their accusers.

The most famous disclosure came in August 1948, when Whittaker Chambers, a repentant Communist, accused Alger Hiss of having been a Soviet spy in the 1930s. When Hiss, who had been a prominent State Department official, denied the charges, Chambers led investigators to a hollowed-out pumpkin on his Maryland farm. Inside the pumpkin were microfilms of confidential government documents. Chambers claimed that Hiss had passed the State Department materials to him in the late 1930s. Although the statute of limitations prevented a charge of treason against Hiss, he was convicted of perjury in January 1950 and sentenced to a five-year prison term.

In 1948, the Justice Department further heightened fears of subversion. It charged eleven officials of the Communist Party with advocating the violent overthrow of the government. After a long trial, the jury found them guilty, and the party officials received prison sentences and heavy fines; in 1951, the Supreme Court upheld the convictions as constitutional.

Such repressive measures failed, however, to reassure the nation. Events abroad intensified the sense of danger. The communist triumph in China in the fall of 1949 came as a shock; soon there were charges that "fellow travelers" in the State Department

A jubilant Harry Truman, on the morning after his 1948 election win, displays the headline blazoned on the front page of the *Chicago Daily Tribune*—a newspaper that believed the pollsters.

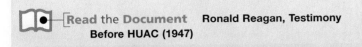

Read the Document Ronald Reagan, Testimony Before HUAC (1947)

Alger Hiss, accused of being a Communist spy by Whittaker Chambers, takes an oath during his August 1948 hearings before the House Un-American Activities Committee. Hiss's conviction on charges of perjury convinced many Americans that internal subversion threatened the nation's survival.

were responsible for "the loss of China." In September 1949, when the Truman administration announced that the Russians had detonated their first atomic bomb, the end of America's nuclear monopoly was blamed on Soviet espionage. In early 1950, Klaus Fuchs—a British scientist who had worked on the wartime Manhattan Project—admitted giving the Russians vital information about the A-bomb.

A few months later, the government charged American Communists Ethel and Julius Rosenberg with conspiracy to transmit atomic secrets to the Soviet Union. In 1951, a jury found the Rosenbergs guilty of espionage, and Judge Irving Kaufman sentenced them to die for what he termed their "loathsome offense." Despite their insistent claims of innocence and worldwide appeals on their behalf, the Rosenbergs were electrocuted on June 19, 1953. Thus by the early 1950s, nearly all the ingredients were at hand for a new outburst of hysteria—fear of Russia, evidence of espionage, and a belief in a vast unseen conspiracy. The only element missing was a leader to release the new outburst of intolerance.

McCarthyism in Action

On February 12, 1950, Senator Joseph R. McCarthy of Wisconsin delivered a routine Lincoln's Birthday speech in Wheeling, West Virginia. This little known Republican suddenly attracted

national attention when he declared, "I have here in my hand a list of 205—a list of names that were made known to the secretary of state as being members of the Communist Party and who nevertheless are still working and shaping policy in the State Department." The charge that there were Communists in the State Department on different occasions with the number changed to 57, then 81—was never substantiated. But McCarthy's Wheeling speech triggered a four-and-a-half-year crusade to hunt down alleged Communists in government. The stridency and sensationalism of the senator's accusations soon won the name **McCarthyism**.

McCarthy's basic technique was the multiple untruth. He leveled a bevy of charges of treasonable activities in government. While officials were refuting his initial accusations, he brought forth a steady stream of new ones, so the corrections never caught up with the latest blast. He failed to unearth a single confirmed Communist in government, but he kept the Truman administration in turmoil. Drawing on an army of informers, primarily disgruntled federal workers with grievances against their colleagues and superiors, McCarthy charged government agencies with harboring and protecting Communist agents and accused the State Department of deliberately losing the Cold War. His briefcase bulged with documents, but he did very little actual research, relying instead on reports (often outdated) from earlier congressional investigations. He exploited the press with great skill, combining current accusations with promises of future disclosures to guarantee headlines.

The secret of McCarthy's power was the fear he engendered among his Senate colleagues. In 1950, Maryland Senator Millard Tydings, who headed a committee critical of McCarthy's activities, failed to win reelection when McCarthy opposed him; after that, other senators ran scared. McCarthy delighted in making sweeping, startling charges of Communist sympathies against prominent public figures. A favorite target was patrician Secretary of State Dean Acheson, whom McCarthy ridiculed as the "Red Dean," with his "cane, spats, and tea-sipping little finger"; he even went after General George Marshall, claiming that the wartime army chief of staff was an agent of the Communist conspiracy. Nor were fellow Republicans immune. One GOP senator was described as "a living miracle in that he is without question the only man who has lived so long with neither brains nor guts."

The attacks on the wealthy, famous, and privileged won McCarthy a devoted national following, though at the height of his influence in early 1954, he gained the approval of only 50 percent of the respondents in a Gallup poll. McCarthy drew a disproportionate backing from working-class Catholics and ethnic groups, especially the Irish, Poles, and Italians, who normally voted Democratic. He offered a simple solution to the complicated Cold War: Defeat the enemy at home rather than continue to engage in costly foreign aid programs and entangling alliances abroad. Above all, McCarthy appealed to conservative Republicans in the Midwest who shared his right-wing views and felt cheated by Truman's upset victory in 1948. Even GOP leaders who viewed McCarthy's tactics with distaste, such as Robert A. Taft of Ohio, quietly encouraged him to attack the vulnerable Democrats.

In the early 1950s, U.S. Senator Joseph McCarthy, a Republican politician from Wisconsin, made a stream of sensational, unsubstantiated, and damaging accusations about alleged communists working in the State Department and other U.S. government agencies and institutions. Sen. McCarthy's prominence suffered a fatal downfall when he maliciously attacked top officials and others in the U.S. Army in 1954, and he was subsequently censured by his colleagues in the U.S. Senate

The Republicans in Power

In 1952, the GOP capitalized on a growing sense of national frustration to capture the presidency. The stalemate in Korea and the second Red Scare created a desire for political change; revelations of scandals by several individuals close to Truman intensified the feeling that someone needed to clean up "the mess in Washington." In Dwight D. Eisenhower, the Republican Party found the perfect candidate to explore what one senator called K_1C_2—Korea, Communism, and corruption.

Immensely popular because of his amiable manner, winning smile, and heroic stature, Eisenhower alone appeared to have the ability to unite a divided nation. In the 1952 campaign, Ike displayed hidden gifts as a politician in running against Adlai Stevenson, the eloquent Illinois governor whose appeal was limited to diehard Democrats and liberal intellectuals. Eisenhower allowed his young running mate, Senator Richard M. Nixon of California, to hammer away at the Democrats on

the Communist and corruption issues, but he himself delivered the most telling blow of all on the Korean War. Speaking in Detroit in late October, just after the fighting had intensified again in Korea, Ike promised if elected he would go personally to the battlefield in an attempt "to bring the Korean War to an early and honorable end."

THE ELECTION OF 1952

Candidate	Party	Popular Vote	Electoral Vote
Eisenhower	Republican	33,778,963	442
Stevenson	Democratic	27,314,992	89

"That does it—Ike is in," several reporters exclaimed after they heard this pledge. The hero of World War II had clinched his election by committing himself to end an unpopular war. Ten days later,

Watch the Video Ike for President: Campaign Ad (1952)

In the 1952 presidential campaign, Republican presidential candidate Dwight D. Eisenhower was the first presidential candidate to make effective use of television "spot," advertising. Eisenhower's televised ads help defeat his Democratic opponent, Adlai Stevenson, in the 1952 election.

he won the presidency handily, carrying thirty-nine states, including four in the formerly solid Democratic South. The Republican party, however, did not fare as well in Congress; it gained just a slight edge in the House and controlled the Senate by only one seat.

Once elected, Eisenhower moved quickly to fulfill his campaign pledge. He spent three days in early December touring the battlefront in Korea, quickly ruling out the new offensive the military favored. "Small attacks on small hills," he later wrote, "would not end the war." Instead he turned to diplomacy, relying on subtle hints to China on the possible use of nuclear weapons to break the stalemated peace talks. These tactics, together with the death of Joseph Stalin in early March, finally led to the signing of an armistice on July 27, 1953, which ended the fighting but left Korea divided—as it had been before the war—near the 38th parallel.

The new president was less effective in dealing with the problem raised by Senator McCarthy's continuing witch-hunt. Instead of toning down his antiCommunist crusade after the Republican victory in 1952, McCarthy used his new position as chairman of the Senate Committee on Government Operations as a base for ferreting out Communists on the federal payroll. He made a series of charges against the foreign affairs agencies and demanded that certain books be purged from American information libraries overseas. Eisenhower's advisers urged the president to use his own great prestige to stop McCarthy. But Ike refused such a confrontation, saying, "I will not get into a pissing contest with a skunk." Eisenhower preferred to play for time, hoping the American people would eventually come to their senses.

The Wisconsin senator finally overreached himself. In early 1954, he uncovered an army dentist suspected of disloyalty and proceeded to attack the upper echelons of the U.S. Army, telling one much decorated general that he was "not fit to wear the uniform." The controversy culminated in the televised Army–McCarthy hearings. For six weeks, the senator revealed his crude, bullying behavior to the American people. Viewers were repelled by his frequent outbursts that began with the insistent cry, "Point of order, Mr. Chairman, point of order," and by his attempt to slur the reputation of a young lawyer associated with army counsel Joseph Welch. This last maneuver led Welch to condemn McCarthy for his "reckless cruelty" and ask rhetorically, as millions watched on television, "Have you no sense of decency, sir?"

Courageous Republicans, led by Senators Ralph Flanders of Vermont and Margaret Chase Smith of Maine, joined with Democrats to bring about the Senate's censure of McCarthy in December 1954, by a vote of sixty-seven to twenty-two. Once rebuked, McCarthy fell quickly from prominence. He died three years later virtually unnoticed and unmourned.

Yet his influence was profound. Not only did he paralyze national life with what a Senate subcommittee described as "the most nefarious campaign of half-truth and untruth in the history of the Republic," but he also helped impose a political and cultural conformity that froze dissent for the rest of the 1950s. Long after McCarthy's passing, the nation tolerated loyalty oaths for teachers, the banning of left-wing books in public libraries, and the blacklisting of entertainers in radio, television, and films. Freedom of expression was inhibited, and the opportunity to try out new ideas and approaches was lost as the United States settled into a sterile Cold War consensus.

While Dwight Eisenhower could claim that his policy of giving McCarthy enough rope to hang himself had worked, it is possible that a bolder and more forthright presidential attack on the senator might have spared the nation some of the excesses of the second Red Scare.

Eisenhower Wages the Cold War

How successful was Eisenhower at dealing with the foreign policy issues facing the United States?

Dwight D. Eisenhower came into the presidency in 1952 unusually well prepared to lead the nation at the height of the Cold War. His long years of military service had exposed him to a wide variety of international issues, both in Asia and in Europe, and to an even broader array of world leaders, such as Winston Churchill and Charles de Gaulle. He was not only an experienced military strategist but a gifted politician and diplomat as well. He was blessed with a sharp, pragmatic mind and organizational genius that enabled him to plan and carry out large enterprises, grasping the precise relationship between the parts and the whole. Above all, he had a serene confidence in his own ability. At the end of his first day in the White House, he confided in his diary: "Plenty of worries and difficult problems. But such has been my portion for a long time—the result is that this just seems like a continuation of all I've been doing since July 1941."

Eisenhower chose John Foster Dulles as his secretary of state. The myth soon developed that Ike had given Dulles free rein to conduct American diplomacy. Appearances were deceptive. Eisenhower preferred to work behind the scenes. He let Dulles make the public speeches and appearances before congressional committees, where the secretary's hard-line views placated GOP extremists. But Dulles carefully consulted with the president before every appearance, meeting frequently with Eisenhower at the White House and telephoning him several times a day. Ike respected his secretary of state's broad knowledge of foreign policy and skill in conducting American diplomacy, but he made all the major decisions himself. "There's only one man I know who has seen *more* of the world and talked with more people and *knows* more than he does," Ike said of Dulles, "and that's me."

From the outset, Eisenhower was determined to bring the Cold War under control. Ideally, he wanted to end it, but as a realist,

he would settle for a relaxation of tensions with the Soviet Union. In part, he was motivated by a deeply held concern about the budget. Defense spending had increased from $13 billion to $50 billion under Truman; Ike was convinced the nation was in danger of going bankrupt unless military spending was reduced. As president, he inaugurated a "new look" for American defense, cutting back on the army and navy and relying even more heavily than Truman had on the air force and its nuclear striking power. As a result, the defense budget dropped below $40 billion annually. In 1954, Dulles announced reliance on massive retaliation—in fact a continuance of Truman's policy of deterrence. Rather than becoming involved in limited wars such as Korea, the United States would consider the possibility of using nuclear weapons to halt any Communist aggression that threatened vital U.S. interests anywhere in the world.

While he permitted Dulles to make his veiled nuclear threats, Eisenhower's fondest dream was to end the arms race. Sobered by the development of the hydrogen bomb, successfully tested by the United States in November 1952 and by the Soviet Union in August 1953, the president began a new effort at disarmament with the Russians. Yet before this initiative could take effect, Ike had to weather a series of crises around the world that tested his skill and patience to the utmost.

Entanglement in Indochina

The first crisis facing the new president came in Indochina. Since 1950, the United States had been giving France military and economic aid in a war in Indochina against Communist guerrillas led by Ho Chi Minh. The Chinese increased their support to Ho's forces, known as the Vietminh, after the Korean War ended; by the spring of 1954, the French were on the brink of defeat. The Vietminh had surrounded nearly ten thousand French troops at Dien Bien Phu deep in the interior of northern Indochina; in desperation, France turned to the United States for help. Admiral Arthur Radford, chairman of the Joint Chiefs of Staff, proposed an American air strike to lift the siege. Although the other Joint Chiefs had strong objections to involving American forces in another Asian war so soon after Korea, hawkish Republican senators were clamoring for action.

Eisenhower decided against Radford's bold proposal, but he killed it in his typically indirect fashion. Fearful that an air attack would lead inevitably to the use of ground troops, Ike insisted that both Congress and American allies in Europe approve the strike in advance. Congressional leaders, recalling the recent Korean stalemate, were reluctant to agree; the British were appalled and ruled out any joint action. The president used these objections to reject intervention in Indochina in 1954. Years later, he stated his reasons more candidly. "The jungles of Indochina would have swallowed up division after division of United States troops," he explained. Equally important, he believed that U.S. involvement in France's war would have compromised the American "tradition of anticolonialism."

Dien Bien Phu fell to the Vietminh in May 1954. At an international conference held in Geneva a few weeks later, Indochina was divided at the 17th parallel. Ho gained control of North Vietnam, while the French continued to rule in the South, with provision for a general election within two years to unify the country. The election was never held, largely because Eisenhower feared it would result in an overwhelming mandate for Ho. Instead, the United States gradually took over from the French in South Vietnam, sponsoring a new government in Saigon headed by Ngo Dinh Diem, a Vietnamese

📖 Read the Document   Dwight D. Eisenhower, Letters on Dien Bien Phu (1954)

A French soldier stands guard over a truckload of Vietnamese nationalists captured in the fighting in Indochina. French efforts to quash the rebellion in Vietnam ended on May 7, 1954, when the Vietminh took the French stronghold at Dien Bien Phu.

nationalist from a northern Catholic family. While Eisenhower can be given credit for refusing to engage American forces on behalf of French colonialism in Indochina, his determination to resist communist expansion had committed the United States to a long and eventually futile struggle to prevent Ho Chi Minh from achieving his long-sought goal of a unified, independent Vietnam.

Containing China

The Communist government in Beijing posed a serious challenge for the Eisenhower administration. Senate Republicans, led by William Knowland of California, blamed the Democrats for the "loss" of China. They viewed Mao as a puppet of the Soviet Union and insisted the United States recognize the Nationalists on Formosa as the only legitimate government of China. While State Department experts realized there were underlying tensions between China and Russia, Mao's intervention in the Korean War had convinced most Americans that the Chinese Communists

were an integral part of a larger Communist effort at world domination. Thus, Truman and Acheson had abandoned any hope of trying to exploit differences between Mao and Stalin by wooing China away from the Soviet Union.

Eisenhower and Dulles chose to accentuate the potential conflict between Russia and China. By taking a strong line against China, the United States could make the Chinese realize that Russia was unable to protect their interests; at the same time, such a hawkish policy would please congressional conservatives such as Knowland. Ultimately, Eisenhower and Dulles hoped that a policy of firmness would not only contain communist Chinese expansion in Asia but also drive a wedge between Moscow and Beijing.

A crisis in the Formosa Straits provided the first test of the new policy. In the fall of 1954, communist China threatened to seize coastal islands, notably Quemoy and Matsu, occupied by the Nationalists. Fearful that seizure of these offshore islands would be the first step toward an invasion of Formosa, Eisenhower permitted Dulles to sign a security treaty with Chiang Kai-shek committing

Feature Essay | America Enters the Middle East

Harry Truman never liked disagreeing with George Marshall. The secretary of state was, in Truman's view, the "greatest living American," and, as the architect of the American victory in World War II, Marshall possessed a stature no civilian—and certainly no accidental president, such as Truman remained in the spring of 1948—could hope to match.

Marshall adamantly opposed an action recommended by several of Truman's closest advisers. The British government had decided to relinquish control of Palestine, the region on the eastern shore of the Mediterranean it had inherited from the Ottoman empire after World War I. The United Nations General Assembly in November 1947 proposed partitioning Palestine into two states, one controlled by the Arab inhabitants of the region, the other controlled by the Jewish inhabitants. The UN plan provoked violence between the Arabs and Jews, with each group struggling to position itself most favorably for the moment the British left.

The U.S. State Department advocated a cautious policy in the evolving situation. Robert Lovett, the American undersecretary of state, told Truman that hasty recognition of the new Jewish state, Israel, would constitute "buying a pig in a poke"—that the United States didn't know what kind of government Israel would have, what the boundaries of the new Jewish state would be, or how Israel's neighbors would respond to the creation of this novel entity.

George Marshall was even more adamant than Lovett. Marshall knew that Truman was being told by his political advisers that recognition of Israel would help him and the Democrats in the upcoming 1948 elections, but the secretary of state thoroughly rejected the idea that politics should influence such a crucial foreign policy decision. "These considerations have nothing to do with the issue," Marshall told the president. "I don't think politics should play any part in this." Clark Clifford was the adviser who made the strongest case for early recognition, and Marshall resented that Clifford was even present at the meetings regarding Israel. The secretary of state told Truman in the bluntest of terms, "If you follow Clifford's advice and if I were to vote in the election, I would vote against you."

"Well, that was rough as a cob," Truman remarked after Marshall left the Oval Office. "I never saw the general so furious." But Truman had reasons for going ahead with recognition, and politics was only one. The Cold War was under way, and Truman feared that the Soviet Union would recognize Israel before the United States did, giving Moscow a potential advantage in the Middle East at a time when that oil-rich region was becoming critical in the balance of international power. Moreover, the Jewish people had been promised a homeland by the British many years before, and Israel was the manifestation of that promise. To be sure, Britain's promises didn't bind the United States, but Britain was America's ally, and Truman felt a certain obligation to follow through on Britain's behalf. Finally, the Jews had suffered horribly during World War II, and although a Jewish state wouldn't bring back the six million slaughtered in the Holocaust, it would provide the Jews of the world a refuge against future threats.

Truman gave Marshall time to cool off, confident that the general's military training would incline him to support—or at least not oppose—his commander in chief once the president made up his mind. And when Truman did choose in favor of early recognition of Israel, Marshall gritted his teeth but indeed held his tongue. On May 14, 1948, fifteen minutes after the official proclamation of the Jewish state of Israel, the United States announced its recognition.

This first American step into the Middle East was followed by others. In 1951, the populist prime minister of Iran, Mohammad Mossadeq, announced a plan to nationalize the Anglo-Iranian Oil Company, a giant firm that held exclusive rights to develop and exploit Iran's richest oil fields. The British government was the principal shareholder in Anglo-Iranian, and the company's identity and presence reminded Iranians of the power Britain had long wielded over their country. Mossadeq's nationalization plan was intended to break Britain's hold forever.

The British government, not surprisingly, resisted the nationalization effort. The British approached the Truman administration about joining in a secret operation to overthrow Mossadeq. Truman had consented to the 1947 establishment of the Central Intelligence Agency, but he never lost his fear that the spy agency would become an "American Gestapo," as he called it, and he rejected the British overture. But after Dwight Eisenhower succeeded Truman in the White House, the British reproposed their plan. They argued that Mossadeq was either a Communist in disguise or the dupe of Communists, and that if he remained in power Iran and its oil would slip into the grasp of the neighboring Soviet Union.

Eisenhower took this possibility very seriously. He couldn't know that things would happen the way the British predicted, but neither could he know that they would not happen that way. At a moment when the Cold War was spreading beyond Europe and becoming a global contest, Eisenhower didn't want to risk letting the Soviets seize Iran.

Accordingly, he approved a joint British–American plan against Mossadeq. Operation Ajax, as it was labeled, called for the constitutional monarch of Iran, the Shah, to demand Mossadeq's resignation. If Mossadeq resisted, as he was expected to do, the CIA and its British counterpart would mobilize mobs in Tehran to force the prime minister from office. A pro-Shah general would send tanks into the streets and complete the coup.

The plan went off with only minor glitches, and the pro-American Shah assumed power. The Eisenhower administration brokered an agreement between the Iranian government and the British over the fate of the Anglo-Iranian Oil Company—an agreement that awarded American companies a share of Iranian production. To keep the Shah in power, the United States sent large amounts of economic and military aid to Tehran. The American aid helped the Shah suppress dissent in Iran but made him increasingly unpopular with the masses of the Iranian people—who over time transferred that animosity to the United States.

Washington won back a bit of credibility with the peoples of the Middle East three years later. The British government had a new enemy: Gamal Abdel Nasser, an Egyptian colonel who seized power in Cairo and nationalized the Suez Canal Company, another vestige of Britain's declining empire. The British talked France and Israel, who had their own reasons for disliking Nasser, into a tripartite operation to overthrow the Egyptian leader. In October 1956 the three countries attacked Egypt near the Suez Canal, hoping the military pressure would result in Nasser's downfall.

Eisenhower refused to back them. The president distrusted Nasser, but

President Harry Truman (left) listened to Secretary of State George Marshall (right) on most matters of foreign policy, but charted his own course regarding Israel.

he didn't think the Egyptian leader's actions warranted a Middle Eastern war. He told the British—the ringleaders of the Suez operation, in Eisenhower's accurate assessment—that they must shut down the nascent war at once. When they hesitated, he threatened to use America's trump cards against the British: oil and the dollar. The president prepared to block oil shipments from the Americas to Britain, and to let the British currency, the pound, decline against the dollar. A loss of American oil would squeeze British industry and transport; a collapse of the pound would ravage British finance.

The British had no choice but to acquiesce in Eisenhower's ultimatum. The Suez war halted almost as soon as it began, causing much soul-searching in Britain, where the fiasco symbolized the end of Britain's pretensions to great-power status. The American role in the war's end momentarily belied the prevalent impression in the Middle East that Washington would always stand with the European imperialists and the Zionists—the label applied to the Israelis by the Arabs—in a crisis.

Yet the good feeling faded before long, and it only underscored the larger reality: that by the end of 1956 the United States had become the most important outside power in the Middle East. How America would play its new role remained to be seen, but henceforward nothing of substance would occur in the Middle East without requiring a significant response from the United States.

QUESTIONS FOR DISCUSSION

1. Why did Truman decide to recognize Israel in 1948?

2. Why did Eisenhower side with the British in Iran but against them when they invaded Egypt together with the French and Israelis during the Suez Crisis in 1956?

the United States to defend Formosa. When the Communists began shelling the offshore islands, Eisenhower persuaded Congress to pass a resolution authorizing him to use force to defend Formosa and "closely related localities."

Despite repeated requests, however, the president refused to say whether he would use force to repel a Chinese attack on Quemoy or Matsu. Instead, he and Dulles hinted at the use of nuclear weapons, carefully stating that their action would depend on whether they considered an attack on the offshore islands part of a larger offensive aimed at Formosa. The Chinese leaders, unsure whether Eisenhower was bluffing, decided not to test American resolve. The shelling ended in 1955, and when the Communists resumed it again in 1958, another firm but equally ambiguous American response forced them to desist. The apparent refusal of the Soviet Union to come to China's aid in these crises with the United States contributed to a growing rift between the two communist nations by the end of the 1950s. Unfortunately, the Eisenhower administration failed to take full advantage of the opportunity that it had helped to create.

Covert Actions

Amid these dangerous crises, the Eisenhower administration worked behind the scenes in the 1950s to expand the nation's global influence. In 1953, the CIA was instrumental in overthrowing a popularly elected government in Iran and placing the shah in full control of that country. (See the Feature Essay: "America Enters the Middle East," pp. 682–683.) Closer to home, in Latin America, Eisenhower once again relied on covert action. In 1954, the CIA masterminded the overthrow of a leftist regime in Guatemala. The immediate advantage was in denying the Soviets a possible foothold in the Western Hemisphere, but Latin Americans resented the thinly disguised interference of the United States in their internal affairs. More important, when Fidel Castro came to power in Cuba in 1959, the Eisenhower administration—after a brief effort at conciliation—adopted a hard line that helped drive Cuba into the Soviet orbit and led to new attempts at covert action.

Eisenhower's record as a cold warrior was thus mixed. His successful ending of the Korean War and his peacekeeping efforts in Indochina and Formosa and in the Suez crisis are all to his credit. Yet his reliance on coups and subversion directed by the CIA in Iran and Guatemala reveal Ike's corrupting belief that the ends justified the means. And despite the 1952 campaign call for the liberation of eastern Europe, Eisenhower accepted Soviet domination of this region, refusing to act on behalf of East German protesters in 1953 or Hungarian freedom fighters in 1956.

Nevertheless, Eisenhower did display an admirable ability to stay calm and unruffled in moments of great tension, reassuring the nation and the world. And above all, he could boast, as he did in 1962, of his ability to keep the peace. "In those eight years," he reminded the nation, "we lost no inch of ground to tyranny. One war was ended and incipient wars were blocked."

Waging Peace

Eisenhower hoped to ease Cold War tensions by ending the nuclear arms race. The advent of the hydrogen bomb intensified his concern over nuclear warfare; by 1955, both the United States and the Soviet Union had added this dread new weapon to their arsenals. With new long-range ballistic missiles being perfected, it was only a matter of time before Russia and the United States would be capable of destroying each other completely. Peace, as Winston Churchill noted, now depended on a balance of terror.

Throughout the 1950s, Eisenhower sought a way out of the nuclear dilemma. In April 1953, shortly after Stalin's death, he gave a speech in which he called on the Russians to join him in a new effort at disarmament, pointing out that "every warship launched, every rocket fired signifies, in the final sense, a theft from those who hunger and are not fed, those who are cold and are not clothed." When the Soviets ignored this appeal, the president tried again in December 1953. Addressing the UN General Assembly, he outlined an "atoms for peace" plan whereby the United States and the Soviet Union would donate fissionable material to a new UN agency to be used for peaceful purposes. Despite Ike's appeal "to serve the needs rather than the fears of mankind," the Russians again rebuffed him. Undaunted, Eisenhower tried once more. At a summit conference in Geneva, Switzerland, in 1955, Ike proposed to Nikita Khrushchev, just emerging as Stalin's successor after a two-year struggle for power, a way to break the disarmament deadlock. "Open skies," as reporters dubbed the plan, would overcome the traditional Russian objection to on-site inspection by having both superpowers open their territory to mutual aerial surveillance. Unfortunately, Khrushchev dismissed open skies as "a very transparent espionage device," and the conference ended without any significant breakthrough in the Cold War.

After his reelection in 1956, the president renewed his efforts toward nuclear arms control. Concern over atmospheric fallout from nuclear testing had led presidential candidate Adlai Stevenson to propose a mutual ban on such experiments. At first, Eisenhower rejected the test ban idea, arguing that it could be effective only as part of a comprehensive disarmament agreement, but the Russians supported it. Finally, in 1958, the president changed his mind after American and Soviet scientists developed a system to detect nuclear testing in the atmosphere without on-site inspection. In October 1958, Eisenhower and Khrushchev each voluntarily suspended further weapons tests pending the outcome of a conference held at Geneva to work out a test ban treaty. Although the Geneva Conference failed to make progress, neither the United States nor the Soviet Union resumed testing for the remainder of Ike's term in office.

The suspension of testing halted the nuclear pollution of the world's atmosphere, but it did not lead to the improvement in Soviet–American relations that Eisenhower sought. Instead, the Soviet feat in launching *Sputnik*, the first artificial satellite to orbit the Earth, intensified the Cold War. (See the Feature Essay in Chapter 29, "The Reaction to *Sputnik*," pp. 694–695.) Fearful that the Russians were several years ahead of the United States in the development of intercontinental ballistic missiles (ICBMs), Democrats criticized Eisenhower for not spending enough on defense and warned that a dangerous missile gap would open up by the early 1960s—a time when the Russians might have such a commanding lead in ICBMs that they could launch a first strike and destroy America. Despite the president's belief that the American missile program was in good shape, he allowed increased defense spending to speed up the building of American ICBMs and the new Polaris submarine–launched intermediate range missile (IRBM).

Nikita Khrushchev took full advantage of the furor over *Sputnik* to put the United States on the defensive. "We will bury you," he boasted, telling Americans, "Your grandchildren will live under communism." The most serious threat of all came in November 1958, when the Russian leader declared that within six months he would sign a separate peace treaty with East Germany, calling for an end to American, British, and French occupation rights in Berlin.

Eisenhower met the second Berlin crisis as firmly as Truman had the first. He refused to abandon the city but also tried to avoid a military showdown. Prudent diplomacy forced Khrushchev to extend his deadline indefinitely. After a trip to the United States, culminating in a personal meeting with Eisenhower at Camp David, the Russian leader agreed to attend a summit conference in Paris in May 1960.

This much heralded meeting never took place. On May 1, two weeks before the leaders were to convene in Paris, the Soviets shot down an American U-2 plane piloted by Francis Gary Powers. The United States had been flying over Russia since 1956 in the high-altitude spy planes, gaining vital information about the Soviet missile program that showed there was little basis for the public's fear that the Russians had opened up a dangerous missile gap. After initially denying any knowledge, Eisenhower took full responsibility for Powers's overflight, and Khrushchev responded with a scathing personal denunciation and a refusal to meet with the American president.

Conclusion: The Continuing Cold War

The breakup of the Paris summit marked the end of Eisenhower's attempts to moderate the Cold War. The disillusioned leader told an aide that "he saw nothing worthwhile left for him to do now until the end of his presidency." But Eisenhower did make a final effort for peace by delivering a somber warning about the danger of massive military spending in his farewell address to the American people. "In the councils of government, we must guard against the acquisition of unwarranted influence, whether sought or unsought, by the military-industrial complex," he declared. "The potential for the disastrous rise of misplaced power exists and will persist."

Rarely has an American president been more prophetic. In the next few years, the level of defense spending would skyrocket as the Cold War escalated. The military-industrial complex reached its acme of power in the 1960s when the United States realized the full implications of Truman's doctrine of containment. Eisenhower had succeeded in keeping the peace for eight years, but he had failed to halt the momentum of the Cold War he had inherited from Harry Truman. Ike's efforts to ease tension with the Soviet Union were dashed by his own distrust of communism and by Khrushchev's belligerent rhetoric and behavior. Still, he had begun to relax tensions, a process that would survive the troubled 1960s and, after several false starts, would finally begin to erode the Cold War by the end of the 1980s.

Russians view the wreckage of the U-2 reconnaissance plane piloted by Francis Powers that was shot down over Soviet territory on May 1, 1960. Although Eisenhower originally disavowed any knowledge of Powers's mission, Khrushchev produced photographs of Soviet military and industrial sites, which he said had been taken by the U-2 pilot. Powers was held in a Soviet prison for two years before he was released in exchange for a Russian spy.

Study Resources

 Take the **Study Plan** for **Chapter 28** *The Onset of the Cold War* on **MyHistoryLab**

TIME LINE

1945 Truman meets Stalin at Potsdam Conference (July); World War II ends with Japanese surrender (August)

1946 Winston Churchill gives "Iron Curtain" speech

1947 Truman Doctrine announced to Congress (March); Truman orders loyalty program for government employees (March); George Marshall outlines Marshall Plan (June); Truman signs National Security Act (July)

1948 Soviets begin blockade of Berlin (June); Truman scores upset victory in presidential election

1949 NATO treaty signed in Washington (April); Soviet Union tests its first atomic bomb (August)

1950 Truman authorizes building of hydrogen bomb (January); Senator Joseph McCarthy claims Communists in government (February); North Korea invades South Korea (June)

1951 Truman recalls MacArthur from Korea

1952 Dwight D. Eisenhower elected president

1953 Julius and Ethel Rosenberg executed for atomic-secrets spying (June); Korean War truce signed at Panmunjom (July)

1954 Fall of Dien Bien Phu to Vietminh ends French control of Indochina

1956 England and France touch off Suez crisis

1957 Russia launches *Sputnik* satellite

1959 Fidel Castro takes power in Cuba

1960 American U-2 spy plane shot down over Russia

CHAPTER REVIEW

The Cold War Begins

 How did the Cold War begin?

The Cold War began as the United States and the Soviet Union discovered that their interests in Europe conflicted. Each feared the other and, acting on its fears, took steps that heightened the other's fears. Atomic weapons made the mistakes of miscalculation far greater than in the past and everyone more fearful. (p. 666)

Containment

 What was containment, and why was it adopted?

Containment was the American policy of preventing Soviet power and influence from expanding. It was adopted to preserve American interests without excessively risking war. (p. 668)

The Cold War Expands

 How did the Cold War expand from Europe to Asia?

The United States and the Soviet Union took opposite sides in the Chinese civil war. Shortly after the Communist victory in China, Communist North Korea battled antiCommunist South Korea. The United States sided with South Korea. The Soviet Union and Communist China backed North Korea. (p. 671)

The Cold War at Home

 How did the Cold War affect life in America?

The Cold War spawned fears of Communist subversion. It led to a campaign to ensure loyalty, and fostered McCarthyism, an exaggerated effort to find Communists in every corner of American life. Although McCarthyism eventually burned itself out, it contributed to Eisenhower's election in 1952, which ended twenty years of Democratic control of the White House. (p. 674)

Eisenhower Wages the Cold War

 How successful was Eisenhower at dealing with the foreign policy issues facing the United States?

When he became president in 1953, Eisenhower was deeply experienced in military and diplomatic affairs. While he failed to halt the momentum of the Cold War, as president he kept the peace for eight years and began to relax tensions with the Soviet Union. (p. 680)

KEY TERMS & DEFINITIONS

Potsdam Conference   The final wartime meeting of the leaders of the United States, Britain, and the Soviet Union was held at Potsdam, outside Berlin, in July, 1945. Their failure to agree about the future of Europe led to the Cold War. p. 664

Iron Curtain   Winston Churchill coined the phrase "Iron Curtain" to refer to the boundary in Europe that divided Soviet dominated Eastern and Central Europe from Western Europe. p. 666

Baruch Plan   In 1946, Bernard Baruch presented an American plan to control and eventually outlaw nuclear weapons. The plan called for UN control of nuclear weapons in three stages before the United States gave up its stockpile. Soviet insistence on immediate nuclear disarmament without inspection doomed the Baruch Plan and led to a nuclear arms race between the United States and the Soviet Union. p. 668

Containment   First proposed by George Kennan in 1947, containment became the basic strategy of the United States throughout the Cold War. Kennan argued that firm American resistance would eventually compel Moscow to adopt more peaceful policies. p. 669

Truman Doctrine   In 1947, President Truman asked Congress for money to aid the Greek and Turkish governments that were then threatened by communist rebels. Truman asserted that the United States was committed to support free people everywhere against Communist attack or rebellion. p. 669

Marshall Plan   In 1947, A massive aid program to rebuild the war-torn economies of Western Europe. The plan was motivated by both humanitarian concerns and fear of communism. p. 670

North Atlantic Treaty Organization (NATO)   In 1949, the United States, Canada, and ten European nations formed this military mutual-defense pact. p. 670

Berlin airlift   In 1948, in response to a Soviet land blockade of Berlin, the United States carried out a massive effort to supply the 2 million Berlin citizens by air. The airlift forced the Soviets to end the blockade in 1949. p. 671

National Security Act   Congress passed the National Security Act in 1947 in response to perceived threats from the Soviet Union after World War II. It established the Department of Defense and created the Central Intelligence Agency (CIA) and National Security Council. p. 671

NSC-68   National Security Council planning paper No. 68 redefined America's national defense policy. Adopted in 1950, it committed the United States to a massive military buildup to meet the challenge posed by the Soviet Union. p. 672

Taft–Hartley Act   This 1947 anti-union legislation outlawed the closed shop and secondary boycotts. It also authorized the president to seek injunctions to prevent strikes that threatened national security. p. 675

McCarthyism   A sensationalist campaign by Senator Joseph McCarthy against supposed communists in government that began in 1950 and ended when the Senate censured him in 1954. p. 677

CRITICAL THINKING QUESTIONS

1. Why was the Soviet Union suspicious of the United States?

2. In what ways did the Marshall Plan demonstrate American generosity? In what ways did it reflect American self-interest?

3. How was the Cold War in Asia similar to the Cold War in Europe? How was it different?

4. To what extent was McCarthyism justified?

MyHistoryLab Media Assignments

Find these resources in the Media Assignments folder for Chapter 28 on MyHistoryLab

The Cold War Begins

■ **Read** the **Document**   *Churchill's "Iron Curtain" Speech (March 5, 1946) p. 667*

Containment

Read the **Document**   *George F. Kennan, "The Long Telegram" (1946) p. 668*

Read the **Document**   *George Marshall, The Marshall Plan (1947) p. 669*

The Cold War Expands

■ **View** the **Closer Look**   *Berlin Airlift p. 672*

■ **View** the **Map**   *The Korean War (1950–1953) p. 673*

The Cold War at Home

Read the **Document**   *Ronald Reagan, Testimony Before HUAC (1947) p. 677*

■ **Watch** the **Video**   *McCarthyism and the Politics of Fear p. 678*

Watch the **Video**   *Ike for President: Campaign Ad (1952) p. 679*

Eisenhower Wages the Cold War

Read the **Document**   *Dwight D. Eisenhower, Letters on Dien Bien Phu (1954) p. 681*

■ **Complete** the **Assignment**   *America Enters the Middle East p. 682*

■ *Indicates Study Plan Media Assignment*

29 Affluence and Anxiety

Contents and Learning Objectives

((•—Listen to the Audio File on myhistorylab   Chapter 29 *Affluence and Anxiety*

Levittown: The Flight to the Suburbs

On May 7, 1947, William Levitt announced plans to build two thousand rental houses in a former potato field on Long Island, thirty miles from Midtown Manhattan. Using mass production techniques he had learned while erecting navy housing during the war, Levitt quickly built four thousand homes and rented them to young veterans eager to leave crowded city apartments or their parents' homes to begin raising families. A change in government financing regulations led him to begin offering his houses for sale in 1948 for a small amount down and a low monthly payment. Young couples, many of them the original renters, quickly bought the first four thousand; by the time **Levittown**—as he called the new community—was completed in 1951, it contained more than seventeen thousand homes. So many babies were born in Levittown that it soon became known as "Fertility Valley" and "the Rabbit Hutch."

Levitt eventually built two more Levittowns, one in Pennsylvania and one in New Jersey; each contained the same curving streets, neighborhood parks and playgrounds, and community swimming pools characteristic of the first development. The secret of Levittown's appeal was the basic house, a 720-square-foot Cape Cod design built on a concrete slab. It had a kitchen, two bedrooms and bath, a living room complete with a fireplace and 16-foot picture window, and an expansion attic with room for two more bedrooms. Levitt built only one interior, but there were four different facades to break the monotony. The original house sold for $6,990 in 1948; even the improved model, a ranch-style house, sold for less than $10,000 in 1951.

Levitt's houses were ideal for young people just starting out in life. They were cheap, comfortable, and efficient, and each home came with a refrigerator, cooking range, and washing machine. Despite the conformity of the houses, the three Levittowns were surprisingly diverse communities; residents had a wide variety of religious, ethnic, and occupational backgrounds. African Americans, however, were rigidly excluded. In time, as the more successful families moved on to larger homes in more expensive neighborhoods, the Levittowns became enclaves for lower-middle-class families.

Levittown symbolized the most significant social trend of the postwar era in the United States—the flight to the suburbs. The residential areas surrounding cities such as New York and Chicago nearly doubled in the 1950s. While central cities remained relatively stagnant during the decade, suburbs grew by 46 percent; by 1960, some sixty million people, one-third of the nation, lived in suburban rings around the cities. This massive shift in population from the central city was accompanied by a **baby boom** that started during World War II. Young married couples began to have three, four, or even five children (compared with only one or two children in American families during the 1930s). These larger families led to a 19 percent growth in the nation's population between 1950 and 1960, the highest growth rate since 1910.

The houses of Levittown spread over twelve hundred acres of former potato fields on Long Island, New York.

The economy boomed as residential construction soared. By 1960, one-fourth of all existing homes were less than ten years old, and factories were turning out large quantities of appliances and television sets for the new households. A multitude of new consumer products—ranging from frozen foods to filter cigarettes, from high-fidelity phonographs to cars equipped with automatic transmissions and tubeless tires—appeared in stores and showrooms. In the suburbs, the corner grocery gave way to the supermarket carrying a vast array of items that enabled homemakers to provide their families with a more varied diet.

A new affluence replaced the poverty and hunger of the Great Depression for most Americans, but many had haunting memories

((•─ Listen to the Audio File   "Little Boxes"

A photograph, for a Levittown house. The Levittown builders applied the principles of mass production used in auto manufacturing to house construction. One important difference was the fact that the product stood stationary while workers came to the site to perform their specialized tasks.

Events abroad added to the feeling of anxiety in the postwar years. Nuclear war became a frighteningly real possibility. The rivalry with the Soviet Union had led to the second Red Scare, with charges of treason and disloyalty being leveled at loyal Americans. Many Americans joined Senator Joseph McCarthy in searching for the communist enemy at home rather than abroad. Loyalty oaths and book burning revealed how insecure Americans had become in the era of the Cold War. The 1950s also witnessed a growing demand by African Americans for equal opportunity in an age of abundance. The civil rights movement, along with strident criticism of the consumer culture, revealed that beneath the bland surface of suburban affluence forces for change were at work.

The Postwar Boom

How did the American economy evolve after World War II?

For fifteen years following World War II, the nation witnessed a period of unparalleled economic growth. A pent-up demand for consumer goods fueled a steady industrial expansion. Heavy government spending during the Cold War added an extra stimulus to the economy, offsetting brief recessions in 1949 and 1953 and moderating a steeper one in 1957–1958. By the end of the 1950s, the American people had achieved an affluence that finally erased the lingering fears of the Great Depression.

of the 1930s. The obsession with material goods took on an almost desperate quality, as if a profusion of houses, cars, and home appliances could guarantee that the nightmare of depression would never return. Critics were quick to disparage the quality of life in suburban society. They condemned the conformity, charging the newly affluent with forsaking traditional American individualism to live in identical houses, drive look-alike cars, and accumulate the same material possessions. Folksinger Malvina Reynolds caught the essence of postwar suburbia in a 1962 song:

> Little boxes on the hillside,
> Little boxes made of ticky tacky,
> Little boxes on the hillside,
> Little boxes all the same.
> There's a green one and a pink one
> And a blue one and a yellow one,
> And they're all made out of ticky tacky,
> And they all look just the same.[1]

---

[1]"Little Boxes," words and music by Malvina Reynolds. Copyright © 1962 Schroder Music Co. [ASCAP]. Used by permission. All rights reserved.

Postwar Prosperity

The economy began its upward surge as the result of two long-term factors. First, American consumers—after being held in check by depression and then by wartime scarcities—finally had a chance to indulge their suppressed appetites for material goods. At the war's end, personal savings in the United States stood at more than $37 billion, providing a powerful stimulus to consumption. Initially, American factories could not turn out enough automobiles and appliances to satisfy the horde of buyers. By 1950, however, production lines had finally caught up with the demand. In that year, Americans bought more than six million cars, and the gross national product (GNP) reached $318 billion (50 percent higher than in 1940).

The Cold War provided the additional stimulus the economy needed when postwar expansion slowed. The Marshall Plan and other foreign aid programs financed a heavy export trade. The Korean War helped overturn a brief recession and ensured continued prosperity as the government spent massive amounts on guns, planes, and munitions. In 1952, the nation spent $44 billion, two-thirds of the federal budget, on national defense.

Although Eisenhower managed to bring about some modest reductions, defense spending continued at a level of $40 billion throughout the decade.

The nation achieved an affluence in the 1950s that made the persisting fear of another Great Depression seem irrational. The baby boom and the spectacular growth of suburbia served as great stimulants to the consumer goods industries. Manufacturers turned out an ever-increasing number of refrigerators, washing machines, and dishwashers to equip the kitchens of Levittown and its many imitators across the country. The automobile industry thrived with suburban expansion as two-car families became more and more common. In 1955, in an era when oil was abundant and gasoline sold for less than 30 cents a gallon, Detroit sold a record eight million cars. The electronics industry boomed. Consumers were eager to acquire the latest marvel of home entertainment—the television set.

Commercial enterprises snapped up office machines and the first generation of computers; industry installed electronic sensors and processors as it underwent extensive automation; and the military displayed an insatiable appetite for electronic devices for its planes and ships. As a result, American industry averaged more than $10 billion a year in capital investment, and the number of persons employed rose above the long-sought goal of sixty million nationwide.

Yet the economic abundance of the 1950s was not without its problems. While some sections of the nation (notably the emerging Sunbelt areas of the South and West) benefited enormously from the growth of the aircraft and electronics industries, older manufacturing regions, such as New England, did not fare as well. The steel industry increased its capacity during the decade, but it began to fall behind the rate of national growth. Agriculture continued to experience bumper crops and low prices, so rural regions, like the vast areas of the Plains states, failed to share in the general affluence. Unemployment persisted despite the boom, rising to more than 7 percent in a sharp recession that hit the country in the fall of 1957 and lasted through the summer of 1958. The rate of economic growth slowed in the second half of the decade, causing concern about the continuing vitality of the American economy.

None of these flaws, however, could disguise the fact that the nation was prospering to an extent no one dreamed possible in the 1930s. The GNP grew to $440 billion by 1960, more than double the 1940 level. More important, workers now labored fewer than forty hours a week; they rarely worked on Saturdays, and nearly all enjoyed a two-week paid vacation each year. By the mid-1950s, the average American family had twice as much real income to spend as its counterpart had possessed in the boom years of the 1920s. From 1945 to 1960, per capita disposable income rose by $500—to $1,845—for every man, woman, and child in the country. The American people, in one generation, had moved from poverty and depression to the highest standard of living the world had ever known.

Life in the Suburbs

Sociologists had difficulty describing the nature of suburban society in the 1950s. Some saw it as classless, while others noted the absence of both the very rich and the very poor and consequently labeled it "middle class." Rather than forming a homogeneous social group, though, the suburbs contained a surprising variety of people, whether classified as "upper lower," "lower middle," and "upper middle" or simply as blue collar, white collar, and professional. Doctors and lawyers often lived in the same developments as salesclerks and master plumbers. The traditional distinctions of ancestry, education, and size of residence no longer differentiated people as easily as they had in the past.

Yet suburbs could vary widely, from working-class communities clustered near factories built in the countryside to old, elitist areas such as Scarsdale, New York, and Shaker Heights, Ohio. Most were almost exclusively white and Christian, but suburbs such as Great Neck on Long Island and Richmond Heights outside Miami enabled Jews and blacks to take part in the flight from the inner city.

Life in all the suburban communities depended on the automobile. Highways and expressways allowed fathers to commute to jobs in the cities, often an hour or more away. Children might ride buses to and from school, but mothers had to drive them to piano lessons and Little League ballgames. Two cars became a necessity for almost every suburban family, thus helping spur the boom in automobile production. In 1948, only 59 percent of American families owned a car; just a few years later, nearly every suburban family had at least one vehicle, and many had several.

In the new drive-in culture, people shopped at the stores that grew up first in "miracle miles" along the highways and later at the shopping centers that spread across the countryside in the 1950s. There were only eight shopping centers in the entire country in 1946; hundreds appeared over the next fifteen years, including Poplar Plaza in Memphis, with one large department store, thirty retail shops, and parking for more than five hundred cars. In 1956, the first enclosed air-conditioned mall, the Southdale Shopping Center, opened outside Minneapolis.

Despite the increased mobility provided by the car, the home became the focus for activities and aspirations. The postwar shortage of housing that often forced young couples to live with their parents or in-laws created an intense demand for new homes in the suburbs. When questioned, prospective buyers expressed a desire for "more space," for "comfort and roominess," and for "privacy and freedom of action" in their new residences. Men and women who moved to the suburbs prized the new kitchens with their built-in dishwashers, electric ovens, and gleaming counters; the extra bedrooms that ensured privacy from and for the children; the large garages that could be converted into recreation rooms; and the small, neat lawns that gave them an area for outdoor activities as well as a new way to compete with their neighbors. "Togetherness" became the code word of the 1950s. Families did things together, whether gathering around the TV sets that dominated living rooms, attending community activities, or taking vacations in the huge station wagons of the era.

But there were some less attractive consequences of the new suburban lifestyle. The extended family, in which several generations had lived in close proximity, was a casualty of the boom in small detached homes. As historian Kenneth Jackson noted, suburban life "ordained that most children would grow up in intimate contact only with their parents and siblings." For many families, grandparents, aunts and uncles, cousins, and more distant relatives would become remote figures, seen only on special occasions.

The nuclear family, typical of the suburb, did little to encourage the development of feminism. The end of the war saw many women who had entered the workforce return to the home, where the role of wife and mother continued to be viewed as the ideal for women in the 1950s. Trends toward getting married earlier and having larger families reinforced the pattern of women devoting all their efforts to housework and child raising rather than acquiring professional skills and pursuing careers outside the home. Adlai Stevenson, extolling "the humble role of housewife," told Smith College graduates that there was much they could do "in the living room with a baby in your lap or in the kitchen with a can opener in your hand." Dr. Benjamin Spock's 1946 best-seller, *Baby and Child Care*, became a fixture in millions of homes, while the traditional women's magazines such as *McCall's* and *Good Housekeeping* thrived by featuring articles on natural childbirth and inspirational pieces such as "Homemaking Is My Vocation."

Nonetheless, the number of working wives doubled between 1940 and 1960. By the end of the 1950s, 40 percent of American women, and nearly one-third of all married women, had jobs outside the home. The heavy expenses involved in rearing and educating children led wives and mothers to seek ways to augment the family income, inadvertently preparing the way for a new demand for equality in the 1960s.

The Good Life?

How did American culture change after the war?

Consumerism became the dominant social theme of the 1950s. Yet even with an abundance of creature comforts and added hours of leisure time, the quality of life left many Americans anxious and dissatisfied.

Areas of Greatest Growth

Organized religion flourished in the climate of the 1950s. Ministers, priests, and rabbis all commented on the rise in church and synagogue attendance in the new communities. Will Herberg claimed that religious affiliation had become the primary identifying feature of modern American life, dividing the nation into three separate segments—Protestant, Catholic, and Jewish.

Some observers condemned the bland, secular nature of suburban churches, which seemed to be an integral part of the consumer society. "On weekdays one shops for food," wrote one critic, "on Saturdays one shops for recreation, and on Sundays one shops for the Holy Ghost." But the popularity of religious writer Norman Vincent Peale, with his positive gospel that urged people to "start thinking faith, enthusiasm, and joy," suggested that the new churches filled a genuine, if shallow, human need. At the same time, the emergence of neo-orthodoxy in Protestant seminaries (notably through the ideas of Reinhold Niebuhr) and the rapid spread of radical forms of fundamentalism (such as the Assemblies of God) indicated that millions of Americans still were searching for a more personal religious faith.

Schools provided an immediate problem for the growing new suburban communities. The increase in the number of school-age children, from twenty to thirty million in the first eight grades, overwhelmed the resources of many local districts, leading to demands for federal aid. Congress granted limited help for areas affected by

defense plants and military bases, but Eisenhower's reluctance to unbalance the budget—along with traditional adherence to state control over public education—blocked further federal assistance prior to 1957, when the government reacted to *Sputnik*. (See the Feature Essay, "The Reaction to *Sputnik*," pp. 694–695.)

Equally important, a controversy arose over the nature of education in the 1950s. Critics of "progressive" education called for sweeping educational reforms and a new emphasis on traditional academic subjects. Suburban communities often had bitter fights; affluent parents demanded kindergarten enrichment programs and grade school foreign language instruction while working-class people resisted such costly innovations. The one thing all seemed to agree on was the desirability of a college education. The number of young people attending colleges increased from 1.5 million in 1940 to 3.6 million in 1960.

The largest advances were made in the exciting new medium of television. From a shaky start just after the war, TV boomed in the 1950s, pushing radio aside and undermining many of the nation's magazines. By 1957, three networks controlled the airwaves, reaching forty million sets over nearly five hundred stations. Advertisers soon took charge of the new medium, using techniques first pioneered in radio—including taped commercials, quiz shows, and soap operas.

At first, the insatiable demand for programs encouraged a burst of creativity. Playwrights such as Reginald Rose, Rod Serling, and Paddy Chayefsky wrote a series of notable dramas for *Playhouse 90*, *Studio One*, and the *Goodyear Television Playhouse*. Broadcast live from cramped studios, these productions thrived on tight dramatic structures, movable scenery, and frequent close-ups of the actors.

Advertisers, however, quickly became disillusioned with the live anthology programs, which usually dealt with controversial subjects or focused on ordinary people and events. In contrast, sponsors wanted shows that stressed excitement, glamour, and instant success. Aware that audiences were fascinated by contestants with unusual expertise (a shoemaker answering tough questions on operas, a grandmother stumping experts on baseball), producers began giving away huge cash prizes on *The $64,000 Question* and *Twenty-one*. In 1959, the nation was shocked when Charles Van Doren, a Columbia University professor, confessed he had been given the answers in advance to win $129,000 on *Twenty-one*. The three networks quickly dropped all the big-prize quiz programs, replacing them with comedy, action, and adventure shows such as *The Untouchables* and *Bonanza*. Despite its early promise of artistic innovation, television had become a technologically sophisticated but safe conveyor of the consumer culture.

Critics of the Consumer Society

One striking feature of the 1950s was the abundance of self-criticism. A number of widely read books explored the flaws in the new suburbia. John Keats's *The Crack in the Picture Window* described the endless rows of tract houses "vomited up" by developers as "identical boxes spreading like gangrene." Their occupants—whom he dubbed the Drones, the Amiables, and the Fecunds—lost any sense of individuality in their obsession with material goods.

Richard Gordon, Katherine Gordon, and Max Gunther were more concerned about the psychological toll of suburban life in their 1960 book *The Split-Level Trap*. They labeled the new life-style "Disturbia" and bemoaned the "haggard" men, the "tense and anxious" women, and the "gimme" kids it produced. The most sweeping indictment came in William H. Whyte's *The Organization Man* (1956), based on a study of the Chicago suburb of Park Forest. Whyte perceived a change from the old Protestant ethic, with its emphasis on hard work and personal responsibility, to a new social ethic centered on "the team" with the ultimate goal of "belongingness." The result was a stifling conformity and the loss of personal identity.

The most influential social critic of the 1950s was Harvard sociologist David Riesman. His book *The Lonely Crowd* appeared in 1950 and set the tone for intellectual commentary about suburbia for the rest of the decade. Riesman described the shift from the "inner-directed" Americans of the past who had relied on such traditional values as self-denial and frugality to the "other-directed" Americans of the consumer society who constantly adapted their behavior to conform to social pressures. The consequences—a decline in individualism and a tendency for people to become acutely sensitive to the expectations of others—produced a bland and tolerant society of consumers lacking creativity and a sense of adventure.

C. Wright Mills was a far more caustic commentator on American society in the 1950s. Anticipating government statistics that revealed white-collar workers (salesclerks, office workers, bank tellers) now outnumbered blue-collar workers (miners, factory workers, mill hands), Mills described the new middle class in ominous terms in his books *White Collar* (1951) and *Power Elite* (1956). The corporation was the villain for Mills, depriving office workers of their own identities and imposing an impersonal discipline through manipulation and propaganda. The industrial assembly line had given way to an even more dehumanizing workplace, the modern office. "At rows of blank-looking counters sat rows of blank-looking girls with blank, white folders in their blank hands, all blankly folding blank papers."

This disenchantment with the consumer culture reached its most eloquent expression with the beats, literary groups that rebelled against the materialistic society of the 1950s. Jack Kerouac's novel *On the Road*, published in 1957, set the tone for the new movement. The name came from the quest for beatitude, a state of inner grace sought in Zen Buddhism. Flouting the respectability of suburbia, the "beatniks"—as middle America termed them—were

 View the **Closer Look**   **A 1950s Family Watching Television**

I Love Lucy was one of the most popular television shows of the 1950s. Manufacturers designed television sets as living room furniture and marketed televisions as promoting family togetherness and facilitating domestic leisure time.

Feature Essay | The Reaction to *Sputnik*

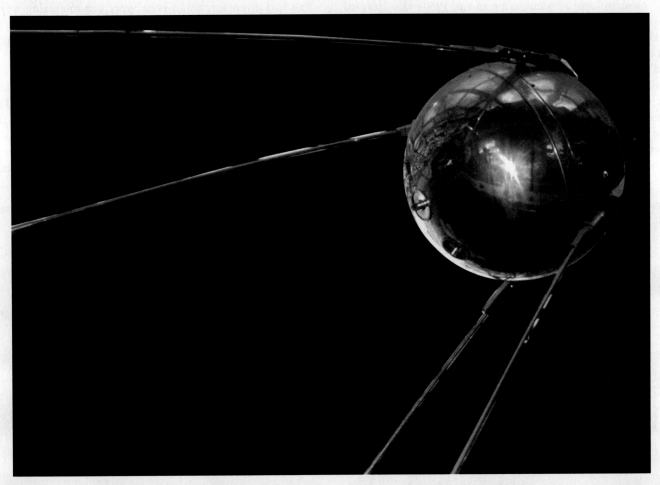

Sputnik was launched into an elliptical low orbit by the Soviet Union on October 4, 1957. The surprise success of the launching of the world's first artificial satellite by the Soviet Union served as catalyst in the United States for major changes and initiatives in national security, education, and space exploration.

On October 4, 1957, the Soviet Union launched *Sputnik*, the world's first artificial satellite. Every 92 minutes, the 184-pound sphere orbited the globe, emitting its distinctive radio signal, "beep...beep...beep." Americans were stunned. The United States had been planning to send up its own satellite as part of the International Geophysical Year established as July 1, 1957, to December 31, 1958. But the Vanguard program, kept separate from the military's quest for an intercontinental ballistic missile (ICBM), was far behind schedule. All American scientists could do was offer their congratulations to the Soviets, while political leaders tried to downplay the feat, with one official dismissing *Sputnik* as "a silly bauble."

Critics of the Eisenhower administration, however, reacted quite differently. A sense of panic gripped the nation. Edward Teller, father of the H-bomb, spoke of a technological Pearl Harbor and raised the fear that the Soviets, with a rocket powerful enough to send *Sputnik* into space, were ahead of the United States in the race for the ICBM. Even more important, many soon began to worry that the Soviets threatened the superiority of the United States in science and technology, areas in which Americans had long felt invincible. Thus Senator Henry Jackson, a Cold War Democrat, called the launch of *Sputnik* "a devastating blow to the prestige of the United

States as the leader in the scientific and technical world."

In responding to *Sputnik*, Americans began to voice doubts about the vitality and quality of their own society. Critics warned of excessive devotion to material objects—cars, appliances, luxury goods—at the expense of traditional American values such as hard work, dedication, and national pride. One senator proclaimed that it was time "to be less concerned with the depth of pile on the new broadloom rug or the height of the tail fin on the car and to be more prepared to shed blood, sweat, and tears if this country and the Free World are to survive." Others worried over the realization that the Soviets were training more scientists and engineers than the United States and called for a complete overhaul of the American educational system. *Sputnik* gave new momentum to reformers who for years had been critical of the trend toward social adjustment in American schools and were crying out for more stress on the basics—reading, writing, and arithmetic.

Events in the first few months following the launch of *Sputnik* did little to calm the nation. In November 1957, the Soviets orbited a second satellite, one weighing over 1,000 pounds and carrying a dog into space. A month later, American scientists readied Vanguard for its first launch at Cape Canaveral in Florida. The slim rocket, carrying a tiny 4-pound sphere as its payload, rose only a few inches off the ground and then toppled over in a cloud of smoke and fire. Reporters covering the event quickly derided Vanguard, referring to it as *"Flopnik"* and *"Kaputnik."*

President Eisenhower then approved plans to let an army team, led by German scientist Wernher Von Braun, attempt to put a satellite into orbit using the reliable intermediate range Jupiter rocket. On January 31, 1958, *Explorer*, the first American satellite, successfully orbited the earth. Much smaller than the original *Sputnik, Explorer* did carry a more sophisticated set of instruments to send back data from space. Informed of the successful launch, President Eisenhower expressed the sentiments of millions of Americans when he exclaimed, "I surely feel a lot better now."

Sputnik served as a catalyst for change that led to many positive developments. The most significant came in the area of national security. Democrats, led by Senator Lyndon Johnson, criticized Eisenhower for cutting defense spending in an effort to balance the budget and warned of a future missile gap, claiming that the powerful rocket that launched *Sputnik* into orbit showed the Soviets were ahead in developing the ICBM. The president responded by increasing the Pentagon budget by several billion dollars and speeding up the American missile program.

His most important action, however, was the appointment of MIT President James Killian to the new post of presidential science adviser. Killian quickly created a President's Science Advisory Committee (PSAC), composed of 17 leading scientists who met regularly to advise Eisenhower on technical issues. "Science," commented *Time* magazine, "has never before been given that kind of attention at that level." Killian and the PSAC persuaded Eisenhower to take a gamble on ICBMs that paid off handsomely. Instead of focusing on liquid-fuel missiles, which took hours to load and could not be placed in hardened sites, the president gave priority to development of solid-fuel missiles—the Minuteman and the Polaris—which could be fired almost immediately and could be protected against attack in underground silos or underwater onboard submarines. By the 1960s, fears of a missile gap evaporated as America's second generation of missiles made the original Soviet ICBMs obsolete.

In 1958, the nation moved quickly to address the other issues raised by *Sputnik*. With strong bipartisan support, Congress acted on long overdue educational reform. The National Defense Education Act (NDEA) helped schools improve and broaden their science and math offerings as academic leaders helped design "new math" and "new physics" courses. The act also created a loan fund to assist needy students in meeting the costs of a college education, as well as establishing graduate fellowships in science, engineering, and foreign area studies. *Sputnik* had allowed those calling for educational reform to break the logjam and upgrade and improve school curriculums as well as make higher education more affordable.

Another important congressional action came with the creation of the National Aeronautics and Space Administration (NASA) in 1958. Concerned by the interservice rivalry that hampered the missile program, its sponsors insisted on a new civilian agency to oversee the nation's space program. While dependent on the military for the rocket boosters, NASA was able to develop its own agenda for space exploration and started a program that would eventually place astronauts in orbit around the Earth and land them on the moon by the end of the next decade.

The reaction to *Sputnik* illustrates the curious way that democracy often works. Advocates of space exploration, educational reform, and intercontinental ballistic missiles had made little headway before October 4, 1957. The Soviet feat in launching *Sputnik* helped arouse the nation, and despite the initial overreaction, led to important advances in all three areas. *Sputnik* thus proved to be like a fire bell in the night, filling the American people with alarm but triggering a positive response that served the nation well.

QUESTIONS FOR DISCUSSION

1. How did the Cold War influence America's decision to invest heavily in space exploration?

2. Why did NASA favor manned space flight over instrument probes?

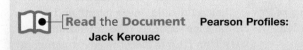

Read the Document   Pearson Profiles:
Jack Kerouac

Novelist Jack Kerouac and his fellow "beat" writers bemoaned the moral bankruptcy of popular culture. They sought not to improve conditions but to find release from the moral and social confines constricting their lives and the literary conventions circumscribing their writing. This photograph of Jack Kerouac was taken by beat poet Allen Ginsberg.

easily identified by their long hair and bizarre clothing; they also had a penchant for sexual promiscuity and drug experimentation. They were conspicuous dropouts from a society they found senseless. Poet Lawrence Ferlinghetti, who held forth in the City Lights Bookshop in San Francisco (a favorite resort of the beats), summed it up this way: "I was a wind-up toy someone had dropped wound up into a world already running down."

The social protest inherent in the books and poems of the beats found its artistic counterpart in the rise of abstract expressionism. Abstract expressionists worked in styles that emphasized individuality and freedom from the constraints of representational, realistic art. Painters Jackson Pollock and Mark Rothko, among others, challenged mainstream America's notions about the form and function of art. For Pollock, the act of creating a painting was as important as the painting itself. Rothko pioneered a style known as color field painting; his works in this style are monumental pieces in which enormous areas of color lacking any distinct structure or central focus are used to create a mood.

Despite the disapproval they evoked from mainstream Americans, the beat generation had some compassion for their detractors. "We love everything," Kerouac proclaimed, "Billy Graham, the Big Ten, Rock and Roll, Zen, apple pie, Eisenhower—we dig it all." Yet, as highly visible nonconformists in an era of stifling conformity, the beats demonstrated a style of social protest that would flower into the counterculture of the 1960s.

Farewell to Reform

What was the primary justification for the passage of the Interstate Highway Act of 1956?

It is not surprising that the spirit of reform underlying the New Deal failed to flourish in the postwar years. Growing affluence took away the sense of grievance and the cry for change that was so strong in the 1930s. Eager to enjoy the new prosperity after years of want and sacrifice, the American people turned away from federal regulation and welfare programs.

Truman and the Fair Deal

Harry Truman was in a buoyant mood when he gave his State of the Union address on January 5, 1949. Heartened by his upset victory in 1948 and by the substantial Democratic majorities in Congress—54 to 42 in the Senate and 263 to 171 in the House—he looked forward to advancing a liberal legislative agenda. As expected, he emphasized traditional New Deal goals: expansion and reform of the farm price-support program, broadened Social Security, an increase in the minimum wage, and repeal of the antiunion Taft-Hartley Act. But he went further, advocating new areas of reform when he declared, "Every segment of our population and every individual has a right to expect from our government a fair deal."

Three reform measures stood out in Truman's plan for a Fair Deal. The first measure called for medical insurance for all Americans, designed to provide a comprehensive solution to the nation's health problem. Equally controversial was the second measure that proposed establishing a compulsory Fair Employment Practices Commission (FEPC) to open up employment opportunities for African Americans. During World War II, President Roosevelt had created a voluntary Fair Employment Practices Committee, but Congress stopped funding, and it expired in 1946. The third measure called for federal aid to education in order to help the states and local school districts meet the demands created by the postwar baby boom. Taken together, these legislative proposals went far beyond the New Deal legacy in an effort to provide greater social justice for all citizens.

Truman's ambitious Fair Deal met with defeat after defeat in Congress. Doctors, led by the American Medical Association, branded the administration's health insurance plan as socialized medicine and lobbied effectively against it. Southern senators threatened a filibuster against the FEPC proposal, quickly ending any chance for action on civil rights. And despite the need for more funding for schools, those favoring local control, especially southern defenders of segregation, were able to defeat measures for federal aid. Thus Congress failed to act on all three of the Fair Deal reforms; it also refused to repeal the Taft-Hartley Act or revise the farm program. Truman's only successes came in expanding Social Security to cover 10 million more Americans and in raising the minimum wage to 75 cents an hour.

The president's failure to enact his Fair Deal program stemmed primarily from political reality. Despite the nominal Democratic control of the House and Senate, a conservative coalition, in the making since 1938, blocked all efforts at further reform. Southern Democrats and northern Republicans combined to defeat any effort to extend government regulation, especially into sensitive areas such as health care and civil rights. At the same time, Truman can be faulted for trying to do too much, too soon. Had he selected one of his proposed reforms, such as federal aid to education, and given it priority, he might have been successful. But attempting to pass such a sweeping program in face of the bipartisan conservative coalition proved hopeless. Yet Truman must be given credit for defending and consolidating the New Deal legacy of the 1930s. By going on the offensive, he blocked any effort by conservatives to undo reforms such as Social Security. Moreover, Truman succeeded in expanding his party's reform agenda. By calling for action on civil rights, health care, and federal aid to education, he was opening up discussion of vital issues that laid the groundwork for legislative action in the future.

Eisenhower's Modern Republicanism

The American people found that moderation was the keynote of the Eisenhower presidency. His major goal from the outset was to restore calm and tranquility to a badly divided nation. Unlike FDR and Truman, Eisenhower had no commitment to social change or economic reform. Ike was a fiscal conservative who was intent on balancing the budget. Yet unlike some Republicans of the extreme right wing, he had no plans to dismantle the social programs of the New Deal. He sought instead to keep military spending in check, to encourage as much private initiative as possible, and to reduce federal activities to the bare minimum. Defining his position as Modern Republicanism, he claimed that he was "conservative when it comes to money and liberal when it comes to human beings."

On domestic issues, Eisenhower preferred to delegate authority and to play a passive role. He concentrated his own efforts on the Cold War abroad. The men he chose to run the nation reflected his preference for successful corporation executives. Thus George Humphrey, an Ohio industrialist, carried out a policy of fiscal stringency as secretary of the treasury, while Charles E. Wilson (the former head of General Motors) sought to keep the Pentagon budget under control as secretary of defense. Neither man was wholly successful, and both were guilty of tactless public statements. Humphrey warned that unless Congress showed budgetary restraint, "We're gonna have a depression which will curl your hair," and Wilson gained notoriety by proclaiming that "What was good for our country was good for General Motors, and vice versa."

Eisenhower was equally reluctant to play an active role in dealing with Congress. A fervent believer in the separation of powers, Ike did not want to engage in intensive lobbying. He left congressional relations to aides such as Sherman Adams, a former New Hampshire governor who served as White House chief of staff. Adams's skill at resolving problems at lower levels insulated Eisenhower from many of the nation's pressing domestic concerns.

Republican losses in the midterm election of 1954 weakened Eisenhower's relations with Congress. The Democrats regained control of both houses and kept it throughout the 1950s. The president had to rely on two Texas Democrats, Senate Majority Leader Lyndon B. Johnson and Speaker of the House Sam Rayburn, for legislative action; at best, it was an awkward and uneasy relationship.

The result was a very modest legislative record. Eisenhower did continue the basic social measures of the New Deal. In 1954, he signed bills extending Social Security benefits to more than seven million Americans, raising the minimum wage to $1 an hour, and adding four million workers to those eligible for unemployment benefits. He consolidated the administration of welfare programs by creating the Department of Health, Education, and Welfare in 1953. Oveta Culp Hobby, the first woman to hold a cabinet post in a Republican administration, headed the new department. But Ike steadfastly opposed Democratic plans for compulsory health insurance—which he condemned as the "socialization of medicine"—and comprehensive federal aid to education, preferring to leave everything except school construction in the hands of local and state authorities. This lack of presidential support and the continuing grip of the conservative coalition in Congress blocked any further reform in the 1950s.

The one significant legislative achievement of the Eisenhower years came with the passage of the Highway Act of 1956. After a twelve-year delay, Congress appropriated funds for a 41,000-mile interstate highway system consisting of multilane divided expressways that would connect the nation's major cities. Justified on grounds of national defense, the 1956 act pleased a variety of highway users: the trucking industry, automobile clubs, organized labor (eager for construction jobs), farmers (needing to speed their crops to market), and state highway officials (anxious for the 90 percent funding contributed by the federal government). Eisenhower's insistence that general revenue funds not be used to provide the federal share—estimated at $25 billion—of the total cost led to the creation of a highway trust fund raised by taxes on fuel, tires, and new cars and trucks. Built over the next twenty years, the interstate highway system had a profound influence on American life. It stimulated the economy and shortened travel time dramatically, while at the same time intensifying the nation's dependence on the automobile and distorting metropolitan growth patterns into long strips paralleling the new expressways.

THE ELECTION OF 1956

Candidate	Party	Popular Vote	Electoral Vote
Eisenhower	Republican	35,575,420	457
Stevenson	Democratic	26,033,066	73

Overall, the Eisenhower years marked an era of political moderation. The American people, enjoying the abundance of the 1950s, seemed quite content with legislative inaction. The president was sensitive to the nation's economic health; when recessions

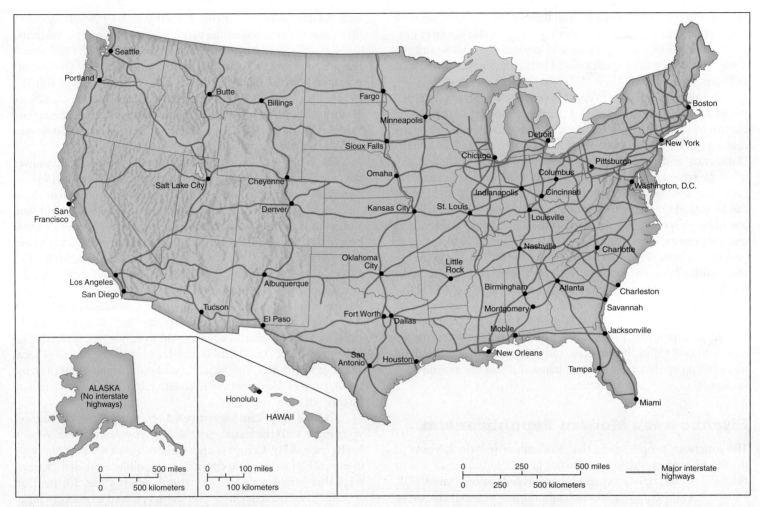

THE INTERSTATE HIGHWAY SYSTEM The 1956 plan to create an interstate highway system drastically changed America's landscape and culture. Today, the system covers about forty-five thousand miles, only a few thousand more miles than called for in the original plan.

developed in 1953 and again in 1957 after his landslide reelection victory over Adlai Stevenson, he quickly abandoned his goal of a balanced budget in favor of a policy advocating government spending to restore prosperity. These steps, along with modest increases in New Deal welfare programs, led to a steady growth in the federal budget from $29.5 billion in 1950 to $76.5 billion in 1960. Eisenhower was able to balance the budget in only three of his eight years in office, and the $12 billion deficit in 1959 was larger than any ever before recorded in peacetime. In this manner, Eisenhower was able to maintain the New Deal legacy of federal responsibility for social welfare and the state of the economy while at the same time successfully resisting demands for more extensive government involvement in American life.

The Struggle over Civil Rights

How did the civil rights movement develop in the 1940s and 1950s?

Despite President Eisenhower's reluctance to champion the cause of reform, powerful pressures for change forced long-overdue action in one area of American life—the denial of basic rights

to the nation's black minority. In the midst of the Cold War, the contradiction between the denunciation of the Soviet Union for its human rights violations and the second-class status of African Americans began to arouse the national conscience. Fighting for freedom against communist tyranny abroad, Americans had to face the reality of the continued denial of freedom to a submerged minority at home.

African Americans had benefited economically from World War II, but they were still a seriously disadvantaged group. Those who had left the South for better opportunities in northern and western cities were concentrated in blighted and segregated neighborhoods, working at low-paying jobs, suffering economic and social discrimination, and failing to share fully in the postwar prosperity. The rising expectations of African Americans in the postwar years led them to challenge the older patterns of racial segregation and inequality.

In the South, conditions were much worse. State laws forced blacks to live almost totally segregated from white society. Not only did African Americans attend separate (and almost always inferior) schools, but they also were rigidly segregated in all public facilities. They were forced to use separate waiting rooms in train stations, separate seats on all forms of transportation, separate drinking

👁 —Watch the Video   **Justice for All: Civil Protest and Civil Rights**

The firebombing of a Greyhound bus carrying white and black civil rights activists challenging illegal segregation on interstate bus routes in the South during 1961 was undertaken by a mob outside of Anniston, Alabama. These civil rights activists barely escaped with their lives from this violent attack on their passive resistance efforts.

fountains, and even separate telephone booths. "Segregation was enforced at all places of public entertainment, including libraries, auditoriums, and circuses," Chief Justice Earl Warren noted. "There was segregation in the hospitals, prisons, mental institutions, and nursing homes. Even ambulance service was segregated."

Civil Rights as a Political Issue

Truman was the first president to attempt to alter the historic pattern of racial discrimination in the United States. In 1946, he appointed a presidential commission on civil rights. A year later, in a sweeping report titled *To Secure These Rights*, the commission recommended the reinstatement of the wartime Fair Employment Practices Committee (FEPC), the establishment of a permanent civil rights commission, and the denial of federal aid to any state that condoned segregation in schools and public facilities. The president's ten-point legislative program proposed

in 1948 included some of these measures, notably the establishment of a permanent FEPC and a civil rights commission. But southern resistance had blocked any action by Congress, and the inclusion of a strong civil rights plank in the 1948 Democratic platform had led to the walkout of some southern delegations and a separate States' Rights (Dixiecrat) ticket in several states of the South that fall.

African American voters in the North overwhelmingly backed Truman over Dewey in the 1948 election. The African American vote in key cities—Los Angeles, Cleveland, and Chicago—ensured the Democratic victory in California, Ohio, and Illinois. Truman responded by including civil rights legislation in his Fair Deal program in 1949. Once again, however, determined southern opposition blocked congressional action on both a permanent FEPC and an antilynching measure.

Even though President Truman was unable to secure any significant legislation, he did succeed in adding civil rights to the liberal agenda. From this time forward, it would be an integral part of the Democratic reform program. Also, Truman used his executive power to assist African Americans. He strengthened the civil rights division of the Justice Department, which aided black groups in their efforts to challenge school segregation and restrictive housing covenants in the courts. Most important, in 1948 Truman issued an order calling for the desegregation of the armed forces. The navy and the air force quickly complied, but the army resisted until the personnel needs of the Korean War finally overcame the military's objections. By the end of the 1950s, the armed forces had become far more integrated than American society at large.

Desegregating the Schools

The nation's schools soon became the primary target of civil rights advocates. The NAACP concentrated first on universities, successfully waging an intensive legal battle to win admission for qualified African Americans to graduate schools and professional programs. Led by Thurgood Marshall, NAACP lawyers then took on the broader issue of segregation in the country's public schools. Challenging the 1896 Supreme Court decision that upheld the constitutionality of separate but equal public facilities (see "*Plessy* v. *Ferguson*: The Shaping of Jim Crow," pp. 460–463), Marshall argued that even substantially equal but separate schools did profound psychological damage to African American children and thus violated the Fourteenth Amendment.

The Supreme Court was unanimous in its 1954 decision in the case of **Brown v. Board of Education of Topeka**. Chief Justice Earl Warren, recently appointed by President Eisenhower, wrote the landmark opinion flatly declaring that "separate educational facilities are inherently unequal." To divide grade school children "solely because of their race," Warren argued, "generates a feeling of inferiority as to their status in the community that may affect their hearts and minds in a way unlikely ever to be undone." Despite this sweeping language, Warren realized it would be difficult to change historic patterns of segregation quickly. Accordingly, in 1955, the Court ruled that desegregation of the schools should proceed "with all deliberate speed" and left the details to the lower federal courts.

"All deliberate speed" proved to be agonizingly slow. Officials in the border states quickly complied with the Court's ruling, but states deeper in the South responded with a policy of massive resistance. Local white citizens' councils organized to fight for retention of racial separation; 101 representatives and senators signed a Southern Manifesto in 1956 that denounced the *Brown* decision as "a clear abuse of judicial power." School boards, encouraged by this show of defiance, found a variety of ways to evade the Court's ruling. The most successful was the passage of pupil placement laws. These laws enabled local officials to assign individual students to schools on the basis of scholastic aptitude, ability to adjust, and "morals, conduct, health, and personal standards." These stalling tactics led to long disputes in the federal courts; by the end of the decade, fewer than 1 percent of the black children in the Deep South attended school with whites.

A conspicuous lack of presidential support further weakened the desegregation effort. Dwight Eisenhower believed that people's attitudes could not be altered by "cold lawmaking"—only

"by appealing to reason, by prayer, and by constantly working at it through our own efforts" could change be enacted. Quietly and unobtrusively, he worked to achieve desegregation in federal facilities, particularly in veterans' hospitals, navy yards, and the District of Columbia school system. Yet he refrained from endorsing the *Brown* decision, which he told an aide he believed had "*set back progress in the South at least fifteen years.*"

Southern leaders mistook Ike's silence for tacit support of segregation. In 1957, Governor Orval Faubus of Arkansas called out the national guard to prevent the integration of Little Rock's Central High School on grounds of a threat to public order. After 270 armed troops turned back nine young African American students, a federal judge ordered the guardsmen removed; but when

📖⊙ Read the Document   *Brown* v. *Board of Education of Topeka, Kansas* (1954)

Demonstrators bearing signs in support of the Supreme Court's 1954 *Brown* v. *Board of Education* ruling to desegregate the nation's schools. The ruling also sparked protests, many of them violent and destructive, from opponents of integration.

👁 ⎯Watch the Video   **How did the Civil Rights Movement Change American Schools?**

Clinton High School, located in a small town of 5,000 in eastern Tennessee, was the first public high school to desegregate. Clinton was also one of the first towns to witness the anger and hatred associated with school integration. On September 1, 1956, the National Guard and state troopers were called in to help control the violent crowds of protestors.

the black students entered the school, a mob of five hundred jeering whites surrounded the building. Eisenhower, who had told Faubus that "the Federal Constitution will be upheld by me by every legal means at my command," sent in one thousand paratroopers to ensure the rights of the Little Rock Nine to attend Central High. The students finished the school year under armed guard. Then Little Rock authorities closed Central High School for the next two years; when it reopened, there were only three African Americans in attendance.

Despite the snail's pace of school desegregation, the *Brown* decision led to other advances. In 1957, the Eisenhower administration proposed the first general civil rights legislation since Reconstruction. Senate Majority Leader Lyndon B. Johnson overcame strong southern resistance to avoid a filibuster, but at the expense of weakening the measure considerably. The final act, however, did create a permanent Commission for Civil Rights, one of Truman's original goals. It also provided for federal efforts aimed at

"securing and protecting the right to vote." A second civil rights act in 1960 slightly strengthened the voting rights section.

Like the desegregation effort, the attempt to ensure African American voting rights in the South was still largely symbolic. Southern registrars used a variety of devices, ranging from intimidation to unfair tests, to deny African Americans suffrage. Yet the actions of Congress and the Supreme Court marked a vital turning point in national policy toward racial justice.

The Beginnings of Black Activism

The most dynamic force for change came from African Americans themselves. The shift from legal struggles in the courts to protest in the streets began with an incident in Montgomery, Alabama. On December 1, 1955, Rosa Parks—a black seamstress who had been active in the local NAACP chapter—violated a city ordinance by refusing to give up her seat to a white person on a local bus. Her action, often viewed as spontaneous, grew out of a long tradition of black protest against the rigid segregation of the races in the South. Rosa Parks herself had been ejected from a bus a decade earlier for refusing to obey the driver's command, "Niggers move back." In 1953, black church leaders in Baton Rouge, Louisiana, had mounted a weeklong boycott of that city's bus system and succeeded in modifying the traditional segregated seating rules.

In Montgomery, the arrest of Rosa Parks sparked a massive protest movement. Black women played a particularly important role in the protest, printing and handing out fifty thousand leaflets to rally the African American community behind Parks. The movement also led to the emergence of Martin Luther King, Jr., as an eloquent new spokesman for African Americans.

King agreed to lead the subsequent bus boycott. The son of a famous Atlanta preacher, he had recently taken his first church in Montgomery after years of studying theology while earning a Ph.D. at Boston University. Now he would be able to combine his wide learning with his charismatic appeal in behalf of a practical goal—fair treatment for the African Americans who made up the bulk of the riders on the city's buses.

The **Montgomery bus boycott** started out with a modest goal. Instead of challenging the legality of segregated seating, King simply asked that seats be taken on a first-come, first-served basis, with African Americans being seated from the back and the whites from the front of each bus. As the protest continued, however, and as they endured both legal harassment and sporadic acts of violence, the protesters began to be more assertive. An effective system of car pools enabled them to avoid using the city buses. Soon they were insisting on a complete end to segregated seating as they sang their new song of protest:

> Ain't gonna ride them buses no more
> Ain't gonna ride no more
> Why in the hell don't the white folk know
> That I ain't gonna ride no more.

The boycott ended in victory a year later when the Supreme Court ruled the Alabama segregated seating law unconstitutional. The protest movement had triumphed, not only in denting the wall of southern segregation, but in featuring the leadership of Martin Luther King, Jr. He had emerged as the charismatic leader of a new civil rights movement—a man who won acclaim not only at home but around the world. A year after the successful bus boycott, King founded the **Southern Christian Leadership Conference (SCLC)** to direct the crusade against segregation. He visited Third World leaders in Africa and Asia and paid homage to India's Mahatma Gandhi, who had influenced his reliance on civil disobedience. He led a triumphant Prayer Pilgrimage to Washington in 1957 on the third anniversary of the *Brown* decision, stirring the crowd of thirty thousand with his ringing demand for the right to vote. His cry "Give us the ballot" boomed in salvos that civil rights historian Taylor Branch likened to "cannon bursts in a diplomatic salute." His remarkable

voice became familiar to the entire nation. Unlike many African American preachers, he never shouted, yet he captured his audience by presenting his ideas with both passion and a compelling cadence. "Though still a boy to many of his older listeners," Branch noted, "he had the commanding air of a burning sage."

Even more important, he had a strategy and message that fitted perfectly with the plight of his followers. Drawing on sources as diverse as Gandhi and Henry David Thoreau, King came out of the bus boycott with the concept of passive resistance. "If cursed," he had told protesters in Montgomery, "do not curse back. If struck, do not strike back, but evidence love and goodwill at all times." The essence of his strategy was to use the apparent weakness of southern blacks—their lack of power—and turn it into a conquering weapon. His message to southern whites was clear and unmistakable: "We will match your capacity to inflict suffering with our capacity to endure suffering. We will meet your physical force with soul force. We will not hate you, but we will not obey your evil laws. We will soon wear you down by pure capacity to suffer."

His ultimate goal was to unite the broken community through bonds of Christian love. He hoped to use nonviolence to appeal to middle-class white America, "to the conscience of the great decent majority who through blindness, fear, pride or irrationality have allowed their consciences to sleep." The result, King prophesied, would be to enable future historians to say of the effort, "There lived

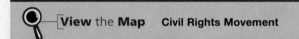

View the Map Civil Rights Movement

Rosa Parks' refusal to surrender her seat to a white man on a Montgomery, Alabama, bus led to a citywide bus boycott that brought Rev. Martin Luther King, Jr., to prominence as a leader of the civil rights movement. Parks remained active in the movement as well; she is shown here being fingerprinted in February 1956 after her arrest for violating an antiboycott law.

Read the Document Student Nonviolent Coordinating Committee, Statement

In February 1960, black students from North Carolina A&T College staged a sit-in at a "whites only" Woolworth's lunch counter in Greensboro, North Carolina. Their act of nonviolent protest spurred similar demonstrations in public spaces across the South in an effort to draw national attention to racial injustice, to demand desegregation of public facilities, and to prompt the federal government to take a more active role to end segregation.

a great people—a black people—who injected new meaning and dignity into the veins of civilization."

King was not alone in championing the cause of civil rights. JoAnn Robinson helped pave the way in Montgomery with the Woman's Political Caucus, and leaders as diverse as Bayard Rustin and Ella Baker were advancing the cause at the grassroots level.

In February 1960, another spontaneous event sparked a further advance for passive resistance. Four African American students from North Carolina Agricultural and Technical College sat down at a dime-store lunch counter in Greensboro, North Carolina, and refused to move after being denied service. Other students, both whites and blacks, joined in similar "sit-ins" across the South, as well as "kneel-ins" at churches and "wade-ins" at swimming pools. By the end of the year, some fifty thousand young people had succeeded in desegregating public facilities in more than a hundred southern cities. Several thousand of the demonstrators were arrested and put in jail, but the movement gained strength, leading to the formation of the **Student Nonviolent Coordinating Committee (SNCC)** in April 1960. From this time on, the SCLC and SNCC, with their tactic of direct, though peaceful confrontation, would replace the NAACP and its reliance on court action in the forefront of the civil rights movement. The change would eventually lead to dramatic success for the movement, but it also ushered in a period of heightened tension and social turmoil in the 1960s.

Conclusion: Restoring National Confidence

In 1959, disturbed by the criticism of American society sparked by *Sputnik*, President Eisenhower appointed a Commission on National Goals "to develop a broad outline of national objectives for the next decade and longer." Ten prominent citizens from all walks of life, led by Henry W. Wriston of Brown University, issued a report that called for increased military spending abroad, greater economic growth at home, broader educational opportunities, and more government support for both scientific research and the advancement of the arts. The consensus seemed to be that rather than a change of direction, all the United States needed was a renewed commitment to the pursuit of excellence.

The 1950s ended with the national mood less troubled than when the decade began amid the turmoil of the second Red Scare and the Korean War, yet hardly as tranquil or confident as Eisenhower had hoped it would be. The American people felt reassured about the state of the economy, no longer fearing a return to the grim years of the Great Depression. At the same time, however, they were aware that abundance alone did not guarantee the quality of everyday life and realized that there was still a huge gap between American ideals and the reality of race relations, in the North as well as the South.

Study Resources

 Take the **Study Plan** for **Chapter 29** *Affluence and Anxiety* on **MyHistoryLab**

TIME LINE

1946 Republicans win control of both houses of Congress in November elections

1947 William Levitt announces first Levittown

1948 Truman orders end to segregation in armed forces

1949 Minimum wage raised from 40 to 75 cents an hour

1953 McDonald's chooses golden arches design for its hamburger shops

1954 Supreme Court orders schools desegregated in *Brown* v. *Board of Education of Topeka*

1955 African Americans begin boycott of Montgomery, Alabama, bus company (December)

1956 Eisenhower signs legislation creating the interstate highway system

1957 Congress passes first Civil Rights Act since Reconstruction

1958 Charles Van Doren confesses to cheating on television quiz show *Twenty-One*

1960 African American college students stage sit-in in Greensboro, North Carolina

CHAPTER REVIEW

The Postwar Boom

 How did the American economy evolve after World War II?

The American economy boomed after World War II, as the nation recovered from the Great Depression and the war. The GNP doubled between 1940 and 1960. Individuals spent heavily on housing, automobiles, and consumer goods, and the government on defense. New communities emerged in the suburbs and the Sunbelt states of the West and South. (p. 690)

The Good Life?

 How did American culture change after the war?

American culture reflected both the promise of material prosperity and the failure of material goods to yield true happiness. More people went to church than ever; more young people went to college. Television provided endless information and entertainment. But suburban life exhibited a shallow sameness that prompted critics to question if it was worthwhile. (p. 692)

Farewell to Reform

 What was the primary justification for the passage of the Interstate Highway Act of 1956?

The Highway Act appropriated funds to construct a 41,000-mile interstate highway system that would connect the nation's major cities to each other. Although the highways would benefit a variety of users, such as the trucking industry, organized labor, state transportation departments, and farmers, the primary justification for passing the law in Congress was national defense. (p. 696)

The Struggle over Civil Rights

 How did the civil rights movement develop in the 1940s and 1950s?

Civil rights became a major issue after World War II. Truman desegregated the military, and federal courts ordered the desegregation of schools. Black activists such as Rosa Parks and Martin Luther King, Jr., led protests against segregation on buses and other public facilities. Students organized sit-ins. (p. 698)

KEY TERMS AND DEFINITIONS

Levittown   In 1947, William Levitt used mass production techniques to build inexpensive houses in suburban New York to help relieve the postwar housing shortage. Levittown became a symbol of the postwar move to the suburbs. p. 688

Baby boom   The rise in births following World War II. Children born to this generation are referred to as "baby boomers." p. 688

Brown v. Board of Education of Topeka   In 1954, the Supreme Court reversed the *Plessy* v. *Ferguson* decision (1896), which established the "separate but equal" doctrine. The *Brown* decision found segregation in schools inherently unequal and initiated a long and difficult effort to integrate the nation's public schools. p. 700

Montgomery bus boycott   In late 1955, African Americans led by Martin Luther King, Jr., boycotted the buses in Montgomery, Alabama, after seamstress Rosa Parks was arrested for refusing to move to the back of a bus. The boycott, which ended when the Supreme Court ruled in favor of the protesters, marked the beginning of a new, activist phase of the civil rights movement. p. 702

Southern Christian Leadership Conference (SCLC)   An organization founded by Martin Luther King, Jr., to fight segregation through passive resistance, nonviolence, and peaceful confrontation. p. 702

Student Nonviolent Coordinating Committee (SNCC)   A group organized by students to work for equal rights for African Americans. It spearheaded peaceful sit-ins and marches in the early 1960s, but later grew more radical and changed its name to the Student National Coordinating Committee. p. 703

CRITICAL THINKING QUESTIONS

1. What are some advantages of suburban life? What are some disadvantages?

2. Did television bring Americans together, or drive them apart?

3. Were the civil rights marchers justified in breaking Jim Crow Laws?

MyHistoryLab Media Assignments

Find these resources in the Media Assignments folder for Chapter 29 on MyHistoryLab

The Postwar Boom

Listen to the **Audio**   *"Little Boxes" p. 690*

The Good Life?

■ **View** the **Closer Look**   *A 1950s Family Watching Television p. 693*

■ **Complete** the **Assignment**   *The Reaction to Sputnik p. 694*

Read the **Document**   *Pearson Profiles: Jack Kerouac p. 696*

The Struggle over Civil Rights

■ **Watch** the **Video**   *Justice for All: Civil Protest and Civil Rights p. 699*

■ **Read** the **Document**   *Brown v. Board of Education of Topeka, Kansas (1954) p. 700*

■ **Watch** the **Video**   *How did the Civil Rights Movement Change American Schools? p. 701*

View the **Map**   *Civil Rights Movement p. 702*

Read the **Document**   *Student Nonviolent Coordinating Committee, Statement p. 703*

■ *Indicates Study Plan Media Assignment*

30 The Turbulent Sixties

Contents and Learning Objectives

((●━ Listen to the Audio File on **myhistorylab**　　**Chapter 30** *The Turbulent Sixties*

Kennedy versus Nixon: The First Televised Presidential Candidate Debate

On Monday evening, September 26, 1960, John F. Kennedy and Richard M. Nixon faced each other in the nation's first televised debate between two presidential candidates. Kennedy, the relatively unknown Democratic challenger, had proposed the debates; Nixon, confident of his mastery of television, had accepted even though, as Eisenhower's vice president and the early front-runner in the election, he had more to lose and less to gain.

Richard Nixon arrived an hour early at the CBS studio in Chicago, looking tired and ill at ease. He was still recovering from a knee injury that had slowed his campaign and left him pale and weak as he pursued a hectic catch-up schedule. Makeup experts offered to hide Nixon's heavy beard and soften his prominent jowls, but the GOP candidate declined, preferring to let an aide apply a light coat of Max Factor's "Lazy Shave," a pancake cosmetic. John Kennedy, tanned from open-air campaigning in California and rested by a day spent nearly free of distracting activity, wore very light makeup. He also changed from a gray to a dark blue suit better adapted to the intense television lighting.

At 8:30 P.M. central time, moderator Howard K. Smith welcomed a viewing audience estimated at seventy-seven million. Kennedy led off, echoing Abraham Lincoln by saying that the nation faced the question of "whether the world will exist half slave and half free." Although the ground rules limited the first debate to domestic issues, Kennedy argued that foreign and domestic policy were inseparable. He accused the Republicans of letting the country drift at home and abroad. "I think it's time America started moving again," he concluded. Nixon, caught off guard, seemed to agree with Kennedy's assessment of the nation's problems, but he contended that he had better solutions. "Our disagreement," the vice president pointed out, "is not about the goals for America but only about the means to reach those goals."

For the rest of the hour, the two candidates answered questions from a panel of journalists. Radiating confidence

Kennedy–Nixon Debate

and self-assurance, Kennedy used a flow of statistics and details to create the image of a man deeply knowledgeable about all aspects of government. Nixon fought back with a defense of the Eisenhower record, but he seemed nervous and unsure of himself. The reaction shots of each candidate listening to the other's remarks showed Kennedy calm and serene, Nixon tense and uncomfortable.

Polls taken during the following few weeks revealed a sharp swing to Kennedy. Many Democrats and independents who had thought him too young or too inexperienced were impressed by his performance. Nixon suffered more from his unattractive image than from what he said; those who heard the debate on radio thought the Republican candidate more than held his own. In the three additional debates held during the campaign, Nixon improved his performance notably, wearing makeup to soften his appearance and taking the offensive from Kennedy on the issues. But the damage had been done. A post-election poll revealed that of four million voters who were influenced by the debates, three million voted for Kennedy.

The televised debates were only one of many factors influencing the outcome of the 1960 election. In essence, Kennedy won because he took full advantage of all his opportunities. Lightly regarded by Democratic leaders, he won the nomination by appealing to the rank and file in the primaries, but then he astutely chose Lyndon Johnson of Texas as his running mate to blunt Nixon's southern strategy.

During the fall campaign, Kennedy exploited the national mood of frustration that had followed *Sputnik*. (See the Feature Essay in Chapter 29, "The Reaction to *Sputnik*," pp. 694–695.) At home, he promised to stimulate the lagging economy and carry forward long overdue reforms in education, health care, and civil rights under the banner of the **New Frontier**. Abroad, he pledged a renewed commitment to the Cold War, vowing he would lead the nation to victory over the Soviet Union. He met the issue of his Catholicism head on, telling a group of Protestant ministers in Houston that as president he would always place country above religion. In the shrewdest move of all, he won over African American voters by helping to secure the release of Martin Luther King, Jr., from a Georgia jail where the civil rights leader was being held on a trumped-up charge.

The Democratic victory in 1960 was paper thin. Kennedy's edge in the popular vote was only two-tenths of 1 percent, and his wide margin in the electoral college (303 to 219) was tainted by voting irregularities in several states—notably Illinois and Texas—which went Democratic by very slender majorities. Yet even though he had no mandate, Kennedy's triumph did mark a sharp political shift. In contrast to the aging Eisenhower, Kennedy symbolized youth, energy, and ambition. His mastery of the new medium of television reflected his sensitivity to the changes taking place in American life in the 1960s. He came to office promising reform at home and advances abroad. Over the next eight years, he and Lyndon Johnson achieved many of their goals. Yet the nation also became engulfed in angry protests, violent demonstrations, and sweeping social change in one of the stormiest decades in American history.

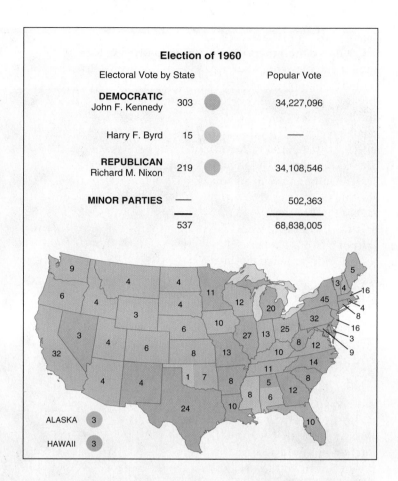

Election of 1960

	Electoral Vote by State	Popular Vote
DEMOCRATIC John F. Kennedy	303	34,227,096
Harry F. Byrd	15	—
REPUBLICAN Richard M. Nixon	219	34,108,546
MINOR PARTIES	—	502,363
	537	68,838,005

Kennedy Intensifies the Cold War

How did the Cold War intensify under Kennedy?

John F. Kennedy was determined to succeed where he believed Eisenhower had failed. Critical of his predecessor for holding down defense spending and apparently allowing the Soviet Union to open up a dangerous lead in ICBMs, Kennedy sought to warn the nation of its peril and lead it to victory in the Cold War.

In his inaugural address, the young president sounded the alarm. Ignoring the domestic issues aired during the campaign, he dealt exclusively with the world. "Let every nation know, whether it wishes us well or ill, that we shall pay any price, bear any burden, meet any hardship, support any friend, oppose any foe," Kennedy declared, "to assure the survival and success of liberty. We will do all this and more."

From the day he took office, John F. Kennedy gave foreign policy top priority. In part, the decision reflected the perilous world situation, the immediate dangers ranging from the unresolved Berlin crisis to the emergence of Fidel Castro as a Soviet ally in Cuba. But it also corresponded to Kennedy's personal priorities. As a congressman and senator, he had been an intense cold warrior. Bored by committee work and legislative details, he had focused on foreign policy in the Senate, gaining a seat on the Foreign Relations Committee and publishing a book of speeches, *The Strategy of Peace*, in early 1960.

His appointments reflected his determination to win the Cold War. His choice of Dean Rusk, an experienced but unassertive diplomat, to head the State Department indicated that Kennedy planned to be his own secretary of state. He surrounded himself with young pragmatic advisers who prided themselves on toughness: McGeorge Bundy, dean of Harvard College, became national security adviser; Walt W. Rostow, an MIT economist, was Bundy's deputy; and Robert McNamara, the youthful president of the Ford Motor Company, took over as secretary of defense.

These New Frontiersmen, later dubbed "the best and the brightest" by journalist David Halberstam, all shared a hard-line view of the Soviet Union and the belief that American security depended on superior force and the willingness to use it. Walt Rostow summed up their view of the contest with Russia best when he wrote, "The cold war comes down to this test of whether we and the democratic world are fundamentally tougher and more purposeful in the defense of our vital interests than they are in the pursuit of their global ambitions."

Flexible Response

The first goal of the Kennedy administration was to build up the nation's armed forces. During the 1960 campaign, Kennedy had warned that the Soviets were opening a missile gap. In fact, due largely to Eisenhower's foresight, the United States had a significant lead in nuclear striking power by early 1961, with a fleet of more than 600 B-52 bombers, 2 Polaris submarines, and 16 Atlas ICBMs capable of delivering more than 2,000 warheads against Russian targets. Nevertheless, the new administration, intent on putting the Soviets on the defensive, authorized the construction of an awesome nuclear arsenal that included 1,000 Minuteman solid-fuel ICBMs (five times the number Eisenhower had believed necessary) and 32 Polaris submarines carrying 656 missiles. The United States thus opened a missile gap in reverse, creating the possibility of a successful American first strike.

At the same time, the Kennedy administration augmented conventional military strength. Secretary of Defense McNamara developed plans to add five combat-ready army divisions, three tactical air wings, and a ten-division strategic reserve. These vast increases led to a $6 billion jump in the defense budget in 1961 alone. The president took a personal interest in counterinsurgency. He expanded the Special Forces unit at Fort Bragg, North Carolina, and insisted, over army objections, that it adopt a distinctive green beret as a symbol of its elite status.

The purpose of this buildup was to create an alternative to Eisenhower's policy of massive retaliation. Instead of responding to communist moves with nuclear threats, the United States could now call on a wide spectrum of force—ranging from ICBMs to Green Berets. Thus, as Robert McNamara explained, the new strategy of flexible response meant the United States could "choose among several operational plans. We shall be committed only to a system that gives us the ability to use our forces in a controlled and deliberate way." The danger was that such a powerful arsenal might tempt the new administration to test its strength against the Soviet Union.

Crisis over Berlin

The first confrontation came in Germany. Since 1958, Soviet Premier Khrushchev had been threatening to sign a peace treaty that would put access to the isolated western zones of Berlin under the control of East Germany. The steady flight of skilled workers to the West through the Berlin escape route weakened the East German regime dangerously, and the Soviets believed they had to resolve this issue quickly.

At a summit meeting in Vienna in June 1961, Kennedy and Khrushchev focused on Berlin as the key issue. The Russian leader called the current situation "intolerable" and announced the Soviet Union would proceed with an East German peace treaty. Kennedy was equally adamant, defending the American presence in Berlin and refusing to give up occupation rights that he considered crucial to the defense of western Europe. In their last session, the failure to reach agreement took on an ominous tone. "I want peace," Khrushchev declared, "but, if you want war, that is your problem." "It is you, not I," the young president replied, "who wants to force a change." When the Soviet leader said he would sign a German peace treaty by December, Kennedy added, "It will be a cold winter."

The climax came sooner than either man expected. On July 25, Kennedy delivered an impassioned televised address to the American people in which he called the defense of Berlin "essential" to "the entire Free World." Announcing a series of arms increases, including $3 billion more in defense spending, the president took the unprecedented step of calling more than 150,000 reservists and national guardsmen to active duty.

Aware of superior American nuclear striking power, Khrushchev settled for a stalemate. On August 13, the Soviets sealed off their zone of the city. They began the construction of the Berlin Wall to stop the flow of brains and talent to the West. For a brief time, Russian and American tanks maneuvered within sight of each other at Checkpoint Charlie (where the American and Soviet zones met), but by fall, the tension gradually eased. The Soviets signed a separate peace treaty that did not affect U.S. occupation rights; Berlin—like Germany and, indeed, all of Europe—remained divided between the East and the West. Neither side could claim a victory, but Kennedy believed that at least he had proved to the world America's willingness to honor its commitments.

Containment in Southeast Asia

Two weeks before Kennedy's inauguration, Khrushchev gave a speech in Moscow in which he declared Soviet support for "wars of national liberation." The Russian leader's words were actually aimed more at China than the United States; the two powerful communist nations were now rivals for influence in the developing world. But the new American president, ignoring the growing Sino-Soviet split, concluded the United States and Russia were locked in a struggle for the hearts and minds of the uncommitted in Asia, Africa, and Latin America.

Calling for a new policy of nation building, Kennedy advocated financial and technical assistance designed to help developing-world nations achieve economic modernization and stable pro-Western governments. Measures ranging from the formation of the idealistic Peace Corps to the ambitious Alliance for Progress—a massive economic aid program for Latin America—were part of this effort. Unfortunately, Kennedy relied even more on counterinsurgency and the Green Berets to beat back the communist challenge in the developing world.

Southeast Asia offered the gravest test. The American decision to back Ngo Dinh Diem (see p. 710) had prevented the holding of

Flames engulf Buddhist monk, the Reverend Quang Duc, who set himself afire at an intersection in Saigon, Vietnam, to protest persecution of Buddhists by Vietnam president Ngo Dinh Diem and his government. Other monks placed themselves in front of the wheels of nearby fire trucks to prevent them from reaching Duc.

their war. They are the ones who have to win it or lose it." But at the same time, Kennedy was not prepared to accept the possible loss of all Southeast Asia. Saying it would be "a great mistake" to withdraw from South Vietnam, he told reporters, "Strongly on our mind is what happened in the case of China at the end of World War II, where China was lost. We don't want that." Although aides later claimed he planned to pull out after the 1964 election, Kennedy raised the stakes by tacitly approving a coup that led to Diem's overthrow and death on November 1, 1963. The resulting power vacuum in Saigon made further American involvement in Vietnam almost certain.

Containing Castro: The Bay of Pigs Fiasco

Kennedy's determination to check global communist expansion reached a peak of intensity in Cuba. In the 1960 campaign, pointing to the growing ties between the Soviet Union and Fidel Castro's regime, he had accused the Republicans of permitting a "communist satellite" to arise on "our very doorstep." Kennedy had even issued a statement backing "anti-Castro forces in exile," calling them "fighters for freedom" who held out hope for "overthrowing Castro."

elections throughout Vietnam in 1956, as called for in the Geneva accords. Instead, Diem sought to establish a separate government in the South with large-scale American economic and military assistance. By the time Kennedy entered the White House, however, the communist government in North Vietnam, led by Ho Chi Minh, was directing the efforts of Vietcong rebels in the South. As the guerrilla war intensified in the fall of 1961, the president sent two trusted advisers, Walt Rostow and General Maxwell Taylor, to South Vietnam. They returned favoring the dispatch of eight thousand American combat troops. "As an area for the operation of U.S. troops," reported General Taylor, "SVN [South Vietnam] is not an excessively difficult or unpleasant place to operate.... The risks of backing into a major Asian war by way of SVN are present but are not impressive."

The president decided against sending in combat troops in 1961, but he authorized substantial increases in economic aid to Diem and in the size of the military mission in Saigon. The number of American advisers in Vietnam grew from fewer than one thousand in 1961 to more than sixteen thousand by late 1963. The flow of supplies and the creation of "strategic hamlets," fortified villages designed to protect the peasantry from the Vietcong, slowed the communist momentum. American helicopters gave government forces mobility against the Vietcong, but by 1963, the situation had again become critical. Diem had failed to win the support of his own people; Buddhist monks set themselves aflame in public protests against him; and even Diem's own generals plotted his overthrow.

President Kennedy was in a quandary. He realized that the fate of South Vietnam would be determined not by America but by the Vietnamese. "In the final analysis," he said in September 1963, "it is

In reality, the Eisenhower administration had been training a group of Cuban exiles in Guatemala since March 1960 as part of a CIA plan to topple the Castro regime. Many of the new president's advisers had doubts about the proposed invasion. Some saw little chance for success because the operation depended heavily on a broad uprising of the Cuban people. Others—notably Senator William Fulbright of Arkansas, chairman of the Foreign Relations Committee—viewed it as an immoral act that would discredit the United States. "The Castro regime is a thorn in the flesh," Fulbright argued, "but it is not a dagger in the heart." The president, however, committed by his own campaign rhetoric and assured of success by the military, decided to proceed.

On April 17, 1961, fourteen hundred Cuban exiles moved ashore at the Bay of Pigs on the southern coast of Cuba. Even though the United States had masterminded the entire operation, Kennedy insisted on covert action, even canceling at the last minute a planned American air strike on the beachhead. With air superiority, Castro's well-trained forces had no difficulty in quashing the invasion. They killed nearly five hundred exiles and forced the rest to surrender within forty-eight hours.

Aghast at the swiftness of the defeat, President Kennedy took personal responsibility for the **Bay of Pigs**. In his address to the American people, however, he showed no remorse for arranging the violation of a neighboring country's sovereignty, only regret at the outcome. Above all, he expressed renewed defiance, warning the Soviets that "our restraint is not inexhaustible." He went on to assert that the United States would resist "communist penetration" in the Western Hemisphere, terming it part of the "primary obligations ... to the security of our nation." For the remainder of his presidency, Kennedy continued to harass the Castro regime, imposing an economic blockade on Cuba, supporting a continuing series of raids by exile groups operating out of Florida, and failing to stop the CIA from experimenting with bizarre plots to assassinate Fidel Castro.

Containing Castro: The Cuban Missile Crisis

The climax of Kennedy's crusade came in October 1962 with the **Cuban missile crisis**. Throughout the summer and early fall, the Soviets engaged in a massive arms buildup in Cuba, ostensibly to protect Castro from an American invasion. In the United States, Republican candidates in the 1962 congressional elections called for a firm American response; Kennedy contented himself with a stern warning against the introduction of any offensive weapons, believing their presence would directly threaten American security. Khrushchev publicly denied any such intent, but secretly he took a daring gamble, building sites for twenty-four medium-range (1,000-mile) and eighteen intermediate-range (2,000-mile) missiles in Cuba. Later he claimed his purpose was purely defensive, but most likely he was responding to the pressures from his own military to close the enormous strategic gap in nuclear striking power that Kennedy had opened.

Unfortunately, the Kennedy administration had stopped direct U-2 overflights of Cuba in August. Fearful that recently installed Soviet surface-to-air missiles could bring down the American spy plane and create an international incident similar to the 1960 U-2 episode (see p. 712), the White House, over the objections of CIA Director John McCone, limited U-2 flights to the air space bordering the island. McCone finally prevailed on the president to resume direct overflights, and on October 14 the first such mission brought back indisputable photographic evidence of the missile sites, which were nearing completion.

As soon as President Kennedy was informed of this development, he decided to keep it secret while he consulted with a hand-picked group of advisers to consider how to respond. In the ExComm, as this group became known, the initial preference for an immediate air strike gradually gave way to discussion of either a full-scale invasion of Cuba or a naval blockade of the island. The president and his advisers ruled out diplomacy, rejecting a proposal to offer the withdrawal of obsolete American Jupiter missiles from Turkey in return for a similar Russian pullout in Cuba. Kennedy finally agreed to a two-step procedure. He would proclaim a quarantine of Cuba to prevent the arrival of new missiles and threaten a nuclear confrontation to force the removal of those already there. If the Russians did not cooperate, then the United States would invade Cuba and dismantle the missiles by force.

On the evening of October 22, the president informed the nation of the existence of the Soviet missiles and his plans to remove them. He blamed Khrushchev for "this clandestine, reckless, and provocative threat to world peace," and he made it clear that any missile attack from Cuba would lead to "a full retaliatory response upon the Soviet Union."

For the next six days, the world hovered on the brink of nuclear catastrophe. Khrushchev replied defiantly, accusing Kennedy of pushing mankind "to the abyss of a world nuclear-missile war."

In the Atlantic, some sixteen Soviet ships continued on course toward Cuba, while the American navy was deployed to intercept them five hundred miles from the island. In Florida, nearly a quarter million men were being concentrated in the largest invasion force ever assembled in the continental United States.

The first break came at midweek when the Soviet ships suddenly halted to avert a confrontation at sea. "We're eyeball to eyeball," commented Secretary of State Dean Rusk, "and I think the other fellow just blinked." On Friday, Khrushchev sent Kennedy a long, rambling letter offering a face-saving way out: Russia would remove the missiles in return for an American promise never to invade Cuba. The president was ready to accept when a second Russian message raised the stakes by insisting that American Jupiter missiles be withdrawn from Turkey. Heeding the advice of his brother, attorney general Robert Kennedy, the president refused to bargain; Khrushchev had endangered world peace by putting the missiles in Cuba secretly, and he must take them out immediately. Nevertheless, while the military went ahead with plans for the invasion of Cuba, the president, heeding his brother's advice, decided to make one last appeal for peace. Ignoring the second Russian message, he sent a cable to Khrushchev accepting his original offer.

On Saturday night, October 27, Robert Kennedy met with Soviet ambassador Anatoly Dobrynin to make clear it was the last chance to avert nuclear confrontation. "We had to have a commitment by tomorrow that those bases would be removed," Robert Kennedy recalled telling him. "He should understand that if they did not remove those bases, we would remove them." Then the president's brother calmly remarked that if Khrushchev did not back down, "there would be not only dead Americans but dead Russians as well."

In reality, John F. Kennedy was not quite so ready to risk nuclear war. He instructed his brother to assure Dobrynin that the Jupiter missiles would soon be removed from Turkey. The president preferred that the missile swap be done privately, but twenty-five years later, Secretary of State Dean Rusk revealed that JFK had instructed him to arrange a deal through the United Nations involving "the removal of both the Jupiters and the missiles in Cuba." In recently released transcripts of his meetings with his advisers, the president reaffirmed his intention of making a missile trade with Khrushchev publicly as a last resort to avoid nuclear war. "We can't very well invade Cuba with all its toil," he commented, "when we could have gotten them out by making a deal on the same missiles in Turkey."

President Kennedy never had to make this final concession. At nine the next morning, Khrushchev agreed to remove the missiles in return only for Kennedy's promise not to invade Cuba. The crisis was over.

The world, however, had come perilously close to a nuclear conflict. We now know the Soviets had nuclear warheads in Cuba, not only for twenty of the medium-range missiles, but also for short-range tactical launchers designed to be used against an American invading force. If Kennedy had approved the military's recommendations for an invasion of Cuba, the consequences might have been disastrous.

The peaceful resolution of the Cuban missile crisis became a personal and political triumph for John F. Kennedy. His party successfully overcame the Republican challenge in the November elections, and his own popularity reached new heights.

👁️ Watch the Video   **President John F. Kennedy and the Cuban Missile Crisis**

The Cuban Missile Crisis occurred in 1962 when U.S. spy planes detected Soviets supplying nuclear warheads being delivered to Cuba.

The American people, on the defensive since *Sputnik*, suddenly felt that they had proved their superiority over the Russians. Arthur Schlesinger, Jr., Kennedy's confidant and later his biographer, claimed that the Cuban crisis showed the "whole world … the ripening of an American leadership unsurpassed in the responsible management of power …. It was this combination of toughness and restraint, of will, nerve and wisdom, so brilliantly controlled, so matchlessly calibrated, that dazzled the world."

The Cuban missile crisis had more substantial results as well. Shaken by their close call, Kennedy and Khrushchev agreed to install a "hot line" to speed direct communication between Washington and Moscow in an emergency. Long-stalled negotiations over the reduction of nuclear testing suddenly resumed, leading to the limited test ban treaty of 1963, which outlawed tests in

the atmosphere while still permitting them underground. Above all, Kennedy displayed a new maturity as a result of the crisis. In a speech at American University in June 1963, he shifted from the rhetoric of confrontation to that of conciliation. Speaking of the Russians, he said, "Our most basic common link is the fact that we all inhabit this planet. We all breathe the same air. We all cherish our children's future. And we are all mortal."

Despite these hopeful words, the missile crisis also had an unfortunate consequence. Those who believed that the Russians understood only the language of force were confirmed in their penchant for a hard line. Hawks who had backed Kennedy's military buildup believed events had justified a policy of nuclear superiority. The Russian leaders drew similar conclusions. Aware the United States had a four-to-one advantage in nuclear striking

The New Frontier at Home **713**

power during the Cuban crisis, one Soviet official told his American counterpart, "Never will we be caught like this again." After 1962, the Soviets embarked on a crash program to build up their navy and to overtake the American lead in nuclear missiles. Within five years, they had the nucleus of a modern fleet and had surpassed the United States in ICBMs. Kennedy's fleeting moment of triumph thus ensured the escalation of the arms race. His legacy was a bittersweet one of short-term success and long-term anxiety.

The New Frontier at Home

What was the "New Frontier," and what did it accomplish?

Kennedy hoped to change the course of history at home as well as abroad. His election marked the arrival of a new generation of leadership. For the first time, people born in the twentieth century who had entered political life after World War II were in charge of national affairs. Kennedy's inaugural call to get the nation moving again was particularly attractive to young people who had shunned political involvement during the Eisenhower years.

The new administration reflected Kennedy's aura of youth and energy. Major cabinet appointments went to activists—notably Connecticut governor Abraham Ribicoff as secretary of health, education, and welfare; labor lawyer Arthur J. Goldberg as secretary of labor; and Arizona congressman Stuart Udall as secretary of the interior. The most controversial choice was Robert F. Kennedy, the president's brother, as attorney general. Critics scoffed at his lack of legal experience, leading JFK to note jokingly he wanted to give Bobby "a little experience before he goes out to practice law." In fact, the president prized his brother's loyalty and shrewd political advice.

Equally important were the members of the White House staff who handled domestic affairs. Like their counterparts in foreign policy, these New Frontiersmen—Kenneth O'Donnell, Theodore Sorensen, Richard Goodwin, and Walter Heller—prided themselves on being tough-minded and pragmatic. In contrast to Eisenhower, Kennedy relied heavily on academics and intellectuals to help him infuse the nation with energy and a new sense of direction.

Kennedy's greatest asset was his own personality. A cool, attractive, and intelligent man, he possessed a sense of style that endeared him to the American public. Encouraged by his wife, Jacqueline, the president invited artists and musicians as well as corporate executives to White House functions, and he sprinkled his speeches with references to Emerson and Shakespeare. He seemed to be a new Lancelot, bent on calling forth the best in national life; admirers likened his inner circle to King Arthur's court at Camelot. Reporters loved him, both for his fact-filled and candid press conferences and for his witty comments. After an embarrassing foreign policy failure, when his standing in the polls actually went up, he remarked, "It's just like Eisenhower. The worse I do, the more popular I get."

The Congressional Obstacle

Neither Kennedy's wit nor his charm proved strong enough to break the logjam in Congress. Since the late 1940s, a series of reform bills ranging from health care to federal aid to education had been stalled on Capitol Hill. Despite JFK's victory, the election of 1960 clouded the outlook for his New Frontier program. The Democrats had lost twenty seats in the House and two in the Senate; even though they retained majorities in both branches, a conservative coalition of northern Republicans and southern Democrats opposed all efforts at reform.

The situation was especially critical in the House, where 101 southern representatives held the balance of power between 160 northern Democrats and 174 Republicans. Aided by Speaker Sam Rayburn, Kennedy was able to enlarge the Rules Committee and overcome a traditional conservative roadblock, but the narrowness of the vote, 217 to 212, revealed how difficult it would be to enact reform measures. The president gave up the fight for health care in the Senate and settled instead for a modest increase in the minimum wage and the passage of manpower training and area-redevelopment legislation.

Kennedy had no more success in enacting his program in 1962 and 1963. The conservative coalition stood firmly against education and health-care proposals. Shifting ground, the president did win approval for a trade expansion act in 1962 designed to lower tariff barriers, but no significant reform legislation was passed. Although the composition of Congress was his main obstacle, Kennedy's greater interest in foreign policy and his distaste for legislative infighting contributed to the outcome. JFK did not enjoy "blarneying with pompous congressmen and simply would not take the time to do it," one observer noted. As a result, the New Frontier languished in Congress.

Economic Advance

Kennedy gave a higher priority to the sluggish American economy. During the last years of Eisenhower's administration, the rate of economic growth had slowed to just over 2 percent annually, while unemployment rose to new heights with each recession. JFK was determined to stimulate the economy to achieve a much higher rate of long-term growth. In part, he wanted to redeem his campaign pledge to get the nation moving again; he also believed the United States had to surpass the Soviet Union in economic vitality.

Kennedy received conflicting advice from the experts. Those who claimed the problem was essentially a technological one urged manpower training and area-redevelopment programs to modernize American industry. Others called for federal spending to rebuild the nation's public facilities—from parks and playgrounds to decaying bridges and urban courthouses. Kennedy sided with the first group, largely because Congress was opposed to massive spending on public works.

The actual stimulation of the economy, however, came not from social programs but from greatly increased appropriations for defense and space. A $6 billion increase in the arms budget in 1961 gave the economy a great lift, and Kennedy's decision to send an astronaut to the moon eventually cost $25 billion. By 1962, more than half the federal budget was devoted to space and defense; aircraft and computer companies in the South and West benefited, but unemployment remained uncomfortably high in the older industrial areas of the Northeast and Midwest.

The administration's desire to keep the inflation rate low led to a serious confrontation with the business community. Kennedy relied on informal wage and price guidelines to hold down the cost of living. But in April 1962, just after the president had persuaded the steelworkers' union to accept a new contract with no wage increases and only a few additional benefits, U.S. Steel head Roger Blough informed Kennedy that his company was raising steel prices by $6 a ton. Outraged, the president publicly called the increase "a wholly unjustifiable and irresponsible defiance of the public interest" and accused Blough of displaying "contempt for the interests of 185 million Americans." Privately, Kennedy was even blunter. He confided to aides, "My father always told me that all businessmen were sons-of-bitches, but I never believed it till now."

Roger Blough soon gave way. The president's tongue-lashing, along with a cutoff in Pentagon steel orders and the threat of an antitrust suit, forced him to reconsider. When several smaller steel companies refused to raise their prices in hopes of expanding their share of the market, U.S. Steel rolled back its prices. The business community deeply resented the president's action, and when the stock market, which had been rising steadily since 1960, suddenly fell sharply in late May 1962, analysts were quick to label the decline "the Kennedy market."

Troubled by his strained relations with business and by the continued lag in economic growth, the president decided to adopt a more unorthodox approach in 1963. Walter Heller, chairman of the Council of Economic Advisers, had been arguing since 1961 for a major cut in taxes in the belief it would stimulate consumer spending and give the economy the jolt it needed. The idea of a tax cut and resulting deficits during a period of prosperity went against economic orthodoxy, but Kennedy finally gave his approval. In January 1963, the president proposed a tax reduction of $13.5 billion, asserting that "the unrealistically heavy drag of federal income taxes on private purchasing power" was the "largest single barrier to full employment." When finally enacted by Congress in 1964, the massive tax cut led to sustained economic advance for the rest of the decade.

Kennedy's economic policy was far more successful than his legislative efforts. Although the rate of economic growth doubled to 4.5 percent by the end of 1963 and unemployment was reduced substantially, the cost of living rose only 1.3 percent a year. Personal income went up 13 percent in the early 1960s, but the greatest gains came in corporate profits—up 67 percent in the period. Critics pointed to the Kennedy administration's failure to close the glaring loopholes in the tax laws that benefited the rich and its lack of effort to help those at the bottom by forcing redistribution of national wealth. Despite the overall economic growth, the public sector continued to be neglected. "I am not sure what the advantage is," complained economist John Kenneth Galbraith, "in having a few more dollars to spend if the air is too dirty to breathe, the water too polluted to drink, the commuters are losing out in the struggle to get in and out of the cities, the streets are filthy, and the schools so bad that the young, perhaps wisely, stay away."

Moving Slowly on Civil Rights

Kennedy faced a genuine dilemma over the issue of civil rights. Despite his own lack of a strong record while in the Senate, he had portrayed himself during the 1960 campaign as a crusader for African American rights. He had promised to launch an attack on segregation in the Deep South, but his fear of alienating the large bloc of southern Democrats forced him to downplay civil rights legislation.

The president's solution was to defer congressional action in favor of executive leadership in this area. He directed his brother, Attorney General Robert Kennedy, to continue and expand the Eisenhower administration's efforts to achieve voting rights for southern blacks. To register previously disfranchised citizens, the Justice Department worked with the civil rights movement—notably the Student Nonviolent Coordinating Committee (SNCC)—in the Deep South. In two years, the Kennedy administration increased the number of voting rights suits fivefold. Yet the attorney general could not force the FBI to provide protection for the civil rights volunteers who risked their lives by encouraging African Americans to register. "SNCC's only contact with federal authority," noted one observer, "consisted of the FBI agents who stood by taking notes while local policemen beat up SNCC members."

Other efforts had equally mixed results. Vice President Lyndon Johnson headed a presidential Commission on Equal Employment Opportunities that worked with defense industries and other government contractors to increase the number of jobs for African Americans. But a limited budget and a reliance on voluntary cooperation prevented any dramatic gains; African American employment improved only in direct proportion to economic growth in the early 1960s.

Kennedy did succeed in appointing a number of African Americans to high government positions: Robert Weaver became chief of the federal housing agency, and Thurgood Marshall, who pleaded the *Brown* v. *Topeka* school desegregation case before the Supreme Court, was named to the U.S. Circuit Court. On the other hand, among his judicial appointments, Kennedy included one Mississippi jurist who referred to African Americans in court as "niggers" and once compared them to "a bunch of chimpanzees."

The civil rights movement refused to accept Kennedy's indirect approach. In May 1961, the Congress of Racial Equality (CORE) sponsored a **freedom ride** in which a biracial group attempted to test a 1960 Supreme Court decision outlawing segregation in all bus and train stations used in interstate commerce. When they arrived in Birmingham, Alabama, the freedom riders were attacked by a mob of angry whites. The attorney general quickly dispatched several hundred federal marshals to protect the freedom riders, but the president, deeply involved in the Berlin crisis, was more upset at the distraction the protesters created. Kennedy directed one of his aides to get in touch with the leaders of CORE. "Tell them to call it off," he demanded. "Stop them."

In September, after the attorney general finally convinced the Interstate Commerce Commission to issue an order banning segregation in interstate terminals and buses, the freedom rides ended. The Kennedy administration then sought to prevent further confrontations by involving civil rights activists in its voting drive.

A pattern of belated reaction to southern racism marked the basic approach of the Kennedys. When James Meredith courageously sought admission to the all-white University of Mississippi in 1962, the president and the attorney general worked closely with Mississippi governor Ross Barnett to avoid violence. A transcript of Robert Kennedy's conversation with Governor Barnett on

Watch the **Video**   **Photographing the Civil Rights Movement**

African American civil rights demonstrators in Birmingham, Alabama, encounter high-velocity fire hoses in response to their nonviolent demonstrations during the spring of 1963. This and other similar photographs of young African Americans being assaulted by the authorities in Birmingham rallied support for the civil rights protestors and their political and economic demands.

September 25 indicates that the attorney general focused on the legal rather than the moral issues involved:

RFK: I think the problem is that the federal courts have acted and when there is a conflict between your state and the federal courts under arrangements made some years ago—

Barnett: The institution is supported by the taxpayers of this state and controlled by the Trustees.

RFK: Governor, you are a part of the United States.

Barnett: ... I am going to treat you with every courtesy, but I won't agree to let that boy get to Ole Miss. I will never agree to that. I would rather spend my whole life in a penitentiary than do that.

RFK: I have a responsibility to enforce the laws of the United States.

Barnett: I appreciate that. You have a responsibility. Why don't you let the NAACP run their own affairs and quit cooperating with that crowd?

Watch the **Video**   Civil Rights March on Washington

The March on Washington, organized by civil rights leaders to maintain political pressure on the Kennedy administration, was held on August 28, 1936. The rally in front of the Lincoln Memorial was highlighted by Martin Luther King, Jr.'s famous "I Have a Dream" speech.

Despite Barnett's later promise of cooperation, the night before Meredith enrolled at the University of Mississippi, a mob attacked the federal marshals and national guard troops sent to protect him. The violence left 2 dead and 375 injured, including 166 marshals and 12 guardsmen, but Meredith attended the university and eventually graduated.

In 1963, Kennedy sent the deputy attorney general to face down Governor George C. Wallace, an avowed segregationist who had promised "to stand in the schoolhouse door" to prevent the integration of the University of Alabama. After a brief confrontation, Wallace yielded to federal authority, and

two African American students peacefully desegregated the state university.

"I Have a Dream"

Martin Luther King, Jr., finally forced Kennedy to abandon his cautious tactics and come out openly in behalf of racial justice. In the spring of 1963, King began a massive protest in Birmingham, one of the South's most segregated cities. Public marches and demonstrations aimed at integrating public facilities and opening up jobs for African Americans quickly led to police harassment and many arrests, including that of King himself. Police Commissioner Eugene "Bull" Connor was determined to crush the civil rights movement; King was equally determined to prevail. Writing from his cell in Birmingham, he vowed an active campaign to bring the issue of racial injustice to national attention.

Bull Connor played directly into King's hands. On May 3, as six thousand children marched in place of the jailed protesters, authorities broke up a demonstration with clubs, snarling police dogs, and high-pressure water hoses strong enough to take the bark off a tree. With a horrified nation watching scene after scene of this brutality on television, the Kennedy administration quickly intervened to arrange a settlement with the Birmingham civic leaders that ended the violence and granted the protesters most of their demands.

More important, Kennedy finally ended his long hesitation and sounded the call for action. "We are confronted primarily with a moral issue," he told the nation on June 11. "It is as old as the Scriptures and is as clear as the American Constitution." Eight days later, the administration sponsored civil rights legislation providing equal access to all public accommodations as well as an extension of voting rights for African Americans.

Despite pleas from the government for an end to demonstrations and protests, civil rights leaders kept pressure on the administration. They scheduled a massive **March on Washington** for August 1963. On August 28, more than 200,000 marchers gathered for a daylong rally in front of the Lincoln Memorial where they listened to hymns, speeches, and prayers for racial justice. The climax of the event was Martin Luther King, Jr.'s, eloquent "I Have A Dream" speech.

By the time of Kennedy's death in November 1963, his civil rights legislation was well on its way to passage in Congress. Yet even this achievement did not fully satisfy his critics. For two years, they had waited for him to deliver on his campaign promise to wipe out housing discrimination "with a stroke of the pen." The executive order on housing, finally issued in November 1962, proved disappointing; it ignored all past discrimination and applied only to houses and apartments financed by the federal government. For many, Kennedy had raised hopes for racial equality that he never fulfilled.

But unlike Eisenhower, he had provided presidential leadership for the civil rights movement. His emphasis on executive action gradually paid off, especially in extending voting rights. By early 1964, 40 percent of southern blacks had the franchise, compared to only 28 percent in 1960. Moreover, Kennedy's sense of caution and restraint, painful and frustrating as it was to African American activists, had proved to be well-founded. Avoiding an early, and possibly fatal, defeat in Congress, he had waited until a national consensus emerged and then had carefully channeled it behind effective legislation. Behaving very much the way Franklin Roosevelt did in guiding the nation into World War II, Kennedy chose to be a fox rather than a lion on civil rights.

The Supreme Court and Reform

The most active impulse for social change in the early 1960s came from a surprising source: the usually staid and conservative Supreme Court. Under the leadership of Earl Warren, a pragmatic jurist more noted for his political astuteness than his legal scholarship, the Court ventured into new areas. A group of

liberal judges—especially William O. Douglas, Hugo Black, and William J. Brennan, Jr.—argued for social reform, while advocates of judicial restraint (such as John Marshall Harlan and Felix Frankfurter) fought stubbornly against the new activism.

The resignation of Felix Frankfurter in 1962 enabled President Kennedy to appoint Secretary of Labor Arthur Goldberg, a committed liberal, to the Supreme Court. With a clear majority now favoring judicial intervention, the Warren Court issued a series of landmark decisions designed to extend to state and local jurisdictions the traditional rights afforded the accused in federal courts. Thus in *Gideon* v. *Wainwright* (1963), *Escobedo* v. *Illinois* (1964), and *Miranda* v. *Arizona* (1966), the majority decreed that defendants had to be provided lawyers, had to be informed of their constitutional rights, and could not be interrogated or induced to confess to a crime without defense counsel being present. In effect, the Court extended to the poor and the ignorant those constitutional guarantees that had always been available to the rich and to the legally informed—notably hardened criminals.

The most far-reaching Warren Court decisions came in the area of legislative reapportionment. In 1962, the Court ruled in *Baker* v. *Carr* that Tennessee had to redistribute its legislative seats to give citizens in Memphis equal representation. Subsequent decisions reinforced the ban on rural overrepresentation as the Court proclaimed that places in all legislative bodies, including the House of Representatives, had to be allocated on the basis of "people, not land or trees or pastures." The principle of "one man, one vote" greatly increased the political power of cities at the expense of rural areas; it also involved the Court directly in the reapportionment process, frequently forcing judges to draw up new legislative and congressional districts.

The activism of the Supreme Court stirred up a storm of criticism. The rulings that extended protection to criminals and those accused of subversive activity led some Americans to charge that the Court was encouraging crime and weakening national security. The John Birch Society, an extreme anticommunist group, demanded the impeachment of Chief Justice Warren. The 1962 *Engel* v. *Vitale* decision banning school prayer incensed many conservative Americans, who saw the Court as undermining moral values. Legal scholars worried more about the weakening of the Court's prestige as it became more directly involved in the political process. On balance, however, the Warren Court helped achieve greater social justice by protecting the rights of the underprivileged and by permitting dissent and free expression to flourish.

"Let Us Continue"

What were Johnson's domestic priorities and what were his achievements?

The New Frontier came to a sudden and violent end on November 22, 1963, when Lee Harvey Oswald assassinated John F. Kennedy as the president rode in a motorcade in downtown Dallas. The shock of losing the young president, who had become a symbol of hope and promise for a whole generation, stunned the entire world. The American people were bewildered by the rapid sequence of events: the brutal killing of their young president; the televised slaying of Oswald by Jack Ruby in the basement of the Dallas police station; the composure and dignity of Kennedy's widow, Jacqueline, at the ensuing state funeral; and the hurried Warren Commission report, which identified Oswald as the lone assassin. Afterward, critics would charge that Oswald had been part of a vast conspiracy, but at the time, the prevailing national reaction was a numbing sense of loss.

Vice President Lyndon B. Johnson moved quickly to fill the vacuum left by Kennedy's death. Sworn in on board Air Force One as he returned to Washington, Johnson soon met with a stream of world leaders to reassure them of American political stability. Five days after the tragedy in Dallas, Johnson spoke eloquently to a special joint session of Congress. Recalling JFK's inaugural summons, "Let us begin," the new president declared, "Today in the moment of new resolve, I would say to all my fellow Americans, 'Let us continue.'" Asking Congress to enact Kennedy's tax and civil rights bills as a tribute to the fallen leader, LBJ concluded, "Let us here highly resolve that John Fitzgerald Kennedy did not live or die in vain."

Johnson in Action

Lyndon Johnson suffered from the inevitable comparison with his young and stylish predecessor. LBJ was acutely aware of his own lack of polish; he sought to surround himself with Kennedy advisers and insiders, hoping their sophistication would rub off on him. Johnson's assets were very real—he possessed an intimate knowledge of Congress, an incredible energy and determination to succeed, and a fierce ego. When a young marine officer tried to direct him to the proper helicopter, saying, "This one is yours," Johnson replied, "Son, they are all my helicopters."

LBJ's height and intensity gave him a powerful presence; he dominated any room he entered, and he delighted in using his physical power of persuasion. One Texas politician explained why he had given in to Johnson: "Lyndon got me by the lapels and put his face on top of mine and he talked and talked and talked. I figured it was either getting drowned or joining."

Yet LBJ found it impossible to project his intelligence and vitality to large audiences. Unlike Kennedy, he wilted before the camera, turning his televised speeches into stilted and awkward performances. Trying to belie his reputation as a riverboat gambler, he came across like a foxy grandpa, clever, calculating, and not to be trusted. He lacked Kennedy's wit and charm, and reporters delighted in describing the way he berated his aides or shocked the nation by baring his belly to show the scar from a recent operation.

Whatever his shortcomings in style, however, Johnson possessed far greater ability than Kennedy in dealing with Congress. He entered the White House with more than thirty years of experience in Washington as a legislative aide, congressman, and senator. His encyclopedic knowledge of the legislative process and his shrewd manipulation of individual senators had enabled him to become the most influential Senate majority leader in history. Famed for "the Johnson treatment," a legendary ability to use personal persuasion to reach his goals, Johnson in fact relied more on his close ties with the Senate's power brokers—or "whales," as he called them—than on his exploitation of the "minnows."

Above all, Johnson sought consensus. Indifferent to ideology, he had moved easily from New Deal liberalism to oil-and-gas conservatism as his career advanced. He had carefully cultivated Richard Russell of Georgia, leader of the Dixie bloc, but he also had taken Hubert Humphrey, a Minnesota liberal, under his wing. He had performed a balancing act on civil rights, working with the Eisenhower administration on behalf of the 1957 Voting Rights Act, yet carefully weakening it to avoid alienating southern Democrats. When Kennedy dashed Johnson's own intense presidential ambitions in 1960, LBJ had gracefully agreed to be his running mate and had endured the humiliation of the vice presidency loyally and silently. Suddenly thrust into power, Johnson used his gifts wisely. Citing his favorite scriptural passage from Isaiah, "Come now, and let us reason together, saith the Lord," he concentrated on securing passage of Kennedy's tax and civil rights bills in 1964.

The tax cut came first. Aware of the power wielded by Senate Finance Committee Chairman Harry Byrd, a Virginia conservative, Johnson astutely lowered Kennedy's projected $101.5 billion budget for 1965 to $97.9 billion. Although Byrd voted against the tax cut, he let the measure out of his committee, telling Johnson, "I'll be working for you behind the scenes." In February, Congress reduced personal income taxes by more than $10 billion, touching off a sustained economic boom. Consumer spending increased by an impressive $43 billion during the next eighteen months, and new jobs opened up at the rate of one million a year.

Johnson was even more influential in passing the Kennedy civil rights measure. Staying in the background, he encouraged liberal amendments that strengthened the bill in the House. With Hubert Humphrey leading the floor fight in the Senate, Johnson refused all efforts at compromise, counting on growing public pressure to force northern Republicans to abandon their traditional alliance with southern Democrats. Everett M. Dirksen of Illinois, the GOP leader in the Senate, met repeatedly with Johnson at the White House. When LBJ refused to yield, Dirksen finally led a Republican vote to end a 57-day filibuster.

The 1964 Civil Rights Act, signed on July 2, made illegal the segregation of African Americans in public facilities, established an Equal Employment Opportunity Commission to lessen racial discrimination in employment, and protected the voting rights of African Americans. An amendment sponsored by segregationists in an effort to weaken the bill added gender to the prohibition of discrimination in Title VII of the act; in the future, women's groups would use the clause to secure government support for greater equality in employment and education.

The Election of 1964

Passage of two key Kennedy measures within six months did not satisfy Johnson who wanted now to win the presidency in his own right. Eager to surpass Kennedy's narrow victory in 1960, he hoped to win by a great landslide.

Searching for a cause of his own, LBJ found one in the issue of poverty. Beginning in the late 1950s, economists had warned that the prevailing affluence disguised a persistent and deep-seated problem of poverty. In 1962, Michael Harrington's book *The Other America* attracted national attention. Writing with passion and

📖●—┤**Read** the **Document**   **The Civil Rights Act of 1964**

President Johnson applies the "Johnson treatment" to Senator Theodore Francis Green of Rhode Island. A shrewd politician and master of the legislative process, Johnson always knew which votes he could count on, those he couldn't, and where and how to apply pressure to swing votes his way.

eloquence, Harrington claimed that nearly one-fifth of the nation, some thirty-five million Americans, lived in poverty.

Three groups predominated among the poor—African Americans, the aged, and households headed by women. The problem, Harrington contended, was that the poor were invisible, living in slums or depressed areas such as Appalachia. They were cut off from the educational facilities, medical care, and employment opportunities afforded more affluent Americans. Moreover, poverty was a vicious cycle. The children of the poor were trapped in the same culture of poverty as their parents, living without hope or knowledge of how to enter the mainstream of American life.

Johnson quickly took over proposals that Kennedy had been developing and made them his own. In his January 1964 State of the Union address, LBJ announced, "This administration, today, here and now, declares unconditional war on poverty in America." During the next eight months, Johnson fashioned a comprehensive poverty program under the direction of R. Sargent Shriver, Kennedy's brother-in-law. The president added $500 million to existing programs to come up with a $1 billion effort that Congress passed in August 1964.

The new Office of Economic Opportunity (OEO) set up a wide variety of programs, ranging from Head Start for preschoolers to the Job Corps for high school dropouts in need of vocational training. The emphasis was on self-help, with the government providing money and know-how so the poor could reap the benefits of neighborhood day care centers, consumer education classes, legal aid services, and adult remedial reading programs. The level of funding was never high enough to meet the OEO's ambitious goals, and a controversial attempt to include representatives of the poor in the Community Action Program led to bitter political feuding with city and state officials. Nonetheless, the **war on poverty**, along with the economic growth provided by the tax cut, helped reduce the ranks of the poor by nearly ten million between 1964 and 1967.

The new program established Johnson's reputation as a reformer in an election year, but he still faced two challenges to his authority. The first was Robert F. Kennedy, the late president's brother, who continued as attorney general but who wanted to become vice president and Johnson's eventual successor in the White House. Desperate to prove his ability to succeed without

Kennedy help, LBJ commented, "I don't need that little runt to win" and chose Hubert Humphrey as his running mate.

The second challenge was the Republican candidate, Senator Barry Goldwater, an outspoken conservative from Arizona. An attractive and articulate man, Goldwater advocated a rejection of the welfare state and a return to unregulated free enterprise. To Johnson's delight, Goldwater chose to place ideology ahead of political expediency. The senator spoke out boldly against the Tennessee Valley Authority, denounced Social Security, and advocated a hawkish foreign policy. "In Your Heart, You Know He's Right," read the Republican slogan, leading the Democrats to reply, "Yes, Far Right," and in reference to a careless Goldwater comment about using nuclear weapons, Johnson backers punned, "In Your Heart, You Know He Might."

Johnson stuck carefully to the middle of the road, embracing the liberal reform program—which he now called the **Great Society**—while emphasizing his concern for balanced budgets and fiscal orthodoxy. The more Goldwater sagged in the polls, the harder Johnson campaigned, determined to achieve his treasured landslide. On election day, LBJ received 61.1 percent of the popular vote and an overwhelming majority in the electoral college; Goldwater carried only Arizona and five states of the Deep South. Equally important, the Democrats achieved huge gains in Congress, controlling the House by a margin of 295 to 140 and the Senate by 68 to 32. Kennedy's legacy and Goldwater's candor had enabled Johnson to break the conservative grip on Congress for the first time in a quarter century.

THE ELECTION OF 1964

Candidate	Party	Popular Vote	Electoral Vote
Johnson	Democratic	43,126,506	486
Goldwater	Republican	27,176,799	52

The Triumph of Reform

LBJ moved quickly to secure his legislative goals. Despite solid majorities in both Houses, including seventy first-term Democrats who had ridden into office on his coattails, Johnson knew he would have to enact the Great Society as swiftly as possible. "You've got to give it all you can, that first year," he told an aide. "Doesn't matter what kind of majority you come in with. You've got just one year when they treat you right, and before they start worrying about themselves."

Johnson gave two traditional Democratic reforms—health care and education—top priority. Aware of strong opposition to a comprehensive medical program, LBJ settled for **Medicare**, which mandated health insurance under the Social Security program for Americans over age 65, and a supplementary Medicaid program for the indigent. To symbolize the end of a long struggle, Johnson flew to Independence, Missouri, so Truman could witness the ceremonial signing of the Medicare law, which had its origins in Truman's 1949 health insurance proposal.

LBJ overcame the religious hurdle on education by supporting a child-benefit approach, allocating federal money to advance the education of students in parochial as well as public schools. The Elementary and Secondary Education Act of 1965 provided more than $1 billion in federal aid, the largest share going to school districts with the highest percentage of impoverished pupils.

Civil rights proved to be the most difficult test of Johnson's leadership. Martin Luther King, Jr., concerned that three million southern blacks were still denied the right to vote, in early 1965 chose Selma, Alabama, as the site for a test case. The white authorities in Selma, led by Sheriff James Clark, used cattle prods and bullwhips to break up the demonstrations. More than two thousand African Americans were jailed. Johnson intervened in March, after TV cameras showed Sheriff Clark's deputies brutally halting a march from Selma to Montgomery. The president ordered the Alabama National Guard to federal duty to protect the demonstrators, had the Justice Department draw up a new voting rights bill, and personally addressed the Congress on civil rights. "I speak tonight for the dignity of man and the destiny of democracy," he began. Calling the denial of the right to vote "deadly wrong," LBJ issued a compelling call to action. "Their cause must be our cause, too. Because it is not just Negroes, but really it is all of us who must overcome the crippling legacy of bigotry and injustice."

Five months later, Congress passed the **Voting Rights Act of 1965**. Once again Johnson had worked with Senate Republican leader Dirksen to break a southern filibuster and assure passage of a measure. The act banned literacy tests in states and counties in which less than half the population had voted in 1964 and provided for federal registrars in these areas to assure African Americans the franchise.

The results were dramatic. In less than a year, 166,000 African Americans were added to the voting rolls in Alabama; African American registration went up 400 percent in Mississippi. By the end of the decade, the percentage of eligible African American voters who had registered had risen from 40 to 65 percent. For the first time since Reconstruction, African Americans had become active participants in southern politics.

Before the 89th Congress ended its first session in the fall of 1965, it had passed eighty-nine bills. These included measures to create two new cabinet departments (Transportation and Housing and Urban Affairs); acts to provide for highway safety and to ensure clean air and water; large appropriations for higher education, public housing, and the continuing war on poverty; and sweeping immigration reform legislation. (See the Feature Essay, "Unintended Consequences: The Second Great Migration," pp. 722–723.) In nine months, Johnson had enacted the entire Democratic reform agenda.

The man responsible for this great leap forward, however, had failed to win the public adulation he so deeply desired. His legislative skills had made the most of the opportunities offered by the 1964 Democratic landslide, but the people did not respond to Johnson's leadership with the warmth and praise they had showered on Kennedy. Reporters continued to portray him as a crude wheeler-dealer; as a maniac who drove around Texas back roads at 90 miles an hour, one hand on the wheel and the other holding a can of beer; or as a bully who picked up his dog by the ears. No one was more aware of this lack of affection than LBJ himself. His public support, he told an aide, is "like a Western river, broad but not deep."

Johnson's realization of the fleeting nature of his popularity was all too accurate. The dilemmas of the Cold War began to divert his attention from domestic concerns and eventually, in the

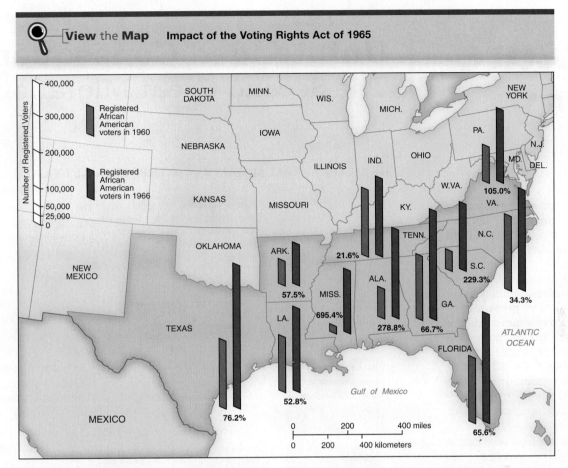

AFRICAN AMERICAN VOTER REGISTRATION BEFORE AND AFTER PASSAGE OF THE VOTING RIGHTS ACT OF 1965 The percentages shown on the map indicate the increase in African American voter registration between 1960 and 1966.

case of Vietnam, would overwhelm him. Yet his legislative achievements were still remarkable. In one brief outburst of reform, he had accomplished more than any president since FDR.

Difficulties abroad would dim the luster of the Johnson presidency, but they could not diminish the lasting impact of the Great Society on American life. Federal aid to education, the enactment of Medicare and Medicaid, and, above all, the civil rights acts of 1964 and 1965 changed the nation irrevocably. The aged and the poor now were guaranteed access to medical care; communities saw an infusion of federal funds to improve local education; and African Americans could now begin to attend integrated schools, enjoy public facilities, and gain political power by exercising the right to vote. But even at this moment of triumph for liberal reform, new currents of dissent and rebellion were brewing.

Johnson Escalates the Vietnam War

How did Johnson's Vietnam policy evolve?

Lyndon Johnson emphasized continuity in foreign policy just as he had in enacting Kennedy's domestic reforms. He not only inherited the policy of containment from his fallen predecessor, but

he shared the same Cold War assumptions and convictions. And, feeling less confident about dealing with international issues, he tended to rely heavily on Kennedy's advisers—notably Secretary of State Rusk, Secretary of Defense McNamara, and McGeorge Bundy (the national security adviser until he was replaced in 1966 by the even more hawkish Walt Rostow).

Johnson had broad exposure to national security affairs. He had served on the Naval Affairs Committee in the House before and during World War II, and as Senate majority leader he had been briefed and consulted regularly on the crises of the 1950s. A confirmed cold warrior, he had also seen in the 1940s the devastating political impact on the Democratic party of the communist triumph in China. "I am not going to lose Vietnam," he told the American ambassador to Saigon just after taking office in 1963. "I am not going to be the president who saw Southeast Asia go the way China went."

Aware of the problem Castro had caused John Kennedy, LBJ moved firmly to contain communism in the Western Hemisphere. When a military junta overthrew a leftist regime in Brazil, Johnson offered covert aid and open encouragement. He was equally forceful in compelling Panama to restrain rioting aimed at the continued American presence in the Canal Zone.

In 1965, to block the possible emergence of a Castro-type government, LBJ sent twenty thousand American troops to the

Feature Essay

Unintended Consequences
The Second Great Migration

This is not a revolutionary bill," President Lyndon Johnson declared when he signed the Immigration Act of 1965 into law. Rarely has a president been so wrong. The changes Congress made in American immigration policy led to a second great migration, larger and even more diverse than the first great migration that took place in the thirty years before World War I. By the end of the century, the second great wave of immigration had profoundly altered the ethnic composition of the United States.

The political leaders responsible for changing immigration policy in the 1960s had very different intentions. Focused on removing long-standing inequities in the law, they sought to replace the national origins system, adopted in the 1920s, which favored people from western Europe, with a new set of criteria designed to bring in newcomers with economic skills the United States needed and to reunite broken families. Above all, the architects of change wanted to end the unfair race-based quotas for people of Asian extraction and the evident discrimination against applicants from eastern and southern Europe. Attorney General Robert Kennedy called the national origins quotas "a standing affront to many Americans and to many countries." At the height of the Cold War, realism seemed to join with idealism in the effort to end a discriminatory immigration policy that smacked of racism.

The legislative process, however, often works in mysterious ways. The bill passed by Congress did end the national origins system, as its framers desired, but reversed the new

THE SECOND GREAT MIGRATION: A THEORETICAL EXAMPLE

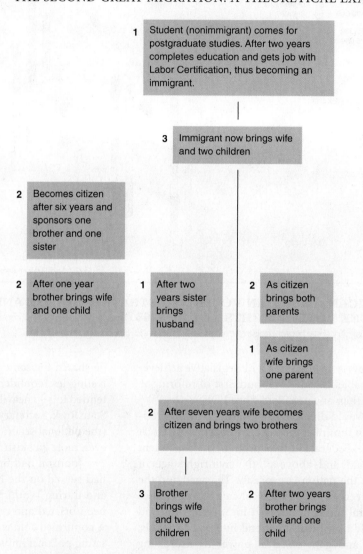

Note: Total is nineteen after original student arrived for postgraduate education ten years earlier.

Source: Adapted from David M. Reimer, *Still the Golden Door*, 2nd ed. (New York: Columbia University Press, 1992), p. 95.

priorities, giving highest preference to family reunification, and less emphasis to job skills and asylum for refugees. As enacted and later amended, the 1965 Immigration Act set an annual limit of 170,000 for immigrants from Europe, Asia, and Africa, and 120,000 for those

from Western Hemisphere countries, with a ceiling of 20,000 for any one country. The total, 290,000, would be only slightly larger than the number admitted under the old system.

By the end of the 1970s, it was clear that the family preferences,

722

which made up nearly 70 percent of the allotted visas, were allowing recent immigrants to bring in large numbers of relatives, instead of reuniting immigrants who had been in the United States for years with their families. The figure, "The Second Great Migration: A Theoretical Example," shows how one postgraduate student with a non-immigrant visa, by adroit use of the available family preferences, could easily gain the admission of eighteen relatives in just a decade. Moreover, once resident aliens became citizens, they could bring in relatives—spouses, children under 21, and parents—without regard to visa limits.

Two significant developments flowed directly from the Great Society's immigration policy. First, annual immigration increased steadily from an average of 250,000 in the 1950s to at least one million by the end of the century. In 1990, in an effort to place "immediate relatives" under an effective limit, Congress approved an overall ceiling of just less than 700,000 immigrants a year, except for refugees. But other legislation allowing undocumented workers to gain legal status, as well as an estimated 300,000 illegal immigrants a year, swelled the actual total to more than one million. In effect, the 1965 legislation had led to a quadrupling of newcomers entering the United States every year.

The other unintended consequence of the 1965 Immigration Act was a rapid shift in the source of the new immigrants. Europe, the traditional place of origin for immigrants, fell from providing 70 percent of newcomers in the 1950s to just 16 percent by the mid-1990s. Latin American immigrants rose from 25 to 49 percent of the total, while Asia supplied 32 percent by the end of the century, up from just 6 percent in the 1950s. This change in the countries of origin was as striking as the similar shift from western to eastern Europe in the first great migration. Where once Germany, Great Britain, and Ireland had furnished the majority of newcomers, by 1989 it was Mexico, the Philippines, and Vietnam that led the list, with no European country among the top ten.

The result was a growing diversity that promised to make the United States a truly multiethnic society in the twenty-first century. By the 1990s, the number of foreign-born Americans had more than doubled to 10 percent of the population. Hispanic Americans were the most rapidly growing segment, replacing African Americans as the nation's largest minority in 2001. Asian Americans, although much smaller in number, grew at a fast pace and had greater success economically than any other ethnic group.

By the end of the century, it was clear that the Immigration Act of 1965 had led to a major shift in the racial and ethnic composition of the United States. The effort to erase past discriminatory and race-based quotas resulted in an unexpected flow of people from Asia and Latin America that ensured the end of traditional European dominance. By 2050, according to Census Bureau projections, the country will be almost evenly divided between non-Hispanic whites and minorities. Social harmony in the twenty-first century will depend on whether the melting pot continues to melt, blending ethnic groups into mainstream America, or whether these groups, as their numbers grow, will shape the society into one that political leaders of the 1960s such as Lyndon Johnson and Robert Kennedy could never have foreseen.

QUESTIONS FOR DISCUSSION

1. How did the 1965 Immigration Act change immigration policy?

2. Why did the Act lead to a major change in the nation's ethnic and racial make-up?

Dominican Republic. Johnson's flimsy justifications—ranging from the need to protect American tourists to a dubious list of suspected communists among the rebel leaders—served only to alienate liberal critics in the United States, particularly Senate Foreign Relations Committee Chairman J. William Fulbright, a former Johnson favorite. The intervention ended in 1966 with the election of a conservative government. Senator Fulbright, however, continued his criticism of Johnson's foreign policy by publishing *The Arrogance of Power*, a biting analysis of the fallacies of containment. Fulbright's defection symbolized a growing gap between the president and liberal intellectuals; the more LBJ struggled to uphold the Cold War policies he had inherited from Kennedy, the more he found himself under attack from Congress, the media, and the universities.

The Vietnam Dilemma

It was Vietnam rather than Latin America that became Lyndon Johnson's obsession and led ultimately to his political downfall. Inheriting an American commitment that dated back to Eisenhower to support an independent South Vietnam, the new president believed he had little choice but to continue Kennedy's policy in Vietnam. The crisis created by Diem's overthrow only three weeks before Kennedy's assassination led to a vacuum of power in Saigon that prevented Johnson from conducting a thorough review and reassessment of the strategic alternatives in Southeast Asia. In 1964, seven different governments ruled South Vietnam; power changed hands three times within one month. According to an American officer, the atmosphere in Saigon "fairly smelled of discontent," with "workers on strike, students demonstrating, [and] the local press pursuing a persistent campaign of criticism of the new government."

Resisting pressure from the Joint Chiefs of Staff for direct American military involvement, LBJ continued Kennedy's policy of economic and technical assistance. He sent in seven thousand more military advisers and an additional $50 million in aid. While he insisted it was still up to the Vietnamese themselves to win the war, he expanded American support for covert operations, including amphibious raids on the North.

These undercover activities led directly to the Gulf of Tonkin affair. On August 2, 1964, North Vietnamese torpedo boats attacked the *Maddox*, an American destroyer engaged in electronic intelligence gathering in the Gulf of Tonkin. The attack was prompted by the belief the American ship had been involved in a South Vietnamese raid nearby. The *Maddox* escaped unscathed, but to show American resolve, the navy sent in another destroyer, the *C. Turner Joy*. On the evening of August 4, the two destroyers, responding to sonar and radar contacts, opened fire on North Vietnamese gunboats in the area. Johnson ordered retaliatory air strikes on North Vietnamese naval bases. Later investigation indicated that the North Vietnamese gunboats had not launched a second attack on the American ships.

The next day, the president asked Congress to pass a resolution authorizing him to take "all necessary measures to repel any armed attack against the forces of the United States and to prevent further aggression." He did not in fact need this authority; he had already ordered the retaliatory air strike

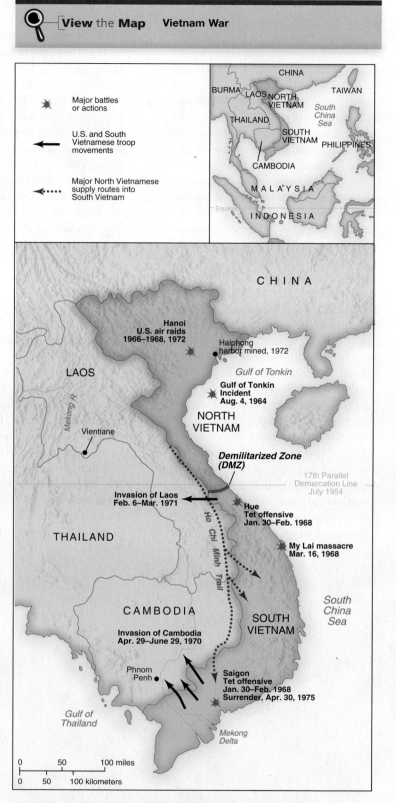

View the Map Vietnam War

SOUTHEAST ASIA AND THE VIETNAM WAR American combat forces in South Vietnam rose from sixteen thousand in 1963 to a half million in 1968, but a successful conclusion to the conflict was no closer.

without it. Later, critics charged that LBJ wanted a blank check from Congress to carry out the future escalation of the Vietnam War, but such a motive is unlikely. He had already rejected immediate military intervention. In part, he wanted the **Gulf of Tonkin Resolution** to demonstrate to North Vietnam the American determination to defend South Vietnam at any cost. "The challenge we face in Southeast Asia today," he told Congress, "is the same challenge that we have faced with courage and that we have met with strength in Greece and Turkey, in Berlin and Korea." He also wanted to preempt the Vietnam issue from his Republican opponent, Barry Goldwater, who had been advocating a tougher policy. By taking a firm stand on the Gulf of Tonkin incident, Johnson could both impress the North Vietnamese and outmaneuver a political rival at home.

Congress responded with alacrity. The House acted unanimously, while only two senators voted against the Gulf of Tonkin Resolution. Johnson appeared to have won a spectacular victory. His standing in the Gallup poll shot up from 42 to 72 percent, and he had effectively blocked Goldwater from exploiting Vietnam as a campaign issue.

In the long run, however, this easy victory proved costly. Having used force once against North Vietnam, LBJ was more likely to do so in the future. And although he apparently had no intention of widening the conflict in August 1964, the congressional resolution was phrased broadly enough to enable him to use whatever level of force he wanted—including unlimited military intervention. Above all, when he did wage war in Vietnam, he left himself open to the charge of deliberately misleading Congress. Presidential credibility proved ultimately to be Johnson's Achilles' heel; his political downfall began with the Gulf of Tonkin Resolution.

Escalation

Full-scale American involvement in Vietnam began in 1965 in a series of steps designed primarily to prevent a North Vietnamese victory. With the political situation in Saigon growing more hopeless every day, the president's advisers urged the bombing of the North. American air attacks would serve several purposes: They would block North Vietnamese infiltration routes, make Hanoi pay a heavy price for its role, and lift the sagging morale of the South Vietnamese. But most important, as McGeorge Bundy reported after a visit to Pleiku (site of a Vietcong attack on an American base that took nine lives), "Without new U.S. action defeat appears inevitable—probably not in a matter of weeks or perhaps even months, but within the next year or so." In February 1965, Johnson cited the Pleiku attack in ordering a long-planned aerial bombardment of selected North Vietnamese targets.

The air strikes, aimed at impeding the communist supply line and damaging Hanoi's economy, proved ineffective. In April, Johnson authorized the use of American combat troops in South Vietnam, restricting them to defensive operations intended to protect American air bases. The Joint Chiefs then pressed the president for both unlimited bombing of the North and the aggressive use of American ground forces in the South. In mid-July, Secretary of Defense McNamara recommended sending a hundred thousand combat troops to Vietnam, more than doubling the American forces there. He believed this escalation would lead to a "favorable outcome," but he also told the president that an additional hundred thousand soldiers might

be needed in 1966 and that American battle deaths could rise as high as five hundred a month (by early 1968, they hit a peak of more than five hundred a week).

At the same time, other advisers, most notably Undersecretary of State George Ball, spoke out against military escalation in favor of a political settlement. Warning that the United States was likely to suffer "national humiliation," Ball told the president that he had "serious doubt that an army of westerners can successfully fight Orientals in an Asian jungle."

Lyndon Johnson was genuinely torn, asking his advisers at one point, "Are we starting something that in two to three years we simply can't finish?" But he finally decided he had no choice but to persevere in Vietnam. Although he insisted on paring down McNamara's troop request, LBJ settled on a steady

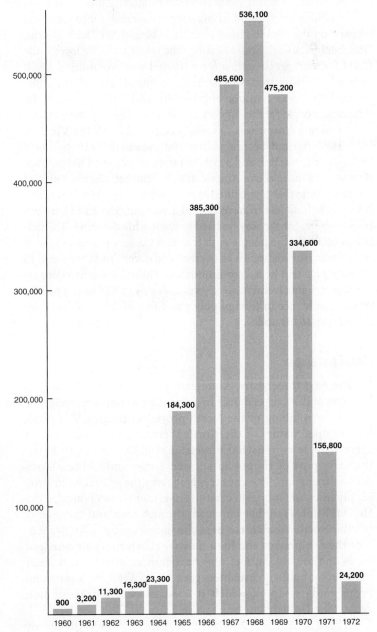

U.S. TROOP LEVELS IN VIETNAM
(AS OF DEC. 31 OF EACH YEAR)

Source: U.S. Department of Defense

military escalation designed to compel Hanoi to accept a diplomatic solution. In late July, the president permitted a gradual increase in the bombing of North Vietnam and allowed American ground commanders to conduct offensive operations in the South. Most ominously, he approved the immediate dispatch of fifty thousand troops to Vietnam and the future commitment of fifty thousand more.

These July decisions formed "an open-ended commitment to employ American military forces as the situation demanded," wrote historian George Herring, and they were "the closest thing to a formal decision for war in Vietnam." Convinced that withdrawal would destroy American credibility before the world and that an invasion of the North would lead to World War III, Johnson opted for large-scale but limited military intervention. Moreover, LBJ feared the domestic consequences of either extreme. A pullout could cause a massive political backlash at home, as conservatives condemned him for betraying South Vietnam to communism. All-out war, however, would mean the end of his social programs. Once Congress focused on the conflict, he explained to biographer Doris Kearns, "that bitch of a war" would destroy "the woman I really loved—the Great Society." So he settled for a limited war, committing a half million American troops to battle in Southeast Asia, all the while pretending it was a minor engagement and refusing to ask the American people for the support and sacrifice required for victory.

Lyndon Johnson was not solely responsible for the Vietnam War. He inherited both a policy that assumed Vietnam was a vital national interest and a deteriorating situation in Saigon that demanded a more active American role. Truman, Eisenhower, and Kennedy had taken the United States deep into the Vietnam maze; it was Johnson's fate to have to find a way out. But LBJ bears full responsibility for the way he tried to resolve his dilemma. The failure to confront the people with the stark choices the nation faced in Vietnam, the insistence on secrecy and deceit, and the refusal to acknowledge that he had committed the United States to a dangerous military involvement were Johnson's sins in Vietnam. His lack of self-confidence in foreign policy and fear of domestic reaction led directly to his undoing.

Stalemate

For the next three years, Americans waged an intensive war in Vietnam and succeeded only in preventing a communist victory. American bombing of the North proved ineffective. The rural, undeveloped nature of the North Vietnamese economy meant there were few industrial targets; a political refusal to bomb the main port of Haiphong allowed Soviet and Chinese arms to flow freely into the country. Nor were the efforts to destroy supply lines any more successful. American planes pounded the Ho Chi Minh Trail that ran down through Laos and Cambodia, but the North Vietnamese used the jungle canopy effectively to hide their shipments and their massive efforts to repair damaged roads and bridges. In fact, the American air attacks, with their inadvertent civilian casualties, gave North Vietnam a powerful propaganda weapon, which it used to sway world opinion against the United States.

The war in the South went no better. Despite the steady increase in American ground forces, from 184,000 in late 1965 to more than 500,000 by early 1968, the Vietcong still controlled much of the countryside. The search-and-destroy tactics employed by the American commander, General William Westmoreland, proved ill suited to the situation. The Vietcong, aided by North Vietnamese regulars, were waging a war of insurgency, avoiding fixed positions and striking from ambush. In a vain effort to destroy the enemy, Westmoreland used superior American firepower wantonly, devastating the countryside, causing many civilian casualties, and driving the peasantry into the arms of the guerrillas. Inevitably, these tactics led to the slaughter of innocent civilians, most notably at the hamlet of My Lai. In March 1968, an American company led by Lieutenant William Calley, Jr., killed more than two hundred unarmed villagers.

The main premise of Westmoreland's strategy was to wage a war of attrition that would finally reach a "crossover point" when communist losses each month would be greater than the number of new troops they could recruit. He hoped to lure the Vietcong and the North Vietnamese regulars into pitched battles in which American firepower would inflict heavy casualties. But soon it was the communists who were deciding where and when the fighting would take place, provoking American attacks in remote areas of South Vietnam that favored the defenders and made Westmoreland pay heavily in American lives for the communist losses. By the end of 1967, the nearly half million American troops Johnson had sent to Vietnam had failed to defeat the enemy. At best, LBJ had only achieved a bloody stalemate that gradually turned the American people against a war they had once eagerly embraced.

Years of Turmoil

Why were there protests during the 1960s?

The Vietnam War became the focal point for a growing movement of youthful protest that made the 1960s the most turbulent decade of the twentieth century. Disenchantment with conventional middle-class values, a rapid increase in college enrollments as a result of the post–World War II baby boom, a reaction against the crass materialism of the affluent society—with its endless suburbs and shopping malls—all led American youth to embrace an alternative lifestyle based on the belief that people are "sensitive, searching, poetic, and capable of love." They were ready to create a counterculture.

The agitation of the 1960s was at its height between 1965 and 1968, the years that marked the escalation of the Vietnam War. Disturbances on college campuses reflected growing discontent in other parts of society, from the urban ghettos to the lettuce fields of the Southwest. All who felt disadvantaged and dissatisfied—students, African Americans, Hispanics, Native Americans, women, hippies—took to the streets to give vent to their feelings.

The Student Revolt

The first sign of student rebellion came in the fall of 1964 at the prestigious University of California at Berkeley. A small group of radical students resisted university efforts to deny them a place to solicit volunteers and funds for off-campus causes. Forming the Free Speech movement, they struck back by occupying administration buildings and blocking the arrest of a nonstudent protester. For the next two months the campus was in turmoil.

In the end, the protesters won the rights of free speech and association that they championed. Their hero was Mario Savio, a student who had eloquently summed up the cause by likening the university to a great machine and telling others, "You've got to put your bodies upon the gears, and upon the wheels, upon the levers, upon all the apparatus, and you've got to make it stop."

The Free Speech movement at Berkeley offered many insights into the causes of campus unrest. It was fueled in part by student suspicion of an older, depression-born generation that viewed affluence as the answer to all problems. Unable to exert much influence on the power structure that directed the consumer society, the students turned on the university. They viewed higher education as the faithful servant of a corporate culture: The university trained hordes of technicians, harbored research laboratories that perfected dreadful weapons, and used IBM punch cards to regiment students. The feeling of powerlessness that underlay the Berkeley riots was best revealed by a protester carrying a sign that read, "I am a UC student. Please don't bend, fold, spindle, or mutilate me."

Student protest found its full expression in the explosive growth of the **Students for a Democratic Society (SDS)**. Founded in Port Huron, Michigan, in 1962, this radical organization wanted to rid American society of poverty, racism, and violence. Although the SDS embraced many traditional liberal reforms, such as expanded public housing and comprehensive health insurance, its founders advocated a new approach called participatory democracy. In contrast to both liberalism and old-style socialism, the SDS sought salvation through the individual rather than the group. Personal control of one's life and destiny, not the creation of new bureaucracies, was the hallmark of the New Left.

In the next few years, the SDS grew phenomenally. Spurred on by the Vietnam War and massive campus unrest, the SDS could count more than a hundred thousand followers and was responsible for disruptions at nearly a thousand colleges in 1968. Yet its very emphasis on the individual and its fear of bureaucracy left it leaderless and subject to division and disunity. By 1970, a split between factions, some of which were given to violence, led to its complete demise.

The meteoric career of the SDS symbolized the turbulence of the 1960s. For a brief time, it seemed as though the nation's youth had gone berserk, indulging in a wave of experimentation with drugs, sex, and rock music. Older Americans believed that all the nation's traditional values, from the Puritan work ethic to the family, were under attack. Not all American youth joined in the cultural insurgency; the rebellion was generally limited to children of the upper-middle class. But like the flappers of the 1920s, the protesters set the tone for an entire era and left a lasting impression on American society.

Protesting the Vietnam War

The most dramatic aspect of the youthful rebellion came in opposing the Vietnam War. The first student "teach-ins" began at the University of Michigan in March 1965; soon they spread

👁 **Watch** the **Video**   **Protests Against the Vietnam War**

Antiwar demonstrators protest in Central Park, New York City on April 15, 1967. Four hundred thousand peace demonstrators, with Martin Luther King, Jr. leading the procession, marched from Central Park to the United Nations to demand a halt to the American bombing of North Vietnam.

to campuses across the nation. More than twenty thousand protesters, under SDS auspices, gathered in Washington in April to listen to entertainers Joan Baez and Judy Collins sing antiwar songs. "End the War in Vietnam Now, Stop the Killing" read the signs.

One of the great ironies of the Vietnam War was the system of student draft deferments, which enabled most of those enrolled in college to avoid military service. As a result, the children of the well-to-do, who were more likely to attend college, were able to escape the draft. One survey revealed that men from disadvantaged families, including a disproportionately large number of African and Hispanic Americans, were twice as likely to be drafted and engage in combat in Vietnam as those from more privileged backgrounds. Consequently, a sense of guilt led many college activists who were safe from Vietnam because of their student status to take the lead in denouncing an unjust war.

As the fighting in Southeast Asia intensified in 1966 and 1967, the protests grew larger and the slogans more extreme. "Hey, Hey, LBJ, how many kids did you kill today?" chanted students as they proclaimed, "Hell, no, we won't go!" At the Pentagon in October 1967, more than a hundred thousand demonstrators—mainly male students but housewives, teachers, and young professionals as well—confronted a cordon of military policemen guarding the heart of the nation's war machine.

The climax came in the spring of 1968. Driven by both opposition to the war and concern for social justice, the SDS and African American radicals at Columbia University joined forces in April. They seized five buildings, effectively paralyzing one of the country's leading colleges. After eight days of tension, the New York City police regained control. The brutal repression quickened the pace of protest elsewhere. Students held sit-ins and marches at more than one hundred colleges, from Cheyney State in Pennsylvania to Northwestern in Illinois.

The students failed to stop the war, but they did succeed in gaining a voice in their education. University administrations allowed undergraduates to sit on faculty curriculum-planning committees and gave up their once rigid control of dormitory and social life. But the students' greatest impact lay outside politics and the campus. They spawned a cultural uprising that transformed the manners and morals of America.

The Cultural Revolution

In contrast to the elitist political revolt of the SDS, the cultural rebellion by youth in the 1960s was pervasive. Led by college students, young people challenged the prevailing adult values in clothing, hairstyles, sexual conduct, work habits, and music. Blue jeans and love beads took the place of business suits and wristwatches; long hair and unkempt beards for men, bare feet and bralessness for women became a new uniform of protest. Families gave way to communes for the "hippies" and "flower children" of the 1960s. A "summer of love" in San Francisco's Haight Ashbury district in 1967 drew hundreds of thousands of young men and women from all across the country to sample free sex, free drugs, and free medical care (the last required to deal with the former two). Underground newspapers proliferated,

rejecting the values and opinions of the media establishment. Experimental art and film smashed the models of highbrow art and Hollywood.

Music became the touchstone of the counterculture. Folksingers such as Joan Baez and Bob Dylan, popular for their songs of social protest in the mid-1960s, gave way first to rock groups such as the Beatles, whose lyrics were often suggestive of drug use, and then to "acid rock" as symbolized by the Grateful Dead. The climactic event of the counterculture during the decade came at the Woodstock concert at Bethel in upstate New York when 400,000 young people indulged in a three-day festival of rock music, drug experimentation, and public sexual activity.

Former Harvard psychology professor Timothy Leary encouraged youth to join him in trying out the drug scene. Millions accepted his invitation to "tune in, turn on, drop out" literally, as they experimented with marijuana and with LSD, a new and dangerous chemical hallucinogen. The ultimate expression of insurgency was the Yippie movement, led by Jerry Rubin and Abbie Hoffman. Shrewd buffoons who mocked the consumer culture, they delighted in capitalizing on the mood of social protest to win attention. Once, when testifying before a congressional committee investigating internal subversion, Rubin dressed as a Revolutionary War soldier; Hoffman appeared in the gallery of the New York Stock Exchange in 1967, raining money down on the cheering brokers below.

"Black Power"

The civil rights movement, which had spawned the mood of protest in the 1960s, fell on hard times later in the decade. The legislative triumphs of 1964 and 1965 were relatively easy victories over southern bigotry; now the movement faced the far more complex problem of achieving economic equality in the cities of the North, where more than half of the nation's African Americans lived in poverty. The civil rights movement had raised the expectations of urban African Americans for improvement; frustration mounted as they failed to experience any significant economic gain.

The first sign of trouble came in the summer of 1964, when African American teenagers in Harlem and Rochester, New York, rioted. The next summer, a massive outburst of rage and destruction swept over the Watts area of Los Angeles as the inhabitants burned buildings and looted stores. Riots in the summer of 1966 were less destructive, but in 1967 the worst ones yet took place in Newark and in Detroit, where forty-three were killed and thousands were injured. The mobs attacked the shops and stores, expressing a burning grievance against a consumer society from which they were excluded by their poverty.

The civil rights coalition fell apart, a victim of both its legislative success and economic failure. Black militants took over the leadership of the Student Nonviolent Coordinating Committee (SNCC); they disdained white help and even reversed Martin Luther King's insistence on nonviolence. The SNCC's new leader, Stokely Carmichael, told blacks they should seize power in those parts of the South where they outnumbered whites. "I am not going to beg the white man for anything I deserve," he said, "I'm going to take it." Soon his calls for "black power" became a rallying cry for more militant blacks who advocated the need for African Americans to form "our own institutions, credit unions, co-ops, political parties" and even write "our own history."

Others went further than calls for ethnic separation. H. Rap Brown, who replaced Carmichael as the leader of the SNCC in 1967, told an African American crowd in Cambridge, Maryland, to "get your guns" and "burn this town down"; Huey Newton, one of the founders of the militant Black Panther party, proclaimed, "We make the statement, quoting from Chairman Mao, that political power comes through the barrel of a gun."

King suffered the most from this extremism. His denunciation of the Vietnam War cost him the support of the Johnson administration and alienated him from the more conservative civil rights groups such as the NAACP and the Urban League. He finally seized on poverty as the proper enemy for attack, but before he could lead his Poor People's March on Washington in 1968, he was assassinated in Memphis in early April.

Both blacks and whites realized the nation had lost its most eloquent voice for racial harmony. His tragic death elevated King to the status of a martyr, but it also led to one last outbreak of urban violence. African Americans exploded in angry riots in 125 cities across the nation; the worst rioting took place in Washington, D.C., where buildings were set on fire within a few blocks of the White House. "It was as if the city were being abandoned to an invading army," wrote a British journalist. "Clouds of smoke hung over the Potomac, evoking memories of the London blitz."

Yet there was a positive side to the emotions engendered by black nationalism. Leaders urged African Americans to take pride in their ethnic heritage, to embrace their blackness as a positive value. African Americans began to wear Afro hairstyles and dress in dashikis, emphasizing their African roots. Students began to demand new black studies programs in the colleges; the word *Negro*—identified with white supremacy of the past—virtually disappeared from usage overnight, replaced by the favored *Afro-American* or *black*. Singer James Brown best expressed the sense of racial identity: "Say It Loud—I'm Black and I'm Proud."

Ethnic Nationalism

Other groups quickly emulated the African American phenomenon. Native Americans decried the callous use of their identity as football mascots; in response, universities such as Stanford changed their symbols. Puerto Ricans demanded their history be included in school and college texts. Polish, Italian, and Czech groups insisted on respect for their nationalities. Congress acknowledged these demands with passage of the Ethnic Heritage Studies Act of 1972. Instead of trying to melt all groups down into a standard American type, Congress now gave what one sponsor of the measure called "official recognition to ethnicity as a positive constructive force in our society today."

Mexican Americans were in the forefront of the ethnic groups that became active in the 1970s. The primary impulse came from the efforts of César Chávez to organize the poorly paid grape pickers and lettuce workers in California into the National Farm Workers Association (NFWA). Chávez appealed to ethnic nationalism in mobilizing Mexican American field hands to strike against grape growers in the San Joaquin Valley in 1965. A national boycott of grapes by Mexican Americans and their sympathizers among the young people of the counterculture led to a series of hard-fought victories over the growers. The five-year struggle resulted in a union victory in 1970, but at an enormous cost— 95 percent of the farmworkers involved had lost their homes and their cars. Nevertheless, Chávez succeeded in raising the hourly wage of farmworkers in California to $3.53 by 1977 (it had been $1.20 in 1965).

Chávez's efforts helped spark an outburst of ethnic consciousness among Mexican Americans that swept through the urban barrios of the Southwest. Mexican American leaders campaigned for bilingual programs and improved educational opportunities. Young activists began to call themselves Chicanos, which had previously been a derogatory term, and to take pride in their cultural heritage; in 1968, they succeeded in establishing the first Mexican American studies program at California State College at Los Angeles. Campus leaders called for reform, urging high school students to insist on improvements. Heeding such appeals, nearly ten thousand students at East Los Angeles high schools walked out of class in March 1968. These walkouts sparked similar movements in San Antonio, Texas, and Phoenix, Arizona, and led to the introduction of

In March 1966, César Chávez, shown here talking with workers, led striking grape pickers on a 250-mile march from Delano, California, to the state capital at Sacramento to dramatize the plight of the migrant farmworkers. With the slogan "God is beside you on the picket line," the march took on the character of a religious pilgrimage.

📖 Read the Document   National Organization for Women, Statement of
Purpose (1966)

Betty Friedan was a writer and a major American feminist during the 1960s and 1970s. She was the founder of the National Organization for Women (NOW), and her book *The Feminist Mystique* helped ignite the "second wave" of American feminism in the 20th century.

bilingual programs in grade schools and the hiring of more Chicano teachers at all levels.

Women's Liberation

Active as they were in the civil rights and antiwar movements, women soon learned that the male leaders of these causes were little different from corporate executives—they expected women to fix the food and type the communiqués while the men made the decisions. Understandably, women soon realized that they could only achieve respect and equality by mounting their own protest.

In some ways, the position of women in American society was worse in the 1960s than it had been in the 1920s. After forty years, a lower percentage of women were enrolled in the nation's colleges and professional schools. Women were still relegated to stereotyped occupations such as nursing and teaching; there were few female lawyers and even fewer women doctors. And gender roles, as portrayed on television commercials, continued to call for the husband to be the breadwinner and the wife to be the homemaker.

Betty Friedan was one of the first to seize on the sense of grievance and discrimination that developed among white middle-class women in the 1960s. The beginning of the effort to raise women's consciousness was her 1963 book, *The Feminine Mystique*. Calling the American home "a comfortable concentration camp," she attacked the prevailing view that women were completely contented with their housekeeping and child-rearing tasks, claiming that housewives had no self-esteem and no sense of identity. "I'm a server of food and putter on of pants and a bedmaker," a mother of four told Friedan, "somebody who can be called on when you want something. But who am I?"

The 1964 Civil Rights Act helped women attack economic inequality head-on by making it illegal to discriminate in employment on the basis of gender. Women filed suit for equal wages, demanded that companies provide day care for their infants and preschool children, and entered politics to lobby against laws that—in the guise of protection of a weaker gender—were unfair to women. As the women's liberation movement grew, its advocates began to attack laws banning abortion and waged a campaign to toughen the enforcement of rape laws.

The women's movement met with many of the same obstacles as other protest groups in the 1960s. The moderate leadership of the **National Organization for Women (NOW)**, founded by Betty Friedan in 1966, soon was challenged by those with more extreme views. Ti-Grace Atkinson and Susan Brownmiller attacked revered institutions—the family and the home—and denounced sexual intercourse with men, calling it a method of male domination. Many women were repelled by the harsh rhetoric of the extremists and expressed satisfaction with their lives. But despite these disagreements, most women supported the effort to achieve equal status with men, and in 1972, Congress responded by voting to send the Equal Rights Amendment to the state legislatures for ratification.

The Return of Richard Nixon

How did the Vietnam War influence American politics?

The turmoil of the 1960s reached a crescendo in 1968 as the American people responded to the two dominant events of the decade—the war in Vietnam and the cultural insurgency at home. In an election marked by a series of bizarre events, including riots and an assassination, Richard Nixon staged a remarkable comeback to win the post denied him in 1960.

Vietnam Undermines Lyndon Johnson

A controversial Vietcong offensive in early 1968 proved to be the decisive event in breaking the stalemate in Vietnam and driving Lyndon Johnson from office. Using deceptive tactics, the North Vietnamese began a prolonged siege of an American marine base at Khe Sanh, deep in the northern interior. Fearing another Dien Bien Phu, Westmoreland rushed in reinforcements, sending more than 40 percent of all American infantry and armor battalions into the two northernmost provinces of South Vietnam.

The Vietcong then used the traditional lull in the fighting at Tet, the lunar New Year, to launch a surprise attack in the heavily populated cities. Beginning on January 30, 1968, the Vietcong struck at thirty-six of the forty-four provincial capitals. The most daring raid came at the American embassy compound in Saigon. Although the guerrillas were unable to penetrate the embassy proper, for six hours television cameras caught the dramatic battle that ensued in the courtyard before military police finally overcame the attackers.

Although caught off guard, American and South Vietnamese forces succeeded in repulsing the **Tet offensive** quickly everywhere except in Hue, the old imperial capital, which was retaken only after three weeks of heavy fighting that left this beautiful city, in the words of one observer, "a shattered, stinking hulk, its streets choked with rubble and rotting bodies."

Tet proved to be the turning point of the Vietnam War. Although the communists failed to win control of the cities and suffered heavy losses, they still held on to most of the rural areas and had scored an impressive political victory. For months, President Johnson had been telling the American people the war was almost over and victory was in sight; suddenly it appeared to be nearly lost. CBS-TV newscaster Walter Cronkite took a quick trip to Saigon to find out what had happened. Horrified at what he saw, he exclaimed to his guides, "What the hell is going on? I thought we were winning the war." He returned home to tell the American people, "It seems now more certain than ever that the bloody experience of Vietnam is to end in a stalemate."

President Johnson reluctantly came to the same conclusion after the Joint Chiefs of Staff requested an additional 205,000 troops to achieve victory in Vietnam following the Tet offensive. He began to listen to his new secretary of defense, Clark Clifford, who had replaced Robert McNamara in January 1968. In mid-March, after receiving advice from the "wise men," a group of experienced cold warriors that included such illustrious figures

as Dean Acheson and Omar Bradley, the president decided to limit the bombing of North Vietnam in an effort to open up peace negotiations with Hanoi. In a speech to the nation on Sunday evening, March 31, 1968, Johnson outlined his plans for a new effort at ending the war peacefully and then concluded by saying, as proof of his sincerity, "I shall not seek, and I will not accept, the nomination of my party for another term as your president."

In the fourteen years since the siege of Dien Bien Phu, American policy had gone full cycle in Vietnam. Even though Eisenhower had decided against using force to rescue the French, his commitment to the Diem regime in Saigon had led eventually to American military involvement on a massive scale. Three years of inconclusive fighting and a steadily mounting loss of American lives had disillusioned the American people and finally cost Lyndon Johnson the presidency. And the full price the nation would have to pay for its folly in Southeast Asia was still unknown—the Vietnam experience would continue to cast a shadow over American life for years to come.

The Democrats Divide

Lyndon Johnson's withdrawal from the presidential race after the Tet offensive set the tone for the 1968 election. LBJ's decision had come in response to political as well as military realities. By 1966, the antiwar movement had spread from the college campuses to Capitol Hill. Chairman J. William Fulbright gave the protests a new respectability when his Senate Foreign Relations Committee held probing hearings on the war, broadcast on television to the entire country. Johnson began to feel like a prisoner in the White House, since in his infrequent public appearances he was hounded by larger and larger groups of antiwar demonstrators, whose taunts and jeers wounded him.

The essentially leaderless protest against the war had taken on a new quality on January 3, 1968, when Senator Eugene McCarthy, a Democrat from Minnesota, announced he would challenge LBJ for the party's presidential nomination. Intellectual, cool, and aloof, McCarthy raised the banner of idealism, telling audiences, "Whatever is morally necessary must be made politically possible." College students flocked to his campaign, shaving their beards and cutting their hair to be "clean for Gene." In the New Hampshire primary in early March, the nation's earliest political test, McCarthy shocked the political experts by coming within a few thousand votes of defeating President Johnson.

McCarthy's strong showing in New Hampshire led Robert Kennedy, who had been weighing the risks in challenging Johnson, to enter the presidential race. Elected senator from New York in 1964, Bobby Kennedy had become an effective voice for the disadvantaged, as well as an increasingly severe critic of the Vietnam War. Unlike McCarthy, whose appeal was largely limited to upper-middle-class whites and college students, Kennedy attracted strong support among blue-collar workers, African Americans, Chicanos, and other minorities who formed the nucleus of the continuing New Deal coalition.

Lyndon Johnson's dramatic withdrawal caused an uproar in the Democratic party. With Johnson's tacit backing and strong support from party regulars and organized labor, Vice President Hubert H. Humphrey immediately declared his candidacy.

Humphrey, a classic Cold War liberal who had worked equally hard for social reform at home and American expansion abroad, was totally unacceptable to the antiwar movement. Accordingly, he decided to avoid the primaries and work for the nomination within the framework of the party.

Kennedy and McCarthy, the two antiwar candidates, were thus left to compete in the spring primaries, requiring agonizing choices among those who desired change. Kennedy won everywhere except in Oregon, but his narrow victory in California ended in tragedy when a Palestinian immigrant, Sirhan Sirhan, assassinated him in a Los Angeles hotel.

With his strongest opponent struck down, Hubert Humphrey had little difficulty at the Chicago convention. Backed by that city's political boss, Mayor Richard Daley, the vice president relied on party leaders to defeat an antiwar resolution and win the nomination on the first ballot by a margin of more than two to one.

Humphrey's triumph was marred by violence outside the heavily guarded convention hall. Radical groups had urged their members to come to Chicago to agitate; the turnout was relatively small but included many who were ready to provoke the authorities in their despair over the convention's outcome. Epithets and cries of "pigs" brought on a savage response from Daley's police. "The cops had one thing on their mind," commented journalist Jimmy Breslin. "Club and then gas, club and then gas, club and then gas."

The bitter fumes of tear gas hung in the streets for days afterward; the battered heads and bodies of demonstrators and innocent bystanders alike flooded the city's hospital emergency rooms. What an official investigation later termed a "police riot" marred Humphrey's nomination and made a sad mockery out of his call for "the politics of joy." The Democratic party itself had become the next victim of the Vietnam War.

The Republican Resurgence

The primary beneficiary of the Democratic debacle was Richard Nixon. Written off as politically dead after his unsuccessful race for governor of California in 1962, Nixon had slowly rebuilt his place within the party by working loyally for Barry Goldwater in 1964 and for GOP congressional candidates two years later. Positioning himself squarely in the middle, he quickly became the front-runner for the Republican nomination. At the GOP convention in Miami Beach, Nixon won an easy first-ballot nomination and chose Maryland governor Spiro Agnew as his running mate. Agnew, little known on the national scene, had won the support of conservatives by taking a strong stand against African American rioters.

In the fall campaign, Nixon opened up a wide lead by avoiding controversy and reaping the benefit of discontent with the Vietnam War. He played the peace issue shrewdly, appearing to advocate an end to the conflict without ever taking a definite stand. The United States should "end the war and win the peace," he declared, hinting he had a secret formula for peace but never revealing what it was. Above all, he chose the role of reconciler for a nation torn by emotion, a leader who promised to bring a divided country together again.

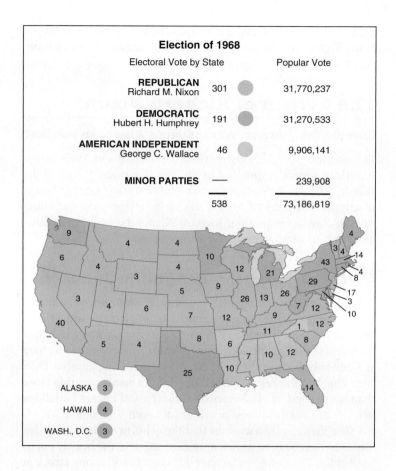

Election of 1968

	Electoral Vote by State		Popular Vote
REPUBLICAN Richard M. Nixon	301		31,770,237
DEMOCRATIC Hubert H. Humphrey	191		31,270,533
AMERICAN INDEPENDENT George C. Wallace	46		9,906,141
MINOR PARTIES	—		239,908
	538		73,186,819

ALASKA 3
HAWAII 4
WASH., D.C. 3

Humphrey, in contrast, found himself hounded by antiwar demonstrators who heckled him constantly. He walked a tightwire, desperate for the continued support of President Johnson but handicapped by LBJ's stubborn refusal to end all bombing of North Vietnam. Only when he broke with Johnson in late September by announcing that if elected he would "stop the bombing of North Vietnam as an acceptable risk for peace" did his campaign begin to gain momentum.

Unfortunately for Humphrey, a third-party candidate cut deeply into the normal Democratic majority. George C. Wallace had first gained national attention as the racist governor of Alabama whose motto was "Segregation now ... segregation tomorrow ... segregation forever." In 1964, he had shown surprising strength in Democratic primaries in northern states. By attacking both black leaders and their liberal white allies, Wallace appealed to the sense of powerlessness among the urban working classes. "Liberals, intellectuals, and longhairs have run the country for too long," Wallace told his followers. "When I get to Washington," he promised, "I'll throw all these phonies and their briefcases into the Potomac."

Running on the ticket of the American Independent Party, Wallace was a close third in the September polls, gaining support from more than 20 percent of the electorate. But as the election neared, his following declined. Humphrey continued to gain, especially after Johnson agreed in late October to end all bombing of North Vietnam. By the first week in November, the outcome was too close for the experts to call.

Nixon won the election with the smallest share of the popular vote of any winning candidate since 1916. But he swept a broad band of states from Virginia and the Carolinas through the Midwest to the Pacific for a clear-cut victory in the electoral college. Humphrey held on to the urban Northeast; Wallace took just five states in the Deep South, but his heavy inroads into blue-collar districts in the North shattered the New Deal coalition.

Conclusion: The End of an Era

The election of 1968 was a repudiation of the politics of protest and the cultural insurgency of the mid-1960s. The combined popular vote for Nixon and Wallace, 56.5 percent of the electorate, signified there was a silent majority that was fed up with violence and confrontation. A growing concern over psychedelic drugs, rock music, long hair, and sexual permissiveness had offset the usual Democratic advantage on economic issues and led to the election of a Republican president.

Richard Nixon's victory marked the end of an era with the passing of two concepts that had guided American life since the 1930s. First, the liberal reform impulse, which reached its zenith with the Great Society legislation in 1965, had clearly run its course. Civil rights, Medicare, and federal aid to education would continue in place, but Nixon's election signaled a strong reaction against the growth of federal power. At the same time, the Vietnam fiasco spelled the end of an activist foreign policy that had begun with American entry into World War II. Containment, so successful in protecting western Europe against the Soviet threat, had proved a disastrous failure when applied on a global scale. The last three decades of the twentieth century would witness a struggle to replace outmoded liberal internationalism with new policies at home and abroad.

Study Resources

 Take the **Study Plan** for **Chapter 30** *The Turbulent Sixties* on **MyHistoryLab**

TIME LINE

1961 JFK establishes Peace Corps (March); U.S.-backed Bay of Pigs invasion crushed by Cubans (April)

1962 President Kennedy forces U.S. Steel to roll back price hike (April); Cuban missile crisis takes world to brink of nuclear war (October)

1963 United States, Great Britain, and USSR sign Limited Nuclear Test Ban treaty (August); JFK assassinated; Lyndon B. Johnson sworn in as president (November)

1964 President Johnson declares war on poverty (January); Congress overwhelmingly passes Gulf of Tonkin Resolution (August); Johnson wins presidency in landslide (November)

1965 LBJ commits fifty thousand American troops to combat in Vietnam (July); Congress enacts Medicare and Medicaid (July)

1966 National Organization for Women (NOW) formed

1967 Israel wins Six-Day War in Middle East (June); Riots in Detroit kill forty-three, injure two thousand, leave five thousand homeless (July)

1968 Vietcong launch the Tet offensive (January); Johnson announces he will not seek reelection (March); Martin Luther King, Jr., assassinated in Memphis (April); Robert Kennedy assassinated in Los Angeles (June)

CHAPTER REVIEW

Kennedy Intensifies the Cold War

 How did the Cold War intensify under Kennedy?

Kennedy increased American support to South Vietnam and pressured the Cuban government of Fidel Castro. Kennedy raised troop levels in Vietnam and authorized the overthrow of Diem. He ordered a covert operation against Castro at the Bay of Pigs (which failed) and delivered an ultimatum to the Soviets to pull their missiles out of Cuba (which succeeded). (p. 708)

The New Frontier at Home

 What was the "New Frontier," and what did it accomplish?

The "New Frontier" was Kennedy's domestic program, and on its most important issue, civil rights, it achieved mixed results. Kennedy supported civil rights, but hesitantly. Black activists, especially Martin Luther King, Jr., pushed the cause of racial equality farther than Kennedy was prepared to take it. (p. 713)

"Let Us Continue"

 What were Johnson's domestic priorities, and what were his achievements?

Johnson's "Great Society" included the 1964 Civil Rights Act and the 1965 Voting Rights Act; Medicare, which provided health insurance for the elderly; and federal aid to education. (p. 717)

Johnson Escalates the Vietnam War

 How did Johnson's Vietnam policy evolve?

Johnson seized upon an ambiguous incident in the Gulf of Tonkin to persuade Congress to grant him authority to escalate American involvement in Vietnam. He initiated a major troop buildup and air attacks against North Vietnam. The escalation produced only a bloody stalemate. (p. 721)

Years of Turmoil

 Why were there protests in the 1960s?

During the 1960s, students protested the war in Vietnam. Many young people also rebelled against the values of their parents, experimenting with new kinds of music, clothing styles, and drugs. Black militants demanded faster progress toward racial equality, and sometimes employed violence to achieve it. César Chávez improved the lot of Mexican American farmworkers. Feminists sought greater equality for women. (p. 726)

The Return of Richard Nixon

 How did the Vietnam War influence American politics?

Johnson's failure in Vietnam discredited his administration and produced desire for change. He abandoned plans to run for reelection in 1968, opening the door to Richard Nixon. (p. 731)

KEY TERMS AND DEFINITIONS

New Frontier President John F. Kennedy's program to revitalize the stagnant economy and enact reform legislation in education, health care, and civil rights. p. 708

Bay of Pigs In April 1961, a group of Cuban exiles, organized and supported by the CIA, landed on the southern coast of Cuba in an effort to overthrow Fidel Castro. When the invasion ended in disaster, President Kennedy took full responsibility for it. p. 710

Cuban missile crisis In October 1962, the United States and the Soviet Union came close to nuclear war when President John F. Kennedy insisted that Nikita Khrushchev remove the 42 missiles he had secretly deployed in Cuba. The Soviets eventually did so, and the crisis ended. p. 711

Freedom ride Sponsored by the Congress of Racial Equality (CORE), freedom rides on buses by civil rights advocates in 1961 in the South were designed to test the enforcement of federal regulations that prohibited segregation in interstate public transportation. p. 714

March on Washington In August 1963, civil rights leaders organized a massive rally in Washington to urge passage of President John F. Kennedy's civil rights bill. The high point was Martin Luther King, Jr.'s "I Have a Dream" speech. p. 717

War on poverty President Lyndon Johnson declared war on poverty in his 1964 State of the Union address. A new Office of Economic Opportunity (OEO) oversaw programs to help the poor. p. 719

Great Society President Lyndon Johnson's name for his version of the Democratic reform program. In 1965, Congress passed many Great Society measures, including Medicare, civil rights legislation, and federal aid to education. p. 720

Medicare The 1965 Medicare Act provided Social Security funding for hospitalization insurance for people over age 65 and the disabled and a voluntary plan to cover doctor bills paid in part by the federal government. p. 720

Voting Rights Act of 1965 The 1965 Voting Rights Act banned literacy tests for voting rights and provided for federal registrars to assure the franchise to minority voters. p. 720

Gulf of Tonkin Resolution After a North Vietnamese attack on an American destroyer in the Gulf of Tonkin in 1964, Congress gave President Lyndon authority in this resolution to use force in Vietnam. p. 725

Students for a Democratic Society (SDS) Founded in 1962, the SDS was a popular college student organization that protested shortcomings in American life, notably racial injustice and the Vietnam War. It led thousands of protests before it split apart in the late 1960s. p. 727

National Organization for Women (NOW) Founded in 1966, NOW called for equal employment opportunity and equal pay for women. It also championed the legalization of abortion and an equal rights amendment to the Constitution. p. 730

Tet offensive In February 1968, the Viet Cong launched a major offensive in the cities of South Vietnam. Although caught by surprise, American and South Vietnam forces quashed this attack. But the Tet offensive was a blow to American public opinion and led President Lyndon Johnson to seek a negotiated peace. p. 731

CRITICAL THINKING QUESTIONS

1. How did American foreign policy in the 1960s reflect the personalities of Kennedy and Johnson?

2. Why did MLK, Jr., command such respect?

3. How did the War on Poverty influence Johnson's handling of the Vietnam War?

4. Why did Americans turn to Nixon in 1968?

MyHistoryLab Media Assignments

Find these resources in the Media Assignments folder for Chapter 30 on MyHistoryLab

Kennedy Intensifies the Cold War

Watch the **Video** Kennedy–Nixon Debate p. 707

Watch the **Video** President John F. Kennedy and the Cuban Missile Crisis p. 712

The New Frontier at Home

Watch the **Video** Photographing the Civil Rights Movement p. 715

Watch the **Video** Civil Rights March on Washington p. 716

"Let Us Continue"

Read the **Document** The Civil Rights Act of 1964 p. 719

View the **Map** Impact of the Voting Rights Act of 1965 p. 721

Johnson Escalates the Vietnam War

Complete the **Assignment** Unintended Consequences: The Second Great Migration p. 722

View the **Map** Vietnam War p. 724

Years of Turmoil

Watch the **Video** Protests Against the Vietnam War p. 727

Read the **Document** National Organization for Women, Statement of Purpose (1966) p. 730

■ Indicates Study Plan Media Assignment

31 The Rise of a New Conservatism, 1969–1988

Contents and Learning Objectives

Reagan and America's Shift to the Right

In October 1964, the Republican National Committee sponsored a televised address by Hollywood actor Ronald Reagan on behalf of Barry Goldwater's presidential candidacy. Reagan's speech had originally been aired on a Los Angeles station; the resulting outpouring of praise and campaign contributions led to its national rebroadcast.

In contrast to Goldwater's strident rhetoric, Reagan used relaxed, confident, and persuasive terms to put forth the case for a return to individual freedom. Instead of the usual choice between increased government activity and less government involvement, often couched in terms of the left and the right, Reagan presented the options of either going up or down—"up to the maximum of human freedom consistent with law and order, or down to the ant heap of totalitarianism." Then, borrowing a phrase from FDR, he told his audience: "You and I have a rendezvous with destiny. We can preserve for our children this the last best hope of man on Earth, or we can sentence them to take the first step into a thousand years of darkness."

Although the speech did not rescue Goldwater's unpopular candidacy, it marked the beginning of Ronald Reagan's remarkable political career. A popular actor whose movie career had begun to fade in the 1950s,

Reagan had become an effective television performer as host of *The General Electric Theater.* His political views, once liberal, moved steadily to the right as he became a spokesperson for a major American corporation. In 1965, a group of wealthy friends persuaded him, largely on the basis of the success of "the speech," to run for the California governorship.

Reagan proved to be an attractive candidate. His approachable manner and his mastery of television enabled him to present his strongly conservative message without appearing to be a rigid ideologue of the right. He won handily by appealing effectively to rising middle-class suburban resentment over high taxes, expanding welfare programs, and bureaucratic regulation.

In his two terms as governor, Reagan displayed natural ability as a political leader. Instead of insisting on implementing all of his conservative beliefs, he proved surprisingly flexible. Faced with a Democratic legislature, he yielded on raising taxes and increasing state spending while managing to trim the welfare rolls. Symbolic victories were his specialty; in one example he managed to confront campus radicals and fire Clark Kerr, chancellor of the University of California, while at the same time generously funding higher education.

Ronald Reagan and his wife Nancy wave to the crowd during the 1980 Republican convention in Detroit.

By the time Reagan left the governor's office in 1974, many signs pointed to a growing conservative mood across the nation. In a popular rebellion against escalating property taxes in 1978, California's voters passed Proposition 13, which slashed property taxes in half and resulted in a gradual reduction in social services. Religious leaders were especially outraged over the 1962 Supreme Court ruling in *Engel* v. *Vitale* outlawing school prayer on the grounds that it was "no part of the business of government to compose official prayers." In the South, where daily prayers were the customary way of beginning the school day, the reaction was intense. One Alabama congressman denounced the Supreme Court justices, proclaiming, "They put the Negroes in the schools and now they're driving God out."

Concern over school prayer, along with rising abortion and divorce rates, impelled religious groups to engage in political activity to defend what they viewed as traditional family values. Jerry Falwell, a successful Virginia radio and television evangelist, founded the **Moral Majority**, a fundamentalist group dedicated to preserving the "American way of life." (See the Feature Essay, "The Christian Right," pp. 756–757.)

The population shift of the 1970s, especially the rapid growth of the Sunbelt region in the South and West (see p. 774), added momentum to the conservative upsurge. Those moving to the Sunbelt tended to be white, middle- and upper-class suburbanites—mainly skilled workers, young professionals, and business executives who were attracted both by economic opportunity and by a political climate emphasizing low taxes, less government regulation, and more reliance on the marketplace. The political impact of population shifts from east to west and north to south during the 1970s was reflected in the congressional gains (seventeen seats) by Sunbelt and far western states after the 1980 census.

Conservatives also succeeded, for the first time since World War II, in making their cause intellectually respectable. Scholars and academics on the right flourished in new "think tanks"; writer William Buckley and economist Milton Friedman proved to be effective advocates of conservative causes in print and on television. **Neoconservatism**, led by Norman Podhoretz's magazine *Commentary,* became fashionable among many intellectuals who were former liberal stalwarts. They denounced liberals for being too soft on the Communist threat abroad and too willing to compromise high standards at home in the face of demands for equality from African Americans, women, and the

disadvantaged. Neoconservatives called for a reaffirmation of capitalism and a new emphasis on what was right about America rather than an obsessive concern with social ills.

By the end of the 1970s, a decade marked by military defeat in Vietnam, political scandal that destroyed the administration of Richard Nixon, economic ills that vexed the country under Gerald Ford and Jimmy Carter, and unprecedented social strains on families and traditional institutions, millions of Americans had come to believe that Cold War liberalism had run its course. Ronald Reagan, as the acknowledged leader of the conservative resurgence, was ideally placed to capitalize on this discontent. His personal charm softened the hard edges of his right-wing call to arms, and his conviction that America could regain its traditional self-confidence by reaffirming basic ideals had a broad appeal to a nation facing new challenges at home and abroad. In 1976, Reagan had barely lost to President Ford at the Republican convention; four years later, he overcame an early upset by George Bush in Iowa to win the GOP presidential nomination handily.

In his acceptance speech at the Republican convention in Detroit, Reagan set forth the themes that endeared him to conservatives: less government, a balanced budget, family values, and peace through greater military spending. Unlike Barry Goldwater, who frightened people with his rigid ideology, Reagan offered reassurance and hope for the future. He spoke of restoring to the federal government "the capacity to do the people's work without dominating their lives." As historian Robert Dallek pointed out, Reagan "assured his listeners that he was no radical idealist courting defeat, but a sensible, thoroughly likable American with a surefire formula for success that would please everyone." In Ronald Reagan, the Republicans had found the perfect figure to lead Americans into a new conservative era.

The Tempting of Richard Nixon

What were the major accomplishments and failures of the Nixon presidency?

Following the divisive campaign of 1968, Richard Nixon's presidency proved to be one of the most controversial in American history. Nixon's domestic policies had limited success, and though his diplomacy broke new ground in relations with China and the Soviet Union and ended American fighting in Vietnam, he was forced to resign the presidency under the dark cloud of the Watergate scandal.

Pragmatic Liberalism

Nixon began his first term on a hopeful note, promising the nation peace and respite from the chaos of the 1960s. Rejecting the divisions that had driven Americans apart, he pledged in his inaugural address to bring the country together. "We cannot learn from one another," he said, "until we stop shouting at one another—until we speak quietly enough so that our words can be heard as well as our voices."

Nixon's moderate language appeared to herald a return to the politics of accommodation that had characterized the Eisenhower era. Faced with a Democratic Congress, Nixon, like Ike, reconciled himself to the broad outlines of the welfare state. Instead of trying to overthrow the Great Society, he focused on making the federal bureaucracy function more efficiently. In some areas he actually expanded federal programs and responsibilities.

On civil rights, for example, Nixon was the first president to adopt affirmative action as an explicit policy. His labor secretary, George Shultz, applied the "Philadelphia plan," which had evolved to ensure the hiring of minority contractors in Pennsylvania's largest city, to other cities and eventually to all federal contracts worth more than $50,000. Nixon also expanded affirmative action to include women, vastly increasing the scope of the policy. The goal, a Nixon executive order explained, was for the federal government to achieve "the prompt and full utilization of minorities and women at all levels in all segments of its work force."

Nixon broke new ground in other areas associated with liberalism. He approved the creation of the Occupational Safety and Health Administration, which assumed responsibility for reducing workplace injuries. He oversaw the establishment of the Environmental Protection Agency (EPA), the federal watchdog on environmental affairs. He signed the Clean Air Act, which provided the basis for tackling smog and other air pollutants. He supported automatic cost-of-living increases to Social Security, ensuring that the elderly not lose ground to the inflation that increasingly vexed the American economy.

Many liberals suspected Nixon's motives, and not without reason. Nixon's liberalism was pragmatic, even opportunistic, rather than principled. In private conversations, he could be demeaning of African Americans, Jews, and other minorities. But, planning big changes in American foreign policy, he chose not to pick fights with congressional Democrats or buck the liberal tide that was still flowing from the 1960s.

He did try to shape that tide. Under the label of the "new federalism," he shifted responsibility for many social programs from Washington to state and local authorities. He developed the concept of revenue sharing, by which federal funds were dispersed to state, county, and city agencies to meet local needs. In 1972, he signed a law that shared $30 billion with local governments over a five-year period. An accompanying ceiling of $2.5 billion a year on federal welfare payments meant that much of the revenue-sharing payments had to be allocated by cities and states to programs previously paid for by the federal government.

Nixon's civil rights policy was similarly calculating. Action by Congress and the Johnson administration had ensured that massive desegregation of southern schools, delayed for more than a decade by legal action, would begin just as Nixon took office. Nixon and his attorney general, John Mitchell, decided to shift the responsibility for this process to the courts. In the summer of 1969, the Justice Department asked a federal judge to delay the integration of thirty-three school districts in Mississippi. The Supreme Court quickly ruled against the Justice Department, declaring that "the obligation of every school district is to terminate dual school systems at once." Thus, in the minds of southern white voters, it was the hated Supreme Court, not Richard Nixon, who had forced them to integrate their schools.

The upshot of Nixon's domestic policies was to extend the welfare state in some areas, reshape it in others, and leave liberals and conservatives alike wondering just where Nixon stood.

Détente

Nixon didn't really care, because foreign policy—not domestic policy—was his pride and joy. Nixon had thought long about the state of the world, and he was determined to improve it. To assist him in this endeavor, he appointed Henry Kissinger to be national security adviser. A refugee from Nazi Germany, Kissinger had become a professor of government at Harvard, the author of several influential books, and an acknowledged authority on international affairs. Nixon and Kissinger approached foreign policy from a practical, realistic perspective. Instead of viewing the Cold War as an ideological struggle for survival with Communism, they saw it as a traditional great-power rivalry, one to be managed and controlled rather than to be won.

Nixon and Kissinger had a grand design. Realizing that recent events, especially the Vietnam War and the rapid Soviet arms buildup of the 1960s, had eroded America's position of primacy in the world, they planned a strategic retreat. Russia had great military strength, but its economy was weak, and it had a dangerous rival in China. Nixon planned to use American trade—notably grain and high technology—to induce Soviet cooperation, while at the same time improving U.S. relations with China.

Nixon and Kissinger shrewdly played the China card as their first step toward achieving **détente**—a relaxation of tension—with the Soviet Union. In February 1972, accompanied by a planeload of reporters and television camera crews, Nixon visited China, meeting with the Communist leaders and ending more than two decades of Sino–American hostility. Nixon agreed to establish an American liaison mission in Beijing as a first step toward diplomatic recognition.

The Soviets, who viewed China as a dangerous adversary, responded by agreeing to an arms control pact with the United States. The **Strategic Arms Limitation Talks (SALT)** had been under way since 1969. During a visit to Moscow in May 1972, Nixon signed two vital documents with Soviet leader Leonid Brezhnev. The first limited the two superpowers to two hundred antiballistic missiles (ABMs) apiece; the second froze the number of offensive ballistic missiles for a five-year period. The SALT I agreements recognized the existing Soviet lead in missiles, but the American deployment of multiple independently targeted reentry vehicles (MIRVs) ensured a continuing strategic advantage for the United States.

The SALT I agreements were most important as a symbolic first step toward control of the nuclear arms race. They signified that the United States and the Soviet Union were trying to achieve a settlement of their differences by peaceful means.

Ending the Vietnam War

Vietnam remained the one foreign policy challenge that Nixon could not overcome. He had a three-part plan to end the conflict—gradual withdrawal of American troops, accompanied by training of South Vietnamese forces to take over the combat role; renewed bombing; and a hard line in negotiations with Hanoi. The number of American soldiers in Vietnam fell from 540,000 in early 1969 to less than 30,000 by 1972; domestic opposition to the war declined sharply with the accompanying drop in casualties and reductions in the draft call.

Renewed bombing proved the most controversial part of the plan. As early as the spring of 1969, Nixon secretly ordered raids on Communist supply lines in neutral Cambodia. Then in April 1970, he ordered both air and ground strikes into Cambodia, causing a massive outburst of antiwar protests at home. Students demonstrated against the invasion of Cambodia on campuses across the nation. Tragedy struck at Kent State University in Ohio in early May. After rioters had firebombed an ROTC building, the governor sent in national guard troops who were taunted and harassed by irate students. The guardsmen then opened fire, killing four students and wounding eleven more. The victims were innocent bystanders; two were young women caught in the fusillade on their way between classes. A week later, two African American student demonstrators were killed at Jackson State

College in Mississippi; soon riots and protests raged on more than four hundred campuses across the country.

Nixon had little sympathy for the demonstrators, calling the students "bums" who were intent on "blowing up the campuses." The "silent majority" to whom he appealed seemed to agree; one poll showed that most Americans blamed the students, not the national guard, for the deaths at Kent State. An "Honor America Day" program, held in Washington, D.C., on July 4, attracted 250,000 people who heard Billy Graham and Bob Hope endorse the president's policies. Nixon's Cambodian invasion did little to shorten the Vietnam War, but the public reaction reinforced the president's resolve not to surrender.

The third tactic, negotiation with Hanoi, finally proved successful. Beginning in the summer of 1969, Kissinger held a series of secret meetings with North Vietnam's foreign minister, Le Duc Tho. In the summer and fall of 1972, the two sides neared agreement, but South Vietnamese objections blocked a settlement before the 1972 election. When the North Vietnamese tried to make last-minute changes, Nixon ordered a series of heavy

The photograph depicts the horror of the Kent State University shooting of thirteen unarmed college students by Ohio National Guardsmen on May 4, 1970. Some of the students who were shot were protesting President Nixon's invasion of Cambodia. In response to the Kent State tragedy, hundreds of high schools, colleges, and universities across America closed due to a student strike.

B-52 raids on Hanoi that finally led to the signing of a truce on January 27, 1973. In return for the release of all American prisoners of war, the United States agreed to remove its troops from South Vietnam within sixty days. The political clauses allowed the North Vietnamese to keep their troops in the South, thus virtually guaranteeing future control of all Vietnam by the Communists.

For two years after the accords the Communists waited, weighing, among other things, the willingness of Americans to continue to support South Vietnam. As Nixon became enmeshed in the Watergate scandal, his grip on foreign policy weakened, and by the time he was forced from office in August 1974, most Americans simply wanted to forget Vietnam. The following spring the Communists mounted a major offensive and in just weeks completed their takeover of Vietnam. Ten years after the American escalation of the war, and after the loss of sixty thousand American lives, the American effort to preserve South Vietnam from Communism had proved a tragic failure.

The Watergate Scandal

Nixon's Vietnam problems and especially his formulation of détente made him sensitive to the unauthorized release of information about American foreign policy. He had good reason for fearing leaks, since they might tip the administration's hand in sensitive negotiations with the Communists. When leaks did occur, Nixon grew outraged and demanded that they be stopped. The White House established an informal office of covert surveillance—the "plumbers," its operatives were called—which began by investigating the national security breaches but, during the presidential campaign of 1972, branched out into spying on Nixon's Democratic opponents and engaging in political dirty tricks.

Five of the "plumbers" were arrested in June 1972 during a break-in at the headquarters of the Democratic National Committee at the Watergate office complex in Washington. The Nixon White House took pains to conceal its connection to what its spokesman dismissed as a "third-rate burglary attempt." Nixon personally ordered the cover-up. "I want you to stonewall it, let them plead the Fifth Amendment, cover-up, or anything else," Nixon told John Mitchell, his former attorney general, and then campaign director.

The cover-up succeeded long enough to ensure Nixon's landslide reelection victory over Democrat George S. McGovern of South Dakota, but in the months after the election the cover-up began to unravel. James McCord, one of the Watergate burglars, was the first to break the silence. Sentenced to a long jail term by Judge John Sirica, McCord asked for leniency, informing Sirica he had received money from the White House and had been promised a presidential pardon in return for his silence. By April 1973, Nixon was compelled to fire aide John Dean, who had directed the cover-up but who now refused to become a scapegoat. Two other aides, H. R. Haldeman and John Ehrlichman, were forced to resign.

The Senate then appointed a special committee to investigate the unfolding **Watergate scandal**. In a week of dramatic testimony, Dean revealed the president's personal involvement in the cover-up. Still, it was basically a matter of whose word was to be believed—the president's or a discredited aide's—and Nixon hoped to weather the storm.

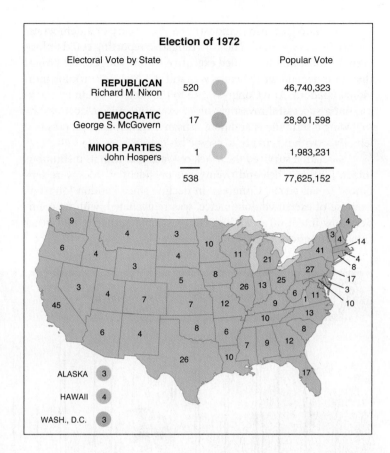

Election of 1972

	Electoral Vote by State		Popular Vote
REPUBLICAN Richard M. Nixon	520		46,740,323
DEMOCRATIC George S. McGovern	17		28,901,598
MINOR PARTIES John Hospers	1		1,983,231
	538		77,625,152

ALASKA 3
HAWAII 4
WASH., D.C. 3

The committee's discovery of the existence of tape recordings of conversations in the Oval Office, made regularly since 1970, proved the beginning of the end for Nixon. At first, the president tried to invoke executive privilege to withhold the tapes. When Archibald Cox, appointed as Watergate special prosecutor, demanded the release of the tapes, Nixon fired him. Yet the new Watergate prosecutor, Leon Jaworski, continued to press for the tapes. Nixon tried to release only a few of the less damaging ones, but the Supreme Court ruled unanimously in June 1974 that the tapes had to be turned over to Judge Sirica.

By this time, the House Judiciary Committee, acting on evidence compiled by the staff of the Senate committee, had voted three articles of impeachment, charging Nixon with obstruction of justice, abuse of power, and contempt of Congress. Faced with the release of tapes that directly implicated him in the cover-up, the president chose to resign on August 9, 1974.

Nixon's resignation proved to be the culmination of the Watergate scandal. The entire episode revealed both the weaknesses and strengths of the American political system. Most regrettable was the abuse of presidential authority—a reflection both of the growing power of the modern presidency and of fatal flaws in Richard Nixon's character. Unlike previous executive branch scandals such as the Whiskey Ring and Teapot Dome, Watergate involved a lust for power rather than for money. Realizing he had reached the White House almost by accident, Nixon did everything possible to retain his hold on his office. He used the plumbers to maintain executive secrecy, and he directed the Internal Revenue Service and the Justice Department to punish his enemies and reward his friends.

But Watergate also demonstrated the vitality of a democratic society. The press showed how investigative reporting could unlock even the most closely guarded executive secrets. Judge Sirica proved that an independent judiciary was still the best bulwark for individual freedom. And Congress rose to the occasion, both by carrying out a successful investigation of executive misconduct and by following a scrupulous and nonpartisan impeachment process that left Nixon with no chance to escape his fate.

The nation survived the shock of Watergate with its institutions intact. John Mitchell and twenty-five presidential aides were sentenced to jail terms. Congress, in decline since Lyndon Johnson's exercise of executive dominance, was rejuvenated, with its members now intent on extending congressional authority into other areas of American life.

View the Closer Look   Watergate Shipwreck

'I HAVE DISCOVERED THAT ACCORDING TO A SECRET TAPE OF JUNE 23, 1972, I **AM** A CROOK.'

This Watergate cartoon by *Milwaukee Journal* cartoonist Bill Sanders, "'I Have Discovered That According to a Secret Tape of June 23, 1972, I AM a crook," was published on August 6, 1974. The title is a play on Nixon's infamous "I am not a crook" speech given in November of 1973 during the height of the infamous scandal. The Watergate scandal revolved around Nixon's participation in the planning and cover-up of a break-in at the Democratic National Committee headquarters.

The Economy of Stagflation

How were oil and inflation linked during the 1970s?

In the midst of Watergate, the outbreak of war in the Middle East threatened a vital national interest: the unimpeded and inexpensive flow of oil to the United States. The resulting energy crisis helped spark a raging price inflation that had a profound impact on the national economy and on American society at large.

War and Oil

On October 6, 1973, Egypt and Syria launched a surprise attack on Israel. The fighting followed decades of tension between Israel and its Arab neighbors, which had grown only worse upon the stunning Israeli victory in the Six Days' War of 1967. In that conflict, the Israelis routed the Arabs, seizing the Golan Heights from Syria, the Sinai Peninsula from Egypt, and Jerusalem and the West Bank from Jordan. The Arabs ached for revenge, and in 1973 the Egyptians and Syrians attacked. Catching Israel off guard, they won early battles but eventually lost the initiative and were forced to give up the ground they had recovered. The Israelis would have delivered another devastating defeat to the Arabs if not for the diplomatic intervention of Nixon and Kissinger, who, despite America's previous strong support for Israel, believed a decisive Israeli victory would destabilize the Middle East even more.

The American diplomatic triumph, however, was offset by an unforeseen consequence of the October War (also called the Yom Kippur War, as it started on the Jewish holy day). On October 17, the Arab members of the **Organization of Petroleum Exporting Countries (OPEC)** announced a 5 percent cut in oil production, and vowed additional cuts of 5 percent each month until Israel surrendered the lands it had taken in 1967. Three days later, following Nixon's announcement of an emergency aid package for Israel, Saudi Arabia cut off oil shipments to the United States.

The Arab oil embargo had a disastrous impact on the American economy. With Arab producers cutting production by 25 percent from the September 1973 level, world supplies fell by 10 percent. For the United States, which imported one-third of its daily consumption, this meant a loss of nearly 2 million barrels a day. Long lines formed at gas stations as motorists who feared running out of fuel kept filling their tanks.

A dramatic increase in oil prices proved to be a far more significant result of the embargo. After the Arab embargo began, OPEC, led by the shah of Iran, raised crude oil prices

THE OIL SHOCKS: PRICE INCREASES OF CRUDE OIL AND GASOLINE, 1973–1985

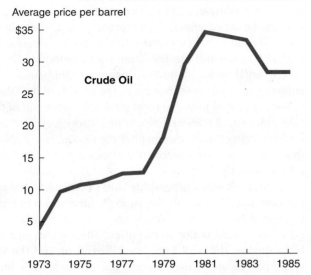

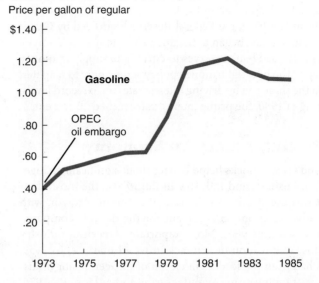

fourfold. In the United States, gasoline prices at the pumps nearly doubled in a few weeks' time, while the cost of home heating fuel rose even more.

Nixon responded with a series of temporary measures, including pleas to Americans to turn down their thermostats in homes and offices and avoid driving simply for pleasure. When the Arab oil embargo ended in March, after Kissinger negotiated an Israeli pullback in the Sinai, the American public relaxed. Gasoline once again became plentiful, thermostats were raised, and people resumed their love affair with the automobile.

The energy crisis, however, did not end with the lifting of the embargo. The Arab action marked the beginning of a new era in American history. The United States, with only 6 percent of the world's population, had been responsible for nearly 40 percent of the world's energy consumption. In 1970, domestic oil production began to decline; the embargo served only to highlight the fact that the nation was now dependent on other countries, notably those in the Persian Gulf, for its economic well-being. A nation that based its way of life on abundance and expansion suddenly was faced with the reality of limited resources and economic stagnation.

The Great Inflation

The price spike from the October War was merely the first of the "oil shocks" of the 1970s. Cheap energy had been a primary contributor to the relentless growth of the American economy after World War II. The GNP had more than doubled between 1950 and 1973; the American people had come to base their standard of living on oil prices that yielded gas at about 35 cents a gallon. Large cars, sprawling suburbs, detached houses heated by fuel oil and natural gas and cooled by central air-conditioning produced a dependence on inexpensive energy that Americans took for granted.

The quadrupling of oil prices in 1973–1974 suddenly put all this at risk. Because oil or its equivalent in energy is required for the production and transportation of manufactured goods, the rising oil prices caused the prices of nearly everything else to increase as well. Most services require energy; they went up as well.

Other factors added to the trend of rising prices. The Vietnam War created federal budget deficits that grew from $63 billion for the entire decade of the 1960s to a total of $420 billion in the 1970s. A worldwide shortage of food, resulting from both rapid population increases and poor harvests around the globe in the mid-1970s, triggered a 20 percent rise in American food prices in 1973 alone. But above all else, the primary source of the great inflation of the 1970s was the six-fold increase in petroleum prices.

The impact on consumers was staggering. The price of an automobile jumped 72 percent between 1973 and 1978. During the decade, the price of a hamburger doubled, milk went from 28 to 59 cents a quart, and a loaf of bread—the proverbial staff of life—rose from 24 to 89 cents. Corresponding wage increases failed to keep pace with inflation; in 1980, the real income of the average American family fell by 5.5 percent.

Often inflation signals economic exuberance, and rising prices indicate a rapid rate of growth. Not so with the inflation of the 1970s, which reflected economic weakness. The great inflation contributed to the worst recession in the United States since World War II. American GNP dropped by 6 percent in 1974, and unemployment rose to more than 9 percent, the highest level since the Great Depression of the 1930s.

President Gerald R. Ford, who followed Richard Nixon into the White House (see p. 749), responded belatedly to the economic crisis by proposing a tax cut to stimulate consumer spending. Congress passed a $23 billion reduction in taxes in early 1975, which led to a gradual recovery by 1976. The resulting budget deficits, however, helped keep inflation above 5 percent and prevented a return to full economic health.

Jimmy Carter of Georgia, who succeeded Ford (see pp. 749–751), had little more success in reviving the economy. Continued federal deficits and relatively high interest rates kept the economy sluggish throughout 1977 and 1978. Then in 1979, the outbreak of the Iranian Revolution and the overthrow of the shah touched off another oil shock. The members of the OPEC cartel took advantage of the situation to double prices over the next eighteen months. A barrel of crude oil now cost more than $30. Gasoline prices climbed to more than $1 a gallon at American service stations, leading to an even greater wave of inflation than in 1973.

Finally, in late 1979, the Federal Reserve Board, led by Carter appointee Paul Volcker, began a sustained effort to halt inflation by mandating increased bank reserves to curtail the supply of money in circulation. The new tight-money policy served only to heighten inflation in the short run by driving interest rates up to record levels. By the spring of 1980, the prime interest rate reached 20 percent.

The Shifting American Economy

Inflation and the oil shocks helped bring about significant changes in American business and industry in the 1970s. The most obvious result was the slowing of the rate of economic growth, with the GNP advancing only 3.2 percent for the decade, compared to 3.7 percent in the 1960s. More important, American industry began to lose its position of primacy in world markets. In 1959, U.S. firms had been the leaders in eleven of thirteen major industrial sectors, ranging from manufacturing to banking. By 1976, American companies led in only seven areas, and in all but one category—aerospace—U.S. corporations had declined in relation to Japanese and western European competitors.

The most serious losses came in the heavy industries in which the United States had once led the world. New steel producers in western Europe, Japan, and the developing world, using more advanced technology and aided by government subsidies, were producing steel far more efficiently than their American counterparts. As a result, by the end of the 1970s, American firms were closing down their obsolete mills in the East and Midwest, idling thousands of workers.

The foreign competition did even more damage in the automobile industry. The oil shocks led to a consumer demand for small, efficient cars. German and Japanese automakers seized the opportunity to expand their once low volume of sales in the United States. By 1977, imported cars had captured nearly a fifth of the American market, with Japan leading the way. In response, Detroit spent $70 billion retooling to produce a new fleet of smaller, lighter front-wheel-drive cars, but American manufacturers barely survived the foreign invasion. Only government-backed loans helped the Chrysler Corporation stave off bankruptcy.

The decline in manufacturing led to significant shifts in the labor movement. The industrial unions such as the United Automobile Workers (UAW) lost members steadily in the 1960s and 1970s. At the same time, public employee unions enjoyed rapid growth and acceptance. The Great Society legislation, the baby boom with the resulting need for many more teachers, and the growth of social agencies on the state and local level opened up new jobs for social workers, teachers, and government employees. By the end of the 1980s, members of public employee unions made up over 20 percent of the AFL-CIO ranks, while the separate National Education Association (NEA) became the nation's largest single union with two million members—600,000 more than the Teamsters. The rise of public employee unions also opened the way for greater participation by African Americans and women than in the older trade and industrial unions.

Just as public employee unions prospered from the shifts in the American economy in the 1970s, so did many American corporations.

The multinationals that had emerged in the boom years of the 1960s continued to thrive. IBM sold computers all over the globe. The growth of conglomerates—huge corporations that combined many dissimilar industrial concerns—accelerated as companies such as Gulf & Western and the Transamerica Corporation diversified by buying up Hollywood studios, insurance companies, and recreational equipment manufacturers. The growth of high-technology industries proved to be the most profitable new trend of the 1970s. Computer companies and electronics firms grew at a rapid rate, especially after the development of the silicon chip, a small, wafer-thin microprocessor capable of performing complex calculations almost instantly.

The result was a geographic shift of American industry from the East and Midwest to the Sunbelt. Electronics manufacturers flourished in California, Texas, and North Carolina, where they grew up around major universities. The absence of entrenched labor unions, the availability of skilled labor, and the warm and attractive climate of the southern and western states lured many new concerns to the Sunbelt. At the same time, the decline of the steel and auto industries was leading to massive unemployment and economic stagnation in the northern industrial heartland.

The overall pattern was one of an economy in transition. The oil shocks had caused serious problems of inflation, slower economic growth, and rising unemployment rates. But American business still displayed the enterprise and the ability to develop new technologies that gave promise of renewed economic vitality.

A New Environmentalism

The oil shocks had another effect: They injected new life into the environmental movement. The high price of gasoline made pocketbook conservationists of millions of Americans who hadn't thought twice about their country's heavy dependence on foreign oil; it also spurred Congress to press automakers to improve the fuel efficiency of the cars they built. The 1975 Energy Policy and Conservation Act set corporate standards for gas mileage; manufacturers who failed to achieve the mandated averages faced stiff fines and other sanctions. Between the high prices and the federal requirements, American drivers began squeezing more miles out of each tank of gas.

Environmentalists and consumers meanwhile began searching for alternative sources of energy. Solar power appealed to some as being clean and endlessly renewable. But it was also expensive (solar panels and related technologies remained underdeveloped) and intermittent (clouds cut off the power). Hydropower—electricity generated by falling water—was better proven and more reliable, but most of the suitable dam sites had already been built upon. Wind power worked in some areas (where the wind blew frequently and without obstruction), but those were precisely the areas where few people lived. Coal power was reliable, proven, and cheap, but it was also dirty (the gases emitted by coal plants fouled the air) and dangerous (to the men and women who mined the coal).

Nuclear power had its advocates. It had been in use in America since the 1950s, and its characteristics were well known. Its fuel—uranium—was essentially inexhaustible, and nuclear reactors, in normal operations, produced no noxious gases. Nor did they produce any "greenhouse gases"—carbon dioxide and other heat-trapping gases—that contribute to global warming, a rise in average temperatures that was just beginning to worry some Earth scientists (and would worry them much more in coming decades).

But nuclear power made many environmentalists nervous. The waste products of the reactors were radioactive, and would remain so for thousands of years. Guaranteeing that the wastes would not contaminate water supplies—for fifty generations into the future—was a daunting challenge. And occasionally nuclear reactors malfunctioned in terrifying ways. In March 1979, a reactor at Three Mile Island, near Harrisburg, Pennsylvania, nearly melted down when cooling systems failed. Tens of thousands of people living in the vicinity fled, and though the reactor didn't explode, as authorities had feared it might, the close call inspired grave second thoughts about nuclear power. A more severe accident at Chernobyl, in the Soviet Ukraine in 1986, released large amounts of radiation into the atmosphere and caused many deaths, reinforcing the fears.

The debate over alternative energy sources was part of a larger debate on the environment. Earth Day, first celebrated in April 1970, became an annual event at which participants considered the effect of human actions on their natural surroundings. Groups such as the Sierra Club and Friends of the Earth lobbied to reinforce antipollution laws, to clean up toxic wastes, and to increase gas mileage standards further. Business associations typically resisted the measures as too restrictive and expensive.

The results were mixed. Congress strengthened the Clean Air Act, and in 1980 it created the federal "Superfund" for toxic cleanups. But oil imports continued to rise, by some 50 percent between 1973 and 1979, to nine million barrels a day, or half what the country consumed.

Private Lives, Public Issues

How did private life change during this period?

Sweeping changes in the private lives of the American people began in the 1970s and continued for the rest of the century. The traditional American family, with the husband as wage earner and the wife as homemaker, gave way to much more diverse living arrangements. The number of working women, including wives and mothers, increased sharply; the wage gap between the sexes narrowed, but women still lagged noticeably behind men in earnings. Then, in the years following 1970, came the emergence of an active gay rights movement as more and more gay, lesbian, and bisexual Americans began to disclose their sexual identities and demand an end to discrimination.

The Changing American Family

Family life underwent a number of significant shifts after 1970. The most notable was a decline in the number of families with two parents and one or more children under 18. By the end of the 1980s, in only one two-parent family out of five was the mother solely engaged in child rearing. A few fathers stayed at home with the children, but in the great majority of these families, both parents worked outside the home.

The traditional nuclear family of the 1950s no longer prevailed in America by the end of the twentieth century. The number of married couple households with children dropped from 30 percent in the 1970s to 23 percent by 2000. The number of unmarried couples doubled in the 1990s, while adults living alone surpassed the number of married couples with children for the first time in American history. "Being married is great," commented demographer William H. Frey, "but being married with kids is tougher in today's society with spouses in different jobs and expensive day care and schools."

The divorce rate, which doubled between the mid-1960s and the late 1970s, leveled off for the rest of the century. Nevertheless, half of all first marriages still ended in divorce. After a sharp fall in the 1970s, the birthrate climbed again as the baby boom generation began to mature. There was a marked increase in the number of births to women over age 30, as well as a very high proportion of children born to single mothers, who composed 7 percent of all households by 2000, a 25 percent increase since 1990. Conservatives, alarmed by the decline of the nuclear family, called for change. "We need to discourage people from living together outside of marriage," observed Bridget Maher of the Family Research Council, "and encourage them to have children within marriage."

For better or worse, the American family structure changed significantly in the last three decades of the twentieth century, with a large number of people either never marrying or postponing marriage until late in the childbearing period. The traditional family unit, with the working father and the mother rearing the children at home, rapidly declined. Most mothers worked outside the home, and many were the sole support for their children. The proportion of children living with only one parent doubled in twenty years. Women without partners headed more than one-third of all impoverished families, and children made up 40 percent of the nation's poor. Although politicians, especially Republicans, refer to family values during campaigns, the fact remains that the American family underwent great stress due to social changes in the last third of the twentieth century, and children suffered disproportionately.

Gains and Setbacks for Women

American women experienced significant changes in their way of life and their place in society in the last quarter of the twentieth century. The prevailing theme concerned the increasing percentage of working women. There was a rapid movement of women into the labor force in the 1970s; six million more married women held jobs by the end of the decade as two incomes became increasingly necessary to keep up with inflation. The trend continued through the 1980s. Fully 61 percent of the nearly nineteen million new jobs created during the decade were filled by women; many of these new jobs, however, were entry-level or low-paying service positions.

Women scored some impressive breakthroughs. They began to enter corporation boardrooms, became presidents of major universities, and were admitted to the nation's military academies. Women entered blue-collar, professional, and small-business fields traditionally dominated by men. Ronald Reagan's appointment of Sandra Day O'Connor to the Supreme Court in 1981 marked a historic first; Bill Clinton doubled the number of women on the Court with his selection of Ruth Bader Ginsburg.

VOTING ON THE EQUAL RIGHTS AMENDMENT By the end of 1974, thirty-four states had ratified the ERA; Indiana finally approved the amendment in 1977, but the remaining fifteen states held out, leaving ratification three states short of the required three-fourths majority.

Yet at the same time, women encountered a great deal of resistance. Most women continued to work in female-dominated fields—as nurses, secretaries, teachers, and waitresses. Those who entered such "male" areas as management and administration soon encountered the so-called glass ceiling, which kept them from advancing beyond midlevel executive status. In 1990, only 4.3 percent of corporate officers were women. Most in business worked at the middle and lower rungs of management with staff jobs in personnel and public relations, not key operational positions in sales and marketing that would lead to the boardroom; women held fewer than 3 percent of the top jobs in Fortune 500 companies. The economic boom of the 1990s, however, led to a steady increase in the number of women executives; in 1998, there was an increase of 514,000.

Even with these gains, however, by 2004 women's wages still averaged only 76.5 percent of men's earnings. A college education helped close the gap, but a woman with a degree made only $600 a year more on the average than a man with a high school diploma. Younger women did best; those between 16 and 24 earned almost 90 cents for every dollar paid to a male in the same age group. Older women, who often had no other source of support, fared poorly; those over the age of 50 earned only 64 percent as much as men their age. Feminists had once hoped to close the gender gap by the year 2000, but experts predicted women would not reach pay equity with men until 2018.

The most encouraging development for women came in business ownership. Often blocked by the glass ceiling and seeking flexible schedules, more and more women went into business for themselves. The number of female business owners increased 40 percent between 1987 and 1992, twice the national rate of business growth. A women's trade group estimated that in 1996 women owned almost eight million businesses, employing more than eighteen million workers—one out of four American workers. A speaker at the first National Women's Economic Summit in 1996 exaggerated only slightly in crediting her group with restoring prosperity, claiming that "the American economy has been revitalized in good measure because of the participation of and contributions of women business owners."

Beyond economic opportunity, the women's movement had two goals. The first was ratification of the **Equal Rights Amendment (ERA)**. Approved by Congress in 1972, the ERA stated simply, "Equality of rights under the law shall not be denied or abridged by the United States or any state on account of sex." Within a year, twenty-two states had approved the amendment, but the efforts gradually faltered just three states short of ratification. The opposition came in part from working-class women who feared, as one union leader explained, that those employed as "maids, laundry workers, hospital cleaners, or dishwashers" would lose the protection of state laws that regulated wages and hours of work for women. Right-wing activist Phyllis Schlafly led an organized effort to defeat the ERA, claiming the amendment would lead to unisex toilets, homosexual marriages, and the drafting of women. The National Organization of Women (NOW) fought back, persuading Congress to extend the time for ratification by three years and waging intense campaigns for approval in Florida and Illinois. But the deadline for ratification finally passed on June 30, 1982, with the ERA forces still three states short. NOW leader Eleanor Smeal vowed a continuing struggle: "The crusade is not over. We know that we are the wave of the future."

The women's movement focused even more of its energies in protecting a major victory it had won in *Roe v. Wade* in 1973. (See the Law and Society essay, "*Roe* v. *Wade:* The Struggle over Women's Reproductive Rights," pp. 760–763.) Right-to-life groups, consisting mainly of orthodox Catholics, fundamentalist Protestants, and conservatives, fought back. In 1978, with strong support from President Carter, Congress passed the Hyde amendment, which denied the use of federal funds to pay for abortions for poor women. Nevertheless, prochoice groups organized privately funded family planning agencies and abortion clinics to give more women a chance to exercise their constitutional right to abortion.

As Presidents Reagan and Bush appointed more conservative judges to the Court, however, prochoice groups began to fear the future overturn of *Roe* v. *Wade*. The Court avoided a direct challenge, contenting itself with lesser actions that upheld the rights of states to regulate abortion clinics, impose a 24-hour waiting period, and require the approval of one parent or a judge before a minor could have an abortion. Abortion became an issue in presidential contests, with the Republicans upholding a prolife position and the Democrats taking a prochoice stand. Bill Clinton's election and appointment of Ruth Bader Ginsburg to the Court appeared to end the danger to *Roe* v. *Wade*, but in 2000 the Court margin in rejecting a Nebraska law forbidding certain late-term abortions fell to a bare majority, 5–4. And even the exercise of the right to abortion proved difficult and sometimes dangerous in view of the often violent protests of prolife groups outside abortion clinics. For many women, abortion was a hard-won right they still had to struggle to protect.

The Gay Liberation Movement

On the night of June 27, 1969, a squad of New York policemen raided the Stonewall Inn, a Greenwich Village bar frequented by "drag queens" and lesbians. As the patrons were being herded into

Read the Document   *Roe* v. *Wade* (January 22, 1973)

Roe v. *Wade* exerted a tremendous impact throughout the country, as only four states had enacted laws guaranteeing a woman widespread access to an abortion at the time of the ruling. The abortion issue continues to be a major source of controversy within U.S. politics and society.

vans, a crowd of gay onlookers began to jeer and taunt the police. A riot quickly broke out. "Beer cans and bottles were heaved at the windows and a rain of coins descended on the cops," reported the *Village Voice*. "Almost by signal the crowd erupted into cobblestone and bottle heaving." The next night, more than four hundred police officers battled two thousand gay demonstrators through the streets of Greenwich Village. The two-day Stonewall Riots marked the beginning of the modern gay liberation movement. Refusing to play the role of victims any longer, gays and lesbians decided to affirm their sexual orientation and demand an end to discrimination against homosexuals.

Within a few days, two new organizations were formed in New York, the Gay Liberation Front and the Gay Activist Alliance, with branches and offshoots quickly appearing in cities across the country. The basic theme of gay liberation was to urge all homosexuals to "come out of the closet" and affirm with pride their sexual identity; instead of shame, they would find freedom and self-respect in the very act of coming out. "Come out for freedom! Come out now!" proclaimed the Gay Liberation Front's newspaper. "Come out of the closet before the door is nailed shut!"

In the course of the 1970s, hundreds of thousands of gays and lesbians responded to this call. They formed more than a thousand local clubs and organizations and won a series of notable victories. In 1974, the American Psychiatric Association stopped classifying homosexuality as a mental disorder, and by the end of the decade, half the states had repealed their sodomy statutes. Gays fought hard in cities and states for laws forbidding discrimination against homosexuals in housing and employment, and in 1980, they finally succeeded in getting a gay rights plank in the Democratic National Platform.

In the 1980s, the onset of the AIDS epidemic (see pp. 748–749) forced the gay liberation movement onto the defensive. Stung by the accusation that AIDS was a "gay disease," male homosexuals faced new public condemnation at a time when they were trying desperately to care for the growing number of victims of the disease within their ranks. The gay organizations formed in the 1970s to win new rights now were channeling their energies into caring for the ill, promoting safe sex practices, and fighting for more public funding to help conquer AIDS. In 1986, ACT UP (AIDS Coalition to Unleash Power) began a series of violent demonstrations in an effort to shock the nation into doing more about AIDS. ACT UP members disrupted public meetings, chained themselves to a New York Stock Exchange balcony, and spray-painted outlines of corpses on the streets of San Francisco to call attention to those who had died of AIDS.

The movement also continued to stimulate gay consciousness in the 1980s. In 1987, an estimated six hundred thousand gays and lesbians took part in a march on Washington on behalf of gay rights. Every year afterward, gay groups held a National Coming Out Day in October to encourage homosexuals to proclaim proudly their sexual identity. In a more controversial move, some gay leaders encouraged "outing"—releasing the names of prominent homosexuals, primarily politicians and movie stars—in an effort to make the nation aware of how many Americans were gay or lesbian. Gay leaders claimed there were more than twenty million gays and lesbians in the nation, basing this estimate on a Kinsey report which had stated in the late 1940s that one in ten American males had engaged in homosexual behavior. A sociological survey released in the spring of 1993 contradicted those numbers, finding only 1.1 percent of American males exclusively homosexual. Whatever the actual number, it was clear by the 1990s that gays and lesbians formed a significant minority that had succeeded in forcing the nation, however grudgingly, to respect its rights.

There was one battle, however, in which victory eluded the gay liberation movement. In the 1992 election, gays and lesbians strongly backed Democratic candidate Bill Clinton, who promised, if elected, to end the ban on homosexuals in the military. In his first days in office, however, President Clinton stirred up great resistance in the Pentagon and Congress when he tried to issue an executive order forbidding such discrimination. The Joint Chiefs of Staff and many Democrats, led by Georgia Senator Sam Nunn, warned that acceptance of gays and lesbians would destroy morale and seriously weaken the armed forces. Clinton finally settled for the Pentagon's compromise "Don't ask, don't tell" policy that would permit homosexuals to continue serving in the military as they had in the past as long as they did not reveal their sexual preference and refrained from homosexual conduct. However disappointed gays and lesbians were in Clinton's retreat, their leaders understood that the real problem was the resistance of mainstream America to full acceptance of homosexuality.

Public attitudes toward gays and lesbians seemed to be changing in the 1990s, but the growing tolerance had definite limits. In a 1996 poll, 85 percent of those questioned believed that gays should be treated equally in the workplace, up from 76 percent in 1992. Violence against gays, however, continued, most notably in the 1998 fatal beating of Matthew Shepard, a 21-year-old gay college student, in Wyoming. The brutal attack spurred calls for hate-crime legislation, and the judge in the case, banning a so-called gay-panic defense, sentenced Shepard's assailant to two consecutive terms of life imprisonment.

The issue of same-sex marriage came to a head at the end of the century. In 1996, President Clinton signed the Defense of Marriage Act, which decreed that states did not have to recognize same-sex marriages performed elsewhere. But in 2000, following a state supreme court ruling, the Vermont legislature legalized civil unions between individuals of the same sex, enabling gays and lesbians to receive all the legal benefits available to married couples. Whether sanctioned by law or not, the number of gay and lesbian households steadily increased; the 2000 census revealed that there were nearly six hundred thousand homes in America headed by same-sex couples. While nearly one-quarter were in California and New York, there was at least one gay or lesbian couple living in 99 percent of the nation's counties.

The AIDS Epidemic

The outbreak of AIDS (acquired immune deficiency syndrome) in the early 1980s took most Americans by surprise. Even health experts had difficulty grasping the nature and extent of the new public health threat. Doctors first noticed a few cases of a rare form of pneumonia and an unusual type of skin cancer in male patients in New York City and San Francisco in 1981. The Centers for Disease Control noted the phenomenon in a June 1981 bulletin, but it was several years before researchers finally identified it as a hitherto unknown human immunodeficiency virus (HIV). HIV apparently originated in Central Africa and spread to the United States, where it found its first victims primarily among gay men.

Initially, AIDS was perceived as a threat only to gay men. With a growing sense of urgency as the death toll mounted, gay men began to practice safer sex, using condoms and confining themselves to trusted partners. It soon became clear, however, that AIDS could not be so easily contained. It began to appear among intravenous (IV) drug users who shared the same needles and eventually among hemophiliacs and others receiving frequent blood transfusions. The threat of a contaminated national blood supply terrified middle-class America, as did the possibility of the spread of AIDS to heterosexuals.

Scientists tried to reassure the public by explaining that the virus could be spread only by the exchange of bodily fluids, primarily blood and semen, and not by casual contact. The death of former movie star Rock Hudson from AIDS in the summer of 1985, however, intensified the sense of national panic. Controversy soon developed over proposals for mandatory blood tests for suspected HIV carriers and for the quarantine of AIDS victims. The integrity of hospital blood supplies caused the most realistic concern; in 1985, a new test finally gave reassurance that transfusions could be performed safely.

The Reagan administration proved slow and halting in its approach to the AIDS epidemic. The lack of sympathy for gays and a need to reduce the deficit worked against any large increase in health spending; what little money was devoted to AIDS went almost entirely for research rather than for educational measures to slow its spread. The only real leadership came from Surgeon General C. Everett Koop, who surprised his conservative backers in 1986 by coming out boldly with proposals for sex education, the use of condoms to ensure "safer sex," and confidential blood testing to help contain the disease.

While the administration dallied, the grim toll mounted. Because the average time between the initial HIV infection and the first symptoms of AIDS was five years and the delay could be as long as fourteen years, efforts at prevention had little immediate impact. In November 1983, there were 2,803 known cases and 1,416 deaths; by the time Hollywood film actor Rock Hudson died from complications of HIV/AIDS in mid-1985, more than 12,000 cases and more than 6,000 deaths had been reported.

Growing public concern finally led to action. In 1987, Reagan appointed a special presidential commission headed by Admiral James Watkins, a former chief of naval operations, to study the

AIDS epidemic. The Watkins report in 1988 criticized the administration's AIDS efforts as "inconsistent" and recommended a new effort that included antidiscrimination legislation and explicit prevention education. Koop responded by sending out a pamphlet titled "Understanding AIDS" to 107 million households, while in the fall, Congress voted to spend $1.3 billion to fight AIDS, with much of the money going for confidential testing and counseling and home care for victims.

Despite the new efforts, the epidemic continued to grow. In 1987, there were 50,000 cases; by mid-1989, the count had reached 100,000. The U.S. Centers for Disease Control and Prevention in Atlanta, Georgia, reported more than 200,000 cases at the end of 1991; the total had increased to more than 500,000 by mid-1996. By then, 345,000 AIDS victims had died, making it the leading cause of death for Americans aged 25 to 44.

The number of those infected with HIV appeared to be stabilizing by the mid-1990s at between 650,000 and 900,000. Yet, what was once known as the gay disease had spread far beyond that one group in society by the end of the century. Minorities and the young were at greatest risk. African American youths made up two-thirds of the new HIV cases among people under 25. "The disease is disappearing from the mainstream" claimed a Washington, D.C., clinic director, "and becoming a disease of kids who are disenfranchised anyway."

The most encouraging development was a fall-off in the death rate from AIDS that began in the mid-1990s. Health officials attributed the decline to heavier spending on treatment and prevention and, above all, to powerful new drug combinations. By 2001, however, the drop in new cases and deaths from AIDS began to level off. "The latest data," commented one expert in August 2001, "suggest that the era of dramatic declines is now over." There was a particularly alarming increase in the number of new cases among young gay men who apparently believed that the new treatment had made the disease manageable. But unfortunately the so-called AIDS cocktail was very expensive, running as high as $15,000 a year, and did not work for everyone. And even more disturbing was the growing realization that AIDS was threatening to decimate the population of developing countries, especially in sub-Saharan Africa.

Politics and Diplomacy After Watergate

Why did the presidencies of Ford and Carter largely fail?

The economic and social disruptions of the era contributed to problems of governance left over from Watergate. Even as many Americans worried about shrinking paychecks and disintegrating families, Congress increasingly challenged the prerogatives of the presidency. This made life in the White House difficult for Richard Nixon's immediate successors—and it made solving America's pressing problems nearly impossible.

The Ford Administration

Gerald R. Ford had the distinction of being the first president who had not been elected to national office. Richard Nixon had appointed him to the vice presidency to succeed Spiro Agnew,

who had been forced to resign in order to avoid prosecution for accepting bribes while he was governor of Maryland. Ford, an amiable and unpretentious Michigan congressman who had risen to the post of House minority leader, seemed ready to restore public confidence in the presidency when he replaced Nixon in August 1974.

Ford's honeymoon lasted only a month. On September 8, 1974, he shocked the nation by announcing he had granted Richard Nixon a full and unconditional pardon for all federal crimes he may have committed. Some critics charged darkly that Nixon and Ford had made a secret bargain; others pointed out how unfair it was for Nixon's aides to serve their prison terms while the chief criminal went free. Ford apparently acted in an effort to end the bitterness over Watergate, but his attempt backfired, eroding public confidence in his leadership and linking him indelibly with the scandal.

Ford soon found himself fighting an equally difficult battle on behalf of the beleaguered CIA. The Watergate scandal and the Vietnam fiasco had eroded public confidence in the government and lent credibility to a startling series of disclosures about past covert actions. The president allowed the CIA to confirm some of the charges, and then he made things worse by blurting out to the press the juiciest item of all: The CIA had been involved in plots to assassinate foreign leaders.

Senate and House select committees appointed to investigate the CIA now focused on the assassination issue, eventually charging that the agency had been involved in no less than eight separate attempts to kill Fidel Castro. The chairman of the Senate committee, Frank Church of Idaho, worried that the revelations would damage the reputations of Democratic Presidents Kennedy and Johnson; he tried to put all the blame on the CIA, likening it to "a rogue elephant on the rampage."

In late 1975, President Ford finally moved to limit the damage to the CIA. He appointed George H. W. Bush, then a respected former Republican congressman, as the agency's new director and gave him the authority both to reform the CIA and to strengthen its role in shaping national security policy. Most notably, Ford issued an executive order outlawing assassination as an instrument of American foreign policy. To prevent future abuses, Congress created permanent House and Senate intelligence committees to exercise general oversight for covert CIA operations.

Ford proved less successful in his dealings with Congress on other issues. Although he prided himself on his good relations with members of both houses, he opposed Democratic measures such as federal aid to education and control over strip mining. In a little more than a year, he vetoed thirty-nine separate bills. In fact, Ford, who as a congressman had opposed virtually every Great Society measure, proved far more conservative than Nixon in the White House.

Carter and American Malaise

Ford's lackluster record and the legacy of Watergate made the Democratic nomination a prize worth fighting for in 1976. A large field of candidates entered the contest, but a virtual unknown, former Georgia governor James Earl Carter, quickly became the

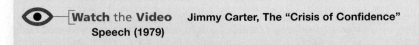

Watch the Video Jimmy Carter, The "Crisis of Confidence" Speech (1979)

As national polls in the summer of 1979 reflected a profound loss of Americans' confidence in the leadership of President Jimmy Carter, the president attempted to rally the nation and redeem his presidency with his nationally televised "Crisis of Confidence" speech.

On television, the basic Carter commercial showed him at his Georgia peanut farm, dressed in blue jeans, looking directly into the camera and saying, "I'll never tell a lie."

Voters took Carter at his word, and elected him over Ford in a close contest. Unfortunately, Carter's outsider status, while attractive in a campaign, made governing as president difficult. He had no discernible political philosophy, no clear sense of direction. He called himself a populist, but that label meant little more than an appeal to the common man, a somewhat ironic appeal, given Carter's personal wealth. "The idea of a millionaire populist has always amused me," commented his attorney general, fellow Georgian Griffin Bell.

Lacking both a clear set of priorities and a coherent political philosophy, the Carter administration had little chance to succeed. The President strove hard for a balanced budget but was forced to accept mounting deficits. Federal agencies fought to save the environment and help consumers but served only to anger industry.

In the crucial area of social services, Joseph Califano, secretary of Health, Education, and Welfare (HEW), failed repeatedly in efforts to carry out long-overdue reforms. His attempts to overhaul the nation's welfare program, which had become a $30 billion annual operation serving some thirty million Americans, won little support from the White House. Carter's unwillingness to take the political risks involved in revamping the overburdened Social Security system by reducing benefits and raising the retirement age blocked Califano's efforts. And the HEW secretary finally gave up his attempt to draw up a workable national health insurance plan.

Informed by his pollsters in 1979 that he was losing the nation's confidence, Carter sought desperately to redeem himself. After a series of meetings at Camp David with a wide variety of advisers, he gave a speech in which he seemed to blame his failure on the American people, accusing them of creating "a crisis of confidence . . . that strikes at the very heart and soul and spirit of our national will." Then, a week after what his critics termed the "national malaise" speech, he requested the resignation of Califano and the secretary of the treasury. But neither the attempt to pin responsibility on the American people nor the firing of cabinet members could hide the fact that Carter, despite his good intentions and hard work, had failed to provide the bold leadership the nation needed.

front-runner. Aware of the voters' disgust with politicians of both parties, Jimmy Carter ran as an outsider, portraying himself as a southerner who had no experience in Washington and one who could thus give the nation fresh and untainted leadership.

THE ELECTION OF 1976

Candidate	Party	Popular Vote	Electoral Vote
Jimmy Carter	Democratic	40,828,587	297
Gerald Ford	Republican	39,147,613	241

Troubles Abroad

In the aftermath of the Vietnam War, most Americans wanted to have little to do with the world. Military intervention had failed in Southeast Asia, and with the American economy in trouble, the country's economic leverage appeared minimal. Moreover, the point of détente was to diminish the need for American intervention abroad by directing the superpower contest with the Soviet Union into political channels.

Yet various groups in the developing world didn't get the message of détente. Central America, for example, witnessed numerous uprisings against entrenched authoritarian regimes. In mid-1979, dictator Anastasio Somoza capitulated to the Sandinista forces in Nicaragua. Despite American attempts to moderate the Sandinista revolution, the new regime moved steadily to the left, developing close ties with Castro's Cuba. In neighboring El Salvador, a growing leftist insurgency against a repressive regime put the United States in an awkward position. Unable to find a workable alternative between the extremes of reactionary dictatorship and radical revolution in Central America, Carter tried to use American economic aid to encourage the military junta in El Salvador to carry out democratic reforms. But after the guerrillas launched a major offensive in January 1981, he authorized large-scale military assistance to the government for its war against the insurgents, setting a precedent for the future.

Carter initially had better luck in the Middle East. In 1978, he invited Egyptian president Anwar Sadat and Israeli prime minister Menachem Begin to negotiate a peace treaty under his guidance at Camp David. For thirteen days, Carter met with Sadat and Begin, finally emerging with the **Camp David accords**. A framework for negotiations rather than an actual peace settlement, the Camp David accords nonetheless paved the way for a 1979 treaty between these principal antagonists in the Arab–Israeli conflict. The treaty provided for the gradual return of the Sinai to Egypt but left the fate of the Palestinians, the Arab inhabitants of the West Bank and the Gaza Strip, unsettled.

Any sense of progress in the Middle East was quickly offset in 1979 with the outbreak of the Iranian revolution. Under Nixon and Kissinger, the United States had come to depend heavily on the shah for defense of the vital Persian Gulf. Carter continued the close relationship with the shah, despite growing signs of domestic discontent with his leadership. By 1978, Iran was in chaos as the exiled Ayatollah Ruholla Khomeini led a fundamentalist Muslim revolt against the shah, who was forced to flee the country.

In October 1979, Carter permitted the shah to enter the United States for medical treatment. Irate mobs in Iran denounced the United States, and on November 4, militants seized the U.S. embassy in Tehran and took fifty-three Americans prisoner. The prolonged **Iranian hostage crisis** revealed the extent to which American power had declined in the 1970s. Carter relied first on diplomacy and economic reprisals in a vain attempt to free the hostages. In April 1980, the president authorized a desperate rescue mission that ended in failure when several helicopters broke down in the Iranian desert and an accident cost the lives of eight crewmen. The hostage crisis dragged on through the summer and fall of 1980, a symbol of American weakness that proved to be a powerful political handicap to Carter in the upcoming presidential election.

The Collapse of Détente

The policy of détente was already in trouble when Carter took office in 1977. Congressional refusal to relax trade restrictions on the Soviet Union had doomed Kissinger's attempts to win political concessions from the Soviets through economic incentives. The Kremlin's repression of the growing dissident movement and its harsh policy restricting the emigration of Soviet Jews had caused many Americans to doubt the wisdom of seeking accommodation with the Soviet Union.

President Carter's emphasis on human rights appeared to the Russians to be a direct repudiation of détente. In his inaugural address, Carter reaffirmed his concern over the mistreatment of

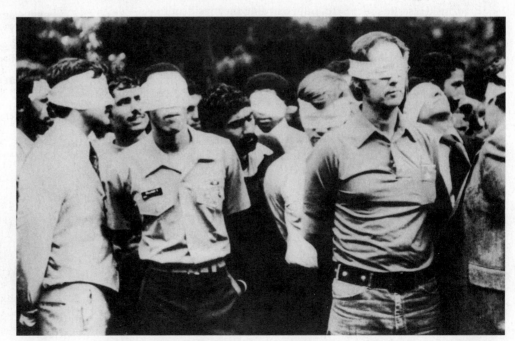

Blindfolded American hostages stand among their Iranian captors after Iranian militants captured the American embassy in Tehran on November 4, 1979. The Iranians' capture of fifty-three Americans as hostages and their violent attacks on the embassy shocked U.S. citizens. The hostage crisis dragged on for the rest of Carter's administration; the hostages were not released until January 1981.

human beings anywhere in the world, declaring that "our commitment to human rights must be absolute." It was easier said than done. Carter withheld aid from authoritarian governments in Chile and Argentina, but equally repressive regimes in South Korea and the Philippines continued to receive generous American support. The Soviets, however, found even an inconsistent human rights policy to be threatening, particularly after Carter received Soviet exiles in the White House.

Secretary of State Cyrus Vance concentrated on continuing the main pillar of détente, the Strategic Arms Limitation Talks (SALT). In 1974, President Ford had met with Brezhnev in Vladivostok and reached tentative agreement on the outline of SALT II. The chief provision was for a ceiling of twenty-four hundred nuclear launchers by each side, a level that would not require either the Soviet Union or the United States to give up any existing delivery vehicles. In March 1977, Vance went to Moscow to propose a drastic reduction in this level; the Soviets, already angry over human rights, rejected the American proposal as an attempt to overcome the Soviet lead in land-based ICBMs.

Zbigniew Brzezinski, Carter's national security adviser, worked from the outset to reverse the policy of détente. Commenting that he was "the first Pole in three hundred years in a position to really stick it to the Russians," he favored confrontation with the Kremlin. Although Carter signed a SALT II treaty with Russia in 1979, lowering the ceiling on nuclear delivery systems to 2,250, growing opposition in the Senate played directly into Brzezinski's hands. He prevailed on the president to advocate adoption of a new MX missile to replace the existing Minuteman ICBMs, which some experts thought were now vulnerable to a Soviet first strike. This new weapons system, together with the planned Trident submarine, ensured that regardless of SALT, the nuclear arms race would be speeded up in the 1980s.

Brzezinski also was successful in persuading the president to use China to outmaneuver the Soviets. On January 1, 1979, the United States and China exchanged ambassadors, thereby completing the reconciliation that Nixon had begun in 1971. The new relationship between Beijing and Washington presented the Soviet Union with the problem of a link between its two most powerful enemies.

The Cold War, in abeyance for nearly a decade, resumed with full fury in December 1979 when the Soviet Union invaded Afghanistan. Although this move was designed to ensure a regime friendly to the Soviet Union, it appeared to many the beginning of a Soviet thrust toward the Indian Ocean and the Persian Gulf. Carter responded to this aggression by declaring a "Carter doctrine" that threatened armed opposition to any further Soviet advance toward the Gulf. The president banned the sale of high technology to Russia, embargoed the export of grain, resumed draft registration, and even boycotted the 1980 Moscow Olympics.

The Soviet action and the American reaction doomed détente. Aware that he could not get a two-thirds vote in the Senate, Carter withdrew the SALT II treaty. The hopeful phrases of détente gave way to belligerent rhetoric as groups such as the Committee on the Present Danger called for an all-out effort against the Soviet Union. Jimmy Carter, who had come into office hoping to advance human rights and control the nuclear arms race, now found himself a victim of a renewed Cold War.

The Reagan Revolution

What was the "Reagan revolution"?

After the turmoil of the 1960s, the economic and political troubles of the 1970s made Americans' turn to conservatism almost inevitable. The Watergate scandal won the Democrats a brief reprieve, but when the Republicans discovered an attractive candidate in Ronald Reagan, a decisive Republican victory was essentially assured.

The Election of 1980

In 1980, Jimmy Carter, who had used the Watergate trauma to win the presidency, found himself in serious trouble. Inflation, touched off by the second oil shock of the 1970s, reached double-digit figures. The Federal Reserve Board's effort to tighten the money supply had led to a recession, with unemployment climbing to nearly 8 percent by July 1980. What Ronald Reagan dubbed the "misery index," the combined rate of inflation and unemployment, hit 28 percent early in 1980 and stayed above 20 percent throughout the year.

Foreign policy proved almost as damaging to Carter. The Soviet invasion of Afghanistan had exploded hopes for continued détente

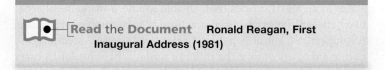

Read the Document   Ronald Reagan, First Inaugural Address (1981)

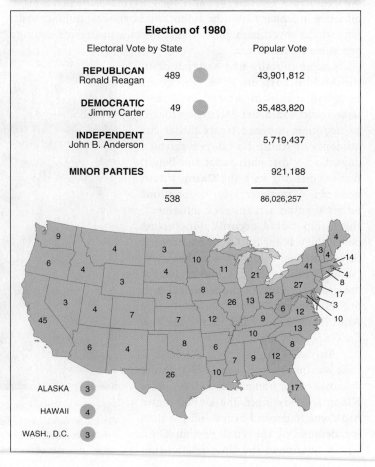

Election of 1980

	Electoral Vote by State		Popular Vote
REPUBLICAN Ronald Reagan	489		43,901,812
DEMOCRATIC Jimmy Carter	49		35,483,820
INDEPENDENT John B. Anderson	—		5,719,437
MINOR PARTIES	—		921,188
	538		86,026,257

and made Carter appear naive. The continuing hostage crisis in Iran underlined the administration's helplessness.

Ronald Reagan and his running mate, George H. W. Bush, hammered away at the state of the economy and the world. Reagan scored heavily among traditionally Democratic blue-collar groups by blaming Carter for inflation, which robbed workers of any gain in real wages. Reagan also accused Carter of allowing the Soviets to outstrip the United States militarily and promised a massive buildup of American forces if he was elected. Carter's position was further hurt by the independent candidacy of liberal Republican John Anderson of Illinois, who appealed to voters disenchanted with Carter but not yet ready to embrace Reagan.

The president fought back by claiming that Reagan was too reckless to conduct American foreign policy in the nuclear age. Charging that the election would decide "whether we have peace or war," Carter tried to portray his Republican challenger as a warmonger. Reagan deflected the charge and summarized the case against the administration by putting a simple question to voters: "Are you better off now than you were four years ago?"

Voters answered with a resounding "no." Reagan carried forty-four states and gained 51 percent of the popular vote. Carter won only six states and 41 percent of the popular vote, while John Anderson received the remaining 8 percent but failed to carry a single state. Reagan clearly benefited from the growing political power of the Sunbelt; he carried every state west of the Mississippi except Minnesota, the home state of Carter's running mate, Walter Mondale. In the South, Reagan lost only Georgia, Carter's home state. Even more impressive were Reagan's inroads into the old New Deal coalition. He received 50.5 percent of the blue-collar vote and 46 percent of the Jewish vote, the best showing by a Republican since 1928. Only one group remained loyal to Carter: African American voters gave him 85 percent of their ballots.

Republican gains in Congress were even more surprising. For the first time since 1954, the GOP gained control of the Senate, 53 to 46, and the party picked up 33 seats in the House to narrow the Democratic margin from 114 to 50.

Though the full implications of the 1980 election remained to be seen, the outcome suggested that the Democratic coalition that had dominated American politics since the days of Franklin Roosevelt was falling apart. In the eight presidential elections from 1952 to 1980, Republican candidates received 52.3 percent of the popular vote, compared with 47.7 percent for the Democrats. Reagan's victory in 1980 thus marked the culmination of a Republican presidential realignment that ended a half-century of Democratic dominance.

Cutting Taxes and Spending

When Ronald Reagan took office in January 1981, the ravages of inflation had devastated the economy. Interest rates hovered near 20 percent, while the value of the dollar, compared to 1960, had dropped to just 36 cents. The new president

blamed what he termed "the worst economic mess since the Great Depression" on high federal spending and excessive taxation. "Government is not the solution to our problems," Reagan announced in his inaugural address. "Government is the problem."

The president embraced the concept of **supply-side economics** as the remedy for the nation's economic ills. Supply-side economists believed that the private sector, if encouraged by tax cuts, would shift its resources from tax shelters to productive investment, leading to an economic boom that would provide enough new income to offset the lost revenue. Although many economists worried that the 30 percent cut in income taxes that Reagan favored would lead to large deficits, the president was confident that his program would both stimulate the economy and reduce the role of government.

The president made federal spending his first target. Quickly deciding not to attack such popular middle-class entitlement programs as Social Security and Medicare, and sparing critical social services for the "truly deserving needy," the so-called safety net, the Republicans concentrated on slashing $41 billion from the budget by cutting heavily into other social services such as food stamps and by reducing public service jobs, student loans, and support for urban mass transit. Reagan used his charm and powers of persuasion to woo conservative Democrats from the West and South. Appearing before a joint session of Congress only weeks after an attempt on his life, Reagan won a commanding 253 to 176 margin of victory for his budget in the House, and an even more lopsided vote of 78 to 20 in the Senate in May. A jubilant Reagan told a Los Angeles audience that he had achieved "the greatest reduction in government spending that has ever been attempted."

Watch the Video   Ronald Reagan on the Wisdom of the Tax Cut

President Ronald Reagan's televised speech to the nation in the 1981 advocating deep personal income taxes to spur economic growth and limit the ability of Congress to spend funds on domestic social programs. President Reagan persuaded Congress to adopt a 25 percent cut in personal income taxes over three years.

The president proved equally successful in trimming taxes. He initially advocated annual cuts of 10 percent in personal income taxes for three consecutive years. When the Democrats countered with a two-year plan that would reduce taxes by only 15 percent, Reagan compromised with a proposal to cut taxes by 5 percent the first year but insisted on the full 10 percent reduction for the second and third years. In July, both houses passed the tax cut by impressive margins.

In securing reductions in spending and lowering taxes, Reagan demonstrated beyond doubt his ability to wield presidential power effectively. As *Time* magazine commented, no president since FDR had "done so much of such magnitude so quickly to change the economic direction of the country."

Unleashing the Private Sector

Reagan met with only mixed success in his other efforts to restrict government activity and reduce federal regulation of the economy. Cutting back on the scope of federal agencies and limiting their impact on American business was a central tenet of the president's political philosophy. To achieve his goal of deregulation he appointed men and women who shared his belief in relying on the marketplace rather than the bureaucracy to direct the nation's economy. To the outrage of environmentalists, Secretary of the Interior James Watt opened up federal land to coal and timber production, halted the growth of national parkland, and made more than a billion acres available for offshore oil drilling. Though Watt was eventually forced to resign, the Reagan administration continued its policy of reducing government intervention in business long after Watt's departure.

Transportation Secretary Drew Lewis proved to be the most effective cabinet member in the administration's first two years. He helped relieve the troubled American automobile industry of many of the regulations adopted in the 1970s to reduce air pollution and increase passenger safety. At the same time, he played a key role in the behind-the-scenes negotiations that led Japan to agree in the spring of 1981 to restrict its automobile exports to the United States for the next three years. This unilateral Japanese action enabled the Reagan administration to help Detroit's carmakers without openly violating its free market position by endorsing protectionist measures.

Lewis gained notoriety in opposing a strike by the air traffic controllers' union (PATCO) in the summer of 1981. The president, denouncing PATCO for threatening to interrupt "the protective services which are government's reason for being," fired the striking workers, decertified the union, and ordered Lewis to hire and train thousands of new air traffic controllers at a cost of $1.3 billion. For the Reagan administration, the price was worth paying to prove that no group of government employees had the right to defy the public interest.

The Reagan administration was less successful in trying to cut back on the entitlement programs that it viewed as the primary cause of the growing budget deficits. Social Security was the greatest offender. A 500 percent increase in Social Security benefits in the 1970s threatened to bankrupt the system's trust fund by the end of the century. Reagan, overconfident from his budget victory, met a sharp rebuff when he tried to make substantial cuts in future benefits. The president then appointed a bipartisan commission to recommend ways to protect the system's endangered trust fund.

In March 1983, Congress approved a series of changes that guaranteed the solvency of Social Security by gradually raising the retirement age, delaying cost-of-living increases for six months, and taxing pensions paid to the well-to-do elderly.

The administration's record in dealing with women's concerns and civil rights proved clumsy and divisive. Although feminist groups were disappointed by the administration's strong rhetorical attacks on legalized abortion, the appointment of Sandra Day O'Connor to the Supreme Court pleased them. By this one shrewd move, Reagan was able both to fulfill a campaign pledge and to make a symbolic gesture to women. His appointments to the lower federal courts were a better indication of his administration's relatively low regard for women. Of the first seventy-two Reagan nominees to the federal judiciary, only three were women; just one of the sixty-nine men was African American.

Read the Document   Ronald Reagan, the Air Traffic Controllers Strike

The Professional Air Traffic Controllers' Organization (PATCO) was one of the few unions to support Reagan in the 1980 campaign. But when PATCO struck in August 1981, Reagan unhesitatingly fired the striking air traffic controllers and refused to rehire them when the strike collapsed.

The administration's civil rights record proved especially revealing. Aware of how few African Americans had supported the GOP in 1980, Reagan made no effort to reward this group with government jobs or favors. Instead, the Justice Department actively opposed busing to achieve school integration and affirmative action measures that resulted in minority hiring quotas.

Reagan and the World

How did Reagan reshape American foreign relations?

Reagan was determined to reverse the course of American policy abroad no less than at home. He believed that under Carter, American prestige and standing in the world had dropped to an all-time low. Intent on restoring traditional American pride and influence, Reagan devoted himself to strengthening America's defenses and recapturing world supremacy from the Soviet Union.

Challenging the "Evil Empire"

The president scored his first foreign policy victory on the day he took office, thanks to diplomatic efforts begun under Carter. On January 20, 1981, Iran released the fifty-three Americans held hostage and thus enabled Reagan to begin his presidency on a positive note.

He built upon this accomplishment by embarking on a major military expansion. Here again he continued efforts begun by Carter, who after the Soviet invasion of Afghanistan had persuaded Congress to fund a 5 percent increase in defense spending. The Reagan expansion went far beyond Carter's. Secretary of Defense Caspar Weinberger proposed a plan that would more than double defense spending. The emphasis was on new weapons, ranging from the B-1 bomber and the controversial MX nuclear missile to the expansion of the navy from 456 to 600 ships. Despite some opposition in Congress, Reagan and Weinberger got most of what they wanted, and by 1985 the defense budget grew to more than $300 billion.

The justification for all the new weapons was Reagan's belief that the Soviet Union was a deadly enemy that threatened the well-being and security of the United States. Reagan saw the Russians as bent on world revolution, ready "to commit any crime, to lie, to cheat" to advance their cause. Citing what he called a "record of tyranny," Reagan denounced the Russians before the UN in 1982, claiming, "Soviet-sponsored guerrillas and terrorists are at work in Central and South America, in Africa, the Middle East, in the Caribbean and in Europe, violating human rights and unnerving the world with violence."

Given this view of Russia as "the focus of evil in the modern world," it is not surprising that the new president continued the hard line that Carter had adopted after the invasion of Afghanistan. Abandoning détente, Reagan proceeded to implement a 1979 decision to place 572 Pershing II and cruise missiles in western Europe within range of Moscow and other Russian population centers to match Soviet deployment of medium-range missiles aimed at NATO countries. Despite strong protests from the Soviet Union, as well as growing uneasiness in Europe and an increasingly vocal nuclear freeze movement at home, the United States began putting the weapons in bases in Great Britain and Germany in November 1983. The Soviets, claiming the move gave them only ten minutes of warning time in case of an American attack, responded by breaking off disarmament negotiations in Geneva.

The nuclear arms race had now reached a more dangerous level than ever before. The United States stepped up research and development of the **Strategic Defense Initiative (SDI)**, an antimissile system based on the use of lasers and particle beams to destroy incoming missiles in outer space. SDI was quickly dubbed "star wars" by the media. Critics doubted that the SDI could be perfected, but they warned that even if it were, the result would be to escalate the arms race by forcing the Russians to build more offensive missiles in order to overcome the American defense system. The Reagan administration, however, defended SDI as a legitimate attempt to free the United States from the deadly trap of deterrence, with its reliance on the threat of nuclear retaliation to keep the peace. Meanwhile, the Soviet Union kept deploying larger and more accurate land-based ICBMs. Although both sides continued to observe the unratified SALT II agreements, the fact remained that between them the two superpowers had nearly fifty thousand warheads in their nuclear arsenals.

Confrontation in Central America

Reagan perceived the Soviet challenge as extending across the globe. In Central America, an area marked by great extremes of wealth, with a small landowning elite and masses of peasants mired in poverty, the United States had traditionally looked for moderate middle-class regimes to support. But these were hard to find, and Washington often ended up backing repressive right-wing dictatorships rather than the leftist groups that raised the radical issues of land reform and redistribution of wealth. Yet it was often oppression by U.S.-supported regimes that drove those seeking political change to embrace revolutionary tactics.

This was precisely what happened in Nicaragua, where the leftist Sandinista coalition finally succeeded in overthrowing the authoritarian Somoza regime in 1979. In an effort to strengthen the many middle-class elements in the original Sandinista government and to avoid forcing Nicaragua into the Cuban and Soviet orbit, Carter extended American economic aid.

The Reagan administration quickly reversed this policy. Secretary of State Alexander Haig cut off aid to Nicaragua in the spring of 1981, accusing the Sandinistas of driving out the moderates, welcoming Cuban advisers and Soviet military assistance, and serving as a supply base for leftist guerrillas in nearby El Salvador. The criticism became a self-fulfilling prophecy as Nicaragua became even more dependent on Cuba and the Soviet Union.

The United States and Nicaragua were soon on a collision course. In April 1983, declaring that "the national security of all the Americas is at stake in Central America," Reagan asked Congress for the money and authority to oust the Sandinistas. When Congress, fearful of repeating the Vietnam fiasco, refused, Reagan opted for covert action. The CIA began supplying the Contras, exiles fighting against the Sandinistas from bases in Honduras and Costa Rica. The U.S.-backed rebels tried to disrupt the Nicaraguan economy, raiding villages, blowing up oil tanks, and even mining harbors. Then, in 1984, Congress passed the Boland Amendment

Feature Essay | The Christian Right

In early 1979, Rev. Jerry Falwell was flying to Lynchburg, Virginia, when he suddenly felt God calling him to enlist "the good people of America" in a crusade to battle permissiveness and moral decay. Falwell, who had built a small church in Lynchburg into a huge religious enterprise with eighteen thousand members, sixty associate pastors, and a television and radio audience of a million and a half, plus fifteen hundred students at Liberty Baptist College, launched his new enterprise on Capitol Hill in April 1979. Announcing that it was time to "fight the pornography, obscenity, vulgarity, profanity that, under the guise of sex education and 'values clarification,'" pervaded public school education, Falwell founded an overtly political organization to purify American society. He invited Roman Catholics, Jews, Protestants, Mormons, and even nonreligious conservatives to join his "Moral Majority."

Falwell's Moral Majority highlighted the emergence in the 1970s of what journalists called the Christian Right. Throughout American history, many church members have been swept up in religious "awakenings." Leaders of the revivals have called Americans back to personal piety and a concern for their society and its changing values. At those times, Christians have been urged to work actively to change their communities.

The Supreme Court's 1962 and 1963 decisions to ban school-sponsored prayer and Bible reading sparked increased political activity among conservative Christians. Many joined organizations working at the local level to gain greater control over public education and the content of textbooks

Ronald Reagan appears with Rev. Jerry Falwell at a Moral Majority rally in Dallas, Texas, in 1980. Falwell's Moral Majority and other similar evangelical groups endorsed conservative positions on a variety of issues, including abortion and school prayer. In his two presidential election campaigns, Reagan vigorously sought the support of Falwell's followers.

and science lectures. Church leaders often encouraged their congregations to become more active in local politics; they endorsed candidates and causes and passed out literature at church services. Conservative Christians also supported candidates who promised measures that would reverse the perceived decline in traditional family values as evidenced by feminism, abortion, and overt homosexuality.

Concern for the changing values of Americana resulted in a new series of revivals. The open-air "camp meetings" of past awakenings developed into gatherings that packed thousands into large arenas for events broadcast by television to extended audiences. A number of Christian preachers used television to broaden their ministries. Several, like Falwell, produced their own weekly or daily television broadcasts. The new television evangelists—dubbed *televangelists*—combined commentary on social, economic, and foreign policy issues with

their more traditional sermons and advice on living the Christian life. The televangelists produced publications and solicited contributions for their ministries. Their mailing lists formed the first "membership roles" of the new Christian Right. Jimmy Carter was one of their earliest national beneficiaries and suffered the consequences.

Carter was a devoted Baptist who taught Sunday school, readily professed his Christianity, and emphasized family values in his speeches. He received the endorsement of some of the televangelists for his campaign to become president of the United States, and the national press began to pay closer attention to his personal religious beliefs. But support from the budding Christian Right was not necessarily an asset; such Christians hold themselves, their preachers, and other Christians to very high standards of moral behavior and ideological purity. When Carter discussed his Christian commitment in an interview in *Playboy* magazine, it cost him some votes in a close election; *Playboy* was the cultural antithesis of the family values advocated by the Christian Right. Other voters feared that Carter was crossing the traditional barrier placed between religion and politics in America.

As president, Carter's actions continually reminded conservatives that he was, after all, a Democrat and a liberal one. Carter was unwilling to reform welfare, to work for the return of prayer in public schools, or to ban abortion. The developing Christian Right wanted more than just Christians in office; they wanted to see their program enacted. They found a new darling—Ronald Reagan.

Reagan was not a practicing Christian, he was divorced, and his children were not the model products of a "family values" home. But he was a bona fide conservative. He knew the right words to answer questions about his faith; and he peppered his speeches with the program of the Christian Right. With his words, Reagan brought the growing power of the Christian Right solidly into the Republican party. Their numbers and the enthusiasm of their individual political workers were sufficient to swing close elections; candidates at all levels sought their endorsement. The Moral Majority, and conservative Christians in general, were energized by the recognition they received while working hard for Ronald Reagan. However, President Reagan paid them for their support with little more than the words in his speeches.

So the Christian Right began to carefully consider the choice of a successor.

Pat Robertson stepped forward. He was the son of a congressman and a Phi Beta Kappa graduate of Washington and Lee University, Yale Law School, and the New York Theological Seminary. He had first joined the Baptist Church but later became a charismatic Christian and one of the most prominent preachers and healers on television with his *700 Club*. Like Falwell, Robertson formed a coalition of religious conservatives from many faiths, with the intent of teaching the members how to be effective in politics. That organization provided the grassroots workers for his effort to win the Republican nomination for president in 1988.

Robertson, however, became the innocent victim of the televangelist scandals—the "fallen angels"—that filled newspapers and television throughout 1987 and 1988. Oral Roberts demanded that his supporters send him $8 million or God would "call him home." Jim and Tammy Bakker, of the *PTL Club*, were accused of sexual, drug, and financial misconduct; Jim Bakker was sentenced to prison. Jimmy Swaggart, famous for his exhortations calling Christians to morally upright lives, was caught with a prostitute. The scandals cut into the income of every religious broadcast, including the ministries of Falwell and Robertson. The Moral Majority folded. Pat Robertson received good seats for his supporters and some attention at the Republican convention; George Bush got the nomination.

By the end of the twentieth century, the Christian Right had grown into a powerful political force but its national program remained unrealized. Conservative Christians had become experts at mobilizing support for national elections and local causes and candidates, but they did not form a mature political entity willing to negotiate, compromise, or trade one goal in order to achieve another. Many religious activists quickly became disillusioned with politics when their candidates could not fulfill all their promises once elected. Likewise, candidates who campaigned on the programs of the Christian Right often lost the support of the general electorate because they were seen as too extreme. Clearly, the ideological purity demanded by the Christian Right was at odds with the pragmatism needed to achieve their goals through the actions of government.

QUESTIONS FOR DISCUSSION

1. What events contributed to the emergence of the Christian Right in the 1970s and 1980s?

2. What challenges did the new movement pose to the liberalism of the 1960s?

3. To what extent do you think overtly religious values should influence political debate and the framing of laws?

View the Map   **Conflict in Central America (1970–1998)**

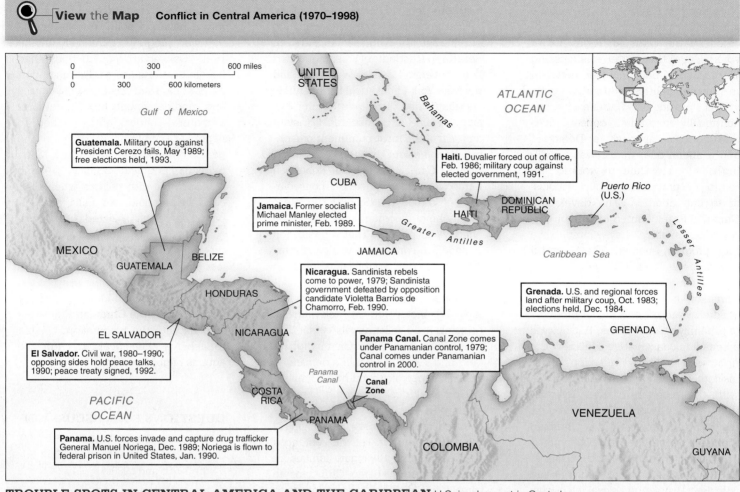

Guatemala. Military coup against President Cerezo fails, May 1989; free elections held, 1993.

Haiti. Duvalier forced out of office, Feb. 1986; military coup against elected government, 1991.

Jamaica. Former socialist Michael Manley elected prime minister, Feb. 1989.

Nicaragua. Sandinista rebels come to power, 1979; Sandinista government defeated by opposition candidate Violetta Barrios de Chamorro, Feb. 1990.

Grenada. U.S. and regional forces land after military coup, Oct. 1983; elections held, Dec. 1984.

El Salvador. Civil war, 1980–1990; opposing sides hold peace talks, 1990; peace treaty signed, 1992.

Panama Canal. Canal Zone comes under Panamanian control, 1979; Canal comes under Panamanian control in 2000.

Panama. U.S. forces invade and capture drug trafficker General Manuel Noriega, Dec. 1989; Noriega is flown to federal prison in United States, Jan. 1990.

TROUBLE SPOTS IN CENTRAL AMERICA AND THE CARIBBEAN U.S. involvement in Central American trouble spots intensified in the 1980s and early 1990s.

prohibiting any U.S. agency from spending money in Central America. The withdrawal of U.S. financial backing left the Contras in a precarious position.

More Trouble in the Middle East

Reagan tried to continue Carter's basic policy in the turbulent Middle East. In April 1982, the Israelis honored a Camp David pledge by making their final withdrawal from the Sinai. Reagan hoped to achieve the other Camp David objective of providing a homeland for the Palestinian Arabs on the West Bank, but Israel instead continued to extend Jewish settlements into the disputed area. The threat of the Palestine Liberation Organization (PLO), based in southern Lebanon and frequently raiding across the border into Israel, seemed to be the major obstacle to further progress.

On June 6, 1982, with tacit American encouragement, Israel invaded southern Lebanon in order to secure its northern border and destroy the PLO. The Reagan administration made no effort to halt the offensive but did join with France and Italy in sending a multinational force to permit the PLO to evacuate to Tunisia. Unfortunately, the United States soon became enmeshed in the Lebanese civil war, which had been raging since 1975. American marines, sent to Lebanon as part of the multinational force to restore order, were caught up in the renewed hostilities between Muslim and Christian militia. The Muslims perceived the marines as aiding the Christian-dominated government of Lebanon instead of acting as neutral peacekeepers, and they began firing on the vulnerable American troops.

In the face of growing congressional demands for the withdrawal of the marines, Reagan declared they were there to protect Lebanon from the designs of Soviet-backed Syria. But finally, after terrorists drove a truck loaded with explosives into the American barracks, killing 239 marines, the president saw no choice but to pull out. The last American unit left Beirut in late February 1984. Despite his good intentions, Reagan had experienced a humiliation similar to Carter's in Iran—one that left Lebanon in shambles and the Arab–Israeli situation worse than ever.

Trading Arms for Hostages

Reagan's Middle Eastern troubles didn't prevent his easy reelection in 1984. Voters gave him credit for curbing inflation, reviving the economy, and challenging Communism; compared to these major

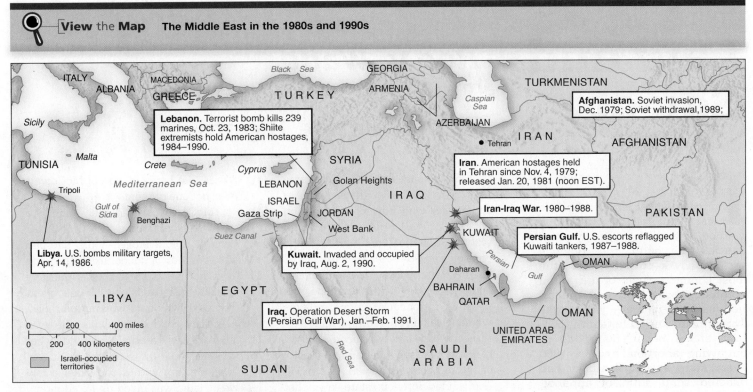

TROUBLE SPOTS IN THE MIDDLE EAST Armed conflict and territorial attacks in this region intensified in the 1980s and early 1990s.

achievements, the miscue in Lebanon appeared minor. Democratic candidate Walter Mondale, formerly Jimmy Carter's vice president, provided a jolt to the campaign by choosing Representative Geraldine Ferraro of New York as his running mate. But even the presence of the first woman on the national ticket of a major American party couldn't dent Reagan's enormous popularity. He swept to victory with 59 percent of the popular vote and carried every state but Mondale's home, Minnesota.

Yet the troubles abroad persisted. Not long after Reagan's second inauguration, his administration's policies in the Middle East and Central America converged in the **Iran-Contra affair**. In mid-1985, Robert McFarlane, who had become national security adviser a year earlier, began a new initiative designed to restore American influence in the troubled Middle East. Concerned over the fate of six Americans held hostage in Lebanon by groups thought to be loyal to Iran's Ayatollah Khomeini, McFarlane proposed trading American antitank missiles to Iran in return for the hostages' release. The Iranians, desperate for weapons in the war they had been waging against Iraq since 1980, seemed willing to comply.

THE ELECTION OF 1984

Candidate	Party	Popular Vote	Electoral Vote
Reagan	Republican	54,455,075	525
Mondale	Democratic	37,577,185	13

McFarlane soon found himself in over his head. He relied heavily on a young marine lieutenant colonel assigned to the National Security Council (NSC), Oliver North, and North, in turn, sought the assistance of CIA director William Casey, who interpreted the Iran initiative as an opportunity to use the NSC to mount the kind of covert operation denied the CIA under the post-1975 congressional oversight policy. By early 1986, when John Poindexter, a naval officer with little political experience, replaced a burned-out McFarlane as national security adviser, Casey was able to persuade the president to go ahead with shipments of TOW antitank missiles and HAWK antiaircraft missiles to Iran.

The arms deal with Iran was bad policy, but what came next was criminal. Ever since the Boland Amendment in late 1984 had cut off congressional funding, the Reagan administration had been searching for ways to supply the Contras in Nicaragua. Oliver North was put in charge of soliciting donations from wealthy right-wing Americans. In early 1986, North had what he later described as a "neat idea" (apparently shared by Casey as well)—he could use profits from the sale of weapons to Iran (charging as much as $10,000 for a TOW that cost the United States only $3,500) to finance the Contras. North's ploy was clearly not only illegal but unconstitutional, since it meant usurping the congressional power of the purse.

Ultimately the secret got out. Administration officials tried to shield Reagan from blame, and even after a congressional investigation it was unclear whether the president had approved the Contra diversion. Reagan's reputation survived the scandal,

Law and Society | *Roe* v. *Wade*
The Struggle over Women's Reproductive Rights

In colonial America, abortion was generally legal as a method of terminating early pregnancies, although the practice was usually kept secret since the most common cause of unwanted pregnancy—sex between unmarried men and women—was illegal. Throughout the nineteenth century, states began restricting or outlawing abortion, and by 1900 every state except Kentucky had enacted some form of antiabortion law. Despite laws criminalizing abortion, the number of illegal abortions each year—whether performed privately by physicians or by unlicensed practitioners—numbered anywhere from 200,000 to 1.2 million. And each year about two hundred of the women who obtained illegal abortions died as a result of the procedure.

Abortion rights advocates mobilized in the 1960s, helped by the growing women's rights movement, the declining health risk involved in the procedure, and the wave of fetal deformities and birth defects that swept the nation in the early 1960s, largely attributable to an outbreak of German measles. Their argument centered on the belief that a woman had the right to control her own body. Just as vocal as abortion rights advocates were those who opposed abortion, believing that human life began at conception and that a fetus's right to life outweighed a woman's right to end a pregnancy. In 1973, in the case of *Roe* v. *Wade*, the U.S. Supreme Court handed down a momentous decision on the abortion debate—a decision that continues to generate controversy more than thirty years later.

On January 22, 1998, Norma McCorvey joined thousands of Americans who braved the freezing weather of Washington, D.C., to protest the Supreme Court decision in the case of *Jane Roe et. al.* v. *Henry Wade*. Exactly twenty-five years earlier the court had sided with Jane Roe, the pseudonym for an anonymous Texas woman seeking an abortion, and overturned a state law that made abortion illegal in all cases except when the life of the mother was at risk. The ruling had voided forty-six state laws that denied or restricted a woman's access to the controversial procedure. Now, Norma McCorvey and other abortion opponents were observing the anniversary of the decision by taking to the streets to demonstrate their opposition. In many ways, McCorvey's presence was unsurprising; she was a "born-again" Christian, an active abortion opponent, and the founder of an antiabortion ministry. In 1997, she had publicly denounced abortion in America as "a terrible, terrible holocaust." Yet, one thing made Norma different from the other protestors: Twenty-five years earlier, she had been Jane Roe.

The intensity of the debate over abortion reached unprecedented heights in the 1970s, and state legislatures began to pay attention to the cries for reform of laws governing abortion. Between 1967 and 1970, twelve states liberalized their laws, usually to permit abortion in cases of rape, incest, or fetal deformity, or to protect the life and health of the pregnant woman. Most states, however, retained their restrictive laws, and by 1973 only four states guaranteed their residents virtually unhindered access to an abortion.

Texas, the home of Norma McCorvey, was not one of them.

McCorvey was largely unaware of these legal struggles. A poor Texas woman from a broken home, she had dropped out of school in tenth grade and married at sixteen. The marriage quickly collapsed, and Norma spent the next five years working odd jobs. Her first child, born while she was sixteen, was eventually adopted by her mother, and her second, the product of a short affair with a co-worker a few years later, was given up for adoption. In late 1969, Norma again became pregnant. Twenty-two years old, depressed and poor, she sought a way to avoid having another child. Her attempt to induce an abortion by drinking castor oil only made her sick. Texas's abortion law, which had stood virtually unchanged since 1857, prescribed a punishment of up to five years in prison for anyone convicted of performing an abortion for reasons other than saving the mother's life. Adoption, it seemed, was her only option.

Surprisingly, her path toward adoption led McCorvey into the struggle for abortion rights. An adoption lawyer referred her to Sarah Weddington and Linda Coffee, two young lawyers who were preparing to challenge Texas's abortion law but needed a pregnant woman willing to serve as the name plaintiff. In December 1969, the three women met for dinner in Dallas. McCorvey agreed to join the lawsuit without much prodding, but had one request: the use of a pseudonym to hide her identity. Three months later, Weddington and Coffee filed a class action lawsuit on behalf of all Texas women against Henry Wade, the district attorney of Dallas County, demanding that he stop enforcing the state's abortion laws; McCorvey, the name plaintiff, was identified only as Jane Roe.

Coffee and Weddington asked the three-judge court of the federal Fifth Circuit to overturn the Texas law on two grounds. First, they claimed, it was written too vaguely to be applied fairly. More significantly, they argued that the Texas law violated a woman's right to privacy. They cited recent Supreme Court decisions articulating a zone of personal privacy; this zone, the justices had admitted, was not explicitly written into the Constitution but could be inferred from a number of amendments. In 1965, the Supreme Court had made their most specific statement on this concept, writing in *Griswold* v. *Connecticut* of a "zone of privacy created by several fundamental constitutional guarantees." In *Griswold*, the justices struck down a one-hundred-year-old Connecticut law forbidding the sale of birth control devices; now, Weddington and Coffee argued that this personal privacy zone included reproductive rights as well.

Texas's lawyers rejected the claims. Jay Floyd of the attorney general's office contended that Jane Roe, whoever she was, had no standing to sue since the law punished only doctors who performed abortions, not the women who received them. Besides, Floyd claimed, Roe had to be so far along in her pregnancy by now that either she had already given birth or would do so fairly soon; thus, regardless of the court's decision, the whole case was moot. Assistant District Attorney John Tolle took a different approach, arguing that the state had the right to protect life in all forms, and hence the fetus was entitled to the full protection of the state. "I personally think and I think the state's position," he concluded, "is that the right of the child to life is superior to that woman's right to privacy."

It took almost a month for the judges to announce their decision. The Texas laws, they ruled, were unconstitutional, "because they deprive single women and married couples of their

Norma McCorvey, the Jane Roe of *Roe* v. *Wade*, with one of her lawyers, Gloria Allred.

right [to privacy], secured by the Ninth Amendment." They also found the statute too vague to be allowed to continue under the Fourteenth Amendment. The law would have to be eliminated. However, the judges refused to issue an injunction ordering the district attorney's office to stop enforcing it immediately; such an action, they announced, would be too intrusive considering that the state had not yet been given the opportunity to revise its laws. Quickly,

the Texas attorney general announced his intention to appeal the case and to continue prosecuting doctors who violated the statute. Weddington and Coffee also appealed, citing the court's refusal to issue an injunction.

For Weddington and Coffee, the decision would mean an eventual appeal to the Supreme Court; for Norma McCorvey it meant only crushing disappointment. McCorvey had never seen herself as a crusader for women's rights, and despite being the named plaintiff she had played virtually no role in the case. She had joined the lawsuit only in the hope of obtaining an abortion, and for six months had drifted across Texas, clinging to the lawsuit as her last chance. Now, she discovered, she had won her case, but without an immediate injunction she would have to deliver the baby after all. The lawsuit, she realized for the first time, was "not really for me. It was about me, and maybe all the women who've come before me, but it was really for all the women who were coming after me." A few months later she had her third baby, whom she gave up for adoption.

In March 1971, the United States Supreme Court agreed to hear the case. Supreme Court involvement prior to a case being argued before an appeals court was an unusual step, but since a constitutional right was at issue, the justices agreed to intervene immediately. Undoubtedly, the growing intensity of the abortion debate also influenced the court; by the time the *Roe* appeal was filed, eleven state courts had abortion cases pending, twenty cases were before three-judge federal panels, and four others were on the Supreme Court docket for consideration.

In the end, the Supreme Court would hear *Roe* v. *Wade* not once but twice. At oral arguments on December 13, 1971, both sides reiterated their positions to the nation's highest court. The justices pondered the arguments and handed down their verdict. Five of the justices favored striking down the Texas law, while only two sided with the state. Due to recent retirements, however, the court was operating with only seven members, two short of its full complement. This fact, combined with general unhappiness with the majority opinion written by Justice Harry Blackmun, led the Court to the unusual decision of putting the case over for reargument the following year.

On October 10, 1972, the two sides rehashed their arguments for a final time. Again, McCorvey remained in Texas while Weddington emphasized her constitutional right to privacy. "We are not here to advocate abortion," she

told the court. "We do not ask this Court to rule that abortion is good or desirable in any particular situation. We are here to advocate that the decision as to whether or not a particular woman will continue to carry or will terminate a pregnancy is a decision that should be made by that individual."

A majority of the justices agreed. On January 22, 1973, the Supreme Court struck down the Texas law by a 7 to 2 vote. Justice Blackmun's eighty-page majority opinion echoed Weddington and Coffee's argument about an implied zone of privacy. "The right of privacy," he wrote, "whether it be founded in the Fourteenth Amendment's concept of personal liberty and restrictions upon state action, as we feel it is, or, as the District Court determined, in the Ninth Amendment's reservation of rights to the people, is broad enough to encompass a woman's decision whether or not to terminate her pregnancy." The fetus, the majority also agreed, had never been given legal recognition as a person, and as such could not expect to receive equal protections.

Once again the verdict was not an unqualified victory for Coffee and Weddington. Blackmun's decision forbade states from restricting abortion in the first trimester of pregnancy and allowed them to regulate it only in the interests of preserving maternal health in the second. However, he recognized a legitimate state interest in protecting "potential life," which he defined as occurring when the fetus had "the capacity for meaningful life outside of the mother's womb." Accordingly, he permitted states to regulate abortion under almost all circumstances during the last trimester. Only Justices Byron White and William Rehnquist sided with Texas. In a scathing dissent, White attacked his brethren for making a decision that should have been left to the individual states, calling the verdict "an improvident and extravagant exercise of the power of judicial review." The Court, he concluded, "apparently values the convenience of the pregnant mother more than the continued existence and development of the life or potential life which she carries."

The ruling set off both celebration and protest. In Texas, Norma McCorvey read about the decision in the newspaper and immediately broke into tears. When Weddington finally reached her a few days later, Norma was thrilled. "It makes me feel like I'm on top of Mt. Everest," she told her lawyer. Many others felt quite differently. John Cardinal Krol, president of the National Catholic Conference, predicted that the Court was ushering in "the greatest slaughter of innocent life in the history of mankind."

The debate over *Roe* v. *Wade* was just beginning. Shocked by the decision, antiabortion forces redoubled their efforts. Although a few chose violence, most opponents of the *Roe* decision turned to lobbying and legislation to undo the verdict. Congressmen introduced hundreds of constitutional amendments limiting abortion, but none were approved. In 1976, Congress did prohibit the use of Medicaid funds for abortions, except when the life of the mother was at risk, and twelve years later, the Department of Health and Human Services banned government-employed doctors from counseling women about abortions. Even the Supreme Court showed a willingness to chip away at its earlier decision. In *Bellotti* v. *Baird* (1979), the Court allowed states to require unmarried minors to get parental consent for abortions, as long as the state offered an alternative procedure such as allowing her to obtain a judge's permission instead. The Court, in *Planned Parenthood of Southeastern Pennsylvania* v. *Casey* (1992), later upheld a Pennsylvania law that placed various restrictions on abortion rights, including a mandatory twenty-four hour waiting period and a requirement that doctors present alternative options before performing the surgery. During the next decade, abortion continued to be the most controversial issue in American politics and law. As of early 2006, the *Roe* decision still held, and abortion remained legal in most cases. But conservatives remained as determined as ever to overturn it.

Throughout the intense debate, no figure remained more central to the struggle than Norma McCorvey. For two decades, many who supported abortion rights admired her as a courageous individual who led American women in their fight to recapture control of their own bodies. Yet, more than twenty years later, McCorvey, who revealed her identity in 1984, stunned her supporters by renouncing her past position and embracing the antiabortion movement. She then became an inspirational symbol to those on the other side of the debate who applauded her wisdom and courage in renouncing the errors of her past. By 1997, she had joined the controversial antiabortion group Operation Rescue and the following year opened her own ministry, "Roe No More." Yet, despite her role as a symbol of this intense struggle, McCorvey remained just a typical American struggling to come to grips with a difficult and complex topic. "Deep inside," she recalled twenty years after Jane Roe had become famous, "I'm still nobody but Norma McCorvey."

QUESTIONS FOR DISCUSSION

1. What is the constitutional basis for the assertion of a woman's right to privacy?

2. Why was Justice Blackmun's opinion so controversial? Why did he limit the right to abortion to the first two trimesters of a pregnancy?

3. To what extent have subsequent court decisions limited a woman's right to abortion? How likely do you think it is that the Court will overturn *Roe* v. *Wade* in the future?

Despite Oliver North's questionable conduct, the public elevated him to near hero status during the televised Iran-Contra hearings. The bemedaled marine testified that he believed his deeds were justified as a defense of democracy.

albeit tarnished. Several of his subordinates, including North and Poindexter, were prosecuted. William Casey might have joined them in the dock but died suddenly of a brain tumor.

Reagan the Peacemaker

Americans' tolerance of Reagan's mistakes in the Iran-Contra affair resulted in part from the progress he was making on the larger issue of U.S.–Soviet relations. Elected as an antiCommunist hardliner, Reagan softened during his second term to become an advocate of cooperation with Moscow.

A momentous change in leadership in the Soviet Union had much to do with the change in Reagan's approach. The illness and death of Leonid Brezhnev in 1982, followed in rapid succession by the deaths of his aged successors, Yuri Andropov and Konstantin Chernenko, led finally to the selection of Mikhail Gorbachev, a younger and more dynamic Soviet leader. Gorbachev was intent on improving relations with the United States as part of his new policy of *perestroika* (restructuring the Soviet economy) and *glasnost* (political openness). Soviet economic performance had been deteriorating steadily, and the war in Afghanistan had become a major liability. Gorbachev needed a breathing spell in the arms race and a reduction in Cold War tensions in order to carry out his sweeping changes at home.

A series of summit meetings between Reagan and Gorbachev broke the chill in superpower relations and led in December 1987 to an **Intermediate Nuclear Forces Treaty**, by which Reagan and Gorbachev agreed to remove and destroy all intermediate-range missiles in Europe. The most important arms-control agreement since SALT I of 1972, the INF treaty raised hopes that an end to the Cold War was finally in sight.

During the president's last year in office, the Soviets cooperated with the United States in pressuring Iran and Iraq to end their long war. Most significant of all, Gorbachev moved to end the war in Afghanistan. The first Soviet units pulled out in April 1988, with the final evacuation due to be completed early the next year. By the time Reagan left office in January 1989, he had scored a series of foreign policy triumphs that offset the Iran-Contra fiasco and thus helped redeem his presidency.

Conclusion: Challenging the New Deal

Though trouble dogged the final years of his presidency, the overall effect of Reagan's two terms was to reshape the landscape of American politics. The Democratic coalition forged by Franklin Roosevelt during the New Deal finally broke down as the Republicans captured the South and made deep inroads into organized labor.

More significantly, Reagan challenged the liberal premises of the New Deal by asserting that the private sector, rather than the federal government, ought to be the source of remedies to most of America's ills. Reagan prudently left intact the centerpieces of the welfare state—Social Security and Medicare—but he trimmed other programs and made any comparable expansion of federal authority nearly impossible. By the time he left office, small-government conservatism seemed the undeniable wave of the American future.

Study Resources

 Take the **Study Plan** for **Chapter 31** *The Rise of a New Conservatism, 1969–1988* on **MyHistoryLab**

TIME LINE

1969 Stonewall Riots in New York's Greenwich Village spark gay rights movement (June); American astronauts land on the moon (July)

1970 U.S. forces invade Cambodia (April); Ohio National Guardsmen kill four students at Kent State University (May)

1971 States ratify Twenty-sixth Amendment to the Constitution, giving 18-year-olds the right to vote (July); President Nixon freezes wages and prices for ninety days (August)

1972 Richard Nixon visits China (February); U.S. and USSR sign SALT I accords in Moscow (May); White House "plumbers" unit breaks into Democratic headquarters in Watergate complex (June); Nixon wins reelection in landslide victory over George McGovern (November)

1973 United States and North Vietnam sign truce (January); Arab oil embargo creates energy crisis in the United States (October)

1974 Supreme Court orders Nixon to surrender White House tapes (June); Nixon resigns presidency (August)

1975 Last evacuation helicopter leaves roof of U.S. embassy in Saigon, South Vietnam (April)

1976 Nation celebrates bicentennial with fireworks, patriotic music, and parade of sailing ships (July); Jimmy Carter defeats Gerald Ford in presidential election (November)

1977 Carter signs Panama Canal treaties restoring sovereignty to Panama (September); Carter orchestrates Camp David accords between Israel and Egypt (September)

1979 Iranian militants seize American hostages Tehran (November); Soviet invasion of Afghanistan leads to U.S. withdrawal from 1980 Moscow Olympics (December)

1980 Ronald Reagan wins presidency over Carter

1981 American hostages in Iran released after 444 days in captivity (January); Sandra Day O'Connor becomes first woman U.S. Supreme Court justice (September)

1982 Equal Rights Amendment fails state ratification (June); Unemployment reaches postwar record high of 10.4 percent (October)

1984 Russia boycotts summer Olympics in Los Angeles (July); Reagan reelected president (November)

1985 Mikhail Gorbachev becomes leader of the Soviet Union (March)

1986 Iran-Contra affair made public (November)

1987 Reagan and Gorbachev sign INF treaty at Washington summit

1988 George H. W. Bush defeats Michael Dukakis decisively in presidential election

CHAPTER REVIEW

The Tempting of Richard Nixon

 What were the major accomplishments and failures of the Nixon presidency?

Nixon opened diplomatic relations with China and initiated détente with the Soviet Union. He withdrew American troops from Vietnam, terminating a quarter-century of American involvement. But his role in the Watergate scandal led to a constitutional crisis that forced him from office in disgrace. (p. 738)

The Economy of Stagflation

 How were oil and inflation linked during the 1970s?

Oil prices jumped dramatically in the 1970s, as a result of growing demand for oil and turmoil in the Middle East. Rising oil prices contributed to the worst inflation in modern American history. (p. 742)

Private Lives, Public Issues

 How did private life change during this period?

The divorce rate rose significantly, and the number of married couples with children declined. More women entered the professions, and *Roe* v. *Wade* guaranteed their right to an abortion. Gay men and lesbians achieved greater freedom than before, though they still lacked rights accorded to heterosexuals. (p. 745)

Politics and Diplomacy After Watergate

 Why did the presidencies of Ford and Carter largely fail?

Ford and Carter had to deal with the aftermath of Vietnam and Watergate and the economic disruptions that followed the oil price rises of the 1970s. Ford alienated many Americans by pardoning Nixon, and Carter fumbled the hostage crisis in Iran. (p. 749)

The Reagan Revolution

What was the "Reagan revolution"?

The Reagan revolution was the return to conservatism in American politics and diplomacy upon Reagan's 1980 election as president. Reagan pledged to reduce the role of government in American life, and restore American honor and confidence abroad. (p. 752)

Reagan and the World

How did Reagan reshape American foreign relations?

Reagan rejected détente and challenged the Soviet Union more directly than any American president in decades. He called for the creation of the SDI missile system, and he waged covert war against leftists in Central America. The Iran-Contra affair, in which Reagan traded arms for hostages, tarnished his reputation, but he also negotiated the INF treaty with the Soviet Union. (p. 755)

KEY TERMS AND DEFINITIONS

Moral Majority In 1979, the Reverend Jerry Falwell founded the Moral Majority to combat "amoral liberals," drug abuse, "coddling" of criminals, homosexuality, communism, and abortion. The Moral Majority represented the rise of political activism among organized religion's radical right wing. p. 738

Neoconservatism Former liberals who advocated a strong stand against Communism abroad and free market capitalism at home. These intellectuals stressed the positive values of American society in contrast to those liberals who emphasized social problems. p. 738

Détente President Richard Nixon and Henry Kissinger pursued a policy of détente, a French word meaning a relaxation of tension, with the Soviet Union to lessen the possibility of nuclear war in the 1970s. p. 739

Strategic Arms Limitation Talks (SALT) In 1972, the United States and the Soviet Union culminated four years of SALT by signing a treaty limiting the deployment of antiballistic missiles (ABM) and an agreement to freeze the number of offensive missiles for five years. p. 739

Watergate scandal A break-in at the Democratic National Committee offices in the Watergate complex in Washington was carried out under the direction of White House employees. Disclosure of the White House involvement in the break-in and subsequent cover-up forced President Richard Nixon to resign in 1974. p. 741

Organization of Petroleum Exporting Countries (OPEC) A cartel of oil-exporting nations. p. 742

Equal Rights Amendment (ERA) A proposed constitutional amendment passed by Congress in 1972 to guarantee women equal treatment under the law. The amendment failed to be ratified in 1982. p. 746

Roe v. Wade The 1973 Supreme Court decision that women have a constitutional right to abortion during the early stages of pregnancy. p. 746

Camp David accords In 1978, President Jimmy Carter mediated a peace agreement between the leaders of Egypt and Israel at Camp David. In 1979, Israel and Egypt signed a peace treaty based on the accords. p. 751

Iranian hostage crisis In 1979, Iranian fundamentalists seized the American embassy in Tehran and held fifty-three Americans hostage for over a year. The hostages were released on January 20, 1981, the day Ronald Reagan became president. p. 751

Supply-side economics The theory that tax cuts would stimulate the economy by giving individuals more incentive to earn more money, which would lead to greater investment and eventually larger tax revenues at a lower rate. p. 753

Strategic Defense Initiative (SDI) Popularly known as "Star Wars," President Ronald Reagan's SDI proposed to construct an elaborate computer-controlled antimissile defense system capable of destroying enemy missiles in outer space. p. 755

Iran-Contra affair The Iran-Contra affair involved officials in the Reagan administration secretly and illegally selling arms to Iran and using the proceeds to finance the Contra rebels in Nicaragua. p. 759

Intermediate Nuclear Forces Treaty (INF) Signed by President Ronald Reagan and Soviet President Mikhail Gorbachev in late 1987, this agreement provided for the destruction of all intermediate-range nuclear missiles and permitted on-site inspection for the first time during the Cold War. p. 764

CRITICAL THINKING QUESTIONS

1. If Nixon hadn't resigned, would he have been impeached? Would that have been a good thing or a bad thing?

2. What did feminism and gay liberation have to do with each other?

3. Should Ford have pardoned Nixon? Why or why not?

4. Which was more scandalous: Iran-Contra or Watergate? Why?

MyHistoryLab Media Assignments

Find these resources in the Media Assignments folder for Chapter 31 on MyHistoryLab

The Tempting of Richard Nixon

■ **View** the **Closer Look**   *Watergate Shipwreck p. 742*

Private Lives, Public Issues

■ **Read** the **Document**   Roe v. Wade *(January 22, 1973) p. 747*

Politics and Diplomacy After Watergate

Watch the **Video**   *Jimmy Carter, The "Crisis of Confidence" Speech (1979) p. 750*

The Reagan Revolution

Read the **Document**   *Ronald Reagan, First Inaugural Address (1981) p. 752*

■ **Watch** the **Video**   *Ronald Reagan on the Wisdom of the Tax Cut p. 753*

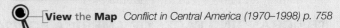**Read** the **Document**   *Ronald Reagan, the Air Traffic Controllers Strike p. 754*

Reagan and the World

View the **Map**   *Conflict in Central America (1970–1998) p. 758*

■ **Complete** the **Assignment**   *The Christian Right p. 756*

■ **View** the **Map**   *The Middle East in the 1980s and 1990s p. 759*

Complete the **Assignment**   Roe v. Wade: *The Struggle over Women's Reproductive Rights p. 760*

Watch the **Video**   *Oliver North Hearing p. 764*

■ *Indicates Study Plan Media Assignment*

32 Into the Twenty-first Century, 1989–2012

Contents and Learning Objectives

"This Will Not Stand": Foreign Policy in the Post–Cold War Era

On the evening of August 1, 1990, George H. W. Bush sat in a T-shirt in the medical office in the basement of the White House. Bush was an avid golfer, but his duties as president kept him from playing as much as he would have liked, and when he did find time to squeeze in a round or some practice, he tended to overdo things. This summer day he had strained a shoulder muscle hitting practice balls, and now he rested on the exam table while a therapist applied deep heat. He planned a quiet evening and hoped the soreness would be gone by morning.

Two unexpected visitors altered his plans. Brent Scowcroft, Bush's national security adviser, and Richard Haass, the Middle East expert of the National Security Council, appeared at the door of the exam room. Bush had known Scowcroft for years, and the look on his face told him something was seriously amiss. Scowcroft's words confirmed the impression. "Mr. President, it looks very bad," Scowcroft said. "Iraq may be about to invade Kuwait."

For months, the Bush administration had been monitoring a territorial and financial dispute between Iraq and Kuwait. Iraqi dictator Saddam Hussein was rattling the saber against the much smaller Kuwait, but Saddam had rattled sabers before without actually using them. The previous week, Saddam had spoken with the American ambassador in Iraq, April Glaspie, who came away from the meeting with the belief that his bellicose talk was chiefly for political effect. The United States had indicated its displeasure with Saddam's threats, and Glaspie judged that he had gotten the message. "He does not want to further antagonize us," she wrote to Washington.

For this reason, Saddam's decision to invade Kuwait at the beginning of August caught the Bush administration by surprise. American intelligence agencies detected Iraq's mobilization; this was what brought Scowcroft and Haass to the White House on the evening of August 1. Haass suggested that the president call Saddam and warn him not to go through with the attack. But even as Bush considered this suggestion, Scowcroft received a message from the State Department that the American embassy in Kuwait had reported shooting in downtown Kuwait City. "So much for calling Saddam," Bush said. Within hours the Iraqi forces crushed all resistance in Kuwait.

Bush, Scowcroft, and other American officials recognized that the Iraqi takeover of Kuwait constituted the first crisis of the post–Cold War era. As Lawrence Eagleburger, the deputy secretary of state, asserted in

President George Bush confers with National Security Council adviser Brent Scowcroft (left), White House Chief of Staff John Sununu (center), and Vice President Dan Quayle (right) at the Oval Office on August 1, 1990, following the Iraqi invasion of Kuwait.

Source: Getty Images/Time Life Pictures.

an emergency meeting of the National Security Council, "This is the first test of the postwar system. As the bipolar world is relaxed, it permits this, giving people more flexibility because they are not worried about the involvement of the superpowers." During the Cold War, a de facto division of labor had developed, with the United States and the Soviet Union each generally keeping its clients and allies in line, typically by threatening to withhold weapons or other assistance. Had the Soviet Union still been a superpower, Saddam, a long-time recipient of Soviet aid, likely would have heeded Moscow's warnings to settle his dispute with Kuwait peacefully. But in 1990 the Soviet system was disintegrating, and the Kremlin's clients were on their own. "Saddam Hussein now has greater flexibility because the Soviets are tangled up in domestic issues," Eagleburger explained. The world was watching. "If he succeeds, others may try the same thing."

It was this belief that shaped the Bush administration's response to the crisis. The president and his advisers understood that they were entering uncharted territory after the Cold War. As the sole remaining superpower, the United States had the opportunity to employ its military and economic resources more freely than at any time in history. But with that freedom came unprecedented responsibility. During the Cold War, the United States could cite the threat of Soviet retaliation as reason to avoid intervening in the affairs of other countries; with that threat gone, American leaders would have to weigh each prospective intervention on its own merits. If one country attacked another, should the United States defend the victim? If the government of a country oppressed its own people, should the United States move to stop the oppression? These questions—and the answers American presidents gave to them—would define American foreign policy in the era after the Cold War.

Bush sensed the importance of the United States' responses, and he responded accordingly. He convened his principal deputies for a series of White House meetings. The particular stakes with Iraq and in the surrounding Persian Gulf were discussed at length. "The rest of the world badly needs oil," Defense Secretary Dick Cheney observed, restating the obvious. Saddam's seizure of Kuwait gave him control of a large part of the world's oil supply, but the real prize was Saudi Arabia. "Saudi Arabia and others will cut and run if we are weak," Cheney predicted.

Bush consulted America's oldest allies. Britain's Margaret Thatcher urged the president to oppose Saddam most vigorously. "If Iraq wins, no small state is safe," the prime minister declared. She offered to help. "We must win this . . . . We cannot give in to dictators."

Bush asked his generals what his military options were. "Iraq is not ten feet tall, but it is formidable," Norman Schwarzkopf, the U.S. commander for the Middle East, replied. American air power could punish Saddam and perhaps soften him up, but ground forces—in large numbers—would be required to guarantee victory.

By August 5, Bush had made up his mind. As he exited the helicopter that brought him back from Camp David to the White House from another high-level meeting, reporters crowded the South Lawn. What was he planning to do? they asked.

"I'm not going to discuss what we're doing in terms of moving forces, anything of that nature," Bush answered. "But I view it very seriously, not just that but any threat to any other countries." Bush was no orator, and these remarks were unscripted. But one sentence summarized the policy that soon began to unfold: "This will not stand, this aggression against Kuwait."

The First President Bush

What were the important issues in George H. W. Bush's presidency, and how were they handled?

Elected on the strength of his association with Ronald Reagan, George H. W. Bush appeared poised to confirm the ascendancy of the conservative values Reagan forced to the center stage of American life. But events, especially abroad, distracted Bush, whose principal contribution proved to be in the area of foreign affairs. Bush brought the Cold War to a peaceful and triumphant conclusion, and he launched America toward the twenty-first century, an era when the United States faced new opportunities and new challenges.

Republicans at Home

Democrats approached the 1988 presidential election with high hopes, having regained control of the Senate in 1986 and not having to face the popular Reagan. But Vice President George H. W. Bush proved a stronger candidate than almost anyone had expected, and in a contest that confirmed the Republicans' hold on the Sunbelt, he defeated Massachusetts governor Michael Dukakis.

Many people expected the policies of the Bush administration to reflect the reputation of the new president—bland and cautious, lacking in vision but safely predictable. At home, he lived up (or down) to his reputation, sponsoring few initiatives in education, health care, or environmental protection while continuing

the Reagan theme of limiting federal interference in the everyday lives of American citizens. He vetoed family leave legislation, declined to endorse meaningful health care reform, and watered down civil rights proposals in Congress. The one exception was the **Americans with Disabilities Act (ADA)**, passed by Congress in 1991, which prohibited discrimination against the disabled in hiring, transportation, and public accommodations. Beginning in July 1992, ADA called for all public buildings, restaurants, and stores to be made accessible to those with physical handicaps and required that businesses with twenty-five or more workers hire new employees without regard to disability.

THE ELECTION OF 1988

Candidate	Party	Popular Vote	Electoral Vote
Bush	Republican	48,886,097	426
Dukakis	Democratic	41,809,074	111

Most of Bush's time on domestic affairs was taken up with two pressing issues: the possible meltdown of the savings and loan industry, and the soaring federal budget deficit. The thrift industry, based on U.S. government-insured deposits, had fallen into deep trouble as a result of lax regulation and unwise, and in some cases fraudulent, loan policies. After record losses of $13.4 billion in 1988, more than 250 savings and loan companies had been forced to close. Bush sought to stanch the bleeding by merging the weakest of the remaining thrifts with the stronger, and by regulating the survivors more carefully. Congress consented, and in August 1989 passed a bill to close or merge more than seven hundred ailing savings and loans and to restructure the federal regulatory system. A new agency, the Resolution Trust Corporation, took over properties on which developers had secured loans many times their actual value, and it gradually sold them off at discount prices. By the time the Resolution Trust Corporation expired in 1992, the cost to the government had passed $150 billion; the eventual bill for the savings and loan cleanup, including interest, was estimated between $500 and $700 billion.

The federal budget deficit posed an even greater challenge. The deficits Bush inherited from Reagan topped $150 billion per year, and conventional financial wisdom dictated that something be done to bring them down. In campaigning for president, Bush had promised "no new taxes," but in the fall of 1990 he broke the pledge. In a package deal negotiated with the leaders of Congress, he agreed to a budget that included new taxes along with substantial spending cuts, especially on the military. The resulting agreement projected a savings of $500 billion over five years, half from reduced spending and half from new revenue generated mainly by increasing the top tax rate from 28 percent to 31 percent and raising the gasoline tax by 5.1 cents a gallon.

Unfortunately for the president, the budget deal coincided with the beginning of a slow but painful recession that ended the Republican prosperity of the 1980s. Not only did Bush face recriminations from voters for breaking a campaign pledge not to raise taxes, but the economic decline led to greatly reduced government revenues. As a result, the deficit continued to soar, rising from

$150 billion in fiscal year 1989 to just under $300 billion in 1992. Despite the 1990 budget agreement, the national debt increased by more than $1 trillion during Bush's presidency.

Ending the Cold War

Bush might have accomplished more in domestic affairs had not the international developments begun during the Reagan years accelerated dramatically. Bush had been in office only months when the communist system of the Cold War began falling apart. In country after country, communism gave way to democracy as the old order collapsed more quickly than anyone had expected.

An early attempt at anticommunist liberation proved tragically abortive. In May 1989, students in China began a month-long demonstration for democracy in Beijing's Tiananmen Square that attracted worldwide attention. Watching American television coverage of Gorbachev's visit to China in mid-May, Americans were fascinated to see the Chinese students call for democracy with a hunger strike and a handcrafted replica of the Statue of Liberty. But on the evening of June 4, the Chinese leaders sent tanks and troops to Tiananmen Square to crush the student demonstration. By the next day, full-scale repression swept over China; several hundred

protesters were killed, and thousands were injured. Chinese leaders imposed martial law to quell the dissent and shatter American hopes for a democratic China.

Bush responded cautiously. He wanted to preserve American influence with the Chinese government. Hence, despite official statements denouncing the crackdown, Bush sent National Security Adviser Brent Scowcroft on a secret mission to Beijing to maintain a working relationship with the Chinese leaders.

A far more promising trend toward freedom began in Europe in mid-1989. In June, Lech Walesa and his Solidarity movement came to power in free elections in Poland. Soon the winds of change were sweeping over the former Iron Curtain countries. A new regime in Hungary opened its borders to the West in September, allowing thousands of East German tourists in Hungary to flee to freedom. One by one, the repressive governments of East Germany, Czechoslovakia, Bulgaria, and Romania fell. The most heartening scene of all took place in East Germany in early November when the new communist leaders suddenly announced the opening of the Berlin Wall. Workers quickly demolished a 12-foot-high section of this despised physical symbol of the Cold War, joyously singing a German version of "For He's a Jolly Good Fellow."

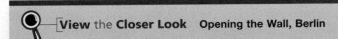

View the **Closer Look**   **Opening the Wall, Berlin**

Germans celebrate the destruction and fall of the Berlin Wall on November 9, 1989. The Berlin Wall had been a hated symbol of the Cold War since its construction by the communist East German authorities in August of 1961.

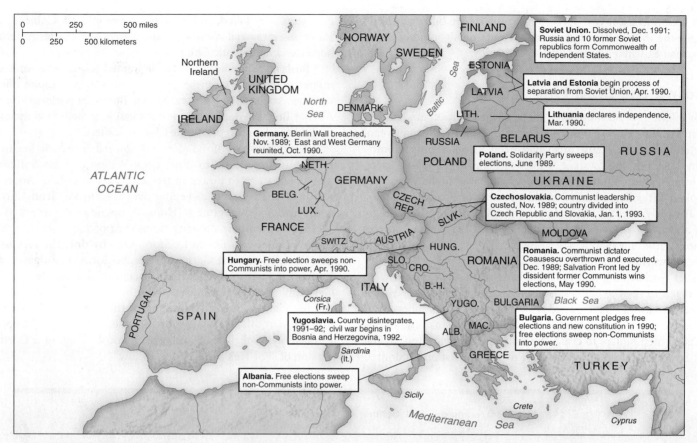

THE END OF THE COLD WAR Free elections in Poland in June 1989 triggered the domino effect in the fall of communism in eastern Europe and the former Soviet Union. Changes in policy came quickly, but the restructuring of social and economic institutions continues to take time.

Most people realized it was Mikhail Gorbachev who was responsible for the liberation of eastern Europe. In late 1988, the Soviet leader signaled the spread of his reforms to the Soviet satellites by announcing that the Brezhnev doctrine, which called for Soviet control of eastern Europe, was now replaced with "the Sinatra doctrine," which meant that the people of this region could now do things "their way." It was Gorbachev's refusal to use armed force to keep repressive regimes in power that permitted the long-delayed liberation of the captive peoples of central and eastern Europe.

Yet by the end of 1991, both Gorbachev and the Soviet Union had become victims of the demise of communism. On August 19, 1991, right-wing plotters placed Gorbachev under arrest. Boris Yeltsin, the newly elected president of the Russian Republic, broke up the coup by mounting a tank in Moscow and demanding Gorbachev's release. The Red Army rallied to Yeltsin's side. The coup failed and Gorbachev was released, only to resign in December 1991 after the fifteen republics dissolved the Soviet Union. Russia, by far the largest and most powerful of the former Soviet republics, took the lead in joining with ten others to form a loose alignment called the Commonwealth of Independent States (CIS). Yeltsin then disbanded the Communist party and continued the reforms begun by Gorbachev to establish democracy and a free market system in Russia.

The Bush administration, although criticized for its cautious approach, welcomed the demise of communism. Bush facilitated the reunification of Germany and offered economic assistance to Russia and the other members of the new CIS. On the critical issue of nuclear weapons, Bush and Gorbachev in 1991 signed START I, agreeing to reduce nuclear warheads to less than ten thousand apiece. In late 1992, Bush and Yeltsin agreed on the terms of START II, which would eliminate land missiles with multiple warheads and reduce the number of nuclear weapons on each side to just over three thousand, a level not seen since the mid-1960s.

The Gulf War

Amid the disintegration of the Soviet system, Iraq in August 1990 invaded Kuwait. Although Bush quickly concluded that Saddam Hussein's aggression must be reversed, actually removing Iraq from Kuwait took time and great effort. The president started by persuading Saudi Arabia to accept a huge American troop buildup, dubbed Desert Shield. This American presence would prevent Saddam from advancing beyond Kuwait into Saudi Arabia; it would also allow the United States to launch a ground attack against Iraqi forces if and when the president determined such an attack was necessary.

While the American buildup took place, Bush arranged an international coalition to condemn the Iraqi invasion and endorse economic sanctions against Iraq. Not every member of the coalition subscribed to the "new world order" that Bush said the liberation of Kuwait would help establish, but all concurred in the general principle of deterring international aggression. Essential to the success of Bush's diplomatic offensive was the support of the

📖 **Read the Document**   **George Bush, Address to the Nation on the Persian Gulf (1991)**

On the evening of January 16,1991, President George H.W. Bush addresses the nation to discuss the launch of Operation Desert Storm.

Soviet Union, which during the Cold War had regularly blocked American initiatives in the United Nations. Soviet leaders may have been sincere in wishing to see Saddam punished, but they also hoped to receive American aid in restructuring their economy.

Congress required somewhat more convincing. Many Democrats supported economic sanctions against Iraq but opposed the use of force. Yet as the troop buildup in the Persian Gulf proceeded—as Operation Desert Shield evolved into what would be called **Operation Desert Storm**—and as the sanctions failed to dislodge Iraq from Kuwait, some of the skeptics gradually came around. After securing UN support for military action, Bush persuaded Congress (with just five votes to spare in the Senate) to approve the use of force to liberate Kuwait.

On January 17, 1991, the president unleashed a devastating aerial assault on Iraq. After knocking out the Iraqi air defense network in a few hours, F-117A stealth fighters and Tomahawk cruise missiles hit key targets in Baghdad. The air attack, virtually unchallenged by the Iraqis, wiped out command and control centers and enabled the bombers of the United States and its coalition partners (chiefly Britain) to demoralize the beleaguered enemy troops.

After five weeks of this, Bush gave the order for the ground assault. Led by General Schwarzkopf, American and allied armored units swept across the desert in a great flanking operation while a combined force of U.S. marines and Saudi troops drove directly into Kuwait City. In just one hundred hours, the American-led offensive liberated Kuwait and sent Saddam Hussein's vaunted Republican Guard fleeing back into Iraq.

In a controversial decision, President Bush, acting on the advice of General Colin Powell, chairman of the Joint Chiefs, halted the advance and agreed to an armistice with Iraq. Critics claimed that with just a few more days of fighting, perhaps even just a few more hours, American forces could have encircled the Republican Guard and ended Saddam's cruel regime. But the president, fearful of disrupting the allied coalition and of having American troops mired down in a guerrilla war, stopped when he had achieved his announced goal of liberating Kuwait. Moreover, he hoped that a chastened Saddam would help balance the threat of Iran in the volatile Persian Gulf region.

Desert Storm brought mixed blessings. It was a great personal victory for George Bush, who saw his approval rating climb to an unprecedented level—nearly 90 percent, higher than for even Eisenhower and Kennedy at the height of the Cold War. American military leaders believed they had finally atoned for Vietnam, a sentiment widely shared by a euphoric public. The United States had deployed more than five hundred thousand troops, as many as were in Vietnam in 1968, and had lost just 146 lives in inflicting a stinging defeat on a dangerous bully. Moreover, the price of oil, which had climbed to nearly $40 a barrel in October, fell back to less than $20, allowing Americans to fill the gas tanks of their cars for just over $1 a gallon.

At the same time, however, Saddam Hussein continued to rule in Baghdad, persecuting Kurds in northern Iraq and Shi'ite Muslims in the south. He survived several attempts on his life and tightened his grip on Iraq, frustrating U.S. efforts to uncover and destroy his suspected chemical, biological, and nuclear weapons facilities. During the next dozen years, many Americans would conclude that if Bush had completed the ouster of Saddam in 1991, he would have spared the United States and the world a great deal of trouble.

The Changing Faces of America

How did the American population shift and grow between 1990 and 2010?

From the *Mayflower* to the covered wagon, movement has always characterized the American people. The final years of the twentieth century and the early years of the twenty-first witnessed two significant shifts in the American population: continued movement internally to the Sunbelt region of the South and West, and a remarkable influx of immigrants from developing nations. These changes led to increased urbanization, greater ethnic diversity, and growing social unrest.

A People on the Move

By the 1990s, a majority of Americans lived in the **Sunbelt** of the South and West. Best defined as a broad band running across the country below the 37th parallel from the Carolinas to Southern California, the Sunbelt had begun to flourish with the buildup of military bases and defense plants during World War II. Rapid population growth continued with the stimulus of heavy Cold War defense spending and accelerated in the 1970s when both new high-technology firms and more established industries were attracted by lower labor costs and the favorable climate of the Sunbelt states. Florida, Texas, and California led the way, each gaining more than two million new residents in the 1970s.

The flow continued at a slightly lower rate over the next two decades. The Northeast and the Middle West continued losing people to the South and West, and in 1994 Texas surpassed New York as the nation's second most populous state. The 2000 census revealed that while all regions had gained population in the 1990s, the South and West had expanded by nearly 20 percent, compared to around 6 percent for the Northeast and Middle West. Phoenix was typical of the phenomenal growth of Sunbelt cities, adding a million residents in the 1990s to grow at a 45 percent rate. "Phoenix is flat and it's easy," explained a geographer who saw no end in sight. "You stick a shovel in the ground and pour a slab and you have a house."

The increasing urbanization of America had positive and negative aspects. People living in the large metropolitan areas were both more affluent and better educated than their rural counterparts. Family income among people living in the bigger cities and their suburbs ran $9,000 a year more, and three-fourths of the urban population had graduated from high school, compared to two-thirds of other Americans. A metropolitan American was twice as likely to be a college graduate as a rural resident. Yet these advantages were offset by higher urban crime rates, longer commuting time in heavy traffic, and higher living costs. Nevertheless, the big cities and their suburbs continued to thrive, accounting for 80 percent of all Americans by 2000.

Another striking population trend was the nationwide rise in the number of the elderly. At the beginning of the twentieth century, only 4.1 percent of the population was aged 65 or older; by 2000, those over 65 made up more than 12 percent of the population, with the nearly four million over 85 the fastest growing group of all. Census Bureau projections suggest that by the year 2030, one out of every five Americans will be over age 65.

Six of every ten older Americans were women, and they tended to have a higher rate of chronic disease and to be worse off economically than men the same age. Many of the oldest old, those over 85, lived in nursing homes and accounted for one-third of all Medicaid payments. Yet only 10 percent of the elderly lived below the poverty line and three-fourths owned their own homes. The annual cost-of-living increases in Social Security payments spared them the worst ravages of inflation. Most impressive of all was their political power: Two-thirds of those over 65 voted regularly, compared to just under half of the entire population. With more than 30 million members, the AARP (formerly known as the American Association of Retired People) proved very effective in Washington in representing the interests of the elderly, particularly in regard to Medicare.

The Revival of Immigration

The flow of immigrants into the United States reached record proportions in the 1990s as a result of the new policies adopted in 1965. (See the Feature Essay in Chapter 30, "Unintended Consequences: The Second Great Migration," pp. 722–723.) The number of arrivals continued to grow during the first decade of the new century, with nearly 8 million immigrants reaching America between the beginning of 2000 and early 2005. By 2005, a record high of 35 million foreign-born persons lived in the United States, constituting 12 percent of the total population.

The new wave of immigrants came mainly from Latin America and Asia. By 2005, over half the foreign-born population of the United States came from Latin America, about one-quarter from Asia, and about one out of seven from Europe. The new immigrants tended to settle in urban areas in six states—California, Texas, New York, Florida, Illinois, and New Jersey. In California, the influx of immigrants from Asia and Mexico created growing pressure on public services, especially during the recessions of the early 1990s and the early 2000s.

The arrival of so many immigrants was bound to lead to controversy over whether immigrants were a benefit or a liability to American society. A study by the National Academy of Sciences in

1997 reported that while government services used by immigrants—schools, welfare, health clinics—cost more initially than was collected from them in taxes, in the long run, immigrants and their families more than paid their way. In regard to employment, immigrants tended to help consumers and employers by working for relatively low wages in restaurants, the textile industry, and farming, but they hurt low-skilled U.S. workers, notably high school dropouts and many African Americans, by keeping wages low. Economist George J. Borjas, a refugee from Cuba, claimed that immigrants from developing countries lacked the education and job skills needed to achieve the level of prosperity attained by newcomers in the past; instead of entering the mainstream of American life, they were likely to remain a permanent underclass.

Emerging Hispanics

People of Hispanic origin became the nation's largest ethnic group in 2002, surpassing African Americans for the first time. The rapidly growing Hispanic population climbed to over 41 million by 2005, accounting for 14 percent of the nation's population. "It doesn't surprise me," commented the leader of the League of Latin American Citizens. "Anybody that travels around . . . can see Latinos everywhere, working everywhere, trying to reach the American dream."

The Census Bureau identified four major Hispanic groups: Mexican Americans, Puerto Ricans, Cuban Americans, and other Hispanics, including many from Central America. Even though most of the Hispanic population was concentrated in cities such as New York, Los Angeles, San Antonio, and Miami, the 2000 census showed a surprising geographical spread. Hispanics made up 20 percent of the population in individual counties in states such as Georgia, Iowa, and Minnesota. "The Latinization of the country is not just happening in New York, Miami, or L.A.," observed a Puerto Rican leader. "Its greatest impact is in the heartland in places like Reading, Pennsylvania; Lorain, Ohio; and Lowell, Massachusetts."

The Hispanic groups had several features in common. All were relatively youthful, with a median age of 22 and a high fertility rate. They tended to be relatively poor, with one-fourth falling below the poverty line, and to be employed in low-paying positions as manual laborers, domestic servants, and migrant workers. Although the position of Hispanics had improved considerably in the boom years of the 1980s and 1990s, they still lagged behind mainstream America. The poverty rate among Hispanics was twice the national average, and family median income in 2005 was $34,000, or roughly two-thirds the level for whites.

Lack of education was a key factor in preventing economic progress for Hispanics. Fewer Hispanics graduated from high school than other minorities, and their school dropout rate was the nation's highest at more than 50 percent. Hispanic leaders warned that these figures boded ill not just for their own group but for society as a whole. "You either educate us," claimed a San Antonio activist, "or you pay for building more jails or for more welfare."

Read the Document Illegal Immigration Reform and Immigrant Responsibility Act of 1996

Newly sworn-in citizens of the United States wave U.S. flags during a naturalization ceremony in Miami on April 28, 2006. Days later, more than one million immigrants participated in a nationwide boycott called "A Day Without Immigrants" to protest the proposed tightening of U.S. immigration laws.

The entry of several million illegal immigrants from Mexico, once derisively called "wetbacks" and now known as **undocumented aliens**, created a substantial social problem for the nation and especially for the Southwest. Critics charged that the flagrant violation of the nation's border with Mexico had led to a subculture beyond the boundaries of law and ordinary custom. They argued that the aliens took jobs from U.S. citizens, kept wages artificially low, and received extensive welfare and medical benefits that strained budgets in states such as Texas and California.

Defenders of the undocumented aliens contended that the nation gained from the abundant supply of workers who were willing to work in fields and factories at backbreaking jobs shunned by most Americans. Moreover, defenders stated, illegal entrants usually paid sales and withholding taxes but rarely used government services for fear of being deported. Whichever view was correct, an exploited class of illegal aliens was living on the edge of poverty. The *Wall Street Journal* summed it up best by observing, "The people who benefit the most from this situation are certainly the employers, who have access to an underground market of cheap, productive labor, unencumbered by minimum wage laws, union restrictions, or pension requirements."

Concern over economic competition from Mexican "illegals" led Congress to pass legislation in 1986 that penalized employers who hired undocumented workers. Congress permitted those aliens who could show that they were living in the United States before 1982 to become legal residents; nearly three million accepted this offer of amnesty to become legal residents. The reform effort, however, failed to stem the continued flow of undocumented workers northward from Mexico in the 1990s and early 2000s—more than five hundred thousand in some years. While experts debated the exact number, the most widely accepted estimates indicated that more than ten million foreigners, mainly from Mexico and Central America, were living illegally in the United States in 2005.

Despite stepped-up border enforcement efforts after the September 11, 2001, terrorist attacks, illegal immigrants continued to move northward from Mexico and Central America. The trip could be dangerous, even lethal. Human-rights advocates estimated that more than three thousand migrants lost their lives attempting to enter the United States illegally between 1997 and 2006. Nineteen Mexican and Central American workers died from suffocation in south Texas in May 2003—nearly one hundred illegal aliens had been jammed into a truck trailer without access to water or fresh air. Yet the movement continued. As one rural Mexican official commented, "There are great problems in the countryside. And that famous American dream keeps calling."

Advance and Retreat for African Americans

African Americans formed the second largest of the nation's ethnic minorities. In 2004, there were just over 39 million blacks in the United States, 13.4 percent of the population. Although the heaviest concentration of African Americans was in northern cities, notably New York and Chicago, there was a significant movement back to the South. This shift, which began in the 1970s and accelerated during the 1990s, meant that by 2000 nearly 54 percent of those identifying themselves as black for the census lived in the sixteen states of the Sunbelt. Family ties and a search for ancestral roots explained much of this movement, but it also reflected the same economic incentives that drew so many Americans to the Sunbelt in the last three decades of the twentieth century.

African Americans made substantial gains in certain areas of life. In 2004, some 81 percent of blacks aged 25 and older had earned a high school diploma, an increase of 8 percent during the previous decade. Eighteen percent of African Americans possessed a college degree, 5 percent more than a decade earlier. The number of black-owned businesses topped 1.2 million, up more than 45 percent since 1997.

Yet in other respects African Americans did less well. The black poverty rate was nearly 25 percent, and the median income for black families was less than two-thirds of that for whites. Blacks remained clustered in entry-level jobs, where they faced increasing competition from immigrants. The African American incarceration rate was much higher than the national average; in 2002, more than 10 percent of black males aged 25 to 29 were in prison, and more than one out of four black men could expect to spend time in a state or federal prison during their lives. Blacks were also more likely to be victims of crime, especially violent crime. Homicide was the leading cause of death among black males between the ages of 15 and 34.

Two events, one from 1991 and the other from 2005, summarized much of the frustration African Americans felt. In March 1991, a bystander videotaped four Los Angeles policemen brutally beating Rodney King, an African American who had been stopped for a traffic violation. The pictures of the rain of blows on King shocked the nation. Nearly a year later, when an all-white jury acquitted the four officers of charges of police brutality, rioting erupted in South Central Los Angeles that for a time threatened the entire city when the police failed to respond promptly. In the aftermath of the riot, which took fifty-three lives (compared to thirty-four deaths in the 1965 riot in the nearby Watts area) and did more than $1 billion in damage, government and state agencies promised new efforts to help the inner-city dwellers. But the efforts produced little effect, and life for many urban blacks remained difficult and dangerous.

A tragedy of a different sort occurred fourteen years later. In August 2005, Hurricane Katrina ravaged the Gulf Coast and broke levees in New Orleans. The high winds and water killed more than a thousand persons, destroyed hundreds of thousands of homes, and forced the evacuation of millions of men, women, and children. Television cameras captured the plight of the several thousand who took refuge in the New Orleans Superdome, only to be stranded when state and federal relief efforts failed. Most conspicuous in the footage was the fact that the vast majority of those suffering the worst in New Orleans were black. Their neighborhoods were the lowest-lying in the city, and hence, the worst flooded. Many lacked the cars necessary to flee the city in advance of the hurricane; others lacked the means to pay for hotels or apartments had they been able to get out. Though the relief efforts were largely color-blind (despite early allegations to the contrary), the entire experience demonstrated that poverty in America most certainly was not.

Americans from Asia and the Middle East

Asian Americans were the fasting-growing minority group at the beginning of the twenty-first century. According to the 2000 census, there were more than 12 million Americans of Asian or Pacific Island descent. Although they represented only 4 percent of the total population, they were increasing at seven times the national rate, and future projections indicated that by 2050 one in ten Americans would be of Asian ancestry.

The Chinese formed the largest single group of Asian Americans, followed by Filipinos, Japanese, Indians, Koreans, and Vietnamese. Immigration was the primary reason for the rapid growth of all these groups except the Japanese; during the 1980s, Asia had provided nearly half of all immigrants to the United States. Though the influx subsequently slowed, the children of the immigrants added to the Asian numbers.

Compared to other minorities, Asian Americans were well-educated and affluent. Three out of four Asian youths graduated from high school, compared to less than one out of two for blacks and Hispanics. Asian Americans also had the highest percentage of college graduates and recipients of doctoral degrees of any minority group; in fact, they were better represented in colleges and universities than the white majority. Many Asians entered professional fields, and in part as a result, the median income for Asian American families in 2004 was nearly 20 percent higher than the national average.

Not all Asian Americans fared so well, however. Refugees from Southeast Asia experienced both economic hardship and persecution. The median family income for Vietnamese Americans fell substantially below the national average. Nearly half the Laotian refugees living in Minnesota were unemployed because they had great difficulty learning to read and write English. Vietnamese fishermen who settled on the Gulf Coast of Texas and Louisiana experienced repeated attacks on their livelihood and their homes. In the Los Angeles riots in 1992, Korean stores and shops became a main target for looting and firebombing.

But the overall experience of Asian Americans was a positive one. They came to America seeking economic opportunity, or as many put it, "to climb the mountain of gold." "People are looking for a better life," a Chinese spokeswoman explained. "It's as simple as that, and we will continue to come here, especially if the situations over there [in Asia] stay tight, or get worse."

The number of Americans from the Middle East grew almost as fast as the number of those from Asia in the 1990s. The 2000 census counted 1.5 million Americans of Middle Eastern ancestry, up from 200,000 thirty years earlier. Most came from Arab countries, as well as Israel and Iran. Concentrated in California, New York, and Michigan, Middle Eastern Americans were well-educated, with nearly half having college degrees. Many Arab Americans felt nervous after the terrorist attacks of September 11, 2001, committed by Arab extremists; some experienced actual violence at the hands of persons who wanted to blame anyone of Arab descent for the shocking mass murders. Yet most Arab Americans carried on as before, pursuing their interpretation of the American dream.

Assimilation or Diversity?

The influx of people from all around the world, not just from Europe, had profound implications for American culture. Traditionally, the favorite American self-image was the melting pot, the title of Israel Zangwill's play written in 1908, at the height of European immigration into the nation. "America is God's crucible, the great Melting-Pot where all the races of Europe are melting and reforming," one of his characters proclaimed. "Germans and Frenchmen, Irishmen and Englishmen, Jews and Russians—into the Crucible with you all! God is making the American!"

The melting pot image carried with it the concept of stripping newcomers of their culture and national traits and casting them into an Anglo-Saxon mold. Dubious for European immigration in view of the way each ethnic group retained its separate identity, this analogy seemed increasingly irrelevant to the Latin American, Asian, and Middle Eastern migration to America in the late twentieth and early twenty-first centuries. Instead of recasting immigrants into an American type, immigration could better be seen as broadening the diversity that had always characterized the United States. Sociologist Amitai Etzioni suggested replacing the melting pot image with a "mosaic" portraying a nation in which ethnic groups retained their own identities "while recognizing that they are integral parts of a more encompassing whole."

The new awareness of ethnic diversity manifested itself in many ways. In public education, blacks led a crusade against Eurocentric curriculums and demanded a new emphasis on the influence of African culture; on college campuses, the call for multicultural courses and separate departments for African American, Asian American, and Hispanic studies created controversy. Citing the forecasts of a declining Anglo dominance and the rise of minority groups in the twenty-first century, ethnic leaders advocated cultural pluralism. Raul Yzaguirre, president of the National Council of La Raza, an Hispanic advocacy group, argued that America had never had a real melting pot in which all races contributed to the mix. "What we've had is a pressure cooker, where everybody has had to come in and become Anglophiles." Yzaguirre claimed that the "new demographics ask America to live up to its own conception of itself as a pluralistic society."

Many Americans found themselves perplexed and uncertain of their cultural identity. A Census Bureau survey, asking people to state their ancestry, revealed that fully one-fourth of Americans listed Germany first, with Ireland and England a distant second and third. Some Hispanics found the census racial classifications—black, Asian–Pacific Islander, white, or American Indian—meaningless. "I don't really consider myself Caucasian," objected Jose Arroyo of San Jose, California. "My roots go down into the Indians of Mexico." People of Arab descent felt equally confused. Maha El-Sheikh, a Californian of mixed Egyptian and Jordanian parentage, resented the fact that "on tests and things like that, I either have to put that I'm 'Caucasian' or I'm 'Asian'—which I'm not. . . . I say I am Arabic—or I leave it blank."

In the 1990s, people of mixed racial parentage demanded that the census for 2000 include a box labeled "multiracial" rather than just the meaningless "other." A group called Project RACE (Reclassify All Children Equally) argued that the four million children of more than a million interracial marriages deserved their own census category. The professional golf champion Tiger Woods—whose ancestry is part black, part Thai, part Chinese, part Native American, and part Caucasian—agreed, saying that as a child he called himself "Cablinasian." Civil rights groups, however, objected, fearing cuts in government benefits to minorities based on the census figures. The Census Bureau compromised in 2000 by adding four new dual-race categories—American Indian–white, American Indian–black, Asian-white, and black-white.

In addition, individuals of mixed ancestry could mark several racial categories, not just one as in the past.

The results were startling. Nearly seven million Americans claimed to be multiracial, with most choosing either black-white or Asian-white. Levonne Gaddy, president of the Association of Multiethnic Americans, was ecstatic. "This is the beginning of our having to redefine this social myth that we call race," she declared. A more neutral Census Bureau official observed, "The nation is much more diverse in the year 2000 than it was in 1990." "That diversity," he added, "is much more complex than we've ever measured before."

Horace Kallen, one of the early critics of Zangwill's melting pot analogy, offered the most appealing image of the nation's diverse heritage. He likened the United States to a symphony orchestra, in which each nationality and ethnic group contributed its "own specific timbre and tonality" to create "a multiplicity in a unity, an orchestration of mankind." As Americans wrestled with the continuing dilemma embodied in the national motto, *E pluribus unum,* the image of a great symphony in which all groups blended harmoniously offered a way to balance the pride individuals find in ethnic identity with the need for national unity.

The New Democrats

What were the accomplishments and failures of the Clinton administration?

The Democrats, victims of the runaway inflation of the 1970s, became the beneficiaries of the lingering recession of the early 1990s. Moving away from its traditional liberal reliance on big government, the party regained strength by choosing moderate candidates and tailoring its programs to appeal to the hard-pressed middle class. These tactics enabled the Democrats to regain the White House in 1992 and retain it in 1996, despite a Republican sweep of Congress in 1994. The key figure in this political shift was Bill Clinton, who overcame some early setbacks to reap the rewards of a sustained economic boom.

 Watch the Video Bill Clinton Sells Himself to America

Twelve years of Republican administrations and economic turmoil left voters ready to make a change. Enter Bill Clinton, Democratic governor of Arkansas, who would best George Bush in the election of 1992 and go on to serve two full terms.

The Election of 1992

The persistence of the recession that had begun two years earlier became a major political issue in 1992. Although mild by postwar standards, the economic downturn that began in July 1990 proved unusually stubborn, especially in states such as California that relied heavily on the defense industry, which was hurt by the end of the Cold War. The recovery, which started just after the end of the Persian Gulf War in the spring of 1991, proved slow and uneven. Unemployment remained high for eighteen months and the gross domestic product rose only an anemic 2.9 percent in the same period.

The political impact was devastating for the Bush administration. Three million Americans joined the ranks of the unemployed, and many were white-collar employees rather than factory workers typically hit by hard times. Although the economy began to advance more briskly in 1992, unemployment persisted as businesses still hesitated to hire new workers. As a result, the average American worker was ready to look beyond the Republican party for relief.

As Bush's popularity plummeted, two men sought to capitalize on the dismal state of the U.S. economy. First, Arkansas governor Bill Clinton defeated a field of five other challengers for the Democratic nomination by becoming the champion of economic renewal. Forgoing traditional liberal appeals to interest groups, Clinton stressed the need for investment in the nation's future—rebuilding roads and bridges, training workers for high-tech jobs, and solving the growing national health care crisis.

Despite his victories in the Democratic primaries, however, Clinton faced a new rival in H. Ross Perot. An eccentric Texas billionaire, Perot singled out the deficit as the nation's gravest problem and agreed to run as an independent candidate in response to a grassroots movement (which he financed) to place his name on the November ballot.

When Clinton and his running mate, Senator Albert Gore, Jr., of Tennessee, succeeded in unifying the Democratic party and gaining agreement on a moderate platform promising economic change, Perot stunned his supporters by suddenly dropping out of the race in July. Clinton immediately became the front-runner, rising from 30 percent to more than 50 percent in the polls, leaving Bush far behind.

A relentless Democratic attack on the administration's lackluster economic performance overcame all the president's efforts to remind the nation of Reagan prosperity and Bush triumphs abroad. Even GOP assaults on Clinton's character, notably his evasion of the draft during the Vietnam War, failed to halt the Democratic momentum. The message that Clinton's political advisers tacked up at the Democratic candidate's headquarters in Little Rock—"The economy, stupid"—provided the key to victory in November. Clinton wound up with 43 percent of the popular vote but with a commanding lead in the electoral college, 370 to 168 for Bush. Perot, who had reentered the race, won 19 percent of the popular vote but failed to carry a single state.

Clinton and Congress

In the White House, Bill Clinton proved to be the most adept politician since Franklin Roosevelt. Born in Hope, Arkansas, in 1946, Clinton weathered a difficult childhood with an alcoholic stepfather by developing skills at dealing with people and using personal charm to achieve his goals. Intelligent and ambitious, he completed his undergraduate work at Georgetown University, studied law at Yale, and spent two years as a Rhodes scholar at Oxford University in England. Entering politics after teaching law briefly at the University of Arkansas, he won election first as Arkansas attorney general and then as governor. Defeated after his first term in 1980, Clinton won the nickname "Comeback Kid" by regaining the governor's office in 1982. He was elected three more times, earning a reputation as one of the nation's most successful young political leaders.

In keeping with the theme of his campaign, Clinton concentrated at first on the economy. The federal budget he proposed to Congress in February 1993 called for tax increases and spending cuts to achieve a balanced budget. Congress was skeptical of such unpopular measures, but Clinton cajoled, shamed, and threatened sufficient members to win approval of $241 billion in new taxes and $255 billion in spending cuts, for a total deficit reduction of $496 billion over four years. This major achievement earned Clinton the confidence of financial markets and helped fuel the economic boom of the 1990s.

Clinton scored another victory when Congress approved the North American Free Trade Agreement (NAFTA) in the fall of 1993. NAFTA, initiated and nearly completed by Bush, was a free-trade plan that united the United States, Mexico, and Canada into a common market without tariff barriers. Clinton endorsed the treaty as a way of securing American prosperity and spreading American values. Critics complained that free trade would cost American workers their jobs as American companies moved production overseas; Ross Perot, the defeated 1992 third-party candidate, predicted a "giant sucking sound" as American jobs went south to Mexico. But Clinton carried the day, winning a bruising fight in the House and an easier contest in the Senate.

Election of 1992

Electoral Vote by State		Popular Vote
DEMOCRATIC Bill Clinton	370	44,908,254
REPUBLICAN George Bush	168	39,102,343
INDEPENDENT H. Ross Perot	—	19,741,065
MINOR PARTIES	—	773,161
	538	104,524,823

ALASKA 3

HAWAII 4

WASH., D.C. 3

Although Clinton's NAFTA coalition included many congressional Republicans, on other issues the GOP staunchly opposed the president. Republicans decried his budget as entailing "the biggest tax increase in the history of the world," and they scuttled an ambitious attempt to revamp the nation's health care system. Leading the opposition was a young congressman from Georgia, Newton Leroy "Newt" Gingrich, who asked all GOP candidates in the 1994 congressional races to sign a ten-point **Contract with America**. The contract consisted of familiar conservative goals, including a balanced budget amendment to the Constitution, term limits for members of Congress, a line-item veto for the president, and a middle-class tax cut. For the first time in recent political history, a party sought to win Congress on ideological issues rather than relying on individual personalities.

A series of embarrassing disclosures involving Bill Clinton's character made this tactic particularly effective in 1994. During the 1992 campaign, the *New York Times* had raised questions about a bankrupt Arkansas land development called Whitewater in which the Clintons had lost a modest investment. Additional scandals cropped up over activities that had taken place after Clinton was elected president. Travelgate was the name given to the firing, apparently at the urging of First Lady Hillary Clinton, of several White House employees who arranged travel for the press covering the president. Then in early 1994, Paula Jones, a former Arkansas state employee, filed a sexual harassment suit against Clinton, charging that in 1991 then-Governor Clinton had made sexual advances to her.

The outcome of the November 1994 vote stunned political observers. The Republicans gained 9 seats in the Senate and an astonishing 53 in the House to take control of both houses. Newt Gingrich, who had worked so hard to ensure the change in leadership in the Congress, became speaker of the House. The GOP also captured 32 governorships, including those of New York, California, and Texas, where George W. Bush, the son of the man Clinton beat in 1992, won handily.

The Republicans claimed a mandate to resume the Reagan Revolution: to cut taxes, diminish the scope of government, and empower the private sector. Clinton and the Democrats managed to keep the Republicans in check on matters of substance, but the Republicans, in turn, contrived to hobble Clinton. The administration and the Republicans collaborated on welfare reform and a modest increase in the minimum wage, but otherwise deadlock descended on Washington.

Clinton turned the deadlock to his benefit in 1996 after the Republicans, having failed to force him to accept cuts in Medicare, college loans, and other social services, refused to pass a budget bill, and thereby shut down the federal government. Clinton proved more deft at finger-pointing than Gingrich and the Republicans did, and he succeeded in persuading voters that they were to blame. He carried this theme into his 1996 reelection campaign. The Republican nominee, Robert Dole of Kansas, lacked Clinton's charisma and failed to shake the impression that the Republicans were flint-hearts who wanted to cut the pet programs of the American people. Clinton won decisively, holding the presidency for the Democrats even while the Republicans continued to control Congress.

Scandal in the White House

Despite Clinton's reelection, rumors of wrongdoing still clung to his presidency. The special prosecutor appointed to probe the Whitewater transactions, Kenneth Starr, turned over stone after stone in search of evidence of malfeasance, until he came across rumors that Clinton had conducted a clandestine affair with a White House intern, Monica Lewinsky.

Clinton initially denied the affair. "I did not have sexual relations with that woman, Miss Lewinsky," he said in January 1998. But Starr subpoenaed Lewinsky, who eventually gave a detailed account of her sexual encounters with the president and provided crucial physical evidence implicating Clinton.

Realizing that he could no longer deny the affair, the president sought to limit the damage. On August 17, 1998, he appeared before Starr's grand jury and admitted to having "inappropriate intimate contact" with Lewinsky. That evening Clinton spoke briefly to the nation. Claiming that he had given the grand jury "legally accurate" answers, the president for the first time admitted to a relationship with Lewinsky that was "not appropriate" and "wrong." He said he regretted misleading the people and especially his wife, but he refused to apologize for his behavior or his false denials.

Clinton's fate hung in the balance. For the first time, some Democrats began to speak out, most notably Senator Joseph Lieberman of Connecticut, who called the president's behavior "disgraceful" and "immoral." But just when Clinton seemed most vulnerable, the special prosecutor inadvertently rescued him. In early September, Starr sent a 452-page report to Congress outlining

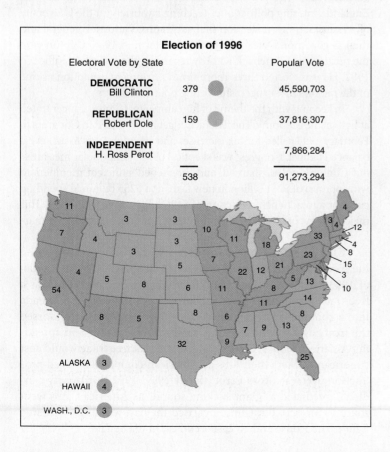

Election of 1996

Electoral Vote by State		Popular Vote
DEMOCRATIC Bill Clinton	379	45,590,703
REPUBLICAN Robert Dole	159	37,816,307
INDEPENDENT H. Ross Perot	—	7,866,284
	538	91,273,294

ALASKA 3

HAWAII 4

WASH., D.C. 3

📖 Read the Document   Bill Clinton, Answers to the Articles of Impeachment

Members of the House Judiciary Committee listen to Clinton's testimony during the hearings on the president's impeachment in December 1998. The Committee sent four articles of impeachment to the full House, and the House adopted two—one count of perjury and one of obstruction of justice. The Senate could not muster the two-thirds majority required for conviction, and so Clinton was acquitted of both articles.

eleven possible impeachment charges against Clinton. The key charge was perjury, and Starr provided painstakingly graphic detail on all of the sexual encounters between Clinton and Lewinsky to prove that the president had lied when he denied engaging in sexual relations with the intern.

Many Americans responded by condemning Starr rather than the president. Shocked by the sordid details, they blamed the prosecutor for exposing families to distasteful sexual practices on the evening news. When Hillary Clinton stood staunchly by her husband, a majority of the public seemed to conclude that however bad the president's conduct, it was a private matter, one to be settled between a husband and a wife, not in the public arena.

Republican leaders ignored the public sentiment and pressed ahead with impeachment proceedings. In December, the House (where the 1998 midterm elections had narrowed the GOP advantage to six) voted on four articles of impeachment, rejecting two, but approving two others—perjury and obstruction of justice—by small margins in nearly straight party-line votes.

The final showdown in the Senate was anticlimactic. With a two-thirds vote required to find the president guilty and remove him from office, there was no chance of conviction in the highly charged partisan mood that prevailed. On February 12, 1999,

the GOP was unable to muster even a majority on the perjury charge, with 45 in favor and 55 opposed. After a second, closer vote, 50 to 50, on obstruction of justice, the presiding officer, Chief Justice William Rehnquist, declared, "Acquitted of the charges."

Clinton had survived the Monica Lewinsky affair, but he emerged from the ordeal with his presidency badly damaged. His final two years in office would be devoted to a concerted effort to restore his damaged reputation. Desperate for a legacy to mark his White House years, Clinton failed to realize that he had already created an enduring one—he would always be remembered as the president who dishonored his office by his affair with a young intern.

Clinton and the World

How did Clinton respond to the Balkan Wars?

Neither Clinton's scandals nor his struggle with Congress allowed Americans to forget about the rest of the world, although many would have liked to do so. The Cold War had ended, and with it America's forty-year struggle with communism. But the post–Cold

War world was plenty threatening, and while the United States was the only superpower still standing, America's power could not preserve Americans from having to make difficult decisions about how to use that power.

Old Rivals in New Light

Inheriting the chaos left by the breakup of the Soviet Union, Clinton concentrated on two issues in dealing with Russia and its neighbors. First, as Bush had done, he strongly supported Russian President Boris Yeltsin. In 1993, Clinton persuaded Congress to provide a $2.5 billion aid package to help Yeltsin carry out his free market reforms of the devastated Russian economy. The Clinton administration backed Yeltsin and his successor, Vladimir V. Putin, despite Russia's continuing brutal war with Chechnya. Although the expansion of NATO to include Poland, Hungary, and the Czech Republic, and plans for a missile defense system created some tension, the Clinton administration succeeded in maintaining good relations with Russia.

Clinton was even more successful on the second big issue left over from the Cold War against the Soviets: preventing the proliferation of nuclear weapons among the former republics of the Soviet Union. With patient diplomacy, Secretary of State Warren Christopher won agreements from Belarus and Kazakhstan to scrap their deadly ICBMs. Ukraine proved more difficult, but in 1994, Clinton persuaded the president of Ukraine to surrender his country's entire nuclear stockpile. Clinton's effort on behalf of nuclear nonproliferation in the former Soviet Union was perhaps his most important, if least heralded, achievement.

The president's policy toward China was more questionable. Clinton ignored China's dismal human rights record and continued Bush's policy of annually extending most-favored-nation status to Beijing. The growing importance of trade with China, whose economic output in 1993 exceeded Britain's, led Clinton to overlook the memory of the Tiananmen Square massacre and the continued persecution of dissidents in China. As trade with China began to rival that with Japan, the president announced a policy of "constructive engagement." It was better, he contended, to keep talking, and trading, with China than to harden Chinese resentment against the West by harping on moral issues. In 2000, Clinton won a notable victory for free trade when the House voted to give China permanent most-favored-nation status.

The Chinese, however, proved to be less than fully cooperative. China ignored U.S. protests of its export of missiles to Iran and nuclear technology to Pakistan, and it continued to stifle dissent at home. China conducted provocative missile tests near Taiwan, which Beijing still claimed for China. When the Clinton administration sent aircraft carriers to patrol the waters off Taiwan, a Chinese official talked casually about raining nuclear bombs upon Los Angeles. Constructive engagement clearly had its limits.

To Intervene or Not

The most difficult foreign policy decisions for the Clinton administration came over the use of American troops abroad. The absence of the Cold War threat, with its implicit need to counter communist rivals, made it much more difficult for the president

and his advisers to decide when the national interest required sending American servicemen and servicewomen into harm's way. Between 1993 and 1999, Clinton opted for foreign intervention in four areas—Somalia, Haiti, Bosnia, and Kosovo—with decidedly mixed results.

Clinton inherited the Somalian venture from Bush, who in December 1992 had sent twenty-five thousand American troops to that starving country on a humanitarian mission. Under Clinton, however, the original aim of using troops to protect the flow of food supplies and relief workers gradually shifted to supporting a UN effort at nation building. Tragedy struck in October 1993 when eighteen American soldiers died in a botched attempt to capture a local warlord in Mogadishu. After television cameras recorded the naked corpse of a U.S. helicopter pilot being dragged through the streets of Somalia's capital, an angry Congress demanded a quick end to the intervention. American forces left Somalia by the end of March 1994 in what was unquestionably the low point of Clinton foreign policy.

The lack of clear criteria governing intervention that had brought on the disaster in Somalia almost led to another fiasco in Haiti. Seeking to halt the flow into Florida of thousands of Haitians fleeing both poverty and tyranny, Clinton worked to compel the military rulers of Haiti to abdicate in favor of the man they had overthrown in 1991, Jean-Bertrand Aristide. After nearly a year of trade sanctions and increasing diplomatic pressure, the president prepared to use force to remove the military regime. At the last minute, a three-member peace mission led by former President Jimmy Carter worked out a compromise that allowed U.S. troops to land unopposed in late September 1994. Aristide returned to Haiti, but he could do little either to restore democracy or achieve economic progress in view of his country's bankrupt treasury, ruined economy, and deep political divisions. By the time Aristide turned over the presidency to his elected successor in 1996, Haiti remained mired in hopeless poverty. The reality of Haiti's plight had frustrated Clinton's effort to use American power righteously.

The Balkan Wars

Two other U.S. interventions, in Bosnia and Kosovo in the Balkan Peninsula, were more difficult but more successful. The breakup of Yugoslavia in 1991 led the Muslim president of Bosnia to ask the European community to recognize the independence of Bosnia-Herzegovina. But Bosnia's ethnic and religious makeup—44 percent Muslim, 31 percent Serb, and 17 percent Croat—contributed to a civil war in which the Bosnian Serbs used the weapons of the former Yugoslavian army to seize more than 70 percent of Bosnian territory. The Muslim and Croatian forces were unable to prevent the Serb bombardment of the capital, Sarajevo, or the Serb policy of "ethnic cleansing"—driving Muslims and Croats from their ancestral homes.

Clinton initially backed a plan to divide Bosnia into ten ethnic provinces. When the Serbs rejected the proposal in the spring of 1993, the president fell back on using American air power to patrol no-fly zones over Bosnia designed to protect UN peacekeeping efforts. Meanwhile, Serb artillery continued to pour a withering fire on the civilian population of Sarajevo, and journalists reported a series of brutal atrocities in which Serb troops slaughtered thousands of Muslim men and raped thousands of Muslim women.

These reports forced Clinton's hand. In the summer of 1995, American planes under NATO auspices began a series of air strikes on the Serb forces that were shelling Sarajevo from the surrounding mountains. The air campaign, which lasted two weeks, along with a major counteroffensive by better equipped Croatian and Muslim forces, led to a cease-fire in October 1995. The three warring factions sent delegations to Dayton, Ohio, to discuss a settlement. After three weeks of talks, U.S. mediator Richard Holbrooke secured agreement to create a weak central government for all Bosnia at Sarajevo and to divide the rest of the country into two parts—a Muslim–Croatian federation with 51 percent of the territory and a Serbian enclave with 49 percent. The Dayton plan called for free elections, the return of refugees to their former homes, and a NATO force to oversee the peace process.

The U.S. intervention in Kosovo was similarly rooted in the breakup of Yugoslavia. Serbian leader Slobodan Milosevic had ended Kosovo's autonomy within Yugoslavia and imposed Serbian

Read the Document The Balkan Proximity Peace Talks Agreement (1995)

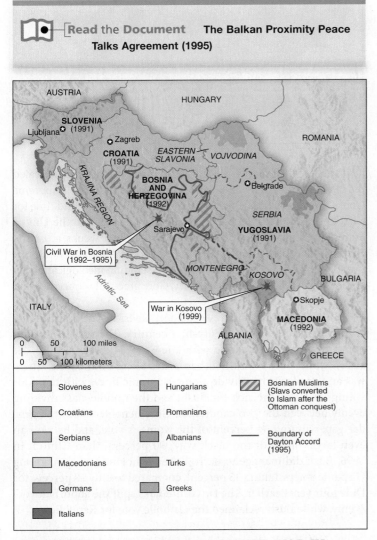

THE BREAKUP OF YUGOSLAVIA/CIVIL WAR IN BOSNIA With the end of the communist regime in Yugoslavia in the early 1990s, the country broke apart into ethnically distinct regions. In Bosnia, Muslims, Croatians, and Serbians fought a bloody civil war rife with atrocities on all sides over the issue of ethnic cleansing.

rule, even though 90 percent of the province's population was ethnic Albanian. When these Kosovars launched a guerrilla war against the Serbian police, Milosevic responded with a campaign of repression that outraged world opinion. Diplomatic efforts failed to achieve a ceasefire, prompting Clinton and the heads of government of other NATO countries in March 1999 to order an aerial assault on Serbia, in an effort to end the persecution of the Kosovars.

At first it appeared that Clinton had miscalculated. The initial air attacks, directed at empty barracks and remote military bases, failed to persuade Milosevic to seek peace. Instead, he stepped up the ethnic cleansing in Kosovo, forcing hundreds of thousands of Kosovars to leave their homes and flee to neighboring Albania and Macedonia. Clinton and the NATO governments shifted the focus of the air assault to Serbia's infrastructure, targeting bridges, oil refineries, and, most important of all, power stations. By the end of May 1999, Serbia had lost 60 percent of its electrical capacity, and domestic pressure on Milosevic began to mount. With Russian diplomats acting as go-betweens, Milosevic finally agreed to halt his attempts to purge Kosovo of its Albanian inhabitants. An agreement signed on June 10, 1999, called for the withdrawal of all Serb forces and placed Kosovo under UN supervision, with NATO troops acting as peacekeepers.

The conflict over Kosovo revealed both the strengths and weaknesses of the United States in the turbulent post–Cold War world. American military power, while great, was limited by a strong desire to avoid risking American lives. Clinton could boast of an amazing result—NATO had waged a 12-week air campaign without the loss of a single pilot. Yet the United States had been unable to prevent Milosevic from uprooting and terrorizing nearly one million Kosovars. When the fighting ended, the Kosovars returned to their devastated homeland, and soon NATO troops had the thankless task of preventing the Albanians from seeking revenge against the Serbian minority in Kosovo.

Republicans Triumphant

How did George W. Bush become president, and what did he do in the White House?

Clinton's eight years in the White House gave Democrats hope that the conservative gains of the 1980s had been only temporary. They pointed to the booming economy of the 1990s and the absence of any serious threat to American security as reasons for voters to leave the presidency in Democratic hands. The election of 2000 proved a bitter disappointment—all the more bitter by reason of the way in which it made Republican George W. Bush president.

The Disputed Election of 2000

If history had been the guide, the prosperity of the 1990s should have guaranteed victory to Clinton's protégé, Vice President Al Gore. The state of the economy generally determines the outcome of presidential elections, and entering 2000, the American economy had never appeared stronger. The stock market soared, spreading wealth among tens of millions of Americans; the federal deficit of the Reagan years had given way to large and growing surpluses.

But Clinton's personal problems muddled the issue. Clinton had survived his impeachment trial, yet the experience tainted his record and left many voters unwilling to reward the Democrats by promoting his vice president.

Certain other domestic problems unnerved voters, as well. The 1995 bombing of a federal building in Oklahoma City by two domestic terrorists killed 168 people and suggested that irrational violence threatened the daily lives of ordinary Americans. This feeling was reinforced by a 1999 shooting rampage at Columbine High School near Denver, which left twelve students and a teacher dead, besides the two shooters, who killed themselves. The apparent conflict between material abundance and eroding personal values resulted in the closest election in more than a century.

The two candidates, Vice President Gore of Tennessee and Governor Bush of Texas, had little in common beyond being the sons of successful political fathers. Gore had spent eighteen years in Washington as a congressman, senator, and vice president. Somewhat stiff and aloof in manner, he had mastered the intricacies of all the major policy issues and had the experience and knowledge to lead the nation. Bush, by contrast, had pursued a business career before winning the governorship of Texas in 1994. Personable and outgoing, Bush had the temperament for leadership but lacked not only experience but a full grasp of national issues. Journalists were quick to seize on the weaknesses of both men, accusing Gore of frequent and misleading exaggeration and Bush of mangling words and speaking only in generalities.

The candidacy of consumer advocate Ralph Nader, who ran on the Green Party ticket, complicated the political reckoning. Nader never seemed likely to win more than a small percentage of the votes, but in a close election a few points could make all the difference. Nader's mere presence pushed Gore to the left, leaving room for Bush among independent-minded swing voters.

The race appeared close until election day, and even closer on election night. Gore seemed the likely winner when the major television networks predicted a Democratic victory in Florida. They reconsidered as Bush swept the South, including the Clinton-Gore home states of Arkansas and Tennessee. After midnight, the networks again called Florida, but this time for Bush, and the vice president telephoned the governor to concede, only to recant an hour later when it became clear that the Bush margin in Florida was paper thin.

There things stuck, and for the next month all eyes were on Florida. Gore had two hundred thousand more popular votes nationwide than Bush, and 267 electoral votes to Bush's 246. Yet with Florida's 25 electoral votes, Bush could win the presidency. Both sides sent teams of lawyers to Florida. Bush's team, working with Florida's Republican secretary of state, sought to certify the results that showed the GOP candidate with a lead of 930 votes out of nearly six million cast. Citing many voting problems disclosed by the media, Gore asked for a recount in three heavily Democratic counties in south Florida. All three used antiquated punch card machines that resulted in some ballots not being clearly marked for any presidential candidate when the chads, the bits of paper removed when a card is punched, were not completely detached from the cards. For weeks the results in Florida, and hence of the entire election, appeared to depend on how one divined the intent of a voter based on hanging, dimpled, or bulging chads.

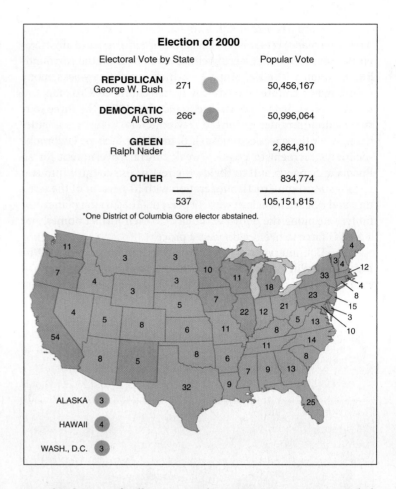

The decision finally came in the courts. Democrats appealed the initial attempt to certify Bush as the victor to the Florida Supreme Court. The Florida court twice ordered recounts, the second time for all counties in the state, but Bush's lawyers appealed to the United States Supreme Court. On December 12, five weeks after the election, the Court overruled the state court's call for a recount, in a five to four decision that reflected a long-standing ideological divide among the nine justices. The next day, Gore gracefully conceded, and Bush finally became president-elect.

Bush's narrow victory revealed deep divisions in American life at the beginning of the twenty-first century. The rural West and South went for Bush, along with a few key Midwest and border states, while Gore won the urban states along both coasts. There was an equally strong divide along economic lines, with the poor voting for Gore, the rich for Bush, and the middle class dividing evenly between the two candidates. Gore benefited from the gender gap, winning 54 percent of the women's vote, and he won an even larger share of the black vote, 90 percent, than Clinton in 1996. Bush did manage to narrow the Democratic margin among Hispanic voters, taking 35 percent, compared to only 28 percent for Dole four years earlier. The two candidates split the suburban vote evenly, while Bush reclaimed the Catholic vote for Republicans.

George W. Bush at Home

Bush's first order of business was a large tax cut, which required intense lobbying from the White House. The president had to win over enough conservative southern Democrats to compensate for losing Republican moderates who insisted on reducing the federal debt before cutting taxes. Bush managed the feat, and in June 2005 Congress passed legislation that slashed taxes by a staggering $1.35 trillion over a ten-year period. Many of the cuts would take effect only in future years, but Congress offered an immediate stimulus to the economy by authorizing rebate payments to tax-payers: $600 for couples and $300 for individuals earning more than $6,000 a year. While critics saw this measure as a betrayal of the long effort to balance the budget, Bush contended that future budget surpluses would more than offset the loss of tax revenue.

A slowdown in the American economy, triggered by the bursting of the 1990s high-tech bubble, soon turned the projected budget surplus into annual deficits. But it failed to halt the Bush administration's tax cut momentum. In 2003, arguing that a fur-ther reduction in taxes would stimulate the stalled economy, Bush prevailed upon Congress to adopt another $350 billion in cuts. Like the 2001 cuts, the new reductions were temporary in order to preserve the possibility of a balanced budget by 2010. Opponents charged that if a future Congress made these tax cuts permanent, as seemed likely, the total cost would rise to nearly $1 trillion. While Clinton had favored a policy of eliminating the deficit, Bush made tax reduction the centerpiece of his economic policy.

Although it took a bit longer, the president also succeeded in persuading Congress to enact a program of education reform. Borrowing the label, "No Child Left Behind," from liberal Democrats, the administration pushed hard for a new policy requiring states to give annual performance tests to all elemen-tary school students. Democrats countered with demands for increased federal funding of public education to assist states and local school boards in raising their standards. Bush shrewdly cultivated the support of Senator Edward Kennedy, a leading liberal Democrat, to forge a bipartisan consensus. The final mea-sure increased federal aid to education by $4 billion, to a total of $22 billion annually, and mandated state tests in reading and math for all students in grades three through eight, and at least once during grades ten to twelve.

By this time the economic slowdown had become a full-blown recession, the first in ten years. A glut of unsold goods forced manu-facturers to curtail production and lay off workers. Unemployment rose, eventually to 6 percent, despite the efforts of the Federal Reserve to stem the economic decline by cutting interest rates. The tax rebates authorized by Congress had boosted the economy slightly during the summer of 2001, but then the September 11 ter-rorist attacks on New York and the Pentagon led to a further decline. In 2002, the economy once again began to recover, only to relapse late in the year amid concern over the threat of war with Iraq.

One of the most troubling aspects of the economic downturn was the implosion of several major corporations and the sub-sequent revelation of shocking financial practices. WorldCom, Inc., a major telecommunications company, became the largest corporation in American history to declare bankruptcy, while a New York grand jury charged executives of Tyco International, a large electronics company, with stealing more than $600 million from shareholders through stock fraud, false expense reports, and unauthorized bonuses.

These scandals, however, paled before the misdeeds of Enron, a Houston energy company that failed in late 2001 as the result of astonishingly corrupt business practices, including fraudulent accounting and private partnerships designed to inflate profits and hide losses. When investors began to sell their overvalued Enron stock, shares that were once worth nearly $100 fell to less than $1. Enron declared bankruptcy and the remaining shareholders lost over $50 billion, while rank-and-file employees lost not only their jobs but much of their retirement savings, invested largely in now worthless Enron stock.

The War on Terror

On the morning of September 11, 2001, nineteen Islamic militant terrorists hijacked four U.S. airliners and turned them to attack targets in New York City and Washington, D.C. The hijackers took over two planes flying out of Boston's Logan Airport en route to California, and flew them into the World Trade Center (WTC) in New York. One plane slammed into the north tower just before 9 A.M., and the second hit the south tower only twenty minutes later. Within two hours, both towers had collapsed, taking the lives of nearly three thousand victims trapped in the buildings or crushed by the debris and more than three hundred firefighters and other rescue workers who had attempted to save them.

In Washington, an American Airlines flight that left Dulles Airport bound for Los Angeles met a similar fate. Taken over by five terrorists, the Boeing 757 plowed into the Pentagon, destroying one wing of the building and killing 189 military personnel and civil-ian workers. The terrorists had seized a fourth plane, United Airlines flight 93, scheduled to fly from Newark, New Jersey, to San Francisco. Over Pennsylvania, as the hijackers attempted to turn the plane toward the nation's capital, the passengers fought to regain control of the plane. They failed to do so, but prevented the plane from hit-ting another target in Washington—perhaps the White House or the Capitol building. Flight 93 crashed in southern Pennsylvania, killing all forty-four passengers and crew as well as the hijackers.

"None of us will forget this day," President Bush told the American people in a televised speech that evening. Bush vowed to find and punish those responsible for the attacks, as well as any who assisted them. "We will make no distinction between those who planned these acts and those who harbor them."

Bush didn't have to look long to discover the master mind behind the September 11 attacks. Osama bin Laden, a wealthy Saudi, released videotapes claiming responsibility on behalf of his terrorist organization, al Qaeda ("the Base" in Arabic). Bin Laden had originally been part of the international Muslim resistance to the Soviet invasion of Afghanistan that had received support and weapons from the CIA in the 1980s. He turned against the United States at the time of the Persian Gulf War, outraged by the presence of large numbers of American troops in his native Saudi Arabia. Evidence linked bin Laden and al Qaeda to the bombing of two American embassies in East Africa in 1998 and an attack on the American destroyer USS *Cole* in Yemen in 2000.

The United States had been trying to neutralize al Qaeda for a decade without success. Ordered out of Saudi Arabia in 1991, bin Laden had sought refuge in the Sudan and later in Afghanistan after the Taliban, another extremist Muslim group, took over that country. In Afghanistan, bin Laden set up camps to train hundreds of would-be terrorists, mainly from Arab countries but including

Feature Essay

An Inconvenient Truth? The Controversy Surrounding Global Warming

Al Gore in a still from *An Inconvenient Truth*, his Oscar-winning documentary about climate change.

When Al Gore lost the disputed 2000 presidential election, he gave such a gracious concession speech that pundits wondered just how badly he wanted to be president. Did he know something they didn't know? Was there life after politics?

For Gore it turned out there was. But if he had expected that the next phase of his career might be less bruising than the slugfest he had just experienced with George W. Bush, he was quickly proven wrong. Gore's new cause was environmentalism, and he discovered that nothing posed greater danger to one's reputation or peace of mind than trying to save the earth.

Gore had become interested in environmental affairs while he was in Congress during the 1970s and 1980s. In 1992 he published *Earth in the Balance*, an environmentalist call to arms. "We must make the rescue of the environment the central organizing principle for civilization," he wrote. As vice president under Bill Clinton, he pushed hard for American approval of the 1997 Kyoto Protocol, which would have committed the United States to substantially reduce greenhouse gases: carbon dioxide and other gases that trap heat in the atmosphere and are responsible, in the opinion of most scientists, for rising global temperatures.

Gore lost the Kyoto fight—badly. The Senate, which has the responsibility to ratify treaties, rejected the Kyoto pact by a vote of 95 to 0. The negative Republican votes were no surprise, but that Democrat Gore—a former senator and the Senate's presiding officer, by virtue of his office as vice president—couldn't muster even one Democratic vote was an embarrassment that would have daunted most politicians.

But Gore wasn't an ordinary politician, and he didn't embarrass easily. Following his defeat by Bush in 2000, he threw himself into the environmental cause, becoming what some of his many critics derided as a one-man-traveling-band in favor of all things green. He wrote a new book, *An Inconvenient Truth*, that described the threat to civilization from global warming as dire and imminent. The book became the basis for a documentary, also called *An Inconvenient*

Truth, that in 2007 won an Academy Award, further irking Gore's critics. President Bush gave the movie the back of his hand; asked whether he would watch it, Bush replied, "Doubt it." The Republican chairman of the Senate Environment and Public Works Committee, Jim Inhofe, who was disparaged in the film, compared it to Hitler's *Mein Kampf*: "If you say the same lie over and over again, and particularly if you have the media's support, people will believe it." Spoofs of *An Inconvenient Truth* on YouTube mocked the film as boring and self-righteous. Gore's critics grew even more incensed when he was awarded the 2007 Nobel Peace Prize for his environmental efforts.

At the heart of the controversy were the substantive questions of global warming: Was the earth's climate really getting hotter, and were human actions responsible? Mountains of data gathered over decades by thousands of scientists suggested that the planet was indeed warming and that human production of greenhouse gases was responsible. But the data and the models the scientists employed weren't definitive or irrefutable. Persons determined not to be persuaded could find plausible grounds for skepticism.

Had the debate involved scientists only, it would have been bitter enough. But the consequences of global warming predicted by most of the scientists—floods, droughts, famine, pestilence—appeared to require a political response. Humans must stop producing so much carbon dioxide, and their governments must make them stop. This would be inconvenient (hence the title of Gore's book and film), and almost certainly expensive. But it had to be done.

So said the convinced. Skeptics disagreed. Many were political conservatives, who didn't like government telling them what to do. Most complained at the expense and trouble. And nearly all bridled at what they deemed the holier-than-thou attitude of Gore and the global-warming believers.

The emotions surrounding the issue made reasoned debate difficult, at times impossible. Liberals often treated the skeptics as ignorant and venal; many conservatives made denial of global warming a litmus test of true conservatism. Many liberals made changes in their own lives, switching to gas-electric hybrid cars, which squeezed more mileage out of each gallon of gas, and recycling household items, to save the energy cost of producing new ones. Cities adopted ordinances to encourage recycling and diminish the "carbon footprint"—the amount of carbon dioxide emitted—of urban activities. But conservatives often derided such measures as liberal hypocrisy—they noted that Gore's globe-spanning travels on behalf of carbon reduction generated huge amounts of carbon—and an affront to the American way of life.

Meanwhile, the evidence mounted. The National Aeronautics and Space Administration (NASA) reported in 2012 that the surface temperature of the earth had been rising since 1880, and that the warming was accelerating, with the ten warmest years of the last century occurring within the last twelve years. The oceans were also warming, which caused sea levels to rise and threaten low-lying areas along the shores. Glaciers and the ice sheets that covered most of Greenland and Antarctica were shrinking. The ice cap over the North Pole retreated farther and faster during the summer. Instances of extreme weather—droughts, torrential rains, record high temperatures—appeared to be increasing, although climate scientists were careful not to claim that any one of these events was a direct consequence of global warming.

Despite the evidence, the controversy persisted. Among conservatives, especially social and religious conservatives, rejection of human-caused global warming seemed to be part of the broader rejection of science that included disbelief in evolution. During the Republican campaign for the 2012 nomination for president, most of the candidates either dodged the issue or denied it. Rick Santorum, former Pennsylvania senator, called the assertion that humans were warming the planet "patently absurd...It's just an excuse for more government control of your life." When Mitt Romney, the front-runner, expressed tepid support for the idea, Rush Limbaugh, the conservative radio host, jibed, "Bye-bye nomination."

Romney's stance on global warming did not kill his hopes of getting the nomination, but the controversy guaranteed that the government would take no serious action to curtail emissions of greenhouse gases. Even environmentalists acknowledged that there was comparatively little the United States could do, given that the greatest growth in carbon dioxide emissions would almost certainly come from China, India, and other developing countries. Those countries weren't likely to agree to emissions caps until their inhabitants' standards of living more closely approximated those of the developed nations. The economic recession in the United States also raised the political cost of new environmental regulations on business that might cause firms to hire fewer workers.

In consequence, the issue of global warming joined such others as health care and Social Security in generating enormous debate but no resolution. One of the strengths of the American political system had always been its checks and balances, with each branch and interest group countering the others until a consensus was achieved. As the earth heated up, many Americans wondered if the old system could meet this new challenge.

QUESTIONS FOR DISCUSSION

1. Why has the issue of global warming become so controversial in the United States?

2. What does the controversy say about the intersection of politics and science in American democracy?

3. Is democracy the best way to resolve debates that turn on technical issues?

View the **Closer Look** World Trade Center, Sept. 11, 2001

This photo depicts the unprecedented deaths and destruction caused by the al Qaeda terrorist attacks on the World Trade Center in New York on September 11, 2011. Nearly 3,000 victims were trapped in the buildings or crushed by the debris and more than three hundred first responders died in their heroic efforts to save the victims.

political coalition resisting the Taliban. Using a variety of methods, ranging from bribes of local warlords to air strikes, American forces quickly routed the Taliban and by December had installed a U.S.-friendly regime in Kabul. Most of Afghanistan, however, remained in chaos, and despite extensive efforts and several near misses, bin Laden avoided capture.

While waging the **war on terror** abroad, the Bush administration also focused on the problem of securing the United States from any further terrorist assaults. At the president's urging, Congress approved a new Department of Homeland Security, combining the Customs Bureau, the Coast Guard, the Immigration and Naturalization Service (INS), and other government bureaus.

A primary focus of homeland security was ensuring the safety of airline travel in the wake of the September 11 hijackings. In November 2001, Bush signed legislation replacing private companies with government employees at all airport screening stations. The airlines were required to replace cockpit doors with secure barriers and to permit armed air marshals to ride among the passengers. The understandable public fear of flying after September 11 nevertheless had a devastating effect on the airline industry, forcing the cancellation of many flights and the laying off of thousands of pilots and other workers. Despite a $15 billion government bailout approved in late September 2001, the airlines continued to experience heavy losses. Several, including United Airlines, filed for bankruptcy. Although air travel began to revive slowly in 2002, the industry, along with other forms of tourism, continued to be a drag on an already sluggish economy.

The war on terror raised an even more fundamental question than economic stagnation. Attorney General John Ashcroft, using new powers granted by Congress under the Patriot Act, conducted a broad crackdown on possible terrorists, detaining many Muslim Americans on flimsy evidence and insisting that concern for national security outweighed traditional civil liberties. Opponents quickly challenged Ashcroft, arguing that the terrorists would win their greatest victory if the United States violated its own historic principles of individual freedom in the name of fighting terrorism. It was a debate that troubled many Americans who had difficulty reconciling the need for security with respect for civil liberties.

Widening the Battlefield

The terrorist attacks on the United States were the catalyst for a major change in direction for American foreign policy. Not only did the Bush administration wage an intensive effort to avenge

recruits from the Philippines, Indonesia, and Central Asia. After the 1998 embassy bombings, President Clinton ordered cruise missile attacks on several of these camps in the hope of killing bin Laden. The al Qaeda leader survived, though, leaving one of the targets only a few hours before the strike.

Bush's determination to go after those harboring terrorists made Afghanistan the prime target for the American counterattack. The president ordered the Pentagon and the CIA, which already had agents on the scene, to launch an invasion of Afghanistan to destroy the Taliban, wipe out al Qaeda, and capture or kill Osama bin Laden.

In early October 2001, the CIA and Army Special Forces began the operation, relying on the Northern Alliance, an Afghan

📖 —Read the Document   George W. Bush, Address to Congress
(September 20, 2001)

As rescue efforts continued in the rubble of the World Trade Center, President Bush toured the site on September 14, 2001. In CNN's televised coverage of the visit, Bush is shown here addressing rescue workers through a bullhorn. Firefighter Bob Beckwith stands beside him.

the September 11 attacks and prevent further assaults, it initiated a new global policy of American preeminence. For the first time since the end of the Cold War, the United States had a clear, if controversial, blueprint for international affairs.

The new administration rejected traditional forms of international cooperation. President Bush withdrew U.S. participation in the Kyoto Protocol to control global warming and announced plans to terminate the 1972 Antiballistic Missile (ABM) treaty with Russia. And he was outspoken in refusing to expose American military personnel to the jurisdiction of the International Criminal Court for possible crimes committed in worldwide peacekeeping efforts.

The new direction of American foreign policy became clear on January 29, 2002, when Bush delivered his second State of the Union address to Congress and the nation. He repeated his vow to punish all nations sponsoring terrorism, and he specified three countries in particular. Iraq, Iran, and North Korea, he declared in a memorable phrase, constituted an "axis of evil." Nine months later, in September 2002, the Bush administration released a fully developed statement of its new world policy, "National Security Strategy (NSS) of the United States." The goal of American policy, Bush's NSS declared, was to "extend the peace by encouraging free and open societies on every continent."

There were two main components of the new strategy, which critics quickly called **unilateralism**. The first was to accept fully the role the nation had been playing since the end of the Cold War: global policeman. The United States would not shrink from defending freedom anywhere in the world—with allies if possible, by itself if necessary. To implement this policy, NSS asserted that the Bush administration would maintain "military strength beyond challenge." "Our forces," the NSS declared, "will be strong enough to dissuade potential adversaries from pursuing a military buildup in hopes of surpassing, or equaling, the power of the United States."

In playing the role of world cop, Bush and his advisers asserted the right to the preventive use of force. Reacting to September 11, the NSS continued, "We cannot let our enemies strike first." Although promising to seek the support of the international community before using force, the NSS stated, "we will not hesitate to act alone, if necessary, to exercise our right of self-defense." In other words, the Bush administration, aware that the United States was far stronger militarily and economically than any other nation, accepted its new role as final arbiter of all international disputes.

Iraq quickly became the test case for this new shift in American foreign policy. After his "axis of evil" speech in January, President Bush focused on what he and his Pentagon advisers called weapons of mass destruction (WMD) that they claimed Saddam Hussein had been secretly amassing in large quantities. The United States demanded that Iraq permit UN inspectors (forced out of the country in 1998) to search for such weapons. Meanwhile, the Bush administration formulated plans for a unilateral American military solution to the Iraq question.

Slowly, but inevitably, the United States moved toward war with Iraq in late 2002 and early 2003. Congress approved a resolution in October authorizing the president to use force against Saddam Hussein's regime. A month later, the UN Security Council voted unanimously to send its team of inspectors back into Iraq, warning Saddam of "severe consequences" if he failed to comply. Despite the failure of the international inspectors to find any evidence of chemical, biological, or nuclear weapons in Iraq, the Bush administration kept pressing for a Security Council resolution authorizing the use of force to compel Saddam to disarm. When France and Russia vowed to veto any such measure, Bush and his advisers decided to ignore the world body and proceed on their own. Preemption would have its first real test.

The ensuing war with Iraq surprised both the backers and the critics of unilateralism. In March 2003, three columns of American troops, a total of sixty-five thousand, began to execute a two-pronged invasion of Iraq from bases in Kuwait. Britain, the only major power to join the United States in the fighting, helped by besieging the city of Basra and taking control of

In a memorable image from the war in Iraq, Iraqi civilians and U.S. soldiers pull down a statue of Saddam Hussein in Baghdad on April 9, 2003. Eight months later, U.S. soldiers captured the former Iraqi president near Tikrit.

southern Iraq. Within two weeks, the U.S. army had captured the Baghdad international airport, and on April 8, just three weeks after the fighting had begun, marines marched virtually unopposed into the heart of the city. The American people watched the televised scene of joyous Iraqis toppling a statue of Saddam in Fardos Square. An Iraqi major summed up the magnitude of his country's defeat: "Losing a war is one thing, but losing Baghdad is another," he explained. "It was like losing the dearest thing in life."

The rapid success of the anti-Saddam offensive seemed to confirm the wisdom of Bush's decision for war. But the subsequent failure to find any weapons of mass destruction led critics to question the validity of the war. In response, the president's defenders emphasized the importance of deposing Saddam by pointing to his brutal prisons and to the killing fields south of Baghdad where thousands of Shi'ite rebels had been slaughtered in 1991.

The problems of restoring order and rebuilding the shattered Iraqi economy quickly overshadowed the debate over the war's legitimacy. Daily attacks on American troops in the Sunni triangle north of Baghdad began in the summer of 2003 and increased in intensity during the fall, killing an average of three American soldiers each week. By October, more troops had died from these attacks than had been killed during the combat phase in March and April. Widespread looting, sabotage of oil pipelines, and difficulties in repairing and operating outdated power plants

and oil facilities made economic recovery very slow and halting. U.S. efforts to involve occupation forces from other UN members yielded only a few troops.

The December 2003 arrest of Saddam, who had eluded capture until then despite determined efforts to find him, revived American optimism. Yet the overall situation remained troubling. Despite slow but steady progress in restoring public services such as electric power and the gradual recovery of the Iraq oil industry, the armed insurrection continued. Mortar attacks on Baghdad hotels, roadside bombs aimed at American armored convoys, and handheld missile attacks on American helicopters made Iraq a very dangerous place. Equally disturbing, conflicts of interest between Shi'ite and Sunni Muslims, as well as the Kurdish demand for autonomy, threatened the American goal of creating a stable Iraqi government.

Bush Reelected

Not surprisingly, the war in Iraq became the central issue in the 2004 presidential race. Bush cast himself as the resolute commander in the war on terror; he and his supporters contended that it would be reckless to change commanders midconflict. Democrats initially favored former Vermont governor Howard Dean, who had opposed the invasion of Iraq and still strongly criticized Bush's conduct of the war. But the nomination ultimately

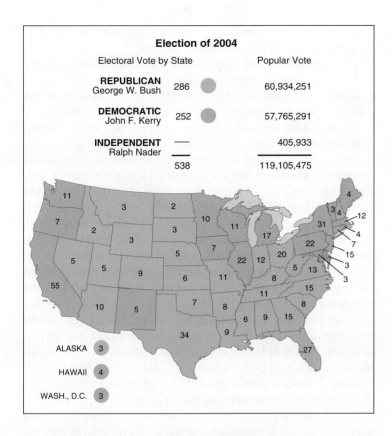

Election of 2004

	Electoral Vote by State		Popular Vote
REPUBLICAN George W. Bush	286		60,934,251
DEMOCRATIC John F. Kerry	252		57,765,291
INDEPENDENT Ralph Nader	—		405,933
	538		119,105,475

ALASKA 3

HAWAII 4

WASH., D.C. 3

went to Senator John Kerry of Massachusetts, a decorated Vietnam War veteran who voted for the war but later criticized Bush for misleading the country regarding the causes of the conflict, and who contended that the war in Iraq, rather than contributing to the war on terror, actually distracted from it.

The campaign was the most vitriolic in years. Democrats accused Bush of having stolen the election of 2000 (with the help of the Supreme Court) and of lying about Saddam's weapons. Republicans called Kerry's belated opposition to the war in Vietnam an insult to those Americans who had died there, and they cited certain of his votes in the Senate as evidence of a fatal inconsistency. Both sides (following the example of Howard Dean in the primaries) employed the Internet to rally the faithful, raise money, and spread rumors.

The strong emotions produced a record turnout: 12 million more than in 2000. Bush won the popular vote by 2.5 percent, becoming the first victor since his father in 1988 to gain an absolute popular majority. The electoral race was comparably close, with 286 for Bush and 252 for Kerry. Taken together with the congressional elections, which increased the Republican majorities in both the Senate and the House of Representatives, the 2004 race confirmed a "red state/blue state" split in America, with the Republicans dominating the South, the Plains, and the Rockies, while the Democrats carried the Northeast, the Great Lakes, and the West Coast.

Despite his modest margin of victory, Bush claimed a mandate. He proposed to privatize part of the Social Security system and promised to stay the course in Iraq. His Social Security plan went nowhere, but the situation in Iraq eventually improved. Following a new round of insurgent attacks, Bush in 2007 ordered an increase in American troop strength; this "surge," combined with

a divide-and-conquer policy toward the insurgents, diminished the violence and made credible Bush's claim that Iraq had turned a corner toward democratic self-government.

Barack Obama's Triumph and Trials

What challenges faced Barack Obama and the American people during the first decade of the twenty-first century?

By then, however, Americans faced a new problem—one that looked much like an old problem. A booming real estate market in the early 2000s tempted banks and other investors to borrow and lend more than was prudent; when the real estate bubble burst in 2007, the financial markets reeled. Wall Street's panic evoked grim memories of the Great Depression of the 1930s and produced a comparable result at the ballot box: the replacement of a Republican president by a Democratic one. That this new president was the first African American to occupy the White House made his accession even more historic. But it didn't make the problems he inherited less daunting.

The Great Recession

Wall Street's troubles reached the crisis stage in the summer and autumn of 2008. Major lenders, including the government-backed twins the Federal National Mortgage Association and the Federal Home Mortgage Corporation (nicknamed Fannie Mae and Freddie Mac), teetered on the brink of bankruptcy. The Bush administration, fearful of the consequences that might follow their collapse, threw the two a life-preserver of federal loans. The panic nonetheless spread, bringing down Wall Street giants Bear Stearns and Lehman Brothers and frightening the administration and Congress into crafting a broader rescue package for the financial sector, totaling hundreds of billions of dollars.

The bailout package averted chaos but left voters shaken. Until this point, the Republican nominee for president, Senator John McCain of Arizona, appeared the favorite in the 2008 contest. His war-hero background from the Vietnam era reassured Americans worried about the ongoing wars in Afghanistan and Iraq. But the floundering economy neutralized McCain's advantage and made voters take a second look at the Democratic candidate, Senator Barack Obama of Illinois. Obama ran a brilliant campaign, summarized in the catchword "Hope" and the promise "Yes, We Can." More important was the fact that he was from the opposite party to that which had held the White House during the boom and bust. Obama garnered 53 percent of the popular vote and defeated McCain handily (See Map: The Election of 2008).

Obama's supporters hoped for great things from the new president. And indeed his inauguration was historic and moving. "God calls on us to shape an uncertain destiny," Obama said. "This is the meaning of our liberty and our creed; why men and women and children of every race and every faith can join in celebration across this magnificent Mall, and why a man whose father less than 60 years ago might not have been served at a local restaurant can now stand before you to take a most sacred oath."

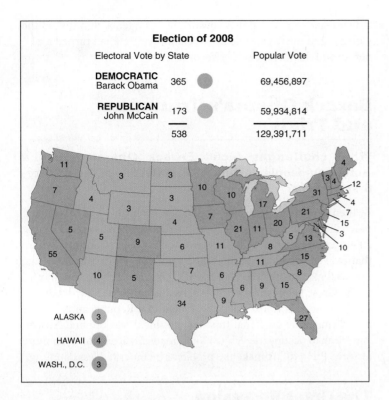

Election of 2008

Electoral Vote by State			Popular Vote
DEMOCRATIC Barack Obama	365		69,456,897
REPUBLICAN John McCain	173		59,934,814
	538		129,391,711

ALASKA 3

HAWAII 4

WASH., D.C. 3

But the warm feeling soon wore off in the cold wind of the bleak economy. The rescue package helped stabilize the financial sector, but unemployment rose inexorably, peaking at 10 percent in 2009 and remaining near there for the next year. Obama and the Democratic majority in Congress pushed through an economic stimulus package, which may have kept unemployment from going even higher but did little to bring it down.

Obama and the Democrats also achieved something Democratic presidents since Harry Truman had been attempting: passage of a comprehensive program of medical insurance for nearly all Americans. But the measure, passed in the face of bitter resistance from Republicans in Congress, prompted a backlash among voters. Together with the lengthening recession, it contributed to the rebuke the Democrats received in the 2010 midterm elections, in which the Republicans reclaimed control of the House of Representatives, gained six seats in the Senate, and carried most of the governor's races.

Obama scored an important success when American special forces killed Osama bin Laden, the al Qaeda mastermind, in 2011. And he withdrew American troops from Iraq and scheduled the removal of troops from Afghanistan, foreshadowing a reduction of the American military role in the Middle East. But instability in Pakistan and the nuclear ambitions of Iran suggested that America's worries about the region were far from over.

New Challenges and Old

Meanwhile, the Great Recession knocked the federal budget wildly out of balance. Government revenues fell as unemployed workers no longer paid income taxes; government spending rose to cover unemployment compensation and other recession-related expenses. By 2011, the annual deficit seemed stuck at more than $1 trillion. Reducing the deficit was the first priority to many voters and elected officials, but if reducing the deficit required laying off government

workers, as it seemed certain to do, it might aggravate the recession. The problem, for the moment, defied solution.

Other problems had deeper roots but no easier solutions. The race question remained alive and contentious, despite the presence of an African American in the White House. **Affirmative action** policies—policies designed to ensure greater participation by minorities—had been under scrutiny for years. The *Bakke* v. *Regents of the University of California* decision of 1978 had allowed the use of race as one factor in determining admission to colleges and universities, so long as rigid racial quotas weren't employed. This dissatisfied many conservatives, who during the 1980s and 1990s attacked affirmative action politically and in the courts. In 1992, Cheryl Hopwood, an unsuccessful white applicant to the University of Texas Law School, challenged her rejection, contending that the school had admitted less-qualified African Americans. In 1996, the Fifth Circuit Court of Appeals decided in her favor, and the *Hopwood* decision raised the hopes of anti–affirmative action groups that the Supreme Court would overturn *Bakke*. But in a 2003 case involving the University of Michigan, the Supreme Court ruled that "student body diversity is a compelling state interest that can justify the use of race in university admissions." In other words, affirmative action in higher education could continue. But the narrowness of the 5–4 vote suggested that affirmative action would continue to spark controversy, as indeed it did.

Even more controversial was abortion. The issue had roiled American politics for decades, but it did so particularly after the 2005 death of Chief Justice William Rehnquist and the nearly concurrent retirement of Associate Justice Sandra Day O'Connor. The two vacancies on the Supreme Court allowed George W. Bush to nominate their replacements. Rehnquist had been a reliable conservative, but O'Connor was a swing vote, and liberals feared that a more conservative successor would tip the balance against abortion rights, among other contentious issues. Yet John Roberts, Bush's nominee for chief justice, and Samuel Alito, the nominee for associate justice, dodged Democrats' questions in hearings, and both nominations succeeded. Almost immediately, the South Dakota legislature essentially banned abortion, hoping to persuade the newly reconfigured court to revisit the 1973 *Roe* decision, which guaranteed abortion rights. South Dakota voters subsequently overturned the state law, but the issue remained highly charged.

Gay rights provoked fresh controversy as gay advocates pushed for equal marital rights. After the Massachusetts Supreme Court in 2004 struck down a state law barring same-sex marriages, gay advocates celebrated, but conservatives in dozens of states pressed for laws and constitutional amendments reaffirming traditional views on the subject and defining marriage as the union of one man and one woman. Nearly all these efforts were successful, suggesting that, on this front at least, the advances gay men and women had achieved since the 1960s had hit a wall. The issue of military service proved similarly controversial. Bill Clinton had achieved a minor breakthrough with the "don't ask, don't tell" policy, which allowed gay service as long as the men and women in question kept their sexual orientation to themselves. Barack Obama campaigned to let gays come out of the military closet, but the Republican party resisted. Finally, however, in the lame duck session of Congress in December 2010, the legislature approved and Obama signed a measure repealing the "don't ask, don't tell" policy and permitting gays to serve openly in the armed forces.

Barack Obama takes the presidential oath of office from Supreme Court Justice John Roberts on January 20, 2011 to become the 44th president of the United States. President Obama's wife, Michelle, is holding the Bible as an estimated 1.8 million people attended the inaugural on the National Mall.

Science and religion continued to battle in America's classrooms. Opponents of evolution revised their challenge to Darwin, replacing creationism with "intelligent design" and demanding that biology classes air this version of their beliefs. School board elections hinged on the issue; Ohio embraced intelligent design only to reject it following an adverse 2005 court decision in a case from the Dover school district. For the moment, the evolutionists held their own, but given that public-opinion polls consistently showed most Americans rejecting evolution in favor of divine creation, the fight was sure to continue.

Doubting the Future

During most of American history, every generation had been better off materially than the generation before. Events of the early twenty-first century called this implicit guarantee into question.

The stubbornness of the Great Recession made Americans wonder whether the economy would ever recover its resiliency. The towering federal deficit imperiled such cherished programs as Social Security and Medicare and put the myriad other contributions the federal government had long made to American life even more at risk.

Demographics didn't help. As the baby boom generation neared retirement, the load on the Social Security system increased. Everyone realized that something would have to be done to keep the pension program afloat, but no one could figure out how to make the necessary changes politically palatable. Middle-aged Americans faced the prospect of delayed retirement, smaller pensions, or both. Not surprisingly, they objected. Younger Americans resisted the tax increases that could have spared their elders such sacrifice.

The trend in health care costs was even more alarming. For years, medical costs had grown rapidly, and as the population aged, the costs appeared certain to claim an ever-larger share of the nation's income. The health care law enacted by Congress at Obama's behest promised to rein in medical costs, but many observers doubted the promises, and the Republicans vowed to repeal it.

Immigration remained controversial. Efforts to reduce the number of illegal entries—by tighter enforcement at the border, by sanctions on employers hiring undocumented aliens, by temporary visas for guest workers—stalled on the opposition of immigrant advocates, businesses, and other groups. The cloud of the Great Recession had at least one silver lining: As jobs grew scarce in America, the flow of illegal immigrants diminished. But no one doubted that the immigration issue would resurface or that it would provoke heated debate.

Environmental problems demanded attention, which they got, and solutions, which they didn't. A broad consensus emerged among the scientific community that global warming had to be addressed, but the proposed solutions—higher mileage standards for automobiles, a "carbon tax" on emissions of greenhouse gases, greater reliance on nuclear energy, among others—were costly, intrusive, unproven, or environmentally problematic in their own ways. And though the scientists mostly agreed that humans were causing global warning, the politicians did not. As on other problems facing the country, the consequence was deadlock.

THE ELECTION OF 2008

Candidate	Party	Popular Vote	Electoral Vote
Obama	Democratic	69,456,897	365
McCain	Republican	59,934,814	173

Conclusion: The End of the American Future—or Not?

From before its eighteenth-century birth as an independent nation, America had been the land of the future. Immigrants to America left their pasts behind as they traveled to the new country; native-born Americans treated the future as though they owned it. And to nearly everyone in the country, the future almost invariably looked bright.

By 2012, however, the American future didn't look bright at all. The terrorist attacks of 2001 had made Americans feel vulnerable; eleven years later they had suffered no comparable assaults, but they still felt vulnerable. They waited in long lines at airport security checkpoints and submitted to personal searches on entering public buildings and gathering places all over the country. The Great Recession darkened America's economic horizons like nothing since the Great Depression, and American officials could not agree on how to restore prosperity. A poll released in 2011 revealed that only 44 percent of Americans believed that the young people of this generation would live better than their parents, the smallest percentage on record.

Not everyone despaired, though. Immigrants still came to America, seeking its promise of a better life for themselves and their children. High-school graduates went to college in search of fulfilling jobs. Young men and women got married and had children, hoping the little ones would fare well in the decades ahead.

Those who knew history tended to be the most optimistic. The country had been through difficult times in the past. The American Revolution, the Civil War, the Great Depression, and two world wars had tested Americans' mettle and faith in the future. Each time the country had survived, typically stronger for the trial. No one could guarantee that America would emerge from its current trials stronger than before, but Americans had never required guarantees.

Study Resources

 Take the **Study Plan** for **Chapter 32** *Into the Twenty-first Century, 1989–2012* on **MyHistoryLab**

TIME LINE

1989 Berlin Wall opens (November)

1990 Saddam Hussein invades Kuwait (August); Bush breaks "no new taxes" campaign pledge, supports $500 billion budget deal (November)

1991 Operation Desert Storm frees Kuwait and crushes Iraq (January–February); Soviet Union dissolves, replaced by Commonwealth of Independent States (December)

1992 Riots devastate South Central Los Angeles after verdict in Rodney King case (May); Bill Clinton elected president (November)

1993 General Motors announces loss of $23.4 billion, the largest one-year loss in U.S. corporate history

1994 Republicans gain control of both houses of Congress (November)

1995 U.S. troops arrive in Bosnia as part of international peacekeeping force (December)

1996 Clinton signs major welfare reform measure (August)

1998 Terrorists bomb American embassies in Kenya and Tanzania

1999 Senate acquits Clinton of impeachment charges (February), Dow Jones Industrial Average goes over 10,000 for first time (March)

2000 Y2K worries prove unfounded; George W. Bush wins contested presidential election

2001 American economy goes into recession, ending the longest period of expansion in U.S. history (March); Terrorist attacks on World Trade Center and the Pentagon (September 11); Anthrax spores found in mail (October); United States military action against the Taliban regime in Afghanistan (October–December)

2002 Department of Homeland Security created (November)

2003 U.S. troops invade Iraq and overthrow Saddam Hussein's regime (March–April); Saddam Hussein captured (December)

2004 Insurgency in Iraq escalates; Global warming gains international attention; George W. Bush reelected (November)

2005 Bush's plan for Social Security reform fails; Hurricane Katrina (August) devastates Gulf Coast and forces evacuation of New Orleans

2006 Proposed constitutional amendment to ban same-sex marriage fails to achieve required two-thirds majority in the Senate

2007 Troop "surge" in Iraq helps calm insurgency (February, to 2008); Real-estate bubble bursts

2008 Oil prices skyrocket before falling back; Federal government takes control of Fannie Mae and Freddie Mac (September); Barack Obama elected president (November)

2009 Recession drives unemployment rate to 10 percent (October)

2010 Health care reform passed (January); Republicans regain control of House (November)

2011 Osama bin Laden killed (May); US troops leave Iraq (December)

CHAPTER REVIEW

The First President Bush

What were the important issues in George H. W. Bush's presidency, and how were they handled?

In domestic affairs, the first President Bush focused on fixing the savings and loan industry and balancing the budget. In foreign affairs, he managed the end the Cold War peacefully and successfully. The Gulf War of 1991 liberated Kuwait and weakened the Iraqi regime of Saddam Hussein, but didn't remove Saddam from power in Baghdad. (p. 770)

The Changing Faces of America

How did the American population shift and grow between 1990 and 2010?

Americans continued to migrate to the Sunbelt in the 1990s and early 2000s, and immigration continued to grow. Hispanics formed the largest segment of the immigrant population and included millions of illegal immigrants. African Americans gained ground economically but still suffered from poverty, as Hurricane Katrina demonstrated. (p. 774)

The New Democrats

What were the accomplishments and failures of the Clinton administration?

Clinton balanced the federal budget and helped revive the economy, which boomed during the 1990s. The North American Free Trade Agreement eliminated tariff barriers among the United States, Canada, and Mexico. But personal scandals led to Clinton's impeachment, which he survived, although not without damage to his own reputation and that of the Democrats. (p. 778)

Clinton and the World

How did Clinton respond to the Balkan Wars?

The breakup of communist Yugoslavia in 1991 led to bloody ethnic fighting. When Serb forces began to commit atrocities first against Muslim Bosnians and then Albanians in Kosovo, Clinton organized military intervention by U.S. and NATO forces that forced the Serbs to stop and led to independence for both Bosnia and Kosovo. (p. 781)

Republicans Triumphant

How did George W. Bush become president, and what did he do in the White House?

George W. Bush became president in an election that turned on a ballot dispute in Florida, which was resolved only by the Supreme Court. As president, Bush persuaded Congress to cut taxes and, after the terrorist attacks of September 11, 2001, to authorize invasions of Afghanistan and Iraq. The war in Iraq bogged down amid an insurgency against the American-supported government in Baghdad. (p. 783)

Barack Obama's Triumph and Trials

What challenges faced Barack Obama and the American people during the first decade of the twenty-first century?

The culture wars between conservatives and liberals continued into the twenty-first century, with abortion, affirmative action, gay rights, and evolution provoking controversy. The Great Recession shook the economy, and Americans wondered how to deal with problems of health care, retirement, illegal immigration, and the environment. (p. 791)

KEY TERMS AND DEFINITIONS

Americans with Disabilities Act (ADA) Passed by Congress in 1991, this act banned discrimination against the disabled in employment and mandated easy access to all public and commercial buildings. p. 770

Operation Desert Storm Desert Storm was the code name used the United States and its coalition partners used in the war against Iraq in 1991 to liberate Kuwait. p. 773

Sunbelt A broad band of states running across the South from Florida to Texas, extending west and north to include California and the Pacific Northwest. Beginning in the 1970s, it experienced rapid economic and population growth. p. 774

Undocumented aliens Illegal immigrants, mainly from Mexico and Central America. p. 776

Contract with America In the 1994 congressional elections, Congressman Newt Gingrich had Republican candidates sign a document in which they pledged support for such things as a balanced budget amendment, term limits for members of Congress, and a middle-class tax cut. p. 780

War on terror Initiated by President George W. Bush after the attacks of September 11, 2001, the broadly defined war on terror aimed to weed out terrorist operatives and their supporters throughout the world. p. 788

Unilateralism A national policy of acting alone without consulting others. p. 789

Affirmative action The use of laws or regulations to achieve racial, ethnic, gender, or other diversity, as in hiring or school admissions. Such efforts are often aimed at improving employment or educational opportunities for women and minorities. p. 792

CRITICAL THINKING QUESTIONS

1. Was the first President Bush lucky or skillful in ending the Cold War so successfully?

2. What do the internal migration to the Sunbelt and the immigration to America from other countries have in common?

3. Do you think President Clinton should have been convicted on his impeachment charges?

4. Many people thought the outcome of the 2000 election was a violation of democracy. Do you?

5. Are you optimistic about America's future, or pessimistic? Why?

MyHistoryLab Media Assignments

Find these resources in the Media Assignments folder for Chapter 32 on MyHistoryLab

The First President Bush

- **View** the **Closer Look** *Opening the Wall, Berlin p. 771*

- 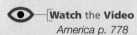 **Read** the **Document**   *George Bush, Address to the Nation on the Persian Gulf (1991) p. 773*

The Changing Faces of America

- **Read** the **Document**   *Illegal Immigration Reform and Immigrant Responsibility Act of 1996 p. 775*

The New Democrats

- **Watch** the **Video**   *Bill Clinton Sells Himself to America p. 778*

- **Read** the **Document**   *Bill Clinton, Answers to the Articles of Impeachment p. 781*

Clinton and the World

- **Read** the **Document**   *The Balkan Proximity Peace Talks Agreement (1995) p. 783*

Republicans Triumphant

- **View** the **Closer Look** *World Trade Center, Sept. 11, 2001 p. 788*

- **Complete** the **Assignment**   *An Inconvenient Truth? The Controversy Surrounding Global Warming p. 786*

- **Read** the **Document**   *George W. Bush, Address to Congress (September 20, 2001) p. 789*

Barack Obama's Triumph and Trials

- **Watch** the **Video**   *The Historical Significance of the 2008 Election p. 793*

■ *Indicates Study Plan Media Assignment*

Appendix

- **The Declaration of Independence**
- **The Articles of Confederation**
- **The Constitution of the United States of America**
- **Amendments to the Constitution**
- **Presidential Elections**
- **Presidents and Vice Presidents**

For additional reference material, go to
www.myhistorylab.com

The Declaration of Independence

In Congress, July 4, 1776

The Unanimous Declaration of the Thirteen United States of America,

When, in the course of human events, it becomes necessary for one people to dissolve the political bonds which have connected them with another, and to assume, among the powers of the earth, the separate and equal station to which the laws of nature and of nature's God entitle them, a decent respect to the opinions of mankind requires that they should declare the causes which impel them to the separation.

We hold these truths to be self-evident: That all men are created equal; that they are endowed by their Creator with certain unalienable rights; that among these are life, liberty, and the pursuit of happiness; that, to secure these rights, governments are instituted among men, deriving their just powers from the consent of the governed; that whenever any form of government becomes destructive of these ends, it is the right of the people to alter or to abolish it, and to institute new government, laying its foundation on such principles, and organizing its powers in such form, as to them shall seem most likely to effect their safety and happiness. Prudence, indeed, will dictate that governments long established should not be changed for light and transient causes; and accordingly all experience hath shown that mankind are more disposed to suffer, while evils are sufferable, than to right themselves by abolishing the forms to which they are accustomed. But when a long train of abuses and usurpations, pursuing invariably the same object, evinces a design to reduce them under absolute despotism, it is their right, it is their duty, to throw off such government, and to provide new guards for their future security. Such has been the patient sufferance of these colonies; and such is now the necessity which constrains them to alter their former systems of government. The history of the present King of Great Britain is a history of repeated injuries and usurpations, all having in direct object the establishment of an absolute tyranny over these states. To prove this, let facts be submitted to a candid world.

He has refused his assent to laws, the most wholesome and necessary for the public good.

He has forbidden his governors to pass laws of immediate and pressing importance, unless suspended in their operation till his assent should be obtained; and, when so suspended, he has utterly neglected to attend to them.

He has refused to pass other laws for the accommodation of large districts of people, unless those people would relinquish the right of representation in the legislature, a right inestimable to them, and formidable to tyrants only.

He has called together legislative bodies at places unusual, uncomfortable, and distant from the depository of their public records, for the sole purpose of fatiguing them into compliance with his measures.

He has dissolved representative houses repeatedly, for opposing, with manly firmness, his invasions on the rights of the people.

He has refused for a long time, after such dissolutions, to cause others to be elected; whereby the legislative powers, incapable of annihilation, have returned to the people at large for their exercise; the state remaining, in the mean time, exposed to all the dangers of invasions from without and convulsions within.

He has endeavored to prevent the population of these states; for that purpose obstructing the laws for naturalization of foreigners; refusing to pass others to encourage their migration hither, and raising the conditions of new appropriations of lands.

He has obstructed the administration of justice, by refusing his assent to laws for establishing judiciary powers.

He has made judges dependent on his will alone, for the tenure of their offices, and the amount and payment of their salaries.

He has erected a multitude of new offices, and sent hither swarms of officers to harass our people and eat out their substance.

He has kept among us, in times of peace, standing armies, without the consent of our legislatures.

He has affected to render the military independent of, and superior to, the civil power.

He has combined with others to subject us to a jurisdiction foreign to our constitution, and unacknowledged by our laws, giving his assent to their acts of pretended legislation:

For quartering large bodies of armed troops among us;

For protecting them, by a mock trial, from punishment for any murder which they should commit on the inhabitants of these states;

For cutting off our trade with all parts of the world;

For imposing taxes on us without our consent;

For depriving us, in many cases, of the benefits of trial by jury;

For transporting us beyond seas, to be tried for pretended offenses;

For abolishing the free system of English laws in a neighboring province, establishing therein an arbitrary government, and enlarging its boundaries, so as to render it at once an example and fit instrument for introducing the same absolute rule into these colonies;

For taking away our charters, abolishing our most valuable laws, and altering fundamentally the forms of our governments;

For suspending our own legislatures, and declaring themselves invested with power to legislate for us in all cases whatsoever.

He has abdicated government here, by declaring us out of his protection and waging war against us.

He has plundered our seas, ravaged our coasts, burned our towns, and destroyed the lives of our people.

He is at this time transporting large armies of foreign mercenaries to complete the works of death, desolation, and tyranny already begun with circumstances of cruelty and perfidy scarcely paralleled in the most barbarous ages, and totally unworthy the head of a civilized nation.

He has constrained our fellow-citizens, taken captive on the high seas, to bear arms against their country, to become the executioners of their friends and brethren, or to fall themselves by their hands.

He has excited domestic insurrection among us, and has endeavored to bring on the inhabitants of our frontiers the merciless Indian savages, whose known rule of warfare is an undistinguished destruction of all ages, sexes, and conditions.

In every stage of these oppressions we have petitioned for redress in the most humble terms; our repeated petitions have been answered only by repeated injury. A prince, whose character is thus marked by every act which may define a tyrant, is unfit to be the ruler of a free people.

Nor have we been wanting in our attentions to our British brethren. We have warned them, from time to time, of attempts by their legislature to extend an unwarrantable jurisdiction over us. We have reminded them of the circumstances of our emigration and settlement here. We have appealed to their native justice and magnanimity; and we have conjured them, by the ties of our common kindred, to disavow these usurpations, which would inevitably interrupt our connections and correspondence. They, too, have been deaf to the voice of justice and of consanguinity. We must, therefore, acquiesce in the necessity which denounces our separation, and hold them, as we hold the rest of mankind, enemies in war, in peace friends.

We, therefore, the representatives of the United States of America, in General Congress assembled, appealing to the Supreme Judge of the world for the rectitude of our intentions, do, in the name and by the authority of the good people of these colonies, solemnly publish and declare, that these United Colonies are, and of right ought to be, FREE AND INDEPENDENT STATES; that they are absolved from all allegiance to the British crown, and that all political connection between them and the state of Great Britain is, and ought to be, totally dissolved; and that, as free and independent states, they have full power to levy war, conclude peace, contract alliances, establish commerce, and do all other acts and things which independent states may of right do. And for the support of this declaration, with a firm reliance on the protection of Divine Providence, we mutually pledge to each other our lives, our fortunes, and our sacred honor.

John Hancock	Thos. Nelson, Jr.
Button Gwinnett	Francis Lightfoot Lee
Lyman Hall	Carter Braxton
Geo. Walton	Robt. Morris
Wm. Hooper	Benjamin Rush
Joseph Hewes	Benja. Franklin
John Penn	John Morton
Edward Rutledge	Geo. Clymer
Thos. Heyward, Junr.	Jas. Smith
Thomas Lynch, Junr.	Geo. Taylor
Arthur Middleton	James Wilson
Samuel Chase	Geo. Ross
Wm. Paca	Caesar Rodney
Thos. Stone	Geo. Read
Charles Carroll of Carrollton	Tho. M'kean
George Wythe	Wm. Floyd
Richard Henry Lee	Phil. Livingston
Th. Jefferson	Frans. Lewis
Benj. Harrison	Lewis Morris

Richd. Stockton

Jno. Witherspoon

Fras. Hopkinson

John Hart

Abra. Clark

Josiah Bartlett

Wm. Whipple

Saml. Adams

John Adams

Robt. Treat Paine

Elbridge Gerry

Step. Hopkins

William Ellery

Roger Sherman

Sam'el Huntington

Wm. Williams

Oliver Wolcott

Matthew Thornton

The Articles of Confederation

Between the States of New Hampshire, Massachusetts Bay, Rhode Island and Providence Plantations, Connecticut, New York, New Jersey, Pennsylvania, Delaware, Maryland, Virginia, North Carolina, South Carolina, Georgia

ARTICLE 1

The stile of this confederacy shall be "The United States of America."

ARTICLE 2

Each State retains its sovereignty, freedom and independence, and every power, jurisdiction, and right, which is not by this confederation expressly delegated to the United States, in Congress assembled.

ARTICLE 3

The said states hereby severally enter into a firm league of friendship with each other for their common defence, the security of their liberties and their mutual and general welfare; binding themselves to assist each other against all force offered to, or attacks made upon them, or any of them, on account of religion, sovereignty, trade, or any other pretence whatever.

ARTICLE 4

The better to secure and perpetuate mutual friendship and intercourse among the people of the different states in this union, the free inhabitants of each of these states, paupers, vagabonds, and fugitives from justice excepted, shall be entitled to all privileges and immunities of free citizens in the several states; and the people of each State shall have free ingress and regress to and from any other State, and shall enjoy therein all the privileges of trade and commerce, subject to the same duties, impositions, and restrictions, as the inhabitants thereof respectively; provided, that such restrictions shall not extend so far as to prevent the removal of property, imported into any State, to any other State of which the owner is an inhabitant; provided also, that no imposition, duties, or restriction, shall be laid by any State on the property of the United States, or either of them.

If any person guilty of, or charged with treason, felony, or other high misdemeanor in any State, shall flee from justice and be found in any of the United States, he shall, upon demand of the governor or executive power of the State from which he fled, be delivered up and removed to the State having jurisdiction of his offence.

Full faith and credit shall be given in each of these states to the records, acts, and judicial proceedings of the courts and magistrates of every other State.

ARTICLE 5

For the more convenient management of the general interests of the United States, delegates shall be annually appointed, in such manner as the legislature of each State shall direct, to meet in Congress, on the 1st Monday in November in every year, with a power reserved to each State to recall its delegates, or any of them, at any time within the year, and to send others in their stead for the remainder of the year.

No State shall be represented in Congress by less than two, nor by more than seven members; and no person shall be capable of being a delegate for more than three years in any term of six years; nor shall any person, being a delegate, be capable of holding any office under the United States, for which he, or any other for his benefit, receives any salary, fees, or emolument of any kind.

Each State shall maintain its own delegates in a meeting of the states, and while they act as members of the committee of the states.

In determining questions in the United States, in Congress assembled, each State shall have one vote.

Freedom of speech and debate in Congress shall not be impeached or questioned in any court or place out of Congress: and the members of Congress shall be protected in their persons from arrests and imprisonments, during the time of their going to and from, and attendance on Congress, except for treason, felony, or breach of the peace.

ARTICLE 6

No State, without the consent of the United States, in Congress assembled, shall send any embassy to, or receive any embassy from, or enter into any conference, agreement, alliance, or treaty with any king, prince, or state; nor shall any person, holding any office of profit or trust under the United States, or any of them, accept of any present, emolument, office or title, of any kind whatever, from any king, prince, or foreign state; nor shall the United States, in Congress assembled, or any of them, grant any title of nobility.

No two or more states shall enter into any treaty, confederation, or alliance, whatever, between them, without the consent of the United States, in Congress assembled, specifying accurately the purposes for which the same is to be entered into, and how long it shall continue.

No State shall lay any imposts or duties which may interfere with any stipulations in treaties entered into by the United States, in Congress assembled, with any king, prince, or state, in pursuance of any treaties already proposed by Congress to the courts of France and Spain.

No vessels of war shall be kept up in time of peace by any State, except such number only as shall be deemed necessary by the United States, in Congress assembled, for the defence of such State or its trade; nor shall any body of forces be kept up by any State, in time of peace, except such number only as, in the judgment of the United States, in Congress assembled, shall be deemed requisite to garrison the forts necessary for the defence of such State; but every State shall always keep up a well regulated and disciplined militia, sufficiently armed and accoutred, and shall provide, and constantly have ready for use, in public stores, a due number of field pieces and tents, and a proper quantity of arms, ammunition and camp equipage.

No State shall engage in any war without the consent of the United States, in Congress assembled, unless such State be actually invaded by enemies, or shall have received certain advice of a resolution being formed by some nation of Indians to invade such State, and the danger is so imminent as not to admit of a delay till the United States, in Congress assembled, can be consulted; nor shall any State grant commissions to any ships or vessels of war, nor letters of marque or reprisal, except it be after a declaration of war by the United States, in Congress assembled, and then only against the kingdom or state, and the subjects thereof, against which war has been so declared, and under such regulations as shall be established by the United States, in Congress assembled, unless such States be infested by pirates, in which case vessels of war may be fitted out for that occasion, and kept so long as the danger shall continue, or until the United States, in Congress assembled, shall determine otherwise.

ARTICLE 7

When land forces are raised by any State for the common defence, all officers of or under the rank of colonel, shall be appointed by the legislature of each State respectively, by whom such forces shall be raised, or in such manner as such State shall direct; and all vacancies shall be filled up by the State which first made the appointment.

ARTICLE 8

All charges of war and all other expences, that shall be incurred for the common defence or general welfare, and allowed by the United States, in Congress assembled, shall be defrayed out of a common treasury, which shall be supplied by the several states, in proportion to the value of all land within each State, granted to or surveyed for any person, as such land and the buildings and improvements thereon shall be estimated according to such mode as the United States, in Congress assembled, shall, from time to time, direct and appoint.

The taxes for paying that proportion shall be laid and levied by the authority and direction of the legislatures of the several states, within the time agreed upon by the United States, in Congress assembled.

ARTICLE 9

The United States, in Congress assembled, shall have the sole and exclusive right and power of determining on peace and war, except in the cases mentioned in the 6th article; of sending and receiving ambassadors; entering into treaties and alliances, provided that no treaty of commerce shall be made, whereby the legislative power of the respective states shall be restrained from imposing such imposts and duties on foreigners as their own people are subjected to, or from prohibiting the exportation or importation of any species of goods or commodities whatsoever; of establishing rules for deciding, in all cases, what captures on land or water shall be legal, and in what manner prizes, taken by land or naval forces in the service of the United States, shall be divided or appropriated; of granting letters of marque and reprisal in times of peace; appointing courts for the trial of piracies and felonies committed on the high seas, and establishing courts for receiving and determining, finally, appeals in all cases of captures; provided, that no member of Congress shall be appointed a judge of any of the said courts.

The United States, in Congress assembled, shall also be the last resort on appeal in all disputes and differences now subsisting, or that hereafter may arise between two or more states concerning boundary, jurisdiction or any other cause whatever; which authority shall always be exercised in the manner following: whenever the legislative or executive authority, or lawful agent of any State, in controversy with another, shall present a petition to Congress, stating the matter in question, and praying for a hearing, notice thereof shall be given, by order of Congress, to the legislative or executive authority of the other State in controversy, and a day assigned for the appearance of the parties by their lawful agents, who shall then be directed to appoint, by

joint consent, commissioners or judges to constitute a court for hearing and determining the matter in question; but, if they cannot agree, Congress shall name three persons out of each of the United States, and from the list of such persons each party shall alternately strike out one, in the petitioners beginning, until the number shall be reduced to thirteen; and from that number not less than seven, nor more than nine names, as Congress shall direct, shall, in the presence of Congress, be drawn out by lot; and the persons whose names shall be drawn, or any five of them, shall be commissioners or judges to hear and finally determine the controversy, so always as a major part of the judges who shall hear the cause shall agree in the determination; and if either party shall neglect to attend at the day appointed, without shewing reasons which Congress shall judge sufficient, or, being present, shall refuse to strike, the Congress shall proceed to nominate three persons out of each State, and the secretary of Congress shall strike in behalf of such party absent or refusing; and the judgment and sentence of the court to be appointed, in the manner before prescribed, shall be final and conclusive; and if any of the parties shall refuse to submit to the authority of such court, or to appear or defend their claim or cause, the court shall nevertheless proceed to pronounce sentence or judgment, which shall, in like manner, be final and decisive, the judgment or sentence and other proceedings being, in either case, transmitted to Congress, and lodged among the acts of Congress for the security of the parties concerned: provided, that every commissioner, before he sits in judgment, shall take an oath, to be administered by one of the judges of the supreme or superior court of the State where the cause shall be tried, "well and truly to hear and determine the matter in question, according to the best of his judgment, without favour, affection, or hope of reward": provided, also, that no State shall be deprived of territory for the benefit of the United States.

All controversies concerning the private right of soil, claimed under different grants of two or more states, whose jurisdictions, as they may respect such lands and the states which passed such grants, are adjusted, the said grants, or either of them, being at the same time claimed to have originated antecedent to such settlement of jurisdiction, shall, on the petition of either party to the Congress of the United States, be finally determined, as near as may be, in the same manner as is before prescribed for deciding disputes respecting territorial jurisdiction between different states.

The United States, in Congress assembled, shall also have the sole and exclusive right and power of regulating the alloy and value of coin struck by their own authority, or by that of the respective states; fixing the standard of weights and measures throughout the United States; regulating the trade and managing all affairs with the Indians not members of any of the states; provided that the legislative right of any State within its own limits be not infringed or violated; establishing and regulating post offices from one State to another throughout all the United States, and exacting such postage on the papers passing through the same as may be requisite to defray the expences of the said office; appointing all officers of the land forces in the service of the United States, excepting regimental officers; appointing all the officers of the naval forces, and commissioning all officers whatever in the service of the United States; making rules for the government and regulation of the said land and naval forces, and directing their operations.

The United States, in Congress assembled, shall have authority to appoint a committee to sit in the recess of Congress, to be denominated "a Committee of the States," and to consist of one delegate from each State, and to appoint such other committees and civil officers as may be necessary for managing the general affairs of the United States, under their direction; to appoint one of their number to preside; provided that no person be allowed to serve in the office of president more than one year in any term of three years; to ascertain the necessary sums of money to be raised for the service of the United States, and to appropriate and apply the same for defraying the public expences; to borrow money or emit bills on the credit of the United States, transmitting, every half year, to the respective states, an account of the sums of money so borrowed or emitted; to build and equip a navy; to agree upon the number of land forces, and to make requisitions from each State for its quota, in proportion to the number of white inhabitants in such State; which requisitions shall be binding; and, thereupon, the legislature of each State shall appoint the regimental officers, raise the men, and cloathe, arm, and equip them in a soldier-like manner, at the expence of the United States; and the officers and men so cloathed, armed, and equipped, shall march to the place appointed and within the time agreed on by the United States, in Congress assembled; but if the United States, in Congress assembled, shall, on consideration of circumstances, judge proper that any State should not raise men, or should raise a smaller number than its quota, and that any other State should raise a greater number of men than the quota thereof, such extra number shall be raised, officered, cloathed, armed, and equipped in the same manner as the quota of such State, unless the legislature of such State shall judge that such extra number cannot be safely spared out of the same, in which case they shall raise, officer, cloathe, arm, and equip as many of such extra number as they judge can be safely spared. And the officers and men so cloathed, armed, and equipped, shall march to the place appointed and within the time agreed on by the United States, in Congress assembled.

The United States, in Congress assembled, shall never engage in a war, nor grant letters of marque and reprisal in time of peace, nor enter into any treaties or alliances, nor coin money, nor regulate the value thereof, nor ascertain the sums and expences necessary for the defence and welfare of the United States, or any of them: nor emit bills, nor borrow money on the credit of the United States, nor appropriate money, nor agree upon the number of vessels of war to be built or purchased, or the number of land or sea forces to be raised, nor appoint a commander in chief of the army or navy, unless nine states assent to the same; nor shall a question on any other point, except for adjourning from day to day, be determined, unless by the votes of a majority of the United States, in Congress assembled.

The Congress of the United States shall have power to adjourn to any time within the year, and to any place within the United States, so that no period of adjournment be for a longer duration than the space of six months, and shall publish the journal of their proceedings monthly, except such parts thereof, relating to treaties, alliances or military operations, as, in their judgment, require secrecy; and the yeas and nays of the delegates of each State on any question shall be entered on the journal, when it is desired by any delegate; and the delegates of a State, or any of them, at his, or their request, shall be furnished with a transcript of the said journal, except such parts as are above excepted, to lay before the legislatures of the several states.

ARTICLE 10

The committee of the states, or any nine of them, shall be authorized to execute, in the recess of Congress, such of the powers of Congress as the United States, in Congress assembled, by the consent of nine states, shall, from time to time, think expedient to vest them with; provided, that no power be delegated to the said committee for the exercise of which, by the articles of confederation, the voice of nine states, in the Congress of the United States assembled, is requisite.

ARTICLE 11

Canada acceding to this confederation, and joining in the measures of the United States, shall be admitted into and entitled to all the advantages of this union; but no other colony shall be admitted into the same, unless such admission be agreed to by nine states.

ARTICLE 12

All bills of credit emitted, monies borrowed and debts contracted by, or under the authority of Congress before the assembling of the United States, in pursuance of the present confederation, shall be deemed and considered as a charge against the United States, for payment and satisfaction whereof the said United States and the public faith are hereby solemnly pledged.

ARTICLE 13

Every State shall abide by the determinations of the United States, in Congress assembled, on all questions which, by this confederation, are submitted to them. And the articles of this confederation shall be inviolably observed by every State, and the union shall be perpetual; nor shall any alteration at any time hereafter be made in any of them, unless such alteration be agreed to in a Congress of the United States, and be afterwards confirmed by the legislatures of every State.

These articles shall be proposed to the legislatures of all the United States, to be considered, and if approved of by them, they are advised to authorize their delegates to ratify the same in the Congress of the United States; which being done, the same shall become conclusive.

The Constitution of the United States of America

PREAMBLE

We the People of the United States, in Order to form a more perfect Union, establish Justice, insure domestic Tranquility, provide for the common defence, promote the general Welfare, and secure the Blessings of Liberty to ourselves and our Posterity, do ordain and establish this Constitution for the United States of America.

ARTICLE I

Section 1

All legislative Powers herein granted shall be vested in a Congress of the United States, which shall consist of a Senate and House of Representatives.

Section 2

The House of Representatives shall be composed of Members chosen every second Year by the People of the several States, and the Electors in each State shall have the Qualifications requisite for Electors of the most numerous Branch of the State Legislature.

No Person shall be a Representative who shall not have attained to the Age of twenty five Years, and been seven Years a Citizen of the United States, and who shall not, when elected, be an inhabitant of that State in which he shall be chosen.

Representatives and direct Taxes shall be apportioned among the several States which may be included within this Union, according to their respective Numbers, *which shall be determined by adding to the whole Number of free Persons, including those bound to Service for a Term of Years, and excluding Indians not taxed, three fifths of all other*

*Persons.** The actual Enumeration shall be made within three Years after the first Meeting of the Congress of the United States, and within every subsequent Term of ten Years, in such Manner as they shall by Law direct. The Number of Representatives shall not exceed one for every thirty Thousand, but each State shall have at Least one Representative; *and until such enumeration shall be made, the State of New Hampshire shall be entitled to chuse three, Massachusetts eight, Rhode-Island and Providence Plantations one, Connecticut five, New York six, New Jersey four, Pennsylvania eight, Delaware one, Maryland six, Virginia ten, North Carolina five, South Carolina five, and Georgia three.*

When vacancies happen in the Representation from any State, the Executive Authority thereof shall issue Writs of Election to fill such Vacancies.

The House of Representatives shall chuse their Speaker and other Officers; and shall have the sole Power of Impeachment.

Section 3

The Senate of the United States shall be composed of two Senators from each State, *chosen by the Legislature thereof*, for six Years; and each Senator shall have one Vote.

Immediately after they shall be assembled in Consequence of the first Election, they shall be divided as equally as may be into three Classes. The Seats of the Senators of the first Class shall be vacated at the Expiration of the second Year, of the second Class at the Expiration of the fourth Year, and of the third Class at the Expiration of the sixth Year so that one third may be chosen every second Year; and if Vacancies happen by Resignation, or otherwise, during the Recess of the Legislature of any state, the Executive thereof may make temporary Appointments until the next Meeting of the Legislature, which shall then fill such Vacancies.

No Person shall be a Senator who shall not have attained to the Age of thirty Years, and been nine Years a Citizen of the United States, and who shall not, when elected, be an Inhabitant of that State for which he shall be chosen.

The Vice President of the United States shall be President of the Senate, but shall have no Vote, unless they be equally divided.

The Senate shall chuse their other Officers, and also a President *pro tempore*, in the Absence of the Vice President, or when he shall exercise the Office of President of the United States.

The Senate shall have the sole Power to try all Impeachments. When sitting for that Purpose, they shall be on Oath or Affirmation. When the President of the United States is tried the Chief Justice shall preside: And no Person shall be convicted without the Concurrence of two thirds of the Members present.

Judgment in Cases of Impeachment shall not extend further than to removal from Office, and disqualification to hold and enjoy any Office of honor, Trust or Profit under the United States: but the Party convicted shall nevertheless be liable and subject to Indictment, Trial, Judgment and Punishment, according to Law.

Section 4

The Times, Places and Manner of holding Elections for Senators and Representatives, shall be prescribed in each State by the Legislature thereof; but the Congress may at any time by Law make or alter such Regulations, except as to the Places of chusing Senators.

The Congress shall assemble at least once in every Year, *and such Meeting shall be on the first Monday in December, unless they shall by Law appoint a different Day.*

Section 5

Each House shall be the Judge of the Elections, Returns and Qualifications of its own Members, and a Majority of each shall constitute a Quorum to do Business; but a smaller Number may adjourn from day to day, and may be authorized to compel the Attendance of absent Members, in such Manner, and under such Penalties as each House may provide.

Each House may determine the Rules of its Proceedings, punish its Members for disorderly Behaviour, and, with the Concurrence of two thirds, expel a Member.

Each House shall keep a Journal of its Proceedings, and from time to time publish the same, excepting such Parts as may in their Judgment require Secrecy; and the Yeas and Nays of the Members of either House on any question shall, at the Desire of one fifth of those Present, be entered on the Journal.

Neither House, during the Session of Congress, shall, without the Consent of the other, adjourn for more than three days, nor to any other Place than that in which the two Houses shall be sitting.

Section 6

The Senators and Representatives shall receive a Compensation for their Services, to be ascertained by Law, and paid out of the Treasury of the United States. They shall in all Cases, except Treason, Felony and Breach of the Peace, be privileged from Arrest during their Attendance at the Session of their respective Houses, and in going to and returning from the same; and for any Speech or Debate in either House, they shall not be questioned in any other Place.

No Senator or Representative shall, during the Time for which he was elected, be appointed to any civil Office under the Authority of the United States, which shall have been created, or the Emoluments whereof shall have been encreased during such time, and no Person holding any Office under the United States, shall be a Member of either House during his Continuance in Office.

Section 7

All Bills for raising Revenue shall originate in the House of Representatives; but the Senate may propose or concur with Amendments as on other Bills.

Every Bill which shall have passed the House of Representatives and the Senate, shall, before it become a Law, be presented to the President of the United States; If he approve he shall sign it, but if not he shall return it, with his Objections to the House in which it shall have originated, who shall enter the Objections at large on their Journal, and proceed to reconsider it. If after such Reconsideration two thirds of that House shall agree to pass the Bill, it shall be sent, together with the Objections, to the other House, by which it shall likewise be reconsidered, and if approved by two thirds of that House, it shall become a Law. But in all such Cases the Votes of both Houses shall be determined by yeas and Nays, and the Names of the Persons voting for and against the Bill shall be entered on the Journal of each House respectively. If any Bill shall not be returned by the President within ten Days (Sundays excepted) after it shall have been presented to him, the Same shall be a Law, in like Manner as if he had signed it, unless the Congress by their Adjournment prevent its Return, in which Case it shall not be a Law.

Every Order, Resolution, or Vote to which the Concurrence of the Senate and House of Representatives may be necessary (except on a question of Adjournment) shall be presented to the President of the United States; and before the Same shall take Effect, shall be approved

---

*Passages no longer in effect are printed in italic type.

by him, or being disapproved by him, shall be repassed by two thirds of the Senate and House of Representatives, according to the Rules and Limitations prescribed in the Case of a Bill.

Section 8

The Congress shall have Power To lay and collect Taxes, Duties, Imposts and Excises, to pay the Debts and provide for the common Defence and general Welfare of the United States; but all Duties, Imposts and Excises shall be uniform throughout the United States;

To borrow Money on the credit of the United States;

To regulate Commerce with foreign Nations, and among the several States, and with the Indian Tribes;

To establish an uniform Rule of Naturalization, and uniform Laws on the subject of Bankruptcies throughout the United States;

To coin Money, regulate the Value thereof, and of foreign Coin, and fix the Standard of Weights and Measures;

To provide for the Punishment of counterfeiting the Securities and current Coin of the United States;

To establish Post Offices and post Roads;

To promote the Progress of Science and useful Arts, by securing for limited Times to Authors and Inventors the exclusive Right to their respective Writings and Discoveries;

To constitute Tribunals inferior to the supreme Court;

To define and punish Piracies and Felonies committed on the high Seas, and Offences against the Law of Nations;

To declare War, grant Letters of Marque and Reprisal, and make Rules concerning Captures on Land and Water;

To raise and support Armies, but no Appropriation of Money to that Use shall be for a longer Term than two Years;

To provide and maintain a Navy;

To make Rules for the Government and Regulation of the land and naval Forces;

To provide for calling forth the Militia to execute the Laws of the Union, suppress Insurrections and repel Invasions;

To provide for organizing, arming, and disciplining, the Militia, and for governing such Part of them as may be employed in the Service of the United States, reserving to the States respectively, the Appointment of the Officers, and the Authority of training the Militia according to the discipline prescribed by Congress;

To exercise exclusive Legislation in all Cases whatsoever, over such District (not exceeding ten Miles square) as may, by Cession of particular States, and the Acceptance of Congress, become the Seat of the Government of the United States, and to exercise like Authority over all Places purchased by the Consent of the Legislature of the State in which the Same shall be, for the Erection of Forts, Magazines, Arsenals, dock-Yards, and other needful Buildings;—And

To make all Laws which shall be necessary and proper for carrying into Execution the foregoing Powers, and all other Powers vested by this Constitution in the Government of the United States, or in any Department of Officer thereof.

Section 9

The Migration or Importation of such Persons as any of the States now existing shall think proper to admit, shall not be prohibited by the Congress prior to the Year one thousand eight hundred and eight, but a Tax or duty may be imposed on such Importation, not exceeding ten dollars for each Person.

The Privilege of the Writ of Habeas Corpus shall not be suspended, unless when in Cases of Rebellion or Invasion the public Safety may require it.

No Bill of Attainder or ex post facto Law shall be passed.

No Capitation, or other direct, Tax shall be laid, unless in Proportion to the Census or Enumeration herein before directed to be taken.

No Tax or Duty shall be laid on Articles exported from any State.

No Preference shall be given by any Regulation of Commerce or Revenue to the Ports of one State over those of another: nor shall Vessels bound to, or from, one State, be obliged to enter, clear, or pay Duties in another.

No Money shall be drawn from the Treasury, but in Consequence of Appropriations made by Law; and a regular Statement and Account of the Receipts and Expenditures of all public Money shall be published from time to time.

No Title of Nobility shall be granted by the United States: And no Person holding any Office of Profit or Trust under them, shall, without the Consent of the Congress, accept of any present, Emolument, Office, or Title, of any kind whatever, from any King, Prince, or foreign State.

Section 10

No State shall enter into any Treaty, Alliance, or Confederation; grant Letters of Marque and Reprisal; coin Money; emit Bills of Credit; make any Thing but gold and silver Coin a Tender in Payment of Debts; pass any Bill of Attainder, ex post facto Law, or Law impairing the obligation of Contracts, or grant any Title of Nobility.

No State shall, without the Consent of the Congress, lay any Imposts or Duties on Imports or Exports, except what may be absolutely necessary for executing its inspection Laws: and the net Produce of all Duties and Imposts, laid by any State on Imports or Exports, shall be for the Use of the Treasury of the United States; and all such Laws shall be subject to the Revision and Controul of the Congress.

No State shall, without the Consent of Congress, lay any Duty of Tonnage, keep Troops, or Ships of War in time of Peace, enter into any Agreement or Compact with another State, or with a foreign Power, or engage in War, unless actually invaded, or in such imminent Danger as will not admit of delay.

ARTICLE II

Section 1

The executive Power shall be vested in a President of the United States of America. He shall hold his Office during the Term of four Years, and, together with the Vice President, chosen for the same Term, be elected, as follows:

Each State shall appoint, in such Manner as the Legislature thereof may direct, a Number of Electors, equal to the whole Number of Senators and Representatives to which the State may be entitled in the Congress: but no Senator or Representative, or Person holding an Office of Trust or Profit under the United States, shall be appointed an Elector.

The Electors shall meet in their respective States, and vote by Ballot for two Persons, of whom one at least shall not be an Inhabitant of the same State with themselves. And they shall make a List of all the Persons voted for, and of the Number of Votes for each; which List they shall sign and certify, and transmit sealed to the Seat of the Government of the United States, directed to the President of the Senate. The President of the Senate shall, in the Presence of the Senate and House of Representatives, open all the Certificates, and the Votes shall then be counted. The Person having the greatest Number of Votes shall be the President, if such Number be a Majority of the whole number of Electors appointed; and if there be more than one who have such Majority, and have an equal Number of Votes, then the House of

Representatives shall immediately chuse by Ballot one of them for President; and if no Person have a Majority, then from the five highest on the List the said House shall in like Manner chuse the President. But in chusing the President, the Votes shall be taken by States, the Representation from each State having one Vote; A quorum for this Purpose shall consist of a Member or Members from two thirds of the States, and a Majority of all the States shall be necessary to a Choice. In every Case, after the Choice of the President, the Person having the greatest Number of Votes of the Electors shall be the Vice President. But if there should remain two or more who have equal Votes, the Senate shall chuse from them by Ballot the Vice President.

The Congress may determine the time of chusing the Electors, and the Day on which they shall give their Votes; which Day shall be the same throughout the United States.

No person except a natural born Citizen, *or a Citizen of the United States, at the time of the Adoption of this Constitution*, shall be eligible to the Office of President; neither shall any Person be eligible to that Office who shall not have attained to the Age of thirty five Years, and been fourteen Years a Resident within the United States.

In Case of the Removal of the President from Office, or of his Death, Resignation, or Inability to discharge the Powers and Duties of the said Office, the Same shall devolve on the Vice President, and the Congress may by Law provide for the Case of Removal, Death, Resignation or Inability, both of the President and Vice President, declaring what Officer shall then act as President, and such Officer shall act accordingly, until the Disability be removed, or a President shall be elected.

The President shall, at stated Times, receive for his Services, a Compensation, which shall neither be encreased nor diminished during the Period for which he shall have been elected, and he shall not receive within that period any other Emolument from the United States, or any of them.

Before he enter on the Execution of his Office, he shall take the following Oath or Affirmation:—"I do solemnly swear (or affirm) that I will faithfully execute the Office of President of the United States, and will to the best of my Ability, preserve, protect and defend the Constitution of the United States."

Section 2

The President shall be Commander in Chief of the Army and Navy of the United States, and of the Militia of the several States, when called into the actual Service of the United States; he may require the Opinion, in writing, of the principal Officer in each of the executive Departments, upon any Subject relating to the Duties of their respective Offices, and he shall have Power to grant Reprieves and Pardons for Offences against the United States, except in Cases of Impeachment.

He shall have Power, by and with the Advice and Consent of the Senate, to make Treaties, provided two thirds of the Senators present concur; and he shall nominate, and by and with the Advice and Consent of the Senate, shall appoint Ambassadors, other public Ministers and Consuls, Judges of the supreme Court, and all other Officers of the United States, whose Appointments are not herein otherwise provided for, and which shall be established by Law: but the Congress may by Law vest the Appointment of such inferior Officers, as they think proper in the President alone, in the Courts of Law, or in the Heads of Departments.

The President shall have Power to fill up all Vacancies that may happen during the Recess of the Senate, by granting Commissions which shall expire at the End of their next Session.

Section 3

He shall from time to time give to the Congress Information of the State of the Union, and recommend to their Consideration such Measures as he shall judge necessary and expedient; he may, on extraordinary Occasions, convene both Houses, or either of them, and in Case of disagreement between them, with Respect to the Time of Adjournment, he may adjourn them to such Time as he shall think proper; he shall receive Ambassadors and other public Ministers; he shall take Care that the Laws be faithfully executed, and shall Commission all the officers of the United States.

Section 4

The President, Vice President and all civil Officers of the United States, shall be removed from Office on Impeachment for, and Conviction of, Treason, Bribery or other high Crimes and Misdemeanors.

ARTICLE III

Section 1

The judicial Power of the United States, shall be vested in one supreme Court, and in such inferior Courts as the Congress may from time to time ordain and establish. The Judges, both of the supreme and inferior Courts, shall hold their offices during good Behaviour, and shall, at stated Times, receive for their Services, a Compensation, which shall not be diminished during their Continuance in Office.

Section 2

The judicial Power shall extend to all Cases, in Law and Equity, arising under this Constitution, the Laws of the United States, and Treaties made, or which shall be made, under their Authority;—to all Cases affecting Ambassadors, other public Ministers and Consuls;—to all Cases of admiralty and maritime Jurisdiction;—to Controversies to which the United States shall be a Party;—to Controversies between two or more States;—*between a State and Citizens of another State*;—between Citizens of different States;—between Citizens of the same State claiming Lands under Grants of different States, and between a State, or the Citizens thereof, and foreign States, Citizens or Subjects.

In all Cases affecting Ambassadors, other public Ministers and Consuls, and those in which a State shall be Party, the supreme Court shall have original Jurisdiction. In all the other Cases before mentioned, the supreme Court shall have appellate Jurisdiction, both as to Law and Fact, with such Exceptions, and under such Regulations as the Congress shall make.

The Trial of all Crimes, except in Cases of Impeachment, shall be by Jury; and such Trial shall be held in the State where the said Crimes shall have been committed, but when not committed within any State, the Trial shall be at such Place or Places as the Congress may by Law have directed.

Section 3

Treason against the United States, shall consist only in levying War against them, or in adhering to their Enemies, giving them Aid and Comfort. No person shall be convicted of Treason unless on the Testimony of two Witnesses to the same overt Act, or on Confession in open Court.

The Congress shall have Power to declare the Punishment of Treason, but no Attainder of Treason shall work Corruption of Blood, or Forfeiture except during the Life of the Person attainted.

ARTICLE IV

Section 1

Full Faith and Credit shall be given in each State to the public Acts, Records, and judicial Proceedings of every other State. And the Congress may by general Laws prescribe the Manner in which such Acts, Records and Proceedings shall be proved, and the Effect thereof.

Section 2

The Citizens of each State shall be entitled to all Privileges and Immunities of Citizens in the several States.

A Person charged in any State with Treason, Felony, or other Crime, who shall flee from Justice, and be found in another State, shall on Demand of the executive Authority of the State from which he fled, be delivered up, to be removed to the State having Jurisdiction of the Crime.

No Person held to Service or Labour in one State, under the Laws thereof, escaping into another, shall, in Consequence of any Law or Regulation therein, be discharged from such Service or Labour, but shall be delivered up on Claim of the Party to whom such Service or Labour may be due.

Section 3

New States may be admitted by the Congress into this Union; but no new State shall be formed or erected within the Jurisdiction of any other State; nor any State be formed by the Junction of two or more States, or Parts of States, without the Consent of the Legislatures of the States concerned as well as of the Congress.

The Congress shall have Power to dispose of and make all needful Rules and Regulations respecting the Territory or other Property belonging to the United States; and nothing in this Constitution shall be so construed as to Prejudice any Claims of the United States, or of any particular States.

Section 4

The United States shall guarantee to every State in this Union a Republican Form of Government, and shall protect each of them against Invasion; and on Application of the Legislature, or of the Executive (when the Legislature cannot be convened) against domestic violence.

ARTICLE V

The Congress, whenever two thirds of both Houses shall deem it necessary, shall propose Amendments to this Constitution, or, on the Application of the Legislatures of two thirds of the several States, shall call a Convention for proposing Amendments, which, in either Case, shall be valid to all Intents and Purposes, as Part of this Constitution, when ratified by the Legislatures of three fourths of the several States, or by Conventions in three fourths thereof, as the one or the other Mode of Ratification may be proposed by the Congress; Provided *that no Amendment which may be made prior to the Year One thousand eight hundred and eight shall in any Manner affect the first and fourth Clauses in the Ninth Section of the first Article*; and that no State, without its Consent, shall be deprived of its equal Suffrage in the Senate.

ARTICLE VI

All Debts contracted and Engagements entered into, before the Adoption of this Constitution, shall be as valid against the United States under this Constitution, as under the Confederation.

This Constitution, and Laws of the United States which shall be made in Pursuance thereof; and all Treaties made, or which shall be made, under the Authority of the United States, shall be the supreme Law of the Land; and the Judges in every State shall be bound thereby, any Thing in the Constitution or Laws of any State to the Contrary notwithstanding.

The Senators and Representatives before mentioned, and the Members of the several State Legislatures, and all executive and Judicial Officers, both of the United States and of the several States, shall be bound by Oath or Affirmation, to support this Constitution; but no religious Test shall ever be required as a Qualification to any Office of public Trust under the United States.

ARTICLE VII

The Ratification of the Conventions of nine States, shall be sufficient for the Establishment of this Constitution between the States so ratifying the Same.

Done in Convention by the Unanimous Consent of the States present the Seventeenth Day of September in the Year of our Lord one thousand seven hundred and Eighty seven and of the Independence of the United States of America the Twelfth* IN WITNESS whereof We have hereunto subscribed our Names,

George Washington
President and Deputy from Virginia

Delaware
George Read
Gunning Bedford, Jr.
John Dickinson
Richard Bassett
Jacob Broom

Maryland
James McHenry
Daniel of St. Thomas Jenifer
Daniel Carroll

Virginia
John Blair
James Madison, Jr.

North Carolina
William Blount
Richard Dobbs Spraight
Hugh Williamson

South Carolina
John Rutledge
Charles Cotesworth Pinckney
Charles Pinckney
Pierce Butler

Georgia
William Few
Abraham Baldwin

New Hampshire
John Langdon
Nicholas Gilman

Massachusetts
Nathaniel Gorham
Rufus King

Connecticut
William Samuel Johnson
Roger Sherman

New York
Alexander Hamilton

New Jersey
William Livingston
David Brearley
William Paterson
Jonathan Dayton

Pennsylvania
Benjamin Franklin
Thomas Mifflin
Robert Morris
George Clymer
Thomas FitzSimons
Jared Ingersoll
James Wilson
Gouverneur Morris

---

*The Constitution was submitted on September 17, 1787, by the Constitutional Convention, was ratified by the Convention of several states at various dates up to May 29, 1790, and became effective on March 4, 1789.

Amendments to the Constitution

AMENDMENT I

Congress shall make no law respecting an establishment of religion, or prohibiting the free exercise thereof; or abridging the freedom of speech, or of the press; or the right of the people peaceably to assemble, and to petition the Government for a redress of grievances.

AMENDMENT II

A well regulated Militia being necessary to the security of a free State, the right of the people to keep and bear Arms, shall not be infringed.

AMENDMENT III

No Soldier shall, in time of peace be quartered in any house, without the consent of the Owner, nor in time of war, but in a manner to be prescribed by law.

AMENDMENT IV

The right of the people to be secure in their persons, houses, papers, and effects, against unreasonable searches and seizures, shall not be violated, and no Warrants shall issue, but upon probable cause, supported by Oath or affirmation, and particularly describing the place to be searched, and the persons or things to be seized.

AMENDMENT V

No person shall be held to answer for a capital, or otherwise infamous crime, unless on a presentment or indictment of a Grand Jury, except in cases arising in the land or naval forces, or in the Militia, when in actual service in time of War or public danger; nor shall any person be subject for the same offense to be twice put in jeopardy of life or limb; nor shall be compelled in any criminal case to be a witness against himself, nor be deprived of life, liberty, or property, without due process of law; nor shall private property be taken for public use, without just compensation.

AMENDMENT VI

In all criminal prosecutions, the accused shall enjoy the right to a speedy and public trial, by an impartial jury of the State and district wherein the crime shall have been committed, which district shall have been previously ascertained by law, and to be informed of the nature and cause of the accusation; to be confronted with the witnesses against him; to have compulsory process for obtaining witnesses in his favor, and to have the Assistance of Counsel for his defence.

AMENDMENT VII

In Suits at common law, where the value in controversy shall exceed twenty dollars, the right of trial by jury shall be preserved, and no fact tried by a jury, shall be otherwise re-examined in any Court of the United States, than according to the rules of the common law.

AMENDMENT VIII

Excessive bail shall not be required, nor excessive fines imposed, nor cruel and unusual punishments inflicted.

AMENDMENT IX

The enumeration in the Constitution, of certain rights, shall not be construed to deny or disparage others retained by the people.

AMENDMENT X*

The powers not delegated to the United States by the Constitution, nor prohibited by it to the States, are reserved to the States respectively, or to the people.

AMENDMENT XI

[ADOPTED 1798]

The Judicial power of the United States shall not be construed to extend to any suit in law or equity, commenced or prosecuted against one of the United States by Citizens of another State, or by Citizens or Subjects of any Foreign State.

AMENDMENT XII

[ADOPTED 1804]

The Electors shall meet in their respective states, and vote by ballot for President and Vice President, one of whom, at least, shall not be an inhabitant of the same state with themselves; they shall name in their ballots the person voted for as President, and in distinct ballots the person voted for as Vice President, and they shall make distinct lists of all persons voted for as President, and of all persons voted for as Vice President, and of the number of votes for each, which lists they shall sign and certify, and transmit sealed to the seat of the government of the United States, directed to the President of the Senate;—The President of the Senate shall, in the presence of the Senate and House of Representatives, open all the certificates and the votes shall then be counted;—The person having the greatest number of votes for President, shall be the President, if such number be a majority of the whole number of Electors appointed; and if no person have such majority, then from the persons having the highest numbers not exceeding three on the list of those voted for as President, the House of Representatives shall choose immediately, by ballot, the President. But in choosing the President, the votes shall be taken by states, the representation from each state having one vote; a quorum for this purpose shall consist of a member or members from two-thirds of the states, and a majority of all the states shall be necessary to a choice. And if the House of Representatives shall not choose a President whenever the right of choice shall devolve upon them, before *the fourth day of March* next following, then the Vice President shall act as President, as in the case of the death or other constitutional disability of the President.— The person having the greatest number of votes as Vice President, shall be the Vice President, if such number be a majority of the whole number of Electors appointed, and if no person have a majority, then from the two highest numbers on the list, the Senate shall choose the Vice President; a quorum for the purpose shall consist of two-thirds of the whole number of Senators, and a majority of the whole number shall be necessary to a choice. But no person constitutionally ineligible to the office of President shall be eligible to that of Vice President of the United States.

---

*The first ten amendments (the Bill of Rights) were ratified and their adoption was certified on December 15, 1791.

AMENDMENT XIII

[ADOPTED 1865]

Section 1

Neither slavery nor involuntary servitude, except as a punishment for crime whereof the party shall have been duly convicted, shall exist within the United States, or any place subject to their jurisdiction.

Section 2

Congress shall have power to enforce this article by appropriate legislation.

AMENDMENT XIV

[ADOPTED 1868]

Section 1

All persons born or naturalized in the United States, and subject to the jurisdiction thereof, are citizens of the United States and of the State wherein they reside. No State shall make or enforce any law which shall abridge the privileges or immunities of citizens of the United States; nor shall any State deprive any person of life, liberty, or property, without due process of law; nor deny to any person within its jurisdiction the equal protection of the laws.

Section 2

Representatives shall be apportioned among the several States according to their respective numbers, counting the whole number of persons in each State, excluding Indians not taxed. But when the right to vote at any election for the choice of electors for President and Vice President of the United States, Representatives in Congress, the Executive and Judicial officers of a State, or the members of the Legislature thereof, is denied to any of the male inhabitants of such State, being twenty-one years of age, and citizens of the United States, or in any way abridged, except for participation in rebellion, or other crime, the basis of representation therein shall be reduced in the proportion which the number of such male citizens shall bear to the whole number of male citizens twenty-one years of age in such State.

Section 3

No person shall be a Senator or Representative in Congress, or elector of President and Vice President, or hold any office, civil or military, under the United States, or under any State, who, having previously taken an oath, as a member of Congress, or as an officer of the United States, or as a member of any State legislature, or as an executive or judicial officer of any State, to support the Constitution of the United States, shall have engaged in insurrection or rebellion against the same, or given aid or comfort to the enemies thereof. But Congress may by a vote of two-thirds of each House, remove such disability.

Section 4

The validity of the public debt of the United States, authorized by law, including debts incurred for payment of pensions and bounties for services in suppressing insurrection or rebellion, shall not be questioned. But neither the United States nor any State shall assume or pay any debt or obligation incurred in aid of insurrection or rebellion against the United States, or any claim for the loss or emancipation of any slave; but all such debts, obligations and claims shall be held illegal and void.

Section 5

The Congress shall have power to enforce, by appropriate legislation, the provisions of this article.

AMENDMENT XV

[ADOPTED 1870]

Section 1

The right of citizens of the United States to vote shall not be denied or abridged by the United States or by any State on account of race, color, or previous condition of servitude.

Section 2

The Congress shall have power to enforce this article by appropriate legislation.

AMENDMENT XVI

[ADOPTED 1913]

The Congress shall have power to lay and collect taxes on incomes, from whatever source derived, without apportionment among the several States, and without regard to any census or enumeration.

AMENDMENT XVII

[ADOPTED 1913]

The Senate of the United States shall be composed of two Senators from each State, elected by the people thereof, for six years; and each Senator shall have one vote. The electors in each State shall have the qualifications requisite for electors of the most numerous branch of the State legislatures.

When vacancies happen in the representation of any State in the Senate, the executive authority of such State shall issue writs of election to fill such vacancies: *Provided*, That the legislature of any State may empower the executive thereof to make temporary appointments until the people fill the vacancies by election as the legislature may direct.

This amendment shall not be so construed as to affect the election or term of any Senator chosen before it becomes valid as part of the Constitution.

AMENDMENT XVIII

[ADOPTED 1919, REPEALED 1933]

Section 1

After one year from the ratification of this article the manufacture, sale, or transportation of intoxicating liquors within, the importation thereof into, or the exportation thereof from the United States and all territory subject to the jurisdiction thereof for beverage purposes is hereby prohibited.

Section 2

The Congress and the several States shall have concurrent power to enforce this article by appropriate legislation.

Section 3

This article shall be inoperative unless it shall have been ratified as an amendment to the Constitution by the legislatures of the several States, as provided in the Constitution, within seven years from the date of the submission hereof to the States by the Congress.

AMENDMENT XIX

[ADOPTED 1920]

The right of citizens of the United States to vote shall not be denied or abridged by the United States or by any State on account of sex.

Congress shall have power to enforce this article by appropriate legislation.

AMENDMENT XX

[ADOPTED 1933]

Section 1

The terms of the President and Vice President shall end at noon on the 20th day of January, and the terms of Senators and Representatives at noon on the 3d day of January, of the years in which such terms would have ended if this article had not been ratified and the terms of their successors shall then begin.

Section 2

The Congress shall assemble at least once in every year, and such meeting shall begin at noon on the 3d day of January, unless they shall by law appoint a different day.

Section 3

If, at the time fixed for the beginning of the term of the President, the President elect shall have died, the Vice President elect shall become President. If a President shall not have been chosen before the time fixed for the beginning of his term, or if the President elect shall have failed to qualify, then the Vice President elect shall act as President until a President shall have qualified; and the Congress may by law provide for the case wherein neither a President elect nor a Vice President elect shall have qualified, declaring who shall then act as President, or the manner in which one who is to act shall be selected, and such person shall act accordingly until a President or Vice President shall have qualified.

Section 4

The Congress may by law provide for the case of the death of any of the persons from whom the House of Representatives may choose a President whenever the right of choice shall have devolved upon them, and for the case of the death of any of the persons from whom the Senate may choose a Vice President whenever the right of choice shall have devolved upon them.

Section 5

Sections 1 and 2 shall take effect on the 15th day of October following the ratification of this article.

Section 6

This article shall be inoperative unless it shall have been ratified as an amendment to the Constitution by the legislatures of three fourths of the several States within seven years from the date of its submission.

AMENDMENT XXI

[ADOPTED 1933]

Section 1

The eighteenth article of amendment to the Constitution of the United States is hereby repealed.

Section 2

The transportation or importation into any State, Territory, or possession of the United States for delivery or use therein of intoxicating liquors in violation of the laws thereof, is hereby prohibited.

Section 3

This article shall be inoperative unless it shall have been ratified as an amendment to the Constitution by conventions in the several States, as provided in the Constitution, within seven years from the date of the submission hereof to the States by the Congress.

AMENDMENT XXII

[ADOPTED 1951]

Section 1

No person shall be elected to the office of the President more than twice, and no person who has held the office of President, or acted as President, for more than two years of a term to which some other person was elected President shall be elected to the office of the President more than once. But this Article shall not apply to any person holding the office of President when this Article was proposed by the Congress, and shall not prevent any person who may be holding the office of President, or acting as President, during the term within which this Article becomes operative from holding the office of President or acting as President during the remainder of such term.

Section 2

This article shall be inoperative unless it shall have been ratified as an amendment to the Constitution by the legislatures of three-fourths of the several States within seven years from the date of its submission to the States by the Congress.

AMENDMENT XXIII

[ADOPTED 1961]

Section 1

The District constituting the seat of Government of the United States shall appoint in such manner as the Congress shall direct:

A number of electors of President and Vice President equal to the whole number of Senators and Representatives in Congress to which the District would be entitled if it were a State, but in no event more than the least populous State; they shall be in addition to those appointed by the States, but they shall be considered, for the purposes of the election of President and Vice President, to be electors appointed by a State; and they shall meet in the District and perform such duties as provided by the twelfth article of amendment.

Section 2

The Congress shall have power to enforce this article by appropriate legislation.

AMENDMENT XXIV

[ADOPTED 1964]

Section 1

The right of citizens of the United States to vote in any primary or other election for President or Vice President, for electors for President or Vice President, or for Senator or Representative in Congress, shall not be denied or abridged by the United States or any state by reason of failure to pay any poll tax or other tax.

Section 2

The Congress shall have the power to enforce this article by appropriate legislation.

AMENDMENT XXV

[ADOPTED 1967]

Section 1

In case of the removal of the President from office or his death or resignation, the Vice President shall become President.

Section 2

Whenever there is a vacancy in the office of the Vice President, the President shall nominate a Vice President who shall take the office upon confirmation by a majority vote of both houses of Congress.

Section 3

Whenever the President transmits to the President pro tempore of the Senate and the Speaker of the House of Representatives his written declaration that he is unable to discharge the powers and duties of his office, and until he transmits to them a written declaration to the contrary, such powers and duties shall be discharged by the Vice President as Acting President.

Section 4

Whenever the Vice President and a majority of either the principal officers of the executive departments or of such other body as Congress may by law provide, transmit to the President pro tempore of the Senate and the Speaker of the House of Representatives their written declaration that the President is unable to discharge the powers and duties of his office, the Vice President shall immediately assume the powers and duties of the office as Acting President.

Thereafter, when the President transmits to the President pro tempore of the Senate and the Speaker of the House of Representatives his written declaration that no inability exists, he shall resume the powers and duties of his office unless the Vice President and a majority of either the principal officers of the executive department or of such other body as Congress may by law provide, transmit within four days to the President pro tempore of the Senate and the Speaker of the House of Representatives their written declaration that the President is unable to discharge the powers and duties of his office. Thereupon Congress shall decide the issue, assembling within 48 hours for that purpose if not in session. If the Congress, within 21 days after receipt of the latter written declaration, or, if Congress is not in session, within 21 days after Congress is required to assemble, determines by two-thirds vote of both houses that the President is unable to discharge the powers and duties of his office, the Vice President shall continue to discharge the same as Acting President; otherwise, the President shall resume the powers and duties of his office.

AMENDMENT XXVI

[ADOPTED 1971]

Section 1

The right of citizens of the United States, who are 18 years of age or older, to vote shall not be denied or abridged by the United States or any state on account of age.

Section 2

The Congress shall have the power to enforce this article by appropriate legislation.

AMENDMENT XXVII

[ADOPTED 1992]

No law, varying the compensation for the services of the Senators and Representatives shall take effect, until an election of Representatives shall have intervened.

Presidential Elections

Year	Candidates	Parties	Popular Vote	Electoral Vote	Voter Participation
1789	George Washington		*	69	
	John Adams			34	
	Others			35	
1792	George Washington		*	132	
	John Adams			77	
	George Clinton			50	
	Others			5	
1796	John Adams	Federalist	*	71	
	Thomas Jefferson	Democratic-Republican		68	
	Thomas Pinckney	Federalist		59	
	Aaron Burr	Dem.-Rep.		30	
	Others			48	

*Electors selected by state legislatures.

Year	Candidates	Parties	Popular Vote	Electoral Vote	Voter Participation
1800	Thomas Jefferson	Dem.-Rep.	*	73	
	Aaron Burr	Dem.-Rep.		73	
	John Adams	Federalist		65	
	C. C. Pinckney	Federalist		64	
	John Jay	Federalist		1	
1804	Thomas Jefferson	Dem.-Rep.	*	162	
	C. C. Pinckney	Federalist		14	
1808	James Madison	Dem.-Rep.	*	122	
	C. C. Pinckney	Federalist		47	
	George Clinton	Dem.-Rep.		6	
1812	James Madison	Dem.-Rep.	*	128	
	De Witt Clinton	Federalist		89	
1816	James Monroe	Dem.-Rep.	*	183	
	Rufus King	Federalist		34	
1820	James Monroe	Dem.-Rep.	*	231	
	John Quincy Adams	Dem.-Rep.		1	
1824	John Quincy Adams	Dem.-Rep.	108,740 (30.5%)	84	26.9%
	Andrew Jackson	Dem.-Rep.	153,544 (43.1%)	99	
	William H. Crawford	Dem.-Rep.	46,618 (13.1%)	41	
	Henry Clay	Dem.-Rep.	47,136(13.2%)	37	
1828	Andrew Jackson	Democratic	647,286 (56.0%)	178	57.6%
	John Quincy Adams	National Republican	508,064 (44.0%)	83	
1832	Andrew Jackson	Democratic	688,242 (54.2%)	219	55.4%
	Henry Clay	National Republican	473,462 (37.4%)	49	
	John Floyd	Independent		11	
	William Wirt	**Anti-Mason**	101,051 (7.8%)	7	
1836	Martin Van Buren	Democratic	762,198 (50.8%)	170	57.8%
	William Henry Harrison	Whig	549,508 (36.6%)	73	
	Hugh L. White	Whig	145,342 (9.7%)	26	
	Daniel Webster	Whig	41,287 (2.7%)	14	
	W. P. Magnum	Independent		11	
1840	William Henry Harrison	Whig	1,274,624 (53.1%)	234	80.2%
	Martin Van Buren	Democratic	1,127,781 (46.9%)	60	
	J. G. Birney	Liberty	7069	—	
1844	James K. Polk	Democratic	1,338,464 (49.6%)	170	78.9%
	Henry Clay	Whig	1,300,097 (48.1%)	105	
	J. G. Birney	Liberty	62,300 (2.3%)	—	
1848	Zachary Taylor	Whig	1,360,967 (47.4%)	163	72.7%
	Lewis Cass	Democratic	1,222,342 (42.5%)	127	
	Martin Van Buren	Free-Soil	291,263 (10.1%)	—	
1852	Franklin Pierce	Democratic	1,601,117 (50.9%)	254	69.6%
	Winfield Scott	Whig	1,385,453 (44.1%)	42	
	John P. Hale	Free-Soil	155,825 (5.0%)	—	

*Electors selected by state legislatures.

Year	Candidates	Parties	Popular Vote	Electoral Vote	Voter Participation
1856	James Buchanan	Democratic	1,832,955 (45.3%)	174	78.9%
	John C. Frémont	Republican	1,339,932 (33.1%)	114	
	Millard Fillmore	American	871,731 (21.6%)	8	
1860	Abraham Lincoln	Republican	1,865,593 (39.8%)	180	81.2%
	Stephen A. Douglas	Democratic	1,382,713 (29.5%)	12	
	John C. Breckinridge	Democratics	848,356 (18.1%)	72	
	John Bell	Union	592,906 (12.6%)	39	
1864	Abraham Lincoln	Republican	2,213,655 (55.0%)	212*	73.8%
	George B. McClellan	Democratic	1,805,237 (45.0%)	21	
1868	Ulysses S. Grant	Republican	3,012,833 (52.7%)	214	78.1%
	Horatio Seymour	Democratic	2,703,249 (47.3%)	80	
1872	Ulysses S. Grant	Republican	3,597,132 (55.6%)	286	71.3%
	Horace Greeley	Dem.; Liberal Republican	2,834,125 (43.9%)	66†	
1876	Rutherford B. Hayes‡	Republican	4,036,298 (48.0%)	185	81.8%
	Samuel J. Tilden	Democratic	4,300,590 (51.0%)	184	
1880	James A. Garfield	Republican	4,454,416 (48.5%)	214	79.4%
	Winfield S. Hancock	Democratic	4,444,952 (48.1%)	155	
1884	Grover Cleveland	Democratic	4,874,986 (48.5%)	219	77.5%
	James G. Blaine	Republican	4,851,981 (48.2%)	182	
1888	Benjamin Harrison	Republican	5,439,853 (47.9%)	233	79.3%
	Grover Cleveland	Democratic	5,540,309 (48.6%)	168	
1892	Grover Cleveland	Democratic	5,556,918 (46.1%)	277	74.7%
	Benjamin Harrison	Republican	5,176,108 (43.0%)	145	
	James B. Weaver	People's	1,029,329 (8.5%)	22	
1896	William McKinley	Republican	7,104,779 (51.1%)	271	79.3%
	William Jennings Bryan	Democratic People's	6,502,925 (47.7%)	176	
1900	William McKinley	Republican	7,207,923 (51.7%)	292	73.2%
	William Jennings Bryan	Dem.-Populist	6,358,133 (45.5%)	155	
1904	Theodore Roosevelt	Republican	7,623,486 (57.9%)	336	65.2%
	Alton B. Parker	Democratic	5,077,911 (37.6%)	140	
	Eugene V. Debs	Socialist	402,400 (3.0%)	—	
1908	William H. Taft	Republican	7,678,908 (51.6%)	321	65.4%
	William Jennings Bryan	Democratic	6,409,104 (43.1%)	162	
	Eugene V. Debs	Socialist	402,820 (2.8%)	—	
1912	Woodrow Wilson	Democratic	6,293,454 (41.9%)	435	58.8%
	Theodore Roosevelt	Progressive	4,119,538 (27.4%)	88	
	William H. Taft	Republican	3,484,980 (23.2%)	8	
	Eugene V. Debs	Socialist	900,672 (6.0%)	—	

*Eleven secessionist states did not participate.
†Greeley died before the electoral college met. His electoral votes were divided among the four minor candidates.
‡Contested result settled by special election.

Year	Candidates	Parties	Popular Vote	Electoral Vote	Voter Participation
1916	Woodrow Wilson	Democratic	9,129,606 (49.4%)	277	61.6%
	Charles E. Hughes	Republican	8,538,221 (46.2%)	254	
	A. L. Benson	Socialist	585,113 (3.2%)	—	
1920	Warren G. Harding	Republican	16,152,200 (60.4%)	404	49.2%
	James M. Cox	Democratic	9,147,353 (34.2%)	127	
	Eugene V. Debs	Socialist	917,799 (3.4%)	—	
1924	Calvin Coolidge	Republican	15,725,016 (54.0%)	382	48.9%
	John W. Davis	Democratic	8,386,503 (28.8%)	136	
	Robert M. La Follette	Progressive	4,822,856 (16.6%)	13	
1928	Herbert Hoover	Republican	21,391,381 (58.2%)	444	56.9%
	Alfred E. Smith	Democratic	15,016,443 (40.9%)	87	
	Norman Thomas	Socialist	267,835 (0.7%)	—	
1932	Franklin D. Roosevelt	Democratic	22,821,857 (57.4%)	472	56.9%
	Herbert Hoover	Republican	15,761,841 (39.7%)	59	
	Norman Thomas	Socialist	884,781 (2.2%)	—v	
1936	Franklin D. Roosevelt	Democratic	27,751,597 (60.8%)	523	61.0%
	Alfred M. Landon	Republican	16,679,583 (36.5%)	8	
	William Lemke	Union	882,479 (1.9%)	—	
1940	Franklin D. Roosevelt	Democratic	27,244,160 (54.8%)	449	62.5%
	Wendell L. Willkie	Republican	22,305,198 (44.8%)	82	
1944	Franklin D. Roosevelt	Democratic	25,602,504 (53.5%)	432	55.9%
	Thomas E. Dewey	Republican	22,006,285 (46.0%)	99	
1948	Harry S Truman	Democratic	24,105,695 (49.5%)	304	53.0%
	Thomas E. Dewey	Republican	21,969,170 (45.1%)	189	
	J. Strom Thurmond	State-Rights Democratic	1,169,021 (2.4%)	38	
	Henry A. Wallace	Progressive	1,157,326 (2.4%)	—	
1952	Dwight D. Eisenhower	Republican	33,778,963 (55.1%)	442	63.3%
	Adlai E. Stevenson	Democratic	27,314,992 (44.4%)	89	
1956	Dwight D. Eisenhower	Republican	35,575,420 (57.6%)	457	60.6%
	Adlai E. Stevenson	Democratic	26,033,066 (42.1%)	73	
	Other	—	—	1	
1960	John F. Kennedy	Democratic	34,227,096 (49.9%)	303	62.8%
	Richard M. Nixon	Republican	34,108,546 (49.6%)	219	
	Other	—	—	15	
1964	Lyndon B. Johnson	Democratic	43,126,506 (61.1%)	486	61.7%
	Barry M. Goldwater	Republican	27,176,799 (38.5%)	52	
1968	Richard M. Nixon	Republican	31,770,237 (43.4%)	301	60.6%
	Hubert H. Humphrey	Democratic	31,270,533 (42.7%)	191	
	George Wallace	American Indep.	9,906,141 (13.5%)	46	
1972	Richard M. Nixon	Republican	46,740,323 (60.7%)	520	55.2%
	George S. McGovern	Democratic	28,901,598 (37.5%)	17	
	Other	—	—	1	

Year	Candidates	Parties	Popular Vote	Electoral Vote	Voter Participation
1976	Jimmy Carter	Democratic	40,828,587 (50.0%)	297	53.5%
	Gerald R. Ford	Republican	39,147,613 (47.9%)	241	
	Other	—	1,575,459 (2.1%)	—	
1980	Ronald Reagan	Republican	43,901,812 (50.7%)	489	52.6%
	Jimmy Carter	Democratic	35,483,820 (41.0%)	49	
	John B. Anderson	Independent	5,719,437 (6.6%)	—	
	Ed Clark	Libertarian	921,188 (1.1%)	—	
1984	Ronald Reagan	Republican	54,455,075 (59.0%)	525	53.3%
	Walter Mondale	Democratic	37,577,185 (41.0%)	13	
1988	George H. W. Bush	Republican	48,886,097 (53.4%)	426	57.4%
	Michael S. Dukakis	Democratic	41,809,074 (45.6%)	111	
1992	William J. Clinton	Democratic	44,908,254 (43%)	370	55.0%
	George H. W. Bush	Republican	39,102,343 (37.5%)	168	
	H. Ross Perot	Independent	19,741,065 (18.9%)	—	
1996	William J. Clinton	Democratic	45,590,703 (50%)	379	48.8%
	Robert Dole	Republican	37,816,307 (41%)	159	
	Ross Perot	Reform	7,866,284	—	
2000	George W. Bush	Republican	50,456,167 (47.88%)	271	51.2%
	Al Gore	Democratic	50,996,064 (48.39%)	266*	
	Ralph Nader	Green	2,864,810 (2.72%)	—	
	Other		834,774 (less than 1%)	—	
2004	George W. Bush	Republican	60,934,251 (51.0%)	286	50.0%
	John F. Kerry	Democratic	57,765,291 (48.0%)	252	
	Ralph Nader	Independent	405,933 (less than 1%)	—	
2008	Barack H. Obama	Democratic	69,456,897 (51.0%)	365	61.7%
	John McCain	Republican	59,934,814 (48.0%)	173	

*One District of Columbia Gore elector abstained.

Presidents and Vice Presidents

	President	Vice President	Term
1.	George Washington	John Adams	1789–1793
	George Washington	John Adams	1793–1797
2.	John Adams	Thomas Jefferson	1797–1801
3.	Thomas Jefferson	Aaron Burr	1801–1805
	Thomas Jefferson	George Clinton	1805–1809
4.	James Madison	George Clinton (d. 1812)	1809–1813
	James Madison	Elbridge Gerry (d. 1814)	1813–1817
5.	James Monroe	Daniel Tompkins	1817–1821
	James Monroe	Daniel Tompkins	1821–1825
6.	John Quincy Adams	John C. Calhoun	1825–1829
7.	Andrew Jackson	John C. Calhoun	1829–1833
	Andrew Jackson	Martin Van Buren	1833–1837
8.	Martin Van Buren	Richard M. Johnson	1837–1841
9.	William H. Harrison (d. 1841)	John Tyler	1841
10.	John Tyler	—	1841–1845
11.	James K. Polk	George M. Dallas	1845–1849
12.	Zachary Taylor (d. 1850)	Millard Fillmore	1849–1850
13.	Millard Fillmore	—	1850–1853
14.	Franklin Pierce	William R. King (d. 1853)	1853–1857
15.	James Buchanan	John C. Breckinridge	1857–1861
16.	Abraham Lincoln	Hannibal Hamlin	1861–1865
	Abraham Lincoln (d. 1865)	Andrew Johnson	1865
17.	Andrew Johnson	—	1865–1869
18.	Ulysses S. Grant	Schuyler Colfax	1869–1873
	Ulysses S. Grant	Henry Wilson (d. 1875)	1873–1877
19.	Rutherford B. Hayes	William A. Wheeler	1877–1881
20.	James A. Garfield (d. 1881)	Chester A. Arthur	1881
21.	Chester A. Arthur	—	1881–1885
22.	Grover Cleveland	Thomas A. Hendricks (d. 1885)	1885–1889
23.	Benjamin Harrison	Levi P. Morton	1889–1893
24.	Grover Cleveland	Adlai E. Stevenson	1893–1897
25.	William McKinley	Garret A. Hobart (d. 1899)	1897–1901
	William McKinley (d. 1901)	Theodore Roosevelt	1901
26.	Theodore Roosevelt	—	1901–1905
	Theodore Roosevelt	Charles Fairbanks	1905–1909
27.	William H. Taft	James S. Sherman (d. 1912)	1909–1913
28.	Woodrow Wilson	Thomas R. Marshall	1913–1917
	Woodrow Wilson	Thomas R. Marshall	1917–1921
29.	Warren G. Harding (d. 1923)	Calvin Coolidge	1921–1923
30.	Calvin Coolidge	—	1923–1925
	Calvin Coolidge	Charles G. Dawes	1925–1929

	President	Vice President	Term
31.	Herbert Hoover	Charles Curtis	1929–1933
32.	Franklin D. Roosevelt	John N. Garner	1933–1937
	Franklin D. Roosevelt	John N. Garner	1937–1941
	Franklin D. Roosevelt	Henry A. Wallace	1941–1945
	Franklin D. Roosevelt (d. 1945)	Harry S Truman	1945
33.	Harry S Truman	—	1945–1949
	Harry S Truman	Alben W. Barkley	1949–1953
34.	Dwight D. Eisenhower	Richard M. Nixon	1953–1957
	Dwight D. Eisenhower	Richard M. Nixon	1957–1961
35.	John F. Kennedy (d. 1963)	Lyndon B. Johnson	1961–1963
36.	Lyndon B. Johnson	—	1963–1965
	Lyndon B. Johnson	Hubert H. Humphrey	1965–1969
37.	Richard M. Nixon	Spiro T. Agnew	1969–1973
	Richard M. Nixon (resigned 1974)	Gerald R. Ford	1973–1974
38.	Gerald R. Ford	Nelson A. Rockefeller	1974–1977
39.	Jimmy Carter	Walter F. Mondale	1977–1981
40.	Ronald Reagan	George H.W. Bush	1981–1985
	Ronald Reagan	George H.W. Bush	1985–1989
41.	George H.W. Bush	J. Danforth Quayle	1989–1993
42.	William J. Clinton	Albert Gore, Jr.	1993–1997
	William J. Clinton	Albert Gore, Jr.	1997–2001
43.	George W. Bush	Richard Cheney	2001–2005
	George W. Bush	Richard Cheney	2005–2008
44.	Barack H. Obama	Joseph R. Biden, Jr.	2008–

Glossary

Abolitionist movement (p. 278) Reform movement dedicated to the immediate and unconditional end of slavery in the United States.

Adams–Onís Treaty (p. 204) Signed by Secretary of State John Quincy Adams and Spanish minister Luis de Onís in 1819, this treaty allowed for U.S. annexation of Florida.

African Methodist Episcopal (AME) Church (p. 134) Richard Allen founded the African Methodist Episcopal Church in 1816 as the first independent black-run Protestant church in the United States. The AME Church was active in the promotion of abolition and the founding of educational institutions for free blacks.

affirmative action (p. 792) The use of laws or regulations to achieve racial, ethnic, gender, or other types of diversity, as in hiring or school admissions. Such efforts are often aimed at improving employment or educational opportunities for women and minorities.

Agricultural Adjustment Administration (AAA) (p. 622) Created by Congress in 1933 as part of the New Deal, this agency attempted to restrict agricultural production by paying farmers subsidies to take land out of production. The object was to raise farm prices, and it did, but the act did nothing for tenant farmers and sharecroppers. The Supreme Court declared it unconstitutional in 1936.

Agricultural Revolution (p. 5) The gradual shift from hunting and gathering to cultivating basic food crops that occurred worldwide from 7,000 to 9,000 years ago. This transition resulted in sedentary living, population growth, and establishment of permanent villages.

Alamo (p. 296) In 1835, Americans living in the Mexican state of Texas fomented a revolution. Mexico lost the conflict, but not before its troops defeated and killed a group of American rebels at the Alamo, a fort in San Antonio.

Albany Plan (p. 96) Plan of intercolonial cooperation proposed by prominent colonists including Benjamin Franklin at a conference in Albany, New York, in 1754. The plan envisioned the formation of a Grand Council of elected delegates from the colonies that would have powers to tax and provide for the common defense. It was rejected by the colonial and British governments, but was a prototype for colonial union.

Alien and Sedition Acts (p. 172) Collective name given to four laws passed in 1798 designed to suppress criticism of the federal government and to curb liberties of foreigners living in the United States.

American Colonization Society (p. 260) Founded in 1817, this abolitionist organization hoped to provide a mechanism by which slavery could gradually be eliminated. The society advocated the relocation of free blacks (followed by freed slaves) to the African colony of Monrovia, present day Liberia.

American Federation of Labor (AFL) (p. 431) Founded by Samuel Gompers in 1886, the AFL was a loose alliance of national craft unions that organized skilled workers by craft and worked for specific practical objectives such as higher wages, shorter hours, and better working conditions. The AFL avoided politics, and while it did not expressly forbid black and women workers from joining, it used exclusionary practices to keep them out.

Americans with Disabilities Act (ADA) (p. 770) Passed by Congress in 1991, this act banned discrimination against the disabled in employment and mandated easy access to all public and commercial buildings.

Antifederalist (p. 150) Critic of the Constitution who expressed concern that it seemed to possess no specific provision for the protection of natural and civil rights. The antifederalists forced Congress to accept a number of amendments known as the **Bill of Rights.**

Anti-Imperialist League (p. 504) This organization was formed in November 1898 to fight against the **Treaty of Paris** ending the Spanish-American War. Members opposed the acquisition of overseas colonies by the United States, believing it would subvert American ideals and institutions. Membership centered in New England; the cause was less popular in the South and West.

Antinomianism (p. 42) Religious belief rejecting traditional moral law as unnecessary for Christians who possessed saving grace and affirming that an individual could experience divine revelation and salvation without the assistance of formally trained clergy.

Articles of Confederation (p. 138) Ratified in 1781, this document was the United States' first constitution, providing a framework for national government. The articles sharply limited central authority by denying the national government any taxation or coercive power.

Ashcan School (p. 533) This school of early twentieth-century realist painters took as their subjects the slums and streets of the nation's cities and the lives of ordinary urban dwellers. They often celebrated life in the city but also advocated political and social reform.

Axis Powers (p. 642) During World War II, the alliance between Italy, Germany, and Japan was known as the "Rome–Berlin–Tokyo axis," and the three members were called the Axis Powers. They fought against the Allied Powers, led by the United States, Britain, and the Soviet Union.

baby boom (p. 688) Post-World War II Americans idealized the family. The booming birth rate after the war led children born to this generation to be commonly referred to as "baby boomers."

backcountry (p. 80) In the eighteenth century, the edge of settlement extending from western Pennsylvania to Georgia. This region formed the second frontier as settlers moved westward from the Atlantic coast into the nation's interior.

Bacon's Rebellion (p. 69) An armed rebellion in Virginia (1675–1676) led by Nathaniel Bacon against the colony's royal governor Sir William Berkeley. Although some of his followers called for an end of special privilege in government, Bacon was chiefly interested in gaining a larger share of the lucrative Indian trade.

Bank of the United States (p. 162) National bank proposed by Secretary of the Treasury Alexander Hamilton and established in 1791. It served as a central depository for the U.S. government and had the authority to issue currency.

Bank war (p. 237) Between 1832–1836, Andrew Jackson used his presidential power to fight and ultimately destroy the second Bank of the United States.

Baruch Plan (p. 668) In 1946, Bernard Baruch presented an American plan to control and eventually outlaw nuclear weapons. The plan called for United Nations control of nuclear weapons in three stages before the United States gave up its stockpile. Soviet insistence on immediate nuclear disarmament without inspection doomed the Baruch Plan and led to a nuclear arms race between the United States and the Soviet Union.

Battle of New Orleans (p. 198) Battle that occurred in 1815 at the end of the War of 1812 when U.S. forces defeated a British attempt to seize New Orleans.

Bay of Pigs (p. 710) In April 1961, a group of Cuban exiles, organized and supported by the U.S. Central Intelligence Agency (CIA), landed on the southern coast of Cuba in an effort to overthrow Fidel Castro. When the invasion ended in disaster, President Kennedy took full responsibility for the failure.

Benevolent empire (p. 273) Collection of missionary and reform societies that sought to stamp out social evils in American society in the 1820s and 1830s.

Beringia (p. 4) Land bridge formerly connecting Asia and North America that is now submerged beneath the Bering Sea.

Berlin airlift (p. 671) In 1948, in response to a Soviet land blockade of Berlin, the United States carried out a massive effort to supply the two million Berlin citizens with food, fuel, and other goods by air for more than six months. The airlift forced the Soviets to end the blockade in 1949.

Bill of Rights (p. 152) The first ten amendments to the U.S. Constitution, adopted in 1791 to preserve the rights and liberties of individuals.

birds of passage (p. 523) Temporary migrants who came to the United States to work and save money and then returned home to their native countries during the slack season. World War I interrupted the practice, trapping thousands of migrant workers in the United States.

Black Codes (p. 371) Laws passed by southern states immediately after the Civil War in an effort to maintain the pre-war social order. The codes attempted to tie freedmen to field work and prevent them from becoming equal to white Southerners.

Bland–Allison Silver Purchase Act (p. 469) This act, a compromise between groups favoring the coinage of silver and those opposed to it, called for the partial coinage of silver. Those favoring silver coinage argued that it would add to the currency and help farmers and workers; those who opposed it pointed out that few other major countries accepted silver coinage. President Rutherford B. Hayes vetoed the Bland–Allison bill in 1878, but Congress overrode his veto.

bonanza farms (p. 409) Huge farms covering thousands of acres on the Great Plains. In relying on large size and new machinery, they represented a development in agriculture similar to that taking place in industry.

bonus army (p. 620) In June 1932, a group of twenty thousand World War I veterans marched on Washington, D.C., to demand immediate payment of their "adjusted compensation" bonuses voted by Congress in 1924. Congress rejected their demands, and President Hoover, fearing that their ranks were infested with criminals and radicals, had the bonus army forcibly removed from their encampment. It was a public relations disaster for Hoover.

Boston Massacre (p. 113) A violent confrontation between British troops and a Boston mob on March 5, 1770. Five citizens were killed when the troops fired into the crowd. The incident inflamed anti-British sentiment in Massachusetts.

Boston Tea Party (p. 115) Raid on British ships in which Patriots disguised as Mohawks threw hundreds of chests of tea owned by the East India Company into Boston Harbor to protest British taxes.

Brown v. Board of Education of Topeka (p. 700) In 1954, the Supreme Court reversed the *Plessy* v. *Ferguson* decision (1896) that established the "separate but equal" doctrine. The *Brown* decision found segregation in schools inherently unequal and initiated a long and difficult effort to integrate the nation's public schools.

Camp David accords (p. 751) In 1978, President Carter mediated a peace agreement between the leaders of Egypt and Israel at Camp David, a presidential retreat near Washington, D.C. The next year, Israel and Egypt signed a peace treaty based on the Camp David accords.

Chinese Exclusion Act of 1882 (p. 405) Legislation passed in 1882 that excluded Chinese immigrant workers for ten years and denied U.S. citizenship to Chinese nationals living in the United States. It was the first U.S. exclusionary law that was aimed at a specific racial group.

Civilian Conservation Corps (CCC) (p. 623) One of the most popular **New Deal** programs, the CCC was created by Congress to provide young men between ages 18 and 25 with government jobs in reforestation and other conservation projects. It eventually employed over three hundred thousand.

Civil Rights Cases (p. 451) A group of cases in 1883 in which the Supreme Court ruled that the **Fourteenth Amendment** barred state governments from discriminating on the basis of race but did not prevent private individuals or

organizations from doing so. The ruling dealt a major blow to the Republican party's earlier efforts to provide protection for African Americans.

Clayton Antitrust Act (p. 554) An attempt to improve the **Sherman Antitrust Act** of 1890, this law outlawed interlocking directorates (companies in which the same people served as directors), forbade policies that created monopolies, and made corporate officers responsible for antitrust violations. Benefiting labor, it declared that unions were not conspiracies in restraint of trade and outlawed the use of injunctions in labor disputes unless they were necessary to protect property.

Coercive Acts (p. 115) Also known as the Intolerable Acts, the four pieces of legislation passed by Parliament in 1774 in response to the Boston Tea Party were meant to punish the colonies.

Columbian Exchange (p. 10) The exchange of plants, animals, culture, and diseases between Europe and the Americas from first contact throughout the era of exploration.

committee of correspondence (p. 114) Vast communication network formed in Massachusetts and other colonies to communicate grievances and provide colonists with evidence of British oppression.

Committee on Public Information (CPI) (p. 577) Created in 1917 by President Wilson and headed by progressive journalist George Creel, this organization rallied support for American involvement in World War I through art, advertising, and film. Creel worked out a system of voluntary censorship with the press and distributed colorful posters and pamphlets. The CPI's Division of Industrial Relations rallied labor to help the war effort.

Common Sense (p. 117) Revolutionary tract written by Thomas Paine in January 1776. It called for independence and the establishment of a republican government in America.

Compromise of 1850 (p. 318) This series of five congressional statutes temporarily calmed the sectional crisis. Among other things, the compromise made California a free state, ended the slave trade in the District of Columbia, and strengthened the Fugitive Slave Law.

Compromise of 1877 (p. 383) Compromise struck during the contested Presidential election of 1876, in which Democrats accepted the election of Rutherford B. Hayes (Republican) in exchange for the withdrawal of federal troops from the South and the ending of Reconstruction.

Comstock Lode (p. 404) Discovered in 1859 near Virginia City, Nevada, this ore deposit was the richest discovery in the history of mining. Named after T. P. Comstock, a drifter who talked his way into partnership in the claim, between 1859 and 1879 the deposit produced silver and gold worth more than $306 million.

conquistadores (p. 16) Sixteenth-century Spanish adventurers, often of noble birth, who subdued the Native Americans and created the Spanish empire in the New World.

conservation (p. 549) As president, Theodore Roosevelt made this principle one of his administration's top goals. Conservation in his view aimed at protecting the nation's natural resources, but called for the wise use of them rather than locking them away. Roosevelt's policies were opposed by those who favored preservation of the wilderness over its development.

Consumer revolution (p. 89) Period between 1740 and 1770 when English exports to the American colonies increased by 360 percent to satisfy Americans' demand for consumer goods.

containment (p. 669) First proposed by George Kennan in 1947, containment became the basic strategy of the United States throughout the Cold War. Kennan argued that firm American resistance to Soviet expansion would eventually compel Moscow to adopt more peaceful policies.

Contract with America (p. 780) In the 1994 congressional elections, Congressman Newt Gingrich had Republican candidates sign a document in which they pledged their support for such things as a balanced budget amendment, term limits for members of Congress, and a middle-class tax cut.

cooperationists (p. 343) In late 1860, southern secessionists debated two strategies: unilateral secession by each state or "cooperative" secession by the South as a whole. The cooperationists lost the debate.

Copperheads (p. 356) Northern Democrats suspected of being indifferent or hostile to the Union cause in the Civil War.

cotton gin (p. 263) Invented by Eli Whitney in 1793, this device for separating the seeds from the fibers of short-staple cotton enabled a slave to clean fifty times more cotton as by hand, which reduced production costs and gave new life to slavery in the South.

Coureurs de bois **(p. 20)** Fur trappers in French Canada who lived among the Native Americans.

"court-packing" scheme (p. 630) Concerned that the conservative Supreme Court might declare all his New Deal programs unconstitutional, President Franklin Delano Roosevelt asked Congress to allow him to appoint additional justices to the Court. Both Congress and the public rejected this "court-packing" scheme and it was defeated.

Crittenden compromise (p. 344) Faced with the specter of secession and war, Congress tried and failed to resolve the sectional crisis in the months between Lincoln's election and inauguration. The leading proposal, introduced by Kentucky Senator John Crittenden, would have extended the **Missouri Compromise** line west to the Pacific.

Cuban missile crisis (p. 711) In October 1962, the United States and the Soviet Union came close to nuclear war when President Kennedy insisted that Nikita Khrushchev remove the forty-two missiles he had secretly deployed in Cuba. The Soviets eventually did so, nuclear war was averted, and the crisis ended.

Cult of Domesticity (p. 274) Term used by historians to characterize the dominant gender role for white women in the antebellum period. The ideology of domesticity stressed the virtue of women as guardians of the home, which was considered their proper sphere.

Dartmouth College **v.** *Woodward* **(p. 218)** In this 1819 case, the Supreme Court ruled that the Constitution protected charters given to corporations by states.

Dawes Severalty Act (p. 397) Legislation passed by Congress in 1887 that aimed at breaking up traditional Indian life by promoting individual land ownership. It divided tribal lands into small plots that were distributed among members of each tribe. Provisions were made for Indian education and eventual citizenship. The law led to corruption, exploitation, and the weakening of Native American tribal culture.

D-Day (p. 654) D-Day (June 6, 1944) was the day Allied troops crossed the English Channel and opened a second front in western Europe during World War II. The "D" stands for "disembarkation": to leave a ship and go ashore.

Desert Storm (p. 773) Desert Storm was the code name used by the United States and its coalition partners in waging war against Iraq in early 1991 to liberate Kuwait.

détente (p. 739) President Nixon and Henry Kissinger pursued a policy of détente, a French word meaning a relaxation of tension, with the Soviet Union as a way to lessen the possibility of nuclear war in the 1970s.

"dollar diplomacy" (p. 566) This policy, adopted by President William Howard Taft and Secretary of State Philander C. Knox, sought to promote U.S. financial and business interests abroad. It aimed to replace military alliances with economic ties, with the idea of increasing American influence and securing lasting peace. Under this policy, Taft worked in Latin America to replace European loans with American ones, assumed the debts of countries such as Honduras to fend off foreign bondholders, and helped Nicaragua secure a large loan in exchange for U.S. control of its national bank.

Dominion of New England (p. 70) Incorporation of the New England colonies under a single appointed royal governor that lasted from 1686–1689.

dry farming (p. 408) A farming technique developed to allow farming in the more arid parts of the West where settlers had to deal with far less rainfall than they had east of the Mississippi. Furrows were plowed approximately a foot deep and filled with a dust mulch to loosen soil and slow evaporation.

Eastern Woodland Cultures (p. 7) Term given to Indians from the Northeast region who lived on the Atlantic coast and supplemented farming with seasonal hunting and gathering.

Emancipation Proclamation (p. 354) On January 1, 1863, President Lincoln proclaimed that the slaves of the Confederacy were free. Since the South had not yet been defeated, the proclamation did not immediately free anyone, but it made emancipation an explicit war aim of the North.

Embargo Act (p. 194) In response to a British attack on an American warship off the coast of Virginia, this 1807 law prohibited foreign commerce.

encomienda **system (p. 19)** An exploitative labor system designed by Spanish rulers to reward **conquistadores** in the New World by granting them local villages and control over native labor.

Enlightenment (p. 87) Philosophical and intellectual movement that began in Europe during the eighteenth century. It stressed the application of reason to solve social and scientific problems.

enumerated goods (p. 67) Certain essential raw materials produced in the North American colonies, such as tobacco, sugar, and rice specified in the **Navigation Acts**, which stipulated that these goods could be shipped only to England or its colonies.

Equal Rights Amendment (ERA) (p. 746) In 1972, Congress approved the Equal Rights Amendment (ERA) to the Constitution, a measure designed to guarantee women equal treatment under the law. Despite a three-year extension in the time allowed for ratification, ERA supporters fell three states short of winning adoption.

"Era of good feeling" (p. 221) A descriptive term for the era of President James Monroe, who served two terms from 1817–1823. During Monroe's administration, partisan conflict abated and bold federal initiatives suggested increased nationalism.

Espionage Act of 1917 (p. 578) This law, passed after the United States entered World War I, imposed sentences of up to twenty years on anyone found guilty of aiding the enemy, obstructing recruitment of soldiers, or encouraging disloyalty. It allowed the postmaster general to remove from the mail any materials that incited treason or insurrection.

Exodusters (p. 406) A group of about six thousand African Americans who left their homes in Louisiana, Mississippi, and Texas in 1879, seeking freer lives in Kansas, where they worked as farmers or laborers.

Farewell Address (p. 171) In this 1796 speech, President George Washington announced his intention not to seek a third term in office. He also stressed federalist interests and warned the American people to avoid political factions and foreign entanglements that could sacrifice U.S. security.

Federal Reserve Act (p. 554) One of the most important laws in the history of the country, this act created a central banking system, consisting of twelve regional banks governed by the Federal Reserve Board. It was an attempt to provide the United States with a sound yet flexible currency. The Board it created still plays a vital role in the American economy today.

Federalist (p. 150) Supporter of the Constitution who advocated its ratification.

Fifteenth Amendment (p. 379) Ratified in 1870, this amendment prohibited the denial or abridgment of the right to vote by the federal government or state governments on the basis of race, color, or prior condition as a slave. It was intended to guarantee African Americans the right to vote in the South.

Fireside chats (p. 621) Radio addresses by President Franklin D. Roosevelt from 1933 to 1944, in which he spoke to the American people about such issues as the banking crisis, Social Security, and World War II. The chats enhanced Roosevelt's popularity among ordinary Americans.

First Continental Congress (p. 117) A meeting of delegates from twelve colonies in Philadelphia in 1774, the Congress denied Parliament's authority to legislate for the colonies, condemned British actions toward the colonies, created the Continental Association, and endorsed a call to take up arms.

Food Administration (p. 579) A wartime government agency that encouraged Americans to save food in order to supply the armies overseas. It fixed prices to boost production, asked people to observe "meatless" and "wheatless" days to conserve food, and promoted the planting of "victory gardens" behind homes, schools, and churches.

Force acts (p. 380) Congress attacked the Ku Klux Klan with three Enforcement or "Force" acts in 1870–1871. Designed to protect black voters in the South, these laws placed state elections under federal jurisdiction and imposed fines and imprisonment on those guilty of interfering with any citizen exercising his right to vote.

Fourteen Points (p. 582) In January 1918, President Wilson presented these terms for a far-reaching, nonpunitive settlement of World War I. He called, among other things, for removal of barriers to trade, open peace accords, reduction of armaments, and the establishment of a League of Nations. While generous and optimistic, the Points did not satisfy wartime hunger for revenge, and thus were largely rejected by European nations.

Fourteenth Amendment (p. 371) Ratified in 1868, this amendment provided citizenship to ex-slaves after the Civil War and constitutionally protected equal rights under the law for all citizens. Its provisions were used by **Radical Republicans** to enact a congressionally controlled Reconstruction policy of the former Confederate states.

Freedmen's Bureau (p. 371) Agency established by Congress in March 1865 to provide freedmen with shelter, food, and medical aid and to help them establish schools and find employment. The Bureau was dissolved in 1872.

freedom ride (p. 714) Bus trips taken by both black and white civil rights advocates in the 1960s. Sponsored by the Congress of Racial Equality (CORE), freedom rides in the South were designed to test the enforcement of federal regulations that prohibited segregation in interstate public transportation.

French Revolution (p. 163) A social and political revolution in France (1789–1799) that toppled the monarchy.

Fugitive Slave Law (p. 319) Passed in 1850, this federal law made it easier for slaveowners to recapture runaway slaves; it also made it easier for kidnappers to take free blacks. The law became an object of hatred in the North.

Ghost Dances (p. 396) A religious movement that arose in the late nineteenth century under the prophet Wavoka, a Paiute Indian. It involved a set of dances and rites that its followers believed would cause white men to disappear and restore lands to the Native Americans. The Ghost Dance religion was outlawed by the U.S. government, and army intervention to stop it led to the **Wounded Knee Massacre**.

Gibbons v. *Ogden* **(p. 219)** In this 1824 case, the Supreme Court affirmed and expanded the power of the federal government to regulate interstate commerce.

Glorious Revolution (p. 70) Replacement of James II by William and Mary as English monarchs in 1688, marking the beginning of constitutional monarchy in Britain. American colonists celebrated this moment as a victory for the rule of law over despotism.

Gold Rush of 1849 (p. 401) Individual prospectors made the first gold strikes along the Sierra Nevada Mountains in 1849, touching off a mining boom that helped shape the development of the West and set the pattern for subsequent strikes in other regions.

Gold Standard Act (p. 486) Passed by Congress in 1900, this law declared gold the nation's standard of currency, meaning that all currency in circulation had to be redeemable in gold. The United States remained on the gold standard until 1933.

Great Awakening (p. 90) Widespread evangelical religious revival movement of the mid-1700s. The movement divided congregations and weakened the authority of established churches in the colonies.

Great Migration (p. 39) Migration of 16,000 Puritans from England to the Massachusetts Bay Colony during the 1630s.

Great Society (p. 720) President Johnson called his version of the Democratic reform program the Great Society. In 1965, Congress passed many Great Society measures, including **Medicare**, civil rights legislation, and federal aid to education.

greenbacks (p. 348) Paper currency issued by the Union beginning in 1862.

Gulf of Tonkin Resolution (p. 725) After a North Vietnamese attack on an American destroyer in the Gulf of Tonkin in 1964, President Johnson persuaded Congress to pass a resolution giving him the authority to use armed force in Vietnam.

Harlem Renaissance (p. 595) An African American cultural, literary, and artistic movement centered in Harlem, an area in New York City, in the 1920s. Harlem, the largest black community in the world outside of Africa, was considered the cultural capital of African Americans.

Hartford Convention (p. 198) An assembly of New England Federalists who met in Hartford, Connecticut, in December 1814 to protest Madison's foreign policy in the War of 1812, which had undermined commercial interests in the North. They proposed amending the Constitution to prevent future presidents from declaring war without a two-thirds majority in Congress.

Hay–Bunau–Varilla Treaty (p. 565) This 1903 treaty granted the United States control over a canal zone ten miles wide across the Isthmus of Panama. In return, the United States guaranteed the independence of Panama and agreed to pay Colombia a onetime fee of $10 million and an annual rental of $250,000.

headright (p. 34) System of land distribution in which settlers were granted a fifty-acre plot of land from the colonial government for each servant or dependent they transported to the New World. The system encouraged the recruitment of a large servile labor force.

Hepburn Act (p. 548) A law that strengthened the rate-making power of the **Interstate Commerce Commission**, again reflecting the era's desire to control the power of the railroads. It increased the ICC's membership from five to seven, empowered it to fix reasonable railroad rates, and broadened its jurisdiction. It also made ICC rulings binding pending court appeals.

Homestead Act of 1862 (p. 402) Legislation granting 160 acres of land to anyone who paid a $10 fee and pledged to live on and cultivate the land for five years. Although there was a good deal of fraud, the act encouraged a large migration to the West. Between 1862 and 1900, nearly 600,000 families claimed homesteads under its provisions.

Homestead Strike (p. 435) In July 1892, wage-cutting at Andrew Carnegie's Homestead Steel Plant in Pittsburgh provoked a violent strike in which three company-hired detectives and ten workers died. Using ruthless force and strikebreakers, company officials effectively broke the strike and destroyed the union.

House of Burgesses (p. 34) An elective representative assembly in colonial Virginia. It was the first example of representative government in the English colonies.

imperialism (p. 492) The policy of extending a nation's power through military conquest, economic domination, or annexation.

implied powers (p. 162) Powers the Constitution did not explicitly grant the federal government, but that it could be interpreted to grant.

indentured servants (p. 55) Individuals who agreed to serve a master for a set number of years in exchange for the cost of boat transport to America. Indentured servitude was the dominant form of labor in the Chesapeake colonies before slavery.

Industrial Workers of the World (IWW) (p. 527) Founded in 1905, this radical union, also known as the Wobblies, aimed to unite the American working class into one union to promote labor's interests. It worked to organize unskilled and foreign-born laborers, advocated social revolution, and led several major strikes. Stressing solidarity, the IWW took as its slogan, "An injury to one is an injury to all."

Intermediate Nuclear Forces Treaty (p. 764) Signed by President Reagan and Soviet President Gorbachev in Washington in late 1987, this agreement provided for the destruction of all intermediate-range nuclear missiles and permitted on-site inspection for the first time during the Cold War.

Iran–Contra affair (p. 759) The Iran–Contra affair involved officials high in the Reagan administration secretly selling arms to Iran and using the proceeds to finance the Contra rebels in Nicaragua. This illegal transaction usurped the congressional power of the purse.

Iranian hostage crisis (p. 751) In 1979, Iranian fundamentalists seized the American embassy in Tehran and held fifty-three American diplomats hostage for over a year. The Iranian hostage crisis weakened the Carter presidency; the hostages were finally released on January 20, 1981, the day Ronald Reagan became president.

Iron Curtain (p. 666) British Prime Minister Winston Churchill coined the phrase "Iron Curtain" to refer to the boundary in Europe that divided Soviet-dominated eastern and central Europe from western Europe, which was free from Soviet control.

isolationism (p. 492) A belief that the United States should stay out of entanglements with other nations. Isolationism was widespread after the Spanish-American War in the late 1890s and influenced later U.S. foreign policy.

itinerant preachers (p. 91) Traveling revivalist ministers of the **Great Awakening** movement. These charismatic preachers spread revivalism throughout America.

Jay's Treaty (p. 164) Controversial treaty with Britain negotiated by Chief Justice John Jay in 1794 to settle American grievances and avert war. Though the British agreed to surrender forts on U.S. territory, the treaty failed to realize key diplomatic goals and provoked a storm of protest in America.

Jim Crow laws (p. 386) Laws enacted by states to segregate the population. They became widespread in the South after Reconstruction.

joint-stock company (p. 32) Business enterprise that enabled investors to pool money for commercial trading activity and funding for sustaining colonies.

Judicial review (p. 188) The authority of the Supreme Court to determine the constitutionality of the statutes.

Kansas–Nebraska Act (p. 321) This 1854 act repealed the Missouri Compromise, split the Louisiana Purchase into two territories, and allowed its settlers to accept or reject slavery by popular sovereignty. This act enflamed the slavery issue and led opponents to form the Republican party.

Kellogg–Briand Pact (p. 638) Also called the Pact of Paris, this 1928 agreement was the brainchild of U.S. Secretary of State Frank B. Kellogg and French premier Aristide Briand. It pledged its signatories, eventually including nearly all nations, to shun war as an instrument of policy. Derided as an "international kiss," it had little effect on the actual conduct of world affairs.

Kentucky and Virginia Resolutions (p. 173) Statements penned by Thomas Jefferson and James Madison to mobilize opposition to the Alien and Sedition Acts, which they argued were unconstitutional. Jefferson's statement (the Kentucky Resolution) suggested that states should have the right to declare null and void congressional acts they deemed unconstitutional. Madison produced a more temperate resolution, but most Americans rejected such an extreme defense of states' rights.

Knights of Labor (p. 431) Also known as the Noble and Holy Order of the Knights of Labor. Founded in 1869, this labor organization pursued broad-gauged reforms as much as practical issues such as wages and hours. Unlike the

American Federation of Labor, the Knights of Labor welcomed all laborers regardless of race, gender, or skill.

Ku Klux Klan (p. 380) A secret terrorist society first organized in Tennessee in 1866. The original Klan's goals were to disfranchise African Americans, stop Reconstruction, and restore the prewar social order of the South. The Ku Klux Klan re-formed after World War II to promote white supremacy in the wake of the "Second Reconstruction."

Lend-Lease (p. 644) Arguing that aiding Britain would help America's own self-defense, President Roosevelt in 1941 asked Congress for a $7 billion Lend-Lease plan. This would allow the president to sell, lend, lease, or transfer war materials to any country whose defense he declared as vital to that of the United States.

Levittown (p. 688) In 1947, William Levitt used mass production techniques to build inexpensive homes in suburban New York to help relieve the postwar housing shortage. Levittown became a symbol of the movement to the suburbs in the years after World War II.

Lewis and Clark Expedition (p. 186) Overland expedition to the Pacific coast (1804–1806) led by Meriwether Lewis and William Clark. Commissioned by President Thomas Jefferson, the exploration of the Far West brought back a wealth of scientific data about the country and its resources.

Louisiana Purchase (p. 185) U.S. acquisition of the Louisiana Territory from France in 1803 for $15 million. The purchase secured American control of the Mississippi River and doubled the size of the nation.

Loyalists (p. 120) Throughout the conflict with Great Britain, many colonists sided with the king and Parliament. Also called Tories, these people feared that American liberty might promote social anarchy.

Manhattan Project (p. 657) In early 1942, Franklin Roosevelt, alarmed by reports that German scientists were working on an atomic bomb, authorized a crash program to build the bomb first. The Manhattan Project, named for the Corps of Engineers district originally in charge, spent $2 billion dollars and produced the weapons that devastated Hiroshima and Nagasaki in 1945.

Manifest Destiny (p. 298) Coined in 1845, this term referred to a doctrine in support of territorial expansion based on the beliefs that population growth demanded territorial expansion, that God supported American expansion, and that national expansion equaled the expansion of freedom.

***Marbury* v. *Madison* (p. 188)** In this 1803 landmark decision, the Supreme Court first asserted the power of judicial review by declaring an act of Congress, the Judiciary Act of 1789, unconstitutional.

March on Washington (p. 717) In August 1963, civil rights leaders organized a massive rally in Washington to urge passage of President Kennedy's civil rights bill. The high point came when Martin Luther King, Jr., gave his "I Have a Dream" speech to more than 200,000 marchers in front of the Lincoln Memorial.

Marshall Plan (p. 670) In 1947, Secretary of State George Marshall proposed a massive economic aid program to rebuild the war-torn economies of western European nations. The plan was motivated by both humanitarian concern for the conditions of those nations' economies and fear that economic dislocation would promote communism in western Europe.

Mayflower Compact (p. 37) Agreement among the Pilgrims aboard the *Mayflower* in 1620 to create a civil government at Plymouth Colony.

McCarthyism (p. 677) In 1950, Senator Joseph R. McCarthy began a sensational campaign against communists in government that led to more than four years of charges and countercharges, ending when the Senate censured him in 1954. McCarthyism became the contemporary name for the red scare of the 1950s.

***McCulloch* v. *Maryland* (p. 219)** Ruling on this banking case in 1819, the Supreme Court propped up the idea of "implied powers" meaning the Constitution could be broadly interpreted. This pivotal ruling also asserted the supremacy of federal power over state power.

Medicare (p. 720) The 1965 Medicare Act provided Social Security funding for hospitalization insurance for people over age 65 and a voluntary plan to cover doctor bills paid in part by the federal government.

mercantilism (p. 67) An economic theory that shaped imperial policy throughout the colonial period, mercantilism was built on the assumption that the world's wealth was a fixed supply. In order to increase its wealth, a nation needed to export more goods than it imported. Favorable trade and protective economic policies, as well as new colonial possessions rich in raw materials, were important in achieving this balance.

Mexican-American War (p. 302) Conflict (1846–1848) between the United States and Mexico after the U.S. annexation of Texas, which Mexico still considered its own. As victor, the United States acquired vast new territories from Mexico according to the terms of the **Treaty of Guadalupe Hidalgo.**

Middle ground (p. 83) A geographical area where two distinct cultures meet and merge with neither holding a clear upper hand.

Missouri Compromise (p. 217) A sectional compromise in Congress in 1820 that admitted Missouri to the Union as a slave state and Maine as a free state. It also banned slavery in the remainder of the Louisiana Purchase territory above the latitude of 36°30´.

Monroe Doctrine (p. 221) A key foreign policy made by President James Monroe in 1823, it declared the western hemisphere off limits to new European colonization; in return, the United States promised not to meddle in European affairs.

Montgomery bus boycott (p. 702) In late 1955, African Americans led by Martin Luther King, Jr., boycotted the buses in Montgomery, Alabama, after seamstress Rosa Parks was arrested for refusing to move to the back of a bus. The boycott, which ended when the Supreme Court ruled in favor of the protesters, marked the beginning of a new, activist phase of the civil rights movement.

moral diplomacy (p. 567) Policy adopted by President Woodrow Wilson that rejected the approach of **"dollar diplomacy."** Rather than focusing mainly on economic ties with other nations, Wilson's policy was designed to bring right principles to the world, preserve peace, and extend to other peoples the blessings of democracy. Wilson, however, often ended up pursuing policies much like those followed by Roosevelt and Taft.

Moral Majority (p. 738) In 1979, the Reverend Jerry Falwell founded the Moral Majority to combat "amoral liberals," drug abuse, "coddling" of criminals, homosexuality, communism, and abortion. The Moral Majority represented the rise of political activism among organized religion's radical right wing.

muckrakers (p. 514) Unflattering term coined by Theodore Roosevelt to describe the writers who made a practice of exposing the wrongdoings of public figures. Muckraking flourished from 1903 to 1909 in magazines such as *McClure's* and *Collier's*, exposing social and political problems and sparking reform.

Mugwumps (p. 448) Drawing their members mainly from among the educated and upper class, these reformers crusaded for lower tariffs, limited federal government, and civil service reform to end political corruption. They were best known for their role in helping to elect Grover Cleveland to the presidency in 1884.

National American Woman Suffrage Association (p. 450, 541) Founded by Susan B. Anthony in 1890, this organization worked to secure women the right to vote. While some suffragists urged militant action, it stressed careful organization and peaceful lobbying. By 1920 it had nearly two million members.

National Association for the Advancement of Colored People (NAACP) (p. 522) Created in 1909, this organization quickly became one of the most important civil rights organizations in the country. The NAACP pressured employers, labor unions, and the government on behalf of African Americans.

National Farmers' Alliance and Industrial Union (p. 472) One of the largest reform movements in American history, the Farmer's Alliance sought to organize farmers in the South and West to fight for reforms that would improve their lot, including measures to overcome low crop prices, burdensome mortgages, and high railroad rates. The Alliance ultimately organized a political party, the **People's (Populist) party.**

National Grange of the Patrons of Husbandry (p. 409) Founded by Oliver H. Kelly in 1867, the Grange sought to relieve the drabness of farm life by providing a social, educational, and cultural outlet for its members. It also set up grain elevators, cooperative stores, warehouses, insurance companies, and farm machinery factories. Although its constitution banned political involvement, the Grange often supported railroad regulation and other measures.

National Organization for Women (NOW) (p. 730) Founded in 1966, the National Organization for Women (NOW) called for equal employment opportunity and equal pay for women. NOW also championed the legalization of abortion and passage of an equal rights amendment to the Constitution.

National Origins Quota Act (p. 603) This 1924 law established a quota system to regulate the influx of immigrants to America. The system restricted the **new immigrants** from southern and eastern Europe and Asia. It also reduced the annual total of immigrants.

National Reclamation Act (Newlands Act) (p. 402) Passed in 1902, this legisaltion set aside the majority of the proceeds from the sale of public land in sixteen Western states to fund irrigation projects in the arid states.

National Recovery Administration (NRA) (p. 622) A keystone of the early **New Deal,** this federal agency was created in 1933 to promote economic recovery and revive industry during the Great Depression. It permitted manufacturers to establish industrywide codes of "fair business practices" setting prices and production levels. It also provided for minimum wages and maximum working hours for labor and guaranteed labor the right to organize and bargain collectively (Section 7a). The Supreme Court declared it unconstitutional in 1935.

National Security Act (p. 671) Congress passed the National Security Act in 1947 in response to perceived threats from the Soviet Union after World War II. It established the Department of Defense and created the Central Intelligence Agency (CIA) and National Security Council.

Nativism (p. 602) Refers to a policy or ideology of preferring native-born residents to immigrants, restricting the rights of immigrants, and opposing new immigration.

natural rights (p. 136) Fundamental rights over which the government could exercise no control. An uncompromising belief in such rights energized the popular demand for a formal bill of rights in 1791.

Navigation Acts (p. 67) A series of commercial restrictions passed by Parliament intended to regulate colonial commerce in such a way as to favor England's accumulation of wealth.

Nazi Holocaust (p. 659) The slaughter of six million Jews and other persons by Hitler's regime.

neoconservatism (p. 738) Former liberals who advocated a strong stand against communism abroad and free market capitalism at home became known as neoconservatives. These intellectuals stressed the positive values of American society in contrast to liberals who emphasized social ills.

neutrality acts (p. 642) Reacting to their disillusionment with World War I and absorbed in the domestic crisis of the Great Depression, Americans backed Congress's three neutrality acts in the 1930s. The 1935 and 1936 acts forbade selling munitions or lending money to belligerents in a war. The 1937 act required that all remaining trade be conducted on a cash-and-carry basis.

New Deal (p. 614) In accepting the nomination of the Democratic Party in 1932, Franklin Delano Roosevelt promised a "new deal" for the American people. After his election, the label was applied to his program of legislation passed to combat the Great Depression. The New Deal included measures aimed at relief, reform, and recovery. They achieved some relief and considerable reform but little recovery.

New Freedom (p. 553) Woodrow Wilson's program in his campaign for the presidency in 1912, the New Freedom emphasized business competition and small government. It sought to rein in federal authority, release individual energy, and restore competition. It echoed many of the progressive social-justice objectives while pushing for a free economy rather than a planned one.

New Frontier (p. 708) The New Frontier was the campaign program advocated by John F. Kennedy in the 1960 election. He promised to revitalize the stagnant economy and enact reform legislation in education, health care, and civil rights.

new immigrants (p. 444) Starting in the 1880s, immigration into the United States began to shift from northern and western Europe, its source for most of the nation's history, to southern and eastern Europe. These new immigrants tended to be poor, non-Protestant, and unskilled; they tended to stay in close-knit communities and retain their language, customs, and religions. Between 1880 and 1910, approximately 8.4 million of these so-called new immigrants came to the United States.

New Nationalism (p. 553) Theodore Roosevelt's program in his campaign for the presidency in 1912, the New Nationalism called for a national approach to the country's affairs and a strong president to deal with them. It also called for efficiency in government and society; it urged protection of children, women, and workers; accepted "good" trusts; and exalted the expert and the executive. Additionally, it encouraged large concentrations of capital and labor.

Niagara Movement (p. 522) A movement, led by W. E. B. Du Bois, that focused on equal rights and the education of African American youth. Rejecting the gradualist approach of Booker T. Washington, members kept alive a program of militant action and claimed for African Americans all the rights afforded to other Americans. It spawned later civil rights movements.

North Atlantic Treaty Organization (NATO) (p. 670) In 1949, the United States, Canada, and ten European nations formed this military mutual-defense pact. In 1955, the Soviet Union countered NATO with the formation of the Warsaw Pact, a military alliance among those nations within its own sphere of influence.

Northwest Ordinance (p. 141) Legislation that formulated plans for governments in America's northwestern territories, defined a procedure for the territories' admission to the Union as states, and prohibited slavery north of the Ohio River.

NSC-68 (p. 672) National Security Council planning paper No. 68 redefined America's national defense policy. Adopted in 1950, it committed the United States to a massive military buildup to meet the challenge posed by the Soviet Union.

nullification (p. 235) The supposed right of any state to declare a federal law inoperative within its boundaries. In 1832, South Carolina created a firestorm when it attempted to nullify the federal tariff.

Ocala Demands (p. 474) Adopted by the Farmers' Alliance at an 1890 meeting in Ocala, Florida, these demands became the organization's main platform. They called for the creation of a sub-treasury system to allow farmers to store their crops until they could get the best price, the free coinage of silver, an end to protective tariffs and national banks, a federal income tax, the direct election of senators by voters, and tighter regulation of railroads.

Old South (p. 248) The term refers to the slaveholding states between 1830 and 1860, when slave labor and cotton production dominated the economies of the southern states. This period is also known as the "antebellum era."

Open Door policy (p. 507) Established in a series of notes by Secretary of State John Hay in 1900, this policy established free trade between the United States and China and attempted to enlist major European and Asian nations in recognizing the territorial integrity of China. It marked a departure from the American tradition of **isolationism** and signaled the country's growing involvement in the world.

Operation Desert Storm (p. 773) Desert Storm was the code name the United States and its coalition partners used in the war against Iraq in 1991 to liberate Kuwait.

Organization of Petroleum Exporting Countries (OPEC) (p. 742) A cartel of oil-exporting nations. In late 1973, OPEC took advantage of the October War and an oil embargo by its Arab members to quadruple the price of oil. This huge increase had a devastating impact on the American economy.

Ostend Manifesto (p. 322) Written by American officials in 1854, this secret memo—later dubbed a "manifesto"—urged the acquisition of Cuba by any means necessary. When it became public, Northerners claimed it was a plot to extend slavery and the manifesto was disavowed.

Overland Trail (p. 401) The route taken by thousands of travelers from the Mississippi Valley to the Pacific Coast in the last half of the nineteenth century. It was extremely difficult, often taking six months or more to complete.

Panic of 1837 (p. 240) A financial depression that lasted until the 1840s.

parliamentary sovereignty (p. 107) Principle that emphasized the power of Parliament to govern colonial affairs as the preeminent authority.

Peace of Paris of 1763 (p. 99) Treaty ending the French and Indian War by which France ceded Canada to Britain.

Pearl Harbor (p. 647) On December 7, 1941, Japanese warplanes attacked U.S. naval forces at Pearl Harbor, Hawaii, sinking several ships and killing more than twenty-four hundred American sailors. The event marked America's entrance into World War II.

Pendleton Act (p. 470) Passed by Congress in 1883 with the backing of President Chester A. Arthur, this act sought to lessen the involvement of politicians in the running of the government. It created a bipartisan Civil Service Commission to administer competitive exams to candidates for civil service jobs and to appoint officeholders based on merit. It also outlawed forcing political contributions from appointed officials. The measure served as the basis for later expansion of a professional civil service.

People's (or Populist) party (p. 474) This political party was organized in 1892 by farm, labor, and reform leaders, mainly from the Farmers' Alliance. It offered a broad-based reform platform reflecting the **Ocala Demands**. It nominated James B. Weaver of Iowa for president in 1892 and William Jennings Bryan of Nebraska in 1896. After 1896, it became identified as a one-issue party focused on free silver and gradually died away.

Perfectionism (p. 275) The doctrine that a state of freedom from sin is attainable on earth.

Philippine-American War (p. 505) A war fought from 1899 to 1903 to quell Filipino resistance to U.S. control of the Philippine Islands. Although often forgotten, it lasted longer than the Spanish-American War and resulted in more casualties. Filipino guerilla soldiers finally gave up when their leader, Emilio Aguinaldo, was captured.

placer mining (p. 404) A form of mining that required little technology or skill, placer mining techniques included using a shovel and a washing pan to separate gold from the ore in streams and riverbeds. An early phase of the mining industry, placer mining could be performed by miners working as individuals or in small groups.

Plessy* v. *Ferguson* (p. 451)** A Supreme Court case in 1896 that established the doctrine of "separate but equal" and upheld a Louisiana law requiring that blacks and whites occupy separate rail cars. The Court applied it to schools in *Cumming* v. *County Board of Education* (1899). The doctrine was finally overturned in 1954 in ***Brown* v. *Board of Education of Topeka.

popular sovereignty (p. 318) The concept that the settlers of a newly organized territory have the right to decide (through voting) whether or not to accept slavery. Promoted as a solution to the slavery question, popular sovereignty became a fiasco in Kansas during the 1850s.

Potsdam Conference (p. 664) The final wartime meeting of the leaders of the United States, Great Britain, and the Soviet Union was held at Potsdam, outside Berlin, in July, 1945. Truman, Churchill, and Stalin discussed the future of

Europe, but their failure to reach meaningful agreements soon led to the onset of the Cold War.

pragmatism (p. 542) A doctrine that emerged in the early twentieth century, built largely on the ideas of Harvard psychologist and philosopher William James. Pragmatists were impatient with theories that held truth to be abstract; they believed that truth should work for the individual. They also believed that people were not only shaped by their environment but also helped to shape it. Ideas that worked, according to pragmatists, became truth.

preemption (p. 207) The right of first purchase of public land. Settlers enjoyed this right even if they squatted on the land in advance of government surveyors.

progressivism (p. 515) Movement for social change between the late 1890s and World War I. Its origins lay in a fear of big business and corrupt government and a desire to improve the lives of countless Americans. Progressives set out to cure the social ills brought about by industrialization and urbanization, social disorder, and political corruption.

Progressive (or "Bull Moose") party (p. 537) Also known as the "Bull Moose" party, this political party was formed by Theodore Roosevelt in an attempt to advance progressive ideas and unseat President William Howard Taft in the election of 1912. After Taft won the Republican party's nomination, Roosevelt ran on the Progressive party ticket.

prohibition (p. 600) The ban of the manufacture, sale, and transportation of alcoholic beverages in the United States. The Eighteenth Amendment, adopted in 1919, established prohibition. It was repealed by the Twenty-first Amendment in 1933. While prohibition was in effect, it reduced national consumption of alcohol, but it was inconsistently enforced and was often evaded, especially in the cities.

Protestant Reformation (p. 21) Sixteenth-century religious movement to reform and challenge the spiritual authority of the Roman Catholic Church, associated with figures such as Martin Luther and John Calvin.

Pullman Strike (p. 476) Beginning in May 1894, this strike of employees at the Pullman Palace Car Company near Chicago was one of the largest strikes in American history. Workers struck to protest wage cuts, high rents for company housing, and layoffs; the American Railway Union, led by Eugene V. Debs, joined the strike in June. Extending into twenty-seven states and territories, it effectively paralyzed the western half of the nation. President Grover Cleveland secured an injunction to break the strike on the grounds that it obstructed the mail and sent federal troops to enforce it. The Supreme Court upheld the use of the injunction in *In re Debs* (1895).

Puritans (p. 37) Members of a reformed Protestant sect in Europe and America that insisted on removing all vestiges of Catholicism from popular religious practice.

Quakers (p. 46) Members of a radical religious group, formally known as the Society of Friends, that rejected formal theology and stressed each person's "inner light," a spiritual guide to righteousness.

Quasi-War (p. 171) Undeclared war between the United States and France in the late 1790s.

Radical Reconstruction (p. 372) The Reconstruction Acts of 1867 divided the South into five military districts. They required the states to guarantee black male suffrage and to ratify the **Fourteenth Amendment** as a condition of their readmission to the Union.

Radical Republicans (p. 369) The Radical Republicans in Congress, headed by Thaddeus Stevens and Charles Sumner, insisted on black suffrage and federal protection of civil rights of African Americans. They gained control of Reconstruction in 1867 and required the ratification of the **Fourteenth Amendment** as a condition of readmission for former Confederate states.

Red Scare (p. 599) A wave of anticommunist, antiforeign, and antilabor hysteria that swept over America at the end of World War I. It resulted in the deportation of many alien residents and the violation of the civil liberties of many of its victims.

Redeemers (p. 383) A loose coalition of prewar Democrats, Confederate Army veterans, and southern Whigs who took over southern state governments in the 1870s, supposedly "redeeming" them from the corruption of Reconstruction. They shared a commitment to white supremacy and laissez-faire economics.

republicanism (p. 132) Concept that ultimate political authority is vested in the citizens of the nation. The character of republican government was dependent on the civic virtue of its citizens to preserve the nation from corruption and moral decay.

Roe v. _Wade_ (p. 746) In 1973, the Supreme Court ruled in _Roe_ v. _Wade_ that women had a constitutional right to abortion during the early stages of pregnancy. The decision provoked a vigorous right-to-life movement that opposed abortion.

Roosevelt Corollary (p. 566) President Theodore Roosevelt's 1904 foreign policy statement, a corollary to the **Monroe Doctrine,** which asserted that the United States would intervene in Latin American affairs if the countries themselves could not keep their affairs in order. It effectively made the United States the policeman of the western hemisphere. The Roosevelt Corollary guided U.S. policy in Latin America until it was replaced by Franklin D. Roosevelt's **Good Neighbor policy** in the 1930s.

Royal African Company (p. 61) Slaving company created to meet colonial planters' demands for black laborers.

Sanitary Commission (p. 360) An association chartered by the Union government during the Civil War to promote health in the northern army's camps though attention to cleanliness, nutrition, and medical care.

Scopes trial (p. 603) Also called the "monkey trial," the 1924 Scopes trial was a contest between modern liberalism and religious fundamentalism. John T. Scopes was on trial for teaching Darwinian evolution in defiance of a Tennessee state law. He was found guilty and fined $100. On appeal, Scopes's conviction was later set aside on a technicality.

Second Continental Congress (p. 117) This meeting took place in Philadelphia in May 1775, in the midst of rapidly unfolding military events. It organized the Continental Army and commissioned George Washington to lead it, then began requisitioning men and supplies for the war effort.

Second Great Awakening (p. 270) A series of evangelical Protestant revivals that swept over America in the early nineteenth century.

second party system (p. 242) A historian's term for the national two-party rivalry between Democrats and **Whigs.** The second party system began in the 1830s and ended in the 1850s with the demise of the Whig party and the rise of the Republican party.

Sedition Act (p. 578) A wartime law that imposed harsh penalties on anyone using "disloyal, profane, scurrilous, or abusive language" about the U.S. government, flag, or armed forces.

Selective Service Act (p. 576) This 1917 law provided for the registration of all American men between the ages of 21 and 30 for a military draft. By the end of World War I, 24.2 million men had registered; 2.8 million had been inducted into the army. The age limits were later changed to 18 and 45.

Seneca Falls Convention (p. 281) The first women's rights convention held in 1848 in Seneca Falls, New York, and co-sponsored by Elizabeth Cady Stanton and Lucretia Mott. Delegates at the convention drafted a "Declaration of Sentiments," patterned on the Declaration of Independence, but which declared that "all men and women are created equal."

settlement houses (p. 457) Located in poor districts of major cities, these were community centers that tried to soften the impact of urban life for immigrant and other families. Often run by young, educated women, they provided social services and a political voice for their neighborhoods. Chicago's Hull House, founded by Jane Addams in 1889, became the most famous of the settlement houses.

Seven Years' War (p. 97) Worldwide conflict (1756–1763) that pitted Britain against France for control of North America. With help from the American colonists, the British won the war and eliminated France as a power on the North American continent. Also known in America as the French and Indian War.

sharecropping (p. 375) After the Civil War, the southern states adopted a sharecropping system as a compromise between former slaves who wanted land of their own and former slave owners who needed labor. The landowners provided land, tools, and seed to a farming family, who in turn provided labor. The resulting crop was divided between them, with the farmers receiving a "share" of one-third to one-half of the crop.

Shays's Rebellion (p. 144) Armed insurrection of farmers in western Massachusetts led by Daniel Shays, a veteran of the Continental Army. Intended to prevent state courts from foreclosing on debtors unable to pay their taxes, the rebellion was put down by the state militia. Nationalists used the event to justify the calling of a constitutional convention to strengthen the national government.

Sherman Antitrust Act (p. 471) Passed by Congress in 1890, this act was the first major U.S. attempt to deal legislatively with the problem of the increasing size of business. It declared illegal "every contract, combination in the form of trust or otherwise, or conspiracy, in restraint of trade or commerce." Penalties for violations were strict, ranging from fines to imprisonment and even the dissolution of guilty trusts. The law was weakened when the Supreme Court, in *United States* v. *E. C. Knight and Co.* (1895), drew a sharp distinction between manufacturing and commerce and ruled that manufacturing was excluded from its coverage. Nonetheless, the law shaped all future antitrust legislation.

Sherman Silver Purchase Act (p. 471) An act that attempted to resolve the controversy over silver coinage. Under it, the U.S. Treasury would purchase 4.5 million ounces of silver each month and issue legal tender (in the form of Treasury notes) for it. The act pleased opponents of silver because it did not call for free coinage; it pleased proponents of silver because it bought up most of the nation's silver production.

social Darwinism (p. 455) Adapted by English social philosopher Herbert Spencer from Charles Darwin's theory of evolution, this theory held that the "laws" of evolution applied to human life, that change or reform therefore took centuries, and that the "fittest" would succeed in business and social relationships. It promoted the ideas of competition and individualism, saw as futile any intervention of government into human affairs, and was used by influential members of the economic and social elite to oppose reform.

Social Gospel (p. 457) Preached by a number of urban Protestant ministers, the Social Gospel focused as much on improving the conditions of life on Earth as on saving souls for the hereafter. Its adherents worked for child-labor laws and measures to alleviate poverty.

Social Security Act (p. 624) The 1935 Social Security Act established a system of old age, unemployment, and survivors' insurance funded by wage and payroll taxes. It did not include health insurance and did not originally cover many of the most needy groups and individuals.

Southern Christian Leadership Conference (SCLC) (p. 702) An organization founded by Martin Luther King, Jr., to direct the crusade against segregation. Its weapon was passive resistance that stressed nonviolence and love, and its tactic direct, though peaceful, confrontation.

Spanish Armada, The (p. 24) Spanish fleet sent to invade England in 1588.

spectral evidence (p. 70) In the Salem witch trials, the court allowed reports of dreams and visions in which the accused appeared as the devil's agent to be introduced as testimony. The accused had no defense against this kind of "evidence." When the judges later disallowed this testimony, the executions for witchcraft ended.

Stamp Act of 1765 (p. 110) Placed a tax on newspapers and printed matter produced in the colonies, causing mass opposition by colonists.

Stamp Act Congress (p. 111) Meeting of colonial delegates in New York City in October 1765 to protest the Stamp Act, a law passed by Parliament to raise revenue in America. The delegates drafted petitions denouncing the Stamp Act and other taxes imposed on Americans without colonial consent.

Strategic Arms Limitations Talks (SALT) (p. 739) In 1972, the United States and the Soviet Union culminated four years of Strategic Arms Limitation Talks (SALT) by signing a treaty limiting the deployment of antiballistic missiles (ABM) and an agreement to freeze the number of offensive missiles for five years.

Strategic Defense Initiative (SDI) (p. 755) Popularly known as "Star Wars," President Ronald Reagan's Strategic Defense Initiative (SDI) proposed the construction of an elaborate computer-controlled, antimissile defense system capable of destroying enemy missiles in outer space. Critics claimed that SDI could never be perfected.

Student Nonviolent Coordinating Committee (SNCC) (p. 703) A radical group advocating black power. SNCC's leaders, scornful of integration and interracial cooperation, broke with Martin Luther King, Jr., to advocate greater militancy and acts of violence.

Students for a Democratic Society (SDS) (p. 727) Founded in 1962, the SDS was a popular college student organization that protested shortcomings in American life, notably racial injustice and the Vietnam War. It led thousands of campus protests before it split apart at the end of the 1960s.

Sunbelt (p. 774) This region consists of a broad band of states running across the South from Florida to Texas, extending west and north to include California and the Pacific Northwest. Beginning in the 1970s, this area experienced rapid economic growth and major gains in population.

supply-side economics (p. 753) Advocates of supply-side economics claimed that tax cuts would stimulate the economy by giving individuals a greater incentive to earn more money, which would lead to greater investment and eventually larger tax revenues at a lower rate. Critics replied that supply-side economics would only burden the economy with larger government deficits.

Taft–Hartley Act (p. 675) This 1947 anti-union legislation outlawed the closed shop and secondary boycotts. It also authorized the president to seek injunctions to prevent strikes that posed a threat to national security.

tariff of abominations (p. 230) An 1828 protective tariff, or tax on imports, motivated by special interest groups. It resulted in a substantial increase in duties that angered many southern free traders.

Teapot Dome scandal (p. 603) A 1924 scandal in which Secretary of the Interior Albert Fall was convicted of accepting bribes in exchange for leasing government-owned oil lands in Wyoming (Teapot Dome) and California (Elks Hill) to private oil businessmen.

Teller Amendment (p. 499) In this amendment, sponsored by Senator Henry M. Teller of Colorado, the United States pledged that it did not intend to annex Cuba and that it would recognize Cuban independence from Spain after the Spanish-American War.

temperance movement (p. 272) Temperance—moderation or abstention in the use of alcoholic beverages—attracted many advocates in the early nineteenth century. Their crusade against alcohol, which grew out of the Second Great Awakening, became a powerful social force.

Ten Percent Plan (p. 368) Reconstruction plan proposed by President Abraham Lincoln as a quick way to readmit the former Confederate States. It called for full pardon of all Southerners except Confederate leaders, and readmission to the Union for any state after 10 percent of its voters in the 1860 election signed a loyalty oath and the state abolished slavery.

Tennessee Valley Authority (TVA) (p. 621) A **New Deal** effort at regional planning created by Congress in 1933, this agency built dams and power plants on the Tennessee River. Its programs for flood control, soil conservation, and reforestation helped raise the standard of living for millions in the Tennessee River valley.

Tet offensive (p. 731) In February 1968, the Viet Cong launched a major offensive in the cities of South Vietnam. Although caught by surprise, American and South Vietnam forces successfully quashed this attack, yet the Tet offensive was a blow to American public opinion and led President Johnson to end the escalation of the war and seek a negotiated peace.

Thirteenth Amendment (p. 371) Ratified in 1865, this amendment to the U.S. Constitution prohibited slavery and involuntary servitude.

Three-fifths rule (p. 146) Constitutional provision that for every five slaves a state would receive credit for three free voters indetermining seats for the House of Representatives.

Trail of Tears (p. 234) In the winter of 1838–1839, the Cherokee were forced to evacuate their lands in Georgia and travel under military guard to present-day Oklahoma. Due to exposure and disease, roughly one-quarter of the sixteen thousand forced migrants died en route.

Treaty of Guadalupe Hidalgo (p. 303) Signed in 1848, this treaty ended the Mexican-American War. Mexico relinquished its claims to Texas and ceded an additional 500,000 square miles to the United States for $15 million.

Treaty of Paris (p. 504) Signed by the United States and Spain in December 1898, this treaty ended the Spanish-American War. Under its terms, Spain recognized Cuba's independence and assumed the Cuban debt; it also ceded Puerto Rico and Guam to the United States. At the insistence of the U.S. representatives, Spain also ceded the Philippines. The Senate ratified the treaty on February 6, 1899.

Treaty of Paris of 1783 (p. 127) Agreement establishing American independence after the Revolutionary War. It also transferred territory east of the Mississippi River, except for Spanish Florida, to the new republic.

Treaty of Tordesillas (p. 18) Treaty negotiated by the pope in 1494 to resolve competing land claims of Spain and Portugal in the New World. It divided the world along a north–south line in the middle of the Atlantic Ocean, granting to Spain all lands west of the line and to Portugal lands east of the line.

Truman Doctrine (p. 669) In 1947, President Truman asked Congress for money to aid the Greek and Turkish governments that were then threatened by communist rebels. Arguing for the appropriations, Truman asserted his doctrine that the United States was committed to support free people everywhere who were resisting subjugation by communist attack or rebellion.

trunk lines (p. 419) Four major railroad networks that emerged after the Civil War to connect the eastern seaports to the Great Lakes and western rivers. They reflected the growing integration of transportation across the country that helped spur large-scale industrialization.

trust (p. 423) A business-management device designed to centralize and make more efficient the management of diverse and far-flung business operations. It allowed stockholders to exchange their stock certificates for trust certificates, on which dividends were paid. John D. Rockefeller organized the first major trust, the Standard Oil Trust, in 1882.

Turner's thesis (p. 411) Put forth by historian Frederick Jackson Turner in his 1893 paper, "The Significance of the Frontier in American History," this thesis asserted that the existence of a frontier and its settlement had shaped American character; given rise to individualism, independence, and self-confidence; and fostered the American spirit of invention and adaptation. Later historians, especially a group of "new Western historians," modified the thesis by pointing out the environmental and other consequences of frontier settlement, the role of the federal government in peopling the arid West, and the clash of races and cultures that took place on the frontier.

Underground Railroad (p. 254) A network of safe houses organized by abolitionists (usually free blacks) to aid slaves in their attempts to escape slavery in the North or Canada.

Underwood Tariff Act (p. 554) An early accomplishment of the Wilson administration, this law reduced the tariff rates of the Payne-Aldrich law of 1909 by about 15 percent. It also levied a graduated income tax to make up for the lost revenue.

undocumented aliens (p. 776) Once derisively called "wetbacks," undocumented aliens are illegal immigrants, mainly from Mexico and Central America.

unilateralism (p. 789) A national policy of acting alone without consulting others.

Vesey conspiracy (p. 254) A plot to burn Charleston, South Carolina, and thereby initiate a general slave revolt, led by a free African American, Denmark Vesey, in 1822. The conspirators were betrayed before the plan was carried out, and Vesey and thirty-four others were hanged.

Virgin of Guadalupe (p. 20) Apparition of the Virgin Mary that has become a symbol of Mexican nationalism.

Virginia Plan (p. 144) Offered by James Madison and the Virginia delegation at the Constitutional Convention, this proposal called for a new government with a strong executive office and two houses of Congress, each with representation proportional to a state's population. Madison's plan also recommended giving the national government veto power over bills passed by the state legislatures. Smaller states countered with the **New Jersey Plan** that gave each state equal representation in Congress.

Voting Rights Act of 1965 (p. 720) The 1965 Voting Rights Act effectively banned literacy tests for voting rights and provided for federal registrars to assure the franchise to minority voters. Within a few years, a majority of African Americans had become registered voters in the southern states.

Wade–Davis Bill (p. 369) In 1864, Congress passed the Wade–Davis bill to counter Lincoln's **Ten Percent Plan** for Reconstruction. The bill required that a majority of a former Confederate state's white male population take a loyalty oath and guarantee equality for African Americans. President Lincoln pocket-vetoed the bill.

Wagner Act (p. 627) The 1935 Wagner Act, formally known as the National Labor Relations Act, created the National Labor Relations Board to supervise union elections and designate winning unions as official bargaining agents. The board could also issue cease-and-desist orders to employers who dealt unfairly with their workers.

War Hawks (p. 195) Congressional leaders who, in 1811 and 1812, called for war against Britain to defend the national honor and force Britain to respect America's maritime rights.

War Industries Board (WIB) (p. 579) An example of the many boards and commissions created during World War I, this government agency oversaw the production of all American factories. It determined priorities, allocated raw materials, and fixed prices; it told manufacturers what they could and could not produce.

War of 1812 (p. 196) War between Britain and the United States. U.S. justifications for war included British violations of American maritime rights, impressment of seamen, provocation of the Indians, and defense of national honor.

war on poverty (p. 719) Lyndon Johnson declared war on poverty in his 1964 State of the Union address. A new Office of Economic Opportunity (OEO) oversaw a variety of programs to help the poor, including the Job Corps and Head Start.

war on terror (p. 788) Initiated by President George W. Bush after the attacks of September 11, 2001, the broadly defined war on terror aimed to weed out terrorist operatives and their supporters throughout the world.

Watergate scandal (p. 741) A break-in at the Democratic National Committee offices in the Watergate complex in Washington was carried out under the direction of White House employees. Disclosure of the White House involvement in the break-in and subsequent cover-up forced President Richard Nixon to resign in 1974 to avoid impeachment.

Whigs (p. 106) In mid-eighteenth century Britain, the Whigs were a political faction that dominated Parliament. Generally they were opposed to royal influence in government and wanted to increase the control and influence of Parliament. In America, a Whig party—named for the British Whigs who opposed the king in the late seventeenth century—coalesced in the 1830s around opposition to Andrew Jackson. In general, the American Whigs supported federal power and internal improvements but not territorial expansion. The Whig party collapsed in the 1850s.

Whiskey Rebellion (p. 170) Protests in 1794 by western Pennsylvania farmers resisting payment of a federal tax on whiskey. The uprising was forcibly suppressed when President George Washington called an army of fifteen thousand troops to the area, where they encountered almost no resistance.

Wilmot Proviso (p. 316) In 1846, shortly after outbreak of the **Mexican-American War,** Congressman David Wilmot of Pennsylvania introduced this controversial amendment stating that any lands won from Mexico would be closed to slavery.

Women's Christian Temperance Union (WCTU) (p. 448) Founded by Frances E. Willard, this organization campaigned to end drunkenness and the social ills that accompanied it. The largest women's organization in the country, by 1898 it had ten thousand branches and five hundred thousand members. The WCTU illustrated the large role women played in politics and reform long before they won the right to vote.

Women's Trade Union League (WTUL) (p. 523) Founded in 1903, this group worked to organize women into trade unions. It also lobbied for laws to safeguard female workers and backed several successful strikes, especially in the garment industry. It accepted all women who worked, regardless of skill, and while it never attracted many members, its leaders were influential enough to give the union considerable power.

Works Progress Administration (WPA) (p. 623) Congress created this **New Deal** agency in 1935 to provide work relief for the unemployed. Federal works projects included building roads, bridges, and schools; the WPA also funded projects for artists, writers, and young people. It eventually spent $11 billion on projects and provided employment for 8.5 million people.

Wounded Knee Massacre (p. 396) In December 1890, troopers of the Seventh Cavalry, under orders to stop the **Ghost Dance** religion among the Sioux, took Chief Big Foot and his followers to a camp on Wounded Knee Creek in South Dakota. It is uncertain who fired the first shot, but violence ensued and approximately two hundred Native American men, women, and children were killed.

XYZ Affair (p. 172) A diplomatic incident in which American peace commissioners sent to France by President John Adams in 1797 were insulted with bribe demands from their French counterparts, dubbed X, Y, and Z in American newspapers. The incident heightened war fever against France.

Yalta Conference (p. 655) Yalta, a city in the Russian Crimea, hosted this wartime conference of the Allies in February 1945 in which the Allies agreed to final plans for the defeat of Germany and the terms of its occupation. The Soviets agreed to allow free elections in Poland, but the elections were never held.

yellow journalism (p. 498) In order to sell newspapers to the public before and during the Spanish-American War, publishers William Randolph Hearst and Joseph Pulitzer engaged in blatant sensationalization of the news, which became known as "yellow journalism." Although it did not cause the war with Spain, it helped turn U.S. public opinion against Spain's actions in Cuba.

yeoman farmers (p. 59, 258) Southern small landholders who owned no slaves, and who lived primarily in the foothills of the Appalachian and Ozark mountains. They were self-reliant and grew mixed crops, although they usually did not produce a substantial amount to be sold on the market.

Yorktown (p. 125) Virginia market town on a peninsula bounded by the York and James rivers, where Lord Cornwallis's army was trapped by the Americans and French in 1781.

Young America (p. 292) In the 1840s and early 1850s, many public figures—especially younger members of the Democratic party—used this term to describe a movement that advocated territorial expansion and industrial growth in the name of patriotism.

Credits

TEXT CREDITS

51 U.S. Bureau of the Census, *Historical Statistics of the United States: Colonial Times to 1970,* Washington, DC, 1975; John J. McCusker and Russell R. Menard, *The Economy of British America, 1607–1789,* Chapel Hill, 1985; 58 The New England Primer; 58 "To My Dear and Loving Husband" by Anne Bradstreet; 170 Adapted from Thomas Jefferson, *Notes on the State of Virginia* (1787); 385 Unknown, "MANY THOUSAND GO," SONG LYRICS (1867). *Atlantic Monthly,* June 1867; 446 U.S. Bureau of the Census, *Historical Statistics of the United States, Colonial Times to 1970, Bicentennial Edition,* Washington, DC, 1975; 454 U.S. Bureau of the Census, *Historical Statistics of the United States, Colonial Times to 1970, Bicentennial Edition,* Washington, DC, 1975; 471 U.S. Bureau of the Census, *Historical Statistics of the United States, Colonial Times to 1970, Bicentennial Edition,* Washington, DC, 1975; 477 U.S. Bureau of the Census, *Historical Statistics of the United States, Colonial Times to 1970, Bicentennial Edition,* Washington, DC, 1975; 503 U.S. Bureau of the Census, *Historical Statistics of the United States, Colonial Times to 1970, Bicentennial Edition,* Washington, DC, 1975; 514 Frank Baum, *The Wonderful Wizard of Oz;* 551 U.S. Bureau of the Census, *Historical Statistics of the United States, Colonial Times to 1970, Bicentennial Edition,* Washington, DC, 1975; 552 Women's Trade Union League (WTUL), "New World Lessons for Old World Peoples," 1912; 554 U.S. Bureau of the Census, *Historical Statistics of the United States, Colonial Times to 1970, Bicentennial Edition,* Washington, DC, 1975; 579 Upton Sinclair, *The Jungle,* 1906; 596 Advertisement in New York World, May 1, 1915; 618 Data from G. M. Gathorne-Hardy, *The Fourteen Points and the Treaty of Versailles (Oxford Pamphlets on World Affairs,* no. 6, 1939), pp. 8–34; Thomas G. Paterson et al., *American Foreign Policy: A History Since 1900,* 2nd ed., vol. 2, pp. 282–293; 654 Data compiled from C. D. Bremer, "American Bank Failure" (New York: Columbia University Press, 1935), p. 42; 655 John M. Allswang, *A House for All Peoples: Ethnic Politics in Chicago, 1890–1936,*1971; 728 Lyrics from the song, "Little Boxes" by Malvina Reynolds © Copyright 1962 Schroder Music Co. (ASCAP). Renewed 1990. Used by permission. All rights reserved; 729 Compiled from U.S. Bureau of the Census, *Historical Statistics of the United States, Colonial Times to 1970, Bicentennial Edition,* Washington, DC, 1975; 762 from *Still the Golden Door,* David M. Reimer. Copyright © 1992 Columbia University Press. Reprinted with permission of the publisher; 765 U.S. Department of Defense.

CHAPTER 1

6 Art Resource, N.Y. 8 © Ivy Close Images / Alamy 11 Art Resource, N.Y. 13 The Bancroft Library 17 © Hilary Morgan / Alamy 19 The Granger Collection, New York-All Rights Reserved 20 North Wind Picture Archives 22 © National Portrait Gallery / SuperStock 24 © The Trustees of the British Museum

CHAPTER 2

29 Ashmolean Museum 33 © North Wind Picture Archives / Alamy 34 The Granger Collection, New York-All Rights Reserved 35 The Granger Collection, New York-All rights reserved 36 Peter Newark American Pictures / Bridgeman Art Library 38 American Antiquarian Society 40 Massachusetts Historical Society / Bridgeman Art Library 45 © British Library Board (Maps K. Top 125.35) 46 © Ivy Close Images / Alamy 47 Library of Congress

CHAPTER 3

55 Fine Arts Museums of San Francisco, Gift of Mr. and Mrs. John D. Rockefeller, III 57 The Granger Collection, New York-All rights reserved 58 The Granger Collection, New York-All rights reserved 63 © AAA Photostock / Alamy 64 Library of Congress 66 The Granger Collection, New York-All rights reserved 69 MPI/Stringer / Getty Images 71 Art Resource/The New York Public Library Photographic Services 72 © joeysworld.com / Alamy

CHAPTER 4

79 Bridgeman Art Library/Virginia Historical Society 82 Atwater Kent Museum of Philadelphia 83 Richard Cummins / Corbis 84 Courtesy of the Pennsylvania Academy of the Fine Arts, Philadelphia. Gift of Mrs. Sarah Harrison (The Joseph Harrison, Jr. Collection) 88 Courtesy of the Library of Congress 91 © Pictorial Press Ltd / Alamy 92 © National Portrait Gallery, London 93 The Trustees of the British Museum 96 Anne S.K. Brown Military Collection, Brown University 98 © Universal Images Group Limited / Alamy

CHAPTER 5

105 New Hampshire Historical Society 107 John Carter Brown Library 109 The Granger Collection, New York-All rights reserved 112 The Granger Collection, New York-All rights reserved 113 Library of Congress 115L Library of Congress 115R American Antiquarian Society 118L Getty Images Inc.-Hulton Archive Photo 118R © Bettmann/CORBIS 119 Atwater Kent Museum of Philadelphia

CHAPTER 6

131 The Library Company of Philadelphia 134 The Maryland Historical Society 135 Art Resource/The New York Public Library, Rare Book Division 136 Courtesy of the Massachusetts Historical Society 138 © rook76 / Fotolia 145 The National Portrait Gallery, Smithsonian Institution/Art Resource, NY. 146T The Granger Collection, New York-All rights reserved 146B © Jon Helgason / Alamy 148 The Historical Society of Pennsylvania 152 National Archives and Records Administration

CHAPTER 19

439 © The Museum of the City of New York, The Byron Collection 440 © G.E. Kidder Smith/CORBIS 442 Library of Congress 446 The Granger Collection, New York-All rights reserved 452 The Granger Collection, New York-All rights reserved 453 Library of Congress 454 CORBIS All Rights Reserved 456 © CORBIS 458L Getty Images/Time Life Pictures 458R Hull-House Collection, HHC-0074-0508-0106-001, University of Illinois at Chicago Library, Special Collections 461 Library of Congress

CHAPTER 20

467 Solomon D. Butcher / Nebraska State Historical Society 471 The Granger Collection, New York-All rights reserved 474 Wisconsin Historical Society 475 Kansas State Historical Society, Copy and Reuse Restrictions Apply 477 The Granger Collection, New York 479L Bettmann / CORBIS All Rights Reserved 484 The Granger Collection, New York-All rights reserved 486 © Everett Collection Inc / Alamy

CHAPTER 21

491 The Granger Collection, New York 495 The Granger Collection, New York-All rights reserved 497 Library of Congress 499 © CORBIS 500L Chicago History Museum 500R United States Military Academy 505 Library of Congress 507 Library of Congress 508 The Granger Collection, New York-All rights reserved 510 The Granger Collection, New York-All rights reserved

CHAPTER 22

515 The Granger Collection, New York-All rights reserved 516 Culver Pictures / The Art Archive at Art Resource, NY 521 Library of Congress 522L © Archive Pics / Alamy 522R MPI/Stringer/ Getty Images 525 © Bettmann/CORBIS 526 Library of Congress 529 The Granger Collection, New York-All rights reserved 532 © PEMCO-Webster & Stevens Collection; Museum of History and Industry, Seattle/CORBIS

CHAPTER 23

537 Library of Congress 538 © Bettmann/CORBIS 540 © CORBIS 542 Jessie Tarbox (1871–1942) / Schlesinger Library, Radcliffe Institute, Harvard University / The Bridgeman Art Library 543 © Niday Picture Library / Alamy 546 Getty Images Inc.-Hulton Archive Photos 548 Courtesy of the Lilly Library, Indiana University, Bloomington, Indiana 551 Library of Congress 552 © Bettmann/CORBIS 556 A'Lelia Bundles/ Walker Family Collection/madamcjwalkder.com

CHAPTER 24

563 From the May 8, 1915, edition of the *New York Tribune* 568 © Lordprice Collection / Alamy 570 Hulton Archive / Getty Images 571 © Niday Picture Library / Alamy 574 U.S. Government Printing Office 576 Library of Congress 577 Chicago History Museum 579 The Granger Collection, New York-All rights reserved 581 Chicago History Museum/Getty Images 582 © World History Archive / Alamy

CHAPTER 25

589 ullstein bild / The Granger Collection, New York-All rights reserved 591 The Granger Collection, New York-All rights reserved 594 The Granger Collection, New York 596 Art Resource/Schomburg Center for Research in Black Culture 598 The Granger Collection, New York-All rights reserved 599 © Bettmann/CORBIS 601 *The Passion of Sacco and Vanzetti,* (1931–1932) by Ben Shahn, from the Sacco and Vanzetti series of 23 paintings. From the collection of Whitney Museum of American Art. Gift of Edith and Milton Lowenthat. Art © Estate of Ben Shahn/Licensed by VAGA, New York, NY 602 Bettmann/CORBIS All Rights Reserved 604 The Granger Collection, New York-All rights reserved 607 The Granger Collection, New York-All rights reserved 609 Bettmann/CORBIS All Rights Reserved

CHAPTER 26

615 AP Images 617 The Granger Collection, New York-All rights reserved 618 Library of Congress 619 © Everett Collection Inc / Alamy 621 © Keystone Pictures USA / Alamy 625T Underwood and Underwood / CORBIS All Rights Reserved 625B Library of Congress 626L © CORBIS 626R Library of Congress 628 The Granger Collection, New York-All rights reserved 632 Franklin D. Roosevelt Library

CHAPTER 27

639 © Hulton-Deutsch Collection/CORBIS 643 Art Resource/ Bildarchiv Preussischer Kulturbesitz 645 © Everett Collection Inc / Alamy 646 © GL Archive / Alamy 651 The Granger Collection, New York-All rights reserved 652 © Universal History Arc / agefotostock 653 Japanese American National Museum 655 The Granger Collection, New York-All rights reserved 657 © Courtesy: Everett Collection Inc. / age fotostock 658 Rue des Archives / The Granger Collection, New York-All rights reserved 660 Underwood & Underwood/Bettmann/ CORBIS All Rights Reserved

CHAPTER 28

665 AP Wide World Photos 668 ullstein bild / The Granger Collection, New York-All rights reserved 672 © Everett Collection Inc / Alamy 676 Bettmann/CORBIS All Rights Reserved 677 Bettmann/CORBIS All Rights Reserved 678 Rue des Archives / The Granger Collection, New York-All rights reserved 679 © Bettmann/CORBIS 681 AP Images 683 Bettmann/CORBIS All Rights Reserved 685 Bettmann/CORBIS All Rights Reserved

CHAPTER 29

689 Magnum Photos, Inc. 690 Magnum Photos, Inc. 693 © ClassicStock / Alamy 694 © NASA Archive / Alamy 696 Alan Ginsberg / Corbis 699 © Bettmann/CORBIS 700 Magnum Photos, Inc. 701 © Everett Collection Inc / Alamy 702 AP Images 703 Bettmann/CORBIS All Rights Reserved

Index

Key terms and the text pages on which the term is defined are highlighted in boldface type. Terms and definitions also appear in the Glossary, pp. G-1–G-11.

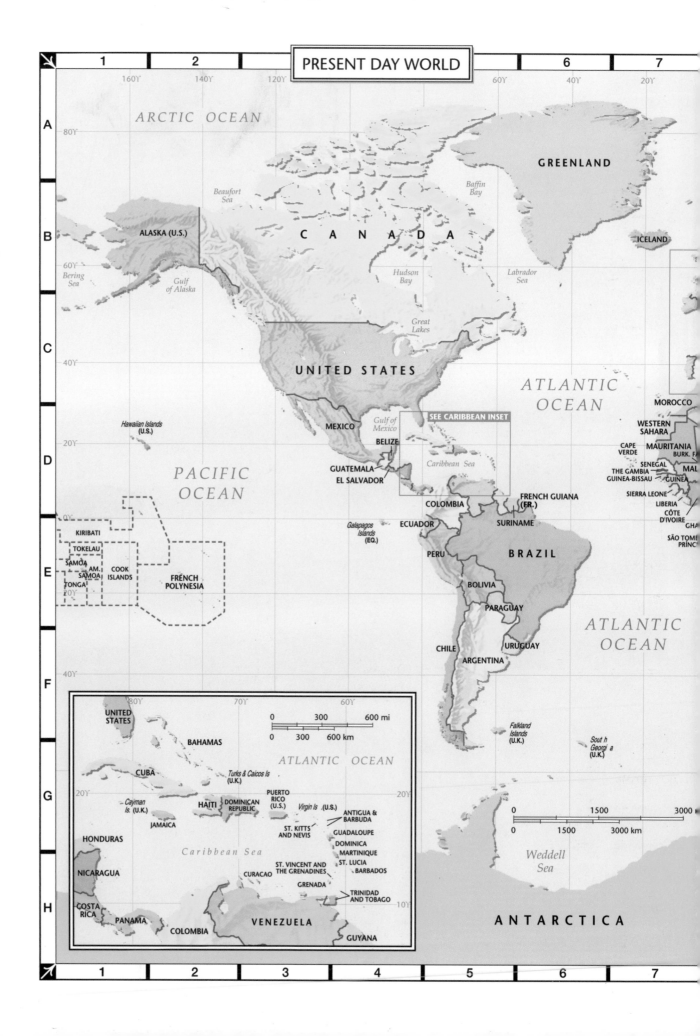

1   **2**   **6**   **7**

160Y   140Y   120Y   60Y   40Y   20Y

A

ARCTIC OCEAN

80Y

GREENLAND

Beaufort
Sea

Baffin
Bay

B

ALASKA (U.S.)

C A N A D A

ICELAND

60Y
Bering
Sea

Gulf
of Alaska

Hudson
Bay

Labrador
Sea

C

40Y

Great
Lakes

UNITED STATES

ATLANTIC
OCEAN

MOROCCO

Hawaiian Islands
(U.S.)

Gulf of
Mexico

SEE CARIBBEAN INSET

WESTERN
SAHARA

MEXICO

CAPE
VERDE

MAURITANIA
BURK. FA

D

20Y

BELIZE

SENEGAL

MAL

PACIFIC
OCEAN

GUATEMALA
EL SALVADOR

Caribbean Sea

THE GAMBIA
GUINEA-BISSAU

GUINEA

SIERRA LEONE

COLOMBIA

FRENCH GUIANA
(FR.)

LIBERIA
CÔTE
D'IVOIRE

GHA

KIRIBATI

Galapagos
Islands
(EQ.)

ECUADOR

SURINAME

SÃO TOME
PRINC

0Y

TOKELAU

PERU

B R A Z I L

SAMOA
AM.
SAMOA

COOK
ISLANDS

FRENCH
POLYNESIA

E

TONGA
20Y

BOLIVIA

PARAGUAY

ATLANTIC

CHILE

URUGUAY

OCEAN

ARGENTINA

F

40Y

Falkland
Islands
(U.K.)

Sout h
Georgi a
(U.K.)

1   **2**   **3**   **4**   **5**   **6**   **7**